D1541724

AMERICAN EMPIRE

AMERICA IN THE WORLD

Sven Beckert and Jeremi Suri, Series Editors

A list of titles in this series appears
at the back of the book.

AMERICAN EMPIRE

EMPIRE

A GLOBAL HISTORY

A. G. HOPKINS

PRINCETON UNIVERSITY PRESS

PRINCETON & OXFORD

COPYRIGHT © 2018 BY A. G. HOPKINS

Requests for permission to reproduce material from this work
should be sent to Permissions, Princeton University Press

PUBLISHED BY PRINCETON UNIVERSITY PRESS
41 William Street, Princeton, New Jersey 08540

IN THE UNITED KINGDOM: PRINCETON UNIVERSITY PRESS
6 Oxford Street, Woodstock, Oxfordshire OX20 1TR

press.princeton.edu

ISBN 978-0-691-17705-2

Library of Congress Control Number: 2017961900

British Library Cataloging-in-Publication Data is available

Acquisitions Editor: Ben Tate
Editorial Assistant: Hannah Paul
Production Editorial: Karen Carter
Jacket Illustration Credit: "It Ought to be a Happy New Year," *Judge* magazine, 1899.
Courtesy of Billy Ireland Cartoon Library & Museum, The Ohio State University
Production: Erin Suydam
Publicity: Sara Henning Stout and Katie Lewis
Copyeditor: Karen Verde
Epigraph Credit: Brian Turner, "*Ashbah*" from *Here, Bullet*.
Copyright © 2005 by Brian Turner. Reprinted
with the permission of The Permissions Company, Inc.,
on behalf of Alice James Books.

This book has been composed in Miller, Coliseum, and Griffon

Printed on acid-free paper. ∞

PRINTED IN THE UNITED STATES OF AMERICA

1 3 5 7 9 10 8 6 4 2

Fired at first sight with what the Muse imparts,
In fearless youth we tempt the height of arts,
While from the bounded level of our mind,
Short views we take, nor see the lengths behind;
But more advanced, behold with strange surprise
New distant scenes of endless science rise!
So pleased at first the towering Alps we try,
Mount o'er the vales, and seem to tread the sky,
The eternal snows appear already passed,
And the first clouds and mountains seem the last:
But, those attain'd, we tremble to survey
The growing labours of the lengthen'd way,
The increasing prospect tires our wandering eyes,
Hills peep o'er hills, and Alps on Alps arise!

—*Alexander Pope, "An Essay on Criticism" (1711)*

CONTENTS

	List of Illustrations	xiii
	Preface	xv
PROLOGUE	Lessons of Liberation: Iraq, 1915–1921	1
CHAPTER 1	Three Crises and an Outcome	10
	The Choice among Alternatives	10
	Beyond "The National Ideology of American Exceptionalism"	15
	Empire: "A Rose by Any Other Name . . ."?	21
	Globalization and Empires	25
	Time and Motion	32
	"The Growing Labours of the Lengthen'd Way"	41
PART I	**DECOLONIZATION AND DEPENDENCE, 1756–1865**	43
CHAPTER 2	The Advance and Retreat of the Military-Fiscal State	45
	Cause and Chronology	45
	A Great Convergence?	48
	The Glorious Revolution, and the Exceptional Military-Fiscal State	53
	The Evolution of Britain's Military-Fiscal State	60
	The New Global Order	64

War, Reconstruction, and Reform 71

Britain: "The Union of Permanence and Change" 76

"A Vast Empire on Which the Sun Never Sets" 83

"The Image of the Past Projected on the Mist of the Unknown" 90

CHAPTER 3 From Revolution to Constitution 95

Harry Washington and the Emerging Global Order 95

Toward "The New Colony-System" 98

John Company at Work 105

A Revolution of Declining Expectations 107

"An Indissoluble Union of the States under One Federal Head" 123

"Spectacles of Turbulence and Contention" 129

"Not an Empire, but the Project of an Empire" 135

CHAPTER 4 The Struggle for Independence 142

Midnight's Children 142

The Rhetoric and the Reality of Revolution 146

Dilemmas of Dependent Development 158

Cultural Continuities 172

"Converting the Forests of a Wilderness into the Favourite Mansion of Liberty" 185

CHAPTER 5 Wars of Incorporation 191

"The Great Nation of Futurity" 191

"The Bright Idea of Property, of Exclusive Right" 194

1812: The Second War of Independence? 208

"America Knows How to Crush as Well as How to Expand" 212

"An Irrepressible Conflict between Opposing and Enduring Forces" 217

"For God's Sake, Let Us If Possible Keep Out Of It"   228

War and Peace Revisited   234

PART II   MODERNITY AND IMPERIALISM, 1865–1914   239

CHAPTER 6   Uneven Development and Imperial Expansion   241

"The Earth, Restive, Confronts a New Era"   241

"Via Pecunia": The Road to Modern Globalization   243

"O, My Brothers, Love Your Country"   249

The Great Deflation   255

Globalization and "New" Imperialism   261

Lions, Jackals, and the Scramble for Empire   267

"This Is a New Age; The Age of Social Advancement Not of Feudal Sports"   281

CHAPTER 7   Achieving Effective Independence   287

"In the Midst of Confusion and Distress"   287

"All Has Been Lost, Except Office or the Hope of It"   289

"Beautiful Credit! The Foundation of Modern Society"   306

The Culture of Cosmopolitan Nationalism   316

From "Union" to "America"   332

CHAPTER 8   Acquiring an Unexceptional Empire   337

"Our World Opportunity, World Duty, and World Glory"   337

The Battle Over the Wars of 1898   339

Don Quixote's Last Ride   343

Mobilizing the Means of Destruction   352

"The Irresistible Tendency to Expansion . . . Seems Again in Operation"   355

"We Come as Ministering Angels, Not as Despots" 362

"Destiny, Divinity and Dollars" 373

CHAPTER 9 Insular Perspectives on an Intrusive World 383

"The Wheels of the Modern Political Juggernaut" 383

Sugaring the Pill 386

Cuba: "A Lot of Degenerates Absolutely Devoid of Honor and Gratitude" 390

Puerto Rico: "Into History as a Picnic" 399

The Philippines: "Land that I Idolise, Sorrow of my Sorrow" 403

Hawai'i: "A People Fast Passing Away" 417

Wars of Choice 427

Intermission Tarzan's Mirror to Modernity 437

PART III EMPIRES AND INTERNATIONAL DISORDER, 1914–1959 441

CHAPTER 10 The Modern Imperial System: From Conquest to Collapse 443

The "American Century"? 443

Isolation or Integration? 446

World War I and the Return to Normality 450

"One of the Greatest Economic Catastrophes of Modern History" 456

The War to Break and Re-Make Empires 465

The Second Colonial Occupation 470

Liberation—Colonial Style 483

The End of the Affair 489

CHAPTER 11 Ruling the Forgotten Empire   494

    Buyers' Remorse   494

    "A Greater England with a Nobler Destiny"   497

    The Modernizing Mission   504

    Owning an Empire: Congress and the Constitution   509

    Lobbies and Liberties   512

    *"A Course of Tuition under a Strong and
    Guiding Hand"*   521

    *"Hardly a Ripple of Failure upon the Stream of
    Our Success"*   530

    Prospective   533

CHAPTER 12 Caribbean Carnival   539

    Pleasure Islands   539

    *Puerto Rico: "An Example of the Best Methods of
    Administering Our Insular Possessions"*   543

    Cuba: "That Infernal Little Republic"   559

    "Now, No Longer Can We Be Unmoved"   588

CHAPTER 13 Paradise in the Pacific   592

    "Where Skies of Blue Are Calling Me"   592

    *"Hawai'i: A World of Happiness in an Island of
    Peace"*   594

    *The Philippines: "Substituting the Mild Sway of
    Justice and Right for Arbitrary Rule"*   607

    "Ours Not to Rest Till Our Banner Wave"   632

    The Insular Empire in Retrospect   635

CHAPTER 14 "The Twilight of Confused Colonialism"   639

    *"Surrendering Authority and Retaining
    Responsibility"*   639

The Global Setting   641

Holding On   643

Protection in the Pacific   649

Coercion and Collaboration in the Caribbean   657

Moving On   662

Progress in the Pacific?   669

Contrasts in the Caribbean   674

Conclusion: "A Shining Example of the American Way for the Entire Earth"   683

PART IV THE OUTCOME: POSTCOLONIAL GLOBALIZATION   689

CHAPTER 15   Dominance and Decline in the Postcolonial Age   691

"The One Duty We Owe to History Is to Rewrite It"   691

Globalization and Empires   692

Postcolonial Globalization   696

The United States: The Aspiring Hegemon   707

Captain America: To Be Continued?   721

EPILOGUE   Lessons of Liberation: Iraq, 2003–2011   730

Notes   739

Index   933

ILLUSTRATIONS

PHOTOS

FIGURE 8.1   The Union of North and South, 1898   371

FIGURE 9.1   José Martí, 1875   398

FIGURE 9.2   General Emilio Aguinaldo, 1899   414

FIGURE 9.3   Queen Liliʻuokalani, c. 1877 (ruled 1891–1893)   424

FIGURE 12.1   Luis Muñoz Marín, c. 1957   555

FIGURE 12.2   Pedro Albizu Campos, 1936   555

FIGURE 12.3   Fulgencio Batista and Ramón Grau San Martín, 1933   583

FIGURE 13.1   Sergio Osmeña, Governor Francis Harrison, and
Manuel Quezon, 1918   614

MAPS

MAP 1.1   The U.S. Insular Empire   14

MAP 3.1   The Mainland Colonies after the Peace of Paris, 1763   108

MAP 5.1   The Continental Expansion of the United States
in the Nineteenth Century   204

MAP 12.1   The Caribbean Islands during the Period of U.S. Rule   542

MAP 12.2   Puerto Rico: Export Crops, Railroads, and
Towns, 1920   544

MAP 12.3   Cuba: Sugar Production (by Province), Towns,
and Railroads, 1924   562

MAP 13.1   Hawaiʻi: Export Crops and Towns in the
Interwar Period   595

MAP 13.2   The Philippines under U.S. Rule   608

TABLES

TABLE 5.1   Statehood as an Index of the Political
Development of the United States   205

TABLE 9.1   Sugar Supplies of the United States, 1870–1906   389

TABLE 11.1 Total Sugar Deliveries for U.S. Consumption by
Country of Origin (%), 1917–1939   517

PREFACE

This book arose from the conjunction of two decisions. The first, my own, brought me to the United States to take up a position at the University of Texas at Austin in 2001. The second, made by others then unknown, was the bombing of the Twin Towers, which occurred on the morning after my arrival. This event, subsequently known as 9/11, had minor as well as major consequences. My own response was among the smallest of the reverberations: I was drawn, like a pin to a magnet, toward the force that had brought down the Towers and riven the world. I then watched, with spectators across the globe, as the attack provoked a massive response. In March 2003, the United States invaded Iraq. At that point, and still largely against my will, I put down the work I was engaged in and turned my attention to understanding Washington's reaction to the first assault on its continental territory since 1812.

The inquiry took me far from my starting point, which was just as well because numerous commentators, who commanded far more knowledge than I did and could write at a speed I could not match, even with artificial propulsion, had plowed through the terrain long before an outsider could reach it. I had to become a fox, as in the fable popularized by Isaiah Berlin, who knows many things, before I could hope to become a hedgehog, who knows one important thing. As I contemplated the huge, impressive, and daunting library of research on the history of the United States, it became apparent that the only possibility I had of making a contribution to the subject was by looking at it from the outside in, instead of from the inside out, while also trying to absorb elements of the national story that fitted my purpose. The resulting study has brought together, in a wholly unpremeditated way, several decades of accumulated knowledge from three diverse fields of history. My interest in globalization has supplied the broad analytical context; my work on Western empires has suggested how imperial expansion transmitted globalizing impulses; my research on the indigenous history of former colonial states, especially those in Africa, has given me an awareness of how different the world looks when viewed from the other side of the frontier.

The dimensions of this endeavor are identified in the Prologue and examined in more detail in chapter 1. My remaining observation on the academic content of the project acknowledges the inherent difficulty that besets all works of synthesis: that of striking a satisfactory balance between generality and detail. George Eliot gave Edward Casaubon his big idea of finding the key to all mythologies, but knew that his procedure of "sifting those mixed heaps of material, which were to be the doubtful illustration of principles still more doubtful," was irredeemably flawed. In his mercurial way, Oscar Wilde also urged writers to be bold and unconventional. He scorned timidity that held "even the courage of other people's ideas" at bay, and mocked "careless habits of accuracy" that stifled imagination. His exhortation, however, was not accompanied by advice on the methodological discipline authors need if imagination is to serve understanding. In grappling with this problem, I have followed a conventional path in formulating a testable hypothesis, defining the terms accompanying it, and considering evidence that extends beyond simple, verifying examples. Nevertheless, the task of specifying and integrating the elements involved in the story remains a work in progress. I am neither a complete fox nor a fully formed hedgehog, but a hybrid whose capacity for further evolution has now reached its limit. If I have failed to be right about all the small things, I hope, nevertheless, to have added a degree of plausibility, and perhaps some illumination, to a few of the big ones. Truth, if it can be found, lies in another country.

My guides to the present country, the United States, have been patient, tolerant, and unreservedly generous with their knowledge. My former colleagues and associates at the University of Texas at Austin responded willingly to my appeals, even when I was no longer on site and able to exercise the power of proximity. George Forgie, Mark Metzler, Marc Palen, and James Vaughn, who took on large chunks of the manuscript dealing with the eighteenth and nineteenth centuries, carried the heaviest burdens. But I owe a great deal, too, to the specialized expertise of Frank Guridy, Mark Lawrence, William Morgan, Bartholomew Sparrow, John Vurpillat, and Ben Brower. I am grateful to the College of Liberal Arts, which gave me a Faculty Research Grant in the spring of 2007, and to the College's Institute of Historical Studies, which awarded me a fellowship in the fall of 2009. The leave granted for these two semesters enabled me to cut into, if not entirely through, some particularly dense problems of interpretation. The administrative staff in the Department of History were unfailingly helpful and, as is the way in Austin, always courteous in responding to requests that were often based on expectations imported from another continent.

My colleagues in Cambridge welcomed me to the American History seminar, which, under Gary Gerstle's leadership, is a source of inspiration as well as information. Seth Archer, Nicholas Guyatt, Andrew Preston, and John Thompson were quickly enlisted to read segments of the manuscript. Their astute comments improved my drafts, even though they may have failed to dislodge all the entrenched positions that authors defend when they reach the final stages of composition. Pembroke College provided a haven for numerous informal discussions; the college Research Fund supported my travel and photocopying needs. Two indispensable experts, Tim Hardingham and Hans Megson, steered me through various incarnations of Windows, including the ultra-stressful experience of Windows 8, with calm authority and saved me, as well as my manuscript, from several impending disasters.

I diluted the demands made on close colleagues by exploiting scholars beyond the universities where I held appointments. Justin duRivage generously allowed me to read his important Ph.D. dissertation on the mid-eighteenth century; Max Edling wrote a publishable memorandum on my efforts to understand the period between the Revolution and the Civil War. William Clarence Smith and Richard Drayton made valuable comments on the chapters discussing the Philippines and the Caribbean, respectively. Ian Phimister kindly read the chapter on late nineteenth-century imperialism; Stephen Sawyer checked my treatment of continental Europe during the same period. Cary Fraser and Gerold Krozewski put their considerable knowledge of decolonization at my disposal. Michael Hunt engaged very willingly in extensive correspondence over the definition of empires and hegemony. If, between us, we have failed to wrestle the problem into submission, we can console ourselves that we are in good company.

Several of the maps that appear here have been constructed from obscure and scattered sources. I should like to express my gratitude to Larry Kessler and Carol MacLennan (Hawai'i), César Ayala (Cuba and Puerto Rico), and William Clarence Smith (the Philippines) for their generosity in placing their specialized cartographical knowledge at my disposal.

Sven Beckert and Jeremi Suri, the editors of Princeton's "America in the World" series, readily gave far more than formal support. Ben Tate, the acquiring editor, provided a winning combination of professional detachment and personal involvement. I am glad to have an opportunity to record my gratitude to all three for helping me to negotiate the final stages of what has become a large and demanding project. I also appreciate my good fortune in being in the safe hands of the production team at Princeton University Press. Their expertise improved my raw text; their experience smoothed the path to publication.

A different expression of gratitude must be extended to the doctors who have seen me through what Byron called one of the "joltings of life's hackney coach." Dr. Scott Shappell, cancer researcher, poet, novelist, and voracious correspondent, was as generous in helping me to comprehend my condition as he was unstinting in responding to everyone who approached him. He retained his commitment to others until shortly before his death from ALS (known in Britain as Motor Neurone Disease) in 2015 at the age of fifty-two. I benefited from the diagnostic expertise of Dr. John Williamson in Austin, and from the surgical skills of the remarkable team at Vanderbilt Medical Center in Nashville, where Professor Joseph Smith, a man for all seasons if ever there was one, somehow managed to appear unhurried in the face of a schedule that would cause others to buckle at the sight of it, while also giving freely of his time to work in Africa. In Cambridge, Dr. Simon Russell dispensed radiotherapy in a spirit of informed cheerfulness that, so far, has kept my instinctive pessimism on the defensive.

Finally, I must thank my wife, Wendy, for her unwavering support in the face of countless revisions of my supposedly realistic writing schedule. Golf widows have no idea how lucky they are. The responsibility for the contents of this book is entirely mine; the credit for making it a better book than it would otherwise have been, and for enabling me to complete it, goes to everyone mentioned here, as well as to the numerous scholars whose contributions are cited in the pages that follow.

Cambridge
July 7, 2017

AMERICAN EMPIRE

LESSONS OF LIBERATION

IRAQ, 1915–1921

They shall not return to us, the resolute, the young,
The eager and whole-hearted whom we gave:
But the men who left them thriftily to die in their own dung,
Shall they come with years and honour to the grave?

They shall not return to us, the strong men coldly slain
In sight of help denied from day to day:
But the men who edged their agonies and chid them in their pain,
Are they too strong and wise to put away?

Our dead shall not return to us while Day and Night divide—
Never while the bars of sunset hold.
But the idle-minded overlings who quibbled while they died,
Shall they thrust for high employments as of old?

Shall we only threaten and be angry for an hour:
When the storm is ended shall we find
How softly but how softly they have sidled back to power
By the favour and contrivance of their kind?

—*Rudyard Kipling, "Mesopotamia," 1917*[1]

"I underestimated the influence of the nationalists."[2]

—*Sir Arnold Wilson, Acting Civil Commissioner
for Mesopotamia, 1918–1920*

Major-General Sir Charles Vere Ferrers Townshend had good reason to wonder at the sudden change of fortune that returned him to Kut-al-Amara so soon after he had left it. Townshend, known as "Lucky" for his exploits in India, had arrived in Basra as commander of the Sixth Division of the Indian Army in April 1915. He was an innovative and energetic member of the military caste that had supported Britain's expansion overseas since the eighteenth century: his distinguished ancestor, Field Marshall George Townshend, had carved a notable career out of the great wars of that period.[3] Townshend himself had risen high in imperial service, aimed to climb higher, and was confident that his new posting would give him the opportunity to do so.[4] Opportunity knocked because British strategists judged that the Ottoman Empire, which had unexpectedly joined the Central Powers in 1914, was likely to fall apart, open the way for further Russian expansion, jeopardize Britain's interests in the region, and threaten its lines of communication with India and East Asia. Townshend's mandate was to clear the region of Turkish forces, encourage an Arab revolt against Ottoman rule, and secure the new oil fields.[5] There was an additional, sub-imperialist agenda. Townshend's expeditionary force was directed by General Sir John Nixon, the Senior Commander of the British Indian Army, who took his orders from the Viceroy.[6] As seen from New Delhi, the opportunity that beckoned was the chance of taking direct control of Mesopotamia.[7]

In June, after early successes against lightly defended positions, the Sixth Division began to move north.[8] On September 29, Townshend occupied Kut, a small town in a loop on the River Tigris, some 180 miles north of Basra.[9] His inclination was to halt at that point, but his superior, General Nixon, ordered him to continue the advance with the aim of taking Baghdad, which was about 100 miles farther north.[10] Leadership was already in question when luck ran out. Townshend never needed the detailed instructions he had drawn up in anticipation of street fighting in Baghdad.[11] Between November 22 and 24, he lost one-third of his force at the fierce battle of Ctesiphen, 20 miles south of Baghdad, and was obliged to retreat to Kut with his 9,000 remaining combat troops. He was pursued and then surrounded by units of the Turkish Sixth Army under the experienced and wily command of Field Marshall Baron Wilhelm von der Goltz.[12]

The siege of Kut, which began on December 5, 1915 and ended five months later, on April 29 the following year, was one of the longest endured by a modern British army; the surrender that followed was regarded as the most humiliating in British military history since Cornwallis capitulated at Yorktown in 1781.[13] There was no pressing need to hold Kut, which had little strategic importance; the more important town of Nasiriya on the Euphrates had already been occupied and the waterways south to Basra secured.[14] The loss of Kut immediately following the disaster at Gallipoli, however, would have further damaged Britain's prestige at a critical point in the wider conflict engulfing the European powers.[15] Accordingly, Kut had to be relieved to save faces and reputations. Initially, Townshend believed that reinforcements from the south would quickly lift the siege. Once he realized that relief was going to be delayed, he proposed to break out from Kut and withdraw toward Basra, where support was available.[16] Nixon, however, ordered him to hold the town while a relief expedition was assembled. Since Townshend could not get out, he dug in. The task of rescuing Townshend and his troops became joined to the larger purpose of upholding Britain's standing as a great power.[17] The outcome depended on whether a relief force could cut through the Turkish cordon before supplies of food and munitions were exhausted.

Three determined attempts were made to relieve Kut in January, March, and April 1916, with increasing numbers of both troops and casualties. The conditions facing the relief forces were appalling: the rainy season had turned the terrain into mud; provisions were limited; medical support was largely absent.[18] Captain Robert Palmer, who participated in two of the attempts, wrote home in January as follows:

> All the same, we were rather gloomy that night. Our line had made no progress that we could hear of; we had had heavy losses (none in our battalion), and there seemed no prospect of dislodging the enemy. Their front was so wide we could not get round them, and frontal attacks on trenches are desperate affairs here if your artillery is paralysed by mirages. The troops who have come from France say that in this respect this action has been more trying than either Neuve Chapelle or Ypres, because, as they say, it is like advancing over a billiard-table all the way.[19]

Palmer also took part in the last attempt to break through the Turkish positions in April, when the losses were so heavy that even the Indian soldiers, who had borne so much so stoically, began to waver:

> That evening . . . D. Coy. had to find a firing party to shoot a havildar, a lance-naik and a sepoy for cowardice in the face of the enemy. Thank goodness North and not I was detailed for it. They helped dig their own graves and were very brave about it. They lay down in the graves to be shot.

This was Palmer's last letter. A few days later, on April 21, he was killed while leading an attack on Turkish trenches. Palmer was twenty-seven years old and had volunteered for military service at the outbreak of the war. He was the son of Lord Selborne, one of the most prominent political figures in Britain.[20]

Townshend's position in Kut deteriorated with each successive failure to recapture the town.[21] In the early stages, assaults had to be beaten back by hand-to-hand combat.[22] Later, when the siege became fully effective, rations had to be divided into ever smaller portions and supplemented with horse meat.[23] By March, malnutrition and disease had reduced the effectiveness of the defenders and depleted their morale. There were instances among the Indian troops of desertions and of soldiers inflicting wounds on themselves in the hope of avoiding further combat. Townshend's communications began to convey signs of emotional strain, and he confessed that "besieged, one is in a constant state of nerves, be your head as cool as an ice box. All watch you and hope for news."[24]

The news, when it came, extinguished hope: it confirmed that the final attempt to relieve Kut had failed. A few days later, on April 29, Townshend surrendered unconditionally to Khalil Pasha, the new commander of the Turkish army, and spent the rest of the war as a prisoner in Constantinople.[25] The British force had sustained 10,000 casualties between the advance on Baghdad and the surrender at Kut; a further 23,000 men were killed or wounded in the effort to relieve the town.[26] Thirteen thousand soldiers and noncombatant auxiliaries were sent into captivity: more than half died on the long, debilitating march north or in Turkish labor camps. Townshend reemerged in 1918, but the public mood, like his luck, soon turned against him.[27] He died in 1924, having lost his confidence, his ambition, and his reputation.[28]

The disaster at Kut led to the appointment of a new commander, General Sir Stanley Maude (nicknamed "Systematic Joe"), who was assigned a massive force of 150,000 troops and given six months to prepare a new offensive.[29] This was to be the mother of all surges. Maude began his advance in December 1916, recaptured Kut in February 1917, and took Baghdad, the great prize, in March. Having occupied Baghdad, Maude continued his methodical progress and was halted only by his death (from cholera) in November 1917, by which time he had annexed large swaths of territory north and east of the city.[30] In the following year, General Sir William Marshall, Maude's successor, extended Britain's control to Mosul, 200 miles north of Baghdad.[31] By then, the Indian Army had 420,000 troops in Mesopotamia.[32]

A week after capturing Baghdad, Maude issued a proclamation containing a phrase that was to become familiar to observers of the invasion of Iraq in 2003: "our Armies do not come into your Cities and Lands as Conquerors, or enemies, but as Liberators."[33] It was then left to Lieutenant Colonel Arnold Wilson, the civil commissioner in Mesopotamia, to confront the eternal conundrum of emerging empire: how to extract legitimacy from the barrel of a gun. Under Wilson's direction, the British imposed a form of direct rule that aroused even more discontent than had the Ottoman administration it replaced.[34] In May 1920, Britain's decision to govern Iraq under the mandate of the League of Nations added widespread militancy to the opposition. Forces generated by political interests, religious leaders, and economic hardship united in calling for independence. The immovable object, in the shape of the autocratic Wilson, known locally as the "Despot of Mespot," stood firm. The result was an uprising that lasted for eight months, took thousands of lives, and cost an estimated £50 million.[35]

Although the "insurgents" (as they were called) were suppressed, Wilson was finally obliged to shift his stance.[36] What T. E. Lawrence described as "a disgrace to our imperial record" prompted a change of policy.[37] Britain's ambitions were scaled down. Administrative order took precedence over political progress; frugality trumped development. In 1921, the British assembled a loose coalition of notables, clerics, officers, and bureaucrats from the old regime and imported a descendant of the family of the Prophet Muhammad to preside, under British tutelage, as the first king of Iraq.[38] In this way, the new state began its inauspicious journey into a future of instability, revolution, and authoritarianism— accompanied and sometimes instigated by periodic foreign intervention. What Maude had called the "tyranny of strangers" was to endure.[39]

*   *   *

It may seem counterintuitive to begin a book entitled *American Empire* by recounting a relatively obscure episode in the history of the British Empire. Townshend himself could scarcely have predicted that his failed expedition would be exhumed, anatomized, and cited in commentaries dealing with America's invasion of Iraq at the beginning of the twenty-first century. Yet, history is rediscovered when the international order is deranged. As novel events strain the explanatory power of customary approaches, commentators whose interest lies in contemporary affairs turn to the past to trace the roots of present discontents. The trauma of "nine eleven" may not have "changed the world," as was claimed at the time, but it undoubtedly galvanized American foreign policy, prompted far-reaching reappraisals of the role of the United States in upholding or disturbing the world order, and generated a now voluminous *genre* of "empire studies."

In this way, the humiliating end to Townshend's career came to be seen as a parable of the rise and fall of empires. The moral of the story, however, was contested. To some observers, the siege of Kut captured more than the Sixth Division. It caught the British Empire at its highest point, which was also the moment when irreversible decline set in and the baton was handed to a new and more vigorous custodian of Western civilization: the United States. From this perspective, Townshend was a prisoner of cyclical forces that were powerful enough to raise up and bring down even the greatest states. The events of 1915, like those that were to follow in 2003, could have only one outcome. All Chinese dynasties eventually lost their "mandate from heaven"; the Greeks taught that *hubris* preceded *nemesis*; Ibn Khaldun charted phases of growth, expansion, and decay; Giambattista Vico identified three repetitive ages; Arnold Toynbee's theory of the rise and fall of civilizations made him a celebrity in the United States.[40] Modern "declinists" continue to take the pulse of the nation at moments of gloom, and reaffirm that the end is nigh.

Other commentators recoiled from an implacable pessimism that foreclosed on the future. In their view, the United States was the legitimate descendant of the British Empire. Townshend's fate signaled the transfer of global responsibilities from an elderly relative to its youthful successor. Political theorists in the United States provided arguments to support the claim that the world needed a dominant leader, a hegemon, to prevent international anarchy. J. A. Hobson had already anticipated the proposition. "Political philosophers in many ages," he observed, "speculated on an empire as the only feasible security for peace, a hierarchy of States conforming on the larger scale to the feudal order within a single State."[41] Moreover, the lessons of history could now be learned: by combining the transforming capacity of advanced technology with the penetrating insights of modern social science, a superpower could disarm dissidents, spread progress throughout the world, and avoid decline. Viewed from this encouraging position, the United States stood at the summit of a process of linear development that had its origins in the optimism of the Enlightenment. Hegel and Marx, in their very different ways, believed that dialectical forces would carry society to higher levels of achievement. For Henry Maine, progress entailed a shift from status to contract. Herbert Spencer linked social development to evolutionary individualism. Talcott Parsons knew how to convert "traditional" into "modern" societies. The "triumphalism" of the 1990s produced the "end of history."[42] Optimists are publicists for swelling national prestige.

In this unexpected way, a consideration of the siege of Kut suggests an agenda that includes many of the key issues in the history of empires. More particularly, the episode and the interpretations placed on it after the invasion of Iraq in 2003 point to the value of placing the United States in a context that is far wider than its national borders. One way of attaining this objective is by inserting the national epic into a global, and specifically imperial, context. Globalization and empires were interlinked throughout the three centuries covered by this study. Empires were both assertive innovators and agents of globalization. Impulses of expansion and contraction moved in unison; chains of cause and consequence ran in both directions. The three principal phases of globalization identified in this study underwent transformative crises at the end of the eighteenth century, the close of the nineteenth century, and in the mid-twentieth century. Each phase had a profound influence on the fortunes and trajectory of empires. Each transition was accomplished through a dialectical process that altered political and economic structures of empire and shifted the geographical distribution of imperial rule. A global view changes the questions asked of some of the central themes in the history of the United States. The answers it provides should engage the interests of two different sets of specialists: historians of the United States and historians of empire.

The history that emerges from these different phases of imperial globalization offers an alternative reading of some familiar applications of the term "empire." The history of Britain's mainland colonies in North America before 1783 can be recast to show how the impulses transmitted by proto-globalization first supported then undermined the imperial expansion promoted by the military-fiscal state. The years between 1783 and 1945, which historians identify primarily as the story of the growth of the nation and its quest for liberty and democracy, can also be drawn into the domain of imperial history. At present, imperialism and empire make only limited appearances, typically in studies of continental expansion and seemingly aberrant episodes, such as the war with Spain in 1898. If the nineteenth century is viewed as a protracted exercise in decolonization, however, the period down to the Civil War can be understood as a search for autonomy, during which the United States remained subject to Britain's informal influence. The years between the Civil War and the Spanish-American War can then be reformulated to emphasize the conjoint processes of nation-building, industrialization, the achievement of substantive independence, and the foundation of an overseas empire.

War with Spain inaugurated a new phase in the history of American empire. The United States became a colonial power in the Pacific and Caribbean; its record in delivering its version of the Western "civilizing mission" is now available for inspection. Yet, the study of U.S. colonial rule between 1898 and decolonization after World War II is one of the most neglected topics in the historiography of the United States and presents research prospects for a new generation of historians. The process of decolonization in the mid-twentieth century was joined to changes in the character of globalization that have shaped the supranational, multiethnic world of today. This new phase, it is argued here, was incompatible with the creation or maintenance of territorial empires. Yet, it is after 1945 that the term American "Empire" makes its final appearance in studies describing the informal and indirect power the United States exercised during the second half of the twentieth century. This apparent paradox is explored at the close of this study, which assesses the limits of U.S. power in an age of postcolonial globalization.

By setting the period as a whole in the context of the Western empires in general and the British example in particular, it is possible to discern common trends in what is otherwise often regarded as a separate national story. The American Revolution can be seen as an extension to the outer provinces of a crisis that was descending on Europe's military-fiscal states in the late eighteenth century. The period after 1783 was not so much a story of the rise of "liberty and democracy" as a struggle between conservatives and reformers over the shape of the post-revolutionary state that reflected similar conflicts in Europe after 1815. The process of building a national-industrial state after 1865 echoed developments in Europe, including their extension into militant imperialism. An examination of the period of colonial rule that followed shows that, after 1898, the insular empire acquired by the United States experienced the same methods of rule as the other Western empires, felt the same oscillations of fortune, and came to an end at the same time, and for the same reasons.

The emphasis on commonalities is not intended to diminish the distinctiveness of the United States. Obvious differences need to be built into the story, though without incorporating the notion of "exceptionalism." Nevertheless, the embedded faculty that Veblen referred to as "trained incapacity" makes it hard for observers to view the world from more than one confined standpoint.[43] Propositions that seem robust, even illuminating, when considered within a national or other specialized context may appear misleading or threadbare when tested in an international or a global setting. One of the principal "lessons of liberation" is that apparent similarities may disguise profound contextual differences. The message from Kut is that the failure to appreciate the fundamental shift in the conditions in which power is now exercised, and the changing nature of power itself, has had immense consequences for order—and disorder—in the world.

The claims made here are confined by the nature of the discipline as well as by the limits of the author. Historical understanding proceeds incrementally. Epiphanies are awaited but rarely arrive. Furthermore, the theme of the book is one facet of U.S. history and not its totality. Even with these qualifications, the subject is still huge and the hazards formidable. Accordingly, ambitious assertions need to be balanced by an admission of the likelihood of error and, beyond that, of the prospect of failure that attends any attempt to reinterpret large-scale historical developments. This being the case, it is as well to acknowledge that if even Odysseus, who could shoot an arrow through holes in a row of axe-heads, required magical assistance to complete his epic journey, lesser voyagers, who lack skill in archery and ready access to the gods, need to be aware that they may be betting hope against probability.[44]

CHAPTER 1

THREE CRISES AND AN OUTCOME

THE CHOICE AMONG ALTERNATIVES

Every generation gets the history it needs. Fashions come and go; some reappear, suitably restyled, long after their original incarnation has been forgotten. The historiographical record indicates that previous trends have boomed for a decade or so before subsiding. The branch of the subject that deals with imperial and global history illustrates the oscillations of the last half century with particular clarity. Modernization theory, which was profoundly ahistorical, gave way to the dependency thesis, which tempted social scientists to embrace the past with unguarded passion. Marxism corrected the over-flexible radicalism of the dependency thesis by reasserting the paramountcy of production over exchange. Postmodernism inverted the prevailing hierarchy of causes by elevating the ideal over the material. Today, historians have resurrected the "totalizing project" and are busily globalizing continents, empires, and islands.

The changing mood of the profession obliges scholars to find their place among shifting priorities. If they fail to move with the times, they risk being trapped, as Marxists used to say, in an "outdated problematic." If they follow fashion, they are in danger of losing their individuality. Those who buy stock at the outset do well. Those who join when the market is at its peak suffer in the collapse that follows. Each fashion appeals because it offers a seemingly comprehensive response to a pressing current issue. Each ends when it is laid low by contrary evidence or is beaten into submission by incessant repetition. After the event, it becomes clear that the issue of the day was not, after all, the riddle of the ages.

The ability to anticipate the next phase of historical studies would greatly ease the difficulty of choosing priorities. Unfortunately, past performance, as financial advisors are obliged to say, does not guarantee future returns.[1] Nevertheless, historians can still use their knowledge of previous and current priorities to help configure their work. It would be unwise, for example, to assign globalization a central place in the interpretation advanced in the present book without recognizing that the term now has a prominent, indeed almost mandatory, place in publications written by historians.[2] Similarly, empire studies have enjoyed a revival that has been stimulated by the collapse of the Soviet Empire and the further rise of the United States, which commentators regard as the superpower of the day, notwithstanding the sudden appearance of China.[3] Accordingly, there is now a danger of repeating a message that has already been received. Once the boredom threshold is crossed, the latest approach becomes redundant. There is a risk, too, of being caught handling an outdated problematic when the mood of the moment changes. If hostility toward globalization gathers momentum, scholars may shift their attention to alternatives, such as nation-states. At this point, however, it is necessary to keep a steady hand, recalling, with Oscar Wilde, that "it is only the modern that ever becomes old-fashioned."[4]

Appearances to the contrary, however, the current problematic has not yet passed its sell-by date. Although the "global turn" has attracted the attention of scholars, it has made only a limited impression on the curriculum, which remains resolutely national.[5] Moreover, publications that respond to the demands of fashion often have more appeal than substance. Some authors have inserted "global" in the titles of books and articles to achieve topicality and add theoretical weight to otherwise orthodox empirical narratives. Others have raised the term to macro-levels that are superficial rather than insightful. As yet, few historians have connected their work to the relevant analytical literature in ways that command the attention of other social scientists.

Despite these weaknesses, which are common to all historiographical trends, there have also been significant advances. Pioneering work during the last decade has established a powerful case for enlarging standard treatments of U.S. history by supplying it with an international context.[6] Research on the non-Western world has shown that globalization had multicentered origins, and was not simply another long chapter in the story of the Rise of the West. Similarly, the realization that globalization can create heterogeneity as well as homogeneity has had the dual effect of showing how localities contributed to global processes and how supranational influences shaped diverse national histories.[7] Other work has opened routes to the past that have yet to be explored. One key question is whether the history of globalization is the record of a process that has grown larger with the passage of time without fundamentally changing its character, or whether it is more accurate to see it as the evolution

of different types in successive sequences.[8] The latter position provides
the overarching context for the interpretation advanced in this study,
which identifies three phases of globalization and explores the dialectical
interactions that transformed them.

The renaissance of empire studies has also left some central questions unresolved. Historians have wrestled with the problem of defining
an empire for so long that it is unlikely they will ever agree on a formula
that commands majority assent. Contributions to the literature by other
commentators have now widened the application of the term to the extent
that exchanges are often at cross-purposes. Comparisons are particularly
vulnerable to definitional differences. If the term "empire" is used in a very
broad sense to refer to great states that exercised extensive international
powers, numerous comparisons can be made through time and across
space. However, if the characteristics of the units chosen for comparison
differ in their essentials, conclusions about commonalities are likely to
be invalid. If the definition is narrowed to suit a particular purpose, potential comparators may fail to qualify, and the resulting study treats singularities without also being able to identify similarities. The definition
adopted here, and discussed later in this chapter, tries to steer a course
between these pitfalls. The hypothesis that empires were globalizing forces
provides a basis for establishing their common purpose. The argument
that globalization has passed through different historical phases anchors
the process in time and suggests how the history of the United States can
be joined to the history of Western Europe, and indeed the world.

The current interest in globalization has had the unanticipated benefit of allowing economic history to re-enter the discussion of key historical issues. Postmodernism and the linguistic "turn" gave historians
a new and welcome focus on cultural influences but also reduced their
interest in the material world. Today, there is a renewed awareness of the
relevance of economic history, but a shortage of practitioners.[9] By reinte-
grating economic themes, the present book hopes to alert a new generation of researchers to the prospects for contributing to aspects of the past
that have been neglected in recent decades. This is not to say that economics should be regarded as the predominant cause of great historical
events, as specialists can easily assume. As conceived here, globalization
is a process that also incorporates political, social, and cultural change.
This comprehensive approach to the subject underlies the interpretation
of the present study and the chronology derived from it.

A consideration of empires as transmitters of globalizing impulses
reveals a further dimension of the past that recent versions of imperial
history have yet to incorporate, namely indigenous perspectives on the

intrusive Western world.[10] With the rise of Area Studies in the 1960s, the old-style imperial history with its focus on white settlers and rulers gave way to new priorities, which concentrated on recovering the indigenous history of parts of the world that had recently gained political independence. Although this work has continued its remarkable advance, it has done so principally by creating separate regional specialisms. The new imperial history, on the other hand, has tended to take a centrist view of empire-building, while exploring topics such as the expansion of the Anglo-world, the creation of racial stereotypes, and the formation of gender roles. The position taken here seeks to integrate the standpoint of the recipients of colonial rule. It will become apparent that the story is not simply one of "challenge and response" but of interactions among interests that were drawn together by the absorptive power of global processes. Globalizing impulses were multicentered. Islands, including those colonized by the United States, were not merely backwaters serving as minor recipients of much larger influences, but cosmopolitan centers that connected entire continents with flows of goods, people, and ideas.[11] They were both turnstiles and manufacturers of globalization. What entered was often processed and altered before it exited. This degree of creativity ought not to be surprising. Borderlands and islands are typically more fluid and often more innovative than established centers, where hierarchy predominates and controls are more readily exercised.

This study combines global, imperial, and insular approaches to compose a history of the United States that builds on, but also differs from, those currently on offer, principally by describing a view from the outside in, rather than, as is more usual, from the inside out.[12] As large claims readily confound those who make them, it is wise to take insurance against the possibility of misfortune. One exclusion clause covers the scope of the book, which does not deal with the totality of U.S. history but with those features judged to be most pertinent to empire-building and decolonization. Accordingly, domestic politics feature principally at the federal level in the nineteenth century, when external influences, especially those from Britain, made themselves felt, but only to a limited extent in the twentieth century, when the United States had gained full control of its own affairs. Other important themes, such as Native American history and the history of borderlands, appear only in relation to issues that directly pertain to the subject examined in this study. Fortunately, these topics and others not mentioned here are being given the prominence they deserve in new accounts of the national story.

A further limit concerns the recipients of U.S. imperialism. The empire considered here is the insular empire acquired after 1898. In 1940,

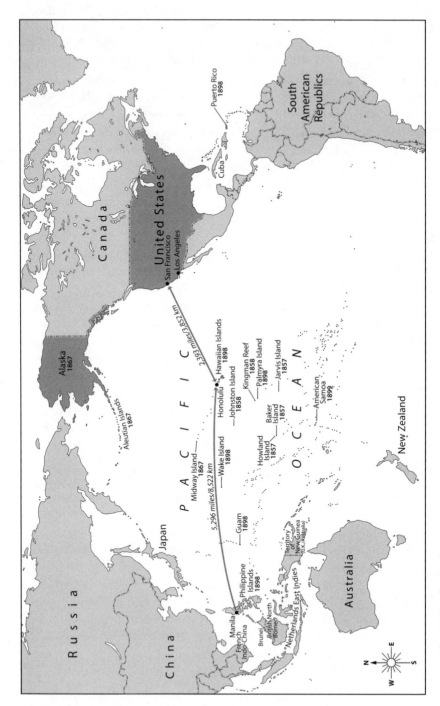

MAP 1.1. The U.S. Insular Empire.

the U.S. Bureau of the Census listed thirteen inhabited overseas territories, which, with Alaska, had a population of 18,883,023.[13] The great majority were islands in the Pacific and Caribbean. Almost 99 percent of the total population was located in the Philippines (16,356,000), Puerto Rico (1,869, 255), and Hawai'i (423,330). These three islands, together with Cuba, form the basis of the U.S. territorial empire considered here. Cuba, which had a population of 4,291,100 in 1940, has been included as an example of a protectorate. The Open Door and dollar diplomacy are not explored in detail, though they undoubtedly merit further examination. One problem arises from the amorphous character of informal influence and the difficulty of tracking it geographically and chronologically. A more prosaic obstacle is that the space required to treat the subject adequately would turn a large study into a forbidding one. On the other hand, the restricted treatment of this theme in the early twentieth century has allowed room for a discussion of U.S. power in the world after 1945, when the debate on informal empire and hegemony imposes itself in a manner that is so weighty as to be unavoidable.

BEYOND "THE NATIONAL IDEOLOGY OF AMERICAN EXCEPTIONALISM"[14]

The emphasis placed here on the global setting requires a reappraisal of the strong national tradition that has long formed the basis of historical studies in the United States, as it has in other independent states. National traditions of historical study arose in the nineteenth century to accompany (and legitimate) new nation-states, and they remain entrenched today in programs of research and teaching throughout the world. The tradition has many admirable qualities that need to be preserved. However, it no longer reflects the world of the twenty-first century, which is shaped increasingly by supranational influences. The national bias can also produce distortions, which are expressed most evidently in the belief that what is distinctive is also exceptional rather than particular. The conviction that the United States had, and has, a unique providential mission has helped to form the character of American nationalism and the content of U.S. history. What the literature refers to as exceptionalism retains a strong grip on popular opinion and continues to influence foreign policy, as it has done since the nineteenth century.[15]

The persistence of a historiographical tradition that is still largely insular ensures that the case for American exceptionalism is largely self-referencing.[16] The consequence is a failure to recognize that distinctiveness is a quality claimed by all countries. Some form of providentialism invariably accompanies states with large ambitions. A sense of mission produces a misplaced sense of uniqueness, which, when allied to material power, translates readily into assumptions of privilege and superiority.

Comparisons, as Marc Bloch pointed out in a classic essay, supply a more convincing means of testing historical arguments than do single case studies.[17] The claim that a particular nation is "exceptional" is demonstrated, not by compiling self-descriptions of the nation in question, but by showing that other nations do not think of themselves in the same way. The common procedure, however, is to ignore competing claims as far as possible and, if challenged, to assert the principle of ideological supremacy.

Yet, Russia's rulers have long attributed semi-divine status to the state and assumed that their purpose is to deliver a special message to the world.[18] The French believe that they are the chosen guardians of a revolutionary, republican tradition. For the historian and patriot, Jules Michelet, the revolution that made France was itself a religion.[19] The concept of *l'exception française* endowed *la grande nation* with the duty of carrying *la mission civilisatrice* to the rest of the world.[20] The poet and philosopher Paul Valéry considered that "the French distinguish themselves by thinking they are universal."[21] They were not alone in this belief, even if Valéry was unaware of the competition. Spanish writers have long discussed their version of *excepcionalismo*. Scholars have traced Japan's sense of distinct cultural identity, *Nihonjinron*, to the eighteenth century, and discovered elements of it long before then. German theorists devised *"den deutschen Sonderweg"* in the late nineteenth century to describe their own country's special path to modernity.[22] The British, unsurprisingly, had no doubt who had reached the summit of civilization first. "Remember that you are an Englishman," Cecil Rhodes advised a young compatriot, "and have consequently won first prize in the lottery of life."[23]

It needs to be said at once that few professional historians, as opposed to members of the public, still subscribe to an undiluted notion of exceptionalism. As some historians have made progress in placing U.S. history in a comparative context, so others have amplified and qualified the founding national saga by exploring every conceivable sub-branch of the subject.[24] It should be acknowledged, too, that an alternative tradition, beginning with Charles Beard and the Progressives, has long challenged the assumption that the United States was an exceptional nation with a unique and unifying providential mission. Skeptics attacked the so-called consensus school, drew attention instead to internal conflicts, and viewed the United States as an expanding power from the outset, first across the continent and then overseas.[25] This perspective was highly influential in the 1960s, following the rise of the New Left and the Wisconsin School.[26] Stimulating new interpretations emphasized the continuous nature of expansion, and viewed the war with Spain in 1898 not as an aberration but as a systemic crisis of capitalism.[27] What followed, according to this interpretation, was not isolationism but informal expansion. A similar approach to the period after 1945 traced U.S. expansion to its culmination in the formation of an empire that, despite outward differences, shared with the European empires it was beginning to replace a desire for global domination.

Radical alternatives, however, have lost visibility since the 1970s and currently remain a minority taste among the present generation of young researchers. The last comprehensive synthesis of U.S. history written from a radical "left" position appeared in 1980.[28] Widespread criticism of its formulaic argument and numerous exaggerations has failed to dent its popularity or its sales, which currently stand at more than two million copies. Despite its manifold weaknesses, this lone work evidently offers successive generations of students a fresh and inspiring approach to U.S. history and meets a need that standard college texts cannot satisfy. The success of *A People's History* is a comment less on the merits of the book than on current orthodoxy, which passes the tests of scholarship but is often safe rather than subversive.

This summary undoubtedly spreads injustice across a vast body of distinguished scholarship. Innovative studies of the highest quality address particular periods, episodes, and themes, but are scattered across an immense and constantly expanding literature. The global turn has yet to become a revolution. Important features of the established historiography remain in place. The result, which can be seen in mainstream texts and syntheses, is a qualified and highly cultivated version of original exceptionalist assumptions.[29] Writing in 1919, the distinguished historian Charles Andrews observed that the "events and persons" of the Revolutionary era "have become in a measure sacrosanct, the objects of an almost idolatrous veneration."[30] What has been called "founders' chic" remains a fashion for all seasons.[31] Heavyweight biographies of the Founding Fathers, which adapt Carlyle's notion of the hero to the needs of a republic, command an insatiable readership.[32] A glance at the titles of authoritative studies of the nineteenth century shows that the theme of liberty and democracy, the presumed outcome of the Revolution, continues to captivate authors and their readership. Historians who chart the swelling role of the United States in international affairs in the twentieth century often find it hard to free themselves from the sense that an expansionist teleology is being fulfilled, even though they may also be critical of its consequences.

The exceptionalist tradition has had a strong influence on the definition and treatment of what is referred to here as the American Empire. Standard histories use the term to refer to two periods covering a half century or longer. The first encompasses the years between 1607 and 1783, when the mainland colonies were part of the British Empire in the New World. All parties accept, minimally, that a formal colonial empire existed during this period. The founding myth emphasizes features that stand in opposition to European, and specifically British, characteristics, notably monarchy, hierarchy, and imperialism, and accentuates qualities of liberty and individualism that are held to distinguish the new republic from the Old World. Although modern research has presented different layers of understanding of the cause and consequences of the Revolution, a new consensus remains elusive and the promising alternatives on offer at present have yet to drive competitors out of circulation.

The second period runs from World War II to the present, and traces the rise of the United States to superpower status. The idea that the United States created an empire in the second half of the twentieth century jars with the notion of exceptionalism and has caused practitioners and scholars to search for ways of squaring the circle. Some theorists of international relations have dealt with the difficulty by applying an alternative term, hegemon, or leader. Other scholars have endowed the language of empire with benign qualities that sought to reconcile global expansion with the principles of liberty and democracy. One influential view portrayed the United States as achieving dominance "by invitation."[33] Another argued, in terms that are familiar today, that the United States possessed an unacknowledged empire that needed both reviving, to protect national interests, and expanding, to realize its potential power.[34] This was the "empire in denial" that ought to reveal itself and embrace what is now termed "offensive realism."[35] Another group, writing from a radical standpoint, applied the term to register their hostility to imperialism. By 1988, "the shelf of recent books devoted to analyzing the post-war American Empire as a successor to other Great Empires of the past" had expanded "at an astonishing rate."[36] Much of this literature remains consistent with the national epic in emphasizing the need to defend and then spread the benefits of political and economic freedom. When the demands of the Cold War called, academia responded by demonstrating that it was not lacking in patriotism.

Between these two periods lies uncertainty. Orthodox accounts of U.S. history after 1783 focus on the expanding national story. Some historians have adopted the epithet "empire" to describe continental expansion during this period, but the application of the term in this context needs careful consideration, as chapter 5 will suggest. External relations receive episodic treatment until 1898, when the United States went to war with Spain and annexed the remnants of her empire. From the standpoint of imperial history, however, the conventional approach is anomalous. Not even the most exceptional states achieved effective independence overnight, and Anglo-settler states typically retained enduring ties with the "mother country."[37] As seen from the perspective adopted here, the nineteenth century can be divided into two parts: between 1783 and 1861, the United States remained dependent on British influence across a range of important material and cultural aspects of life; after 1865, effective independence became an increasing reality, and was sealed and celebrated in 1898. Accordingly, the nineteenth century as a whole merits inclusion in this study as the first important example of a newly decolonized state grappling with continuing imperial influences before eventually shedding them.

The concept of effective independence is indicative rather than precise, but is nevertheless a marked improvement on the alternative, which assumes, by default, that formal independence devolves full control over state sovereignty. Studies of decolonization commonly attempt to distinguish between the two. The formal transfer of power is heralded by official pronouncements and constitutional changes, and is immediate and highly visible; effective devolution traces the typically protracted and fraught process by which political, economic, and cultural links with the ex-colonial power were uncoupled or significantly modified. In a globalized world, the transfer of power is rarely complete: integration inevitably qualifies national sovereignty to some degree, while embedded institutions and established foreign relations have qualities of persistence that carry them forward, even when they are unwanted. The term "neocolonialism" is often applied to cases where the appearance of power, but not its substance, has been transferred. Complete sovereignty, on the other hand, is an exceptional state and not always a desirable one because, in the form of autarchy, it is often associated with poverty rather than with affluence. As applied in this text, the concept of effective independence occupies the generous space between these extremes.

The war with Spain in 1898 used to be seen as a "great aberration" that briefly interrupted the steady growth of republican ideals.[38] Revisionist research has abandoned this explanation, but has yet to weld the many different accounts now available into a coherent alternative. Moreover, although historians have studied the Spanish-American War in considerable detail, their interest flags with the peace settlement. "Normal service" resumes after 1900, when the large themes of domestic history again command attention. It is not until World War I that leading texts begin to allot substantial space to international relations, and only after World War II that a new type of American "empire" comes into view. Meanwhile, a different set of historians has produced a remarkable array of detailed studies of the islands that fell under U.S. rule, though these have yet to be coordinated and made accessible to a wider audience.[39]

It is worth pausing to consider the significance of these omissions. Despite contributions from Progressives and their successors, several generations of historians have either marginalized the insular empire created in 1898 or disguised it by referring to "expansionism."[40] Books on the subject are few in number and have rarely achieved popularity; the exceptions have fitted into the national epic either by identifying the "mystique of freedom" as the central theme of America's "experience with dependencies," or by acknowledging that any sins committed in the course of colonial rule were redeemed subsequently by good works.[41] Most of the early studies of the period of colonial rule have suffered the ultimate scholarly fate of death by neglect, and are now entombed in the lowest reaches of university libraries. Nevertheless, the literature includes pioneering work that deserves credit for opening the subject for inspection, even if historians subsequently decided to look in other directions.[42]

In 1926, Parker T. Moon produced the first comprehensive scholarly account of the imperial systems that arose at the close of the nineteenth century. Moon reflected the prevailing wisdom of the day in assuming that the United States was an exceptional power whose motives and performance set standards that other colonial states were unlikely to match. He judged that the record of the United States as a "non-aggressive nation" was superior to that of the European powers in advancing education and preparing the way to self-government.[43] Julius Pratt, reflecting in 1951 on the period of U.S. colonial rule, took a similar view, claiming that, in general, American imperialism had been "benevolent," and that "those who have fallen under the guardianship of the United States have fared well in the main."[44] Although Pratt's study lacked the incisiveness of his earlier, innovative book, *Expansionists of 1898* (1936), it offered an admirably clear account of all the subordinate territories of the United States. Whitney Perkins's weighty survey of colonial policy and management, published in 1962, made little impression at the time, perhaps because his approach did not reflect the mood of the moment, but it was packed with carefully researched information that remains invaluable today.[45] Extraordinary though it may seem, more than half a century later this book remains the last attempt to produce a comprehensive assessment of U.S. colonial rule in the twentieth century.

Dissenters also made their voices heard. In 1925, the remarkable Scott Nearing offered a broad interpretation of American imperialism in *Dollar Diplomacy* that gave scholarly currency to the phrase first used by President William H. Taft.[46] Nearing anticipated many of the findings of later scholars, especially those associated with the New Left, in emphasizing the interplay of "military power and economic advantage" and the paramountcy of financial interests in creating an empire that was both formal and invisible.[47] He drew attention, too, to continuities in American imperialism, notably Westward expansion and the subjugation of Native American peoples, which historians of imperialism have only recently rediscovered. Leland Jenks, writing with characteristic verve and insight about Cuba in 1928, had little time for what he called "the selective perceptions of idealists," and took a hard-headed view of American purposes.[48] For him, the story was one of "excellent intentions, of ineptitude and misunderstanding, of meddlesome helpfulness, and of a somewhat pettifogging support of American 'interests' on the part of Washington."[49]

At this point, it is worth referring to the exclusion clause cited earlier: the present study lacks the scope, and the author the ability and authority, to offer a new master narrative of U.S. history. The foregoing historiographical sketch serves a more limited function. The discussion of the exceptionalist tradition and its offshoots is not a preface to yet another extended criticism of its failings, but is intended to establish a starting point for the more challenging task of offering an alternative reading of themes that fall under the broad heading "American Empire." The question immediately arises as to whether it is possible to integrate different eras and themes in a coherent explanation of this subject that is consistent with its many particularities. This question, however, leads to another that has a prior claim: the need to grapple with the problem of defining the term "empire."

EMPIRE: "A ROSE BY ANY OTHER NAME . . ."?

A rose will indeed smell as sweet if given another name. Sweetness, however, is an insufficient definition of a rose. Some roses have little scent; some flowers of a different species may smell just as sweet as a rose. As with roses, so with empires: a common feature may be insufficient to distinguish empires from other types of polity, or one type of empire from another. Historians, however, cannot define empires with the precision that botanists can name plants. A general characteristic of empires that identifies their expansive, multiethnic qualities may be sufficient to separate them from compact, homogeneous states, but still groups together too many flowers that are not roses. At this point, the search for an acceptable definition can easily end in frustration. One response is to assert that "it makes very little difference" whether a dominant state is called an empire, a hegemon, or something else.[50] The conclusion has the attraction of allowing commentators to escape further intellectual torment. It is also unsafe because the choice of terms has a crucial influence on the way arguments are framed and, where relevant, on the policy recommendations derived from them.

At one time, historians thought they knew what an empire was. Down to the eighteenth century, "empire" referred to rule over extensive territory; in the second half of the century, and thereafter, the term was applied to a collection of possessions united by command rather than community.[51] The belief that Britain was an empire gave way to the idea that it had an empire.[52] The boundaries of this empire were defined by the constitutional relationship that joined the component territories to a central authority. Admittedly, the relationship varied, and in the British case covered numerous possibilities, from dominions to protectorates. Moreover, the emphasis on formality bypassed the question of how far official authority translated into effective control. Nevertheless, scholars could take reassurance from opening a map and seeing at a glance exactly how far the imperial writ extended.

The age of innocence ended abruptly in 1953, when a now celebrated essay introduced the concept of informal empire.[53] The idea itself was not new: some scholars had already referred to an "invisible" empire; Lenin had included "semi-colonies" in his theory of capitalist imperialism.[54] In 1953, however, a new generation received the history it needed to understand the novelties of the time. By then, the United States had imprinted itself on Britain to an extent that was unprecedented and unexpected. Between 1941 and 1945, Britain's new ally gave a demonstration of its shattering military power that was both comforting and unsettling. The ex-colony was coming back, if not striking back. The former periphery was beginning to influence the center in ways that, arguably, constituted an incursion into national sovereignty. It was a moment to rethink established approaches to the history of empire.

The rethinking that occurred permanently changed the course of imperial studies. According to the new interpretation, empires were not only visible constitutional entities, but could also be invisible spheres of influence that might also qualify for a new status, that of informal empire. Two important innovations followed this insight. One caused scholars to rearrange the chronology of imperialism. Orthodox accounts had long divided imperial history into two main stages: an era of mercantilist empires, which ended in the late eighteenth century, and a sudden burst of "new" imperialism at the close of the nineteenth century. In between lay a period of imperial quiescence. The notion of informal empire bridged the gap. Constitutional definitions obscured the fact that imperial expansion had a continuous history. Far from resting between engagements, imperialism was operating informally in ways that previous observers had failed to see. The other innovation redrew the map of empire. New research into examples of informal empire incorporated large parts of the world that had previously been excluded from the study of nineteenth-century imperialism. Latin America, the Middle East, and China entered the stage—and have never left it.

The voluminous debate stimulated by this transformative interpretation continues, though in a more stately fashion than it did at the outset. Among the unresolved issues, the problem of defining informal empire is particularly relevant to the present discussion. Gallagher and Robinson deployed a method that might be termed "scientific hyperbole" to establish their claim that informal empire deserved to rank with its formal complement. Having launched the idea, however, they did not spend much time refining it. Large areas of uncertainty quickly opened up. In some applications, informal influence appeared as a junior associate of assertive imperialism; in others, it became synonymous with the status of informal empire. The stronger claim remains elusive. The proposition that imperialism involves the exercise of power in international relations to diminish the sovereignty of independent states requires an assessment of the components of sovereignty and some measurement of the extent to which outside influences have been able to compromise them. Historians have struggled to meet these conditions. They accept that the concept of empire is no longer confined by constitutional certainties, but are aware, too, that its new, enlarged boundaries remain imprecise.

Ambiguities of terminology multiplied after the traumatic events of 9/11 and the subsequent invasion of Iraq, when the term "empire" made a dramatic entry into the public domain. A special edition of *The National Interest*, published in the heady spring of 2003, made the point particularly clearly. James Kurth declared in the opening essay that "today, there is only one empire—the global empire of the United States."[55] Philip Zelikow was equally forthright in the article that followed: "let us stop talking of American empire, for there is no such thing."[56] Other contributors represented more nuanced positions. Jack Snyder used the term "empire" to refer mainly to informal control; Stephen Peter Rosen drew attention to the ambiguities involved in applying the term to the United States, but applied it nevertheless.[57] The judgments of this selection of notable social scientists are representative of innumerable similar statements covering a wide range of possible definitions. As empire became the buzzword of the day, a legion of new experts, bearing the gift of instant authority, pronounced on the subject without burdening their readers with definitional difficulties.[58]

Historians whose interests lay in the United States also grappled with the problem of definition. Niall Ferguson and Bernard Porter agreed, from very different perspectives, that the United States was an empire that ought to acknowledge its status.[59] Porter took the definition to its limits by claiming that the United States was a "super-empire" that "exceeds any previous empires the world has ever seen."[60] John Lewis Gaddis, referring to the Cold War, concluded that the United States was an empire because, as a single state, it was able to influence the behavior of other states, whether by coercion or persuasion.[61] Paul Kennedy, though more circumspect, considered the United States in 2002 to be "an empire in formation."[62] Against this position, Arthur Schlesinger was adamant that the United States failed to meet the standards required for imperial status because it did not exercise "political control" over the "domestic and foreign policies of weaker countries"; informal influence, in his view, was an insufficient qualification.[63] Anthony Pagden was equally convinced that the term was a misnomer and that analogies between the United States and previous empires were misplaced.[64] Michael Hunt suggested that "empire" failed to capture the full extent of U.S. power and that "hegemony" might be a more accurate description.[65] Charles Maier surveyed various possible definitions and concluded with an ambiguity of his own, namely that "the United States reveals many, but not all . . . of the traits that have distinguished empires."[66] Dane Kennedy used the term but recognized the significant differences between British and American "empires" and the need to match terms to circumstances.[67]

Variations of this order, when applied to the same phenomenon, are invitations to misunderstanding. To refer to the United States as a quasi-empire, a virtual empire, a super-empire, or an empire of an unprecedented kind is to expand the original formulation while simultaneously amplifying its imprecision. Commentators who begin with very general or very different definitions have no difficulty finding weighty reasons for validating or vilifying the state in question. British authorities reached back to the classical world to cull attributes that justified the Pax Britannica.[68] The Victorians admired Greece for its creativity and colonies of settlement; they turned to Rome for lessons on how to govern subject peoples.[69] These twin towers of Western civilization achieved unrivaled positions in the thinking of the time. As Sir Henry Maine, the distinguished jurist, put it, in a phrase long quoted with approval, "except the blind forces of nature, nothing moves in this world which is not Greek in its origin."[70]

Contemporary American commentators, on the other hand, cited classical sources to contrast Britain's empire of brutality with the consensual extension of liberty across the United States.[71] They used the same sources in the twentieth century to endorse the Pax Americana. The events of 9/11 and the invasion of Iraq that followed produced a veritable frenzy of comparisons.[72] Commentators of various persuasions delivered the Rome of military steel and stern purpose (the Pentagon's Rome), the Rome of a strong state (Roosevelt's or Bush's Rome, according to taste), the Rome of privatization (Reagan's Rome), the Rome of inward-looking myopia addled by corruption (the Rome of a Congress enamored of earmarks and add-ons), and, inevitably, the Rome of pride followed by the Rome of imperial overstretch, ruin, and retribution. All these Romes, freshly laundered, were pressed enthusiastically into political and polemical service.[73] Greece, the smaller, less assertive power, stood in the wings, awaiting the call to deliver democracy, the gift of the gods, to the world.

The infinite malleability of analogies with the classical world should induce skepticism about their value. An established procedure reconstructs the history of Greece and Rome by applying the language and approaches devised for studying modern empires, and then treats the results as independent confirmation of the present.[74] The concepts of Hellenization and Romanization, for example, derive from the nineteenth-century notion of the civilizing mission, which assumes the superiority of the colonizing power and, conversely, the inferiority of those subjected to it. The comparisons typically drawn between classical and modern empires are therefore far less independent than their advocates believe. The methodology guarantees gratifying results, but at the price of abandoning claims to objectivity.

GLOBALIZATION AND EMPIRES

No matter how it is viewed, "empire" is a term that frays at the edges. Imprecision, however, is an inescapable characteristic of all holistic terms, such as state and class, as well as empire. Commentators have defined empires in different ways since classical times partly because empires have changed their structure and function.[75] Accordingly, there is no prospect of reaching an agreed definition that fits all cases, except at the highest level of generalization, which is helpful only for the broadest of purposes. The only reasonable requirements are that definitions are aligned with the purpose of a particular enquiry, and that ideological and other presuppositions are acknowledged, so that, as Hobson put it, "masked words" do not conceal "brute facts."[76] The interpretation advanced in the present study does not depend on a judgment about the malign or benign consequences of empire. The purpose of the terms adopted here is solely to group properties that identify different types of empire and distinguish empires from hegemons.[77]

The same comments apply to the more recent term, "globalization."[78] Definitions abound; all of them are open to criticism. There is general agreement that globalization involves the increase and extension of the flows and velocity of goods, people, and ideas across the world, but continuing uncertainty about how the process can be measured satisfactorily and fitted to an appropriate chronology.[79] Economists have made the most progress in this regard. By tracing the convergence of factor and commodity prices in world markets, they are able to date the decisive advance of globalization to the mid-nineteenth century.[80] They note, too, that the expansion of trade and other flows is an insufficient measure: integration has to have a transforming effect by, for example, raising living standards. The principal drawback of this approach is that it excludes noneconomic considerations. Other means of achieving increasing integration can also have transformative consequences. Imperialism can bring far-reaching political changes; movements of people, whether as free settlers or slaves, create new societies as well as develop new economies; flows of ideas, whether spiritual or secular, can convert belief systems and alter aspirations. Globalization is applied here in this wider, comprehensive sense. Accordingly, the analysis that follows lacks the precision that might accompany a more specialized inquiry. On the other hand, it has the potential to encompass larger developments that might otherwise be seen imperfectly or not at all. This conception treats globalization as a process that can produce different outcomes. Unlike modernization theory or the dependency thesis, it is not a theory that claims predictability, which is why it has been attached, with equal conviction, to conflicting views of its consequences.

As a process, globalization needs an impulse to give it a trajectory. The evolution of empires, specifically Western empires, is the impulse that best fits the historical evolution considered here. Empires were not, of course, exclusive agents of globalization. They shared the role with diaspora, mercantile networks, and universal systems of belief, such as Islam, in ways that were both complementary and competitive. Nevertheless, the British Empire, the greatest of the modern empires, gave globalization unrivaled impetus by annexing territory throughout the world and extending its influence informally into Latin America, the Ottoman Empire, and China. Its all-embracing character serves as a template for the definition that follows, and is further justified by its acknowledged importance in the history of the United States. Admittedly, empires could be restrictive as well as expansive, and their writ did not cover all parts of the globe. Yet, it is as well to remember that, even in the twenty-first century, national governments continue to restrict the free flow of goods, people, and services, and large swaths of territory remain insulated from globalizing influences.[81] Accordingly, the incomplete character of the process is not a disqualification: empires can still serve as exceptionally valuable means of reconstructing the history of globalization since the eighteenth century. In doing so, they also offer a way of drawing the United States into the story of the transformations that changed the world.

In the most general terms, an empire is a species of the genus expansion. An expanding state or society is not necessarily an imperialist one: goods, people, and ideas can flow across borders without one state seeking to dominate or subordinate another. Imperialism, however, expresses an intention to dominate other states or peoples. It joins expansion to empire but can subsist without it.[82] Successful imperialism, where an imperialism of intent becomes an imperialism of result, has three possible outcomes. One is the creation of a formal empire, whereby the dominant power annexes territory by force or negotiation and abolishes the constitutional independence of the polity concerned. Subordination enables the dominant power to manage the internal and external policies of the dependency to ensure, as far as possible, that they reflect its own priorities. The second outcome is the creation of informal influence or possibly even informal empire, whereby the constitutional independence of the satellite is untouched but the dominant power is able to diminish or reshape other elements of sovereignty, again within limits, to suit its own interests. The third possibility is that imperialist actions lead to the incorporation of territory and the assimilation of its people on a basis of equality, in which case the outcome is a unitary state or a nation-state.

Formal empires were extensive, multiethnic polities dominated by one state or *ethnie* that ruled separate, subordinate states, provinces, or peoples. Empires of this type exercised integrative functions that distinguished them from assertive states that conquered rivals and then either withdrew or failed to establish permanent control. Radial lines joined the imperial power to its satellites and became channels for flows of goods, people, and ideas that reflected the priorities of the center. Integration was not the work of a moment, which explains why empires had to be sufficiently durable to acquire the name. Formal empires used force to annex territory and manage subordinates. They also deployed the negotiating skills needed to maintain allies and secure obedience over diverse and distant subjects. Toleration of diversity was the necessary price central authority paid to achieve the degree of integration that met its needs.[83]

The resulting relationship between the imperial center and its colonies was mutual but unequal. Without a degree of cooperation, empires would have been ungovernable. Without constitutional inequality, they would have become states with citizens enjoying equal rights rather than states with subjects held in conditions of subordination. The degree of mutuality or congruence varied from colony to colony and through time. A high degree of mutuality encouraged collaborative techniques of control based on the use of strategically placed intermediaries; a low degree of mutuality obliged the imperial power to rely to a greater extent on coercion. Empires ended when intermediaries ceased to cooperate or when the costs of coercion proved too burdensome. Visible manifestations of decline were reflections of underlying changes in the conditions that had brought the imperial state into being.

Two additional features of empires are central to the argument that follows and need identifying at this point. The first emphasizes the territorial character of formal empires: the imperial authority claimed ownership as well as use of the lands it acquired.[84] The "maritime empires" were not set on ceaseless circumnavigation. Oceanic voyages were a means of reaching land, securing bases, and prospecting inland, where it was possible to do so. Technology, not ambition, set the limits to their achievements. By the eighteenth century, the acquisition of large tracts of territory beyond Europe had become a prominent and enduring feature of Western empires. New property rights attracted settlers from Europe by opening the way for permanent land transfers. Until the late nineteenth century, most commentators still thought of colonies in the classical sense, as being settlements of people.[85] Settlers were powerful agents of integration, and their presence, even as minorities, greatly influenced economic development, political relations, racial attitudes, and legislation in what became known as colonies of settlement. Territorial control grew in importance in the nineteenth century in parts of the imperial world where colonial policy limited white settlement and confirmed the property rights of indigenous people. Colonial governments there were heavily involved in clarifying land law, encouraging export crops, overseeing mining operations, managing labor supplies, and constructing roads and railroads. They promoted a degree of cultural assimilation, through missionaries and education, and set about introducing political institutions that would encourage local elites to cooperate with their foreign rulers.

It could be argued that the means by which authority is established are secondary to the fact that imperialism traces the exercise of asymmetrical power in international relations. The means of applying power, however, provide a key to the character of an empire and its place in history. The Western states that created, managed, and eventually dissolved empires between the mid-eighteenth century and the mid-twentieth century established territorial empires because they fitted their stage of development. The ensuing pattern of integration amounted to a development plan for the world. The "civilizing mission" that followed was an unprecedented exercise in social engineering that could be undertaken only after a significant measure of territorial control had been established.

The second feature concerns the role of empires in supplying public goods (externalities). The concept of public goods refers to a wide range of services, such as administration, security, infrastructure, and the provision of legal, educational, and monetary systems. Public goods are inclusive ("non-excludable," in economists' terms) because they confer benefits that can be enjoyed by those who do not contribute to the cost of provision, as well as by those who do. They are also noncompetitive ("non-rivalrous") in that benefits are realized not only by those who pay for them but also by those who do not. National defense benefits everyone, whether or not they pay taxes. Governments provide public goods because private enterprise is unable or unwilling to do so. Accordingly, the supply of public goods involves taxation, subsidies, and, in some cases, changes in property rights. The East India Company, for example, provided public goods while Britain's interest in India was limited, but was brought under government control once the task exceeded its capacity. The Industrial Revolution and the rise of nation-states increased the demand for public goods—and with it the importance of governments.

States of all kinds supply public goods. Empires, however, had a distinctive role in this regard. As leading agents of globalization, they spanned diverse regions and continents, and extended public goods across existing boundaries. Technological advances encouraged the idea that world trade could increase and development could become cumulative. The benefits of what became known as progress, however, depended on the provision of public goods. Seen from this perspective, imperialism was a form of enforced globalization that sought to increase international integration by delivering public goods to newly colonized regions. Empires enjoyed advantages of economies of scale in providing some public goods, notably protection. They mobilized formidable military power, possessed bases across the world, and could call upon accumulated managerial experience. On the other hand, the cost of protection and other services had to be met without causing disaffection at home or, ultimately, in the dependencies. This imperial dilemma shaped the trajectory of the Western empires from their rise to their demise.

A final consideration concerns the relationship between empires, as defined here, and hegemons, as defined in the literature on international relations.[86] The Greek concept of *hegemonia* established itself as the most influential alternative in the 1970s, since which time specialists in international relations have used the term to refer to political and other forms of leadership exercised by a single state.[87] The theory holds that a hegemon is an essential guarantor of international order. Its exceptional ability to supply public goods enables it to deploy powers of direction and persuasion throughout the world.[88] Moreover, in pursuing its own priorities, a hegemon bestows wider benefits that confer moral legitimacy on its leadership and ensure that its actions are not dictatorial. Without a hegemon, the argument runs, the world would lapse into disorder.

This justification has the special advantage of presenting hegemony as the smiling face of dominance. If justice, or even gratitude, existed in international affairs, the prize of eternal life would reward the hegemon's benevolence. In reality, the hegemon suffers a fate that is appropriately Greek in its tragedy. As charity spreads abroad, it drains the hegemon of resources and energy, and creates opportunities for other states to emerge as rivals. If the hegemon continues to promote liberal policies, the gains may accrue disproportionately to competing powers. If the hegemon retreats into protectionism, the liberal international order as a whole is likely to suffer. When the system fragments, disorder follows; ultimately, war may bring the hegemon's reign to a cataclysmic conclusion. Altruism brings heavy burdens.

This dispiriting sequence raises the question of whether the potentially suicidal consequences of success can be avoided, and, if so, how.[89] Although theorists of international relations have devoted a great deal of energy to finding the answer, their solutions have fallen short of the scientific certitude they have sought.[90] Critics have attacked both the assumptions underlying the theory and its application.[91] Some analysts have revised standard interpretations of Thucydides, which treat *The History of the Peloponnesian War* as a founding text of almost biblical stature.[92] Thucydides, it now appears, was not establishing timeless principles of international relations, but offering a rich description and a sense of the contingency of explanatory variables that are closer to the historian's art than to the theorist's science. Given that Thucydides saw himself as a historian, this finding aligns revisionist thinking with his self-description. The notion that the international system is inherently "anarchic" has also been contested because it understates cooperative in-clinations among states and elevates the importance of the hegemon as the presumed guarantor of order.[93] Empirical studies of the life cycles of Britain and the United States have failed to deliver convincing recom-mendations about the causes of hegemonic stability and decline.[94] Some scholars deny that Britain qualified for hegemonic status in the nine-teenth century, despite managing a vast empire.[95] Others have argued that peace in the nineteenth century was preserved by strong coalitions rather than by single hegemons, which in any case were not noted for benevolence and could be disruptive rather than stabilizing influences.[96] The flaws in the theory, like the quest for scientific certainty, derive ulti-mately from its purpose, which in retrospect can be seen to have been a sustained attempt to objectify the global role of the United States during the Cold War.[97]

Shorn of this particular application, however, the term "hegemony" still has a place in the language of international relations. As agents of global-ization, hegemons and empires seek to manage the "rules of the game" that other states are expected to follow in the international arena.[98] Both possess impressive economic and military power, but exercise it in dif-ferent ways. Hegemons are leaders, not rulers, and hope to achieve legit-imacy through persuasion, though they may resort to coercion.[99] They supply public goods, but possess little territory beyond their own bor-ders. They aim to influence the external policy of other states but have only a limited interest in directing internal policy. Britain, among other Western states, had a territorial empire and exercised managerial powers over domestic politics. Whether or not the British Empire was also he-gemonic does not affect the argument advanced here, and is a question that can be left to specialists in international relations who first raised it.

It follows from the definition used here, however, that the United States also had an empire between 1898 and 1959. This is the long for-gotten insular empire, which is featured in the second half of this study. After 1945, the United States became a world power without having extensive territorial possessions. It ceased to be an empire, even though commentators, impressed by its economic and military might, attached the imperial label to it during this period.[100] From that point onward, the United States is better described as a hegemon, or more accurately an aspiring hegemon, a leading power that aimed to achieve the degree of dominance that met its priorities. As the next section will show, fundamental changes in the global order underlay these semantic differences and shaped the possibilities open to the two dominant powers: Britain built an empire; the United States sought hegemony.

TIME AND MOTION

It is now evident that globalization sprang from multiple centers of origin and had roots that antedated the twentieth century.[101] As yet, however, agreement on the longevity of the process has not been matched by a discussion of periodization that is sufficiently detailed to represent different phases in its trajectory. The analysis advanced here identifies three overlapping sequences, termed proto-globalization, modern globalization, and postcolonial globalization, which encompass the last three centuries.[102] The terms and the periodization relate primarily to Western Europe and the United States, the regions covered by this study, though with some chronological adjustments the categories could also be applied to other parts of the world. Each phase advanced through a dialectical process: successful expansion created countervailing or competing forces; the struggle between them culminated in successive crises, which occurred in the late eighteenth and late nineteenth centuries, and the mid-twentieth century. These were transformative events. Each ushered in a new phase that resolved one major conflict before eventually giving rise to another.

Montesquieu provided a fundamental insight into the dynamic involved in this dialectic when he formulated the principle that changes in the scale of institutions required corresponding changes in their structure.[103] Montesquieu shared with other political philosophers of his age a concern with the problem of reconciling liberty and security in ways that avoided the extremes of anarchy and authoritarianism.[104] Small states, in his view, were particularly well suited to nurturing republican civic virtues, which flourished in conditions that allowed personal relations to predominate. States of moderate size tended to be both hierarchical and monarchical but could nevertheless preserve the liberty of their citizens, providing that their constitutions were designed to control the abuse of power. The larger a state became, however, the more it was inclined to develop despotic tendencies. Its composition became more diverse, interpersonal relations weakened, and private interests took precedence over the public good. The merits of small states were offset by their inability to ward off external predators. Large states, on the other hand, bought security at the cost of liberty and were liable to be brought down by internal corruption or excessive military expenditure. Montesquieu concluded that states of moderate size, of which Britain was the prime exemplar, were those best fitted to achieve the optimum balance between liberty and order. The ramifications of this argument had particular relevance for the United States. Montesquieu suggested that the dangers associated with large states might be controlled by adopting a federal rather than a unitary form of government and by inserting checks and balances to prevent the growth of autocracy.[105] These ideas, mediated by Hume and taken up by Madison, influenced the shape of the Constitution the United States adopted in 1788.[106]

Montesquieu classified empires among the large states with tendencies toward despotism. He distinguished, however, between territorial and maritime empires. He considered that the former, which included Rome and Spain, were predatory and oppressive, whereas the latter, such as Britain, had positive qualities because of their commercial potential.[107] Montesquieu also allowed for the possibility that expansive republics could be both durable and progressive, which helps to explain why his work was so influential among the founders of the United States.[108] His optimism about the benefits of trade placed him with subsequent advocates of laissez-faire, notably François Quesnay and Adam Smith, though, like them, Montesquieu thought that government regulation had its place, especially in upholding the security of the state.[109] Empires, like other states, had dynamic as well as organic qualities. Fluctuating fortunes followed from unanticipated and often uncontrollable shifts in size or structure. The consequences were diverse, sometimes ambiguous, and rarely predictable with any degree of precision.

Montesquieu's most famous work, *The Spirit of the Laws*, was published in 1748, shortly before his death in 1755. The Seven Years' War, the first global battle for empire, had yet to take place; Britain had still to annex extensive territory in India; the mainland colonies remained modest settlements nestling on the east coast. Still further ahead lay a world of towns, industries, and nation-states. Montesquieu's basic insight joining size and structure retains its value, but needs to be related to novel circumstances that not even a thinker of his perspicacity could have envisaged. The interpretation advanced here offers one possible template for developments that appeared after the transformation of the world Montesquieu was familiar with. The signposts that follow identify the three crises that form the core of the book and provide an abbreviated guide to the argument laid out in detail in the chapters that follow. In one form or another, these crises are familiar entries in histories of the period concerned. The analysis offered here seeks to place them in a wider context than the one they habitually occupy and to suggest some fresh ways of looking at their causes and consequences.

The term "proto-globalization," which is discussed in chapter 2, is used here principally to refer to military-fiscal states in the seventeenth and eighteenth centuries. These were dynastic states dominated by landed elites who drew their wealth and position from economies that were based primarily on agriculture but had also sprouted substantial market sectors that included handicrafts as well as food products. Military imperatives encouraged expansion and centralization to secure and administer the growing revenue needs of the state. These ambitions acquired a maritime dimension as technological improvements carried oceanic exploration across the globe. Proto-globalization reached its highest stage of development in the second half of the eighteenth century, when a series of wars among the leading military-fiscal states reverberated around the world and ended in large-scale mutual destruction. What followed, however, was not simply the story of the "rise of liberalism." After 1815, the victors made strenuous efforts to restore the prewar order. The first half of the nineteenth century was characterized by an intense and continuing struggle between conservatives and reformers. By 1848, moreover, conservative forces were in the ascendant nearly everywhere, with the partial exception of Britain. Even in Britain, political reform arrived late and did not disturb the dominance of the landed interest. Similarly, it was not until the adoption of free trade in 1846 that international economic policy broke decisively with the mercantilist system.

The crisis of the late eighteenth century was essentially fiscal in origin. Fiscal imperatives arising from a costly arms race and related expenditure on public goods intensified the search for new and increased taxes. European governments treated imperial possessions as key contributors to pressing revenue needs. Increased tax demands at home and abroad, however, provoked discontent that was subsequently converted into political claims for government accountability and reform. Adam Smith observed the dialectical process at work in the mainland colonies. As chapter 3 shows, mercantilism helped the fledgling settlements to increase in size and wealth in the course of the century. The success of the colonizing venture, however, not only raised the revenue potential of the colonies, but also uplifted the aspirations of the settlers and provided them with the means of realizing them. The home government could control discontent in its inner provinces, including Scotland and Ireland, but struggled to manage distant settlements across the Atlantic. What followed in 1776 was a revolution of falling expectations. It was a protest against both the unexpected increase in revenue demands and the unwelcome imposition of controls on the expansion of inland settlement. This argument joins developments in Britain to those in the colonies, and revives an interest in material explanations of the Revolution, which in recent years have received less attention than intellectual and cultural considerations. Events in the mainland colonies need to be seen in a European and global context. The British government's struggle to impose its will on the mainland colonies and the decision to advance into India were both products of the imperative that joined fiscal needs to the stability of the state.

After 1783, historians of empire hand the study of the United States to a new set of specialists, who tell the national story. By all accounts, the American Empire had come to an end. Yet, formal decolonization does not necessarily signify the passing of imperial influence. The evidence presented in chapter 4 suggests that the United States had still to attain effective independence by the time the Civil War began in 1861. British influence in particular featured prominently in the economic, political, and cultural life of the new Republic. Standard approaches to the period that focus on nation-building may miss wider considerations. Seen from an imperial perspective, the United States appears in a new guise as the first important exemplar of Britain's emerging global informal influence and also the first to devise and dispute strategies for achieving genuine independence. The mounting quarrel between North and South over the character of the new state reflected the contest between progressive and conservative forces in Europe after 1815. Northern interests advocated ideas of development that ranged from tariff protection to ambitions for attaining cultural independence The political dominance of Southern interests, however, entrenched a dependent free-trading relationship with Britain and a matching sense of cultural affiliation.

Continental expansion, as chapter 5 recounts, is best understood in the context of the expansion of settler societies in other parts of the world. The westward movement gave vent to the demand for land that Britain had attempted to curtail, but also increased competition between Northern and Southern interests. The Civil War, the culmination of these tensions, was a secessionist movement that foreshadowed similar episodes that were to mark the history of many other newly independent states. Cotton was to the South what oil was to Biafra. The war also echoed the conflicts in Europe that erupted in the revolutions of 1848 and the military campaigns that assembled Germany and Italy in the 1860s. Self-determination and individual rights were watchwords on both sides of the Atlantic. The Civil War broke a state to build a nation.

The second great crisis, which struck in the late nineteenth century, and is the subject of Part II, arose from what is termed here "modern globalization," which was the product of two well-known processes: the spread of industrialization and the creation of nation-states. Military-fiscal states battled on, in some cases down to World War I, but lost ground to forces that aimed to reshape the economy, society, and the state itself. Nation-states sought fiscal unity to raise the revenues needed to bind new social groups together. Warfare states added welfare to their mandate; parliamentary government replaced dynastic control of revenues and policy.

Chapter 6 traces the process of uneven development that manifested itself in the contrast between Britain, which had become an industrial power with an unmatched financial and service sector, and states in continental Europe such as Italy and Spain, which remained largely rural. Political development was similarly uneven: Britain had a well-developed sense of nationality and had moved slowly but significantly in the direction of political reform; a number of other countries were recent creations in which provincial loyalties remained dominant and traditional political hierarchies, though increasingly challenged, still held power. The transition to modern globalization, as the name implies, was associated with increasing global integration as technological improvements cut the costs of production, distribution, and coercion. Britain again led the process by expanding world trade, encouraging international specialization, advertising preferred forms of constitutional government, and raising aspirations. The British Empire became the principal mechanism for managing multilateral exchanges, policing financial flows, and enforcing order on the high seas. Free trade carried Britain's empire of influence well beyond the formal empire. As the century advanced, influences that had already penetrated the United States extended to the Ottoman Empire, Latin America, and East Asia.

The conversion of military-fiscal states to liberal constitutions and modern economies was a stressful process that swept the European states into major crises in the late nineteenth century. Industrializing states grappled with large-scale class conflict for the first time; rural states faced new competition from imported agricultural products. The strains of the transition were exacerbated by a long period of deflation, which depressed expectations and increased unemployment during the last quarter of the century. These pressures tested the unity of the embryonic nation-state. Politicians charged with the duty of upholding civil order and maintaining social cohesion experimented with a range of possible solutions, including welfare reform, repression, and imperialism. Chapter 6 concludes by setting out a typology that links uneven development in Europe to the dramatic imperial ventures that ended in the occupation and annexation of large parts of the world at the close of the century. Imperialism, formal and informal, was the leading globalizing agent of its time.

These developments are integral to an understanding of the history of the United States after 1865, and are not merely background information to a wholly different story of the rise of an independent republic. Chapter 7 argues that the Civil War was followed by a determined effort to construct a nation out of the wreckage of the federal union. Nation-building at home was undertaken at the same time as Germany and Italy were being united; Austria, France, and Japan were being restructured; and Britain was extending the franchise and contemplating the feasibility of creating an imperial federation. Similarly, rapid economic development in the United States from the 1870s, exacerbated by sudden downturns and deflation, produced conflicts between capital and labor, generated unprecedented problems of urban unemployment, and stimulated instances of violent anarchism. Simultaneously, rural distress arising from the loss of foreign markets and deflation fed into a large-scale populist movement that challenged the power and policies of the dominant Republican Party. Although the United States had achieved an exceptional degree of effective independence by the close of the century, the postwar settlement that underpinned it was threatened from within. The success of the forces that had transformed the old structures had in turn created new challenges.

After a short war with Spain in 1898, the United States acquired a territorial empire, consisting primarily of the Philippines, Puerto Rico, and a protectorate in Cuba, and annexed the independent state of Hawai'i. Although the war itself has been the subject of innumerable studies, few historians place the event in the wider setting formed by "new imperialism," even though the imperial expansion of the United States occurred at the same time as the European powers were occupying extensive territories in Africa and Asia. Chapter 8 advances an explanation that places the United States in the typology of uneven development offered in chapter 6. In the United States, imperialism was part of the process of nation-building. It sealed the unity of the Republic at a moment when it was again under threat, and in doing so celebrated the achievement of effective independence. Internal tensions were calmed; capitalism was saved from its own excesses.

Chapter 9 offers an insular view of imperialist encroachments. The analysis, though preliminary, shows how the islands had become entangled in the process of globalization and how the consequences contributed to their loss of independence. Although this perspective has long been a standard part of assessments of the partition and occupation of other parts of the world, studies of the war of 1898 rarely give it the importance it merits. Historians of the United States focus on events within the Republic. Historians of European imperialism leave the insular possessions to historians of the United States. Specialized research examines the islands in detail but generally treats them as separate entities. The account offered here should enable historians of nineteenth-century imperialism to add the islands acquired by the United States to their standard list of illustrations.

After 1898, the insular empire disappears from view, though this is the moment when the real American Empire, the tangible territorial empire, was established. Chapters 10–14 attempt to resuscitate a subject that has been left to wither from neglect. Chapter 10 complements chapters 2 and 6 in setting the scene for the more specialized chapters that follow. The discussion of the international order emphasizes the continuing importance of Britain, and to a lesser extent France, as the leading imperial powers, and disputes claims that an "American Century" arose before Henry Luce envisaged it in 1941. Instead, the argument stresses the continuities rather than the contrasts in the periods before and after World War I. The peace settlement confirmed imperial borders and endorsed the imperial mission. The classic exchange of manufactures for raw materials remained the basis of colonial development. Racial prejudice continued to guide colonial policy. Politicians regarded the possibility of transferring colonial territories from one power to another as a wholly acceptable feature of diplomacy, as it was in the eighteenth and nineteenth centuries.

Nevertheless, intimations of changes that were to produce a third phase, postcolonial globalization, appeared during the interwar period. A rash of nationalist demonstrations erupted during and immediately after World War I. A more significant challenge arose in the 1930s. The world slump provoked major protests throughout the Western empires; new political movements arose to organize discontent and direct it against colonial rule. The imperial dialectic arising from globalization had again turned success into failure. The expansion of export crops, which colonial rule had encouraged, had jeopardized living standards and subsistence.

Colonial subjects translated liberal advertisements for the civilizing mission into demands for political progress. World War II brought more disruption but in the short run helped to postpone decolonization until the late 1950s. Unexpected help came from the United States, which finally emerged as the leader of the Free World and in this capacity acted to restore the imperial order as a bulwark against the expansion of communism and what later became known as the "Evil Empire."

Chapters 11, 12, and 13 place the interpretation presented in chapter 10 against the record of U.S. rule in the insular empire. Chapter 11 views the imperial world from Washington, draws comparisons with the policies of other Western imperial powers, and compiles an agenda to assist future research. Chapters 12 and 13 underline the diversity and individuality of the islands and direct attention to local agency. Here, too, the argument is no more than a preliminary attempt to sketch the comparative context, which other scholars with appropriate skills will be able to develop.

The American Empire undoubtedly had a number of distinctive features, notably the lack of a bipartisan policy and the insignificant place of the islands in the deliberations of Congress and in the U.S. economy. Nevertheless, the history of U.S. colonial rule, far from being exceptional, provides a faithful illustration of the general argument advanced in chapter 10. Despite their modest size, the islands represented all the types of colony found in the British and French empires. Colonial administrators adopted direct and indirect methods of rule, and experimented with policies of assimilation and association. Racial prejudices, embedded by long experience of "Indian Wars" and Southern slavery, ensured that policy was infused with paternalism and stiffened with coercion. The orthodox assumptions of development policy, which relied on the expansion of export crops—especially sugar—and cheap labor, continued to prevail. Tariff policy remained the tool of rival lobbies whose mandate was to represent domestic interests in Washington. Contradictory policies espoused by Democrats and Republicans, lack of money, and lack of interest frustrated long-term plans for achieving economic and political progress. The trajectory of the U.S. Empire closely followed that of the European empires, culminating in widespread anti-colonial demonstrations in the 1930s. Viability and democracy, the slogans of the day, were never translated into reality. In the 1940s and 1950s, when Washington devised ways of transferring responsibility while retaining influence, the mission was still unaccomplished.

Decolonization, which is discussed in chapter 14, resulted from the transition from modern to postcolonial globalization. An imperial dialectic was again in operation: global integration of the kind that had fitted the needs of national-industrial states since 1850 had served its purpose. It had also ceased to be feasible. In 1945, however, policy-makers in Washington and London saw a different future. Following the war, the victorious allies reconstructed the imperial order, as they had done after 1918. The mission was reaffirmed; opposition was forcefully suppressed. After the mid-1950s, however, empires lost legitimacy. Imperial policy was obliged to adapt to changing circumstances: shifts in the world economy; the needs of the Cold War; the costs of holding on; the demands for self-determination. The literature allows the United States scarcely any role in this drama, apart from prosecuting the Cold War and contributing to the decolonization of other Western empires. Yet, the United States decolonized its own insular empire at exactly the same time as the European powers were uncoupling their colonies. In doing so, the Republic went through the same sequence of repression and concession. The United States, moreover, had the additional problem of managing internal decolonization. After World War II, Washington could no longer ignore increased pressure from African Americans and Native Americans for improved civil rights.[110] Federal and state governments responded, as in the case of the insular empire, first by suppressing "agitators" and then by giving ground. By the 1970s, it was clear that the era of great empires had passed, even if the Soviet Empire had yet to fall. It should be apparent, too, that the role of the United States in this process ought to be recast to give full weight to its own experience as an imperial power.

The outcome, the spread of postcolonial globalization, is discussed in chapter 15.[111] In the 1950s, the established pattern of colonial exchange, which traded manufactured goods for raw materials, started to fragment. Alternative forms of specialization and integration made their appearance. Inter-industry trade drew advanced economies together; finance and commercial services displaced old manufacturing occupations; manufacturing clusters arose in former colonies in Asia. World trade no longer radiated from imperial centers but formed new regional connections. Supranational commercial and political organizations with the potential to challenge the sovereignty of the nation-state appeared. The belief in white supremacy that had justified imperialism and facilitated colonial rule began to dissolve. Ideas of racial equality spread. Self-confidence accompanied self-determination. By the 1960s, the conditions that had favored the creation of territorial empires had receded. Power in international relations had to be exercised in other ways. Strategy had to be realigned to fit new structures, as Montesquieu had observed. The United States was neither a new Rome nor a new Britain. After 1945, the Republic was an aspiring hegemon, not a territorial imperial power. Failure to see, and act on, the distinction has provided a fresh setting for the performance of a timeless Greek tragedy.

"THE GROWING LABOURS OF THE LENGTHEN'D WAY"[112]

This study has stretched the author and it may well stretch the reader, too. This is partly because the history that follows this introductory chapter covers nearly three hundred years and extends across the Atlantic and into the Pacific, and also because it seeks to unite two sets of literature that have yet to be integrated systematically: the history of the United States and the history of other Western empires. Historians of the United States will be asked to engage with three substantial chapters dealing with developments outside the United States, as well as tolerate a synthesis and reinterpretation of themes they will be familiar with. Historians of empire face the task of finding their way through a selection of the many intricacies of U.S. history, while also reappraising some well-known features of European imperialism. Stereotyped or unduly shortened versions of history will not serve the purpose, which requires sufficient detail to support large claims about the trajectory of the leading Western powers from the eighteenth century onward. If a supranational world is to have a supranational history, specialists who are separated by time and place need to give parity to other regions if they are to avoid the danger of attaching them to an amplified version of the existing national story. The history offered here does not presume to meet this goal. It does attempt, however, to point in the right direction.

All authors are obliged to make claims that justify their efforts. If they fly too high, ambition may bring them down. If they keep their eyes on the ground, caution prevents them from seeing the stars. Ambition can be tempered by recognizing that the size of the problem far exceeds the skill of any single author, and by acknowledging the achievements of previous scholars.[113] Caution can be adjusted to fit Longfellow's advice on the art of composition:

> If you would hit the mark, you must aim a little above it;
> Every arrow that flies feels the attraction of earth.

PART I

DECOLONIZATION
AND
DEPENDENCE

1756–1865

CHAPTER 2

THE ADVANCE AND RETREAT OF THE MILITARY–FISCAL STATE

CAUSE AND CHRONOLOGY

The period between the Seven Years' War and the American Civil War cuts across some familiar historical divisions. Historians of the United States generally use 1783 or, less frequently, 1812, as their points of arrival or departure. The majority of specialists on eighteenth-century Europe halt in 1789 or 1815. Historians of the nineteenth century typically begin in 1815 and finish in 1914. A few scholars specializing in British history favor a "long" century that starts with the English Civil War and ends with the Great Reform Act of 1832, but the justification for the extension is too specialized to capture large themes, such as the changing character of globalization. These divisions serve purposes that are not in question here, but they have insufficient scope to represent the substance of this chapter. Historians of empire, meanwhile, have begun to find a broad degree of unity in the period 1750–1850 that stretches far beyond Europe, and accordingly diverges from the accepted divisions of national history. This chapter, which introduces part I of this study, suggests how developments in Western Europe, and in Britain in particular, can be joined to the evolution of both empire and the United States. The link is made by emphasizing the continuing vitality of the military-fiscal state and its efforts both to promote globalization and to deal with its consequences. It is the persistence of the old rather more than the shock of the new that gives the period its unity.

The first part of the chapter deals with the eighteenth century, when the mainland settlements were still under Britain's formal control. The focus on Britain's policy and presence during the colonial era is, self-evidently, necessary and also familiar. Recent research, however, makes it possible to take a fresh look at Britain's role in causing the Revolution. The second part of the chapter, which reconsiders some standard characterizations of Britain and continental Europe during the first half of the nineteenth century, is rarely incorporated into studies of U.S. history and so needs an explicit justification. With the attainment of independence in 1783, historians part company. One branch of the profession tells the story of the new nation; the other follows the course of empire elsewhere.[1] An understandable preoccupation with domestic developments in the new Republic has reduced the attention paid to Anglo-American relations. The Atlantic world, which historians of the eighteenth century have done so much to reconstruct, loses visibility at a moment when its importance was increasing.[2] Accordingly, a summary of an assumed "background" to events in the United States will not meet the needs of the case. What is required is a restatement of the external developments that influenced the mainland colonies and the Republic between the Revolution and the Civil War.

Seen in a global perspective, the American Revolution was one of a set of convulsions that overturned established polities across the world during this period.[3] Virtually all of Europe's military-fiscal states, including Britain, experienced destabilizing crises in the late eighteenth century. The British variant, however, developed a distinctive reciprocal relationship with imperialism and empire that entailed far-reaching global consequences, notably the loss of the mainland colonies, the advance into India, and involvement in long wars with France. The fiscal crisis in Britain can be seen as a challenge to the settlement that followed the Glorious Revolution of 1688 and a direct threat to the structure of power that had survived Jacobite rebellions and the strains of repeated continental wars.

The mainland colonies, though distant, were directly affected by these developments because they were viewed as British provinces overseas. They were places where, as John Stuart Mill later described the West Indies, Britain found it "convenient to carry on the production . . . of tropical commodities," and where settlers considered themselves to be citizens as well as subjects.[4] Accordingly, the colonies were regarded as sources of revenue that could be expanded to help resolve Britain's budgetary difficulties. The objections of the colonists were those articulated by reformers and radicals in Britain; the reforms they advocated were those championed by the inner provinces, too. The debate that followed divided the ruling oligarchy over whether imperial policy should be extractive or developmental. The crucial decision to opt for the former led to conflict and eventual secession. The colonists had to be confronted. If the outer provinces across the Atlantic succeeded in defying the king and his ministers, the Home Counties would demand similar concessions.

Hierarchy would crumble; harmony would dissolve. England's Augustan Age would end prematurely.

The wars that followed the revolt of the mainland colonies and the French Revolution brought down the overseas empires of the great continental powers and reshaped much of Europe. Against expectations, however, the military-fiscal state survived these traumas. The peace settlement in 1815 entrenched the power of the victors. Liberal voices were raised; conservative responses prevailed. The years down to the middle of the century were characterized by determined attempts to restore the world that existed before 1789. Efforts to dismantle military-fiscal states, though visible and vigorous, were halted in 1848. The reaction that followed ensured that the battle for reform continued for the rest of the century. By 1850, just one major European power, Britain, had achieved significant liberal reform, though only after a long struggle.

After 1815, Britain, the superpower of the day, began to formulate the world's first development program. This was a comprehensive design aimed at promoting international trade, institutional reform, and cultural conversion. The foreign and imperial policies of successive governments reflected the ambivalence of Britain's position as a mercantilist state that was beginning to experiment with policies of freer trade from the 1820s. Mercantilist regulations sheltered modern manufacturing; revenue needs continued to act as an incentive for acquiring taxable territories and establishing formal rule. Simultaneously, policy-makers began to test techniques of informal influence, which were applied to countries that were independent but susceptible to foreign pressures. Technological constraints, however, curbed the penetrative capacity of even the greatest of the Western powers until the second half of the century, when the transition from proto-globalization accelerated. There was, however, one country where conditions favored the new policy: the United States. The Republic became the most important, and also the most neglected, example of Britain's informal influence during the first half of the nineteenth century, and is thus the most deserving of attention.

There is, then, still a story to be told, notwithstanding the extensive and admirable literature that is available on the period under review. It is a story that requires an understanding of how Britain's military-fiscal state sustained Anglo-American relations while also beginning the transition from formal to informal means of influence. The implications of this analysis for understanding the evolution of the United States will be noted at the close of the chapter and explored in the three following chapters, which examine the economic, political, and cultural ties that joined the two countries down to the Civil War.

A GREAT CONVERGENCE?

In its simplest form, the concept of the military-fiscal state describes the transformation of the military potential of states in Western Europe from the fifteenth century onward following the addition of gunpowder to the armory of coercion.[5] Cervantes, writing at the beginning of the seventeenth century, thought that "these devilish engines of artillery" were altering society as well as military capacity.[6] By the mid-eighteenth century, what Gibbon called "the mischievous discovery" had profoundly influenced state structures across Europe.[7] The cost of the new technology and the large armies associated with it meant that monarchs could no longer "live of their own."[8] The pressure to increase revenues obliged governments to create effective bureaucracies, to strike deals with private entrepreneurs by franchising commercial rights, and above all to find ways of ensuring that the central authority secured and retained a monopoly of armed force. The result was a trend toward centralization and "absolutism" within states, and pressure to define external borders and capture taxable potential. Consequently, the gunpowder revolution raised the political stakes, especially for states that were contiguous or within striking distance of each other. Governments that could mobilize the substantial resources needed to invest in artillery and specialized manpower became potential predators; those that failed to keep pace became potential victims. The ensuing arms race was an important element determining state formation and the balance of power in Europe from the sixteenth century onward. Command of the latest means of destruction funded the emergence of the eighteenth-century security state and the creation of clients and satellites among lesser powers that were unable to compete with their fitter rivals.

The search for revenue stimulated territorial expansion, which typically required military support. The principal aim was to annex taxable peasants and trade, both to supplement local sources of revenue and to avoid impositions that would alienate domestic taxpayers, especially landed property owners. States that mastered the new conditions, such as Sweden under Gustavus Adolphus, Russia under Peter the Great, France under Louis XIV, and Prussia under Frederick the Great, became regional powers with pan-European ambitions; smaller states that were unable to compete with the leaders were obliged to seek shelter, either with or from them. Foreign policy, shaped by fiscal capacity, became a gamble on the likely costs and benefits of military action. Victory alone did not guarantee success; costly victories could amplify the budgetary problems they were supposed to solve. Defeat came at an even higher price: depleted resources, increased indebtedness, and loss of prestige. A political economy that subordinated fiscal probity to military needs was programmed to experience recurring crises, which attained devastating proportions at the close of the eighteenth century.

Following the "global turn" in historical studies, the boundaries of research on the history of military-fiscal states have been pushed far beyond Western Europe.[9] The new literature emphasizes the longevity and intimacy of the links between Asia and Europe and identifies similarities in their institutional and entrepreneurial attributes. Research has shown, for example, that China provided the dynamism behind the growth of extensive trade and other relations that connected much of Asia before the "coming of the Europeans," and that subsequent links with the Spanish Empire created a "Pacific complex" that the traditional focus on the Atlantic has long underestimated.[10] An awareness of global connections has encouraged historians to identify broad global resemblances arising from common causes. A comparison of a selection of countries in Europe and Asia has shown that they all experienced administrative centralization, increasing political and cultural integration, commercialization, and territorial expansion in the centuries before 1800.[11] Complementary studies have identified successive waves of rebellions and revolutions that overturned governments from England to China.[12] Specifically, it has been argued that modernity arose from conflict among the military-fiscal states that reached their highest stage of development in the eighteenth century.[13] Confidence in these conclusions has inspired the claim that the conception of a "world crisis between 1760 and 1840 has rapidly gained the status of a testable hypothesis."[14] Whether or not this is the case, the hypothesis has the merit of encouraging historians to cross conventional divisions, most of which derive from the habit of fitting national boundaries on societies that had yet to become nation-states.

The most prominent line of inquiry emerging from these initiatives relates to the debate over what has become known as the "great divergence," which has reappraised the causes and timing of the different development paths taken by Asia (represented principally by China) and Europe (represented principally by Britain).[15] While the debate ranges far beyond considerations of governance, it is generally agreed that state capacity and policy were essential ingredients, whether they contributed to the problem or to the solution. Military-fiscal states have now been associated not only with the Manchus but also with the Mughals, the Ottomans, and the Romanovs, among other candidates, and have provided a basis for comparing political and economic trends in Western Europe with those elsewhere.

Current work explores developments over which both Western and non-Western societies had little or no control, such as demographic and climatic changes and the fortuitous distribution of natural resources.[16] Considered from this position, the great divergence was not the result of the steady accumulation, over many centuries, of exclusive preconditions that were assigned, providentially, to a minuscule fragment of the world, but was a relatively recent development. It appeared at the close of the eighteenth century, manifested itself fully in the nineteenth and twentieth centuries, and is currently giving way to a new era of convergence. The period known as "early modern" is being questioned; the Middle Ages are on course to lose their middle and to age faster than medievalists have traditionally allowed.[17]

Exactly why the divergence occurred at all remains an enigma. One formulation suggests that the growth of population in Europe after 1650 combined with deteriorating climatic conditions produced an energy crisis that led to reduced living standards in the second half of the eighteenth century.[18] These conditions encouraged the development of new sources of energy, especially coal-mining, in regions such as Britain, which had access to the necessary resources. It was this "lucky strike" that finally produced the great divergence. A complementary argument revives the long-standing claim that the main feature distinguishing Europe from Asia was the possession of overseas colonies, which supplied the food needed to overcome the energy deficiency and the wealth needed to support a manufacturing economy.[19] On this view, a largely fortuitous encounter threw out possibilities that enabled parts of Europe to pull ahead of the rest of the world.

These developments present promising opportunities for advancing global history, while also helping to rescue Asia from the "enormous condescension" of Western posterity. However, they also raise questions about the basis of comparison. Evidence establishing similarities among pre-industrial states is accurate only at a high level of generalization. Once the focus is narrowed, important differences appear. It becomes apparent that the genus, "military-fiscal state," produced species with varying resources, governmental structures, policies toward finance, taxation, and debt, and attitudes toward science, technology, and the use of military force that were significant enough to have major causal consequences.[20] It has been argued, for example, that Chinese governments never developed the fiscal capacity needed to mobilize resources for state purposes, though it remains uncertain whether or not this was a conscious choice.[21] A comparative study suggests that Manchus and Mughals established military-fiscal states that could guarantee security without the need to invest permanently in costly military improvements, whereas the rivalries that constantly beset European states compelled them to engage in an arms race that required increasing political centralization and innovative ways of raising revenue.[22] According to this interpretation, the military-fiscal state that was present in Western Europe in the eighteenth century did not appear in China until the nineteenth century, when a combination of internal revolts and external incursions compelled the authorities to institute far-reaching reforms.[23] Similarly, it could be held that the Western version of the military-fiscal state did not reach India until the close of the eighteenth century, when the British army imposed foreign rule and British officials improved the efficiency of the tax-gathering machinery. Once established, imperial military fiscalism had a life span that far outreached its domestic progenitor. Arguably, its legacy is still present in Pakistan.[24]

The appealing clarity of the original notion of military fiscalism has also drawn fire from specialists on European history.[25] While there is broad agreement that the military-fiscal state was the predominant form of political organization in Europe in the eighteenth century, critics have objected to the alleged technological determinism of the argument. The availability of military technology is insufficient to explain its differential adoption, which required political intervention. Political and other economic and social considerations, in turn, may have reversed the direction of causation: favorable institutions and thriving commerce may have been responsible both for the willingness of states to adopt new military hardware and for their ability to do so. The accumulation of research has drawn attention to the considerable diversity of the states mustered under a common label. Centralization did not lead inevitably to absolutism; absolutism was itself a malleable condition; absolutist states were rarely the most efficient means of raising revenue.[26]

Europe's military-fiscal states undoubtedly displayed marked variations in the eighteenth century.[27] Sweden lacked adequate borrowing facilities, relied on subsidies from France and Britain, hired mercenaries when it could afford them, and supplied them to others when it was able to do so.[28] The French military-fiscal state lacked a central budget and denied its "absolutist" monarchs full control over state revenues. The crown had recourse to various expedients, some of them desperate; the government's credit-worthiness was regularly in doubt; lack of funds inhibited the capacity of the French military at crucial moments.[29] Spain's record defies all stereotypes.[30] Spain was neither an absolutist state nor in decline in the eighteenth century. The size of the military was limited; governments distrusted public debt; regional authorities and colonial elites controlled a substantial proportion of total tax revenues. Despite (or because of) these qualities, Spain presided over a rich and dynamic empire.

For current purposes, the most important of the resemblances among European military-fiscal states can be seen in what might be called the "great convergence," which drew the large imperial states toward a common fiscal fate that had far-reaching political repercussions. In the course of the eighteenth century, all the great military-fiscal states ran into serious, and in some cases terminal, difficulties as the cost of the long wars they fought exceeded their financial resources. The Seven Years' War undermined French finances. France lost an empire, spent large sums on building a new navy in the hope of regaining it, and then wrecked her fiscal health by declaring war on Britain in 1778. One consequence was to help the mainland colonies gain their independence; another was to prepare France for its own revolution in 1789. Increasing debt eventually obliged the monarchy to institute fiscal reforms that raised tax levels and imposed new direct taxes on the privileged classes.[31] The political elite fractured; some segments turned against the king; underprivileged taxpayers saw an opportunity and took it.

Spain retained her empire in 1763, but heavy expenditure during the war impelled her to initiate reforms aimed at increasing imperial revenues.[32] Spain, like France, supported the American Revolution and joined the war against Britain in 1779. Unlike France, however, Spain had access to the considerable resources of New Spain, which she exploited effectively.[33] Nevertheless, in 1779 Madrid was forced to raise taxes and increase the national debt. By the close of the century, the drain of funds to meet mounting liabilities had alienated key colonial interest groups, whose resistance to imperial impositions then fueled the movements for independence.[34]

The Dutch, having suffered during the wars with Britain in the seventeenth century, avoided major expenditure for most of the eighteenth century by exchanging combat for neutrality until they, too, decided to support the American rebels. The fourth Anglo-Dutch War, fought between 1780 and 1784, destroyed Dutch naval power, completed the decline of the Dutch East India Company, and greatly weakened the state. The end came with the French Wars, which terminated the independence of the Netherlands and subsequently placed most of the Dutch colonies in British hands.

The success of the American Revolution owed a great deal to the intervention of European imperial powers whose interest lay, not in setting subject peoples free, but in overturning British supremacy.[35] The struggle for paramountcy then turned into the turmoil of the French Wars, which brought down France and Spain, as well as the Netherlands—and left Britain as the only power standing with the prospect of organizing a new international order after 1815.

THE GLORIOUS REVOLUTION, AND THE EXCEPTIONAL MILITARY-FISCAL STATE

The particularities of Europe's military-fiscal states, far from being mere embellishments, had the potential to cause individual countries to diverge from what otherwise might have been a common trajectory. The differences in the case of Britain were sufficient to have shaped its distinctive contribution to political, economic, and imperial development.[36] They account for Britain's survival and continuing expansion while rival European powers fell into decline or disaster. As a military-fiscal state, Britain faced much the same problems as states on the European continent did. Britain, however, produced a uniquely effective response to the political and fiscal problems of the age. Distinctive solutions enabled the newly-United Kingdom to compete successfully with larger, more populous neighboring powers and to extend its influence overseas.[37] Britain, in short, was a military-fiscal state like no other.[38]

Britain was exceptional in achieving a high degree of political centralization and fiscal unity while also managing to curb the absolutist tendencies of ambitious monarchs. By contrast, the majority of European military-fiscal states were ruled by dynasties that were largely unconstrained by parliamentary controls and had yet to achieve the same degree of fiscal unity. In this respect, the compact nature of the state was an advantage in assisting effective government and efficient tax-gathering.[39] Parliament held ultimate control over the nation's purse and used its authority to squeeze more revenue per head from its generally compliant citizenry than other European states managed to do. The division of power between the monarch and parliament contained areas of uncertainty that took time to clarify. Nevertheless, dissent was kept within bounds: memories of the Civil War, fears of Stuart pretensions, and the imperative of upholding the creditworthiness of the government restrained the ambitions of wilder members of the political elite. In France, on the other hand, Louis XV could never be quite sure of either his nobles or his credit.[40]

Although the American rebels eventually condemned George III's impositions as acts of tyranny, before the Revolution they shared Montesquieu's opinion that Britain was the freest of nations. Voltaire thought that "the English are the only people on earth who have been able to prescribe limits to the power of kings by resisting them."[41] Diderot, who criticized Britain's policy toward the mainland colonies, nevertheless judged that the constitution established after the Glorious Revolution was "the happiest possible outcome" because "there liberty has ended in triumph."[42] Johann Archenholz, a Prussian soldier and historian who lived in England in the 1770s, provided a fulsome summary of Anglophile opinion by proclaiming that Britain had been elevated to "one of the first powers in the world by bravery, wealth, liberty, and the happy consequences of an excellent political system."[43]

Britain was distinctive, too, in having a highly productive capitalist agriculture, substantial manufacturing output, extensive foreign and colonial commercial ties, an efficient distribution system, and an unrivaled financial sector.[44] These features were present long before industrialization transformed the economy. By the mid-eighteenth century, the economy had evolved to the point where handicrafts, which supplied the bulk of manufactured goods for both domestic and overseas markets, accounted for as much as one-third of the labor force; services for only slightly less; agriculture for only slightly more.[45] Since manufactures required markets overseas as well as at home, important segments of the service sector became specialized in international finance and distribution. The expanding overseas commitment provides the context for understanding the great imperial events of the eighteenth century, which were already under way when Smith produced *The Wealth of Nations* in 1776—coincidentally in the same year as Gibbon's *Decline and Fall* and the Declaration of Independence.

The military component of the British fiscal state also differed from its continental neighbors in being heavily weighted toward the navy rather than the army.[46] Other states, of course, maintained navies, but none spent as much as Britain did in preparing for war at sea. By 1795, the fleet had two and a half times the tonnage it had in 1705; by 1805, Britain's navy was the largest and most powerful in the world.[47] Naval demands stimulated the economy by boosting shipbuilding, the armaments industry, ships' chandlers, and sectors of agriculture that served ports and supplied provisions for the fleet.[48] The strategy that defended the British Isles also placed them in an unrivaled position to encompass the world. The navy, moreover, followed the Greek tradition in embodying the defense of liberty.[49] Armies, on the other hand, were more readily associated with Rome's imperial reach as well as with the capacity to enter the citadels of power. Appropriately, colonial armies represented the full might of Britain's military-fiscal state in India and North America.

The Glorious Revolution, once seen as the source of Britain's distinctive progressive qualities, has lost some of its luster.[50] One branch of revisionist scholarship holds that it fails to qualify as a revolution because it was undertaken to defend the existing Protestant order and thus to preserve the status quo rather than to change it.[51] According to this account, success in 1688 perpetuated an *ancien régime* that survived until the 1830s. This interpretation complements studies of intellectual history that have emphasized how conservative political theorists drew on classical thinking to fend off radical change and reinforce political stability.[52] Advocates revived classical ideals of civic virtue to provide a moral code that was designed to restore coherence and order to a society that had experienced the upheaval of civil war and remained on the brink of instability. Other critics, taking a view beyond intellectual history, have drawn attention to important fiscal and naval reforms undertaken after the Civil War that anticipated changes traditionally associated with the Revolution of 1688.[53]

A vigorous post-revisionist reaction to these views reasserts the importance of the Revolution in determining economic policy.[54] According to this position, the Revolution was primarily a struggle between two different conceptions of modernity. James II and William III appear as modernizers who wanted to build a strong, centralized state but had different conceptions of its character. James aimed to restore absolutism; William, though no democrat, favored a more participatory state. Tories who backed James held the traditional position that value derived from land. Whigs who supported William adopted John Locke's argument that labor was the source of wealth. James appealed to large landowners who also wanted to retain protective tariffs, while supporters of the Revolution favored commerce, manufactures, financial institutions, and freer trade. Both views had implications for Britain's role in the wider world. If wealth was based on land, a fixed resource, overseas policy ought to aim for territorial acquisition; if prospects for increasing trade were limited, assertive mercantilist policies were needed to secure as much of it as possible. On the other hand, if commerce was the product of mobile labor and nimble entrepreneurship, there was considerable potential for growth. Accordingly, policy should aim to expand overseas trade without necessarily tying it to territorial aggrandizement or mercantilist restrictions.

Each of these standpoints illuminates important dimensions of the Glorious Revolution. Neither, however, can be accepted without qualification. An emphasis on the centrality of religion and other intellectual influences is achieved at the cost of minimizing the role of other considerations, not least financial innovation and, later, the Industrial Revolution. The claim that the century was marked by the persistence of an ancien régime underplays the extent to which *les anciens* both adapted to and promoted change. On the other hand, to identify some of the material antecedents of the Revolution is not necessarily to diminish the significance of the event itself, while to claim that William of Orange and James II were both "modernizers" is to suggest, however inadvertently, that they were anticipating ideas that were not expressed as policy goals until the nineteenth century. The distinction between land and labor is too sharp to capture the reality that value arose from combining both factors of production, as Whig magnates and Tory gentry surely understood. The association of Tories with mercantilism and Whigs with free, or at least freer, trade runs into the comparable problem that the difference was one of emphasis at best: mercantilist regulations prevailed throughout the century because all parties recognized their value in meeting essential strategic and revenue needs and in conciliating powerful interests. Moreover, as Adam Smith himself acknowledged, mercantilism had promoted commercial expansion. Even as late as 1846, Sir Robert Peel split his party and wrecked his career by taking a different view.

The innovations associated with the Glorious Revolution were nourished by a society that had yet to incorporate the assumption that cumulative economic development was a norm. Capitalist enterprise, though everywhere in evidence, had still to transform the rural basis of society. The industrial "revolution" escaped even Adam Smith's eagle eye for the very good reason that, at the time of his death in 1790, steam-powered, machine production had only just been introduced. Agriculture remained the matrix within which all other activity was set, at least until the second quarter of the nineteenth century. The privileged landed oligarchy that ran Britain presided over a society with massive social and regional inequalities. The new "monied men" in the City of London won gentlemanly status and access to political influence because they provided vital support for the political system. Directly or indirectly, everyone battled with the seasons, the uncontrollable determinants of economic life, which influenced consumption, revenue, civil order, life, and death. For the majority of the population, life itself remained short; for some it was nasty and brutal too.

After 1688, Britain became, not a welfare state, but a warfare state in a century noted for its devastating wars.[55] Expenditure on defense accounted for a large and increasing share of the national budget throughout the eighteenth century and had wide-ranging repercussions on the domestic economy.[56] If the continental commitment weakened from the 1760s, as George III became fully indigenized, the wars that accompanied imperial expansion kept large numbers of troops overseas, not least because the monarch was anxious to demonstrate the extent of his patriotic commitment to Britain.[57] Indeed, the price of victory in the Seven Years' War was the need to find the means of controlling the extensive new territories added to the empire in North America and India. Accordingly, securing the revenue to meet military expenditure remained a priority for successive governments, irrespective of their political preferences. Continuing fears that the king might use compulsion to dispense with parliamentary restraints ensured that the army remained small in peacetime but expanded to meet the demands of war. By the end of the French Wars, the British army contained a total of 250,000 troops, though this number was less than half the size of Napoleon's *Grande Armée.*

In the course of the century, Britain evolved from being a set of small offshore islands on the edge of Europe to becoming the manager of a global mercantilist system that encompassed an expanding empire.[58] It has long been established that mercantilism was neither an abstract theory nor a fixed commercial practice inherited from the Middle Ages, but a contested and evolving set of regulations that grew in range and complexity in the second half of the seventeenth century and throughout the eighteenth century.[59] The aim of commercial regulation was to raise revenue to fund the state and reward its principal supporters. Bargaining among key interest groups produced rent-sharing agreements: governments acquired income from the sale of monopolies; merchants profited from the protection they gained.[60] By the time Adam Smith penned his famous critique of monopolies in 1776, mercantilism shaped all aspects of overseas commerce: the Navigation Acts nurtured English shipping and encouraged a cluster of related investments; an array of import tariffs generated revenue and sheltered domestic manufactures; the East India Company, the most visible symbol of monopolistic restraints on trade, dominated Britain's interests in India and China.[61]

These developments made Britain unique among European powers and placed a distinctive and an enduring imprint on international policy, the economy, and public attitudes. Overseas trade grew at an increasing pace: the value of Britain's exports increased nearly eightfold between 1699 and 1701, and 1772 and 1774, and by the close of the century had become a significant component of national income.[62] The rising trend was accompanied by a dramatic change in Britain's main trading partners: in 1700, Britain conducted about 85 percent of its total trade with continental Europe; by 1800 the figure had fallen to about 25 percent.[63]

The majority of Britain's imports came from the West Indies and Asia, followed by North America; most of its exports went to North America and the West Indies, followed by Asia.[64] The need to settle the balance of payments by using surpluses earned in the New World to cancel deficits with Asia gave Britain a long-term commitment to influencing, and if possible managing, the international order. A combination of financial innovation and mercantilist regulations enhanced the dominance of London, which remained the principal center of finance, commercial services, and overseas trade throughout the century and beyond, notwithstanding the expansion of provincial ports, such as Bristol and Liverpool. The Atlantic colonies provided protected markets for British manufactures, led by woolens and metal goods; supplied otherwise unobtainable items of consumption, such as sugar and tobacco; and gave a huge boost to the financial and service sectors.[65] Britain's grip on the trade in tropical imports also enabled it to dominate the reexport trade to continental Europe, and thereby bypass the protective tariffs that hampered exports of manufactured goods.

Public revenues increased commensurately throughout the century. They underpinned the state by providing most of the funds needed to service the public debt and by financing the eight major wars that Britain fought between 1689 and 1815.[66] In the century down to the French Wars, indirect taxes (mainly excise and stamp duties) supplied about 75 percent of all tax revenues.[67] Most of the liability fell on goods and services produced for domestic consumption and on the mass of the population. Shipping, exports of services, and a large number of manufactures destined for overseas markets escaped taxation in conformity with the mercantilist principle of aiming for a favorable balance of trade. By 1789, British citizens had the highest per capita tax burden in Europe. The regressive character of the system remained unchanged until 1793, when war with France obliged the Prime Minister, William Pitt, to tax the wealthy.[68] As he put it in 1795: "In a war for the protection of property it was just and equitable that property should bear the burden"—or at least a small part of it.[69] Necessity, not a concern for equality, fathered this invention, too.

Additional needs were met by borrowing, which held down the land tax, reconciled the landed oligarchy to fiscal innovation, and enabled the "monied" men of the City to win social acceptance as well as great wealth.[70] By the beginning of the Seven Years' War, Britain was able to raise long-term loans of unspecified duration by issuing government stock, and to meet short-term needs by selling Treasury bills. The success of these devices was apparent: government issues were well-subscribed;

interest rates remained low; inflows of foreign investment showed that confidence in the British credit system had spread abroad. The pound sterling, though under pressure at moments of wartime emergency, remained steady; confidence in the stability of Britain's political system held firm, despite the profound anxieties that accompanied the long years of war.

An older orthodoxy held that these distinctive attributes came together, whether fortuitously or through a series of striking technological innovations and judicious political decisions, to produce the world's first industrial revolution, which in some formulations became a proxy for what is now summarized as "modernization."[71] Recent thinking has given plausibility to the idea that development prospects were indeed more favorable in Britain than they were elsewhere in Europe.[72] The only comparable state, the Dutch Republic, which pioneered a number of innovations that Britain developed subsequently, was unable to sustain its position in the eighteenth century.[73] Fortunately, the vast literature on this equally vast and enigmatic problem lies beyond the subject matter of the present chapter.[74] To avoid misunderstanding, however, it should be noted that the claims made here about Britain's exceptional qualities as a military-fiscal state are independent of any larger assertions about their connections to the industrial revolution or modernization.[75] What can be said, in relation to the present context, is that mercantilism can no longer be dismissed as being an unqualified drag on development.[76] Colonial trade, in conjunction with exports of British goods and services, was vital in helping Britain to fund the massive resources needed for the French Wars, to dispense with foreign borrowing, and to exchange its status as a net debtor to that of a net creditor in the 1790s.[77]

Whether "Glorious" or not, the Revolution of 1688 deserves to retain its title as a label for events that had a decisive influence on the course of British history. It did more than merely accelerate reforms that were already under way. The decision to remove James II was vital to the aim of making the monarch accountable to parliament, as well as to safeguarding the Protestant succession. The accession of foreign-born monarchs gave Britain a commitment to continental Europe that influenced foreign policy throughout the century—and beyond.[78] The obligation compelled parliament to find permanent means of replacing the hand-to-mouth expedients that had traditionally provided short-term finance for the needs of state. The Bank of England and the national debt were founded after the Revolution and not before; the development of the stock market, improved means of payment through currency reform and bills of exchange, and the rise of private institutions, such as insurance companies, all followed. The prospect of war with larger neighbors encouraged Britain to strengthen its defenses, initially by extending the military-fiscal state to Scotland and Ireland, and later in the century by tapping the overseas empire for additional revenues. The Revolution confirmed the Protestant ascendancy in Ireland and the mainland colonies, and endorsed the dominance of the Presbyterian Church of Scotland, which opened the door to Union with England in 1707.[79] These institutional innovations transformed Britain's fiscal and financial prospects from the 1690s and set public finance on a secure, long-term footing.[80] They underpinned the Revolution settlement, funded an assertive foreign policy, facilitated domestic transactions, and made the City of London a world financial center.[81] The authors of these far-reaching institutional innovations were not planning to deliver modernity in their time. What they were doing, though this, too, is unlikely to have been a blueprint for the century, was to bring the military-fiscal state to its highest stage of development.

THE EVOLUTION OF BRITAIN'S MILITARY-FISCAL STATE

The crisis that shook imperial Britain in the closing decades of the eighteenth century had its roots in the settlement that followed the events of 1688. As the new order unfolded, it affected, and to a degree incorporated, increasing numbers of citizens, regions, and eventually continents. The chosen path was precarious. Blackstone's description of a "polite and commercial people" applied to the manners of the upper class, who set standards for those below them, and identified the sense of deference and compliance that enabled British governments to extract so much tax from so many underprivileged citizens.[82] The belief that the Augustan Age was one of social tranquility and political stability, however, no longer fits the findings of research.[83] Urbane classicism contrasted with urban dissent; regional movements for political reform spilled over the boundaries of deference and compliance.

Discontent took various forms and had correspondingly varied causes. What can be said, however, is that the fiscal innovations embedded by the Glorious Revolution and the wars they facilitated were directly or indirectly implicated and became more contentious as the century advanced.[84] Questions of revenue, tax, and expenditure touched all aspects of society. They stimulated a long-running discussion of the consequences of extending credit, and its corollary, debt, that stretched far beyond the square mile of the City of London. The provinces were drawn into the new fiscal system, as were Scotland, Ireland, the West Indies, and the mainland colonies.[85] The chief concern, especially after the Seven Years' War, was the state of public finances, particularly the national debt.[86] As the debt rose to unprecedented levels and tax rates increased, public reactions became more overt and more assertive. From the 1770s, too, the expansion of private credit coupled with increasing numbers of bankruptcies enlarged the frame of reference and ensured that fiscal and financial issues remained at the forefront of party politics and public discussion.[87]

An aversion to taxation, criticism of corruption at the heart of government, and hostility to the threat of a well-funded and overbearing state were highly developed British sentiments in the eighteenth century. Taxation was an especially sensitive subject because it had the potential to challenge government by oligarchy. In 1689, the Bill of Rights had established the principle that the taxation of British subjects required the consent of a representative parliament. In doing so, it opened the way to fresh interpretations of the concept of representation and thus raised unsettling constitutional issues. Contemporaries also viewed finance and money as matters of ethics and religious principle. The association of debt with moral decay and the corrosion of the organic unity of society was not easily shed; the taint of the usurer who "cometh between the bark and the tree" persisted. Literature and poetry were full of references to these questions, which commentators regarded as penetrating to the heart of society.[88]

Despite the oligarchic character of the Hanoverian ruling elite, the political nation spoke with many voices and was able to make them heard. The electorate was larger, more diverse, and more involved than was once thought. The high politics of the time were expressions not only of interests but also of principles.[89] Party allegiances counted, even if they were fluid.[90] At the outset of the period, Whigs, who drew support from large landowners and the new "monied" interest, were committed defenders of the Glorious Revolution and the Protestant succession, and advocates of religious toleration. Tories, who represented a large section of the smaller gentry, were associated with High Church Anglicanism and included some who sympathized with the Stuart cause. Following the Revolution, the Whigs regained control of the East India Company, which James II had planned to use as a means of extracting revenues from the empire. Whig managers won over important merchants, who were previously designated interlopers, and found places for them in a new East India Company, which merged with its older rival in 1709.[91] The amalgamation enlarged a monopoly, but one under the eye of parliament rather than the control of the king.

The settlement that followed the Glorious Revolution aroused strong opposition, provoked widespread controversy, and carried significant political risks. Whigs and Tories competed to impose different interpretations of its legacy; Jacobites, supported by France, planned to subvert it. The outcome of the Revolution evoked a powerful response from segments of the landed interest who feared that old money would give way to new and that political power would migrate from the trusted to the untried. Critics claimed that assertive mercantilism would lead to dangerous foreign entanglements and unnecessary wars. Uncontrollable budgetary deficits would destabilize the state and result in authoritarian rule, which would destroy civil liberties and erode the moral basis of society. The mounting cost of the War of the Spanish Succession (1701–1714) confirmed their fears. The ensuing reaction installed a Tory government in 1710 and led to the Treaty of Utrecht in 1713, which brought the war to an end.

The Tories' moment passed almost as soon as it appeared. The accession of George I in 1714 returned the Whigs to power; the Jacobite rising in the same year discredited the Tories, innocent and compromised alike, and ensured their exclusion from government. The large Whig landowners and their allies in the City of London proceeded to implement policies that kept them in power for several decades.[92] A network of patronage delivered electoral support; the City supplied public credit; the tax burden shifted from the land to the mass of consumers. An expansive commercial policy, supported by a well-funded navy, opened markets across the world. The East India Company's shareholders, who included an influential parliamentary contingent and valuable connections at court, oiled the wheels of government while benefiting from the company's commercial monopoly and their own limited liability. The company's small but well-directed organization in London was complemented by looser arrangements abroad, where official agents shared markets with franchised private traders, including some who were backed by the City of London.[93] With all its faults, later pilloried as "Old Corruption," Walpole's plutocratic "system" held the country together and provided the political stability and confidence that encouraged economic growth.[94]

The realization that Walpole's Whigs were close to installing their version of the Glorious Revolution prompted critics to reformulate the politics of opposition. The opportunity gave Henry St. John, Viscount Bolingbroke, formerly an ultra-Tory partisan, both voice and influence.[95] Bolingbroke was a senior but erratic politician and erstwhile Jacobite who fled to France after the rebellion of 1715, but was later readmitted to the royal circle. On his return, he positioned himself as the champion of the landed interest and its privileges, irrespective of party affiliations. The danger, as he saw it, was that Walpole's effective political organization would destroy Britain's essentially rural order and the political stability it underwrote. Bolingbroke formed what became known as the "country party" to challenge the Whig oligarchy, its "monied," mercantile supporters, and its foreign policy, which in his view departed from the principles of 1688. To achieve his purpose, Bolingbroke formulated novel principles that were to become durable features of the political system: the idea that governments needed a permanent opposition to safeguard liberty, and the notion of a "patriot king" who would stand above party and act in the interests of the whole kingdom.[96]

Beyond Westminster and Whitehall, those who were "virtually" represented by their betters were also capable of representing themselves and did so, despite punitive deterrents symbolized by the Game Laws and the Riot Act. Hardship, brought about by food shortages, unemployment, and tax increases, was one powerful incentive to protest; resentment at impressment and service in the militia was another; a miscellany of other frustrations, from smuggling to turnpike tolls, extended the list. The excise crisis was an early indication of the extent and effectiveness of dissent "from below."[97] In 1733, Walpole thought that he could conciliate landowners by shifting the tax burden toward consumers without suffering immediate political consequences because only a minority of those affected had the right to vote. This was a miscalculation. The response to what Dr. Johnson described in his *Dictionary* as "a hateful tax levied upon commodities" was immediate and vociferous. Tradesmen and consumers demonstrated their displeasure; parliament was swamped with petitions; the proposed tax was quickly withdrawn. Although Walpole managed to secure reelection in the following year, his majority was greatly reduced and his credibility damaged. The episode was an early indication of difficulties that were to multiply after the Seven Years' War, when the issues of taxation and parliamentary reform became permanent as well as highly contentious.

Governments, even in an undemocratic polity, had to take account of party differences and bear in mind that "the condition of the people" mattered. They also had to remain alert to threats, real and prospective, from beyond the political nation. France and "popery" were dangers and at times obsessions that came together in the Jacobite rebellions of 1715 and 1745, and remained powerful enough to spark the Gordon Riots in 1780, when "King Mob" also took the opportunity to strike blows at the Bank of England, Newgate Prison, and the Fleet. Although the great majority of the population decided against returning to Roman Catholicism, the Anglican Church and its supporters were challenged by the growth of dissenting denominations, led by Methodists, from the 1730s onward. The Great Awakening, which encompassed the American colonies, as well as parts of continental Europe, presented a pacific but increasingly effective challenge to orthodoxy. Even if the established political and religious hierarchy remained unreformed, the spiritual life of the nation could still be cleansed and emancipated.

The Whig supremacy depended on matching the costs of unavoidable wars in Europe to resources provided by taxation and borrowing. Taxation had to be held at levels that would fall short of provoking protest and resistance; borrowing added to the national debt and aroused political opposition. In principle, the needs of opulence and defense could be reconciled; in practice, too many variables were involved to allow the outcome to be calculated. Harvests were unpredictable; global trade was risky; warfare wrecked fiscal planning. What is certain is that the stakes rose as the century advanced. Taxation reached protest point; the national debt reached record levels. In the second half of the century, the English provinces felt the full weight of the new fiscal system, as did Scotland, Ireland, the West Indies, and the mainland colonies.[98] Moreover, the continuing expansion of private credit accompanied by increasing numbers of bankruptcies enlarged the frame of reference and ensured that financial questions remained at the forefront of party politics and public discussion.[99] The incipient crisis was made manifest by a period of almost continuous warfare, which began in 1739 and culminated in the Seven Years' War (1756–1763).[100] The demands of war finance strained the interlocking elements of Walpole's political system, brought the long period of Whig dominance to an end, and found full expression in the conflict with the mainland colonies, which is explored in chapter 3.

THE NEW GLOBAL ORDER

Contemporaries were well aware that the great events taking place around them had global ramifications.[101] Impressions of the world beyond Britain, though often hazy and invariably imperfect, nevertheless reflected the growing volume of information gathered, recorded, and reported in the course of the century.[102] People, trade, and ideas were on the move in the eighteenth century to an astonishing extent, despite the fact that the age had yet to contemplate the marvels of telegraphs, steamships, and submarine cables. The questing, classifying curiosity of the Enlightenment drove European adventurers and scientists to the outer reaches of the world and into regions tentatively mapped but little explored. Reciprocally, the discovery of new flora, fauna, and people contributed to the Enlightenment by inspiring new thinking and extending its range.[103] Empires were the ubiquitous agents of this process. Whether as sponsors, pioneers, or facilitators, they helped to create a truly global Enlightenment.

The discovery of diversity encouraged a quest for unity. Carl Linnaeus's exploration of Lapland in 1732 laid the foundation for his celebrated system of plant classification; Alexander von Humboldt's extensive travels through South America in 1799–1804 produced the first full account of the continent's geography, climate, and resources. Linnaeus devised a unified, hierarchical taxonomy that in principle was applicable globally. Von Humboldt's major work, appropriately entitled *Cosmos* (1845–1862), treated the universe as a set of interacting units that integrated science and culture. Knowledge of all kinds spread internationally among Europe's political classes and intellectuals, and to a limited but increasing extent beyond them. The growth of the public sphere promoted wider discussion of the issues of the day.[104] The circulation of printed material in the vernacular increased, as did the custom of public debate and the sites of concourse, which ranged from coffeehouses to literary societies and political clubs.

By 1750, the empire had turned London into a cosmopolitan center, where City bankers and merchants from continental Europe collaborated and competed with their English equivalents.[105] London, the imperial hub, also helped to make the empire cosmopolitan: by the middle of the century nearly one-third of the population of the mainland colonies originated outside England, principally in Scotland and Ireland. Knowledge of different parts of the empire, however fragmentary, also circulated among its constituents. American colonists were aware that they were part of a global empire and were keen consumers of Indian (and Chinese) goods, though by the 1770s they had concluded that annexations in India were corrupting Britain and were likely to have a similar effect on the Atlantic empire.[106] Overseas connections spread far beyond the boundaries of the British Empire. Informal links with other European empires, supplemented by private networks that extended into independent states, created a global system of communications that was as extensive as the technology of the time allowed.[107] Before the close of the century, Jeremy Bentham was already thinking in global terms as he worked toward creating a "universal jurisprudence."[108]

Unprecedented global flows, combined with the upheaval brought by war and revolution, compelled contemporaries to reappraise the changing character of the world around them.[109] The term "empire" was enlarged in the course of the eighteenth century to refer not only to a sovereign state and a single community, even one "writ large," but also to the increasingly diverse lands Britain ruled overseas.[110] The acquisition of new territories raised fundamental questions of authority.[111] Was sovereignty indivisible, as Blackstone theorized and Burke argued, or could it be adapted to create a form of integrated union, as Smith speculated, or even devolved, as Hume was inclined to think?[112] According to Blackstone, divided sovereignty was a recipe for anarchy; according to Hume, it was a solution to problems that, if left unattended, would produce the same result. These questions applied to the newly united kingdom as well as to the colonies because the status of both remained uncertain. Union with Scotland was recent and still contested. Ireland was neither fish nor fowl. The constitutional standing of the colonies remained ambiguous in crucial respects.[113] Britain was an imperial state but had yet to become a nation-state with clearly defined subordinate colonies. Questions respecting political affiliations, rights, and duties applied to the home countries as well as to distant colonies, which is why the empire needs to be considered as an entity if issues of sovereignty are to be understood.

The extension of British rule overseas inevitably led to a consideration of the desirability of imperial expansion. Advocates of assertive expansion, such as William Pitt, the Elder, stressed not only the material advantages and patriotic merits of strengthening the institutions of state, but also moral duty, whether to spread "liberty," Protestantism, or more generally what was later called "improvement." In the eyes of William Robertson, among others, overseas expansion was providentially ordained because only Europe had achieved the level of civilization needed for the task.[114] Opponents emphasized the damaging consequences, at home and abroad, of extending the empire. The implication of Gibbon's great work was that unchecked expansion eventually led to militarism, despotic rule, corruption, and decadence. Smith echoed these concerns; Hume became convinced; Burke put the case into political form; Bentham carried the message into the nineteenth century; continental luminaries, such as Diderot and Kant, gave similar views powerful expression.[115] On this interpretation, the material benefits of empire were limited, where they existed at all, and were far outweighed by the cost of allowing degenerate influences to sap the health of the home country.

Although discussions of sovereignty and analyses of empire are commonly traced to their intellectual origins, they also drew on two proximate material sources, Scotland and Ireland, which exemplified the expansion, in different imperial forms, of the military-fiscal state.[116]

Burke's distinctive contribution to the debates on America and India owed much to the fact that he began life effectively as a colonial subject.[117] He was born in Ireland and grew up in Dublin but was also an Anglican who made his career in England. His perspective on the issues of the day, like his accent, reminded his audience that the empire began at home before it became a global enterprise. The Union of the Kingdoms in 1707 (following the Union of the Two Crowns in 1603) joined Scotland and England. The conquest of Ireland in 1649–1653 gave England effective control of the island; the suppression of the Jacobite rebellion in 1691 confirmed it.[118] These events stimulated a long-running debate about the morality of colonial rule, techniques of management, attitudes toward subject peoples, and the costs and benefits of empire, all of which were carried forward and applied to annexations made overseas in the nineteenth and twentieth centuries.[119] Neither Scotland nor Ireland provided an exact template for future colonial rule; between them, however, they covered the options.

Scotland served as a model for colonies that were acquired principally by negotiation and depended on local magnates to manage indigenous populations.[120] The Act of Union was as much a bargain as an imposition.[121] Scots gave up their parliament and their independence in matters of foreign policy, but gained representation in Westminster and retained key legal, financial, educational, and religious institutions. Britain increased the market for its goods and eliminated the worrying prospect that Scotland might enter an alliance with France. The administration of the Act was facilitated by a new generation of intermediaries, such as the enterprising government contractor, Sir Lawrence Dundas, who spotted opportunities and knew how to take them.[122] Scottish landowners were confirmed in their property rights; Scottish merchants gained from free trade with England and the empire. The East India Company insisted on retaining its monopoly and ensured that the Company of Scotland Trading to Africa and the Indies was dissolved; in exchange, the Company opened its doors to Scottish merchants.[123] The English woolen industry also took care to protect its interests; Scottish entrepreneurs responded by developing complementary manufactures. Anglicization went far enough to produce a top echelon of political and business leaders but not so far as to provoke a militant reaction among the population at large. Political subordination was consistent with a continuing sense of Scottish identity and indeed helped to strengthen it.[124] Cultural union was facilitated by a shared commitment to Protestantism, which expressed itself in Scotland's overwhelmingly loyal response to the Jacobite rebellions of 1715 and 1745, and later to the American Revolution.[125] Economic union was reinforced by a joint interest in the empire, which enterprising Scots developed through settlement, business, and the professions.[126] Scotland's notable contribution to the armed services, an uncompromising manifestation of its support of the Union, made it the Punjab of the north.[127] The sense of "Britishness" that emerged in the second half of the century owed much to a common Anglo-Scottish commitment to the Glorious Revolution and the opportunities it created, even though the English component was the dominant one.[128] Faith, monarchy, and empire continued to hold Scotland to the Union throughout the colonial era.

The colorful history of the Johnstone family, whose home was in Eskdale, Dumfriesshire, illustrates how readily well-placed Scots grasped the opportunities created by Union and empire.[129] Sir James Johnstone, who became the third baronet in 1727, was the head of an ancient family but one burdened by debts attached to Westerhall, the family estate. Status and antiquity, however, gave the family two privileged resources: education, which enabled junior members to join the "unprosperous" professions, and "name recognition," which provided access to influential connections.[130] James and his wife, Barbara, who came from an undistinguished branch of the Scottish aristocracy, had fourteen children, eleven of whom survived to adulthood in the 1740s and 1750s. By midcentury, when the children began to make their way, the collapse of the Jacobite rebellion had confirmed the security of the Union, and the impending defeat of France was about to ensure Britain's dominance in British North America and rule over large swaths of India. The new generation of Johnstones helped to speed the process of imperial globalization that, reciprocally, shaped their lives in ways that could scarcely have been imagined half a century earlier.

The Johnstones became entrepreneurs of the new imperial age, capitalizing on their connections and building a global network based on what was, literally, an extended family. Several of the seven brothers built careers in the army or navy. One, Alexander, served in North America, reached the rank of colonel, and bought a sugar plantation in Grenada and, with it, several hundred slaves. Three brothers made their way to India. The most successful, John, made his fortune as a merchant and tax collector for the East India Company before returning to Scotland, where he became a northern nabob complete with Indian servants, and, appropriately, a member of parliament (M.P.) too.[131] William Johnstone, who was one of Adam Smith's most talented students, became a successful lawyer, but outshone his siblings by making a spectacular marriage.

His union with Frances Pulteney, an English heiress, made him, reputedly, the richest commoner in England, as well as one of the leading investors in North America.

William and his nabob brother, John, hit the jackpot. Union with England opened the road south; imperial expansion revealed even wider vistas. The success of the two brothers supported other members of the family and kept the estate at Westerhall afloat. Their four sisters also made their marks. Two of them, Barbara and Margaret, parted from the Johnstone tradition of loyalty to the Union by supporting the Jacobite cause. Betty and Charlotte, however, remained in Scotland, where they led lives that were less flamboyant than those of their sisters but of greater consequence. Betty, who was unmarried, ran the family "business" from its headquarters at Westerhall for much of her long life, which stretched from 1728 to 1813. Charlotte assisted her until her marriage and early death in 1773. The sisters wrote innumerable letters reporting military and commercial information, galvanizing existing connections and generating new ones, and ensuring that the Johnstone global network continued to hum. The Johnstones exemplify, as well as any single family can, the great events of the age: its constant warfare, expanding commercial prospects, fluctuating imperial fortunes, and political hazards. In 1759, Adam Smith commented that "the industry of mankind" had "entirely changed the face of the globe."[132] The Johnstones, to adapt Marx and Engels, played "a most revolutionary part" in the process.[133]

Ireland, on the other hand, was a colony of conquest populated by settlers from the mainland who dispossessed indigenous landowners.[134] Like Scotland, Ireland was brought into the military-fiscal state but the terms of incorporation were different, apart from the fact that both countries were denied an independent foreign policy. Religious affiliation had a determinative influence on attitudes and policy. London viewed Ireland's Roman Catholics, the majority of the population, as being disloyal and incipiently rebellious, and treated them accordingly.[135] Penal laws enforced discrimination, which was validated by an image of Ireland as a country that was backward to the point of barbarity. Absentee landlords and limited export opportunities constrained development and provoked rural protests; political and economic discrimination stoked resentment among both Catholic and Protestant elites.

Although the Irish parliament survived, its legislative scope was limited, and the Lord Lieutenant of Ireland (also known, prophetically, as the Viceroy) exercised power in much the same way as a colonial governor. The Lord Lieutenant's intermediaries enjoyed commensurate status and power, though none of the "new men" could match the wealth and influence of William Conolly, who far outdistanced his counterpart in Scotland, Lawrence Dundas.[136] Conolly was a man of the times, if not for all seasons. His father, Patrick, converted to Anglicanism; William became a Whig. He was visibly on the right side of the Glorious Revolution, which he celebrated by buying, at sale prices, lands confiscated from the supporters of James II. In due course he became Speaker of the Irish House of Commons and Revenue Commissioner. At his death in 1729, he was reputed to be the richest man in Ireland.

During his time in office, Conolly instituted improvements in tax-gathering that were carried forward after his death. Ireland and Scotland performed different fiscal functions. Whereas Scotland was a recruiting ground for the British army, Ireland supplied the revenues that paid for a large proportion of the army garrisoned on the island.[137] The scale and reach of the state increased as the century advanced. The Irish national debt was established in 1716 largely to help pay for the garrison; per capita tax revenues rose thereafter. Most taxes derived from customs duties because consumer expenditure was too limited to yield the sums required. However, unlike Scotland, Ireland suffered from the Navigation Acts, which discriminated against her exports and restricted tax revenues from overseas trade. Pressure for reform in Ireland built up from the 1760s, just as it did in England and the mainland colonies. The American Revolution strengthened the hand of Irish reformers and obliged the British government to concede greater degrees of free trade and legislative independence in the 1770s and 1780s, and to reduce substantially the discrimination suffered by Roman Catholics. Given that these reforms were designed to uphold British rule, they could never satisfy the republican movement, which gathered strength in the 1790s and mounted a nationwide rebellion against British dominance in 1798.

The American Revolution, when it came, was a challenge from afar that will be discussed in chapter 3. The prospective Irish Revolution was in Britain's backyard. It was also more radical. As the United States turned away from the ideals of the French Revolution in the 1790s, Ireland turned toward them. The British government, at war with France, took no chances. The rebellion was suppressed with great force. The Act of Union, which confirmed Britain's suzerainty, followed in 1801.[138] Scots found Union sufficiently malleable and advantageous for it to survive the end of empire.[139] Large numbers of rural poor, faced with dispossession, rising population, and limited opportunities, took the exit option and emigrated. Scots went willingly to the empire; Irish took refuge in a friendly republic, the United States.[140]

WAR, RECONSTRUCTION, AND REFORM

The military-fiscal states that carried proto-globalization to its highest point of development in the late eighteenth century suffered widespread damage from revolutionary movements and extended warfare between 1776 and 1815. The wounds, however, were not fatal. The survivors limped into the nineteenth century; fractured remnants began to assemble a future. To the representatives of conservative and authoritarian forms of government, the end of the French Wars was an opportunity to reestablish the pre-revolutionary order; to liberal reformers and radicals, it was the moment to carry forward or initiate changes that would transform politics and society.

The reconstructed military-fiscal states and their imperial extensions reached their zenith with Napoleon Bonaparte, who developed a form of populist absolutism that advertised freedom but exercised imperial rule. The empire he created in Europe, though short-lived, has been neglected by historians of imperialism, just as historians of France studying Napoleon's empire have generally bypassed the wider literature on Europe's expansion overseas.[141] Yet, Napoleon demonstrated, with military decisiveness, how a republic could become an empire. He personified Hegel's "Hero," promoted an imperial cult that elevated martial values, assigned power to himself, and justified authoritarian government as a necessary means of bringing development to backward peoples. He wrapped imperial expansion in a civilizing mission derived from Enlightenment theories of progress, and validated his conquests by asserting that the world needed to be rescued from barbarism, degeneracy, and sin, preferably by making it more French. According to Jules Michelet, the new religion of France was liberty, a cause that was universal, eternal, and morally superior to the grasping commercialism that characterized British expansion.[142] At that moment, the French saw themselves as creating a new Rome that would control and reshape the European order and beyond that, the world. These ambitions had momentum. Although Napoleon's global aspirations were halted in Egypt in 1798, his plans for a new Europe under French domination were not frustrated until 1815. Similar claims were to appear under other flags in the nineteenth and twentieth centuries.

In managing conquered territories, the emperor and his advisors distinguished among incorporated states, satellites, and allies, sought out collaborators, applied techniques of direct and indirect rule, and imposed the Napoleonic Code to reform existing legal systems. Napoleon's imperial representatives showed a very modern awareness of the power of symbolism in art, architecture, styles, and public displays, and demonstrated, to their own satisfaction, the matchless superiority of French culture.[143] They also dealt with different types of resistance, including "insurgents," established networks of informers, and created paramilitary units (*gendarmeries*) to control the populace.[144] These features anticipated much that was to come later in the century, when other Western states joined the imperial club and adopted similar policies. Most of the new European imperial states were, in some way, former French colonies. From this perspective, nineteenth-century imperialism can be viewed as the ex-empire striking back in Europe before striking out in the wider world.

The most dramatic consequence of the French Wars was to disrupt the military-fiscal states of continental Europe and to offer a new set of governing principles that were to reverberate through the nineteenth century.[145] In proclaiming liberty, the French Wars set in train a series of convulsions that included the decolonization of Austrian territories in the South Netherlands and parts of Germany, the occupation of Spain and parts of Italy, and the exodus of the Portuguese monarchy to its refuge in Brazil. In imposing autocracy and creating new imperial states, Napoleon provoked the formation of what were, in effect, anti-colonial resistance movements. The German states were first trampled over in the 1790s and then pushed into an unwanted confederation.[146] The resulting proto-nationalist reaction eventually led to the unification of Germany under Prussian leadership. The effects of the long wars were also felt in the far north and south of the continent. The Nordic countries experienced political upheaval and economic disruption; the Italian states were freed from Austrian rule but placed under French colonial control. Resistance movements made their appearance in both regions. Norwegians fought against the imposition of Swedish control; *patrioti* in Italy rose against both Austrian and French rule and thereby laid the foundation for the *Risorgimento*; guerrilla activity in Spain helped to defeat the French army and opened the way for a new era of postcolonial politics.

This was the age of romantic, and often unrealistic, national aspirations, when Lord Byron, who "dream'd that Greece might still be free," inspired Europe's elites to treat self-determination as an international cause.[147] Shelley's idealization made liberty the "lightning of the nations"; Greece was the source of "prophetic echoes" that "flung dim melody" across Europe.[148] Mazzini and Garibaldi became not just national but international heroes who motivated volunteers from other European countries to join the cause of liberation. Mazzini developed a close relationship with William Lloyd Garrison, who founded the American Anti-Slavery Association in 1833 and remained one of the most prominent campaigners against slavery in the United States until abolition was achieved in 1865.[149] Mazzini wanted to free Italy from monarchy and foreign rule; Garrison wanted to free the United States from patriarchy and slavery. Both held that national unity was essential if free institutions were to flourish. Both looked even further ahead: Garrison to the time when social reform would make the United States the moral capital of the world; Mazzini to when the Old World, borrowing from the New, would create a republican united states of Europe.[150] Few foreign nationalists, however, matched the popularity of Lajos Kossuth, who led the Hungarian independence movement. When Kossuth arrived in the United States in 1851, he was treated as a public celebrity and received fulsome commendations from, among others, Abraham Lincoln.[151] In death, Lincoln himself became the "Great Emancipator" who inspired progressives across the world.[152]

The collapse of Napoleon's empire in 1815 was followed throughout Europe by a contest between conservatives, liberals, and radicals that extended to World War I, and in some cases even further into the twentieth century. Conservative forces led by Austria, which had turned itself into an empire in 1804, set about reestablishing the old order. Moderate progressives, headed by Britain, aimed to install constitutional governments that, ideally, would remain monarchies. Republicans, whose triumphs had been overshadowed by defeats, cherished hopes of a future realized by the United States, which had escaped both empire and recolonization. Conservative interests scooped the rewards of victory. As Victor Hugo saw it, the Battle of Waterloo was "intentionally a counterrevolutionary victory."[153] Honoré de Balzac, on the other hand, welcomed the new lease on life. He was horrified at the prospect of "elected power extended to all" and placed his faith in "two eternal truths: Religion and Monarchy."[154] In the short run, God appeared to be on his side. Louis XVIII became King of France; Ferdinand VII regained the throne of Spain. The Austrian Empire, guided by Metternich, recovered some lost territories in Italy. Prussia, under Frederick William III, embarked on military reforms in 1806, joined the anti-French coalition in 1813, and made territorial gains in 1815.[155] Tzar Nicholas I crushed moderate reformers in 1825 and went on to set new standards for reactionary rulers. Sweden and Norway were united under Charles XIII; Frederick VI retained the throne of Denmark. The two parts of the Netherlands were joined to form the United Kingdom of the Netherlands under the rule of an exemplary conservative, William I. Some monarchies made limited concessions to constitutional demands; the majority took the opportunity to reimpose authoritarian regimes.

The peace settlement began to unravel shortly after 1815, as liberals and radicals pulled the seams of the reconstituted monarchical order. In France, the Bourbon restoration ended with the Revolution of 1830. The monarchy survived under Louis-Philippe, who was obliged to make a number of constitutional concessions, but was brought down again in 1848 before reappearing in 1852 in the shape of the Second French Empire under Napoleon III. The Austrian Empire struggled to match the rising power of Prussia but retained control of its diverse provinces through a combination of repression, censorship, and ethnic manipulation. The newly united Netherlands came apart in 1830 when, with British support, the southern provinces became the constitutional monarchy of Belgium. Spain endured the reactionary policies of Ferdinand VII, whose turbulent reign culminated in the so-called Ominous Decade that ended with his death in 1833. All things being relative, however, this was a time of sunny optimism compared to the years of civil war, regencies, and military rule that followed down to the Catalan Revolt of 1846.[156]

Unrest culminated in the revolutions of 1848. Nearly every state in Europe was disrupted.[157] Denmark, the Netherlands, Spain, Portugal, and Russia reverberated from the side effects. The risings had a number of common features, even though they had multiple causes and independent centers of origin. They expressed long-standing and widespread discontent with the absolutist and quasi-absolutist governments installed in 1815. They drew upon the middle classes, urban workers, and peasants, albeit in different proportions. They demanded reform, whether to extend the political arena, to limit state power, to deal with urban social problems, to remedy agrarian grievances, or to meet provincial and ethnic claims.[158] They also had a significant imperial dimension.[159] Discontent in the leading imperial states was fueled by tax burdens arising from military expenditure, which had been incurred to control provincial dissident movements, including demands for self-determination. France had accumulated large costs in conquering Algeria, Prussia in dealing with the claims of Silesia, Saxony, and Schleswig-Holstein, and Austria in trying to control Hungary, Lombardy, and Venice. Britain escaped partly because domestic reforms had made progress and partly because the government was able to shift military and allied costs to the overseas empire.[160] Free trade cut subsidies to export producers, emigration dealt with "agitators," retrenchment in the colonies combined with new taxes reduced the fiscal burden on domestic taxpayers. Although the strategy generated its own costs in the form of widespread colonial discontent, it helped Britain to avoid revolution in 1848.

In the short run, the revolutionaries were contained, though they won a number of concessions: slavery was abolished in the French Empire, as was serfdom in Austria, Hungary, and, later, in Russia; liberal constitutions replaced absolutism in Denmark, The Netherlands, and Piedmont. As the risings were being suppressed, a counterrevolution was set in motion across Europe to reassert the power of the landed order and reaffirm the principle of dynastic government. In 1849, Fyodor Dostoyevsky was sent to Siberia for transgressing Russia's stern censorship laws. In the same year, Victor Hugo's advocacy of universal suffrage and free education, and subsequent opposition to Louis Napoleon's coup, led him into exile. Police forces were expanded and reshaped to deal with "terrorism"; alliances with religious authorities were strengthened; education and the press were brought under firm control. By mid-century, resurgent military elements had become predominant in a number of European states, though not in Britain. Tzar Nicholas I, who regretted that he had not been given the leading role in suppressing the revolutionary movement, took his next chance to consolidate Russian autocracy by waging war in the Crimea in 1854. The history of the military-fiscal state had yet to reach its final chapter.

The revolutions of 1848 were closely watched in the United States, where tension between North and South was rising. One influential interpretation held that the events of 1848, though partly inspired by the Revolution of 1776, were evidence of Europe's failure to install democratic forms of government.[161] Another, which appealed to observers in both the North and the South, regarded the uprisings as evidence that the principle of self-determination was gathering legitimacy.[162] The reaction that followed the attempted revolutions in Europe gave comfort to conservatives, who concluded that history was still on their side, but alarmed liberals, who feared that Southern states would exercise their power in Congress to introduce repressive measures, as indeed they did in 1850, when the Fugitive Slave Act was passed.[163] The revolutions of 1848 left a deep impression on Abraham Lincoln, who was then a fledgling congressman from Illinois. Lincoln's vision was both local and international. His frequent references comparing the nation to a house underlined its domestic, family qualities. His admiration for Mazzini, Garibaldi, Cavour, and the big celebrity of the day, Kossuth, confirmed his belief that liberation, though variously defined, was a universal cause. Popular revolution, the means of attaining freedom, was a "sacred right," providing it avoided radicalism, as it had done in the United States.[164] Europe reciprocated in an unanticipated way: Britain exported dissidents to the empire; many thousands of political refugees from continental Europe made their way to the United States, where large numbers of them joined the Republican Party, supported abolition, and volunteered for service in the Union army in 1861.

BRITAIN: "THE UNION OF PERMANENCE AND CHANGE"[165]

Lord Liverpool's Foreign Secretary, George Canning, summarized the postwar issues and opportunities in appropriately global terms when he observed in 1825 that Britain needed to chart a course between a "league of worn out" monarchies in continental Europe and new "youthful and stirring" republics headed by the United States.[166] According to opinion in governing circles, absolutist states had no future and were potentially destabilizing, while republics were old-fashioned devices, where they were not anarchic. Britain viewed the continuing turmoil and attendant uncertainties on the continent of Europe with alternating apprehension and dismay, given its abiding interest in ensuring the maintenance of a balance of power that would prevent one or more large states from threatening national security. The United States, which continued to defend the institution of slavery, was frequently cited—with considerable relish—to illustrate the point that republics were ill-suited to the needs of the modern world.[167]

The defeat of France in 1815 gave Britain the opportunity to devise a moderate peace settlement that would reestablish stability in Europe.[168] Direct intervention on the continent was unwise as well as impractical, but Britain assumed the leading role in the diplomacy of the postwar period. The Duke of Wellington remained on the continent until 1818 as commander of the allied forces with a mandate to add steel to influence. Britain backed diplomacy with large loans and subsidies to help install the restored monarchical governments. The most considerable achievement was the work of Wellington and Alexander Baring, who devised and implemented a plan to resuscitate French public finances by reforming them along British lines.[169] The scheme was not as magnanimous as Marshall Aid: reparations had to be paid, and were. Nevertheless, the idea of securing peace through provision contained an element of farsightedness that suggests that the duke should be celebrated for more than his success on the battlefield.

The complement to Britain's European strategy reaffirmed the traditional policy of compensating for its limits as a land power by strengthening its position overseas. The United States had an increasingly important part to play in realizing Britain's vision of the new world order, especially after the conclusion of the War of 1812 in 1815, just six months before the Battle of Waterloo ended hostilities in Europe. From then on, the United States offered a large and growing market for British goods and a profitable home for British investment. At the same time, republican government served as a political antonym against which Britain could measure the progress of its own monarchical model of the ideal polity. Britain's leaders might not be "youthful" but they could still stir themselves to reform the state by promoting a unifying, Christian version of moral rearmament designed to avoid revolution and the dangerous temptations of republicanism.

The outcome was different in Britain partly because the monarchical order had already ceased to qualify as an ancien régime, and partly because the islands had escaped invasion and were the least scarred of the victors of 1815. Nevertheless, the social forces contesting change resembled those competing for supremacy on the continent of Europe, even though the confrontation was on the whole less stark and less brutal than it was across the Channel. The reforms that followed the French Wars, however, were not simply early expressions of secular liberalism that swelled to fulfillment in the second half of the century, when the principles of free trade, the market economy, and minimal government became orthodoxies. Initially, Lord Liverpool, who was Prime Minister between 1812 and 1827, hoped to carry forward Pitt's neoconservative legacy by reinforcing the military-fiscal state and safeguarding monarchical government.[170] It soon became apparent, however, that a change of course was essential to meet the urgent needs of peace and to deal with the revival of political demands that had been postponed by the wartime emergency. If Tories were prepared to contemplate minimal change, Whigs showed greater willingness to present themselves as the party of reform, and proved the point when they held office between 1830 and 1841. Yet, not even Whigs could be called "liberals." They embodied the values of the eighteenth-century landed interest: they saw themselves as "the people's aristocrats" and hoped that paternalism applied to reform would enlarge the circle of deference needed to keep them in power.[171] It was not until the 1850s that the last Whig government gave way to the new Liberal Party and a closer alliance with the middle classes.

The teachings of Adam Smith and Jeremy Bentham were well represented in the debates that followed, as were those of Benjamin Constant and Henri de Saint Simon in France.[172] At the outset, however, they had to contend with an influential alternative ideological influence on policy propounded by evangelicals such as William Wilberforce, Thomas Chalmers, and their disciples.[173] Evangelicals advocated a brand of conservative, Christian political economy that resonated in a country that was profoundly religious and becoming more so. Britain's "Second Great Awakening" complemented the evangelical revival in the United States, which was energized by the fear of importing malign influences from France.[174] There was an unprecedented expansion in church-building after 1815 to meet the needs of an increasing population. By the middle of the century about half the adult population attended church.[175] The American Revolution had spread anxiety and uncertainty; the French Revolution had inspired fear and occasionally panic. If the Jacobins helped to create the Victorian Sabbath by frightening the English into attending their local churches, as has been suggested, the Lord's Day Observance Society, founded in 1831, did much to keep them there.[176]

The world had been turned upside down: righting it called for spiritual renewal to atone for sins that were the wages of corruption and decay. Evangelical activists held paternal or authoritarian attitudes toward the role of government, but supported reforms that fitted their ideas of the natural social order. They sanctified legitimate economic activities to the point where phrases such as the "sacred laws of political economy" and the "gospel of free trade" became common currency.[177] The aim of political action was to restore what had been lost, not to create new uncertainties and attendant temptations. The gloomy predictions of Thomas Malthus, who saw the "glimmer of twilight" more often than a "glad confident morning," provided support for a view of the world that rejected the idealism and optimism of the Enlightenment.[178]

Political reform was strongly advocated and strongly resisted, as it had been in the 1760s and 1770s.[179] The onset of the French Wars concentrated minds on survival but did not destroy radical activism. The immediate fear of the spread of revolution caused the British government to take action against presumed subversive elements, but it was the threat of invasion, especially after the rise of Napoleon, that produced national solidarity.[180] Even so, unity remained ambivalent, and patriotism was often divided between loyalist and radical affiliations.[181] Pitt's skilled pragmatism steered the country through most of the conflict with France, but the hardships of war also helped to produce the Luddite movement in 1811. The expectations aroused by the long-awaited peace in 1815 revived the reform movement. In 1819, demonstrators in Manchester demanding increased participation in the electoral process were suppressed by force and with loss of life in what became known as the Peterloo Massacre.

More than a decade later, the Great Reform Act was passed following an extended battle that moved from the streets to parliament, where it was resisted almost to the last grandee. The debate was infused with religiosity.[182] Apocalyptic visions abounded: evangelical Anglicans regarded the constitution as a covenant with God; dissenters wanted to breach the secular citadel of the established Church; a pre-liberal, highly charged Gladstone viewed the issue as a "holy war." Imperial considerations also played an important part in the debate.[183] Parliamentary reform drew support from complementary movements to abolish slavery and eliminate the East India Company's monopoly of trade with China. Tory opposition to reform was motivated partly by the consequences it might have for representing imperial interests in parliament and concern that it would spread demands for change throughout the empire. Absentee planters and British investors, who were worried about the loss of their "property" in slaves, were won over by an offer of generous compensation. A large proportion of the £20 million voted by parliament was paid, not to planters in the West Indies, but to claimants in Britain, principally in London and its environs. The recipients included more than one hundred M.P.'s, a selection of the nobility, sundry Anglican divines, a clutch of City bankers, and a number of leading merchants in Liverpool and Glasgow, as well as members of the middle class and a significant number of "widows and orphans."[184] Advocates presented the case for compensation in terms of Christian political economy: the need to redeem the sin of the nation. Slaves, though formally freed, received no compensation. The islands lacked competitive alternatives to sugar, were overtaken by producers elsewhere, and languished for decades thereafter.

After mounting pressure, the Duke of Wellington met his own Waterloo when his uncompromising opposition to reform compelled his resignation as Prime Minister in 1830. "The mischief of the reform," he wrote ruefully to a fellow Tory in 1833, "is that whereas democracy prevailed heretofore only in some places, it now prevails everywhere."[185] This was an exaggeration arising from the disappointment of defeat: in reality, the Reform Act enfranchised only a small proportion of the potential electorate, and the political authority of the landed interest remained intact.[186] The Duke's comment nevertheless pointed to developments that were to swell as the century advanced: the incremental growth of pressure for change, the increased prominence attached to national as well as to local politics, and the sharper definition given to parties and partisanship.[187] It was at this time that the terms "reform" and "radical" became clearly differentiated.[188] Reformers were moderates who drew more hope than satisfaction from the Act of 1832; radicals represented those who remained outside the formal political arena and were thought to be potential subversives. Diverse though it was, the reform movement was united by the belief that amelioration, or "improvement," was necessary to blunt the edge of radicalism and forestall revolution.

Radical claims progressed, as the Duke of Wellington feared that they would, and found militant expression in the 1840s in the Chartist movement, which called for voting rights for all adult males. In the short run, the Chartists failed, as did most contemporary radical movements on the continent of Europe. Radicalism then entered a temporary decline. There was no populist "green uprising" in Britain, as there was in the United States at this time; an urban, "brownfield" uprising was postponed; the political power of large landowners remained unimpaired until the Reform Act of 1867 approved a sizeable extension of the electorate.[189] Nevertheless, reform had advanced just far enough by mid-century to enable Britain to escape one of the many revolutions that engulfed European governments in 1848 and to make its claim to be the standard bearer of nonrevolutionary progress credible. Britain's rulers had decided not to "hunt abroad after foreign affections," as Burke put it, but to improve "legitimate and home-bred connections," thereby hoping to preserve them.[190]

The economic measures that accompanied political reform began as adjustments to the mercantile system.[191] Mercantilist regulations had nurtured the growth of the most dynamic sectors of the economy—the cotton industry and the City of London—whose representatives were reluctant to see them dismantled. Reform, when it came, was more the product of necessity than of choice, and was partly motivated by the desire to prevent radicalism from turning to revolution. Governments had to devise ways of reducing the national debt, of securing new sources of food, and of dealing with bouts of unemployment in the textile industry. These pressures led to two decisions that accelerated the transition to an economy that had the potential to shape a new international order: the return to the gold standard and the adoption of free trade.

In 1819, Lord Liverpool's Conservative government began the process of reestablishing the gold standard after it had been suspended, following the exigencies of war, in 1797. The decision was a clear signal that the administration intended to restore sound money and all that it stood for: fiscal responsibility, good government, and social stability. The huge national debt incurred during the French Wars had to be attacked with the aggression that only peacetime conditions allowed. In 1815, Britain's per capita public debt was not only the highest in Europe but also the highest in its history, and debt service accounted for 60 percent of all tax receipts.[192] Public expenditure was cut; inflation was squeezed out of the system. The return to gold prepared the way for the City of London to realize its full economic potential, and that of the pound sterling, by becoming the world's warehouse and banker. Evangelicals approved the decision on the grounds that it would curb speculation, reduce the temptations of self-indulgence, reassert social order, and thereby underpin the morality of pious restraint. Farsighted policy-makers, like William Huskisson, regarded the gold standard as an essential means of disciplining the economy in the absence of mercantilist regulations.

The reintroduction in 1815 of the Corn Laws, which had been suspended during the French Wars, was an early indication that Lord Liverpool's Tory government intended to restore the prewar order.[193] The tariff on imported corn, its advocates claimed, not only protected domestic grain-farmers, but also safeguarded the staple food of Britain's households.[194] In addition, as Robert Torrens argued later, the Corn Laws were an essential support of Britain's status as a great power. The argument for free trade also had able advocates, among them William Huskisson, who used his position as president of the Board of Trade to reduce the import duty on corn in the 1820s.[195] By then, Robert Peel, who was Home Secretary in the Tory government, was also in favor of free trade. The 1830s saw an increasingly open and vigorous debate between free traders and protectionists. Peel, as Prime Minister, introduced the first repeal bill in 1842; the measure finally passed, after a series of epic debates, in 1846.[196]

By 1846, the pressures for change had risen to steaming point.[197] In the late 1820s, there were indications that population growth was beginning to outstrip supplies of basic foods. By then, too, the most important of the new manufactures, cotton textiles, had begun to experience the first of a series of crises of overproduction that Marx and Engels were shortly to catalogue. These developments presented governments of the period with a set of social and political challenges that culminated in the upheaval threatened by the Chartist movement. Without cheap imports of corn, bread supplies for a growing population would be inadequate and costly. Without new markets abroad, the textile industry would continue to suffer bouts of unemployment on a scale that endangered civil order. The Chartists, however, were not the vanguard of a new industrial working class, but the final major upsurge of eighteenth-century radicalism. They aimed their message at the state, not at employers.[198] Their principal concern was with what they saw as legislative oppression authorized by a parliament that represented property rather than people.

Peel held no brief for what he referred to as Britain's "artificial" industrial condition, even though he was the son of a successful textile manufacturer.[199] His aim was to place economic progress on a broad base that would deliver social contentment to the majority and not just wealth to the few. He had long considered repeal of the Corn Laws to be inevitable, given the needs of an expanding population; his concern was to manage the politics and the timing of parliamentary action.[200] Dissenters applied a different argument to a similar end: they supported repeal because they thought, mistakenly as it turned out, that free trade would correct the artificial degree of overproduction stimulated by mercantilism, and so limit the corrosive consequences of excessive consumption. Gladstone, who had opposed the Reform Act in 1832, redirected his fervor to support repeal, which he viewed as an act of penitence for past sins. Morality and practicality came together, too, in the optimistic thinking of Richard Cobden, the key figure in the movement for repeal and the main spokesman for the Anti-Corn Law League.[201] Cobden regarded free trade as a universal moral principle. Once adopted, it would raise both the standard of living and the standard of morality, and—for good measure—would deliver world peace, too. Its counterpart, minimal government, would be the parsimonious means of preserving individual liberties. By the time Cobden died in 1865, free trade had entered national life as a symbol of liberty, individual choice, and moral rectitude. It had won the support of consumers, received the blessing of religious authorities, and become an accepted part of the public interest.[202]

Peel succeeded because he was able to present abolition as being in the national interest. Repeal would moderate the tensions between agriculture and industry and avert class conflict. A policy of amelioration would curb revolutionary tendencies, which were palpable in 1845, and allow reform without subverting the constitution. Repeal was followed by complementary measures taken between 1846 and 1851 to limit imperial preference and abolish the Navigation Acts. The demise of the Navigation Acts in 1849 was not, as once thought, symbolic, nor did it follow inevitably from the repeal of the Corn Laws. The Acts, which had been inherited from the seventeenth century, remained substantially intact, and were defended vigorously by a powerful alliance of shipowners, landowners, and sections of the City.[203] Indeed, the protectionist cause revived in the late 1840s, included a campaign to reintroduce the Corn Laws, and remained Conservative Party policy until 1852.[204] A similar struggle marked the end of the duties that gave preferential treatment to imports of sugar from the empire. The Sugar Duties Act reduced the level of protection in 1846, but it was not until 1851 that the tariff on imported sugar was equalized.[205] The reforms passed, but the intensity of the struggle was a measure of the continuing weight of mercantilist influences on "liberal" Britain.

The issues at stake were momentous; the interested parties were divided and uncertain.[206] Segments of the landed interest had diversified their investments and were no longer solidly behind the Corn Laws; manufacturers in Manchester and Liverpool had turned in favor of free trade; the City of London, though split on the issue, had become attracted to the opportunities that free trade offered. Among the public at large, the Corn Laws had become an unpopular symbol of what Cobden called "aristocratic misrule."[207] The peers in the House of Lords learned from the experience of reform in 1832 and decided, reluctantly, to accept the possibility of economic loss in return for the probability of securing political stability.[208] Domestic reforms had the additional merit of demonstrating that the monarchical system, suitably updated, was the best means of dealing with the challenges of the new century. As the century advanced, they became international advertisements for the British "middle way" of combining liberty and order.

By about 1850, political and economic reforms had dismantled most of Britain's military-fiscal state.[209] The monarchy had been elevated above party politics to become a pristine symbol of national unity. A liberal ethos, represented in parliament by a succession of Liberal governments, had succeeded in shaping a concept of patriotism that emphasized respect for the constitution, liberty, and free trade.[210] The East India Company, the greatest single symbol of mercantilist cronyism, had lost its commercial monopolies and was shortly to be liquidated.[211] Complementary reforms of the civil service, the armed services, public health, labor conditions, and education either were being implemented or were in sight. Evangelical energies had flagged, but a broader Christian humanitarianism incorporating utilitarian principles represented the values of the wider population, not least because it took a less censorious view of consumer goods.[212] "Old Corruption" had given way to new probity. Georgian excesses lay in the past or out of sight; Victorian respectability had arrived.

"A VAST EMPIRE ON WHICH THE SUN NEVER SETS"[213]

George Macartney made his famous observation in 1773, when British statesmen still felt the glow of victory after the Seven Years' War. Although the loss of the American colonies dissipated the warmth, Macartney was correct in supposing that "nature" had "not yet ascertained" the bounds of the empire.[214] The political reaction to defeat in North America did not entail the rejection of imperial ambitions: Britain gained territory across the world during the long French Wars that followed the loss of the American colonies. When peace returned to Europe in 1815,

Britain was the only European power left with substantial overseas possessions and the naval capacity to police the oceans. [215] The long peace in Europe that followed victory over France allowed Britain to shift resources into overseas expansion.[216] The years that followed saw the continuation of assertive policies across the world combined with efforts to establish pacific relations by means of commercial treaties.

Other European powers were unable to challenge Britain's imperial progress. By the 1830s, when the term "decolonization" was coined, the mortality of empires was everywhere in evidence.[217] Spain had been damaged by war, occupation, and revolution, and in 1815 retained only the Philippines, Cuba, and Puerto Rico, and was about to lose Mexico. France had been vanquished and was reassigned some of her tropical islands and enclaves only because the gesture suited British policy. The invasion of Algeria in 1830, a belated attempt by Charles X to boost his fading popularity, provoked resistance that entangled French troops and limited French control for decades to come. The Netherlands, which also had been greatly weakened by the European war, recovered her possessions in Indonesia with Britain's approval and implied protection. The Portuguese royal family, which had been snatched from Napoleon's grasp by the British navy, was evacuated to Brazil, its most important colony, which nevertheless became independent in 1825.[218] The Austrian and Russian empires survived the long wars but were exposed thereafter to persistent challenges from dissident elements. "Every empire," Adam Smith observed, "aims at immortality," yet "have all hitherto proved mortal."[219] Only Britain, it seemed, had defied, or at least postponed, Smith's law.

Britain's position as the unrivaled international "superpower" of the time represented a remarkable reversal of fortune after the setback caused by the loss of the mainland colonies and the long and desperate struggle with France.[220] Defeat at the hands of the colonists was undoubtedly a blow to Britain's prestige, but the event proved to be an interruption rather than a turning point.[221] The temptations of soul-searching were cut short by the need to focus on the French threat. Britain's economy continued to expand, notwithstanding the hazards of war: overseas commerce increased much faster between 1773 and 1819 than between 1773 and 1793, mainly as a result of the rise of cotton manufactures and increased trade with Asia and the New World.[222] Britain's share of world shipping, which stood at about 25 percent in 1780, had risen to 42 percent by 1820.[223] By then, too, Britain had ceased to be a net debtor to the world and had become its chief creditor; the United States was to make the same transition in 1918.[224]

Canning's expansive conception of global problems produced a correspondingly spacious solution.[225] After 1815, Britain formulated a program for a new international order. The plan was not drawn up as a formal part of the peace settlement, as was the case after World War II, but evolved by experiment between 1815 and 1846. Accordingly, the totality achieves coherence only in retrospect, though the principal elements were clear to contemporaries, were widely publicized and debated, and were driven forward by well-organized pressure groups. International economic policy aimed to capitalize on Britain's dominance in finance and shipping. London was to become the "emporium of the East," as Henry Dundas put it, and to corner the large and highly profitable reexport trade in tropical products in particular.[226] Overseas investment and commercial services would secure raw materials, notably cotton, and open new markets for manufactured textiles. The political component of the plan called for the creation of a string of cooperative and stable governments across the globe, some as way stations, others as focal points for the dissemination of British influence into the interior of continents that were still largely unknown.

These aims were to be achieved by diplomacy, where possible, and by force, where necessary. Ideally, "hearts and minds" would be won by demonstrating the success of British values. Advocates hoped that this set of part-religious, part-secular universal beliefs would validate the British mission and create what the World Bank would later call "like-mindedness." The strategy was most successful in countries of recent settlement, where comparable institutions and ties of "kith and kin" smoothed relations.[227] The problem was that, with one exception, these settlements were still at an early stage of development. The exception was the United States, which developed a complementary export economy based on cotton, and where Southern dominance of Congress ensured that import tariffs remained low. Elsewhere, in Asia, Africa, and the Middle East, "like-mindedness" provided a measure of commonality that lubricated the international system but could not guarantee to deliver the institutional changes needed to meet the requirements of commercial expansion.

Such an ambitious international strategy could not be realized within the confines of the military-fiscal state, but required a gamble for growth that committed Britain to expand its already considerable role as a world power. There were few gamblers in office, however, until Peel placed his bet in 1846. The promotion of trade within the mercantilist system marched in step with Britain's military, which continued to collect stretches of territory in India. Where "barbarous" nations obstructed progress, the navy opened the way for British commerce. By 1815, Britain had added to the extensive territory it already held in India, had retained the West Indies and what was to become Canada, and had acquired footholds in Cape Town and Singapore, besides staking an exclusive claim to Australia.

At the beginning of the century, Henry Dundas, the arch-Tory president of the Board of Control, intended to use the East India Company to develop both empire and trade. In 1813, however, his son, Robert, who had replaced him as president of the Board, secured the abolition of the Company's monopoly on trade with India.[228] Pressure for change came from provincial manufacturers and powerful City figures, such as Francis Baring, who were keen to capitalize on the opportunities territorial possession offered.[229] In 1833, after further lobbying, the Company lost its monopoly of the China trade as well. In the 1830s, too, Edward Gibbon Wakefield advanced a scheme for extending the formal empire through a combination of state sponsorship and private enterprise.[230] His essentially conservative plan for reproducing Britain's social hierarchy overseas suited the mood of the times and was much discussed in the 1830s as a way of dealing with increasing population, unemployment, and "surplus" capital. Wakefield also envisaged a special relationship with the United States: "Americans would raise cheaper corn than has ever been raised; and, no longer wanting a tariff, might drive with the manufacturers of England the greatest trade ever known to the world."[231]

Shafts of Smithian optimism began to brighten the Malthusian gloom. In 1833, Thomas Babington Macaulay, the Whig politician and historian, felt confident enough to speak of "an empire exempt from all natural causes of decay."[232] The loss of the American colonies had been accepted; its consequences had been absorbed. Macaulay looked to new horizons, above all in India, and took inspiration from fresh motives. "To have found a great people sunk in the lowest depths of slavery and superstition, to have so ruled them as to have made them desirous and capable of all the privileges of citizens, would indeed be a title to glory all our own." Admittedly, "unforeseen accidents" could still "derange our most profound schemes of policy." Nevertheless, Britain had nurtured an exceptional polity that had transmitted an enduring legacy in "the pacific triumphs of reason over barbarism" and created an "imperishable empire of our arts and our morals, our literature and our laws."

Herman Merivale, professor of Political Economy at Oxford University, went a step further. In 1841, he laid out an ambitious plan for a limitless, free-trade empire based on international specialization.[233] The abolition of slavery within the British Empire in 1833, he argued, opened the way for the "reconstruction and great extension of the British dominion beyond the seas, on principles of internal self-government and commercial freedom."[234] The new *imperium* would be at least as impressive as the old one: "empires as vast and wealthy still remain to be founded, and new branches of commerce as extensive and as prosperous to be created."[235] By then, too, Macaulay had realized that free trade had the potential to tie the United States to Britain in what he judged would be a mutually advantageous relationship. In 1842, he looked forward to the time when, after repeal of the Corn Laws, Britain could "supply the whole world with manufactures, and have almost a monopoly of the trade of the world," while "other nations were raising abundant provisions for us on the banks of the Mississippi and the Vistula."[236]

Missionary and humanitarian organizations, which had combined to end Britain's participation in the slave trade in 1807, also endorsed these increasingly spacious conceptions of Britain's world role.[237] The American Revolution had created a crisis of legitimacy for Britain's vaunted "empire of liberty." The purpose of empire had to be rethought and its moral authority reestablished.[238] Evangelicals interpreted the loss of the mainland colonies as being God's judgment on the sin of slavery and viewed abolition as a means of atonement; humanitarians drew on Enlightenment principles to appeal to universal rights. The application of the concept of freedom, however, required discrimination to avoid the anarchic implications of French radicalism.[239] Abolition served the purpose because it opened the way to the civilizing influence of Christian missions.[240] Equality of souls did not imply equality of wealth or social standing; unsettling consequences, if they arose, would disturb societies overseas without affecting Britain. Once started, however, the movement acquired popular momentum that quickly extended below the elite leadership, attracted women as well as men, and reached far beyond the capital.[241] After the objections of pro-slavery patriots had been overcome, this version of freedom contributed to the creation of a more inclusive political community, which in turn helped to shape Britain's national identity.[242]

The Act of 1833 emancipating slaves within the British Empire encouraged evangelicals and humanitarians to engage in an international campaign to abolish slavery and promote economic development through what became known as "legitimate" commerce. Abolition became part of the wider European and trans-Atlantic movements to reform military-fiscal states and dispossess their privileged beneficiaries. The success of the British campaign, combined with slave resistance in the South and the active advocacy of freed slaves in the North, galvanized abolitionists in the United States and added greater vigor and urgency to their cause.[243] In the 1840s, the movements to secure Irish independence and repeal the Corn Laws gave abolitionists in the United States further evidence of the power of popular politics. William Lloyd Garrison, the leading figure in the American Anti-Slavery Society, drew the moral that democracy could be made to work, despite Tocqueville's cogent fear that the majority could become "tyrannical" by approving or ignoring blatant violations of natural rights. Cobden saw the repeal of the Corn Laws as a step toward global integration and, ultimately, world peace.[244] Both men were agents of a new cosmopolitan morality that became operational through what today would be called International Non-Governmental Organizations (INGOs).

If souls were to be saved, stomachs had to be filled. "The bible and the plough" became the catchphrase of the civilizing mission. Christian missions, which had established stations overseas in the 1790s, increased their funding, expanded their presence, and experimented with new export crops.[245] In complementary fashion, industrial capitalists, who had played little part in the early stages of the abolitionist movement, became more involved in the new economy as their stake in the mercantilist system diminished. In the 1830s, the firm that pioneered the substitution of vegetable oils for animal fats in the manufacture of candles appealed to its customers to "buy our candles and help stop the slave trade."[246] A limited number of bilateral free-trade treaties were negotiated with the powerful and imposed on the weak, and gave employment to peripatetic diplomats, such as Sir John Bowring.[247]

Beyond Europe and the United States, Cobden's pacific ideal was frequently translated into assertive action. Empires were inherently violent creations, and the military were in the vanguard that created the British Empire, even where free trade was not the immediate cause of action. The Royal Navy acted vigorously to halt the international slave trade, which had expanded during the first half of the century, to eliminate piracy, and to extend free-trade agreements of the type signed with the Ottoman Empire in 1838.[248] The impetus given to the conquest of India continued after 1815 down to the acquisition of the Punjab in 1849.[249] Britain fought large and costly wars with Burma in 1823–1826 and 1852–1853 to secure northeast India, and with Afghanistan in 1839–1842 to consolidate its position in the northwest. War with Persia in 1856–1857 fortified the treaty that had been signed in 1841; wars with China in 1839–1842 and 1856–1860 secured extraterritorial rights in designated ports and legalized the opium trade. Gunboat diplomacy in the 1850s and 1860s committed coastal states in Africa to sign treaties that suppressed the slave trade and encouraged the development of "legitimate" commerce. The use of force against indigenous peoples accompanied the spread of colonial settlement in Canada, South Africa, Australia, and New Zealand with the aim of creating a Greater Britain that would extend the power of the homeland to the wider world.

Bruising encounters with non-Western societies brought a growing awareness of differences among the peoples of the world. This perception, combined with increased confidence in Europe's capabilities, gradually altered attitudes toward non-Western societies. At the close of the eighteenth century, a range of formidable Enlightenment figures, including Diderot, Kant, Herder, Hume, and Bentham, had formulated a universal conception of humanity that rejected imperial domination.[250] By the mid-nineteenth century, this tolerant, cosmopolitan view of the world had to compete with a distinction between the civilized and the savage that elevated the former and stripped the latter of the nobility Rousseau had conferred.[251] John Stuart Mill, an ultra-liberal in other respects, elaborated a case first formulated by his father in the 1820s in favor of a paternal, interventionist empire, even as Cobden was promoting the ideal of a pacific world order.[252] The original "empire of liberty" was intended to embrace Britons at home and overseas. Where "barbarians" were concerned, Mill held that "despotism" was a "legitimate mode of government," provided that "the end be their improvement."[253] As Bentham gave way to Mill in Britain, so Benjamin Constant's anticolonialism was followed by Tocqueville's ardent support of French imperialism, which in turn was in sight of de Gobineau's theory of the Aryan master race.[254] The Enlightenment had seen the potential in environmental change; the new biology emphasized the limits that nature had placed on nurture.

Britain's vision of world development was outlined but not realized during the first half of the century. Despite the roll call of annexations and treaties, what Adam Smith called "the project of an empire" had still to realize its full potential.[255] The "golden dream" lived on, but became a reality only after Britain had found the means of overcoming what he termed the "mediocrity of her circumstances."[256] Not for the last time, the planners of the day found that they had underestimated the difficulties of exporting Western values and institutions to non-Western societies, and overestimated the welcome they expected their policies to receive. Few indigenous societies were keen to cooperate in their own subordination, notwithstanding the repeated assurances of those who claimed to be liberating or otherwise improving them. Among settler societies, only the United States had reached the size needed to support a large volume of foreign trade. By the time of his death in 1865, Cobden had lost some of his faith in the pacific, cosmopolitan instincts of the middle classes and had lost popularity himself for his opposition to the Crimean War and the bombardment of China.

Nevertheless, powerful interests, secular and spiritual, had by then acquired a stake in a forceful, free-trading empire that, with Cobden and Mill's endorsement, had also become a thoroughly moral undertaking. With the assistance of Samuel Cunard, Isambard Kingdom Brunel, Hiram Maxim, and others, it would shortly become a feasible one, too. Some promising signs had already appeared. None had more potential than the burgeoning informal relationship that Britain had already established with its ex-colony, the United States.

"THE IMAGE OF THE PAST PROJECTED ON THE MIST OF THE UNKNOWN"[257]

Coleridge's vision of the future, "seen with a glory round its head," was one of continuity dissolving into a blend of expectation and uncertainty. His understanding of the era he lived through captures the central point of the interpretation advanced in this chapter: despite revolutions and wars, the world Coleridge knew was not transformed during his lifetime. Since all ages are ages of transition, portents of change were everywhere in evidence. Modern manufacturing had begun; reform movements clamored for political change. Taken as a whole, however, agriculture still dominated Western Europe's economies, and dynasties still ruled its polities. This was the case even in Britain, the most advanced of the new manufacturing economies, where politics remained in the hands of the landed interest. Viewed from the perspective adopted here, Palmer's heroic *Age of Democratic Revolutions* and Hobsbawm's pioneering *Industry and Empire* both read rather too much of the future into the past.[258] In this instance, Coleridge's sense of the union of past and present provides a more accurate guide to processes whose potential had not yet been realized.

The Glorious Revolution inaugurated a new phase in the evolution of the military-fiscal state. The events of 1688–1689 were products of an accommodation between those who, in Burke's formulation, had "a disposition to preserve and an ability to improve."[259] The landed oligarchs devised the settlement that followed the removal of James II to ensure that wealth and position inherited from the past would be extended into an indefinite future. To achieve their aim they were obliged to introduce constitutional and fiscal reforms that put Britain on a war footing to meet expanding continental and global commitments. Europe's military-fiscal states reached their highest stage of development in the late eighteenth century. Political centralization and mercantilist regulations increased trade and revenues, and funded military expansion. The outcome was a set of competing warfare states whose costly conflicts drove them toward bankruptcy. The revolutions that followed in Europe and the New World had multiple causes. They also had a common denominator: self-induced fiscal blight. The consequences of rising state debts were widely felt. They produced hardship, unrest, and protest, fractured ruling classes, and stimulated new thinking about political and economic reform that entered the rhetoric of revolution and was carried forward into the nineteenth century. Britain, the only major European power to escape revolution, did so at least partly because it possessed the most advanced fiscal and financial system of the time and could mobilize the national debt to shunt debt service into the future.

In the 1740s, Montesquieu observed how territorial expansion created problems of political control that established institutions of government could solve only by embracing major structural change. Expansion placed added demands on expenditure to provide what are now called public goods, principally in the form of protection costs. A commensurate increase in revenues was needed to pay for them. Repeated warfare guaranteed that expenditure would rise: victory was costly; defeat was disastrous. Economic constraints and widespread tax evasion ensured that revenues would struggle to keep pace with demand. Montesquieu feared that the institutional changes needed to manage polities of increasing size would lead to despotism. Centralizing tendencies were certainly widespread in the eighteenth century and accusations of despotism also mounted as the century advanced. Ultimately, however, the process of expansion imposed its own limits: the further states reached, the more tenuous their grasp became. Spain, Britain, and France claimed sovereignty in the New World, but technological and other constraints prevented them from exercising it fully. The decolonizing movements of the late eighteenth century arose from convulsions of military-fiscal states that could no longer control the territorial and commercial expansion they had initiated. The protection afforded by isolation made it possible for the mainland colonies to turn dissent into secession. Under conditions of proto-globalization, the "tyranny of distance" ruled more effectively than any human despot.[260]

The causes of the American Revolution have been studied to the point where repetition far exceeds novelty. Ambitious claims, accordingly, should be treated with caution and even skepticism. The modest

suggestion made here, and explored further in chapter 3, is that current appraisals of the Revolution can be enhanced by placing them in
the broad context of the evolution of Britain's military-fiscal state. This
perspective allows one of the best known features of the Revolution, the
controversy over taxation, to be related both to the survival of the unreformed polity in Britain and to widening divisions within the ruling oligarchy about the purposes of empire. The crisis at the center of Britain's
military-fiscal state provided the momentum that turned preconditions
into causes and rebellion into independence.

When peace returned in 1815, the victorious powers set about restoring the order that the French Revolution and Napoleonic imperialism
had torn apart. The history of the nineteenth century is not that of the
inexorable rise of liberalism, or "secular modernism," set against a background of waning conservatism. Continental monarchs allied to large
landowners endeavored to reestablish absolutism; governments everywhere perpetuated mercantilist regulations. In Britain, absolutism had
ceased to be on the agenda. Nevertheless, the monarchy joined with the
landed interest to repel challenges to the established political system and
to uphold mercantilism. The Battle of Waterloo was fought to defeat republican imperialism, not to open the door to political reforms of the
kind advocated by the radical Whigs in the 1760s or the champions of
Adam Smith's teachings. By 1850, liberal forces had suffered serious reverses, except in Britain, and even there the military-fiscal state survived
until the last moment.

Changing circumstances, however, altered policies. International conditions after 1815 gave Britain, the new superpower, an exceptional opportunity to shape a world order that fitted its priorities. Domestic pressures ensured that Britain took them up. Population growth increased
the need for imported food; new manufactures needed foreign markets;
revenues had to be boosted to reduce the national debt and preserve what
one observer called "the vital existence of this mighty empire."[261] Politicians and pundits developed a vision of global development that would
expand international commerce, promote cooperative governments in
distant parts of the world, and nurture a new generation of cosmopolitan elites. This was neither a period of imperial quiescence, as was once
believed, nor the moment when formal rule was adroitly exchanged for
informal influence. The loss of the mainland colonies prompted moves,
not to abandon the empire, but to reposition it and make it function
more effectively.

Britain consolidated its position at home by negotiating a settlement
with Scotland and imposing one on Ireland. Overseas, Britain contin-

ued to enlarge its territorial empire in India and to develop colonies of white settlement. By 1850, the largest and most valuable colonies held by European powers were in British hands. At a time when mercantilists and free-traders competed for control of policy at home, it should be no surprise to find that both influences were felt abroad in the territorial empire and in efforts to turn independent states beyond Europe into obedient clients. As Britain extended mercantilist regulations to its territorial gains, so it experimented with free-trade treaties and attempted to exercise informal influence in the new Latin American republics. Doors that would not open readily were given a shove, as in China, or unlocked by a combination of menace and persuasion, as in the Ottoman Empire. Impressive though the new imperial ventures were, results fell far behind ambitions. Before 1850, technological constraints hampered international communications, resistance checked foreign intrusions, and limits to resources and markets curbed the export potential of new territories.

The relevance of these developments to the history of the United States has yet to be fully appreciated. The mainland colonies were extensions of Britain's military-fiscal state; the new republic grappled with the problem of how much of its colonial inheritance to keep and how much to abandon. In this regard the political economy of the new state replicated the contest between conservative and liberal forces that was shaping the history of Europe. These trends did not merely evolve in parallel: they were interconnected. Attitudes and policies associated with Tories and Whigs resurfaced across the Atlantic, albeit applied to different circumstances. The persistence of monarchy in Europe encouraged conservatives in the United States who wanted to perpetuate aristocratic, patriarchal rule. Conversely, the example of the United States gave hope to republicans and reformers in Europe. Ideas of romantic and ethnic nationalism, originally conceived in Europe, inspired competing schemes of nation-building among patriarchs and republicans in the United States. The political and economic dominance of Southern states and their allies ensured that conservative, landed interests prevailed in the United States, as they did in Europe. The Republic, like other settler states, was unable to shake off its dependence on the former colonial power after 1783, not least because the relationship benefited the "power elites" of the day. The United States became an advertisement for expansion through influence, or soft power, and a precursor of the techniques that Britain was to extend to other parts of the world in the second half of the century.

An emphasis on the wider context undoubtedly diminishes the importance historians of the United States attach to the national narrative.

Yet, the larger perspective also alters the narrative by showing how a process that was common to the Western world, notwithstanding its diversity, helped first to create the United States and then to shape its history as an ex-colonial state. All Western states were entering, willingly or not, a "great transition," which ultimately transported them from a form of proto-globalization based on agriculture, commerce, and dynastic rule to a full-blown form of modern globalization characterized by industrialization, financial services, and nation-states. To exclude the United States from this common undertaking is not only to minimize its role in the process but also to shrink the scale of the process itself. Moreover, the global context reveals distinctive features of the history of the United States that have yet to attract attention. The Republic was the first of the modern ex-colonial states to try to turn formal independence into effective independence. In making the attempt, the Founding Fathers and their successors experimented with novel styles of government and plans for economic development that were to influence the leaders of the second and final wave of decolonization after 1945. Far from being conducted in isolation, these ventures drew on, and contributed to, comparable undertakings in Western Europe.

Lord Macartney was right. The sun had yet to set on the British Empire, even after the loss of the mainland colonies. It rose again, not only in the East, but also, in defiance of planetary laws, in the West across the Atlantic. How these trans-Atlantic ties influenced the history of the United States in the period down to the Civil War is the subject of the next three chapters.

CHAPTER 3

FROM REVOLUTION TO CONSTITUTION

HARRY WASHINGTON AND THE EMERGING GLOBAL ORDER

George Washington is assured of a starring role in all accounts of the American Revolution; Harry Washington is virtually unknown.[1] Yet Harry deserves recognition too, even though his hand was only one of many on the wheel of history. His extraordinary story is compelling in itself; it also offers a fresh insight into the upheaval in imperial relations that brought the eighteenth century to a close.

Harry Washington was one of George Washington's slaves. He was born in the Gambia around 1740, shipped across the Atlantic in the early 1760s, and bought by George Washington in 1763 to work for the aptly named Dismal Swamp Company in Virginia. George managed the company until 1768, when control passed to his brother, John. Harry attempted to escape in 1771 but was recaptured and thereafter worked as one of John Washington's house servants. A second opportunity to secure his liberty arose in 1775, when Lord Dunmore, the Governor of Virginia, issued a proclamation offering freedom to slaves who joined the British army.[2] Dunmore was in dispute with the colonists over the taxes needed to fund operations against the Shawnee and saw an opportunity to strengthen his hand against dissident elements without incurring further expenditure. Harry, with several hundred other slaves, took his chance and joined the British in 1776. He became a corporal in a unit of the Black Pioneers, served in Charleston in 1781, and ended up in New York with the defeated British forces in 1782.

Under the terms of the peace settlement signed in 1783, escaped slaves were to be returned to their masters. However, General Sir Guy Carlton, the Commander-in-Chief of British forces, refused to comply with the requirement, despite persistent efforts made by George Washington and other leading political figures to reclaim their human property.[3] A total of about 20,000 slaves defected to the British in the course of the war; about 12,000 survived or escaped recapture.[4] The majority of the survivors were evacuated with the remaining British troops in 1782–1783 and made their way to the West Indies, British North America, and Britain.[5] Some moved on from these intended places of refuge and settled in Africa; others found even more distant homes in India and Australia. The first fleet to reach New South Wales in 1788 contained eleven black convicts who were freed slaves from the former mainland colonies. In this way, a handful of colonial subjects emerged from the demise of one empire to help found another. Australian citizens may be surprised to learn that their country began as a multiracial society and that the origins of its settlers are global, and not exclusively British.

Harry, too, eventually traveled beyond his intended destination. In 1783, he was sent to Nova Scotia with several thousand other loyalists, the majority of whom were white.[6] However, the authorities in Nova Scotia failed to match the honorable action of the British officer who had refused to return Harry to his distinguished owner. The settlement was underfunded, and the minority of black immigrants had difficulty securing the land grants they needed to ensure self-sufficiency. After years of frustration and hardship, Harry, with his wife, Jenny, and 1,200 other freed slaves, volunteered in 1791 to help found a settlement in West Africa. The settlement, which became Freetown in the following year, was managed by the Sierra Leone Company, a new venture organized by the leading humanitarians and abolitionists of the day: Granville Sharp, Thomas Clarkson, and William Wilberforce.[7] Although Harry and his compatriots had moved to another continent, they soon found that they had not distanced themselves from the problems that had driven them from North America. The new settlement lacked adequate finance; promised land grants were slow to appear; rents were oppressive; the justice system was discriminatory; the administration was authoritarian. In April 1799, a group of settlers, including Harry Washington, took advantage of the Governor's temporary absence to appoint administrators who would deal with their grievances. On his return, the Governor reacted, first with discipline and then with force. Local rulers had only just quelled a series of long-running slave rebellions in the region, and the British had no intention of allowing a further outbreak of unrest to spread.[8] Harry Washington was among those tried for rebellion, convicted, and exiled to a remote part of the settlement, where he died as one of the almost forgotten leaders of a free community.

There are many ways of explaining the American Revolution, each with its own claims to validity. Materialism and ideology have contended for primacy; the view from below has been set against the view from above. The story has been carried from the East Coast into the vast interior, where advancing settlers met the indigenous inhabitants of the continent. The next step, which lies in an unspecified future, will be to compare the results of this approach with studies of imperial expansion in other parts of the world, where similar interactions are established features of the literature on empire. Nevertheless, revisionist scholarship has failed to dislodge the most popular treatment, which tells the saga of how a new and exceptional nation achieved and spread liberty and democracy.[9] Harry's story stands apart from this now hallowed account of the founding of the Republic. His biography draws attention to losers and not just winners, to the divisions that produced what began as a civil war, and to notions of freedom that spread far beyond the elites who articulated them so powerfully.

The fortunes of empire also gave Harry's life an additional, global dimension that is best seen from an imperial standpoint. This approach does not represent a willful attempt to revive an older account of the Revolution; nor does it stand in opposition to the view from within.[10] Rather, it complements research on the internal features of the Revolution that specialists have explored so capably, and joins a growing trend in placing the event in a perspective that spans the Atlantic and ventures into the Pacific.[11] Considered from this position, the American Revolution appears as one among a series of imperial revolutions across the world. Its importance is not to be denied; nor, however, should it be exaggerated by projecting the superpower status attained by the United States in the twentieth century on the past. It is salutary to remember that, at the close of the eighteenth century, Haiti was the richest colony in the Atlantic and that the population of Mexico alone equaled that of the United States and provided Spain with more revenue from taxation than all thirteen mainland colonies raised for Britain.[12] Harry's story draws attention to some of the wider ramifications of what traditionally has been seen as a national event. It joins the American Revolution to the crisis of the military-fiscal state discussed in chapter 2, and illustrates the emerging paradox of empire, whereby British colonial policy attempted to marry humanitarian endeavor with authoritarian control in the nineteenth century.

The Revolution was the product of a dialectic whereby the success of the military-fiscal state in promoting development generated forces that had the capacity both to challenge the established order in Britain and to resist the imperial presence in the New World. Military-fiscal states were highly geared in the sense that their investment in warfare far exceeded the financial resources at their disposal. Fiscal imperatives arising from massive and invariably underestimated war expenditures compelled often desperate searches for new and increased taxes. Taxation, however, touched minds as well as pockets and became joined to wider issues of sovereignty and representative government. The crisis of the military-fiscal state in the late eighteenth century converted fiscal issues into tests of government authority. Assertive policies, devised by centralizing governments, drove the final confrontation, which ended British rule in the mainland colonies while expanding it into India.

The revolt against British rule hurried the leaders of the United States into a bold experiment with a federal constitution in a bid to solidify the new state. The Constitution established rules of political conduct that were to guide the Republic down to the Civil War, and for this reason its consequences occupy a central place in studies of the period. The Revolution settlement was also the first important attempt by a major decolonized state to establish conditions that would not only sustain political viability but also foster economic development. The achievement of formal independence, however, was not the end of the "empire story." The extent to which the United States was able to convert formal independence into effective independence is the subject of the next chapter. In preparing the way for this assessment, the discussion here also aims to alert historians of empire to the merits of adding the United States to the long list of ex-colonial states that struggled to make the transfer of power a reality.

Zachary Macaulay, the Governor of Freetown, captured part of the wider story in 1793, when he observed of the rebellions along the west coast of Africa that: "The present combination of African chiefs to crush these people and the gallant struggle it is likely they will make for their liberty will form a parallel to the history of Europe at this moment."[13] Macaulay's prophecy was fulfilled. The revolutions in Europe and the New World were precursors of subsequent decolonizing movements, as expanding aspirations, claims based on universal rights, and economic grievances ran into uncomprehending colonial policies, which progressed from initial coercion to eventual capitulation. Harry Washington and many thousands like him were actors in a vast human drama, which in retrospect can be categorized impersonally as the culmination of proto-globalization in the Western world.

TOWARD "THE NEW COLONY-SYSTEM"[14]

Walpole's strategy for defending the Revolution of 1688 and the Hanoverian succession depended on limiting warfare and the damaging costs it incurred.[15] Overseas and imperial trade, which generated profit and revenue, were intimately linked to policy toward Europe, which ran at a loss. The one funded the other; the success of both was necessary to preserve Britain's independence and the political stability that were essential to London's ability to raise long-term loans. The national credit card issued by the City allowed payment to be postponed but could neither dampen criticism of rising public debt, nor mitigate the short-term costs of war, which were felt in losses of men and materials, shortages of food supplies, and interruptions to business. The centrality of these issues can be seen in the evolution of the word "budget," which first entered political debate during the excise crisis of 1733. By 1764, when George Grenville proposed additional taxes for the mainland colonies, the term had become a staple of rival party programs. In that year, David Hartley published a popular pamphlet entitled, *The Budget*, addressed to "The Man who Thinks Himself a Minister," which set the tone for innumerable future exchanges on the subject.[16]

In 1739, Walpole lost his balance. He became a reluctant participant in what was intended to be a short war with Spain that developed into a long conflict with additional adversaries.[17] The War of the Austrian Succession, which began in the following year, included France, drew Britain into continental Europe to defend Flanders and Hanover, and spread across the world. The Treaty of Aix la-Chapelle in 1748 ended one war but incubated another by commissioning a settlement of postwar boundaries in North America. The acrimonious negotiations over disputed land in the "backcountry" that followed led to a resumption of hostilities in 1754 and culminated in the Seven Years' War (1756–1763), which specialists judge to be the first truly global war for empire.[18] The strains of the conflict brought down Walpole and gave William Pitt, one of his most assertive critics, the opportunity to direct the war effort.[19] Pitt brought new vigor to the task and, equally important, new money too. The combination helped Britain to secure victory in 1763. Pitt gambled that the expansion of trade and empire would pay for the war, enhance Britain's power, and secure the votes of grateful electors. In the event, the road to peace was paved with unexpected hazards as well as optimistic intentions.

Protracted international conflict brought ambiguous consequences. The war effort, combined with loyalist propaganda, helped to foster a sense of national purpose and solidarity that generated enthusiasm for the imperial cause and set temporary limits to party rivalries.[20] The army ceased to be seen as a threatening extension of royal authority and came to symbolize the defense of the nation as a whole.[21] John Bull, who began his career in 1712 as a figure of fun, evolved in the 1760s as a steadying symbol of the distinctive virtues of free-born Englishmen.[22] The empire became a unifying national cause associated with Britain's providential, Protestant mission.[23] The warfare state made the English empire British, even though it was still managed by a board of directors based in London. In the short run, however, the fortunes of war brought disappointment and distress that were capable of toppling governments, as Walpole discovered. The loss of Minorca in 1756 prompted widespread demonstrations; the execution of Admiral John Byng in 1757 led to public protests against the management of the war effort; the revival of the militia—a form of conscription—in the following year was deeply unpopular.

By 1757, when Pitt emerged from the ranks of the Patriot Whigs, economic development had begun to alter the political map. Pitt drew part of his strength from a stratum of manufacturers and merchants who had grown in number and influence in London and the provinces since 1688, and from a broader public that gave him the title of "The Great Commoner."[24] These groups turned to Pitt to champion their interests against the Whig magnates and City elite, to end corruption and waste in government, and to create lucrative openings in overseas trade. They looked forward, not back, and regarded their political opponents as closet absolutists who were working to betray the Revolution of 1688. Pitt rapidly expanded the defense budget. Subsidies to European allies, notably Prussia, tied down French forces on the continent and allowed Britain to make colonial gains overseas, which in turn sapped French power at home. Increased financial support for the colonists in North America contained and eventually helped to defeat France there. France was to be eliminated as a competitor; Britain was to become the first undisputed superpower.[25] The circle was to be squared: wealth derived from controlling the highly prized colonial trades would pay for the aggressive policies needed to acquire them. Britain would dominate the peace settlement, secure the Hanoverian monarchy, entrench the Protestant succession, and expand overseas trade and empire. The Patriot Whigs and their progressive allies in government would garner the rewards of success: permanent power and popularity.

The accession of George III in 1760, followed by the prospect of peace, initiated a reaction that brought to prominence new leaders who opposed Pitt's extravagant foreign policy and program of moderate political reform.[26] Tories and conservative Whigs rallied around the court and the aristocracy; new ministers, headed successively by Lord Bute, George Grenville, and Lord North, took charge of government business. From their elevated perspective, it appeared that the radical Whigs were subverting the principles of the Glorious Revolution and threatening the stability of the state. The new ministry applied conservative policies to achieve austerity in government and increase revenues from taxation. The aim was to cut the national debt, eliminate profligacy, restore probity to public life, and halt the drift to seditious radicalism. Accordingly, the government moved swiftly to bring the war to a close. In 1763, the Peace of Paris preserved the Hanoverian succession, expelled France from North America and India, and confirmed Britain's dominance as the unmatched imperial power of the time.

Pitt judged that the settlement made too many concessions and missed an exceptional opportunity to destroy French military power permanently.[27] Tories and conservative Whigs, however, were preoccupied with the huge costs of victory. The national debt, which had already expanded during the War of the Austrian Succession, nearly doubled between 1756 and 1763.[28] Peace would stem the hemorrhage; new taxes would pay down the debt. Fiscal reform would induce moral reform; the natural balance of society would be restored. Bolingbroke's vision, it seemed, could still be made a reality. The political costs of increasing taxes, however, were a pressing and unremitting concern. As the tax burden in Britain was already heavy, the potential for political damage was extensive. Moreover, the spoils of war added to the costs of peace by increasing the funds needed to control the vast new territory in North America allocated to Britain under the terms of the peace treaty.[29] In 1763, the City sought assurances that interest on the national debt would continue to be paid in full.[30] Parliament was caught: members dared not jeopardize their ability to raise future loans, yet were unwilling to inflict political damage on themselves by increasing domestic taxes.

Pitt's Patriot supporters, headed by the radical populist John Wilkes, alarmed the authorities by carrying opposition to the new government from parliament to the streets of London.[31] Wilkes created a political organization that mobilized tradesmen, artisans, and others who had been excluded from national politics. His program, which advocated press freedom, religious tolerance, open government, and an enlarged franchise, had wide appeal to an extent that also made him a hero in the cause of liberty in the mainland colonies, where his example provided encouragement to critics of British rule. The government hounded Wilkes and brought the strong arm of the law to bear on him and the stronger arm of military force to deter his followers, though with limited success. In the end, Wilkes deterred himself: advancing years eventually turned him toward a form of conservatism that was as robust as the radicalism of his youth, though not before his criticism of the established order had taken root. Wilkes's example confirmed the government's belief that radical challenges to authority had to be suppressed. Compromise and concession would be taken as signs of weakness and would embolden subversive claims.

Wilkes was far from being a lone voice. Attacks on over-centralized government, high taxes, corruption, and criticism of policies toward India and the mainland colonies all grew in scale and volume from the 1760s. Proximity enabled the London "mob" to sit on the doorsteps of power, but the amorphous "middling sort" also made their presence felt. Christopher Wyvill's Yorkshire Association, which had branches in twenty-one counties, pressed for parliamentary reform and greater accountability in the late 1770s and early 1780s. Groups of dissenters and reformers, including such notable public figures as Richard Price, Joseph Priestley, and Mary Wollstonecraft, formulated and publicized plans for a better world. Benjamin Franklin, who attended a number of their meetings, referred to his coffeehouse companions in what he called the "Club of Honest Whigs" as "such Good Creatures in the midst of so perverse a Generation."[32] In reality, the "Good Creatures" did not act as one, and there was no "great convergence" of elite and popular politics. Nevertheless, governments of all stripes were put on notice that the demand for reform was widespread and was unlikely to be wished away.

At this point, government ministers formulated a bold response to the revenue problem. They devised a plan to satisfy the City while also avoiding the political consequences of galvanizing radicalism at home: the empire was to be taxed instead. A similar strategy was to be deployed in 1848, when efforts to shift a weighty fiscal burden from the metropolis to the empire helped the British government to maintain political stability within the United Kingdom, when much of the rest of Europe was in a state of upheaval.[33] To its advocates, the proposal was just and reasonable. Although the mainland colonies had contributed to the war effort by paying additional taxes, their load was far lighter than was carried by their counterparts in Britain. Moreover, parliament had agreed to reimburse more than 40 percent of the military costs the colonies had incurred.[34] In 1763, Grenville and his colleagues, with what they thought was a promising solution in sight, set about creating an authoritarian tributary empire, which Burke referred to as "a new colony-system."[35] Plans were drawn up to secure the political control needed to keep revenues flowing by stationing a large standing army in North America. New taxes were imposed; the customs service was expanded; the navy was deployed to help enforce tax collection.

Radical Whigs responded with as much vigor as their minority status allowed.[36] Some of the most eminent and astute political figures of the day attacked the new colonial policy. In addition to Pitt, Edmund Burke, Charles James Fox, and the Marquis of Rockingham were all persistent critics of government policy who opposed the new taxes and urged conciliation. Senior army officers, headed by General Henry Conway, joined them.[37] Pitt, in opposition, defended Wilkes, argued against parliamentary taxes on the mainland colonies, and helped to secure the repeal of the Stamp Act. He and his supporters hoped to manage the empire of settlement in such a way as to guarantee unity, or at least peaceful coexistence.[38] The government's extractive and coercive measures ran counter to the radicals' vision of a growing, prosperous, and cooperative outer province of Britain that had the potential to provide a limitless market for British manufactures. Their empire was primarily one of trade in which low and progressive rates of tax would lift purchasing power and benefit all parties. Revenues would rise because prosperity would increase; fiscal probity would be achieved by ending corruption; moderate parliamentary reform would provide the votes needed to consign Tories and conservative Whigs to political oblivion. The efforts of the Pittites, however, could not divert the government from its fixed course, and by the time Pitt again took office, briefly, in 1766–1768, he was too ill to direct affairs of state effectively.

By that point too, the fiscal consequences of warfare had joined wider assessments of imperial policy. The view that empire was a providential expression of national greatness maintained its hold on patriotic opinion. Nevertheless, criticism swelled as Britain's presence in India and its policy toward the mainland colonies approached their turning points. Commentators in Scotland and Ireland, who had firsthand experience of living under semicolonial and colonial conditions, formulated particularly wide-ranging and increasingly censorious appraisals of Britain's actions overseas. The idea that the Glorious Revolution inaugurated a new era of progress that had spread or would spread to the empire was a familiar theme in the writings of the luminaries of the Scottish Enlightenment. David Hume, Adam Ferguson, and William Robertson, like Adam Smith, approved of commercial society, which they equated with civilization and contrasted with a preceding state of savagery. They regarded the formation of the Union as a progressive act and favored benign expansion driven by what Robertson called "the gentle pressures of commerce."[39] In 1754, Hume was willing to approve of "British dominion," where it was maintained by "mild government and great naval force."[40] Problems arose when the pressure ceased to be gentle and government was no longer mild. This happened, according to Ferguson, when commercial society developed more vices than virtues, and lost sight of values such as public duty that, ironically, were one of the attributes of "barbarous" people. At this point, the fate of Rome beckoned.

As the military-fiscal state entered what critical observers thought was a path of self-destruction in the second half of the century, commentaries on empire took a pessimistic turn. Swift's distinctive voice had already registered his searing critique of Britain's indifference to the plight of Ireland's rural poor. Burke's condemnation of the violence and loss of civil liberties that accompanied foreign rule followed. Burke, however, struck a characteristically moderate if also ambivalent position: he argued the case for reform, while holding that Ireland could prosper only if it retained its links with England. David Hume's reaction to the rise of the over-mighty state was unqualified. He deplored the aggressive mercantilism and political irresponsibility that had allowed the English public debt to reach what he judged, in the 1760s, to be unsustainable levels. In his opinion, England had turned away from progress and had become "sunk in Stupidity, Barbarism and Faction."[41] In 1768, Hume advocated giving the mainland colonies independence long before the colonists themselves did, judging that it would be best to "let them alone to govern or misgovern themselves as they think proper."[42] How can anyone expect, he asked rhetorically, "that a form of Government will maintain an Authority at 3,000 Miles distance when it cannot make itself be respected or even treated with common Decency at home?"[43] Analogies with Rome, made topical by Gibbon after the publication of the *Decline and Fall of the Roman Empire* in 1776, influenced all parties to the debate thereafter.[44] By the turn of the century, the colorful Scot, William Playfair, advertised the extent of Gibbon's influence in his own study of decline and fall, which deplored the loss of civic virtue brought by conquests, excessive consumption, and indebtedness.[45]

Francis Hutcheson's utilitarianism, which greatly influenced both Hume and Smith, had subversive implications. If the duty of government was to seek the greatest happiness of the greatest number, what actions were citizens entitled to take if the principle was either not followed or not realized? Hutcheson answered the question by recognizing the right of rebellion against governments that did not act for the common good. Empires were especially suspect. In Hutcheson's judgment, nothing has

> occasioned more misery in human life than a vain and insolent ambition both in princes and popular states of extending their empires, and bringing every neighbouring state under subjection to them; without consulting the real felicity either of their own

people or of their new acquisitions. In short, in foreign as in colonial policy that is best which considers most fully the welfare of
all mankind.[46]

Such arguments helped to galvanize the movement associated with
Thomas Muir, the Scottish radical, who campaigned with the Friends of
the People for a reformed monarchy and increased political representation in the 1790s.[47] They also inspired subsequent anti-imperial movements that eventually contributed to the formulation of the concept of
human rights after World War II. Twentieth-century colonial nationalism owes much to eighteenth-century Glasgow.

JOHN COMPANY AT WORK[48]

India felt the drive for revenue before it reached the mainland colonies.
By the middle of the century, the East India Company had established
a stake in India that matched its standing as the holder of the military-
fiscal state's principal global franchise.[49] The Company flew its own flag
and had its own administration, courts, and coinage.[50] It maintained its
own fleet and supported its own army, which increased rapidly after 1763
to reach nearly 70,000 men by 1780. It developed a distinctive, justificatory ideology of superiority, and had hopes of spreading a moral code
based on the Protestant ethic.[51] Its experiments in ruling "alien peoples"
had a profound influence on colonial administration throughout the
British Empire in the nineteenth and twentieth centuries.[52] The Company's preparations for assuming a larger political role acquired greater
urgency in the 1750s, when it ran into financial difficulty following the
decline of trade with Gujarat and a rise in military expenditure after the
outbreak of the Seven Years' War. London's need for revenue matched
the Company's need to find new ways of improving its fortunes. In 1757,
Robert Clive's victory over the Nawab of Bengal at the Battle of Plassey
opened the way to a solution.

Current explanations of Britain's advance into India tend to emphasize developments on the periphery. A consideration of the strengths and
weaknesses of the states that were emerging from the decline of the Mughal Empire is one element; the role of the East India Company's local officials, notably Robert Clive, is another.[53] Specialists have long discussed the
relative weight to be attached to these two causes, which became joined in
conflict in 1757.[54] The approach from the periphery is indispensable and
illuminating. However, it captures only part of the story, which needs to be
placed in the wider context provided by geopolitical and fiscal calculations

in London.[55] The turn to empire was controversial. Pitt and the radical
Whigs envisaged an empire of trade rather than of territory; the directors
of the East India Company were wary of the costs involved in tangling
with increasingly fraught relations among the states that emerged from
the decline of the Mughal Empire. Nevertheless, Pitt had a war to win
and Britain's agent in India, the East India Company, had an obligation to
prosecute it and to find the money to do so. The need to capture a strategic resource, saltpeter (potassium nitrate), which had the potential to win
the war as well as to turn a profit, was an additional motive for action.[56]
Private traders, including those with links to the City of London, wanted
an end to the uncertainties that inhibited trade. War was risky but ultimately unavoidable because Britain's global commercial supremacy depended on restraining and preferably defeating its main rival, France.

These imperatives created the conditions in which Clive and other
ambitious officers could see chances and take them. Clive's initiative was
intended to create a tribute-paying territorial empire. Pitt hoped that
commercial priorities could be restored with peace; the directors of the
East India Company concurred. As the cost of securing the modest territory around Calcutta that Clive had acquired quickly exceeded his optimistic estimates, the directors of the Company resolved to limit further
expansion. With his plans to use Plassey as the bridgehead for invading
India thwarted, Clive began a campaign to dislodge the Company's directors in London. In 1762, following the departure of Pitt and Newcastle
from office, Lord Bute and his conservative allies took charge of policy.
In 1763, when George Grenville was appointed to follow Bute as prime
minister, the political balance shifted decisively toward Clive. In the following year, the faction backing Clive succeeded in appointing an ally as
chairman of the Company.[57] Grenville's influence then secured Clive's return to Bengal with a comprehensive mandate for dealing with renewed
opposition from the Nawab and his supporters.

Bengal was to be brought fully under the control of the East India
Company. Its vast revenues, after expenses, were to be transferred
through the Company to Britain, where they would help to pay down
the national debt, ease the tax burden, take the edge off radical claims,
and strengthen the hold of the landed oligarchy. The undertaking was
to be justified on the grounds that the Nawab and his government were
corrupt and inefficient, and Indian society was in need of reform. These
were audacious claims, given that the British government was resolute
in resisting reform at home. They nevertheless laid the foundation for
the idea of the "civilizing mission," which became part of the conventional wisdom of imperialism in the nineteenth century.

In 1765, Clive appeared to have hit the jackpot: the Mughal Emperor issued a *diwani* (grant) that gave the Company rights to tax revenues from Bengal, the richest province in the empire, and also from Bihar and Orissa. Since revenues from Bengal alone amounted to about one-quarter of Britain's public revenue, it looked as if conservative plans for an extractive, territorial empire were about to be realized.[58] Once again, however, expectation outpaced reality. By the close of the 1760s, it was evident that the "Indian solution" was not going to resolve the revenue problem. A contemporary historian reported that, in 1768, "those who recently contemplated India as a never-failing source of riches, and as a territory sufficiently opulent to provide for all the exigencies of Great Britain, now considered it as a precarious, and perhaps unprofitable tenure."[59] By 1772, continuing military expenditure, the need to hold dividend payments at levels that would retain the loyalty of important investors, and a substantial mandatory annual payment to the British government, had brought the Company close to bankruptcy.[60] Creative accountancy could no longer disguise reality.[61] No government was willing to raise land taxes; excise taxes had exceeded resentment point; Scotland and Ireland had already been squeezed. Additional sources of revenue would have to be found and robust means applied, if necessary, to secure them. The mainland colonies were the only remaining possibility with the potential to meet the need.

A REVOLUTION OF DECLINING EXPECTATIONS

The explanation of the American Revolution offered here seeks to join materialism and ideology. Marx correctly emphasized the part played by specific socioeconomic groups, though, in the case of the American Revolution, class relations were imperfectly formed and living standards were improving, not declining. Tocqueville rightly drew attention to the importance of the link between increasing aspirations and material progress, though his argument was incomplete. The combination, he claimed, fueled a desire for change that could lead to revolution. "For it is not always when things are going from bad to worse that revolutions break out."[62] On the contrary, "a grievance comes to appear intolerable once the possibility of removing it crosses men's minds."[63] More particularly, crises of authority surfaced when governments sought to ameliorate the conditions they had created, or when expanding expectations were checked, whether by circumstance or policy.[64] At that point, "dazzled by the prospect of a felicity undreamed of hitherto and now within their

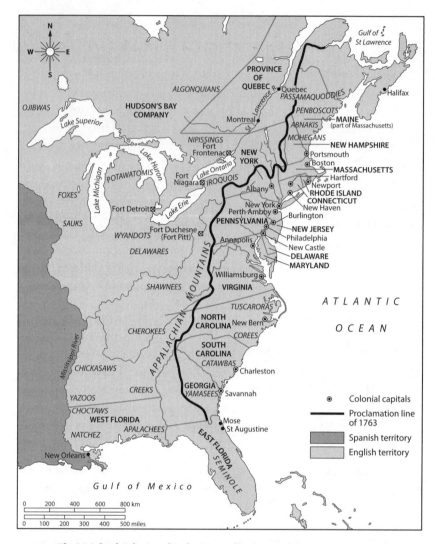

MAP 3.1. The Mainland Colonies after the Peace of Paris, 1763.

grasp," people readily became "blind to the very real improvement that had taken place and eager to precipitate events."[65] The American Revolution was made possible by increased resources, rising living standards, and boundless prospects; it was made certain by a rapid downturn in expectations brought about by British policy. The deprivation felt by the colonists was real, but it was relative rather than absolute.

This claim is wholly compatible with the view that idealism, whether political or religious, was an inspiration to action. Key figures in the Rev-

olution believed that they had a special opportunity to create a virtuous republic that would marry individual freedom to civic responsibility
and halt the drift to decadence that appeared to be corroding British
society.[66] Political idealism, however, had institutional underpinnings.
The mainland colonies, unlike Western Europe, were land-surplus
economies, where settlers had the prospect of acquiring land cheaply.
In these circumstances, it was possible to envisage a society of cohesive
rural communities that could play a crucial part in restoring organic harmony to the social order. Equally, it was necessary for political leaders
to recognize that a society composed largely of independent farmers, as
opposed to tenants, wielded significant bargaining power. Accordingly,
colonial legislatures introduced progressive elements into the tax system
and endorsed reforms that ended entail and primogeniture.[67] Environmental circumstances provided colonists with greater opportunities than
were available in Europe and fostered a concept of liberty that was correspondingly spacious in protecting the property rights of the many rather
than of the few.

Religious inspiration also contributed to the Revolution, though the
Great Awakening is no longer seen to have been a prime mover in the
events leading to the break with Britain. The movement, which began in
the late 1730s, left too many colonies untouched for it to achieve proto-
national status. Moreover, by the time the Revolution was under way,
religious fervor had subsided and evangelicals, though present, were not
a dominant influence among the revolutionary leaders.[68] The Awakening's main connections lay elsewhere.[69] Nevertheless, the principle of
religious liberty helped to unite the colonists against arbitrary power
of any kind, while the impetus evangelicals generated created a form of
spiritual secession that passed power to the people before political independence became a serious prospect. In questioning established hierarchies, evangelicals opened up a new front in the campaign for individual
rights. They challenged Reformed Calvinists (Puritans) in New England
as well as Anglicans in Virginia, both of whom sought to impose uniformity of faith on their communities.[70] In this respect, the Awakening prefigured subsequent developments in other parts of the British Empire,
where local variations on the Christian message gave vent to a desire for
spiritual autonomy in a situation of continuing political subordination.
As the rebel cause developed, political claims won spiritual endorsement.[71] Other causes, however, had already moved the rebels to act.[72] It
was only after the break with Britain that religious leaders justified the
Revolution by presenting it as part of a providential plan for saving the
world.[73] Rather than religion inciting the Revolution, it was the success

of the patriots in securing independence that promoted the religiosity that colonized the new Republic from that time onward.

A remarkable expansion of the mainland colonies underlay these political and religious developments.[74] A combination of natural increase and immigration led to rapid population growth: in 1700 the settler population was estimated at about 273,000; by 1770 it had risen to about 1,719,000.[75] As the original settlements filled up, they also filled out. By 1776, the year of the Declaration of Independence, the thirteen colonies stretched some 1,250 miles from Maine (then part of Massachusetts) to Georgia, which became a crown colony in 1752. Adventurous frontiersmen had pushed inland to the Appalachian fringe, where the prospects of turning sand into gold met the claims of Native Americans, whose sand was already gold enough.

Weight of numbers transformed the prospects for white settlement. They removed the tentative, uncertain character of the early settlements and made possible a massive rise in output.[76] Domestic production responded to the growth of population; exports, headed by tobacco, rice, and indigo, provided the foreign exchange needed to purchase imports. Staple exports, notably from the southern colonies, tied overseas trade to Britain, which in return supplied consumer goods that the colonists could not manufacture locally. In the short period between 1740–1743 and 1770–1774, the value of Britain's imports from the mainland colonies doubled, while her exports to them more than tripled.[77] Bilateral relations were joined to a pattern of multilateral settlements that extended the colonies' links with Britain. New England developed substantial exports of food to meet demand in the West Indies, which produced sugar for the British market. Britain, in turn, relied on reexports of colonial imports to help settle its deficits with continental Europe. The resulting pattern of export growth was reproduced elsewhere in the course of the nineteenth century, when it became established as the classic form of colonial exchange.

Adam Smith identified the basic reason for the successful development of the mainland colonies: "The purchase and improvement of uncultivated land is there the most profitable employment of the smallest as well as the largest capitals and the direct road to all the fortune . . . which can be acquired in that country."[78] In contrast to Europe, "such land is . . . to be had for almost nothing."[79] There was an additional bonus: "in consequence of the moderation of their taxes," colonists in North America were able to retain "a greater proportion of this produce."[80] In the course of the century, these incentives worked their magic: output per head increased; living standards rose.[81] One estimate suggests that by 1774, per capita incomes in the mainland colonies were more than 50 percent higher than in Britain.[82] Although calculations of this kind and for this period have to be regarded as orders of magnitude, the trend is clear. Fortunately, independent sources confirm improvements in welfare. A comparison of the heights of American and British soldiers has shown that colonials were taller and healthier because their standards of nutrition, which were mainly a function of disposable incomes, were higher.[83] The huge increase in consumer imports provides equally impressive, if less direct, evidence of rising standards of living. The main towns, such as Boston, Philadelphia, and New York, not only set standards of affluence in displaying fashions and household goods, but also served as centers of diffusion for items such as textiles, ceramics, and metal products, which spread into the countryside and beyond the circles of privilege.[84]

The prevailing pattern of consumption, detailed in the list of imported goods, was characteristic of settler societies whose aim was to mobilize the opportunities of the frontier to reproduce the customs of the metropolis. Colonial consumers were predominantly British in origin. On the eve of the Revolution, one estimate suggests that more than 60 percent of the population of the mainland colonies was English, nearly 80 percent was British, and 98 percent was Protestant.[85] Typical newcomers were craftsmen from the south of England and farming families from northern England and Scotland, whose modest prospects had been curtailed by a combination of unemployment and improving landlords.[86] The majority established independent household farms, produced for the market in varying degrees, and by the close of the century had achieved a level of individual property ownership that was far higher than it was in Britain.[87] The new owners expected that the gains they had hewn from the frontier would be protected, and they regarded Britain as their defender of last resort.

Material improvement was an aim shared by most colonists; status was particularly important to elites, who were concerned to overcome the sense of inferiority they felt as outer provincials. London was their magnet. They visited the capital to refresh their knowledge of styles and standards, and sent their sons to be educated there.[88] While defining their identity by association with the metropolis, they distanced themselves from Native Americans, who were deemed to be savages, as well as from the rough and ready frontiersmen, who also fell short of civilized standards. In the 1780s, George Washington called white settlers on the Western borderlands "worthless fellows," "our own white Indians," and a "parcel of banditti who will bid defiance to all authority."[89] Violence was endemic in the Wild East long before it galloped westward.[90] Before

1776, abundant opportunities helped to generate rising incomes, though also regional disparities. Coastal towns had the highest incomes and the greatest concentrations of wealth; the long backcountry frontier was a region of risk and poverty.[91] Material success, which was especially visible in the towns of the North and the plantations of the South, encouraged the elite to believe, with John Jay, that "those who own the country are the most fit persons to participate in the government of it."[92]

This proposition, which reaffirmed a fundamental principle shared by Tories and conservative Whigs in Britain, was a further indication that the leaders of the settler majority aimed to Anglicize colonial America rather than to begin the world anew in the radical sense that Tom Paine was to advocate.[93] Puritans in New England wanted an opportunity to establish purified versions of church and state that the Commonwealth had promised and the Restoration had disavowed. Landowners in the South hoped to create a neo-feudal order that was safe from radical and, above all, leveling movements. Regicides and royalists played out in politics the divisions that had ended in civil war in the 1640s.

Differences of wealth and status were to influence attitudes toward the Revolution, but in mid-century they did nothing to qualify the intense loyalty to the crown that was apparent throughout colonial society. Benjamin Franklin and John Hancock, two eminent figures who later signed the Declaration of Independence, considered themselves greatly honored to have been able to attend the coronation of George III in 1761. Franklin was then an ardent monarchist who regarded the British Empire as the vector of progress in international affairs. Under the new king's "virtuous and wise" rule, Franklin wrote, "faction will dissolve and be dissipated like a morning fog."[94] Further down the social order, popular celebrations of military successes during the Seven Years' War expressed the fervent loyalty of colonial subjects and their pride in Britain's global reach. In 1760, a contributor to the *Maryland Gazette* could scarcely contain his enthusiasm for Britain's achievements:

> From Pole to Pole my rambling Muse shou'd rove,
> And where o'er th' astonished World she drove,
> In ev'ry climate as she past along,
> Great GEORGE's triumphs should adorn her Song.[95]

Franklin's fog never dissipated. Soon after the coronation, events began to move at a pace that matched that of the second great decolonization after 1945: disagreements turned to dissent in the 1760s; the Declaration of Independence was signed and proclaimed in 1776; political independence was achieved in 1783. A retrospective view can easily find distant antecedents. For present purposes, the most significant can be traced to the Glorious Revolution, which produced complementary demonstrations in the mainland colonies, where settlers opposed the extractive plans of the Stuarts and feared the reintroduction of Roman Catholicism as the official state religion.[96]

In the 1690s, the colonists were able to win political concessions from the new monarchy, which needed the support of the mainland settlements in the long wars with France that followed the Glorious Revolution. The colonists benefited, too, from the confirmation of the Protestant supremacy, which they used to discriminate further against Catholics. Walpole and his successors, Henry Pelham and the Duke of Newcastle, endorsed a restrained style of imperial government that allowed mercantilist regulations to be applied with a light hand. On occasion, Walpole went even further: in 1741, when colonial affairs complicated European politics, he declared that "it would be better for England if all the Plantations were at the Bottom of the sea."[97] In 1775, Burke adopted a more conciliatory tone in characterizing the period before 1762 as one of "wise and salutary neglect."[98] By then, the mainland colonists had acquired degrees of effective self-government through local assemblies, and communications with London had come to rely increasingly on informal religious, commercial, and family networks.[99] In these ways, the Glorious Revolution helped the colonists become accustomed to a degree of political and economic freedom that became integrated into their lives and expectations. Arguably, too, the light hand of government had allowed the economic development of the colonies to reach the point where they had the power to challenge what they still regarded as the mother country.

Yet, these developments were permissive rather than determinative.[100] In 1763, the colonists expected that the British government would reward the loyalty they had shown during the long mid-century wars. They had contributed men, money, and materiel to the defeat of France and they looked forward to sharing the "blessings of peace and the emoluments of victory and conquest."[101] They anticipated that Britain would confirm and further extend the informal political and commercial benefits conferred by the period of "salutary neglect" and that they would become joint partners in an enterprise that would expand the empire across the continent. Additionally, the elite hoped that long service in what had become a national cause would enable them to exchange their status as provincials for the respect that equality with England's gentlemen would confer.

They were soon disillusioned. The fiscal imperatives that drove the search for revenue in India applied equally to the mainland colonies.

The period following the Seven Years' War witnessed a series of well-known economic and political impositions, which began with the Sugar Act (1764), the Currency Act (also in 1764), and the Stamp Act (1765), continued with the Townshend Acts (1767), and culminated in the Tea Act (1773) and the Coercive Acts (1774). Vigorous opposition forced the repeal of the Stamp Act and some of the Townshend duties (in 1766 and 1770 respectively), but ultimately failed to deflect the government from its uncompromising policy. The reassertion of Britain's imperial power punctured the colonists' elevated expectations and eroded their loyalty. New taxes hit pocket books; new controls curtailed acquired freedoms. Had all the British government's policies been applied effectively, the colonies would have lost the considerable degree of fiscal autonomy their assemblies had won, and parliament would have been able to enforce the power of the purse. Under the Townshend Acts, for example, revenues gathered from new taxes were used to pay the salaries of an increased number of British colonial officials, to maintain a large army in North America to police the territory won from France in 1763, and to ensure that the colonists conformed to imperial policies. Imposition followed by coercion led to attempts at conciliation, but only at the point where, as Tocqueville observed of the French Revolution, government concessions were read as signs of weakness that stiffened colonial resistance.

The colonists' principal economic aim was to secure a greater degree of autonomy while remaining in the empire. The expansion of the colonies by mid-century had realized some of the continent's potential and indicated that much more lay to hand. A sense of Manifest Destiny had taken hold long before the term was invented. At that point, British policy began to cut into past achievements and reel in hopes for the future by reclaiming control over commercial, monetary, fiscal, and settlement policies. The end of the Seven Years' War inaugurated a period of tight money and deflation. Wartime demand, which had kept the economy buoyant and spirits high, had also expanded credit, encouraged a property boom, and generated inflation. A postwar slump followed the peace. Stricter mercantilist regulations squeezed business profits; austerity prompted creditors to call in debts. The colonists protested, negotiated, and then turned reluctantly to political independence as a means of reaching goals that British policy had closed.

It is hard to draw a single line of causation through all thirteen colonies because the results of British policy varied both regionally and socially. Attempts to measure the general effects of mercantilism, for example, appear to have reached the limits of quantification.[102] Adam Smith's assessment remains the safest guide: mercantilist regulations were consistent with economic growth but inhibited future development. Collectively, however, there is no doubt about the pervasive consequences of Britain's reinvigorated imperial policy. Detailed studies of Massachusetts and Virginia, two of the wealthiest colonies that were also in the vanguard of the Revolution, have demonstrated how the reassertion of British power both damaged and divided established interests. Adversity was not uniform but it was ubiquitous; benefits, if they existed, were neither readily found nor widely advertised.

Boston was the largest port in New England and one of the largest in the thirteen colonies.[103] It was also a major center of opposition to British policy after 1763 and host of the celebrated Tea Party. Boston's merchants had prospered in the era of salutary neglect and had taken advantage of the easy credit offered by London houses during the war years. Smuggling was major business (as it was in Britain) and accounted for about three-quarters of the tea consumed in the mainland colonies. Most tea imports were shipped from sources in the Netherlands, where low taxes reduced purchase costs. Additional profits came from smuggling foodstuffs to the French Indies, especially during the war years, which made the trade doubly illegal. Boston's merchants funded these and other trades with commercial credits advanced by London houses. The merchants, though not rampant free-traders, wanted a commercial system that was adapted to local needs.[104] Some sought opportunities to develop the port's modest trade with continental Europe; others hoped for protection for local manufactures. Consequently, Britain's attempt to enforce mercantilist regulations after 1763 threatened established commercial relations, legal and illegal, and blocked plans for a more expansive future.

The Townshend Duties, which imposed a tax on tea in 1767, set off a fresh round of demonstrations, but these failed to deter the British government, which proceeded to pass the Tea Act in 1773. By the early 1770s, the government had become fully aware of the East India Company's desperate financial position, and in the absence of alternatives applied what turned out to be a desperate remedy. The Tea Act provided further support for the Company by allowing it to export tea directly to the colonies and benefit from tax concessions on shipments. For a short while, tea imported legally became cheaper than smuggled tea. Protests resumed, however, because the new arrangements threatened to undercut the smuggling trade, bypassed Boston's established importers, and consigned shipments of tea to a few importers, who were selected principally for their loyalty to the crown. By the time parliament repealed the Tea Act in 1778, it had stimulated sufficient resentment to help set the Revolution in motion.

The postwar slump and ensuing deflation prompted London creditors to call in their debts. In Massachusetts, the largest debtor among
the northern colonies, the squeeze was felt at all levels of society because
credit had percolated from import merchants to shopkeepers and artisans. Boston's paper money had already been regulated by the Currency
Act of 1751, which sought to protect creditors from depreciating currency. The Currency Act of 1764 extended these provisions to the other
mainland colonies but was also the object of protests in Boston, which
suffered from the tightening of the money supply. Unredeemed debt was
considered a deeply moral failing that damaged not only financial well-
being but also the aspirations of the elite.[105] In 1767, John Hancock, the
leading merchant in Boston, exposed his sensitivities in a letter to one
of his suppliers in London: "I look on myself [as] a Man of Capital &
am not to be put on a footing with every twopenny shopkeeper that addresses you."[106] The danger, which came closer in the 1760s, was that he
and others like him would find themselves reduced to an undesirable
state of two-penny equality. Hancock weighed his options until, loaded
with British impositions, they settled. The loyalist who had attended the
coronation of George III was on his way to becoming a Patriot hero.

Boston's large merchants, who were most affected by the impositions,
were also leaders of the movement that opposed Britain's assertive policies.[107] They were active, too, in the Sons of Liberty, which was founded in
Boston in 1765, though some of the most prominent businessmen distanced
themselves from its populist image and unrestrained tactics. The Sons of
Liberty began by demonstrating against the Sugar, Currency, and Stamp
Acts, and went on to organize or participate in subsequent protests: non-
importation agreements halted the entry of British goods in 1765–1766,
1767–1768, and 1773–1774; the Tea Party in 1773 became a dramatic and
highly publicized statement of opposition to British policy. These episodes generated a sense of solidarity among consumers and confirmed
Boston's image as a center of resolute patriotic commitment.[108]

Opposition to British policy, however, was neither united nor consistent.[109] Protests exposed differences of interest among diverse groups
of participants. Large merchants supported the non-importation agreements partly because they could unload stocks of goods at high prices
and eliminate smaller competitors; shopkeepers, on the other hand,
suffered from a shortage of goods, rising prices, and falling sales. Intim-
idation and violence were deployed to enforce the agreements, which
nevertheless suffered from lack of solid support.[110] Some large merchants remained loyal to the crown; others favored the non-importation
agreements in public while acting against them in private by continu-

ing to import British wares. When the Stamp Act was repealed and the Townshend duties modified, opposition to British policy quickly wilted. Popular radicalism, which was highly visible in key centers, such as Boston, Philadelphia, and New York, had its own priorities, strategies, and solutions.[111] Initially, Boston's large merchants attempted to harness urban discontent for their own purposes. Later, experience of the uncontrolled consequences of what contemporaries referred to as the "mob" prompted the merchants to distance themselves from an insurgency they could no longer control. At such moments, interest trumped principle, and Adam Smith was shown to be a surer guide than John Locke to the causes of the Revolution. Locke, however, still had a voice in the proceedings. Once the colonists realized that they would have no place as equal citizens in Britain's developing concept of national identity, they turned to the doctrine of natural rights to validate their claims.[112]

Virginia was the largest exporter among the mainland colonies trading with Britain, and the largest debtor too.[113] A good deal of the colony's wealth depended on tobacco, which by the middle of the century accounted for about 85 percent of its exports to Britain and provided the purchasing power needed to satisfy the demand for British manufactures. Tobacco also shaped the colony's social structure and values. Large planters created an economy based on slave labor, which grew from a force of fewer than 20,000 in 1700 to reach almost 200,000, amounting to about 40 percent of the colony's total population, in 1776. By then, approximately half of the white households in Virginia owned slaves; the remainder depended mainly on family labor. Slaves transformed the social landscape: hierarchy became aligned with race as well as wealth; marked income inequalities, within and between racial groups, translated into visible differences of rank; political power settled comfortably in the hands of members of the rich, white elite. As the demand for tobacco grew and export production expanded, living standards among both planters and smaller farmers rose. The period between 1730 and 1760, far from being one of increasing immiseration, was a "golden age" for the planters of Virginia and Maryland.[114] Economic dependence arising from international specialization brought prosperity, and with it confirmation of Virginia's long-standing loyalty to the crown and adherence to the values of the metropolis. As one commentator noted, Virginians were "distinguished for their imitations of the people of Great Britain, which extended to every particular of their furniture, dress, and manners."[115]

Dependence, however, also brought vulnerability.[116] The market for tobacco was subject to pronounced swings arising from unpredictable and uncontrollable variations in supply and demand. As production increased, the consequences of market fluctuations multiplied. The magic of cheap credit, conjured into being by the financial revolution, gave the export sector an additional boost from the 1740s, when enterprising Glasgow merchants entered the trade and greatly increased the volume of credit available.[117] By mid-century, the colony's tobacco planters were immersed in commercial debt that they were unable to insure. Virginia, like Massachusetts, was then struck in the early 1760s by the postwar slump and Britain's new program of imperial austerity. As deflation squeezed incomes, creditors began to call in debts. George Washington and Thomas Jefferson, who both farmed tobacco, were among Virginia's numerous distinguished debtors of the period. Washington, who acquired estates and slaves through marriage, fell into debt in the 1760s; Jefferson, who was permanently in debt, combined a taste for luxury with an aversion to the banks that underwrote his extravagant lifestyle. Personal experience of the tobacco market convinced them that the mainland colonies needed to be freed from the excesses of economic dependence, though they had different ideas about how this might be achieved. Although the postwar slump eased by the middle of the decade, the problem of indebtedness remained, and the flow of credit resumed when exports recovered in the late 1760s. A deeper crisis struck in 1772, when the collapse of several London banks caused widespread panic and led to a renewed effort by creditors to collect outstanding debts.[118] By 1776, the mainland colonies owed British merchants some £6 million, which was about twice the annual value of colonial exports.

Faced with these challenges, Virginians explored a range of possibilities, most of which were being tried in other mainland colonies too. The soft option of printing paper money had helped Virginia to meet its tax liabilities during the Seven Years' War but was no longer available. When peace returned, creditors in London and Glasgow persuaded parliament to protect their sterling investments. The result was the Currency Act of 1764, which prevented the mainland colonies from paying debts in depreciated currency.[119] Although the Act was amended in 1773, by then Virginia's debtors had become alienated from the commercial system they had willingly embraced in better times. Virginians also participated in the non-importation agreements, which they regarded as a means of reducing outstanding debts by cutting purchases of consumer imports. In 1769–1770, however, the agreement attracted only limited support because many smallholders withheld their cooperation. The boycott was more effective in 1774 because the economic crisis of 1772 affected a wider range of producers. Even so, support waned as the crisis receded, as it did in Massachusetts, and there was insufficient political momentum to carry the movement forward. Non-export agreements were also tried in an attempt to raise prices, but support was uneven and Virginia was unable to influence market conditions as a whole to the degree needed to produce the desired result. Dissatisfaction with the hazards of monoculture prompted a number of farmers, including George Washington, to diversify their output, notably by cultivating grain, but the returns could not match those of tobacco's "golden age."

There was one other option: territorial expansion.[120] Virginians were already prominent speculators in Western lands and hoped that victory in the Seven Years' War would give full legal recognition to their claims and open Ohio and Kentucky in particular to new investment.[121] The removal of the French threat emboldened investors by reducing their dependence on British military support. Washington and Jefferson, two of many disenchanted tobacco farmers, were prominent among the claimants. Other parties, however, had competing ideas. Native Americans treated the advent of peace as an opportunity to reassert their rights over the disputed territory and demonstrated the seriousness of their intent in the conflict known as Pontiac's War, which broke out in 1763.[122] Seen from the British viewpoint, the Peace of Paris gave the government a chance to control the costs of colonial administration by limiting frontier disputes and confining colonists to areas that were within taxable reach.

The result was the Proclamation Line, which the Privy Council issued in 1763 with the aim of halting settlement beyond the Appalachians. The Proclamation established a formal distinction between Native Americans, who were under royal protection, and colonists, who were the king's subjects. The Line imposed limits that were potentially ruinous for existing investors, who were unable to register titles to land they thought they owned, and frustrated the expectations of those who were keen to follow them. Subsequently, Britain adjusted the Line to include some of the land occupied by colonists who continued to trek westward but refused to recognize the legality of the substantial claims made by absentee speculators.[123] Continuing conflict with Native Americans culminated in 1774 in Dunmore's War, which was an attempt by Virginians to seize land from the Shawnee that could not be acquired peacefully.

On the eve of the Revolution, the Proclamation Line remained a major cause of dissent between Britain and influential colonists whose ambitions had been checked.[124] The empire had reached the limits of effective control. The Commander-in-Chief of British forces in North America, General Thomas Gage, concluded that increasing lawlessness on the frontier called for a powerful military response.[125] At this point, both parties were set on confrontation. One of the first acts of Virginia's independent government in 1776 was to declare the frontier open.

It is no longer plausible to cite Virginia as an example of colonial solidarity in the face of British oppression. Virginia, like Massachusetts, was torn by discord arising from competing interests.[126] Elite planters, late converts to the Patriot cause, attempted to lead and then to control the various protest movements as they swelled into rebellion. The elite had lost face as well as money. Debt transformed what they regarded as relations among gentlemen and reduced their highly prized status. As they saw it, their misfortune arose from a conspiracy of British merchants, who were linked, indirectly, to the crown. This reasoning turned personal difficulties into public politics. The "common cause," however, remained an unachieved ideal, even after the conflict with Britain had begun. The large planters were unable to rely on yeomen and poor rural households, whose reaction to the economic difficulties of the times reflected their own priorities. Yeomen and small farmers refused to join the new companies of "minutemen" organized by the elite and showed little support for the militia. Many large planters were themselves reluctant to serve outside the colony in case their absence exposed their property to looting and encouraged slaves to abscond. Slave revolts in the Caribbean in 1772 provided unsettling news on the mainland; rumors that the British intended to end slavery helped to steer slaveholders toward the rebel camp.[127] In 1775, Lord Dunmore's offer of freedom to slaves who joined British forces turned anxiety into action. Even so, there were few indications that widespread resentment had been transformed into a proto-nationalist consensus.[128]

While the majority of colonists overcame their differences sufficiently to support the Revolution, there were others who stood aside or were hostile to it.[129] Very approximate calculations suggest that about 15–20 percent of the colonists stayed loyal and that about 30 percent remained neutral. Of the loyalists, some 25,000 fought on the British side. A total of about 60,000 loyalists (white, black, and Native American) emigrated, most of them to Canada.[130] Some feared that the rebellion would lead to anarchy; others left in search of a better life. The Revolution was no exception to the rule that civil wars split families. Benjamin Franklin was permanently estranged from his son, William, the last colonial governor of New Jersey and an ardent loyalist, who ended his life in exile in London.[131] Tens of thousands of African slaves escaped; some 20,000 enlisted in the British army in return for freedom, among them Harry Washington; a much smaller number joined the rebel cause for the same reason. The majority of Native American polities aimed for neutrality but were eventually drawn into the conflict. Most of the estimated 12,000 Native Americans who became combatants joined the British side, which they judged offered the best chance of saving their lands. The judgment was correct, as far as it went, but it also ensured that they ended on the losing side. Under the provisions of the Treaty of Paris in 1783, the British abandoned their Native American allies and transferred their claims to disputed territories to the United States. The next gun that fired signaled the start of the great land rush.[132]

The richest colonies in British America remained loyal. The planter elite in the Caribbean, like many planters in the Southern colonies, specialized in agricultural exports produced by slave labor.[133] Like the mainland colonies, they too were tied to the Atlantic system and to the British economy by networks of credit and debt that connected them to the City of London's financial resources. Yet, Britain's colonies in the West Indies remained steadfastly loyal. The history of the Lascelles family helps to explain the different outcomes.[134] Henry Lascelles began as a merchant trading to the West Indies early in the eighteenth century; his son, Edwin, expanded the business in the second half of the century into banking, acquired extensive plantations, and owned almost 3,000 slaves. The Lascelles were cosmopolitans: the family home in Yorkshire was matched by a second base of almost equal importance in Barbados. They made their way by creating an international network of commercial alliances, political connections, and ties of marriage. They added their own considerable financial expertise by introducing new types of mortgages and security, reforming estate management, and altering the prevailing system of accounting. In effect, they were venture capitalists who specialized in taking over faltering businesses and turning them around. As bankers, they loaned money to the government at moments of need; as members of parliament, they lobbied for legislation to support their business interests; as one of the wealthiest families in England, they made their way from gentry to nobility, a feat of upward mobility that reached its summit in 1790, when Edwin Lascelles was created the first Baron Harewood.

The islands remained loyal because most plantation owners were either absentees or sojourners. The transients were Caribbean nabobs whose aim, like their counterparts in India, was to buy their way into the upper reaches of British society. They were capitalists who wished to become English gentlemen. The success of the few, however, was offset by a decline in the status of the majority. After the American Revolution, attitudes in the metropolis toward the planters changed: despite their wealth and loyalty, they came to be seen as subjects rather than as citizens.[135] Even if their goals had been different, the Caribbean islands lacked the resources to support a unilateral declaration of independence. The British navy was their only defense against foreign predators and their everlasting fear of slave rebellions. Planters on the mainland, on the other hand, were capitalists who were neither absentees nor transients, but settlers who were embedded in the land they had acquired and developed. They, too, aimed for gentlemanly status but their ambitions had a home-grown quality, and the resources at their disposal enabled them to translate their dreams into reality.

The triumphant conclusion to the Seven Years' War ended a period during which Britain was regarded on both sides of the Atlantic as the exemplar of the Roman virtues of fortitude and selfless service to the state. When peace came, the battle lines of debate hardened. The entity referred to as "British policy" was in reality the product of fierce and divisive debate about appropriate conduct in dealing with both the mainland colonies and India. In the end, however, political leaders in the United Kingdom closed ranks to resist challenges to parliamentary sovereignty, wherever they arose—including radical threats at home.[136] If the will of parliament was flouted, the political order installed in 1688 would be at risk and, with it, the position of the landed oligarchy, who were the main beneficiaries of the Glorious Revolution. The City of London, though initially sympathetic to the claims of the colonists, also turned against them in the 1770s as anxiety about debt service grew.[137] Gibbon supported the war against the rebellious colonists on the grounds that Britain had the right to defend its possessions. Dr. Johnson condemned the rebels unreservedly. By the 1770s, the American colonists had changed their image of Britain. In their eyes, Britain had become the Rome of tyranny and corruption, and George III had metamorphosed into a Hanoverian Nero. On one side of the Atlantic, the classical model gave credibility to an unprecedented act of separation by locating it in a preordained historical process. On the other side, it reinforced conservative, authoritarian tendencies and helped to launch a program of moral rearmament aimed at rescuing the new Rome from its unwanted but predicted fate. The formation of the Society for the Abolition of the Slave Trade in 1787 was the most significant indication of the changing mood; Burke's celebrated prosecution of Warren Hastings, Governor-General of India, in the following year was the most dramatic.

The colonists did not seek political independence before 1776, despite the provocations of British policy. The First Continental Congress, which met in 1774, deliberated on how to avoid a break with Britain. John Galloway, the delegate from Pennsylvania, presented a plan for home rule within the empire that failed by only one vote. In 1775, Congress still hesitated to take the final step, even though war had broken out and battles had been fought at Lexington and Concord. The Olive Branch Petition the Congress submitted in July of that year drew attention to the extent to which the threat from France had been succeeded by a "domestick danger . . . of a more dreadful kind," but emphasized the continuing loyalty of His Majesty's "still faithful colonists."[138] The olive branch provoked the British government into renewed assertions of militancy, at which point all prospect of compromise disappeared. After a lengthy debate, the Second Congress, which convened in 1776, finally approved the Declaration of Independence. Most of the signatories were reluctant to part from Britain, but felt driven to make the break. Benjamin Franklin expressed his feelings a few weeks later in a private letter to a friend, Sir Richard Howe: "Long did I endeavour with unfeigned and unwearied zeal to preserve from breaking that fine and noble China vase the British Empire."[139] Admiral Howe, who commanded the British fleet in North America in 1776–1778, had sympathized with the colonists from the outset of their dispute with Britain. In 1776, he did his duty, but also with regret.

"AN INDISSOLUBLE UNION OF THE STATES UNDER ONE FEDERAL HEAD"[140]

George Washington, commenting on the achievement of independence in 1783, was well aware of the fragility of the new state and of the defects of its provisional system of government. His reference to an "indissoluble union" was not a celebratory effusion prompted by the creation of the United States, but one of several earnest recommendations for creating a state that would be viable and permanent. His anxieties persisted throughout the 1780s. The mainland colonies had managed the war against Britain through a representative body, the Continental Congress, which they converted into a Confederation in 1781. The Confederation, however, lacked the authority needed to manage the peace. Instability hovered throughout the 1780s. War had devastated the economy.[141] Indebtedness hampered reconstruction. The tax burden was heavier than it had been under British rule.[142] Real per capita incomes fell by about 30 percent between 1774 and 1790.[143] Popular discontent produced sporadic outbreaks of violence.[144] Fear that another European power, or Britain itself, might try to recolonize the continent weighed upon the shoulders of the Republic's presidents at least until the end of the War of 1812.

Carl Becker, writing in 1909, summarized what he saw as the two principal issues linking the Revolution and the subsequent political settlement: the first was securing Home Rule; the second was determining who should rule at home.[145] Once the prospect of Home Rule had been upgraded to independence in 1783, the question of who should rule at home became the substance of politics in the nineteenth century. The sequence set a pattern that decolonizing states followed in the twentieth century, when the unity achieved by opposition to the imperial power had ceased to hold anti-colonial movements together, or, as Becker phrased it, after "the stress of military invasion and loyalist conspiracy" had eased.[146] There was, however, a third, related question that concentrated the minds of the Republic's leaders during the 1780s: how to rule at home. After much debate, conducted amidst the anxieties that Washington had enumerated, a resolution of this issue was reached in 1788, when the majority of the mainland states ratified a new federal constitution, which became the Republic's fundamental and enduring instrument of government in the following year.[147]

The U.S. Constitution was one of the great political compromises of the modern era.[148] It established a federal government with the power to collect taxes, contract sovereign debts, regulate interstate and international relations, and raise an army. The reach of the federal government, though greatly extended, was also checked by provisions that confirmed the right of constituent states to decide their internal affairs. The Constitution provided for a president, two houses of Congress, and a judiciary headed by a Supreme Court. The president was to be selected by an electoral college rather than by popular vote. Membership of the Senate was determined by the number of states, which were allocated two seats each irrespective of their size, and by state legislatures rather than by direct election. Seats in the House of Representatives were apportioned according to the size of the population and filled by election. Judicial nominations were made by the president but were subject to the "advice and consent" of the Senate. The Constitution provided defenses against the emergence of autocracy by separating executive and legislative powers, limiting the reach of the central government, and guaranteeing the rights of member states. The provisions of the Constitution were further protected from sudden or arbitrary revision by a requirement that amendments needed a majority of two-thirds of both houses and three-quarters of all the states.

Although the federation was a departure from Britain's unitary state, it drew on familiar precedents, including the Union of England and Scotland in 1707.[149] The aim of forming "a more perfect union," which appears in the Preamble to the Constitution, was borrowed from a letter written by Queen Anne in 1706 urging the Scottish parliament to approve a closer association with England.[150] The debate also called on European political thought, especially Montesquieu's ideas about the separation of powers, the checks and balances needed to prevent despotism, and the appropriate size of states founded on republican principles.[151] Montesquieu had argued that unitary republics should be of "moderate size," like Britain, but he allowed that some federations might be able to combine good government with adequate defense.[152] Hume developed the idea; Madison turned it into practical politics by claiming that the interaction of competing factions in a large federation would assist stability and prevent the emergence of autocracy.[153] If a reputable theory of large federations had not existed, it would have been necessary to invent it because the scale and diversity of the mainland colonies precluded the possibility of establishing a unitary state. The alternative, which was to create a still undecided number of independent and competing states, was an unthinkable prospect that nevertheless had to be thought about.

The motives behind the provisions of the Constitution have been endlessly debated. At the triumphalist end of a long continuum, the Constitution has been hailed as the culmination of trends that led from monarchy to democracy. At the other end, marked "betrayal," it has been seen as a counterrevolution that frustrated the movement for radical change.[154] The full determination of these issues can be left to the specialists concerned. The interest here is in placing the Constitution in the context of the pressing need to secure the viability of the new state and to prepare the way for economic development.

Seen from this perspective, the Constitution provided the minimum condition for viability by creating what has been called a "peace pact" among the constituent states.[155] Despite considerable differences and mutual suspicions, the states compromised because a federation was preferable to the likelihood of interstate conflict and the menacing prospect of re-annexation by foreign powers. The federal government was designed, not as the basis of a national government, but as the means of ensuring stability and harmony among the Republic's diverse constituents. The continuing sense of insecurity was heightened by populist protests against taxation, fears in Southern states about their ability to control slave revolts, and concerns about the evident determination of Native Americans to halt westward expansion.[156] Viability was a precondition of economic development. Uncertainty worried property holders of all kinds. Investors needed assurance that irresponsible policies would not devalue their holdings as had happened under the Confederation, when a number of states tried to print their way out of debt.

Accordingly, financial considerations weighed heavily upon the framers of the Constitution. Without the means of enforcement, the "peace pact" would fail. Local resistance to taxation combined with irresponsible fiscal policies had shown that the states in the Confederation could not be trusted to provide the necessary funding.[157] Confidence among bond holders was vital to attract the investment the Republic needed.[158] Holders of real estate wanted guarantees of the physical security of their property, which underpinned its value. As the United States had the largest percentage of independent land holders in the Western world, their interests had to be given high priority. Opposition to British policies had been based on the defense of property rights; the Revolution settlement confirmed the security of all those invested in the new Republic.

The outcome of these concerns was the installation of elements of a military-fiscal state imported from Britain.[159] Among the available options, the British example recommended itself not only through its familiarity but also by its record in helping to make the United Kingdom the most progressive state in Europe as well as one of the most formidable. Just as the American Revolution was itself an offshoot of the developing struggle in Britain for control of the legacy of the Glorious Revolution, so the settlement that followed independence was the heir to much that had transpired in 1688. The American Revolution, it might be said, was an English revolution that did not happen, or rather that had to await the end of the long French Wars before taking an evolutionary course.

Scholars who are preoccupied with the novelties of nation-building can easily underestimate these colonial continuities. The Revolution was an Anglo-settler revolt led principally by gentlemen of property. It was undertaken to preserve what Burke referred to as "ancient, indisputable laws and liberties."[160] The Constitution ensured that arbitrary power would be brought under control; a Bill of Rights, derived from the English precedent of 1689, followed in 1789.[161] The majority of those who formulated the Constitution were men of the Enlightenment. They were elitist, cosmopolitan, well read, and committed to the application of reason to the issues of the day. They were wary of political parties, or "factions," as Madison called them, which they thought would encourage stereotyped thinking rather than open-minded discussion among informed leaders of opinion.[162] They hoped that the people's representatives would be, as they thought of themselves, well-informed and capable of rising above local interests. They exemplified what might be called the first phase of independence, which in the twentieth century, as in the eighteenth, was led by educated elites. Their sensibilities allied to their global outlook were strikingly at variance with the adulation accorded to them in the twenty-first century by commentators who eschew compromise, prefer instinctive certainties to reasoned reflection, and equate elites with books—and often have a low opinion of both.

Transplants from Britain were adapted to local circumstances. The most visible institutional change advertised the advent of republican government by substituting a president for a monarch. Even so, the debate over the Constitution included the possibility of providing for an elective monarchy. The notion of a "patriot king," borrowed from English political discourse, appealed to those who thought that the head of state should stand above party as the emblem of national unity.[163] Experience of monarchy had shown how reverence for traditional authority could be used to foster a sense of national identity. In the end, the founders opted for a president who was elected for an initial term of four years, but could be reelected, in principle, in perpetuity.[164] Nevertheless, the president was endowed (and burdened) with ceremonial as well as executive functions, and was expected to be the guardian of civic virtues that stood above politics. As befitted its lofty status, the presidency began with a full complement of courtiers, parades, lavish receptions, and even *levées*.[165] Although monarchical pretensions receded with time, President Andrew Jackson's style of rule in the 1830s led his Whig opponents to claim that the office was becoming an "elective kingship."[166] Congress, which consisted of a Senate and a House of Representatives, came sufficiently close to replicating the Lords and Commons for Nicholas de Condorcet, a long-standing supporter of the American Revolution, to deplore the perpetuation of what he called "antiquated English notions."[167] In his view, bicameralism symbolized hierarchy, whereas unicameralism represented equality.

A further qualification to British precedent limited the military element of the new federation. Member states were anxious to restrict the size of the armed services to avoid the potential abuse of federal power; geographical advantages ensured that their concerns were met. In the absence of powerful contiguous neighbors, the United States was in the fortuitous position, denied to states in Europe, of being able to economize on defense costs. Should the potential threat from European powers materialize, the federal government anticipated calling on the militia to amplify a small standing army. At this point the "right to bear arms" would find its fullest expression in serving the public interest.[168] The navy was not only small but was also inadequate, as became evident immediately after independence and during the War of 1812. Thereafter, the United States benefited from a proxy force, the Royal Navy, which provided the best possible deterrent until the close of the nineteenth century, when the Republic built its own modern battleships. Common features survived these differences. Fear of the abuse of central power was also a major concern in Britain, which held the regular army at modest levels that were expanded only in time of war. The central feature of both systems was that each had the ability to mobilize the degree of force required to meet the needs of state. In both cases, "defense" accounted for the largest share of public expenditure by far; debt service, incurred mainly to pay for the army and navy, came next.[169] Military and foreign affairs accounted for no less than four-fifths of federal expenditure between 1783 and 1861.[170] The Tax Britannica funded the Royal Navy and global expansion; the Pax Americana began by financing extensive territorial acquisitions in North America.

The fiscal institutions of the new state were also modeled on the British example. The Constitution enabled the federal government to establish a considerable degree of fiscal unity, which was a central precondition of nation-building. The first Bank of the United States, based on the Bank of England (1694), was established in 1791 with the power to raise money for government purposes, settle war debts, issue notes, and exercise a measure of control over state banks.[171] The new national debt was funded by bonds that paid interest and deferred payment of the principal. The government's credit rating improved; borrowing costs fell. The tax system was reformed. Interest on the public debt was increasingly paid by taxing imports instead of perpetuating the regressive land, poll, and excise taxes that were guaranteed to provoke popular discontent. When supporters of the Whiskey Rebellion in western Pennsylvania threatened to break away from the Republic in 1794, Washington had the resources to mobilize a militia and restore order.[172] Successive governments acquired a commitment to expanding overseas commerce, which became the main source of federal revenues and eased the political problems of raising taxes from other sources. Import taxes had an additional, compelling merit: they bypassed the issue of slaveholding.[173] Had the tax burden been placed on property, which included slaves, slave owners would have been heavily penalized. Anti-federalists formulated a concept of liberty that emphasized individual rights (of white citizens) and hostility toward "big" government. The reality was that a minimal federal government also benefited large wealth holders, who were in a position to control, and sometimes enlarge, state governments.

For all its success in drawing disparate interests together, the Constitution put aside two problems that would fester and eventually poison the body politic. It bypassed the question of secession.[174] If power was ultimately vested in the people, advocates could claim that a decision to leave the federation was not an act of rebellion but the exercise of a constitutional right. Minimally, it gave secession a measure of respectability when the issue became practical politics during the first half of the nineteenth century.[175] New York, Virginia, and Rhode Island insisted on preserving an explicit right to secede before they ratified the Constitution.

The other invisible subject was slavery, which was bundled with property rights and left to the determination of the constituent states. Had the framers confronted the issue, several Southern states, including Virginia, the wealthiest of the ex-colonies, and South Carolina, would have refused to join the proposed federation.[176] The need to include the South and win support for creating a central government obliged Madison and his colleagues to make concessions to Southern interests: slaves, who were denied the vote, were counted as three-fifths of a person for purposes of apportioning seats in the House among the constituent states; imports of slaves were permitted for an additional twenty years (to 1807).[177] To prevent Northern states from being consistently out-voted, Southern states agreed that each state should have equal representation in the Senate. Neither side foresaw that uneven development—stimulated by westward expansion, the growth of manufacturing in the North, and the cotton boom in the South—would unsettle the balance between the parties. As a result, the nominal presence of slaves as fractions of reality gave Southern states greater influence on the federal government than the number of white voters in the region warranted. The flexibility of the concept of liberty again demonstrated its broad appeal: the rights of slaves could be denied on the grounds that granting them would infringe on the liberty of slaveholders.

The successes, ambiguities, and failings of the Constitution guided the history of the Republic down to the Civil War. They stood at the center of political debate, influenced the formulation of competing economic policies, and helped to shape the affiliations and identities that formed the embryonic culture of the nation. The colonists joined hands in 1787, not because they had become united, but because they feared the consequences of disunity. They created a state, not a nation. Without viability and development, they had a past but not a future. Liberty, however understood, depended on success in achieving these prior, ambitious aims.

"SPECTACLES OF TURBULENCE AND CONTENTION"[178]

As soon as the Constitution had been ratified, the interpretation of the compromise it embodied became a matter of public discussion, political debate and, ultimately, national conflict. By the mid-1790s, the startling growth of the federal government was visible from all angles. Federal tax revenues were twelve times greater than those of the constituent states combined; expenditure was more than seven times greater.[179] Federal borrowing capacity had taken the public debt to more than $80 million; the states had raised less than $4 million. Public order, the first requirement of stable government, was guaranteed by the U.S. Army which, though small, was well funded and easily able to suppress Fries's Rebellion in 1799.[180] The Alien and Sedition Acts, passed in 1798, added the weaponry of the law to the expanding armory of state power. These developments, welcomed in some quarters, caused consternation in others. The optimistic assumption that gentlemanly leaders would resolve differences through reasoned and informal discussion did not outlast the century. By 1800, fluid factions had begun to take shape as embryonic political parties.[181]

In this development, as in so many others, the Old World left its imprint on the New. Contemporaries well understood that the basic questions relating to the extent and purpose of government authority had been inherited from the British past. Commonalities of political expression were evident. In the 1780s, the principal proto-parties drew on Whig and Tory discourse to formulate different visions of the Republic's future and of the means of turning ideals into realities. In 1800, Charles Pettit, a prominent Philadelphia merchant, summarized the widespread acceptance of trans-Atlantic continuities in a pamphlet he contributed to the election campaign of that year. There was no need to explain the terms "Whig" and "Tory," he said, because "they have borne so conspicuous a part in history, especially in that of England, that you cannot mistake their Common meaning."[182] Charles Beard suggested a broader categorization of these positions, which he personalized as the Hamiltonian and Jeffersonian persuasions.[183] These familiar terms remain the most useful shorthand guides to political opinion. They can be applied to the nineteenth century; their underlying attitudes still resonate today.

Hamiltonians were Tories in their political inclinations but progressive Whigs in matters of economic reform. The first two presidents, George Washington and John Adams, and the Secretary of the Treasury, Alexander Hamilton, were the leading figures among those who thought that government was more of a solution than a problem. They believed that a strong federal administration funded by revenue tariffs, managed by responsible elites, and nurturing progressive reforms was essential if the United States was to secure full independence. Governing elites required the consent of the governed but were wary of popular radicalism, which posed a potential threat to property and stability. Hamiltonians put their faith in the capacity of a central authority to integrate the diverse communities that formed the new Republic and to create

conditions that would allow liberty to flourish. They departed from the
orthodox view that republics based on cooperation and commerce were
ill-equipped to deal with threats from martial states. On the contrary,
they argued, a peacetime army under the control of Congress was essential to defend the Republic from external aggressors, and so was a means
of protecting rather than threatening civil liberties.[184]

Hamilton used his financial expertise and position as Secretary of
the Treasury and powers under the Constitution to transplant key features of Britain's military-fiscal state.[185] He and his associates founded
the First Bank of the United States, established the national debt, a
federal tax system, a monetary union based on a uniform dollar currency, a securities market, and drew up plans for developing domestic
manufactures.[186] Internal free trade preserved the potential for market
expansion; the federal government's extensive land holdings provided
the ultimate security for government debt. In Hamilton's view, only a
government with authority and resources could attract the long-term
investment needed for economic development. Following British precedent, Hamiltonians claimed that finance had become virtuous because
it had enabled the state to survive the ultimate test of war. According
to their advocates, Hamilton's reforms were not merely consistent with
republican values but were also essential to realizing them. Investment
in public debt, as Hamilton learned from Britain's experience, would pay
political dividends, too, because it would give stockholders a compelling
reason to support the government of the day. By attaching business interests to the federal government, so the argument ran, the Hamiltonian
financial program would ensure that the Republic would be committed
to peace and thereby keep official expenditure under control. This priority implied that foreign policy and attitudes toward continental expansion would be cautious and restrained. At the same time, stability
and peace would support economic development, which the public debt
would promote by expanding credit and the money supply. In Hamilton's
view, the United States needed to diversify into manufactures if it were to
shake off its dependence on British imports. However, Hamilton favored
subsidies in the form of bounties rather than protective tariffs, which he
feared would discourage imports and so erode the tax revenues that were
needed to fund the public debt.[187]

The Federalists' centralizing policies and fiscal reforms, combined
with their commitment to the British connection, provoked mounting
opposition during the 1790s. Thomas Jefferson came to believe that
Hamilton's fiscal program was designed to undermine the Republic and
install a new monarchical order. In 1794, John Taylor, the prominent

senator from Virginia, seasoned his own complaint with some nicely judged sarcasm: "Is it not time," he asked, "to enquire whether the constitution was designed to beget a government or only a British System of finance?"[188] His question was answered by a political reaction led by a coalition of Southern interests, New England merchants, backcountry voters, and anti-Federalist remnants who gathered under the leadership of Thomas Jefferson and James Madison to form the Republican Party in the early 1790s.[189]

Jeffersonians were progressive Whigs to the extent that they favored increased public involvement in the political process, but "country" Whigs to the extent that their agrarian vision had much in common with the decentralized ideology associated with Bolingbroke earlier in the century.[190] Thomas Jefferson and James Madison, who became the third and fourth presidents of the Republic, believed that government (or at least central government) was more of a problem than a solution. They opposed the growth of federal power, criticized the elevation of what they regarded as a narrow and largely unchanged pro-British hierarchy, and devised an approach to development problems that differed markedly from the formula put forward by the Hamiltonians.[191] Jeffersonians sought to sever ties with Britain on the grounds that continued collaboration would perpetuate a state of dependence and encourage corrupting influences to seep into the Republic. From their perspective, developments in Britain revealed the face of a future they wished to forestall. The agrarian order, the natural basis of society, was being eroded. The new "monied interest" had diminished the political authority of large landowners; the land tax had turned independent yeomen into tenants; government, pumped up by borrowed money, had become autocratic; debt had corroded the social order; excess had produced decadence.

Armed with this analysis, Jeffersonians aimed to establish a revitalized version of the natural order that was disappearing from Britain.[192] Their view of social evolution followed the stages of growth outlined by the Scottish Enlightenment, which began with hunting and gathering and culminated in agrarian, mercantile societies. Each stage had a civilizing influence but also carried the risk of decay. The aim of policy was to hold growth at the point before corruption set in. If this goal could be reached, Jeffersonians believed, North America could be populated with clusters of small-scale, self-perpetuating agrarian communities.[193] Abundant resources gave material substance to the Arcadian element in this vision. The availability of land would enable large landowners to revitalize their fortunes and halt the attrition of the yeomanry. Property rights, extended across the social order, would give the majority of the population a stake in upholding law and order. Increased political participation in a well-ordered agrarian society would restore the authority of the landed elite, check autocracy, and eliminate corruption.

These multiplying Edens would raise both the standard of living and the standard of morality. Jeffersonians recognized the central importance of the market, and advocated free trade as a means of encouraging agricultural exports and expanding domestic demand for local products, including artisanal handicrafts.[194] Protestantism, also suitably decentralized, would provide the moral code that would enable rural communities to coalesce into an organic whole. The vision was spacious beyond limit: territorial expansion would spread white settlement and create a vast collection of Anglo-Saxon republics. New states, though varying in size, would replicate the originals by acquiring identical constitutional rights and institutions. The federal government would be contained; civic virtue would flourish; the public voice would be heard.[195] The bounty of the New World would allow Montesquieu's ideal republic to be realized.

Bounty, however, brought its own problems. The Revolution settlement contained an additional dimension that stretched far beyond the preoccupations and ruminations of elites: the involvement of the wider population in the political process. The United States was not a democracy, as the term would be understood today. The electorate was confined to white, adult males who met a mixture of property and educational qualifications; women, slaves, and various other minorities were denied the right to vote. Nevertheless, in the late 1780s a remarkably high proportion (estimated at about 80 percent) of the potential electorate of white, adult males were qualified to vote, and the majority did so.[196] In expanding the political arena, the founders of the United States realized in the New World what radical Whigs had hoped to achieve in Britain. Independence opened the way to progressive policies; material conditions ensured that public participation would increase.

In this matter, too, American democracy was founded on British practice, which linked voting rights to property qualifications. The principle was established long before 1783: in the 1720s about 60 percent of white, adult males in the mainland colonies were already entitled to vote.[197] More adult males were enfranchised in the United States than in Britain, not because of differences of ideology, but because the greater availability of land in the New World enabled a higher proportion of settlers to acquire property. In contrast to crowded Europe, settlers in North America had a ready exit option: they could escape government authority, if it became onerous, by migrating.[198] Accordingly, the political contract had to include terms that would persuade citizens to remain in place and pay their taxes.[199] Republican ideals were sincerely held; realities ensured that they became operational. The first states to abolish voting qualifications were not the original Thirteen Colonies, where republican principles were well understood and clearly articulated, and where opposition to British rule was most pronounced, but rather the new states that needed to retain sparse and mobile populations.[200]

Federal and state governments had to contend with a vigorous style of politics "from below," which was derived from English festivals, patriotic celebrations, and political demonstrations.[201] Popular protests, rural and urban, pacific and violent, had been prominent in mobilizing resistance to Britain in the early days of the revolution, and they remained a permanent, if discontinuous, element in postcolonial politics.[202] The problem, as seen from the perspective of the elites who controlled the two main parties, was how to manage the enlarged *demos* in the absence of a dynastic hierarchy of the kind that ruled Britain.

Both Federalists and their opponents equated political rights with property. Those without property were uncertain and potentially wayward elements because they lacked a stake in society and were liable to express themselves in disturbing ways. The founders dealt with the potential challenge from below in part by inserting provisions in the Constitution that were designed as barriers not only to autocracy but also to the unbridled will of the demos.[203] In Madison's judgment, direct democracy was unworkable in populous and extensive societies, which is why he favored a federal republic and elected representatives.[204] Even so, checks were needed to prevent the polity from being driven off the approved path of republican virtue, which included upholding the sound-money policies that were essential to the successful launch of the new state. Besides the safeguards embodied in the Constitution, the founders placed their faith in the emergence of what Jefferson called a "natural aristocracy" characterized by "virtue and talents."[205] Superior qualities would enable the elite to rest their authority on the willing deference of the majority. Such leaders would have the wealth necessary to provide the leisure needed for public service. They would stock the Senate and apply their wisdom to upholding civic values. Public opinion would be guided by enlightened thinkers, such as themselves, which is why Jefferson emphasized the importance of education in producing an informed, participatory electorate.

Initially, Republicans were more sympathetic to the claims of the demos than were Federalists. In 1789, the French Revolution added inspiration to their inclinations. All talk of what Madison briefly called "sister republics" ended, however, with the onset of the Reign of Terror in 1793.[206] Robespierre's notion that terror was a precondition of virtue alarmed those who were planning to take a pacific route. Hamilton feared that French influence had "unhinged the orderly principles of the People of this country," and that "anarchy" would follow.[207] The ensuing reaction caused Jeffersonians to temper their Francophile leanings and idealistic advocacy of democratic republicanism, and allowed the federal government to strengthen its grip on dissident movements.

In this matter, Britain and the United States moved in harmony. With the example of the French Revolution before them, both countries adopted a form of "new conservatism" in defense of property, Protestantism, and ordered liberty.[208] Condorcet, writing from afar, deplored what he regarded as the oligarchic, anti-democratic direction taken by the American Revolution.[209] Political leaders in the United States disowned Tom Paine, the most radical of the revolutionaries of 1776, who died in obscurity in 1809.[210] The role of the crowd in public commemorations of the Revolution was minimized for half a century.[211] Despite their continuing differences, the elite parties entered a tacit agreement to exclude radical programs from official politics, which down to the Civil War became a debate about how far the reforming inclinations of progressive Whigs were compatible with the conservative aims of the Whig establishment. The eventual outcome was a form of populist nationalism that prefigured the politics of other modernizing and newly independent states in the nineteenth and twentieth centuries. Intimations of this development came in 1800 following the defeat and rapid collapse of the Federalists and the election of Thomas Jefferson as president.

"NOT AN EMPIRE, BUT THE PROJECT OF AN EMPIRE"[212]

Adam Smith chose to conclude *The Wealth of Nations* by reflecting on the high cost of maintaining the American empire and on Britain's inability to rule the mainland colonies effectively. The colonies were "supposed to be provinces of the British Empire." In practice, however, they were "not an empire, but the project of an empire" because Britain had yet to establish its claims to sovereignty on the American mainland.[213] In Smith's view, the colonies had failed to pay their fair share of the costs of defense against foreign aggressors and had become a burden on the Exchequer and taxpayers in Britain. The benefits of empire accrued to a minority of influential pressure groups headed by the East India Company. The increased national debt hampered the growth of the domestic economy; mercantilist regulations guarded by antique monopolies retarded the expansion of international trade. "If the project cannot be completed," Smith concluded, "it ought to be given up," and Britain should "accommodate her future views and designs to the real mediocrity of her circumstances."[214] Smith's phrasing was not intended to minimize Britain's economic achievements but rather to recognize the immensity of the managerial problems they had generated in extending political and commercial affairs over huge distances and often engaging with markedly different cultures.[215] Britain's global reach had led to what would later be termed "imperial overstretch."

Smith's analysis, with its emphasis on fiscal probity, merged with other sources and entered studies of the Revolution through the familiar maxim: "no taxation without representation." Although the formula is still frequently cited, it has been overshadowed in recent decades by illuminating contributions to intellectual and cultural history. The account offered here seeks to regain prominence for Smith's assessment, but also to place it in the wider context of the fiscal crisis of the late eighteenth century. The case rests, not on a priori reasoning, but on a review of the evidence from the perspective of economic history, which has long been out of favor and is only now being revived.[216] In the eighteenth century, the military imperative guaranteed the likelihood of a disastrous outcome by making revenue dependent on expenditure. Policy was based on a calculation, more often a gamble, that money spent on the military would yield profits and revenues in excess of costs. Montesquieu observed the resulting arms race at first hand: "A new distemper has spread itself over Europe, infecting our princes, and inducing them to keep up an exorbitant number of troops. It has its redoublings, and of necessity becomes contagious. For as soon as one prince augments his forces, the rest of course do the same; so that nothing is gained thereby but the public ruin."[217]

The British state, though modest in size, was able to extend its reach further than its larger rivals because it had attributes that were particularly well suited to seaborne enterprise, the most notable being an unparalleled navy, competitive manufactures that were in demand in the New World, and an innovative range of financial and commercial services. The national debt was a facility that Britain's major rivals could not match. It served as the government's credit card, helped to fund defense, and promoted an assertive foreign policy. This combination of assets propelled expansion and reoriented Britain's overseas trade from Europe to the wider world. The costs of the achievement, however, added to the commitment to uphold the Hanoverian cause in Europe, increasing both the national debt and the accompanying tax burden. The Seven Years'

War brought these issues to the forefront of political debate and public sensitivity. Radical Whigs argued that freer trade and further commercial expansion would reduce public debt and ease the weight of taxation. Tories and conservative Whigs planned to achieve the same result by raising the amount of tax drawn from the colonies. When the conservatives took power in the early 1760s, they exerted pressure on both India and the mainland colonies in an attempt to generate the necessary additional revenue. If the plan succeeded, taxpayers in Britain would be spared additional impositions, the reform movement would be blunted, and government ministers would continue to enjoy the benefits of office. The policy would later be known as social imperialism—the device of levying an "imperial tribute" to quell discontent at home.

Fiscal problems quickly became political issues because the authority to tax raised questions about the legitimacy of government and tested the state's exercise of claimed sovereign rights. Radicals in Britain and the mainland colonies had similar programs and drew on similar sources to validate their demands for reform. Pitt's forceful speeches in parliament declaring the new taxes levied on the mainland colonies to be unconstitutional and calling for greater accountability at home, the elimination of wasteful government expenditure, and reform of mercantilist regulations could well have been written for, or even by, the leaders of the loyal opposition in the Atlantic provinces.[218] As it turned out, George III and his ministers persisted with coercion for too long and left conciliation too late. Nevertheless, their policy was informed by reason and was not simply the product of patriotic obstinacy. If sovereignty was indivisible, as Blackstone and other authorities argued, constitutional concessions made to the outer provinces could scarcely be resisted at home, where similar claims were being voiced. Changes of the extent the radicals called for had to be resisted because they would have altered the distribution of power entrenched by the Glorious Revolution. As otherwise mundane matters of revenue, taxation, and expenditure scaled constitutional heights, reformers turned to philosophical authority to establish the credibility of their programs and ultimately to validate rebellion against the crown. The arguments had long been to hand. They were taken up, publicized, and joined to political advocacy when government impositions stretched established loyalties beyond tolerable limits.

The conservative plan for an extractive empire failed. Mounting expenditure in India exceeded revenues and ensured that pressure continued to be applied to the mainland colonies. As it became clear that Pitt and the radical Whigs were unlikely to regain power, the colonists came to the conclusion that reform would be stifled. With constitutional means of redress closed, and government policy vacillating but ultimately resolute, opposition in the colonies turned reluctantly to independence and the means of achieving it. The strategy, as it evolved amidst the turmoil of conflict, was to secure political independence first and to deal with issues of economic development and national identity later. Kwame Nkrumah had exactly the same idea in the 1940s, when he adapted a phrase from the Sermon on the Mount to produce a commandment of his own: "Seek ye first the political kingdom," he urged his followers in the Gold Coast, "and all things will be added unto it."[219] The injunction reverberated throughout Africa and encouraged other leaders to adopt the same priority. British policy was caught, as it was in the eighteenth century, between repression and retreat, and tried the first before having to settle for the second. In this instance, to amend Voltaire, history was a pack of tricks played by the dead upon the living.

The break with Britain took the form of secession rather than revolution. It began as a divisive civil war within the empire and added an international dimension only after France joined the conflict in 1778. The colonists were not revolutionaries in the sense of wishing to overturn the structure of government and society in Britain: their aim was to check parliament's legislative reach by recalling it to what they held to be its traditional constitutional limits. Even so, secession was a last resort: it was the act of British patriots overseas who felt driven to turn themselves into American patriots in the New World. The assumption that the colonists were nationalists, or even proto-nationalists, is wide of the mark, though it was for long a perennial entry in mainstream histories and is still repeated in studies that view the past with more commitment to national mythology than to the exercise of appropriate scholarly skepticism.[220] The Revolution was an example of decolonization before nationalism. It had a popular base as well as elite leadership, but little sense of national identity.[221] It was the work of a coalition of the willing, the unwilling, and the indifferent. Its character was shaped by a mixture of motives, some of them conflicting. Interstate rivalries were endemic; suspicion of centralized authority hampered coordination; elites and populists tussled for control; inherited ties continued to dilute alternative affiliations.[222] The success of the rebellion was the more remarkable for managing to draw support from thirteen diverse mainland colonies, despite being hastily assembled and frugally funded.

At the moment of independence, however, the secessionists had still to construct a state before they could contemplate forming a nation. In Britain, which was already a state, the experience of war with the colonies and France had the effect of further strengthening an emerging sense of national identity and promoting neoconservative attitudes and policies. In the United States, the Constitution created a federal government that succeeded in holding the Union together until 1861. James Madison, faced with the task of devising a form of government that would be acceptable to all the mainland colonies, recommended federalism after studying the experience of the Dutch Republic.[223] The example appeared to be well chosen: the United Provinces, as they were also known, had been in existence since 1581 and survived until the French army overturned the government in 1795. Imperial and postcolonial federations, however, have had varied constitutions and checkered histories. The Canadian and Australian federations endured because settlers there had a sufficient measure of ethnic cohesion, "race patriotism," and loyalty to the crown to transcend regional affiliations.[224] The Central African and West Indies Federations, on the other hand, were short-lived because they were products of political desperation that joined constituents who had little in common. The history of the U.S. federation, which is discussed in the next chapter, lay between these possibilities. The Civil War anticipated the fate of other decolonized states that succumbed to centrifugal forces in the mid-twentieth century; the changes that followed succeeded in keeping the Republic together.

In its widest setting, the Revolution was the product of a dialectical process that gave proto-globalization impetus. Britain's version of the military-fiscal state promoted economic growth, even though it reached limits that ultimately constrained enterprise. A combination of chartered companies and private traders created an extensive international network of exchanges that linked Asia to Europe and Europe to Africa and the New World. Proto-globalization had sufficient penetrative depth to mark the societies it touched, even though it lacked the transforming power delivered by industrialization in the nineteenth century. Economic development and increasing numbers carried the mainland colonies beyond the control of central government. The success of economic growth under the aegis of mercantilism filled the colonies with settlers, expanded the export sector, and increased the flow of finance from the City of London. It also gave the colonists a degree of heft that made resistance possible and political independence feasible. Economic expansion lifted living standards and raised expectations. Consumer goods began the long march from luxuries to necessities; open lands were a visible and compelling inducement drawing the frontier westward.

From a British viewpoint, the prosperity of the mainland colonies made them an irresistible source of taxation. Increased specialization and growing reliance on external sources of funding, however, exposed the colonists to variations in market demand and policy changes in Britain that were beyond their control. The economic uncertainties that followed the Seven Years' War, combined with unexpected tax demands and a sterner regulatory regime, produced a period of austerity that subjected debtors to the demands of external creditors. It may be anachronistic to suggest that Tom Paine was the first dependency theorist, but he nevertheless understood the global ramifications of what he termed, explicitly, "dependence."[225]

The reassertion of central control was the more unwelcome because it contrasted with the preceding period of "salutary neglect," when the colonists had become accustomed to exercising a measure of internal self-government. When the era of informal collaboration broke down in the 1760s, it took with it the colonists' aspirations: tempting vistas of opportunities inland were closed; hopes among elites for parity of status with their peers in Britain were crushed.[226] No new collaborators could be found; coercion, as critics of government policy pointed out, was bound to fail, given the technological limits of the time. At this point, and in accordance with Tocqueville's theory of revolution, Britain's empire on the American mainland subsided under the weight of falling expectations.

At one level of generalization, the American Revolution can be seen as a struggle over the contested legacy of the Glorious Revolution. At a further remove, it illustrates the accuracy of Montesquieu's insight: changes in scale required corresponding changes in structure, which Britain was unable to engineer. As Burke put it in 1774, "no contrivance can prevent the effect of . . . distance, in weakening government."[227] "In large bodies," he added, as if confirming Montesquieu's dictum, "the circulation of power must be less vigorous at the extremities."[228] Distance assisted the mainland colonies to escape British rule; proximity helped to give Scotland a sizeable stake in Union and empire, while also enabling Britain to hold Ireland, its first settler colony in the Atlantic, in a reluctant and resentful embrace. It was not until the second half of the nineteenth century that technological innovation enabled Britain to extend its political capacity to cover its economic interests, and thereby overcome the "tyranny of distance."

The contest between conservatives and liberals in Europe had clear echoes in the United States, despite differences in particularities. The United States was too encumbered by its British heritage to "begin the world anew," as thoroughgoing radicals had hoped. Although the new republic dispensed with the monarchy, it acquired the problem that European states also faced in the nineteenth century: whether to recreate a version of the military-fiscal state or to found a "virtuous" republic.

Hamilton was unable to realize the whole of his plan for reproducing a strong state derived from the British model. Federalism limited centralization; modest defense needs kept the military in its place. Nevertheless, the institutions he transplanted survived to form the basis of what became a much larger and more active federal government than anti-federalists had envisaged.

"Vice," in the shape of material aspirations, had long lapped at the foothills of John Winthrop's "City upon a Hill," and economic development in the eighteenth century raised the water level still further. Idealists, however, were convinced that conditions in the New World would enable them to establish a God-fearing polity uncontaminated by the corrupt world of Europe. Reformers in Europe also proclaimed a new moral order, which many of them believed was endorsed by biblical authority. The distinctive feature of the contest was that the United States was the first decolonized state in the British Empire to grapple with these visions of the past and the future, Accordingly, the Republic's experiments in state formation repay attention, not only from the familiar standpoint of the United States's own history, but also from the neglected perspective of imperial history.

Harry Washington, whose story opened this chapter, illustrates the conundrum facing Europe's military-fiscal states after they had been shaken, and some toppled, by revolution: whether to deal with claims for expanded political rights by suppression or by concession. Harry exchanged slavery in Virginia for the promise of liberty in Nova Scotia, and then found himself subjected to Britain's new, authoritarian style of humanitarianism in Sierra Leone, where he rebelled once more and established his own mini-republic in the hinterland. We do not know how successful his small community was in balancing virtue and vice. We do know that the United States struggled to match its governmental structure to increasing size and growing diversity, as Montesquieu predicted would be the case with large polities, and ended the experiment in the conflagration of civil war in 1861. The route leading to this outcome, like the contest itself, mimicked events among states in Europe, which also strove to resolve the competition between conservative and liberal forces without resorting to outright conflict—and frequently failed to do so.

CHAPTER 4

THE STRUGGLE FOR INDEPENDENCE

MIDNIGHT'S CHILDREN[1]

"A moment, which comes rarely in history, when we step out from the old to the new, when an age ends, and when the soul of a nation, long suppressed, finds utterance."[2] Jawaharlal Nehru caught the moment, the sense of a "tryst with destiny," that marked India's transition from colonial rule at the stroke of midnight on August 15, 1947. John Quincy Adams, commemorating the tenth anniversary of American independence in 1793, had a similar awareness of the "sublime purpose" that culminated in the creation of the Republic.[3] Both orators looked forward as well as back. Beyond the difficulties that lay ahead, "Visions of Bliss," as Adams called them, beckoned. For Nehru, the challenge of the future was to bring "freedom and opportunity to the common man," to "end poverty and ignorance and disease," and "to build up a prosperous, democratic and progressive nation." Adams nourished the "sanguine hope" that the "fair fabric of universal Liberty" would "rise up on the durable foundation of social equality." "The achievement we celebrate today," Nehru concluded, in spacious terms that Adams also employed, "is but a step, an opening of opportunity, to the greater triumphs and achievements that await us. Are we brave enough and wise enough to grasp this opportunity and accept the challenge?"

Adams and Nehru expressed the idealism and sense of achievement, pride, and mission shared by all anti-colonial movements at the point of transition to independence. The comparison cannot be stretched beyond modest limits because the two cases were separated by context and structure, as well as by time. Nevertheless, the juxtaposition has the merit of encouraging a review of the historiography of the first phase of American independence and suggesting how it might be turned in a new direction.

At present, the literature on the post-Revolutionary era is generally limited to the North American continent. Leading studies, though deeply researched and admirably executed, explain the principal developments of the period without assigning much weight to external influences.[4] Historians of the British Empire detach themselves from the United States after 1783 and turn their attention to parts of the world that either remained in the empire or became incorporated into it. Simultaneously, historians of the mainland colonies hand responsibility to a fresh set of specialists, who concentrate on domestic developments during the nineteenth century. The resulting historiography is daunting in size and impressive in quality. In emphasizing the distinctiveness of the American experience, it has now added histories "from below," rescued women from the obscurity long conferred to them, found a place for Native Americans in the national saga, and made room for the contribution of African Americans. The transition is wholly in line with the historiography produced by other ex-colonial states, though the analogy is rarely drawn. All of Britain's former colonies have rewritten their historical legacy in ways that have minimized the imperial connection and highlighted local origins and initiatives.

These welcome amplifications come with costs. The most striking consequence of the focus on domestic history is the virtual elimination of contemporaneous developments in Europe and the retreat into invisibility of the Atlantic complex that historians of the eighteenth century have done so much to recreate. A historiography that is confined to national borders rations the pool of available ideas and is inclined to be self-referencing. This tendency may help to explain why surveys of the period between 1783 and 1861 have enlarged rather than replaced the original "master narrative," which remains in essence the story of the spread of liberty and democracy, albeit now with added setbacks and qualifications. Most accounts of the period follow familiar signposts, which begin with the "Jeffersonian Revolution," proceed to the "Era of Good Feelings," and enter the "Age of Jackson," while managing the "Market Revolution." The route provides a clear view of the problems, personalities, and events of the period, but does so largely within an insular context.[5]

As noted in chapter 1, historians of empire survey these issues from a different angle by distinguishing between formal independence and the effective transfer of power. The aim of the present chapter is to show that Britain's ability to exercise what has been termed "structural power" had a profound influence on the evolution of the Republic.[6] The argument does not assume that the relationship was exploitative. As "enforced bilateralism" was no longer a possibility after independence, the issue of exploitation either ceases to be applicable or grows in complexity, and in any case falls beyond the remit of this study.[7] The concept of structural power, however, is relevant because it set the broad parameters, or "rules of the game," governing international relations and shaped the options open to the leaders of the new Republic. Within these parameters, the parties concerned exercised "relational power" to negotiate outcomes.[8] The discussion that follows examines structural power in Anglo-American relations in three areas: political choice, economic development, and cultural aspirations. Taken together, these themes suggest that the example of the United States can be added to existing studies of Latin America, Asia, and Africa, which were to face similar challenges in trying to make independence a reality.

Policy debates in the United States during the first half of the nine-teenth century adapted and reproduced contemporary struggles in Europe over conservative and progressive values. The United States, however, was distinctive in being a former colony and the owner of a vast underdeveloped estate. Effective independence required a political system that would hold together a clutch of diverse and scattered ex-colonies and defend them from predators. Competition between federalist and anti-federalist factions, however, evolved in ways that jeopardized the quest for unity. Many contemporaries, and numerous historians, have seen the political disputes of the period through the eyes of a succession of presidents who were either advocates or opponents of "big government." This struggle, however, was overlaid by the battle for an even larger prize: command of government resources, irrespective of their provenance. Governments in ex-colonial states, and in underdeveloped countries generally, offer unequaled prospects of escaping poverty and unemployment through the control they exercise over appointments, contracts, and supporting services. In the United States, too, political parties of different persuasions competed for access to federal assets, which institutions imported from Britain's military-fiscal state had greatly enlarged, while also striving to boost the state governments that were the basis of their political power. One result of competitive politics was an increase in patronage, which contemporaries named the "spoils system."[9] A further consequence was what historians of decolonization refer to as the "green uprising," whereby the political arena expanded into the countryside and provided an outlet for new forms of populism.

Political battles took place within an economy that was still underdeveloped, notwithstanding claims that the period experienced a "market revolution."[10] The rural order remained the matrix within which all other activities were set, as it was in Europe. This setting gave rise to an intense debate over economic policy that matched the contest in Europe between protectionists and free-traders. One view held that the introduction of an industrial, urban economy was essential if the United States was to achieve effective independence. The alternative claimed that the predominantly rural character of the United States was not only consistent with economic growth but would also maintain social order, realize republican values, and secure the independence of the polity. Britain's substantial informal presence, manifested in expanding capital flows and commercial connections, influenced the shape of these programs as well as the fortunes of the political parties that championed them.

Contemporaries in the United States gave considerable thought, as they did in Europe, to questions of sovereignty and national identity in an age when some dynastic states had been overthrown and the survivors were besieged by reformers and radicals. The debate in the United States was also shaped by its status as an ex-colonial state based on white settlers. In the Republic, as in Britain's dominions, long-standing continuities hampered the evolution of what specialists on decolonization call a "counterculture."[11] A sense of national identity was not "present at the creation," but was rather the product of protracted endeavor, just as it was elsewhere. Cultural deference was not easily overcome, not least because many opinion-leaders continued to find it congenial. Additionally, the form of federalism adopted by the United States confirmed the status of the constituent states as the primary political units in the Union. By 1861, strong regional identities had been strengthened to the point where they outweighed claims for unity based on common cultural affiliations. Divergence, not convergence, was the most striking feature of the period.

These lines of inquiry enhance rather than diminish the distinctiveness of the great experiment the United States embarked on after 1783. The founders devised a form of government they hoped would maintain the viability of the new state. Their successors undertook an unprecedented venture in what, much later and in different circumstances, would be called "nation-building" within a federal constitution. They advocated principles of natural rights that became orthodoxies after World War II, when they were reshaped as human rights. They formulated and debated economic policies that became staples of economic discourse among colonial nationalists in the twentieth century. They engaged with contending claims of assimilation and pluralism that the globalized world wrestles with today. The experiment they initiated was as bold as it was novel; its full significance can be appreciated once it is placed in the wider setting provided by contemporary movements elsewhere in the Western world. Senator William H. Seward saw the significance of these developments in 1853, when he referred to the War of

Independence as being "the first act in the great drama of decolonization on this continent."[12]

THE RHETORIC AND THE
REALITY OF REVOLUTION

The rhetoric of the Revolution did not wither away in the nineteenth century; it remained, and remains, a powerful electoral weapon. Nevertheless, as the realities of state formation intruded upon the ideals of the founders, the divisions between Hamiltonians and Jeffersonians lost some of their clarity. Nehru experienced a similar transition after India gained independence and the new government shifted its attention from opposing colonial rule to grappling with diverse domestic claims. Nkrumah, in turn, having sought and found "the political kingdom," discovered that "all things" were not easily "added unto it."[13] Policy in the new Republic evolved with the educative effect of experience and with the changing size and composition of the state itself. Effective independence was not attached to the new Constitution in 1787, but was a "work in progress."

Hamiltonians and Jeffersonians agreed that the United States needed to free itself from continuing dependence on Britain but had conflicting ideas of what the Republic should become.[14] Hamilton and his successors envisaged a society with an expanding manufacturing sector, a strong urban middle class, and an elite leadership that was as well informed and as rational as they considered themselves to be. They hoped to emulate Britain's example of successful development by adapting it to conditions in the New World. They recognized that good relations with the former colonial power were essential if the economy was to benefit from the foreign capital and markets it needed. Contrary to a familiar stereotype, however, Hamilton was keenly aware that borrowing had to be kept under firm control and debts repaid on time. Accordingly, he held a guarded view of territorial expansion because he feared that rising costs would impinge on revenues, affect the Republic's defense budget, and damage its credit rating.

Jeffersonians, on the other hand, aimed to strengthen agrarian communities, diffuse political authority, and provide it with a popular base. Jefferson's notion of an empire of liberty favored territorial expansion to create a multiplicity of small republics that would be capable of realizing civic virtues. The patriotic spirit found in representative republics would ensure that civic virtues would flourish, even in large states.[15] This was to be an "empire" (an extended sovereign state) of constitutional but not social equality: in legal terms, each new state would be a replica of the original; in social terms, it would mix plantations and slave labor with independent farmers—the sturdy yeomen who were fast disappearing from Britain.

The central political question after independence was how to mobilize the resources of the new federal government and the votes of the expanding electorate to realize one program and marginalize the other. Rhetoric ensured that the parties remained far apart. Realities brought them to a common understanding that the federal government needed sufficient power to finance essential public goods.[16] Tocqueville thought that the United States was so decentralized that it did not constitute a state at all, at least in the sense understood in Europe. The judgment was one of his many felicitous exaggerations: the federal government was far more active during the first half of the century than he allowed or historians have traditionally acknowledged.[17] The army, which continued to be funded by institutions that Hamilton had put in place, played its part in extending the borders of the state and removing Native Americans to make room for white settlers. The resolution of disputes among states over land rights transferred territory, estimated in 1790 to be more than 228 million acres, to the federal government.[18] Other innovations included a land office, a national legal system, a postal service, and a patent office. In addition, the federal authorities financed transport improvements and subsidized exploration. Slavery became a national institution fully protected by the Constitution.[19] The federal government used its power to perpetuate an internal slave market, close escape routes, pursue fugitives, enforce contracts for hire and sale, and offer slaves as collateral for loans.[20] Arguments about the scope and scale of central authority continued, but the idea that its key institutions could be dismantled was either abandoned or shown to create problems rather than solutions.

Most research on the growth of state power in the nineteenth century has focused on the federal government, principally because the diversity of the constituent states makes generalization about them hazardous. The Federation contained twenty-four states in 1821; by 1861, the number had increased to thirty-four. Recent work, however, suggests that relations between federal and state governments need to be rethought.[21] The Constitution placed formal limits on the authority of the federal government and left all other matters to the states. Devolution gave the states wide-ranging powers over almost all aspects of life—from slavery to morality. Furthermore, many states chose not to emulate the federal government in enacting a Bill of Rights but operated instead through a royalist doctrine, imported from eighteenth-century Britain, known as "police power." This principle empowered the monarch to intervene in civil affairs on behalf of his subjects. The Bill of Rights inserted a wedge of Lockean liberalism into the federal Constitution; "police power" injected the constituent states with a measure of Hobbesian authority. Some of the states were small; others were thinly populated. Within their boundaries, however, they commanded extensive powers.

State governments were especially prominent in exercising coercive powers and promoting economic development. State militias policed the laws governing slavery in the South and supplemented the small federal army in supporting settlers in the borderlands. The need for revenue allied to electoral pressure to provide opportunities and employment drove the states into innovations in banking and taxation.[22] Large numbers of banks and chartered companies appeared during the first half of the century. State banks succeeded in issuing government loans by devising novel ways of linking taxation to the beneficiaries of expenditure. The tax revenues and investment earnings derived from bank profits became major contributions to state budgets. The states were especially active in developing canals, roads, and railroads, where the federal government's powers were limited. Between 1787 and 1861, the states spent more than seven times as much as the federal government on infrastructure projects.[23] The picture that emerges is not that of feeble states whose highest aspiration was to fend off the overweening power of the federal government, but of robust polities that had ambitions of their own and at least some of the power needed to achieve them.

All political parties came to accept, with varying degrees of enthusiasm, the need to accommodate an increasingly numerous and diverse electorate. Jeffersonians abandoned their early support for the French Revolution as the full implications of radical republicanism, dramatically reinforced by the revolution in Haiti, became apparent. Instead, they cultivated a form of conservative, agrarian populism that linked liberty to states' rights, and embraced the idea of manifest destiny, which opened opportunities for private initiatives.[24] The classical concept of civic virtue became a means of validating individual rights rather than public duties.[25] Specialists on the period tend to see the expansion of political participation as a major advance in the creation of a distinctive American democracy. Specialists on decolonization are likely to view it as an early example of the green uprising, whereby politics extended beyond the arena bounded by urban elites to encompass large swaths of the rural population.[26] Jackson and Gandhi, otherwise a most unlikely pairing, had this in common, if almost certainly nothing else.

The battle between the two major parties had a clear outcome: Jeffersonians and their successors, the Jackson Democrats, controlled Congress, staffed the Supreme Court, filled senior positions in the cabinet and the armed services, and held the presidency for the greater part of the period down to the Civil War.[27] Slaveholders occupied the office of president for fifty of the sixty-two years between 1788 and 1850; twenty of the thirty-five Supreme Court judges between 1789 and 1861 were from Southern states.[28] This was not a "slave conspiracy," as some contemporaries claimed, but an open exercise of power validated by the Constitution of 1787. Nor can the green uprising be considered a synonym for the spread of democracy. It is true that the idea of democracy had evolved in the course of half a century: Madison was among those who defined democracy by the principle of direct representation, which he judged to be unworkable in large states, whereas Tocqueville equated democracy with all forms of representative government.[29] It is also the case that a high proportion of white adult males were qualified to vote, and that a large number did so.[30] Nevertheless, it is equally clear that the states, which administered elections, imposed a plethora of restrictions that limited the voting rights of the poor, women, African Americans, and Native Americans, among others.[31] Although the United States was a republic and most of Europe was monarchical, both political systems facilitated the rise of oligarchies and accompanying dynastic pretensions.

Jeffersonians and Democrats drew most of their support from states in the South, where slaveholding predominated.[32] They owed their economic power, as the next section of the chapter will show, to the expansion of a slave-based economy. They owed much of their political power to rights granted by the Constitution. The provision that allocated two senators to each state, irrespective of size or population, allied to an informal agreement to maintain parity in the interests of peace, guaranteed that the South would have equal representation with other states in the Upper House. As Jeffersonians and Democrats controlled the federal government for most of the period, they were able to dispense sufficient patronage to ensure that they could normally count on additional votes from Northern Democrats to secure a Senate majority.

The political balance in the House of Representatives was more complicated. The three-fifths clause (whereby five slaves counted as three whites in determining the number of seats) added considerable bulk to the Southern vote.[33] It is unlikely that the clause delivered the controversial presidential election of 1800 to Jefferson, as is often claimed, but it helped subsequently to inaugurate a series of presidents from Virginia in particular and the South in general.[34] Unlike their opponents, Southern Democrats were bonded by self-interest, single-minded in their determination to preserve slavery, and respectful of party discipline. Moreover, in Martin Van Buren, President Jackson's main agent in the North, they had a skilled political broker who created a "white alliance" that succeeded in preventing slavery from becoming a combustible political issue.

Nevertheless, Southern dominance was provisional and depended on astute political management. A crisis over a proposal to admit Missouri to statehood in 1819 tested the strength of the uncomfortable compromise between North and South over the issue of slavery.[35] Until then, the political balance had been maintained by an informal agreement that admission to the Republic would preserve parity between "slave" and "free" states. In 1803, however, the Louisiana Purchase had opened up a vast territory, which in due course was to be partitioned and incorporated as states of the Union. Since the number of future states had yet to be decided, the potential for engineering a fundamental shift in political power lay to hand should ambition or desperation cause it to be activated.[36] Missouri Territory was a prospective slave state. Had its application been successful, the principle of balance would have been abandoned and Southern states would have gained a decisive political advantage. After protracted negotiations, the issue was resolved in 1820 by a deal known as the Missouri Compromise, which allowed Maine (then part of the free state of Massachusetts) to join Missouri as a new state, and divided the Great Plains between the South, where slavery was permitted, and the North, where it was banned. The episode confirmed the South's existing constitutional rights, extended them to a large section of inland territory, and sustained the balance between North and South until the 1850s.

The Hamiltonian-Federalists were not run out of town. After Jefferson's election in 1800, however, they were in a state of disarray that prefaced a long period of decline. Their elitism removed them from the new era of mass politics; their opposition to war with Britain in 1812 labeled them as being unpatriotic and ruined their chances of recovery.

Jefferson's election as president in 1800 has long been seen as a moment of transition from conservative institutions inherited from Britain to progressive changes leading to (or embodying) democratic capitalism.[37] However, the "Jeffersonian Revolution," as it is known, fell short of the claims that have been made on its behalf. Jefferson entered office with a commitment to realizing his vision of an expanding agrarian society, while also halting the drift toward over-centralized government, cutting back the burgeoning financial sector, and minimizing the British connection.[38] His policy of territorial expansion was strikingly successful: the Louisiana Purchase in 1803 doubled the size of the United States;

Lewis and Clark's expedition, which set out from St. Louis on the Mississippi in 1804, opened even wider horizons when it reached the Pacific in 1806; the army was mobilized to clear paths for European settlement by compelling Native Americans to trek westward.

The cost of these ventures, however, limited Jefferson's scope for fiscal reform. Although he managed to shrink the national debt, the achievement was not a break with past profligacy but a continuation of the prudent policies Hamilton had put in place in the 1790s.[39] An immediate result was to reduce the Republic's military capacity and compromise its ability to respond to external threats. A longer-term consequence stemmed from Jefferson's decision to repeal a number of internal taxes. This move, too, extended Hamilton's policy of shifting the burden of taxation to import duties. The result, however, was to make the Republic more, not less, dependent on commercial relations with Britain, the former colonial power and major trading partner, and to diminish the prospects of securing economic independence.[40] Jefferson's hazardous experiment with discriminatory tariffs, despite his expressed hostility to mercantilism, demonstrated that the United States lacked the power to coerce the former colonial power.[41] His anti-British stance prompted him to oppose the renewal of Jay's Treaty in 1806, but the outcome damaged the fortunes of American rather than British merchants. In the following year, Jefferson imposed an embargo on U.S. exports in retaliation against the effects of the British navy's blockade of Europe and failure to respect the neutrality of American shipping during the French Wars.[42] The decision proved to be a major miscalculation: the threat to British trade had no influence on British policy, and the failure of Jefferson's assertive policy contributed to the indecisive war with Britain that began in 1812.[43]

James Madison, who became president in 1809, shared Jefferson's antipathy toward both the Federalist program and the persistence of British influence.[44] He allowed the charter of the First Bank of the United States to expire in 1811, when it was presented for renewal, and took the country into war with Britain in the following year. As a result, the war effort was hampered by inadequate funding and exacerbated by rising inflation. Madison was then compelled to adopt Federalist policies he had previously disowned.[45] He endorsed the foundation of the Second National Bank in 1816, approved a range of protective tariffs in the same year, copied the British practice of issuing long-term bonds, and accepted the need to expand the army and navy.

After Madison left office in 1817, James Monroe, Madison's successor and president from 1817 to 1825, ensured that the fiscal institutions restored during the war were carried into the peace. Monroe presided

during what has become known as the Era of Good Feelings, a term
coined in 1817 to capture the mood of unity that marked the conclusion
of the war with Britain. Monroe was a planter and slaveholder from Virginia, but he was also a member of an older generation and the last of
the Founders to become president. He shared Washington's belief that
government by like-minded elites would prevent divisive, factional politics. This spirit prompted him to appoint John Quincy Adams, a former
Federalist, as his Secretary of State. It also enabled him to view the ex-
piration of the Federalists, which by 1820 had produced what was effectively one-party government, as a step toward balanced government by
reasonable men. The end of faction, however, did not extend the Era of
Good Feelings, which was one of the shortest "eras" on record. In 1819, a
financial panic produced an economic crisis; in the following year, Missouri's application for statehood led to a political crisis.

The one-party state was interrupted in 1825, when John Quincy
Adams, a former senator from Massachusetts, became president.[46]
Adams had been a prominent Federalist and he retained strong Hamiltonian inclinations, though as President Monroe's Secretary of State
he had pursued a Jeffersonian policy of territorial expansion, notably by
negotiating the acquisition of Florida from Spain in 1819.[47] Adams owed
his election in 1824 to mounting discontent stemming ultimately from
the War of 1812. Once in office, he attempted to implement a program of
government-led development, but his efforts were blocked by Congress,
which remained under Southern control, and in 1828 he failed in his attempt to win a second term. From then until the Civil War, Jeffersonians
and their successors in the Democratic Party succeeded in halting ambitious development plans predicated on greatly expanded federal power.

The issues engendered by war, economic development, and population growth prepared the way for a fresh political initiative. Came the
hour, came the man—in this case on horseback. General Andrew Jackson rose from poverty in the backcountry of Tennessee to become the
dominant political figure of the 1820s and 1830s.[48] He was already well
known when he contested the presidential election of 1824; he was president between 1829 and 1837; his successor and long-standing ally, Martin Van Buren, held the office between 1837 and 1841.[49] Jackson served in
the Revolutionary War while still a teenager, and achieved heroic stature
during the War of 1812. His credentials as a nationalist of a specifically
anti-British stance were unrivaled. His Anglophobia, exacerbated during
the wars with Britain by the brutal treatment he suffered and by the loss
of family members, exceeded even Jefferson's. Like Jefferson, he nurtured a deep suspicion of imported financial institutions and feared the

consequences of an unrestrained "monied interest," not least because he, too, had experienced the privation and humiliation of indebtedness.[50] He was also a realist. His territorial ambitions and ruthless policy in dealing with Native American peoples guaranteed his popularity among land-hungry settlers. His hostility toward the federal government was adjusted to fit his own priorities. When federal initiatives threatened his power base in Tennessee, his opposition was unqualified; when he occupied the White House, federal power served his purposes.

The defeat of Adams in the presidential election of 1828 symbolized the changing of the guard. Jackson was the first president to come from a frontier state rather than from the East Coast elite. The power of the people was felt at his inauguration in 1829, when what spectators described as a "mob" overran the White House. Under the guidance of Martin Van Buren, the Jeffersonians turned themselves into the Democratic Party.[51] Members of the old elite who were regarded as "placemen" were cleared out of the federal administration; new men arrived; the spoils system was born. Attitudes toward government changed; civic virtue was reconfigured to make public service a right rather than a duty. Assertive policies, wielded by a man of action, appealed to Southern slaveholders and to a growing constituency of mobile settlers who coveted Native American lands. Jackson's anti-intellectualism, a marked departure from the informed cosmopolitanism of the Founding Fathers, also pointed the way to the future. By the close of the 1820s, Jackson's popularity far exceeded that of the urbane but pallid Adams, whose bookish inclinations and honed diplomatic skills identified him as an elitist who was at home in the eighteenth century but appeared increasingly at sea in the turbulent world around him. The two minds never met. Jackson regarded Adams as an aristocratic extremist who was set on imposing big government; Adams, whose droll sense of humor passed Jackson by, thought that the real aristocrats were Southern slaveholders.

Few presidents have been more enduringly controversial than Jackson. For present purposes, however, specialists can be left to debate the long-running question of whether he was the herald of democracy who sharpened his sword to defend the great rural majority, or an authoritarian white supremacist who tried to countermand the waves of progress.[52] An alternative way of looking at Jackson's place in U.S. history that fits the story of decolonization told here is to see him as one of the first leaders of the green uprising that spread along settler frontiers in the nineteenth century. Jackson did little to extend the right to vote, as is often claimed, because the franchise was already widespread.[53] His achievement was to mobilize the enlarged electorate behind a populist agenda that revitalized Jeffersonian principles of states' rights, territorial expansion, and minimal government, and fed upon hostility to foreign influences.

The comparison worth exploring in this connection is with contemporary leaders, such as Juan Manuel de Rosas and José Antonio Páez, who achieved power in the new Latin American Republics.[54] These were also men on horseback, veterans of wars against a colonial power, and landowners with territorial and political ambitions. Like Jackson, they too were quick of temper and quick on the draw. Their charismatic appeal combined martial notions of honor with the common touch.[55] Such men came to prominence by taking advantage of the extreme political fluidity of the postcolonial era to build followings that could capture and reshape the state. They were the gatekeepers who opened doors to government resources. Patronage, or the "spoils system," greased the wheels of their party organizations; large gestures kept them in motion. They cleared indigenous societies from the path of "modernization" and helped to create new agricultural export economies, which then became the material sources of their political standing. In 1844, a "special agent" of the State Department in Buenos Aires made the point, even if he stretched it a little, by calling Rosas "a real General Jackson of a fellow."[56] Although Jackson may not have been a *caudillo*, he undoubtedly displayed *caudillesque* qualities. His opponents accused him of having monarchical ambitions and referred to him as King Andrew; *El Supremo*, the republican style, suited him better.[57]

Once in office, the Jackson Democrats pursued a populist agenda that produced three of the principal political crises of the period: an attack on inherited tariff policy, an assault on the National Bank, and an effort to eliminate the national debt. These much-studied episodes are commonly regarded as the most sustained attempts made during the first half of the century to root out corrosive foreign influences and to move decisively toward a self-sufficient and self-sustaining polity. They undoubtedly illustrate Jackson's priorities, which were descended from the Jeffersonian tradition, and his capacity for decisive action. They also demonstrate the extent to which political self-interest and economic realities diluted proclaimed radical ambitions.

The first of the weighty economic issues Jackson tackled on taking office in 1829 was the federal import tariff approved by his predecessor, John Quincy Adams, in the previous year.[58] Protective tariffs, which had become a key element in the Hamiltonian platform of national development by the 1820s, provided a substantial part of the revenue needed to service the national debt and reward electoral support through government largesse. The tariff of 1816 had raised rates; the tariff of 1828, known to its vociferous opponents as the "Tariff of Abominations," increased them further. These measures helped to solidify support for Federalist policies in the North and attract support from the Midwest. Between them, the two regions received more than two-thirds of all federal spending in the 1820s.[59] The attack on the Tariff of Abominations came mainly from the South, and particularly from South Carolina, which had been devastated by the postwar economic crisis. The state challenged the right of the federal government to impose a tariff that exceeded the level needed for revenue purposes. A tense confrontation, which became known as the Nullification Crisis, followed.[60] At one point, the dispute threatened to split the Union, and was settled only after the rattle of sabers produced a compromise in 1833.

Jackson's decision to distance himself from South Carolina was crucial to the outcome. His loyalty to his fellow Southerners took second place on this occasion to ensuring that the Democrats retained their hold on federal power.[61] An astute maneuver, masterminded by the wily Van Buren, delivered the political backing Jackson needed. The final agreement, which provided for the phased reduction of the tariff during the next decade, put tariffs on a downward path (with a short interlude between 1842 and 1845) until the Civil War.[62] The distinguished economist, Alfred Marshall, writing in 1919, judged that the tariff "went very far in the direction of free trade."[63] The result strengthened commercial bonds between Britain and the South, while helping the Democrats to retain their hold on Congress and the presidency.

In 1830, the president vetoed a bill that proposed federal funding for transport improvements, not because he opposed either economic development or all federal funding, but because he saw a way of curtailing the power of his political opponents in Congress.[64] Jackson claimed that the proposed interstate road link was an unconstitutional extension of federal authority; transport policy, he asserted, was best determined by individual states.[65] These arguments appealed to Democrats, who feared the spread of federal power and its possible consequences for slaveholders. They resonated, too, with farmers in the Midwest, who were happy to attack "big government" as long as transport improvements came their way. Jackson's gambit succeeded. The Midwest severed its political alliance with the North and shifted its allegiance to the South. Falling transport costs and expanding overseas markets gave the Midwest a stake in low tariffs that lasted until the eve of the Civil War.[66] The issue was not the principle of import tariffs, which Hamilton had established, Jefferson had endorsed, and Jackson needed, but their level, which mattered for political as well as for economic reasons. Once the compromise had been reached, Jackson had no difficulty approving federal funding for less sensitive projects or providing subsidies for private contractors undertaking transport improvements.[67]

While agreement on the tariff was being negotiated, Jackson pressed ahead with his plan to remove government business from the Second Bank of the United States.[68] He characterized the Bank's largely Northern supporters as agents of corrupt "court" interests, and presented himself as the champion of "country" values. He attacked the Bank for being a constraint on liberty, and castigated what he called the "monied aristocracy" and the foreign (principally British) stockholders who held about 25 percent of the Bank's shares.[69] He appealed to the "humbler members of society" who were unlikely to sympathize either with the rich and powerful or with foreign investors. At the same time, his advocacy of states' rights won support among debtors and prospective borrowers, particularly in the South and Midwest, who resented the Bank's ability to impose monetary discipline on the two hundred or so largely unregulated state banks.[70] When the Bank's charter was presented for renewal in 1832, Jackson refused to extend it and transferred government deposits to various state banks instead. When the charter expired in 1836, the Second Bank of the United States found a home, in reduced circumstances, as a private bank in Pennsylvania before being quietly liquidated in 1841.

The demise of the Bank appears to be a straightforward example of the application of a long held political principle. Unlike Jefferson, however, Jackson was not opposed to all banks: his objection was to what he saw as the unchecked growth of a national corporation that had become a rival power center with roots in the North.[71] Taxes on local banks boosted state revenues, whereas a federal bank contributed to the federal government.[72] Jackson's triumph, however, was short-lived. The removal of the Bank of the United States led to a competitive boom among state banks that contributed to a major financial crash in 1837, which in turn cost Martin Van Buren, Jackson's chosen successor, his chance of being reelected in 1840.[73]

Jackson succeeded in paying off the national debt in 1835. His remarkable achievement, unprecedented in U.S. history, lasted for just over one year. Thereafter, federal borrowing resumed and has continued to swell ever since. In Jackson's view, the debt bound the majority to the few and tied the country to foreign financial interests. Only after the debt was eradicated would it become possible to create a truly free, self-sufficient, and virtuous republic administered by a modest and therefore a benign government. It was also the case that the debt served Northern financial interests and gave Federalist-Whigs opportunities to spread political favors. Central government could not be pared back, however, without also diminishing its borrowing capacity, including the ability to attract foreign capital, which was essential for state-building. The federal government's borrowing capacity was formally restored in 1846, when the Treasury Department was authorized to issue short-term notes and long-term bonds, both of which were vital to funding the annexation of Texas and the war with Mexico.[74] Jeffersonians were big spenders, even if, like Hamiltonians, they tried to repay what they owed.

The conditions underpinning the dominance of the South were subject to change; the dynamic of development ensured that they did. Population growth in the North and Midwest began to shift the balance of power. When Jefferson became president in 1800, there were 106 seats in the House of Representatives; in 1840, when the Whigs gained control of the House and the presidency for the first time, the number had risen to 242. In 1790, Southern states could count on 46 percent of the seats in the House; in 1860, their share had fallen to 35 percent. Southern control of Congress depended increasingly on the alliance with the Midwest, which still enabled the Democrats to command three-quarters of the seats in the House and two-thirds of the Senate in 1850.[75] Nevertheless, Van Buren's carefully crafted political alliances with states outside the South began to unravel after he left office in 1841. A new generation of manufacturers and artisans, who produced for the domestic market and supported protection rather than free trade, diluted the influence of the South's traditional Northern allies headed by bankers and merchants with investments in the cotton industry.[76] Many of these entrepreneurs had evangelical and humanitarian sympathies, and joined labor reformers, feminists, and others to advance the cause of abolition.[77] Equally, if not more important, the growth of settlements of free farmers in the Midwest began to increase the opposition to Southern schemes to extend the plantation system into new territories.[78]

The Federalists were slow to adjust to the green uprising, but remnants of the party modified their elitist predilections and British sympathies in 1834, when they regrouped under the banner of the Whig Party, reinvented themselves as tribunes of the people, embraced the idea of American exceptionalism, and joined protectionism to nationalism.[79] Although the party split in 1852 over a combination of ethnic divisions and the issue of slavery, the majority joined with Northern Free Soilers to form the Republican Party in 1854.[80] The party aimed to defend Hamilton's legacy from Jackson's challenge by appealing beyond its elitist image to new social groups, and by promoting the cause of free labor and free land in the expanding Midwest.[81] At the same time, a progressive wing of the Democrats, known as Young America, tested the unity of Jacksonian orthodoxy by advocating economic expansion and state-sponsored public utilities as means of appealing for support in the Midwest.[82] By the 1850s, reforming elements in both parties saw themselves as "moderns" who were in sympathy with the revolutions of 1848.[83]

Greater divisions, explored in chapter 5, lay ahead. Meanwhile, the assessment presented here suggests the need to reconsider some standard approaches to the politics of independence. The main theme of the period is not the rise of liberal democracy, as portrayed in the "Jeffersonian Revolution" and its Jacksonian sequel, but the confirmation and extension of a slaveholding polity dominated by Southern interests. Jackson and his successors sought, not to abolish federal power, but to harness it to their own purposes while enlarging their regional patrimonies. Hamiltonians and Jeffersonians aimed to secure effective independence from Britain, but neither succeeded. Before 1861, the Jeffersonian persuasion prevailed, and in doing so made the Republic more, not less, dependent on the ex-colonial power, as an examination of economic relationships will illustrate.

DILEMMAS OF DEPENDENT DEVELOPMENT

It is evident that political independence was closely tied to economic development and that the two are not easily disentangled. Nevertheless, the economic policies and outcomes of the period had additional features that require attention in their own right. Admirable research by economic historians has revealed the main trends and given them quantitative precision within the limits of the data available.[84] The predominant approach to the subject has set out to explain the emergence of what became, in the twentieth century, a gigantic and largely self-sufficient economy. The perspective taken here is rather different: it views the United States during this period as an example of one of the first attempts to transform an underdeveloped economy in conditions of continuing quasi-colonial influence.

All political parties recognized the importance of "delivering the goods" to an expectant citizenry and freeing the United States from dependence on the former colonial power. The central issue, set out in the 1790s and debated throughout the century, was how best to achieve these goals.[85] In a series of remarkable exchanges, Hamilton and Jefferson laid down the basis of what were to become enduring arguments about the role of government in economic development, the relative advantages of manufacturing and agriculture, the benefits and perils of banks and credit instruments, and the merits of protection and free trade.[86] As outlined earlier, Hamilton's economic nationalism aimed to promote manufactures by a combination of government action, individual enterprise, and new credit instruments.[87] Jefferson's vision of an independent state, on the other hand, joined the physiocrats' emphasis on the self-sustaining agrarian basis of the economy with Smith's depiction of expanding markets. The contest between these two programs made the United States the largely unacknowledged precursor of policies that ex-colonial states and the World Bank were to grapple with in the second half of the twentieth century.

Hamilton's "Report on Manufactures," submitted to Congress in 1791, was a pioneering work that influenced Friedrich List's program for encouraging industries in "late start" countries and contributed more to the history of modern development policies than scholars have acknowledged.[88] Hamilton's aim was to "render the United States independent of foreign nations for military and other essential supplies."[89] To this end, he emphasized the role of domestic manufacturing in adding value through linkages with the rest of the economy and thereby eliminating "dependence of any kind."[90] He further argued that agriculture and industry, far from being "in opposition," as was commonly claimed at the time, were complementary, and that mutual benefits would draw North and South together.[91] This was a matter of great importance, given that his ultimate aim was to demonstrate that "not only the wealth, but the independence and security of a country appear to be materially connected with the prosperity of manufactures."[92]

Hamilton accepted that commercial and financial ties with Britain would remain vital to the prosperity of the Republic, but hoped to direct them in ways that fostered national development. In 1794, he helped to mastermind Jay's Treaty, which reestablished trade with Britain after the disruption of the revolutionary years. The treaty modified the mercantilist system by granting trade between the two countries most-favored-nation status, and opened a limited number of imperial markets to the United States.[93] Jay's Treaty was controversial in the United States because it was seen as subordinating American economic interests to the former colonial power.[94] Future trends were clear to Bentham before the treaty was signed: "Before the separation," he observed of the former colonies in 1793, "Britain had a monopoly of their trade: upon the separation of course she lost it. How much less is their trade with Britain now then? On the contrary it is much greater."[95] There was widespread opposition: Jeffersonians favored an alliance with France; Southern states were incensed that the negotiations had failed to secure compensation for slaves who had escaped during the war. In the end, the Senate approved the treaty by a slim majority. Facts had to be faced: the United States was obliged to recognize its continuing dependence on trade with Britain and indirectly to acknowledge that its prosperity and security rested on a guarantee provided by the Royal Navy.[96] Madison summarized the position in 1823: "With the British fleets and fiscal resources associated with our own we should be safe against the rest of the World."[97]

After the War of 1812, Hamilton's program was adapted to include tariff protection and carried forward by Henry Clay, one of the most prominent political figures in the United States during the first half of the nineteenth century.[98] By then, Hamilton's reservations about extending the Republic inland had been overtaken by economic growth, which boosted population and manufacturing in the North, and the acquisition of vast new lands, which encouraged free settlers to move into the Midwest. Thereafter, expansion became largely self-propelling. These developments improved the outlook for import-substituting industries and strengthened support for Clay's proposed "American System" (named in opposition to the "British System"), which laid the foundation for what became the economic policy of the Whig-Republicans. The American System aimed at achieving national economic independence through neomercantilist policies of tariff protection, transport improvements, and managed land sales.[99] Britain's aim, so Clay claimed in 1820, was to maintain the United States as "independent colonies of England—politically free, commercially slaves."[100] Twelve years later, Clay remained convinced that the United States had still to break free from what he called "the British colonial system."[101] The mercantilist empire had tied the colonies to the metropolis on unfavorable terms in the eighteenth century; the new danger was that the South's demand for either low tariffs or free trade would bind the country even more tightly to the old colonial power long after political independence had been declared. According to Clay, the version of free trade advocated by the South, if adopted, would lead "substantially to the recolonization of these States, under the commercial dominion of Great Britain."[102] The route to independence, Clay held, lay through protecting infant industries in the United States by imposing tariffs on imported manufactured goods.

Hamilton's agenda and Clay's American System received powerful support from Henry Carey, whose father, Mathew, had been a consistent advocate of protection since the 1790s.[103] Henry Carey, who (like his father) achieved prominence as a public commentator, was regarded as the foremost economist in the United States in the mid-nineteenth century.[104] He began by favoring free trade but in the 1840s embraced the protectionist cause with the zeal of the converted, attached himself to the Whig-Republicans, and ended his public career as President Lincoln's chief economic advisor. Once converted, Carey never missed an opportunity to denounce what he called the British system of "free trade despotism," which "has shown itself the faithful ally of the men who teach that slavery is the natural condition of the laboring man, whether black or white."[105] Free trade, in Carey's judgment, was no more than a plot to keep the United States dependent.[106] He welcomed the protective tariff of 1842 as "a new Declaration of Independence" and dismissed the original as "a mere form of words."[107] In Carey's view, Britain's adoption of free trade in 1846 reinforced the dependence of the United States on the former colonial power. Indeed, "with slight exception we have been governed by the great capitalists of Britain and have the precise system . . . required for retaining the colonies in a state of vassalage."[108] If the United States was to become "really independent" and (using Jackson's term) "Americanized," it needed to nurture its infant industries behind protective tariffs.[109] These remarks were made, not in 1845, but in 1865. If Carey was right, the United States was still in thrall to Britain at the end of the Civil War.

Jefferson and his successors looked forward (and back) to a world of agrarian prosperity sustained by sturdy, independent Anglo-Saxon yeomen (and sturdy, dependent slaves).[110] Although they idealized pre-industrial society and favored self-reliance, they accepted that a market economy was necessary to sustain the vitality of the rural community.[111] However, they abhorred the national debt and regarded the "monied interest" as the devil's favorite emissary.[112] They were hostile, too, to the large-scale and predominantly urban manufacturing industry Hamilton wished to promote, though they accepted the need for artisans who would produce for the local community and help, as the *Aurora* put it in 1802, to avoid "dependence of any kind."[113] Their ultimate aim was to create a large, self-sufficient domestic economy that would eliminate reliance on British trade and finance.

Until this day was in sight, Jefferson and his successors had to adjust their ideals to changing realities. They borrowed extensively to finance territorial expansion. By 1816, they had accepted, in Jefferson's words, that "manufactures are now as necessary to our independence as to our comfort."[114] They acknowledged that a thriving agricultural economy needed overseas markets, even though international specialization led to domestic inequalities that marred the prospects of creating a harmonious rural social order. This imperative, in turn, ensured that Jackson Democrats became committed advocates of free trade, which would guarantee favorable access to foreign markets for cotton exports and, reciprocally, low tariffs on imported manufactures.[115] The South became a semicolonial economic enclave with an increasing allegiance to the British connection. Commentators in the Southern states agreed that the region had become a dependent economy, but were divided in their assessment of the consequences. They compromised by settling for the benefits while blaming outsiders for the defects.[116] Prosperity made dependence bearable.

The struggle between these two perspectives centered on tariff policy, which, as we have seen, also featured prominently in the political and ideological debates of the period. The tariff compromise reached in 1833 halted the advance of Clay's American System and helped to perpetuate the low-tariff (or at least lower-tariff) colonial economy he had campaigned against so ardently. Consequently, the protective effects of the tariff were modest.[117] Nevertheless, as population increased in the northeast, manufactures expanded without a substantial degree of protection. Cotton exports from the South also rose noticeably from the 1820s, despite complaints from growers that high tariffs on imported consumer goods were a disincentive to enterprise.[118] The real significance of the tariff was that it held the Republic together by supplying about half of all federal receipts throughout the nineteenth century.[119] Loans provided the second largest contribution; the two combined accounted for about 90 percent of total federal revenues between 1790 and 1860. Excise and poll taxes were harder to collect and liable to provoke political discontent; the economy, and the country, were not ready for income tax until 1913. The greater part of federal expenditure was devoted to state-building, and to the military in particular. All federal governments, irrespective of their formal positions and contrasting rhetoric, used tariff revenues and borrowed money to acquire territory across the continent. While government finances remained reliant on the fortunes of international trade, the level of the tariff could be, and was, fiercely contested; its existence, however, was beyond dispute.

The political power of the South was based on cotton, which was the leading export from the United States between 1803 and 1937.[120] Between 1820 and 1860, the United States accounted for 80 percent of global production of raw cotton; 75 percent of the total was exported; more than 50 percent of this was shipped to Britain.[121] In 1830, cotton, tobacco, and rice, mostly from Virginia and the Carolinas, accounted for two-thirds of the value of all U.S. exports. Cotton production expanded through a combination of supply-side improvements, beginning with the cotton gin, and rising demand in Europe. As output grew, slave labor increased: in 1760, there were fewer than 400,000 slaves in the mainland colonies; in 1860, there were nearly 4 million. Improved transport facilities, starting with roads and canals and continuing in the 1840s with railroads, extended the land under cotton cultivation in the South and connected the Midwest to the international economy. The prairies were the principal beneficiaries of the large, new grain market that opened after 1846, when Britain adopted free trade. Grain exports from the Midwest rose from a modest 2 million bushels in 1840 to reach 32 million in 1860. Given this rate of growth, the new barons of the prairies looked forward with confidence to making the region the "granary of the world."[122]

Before 1846, the contest between protectionists and free-traders was moderated to a degree by sporadic attempts to negotiate a reciprocity treaty with Britain in the hope that mutual revisions in tariff levels would open up protected imperial markets.[123] Jay's Treaty expired in 1806 and was not renewed; thereafter, Britain treated the United States as a foreign country for tariff purposes. Following the Reciprocity Act of 1815, the United States made a number of reciprocal agreements with other countries. The big prize, however, was to obtain agreement with Britain. This result failed to materialize, despite persistent efforts. The British made minor concessions but held fast to the principle of imperial protection. As Lord Castlereagh, the British Foreign Secretary, observed in 1819, to accede to the American proposals would be to "effect an entire subversion of the British colonial system."[124] His successors concurred. An alternative strategy was for the United States to develop markets outside the imperial network, but this goal could not be achieved without first producing a range of manufactured goods at competitive prices, as Henry Clay repeatedly pointed out.

Britain remained the Republic's principal trading partner and chief source of overseas finance during the first half of the century. Commercial connections between the two countries strengthened after independence and expanded further as mercantilist restrictions were dismantled.[125] Down to the Civil War, the United States remained strongly oriented toward overseas trade (measured by per capita imports and exports). Comparative advantage produced a typical colonial pattern of export dependence based on agricultural products. The United States ran deficits on merchandise trade, which were offset partly by invisible earnings (principally shipping services) and capital imports. Exports (and reexports) from the United States to Britain rose from 35 percent of the total in 1795–1801 to 42 percent of a much larger total in 1849–1858.

This share, though sizeable, underestimates the increasing importance of the British connection. In the years between 1849 and 1858, the United States also sent 23 percent of its total exports to the West Indies, mainly to British colonies there, and an additional 8 percent to British North America (Canada). Moreover, with the development of steamship services from the 1840s, the United States lost its place in the carrying trade. In 1864, representatives of American shipping interests lamented that "we are at the present time totally dependent upon foreign flags for the transportation of our citizens, our correspondence, and our merchandise to and from every country (except Cuba and Panama) upon the globe."[126] Most of the "foreign flags" were British.

British lines of credit, which were cheaper than those offered by competitors on the continent of Europe, continued to connect the City of London to American merchants after the Revolution, as before.[127] The history of the House of Brown illustrates both the enduring character of British influence and the way it mingled with American interests to produce a cosmopolitan network that fitted the requirements of international business.[128] Alexander Brown, an Ulster linen merchant, emigrated to the United States at the close of the eighteenth century, settled in Baltimore, and established the House of Brown in 1800. The dynasty he founded, along with various subsidiaries and associated family networks, functioned as a transnational organization helping to integrate the expanding Anglo-American commercial world in much the same way as the Lascelles family had done in the eighteenth century.[129] Brown's expanded to become one of the leading import and export businesses in North Atlantic trade during the first half of the nineteenth century. From the 1830s, the firm concentrated on finance, which it managed from branches in New York, Philadelphia, Liverpool, and London, and became a leading broker supplying short-term commercial advances, providing letters of credit, and negotiating bills of exchange. Brown's was nearly brought down by the financial crisis of 1837, when it had to approach the Bank of England for support. It was a measure of the firm's importance by then that the Bank agreed to an advance of £2 million, of which £1 million was taken—and repaid within a few months.

Brown's escape was followed by further expansion and wider recognition: Alexander's son, William, became a Liberal M.P. in 1846 and received a knighthood in 1863. The union of international capitalism and gentility was complete: no more Ulster linen had to be displayed or washed in public. Even greater distinction lay ahead. The firm's connections with the Bank of England were considerably strengthened in 1887, when Sir Mark Collet, a partner in Brown Shipley, was appointed

Governor; his grandson, Montagu Collet Norman, who joined the firm in the same year, succeeded him as Governor of the Bank in 1920 and retired as Lord Norman in 1944.

The reach of British capital extended far beyond the need for short-term commercial credit. The City of London was involved from the outset in an enduring commitment to state-building in the United States, as it was later in the dominions and the Latin American republics.[130] Stock and bond markets were formed in New York in 1792 and became formalized as the New York Stock Exchange in 1817. Nevertheless, the local capital market, though increasingly well integrated and drawing on a rising pool of investment, was too small to service the expanding needs of the Republic, which were met principally by British merchant banks.[131] Consequently, links between the City and the United States became stronger after independence than they had been in colonial times. An informal, trans-Atlantic financial alliance emerged with the aim of maintaining good relations between the two countries. Politicians stirred the pot of Anglophobia for electoral purposes; bankers joined forces to keep the lid on.[132]

Long-term foreign investment in the Republic underwent a twelve-fold increase between 1789 and 1853.[133] Britain supplied more than 75 percent of the total, most of which went to federal and state governments to finance improvements in canals, roads, and railroads, and to expand administrative services.[134] The City helped to fund the First National Bank and its successors. In 1803, about two-thirds of the Bank's stock was held abroad, mostly in Britain. In the same year, more than half the U.S. national debt was in foreign, and predominantly British, hands.[135] The proportion fell to about one-third in 1828, three-quarters of which was held by British investors. In 1835, President Jackson capitalized on the decline by liquidating the national debt in the hope of eliminating foreign financial influences. Nevertheless, the bond holders soon returned. By 1853, half the national debt was again held abroad, nearly all of it by British investors. With considerable help from the City of London, the United States ended the nineteenth century as the world's largest debtor. In this case, the status recognized the Republic's credit-worthiness, not its profligacy.

The City firm of Baring Brothers, founded in 1762 by Francis Baring, was the most important of the merchant banks mobilizing long-term capital for the United States and organizing loans for exceptional needs, especially territorial expansion.[136] Barings, like Brown's, created an Anglo-American network that straddled the Atlantic and extended into Asia.[137] The firm became involved in North American finance during the 1770s by helping to fund and supply Britain's war effort against the rebellious colonists. After 1783, Barings assisted the new government to settle its war debts, and in turn benefited from the assurance of stability contained in the Constitution of 1787 and the confidence generated by Jay's Treaty in 1794, which confirmed that debts incurred to British creditors before independence would be repaid. In a remarkable tribute to the power of capital to flow over even the newest and most sensitive of political frontiers, Barings took the lead in negotiating the Louisiana Purchase, which doubled the size of the United States in 1803.[138] The firm then supplied the greater part of the $11.5 million needed to complete the deal (repayable at 6 percent over fifteen years). The U.S. government reciprocated by appointing Barings its official agent in London.

Even after Jefferson had been elected president and anti-British rhetoric infused political sentiment, the market reckoned that radicalism of the kind that would endanger property rights had already been shown the door. The market judged correctly. Barings went on to supply the funds needed to meet interest payments owing to bond holders during the War of 1812 and helped to broker the peace in 1815. They provided the first loans to state governments in the 1820s, financed railroad-building from the 1840s, and funded the federal government's "war of choice" against Mexico in 1846.[139] During the first half of the century, the viability and development of the new state owed a great deal to the financial support of the City of London.

In due course, Barings followed Brown's in adding social distinction to financial success. As revolutionaries were felling financiers in France, British governments were elevating luminaries in the City of London. Francis Baring became a baronet in 1793 and an M.P. in the following year. Alexander, his son and successor, achieved eminence on both sides of the Atlantic. In 1796, he bought 1.25 million acres in Maine from one of the wealthiest merchants on the East Coast, and sealed the compact two years later by marrying his daughter. Having masterminded the Louisiana Purchase and having steered the firm through the conflicted loyalties of the War of 1812, Alexander devoted himself increasingly to politics in Britain. As an M.P. from 1806 to 1835, he supported free trade as firmly as he opposed radical political reform. By the time he was elevated to the House of Lords in 1842 as the first Baron Ashburton, his conservative inclinations were as visible as his vast estates.

Commercial and financial flows across the Atlantic exposed the United States to fluctuations in international trade transmitted by impulses that were beyond its borders and largely beyond its control. George Washington had advised his successors to maintain diplomatic neutrality; Jefferson followed his lead by pledging in 1801 to avoid "entangling alliances."[140] Neither, however, could command the consequences of economic integration with the outside world, nor do much to moderate their domestic effects. In theory, the South had the potential to realize monopoly profits from its control of Britain's cotton supplies. In practice, cotton producers were unable to turn economic power into political action. Export taxes, which would have increased cotton prices, were prohibited by the Constitution.[141] A producers' cartel, which could have raised prices by regulating supplies, never became operational.[142] Cotton prices were set competitively by auction and reflected demand in Europe, as well as inevitable variations in supply caused by weather conditions. Farmers in the Midwest were in an even weaker position because wheat, the second most important U.S. export, provided less than 5 percent of the British market between 1830 and 1850.[143] Exporters in the two regions were price-takers rather than price-makers, albeit for different reasons, and were recipients of shocks from two distant sources: the heavens and external demand.

The economic expansion under way in the second half of the eighteenth century was interrupted by the devastation caused by the Revolutionary War. After 1783, however, commercial relations between the United States and Britain were swiftly reconnected. Josiah Wedgwood's factory symbolized the speed of the adjustment in 1783 by deleting designs showing George III and substituting George Washington instead.[144] Fortuitously, the long wars between Britain and France that began in 1793 preoccupied the great powers, expanded demand for U.S. exports, and brought a degree of prosperity that helped to ease the transition from colonial rule.[145] Although the conflict disrupted Europe's international trade, the most serious effects in the North Atlantic were confined to the years between 1807 and 1814, when trade embargoes were in force.[146] The limited effect of Jefferson's embargo in 1807, however, contrasted with the considerable success of the British blockade in 1814. The disparity between the two powers at this time was as evident as the dominance of the Royal Navy was complete. Adversity, however, had at least one benign outcome: the shortage of manufactured imports encouraged the rapid growth of the New England textile industry.[147] The United States has claims to being the first ex-colony to develop modern import-substituting manufactures under the duress of war; other colonies took the same route during the world wars of the twentieth century.

The War of 1812, combined with the extended conflict in Europe, which also ended in 1815, had far-reaching domestic consequences. A postwar boom in the United States between 1815 and 1818 was followed by a financial "panic" in 1819.[148] The decision not to renew the charter of the Bank of the United States in 1811 paved the way to competitive lending, easy money, and a land boom, which in turn was encouraged by the demand for agricultural products in war-ravaged Europe. When the war ended, the recovery of European agriculture reduced the need for foodstuffs from the United States, while the resumption of imports of cheap manufactures retarded the growth of infant industries. The market for raw cotton contracted too, as British manufacturers located cheaper sources in Asia and as the postwar boom turned into a slump in Europe. U.S. merchant shipping, which had expanded during the long French wars, also suffered. At this point, the Bank of the United States, which had been reconstituted in 1816 to meet the needs of war finance, first ran a loose-money policy that stoked land prices and then, in 1818, tightened the money supply. Cotton prices, which had reached exceptional heights, crashed in the same year. The economic effects, in short order, were deflation, default, rising unemployment, and widespread distress.

The effects of the depression touched all aspects of life in the 1820s, and some stretched into the next decade. The crisis sharpened the debate between the advocates of "sound" and "soft" money, between protectionists and free traders, and between proponents and critics of federal power and states' rights. The immediate consequences of popular discontent included mounting support for Andrew Jackson's bid for the presidency in 1824 (which he only just lost to John Quincy Adams) and his election in 1828. In these ways, the gyrations of the international economy reached deep inland and far down the social order, while also influencing the highest levels of domestic politics.

The recovery that began in the mid-1820s lasted until 1837, when a new "panic" struck the United States, and was followed in 1839 by a second crisis, the cumulative effects of which were felt in five years of deflation and depression.[149] The revival of exports, combined with public spending on infrastructure, attracted flows of capital from the City of London. At the same time, President Jackson's decision in 1832 not to renew the charter of the Second Bank of the United States provided opportunities for a multiplicity of private banks to compete in offering soft loans. A land boom, similar to that of 1815–1819, followed. In this case, it was not the end of a war that brought the good times to a close, but the end of a good run of harvests in Britain. Agricultural prosperity had reduced the cost of foodstuffs and lifted effective demand for consumer goods, notably textiles. As the price of U.S. cotton rose, the value of land and slaves increased. The plantation system became more profitable; its advocates became more confident. The export of capital from Britain, however, reduced the Bank of

England's sterling reserves, and the poor harvests that followed the good years increased the import bill. Officials at the Bank responded by raising interest rates in 1836 to stem the outflow and prevent pressure on the balance of payments. Banks in New York, which shadowed rates in London, followed suit. The boom ended abruptly. Raw cotton prices collapsed, land values fell, creditors scrambled to call in loans, innumerable businesses ceased to trade, nearly half the banks in the United States went into liquidation, unemployment rose to levels that provoked civil disorder. The appearance of state governments in the roll call of chronic debtors was a novel feature of the panic of 1837 and a measure of the development of the economy since 1819. No fewer than eight states and the Territory of Florida defaulted on their debts.

Friedrich List, writing in 1844 with this episode among others in mind, denounced what he called the "insane doctrine" advanced by the advocates of free trade and took aim in particular at the City of London, "the treasure house of all great capital," which "by loans and the receipt of interest on them makes all the peoples of the earth her tributaries."[150] When the Bank of England adjusted interest rates, the repercussions of the changed cost of borrowing were felt in countries like the United States that remained dependent on British finance. British policy, List argued, took no account of American interests yet exercised a powerful influence over the value of land and labor in what was formally an independent country. List even suggested that, if the United States decided to abandon its ambition of becoming a modern manufacturing country, it would be better off within the British Empire, where it would be sheltered by the mercantilist system.

The internal consequences of the financial crises of 1837 and 1839 extended far beyond the events themselves. They help to explain the rejection of Martin Van Buren, the Jacksonian candidate, and the election of William Henry Harrison, an advocate of Clay's American System, as president in 1840.[151] Harrison died shortly after taking office and his successor, John Tyler, unexpectedly abandoned radical Whig policies, partly in response to public hostility toward official profligacy, which increased the appeal of Jeffersonian measures aimed at reducing federal government expenditure and controlling state budgets.[152] Nevertheless, Tyler felt obliged to sanction the tariff of 1842, which raised import duties, because it was the only acceptable way of increasing revenue and restoring the health of public finances.[153] The crisis and its remedy disrupted the social order. Widespread riots challenged state governments, which responded initially with martial law and brutal suppression, and subsequently by creating professional police forces. Several thousand debtors and job-seekers migrated to Texas, where they strengthened the political base of the independent, slaveholding republic, which entered the Union as a new state in 1846. The Mexican-American War of 1846–1848, which was related to the annexation of Texas, was also linked to the depression.[154] The war undoubtedly gave vent to President James Polk's bellicose instincts, but he was responding, in turn, to the public's desire for better times, which a fresh land grab appeared to offer.

The City of London was left swinging in the wind, and with time to ruminate on the consequences of joining a spirit of "irrational exuberance" to a misunderstanding of the U.S. Constitution. The federal government was no more inclined to bail out defaulting states than the British government was willing to subsidize investors who backed lame horses. The City responded to its predicament by mounting a substantial publicity campaign that advertised the merits of fiscal probity and underlined the consequences of the cessation of foreign lending. By the early 1850s, most of the defaulters had resumed payment.[155] Mississippi, which failed to pay (and has still not paid), was excluded from the British capital market. Coincidentally or not, it remains the poorest state in the Republic today.[156]

The United States was too big to fail. Investment opportunities reappeared in the late 1840s, following Britain's adoption of free trade in 1846, war with Mexico in 1846–1848, and the acquisition of California in 1848. As the economy regained momentum, the City again became fully committed to the success of the republican "project." The reductions embodied in the Walker Tariff, passed by Congress in 1846 and supported by British business interests, were designed explicitly to give grain farmers in the Midwest an opportunity to enter the Atlantic export economy on advantageous terms.[157] Grain exports boomed in the 1850s, land values rose, and banks once more advanced money on the assumption that, this time, "it was different." It was not. In 1857, there was another "panic" that repeated the central features of the boom-bust cycles of 1819 and 1837.

This episode, like its predecessors, had both prominent external causes and profound internal consequences.[158] Grain prices had been boosted by the disruption to European agriculture caused by the Crimean War. With the advent of peace in 1856 and the recovery of domestic production, the demand for external supplies eased. Grain prices in the United States dropped; debtors had difficulty servicing their loans; banks recalled advances; bankruptcies and unemployment followed. The political consequences were equally far-reaching. The South, which on this occasion was not directly affected by the depression, used the episode to advertise the strength and superiority of slave society. Republicans in the North, which was affected, responded by sharpening the arguments in favor of free labor as an integral part of a free society, revived the arguments for tariff protection, and blamed a Southern "slave conspiracy" for retarding the Republic's economic development.

The preceding discussion has concentrated on external features of the Republic's development and has deliberately left aside important themes, such as manufacturing and the internal market, which a broader account of the economic history of the period would need to cover. Nevertheless, the argument outlined here ought to refer to the "market revolution" that has been claimed for this period because it has a bearing on the question of economic independence.[159] There was an undoubted surge in economic activity between the 1800s and the Civil War.[160] Agricultural output rose; plantations in the South increased their exports; household production in the northeast became more market-oriented; manufacturing expanded; inequalities of income and wealth grew. Wage and slave labor both rose in importance; artisans were gradually replaced by outworkers producing piece goods; a market in land joined the market for goods. An expanding population enlarged the towns and carried the western frontier far across the Appalachians. The effect of these trends on economic development, however, remains unclear. One estimate suggests that per capita GDP increased at more than 1 percent annually, which is the rate economists regard as qualifying for "modern" economic growth.[161] Different evidence shows that there was a decline in the height of adult men from the 1830s as a result of poor nutrition, as food supplies failed to keep pace with population growth.[162]

Even if an optimistic view of economic progress during the first half of the nineteenth century is adopted, the idea of a "market revolution" remains problematic.[163] As deployed so far, the concept lacks analytical rigor and statistical underpinning. It also implies more than was delivered. Developments that stand out when considered within particular chronological limits become less visible when compared to previous and later periods. The rural origins of American capitalism have been traced to the eighteenth century, when farming households increased their commitment to the market.[164] Modern manufacturing did not grow fast enough to transform what was still an agrarian economy, even in the North.[165] Moreover, down to the 1830s, at least, there is evidence that parts of the advanced sectors of the Northern economy were managed by merchants who aimed at preserving control rather than by industrial capitalists bent on maximizing profits.[166] Fiscal unity was still incomplete; the banking system was unable to meet the demand for investment capital.[167] The full integrative effects of transport improvements were felt after 1850, not before.

In debates of this kind, much depends on the definition of terms. Economic growth can occur without requiring a revolution. Arguably, a "revolution" involves the structural transformation of the economy, which occurred only after the Civil War. It was then that the expansion of industrial manufactures became "more dramatic," and a century of "great inventions" initiated a "revolution" in economic potential and performance.[168] During the period considered here, the economy remained predominantly rural, as it was in most of Europe, and the growth of the market was insufficiently revolutionary to allow the United States to declare economic independence.

CULTURAL CONTINUITIES

In 1783, the new Republic's leaders faced a problem that all ex-colonies are obliged to confront: the need to create a counterculture that would distinguish the new state from the former ruling power.[169] At that moment, the United States was not a nation and was barely a state, and its disparate polities and uncertain borders were unpromising conditions for what would later become known as "nation-building." Where colonial rulers presided over densely populated indigenous societies, cultural differences were already well defined. In these circumstances, leaders of newly independent states had little difficulty in distinguishing between their own society and that of the former colonial power. Their problem was to coordinate or neutralize competing ethnic groups, each of which sought to shape national identity in ways that expressed their own culture and interests. Colonies of white settlement faced a different challenge. Leaders in those states had to derive cultural independence from what was, in many respects, an extended version of British society. They could define themselves against indigenous people, but an effective external antonym was neither readily available nor easily summoned because the legacy of ethnic attributes and reference points persisted well beyond the period of colonial rule. This was the case with the Dominions; it applied to the United States, too, despite the fact that the colonists had fought a war to secure their independence.

An older historiography assumed that a sense of national identity embodying liberal-capitalist values emerged at an early date and was fully formed, or at least largely unproblematic, by the nineteenth century. According to this view, immigrants were poured into a melting pot and stirred into a novel form of civic identity.[170] Current scholarship, however, suggests that, at the moment of independence, most settlers in the mainland colonies still considered themselves to be British Americans.[171]

Some colonists saw themselves as members of a transnational Atlantic complex; others envisaged being part of what was becoming a continental society; a sizeable minority retained ties of kin and culture with Spain and France.[172] This degree of variety reflected the fact that the idea of the state was itself in flux at this time. For Hamilton, the state was a bounded entity held together for reasons of security by a central government. For Jefferson, it was a set of inherently pacific, self-governing republics that by multiplying would become a transcendent world society.[173] The junction between the two was not easily made. More important still, the Constitution, by entrenching the states, helped to solidify the distinction between the federal state and different senses of nationality that adhered to its constituents.

Cosmopolitan and provincial affiliations were formed long before a specifically American sense of nationality emerged. It was only after the settlers parted from their Anglo-Saxon core that they began to mold the Republic in their own image. American identity was then shaped, not by the melting pot, but by a process of ethnogenesis.[174] Students of ethnicity have identified a typical sequence that begins with migration from a center of origin, continues with fission from the primary group, develops in time into distinctiveness, and produces a strategy of assimilation, whereby a dominant *ethnie* persuades or coerces others to conform to its values and customs. Specialists agree that nations arise from an ethnic nucleus; the United States was no exception.[175]

In 1776, the ethnic core was approximately 60 percent English, 80 percent British, and 98 percent Protestant.[176] Following independence in 1783, the leaders of the Republic proceeded to extend the ethnic base to encompass other groups. The quest was not for exclusivity: multiple affiliations were, and remain, ineradicable facts of social life, especially in federations. The aim was rather to attach sufficient loyalty to the new state to generate the degree of unity needed to guarantee its viability. The colonists took the first steps in the seventeenth century, when the Indian wars created the need for antonyms to help create an alternative white-American identity.[177] Persistent warfare with Native Americans ensured that their visibility as a perceived threat remained present throughout the nineteenth century. The expansion and prosperity of slaveholding, combined with a fear of slave rebellions, helped in the same way to define a white culture of racial superiority and economic dominance.

A sense of the unity and preeminence of the white race, though a necessary component of nation-building, was scarcely sufficient. The expatriated British ethnie also had to establish its authority over other white ethnic groups. Anglo-conformity was to be achieved by a process of assimilation that foreshadowed the policies of "Americanization" that were applied to the insular empire in the twentieth century. Assimilation had to appear desirable and be attainable, but at the same time confer a sense of achievement and exclusivity. The balance was not easily struck. Not everyone could join the elite because entry depended on distinctive material success. In principle, however, all could join the elect by committing to one of several evangelical denominations. In practice, religious differences were not easily overcome. Roman Catholics were refused admission to the Anglo-club because their beliefs were inconsistent with the fundamental values attached to membership. Catholics nevertheless served a purpose. The discrimination they suffered established a boundary that reinforced the Protestant core while also defining one of the key qualifications needed for admission.

Policies of assimilation had three main ideological agencies: a cult of the founders, Anglo-Saxon mythology, and evangelical Protestantism. All societies create myths of origin to provide a set of primary values, anchor them in antiquity, and endow them with legitimacy. The fact that the mythology is vague and untestable is a strength rather than a weakness: it can never be disproved, it is enduring, and its generalities give it sufficient flexibility to adjust to changing times.

Commentators and propagandists made strenuous efforts after 1783 to promote the Founding Fathers, especially George Washington, to the status of symbols of national unity.[178] In this initiative, as in others, the United States developed a strategy that all newly independent states were to adopt. The founders became venerated exemplars of moral conduct and champions of liberty. The degree to which this publicity penetrated the citizens of the Republic is not easily gauged, though it probably helped to solidify support for the Constitution. Jefferson thought that each generation needed to consider revising the Constitution; Madison sympathized but concluded that the recommendation was likely to open the door to instability. Instead, he advanced the idea of tacit consent, whereby pacific acceptance was a sufficient indication of political contentment. This doctrine had the advantage of reconciling liberty with slavery because slaves were judged by their presumed passivity to consent to their condition. The problem with this formula was that, in securing support for the Constitution in the short term, it entrenched the long-term issue—slavery—which eventually had to be resolved on the battlefield.

"Anglicization," as it began to be called in the eighteenth century, was a notable Anglo-Saxon derivative that Britain applied throughout the empire after 1783.[179] The centrality attached to the Anglo-Saxon origins

of American society exercised a powerful intellectual influence throughout the nineteenth century, and in a generalized and diluted form shaped
or confirmed attitudes at all levels of society. According to its proponents,
the Anglo-Saxon heritage was one of exceptional attributes that needed
to be preserved or, where abandoned, recovered. Anglo-Saxons were distinctive and superior because they had invented universal liberties, created embryonic democracies, and demonstrated the organizational skills
needed to make these qualities operational.

Anglo-Saxon mythology was a means of creating unity among a diverse white population and shaping it to Anglo-values. Ralph Waldo
Emerson was one of the foremost exponents of the American version,
which he traced to its English roots and then transported to the United
States.[180] Emerson's mystical notion of the virtuous and virile Saxon
merged easily with the romantic nationalism propounded by Herder and
Hegel, who viewed nations as organic growths that reached their desti-
nies by creating strong, independent states. The particular instruments
of Anglo-American destiny were the urban elites on the East Coast
and their imitators in newer towns, such as Chicago and Los Angeles.[181]
Their appointed subalterns were the yeomen who were disappearing
from Britain but were being revitalized in the New World, where they
became both custodians and agents of true, organic values.[182] Emerson's
concept of ethnicity, however, met competition in the South, where an
alternative notion of the Anglo-world had gained ground by the mid-
nineteenth century. Southern commentators presented growing regional
differences as a contest between Northern Anglo-Saxons and Southern
Anglo-Normans.[183] This formulation pitted Puritans of humble origin
against cavaliers of superior stock and predicted that, in the event of a
contest between them, nobility would triumph over the lower orders.[184]

Evangelical Protestantism became the spiritual arm of secular Anglo-
Saxonism.[185] A strong sense of religiosity allied to a powerful belief in
destiny arrived in New England with the Pilgrim Fathers. Successive
renewals maintained the momentum of the initial impetus. The Great
Awakening in the 1730s and 1740s brought Presbyterians, Baptists, and
Methodists to the forefront of American Protestantism.[186] A further
surge in religiosity, led by Methodists and Baptists and known as the Second Great Awakening, began in New England in the 1790s and spread
along the routes taken by canals, roads and, later, railroads. According
to one leading authority, this revival "did more to Christianize American
society than anything before or since."[187] Church membership doubled
between 1776 and 1850.[188] By the mid-nineteenth century, evangelicals
had gained significant political influence in both Britain and the United

States: they inspired the temperance movement and joined other groups to campaign on the issues of slavery and women's rights.[189]

Evangelicals replaced hierarchy with self-reliance supported by direct, personal spiritual communion guided by biblical precepts. Virtuous habits and good works expressed piety; personal guilt symbolized the sins of the wider community as well as of the individual; public confession offered the prospect of redemption for both. Providentialism bestowed certainty and reassurance. Events that could not be fully understood or that produced malign outcomes could be attributed to the will of God, whose ways and wonders often remained mysterious, but whose ultimate purpose was not to be doubted. Providentialism developed from British roots but acquired a specifically American character in the eighteenth century, when it became necessary to devise a justificatory ideology for the Revolution.[190] God's purpose revealed itself after 1783. The Revolution was an act of divine intervention: the United States had been created to fulfill His will, which was to spread liberty and democracy across the world. Material ambition and spiritual commitment were harmonized in the concept of manifest destiny, which was applied enthusiastically to continental expansion after 1783.

American Protestants strove to create a Christian commonwealth united by a shared religious vision that would absorb or override the evident divisions within the Republic. Proselytizing missions began to stitch separate communities together. An interdenominational Protestant alliance spread Anglo-values through public schools and voluntary associations.[191] The endeavor also created a degree of uniformity in matters of public choice. The influence of the Enlightenment, which had inspired Deists, like Jefferson, and Unitarians, like Priestley, receded. Deism was absorbed into organized religion, where it contributed to the growth of a generalized civic faith that the existence and progress of the United States were in accord with the will of God. These developments left little room in political debate for free-thinkers.[192] The rhetoric of republicanism survived, but the concept of civic virtue moved away from the formal political sphere and into an increasingly close association with religion, where it found greater informal expression through churches, schools, and families.[193] In the South, in particular, civic virtue was infused with a form of new Romanticism that emphasized the organic quality of the social order and the need, accordingly, to conserve the past and to preserve it for the future.[194]

Influential interpretations suggest that the Second Great Awakening was a response to the American Revolution and the market revolution, though specialists are sharply divided about the nature of both relationships.[195] The American Revolution had rejected centralized, monarchical government and the hierarchical authority of the established Anglican Church. The resulting crisis of legitimacy was only partly overcome by the Constitution, which was a man-made document that, in principle, could also be unmade. American Protestantism, with its ability to discern God's ultimate purpose, presented a compelling resolution of the problem: the Lord became sovereign. However, if the American Revolution created the need, the French Revolution, combined with militant dissent at home, stimulated the solution.[196] American observers recoiled in horror at the sight of radical anti-clericalism in France, particularly when it was allied to an assault on property rights. Their reaction gave impetus to the Protestant revival. It prompted leaders in the United States, such as John Quincy Adams, to distinguish between virtuous and villainous republics and to point the way toward a specific form of American nationalism that carried the indelible imprint of evangelical Protestantism. The result was a rejection of the secular Enlightenment, an abiding suspicion of European theorists and intellectuals generally, and a fear of radical change reinforced by a persistent belief that foreign conspirators were scheming to bring down the Republic. These elements combined to validate a distinctive form of republicanism that had God's blessing and a special mandate to fulfill His purpose. "Philosophers," declared Congressman Robert Harper in 1798, "are the pioneers of revolution."[197] It is no wonder that Tom Paine, once a hero, was ostracized.[198]

American Protestants also had to deal with unsettling socioeconomic changes brought about by economic growth. Methodists and Baptists, who were the most numerous of the evangelical denominations, responded by strengthening the bonds between religion and capitalism. Individual responsibility in religion joined with economic self-interest, which in turn endorsed consumer choice and the unfettered, decentralized operation of the market.[199] Individual enterprise applied to abundant resources, providentially bestowed, created a new politics of emulation that was bounded by biblical morality rather than by classical thought, which held that virtue was incompatible with acquisitiveness. Preoccupation with economic growth overtook concern for equality.[200] The resulting blueprint validated the route to success while ensuring that failure was the responsibility of those who stumbled on the journey.[201] In these ways, the opportunities, uncertainties, and discontents brought by economic change were channeled into popular religion and away from what later became known elsewhere as the politics of envy.[202]

The rejection of monarchy and the hierarchy that accompanied it gave particular urgency to the need to install a new elite, the "natural aristocrats," as Jefferson called them, who would embody the values of the Republic and provide a steadying sense of order and unity. The continuing vitality of the Anglo-tradition, however, limited efforts to achieve cultural independence, as it did in the remaining colonies of settlement in the British Empire. The Revolution undoubtedly generated a degree of Anglophobia, which was especially visible in the foreign policies of Jefferson and Jackson, but Anglophilia, an understated influence, was present as well and gained strength once the divisions caused by the War of 1812 had healed.[203] The coronation of Queen Victoria in 1838 produced huge enthusiasm in the Republic and moved one American correspondent to compose the unmelodic and short-lived term "Reginamania."[204] When the Prince of Wales visited the United States in 1860, 250,000 people lined the streets of New York to greet him.[205] Reciprocally, the British public received the "melancholy intelligence" of the assassination of President Lincoln in 1865 with shock, revulsion, and grief.[206]

Reverence for tradition in the United States derived from a need for reassurance that the novelties of the present were unable to supply. In this respect, the merits of the Revolution were offset by its shortcomings. Monarchy was appealing because it embodied the desirable qualities of permanence and order, but no longer threatened to impose authoritarian rule. Monarchy, however, had been abandoned, and elected presidents came and went without being able to represent the ties that kept the present in touch with the past. Similarly, devolved Protestantism responded to local needs but lacked the wider sense of commonality that the established Anglican Church symbolized. Nevertheless, there was no alternative to treating Britain as the center of origin and source of values, real and imagined. Tradition in the United States was invented by applying polish to an adapted version of the British model. As Emerson observed in 1847: "The American is only the continuation of the English genius into new conditions, more or less propitious."[207]

Everything that could be copied was copied—and then enlarged.[208] The English language and accent were assiduously cultivated in Ivy League universities and colleges, which trained English-style gentlemen to become guardians of virtue and honor.[209] Foreign immigrants were encouraged to accept English as the national language, to Anglicize their family names, to convert to American Protestantism, and to participate in what later became known as "cultural uplift," which sought to instill elite values into aspiring "under-people."[210] Shakespeare, later regarded by Walt Whitman as being a representative of feudal literature, was widely taught, read, and performed.[211] The classical inheritance not only lived on but expanded, as it did in Britain in the nineteenth century. Universities and colleges extended their teaching beyond the study of grammar to cull moral guidance from Greek and Roman masters.[212] Artists were taught to follow the precepts of Joshua Reynolds, who held that they should attempt to match the famous works of classical antiquity. Trends moved in parallel in both countries. Codes of conduct gradually became less patriarchal and more middle class; a new stratum of urban gentry emerged in the United States, as it did in England; male and female roles underwent a similar evolution.[213]

Leading figures in the Republic recognized that language was a crucial ingredient of nationality and one of the keys to achieving cultural independence. Thomas Jefferson and Noah Webster differed in their politics but were united in their ambition to oversee the creation of a new American language.[214] Webster, who was keenly aware of the links between language, values, and behavior, set himself the task of producing a national language that would overcome linguistic divisions within the United States and separate the Republic from its British origins.[215] His innovative *American Spelling Book*, published in 1783, amended arcane aspects of the English language. He then labored on his famous *Dictionary*, a work of astounding dedication and immense learning, which was published in 1828. By then, however, Webster had parted company with his revolutionary zeal.[216] He had retreated from his youthful plans for producing an independent American version of English and had become preoccupied by what he regarded as the waning of republican ideals and the excesses of liberty. In 1808 Webster turned to evangelicalism, which he saw as providing a set of universal rules of conduct, and he regarded his *Dictionary* as a source of definitions that would help to underwrite social order. In 1828, however, Webster's *Dictionary*, with its modest adaptations of British English, won few adherents. By the time Webster died in 1843, his great work had not yet achieved popularity. Joseph Worcester's *Dictionary* of 1830 was the leading authority down to the 1860s, not least because it held fast to British English.[217] Though a canonical figure today, Webster struggled for recognition during his lifetime.

Emerson's quest for literary independence was similarly frustrated.[218] In 1837, he confidently proclaimed that "our day of dependence, our long apprenticeship to the learning of other lands, draws to a close."[219] His "declaration of literary independence" created a stir because it advertised the extent to which the United States still relied on British sources of inspiration.[220] Tocqueville made the same point in 1840: "American authors may truly be said to live rather in England than in their own country, since they constantly study the English writers and take them every day for their models."[221] Emerson's appeal for cultural originality had a muted response, partly because it was more of a flourish than a program, but mainly because he himself had been marinated in the English classics and was unable to extend his thinking very far beyond them.[222] In 1856, he produced *English Traits*, which lauded English virtues and power with a degree of deference that Australians would later capture in the inimitable phrase "cultural cringe."[223] Herman Melville illustrates the persistence of literary dependence from a different angle. Melville, who published *Moby-Dick* in 1851, is now regarded as one of the most original American writers of the nineteenth century. At the time, however, his allegorical reflections on democracy, racism, and imperialism puzzled critics and deterred readers. Far from being lauded, he ended his life in obscurity.[224]

In these circumstances, it is not surprising to find that the two most popular authors of the period, James Fenimore Cooper and Henry Wadsworth Longfellow, also drew on European sources to create a brand of literature that aimed at shoring up white solidarity and providing psychological support at a time of great social unease. Fenimore Cooper laid the foundation of popular literary patriotism in the 1820s by producing American versions of the historical romances of Walter Scott.[225] His vision, like Scott's, was of a stable and orderly society governed by a natural aristocracy.[226] The attraction of his novels lay in conveying a sense of reassurance in an age of dissension, when national unity was deeply desired but largely absent. Fenimore Cooper invoked a sense of social solidarity that supposedly existed during the Revolution, was in danger of being lost, but could still be recaptured. In the same spirit, he fashioned the legend of the frontier, where rampant violence was ultimately governed by an innate sense of moral justice that produced harmonious outcomes. His novels captured the realities of an insecure world and resolved them in an imagined sense of national unity that drew as much on Anglo-values as on qualities made manifest by life in America. Some critics even called him an Anglo-maniac.[227] Although the charge was too crude to be fair, it nevertheless identified a strand of dependence that characterized his work.

Longfellow was so steeped in the classics that Walt Whitman referred to him, dismissively, as being a mere imitator of European forms.[228] "The Song of Hiawatha," published in 1855, purported to base American literature on indigenous sources, but its main purpose was to provide an allegory that fitted the predicament of white Anglo-Saxon society at a time of socioeconomic upheaval. Longfellow constructed a composite picture of Native Americans that transformed them from hostile savages into restrained and therefore unthreatening noble beings. "Hiawatha" was an immediate success. Performances promoted a sense of community among white audiences who empathized with the evocation of ancient harmonies and the plight of suitably sanitized Native Americans—without having to engage with them. As the saga ends, Hiawatha, the disappearing Indian, welcomes the white man to his country and accepts Christianity before departing, contentedly, for a better place. Redemption brought reassurance: Indians could be tamed; disparate whites could achieve tranquility in unity.

Architecture was the most visible statement of cultural aspirations in the Republic. Colonial styles lingered long after independence in both private and public designs. The Boston business elite invested in country estates to emulate English landowners and establish their leadership in what purported to be a non-hierarchical society; Southern planters maintained grand Georgian estate houses.[229] Asher Benjamin adapted late-colonial architecture to create the Federal style, but without removing the imprint of its origins and, unlike Noah Webster, without wishing to do so.[230] Public buildings presented unrivaled opportunities to advertise the Republic's official aspirations. Here, too, British influence, expressed in the classical tradition, left a permanent impression on the landscape.

By the mid-nineteenth century, the Greek Revival, which symbolized harmony and democracy, had made its mark on churches, courthouses, banks, and libraries, and had influenced the houses of Southern planters, New England mill owners, and even the new frontier-rich.[231] State capitols were nearly all modeled on Greek temples, following the example set by Washington, with a few Roman basilicas added for variety. Classical place names spread west and south from New England throughout the nineteenth century.[232] In the 1850s, the Gothic Revival, also imported from England, became the leading style in the northern states until the close of the century, and extended, for good measure, to the introduction of medieval jousting tournaments.[233] The Gothic style in architecture appealed partly because it fitted the trend toward Anglo-Saxon racial unity, but also because the Greek model included slavery, as well as a short-lived and limited form of democracy. Gothism enabled the northern states to distance themselves from slaveholding at a time when the abolitionist movement was becoming influential. Thereafter, the Greek Revival lingered as a regional style in the South.

Far less is known about the culture of the "under-people," though it is apparent that the spoken word deviated from the prescriptions of both Webster and Worcester. Minstrel shows depicting African Americans as amiable buffoons who had a sentimental attachment to life on the plantation became popular in the North from the 1820s (when Thomas Rice invented the figure of Jim Crow) because they enabled white audiences to identify with each other and to confirm their belief in their own superiority.[234] Minstrelsy appealed initially to white working men but by the 1850s had become an accepted part of middle-class entertainment, too, and in Southern as well as in Northern states. Apart from minstrelsy, home-grown music made little progress.[235] One of the most famous groups of the 1830s and 1840s, the Hutchinson Family Singers, had no success with local songs and gained popularity by copying Tyrolean folk music, complete with full yodeling, which had been popularized by a visiting troupe from Austria.[236] The Hutchinsons added local content to the imported format to voice their commitment to temperance and abolition, but they still performed in Tyrolean costume—thus adding a new dimension to the concept of hybridity.

Half a century after independence had been achieved, these adaptations of imported cultural influences, combined with the formative novelties of a new frontier, had created characteristics that were recognizably American. Tocqueville, writing in the 1830s, identified many qualities that are familiar today. He noted the openness, generosity, and lack of deference that sprang from the "equality of social conditions" and the combination of self-reliance and opportunity that produced a "restless" mobility rarely seen in Europe.[237] He was also struck by the extent to which Americans prized material success: "I know of no country," Tocqueville observed, "where the love of money has taken stronger hold on the affections of men."[238] At the same time, he had no doubt that religious conviction was "one of the most prominent" causes of the "maintenance of the political institutions" of the Republic. Of the evident preference for the "practical" over the "theoretical," he commented: "democratic nations will habitually prefer the useful to the beautiful and they will require that the beautiful should be useful." He drew attention, even at this early date, to the presence of an "obnoxious" and a "boastful" patriotism amidst the signs of equality he admired. Bringing all the objectivity of a French aristocrat to bear on the issue of national prejudice, Tocqueville also censured "the English" for having an attitude of "contemptuous and ignorant reserve" toward the rest of the world.

Yet, the nascent sense of cultural identity that Tocqueville observed had still to be fused in allegiance to the Union as a whole.[239] Tocqueville himself habitually referred to the citizens of the United States as "Anglo-Americans" or "the English race in America," both phrases that captured the sense of a nationality that was still only half-formed. The assumption that nationalism develops in a linear direction beginning with an embryo and ending in maturity, though implicit in many treatments of the subject, does not fit the course taken by the United States. The growth of national identity in the Republic was protracted and marked by setbacks and deviations. By the 1850s, Anglo-Americans were growing apart rather than together. While the theory of Anglo-Saxondom served as a legitimating ideology, it also perpetuated transatlantic connections that inhibited the development of a wholly independent myth of origin. Unlike the Yoruba, Anglo-Americans could not claim to have come "out of a hole in the ground." Even though George III was demonized and the Founding Fathers deified, many of the old bonds survived and new connections were added after independence.[240] Indeed, the success of the American branch in propagating the Anglo-Saxon myth gave favorable publicity to its parental origins, which provided the indispensable seal of authenticity.[241]

The attempt to forge a sense of national unity through the medium of religion had similarly limited results, notwithstanding the earnest efforts of its evangelical agents. The message undoubtedly traveled across social and political boundaries.[242] It attracted white Americans in general, immigrants whose origins lay outside the Anglo-Saxon orbit in particular, African Americans, and women. Yet, the appeal of Protestant unity was not strong enough to overcome persistent divisions in the Republic. Part of its success lay in endorsing them: in escaping the grip of religious hierarchy, the Republic opened the door to a contest for dominance among denominations and individual churches.[243] As a result, the populist, libertarian emphasis on decentralization and individual rights, though contained within a broad Christian message, set in train centrifugal as well as cohesive forces. Competition for adherents tended to produce teachings that reflected the interests of the communities served. The evangelical commitment to abolition, for example, wavered as it traveled from north to south; once arrived, it adjusted to local conditions, absorbed their intellectual justification, and aligned itself with the existing order.[244] To some extent, this development was an inevitable consequence of the territorial expansion of the Republic and of unstable conditions on the frontier. But it was also underwritten by the evangelical message of devolved personal responsibility, which tended to endorse a truncated form of civic identity that was local rather than national.

Furthermore, some religious groups in regions west of the Appalachians supported the Republic less because they were concerned with liberal rights than because they believed they were people chosen for a different purpose.[245] The evangelical message appealed to many who had failed to gain, or had yet to gain, from the opportunities created by the Revolution, and to those who, like the Mormons, sought to distance themselves from the excesses of the market society. Others still, like those moving south to Texas, wanted to reestablish a slaveholding society in territory still untouched by the abolitionist movement. These groups, like the Afrikaners in the 1830s and 1840s, trekked away from the precepts of the Enlightenment, not toward them. Members of these communities applied their religious commitment in ways that were unlikely to put them on a path to assimilation; some were unlikely to be among the acolytes of capitalism. For these groups, the Second Great Awakening was not a means of forging national unity, still less an exercise in social control, but a way of establishing their own independence.

A further, powerful reason why an emerging sense of American identity did not translate into a commitment to the wider nation was that the Republic itself was evolving. In 1783, it was just possible for an optimist to think that the existing Anglo-core could absorb settlers from other parts of Europe.[246] Thereafter, however, the obstacles to assimilation grew significantly. An upsurge in the white population raised the total from 4.5 million in 1800 to 35 million in 1860.[247] A high proportion of the increase resulted from immigration, which also added to ethnic diversity, especially with the arrival of large numbers of Irish Catholics and German-speaking immigrants in the 1840s and 1850s. Settlement no longer nestled on the East Coast but spread across the continent. The extensive territories grasped as a result of the Louisiana Purchase and the Mexican-American War incorporated Spanish- and French-speaking Catholics into the Union. The newcomers amplified the linguistic dissonance that already existed: one estimate suggests that only about half the population of states in the southeast spoke English as a first language during this period.[248] The Republic faced an intractable dilemma: an expanding territory and population were essential to national security and economic development, but they also posed unforeseen problems of identity and affiliation. Outbursts of assertive ethnic nationalism of the kind expressed by the American Party (also called the Know-Nothings) in the 1840s and 1850s signified the perceived failure of the assimilationist agenda.[249]

A recent study has argued that North and South "were divided by a common nationalism."[250] The view taken here, and considered further in the chapter that follows, is that, before the Civil War, there was little common nationalism to divide. The profound political and economic changes discussed earlier widened the divide between North and South. Improved communications, while assisting economic integration, also advertised regional antipathies. Samuel Morse hoped that telegraphy would make "one neighbourhood of the whole country."[251] In 1854, Henry Thoreau commented that "we are in great haste to construct a magnetic telegraph from Maine to Texas; but Maine and Texas, it may be, have nothing important to communicate."[252] What they did communicate, it might be added, did little to create a sense of national unity. Instead, there were two competing versions of the form the Union ought to take. No comprehensive sense of nationalism could be implanted until that issue was resolved.

"CONVERTING THE FORESTS OF A WILDERNESS INTO THE FAVOURITE MANSION OF LIBERTY"[253]

Notable historians have described the struggle to control the direction of the United States during the first half of the nineteenth century in a degree of detail that does not need to be recycled here.[254] The account offered in this chapter has attempted to place the familiar narrative of domestic events in the context formed by larger considerations of decolonization and nation-building. Seen from this angle, historians may have exaggerated both the revolutionary consequences of the period following independence and their insular qualities. Connections with the former colonial power not only persisted after 1783, but also increased in importance. The issues facing the United States, though distinctive in their particulars, had parallels in Europe, where constitutional reform, economic development, and nation-building were central themes in the history of new or newly reconstituted states during the post-Napoleonic era.

The Founding Fathers and their successors pursued a range of policies aimed at answering these questions. Political viability was dealt with by installing a federal system of government that incorporated elements of Britain's military-fiscal state. The federal government provided a sovereign presence of sufficient authority to guarantee the security of the new Republic and conduct the nation's growing business, while also devolving power in internal affairs to the constituent states. As the price of agreement, however, the founders were obliged to include provisions in the Constitution that eventually undermined the stability it was intended to achieve. By defining property to include slaves, and assigning slaves to have a notional vote, the Constitution helped to tilt the political balance in favor of Southern states. By linking federal power to the number of states and voters, the Constitution set the scene for factions and parties to compete in controlling territory and determining statehood. Competitive expansion across the continent, partly funded by British capital and backed by the Royal Navy, provoked a series of crises that nearly wrecked the Union, even before the Civil War. The sense that the Federal Republic was an artificial marriage of those whom God had intended to keep apart became a familiar feature of discussions across the political spectrum. By 1861, the South wanted independence, not from Britain, but from the North.

The quest for economic independence was similarly frustrated. Rifts developed, as they were to do in other newly independent states, between political parties that accepted a neocolonial relationship and those that wanted to break it. Differences in economic policy became highly divisive, despite the growth of regional complementarities. The South became increasingly committed to a free-trading relationship based on exports of slave-grown cotton. The North pursued a mercantilist policy but was unable to secure the high tariffs needed to speed the extension of the market and the development of manufacturing.[255] The United States remained heavily dependent on Britain, which supplied capital for the production and distribution of raw cotton, and provided its largest market. Ties between the former colonial power and its ex-colony grew even closer after Britain adopted free trade and the Midwest entered the international economy as a supplier of grain. These trends in specialization foreshadowed the export economies that were just beginning to emerge in other regions of white settlement. The demand for raw materials and reciprocal supplies of manufactures produced oscillations in foreign trade and investment that were felt across the globe. The consequent booms, slumps, and financial "panics" affected the welfare of all participants and influenced the political fortunes of the parties representing them.

Policies of cultural assimilation designed to create a national identity for the new state struggled to compete with enduring international, ethnic, and regional affiliations. The merits of the literary and artistic achievements of the period are not in question. Inevitably, however, they bore the marks of their time and of Anglo-modes and standards in particular.[256] The content could be changed, but the form remained an export version of the British template. Declarations of cultural independence were expressions of intent, not of attainment. The Anglo-Saxon model, though the most feasible basis for assimilation, necessarily compromised ambitions for cultural independence. The rejection of the monarchy and the established Church devolved authority but also removed powerful symbols of national unity. Britain's informal influence extended to consumer tastes and diverse forms of artistic expression, which continued to follow the lead of the former "mother country." The antonyms needed to fashion an independent sense of nationality were found at home rather

than abroad in the growth of distinctive identities that had their outcome in the conflict between North and South. By 1861, efforts to create
a counterculture had not yet reached the point where a sense of national
identity was able to rise above alternative visions of the future. Ambrose
Bierce, writing after the Civil War, caught the ambiguities of the transition that characterized a land of diverse immigrants when he defined
an alien as "an American sovereign in his probationary state."[257]

The interpretation offered here assigns the Republic a significance
it has so far lacked. The United States was the first country to gain independence at a time when the mercantilist empires, having reached
the "highest stage" of imperialism before the nineteenth century, were
beginning to unravel. This perception suggests that the history of the
United States between 1783 and 1861 can be recast as an anticipation
of what became the classic postcolonial dilemma: how to make formal
independence effective. Histories of the United States that emphasize its
insular and "exceptional" nature might gain from taking greater account
of the continuing importance of British and wider European connections
during this period.

The Atlantic complex, far from withering away, as its limited presence
in standard historical accounts suggests, underwent a transformation
that greatly enhanced Britain's penetrative power. The continuation of
imperialism after formal decolonization was apparent in the elements of
neocolonialism that marked the relationship between Britain and her ex-
colony. The obvious, though still neglected, comparison is with Britain's
other colonies of white settlement, which achieved self-government but
remained dependent on Britain in the political, economic, and cultural
spheres surveyed here.[258] The comparison is suggestive but needs balancing by evident differences. The United States was not only formally
independent in foreign affairs, but also had advantages of scale and resources that Britain's dominions lacked, and was able to contribute a
much larger proportion of total capital formation from domestic sources.
Moreover, the thesis that dependence entails exploitation and underdevelopment fails to recognize the variety of types of dependence and,
consequently, the diversity of possible outcomes. Specialization brought
benefits to both Britain and the United States. The Republic, like Britain's dominions, gained from exporting agricultural exports and importing manufactured goods and capital, just as Britain gained by importing
raw cotton and drawing income from foreign investment.

To accept that the relationship was mutually advantageous, however, is not to conclude that it was one of equality. Conditions in Britain
had greater influence on the United States than "King Cotton" and his

associates had on Britain. The capital supplied by Britain was crucial not only to the development of key export sectors in the United States and the domestic activities linked to them, but also to the formation and trajectory of the polity itself. Commentators of all persuasions were keenly aware of the significance of continuing British influence and wrestled unsuccessfully with the ambiguities it produced. They understood that foreign capital and markets were essential to economic development, but resented the constraints that dependence imposed on the political liberties they prized. The resulting sense of subordination was insufficient to qualify the United States for membership of Britain's informal empire, but it helped nevertheless to shape the priorities of the Republic's leaders across the spectrum of politics, business, and culture.

A further, largely unnoticed, feature of the history of the United States during this period can be found in comparable developments in the larger entity of Western Europe, which were outlined in chapter 2. There, too, newly liberated states searched for ways of securing their viability in the aftermath of Napoleon's compulsory, if also temporary, unification of large parts of the continent. They engaged in a prolonged struggle to determine whether the military-fiscal order was to be reinstated, adapted, or abolished. They carried forward experiments with different types of government, including federalism, and disputed the appropriate balance between central and provincial interests, and between "absolutism" and forms of representative government. They pondered the relative merits of manufacturing and agriculture, engaged in an international debate over the respective advantages of mercantilism and free trade, and discussed the need for social reforms, including the institution of slavery. They, too, reappraised the basis of national unity in an age of increasing political participation and growing uncertainty about dynastic legitimacy. All parties worried about the phenomenon of the age—national indebtedness. Jackson was not alone in trying to shrink the public debt. After 1815, successive British governments also set out to reduce the national debt, cut taxes, and prune the public sector. For Gladstone, as for Jackson, financial institutions helped to shape the values that governed the well-being of society. Sound money produced sound citizens; balanced budgets, household and national, produced balanced people.

Admittedly, the United States did not have to deal with "feudal residues." Nevertheless, the Republic witnessed a contest between a Southern plantation aristocracy and a Northern mercantile elite that can be compared to the struggle between conservatives and reformers in Europe. After 1800, moreover, political parties adapted their programs to meet the changing circumstances of the post-revolutionary world, as they did in Europe. Hamiltonians ceased to be in a position to realize their hopes of recreating a military-fiscal state under the direction of a patrician elite. Power passed to Jefferson and his successors, who harnessed the resources of the federal government, entrenched states' rights, and encouraged a "green uprising" that carried politics beyond elite circles. Jackson's distinctive contribution was to mobilize forms of populism by combining the selective use of federal institutions with the extension of state power. This achievement had parallels in Europe with the increasing power of governments, the gradual spread of adult male suffrage, and the growth of populist movements in both town and country that made their mark in France after 1789, in Britain following the rise of Chartism in the 1840s, and in Russia and with the rise of the *Narodniki* in the 1860s—to cite just three examples. These movements, which appealed to communitarian ideals rather than to class interests, were all manifestations of what Fichte called "the Spring-time of nations."[259]

The two main political parties underwent a further evolution in the 1840s and 1850s to meet the claims of new or enlarged socioeconomic groups. The Whigs turned themselves into Republicans and abandoned their elitist orientation; the New Democrats expanded the party's agrarian platform and embraced markets and internationalism. The assimilationist policies promoted in the United States to replace traditional forms of legitimacy, neutralize divisive social forces, and incorporate the demos into a national entity complemented measures adopted by European political parties for the same purpose. To refer to these developments as the rise of liberal democracy is to adopt a generous definition of terms and to exaggerate the degree to which the future can be seen in the past. Progressive means could also serve conservative ends. Low tariffs were adopted to minimize Northern power and encourage export-dependence. Political rights built on those already present under colonial rule: the franchise was extensive because land was abundant. Without representation, there would have been no taxation. With notable exceptions, the chosen representatives regarded political office as a means to private profit.[260] The ideal of civic virtue had been overtaken by the lure of material improvement. The predominant political interest in the United States during this period was a slave-owning plantocracy, which managed the institutions imported from Britain and inscribed in the federal government, while also consolidating extensive state powers. Liberty gave citizens of the Republic not one layer of government but two. In the United States, as in Europe, movements of reform during this period took second place to conservatism. "Modernity" lay in the future.

Becoming American after 1783 was no less fraught than becoming Indian was after 1947.[261] Indeed, in important respects the founders of the United States faced circumstances that were at least as daunting as those confronting India's rulers because the borders of the Republic were rolling frontiers, and its Anglo-ethnic core was shortly to receive substantial flows of immigrants from different parts of Europe. Both ex-colonies were large and potentially powerful polities; both embarked on independence as uncertain, fragile states and endured political and human catastrophes under the strains of size and diversity: "Mother India" was partitioned at the outset; the United States imploded later into civil war. Despite its obvious limits, the analogy with India makes the point that the United States was once a newly decolonized state too, and suggests that the national story can be reappraised by being set in an imperial context.

Despite intimations of an emerging sense of commonality, the United States was unable to achieve effective independence during the first half of the nineteenth century. The conflict between incompatible programs was a manifestation of the strain of the transition from proto-globalization to its modern successor. Few countries, apart from Britain, managed to synthesize the contending forces peacefully. Some, such as France and Spain, were marked by successive revolutions. The experiment created imbalances in the United States that turned what began as a weak state into a failed state in 1861, thereby fulfilling the fears George Washington expressed in his Farewell Address.[262] Long before the Civil War, John Quincy Adams had tuned his early rhetoric to reality sufficiently to foretell the disaster that lay ahead. A century later, Jawaharlal Nehru learned how hard it was to create a secular, democratic state in one characterized by contending religious commitments and entrenched social hierarchies. In the United States, as in India, inherited continuities retarded change.[263] No established connection with the United States was more persistent or more pervasive than Britain's informal influence. The "tryst with destiny" was never abandoned, but it required a commitment that spanned the greater part of the nineteenth century before effective independence could be declared. Destiny, as Adams and Nehru both found, was a horizon that receded as it was approached.

CHAPTER 5

WARS OF INCORPORATION

"THE GREAT NATION OF FUTURITY"[1]

John L. O'Sullivan offered a preview of the notion of "manifest destiny" when he declared in 1839 that the United States had a "blessed mission to the nations of the world."[2] Those who had fallen or had never been raised were "shut out from the life-giving light of truth." Hope, however, came with help, and the helpers, being "God's chosen agents," combined power with purity: "It is our unparalleled glory that we have no reminiscences of battle fields nor have the American people ever suffered themselves to be led on by wicked ambition to depopulate the land, to spread desolation far and wide."

Evidently, there was a degree of selective perception in these remarks, even though they were written before the Mexican War and the Civil War that followed soon afterward. A retrospective view shows that, unexceptionally, the United States exemplified the proposition that wars build states and nations.[3] It did so, however, on the run. From the eighteenth century on, Europeans constructed states and subsequently nations from societies that were mainly settled. The United States entered the same process in conditions of fluidity: people and borders in the New World were both highly mobile. The difference had important consequences for foreign policy. European states fought each other to repeated standstills; being contiguous, however, they also cultivated negotiating skills aimed at averting or at least minimizing the frequency of conflict. The United States, on the other hand, faced no threat from any comparable power between the War of 1812 and the bombing of Pearl Harbor in 1941. Between these dates, the Republic fought many small wars against states that were under-resourced. The experience nurtured a belief in the efficacy of force that has survived to the present.[4]

Despite the impetus provided by the trend toward writing transnational history, the historiography of U.S. relations with the rest of the world remains conspicuously uneven.[5] As late as 2000, one leading authority could still refer to the study of foreign policy during the period 1815–1861 as being "a great American desert," and another to the period before 1914 as a whole as being "something of a 'wasteland.'"[6] Fortunately, a handful of explorers have trailed through this seemingly barren landscape and left signposts for others. The main route points to the long-standing character of expansionist policies and their links to state-building. International relations, like imperialism, began at home, and were entwined with the Republic's history from the outset.

The Founding Fathers and their successors soon discovered that they could neither insulate themselves from the intrusive realities of Europe's major powers nor banish partisan interests from foreign policy.[7] Washington's celebrated "Farewell Address" appealed for "tranquillity at home" and neutrality in foreign relations.[8] After 1783, however, fear of recolonization ensured that the United States remained entangled with Britain, France, and Spain, which retained substantial interests in the North American continent. After 1815, when this anxiety faded, considerations of international commerce and moral reform came to the fore.[9] Research has also expanded the traditional content of foreign policy to embrace relations among states within the continent. On this view, the history of the Republic is not that of an emerging nation-state with regional differences but of a set of separate states with diverse interests and alliances mediated by a contested federal government.[10] Revisionist work of a different kind has brought Native Americans into the conventional narrative. Scholars in the United States have joined the global research effort to rebalance approaches to the past by amplifying the role of indigenous peoples in polities previously dominated by the story of white settlers. As this long neglected dimension of "national" history has come into focus, more attention has been paid to how the "great land rush" affected existing relations between advancing settlement and independent Native American states after 1783.[11]

Despite the inviting possibilities now on offer, the present study needs to hold to a line of inquiry that is closely related to its main theme if it is to avoid being sunk by excess freight. Accordingly, this chapter focuses on features of foreign policy that illuminate the entangled questions of independence, imperialism, and empire. The starting point situates the United States in the context of the development of settler societies in the nineteenth century. Territorial expansion across North America was a form of settler imperialism involving conflict with indigenous societies and neighboring states, as well as discord among the settlers themselves. The closest comparison is with segments of the Anglo-world that remained within the British Empire and became self-governing dominions.[12] The analogy may seem obvious, but U.S. historians have only recently begun to explore the literature on other settler societies.[13]

The comparison yields contrasts as well as similarities. The desire for land and the consequent subordination of indigenous peoples were common features of all settler states. The United States, however, was distinctive because the frontier was driven forward by the lure of abundant resources, by substantial increases in immigration, and by internal political rivalries of the kind that were unfettered by imperial restraints. The three principal wars considered here—the War of 1812–1815, the Mexican war in 1846–1848, and the Civil War in 1861–1865—were all concerned with controlling or acquiring territory for the purpose of state-building. The years between these conflicts, far from being pacific, saw the continuation of the long-running "Indian Wars." The satirist Ambrose Bierce defined war as "a by-product of the arts of peace."[14] Where state-building was concerned, peace was a by-product of the arts of war.

Chapter 4 showed that Britain's political, economic, and cultural influences helped to shape the state-building project during the first half of the nineteenth century. The present chapter takes a complementary view of the wars of incorporation that were fought during the same period. Wounded feelings and disputed borders ensured that relations between Britain and the new Republic were often strained during the early decades of independence: in 1812 tensions even led to hostilities, despite a lack of enthusiasm on both sides. Nevertheless, coffeehouse talk about recovering the mainland colonies after 1783 never became British policy and subsided after 1815. Successive governments in London recognized that Britain's long-term interest lay in working with rather than against the new Republic.[15]

The opportunities offered by territorial expansion infused diplomatic neutrality with a strong dose of mutual self-interest. The Royal Navy shielded the United States from foreign predators; the glue of informal influence spread over the Republic and stuck both parties together. British finance supported the drive westward and helped to fund the Mexican War. Britain's growing demand for raw cotton underpinned the increase of both wealth and slave labor in the Southern states and indirectly fueled the expansionist ambitions of King Cotton. Britain's anxious neutrality during the Civil War expressed concerns about how best to safeguard its massive economic commitments in both North and South. Informal influence delivered its own set of problems. Nevertheless, the implications of Bentham's assessment, made in the 1790s, became clear as the nineteenth century unfolded: informal influence was more effective than formal rule because it was both cheaper and more acceptable to the recipients.[16] Britain was better off without the mainland colonies than with them.

"THE BRIGHT IDEA OF PROPERTY, OF EXCLUSIVE RIGHT"[17]

When Hector St. John de Crèvecoeur, aristocrat, emigré, farmer, and commentator of inconsistent opinions, delivered his tribute to farming in 1782, his primary reference was to the mainland colonies and to New England in particular. Settlers there acquired "exclusive rights," which promoted independence and enterprise: "the idle may be employed, the useless become useful, and the poor become rich." These qualities, fortified by a larger sense that settlers were agents of a destiny approved by God—and possibly Mammon too—helped to produce the American ambition of "making good" in a world of unlimited opportunity. Frederick Jackson Turner's notion that the frontier shaped character as a means of shaping nations was embedded in the American psyche long before his own celebrated formulation appeared in 1893.[18]

Crèvecoeur's endorsement of physiocratic and Smithian principles applied far beyond New England and the mainland colonies. Nineteenth-century commentators routinely compared the United States to other parts of the Anglo-world.[19] A distinguished cast of observers, including Goldwyn Smith, John Stuart Mill, Charles Dilke, and James Bryce, offered their thoughts on particular aspects of the relationship. Their underlying assumption was that Greater Britons formed an extended community. Settler states were separated geographically (apart from Canada and the United States, which were divided by proximity), but were joined by common interests and a sense of mutuality that came from belonging to the Anglo-Saxon world. The United States was regarded as a close relative, even though it had severed constitutional ties with Britain. The attachment grew even stronger in the second half of the nineteenth century, when notions of racial solidarity reinforced the sense of unity.

The American dream was just one version of aspirations that were shared by several million hopefuls who migrated from Old Europe to "neo-Europes" in other parts of the world in the nineteenth and twentieth centuries.[20] With the partial exception of South Africa, the countries settled by Greater Britons began as Anglo-Saxon, and specifically British, settlements headed by propertied, Protestant elites, whose primary aim was to achieve what the Victorians termed "improvement." Their ambition was less to undertake a radical transformation of society than to reproduce a good deal of what they were familiar with, though with themselves at the top of the social scale rather than among the lower orders. They, too, set out to escape oppression and poverty, and to build a new life by acquiring land that was scarce at home and abundant elsewhere. The notion of "manifest destiny" formulated in the United States in the 1840s had compelling counterparts in the dominions, which produced their own providential and guiltless justifications for assertive expansion.[21] Grueling experiences on frontiers far beyond the United States bonded settlers in what Australians called (and still call) "mateship," which venerated qualities of independence, comradeship, and rugged masculine virtues.[22]

Two of Horatio Alger's youthful heroes "made good" in Australia, where they might almost have rubbed shoulders with Wilkins Micawber, whose long awaited *dénouement* demonstrated that riches could materialize from rags and respect from rejection.[23] Jack London, having failed to strike it lucky in the Klondike, made his fortune writing about it. *The Call of the Wild* showed how the freezing frontier of northern Canada tested and transformed character.[24] The same formula was applied to the swelling numbers of settlers who were either attracted to, or could not escape, the New World's new towns, where urban man embraced rural values derived from a way of life he had rarely experienced. Women, the unsung heroines of the frontier, were expected to conform to this patriarchal formula, though their resistance eventually produced an alternative vision that challenged masculine claims to dominance.[25] The towns also attracted some of Horatio Alger's protagonists, who joined with Samuel Smiles in encouraging self-help through determination and hard work. Elemental demands, both rural and urban, provided evolutionary stimulus: the puny gained stature; progress gained momentum; individuals gained the strength needed to advance the cause of liberty.

Frontier societies were also in the vanguard of movements to establish various forms of democracy in the nineteenth century. Borderland conditions weakened the ability of centralized elites, whether established or aspiring, to control mobile, fluid societies, and allowed political programs supporting representative government to gain ground. As noted in chapter 4, civil authorities in the United States conferred rights in exchange for taxes partly because the favorable land-labor ratio created opportunities for prospective taxpayers to escape government demands. Democracy, however, was not a singular notion that emerged from one center of origin, but a constellation of evolving ideas and often anomalous practices that appeared at different times and in different places throughout the world.[26] Accordingly, the conventional story of the "spread of liberty" needs amending. Although voting rights were common throughout the

Republic, by 1828 only eight states had introduced universal suffrage for free white men.[27] Women, Native Americans, and slaves were still excluded from the franchise. In some respects, the dominions were ahead of the United States, despite being late-start countries within the British Empire. New Zealand extended voting rights to women in 1893, Australia followed in 1894–1908, Canada in 1916–1918, the United States in 1920, and Britain, belatedly, in 1928. Australia led the way in introducing the secret ballot in 1856–1859. Britain, New Zealand, and Canada followed in the 1870s; the United States in 1884–1892.[28] Adult Maori men were enfranchised in New Zealand in 1867. Native Americans in the United States acquired citizenship in a gradual and haphazard manner, but were not granted the same right until 1924.[29] The constitution the United States formulated for Hawai'i in 1898 ensured that voting rights were restricted to white males who owned property.[30]

Settlers carved new societies out of backcountry, outback, bush, and veldt. They had similar debates about how to develop natural resources, how to balance competing agrarian and urban interests, and how to devise forms of government that would fit their new circumstances.[31] They instigated a "green revolution" that was unprecedented in its scale and global reach. The application of mobile, immigrant labor to abundant land transformed property rights by converting common land into individual freeholds.[32] The outcome was a set of dependent export economies that shipped agricultural products to the imperial metropolis in exchange for capital investment and manufactured goods. This momentous development hastened the integration of the world economy and tied the fortunes of specialized producers to the irregular beat of international demand. Crèvecoeur's observations of New England in the 1790s applied on a much larger scale than he envisaged: in the nineteenth century, export agriculture became the basis of settler states globally.

Land policy was a central consideration in all countries of white settlement, whether or not they were independent. The doctrine of *terra nullius* was widely invoked to dignify expropriation with legality.[33] Edward Gibbon Wakefield's plans for "systematic colonization," which were highly publicized in the 1830s and 1840s, shared some of Jefferson's and Jackson's agrarian idealism while borrowing elements of Clay's "American System."[34] At the same time, Wakefield aimed to replace the development model adopted in the United States, which he associated with slave labor, and he joined William Cobbett (who knew America well) in seeking to recreate a social order that was hierarchical as well as free.[35] The long-running discussion of the merits of free trade and protection also drew on the experience of different settler societies. John A. Macdonald's "national policy," which was adopted in Canada in the 1870s, applied the American experience of protectionism to promote industrial development, while advancing the agrarian ideal as a means of attracting settlers to the Western plains.[36]

New property rights were established at the cost of displacing, liquidating, or otherwise controlling indigenous peoples who stood in the way of the rolling frontier. Research on the history of indigenous societies in the United States has now reached the point where it can be related to similar encounters elsewhere, though this is a task for future research.[37] The impressive literature now available has changed traditional perspectives on the history of North America. Before the start of the nineteenth century, European settlements on the mainland were at the edge of events, not at their center. Revisionist historians have reproduced a sequence that is well known to specialists on other parts of the world. Early scholarship began by criticizing pejorative, unexamined assumptions, moved on to recreate a hitherto unknown history of indigenous peoples, and has now reached a stage where critical evaluation has provided the basis for nuanced interpretations. An extensive precolonial past has been revealed. Economies were complex; political systems included confederations and "empires."[38] Native Americans were not simply victims but agents with the capacity to shape events. They traded, raided, and fought one another, and also held slaves.[39] Historians who are familiar with the extensive research undertaken on Africa and Asia since the 1960s will have no difficulty recognizing either the evolution of these approaches or their findings.[40]

The "Indian Wars" in the United States were paralleled by the advance of settlers in the Canadian prairies; the decimation of the aboriginal people of Australia was matched by the defeat of the Maori in New Zealand. The demographic pattern was essentially the same in all cases: imported diseases were the first and most devastating cause of mortality; death through conflict grew in importance in the nineteenth century. The need to put numbers to these trends is as compelling as it is hazardous.[41] References to "millions" of Native Americans in North America before the "colonial encounter" provide an order of magnitude so broad that it is hard to know what inferences can be drawn from it, apart from the fact that numbers fell dramatically after 1500 from uncertain starting points.[42] Figures for the nineteenth century are rather more accurate and show a continuing decline: in the case of the United States, the Native American population fell from about 600,000 in 1800 to about 250,000 a century later. Similar trends were found elsewhere: by 1900, the "First Peoples" of Canada numbered about 120,000; aborigines in

Australia were down to 50,000, and Maori in New Zealand, to 40,000. The low point in all cases was reached in 1900. Indigenous populations recovered in the twentieth century as infant mortality declined, and they continue to expand in the twenty-first century.

Before the nineteenth century, contact between European and indigenous societies mixed conflict with a degree of social fluidity and cooperation on frontiers in Africa and India, as well as North America.[43] Thereafter, all neo-European societies developed a sense of racial superiority that lasted throughout the colonial era and in varying degrees beyond it. The dominions devised policies of assimilation and segregation that complemented those put in place in the United States. Negative stereotypes of societies beyond the frontier reinforced a developing ideology of white supremacy that helped to shape national identities throughout the Anglo-world.[44] Supremacy and certainty produced the "civilizing mission," which was a common feature of all these frontiers. Canada's destiny carried missionaries and humanitarians, "the bible and the plough," in the phrase of the day, to the far north; Afrikaners cited the authority of the Dutch Reformed Church to justify their doctrine of racial superiority, and trekked inland to prove it. Guns were the ubiquitous means of ensuring the advance of civilization.

Commonalities must be emphasized to ensure that the Republic is placed in its much wider setting and not treated as if its experience were unique. Nevertheless, the United States, it need hardly be said, was neither Canada nor Australia. The history of British settlement in the colonies that became the United States is far longer and the scale of activities much greater than it was in other areas of white settlement.[45] Relations between settlers and government differed too: after 1783, the United States was free to devise its own policies toward indigenous peoples, whereas the dominions remained within the imperial orbit.

Conflict over land rights was present from the outset of European settlement in the mainland colonies in the sixteenth century and became a permanent, if also an irregular, feature of the expansion of the United States down to 1924, when the last of the Apache "die-hards" surrendered. It is true that swaths of territory were acquired by means other than war: the vast Louisiana Purchase was transferred to the United States in 1803; Florida was bought in 1819; the Oregon Cession was negotiated in 1846; Alaska was purchased in 1867. Nevertheless, the land then had to be occupied, and it was this process that produced protracted conflict. The swelling European presence added to the complexity of existing intertribal relations by drawing Native Americans into great-power rivalries.[46] Tribal groups split; intertribal alliances rose and fell with the fortunes of war.[47] In North America, as in Africa, Asia, and Australasia, local polities allied with the European states they judged most likely to advance their interests. The onset of the Seven Years' War marked the beginning of a new phase of intensified hostilities.[48] What has been called the "long war for the west" ran from 1754 to 1815 and continued sporadically for the greater part of the nineteenth century.[49] What might be called the "long war for the south" encompassed three conflicts in Florida with the Seminole—in 1818, 1835–1842, and 1855–1858—and ended with their removal to western reservations.[50] Hostilities promoted intransigent attitudes. In 1776, Jefferson set the tone for the future by referring in the Declaration of Independence to "merciless Indian savages, whose known rule of warfare is undistinguished destruction of all ages, sexes and conditions."[51]

Jefferson's characterization and the animosity that accompanied it reflected the diplomatic alignments of the time: most Native American polities favored Britain, not because they were empire loyalists, but because they had an even greater fear of the advancing line of settlers and the "near bedlam" that accompanied them.[52] The American Revolution turned the "peace" that followed the Treaty of Paris into another international conflict. Independence in 1783 removed constraints on Western settlement and amplified the unruly conditions on the frontier. After the War of 1812, and with the assistance of Britain's benign neutrality, settlement spread west and south with government approval and with only indigenous resistance to halt the flow. The Indian Removal Act, passed by President Andrew Jackson's administration in 1830, marked a break with previous policies of assimilation and opened the way to what became forced relocation. The most notorious case was that of the Cherokee, who were moved some 800 miles west to Oklahoma in 1838 on what became known as the Trail of Tears.[53] Additional compulsory removals, though less dramatic, continued during the course of the century.

Expeditions and skirmishes, which arose partly from the policy of relocation, became annual events; warfare, sometimes prolonged, affected much of the country.[54] The Second Seminole War (1835–1842) in Florida was one of the most challenging the U.S. Army faced; the Great Sioux War (1876–1877) in Dakota, which saw the annihilation of the Seventh Cavalry and the death of Colonel George Armstrong Custer in 1876, was the most publicized. The pace of expansion accelerated in the second half of the century, as railroads opened the West and immigrants arrived in growing numbers in the hope of making their fortunes from gold and silver, as well as from ranches and farms. Conflicts proliferated, especially in the Southwest and Far West. Resistance and the violence needed to crush it continued to the end of the century, and even beyond. The contest became increasingly one-sided. By 1890, the most formidable opposition had been overcome. The Comanche were defeated in 1875, the Sioux in 1877, the Ute in 1880, and the Apache in 1886. The last Medal of Honor in the long campaign to subdue indigenous Americans was awarded after the defeat of the Ojibwe in 1898.[55] By then, too, buffalo herds had been decimated and the remaining Native Americans had been rounded up and confined to reservations on poor-quality land.[56]

Changes in the legal status of Native American peoples accompanied the acquisition of their territory. The new federal government assumed the sole right to negotiate treaties and make other formal arrangements with Indian authorities. In the early decades of independence, the United States followed British precedent in treating indigenous states as sovereign entities and according them a position of "measured separatism," whereby internal matters were protected from federal intervention.[57] Native Americans were regarded as citizens of other governments and were denied voting rights in the Republic unless they paid taxes, which very few did. Nevertheless, Washington and Jefferson assumed that a process of evolution would eventually lead to assimilation, and that the "civilized Indian" would then qualify for voting rights.

These formalities were increasingly at odds with realities on the ground, as the effective independence of Native American states shrank before the advancing ranks of settlers. After the Civil War, Congress made national unity the centerpiece of its program of modernization. Southern states were reintegrated; a series of measures were passed to assimilate Native Americans into the larger society that was engulfing them. The Fourteenth Amendment, which was ratified in 1868, confirmed that Native Americans who retained tribal ties were excluded from voting and citizenship.[58] In 1871, the Indian Appropriation Act determined that Native American states would cease to be treated as distinct polities and would be dealt with in the future by statute rather than by treaty. The Act opened the way for the federal government to intervene formally in what previously had been the internal affairs of sovereign states.[59] The Dawes Act, which followed in 1887, reallocated tribal lands by creating small, individual plots and allowing the sale of freeholds. The intention was to produce self-sufficient yeomen farmers and pace-setting, middle-class individualists.[60] By the turn of the century, it was apparent that the Act had become an early example of failed social engineering. It further undermined the political economy of hunting, fragmented kinship systems, and produced a set of poverty-stricken Bantustans.[61] Tribal members could obtain citizenship by meeting various tests of eligibility, which an increasing number managed to do. By 1924, when Congress passed the Indian Citizenship Act, the majority of Native Americans (about 175,000) had already qualified; the Act enfranchised the remainder (about 125,000). Improved status came at a high cost: the "vanishing Indian" disappeared from view, not because assimilation had succeeded in producing anonymity, but because the indigenous population had declined to the point where it was small enough to be isolated, bypassed, and forgotten.[62]

Edmund Burke predicted what would happen if Britain persisted with attempts to control the movement of settlers by legislative command. Speaking in 1775, he claimed that eager migrants "would become hordes of English Tartars . . . pouring down on your unfortified frontiers as a fierce and irresistible cavalry."[63] Burke recommended that settlers and government should advance together in a coordinated manner to ensure legislative and civil order. After 1783, the new Tartars foraged ahead of civil authority, while also benefiting from government support, and dispensed their own rough justice on Burke's "unfortified frontiers."[64] Violence, official and privatized, became decentralized. Fear of the "tyrannical state," originally derived from a particular view of British policy toward the mainland colonies in the 1760s and 1770s, entered public consciousness—and stayed there. The "right to keep and bear arms," the product of necessity and the complement of fear, became an individual right authorized by the Second Amendment to the Constitution in 1791.[65] Physical expressions of personal will, cast as rights, attracted approbation; concepts of duty shrank to minimize their connection to state power. Formal endorsement combined with frontier conditions ensured that values associated with "martial manhood" overpowered those of "restrained manhood," its pallid cousin.[66]

The process of internal colonization that delivered virtually free land to eager settlers contributed powerfully to the symbolism of white supremacy. Commentators depicted Native Americans as obstacles to be cleared, by force if necessary, if civilization were to prevail. Stereotypes of those who resisted progress multiplied, hardened, and justified, in the minds of policy-makers, applying a strategy of total war to civilians and their means of livelihood. Official reports and press commentary concurred in portraying Native Americans as backward savages who did not deserve to remain in charge of the rich resources providence had entrusted to them. Henry Cabot Lodge judged Native Americans to be "cunning, treacherous, and cruel"; Theodore Roosevelt called them "squalid savages."[67] Henry Longfellow was on hand to add his characteristic drumbeat to the political rhetoric of the time by depicting the "savage and unmerciful" Sioux chiefs who

muttered their woes and griefs
and the menace of their wrath.[68]

Once the "savages" had been tamed, enterprising promoters could display them in exhibitions, circuses, and Wild West shows as relics of a doomed species whose function was to prepare the way for the dashing representatives of modernity.[69] When William Cody (Buffalo Bill) brought Sitting Bull under contract in 1885, the allegory of white dominance was complete.[70] For the lucky few, there was life after loss: it was called show business.

The obverse of the denigration of Native Americans was the creation of icons of white supremacy. Lieutenant-Colonel Custer achieved in death the fame that eluded him in life.[71] Custer, like Major-General Charles Gordon, whose life ended in Khartoum ten years later, was a uniformed adventurer of uncertain judgment. Despite their flaws, both men attained the status of martyrs to the cause of civilization and progress and were memorialized as heroes who exemplified the highest ideals of the Anglo-Victorian gentleman. Their symbolic value lay in setting standards of courage, duty, and honor for others to emulate. Walt Whitman commemorated Custer's death with a sonnet shrouded in medieval chivalry:

> Now ending well in death the splendid fever of thy deeds,
> (I bring no dirge for it or thee, I bring a glad triumphal sonnet,)
> Desperate and glorious, aye in defeat most desperate, most glorious,
> After thy many battles in which never yielding up a gun or a color
> Leaving behind thee a memory sweet to soldiers,
> Thou yieldest up thyself. [72]

Lodge and Roosevelt added to the mythology by including Custer in their roster of American heroes who "showed that they knew how to live and how to die."[73] In 1941, Hollywood amalgamated diverse and supposedly uncivilized peoples in its most popular recreation of Custer's last stand.[74] The appearance of several hundred Filipino extras in the guise of savage Indians is one of the little-known improbabilities of "They Died with their Boots On," which starred the ultra-white Errol Flynn as Custer and the Mexican American Anthony Quinn as Crazy Horse.[75] Specificities were unimportant. It was enough to be alien at a time when aliens did not have to come from another planet.

Long before Errol Flynn and Anthony Quinn faced each other on screen, the frontier they fought over, like its original inhabitants, had almost disappeared. The census of 1890 reported that the familiar line of settlement spreading westward was no longer clearly visible: the "shining sea" of the Pacific had been reached; increasing numbers of migrants were grouped in urban clusters; "satanic mills" had made their appearance. This perception was the foundation of Turner's famous lament, published in 1893, commemorating the demise of qualities of individualism, resilience, and fortitude developed on the frontier.[76] Turner's essay complemented numerous other gloomy commentaries in the 1880s and 1890s on persisting economic depression, unrestricted immigration, and social unrest.[77] Turner was looking back in nostalgia; he left the remedies, if they could be found, to others. Some observers, inspired by the closing of the century as well as of the frontier, offered apocalyptic visions of overpopulation, anarchy, and socialism.[78] Others attached Turner's analysis to their own programs of overseas expansion. The frontier experience and its well-practiced methods of dealing with indigenous people could be reproduced abroad, revitalized on ever more distant borderlands, and then repatriated to stiffen the spines of the feeble and the morals of the lapsed.[79]

The "frontier spirit" had already spilled into filibustering expeditions that reached their peak in the 1850s, when the notorious William Walker staged a coup in Nicaragua, and manifested his own destiny in front of a firing squad in Honduras in 1860.[80] Filibustering expressed a spirit of aggressive expansion and applied it to nearby foreign countries. After the Civil War, and the demise of Southern ambitions for extending plantation slavery, the federal government was able to harness expansionist instincts and place them within legal bounds. A major opportunity arose in 1898, when the ethos of continental expansion was joined to war with Spain. The military strategy used against Native Americans was deployed in the Philippines in and after 1898.[81] No fewer than twenty-six of the thirty generals who served in the Philippines between 1898 and 1902 had participated in campaigns against Native American peoples.[82] Military operations included civilians as targets and involved the unavoidable "attendant cruelties," as Theodore Roosevelt called them, that had marked the Indian Wars and the Civil War.[83] Filipinos, like Native Americans, had to be subjugated before they could be civilized. American troops learned that "Filipinos were savages no better than our Indians," and had to be treated similarly.[84] Roosevelt compared Emilio Aguinaldo, the leader of the independence movement, to Sitting Bull: both needed to be eliminated so that "one more fair spot of the world's surface" could be "snatched from the forces of darkness."[85]

Continental expansion produced results that exceeded even the optimistic expectations of the founders. In 1783, the United States covered

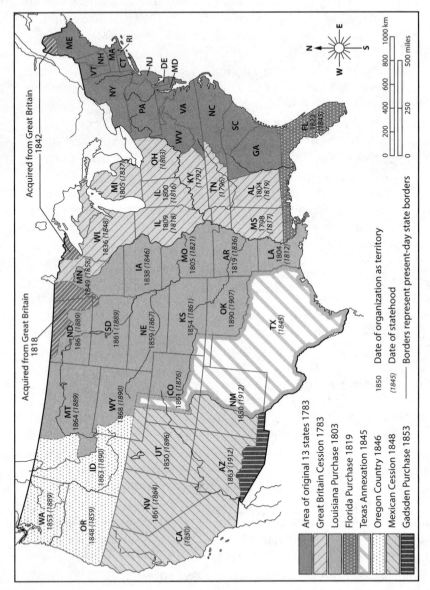

MAP 5.1. The Continental Expansion of the United States in the Nineteenth Century.

Acquired from Great Britain 1842

Acquired from Great Britain 1818

ME

VT NH MA CT RI
NY
PA NJ DE MD
WV VA
NC
SC
GA
FL 18 22 (1845)

OH (1803)
MI 1805 (1837)
IL 1800 (1816)
KY (1792)
TN (1796)
AL 1804 1819
IL 1809 (1818)
MS 1798 (1877)
LA 1804 (1812)
AR 1819 (1836)
MO 1805 (1821)
OK 1890 (1907)
KS 1854 (1861)
NE 1859 (1867)
IA 1838 (1846)
WI 1836 (1848)
MN 1849 (1858)
ND 1861 (1889)
SD 1861 (1889)
TX (1845)
NM 1850 (1912)
CO 1861 (1876)
WY 1868 (1890)
MT 1864 (1889)
UT 1850 (1896)
AZ 1863 (1912)
NV 1861 (1864)
CA (1850)
ID 1863 (1890)
OR 1848 (1859)
WA 1853 (1889)

N E S W

0 200 400 600 800 1000 km

0 250 500 miles

Area of original 13 states 1783
Great Britain Cession 1783
Louisiana Purchase 1803
Florida Purchase 1819
Texas Annexation 1845
Oregon Country 1846
Mexican Cession 1848
Gadsden Purchase 1853

1850 Date of organization as territory
(1845) Date of statehood
—— Borders represent present-day state borders

TABLE 5.1. STATEHOOD AS AN INDEX
OF THE POLITICAL DEVELOPMENT
OF THE UNITED STATES

1787	Delaware, Pennsylvania, New Jersey	1845	Florida,* Texas*
1788	Georgia,* Connecticut, Massachusetts, Maryland, South Carolina,* New Hampshire, Virginia,* New York	1846	Iowa
1789	North Carolina*	1848	Wisconsin
1790	Rhode Island	1850	California
1791	Vermont	1858	Minnesota
1792	Kentucky	1859	Oregon
1796	Tennessee*	1861	Kansas
1803	Ohio	1863	West Virginia
1812	Louisiana*	1864	Nevada
1816	Indiana	1867	Nebraska
1817	Mississippi*	1876	Colorado
1818	Illinois	1889	Montana, North Dakota, South Dakota, Washington
1819	Alabama*	1890	Idaho, Wyoming
1820	Maine	1896	Utah
1821	Missouri	1907	Oklahoma
1836	Arkansas*	1912	New Mexico, Arizona
1837	Michigan	1959	Alaska, Hawai'i

*States that joined the Confederacy

slightly less than one million square miles, consisted of thirteen states, and had a white population of just over three million. In 1900, the area had reached nearly four million square miles, had grown to forty-five states, and the population had risen to 76 million. The spatial and chronological dimensions of this immense development are set out in map 5.1 and table 5.1. The dominions were unable to match this rate of growth. Canada covered about the same area and Australia was not much smaller, but neither supported comparable populations. In 1900, the combined white population of the four countries referred to here as dominions—Canada, South Africa, Australia, and New Zealand— amounted to approximately 10 million, which was only about 13 percent of the total present in the United States. Various hypotheses have been advanced to account for the difference.[86] The most persuasive inter- pretation builds on Adam Smith's insight in emphasizing inequalities in resource endowments.[87] Settlers in the United States took hold of rich agricultural lands and abundant reserves of minerals, which in turn attracted large-scale immigration and the capital needed to activate the factors of production. These unmatched resources could be mobilized cheaply because they had been seized from the original owners, who thereby provided a gigantic subsidy for developing the national economy.

Europeans who emigrated to states that became dominions had similar access to land, but the resources at their disposal either were far less valuable or incapable of being exploited by the technology available in the nineteenth century. Substantial migration to the dominions did not get under way until the mid-nineteenth century. Even so, frontiers in the dominions were never as extensive or as well manned as they were in the United States. Limited resources, climatic conditions, and distance (especially in the case of Australasia) constrained population growth, which in turn hampered the expansion of the domestic market and local industries. Despite these disadvantages, by 1900 rates of growth and living standards in the dominions were roughly comparable to those in the United States, and business enterprise was no less dynamic. The dominions, however, were unable to match the scale of the U.S. economy, and their ability to influence international affairs was correspondingly far more limited.[88]

Accessibility from Europe and economic potential explain the longevity of the settler frontier in the United States, its transcontinental momentum, and the intensity of the conflict with Native Americans. The frontier myth and its stock of stereotypes had time to become embedded in the minds of successive generations. Mythology rationalized conquest and validated contests with the "forces of darkness" elsewhere in the world, too. Additional considerations, however, are needed to explain the way in which the West was won—and spun. After 1783, the United States was able to determine its own policies, though within constraints set by the embryonic nature of the state-building project. A pervasive belief in the despotic potential of central government ensured that the standing army maintained by the United States was too small to control the rapidly expanding frontier. Semi-franchised violence met the needs of the time: state militias, which were rarely motivated by national concerns, and private guns, which were readily deployed outside the law.[89] Settlers who trekked west and south considered that they were responding to heaven-sent opportunities that justified the use of force against "primitive" peoples.[90] Conflict was elevated to the status of "sacred violence" in pursuit of God's providential mission, while being romanticized to justify or disguise its brutalities.[91] Paul Kruger's concept of "sacred history," which bestowed divine validation on the *Voortrekkers'* struggle to reach the Promised Land, emerged from a similar process of frontier conflict. The result in the United States was not only the proliferation of weaponry but also the creation of a pervasive and enduring gun culture, which contributed to the conviction that the values of "martial manhood" were applicable to international problems that had little or no connection to conditions on the nineteenth-century frontier.

Circumstances in the dominions (with the partial exception of South Africa) differed from those in the United States in ways that altered the scope for action. In Canada, for example, ecological conditions, combined with the relatively small numbers of European settlers and the protracted process of development, made relations with First Peoples more peaceful than they were south of the border.[92] The Canadian frontier was shaped initially by a quest for trade rather than for land. Disputes arose, but merchants did not set out to annihilate their suppliers or customers. Settlers in the colonies south of the St. Lawrence River, on the other hand, were embroiled in hostilities from the outset because they coveted fertile land that was already claimed by indigenous people. In Canada, moreover, the law arrived before settlement expanded. In the mainland colonies, settlers established frontiers and provided their own protection before government agencies appeared. Despite their cultural differences, French and English settlers in Canada both feared what they regarded as the anarchy of "mob rule" to the south far more than the prospect of "tyrannical monarchy" in their own country. Loyalists who emigrated to Canada from the United States at the time of the Revolution reinforced this attitude, which expected government, rather than private agents, to provide civil order.[93] The untamed West encouraged privatized violence; the more ordered North was managed by the Royal Canadian Mounted Police.[94]

The possession of lethal weapons in the dominions was regarded less as a right than as a privilege; when national interests were at stake, "bearing arms" became a duty. Frontiers were well stocked with guns, but the dominions never developed a gun culture, nor did firearms carry an aura of religious sanction, as they did in the United States.[95] In this regard, the difference between the Republic and the dominions was not that the latter became secular, though that was undoubtedly a long-term trend, but that they turned away from evangelical fundamentalism in the course of the nineteenth century and toward liberal forms of Christianity, principally within Protestantism.[96] Amidst the broad similarities that characterized settler societies, there was also room for a parting of the ways.

1812: THE SECOND WAR OF INDEPENDENCE?

In 1812, Britain and the United States again went to war, though for the last time, in what many American contemporaries called the "Second War of Independence."[97] Detailed discussions of the causes and consequences of the war are readily available and can be followed in other studies.[98] It is sufficient for present purposes to focus on two questions: the extent to which the war added to the process of territorial incorporation, and how far it can be said to have increased the Republic's effective independence.

The war had multiple causes that are not easily evaluated. Realities were mixed with perceptions and misperceptions, and were then reordered as fortunes on the battlefield fluctuated. The broad context was formed by the global ramifications of the French Wars, which introduced the prospect of changing the balance of power in North America. Both Britain and the United States were alert to the possibilities, but neither pursued grand designs for annexing territory that had already been assigned. Britain was far too involved with the desperate struggle in Europe to contemplate crushing "an emerging rival," as has been claimed.[99] The Republic was still at an early stage of its political and economic development, and was regarded in London less as a rival than as a promising recipient of Britain's informal influence. For their part, Madison and Congress aimed to expand to the west and south rather than to the north because they realized that the annexation of British North America, even if it were possible, would be likely to produce a new set of states opposed to slavery.[100] Westward expansion fitted the Republic's limited military resources and offered the prospect of creating additional slave states at a moment when opposition, in the shape of the Federalist Party, was in disarray.[101]

The immediate causes of the war arose from disputes over the neutrality of U.S. shipping, the impressment of American sailors by the Royal Navy, and frustration over the continuing resistance of Native Americans to the westward advance of the frontier. The Royal Navy's blockade in Europe damaged U.S. trade and prompted Jefferson to retaliate by imposing an embargo on U.S. exports in 1807.[102] Negotiations failed to resolve the dispute. U.S. exports suffered; discontent, especially in East Coast ports, rose to the point where political action was imperative. Madison was not alone in worrying that the fragile independence of the United States was at risk.[103] In these fraught circumstances, the mistrust that was a residual feature of Anglo-U.S. relations after 1783 allowed both sides to place war on the agenda of possibilities, though neither party wished to see it become a reality.[104]

National perspectives have greatly influenced the debate on the outcome of the conflict. Most U.S. historians adopt the view that the war
effort was at least a qualified success; confident interpretations hold
that the Republic emerged in 1815 with strengthened national unity and
greater self-assurance.[105] The Era of Good Feelings signaled the end of
partisan politics; the Monroe Doctrine was a declaration of independence in foreign policy and a warning to European powers that the age
of empire-building in the Western Hemisphere was over. The smaller
contingent of British historians interested in the war has tended to take
the opposite position, claiming that, on balance, Britain won the conflict
on land and at sea. The British contribution, however, has focused on
the military struggle and has left the domestic ramifications in the New
World to other scholars.[106] Historians of Britain who assess the consequences of the war assume that developments at home were affected far
more by the seismic conflict on the continent of Europe than they were
by the minor contest across the Atlantic.

The Treaty of Ghent, signed at the close of 1814, left borders in North
America where they had been at the start of the war. Both protagonists,
however, gained from the settlement: Britain succeeded in defending
what was to become Canada; the United States obtained access to disputed territory in the Ohio Valley. The real victors were the Canadians,
who repelled American invaders and began to forge a sense of national
identity while simultaneously strengthening their ties to Britain.[107]
Thereafter, the United States recognized political realities and took care
not to support the ineffective revolt that broke out in Lower Canada in
1837.[108] The remaining border issues were determined by diplomacy
rather than by force. The Webster-Ashburton Treaty settled the northeast boundary in Maine in 1841. Ashburton was the title taken by Alexander Baring of Barings Bank, which had been the official agent of the
United States in London since 1803.[109] Daniel Webster, the U.S. Secretary of State, included among his qualifications those of being a bank
director and paid consultant to Barings. The negotiations were congenial.[110] The northwest border in Oregon, which Webster and Ashburton
failed to resolve, was agreed by negotiation in 1846. By then, both parties
were keen to ensure that the prairies concentrated on producing wheat
to take advantage of the repeal of Britain's restrictive Corn Laws.[111] The
outcome reflected Britain's wider imperial priorities and its ability to
draw the Midwest on both sides of the boundary into its widening sphere
of economic influence.[112] Finally, in 1871 the United States gave effective
recognition to Canada in the Treaty of Washington, which resolved the
remaining territorial issues between the two countries.

As Canadians won the security needed to enable them to build a country, Native Americans lost the right to retain theirs. In 1810, the Shawnee leader, Tecumseh, assembled a pan-Indian alliance extending from the Great Lakes to the Deep South in an attempt to preserve Native American lands from acquisitive settlers. The alliance was, in effect, a declaration of independence and a gamble on the favorable consequences of a British victory. Although the alliance helped Britain to retain parts of what became southern Canada, the Shawnee were denied their reward. In 1815, Britain and the United States abandoned their respective native allies in the interests of what they regarded as a greater harmony: the need to restore cooperative relations and inaugurate their own "Era of Good Feelings." Disagreements remained: competition between advocates of republican and monarchical forms of government persisted, as did resentment in the United States at Britain's continuing influence on the Republic.[113] The trend, however, was toward cooperation.[114] After 1815 France ceased to be a major threat; Spain entered the peace with her power greatly reduced and her empire in revolt. The removal of external constraints allowed Madison, and his assertive successors, Jackson and Polk, to realize Jefferson's vision of extending the republic of white settlement across the continent.[115]

The principal political result of the conflict in the United States was the consolidation of anti-liberal interests, especially in Southern states. The wider unity forged by the necessities of war fractured on the return of peace. Good Feelings gave way to Strained Feelings. Sectional differences became more marked. The escape of thousands of slaves during the war unnerved owners and reinforced their determination to defend states' rights.[116] The Missouri Crisis, which came close to splitting the Union in 1820, was an early indication of divisions that were to widen. Proposals to allow (white) women to vote were put aside.[117] Schemes for repatriating African American slaves replaced prospects, derived from Enlightenment principles, that they might eventually be assimilated within the United States.[118] "Separate development," as it was later called in South Africa, became the logical complement to plans for Anglo-Saxon dominance. The acrimonious debate over the embargo was carried into the postwar period, emerged in the intense struggle over the tariff, and reinforced the South's resolve to unite behind the cause of free trade.[119]

As the Republic went on the war path to advance its western frontier, it did so with the discreet support of British finance and an indirect guarantee of protection from the British navy. Both were needed. The war had damaged the economy. International trade had been disrupted; the federal government was heavily indebted and unable to meet its obligations.[120] Much of the Republic's navy had been destroyed; the army had demonstrated the inadequacy of its officers and training. None of these developments signaled the imminent achievement of national unity or independence. As the editor of the *North American Review* observed at the close of 1864: "the War of 1812, though dividing us politically from England, left us still provincials."[121] "And this is natural," he added, "for nationality is not the growth of a night; it is not to be created by a declaration of independence; it is not of regular procedure, or the product of calculable forces."[122] It took a third war, the Civil War, to separate the United States "as a nation, not only from our own past, but also from the Old World."[123]

The Monroe Doctrine, which was proclaimed in 1823, has long been regarded as a declaration of independence in foreign policy, and has now assumed "the status of holy writ."[124] The president's annual message to Congress included a passage aimed at preventing European powers from undertaking "future colonization" in the Americas, and warning that such action would be considered "dangerous to our peace and safety."[125] Monroe's pronouncement, however, fell short of being a "ringing affirmation of U.S. pre-eminence in the Western Hemisphere."[126] The statement was made in the aftermath of the French Wars, when the European powers were again at liberty to turn their attention to the wider world and to the Americas in particular. The immediate concern, which was shared by Britain, was that Spain would attempt to reestablish its position in Latin America. Monroe's admonition, however, was an assertion of an ideal, not a program of action, and it had no immediate impact. Congress failed to support it, even as a statement of intent. The United States lacked the capability to direct events. It was Britain's navy and diplomatic weight that determined whether the principle of non-intervention would be upheld or breached. It was not until the close of the century, when the United States needed a policy to validate the exercise of its greatly increased power, that Monroe's address was re-advertised and elevated to the status of being an eternal and inviolable doctrine.[127]

The Monroe Doctrine also suited Britain's evolving interests, which were aligned with those of the United States to the point where both powers almost agreed in 1823 to issue a joint declaration opposing foreign annexations in the Western Hemisphere.[128] The British had abandoned any thoughts they once had of recolonizing the United States or taking over Spain's crumbling empire in Latin America.[129] Britain's aim in the Americas was to develop informal influence, which it did, highly successfully, in the course of the century. The United States, on the other hand, retreated from Jefferson's spacious hemispheric vision.

With the acceptance of British Canada in the north and the recognition of new states in Latin America in 1822, Washington acknowledged that the United States would be unable to monopolize the future of the New World. Old World diplomacy and its intrigues could not be kept at bay: the Americas were to enter international affairs with their own share of competing states. The United States had to tailor its ambitions to its limited means.[130] This realization encouraged the United States under Presidents Jackson and Polk to pursue a program of assertive expansion within one continent.[131] Southern states rallied behind a policy that offered the prospect of extending slavery to the Great Plains south of the line sanctioned by the Missouri compromise. From this perspective, the Monroe Doctrine was a warning to Spain against attempting to reassert control over Florida and Texas.[132] Their future had already been mapped.

"AMERICA KNOWS HOW TO CRUSH AS WELL AS HOW TO EXPAND"[133]

Walt Whitman published his passionate plea urging that Mexico be "thoroughly chastised" shortly before the United States declared war in May 1846. The bulk of the literature refers to the conflict that followed as the Mexican-American War; Mexicans saw it as an unwarranted invasion—and still do. Ulysses Grant, then a junior officer, agreed: "We were sent to provoke war," he observed years later, "but it was essential that the Mexicans should commence it."[134] The defeat of Mexico in 1848 was followed by the cession of about half of its territory covering most of what was to become California, Utah, Nevada, New Mexico, and Arizona. Mexico also agreed to recognize the cession of Texas, "a territory larger than the Austrian Empire."[135] President James Knox Polk had originally offered to buy the land he coveted; when his offer was refused, he launched the most successful war of incorporation in U.S. history.

Placed in the longest perspective, the origins of the invasion of Mexico can be traced to the crisis that struck Europe's military-fiscal states at the end of the eighteenth century and the consequent French Wars, which brought down the Spanish Empire and also created the circumstances that led to the War of 1812. Mexico, Spain's most important colony in the New World, achieved independence in 1821 after a long and debilitating conflict. The divisions that marked the struggle against Spain continued during the unstable peace that followed. As in Spain itself, monarchists clashed with republicans, clerics with laity, and centrists with provincials. Amidst the ensuing turmoil, which was intensified by Spain's efforts to regain Mexico in the 1820s, the new government invited settlers from the United States to occupy parts of its sparsely populated province of *Coahuila y Tejas* in exchange for generous land grants. The authorities calculated that newcomers with a stake in the country would act as a buffer against marauding Comanche and potentially marauding white expansionists from the north. The calculation was mistaken: before long, the Mexicans realized that they had opened the gates to a Trojan horse.

As we have seen, the War of 1812 sharpened the differences between North and South, encouraged slave-owning states to use their political power to strengthen states' rights, and added impetus to territorial expansion.[136] Greed and fear, ever on hand, supplied the motives. The rapid expansion of cotton exports from the 1820s offered evidence that the slave system, far from withering away, was resilient and dynamic.[137] At the same time, the increasing assertiveness of the abolitionist movement alarmed slave-owners everywhere.[138] Britain's decision in 1807 to make it illegal for British subjects to participate in the slave trade, followed in 1833 by the abolition of slavery within the British Empire, removed the principal international slave dealer from the business and placed a large question mark over the future of the "peculiar institution." From the 1830s, too, abolitionists in the United States made headway with an argument claiming that the Constitution guaranteed freedom for the whole nation.[139] On this view, freedom was the norm and slavery the exception. The federal government had no right to alter the status of slaves within individual states, but neither did it have the right to extend slavery beyond those states.

In addition, demographic changes had begun to encroach on the political power of the South, as population growth enabled Northern states to increase their presence in the House of Representatives. These incentives prompted slave interests in the United States to "get their retaliation in first," by spreading west below the Missouri Line and south toward Mexico and the Caribbean. The political benefits of expansion were, in principle, considerable. Each new slave state would add two seats in the Senate and also help to compensate for the increasing presence of the North in the House. Cuba served both purposes: it was the richest island in the Caribbean and was also well populated. If incorporated as a state, Cuba would deliver two senators and as many as nine representatives. Predictably, numerous schemes for acquiring the island, either by purchase or force, were touted during the first half of the nineteenth century. Some were official; others were private, filibustering ventures.

By the 1840s, emboldened advocates of a Southern, slave-owning empire had embraced a spacious design for taking over parts of Central

America and the Caribbean.[140] Although their plans for appropriating Cuba from Spain were frustrated, expansionists reckoned that they stood a better chance of recolonizing Mexico, which had dispensed with its imperial protector and was vulnerable to foreign incursions. Settlers in Texas had made only a tentative start to their challenging venture when the Mexican government decided in 1830 to tighten central control over the outer provinces, prohibit further immigration, and enforce the anti-slavery legislation it had passed during the 1820s. These moves, which threatened to undercut the basis of the new settlements, led to a speedy deterioration in relations between the parties. After a long wrangle, the settlers issued a unilateral declaration of independence in 1836 and converted Texas into a republic. Most of the new republic's leaders hoped for incorporation, but at that stage neither Whigs nor Democrats wanted to receive a gift that was likely to upset the Missouri Compromise and possibly lead to war with Mexico.[141] Other political figures in Texas aimed to secure international recognition to bolster the republic's independence. This plan made some progress: the United States recognized the republic in 1837, France in 1839, and Britain in 1840.

International recognition, however, did not confer viability. The "panic" of 1837 produced a new contingent of settlers who ignored Mexican policy and migrated from Southern states to escape unemployment and indebtedness. However, the numbers of newcomers remained low and the plantation economy made slow progress. In the late 1830s, the Republic contained only about 30,000 white settlers and 11,000 slaves. The rudimentary Texas government had to deal with increased raids from Comanche and Apache bands, and ward off the efforts of the Mexican government to recapture its territory. The Republic lacked its own banks and currency, borrowed when and where it could, and descended into debt.[142] The cavalry came over the hill in 1845, when Texas was incorporated as the twenty-eighth state of the Union. Detailed studies have unraveled the labyrinthine politics that led to Washington's reversal of policy.[143] In essence, President John Tyler, a Virginian and a committed advocate of states' rights, adopted the Texas cause and made it a central issue in 1843–1845; his successor, James K. Polk, carried Tyler's policy to completion, despite rising opposition from the Whigs and their formidable leader, Henry Clay. The treaty to incorporate Texas as a full state, rather than as a transitional territory, failed to attract the two-thirds majority needed for Senate approval; the proposal was passed as a joint resolution of both Houses instead. The precedent was invoked in 1898, when the bid to annex Hawai'i ran into similar objections.

A medley of motives underlay these decisions. Tyler was an expansionist and a slaveholder who embraced the notion of manifest destiny. He also lacked a secure political base and hoped that the annexation of Texas, which was a popular cause in the South, would provide one. Polk was a Jackson Democrat from, appropriately, Tennessee and, like Tyler, a slaveholder and an expansionist. Unlike Tyler, however, Polk had strong support from a loose coalition of Southern expansionists, Texas bond holders, and slave owners in states that had suffered from the panic of 1837 and hoped that rising demand following annexation would boost the price of slaves. Diverse though they were, expansionists shared a growing anxiety that Britain, having formally abolished slavery in the West Indies in 1834, intended to spread the policy to the mainland.[144] Southern leaders claimed that, if Texas remained independent, it would fall into Britain's sphere of influence and be compelled to abolish slavery. Incorporation would eliminate the danger. To mollify opposition in the North, advocates of annexation argued that expansion would help to diffuse slaves across Central America and contribute to the creation of an almost all-white Republic, whereas abolition would destabilize the United States and drive many ex-slaves northward. To comfort moralists, propagandists portrayed Mexico as being a backward, uncivilized state, even though (or perhaps because) it had already abolished slavery. In the end, Whig appeals to classical republican beliefs, which linked unrestrained territorial expansion to the dissolution of civic virtue, were overwhelmed by quasi-religious invocations to manifest destiny and the realization of individual liberty in new pastures.[145]

Britain, the major foreign power in the region following Spain's withdrawal, was closely involved in these events. The British, however, were not preoccupied with schemes to stem the advancing American presence, as was once believed.[146] Britain's connections with Texas were minimal; its main interest lay in Mexico, where the City of London's considerable investments were at risk. Mexico had already defaulted on its external debt in 1827, and Britain had no wish to jeopardize the repayment scheme negotiated in 1830. This priority gave the British government a diplomatic interest in urging restraint on all parties.[147] Although Lord Palmerston thought that Texans were a "band of outlaws," the Foreign Office made no objection to the declaration of independence in 1836 because the act posed no threat to British interests.[148] Britain recognized the Republic in 1840, when it became clear that Mexico was unable to reclaim the territory and when the Texas authorities agreed to accept a proportion of the Mexican debt owed to British bond holders.[149] This was as far as Britain would go. In 1840, when a representative from Texas offered Britain a favorable commercial agreement in exchange for guaranteeing the state's public debt, the Foreign Office refused, even though the proposal was phrased in terms that amounted to a definition of informal empire: "they nevertheless give to England all the benefits of a Colony without the Expense of its Civil government, or a responsibility for its National Defence."[150] Texas had little to offer except debts that were unlikely to be repaid, and Britain had no wish to risk disturbing its much larger interests elsewhere in the United States.

Texas debt soon descended to junk status, and in 1845 Britain advised Mexico to acquiesce in the loss of its province in the expectation that the United States would agree to take over the debts of the new republic when it joined the Union.[151] Although Congress gave no formal guarantee, debt prices recovered after 1845 on the assumption that the federal government would act to protect its own credit rating if Texas threatened to default. The final settlement reached in 1850 justified the expectation and placed Texas bond holders in much the same position as the creditors of other indebted states of the Union after the panic of 1837.[152] Incorporation also eased Britain's concern that Texas might further destabilize Mexico and damage the City's interests there if it remained an independent republic. Accordingly, Britain tried to limit Mexico's response to northern aggression while hoping that opposition among Whigs and some Democrats to the prospect of war would halt the expansionists.[153]

Restraint was not forthcoming. President Polk was determined to press ahead with annexation; Mexico felt obliged to defend its sovereignty.[154] The declaration of an independent republic in Texas ran along a crooked path to annexation. Incorporation into the Union led more directly to a war of choice prompted by expansionists in the United States.[155] The invaders portrayed themselves, not as conquerors, but as liberators whose mission was to bring progress to a society hampered by inept, corrupt government. While it lasted, the war generated popular enthusiasm and its complement of heroes, none greater than General Winfield Scott, who followed the approximate route taken by Hernán Cortés in 1519, defeated Mexican forces in a series of minor battles, and captured Mexico City in 1847.[156] By then, however, the state had already been greatly weakened by devastating Comanche raids, which prepared the way for defeat and enabled Scott to gather the spoils of victory.[157] Scott's army, which numbered only about 6,000 men at the outset of the war, quickly swelled to about 115,000 as volunteers, mainly from Southern states, hastened to enlist. His conquistadors, like their predecessors, were adventurers with a purpose: they were attracted by the prospect of new opportunities of gaining wealth, especially by acquiring land.[158] Many died, principally from disease; most of the survivors were disillusioned; some deserted; others sought compensation by looting local villages.

Victory encouraged Polk and his advisors to consider several grandiose options for postwar Mexico, including annexation, partition, and protectorate status. In the end, opposition from the Whig majority in Congress led the president to abandon these larger ambitions. Nevertheless, in 1848, when the Treaty of Guadalupe Hidalgo brought the war to an end, it was evident that the Texas sun was beaming on the Southern strategy.

"AN IRREPRESSIBLE CONFLICT BETWEEN OPPOSING AND ENDURING FORCES"[159]

The history of the United States reaches great peaks of interest whenever wars are fought. The Civil War, however, is the incomparable Everest that has attracted more scholarly mountaineers than any other single episode of armed conflict, either before or after independence.[160] When Senator William Henry Seward, speaking in 1858, referred to the "irrepressible" character of the impending conflict, he identified a problem that has attracted and baffled historians ever since. Walt Whitman, writing during and after the war, laid out other themes that subsequent commentators have pursued and extended.[161] Whitman began with the naïve enthusiasm of a young poet who thought of war as a purifying force that would speed the progress of modernity and democracy; he continued with sobering reflections on the ugly realities of death and destruction; he ended with the hope that peace would bring national reconciliation.

Today, every conceivable cause and consequence, it seems, has been explored, and every possible detail has been gathered to support, qualify, or refute whatever generalizations the bold and the unwary have ventured. The large majority of studies, however, have treated the Civil War as a national event. The international dimension of the conflict, which Oscar Wilde regarded—with the example of Ireland in mind—as "a struggle for autonomy, self-government for a people," has only recently begun to attract the attention it deserves.[162] This perspective, which coincidentally fits the remit of the present study, makes it possible not only to place the Civil War in the wider context shaped by the modernizing movements of the nineteenth century, but also to explain the apparent ambivalence of British policy, which historians of the period have often found puzzling.

Seen from an international standpoint, the issues leading to the Civil War echoed the contemporary struggle, outlined in chapter 2, between conservative and progressive forces in post-Napoleonic Europe. To be sure, there were few monarchists in the United States and even fewer slaves in Europe. Nevertheless, the contest between defenders of dynasties and advocates of "improvement" reappeared in the New World in recognizable forms. The central issue, as in Europe, was how to define and control the state structures that had emerged from the revolutionary wars of the late eighteenth century. North and South grounded their claims to legitimacy in increasingly divergent interpretations of the Constitution backed by moral imperatives of the kind that were familiar to political leaders and commentators in Europe. They called upon universal principles, biblical authority, and the historical record. They sought unity in half-formed, half-imagined concepts of ethnicity. They summoned visions of a providential destiny that would lead to a Promised Land of peace, liberty, and independence. They were united in opposing the "excesses of democracy" represented by radicalism.[163]

By the 1850s, Southern states had developed a distinctive approach to the Republic's future.[164] The Missouri Crisis had prompted the region to reaffirm an interpretation of the Constitution that gave clear precedence to states' rights. Continuing concern over slave rebellions, brought to panic level by Nat Turner's revolt in Virginia in 1831 and sustained by Britain's decision in 1833 to abolish the slave trade throughout the British Empire, induced slave owners to reinforce their defenses against abolitionist attacks and develop a justificatory ideology that endowed paternalism with an improving purpose.[165] Commentators in the South based their claim for self-determination on a mystical reading of history that contrasted Southern Anglo-Normans with Northern Anglo-Saxons.[166] In this telling, the Normans were cavaliers of superior breeding, while the Saxons were cast as puritans of humble origin who had become money-grubbing and ambitious but remained dishonorable and cowardly.[167] It followed that any conflict between the two nationalities was bound to result in the triumph of nobility over the lower orders. According to this ultra-romantic appeal to the past, the upheavals of the late eighteenth century had destroyed the organic unity of society and given ordinary citizens ideas that were above their station. Abolitionists, like William Lloyd Garrison and his European allies, were subversives who wished to destroy the liberties of the South.[168] Modern industries and rootless urban workers threatened social order. A radical underclass, in which free African Americans and former slaves were prominently represented, confirmed this impression by campaigning not only for abolition but also for a wide range of progressive reforms, including some that would later be categorized as human rights.[169]

In resisting this challenge, spokesmen for the South appealed to biblical authority to prescribe rules of conduct that would help to avert the decay that had overtaken the former great states of Western Europe.[170] The dynastic principle was invoked to provide the necessary leadership. In this patriarchal, Walter-Scottish view of the world, aristocratic supremacy was essential to ensure social harmony and political stability. What Karl Marx termed the Southern "plantocracy," like the monarchical dynasties of Europe, saw itself as defending order and stability against the anarchic consequences of allowing the "tyranny of the majority" to take control of the polity.[171] Bolingbroke's country party stirred; a patriarchal version of Jefferson's agrarian ideal found zealous champions.

The upshot was the propagation of a form of regional "nationalism" that opposed the federal model espoused in the North. The fragility of the Republic became the subject of everyday discussion; the idea that the states were "natural," whereas the Union was an "artificial aggregation," was widely debated.[172] The evolution of John C. Calhoun's political thought symbolized the wider drift toward confrontation.[173] Calhoun, who was one of the most influential Southern politicians and thinkers of the time, started his public career by supporting the nationalist program advanced by Henry Clay. After 1830, he reversed course and became a fervent advocate of states' rights. His hostility to the idea of national unity was uncompromising. "I never use the word 'Nation' in speaking of the United States," he declared in 1849. "I always use the word 'Union' or 'Confederacy.' We are not a Nation, but a Union, a Confederacy of equal and sovereign States."[174]

Political leaders in the North were equally committed advocates of self-determination. Northerners had their own providential vision of the spread of republican values, which grounded universal human rights, expressed in the idea of liberty, in Protestant teaching.[175] Christian humanists, united behind a belief in the moral equality of man, grew in influence from the 1830s. The abolitionist movement, which took shape in the North in the 1830s, gained confidence from the abolition of slavery in the British Empire. Northern liberals also drew support from related international movements, which campaigned to improve labor conditions and education, and to promote temperance.[176] The revolutions of 1848 aroused interest and sympathy throughout the North. Lincoln regarded events in Europe as being part of "the general cause of Republican liberty."[177] Lincoln, himself a man of faith, drew upon these values

to unite the Northern Anglo-Saxon ethnie in support of a concept of independence defined by the sanctity of the Union.[178] By the 1850s, commentators and spokesmen in the North had developed a specific and
assertive sense of nationality that contrasted freedom with slavery, democracy with despotism, and energy with indolence.[179] In juxtaposing
two opposed notions of self-determination and subjecting them to the
trauma of civil war, the conflict between North and South complemented
similar catastrophes that were taking place in Europe.

These contrasting positions need refining. The Civil War, though "ut-
terly memorable," cannot be reduced to a struggle between "Cavaliers
(Wrong but Wromantic) and Roundheads (Right but Repulsive)."[180]
Southern leaders did not see themselves as living in the past, but as using
it to shape the future. They had developed the world's largest and most
efficient cotton industry on the basis of slave labor, which was protected
by the Constitution and defended by the federal government.[181] They had
abandoned mercantilism in favor of free trade, and they had prospered
greatly in consequence. As specialized producers of an indispensable raw
material, the cotton states were linked to manufacturers in New England
and Britain, the world's most advanced industrial economy.[182] Admittedly, Marx's "plantocracy" was by no means monolithic: the majority
of slaveholders in the South had no more than five slaves.[183] Nevertheless, political power was wielded by a minority of large slaveholders, who
strengthened their control over slaves and smallholders after the panic
of 1837 and the depression that followed.[184] In the 1850s, the slave economy experienced what turned out to be its final boom. Emancipation
in the Caribbean, far from demonstrating the superiority of free labor,
had led to a fall in output that strengthened the demand for cotton from
Southern states.[185] Slavery continued to support thriving economies in
Cuba and Brazil.[186] The Mexican War, which had delivered new territories with the potential to become slave states, had encouraged Southern
leaders to devise even more ambitious plans for spreading the plantation
system into Central America.[187] Political liberalism was in retreat after
1848, while the advent of economic liberalism, in the guise of free trade,
boosted the use of unfree labor throughout the international economy.[188]
Ambitious spirits hoped that Southern nationalism could be extended
across the United States to become the dominant republican ideology.[189]

Some revisionist accounts have gone so far as to portray the relationship between South and North as that of two dynamic forms of capitalism
rather than as a contest between backwardness and modernity.[190] At this
point, however, a line needs to be drawn between industrial and commercial capitalism. If power-driven manufacturing and wage labor are

taken to be hallmarks of modern capitalism, as a long tradition claims, the South clearly fails the test.[191] A more telling qualification (since definitions invite endless wrangles) points to the limited development potential of plantation capitalism in the South. An economy based on slave labor skewed the distribution of income toward luxury consumption and hampered the growth of a mass market.[192] Slave societies, moreover, had great difficulty attracting new settlers, who went in increasing numbers to the North and Midwest. Partly for this reason, the South had far fewer towns than the North and a corresponding deficiency of financial and commercial services.[193] Manufacturing had made a modest start in Virginia and Georgia, which had a number of cotton mills, but the Southern states as a whole accounted for only about 10 percent of all U.S. output of manufactures.[194] The South had capitalized on the fact that slave products were more profitable than the alternatives. It was not, however, a society on the verge of an industrial revolution.

The stereotype of the thrusting, modernizing North also needs qualification. Although manufacturing expanded in parts of New England during the first half of the century, the developments of the period did not amount to a "market revolution."[195] Much of the North remained rural; manufactures had not yet become competitive in international markets.[196] Merchants and bankers in New York and Philadelphia conducted substantial business with the cotton states and had a sizeable stake in the continuing prosperity of the slave economy. Northern banks supplied most of the finance for the internal slave trade, which expanded rapidly from the 1820s, and became vital to the Southern economy after 1808, when U.S. citizens were barred from participating in the international slave trade. Several hundred thousand "surplus" slaves were transferred from Maryland and Virginia to the Lower South to ensure that cotton supplies met international demand.[197] Northern finance and Southern agriculture fitted together. The principal economic incompatibility lay elsewhere: between small farmers in the North, who wanted to preserve opportunities for homesteaders, and large farmers in the South, who wanted to extend the plantation system.[198]

Abolition was not a compelling priority in the North outside the limited ranks of the committed, even though the anti-slavery movement had grown in visibility and influence.[199] Racial discrimination was widespread, even in "free" states.[200] Lincoln's position seems to have reflected that of the wider public, insofar as it can be gauged.[201] He was opposed to slavery as an institution, but favored amelioration rather than immediate abolition. His ultimate hope was that slavery would wither away in accord with God's plan for the United States, but he was also prepared to consider various resettlement schemes to speed the process on its way. Caution toward the current status of slaves, however, contrasted with an increasingly resolute position on the question of the future of slavery. Opposition in the North to expanding the institution into the Republic's new territories, and beyond, became a sticking point—and one that held when the prospect of war materialized.

When qualifications have been made and refinements put in place, it remains the case that the Civil War was the product of growing differences between two powerful and expanding regions of the Union. Economic causes, though out of favor for some time, have an important place in the story.[202] Admittedly, the North's complementary and profitable relationship with the South provided little incentive for attempting to transform the plantation economy. Other economic issues, however, greatly heightened the tension between the regions.[203] Although most of these were long-standing, they took on added urgency following the panic of 1857, which affected the North far more than the South.[204] Uncertainty over the future of the Western territories (following the Dred Scott case in 1857) led to a loss of confidence, the bankruptcy of railroad and land speculators, and a run on East Coast banks.[205] Southern propagandists were quick to contrast the robustness of their own economy with the frailty that, so they claimed, was endemic to Northern banking and manufacturing.

Northerners responded by renewing their attempts to persuade Congress to install policies that safeguarded their interests. The tariff question was a particularly acrimonious cause of dispute: manufacturers in the North wanted a high import tariff to protect their output from British imports; planters in the South and farmers in the Midwest favored free trade to expand their export markets and to maintain low tariffs on consumer imports. Northern and Midwestern interests eventually agreed on a compromise tariff in 1857, but the proposal was defeated by the Southern lobby. Representatives from states in the North and Midwest pressed for legislation to allow households to acquire free land, but were frustrated by opposition from the South, which was determined to preserve opportunities for the plantation system.[206] When Congress finally passed the Homestead Bill in 1860, President James Buchanan, a Democrat, vetoed it.[207] Southern interests and their allies also continued to oppose federal subsidies for national transport improvements. The Pacific Railroad Bill passed the House in 1860, but was defeated in the Senate by the Democrats and their allies.[208] Similarly, in 1860, when business interests in the northeast tried to resurrect the National Bank, a long-cherished Whig cause, they were unable to secure sufficient support in Congress.

Slavery was the issue that towered above all others. The principal threat, as seen by observers in the North, was that the institution would spread into Western territories as well as further into the Deep South and even into independent states in Central America and the Caribbean. Transport improvements in the 1840s and 1850s had created the prospect of a united labor market linking the East Coast to the Midwest and the Far West. If slavery took hold there, the region would cease to attract settlers because it would depress the wages of free laborers and stunt the economic potential of a large segment of the continent. The discovery of gold in California in 1848 produced a fierce contest between pro-slavery Democrats, who wanted to import slaves and turn them into miners, and a mixture of free-soilers and abolitionists.[209] Although California banned slavery in 1850, the struggle between the parties continued throughout the decade, when pro-slave interests worked to divide the state in the hope of controlling the southern half.[210] At the same time, the South's ambitious plans for expanding into Central America and the Caribbean promised to deliver a huge new resource base that would strengthen the position of the cotton states within the Union.[211] The pro-slavery "conspiracy," as Lincoln called it, would enable what was originally a slave enclave to take over the Union, transform its character, and ultimately destroy the republican ideals that the founders had fought to establish.

Southern observers, on the other hand, viewed these developments as a mirror image. From their perspective, the threat to the Union came from the disruptive consequences of the rise and encroachment of Northern power. Economic development in the North nurtured an incipient conflict between capital and labor that could tear the Union apart. Militant abolitionists were trying to subvert an institution that was protected by the Constitution and defended through the principle of states' rights. Moreover, the internal slave trade had become essential to the vitality of the production system.[212] Any dilution of these rights would necessarily increase the power of the federal government. Yet, the growth of population in the North was steadily shifting representation in the House away from the South. A resurgent, centralized autocracy was only a short step ahead of the "tyranny" that the Revolution had overthrown at such cost. Southerners regarded their own expansive response to these challenges as being necessary to uphold the ideals of the founders, and Jefferson's authority in particular.[213] The South had to break out before the North broke in.

The differences between North and South manifested themselves in a series of well-known political crises. The first of these, the Missouri Crisis (discussed in chapter 4), ended in 1820 in a compromise between slave and free states that succeeded in keeping the Union together. The agreement held, though amidst gathering tension, and was extended by the Compromise of 1850. The Compromise, however, turned out to be a temporary fix because the key issues were unresolved.[214] Leaders in the South were concerned that the agreement did not explicitly confirm their claimed right to extend slavery to new territories. In 1854, the Kansas-Nebraska Act took the question of slavery out of the hands of the federal government, devolved it to the localities, and ended the precarious balance between free and slave states. Three years later, a crucial ruling by the Supreme Court in the celebrated case of Dred Scott preserved Southern interests by making slaveholding legal in all territories.[215] The trend, however, was against the South: by 1861, the number of "free" states had increased to nineteen, while the total number of "slave" states stood at fifteen.[216] Political conflict at the top was matched by increased lawlessness on the ground, as opposed factions attempted to settle the slavery issue by direct action.[217] The Fugitive Slave Act, which was part of the Compromise of 1850, was a particular cause of dissension because it prompted abolitionists to defy the requirement to return escaped slaves to their owners. In these ways, the compromise planned in 1850 became the confrontation that ended in war in 1861.

These developments occurred at a time of shifting political fortunes.[218] Although remnants of the Federalists had regrouped as Whigs in 1834, they split after the passage of the Kansas-Nebraska Act over questions of slavery and territorial expansion.[219] The Democrats were also beset by divisions in the 1850s, when they were challenged by Young America, a modernizing wing of the party, and began to lose support among their allies in the North. The party "system" regained a measure of stability with what turned out to be a historic event: the foundation of the Republican Party in 1854 with an almost exclusively Northern base and a commitment to oppose the expansion of slavery.[220] While the Democrats remained in disarray, the Republicans made a pivotal breakthrough in the mid-term elections of 1858: they won control of the House and gained seats in the Senate.[221] Two years later, and with more than 80 percent of the electorate voting, the Republican Party achieved majorities in both Houses, and the party's nominee, Abraham Lincoln, won the presidential election without needing (or securing) the backing of a single state in the South.[222] The South had run out of political options.

The Republicans did not interpret their electoral success as authorizing abolition, still less as a mandate to go to war. Although there were "Fire-Eaters" on both sides, the general mood was one of uncertainty about the future accompanied by a reluctance to contemplate a military solution to the problems dividing the Union.[223] Some historians have suggested that war was not inevitable and might have been avoided, even at this late stage.[224] Arguments about the contingency of events, however, while properly identifying the role of chance and individual intervention, are causal only in a limited sense. Developments between the election of 1860 and the outbreak of war in the following year unfolded within narrowing parameters. The war was not inevitable until it happened, but the chances of it happening increased rapidly during this period. The fire had been laid. Either party could have set light to it by accident or premeditation. Declarations of secession by seven Southern states between December 1860 and the formation of the Confederate States of America in February 1861 reduced the options almost to invisibility. In April, a minor engagement at Fort Sumter, South Carolina, between Federal troops and forces representing the Confederacy applied the touch paper.

"At last," proclaimed Henry Timrod, "we are a nation among nations."[225] Timrod, the most notable Southern poet of his day, penned his poem, tellingly entitled "Ethnogenesis," in February 1861, two months before the outbreak of the Civil War. His intention was to celebrate, not the Union of all the states, but the union of the South. In his eyes, the South had a distinctive ethnic affinity that was the basis for national unity. Secession, so its advocates claimed, would realize the principle of self-determination that European states had long struggled to achieve. Greek independence had fallen short of Lord Byron's idealistic expectations; the Hungarian cause had been crushed, with Lajos Kossuth's beguiling rhetoric, in the Revolution of 1848.[226] Yet, political failure had not eliminated the appeal of romantic nationalism, and Timrod was among those who remained captivated. This time, with the cause founded on the bonding principle of racial unity, he believed the outcome really would be different.

The war that followed dragged on for exactly four years, until General Robert E. Lee surrendered the main Confederate force to Lieutenant-General Ulysses S. Grant in April 1865. Detailed research has now charted the devastating scale of the conflict.[227] The accepted figure of 620,000 deaths has been raised to about 750,000 out of three million combatants and a total population of 31 million.[228] Deficiencies in the evidence suggest that these figures still understate losses on the Confederate side. Large stretches of the South, where most of the fighting took place, were left in a ruinous state; the "collateral damage" to civilians, though extensive, defies precise estimation. Nevertheless, even a cautious conclusion indicates that "the human cost of the Civil War was greater than historians have long believed."[229] The economic losses were extensive and enduring. The per capita cost of the war was three times as high for the South as for the North. Consumption in the North regained prewar levels by 1873; in the South, it remained below those levels until the end of the century. By 1900, per capita incomes in the Southern states were still only two-thirds of the national average. Poverty in the region persisted well into the twentieth century.

The outcome of the war confirms that the growing divergence between the two regions cannot be reduced to shades of emphasis between two "modern" states or two comparable forms of capitalism. The North not only had greater resources and a larger population than the South, but also mobilized them more effectively. The North had more capable civilian leadership, better generals, and a superior navy.[230] With the assistance of its advanced financial institutions, the North met more than one-fifth of its war costs by taxation and settled additional bills by issuing Treasury bonds, which were subscribed locally. Above all, the North benefited from widespread and sustained public support. Public opinion was ambivalent on the question of abolition, as opposed to amelioration, but it rallied to the call to save the Union.[231] Although New York City had little sympathy for the anti-slavery movement and continued to vote for the Democrats, the state as a whole made a huge contribution to the war effort by supplying manpower and munitions.

Maine, on the other hand, firmly opposed slavery, even though abolition ran counter to its economic interests. In the Far West, California was greatly exercised by the prospect, which the Republicans took care to emphasize, that slavery might enter states as well as territories. The crucial shift of opinion occurred in the Midwest, which severed its political alliance with the South at the close of the 1850s. Free trade had not lost its appeal, but other considerations directed the region toward the Republicans. The Midwest had become increasingly integrated with the East Coast and benefited from expenditure derived from the import tariff. Farmers were drawn to the party's support for smallholders and opposition to the spread of plantation slavery. Abolitionists had succeeded in winning converts, especially in the burgeoning towns of the Upper Midwest. African Americans throughout the North rallied to the Union cause, which they identified with abolition. Lincoln needed their active service. By 1865, about 200,000 African Americans had enlisted in the army and navy; 40,000 died in battle and from disease.

The war revealed the limits of Southern modernity. The tax basis of the Southern states was too narrow to fund a major conflict.[232] The Confederacy raised only about 5 percent of its revenues from taxation, and found it almost impossible to borrow, either at home or abroad.[233] States that had defaulted on their debts in the panic of 1837 were not well placed to raise new money in Europe.[234] The blockade imposed by the Northern navy eviscerated cotton exports, deprived the Confederacy of its main source of revenue, and reduced regional imports of essential food supplies.[235] The Confederacy's expenditure was met increasingly by issuing inflationary paper currency. Policy as well as resources influenced fiscal decisions. Slave owners refused to vote for a war tax and contributed little from their own pockets. Moreover, the ethnie that Henry Timrod invoked was too small to bid successfully for self-determination.[236] The proponents of a slave state were headed by an oligarchy of plantation owners who were determined to preserve their massive investment in slaves, but who represented few other interests apart from their allies among the commercial elite.[237] Even so, the masters of the "Big Houses" exempted themselves from conscription and supplied few volunteers for military service.[238] Their concept of citizenship excluded some four million African Americans and more than three million white women.[239] Small farmers and poor whites were similarly disengaged. Their instinctive republicanism had little affinity with the patriarchal pretensions of the large planters.[240] Outside the cotton belt, support for a prospective slave empire ebbed. The Upper South and the border states viewed the ambitions of the plantocracy with a mixture of concern and indifference. Virginia, which feared that further territorial expansion would depress land values in the old plantations, was a reluctant supporter of secession; the western part of the state favored the Union.[241] When war was declared, four "slave states" (Delaware, Maryland, Missouri, and Kentucky) refused to join the Confederacy.

Indications of resistance to the draft and evidence of desertion appeared as early as 1862. Food riots and anti-war protests, especially by soldiers' wives, became more frequent in the years that followed as the agricultural basis of the Confederacy disintegrated.[242] Despite a shortage of manpower, slaves were excluded from armed service until the desperate final stage of the war in case they turned their guns on their owners.[243] Unsurprisingly, hardly any slaves joined the Confederate army; most adopted forms of passive resistance; some escaped, if they could.[244] After Lincoln issued the Emancipation Proclamation in January 1863, Confederate dollars, which had previously exchanged at par, rapidly depreciated against both gold and Southern banknotes.[245] Before the

Battle of Gettysburg in July 1863, foreign investors gave the Confederacy a 42 percent chance of winning the Civil War.[246] Following the defeat at Gettysburg and the fall of Vicksburg immediately afterward, the odds fell to 15 percent and declined further from then on. What is remarkable, notwithstanding the undoubted commitment of the front-line troops, is that the South sustained its war effort for as long as it did.[247]

"FOR GOD'S SAKE, LET US IF POSSIBLE KEEP OUT OF IT"[248]

Lord John Russell's appeal to the House of Commons, cited above, was made shortly after the Civil War began, and it set the course of British policy toward the conflict. It was the government's duty, Russell declared, "to use every possible means to avoid taking part in this lamentable contest." Only "the imperative duty of protecting British interests in case they are attacked justifies the Government in interfering at all." The war generated problems that caused Russell's firm line to waver, while the "duty of protecting British interests" produced more than one diplomatic crisis. The most serious of these, the "Trent Affair," occurred in November 1861, when a U.S. naval vessel intercepted a British ship and took custody of two Confederate diplomats who were on board.[249] A red mist descended on both sides of the Atlantic; bellicose sentiments rose almost to action point. Yet, the affair was defused and Russell's policy of neutrality held, even though there was a moment when he himself came close to abandoning it. British policy during the Civil War was not so much an example of the advantages of "splendid isolation" as an illustration of the merits of anxious inaction.

At the outset of the war, official neutrality was tilted toward the Confederacy.[250] In the absence of a clear undertaking that the Union intended to abolish slavery, the British government was inclined to think that the North was engaged in a war to suppress a legitimate claim to self-determination. A cabinet that represented landed privilege readily identified with large planters.[251] Experience of Napoleon Bonaparte's imperial ambitions had persuaded British governments of the wisdom of supporting the aspirations of small states that hoped to become independent, providing they could demonstrate their viability. The policy appeared to be working in South America. Palmerston was among those who saw the advantage to Britain of dividing the United States. The South was confident that the influence of "King Cotton" would be irresistible.[252] In 1860, raw cotton accounted for almost 60 percent of the value of all U.S. exports and was vital to the British textile industry.

Moreover, diplomats from the Confederacy stressed their commitment to free trade and opposition to the high rates imposed by the Morrill Tariff (1861), which British observers regarded as an unfriendly Northern measure.[253] The leaders of the Confederacy calculated that, sooner rather than later, Britain would support their bid for independence. The Confederacy's early victories appeared to confirm the assumption in both London and Richmond, Virginia, that the South was destined to prevail on the battlefield.[254]

Lincoln himself was sufficiently concerned by the progress of the Confederacy, especially after the defeat of Union forces at Bull Run in July 1861, to turn to Giuseppe Garibaldi for help by offering him the position of Major-General in the Union Army.[255] Lincoln's approach, though containing a trace of desperation, was not entirely wayward. Garibaldi, then at the height of his fame, was a heroic figure of international standing. By attaching him to the Union cause, Lincoln hoped to rally support in Europe and forestall recognition of the Confederacy. This was an offer that Garibaldi could, and did, refuse. Garibaldi's sympathies lay with the North, but his main concern was to end slavery throughout the Southern Hemisphere, and he had no interest in becoming an elevated mercenary in a civil war. Consequently, he asked Lincoln to confirm that the purpose of the war was to abolish slavery. At that point, however, the president was unable to give Garibaldi the assurance he needed, and in September the offer of service lapsed.

Like Garibaldi, British observers had a limited appreciation of the president's political difficulties. Lincoln had no mandate to abolish slavery. He had to take care not to step ahead of public opinion in the North or to alienate the border states, whose continued allegiance to the Union was essential. Accordingly, the North's advertised defense of the war rested on the need to maintain the territorial integrity of the Union. As Garibaldi pointed out, the claim was not one to engage the active support of outsiders who identified with independence movements.

Self-help served Lincoln rather better than foreign aid. By the opening months of 1862, the Union Navy's blockade of Confederate ports had greatly reduced the South's overseas trade and largely eliminated the coastal trade.[256] In April, the fall of New Orleans, the principal Southern port, further isolated the South. The loss of cotton exports greatly diminished the Confederacy's revenues; the disruption of inter-regional trade produced shortages of foodstuffs and other supplies; the South's inadequate railroad system began to disintegrate under the strain of handling extra freight. Nevertheless, by September the direction of the war was still unclear and Lincoln was obliged to accept that a further initiative was needed to give momentum to the Union cause and deter European powers from recognizing the Confederacy. Accordingly, in January 1863 Lincoln issued the Emancipation Proclamation, which had the intention of freeing slaves in states that were still at war with the federal government.[257] The announcement dismayed some of his Northern supporters, but had the compensatory effect of boosting his popularity among African Americans in the North and encouraging resistance among slaves in the designated Confederate states. The institution of slavery was not abolished until Congress approved the Thirteenth Amendment in January 1865, shortly before the war ended.[258]

Initially, however, the Emancipation Proclamation provoked skepticism and even apprehension in government circles in Europe. Most commentators did not understand the constitutional limits to the president's powers and were suspicious of a measure that did not free all slaves throughout the United States. Others were concerned that the proposal would nevertheless be sufficiently sweeping to incite a race war that could spread across the continent and into the Caribbean.[259] These considerations prompted Britain and France to consider mediating between the two parties. Both countries thought that it was too late to save the Union and doubted whether further military action would succeed in abolishing slavery. Their aim was to end the war by recognizing the independence of the Confederacy. Britain wanted to return to "business as usual"; Napoleon III saw an opportunity to revive the French Empire by taking a stake in Mexico. The British cabinet divided and debated, but eventually reached agreement in November 1862, after considering a magisterial memorandum written by Sir George Cornewall Lewis, the Secretary of State for War.[260] Lewis argued that recognition of the South in effect meant war with the United States, which would be disastrous from every point of view. He recommended maintaining the current policy of non-intervention on the grounds that it met Palmerston's test of pragmatic wisdom. The Confederacy, Lewis claimed, had yet to demonstrate either military superiority or political viability. The case for independence had not been proved and it was not in Britain's power to determine the outcome. Lewis's advice was in accord with the ground rules Britain had advocated to manage the international order after 1815.[261] France, Austria, and Spain thought that international law should allow intervention to defend dynastic legitimacy; Britain espoused non-intervention so that claims for self-determination could be heard and tested.

Lewis's memorandum settled policy for the remainder of the war. Foreign observers became convinced that Lincoln's commitment to abolition was genuine; North America was not consumed in a racial conflagration. There was positive news too: an inflow of foreign aid, in the shape of several hundred thousand European volunteers, added weight to the Union Army; victory at Gettysburg in July 1863 greatly diminished the chances of the Confederacy gaining recognition.[262] The British government, alert to the need to back the winning side, decided that the South's bid for independence would fail. Britain adhered to neutrality, as Russell had initially recommended, but now with a bias toward the North, which appeared to have might, as well as right, on its side.

Neutrality was determined partly by assessments of the mood in the country and partly by applying Palmerston's principle of cleaving to what he famously called Britain's "eternal and perpetual" interests.[263] The Civil War engaged but also divided public opinion in Britain. Misunderstanding of the circumstances leading to war, compounded by competing propaganda claims, supported the convictions of some and the doubts of others.[264] Unsurprisingly, historians have had great difficulty in linking attitudes toward the war to occupational and social categories. Cobden's uncertainties illustrate the dilemmas public figures faced, though few were as conflicted as he was.[265] On the one hand, Cobden favored free trade, which aligned him with the South; on the other, he supported human rights, which drew him to the North; he then needed a third hand to satisfy his commitment to peace, which led him toward neutrality.

In the broadest terms, however, the Confederate cause tended to receive a sympathetic hearing from aristocrats, gentry, Anglican clergy, and members of the older professions, who stood for tradition, hierarchy, and paternal control.[266] Lord Palmerston, who was prime minister for the duration of the Civil War, looked askance at republican forms of government, distrusted democracy, and saw advantages to Britain in a weaker Union, but was also committed to the abolition of slavery. Lord John Russell, who was Foreign Secretary throughout the war years and had an impressive record as a liberal reformer, was willing at one point to recognize the independence of the Confederacy. Gladstone, who was Chancellor of the Exchequer and on his way to becoming one of the most noted reformers of his day, gave public support to independence for the Confederacy in 1862. He shared with Russell a belief in the right of self-determination, supported the *Risorgimento,* and denounced the Opium Wars as blatant incursions into China's sovereignty. Yet, he came from a family of former slave owners and did not rank abolition as a high priority.

Union supporters were found more readily among middle-class businessmen and manufacturers, wage-earners, and dissenting ministers, who backed a liberal agenda of electoral reform, free trade, and individual rights.[267] The majority of intellectuals, headed by John Stuart Mill, also favored the North.[268] Thomas Carlyle, who was an uncompromising defender of the Confederacy, admitted after the war that he had "not seen into the bottom of the matter."[269] Divisions opened up, however, even in Lancashire, which was the home of the cotton textile industry and the region most directly affected. Some shipowners and brokers in Liverpool urged the government to support the Confederacy; many mill-owners and textile workers in Manchester were inclined to back the Union, despite the hardship brought by the shortage and high price of raw cotton. Once existing stocks had been drawn down, unemployment and distress followed, reaching their deepest levels at the close of 1862.[270] Manchester adapted, though with difficulty. India, encouraged by the high price of cotton, became the textile industry's largest supplier; innovative engineering improved processing techniques; large firms took charge of cotton spinning. Industrial wage-earners who supported the Union did so because they viewed the abolition of slavery as part of an international movement to improve working conditions, whether in field or factory.

Behind public opinion stood Britain's "eternal and perpetual" interests, which were decisive in confirming Russell's policy of neutrality. The leaders of the Confederacy lost sight of the fact that Britain's international connections extended far beyond the cotton states in the South. Most of Britain's exports to the United States were shipped to the North; substantial imports of corn came from the Midwest. More important still, Britain's massive investments in the United States were divided between the North and South, which helps to explain why the City of London gave strong backing to a policy of neutrality.[271] Although the war brought about a decline in British exports to the North as well as to the Confederacy, Britain was able to adjust by expanding trade elsewhere, notably with France, Germany, and India.[272] The Lancashire textile industry undoubtedly experienced considerable difficulties, but the value of Britain's foreign trade as a whole was scarcely affected. "King Cotton," it turned out, was a Pretender.

Recognition of the Confederacy would have brought war with the Union, which would have placed all of Britain's trade and investment with the United States at risk, threatened Canada and the British West Indies, and loaded a heavy burden on the budget. The political costs would also have been weighty. Relations with the United States had greatly improved since the War of 1812. No vital national interest was at stake, and the beat of the public pulse was well below intervention point.[273] Britain's priorities lay in monitoring troubling events in Europe and ensuring the security of the empire.[274] The years of the Civil War witnessed the unification of Italy in 1861, a military coup in Greece in 1862, an uprising in Poland in 1863, and war between Denmark and

Prussia in 1864. Imperial commitments included naval intervention in China to suppress the Taiping Rebellion, military operations in Afghanistan, consolidating the administration of Burma, and dealing with a rebellion in Jamaica. Important though it was, the United States still lay the edge of Britain's global vision.

These broader perceptions brought about a meeting of minds. As the war progressed, Cobden resolved the ambiguities attached to his support of the Union. He gave abolition precedence over free trade and accepted the reality of a conflict that was beyond arbitration. Like many of the textile workers he knew from his time as a manufacturer in Manchester, Cobden regarded the Union as a force for progress. As he saw it, the decisive political struggle was not between capital and labor, but between a militant landed aristocracy and what he hoped was a pacific and productive "middling sort." The future he envisaged was one in which liberal reforms would not only bring international development but also would create a harmonious global society.

The French invasion of Mexico in 1862 was an annex to the Civil War that illustrated Cobden's analysis of the forces determining world affairs with particular clarity. The American Civil War provided Napoleon III with an opportunity to intervene in another civil war, one that was under way in nearby Mexico. With the United States tearing itself apart, Napoleon saw that an alliance with an independent but subordinate Confederacy would assist his plan to restore the French Empire in the New World. The Mexican civil war, which, broadly speaking, pitted monarchist conservatives against republican progressives, ended in 1861 with the installation of Benito Juárez, leader of the liberals, as president. One of the new president's first decisions was to suspend payment on Mexico's substantial external debts, accumulated from a long series of wars, and to divert the money to internal reconstruction. Britain, France, and Spain, the leading creditors, reacted in December 1861 by mounting an expedition to enforce debt collection. At this point, the allies fell out. Britain, the largest creditor, and Spain wanted to control the customs revenue and help to revive trade. When it became clear that Napoleon intended to pursue his grandiose plans for imperial expansion, Britain and Spain withdrew. The French and their conservative Mexican allies dislodged Juárez in 1863 and installed Archduke Maximilian, the younger brother of the Emperor Franz Joseph I of Austria, as Emperor of Mexico in the following year.[275]

The improbabilities in this scheme were soon revealed. Maximilian was unable to control Mexico, and the North won the Civil War. Juárez was restored to power in 1867; French troops withdrew. Maximilian's last official engagement was with a firing squad in June of that year. In 1864,

Cobden had condemned the invasion of Mexico, which, he thought, "involves not only want of wisdom, but breach of faith."[276] From Cobden's perspective, Napoleon III, Mexican landowners, Southern planters, and Britain's still powerful landed interest were all obstacles to progress. The future lay with liberal progressives, like Lincoln, Juárez, and, following a "union of sentiment," Gladstone, even though, as Cobden acknowledged, republicanism was too alien a prospect to tempt Britain's middle classes to abandon the monarchy.[277]

The future, however, was by no means assured in 1865, when the Union prevailed over the Confederacy. Historians writing from a national perspective are sometimes inclined to attribute greater international influence to the Northern victory than is warranted. Lincoln's success undoubtedly had a direct effect on events in Mexico. Other connections, however, cannot carry the weight that has been placed on them.[278] Claims that the Civil War "changed the world," and had a particular influence on the Reform Act of 1867 in Britain, minimize the forces that were already moving in this direction in the countries concerned and underestimate the extent to which Lincoln himself drew on the Old World to remake the New. Monarchies remained in place in Britain, Austria, and Russia, to name just three of a number of leading Western states, and gained eminent recruits in Wilhelm I, who became emperor of the new Germany, and Victor Emmanuel II, who became king of the new Italy. Most of these states were deeply suspicious of progressive politics. Britain did indeed widen the franchise in 1867, but the reform had very little to do with either the Civil War or the desire for greater democracy.[279] On the contrary, the Act of 1867 was designed to protect the established order by managing what John Stuart Mill referred to as the "collective mediocrity" of the commonality.[280] British liberals regarded the Civil War less as an advertisement for democracy than as a warning of impending anarchy. The route forward, in Mill's judgment, was the one mapped by Edmund Burke, which commended itself by its record in averting both revolution and civil war.

WAR AND PEACE REVISITED

War built the United States and eventually helped to make effective independence a reality. Even where land was purchased rather than annexed, warfare followed to make occupation secure. Territorial expansion and rich resources attracted increasing numbers of settlers and provided the material basis for extending political power. Contrary to an influential view, however, war did not build the nation until after 1865. The War of

1812, like the Revolutionary War before it, was not only a war against Britain but also a civil war that was fought to determine the distribution of power within North America. Solidarity in the face of foreign aggression, though undoubtedly present, faded with the arrival of peace. Far from installing national unity, the war helped to create an "Era of Strained Feelings," in which sectional differences became more sharply delineated. The invasion of Mexico in 1846 showed how marked these differences had become. Whig opposition made it clear that the war was not one of national unity. Southern expansion for the explicit aim of adding new territories to the Union alarmed the North and set the scene for confrontations in the 1850s that were the prelude to the third Civil War fought between 1861 and 1865. This devastating conflict did finally create conditions for constructing national unity. Even so, the process, which is discussed in chapter 7, remained uncertain, protracted, and traumatic.

Federations had a distinctive role in the history of empires because they appeared to offer a solution to otherwise intractable problems of managing a wide range of constituent territories and ethnic groups. The British tried various forms of federation in the West Indies from the seventeenth century onward in an attempt to reduce costs and ensure the viability of the islands; they contemplated a federal answer to the question of how to administer the mainland colonies; they created the Canadian Confederation in 1867 to assist economic integration and provide defense. As decolonization gathered pace after World War II, Britain devised federations in Pakistan, Malaya, Central Africa, and the West Indies, either to hold large colonies together or to give small ones credibility. Once foreign rule ended, however, alliances achieved in the face of colonial oppression readily broke up, and new federations quickly foundered in the face of regional opposition. One response, typified by India and Nigeria, was to appease provincial interest groups by creating additional states within unchanged borders. A rarer option, but one that was available to the United States and a few other countries of white settlement in the nineteenth century, was to expand beyond existing frontiers.

Madison thought that a federation would make it hard for large numbers of citizens to subvert the Constitution. "The influence of factious leaders," he judged, "may kindle a flame within their particular States, but will be unable to spread a general conflagration through the other States."[281] The history of the United States after 1787 shows that Madison's imaginative prediction was mistaken.[282] Territorial incorporation within a federal arrangement encouraged political diversity, but increasing size and improved communications also enabled sectional interests to grow and combine. Strenuous efforts were made to maintain a balance among "factious leaders." A series of compromises succeeded in holding the Union together for more than half a century. Ultimately, however, sectional differences developed to the point where a "general conflagration" consumed the Union.

The record of decolonization since the Civil War has shown that newly independent states, carved from inherited imperial boundaries and often without accepted legitimacy of their own, were prime candidates for political instability. Postcolonial federations seem to have endured either where there was already sufficient homogeneity to keep provincial aspirations within constitutional limits, or where, as Madison hoped, heterogeneity was sufficiently divided to make an assault on central government futile. Canada illustrates the first case; India, a quasi-federation, the second, though neither has won immunity from other forms of unconstitutional action. The United States did not fit either category. North and South were separated by differences of ethnicity, values, and geography. A fundamental disagreement over the interpretation of the Constitution encouraged regional interests to coalesce sufficiently to form two sets of opposed states that made a contest for control of the Republic feasible. The contrast between West and East Pakistan, though more extreme, was of a similar order. Size alone, however, was insufficient to support secession: resources were essential. East Pakistan, which became Bangladesh, had a larger population than West Pakistan. The South had cotton, which underpinned its bid for independence. Biafra, the secessionist state in Nigeria, had oil. Both regions fatally overestimated the value of their main resource; both were outnumbered and outgunned. King Oil, like King Cotton, promised far more than could be delivered.

Wars of incorporation accompanying territorial expansion were common elsewhere in the Anglo-world, as settler societies seized large tracts of land from indigenous people. No other settler states, however, fought among themselves to the extent that citizens of the United States did. Not even the Anglo-South African War of 1899–1902 came close to matching the death toll of the Civil War. Assertive territorial expansion qualified as being imperialist because it aimed at dispossession and dominance. An imperialism of intent, however, produced different outcomes. Settlers within the British Empire acted as an advance guard extending the area under British rule and limiting the rights of the indigenous people they controlled. The United States was in a different position. After 1783, the Republic was engaged in strengthening its base, not in extending the British Empire. Expansion had the potential to create an independent territorial empire on the North American continent. In practice, the resulting structure reproduced states with broadly equal rights under a federal system of government, even though statehood generally followed a period of administration directed by Washington.

Native Americans were deprived of their land and rights, as were indigenous societies elsewhere, and successive governments experimented with policies of assimilation and association in attempting to deal with the resulting inequalities. Nevertheless, it is hard to argue that the United States created a continental empire in the nineteenth century. Characterizations of the polity need to take account not only of intent but also of scale, and Native Americans represented only a tiny fraction of the total population. This conclusion is not to be read as an implied defense of imperialism. States other than empires can violate human rights and perpetuate gross inequalities, and habitually do so. It is rather to suggest the need to pause before equating imperialist expansion on the North American continent with the formation of the type of territorial empire discussed in this study.

The long and almost continuous tradition of warfare that is central to the history of the United States provided opportunities for applying military energies to patriotic purposes. The Civil War and the period of Reconstruction put more guns into circulation; the application of industrial techniques to the production of weapons reduced their cost and increased their effectiveness.[283] Martial values became embedded in the concept of liberty in the United States to a degree that made the use of force to advance national values seem natural and therefore normal. Slavery, segregation, and the "Indian Wars" inculcated attitudes of racial supremacy that made it easy to present the imperialism of 1898 as a national duty expressed through the civilizing mission.

Yet, there were clear limits to these tendencies before the Spanish-American War. William H. Seward, the influential Secretary of State between 1861 and 1869, and the most prominent expansionist holding office before the 1890s, viewed the purchase of Alaska in 1867 as a step toward realizing much larger ambitions, starting with neighboring British Columbia and encompassing Mexico, Hawai'i, Panama, the Danish West Indies, and points beyond. These plans remained on the drawing board. Congress agreed to purchase Alaska only reluctantly and after considerable delay. Opponents dubbed the acquisition "Seward's folly"; the name stuck.[284] In 1871, the United States formally abandoned its long-standing ambition to acquire or otherwise absorb Canada.

The best known and the most dramatic episode of overseas expansion was Commodore Matthew Perry's bombardment of the port of Tokyo in 1852, which opened Japan to outside influences. Perry followed this action with a recommendation that the United States should annex Formosa.[285] President Franklin Pierce and Congress, however, were uninterested in acquiring the island, which they regarded as a costly irrelevance. Similarly, President Ulysses Grant's proposal to annex Santo Domingo in 1870–1871 ran into insuperable opposition from anti-annexationists, even though the local *caudillos* had invited the United States to purchase the island. Schemes for taking over Cuba also had a long history that suggests steadiness of purpose. None of them, however, succeeded. Aside from Spain's opposition, sectional divisions within the United States made it impossible to form a united front on the issue.

Territorial expansion undoubtedly helped to shape predispositions that were expressed in the 1890s, when the United States founded an overseas empire. Predispositions, however, were insufficient causes of actions. The danger of emphasizing long-run continuities, or the "years of preparation," and treating them as culminating in the war with Spain is that it diminishes the distinctiveness of different events and risks eliding causes that require separate appraisal.[286] As chapter 8 will show, the drama of 1898 was not simply a contingent consequence of long-standing impulses.

Placed in the widest perspective, the series of conflicts that culminated in the Civil War were extensions of the contest between conservatives and progressives that also drove European politics during the first half of the nineteenth century. Reform sometimes issued from opposed motives. Alexander II ended serfdom in 1861 to save the monarchy; Lincoln liberated slaves in 1865 to save the Republic. As Lincoln drew inspiration from Mazzini and Garibaldi, so the Confederacy represented the conservative forces that mounted counterrevolutions in Europe after 1848. Placed in the longest perspective, the Civil War was the ultimate resolution in the United States of the crisis that overtook Western military-fiscal states at the close of the eighteenth century. In 1861, the North aimed to forge a nation-state, whereas the South hoped to establish a slave empire. Had the Confederacy won the war and realized its ambition, the resulting polity would have been imperial in substance as well as in intent.

In thwarting this ambition, the defeat of the Confederacy also destroyed the neocolonial relationship that bound Britain and the South. Henry Carey, though admittedly a partisan commentator, saw the connection very clearly, even if he exaggerated it: "to British free trade it is," he wrote in 1865, "that we stand indebted for the present Civil War."[287] Until then, Britain was the "indispensable nation." The former colonial power was the main source of external finance, the principal foreign market, and the defender of last resort. Britain's demand for cotton supported the wealth and political dominance of the South; its conversion to abolition helped to undermine the edifice. What Victor Hugo called "that malady of progress, civil war," obliged both parties to rethink their long-standing relationship after 1865.[288]

PART II

MODERNITY
AND
IMPERIALISM
1865–1914

CHAPTER 6

UNEVEN DEVELOPMENT AND IMPERIAL EXPANSION

"THE EARTH, RESTIVE, CONFRONTS A NEW ERA"[1]

Walt Whitman was one of many notable commentators who realized that the transformation occurring around him was not only unprecedented but also unbounded.[2] The revolution he observed was principally the liberation of the "common man" from subservience. Prominent figures elsewhere were preoccupied with the conversion of agricultural to industrial economies. Others still, focused on the way dynastic states were being molded into nation-states. All of them sensed, with Whitman, that the changes they saw unfolding in the second half of the nineteenth century had the potential to straddle the world, and that there might eventually be, as he put it, "one heart to the globe." These profound economic, political, and social developments can be analyzed from a variety of standpoints. The approach taken here treats them as marking the transition from proto-globalization to modern globalization.[3] By extension, imperial expansion, which reached its height at the close of the century, can be seen as an offshoot of the process. Empire-building was an exercise in compulsory globalization.

The rivalry between conservatives and reformers, made militant by the French Revolution, ran through the nineteenth century before culminating in another revolutionary war, that of 1914–1918. Put in the most general terms, the contest pitted the representatives of the land against those of the town. The novelty of this age-old competition was that, by 1918, the land had lost. Before about 1850, as chapter 2 showed, the balance between contending interests in Europe still favored the land. Military-fiscal states were reconstructed after the French Wars; progressive reform movements were held in check. In the second half of the century, the forces thrusting modern globalization forward began to overtake traditional sources of wealth and power. Incomes derived from industry, finance, and commercial services surpassed those from agriculture. Fiscal unity increased the resources available to central governments. Borrowing costs fell; money became available to fund welfare spending and integrate new social groups into new relationships in what were often new nations. The extension of voting rights eroded the established basis of political authority and imposed parliamentary controls on monarchical predilections. The process of transformation was protracted and incomplete, even by 1914. The social upheaval it entailed far exceeded the calming effects of increased welfare expenditure. Discord between capital and labor, as well as between town and country, threatened to destabilize the transition from within. Rivalry among states at different stages of transition menaced it from without.

The forces unleashed by this version of modernity spread their influence across the world during the second half of the century. States, economies, and cultures everywhere were affected; some were transformed. Western expansion, propelled as much by ideas as by technology, took both pacific and assertive forms. Imperialism was a particular species of this "great transformation" that was imposed either by military force or by reducing the options open to recipients. The outcome was an imperialism of result that realized the declarations of intent made earlier in the century, when the penetrative power of the West was still limited. In some cases, the upsurge of assertive expansion incorporated new territories and old states into a formal empire; in others, it led to the exercise of informal sway, or "soft" power. Both strategies were means of securing the degree of integration that the shift to modernity required and of managing the strains it inevitably generated. As Western nation-states extended their influence across the world, growing tensions between interlocking empires, antique and modern, became critical points of international conflict. Satellites were swept up in the contest; polities that had relied on isolation to guard their independence found that no hiding place was beyond reach.

The transition from one form of globalization to another was uneven. As there were leaders and laggards in economic development and the formation of nation-states, so there were early-start and late-start imperial powers.[4] Britain stood at one end of a continuum as an example of a country at an advanced stage of development that had extensive international commitments and powerful economic motives for expansion. Italy, at the other end, represented late developers with little international involvement beyond Europe and a preoccupation with nation-building that gave imperial aspirations a predominantly political character. Britain, the superpower of the time, led the way at home and abroad. Its development program set the standard for the ambitions of other modernizers; its justificatory ideology provided norms for prospective imperial powers; its techniques of colonial management were blueprints that were envied, copied, or adapted. The view that Britain was in some sense "in decline" from the late nineteenth century needed revising. Its economic dominance was challenged but not toppled, and in 1914, no rival came close to matching the scale of its territorial empire or the extent of its informal influence.

The discussion that follows prepares the way for the analysis of new imperialism in the United States that occupies chapters 7, 8, and 9. Generally speaking, the literature on the United States makes little reference to the admittedly vast library on European imperialism; specialists on Europe complement the omission by excluding consideration of the territories in the Caribbean and Pacific annexed by the United States after the Spanish-American War of 1898. The argument developed in the course of the next three chapters is that current explanations of U.S. imperialism at this time are truncated because they fail to recognize that the Republic shared both cause and chronology with other members of the Western imperial club.

It was at this time that the terms "modernist" and "modernity" entered the arts and social sciences, and the label "modern" was attached to the world that was emerging in the late nineteenth century. For Charles Baudelaire, writing in 1860, modernity was the "transient, the fleeting, the contingent," inspired by the hurry and artificiality of city life.[5] Walt Whitman, writing at the close of the Civil War, envisaged a broader, progressive movement:

> Years of the modern! Years of the unperform'd!
> Your horizon rises—I see it parting away for more august dramas;
> I see not America only—not only Liberty's nation, but other nations preparing;
> I see tremendous entrances and exits—I see new combinations—I see the solidarity of races;
> I see that force advancing with irresistible power on the world's stage.[6]

"VIA PECUNIA": THE ROAD TO MODERN GLOBALIZATION[7]

The full potential of the global developments Britain had initiated was realized after 1850. Shortly before then, François-René de Chateaubriand had already envisaged a future shaped by new forms of communication, "which will have made distances disappear," and when "it will not only be commodities that travel, but also ideas which will have wings."[8] Far-reaching technological and institutional innovations transformed the means of production, the means of distribution, and the means of destruction, and greatly enlarged the capacity of the state. Unprecedented flows of trade and finance connected industrial centers in Western Europe to regions specializing in agricultural and mineral products. By 1900, the classic division of labor first advocated by Adam Smith had integrated the world to a degree previously only imagined.[9]

Factory production created a mass market for manufactured goods. Industrialization and urbanization generated new social formations and new political organizations to represent them. Population growth supplied cheap labor for factories at home and emigrants for global settlement. In the century after 1815, approximately 50 million migrants left Europe to start new lives overseas. Improvements in medical knowledge increased the survival rate of European soldiers and settlers in the tropics. Railroads, steamships, telegraphs, and submarine cables reduced the cost of moving goods, people, and ideas; the emergence of an international press delivered "news from nowhere" to the world.[10] The mechanization of armed force cut the costs of coercion by introducing weapons that could fire rapidly, repeatedly, and accurately. Fiscal unity eliminated provincial patrimonies, increased the tax revenues of the central government, and signaled the shift from military-fiscal states to those capable of combining warfare with welfare.[11] The first international organizations sponsored by governments made their appearance in the 1860s to coordinate postal, telegraphic, and health services.[12] By the late nineteenth century, the Western powers commanded a degree of penetrative power that made territorial expansion much easier and far cheaper than it had been at the start of the century.[13]

The Great Exhibition held in London in 1851 was the first large-scale, truly international event of its kind. Its successor, which was held in 1862, drew six million visitors and attracted exhibits from thirty-six countries. The displays included Charles Babbage's analytical engine, the use of *caoutchouc* to produce rubber, and an introduction to the Bessemer process for manufacturing steel. Tennyson's poem, written for the opening ceremony, must count as one of the first odes to globalization:

> O ye, the wise who think, the wise who reign,
> From growing commerce loose her latest chain,
> And let the fair white-winged peacemaker fly,

To happy havens under all the sky,
And mix the seasons and the golden hours,
Till each man find his own in all men's good,
And all men work in noble brotherhood,
And ruling by obeying nature's powers,
And gathering all the fruits of earth and crown'd with all her
    flowers.[14]

The crisis years of the 1840s had receded. The economies of Europe
had revived; the tensions generated by nationalism lay in the future. In
mid-century, Tennyson reflected a degree of optimism that joined the
enlightened self-interest of Adam Smith and the free-trade idealism of
Richard Cobden to produce a vision of a liberal world order that would
deliver prosperity and peace.[15] Karl Marx considered the exhibition of
1851 to be a crass example of commodity fetishism. Tennyson thought he
had better information:

And praise th' invisible universal Lord,
Who lets once more in peace the nations meet

Just beyond the expanding reality made possible by Western technical
mastery lay the volcanic exploits of Jules Verne's *A Journey to the Centre
of the Earth* (1864) and the submarine adventures of *Twenty Thousand
Leagues under the Sea* (1869). By 1873, Verne was able to send a resourceful English gentleman, Phileas Fogg, *Around the World in Eighty Days*,
notwithstanding delays caused by errors, accidents, and the machinations of unfriendly parties. From the 1870s, world fairs became regular
features of the international scene as the leading countries jostled for opportunities to advertise their scientific and commercial achievements.[16]
Standard displays set modern wonders against "primitive" cultures,
which the organizers represented in a manner designed to exceed stereotyped expectations. The perils and promise of an emerging brave new
world conjured political fantasies into virtual existence: Samuel Butler
expressed a cheerless view of the dehumanizing consequences of technological progress in *Erewhon* (1872); William Morris offered an alternative romantic vision of a socialist utopia in *News From Nowhere* (1890).[17]
    Economists, too, participated in the growing mood of optimism after
1850 and deferred their second thoughts until after World War I. Marxists dissented, but their judgment was increasingly challenged by what
became known in radical circles as "bourgeois" economics. The technological advances that brought railroads to India in 1852 and refrigeration
to New Zealand thirty years later also expanded the horizons of a new

generation of liberal economists who disputed the orthodox claim that there was a long-run tendency for profit rates to fall. Setbacks, in their view, were temporary features of the business cycle, which itself was an integral part of the new, industrializing world. Real wages, similarly, ceased to be treated as if they were a function of Malthusian constraints. Progress was not just possible, but likely. The poor were present in abundance, but not necessarily in perpetuity.

The growing band of optimists codified and gave rigor to the concept of free trade, which was based on the fundamental principle that prices should be determined by market forces acting without government interference.[18] The idea proved powerful and durable. In the 1980s, the World Bank summarized its version of the doctrine in the phrase "getting prices right." Adam Smith had laid out the advantages of specialization, Ricardo developed the theory of comparative advantage, Cobden turned the concept into practical politics and made it a moral imperative. Having discarded the Corn Laws and other mercantilist restrictions, Britain had a strong incentive to persuade its trading partners to agree to complementary measures.[19] At the close of the century, Alfred Marshall applied the principles of neoclassical economics to uphold free trade at a time when tariff reformers were attacking orthodoxy.[20] By then, God had parted from Mammon. Christian political economy, which had been so influential during the first half of the century, had been dethroned. Economics, so its proponents claimed, had become a science.

The expansion of trade in the 1850s and 1860s created conditions that encouraged international tariff levels to fall.[21] As increasing opportunities appeared in the British market, other developing countries reduced their tariffs, too. Additionally, the Foreign Office negotiated reciprocal treaties that created a maze of specific commodity agreements across the European continent.[22] Richard Cobden's career as an unofficial diplomat touched its highest point in 1860, when Britain and France signed the Cobden-Chevalier Treaty, which Cobden regarded as a blow struck on behalf of pacific business interests against the institutional structures supporting militarist aristocracies.[23] The year 1867, when the Reform Act in Britain and the Reconstruction Act in the United States became law, was one for liberals on both sides of the Atlantic to savor.[24] Democracy, it seemed, could succeed; high culture could be diffused without standards being lowered.

Economic historians have added precision to these generalizations. The troubled 1840s were followed by renewed expansion in the 1850s and 1860s. Assessments of the years of the most intense imperial rivalry between 1870 and 1914 confirm that the period experienced "unprecedented" increases in wealth and incomes, as measured by Gross Domestic Product (GDP) throughout Western Europe and the United States.[25] If the GDP of colonies is added to that of the metropoles to produce an "imperial GDP," the British economy was the largest in the developed world in 1913. The United States followed; Germany, Russia, and France were some way behind. Since there was also a considerable increase in Europe's population as a result of declining infant mortality, the growth in GDP indicates that productivity (output per head) was rising, too. This development was associated with a broad shift away from agriculture and into industry and services, and with an increasing degree of economic integration. Recent research has confirmed the general trend that impressed Norman Angell in 1910: falling transaction costs eroded price differences; migration to centers of demand initiated a movement toward equalizing real wages; interest rates began to come into line; bond spreads fell. Modern globalization had arrived.[26]

Aggregate trends masked considerable variety. The growth of GDP in northwest Europe exceeded that of southern Europe (including France), which in turn was ahead of eastern Europe.[27] Although differences in per capita GDP tended to narrow as the period advanced, the gap remained substantial: in 1913 Italy's per capita GDP was still only about half that of Britain. Growth rates were correlated with sectoral change: early-start countries that shifted out of agriculture and into industry and services did better than late-starters, principally because the value added through agricultural activities was relatively low.[28] Britain, where only 12 percent of the labor force was in agriculture in 1913, led the field; eastern Europe brought up the rear.[29] When development economics became a recognized specialty in the 1940s, the first countries to be designated as "underdeveloped" were not in the tropics, but in southeast Europe.

Trends presented here as retrospective reconstructions preoccupied the great thinkers of the prewar era. Karl Marx famously identified class conflict in the modern world, though his main interest was in the struggle between the bourgeoisie and the proletariat that lay ahead. It was Cobden who pinpointed the contemporary battle between a militant landed aristocracy and a pacific middle class, and Herbert Spencer who subsequently elaborated the distinction and placed it in the context of "the survival of the fittest." The fittest, in Max Weber's view, were the modernizers who had emerged from "tradition" and were busy shaping the reformed, rational, bureaucratic states he saw appearing around him. Gaetano Mosca and Vilfredo Pareto were concerned with the management of Weber's new states at a time when landowners, who had long monopolized political power, were losing their authority and legitimacy to new, unstable elites. Robert Michels, reflecting on the consequences of elite rule in a new democratic era, resolved the problem of governance to his own satisfaction by discerning an "iron law" of oligarchy, which, he held, would eventually overtake all elected authorities. Nevertheless, the "feudal residues" Weber had identified were not quite finished. They were capable of striking back and did so, according to Joseph Schumpeter, during World War I.

The intellectuals who produced these sweeping assessments were concerned with the adverse consequences of the new order as well as with its progressive potential. Doubts multiplied as the century advanced. Like the sorcerer's apprentice in Goethe's poem, progressives on both sides of the Atlantic realized that they had helped to create an enchanted broom with a will of its own. John Stuart Mill, a central figure in the reform movement, pronounced himself "startled" by Tocqueville's warning that "the tyranny of the majority" could be "more efficient than any despot."[30] Emerson agreed; Thomas Arnold needed no persuasion; James Stephen thought that coercion was required to keep disruptive forces in check. At the close of the century, Brooks Adams, peering across the United States from his redoubt in Boston, recoiled both from the toiling urban masses and from the "usurious mind" that had produced them. Divisions between capital and labor grew as industrialization spread. Concentrations of population made political mobilization easier; levels of literacy improved; the scope of the print media widened. The extension of the franchise posed the question of how to control the emancipated "masses" and their worrying bouts of irrational behavior.

The ultimate danger was that the multiplying demos might sweep away the institutions that held society together. Ill-informed public opinion could threaten free speech; ignorance could destroy high culture; property rights, the bulwark of social order, could be imperiled. An influential segment of the Western literati added to their reputations by recommending ways of escaping these unwelcome prospects. In Britain, Thomas Carlyle put his faith in heroic figures to control the chaos of modern society; Thomas Arnold set out to train a new generation of Christian gentlemen who would guard the flame of tradition; William Morris and John Ruskin attempted to create an alternative culture by reinventing a medieval world of Gothic art, architecture, and literature. Equally concerned imitators in the United States reproduced Gothic styles; enthusiasts in Maryland organized pageants and jousting tournaments. Other members of the intelligentsia remained at their desks devising ways of averting what they saw as impending disaster. Politicians cast about eagerly and sometimes desperately for ideas about how to prevent rapid socioeconomic change from destroying political stability and social privilege.[31]

"O, MY BROTHERS, LOVE YOUR COUNTRY"[32]

Nation-building seemed to be a large part of the solution to the problems of transition. Giuseppe Mazzini's invocation, addressed to workers in Milan in 1848, held out the prospect of realizing democratic principles through the agency of the nation-state. Luminaries and politicians elsewhere in Europe also took to the new idea of nationality, even if their motives were often pragmatic rather than idealistic. They, too, regarded the nation-state as the means of drawing together the restless and often rootless social forces arising by population growth, industry, and urbanization. Nationalism was an instrument that united disparate social elements that might otherwise have felt alienated and abandoned. It did so by appealing to a sense of ethnic unity that rose above class, gender, religion, and region. Ethnic unity itself was scarcely a new phenomenon. Historically, however, it had found political expression through hierarchical, typically dynastic, agencies. The novelty of the nineteenth century, as Benjamin Constant saw in 1819, was to link collective identities to various forms of representative government.[33] Self-determination, however, was not an exclusive concept. Rights claimed for ethnic groups coexisted with, and gained from, a sense of transnational unity derived from universal principles and disseminated through increasingly effective channels of communication.

Elements of the old order still had important parts to play in validating the new. A conservative style of romantic nationalism looked to the past more than to the future. National-industrial states adapted the monarchies that emerged from the French Wars by elevating them above politics, where they could be seen but less often heard, and also aligned themselves with the prevailing branch of Christianity to secure spiritual endorsement. They harnessed new technologies of communication to amplify their claims to lead the chosen ethnie through the turmoil of the times. They competed with liberals to promote the professional study of history and to direct it into codified versions of the past that suited their purposes.

Political parties found themselves compelled to invent ways of appealing to newly enfranchised groups that lay beyond constituencies long bound by privilege. Most observers, at least outside Austria and Russia, realized that there could be no return to exclusive aristocratic rule, or to what Mill called dogma and superstition. The way forward, as seen from on high, lay in adapting mediocrity to elite rule. Educational programs aimed to moderate the materialistic instincts of the masses and instill respect for quality.[34] Issues that cut across class and regional divisions were elevated into matters of national importance. Political outreach extended the appeal of traditional parties. Conservatives presented themselves as the standard-bearers of order and national unity in an attempt to win voters who feared socialist leveling policies. Liberals responded by devising ameliorative forms of capitalism that charted a middle course between conservatism and radicalism.[35]

Nevertheless, the stresses imposed by rapid socioeconomic change and intensified by bouts of economic depression found expression in the resurgence of radical political movements during the last quarter of the century. Rural populism, though a spent force in Britain, gained visibility and varying degrees of vehemence in France, Germany, Russia, the United States, Canada, Australia, and New Zealand, which still depended heavily on agricultural exports. Urban activists also made their mark. Trade unions increased in size and assertiveness. Marxist influences were prominent in Germany and France; the British Labour Party was founded in 1900; the Socialist Party of America in the following year. Radicalism became fully globalized. It was not only capital that "knew no frontiers": trade unions exchanged advice across borders on matters such as organization, funding, and tactics.[36] "Anarchists," later called "terrorists," established networks that enabled their agents to exchange information, techniques, and personnel around the globe.[37]

The authorities in Europe responded by creating countervailing organizations of their own. The Metropolitan Police in Britain formed a Special Branch in 1883, initially to deal with Irish terrorists and subsequently to handle other militant dissidents, including suffragettes. President Theodore Roosevelt incorporated the long-standing but still embryonic Secret Service into a new organization, the Federal Bureau of Investigation (FBI), in 1908. As trade unions and anarchists became transnational, so too did the new security state, which formed connections that later became Interpol.[38] Amelioration accompanied suppression. Remedial programs created an international market for progressive policies.[39] Progressives in the United States borrowed ideas of municipal reform from Britain, town planning from France, social insurance from Germany, and welfare from Australia and New Zealand.[40] A few schemes found their way into policy; most were rejected, though some reappeared in the 1930s in Franklin Roosevelt's New Deal. Despite irreconcilable differences, Right and Left converged on the belief that the problems of the day called for increased state action. Bismarck, the conservative, and

Giolitti, the liberal, had very different views on entitlement, but both agreed that government intervention was necessary, whether to assist the development of business or to alleviate social distress.[41] Reform, though unpalatable to some, was judged to be preferable to the socialist alternative, which was unacceptable to the many.

Politicians and opinion leaders searching for ways to defeat socialism fastened upon the notion of race, which became the "big idea" of the time in Europe, the United States, and other countries of white settlement.[42] The issue recommended itself: it provided a means of consolidating national unity by appealing above (or below) class, region, and religion; and it elevated the national ethnie beyond all comparators, especially those soon to be labeled "primitive" peoples. Theories of racial attributes, though commonly assigned to Darwin, had earlier, independent origins.[43] The popularized idea of the survival of the fittest derived from Spencer, who was strongly opposed to war and imperialism, which he regarded as retarding what he referred to, approvingly, as "the brotherhood of nations."[44] The theory came in different forms. One version held that race was immutable but that character was adjustable and could be replenished, if drained, by being tested and honed on frontiers where the civilized world met the primitive. Another variation of the big idea held that the hierarchy of races had not been fixed at the creation and could be reordered, in which case the currently dominant Anglo-Saxons needed to control lesser peoples while they could, and use the opportunity to restore their own vitality.

The doctrine of Anglo-Saxonism was the most commanding of the pan-national racial theories.[45] The idea of an Anglo-Saxon race had long been in circulation, but it reached its highest point on the scale of ideological appeal in the late nineteenth century, when its assumptions were treated as unquestioned facts throughout the Anglo-world and had particular resonance in the United States. According to the theory, Anglo-Saxons constituted a vigorous, innovative race that had emerged from Teutonic forests at a time too distant to be properly researched (or disproved).[46] Gifted, long-sighted observers could nevertheless discern the distinctive qualities that enabled Anglo-Saxons to prosper while weaker races fell back in the evolutionary struggle. Anglo-Saxons were superior in physical endowment, mental ability, and moral probity. They were instinctive advocates of liberty and possessed the organizational talents needed to convert principle into practice. These attributes elevated them to a level of civilization so unprecedented that it qualified them to improve the world. Other races had inferior characteristics: Russians were naturally inclined toward despotism; Germans had fallen from Teutonic heights and were slipping into autocratic rule; "Latinate" peoples were lazy and corrupt. Others still, beyond the European pale, suffered from a combination of all these debilitating characteristics.

The Anglo-Saxon version of race theory found authoritative expression in the work of James (later Lord) Bryce, the jurist and polymath, who set out his thoughts on Anglo-American relations in two weighty volumes, entitled *The American Commonwealth*, which were published in 1888.[47] Bryce held that people were stratified by race and ordered by rank. Anglo-Saxons were self-evidently the superior race; the elite among them needed to take command of the populace. When Frederick Jackson Turner, a Midwesterner, struck a blow against the urban northeast by claiming that the frontier had formed the rural values that shaped the nation, Bryce countered that it was Teutonic qualities, imported across the Atlantic, that had molded the environment.[48] Bryce's teaching appealed to the powerful on both sides of the Atlantic and supplied ammunition for use against rural insurgents, urban malcontents, and political dissidents. Boston Brahmins, like Brooks Adams, took up the cause and placed it in a wide-ranging account of the rise and fall of civilizations that ended with an appeal for a joint Anglo-American mission to save the world.[49] By the close of the century, residual Anglophobia in the United States had been joined by what Albert Dicey, the distinguished constitutional expert, called "Americomania."[50] The spirit of reconciliation extended well beyond diplomatic and intellectual circles. There was widespread public mourning in the United States when Queen Victoria died in 1901; Britain reciprocated when President McKinley was assassinated a few months later.[51]

Anglo-Saxons, however, also worried that their superiority might not endure. Theories of degeneration gained popularity and credibility during the last quarter of the century.[52] Their pseudo-scientific basis gave them authority; their predictions activated elemental fears. According to the "law of entropy," all "civilizations," including the Anglo-Saxons, were doomed to lose energy and be overtaken by more vigorous races. Detailed research proceeded to identify inferior classes as well as inferior races. Scientific studies purported to show that low intellect, criminal behavior, poverty, and general fecklessness were congenitally determined.[53] Urbanization was severing the ties that bound rural societies together; miscegenation was diluting racial purity. Gibbon's barbarian hordes were again swamping the civilized world, even as the moral order atrophied the hands of those charged with the task of repelling them. Put another way, globalization was mixing people as never before and challenging politicians to devise new ways of creating identities that could be attached to the state.

Those given to anxiety could turn to Brooks Adams, Benjamin Kidd, and Charles Pearson, whose versions of race theory achieved considerable popularity in the 1890s. Brooks Adams, whose pessimistic disposition found expression in his obscure, quasi-Hegelian concept of "cosmic dynamics," traced shifting energy levels from China to Britain and on to the United States, which had the obligation to lead the struggle to survive as the fittest.[54] Kidd held that a national effort was needed to avoid degeneration, and conjured up the prospect of China dominating the world. If his forecast caused concern in London, it was welcomed in Beijing, where the embattled Qing dynasty sponsored translations of his work.[55] Pearson was an Australian of British origin who used his considerable knowledge of the United States to help frame legislation that eventually became known as the "white Australia" policy.[56] His message that the white race was losing ground to yellow and black races, and would eventually be overtaken, resonated across the Anglo-Saxon world. Gladstone was impressed; Roosevelt was converted.

Hope was not abandoned. Not all theorists believed that Anglo-Saxon dominance would be lost, and those who did allowed for a lengthy timetable. Meanwhile, there was work to be done either to avert or postpone decline. Eugenics became an international enterprise promoted by intellectuals who were intent on preserving the strength of the master race.[57] Frances Galton, the Victorian polymath, invented the term in 1883; Charles B. Davenport became its leading exponent in the United States. Davenport's views on the need to maintain the purity of the Anglo-Saxon "germ plasm" influenced the activities of the Immigration Restriction League (1894) and provided scholarly support for laws permitting forced sterilization.[58] If scientists could manage nature, politicians could more easily control nurture, providing they were given the necessary authority.

The process of cultivating ethnic solidarity within established, disputed, and contiguous borders ensured that nation-building in Europe was inherently assertive. As warfare became industrialized, participation in international affairs, whether for acquisition or survival, called for big government and extensive fiscal resources. Central control of tax revenues opened the way to the large-scale use of force. Warfare, embellished with philosophical and religious justifications, became not only the means of nation-building but also the ultimate expression of nationality. The drive for Italian independence prompted even Giuseppe Verdi to douse his habitual moderation in patriotic zeal. When prompted in

1848 by his librettist, Francesco Maria Piave, for an overdue score, Verdi replied: "You talk to me about music! What has got into you? Do you think that I want to bother myself now with notes, with sounds? There cannot be any music welcome to Italian ears in 1848 except the music of the cannon!"[59]

In the 1840s, Mazzini had already distinguished between patriotism and nationalism and warned of the aggressive qualities of the latter. In the 1880s, with abundant evidence to hand, Nietzsche issued his disquieting judgment that the beginning of everything great was soaked in blood, and predicted that the cult of the nation-state would drive Europe into a new form of total war.[60] Others continued to place their faith in the triumph of cosmopolitan values. In 1910, Norman Angell produced his influential analysis, *The Great Illusion*, which updated Cobden's belief in the benign consequences of free trade.[61] Angell emphasized the extent to which international finance had come to dominate the globalized world of the early twentieth century. Financial integration had reached the point where war would damage all parties. Conflict, accordingly, had become irrational, though not inconceivable. Shortly afterward, the irrational element, which Schumpeter identified with atavistic social forces, carried Europe into World War I. Belief in progress fell in the trenches. Cobden's expectation that expanded commerce would deliver Kant's perpetual peace retreated into obscurity. In 1915, Thomas Hardy expressed more hope than confidence that fundamental human values would survive "The Breaking of Nations":

> Yet this will go onward the same
> Though dynasties pass.[62]

By the end of the war, hope had ebbed. As Voltaire's *Candide* exchanged optimism for pessimism, so too a generation of pundits added to postwar miseries by predicting the inexorable decay of what had formerly been known as the civilized world. Oswald Spengler, historian, philosopher, and Prussian nationalist, caught the mood of the moment in *The Decline of the West*, which was published in 1918.[63] Western civilization had passed its peak. The racial energy that had carried it forward had dissipated; its compass was set for Valhalla. New, vigorous, 'colored' nations would fill the void. In 1920, H. G. Wells reflected on a world that had been bound closely together by economic and technical forces but torn apart by nationalism. For Wells, nationalism was an irrational force that was incompatible with the trend toward globalization: it "must follow the tribal gods to limbo," or make way for a federal world government.[64]

This was a thought too far: the "tribal gods" remained in place and continued to claim their sacrificial victims during the twentieth century.

THE GREAT DEFLATION

Adverse economic developments appeared at the moment Western political leaders were trying to create a sense of national unity that would draw different ethnic and regional groups together and overcome, or at least mute, emerging class antagonisms. The balance between economic change and political stability was already unsteady when material developments arising from what Marx called "commodity fetishism" escaped the guiding hand of Providence during the last quarter of the century. Policy-makers had gambled that the benefits of free trade and the gold standard would encourage development, raise living standards, and ease the transition to national-industrial societies. Britain's exceptional role in promoting international investment helped to make the pound sterling the preferred international currency and provided a powerful motive for encouraging other states to adopt the gold standard. In the 1870s, the major European countries and the United States followed Britain's example, even as they retreated from free trade.[65] By 1912, more than forty countries, including numerous colonies, were members of the gold-standard club. The gold standard helped to create an integrated international economic order. Countries that agreed to make their currencies convertible into gold at a fixed rate reduced fluctuations in exchange rates and improved their credit ratings.[66] Sound credit gave access to the London capital market, which was a vital aid to developing countries that had yet to reach the stage where their own capital resources could meet their needs.

The discipline of the gold standard prevented what would later be termed deficit spending, whereby governments could print money to fund favored projects or to reduce debt payments. Membership of the gold-standard club gave foreign investors and merchants confidence that their property was secure, that debts would be repaid in sound money, and that financial risks attached to long-term development projects would be minimized. Policy-makers did not foresee that the gold standard would also be inflexible at times of depression and deflation, and that abiding by the "rules of the game" could contribute to social distress and political instability. "Quantitative easing," as it is termed today, was not on the menu. In the late nineteenth century, a long, if also discontinuous, economic depression sharpened conflicts between capital and labor, between creditors and debtors, and between town and country. Embryonic, semi-united nation-states came under intense pressure to hold alienated and potentially anarchic segments of society together. The outburst of imperialism that reshaped much of the world at the close of the century was a dramatic expression of these fears, forcefully expressed.

The case must now be stated with some care. Historians used to refer to "the Great Depression of 1873–96" as if it were a coherent period characterized by widespread gloom and almost unrelieved doom. Research in economic history has shown that the depression was neither as continuous nor as comprehensive as was once thought, and that living standards in Europe as a whole rose over the longer period to 1914.[67] As historians have disaggregated the period and dispensed with its traditional name, economists studying what is known as "the classical gold standard" have given the years between 1870 and 1913 a degree of unity that obscures the diversity suggested by other indices of economic performance.[68] The classificatory difficulties arising from different specialized inquiries need to be seen in a broad context. There remains general agreement that the rate of growth of world trade slowed during the last quarter of the nineteenth century, which saw periods of falling prices, mounting unemployment, and rising rural and urban discontent throughout Western Europe and the United States.[69] Contemporaries had no doubt that they were living through a time of depression. The term itself came into widespread use during the last quarter of the century: Presidents Grant and Hayes used it in expressing their concern for the health of the U.S. economy in the 1870s; Lord Salisbury set up a *Royal Commission on the Depression in Trade and Industry* in 1885 to study the problem in Britain; academic and trade journals commented on it regularly; Thorstein Veblen imported it into his *Theory of Business Enterprise*, published in 1904.

National traditions of historical scholarship have also obscured some of the international connections that made the depression such a dramatic expression of globalization.[70] Specialists on European history are inclined to begin with the banking panic in Vienna in 1873; historians of the United States start with the failure of Jay Cooke and the Northern Pacific Railroad in the same year. From the perspective of the present chapter, however, it is the connection between these events that needs emphasizing.[71] The banking crisis in Vienna followed from the collapse of a land boom in the newly formed Austro-Hungarian Empire. The inability to service loans contracted to purchase land was directly related to falling export earnings in Russia and Central Europe following competition from wheat imports from the United States. A surge in imports into Britain, a major consumer, had a particularly damaging effect on continental producers. The Bank of England, effectively the lender of last resort, responded to the credit crisis by raising its lending rate. Tighter credit then led to the downfall of Jay Cooke and other banks in the United States that had issued loans on excessively optimistic assumptions about the strength of future export earnings. In this respect, the crisis of 1873 was similar to those that had occurred earlier in the century.[72] The difference was that free trade and improved international connections had increased the number of participants and the scale of their activities. "Irrational exuberance" had long been an ingredient of financial bubbles. In the late nineteenth century, it became a global phenomenon.

The period between 1873 and 1896 did have one clear, unifying feature: it was a time of deflation.[73] World prices fell, partly because of improvements in productivity, and partly because the money supply was constrained by a shortage of gold following the adoption of the gold standard. The deflation of the time had some benign features: rising output combined with productivity gains benefited consumers by cutting prices. There were malign outcomes too, which were expressed in a sequence of financial crises, periodic bouts of depression, and widespread indebtedness. Some comparative research has suggested that, on the whole and allowing for regional variations, the gains outweighed the losses: rising output and falling prices were consistent with a measure of real growth in GDP during the last quarter of the century.[74]

New research has brought a welcome degree of rigor to the debate. Nevertheless, the conclusion that the deflation of the period was "good" rather than "bad" invites a measure of skepticism.[75] The argument accepts that contemporaries in Europe and the United States were convinced that they were living through a period of depression, but suggests that they were suffering from a "money illusion": wage rates declined but were compensated by falling commodity prices. An illusion that lasted for more than twenty years raises the question of why it took so many people so long to adjust to claimed reality that they persisted with widespread strike action and militant rural protests. False consciousness has its limits. An assessment of the net barter terms of trade is an incomplete guide to farmers' welfare. Even if output rose, it would be necessary to compute costs to arrive at an estimate of productivity.[76] Any generalization on this subject would have to take account of regional specialization and varying levels of commitment to the international market.[77]

Two additional features, declining expectations and rising volatility, need to be incorporated into the analysis. Although GDP in Europe and the United States grew during the period as a whole, the rate of growth was low and inconsistent. There were thirteen years of negative rates of growth in per capita GDP in Europe between 1871 and 1905, and only one occasion when a sequence of positive rates extended to five years.[78] This record was in marked contrast to the 1850s and 1860s, when high rates of growth generated confidence and lifted expectations that "improvement," as it was called, would in the future be continuous. Between 1873 and 1896, uncertainty ruled and falling expectations produced a sense of relative deprivation that turned readily into discontent, as it had done with equally dramatic consequences in the mainland colonies during the 1760s.

Volatility produced sudden crises, often followed by short-term depressions, which were scattered throughout the last quarter of the century.[79] The integration of the international economy meant that crises tended to be contagious: in 1890, the Baring Crisis spread from Argentina to other Latin American states and affected countries as far apart as the United States and Australia, as subsequent credit restrictions took effect.[80] Short-term crises stemmed either from reduced inflows of foreign capital or from cyclical downturns, typically manifested in falling demand for exports. Prices, and sometimes incomes too, declined; debt obligations remained constant. The consequent need to reduce costs and increase productivity had painful consequences. In the short run, profits went down and unemployment went up.[81]

Volatility also nurtured indebtedness. Debtors faced bankruptcy; creditors had difficulty securing repayment, especially in countries that were not on the gold standard. One estimate suggests that seventeen "peripheral or less-developed countries" were unable to service their external debts in the mid-1870s alone.[82] Contemporaries recognized the extent of the problem and initiated the first systematic attempts to deal with it: British investors established the Council of Foreign Bondholders in 1868; an international consortium of creditors formed the Ottoman Public Debt Administration in 1881.[83] In the absence of international rescheduling agreements of the kind that came into operation after World War II, the imperial powers became the debt-collecting agencies of the time.[84]

The perception that new, industrializing societies were entering an economic crisis also inspired the theories of imperialism that were formulated at this time. The first attempt to devise a coherent economic explanation accompanied the occupation of Egypt in 1882; the most influential interpretation followed the Anglo-South African War of 1899–1902.[85] These assessments and their many variants, though well-known and much discussed, have generally been treated in a national context.

Contemporary analysts, however, thought that the problems confronting the Western world during the last quarter of the century had common origins and global ramifications. This belief stemmed partly from the widespread assumption, derived from classical economics, that profit rates would decline with the passage of time, at which point capital would lack domestic investment opportunities. The sequence of depressions that struck after 1873 indicated that the moment had arrived, and that imperialism was an attempt to find new ways of employing "surplus" capital profitably. Experience enhanced theory. The global character of the crisis created domestic strains that demanded attention; the intellectuals of the day set themselves the task of producing solutions that met national needs.

Radicals, influenced by Marx, regarded imperialism as a desperate attempt to stave off the inevitable collapse of capitalism. The prospect of socialism, however, galvanized liberals into producing alternatives. In Britain, J. A. Hobson argued that the answer lay in the redistribution of domestic purchasing power, which would reopen profitable opportunities at home and eliminate one of the principal motives for imperialism. Other influential liberal thinkers held that imperialism was a solution rather than a problem. The distinguished German economist, Wilhelm Roscher, emphasized the economic potential of colonies as markets and regions of settlement.[86] Roscher was followed by Gustav von Schmoller, whose advocacy molded national interest, economic advantage, and a version of the civilizing mission into a form that gave the imperial project respectability.[87] In France, another noted economist, Paul Leroy-Beaulieu, exemplified the shift of liberal opinion from cosmopolitanism to imperialism. The first edition of his celebrated *De la colonisation chez les peuples modernes*, published in 1874, focused on Algeria and assumed that colonization was primarily a matter of white settlement. The second edition, which appeared in 1882, had a strident tone, stressed the importance of investment opportunities and the need for space for France to expand, and justified the right of civilized people to control "barbarians" and "savages."[88] In the United States, the financial expert, Charles Arthur Conant, had no doubt that overseas investment, by imperialist means if necessary, was essential "if the entire fabric of the present economic order is not to be shaken by a social revolution."[89]

Viewed from an international perspective, the striking feature of the response was the commitment of Europe's elites to rescuing capitalism from its apparently self-induced difficulties. Even those who judged that imperialism offered a solution agreed with Hobson that capitalism needed modifying. Liberals in Europe, sometimes acting in association with conservatives, produced the welfare state; Progressives in the United States moved in the same direction, though without traveling quite so far.

The "great deflation" and the volatile conditions that accompanied it provoked what has been called a "backlash" against globalization during the last quarter of the century.[90] Free trade exposed Western Europe's grain farmers to damaging competition, especially from Russia, the United States, and Canada, and its nascent manufacturing industries to cheaper imports, particularly from Britain. Countries that had adopted the gold standard at a time of deflation suffered the disciplinary consequences: reduced liquidity, increased unemployment, and indebtedness among key business interests. With the exception of Britain, the principal European countries responded to what they had come to see as the adverse consequences of free trade by adopting protective tariffs, while the United States increased the import tariffs it had already put in place.[91] The trend began in the 1870s and continued to the end of the century, by which time only a handful of European countries retained open economies.[92]

The problems ascribed to the gold standard were more intractable. Countries that broke the "rules of the game" were liable to be penalized by being excluded from access to low-cost credit and relegated from the premier league of leading states.[93] The only serious alternative was to revert to the bimetallic standard that had prevailed in much of Europe earlier in the century.[94] Advocates of a dual standard based on silver and gold argued that a fixed exchange rate between the two metals combined with unlimited legal tender would guarantee monetary stability while also improving liquidity. Despite the technical complexity of the debate, bimetallism became a major political issue and a popular cause in Germany, France, the United States, and even Britain during the 1880s and 1890s. The option was not eliminated until the turn of the century, when new supplies of gold removed the constraint on liquidity and enabled "gold bugs" to defeat "silverites" in the principal gold-standard countries.[95]

As currently expressed, the notion of a backlash nevertheless needs amending and expanding. The present argument is too Eurocentric. The Western powers were redirecting globalization and not simply restricting it. The rise of tariff protection in Europe and the United States helped to drive exports of manufactures to other parts of the world, where political authorities could be persuaded or compelled to conform to free trade. The most extensive and most violent backlash occurred, not in the West, but on the frontiers of the world the West was trying to integrate.[96] If nineteenth-century imperialism is itself viewed as a globalizing force, the unprecedented expansion at the close of the century can be interpreted as a renewed thrust to incorporate regions beyond Europe through the agency of new or revitalized nation-states.[97]

The resistance Western powers encountered amounted to a global protest against the terms of incorporation. Viewed from the other side of the frontier, "improvement" came at a heavy cost. Free trade damaged the interests of key business groups; the abolition of state monopolies reduced public revenues and jeopardized the political control of central governments. The drive for export crops and minerals had implications for rights over land and labor; the inflow of manufactured goods brought unemployment to local artisans. The internal distribution of wealth shifted; core values upholding the social order were challenged. Modern globalization was an expansive process that compressed the institutions that fell under its influence. When they buckled, the Western powers intervened to restore "law and order" as a prelude to introducing "civilization." When the World Bank realized the full implications of "getting prices right" in the 1980s, it adopted a new doctrine summarized as "bringing the state back in." In the late nineteenth century, the solution took the form of colonial governments, which guaranteed the fiscal probity of new satellites in Africa and Asia.

GLOBALIZATION AND "NEW" IMPERIALISM

To those in need, imperialism appeared to be the magic bullet that would provide a one-shot solution to pressing problems. By the 1820s, Europe's empires, with the exception of Britain's, had been immobilized or amputated; some had been liquidated. Nevertheless, imperial aspirations and the concomitant quest for "immortality," as Adam Smith put it, remained undiminished.[98] The critic who urged France in the 1830s to "decolonize" by abandoning the attempt to annex Algeria was to be disappointed. His recommendation was ignored and his signal contribution to the language of empire fell out of circulation. In 1839, an official pronouncement declared Algeria to be "a land forever French," and so it remained until 1962.[99] As expansionist policies prevailed, another linguistic novelty of the 1830s, "*l'impérialisme*," took hold. By the 1870s, the term had become Anglicized and was widely used by both advocates and critics of the quickening pace of empire-building.[100] Established imperial states, headed by Britain, held on to their possessions if they could and added to them when possible; newcomers like Germany, Italy, Belgium, Japan, and the United States applied to join the imperial club as soon as they felt ready for membership. "Decolonization" did not reappear until the close of the 1950s, when it was revived as a way of rationalizing the impending loss of an *Algérie* that was ceasing to be *française*.[101] Other Western imperial centers speedily adopted the term, which became the generic descriptor of the second great transfer of power that occurred in the 1960s.

Territorial acquisitions, large though they were, formed part of an even wider expansionist trend that encompassed the world in the second half of the nineteenth century and included the exercise of what has been called "informal influence" in countries that were not formally annexed.[102] Influence of this kind is not easily measured, and the claim that there was an informal "empire" that matched the formal, constitutional empire inflates reality. Nevertheless, it is clear that the imperial powers, most notably Britain, exercised considerable informal influence over the substantial Ottoman and Chinese empires and the shrinking Persian Empire, and reached into a variety of states, stretching from republics in Latin America to Siam, which were formally independent but unable to resist incursions into their sovereignty. To the dismay of Cobden and his international disciples, the pursuit of cosmopolitan ideals ran alongside a continuing commitment to empire, and free trade proved compatible with the exercise of force. Taken together, formal and informal means of dominance carried the European empires to their fullest extent, or in Lenin's phrase, their highest stage, in 1914, when one empire, Austro-Hungary, prepared to go to war over Serbia, a former province of another, that of the Ottomans.

Contemporaries had no doubt that developments in the Western world during the last quarter of the nineteenth century were linked to overseas expansion and what became known as "new" imperialism, though they disagreed about the nature of the connection. John Seeley, the founder of the modern study of imperial history, saw the novelty in the decision to acquire large parts of the world that were unsuited to white settlement.[103] For Seeley, colonies were, in the Greek sense, diffusions of people from the homeland; empire, the result of conquest, was an altogether more dubious entity.[104] India, in his view, was a warning light, not a beacon of hope. Marxists used the term "new imperialism" to refer to a crisis of accumulation arising from mature industrial capitalism. Advocates of the new type of empire defended territorial acquisitions by emphasizing the duty of extending the civilizing mission to conquered people. Scholars writing in the twentieth century elaborated these positions. Radicals updated the concept of capitalism to incorporate its latest global manifestations. Liberals compiled a comprehensive assortment of alternatives that gave prominence to principles, politics, and personalities.[105]

The new imperialists faced vocal opposition. In Britain, the Cobdenite tradition, though weakened, remained alive in the Gladstonian wing of the Liberal Party. The labor movement hoped that international solidarity among the working classes would trump national affiliations. A segment of conservative opinion held that mingling with other races would weaken British character.[106] Republicans, humanitarians, and socialists expressed similar views on the continent of Europe. Jean Jaurès, the French socialist leader and pacifist, mobilized his party against imperialism from the 1890s until his death in 1914. The outspoken radical deputy, Paul Vigné d'Octon, organized a persistent campaign against colonial abuses from the 1890s to the 1940s.[107] The Anti-Imperialist League founded in the United States in 1898, and headed by luminaries such as former President Grover Cleveland and Mark Twain, deployed variations on similar arguments.[108] Dissenters, however, were unable to compete with the strident appeal of nationalism, which succeeded in making imperialism a popular cause and attaching it to the fate of the *patrie*. Jean Jaurès was assassinated by a French nationalist whose zeal had been fired by the loss of Alsace-Lorraine.

Popular forms of cultural expression drew on these theories to underscore the supremacy of the white race and consolidate national unity. Generalized notions of racial superiority were distributed through expanded channels of mass communication and appeared in literature, theater, newspapers, and advertisements.[109] Explorers became celebrities. Carl Peters, the eccentric, Pierre de Brazza, the romantic, and Henry Morton Stanley, the showman, brought the exotic to Europe and helped to make it big business. Their travelers' tall tales accompanied the age of the Great Imperial Novel, which extended from Robert Louis Stevenson to Rudyard Kipling in Britain and reached its high point in France in the work of Pierre Loti.[110] The imperial novelists shared a fascination with the globalizing consequences of the spread of technology, commerce, and people. Their work also tracked shifts in international relations. Down to the 1870s, British adventure stories were set in exotic surroundings that included the empire but extended far beyond it.[111] By the 1890s, the imperial theme with didactic overtones had become predominant. After the Anglo–South African War, the literature became more defensive and displayed a new interest in spies and invasions, while continuing to emphasize the martial qualities needed to dispatch them.[112]

The outstanding representative of the not-so-great but highly influential imperial novel was G. A. Henty, who traversed the British Empire and much of the globe as a war correspondent. Henty, though scarcely known today, became an industry and ultimately an institution, and he remained a hero to generations of schoolboys for half a century.[113] His tally of 122 novels covered imperial and military exploits across the world; in the early 1890s, his books were selling at the rate of about 200,000 a year.[114] Henty aimed to cultivate a form of civilized patriotism based on Christianity, duty, and honor. His stories emphasized the superiority of the British "race" and the value of the empire, which he portrayed as a vehicle for spreading progress and sustaining the virtues of resourcefulness, energy, and valor that underpinned national greatness. Authors in the United States caught up with the imperial trend following the outbreak of the Spanish-American War and produced patriotic effusions written to Henty's formula, though some were expansive enough to include the Anglo-Saxon alliance in the victory festivities.[115]

The new means of communication also became effective channels for religious enterprise. Steamships ferried Christian missions to the expanding frontiers of empire; railroads carried them across it; cheap print spread the Word to the societies they reached. A third Great Awakening at the close of the century revived evangelical enthusiasm and infused missionary enterprise with a crusading spirit that roused the West to counter resurgent forms of Islam.[116] In authorizing the invasion of Egypt in 1882, Gladstone persuaded himself that he was sanctioning "an upright war, a Christian war."[117] In Britain, where heathens abounded, the mission founded by William Booth in 1865 became the Salvation Army in 1878. In 1880, the pacific army was established in the United States, where its teaching and growing preoccupation with social welfare complemented Josiah Strong's urgent appeal to save souls from sin, and society from breakdown.[118]

Encounters with heathens abroad reaffirmed national values. In replacing lost energy, imperialism prepared the white race for an extended period of world dominance. The road to Mandalay combined healthy adventure with testing responsibilities. Character was shaped on exotic frontiers and duty performed in trying circumstances "somewheres east of Suez, where the best is like the worst."[119] Demonstrations of assertive imperialism promoted the ideal of the muscular, martial Christian whose success in overcoming adversity would help to avert or at least postpone the degenerative tendencies that threatened the white race.[120] The occupation of Africa burnished the image of the civilized, saintly warrior. It created a spectacular "martyr" in Gordon of Khartoum, whose celebrity status, achieved through his death in 1885, stirred others to work for

Christ and the empire.[121] It made the durable Jean-Baptiste Marchand, who fought his way across Africa and also through World War I, a national hero in France.[122] Across the Atlantic, Colonel George Armstrong Custer attained national status as the embodiment of the selfless, gentlemanly hero following his death at the hands of the Sioux in 1876.[123] Not all heroes died in battle. David Livingstone's death from malaria and dysentery in 1873 enshrined his memory in mythologies of courage, self-sacrifice, and service that inspired subsequent generations.[124] Henry Morton Stanley lived to tell tall tales. Both men were eulogized for the qualities they were thought to exemplify: fortitude in the face of hardship; dedication to causes that rose above self-interest.

Other European imperial powers joined Britain in demonstrating the continuing strength of their religious commitment and proselytizing ambitions. France was a particularly enthusiastic participant in the crusade to evangelize Africa. The energetic and long-serving Cardinal Charles Martial Lavigerie, who founded the White Fathers in 1868 and the White Sisters the following year, had dreams of establishing a Christian kingdom in tropical Africa.[125] He cooperated with the French Army in the occupation of Tunisia in 1881, launched an anti-slavery campaign in 1888, and worked tirelessly to bridge the divisions between church and state in France.[126] By the turn of the century, mission and empire had become fused. For the Church, empire became a means of countering anti-clericalism and joining an alliance to defeat socialism.[127] Cooperation among Christians, however, was limited by long-standing denominational differences and intensifying national affiliations. Protestant evangelicals in Britain and the United States were inclined to treat Roman Catholics as exceptionally obdurate heathens. The ensuing competition for souls partitioned the colonial world between branches of the Christian faith in much the same way that protectionists sought to divide markets and raw materials. In these circumstances, the Christian commonwealth was unable to function as an effective transnational organization.

This is not to suggest that the missions were simply tools of imperialism.[128] Nevertheless, evangelical opinion came to regard government, and colonial government in particular, as a power that could work for the Lord.[129] A providential alliance of church and state joined forces in the formidable task of eradicating sin, which was present in its most abhorrent form in the slave trade and the institution of slavery.[130] By the close of the century, the attitudes and activities of the missions were tinged with the sense of racial superiority and its offshoot, paternalism, that characterized the mood of the era. The British were convinced that their Protestant empire was God's chosen agent in the battle to achieve spiritual and material progress.[131] In 1900, Britain provided far more Protestant missionaries to carry the Word overseas than any other country, including the United States.[132] Arthur Benson's text, written in 1902 for Elgar's "Coronation Ode," left no doubt where the "land of hope and glory" was or who was the "Mother of the free" and the guardian of "Truth and Right." Mortals contributed what they could, but it was "God who made thee mighty."

One organization that achieved striking success in maintaining international cooperation while serving national interests was the Boy Scouts and their sisters, the Girl Guides.[133] The Scouts were founded in 1908 by Robert Baden-Powell, who drew on his experience as a military officer in colonial Africa to import some of the qualities he admired in Zulu warriors. The Guides (originally called Scouts until the Boys objected) were founded in the following year.[134] Despite some gendered differences, both organizations aimed to instill values that would deliver patriotic service to the state.[135] Outdoor pursuits, team sports, and a strong Christian ethos were the chosen means of developing the qualities of discipline, self-reliance, and honor that would uphold social order and forestall racial degeneration.[136] The movement spread internationally and at remarkable speed. By 1914, the Scouts were established in most of the leading countries from the United States to Japan and from Tzarist Russia to New Zealand. National branches acquired local character: French Scouts (*éclaireurs*) were conservative and strongly Catholic; U.S. Scouts had links with the National Rifle Association (1871). In all cases, however, the success of the Scouts and Guides lay in their appeal as powerful aids to nation-building.[137] Theodore Roosevelt was one of many eminent figures who supported the movement and applied its principles with enthusiasm to his own outdoor adventures, which ranged from disciplined hunting expeditions to leading the filibustering Rough Riders in the invasion of Cuba. Although historical research has treated the Scouts in their national setting, other authorities have recognized the movement's long-standing contribution to the process of globalization. The World Organization of the Scout Movement, founded in 1922, is now a designated International Non-Governmental Organization, and thus qualifies for the unpoetic acronym, INGO.

By 1914, Britain had drawn lines in the sands and forests of Africa, across the Himalayas from Afghanistan to Burma, through the forests of Malaya, and over the South China Sea to North Borneo and New Guinea, and had extended frontiers of settlement in Canada, South Africa, Australia, and New Zealand to create a "Greater Britain" that was bound together as much by informal networks as by constitutional ties.[138] France had created an empire in North and West Africa, attached Madagascar, and annexed Indo-China. Germany, Italy, and Belgium had acquired colonies in Africa; Portugal had greatly magnified its existing holdings there. The Netherlands had stretched its possessions in Indonesia to include Aceh in the west and New Guinea in the east; Japan had defeated China and appropriated Korea; Russia's eastward progression had reached Manchuria. The United States had become the leading exponent of insular imperialism, having annexed or otherwise acquired Hawai'i, the myriad islands of the Philippines, and remnants of the Spanish Empire in the Caribbean. The North Pole had been conquered; the penguins of Antarctica had become subject to Western territorial claims.[139] Few scraps were left, even for undernourished predators.

LIONS, JACKALS, AND THE SCRAMBLE FOR EMPIRE[140]

Lenin, who had a point to make, coined the phrase the "imperialism of the jackals" to describe the minor powers that fell upon the scraps left by the lions of the international order.[141] His anthropomorphic metaphor had a pejorative purpose, but his recognition of the diverse features of contemporary imperial powers, though now neglected, remains suggestive. Historians agree about a broad range of causes of "new" imperialism, but dispute their relative importance. The most venerable distinction places economic and political interpretations in opposition to one another; the most influential blends them into an amalgam. Methodologically, these options are often presented as a choice between monocausal and multicausal interpretations. The former, however, excludes too much that is relevant, while the latter fails the test of selectivity that all interpretations need to pass.

In principle, comparative analysis provides a way of resolving these dilemmas.[142] In practice, national studies continue to dominate the literature. Consequently, it is still unclear whether all Western imperial states were driven by similar impulses, in which case the differences among them were those of scale, or whether the imperialism of the strong was qualitatively different from that of the weak.[143] Although this question is too large to be treated adequately here, it can be recast to suggest a classification that relates motives to state structures. This approach opens the possibility of including states outside Europe, including the United States, thereby freeing the Republic from the insularity that has characterized the literature on the War of 1898 and its colonial aftermath.

The old, new, and reconstructed states of Europe underwent generally similar processes of transformation, but they did so at different speeds and with varied results. The differences are not easily measured. National unity is not susceptible to precise calculation. National identities can be consistent with other loyalties or in conflict with them. Economic growth can divide as well as integrate. Broad measures of economic development identify leaders and laggards but do not translate directly into causes of imperialism.[144]

Fiscal unity is a suggestive and neglected indicator in this connection because it serves as a measure of political and economic unity and state capacity.[145] Evidence of a common currency, tax compliance, and a national bank with central banking functions provides a guide to the extent of control exercised by central governments, the revenue potential of the state, and its ability to wage war and annex territory.[146] Admittedly, fiscal unity is a permissive rather than a prescriptive consideration. A high degree of fiscal unity may be present in a country with limited resources or in one with plentiful resources but little inclination or opportunity for imperial expansion. Nevertheless, fiscal unity is a useful measure of potential because it distinguishes between countries that lacked the capacity to engage prominently in imperial expansion, even if they wanted to, and those that could mobilize the necessary means should they choose to do so.

The purpose of adopting this measure is not to demonstrate the uncontroversial proposition that lions had the fiscal strength to be successful empire-builders while jackals had to scramble for the leftovers, but to suggest that the two had a different spread of motives. Economic impulses were more prominent among early-start modernizers than among late-starters. The former were more likely to have achieved a considerable degree of national unity and to have incorporated influential manufacturing, commercial, and financial interests. The latter, being at an earlier point of transition, lacked equivalent fiscal strength and attached greater priority to achieving political unity as a precursor to securing the level of economic development that had been attained elsewhere. The distinction needs fine-tuning to take account of the particularities of the mixed band of late-starters. Nevertheless, even as it stands, the categorization has the merit of directing attention to the protracted nature of the adjustment from proto- to modern globalization, and to corresponding shifts in the motives for empire-building.

It is a striking and an under-appreciated fact that most of the states that were to acquire empires for the first time in the late nineteenth century were late-start modernizers that were constructed or reconstructed through war and revolution within a span of a decade. Italy became independent in 1861; the United States, though already formally independent, was not effectively united until after the Civil War of 1861–1865; Japan was restructured following the Meiji Restoration in 1868; the German states came together in 1871.[147] Belgium was exceptional. It joined the scramble for overseas territories for the first time in the 1880s, but had begun to promote industrialization and political reform in the 1830s under the aegis of the newly installed constitutional monarchy. Belgium's involvement in imperialism, however, was largely an expression of the idiosyncratic whims of King Leopold II, who benefited from the benevolent neutrality of Great Britain. Had Britain not provided a guarantee against the predatory intentions of France and Germany in 1870, Belgium would almost certainly have lost its independence, in which case King Leopold would not have been in a position to carve out an additional kingdom for himself in the Congo.

Powers that had long histories of imperial rule and were still struggling to come to terms with political reform and modern industry found themselves handicapped in the race for empire. Spain did not emerge from a long period of turmoil until 1876, following the conclusion of the Third Carlist War, when the monarchy succeeded in holding civil war at bay while presiding over an unsteady political compromise. The Spanish economy failed to catch up with the industrial powers and remained primarily agricultural. Fiscal unity was similarly delayed. The Bank of Spain (1856) did not secure a monopoly of note issues until 1874 and did not begin to function regularly as a bank of last resort until 1921. Spain never joined the gold standard, initially because of limited reserves and subsequently because of policy failures.[148] The United States annexed the remnants of the Spanish Empire in 1898; Spain lacked the power to win adequate compensation elsewhere.

Portugal's long history of internal strife and insecurity extended into the twentieth century, when King Carlos I was assassinated in 1908 and a republic declared in 1910. Portugal, like Spain, remained a predominantly agricultural country with limited fiscal resources. The Bank of Portugal, though founded in 1846, did not acquire control of note issues during this period. The country joined the gold standard in 1854 but abandoned it in 1891 following a series of defaults on repayments of foreign loans; it was unable to resume international borrowing until 1902.[149] In contrast to Spain, Portugal was able to extend its coastal colonies in Africa at the close of the century, but did so, not as a result of a newfound economic impetus, but principally because, like Belgium, it enjoyed the benign neutrality of Great Britain.

The Netherlands was also a late-starter with an established empire: modern industry did not take root until the last quarter of the century.[150] The Netherlands, however, was ahead of Spain and Portugal in having a strong commercial and financial sector and a National Bank that became truly national after the Bank Act of 1863. Moreover, liberal forces scored a rare success in 1848, when a group of patrician financiers averted the imminent threat of revolution, installed a reformed, monarchical constitution, and began to turn the economy toward modern industry.[151] In these circumstances, commercial interests were able to influence the government's decision to extend its hold over Indonesia during this period.[152] Nevertheless, the Netherlands lacked the power to act globally. Dutch involvement in "new imperialism" was confined to Indonesia and supported by a division of spheres of influence agreed with Britain in 1824.

Austria, another late-start modernizer with a multinational territorial empire, initiated a major constitutional change in 1867, when the Austro-Hungarian Empire was formed. The innovation, however, was less a sign of burgeoning strength than a reaction to defeat at the hands of Prussia in 1866. Nonetheless, the new constitution opened the way to monetary union, a common currency, and a central bank.[153] Trade increased; tax revenues rose. The empire had sufficient capacity to pursue expansionist territorial claims in south-eastern Europe, despite spending a smaller proportion of the imperial budget on defense than other European countries did. Expansion, however, provoked resistance among ethnic minorities that the empire had neither the resources nor the skill to control. This exercise in "new" imperialism culminated in the assassination of the Archduke Franz Ferdinand in 1914. The Emperor was not entirely uncomprehending, but he presided over a union that had failed to reconcile absolutist habits with democratic aspirations. On the morning of his fatal visit to Serbia, the Archduke responded angrily to a mismanaged attempt to assassinate him: "I have come to visit Sarajevo," he commented, "and am greeted with bombs, it is outrageous."[154] As Karl Kraus, the writer and satirist, commented: "In Berlin, things are serious but not hopeless. In Vienna, they are hopeless but not serious."[155]

The adjustments needed to distinguish causation among the imperial powers can be illustrated in greater detail by three examples: Britain, the exceptional, first-start modernizer and the lion of the empire-builders; Italy, one of the "jackals," and a late-start power; and France, which occupied an intermediate position. Britain had strong economic motives for imperial expansion; Italy was driven mainly by political imperatives; in France, *la monnaie* and *la gloire* rubbed shoulders without achieving a wholly harmonious partnership.

As the first of the early-start modernizers and an established imperial power, Britain was in a position to follow an evolutionary path that greatly eased the transition from the military-fiscal regime. The East India Company, the last symbol of mercantilism, was liquidated in 1858. The alarm bells rung by the Chartist crisis, resurgent radicalism, and the rise of trade unions undoubtedly concentrated the minds of those in government. The debate in Britain, however, was far less divisive than it was elsewhere in Europe. British governments, unlike many others, did not have to deal with assertive rural populism in the late nineteenth century: distress in the countryside had already harried the unemployed into overcrowded towns and hurried many others into emigration, principally to the "white" empire and the United States.[156] A series of reforms, continuing those enacted during the first half of the century, further enlarged the franchise, reorganized the civil service, the universities, the military, and the colonial service, improved working conditions, and blunted the edge of extreme radicalism.

This is not to suggest that complacency was the order of the day. Recurring bouts of unemployment and strike action had significant political consequences at the close of the century: the rise of the Labour Party drove property owners into the Conservative Party and pushed the Liberals into sponsoring welfare reforms. The appearance of powerful foreign competitors increased the appeal of empire and cast doubt on the relevance of the notion of "splendid isolation" which by 1900 had more isolation than splendor about it. As the author of the phrase acknowledged, it was a state that could be ended swiftly—and soon was.[157] In the 1890s, the pacific, cosmopolitan internationalism championed by Gladstone and Bright shriveled before the fiery imperial rhetoric that had enhanced the appeal of the Conservatives. Younger members of Gladstone's party responded by forming a splinter group of Liberal imperialists, who aimed to show that they, too, could harness the empire to the cause of national unity. Until costs and casualties sobered spirits, popular imperialism—jingoism—garnered votes.[158]

National identity was a permanent work in progress, and different interests competed to shape John Bull's character, even as his symbolic importance grew.[159] Nonetheless, as a small, unitary state, Britain had the advantage of being able to capitalize on a sense of national identity that had been developing since the seventeenth century and been greatly strengthened by the wars of the eighteenth century and the victories that accompanied them.[160] Ethnogenesis in the United Kingdom took the form of layered identities rather than a standardized process of assimilation. "Englishness" and its familiar representative, the English gentleman, developed in the south; the Scots and Welsh were encouraged to reinforce or invent their own traditions.[161] Regional distinctiveness offered enough to local aspirations to deflect radical claims, while leaving space for the overarching concept of "Britishness" to unite them. To be British was to subscribe to monarchy, Protestantism, and empire; to adopt or respect the masculine, muscular qualities that helped to sustain them; and to be ready to defend the distinctive liberties embodied in Britain's long tradition of parliamentary government.[162] The death of the Duke of Wellington in 1852 accelerated a process of myth-making at home that had begun with Nelson and continued overseas with the passing of David Livingstone and General Charles Gordon in Africa in 1873 and 1885. Irish, Scots, and English, secular and spiritual alike, came together as Britons under the Union Flag.[163] Myriad agencies reinforced British identity among the wider population: schools, pageants, statues, the arts, newspapers, and novels all served to instill a bond that was strong enough to overcome the divisive forces that tested national unity at the close of the century.

When these political and cultural influences have been acknowledged, it remains the case that Britain's global interests, within and beyond the empire, were predominantly economic. By 1850, the industrial revolution had reached an advanced state. In 1844, the Bank Charter Act strengthened fiscal unity by curtailing the role of country banks and giving the Bank of England control over the issue of new notes. In 1866, the Bank assumed the key function of a central bank—that of being the lender of last resort.[164] After arable farming lost its long-standing protection in 1846, industry and finance took full advantage of the spread of free trade, the extension of the gold standard, and the status of the pound sterling as the accepted global currency. Britain was already becoming a "mature creditor": by the close of the nineteenth century, much of its wealth and power rested on its capital, its credit—and its navy.[165] Several late-starters, such as Switzerland and Denmark, had higher rates of growth; some, such as the Netherlands, derived a larger share of GDP from foreign trade. Countries with small economies, however, could not convert their economic success into the degree of political might needed to compete with larger powers. Countries with large economies, such as Germany and France, eventually became competitors but were unable to dislodge Britain from its position as the unrivaled global power of the day.

Britain's welfare depended on foreign trade and investment to a degree that no other power came near to matching. The scale of Britain's global commitments was equaled by their complexity. The intricacy of the international network of exchanges that ultimately determined the balance of payments ensured that dislocation affecting one segment would damage the system as a whole. Consequently, Britain was inextricably involved in "new" imperialism, whether to defend spheres of influence from foreign claimants, who might also impose discriminatory tariffs, or to impose "law and order" on regions where resistance to foreign impositions jeopardized the country's own direct interests. The familiar argument that Britain was a passive, declining power in the late nineteenth century understates its industrial performance and fails to take full account of its exceptional role as financier to the world.[166] The arteries had not hardened; the blood still ran freely. Available supplies of energy were sufficient to prevent "cosmic dynamics" from activating the "law of entropy."

Key policy issues, such as bimetallism and tariff revision, focused on the economy. Advocates of policy reform mustered different sets of supporters but were connected by a common assumption: the belief that the open economy Britain had established after 1846 no longer served its interests.[167] Members of the Conservative Party, representatives of the Lancashire textile industry, and even a small number of City bankers were prominent among those who hoped to see Britain's international economic policy revised. The reaction against free trade had particular appeal at a time when the rest of the developing world, including former colonies such as the United States and Canada, was becoming protectionist, and manufactures from the United States and Germany were flowing into Britain.[168] The issue assumed national importance in the 1890s, when it was joined to plans to give the empire an enlarged role in Britain's political economy. Imperial preference, so advocates claimed, would create a huge free-trade area within the empire and allow a degree of protection, or "fair trade," beyond it. An imperial federation would strengthen links among constituents and create a mega-polity that would enable a Greater Britain to match the advance of large states, such as the United States and Germany.[169] The movement reached its high point in 1903, when Joseph Chamberlain resigned his position as Secretary of State for the Colonies to campaign for the creation of an imperial economic bloc that would make these ideas operational.[170] Technology had overcome the "tyranny of distance"; Adam Smith's tentative suggestions for incorporating the mainland colonies into the United Kingdom appeared to be a practical proposition.[171] A rejuvenated empire, allied to an even wider grouping of Anglo-Saxon peoples, would have the vitality and power to repel boarders, barbarians, and unfriendly newcomers, and enable Britain to survive among the fittest.

Ultimately, the challenge to orthodoxy failed. When put to the test in the general election of 1906, the Liberal Party and free-trade sentiment prevailed. By then, too, support for bimetallism had waned. Tariff reform alienated more interests than it attracted. The prospect of increased taxes on imported foods was unpalatable to all but the rich; the likelihood of paying higher prices for imported raw materials was unpopular with segments of industry. Schemes for imperial federation raised unresolved constitutional questions and failed to take account of nationalist sentiment in the dominions.

The outcome, however, does not imply either that the empire was a declining economic asset or that it was ceasing to be an important component of Britain's national identity. Free trade and the gold standard were essential props of Britain's overseas investments and services, which had a vital role in financing global development. Free trade prevailed because protection would have harmed Britain's network of multilateral settlements. Britain could absorb only a proportion of colonial exports, which needed other markets in the developed world. The gold standard prevailed because it provided confidence that fiscal responsibility would be maintained beyond as well as within the empire, and that debts would be settled in sound money.

Accordingly, British policy-makers recognized the need for developing countries, including the United States, the dominions, and India, to fix import tariffs at levels that would generate sufficient income to service their external debts. Such tariffs might also protect domestic manufactures and thus hamper British exports, but that was the price to be paid for upholding Britain's position as financier to the world.[172] One consequence of this understanding was to push Britain's manufactured exports into accessible markets, which increased the political pressure on underdeveloped countries. Imperial federation remained unattained and unattainable, but continuing expansion ensured that by 1914 Britain controlled more territory than the rest of the Western empires combined. Even so, the formal empire was still not large enough to encompass all of Britain's global economic interests.

On the eve of World War I, Britain, the first of the "early-start" modernizers, was not only the most heavily industrialized of the major European economies, but also the one with the largest service sector, the greatest commitment to overseas trade and investment, and the most advanced financial and fiscal system. In 1913, the value of merchandise exports from Britain ranked ahead of that of Germany, if only just, and was almost twice as large as that of France. Britain's domination of foreign investment was unassailable. In 1914, Britain accounted for a staggering 42 percent of global foreign investment, which represented no less than 32 percent of national wealth.[173] France held 20 percent of global foreign investment, and Germany, 13 percent. Furthermore, approximately 90 percent of British foreign investment was placed outside Europe, whereas more than half of French and German foreign investment remained within the continent. In 1913, nearly half of the British total was invested in the empire and a further 20 percent in the United States.[174] These facts alone suggest that Britain was a uniquely expansive power with an abiding commitment to ensuring that the international order ran smoothly and in ways that suited its interests.

Italy sat uncomfortably at the other end of the spectrum. Aspirations arrived with Mazzini long before national independence and economic modernization.[175] The new Italy, the only authentic claimant, hoped to become the new Rome; *fortuna* determined a different destiny.[176] In the late nineteenth century, the country remained predominantly rural and overwhelmingly poor.[177] Agriculture, though responsive to market opportunities, still awaited a revolution in productivity. Meanwhile, despite the persistence of high rates of infant mortality, population density kept unemployment high and living standards low. Modern manufactures began to make an impression in the 1890s, but were restricted to a few centers in the northwest, notably Milan, Turin, and Genoa. Foreign trade and investment were limited in size and confined to Europe and the Mediterranean littoral. Agriculture supplied more than 80 percent of Italy's exports in the late nineteenth century; manufactures accounted for just over 50 percent of the country's imports. Foreign investment added dependence to underdevelopment. Italy relied heavily on capital flows from abroad, which were supplied mainly by British investors. Cyclical variations in economic performance were determined largely by decisions made in the City of London, where Italy was regarded as one more periphery in a world of peripheries.[178]

The immediate and most pressing problem was political. The Kingdom of Italy had been formed in 1861 but was incomplete until Venice was incorporated in 1866 and Rome in 1870. Like the United States in 1783, Italy was a state that had yet to become a nation. The country had been assembled from a collection of diverse polities that had deep-rooted identities, distinct dialects, and varying views of the world. The Risorgimento began as an anti-colonial resistance movement after 1815, when Austrian control was re-imposed in the north of the country and Bourbon rule restored in the Kingdom of the Two Sicilies in the south. The struggle that followed exemplified the wider conflict between conservatives and reformers in Europe. Parallel opposition movements in the north and south of the country, made famous internationally through the dramatic actions of Mazzini and Garibaldi, coalesced sufficiently to overcome the defeat of revolutionary forces in 1848 and achieve formal independence. Unity, however, was tenuous. Powerful interests opposed unification.[179] The political elite of rich landlords in the rural south rejected both Bourbon absolutism and the centralizing tendencies inherent in a national government.[180] They had their own aspirations for national unity but lacked the power to impose them. Accordingly, they cooperated with the new order to the extent of endorsing the constitutional monarchy installed by northern interests because it offered protection from radicalism. The impetus behind the success of the Risorgimento came from Piedmont-Savoy, the most advanced region, which had the resources to support the movement, the fiscal base needed for military expenditure, and the political skill, in the shape of Camillo, Count of Cavour, to coordinate them.[181] Cavour's influence began the process of fiscal integration. A national currency, the lira, was established in 1862, and a central bank in 1893. The tax base, however, was limited, and tax-gathering was inefficient.

The monarchy was the only institution that could serve as a symbol of national unity apart from the Vatican, which was wary of endorsing a centralized, secular authority. The monarch came from the ancient House of Savoy in the far northwest of the country. The first incumbent, Victor Emmanuel II (1861–1878), former King of Piedmont-Sardinia, was provincial by inheritance and absolutist by inclination. The new representative institutions embodied formal sovereignty but lacked effective authority.[182] The national government became a resource for sectional and regional interests. Governments acquired a record of instability and corruption; faith in democracy faded; Mazzini's radical expectations ebbed. The Risorgimento was a beginning that ended by confirming the power of a narrow oligarchy.[183] Economic problems multiplied too. Government debt mounted; agricultural distress increased from the 1870s as prices fell and the sector failed to compete in international markets; emigrants became Italy's most successful export.[184] Protectionist measures introduced after 1878 provided a modest stimulus to manufactures but failed to correct the underlying problem of low productivity in agriculture. In the 1890s, urban unrest fueled socialism and anarchism.

The political response to these accumulating problems was to redouble the effort to promote the monarchy as a symbol of national unity.[185] Unfortunately, Umberto I (1878–1900), though more adaptable than his father, was unsuited to be the noble warrior-leader the Roman image demanded and Francesco Crispi, the leading politician of the time, desperately needed.[186] Crispi's battle plan, a stratagem with many precedents, was to unite Italy behind a short, cheap, successful war. One bad idea, war with France, was followed by a worse one: war with Germany.[187] Both were rejected in favor of an imperial venture in Africa. This supposedly soft option was linked to the hope that colonies of settlement would attract the emigrants who were flowing to the United States and Latin America, and create a Greater Italy modeled on that of Greater Britain.[188] A brief campaign to annex Ethiopia in 1887 failed; a more ambitious effort in 1896 was badly supplied, incompetently led, and ended in inglorious defeat. Italy's sole success, which turned Eritrea into a colony in 1890, was won with British connivance. Subsequent gains, in Somalia (Benadir) in 1905 and Libya (Tripolitania) in 1912, were driven principally by the need to repair the damage to national prestige caused by the disaster in Ethiopia.

The imperial option was a failure. The new colonies had few resources and were unattractive to emigrants. Even Eritrea, the most promising of an unappealing selection, counted only about 4,000 Italian settlers and officials in 1914. The Greater Italy, the successful Italy, was the globalized Italy in the New World. The new Rome itself fell to a combination of distant African "barbarians" and proximate Italian anarchists. Crispi lost power; Umberto lost prestige. Unrest, unassuaged, turned the knives on Caesar. An attempt on the king's life made with a dagger failed in 1897; he was killed by four shots in 1900, after the weaponry had been updated. The Italian bourgeoisie did not "play a most important part" in urging governments to secure markets, raw materials, and investment opportunities. Economic motives scarcely registered. A few specialized business interests attached themselves to a movement that was already under way, but most of their energies went into trading political support for lucrative military and associated contracts.[189] Political imperatives drove Italian imperialism. The paramount need was to hold the fragile state together. An assertive foreign policy was the chosen means; a future of wealth and grandeur was the predicted result. Pride came before the fall; illusion preceded both.

In terms of development, as well as geography, France lay between Britain and Italy. By the 1870s, sizeable manufacturing centers in towns such as Lille and Lyon, in ports such as Marseilles and Bordeaux, and in the capital, Paris, produced a range of goods, from textiles to metal wares, that were typical of the first stage of industrialization.[190] The matrix, however, was still overwhelmingly rural. About 50 percent of the working population was employed in agriculture in 1870 compared to about 28 percent in manufacturing.[191] These figures put France ahead of Italy but a long way behind Britain. France had also developed a sizeable export sector: in 1913, French exports were three times the value of exports from Italy, though still only half those of Britain. Exports from France, like those from Italy, were sent mainly to other European countries, though French goods entered global markets too. French financial institutions were far more advanced than Italy's and supported considerable foreign investment, though most of it went to destinations in Europe, especially Russia, Spain, and Italy.[192] Again, however, the scale, range, and competitiveness of French financial institutions could not match those of the City of London.

France, a late-start power with a long imperial history, experienced kings, republics, an emperor, revolutions in 1830 and 1848, a coup in 1851, and defeat at the hands of Prussia in 1870 before initiating a series of fiscal reforms as part of a program of national renovation.[193] In this case, reform did not require major institutional change: the French National Bank, founded in 1800, had already secured a monopoly of note issue in 1848. The growth of capital exports had reached the point where France took the lead in 1865 in forming the Latin Monetary Union to ensure that borrowers would service their debts in sound money.[194] This was not a move that Italy could have contemplated. Equally, however, it was not one that France was strong enough to sustain. A comparison with sterling and the gold standard underlines Britain's predominance in international finance. After 1870, innovation was achieved primarily through the improved efficiency of tax-gathering, which captured the provinces in a national net and produced a rapid rise in revenue. Once the large bill for reparations had been settled, most of the increase was spent on domestic welfare measures relating to education, public works, and agriculture. A smaller tranche was directed to the defense budget, which supported France's imperial ambitions during the last quarter of the century.

Economic and political developments intersected. French leaders compared their country, not to Italy, but to Germany. After 1880, the pace of economic growth in Germany exceeded that in France, as did per capita GDP, despite the fact that the German population was expanding rapidly, while the rate of increase in France was the lowest in Europe. Changing economic and demographic relativities produced apprehension; the defeat of French troops at the hands of Prussia in 1870 produced catastrophe. Napoleon III was captured at Sedan; the Second Empire collapsed. This was a reversal of fortune that France, once the most populous and powerful of European states, struggled to overcome down to and beyond 1914. For one set of patriots, the disaster was a chance to deal with a malaise that was destroying the body politic; for another, it was an opportunity to strengthen national unity, which was still a work in progress. Conflict between the two positions began with the creation of the Paris Commune in 1871 and became what was effectively a civil war, though one confined largely to the capital. The Commune dramatized the rift between urban radicalism and rural conservatism. It was approved by Marx, condemned by the Vatican, and suppressed with considerable bloodshed. As the leaders of the Third Republic emerged from the wreckage to resume the task of holding the country together, they were presented with a new set of problems arising from the series of economic depressions that began in 1873.

Although the Third Republic started shakily, it achieved a measure of stability after a "holy alliance" of industrialists, landowners, and the Catholic Church came together in the course of the turbulent 1880s to consolidate political support for the central government.[195] The need to defuse rural and urban unrest and avert the calamitous prospect of another revolution from below forced the warring parties to think beyond their sectional interests. The compromise was sealed by a shift to protection that began in the 1880s and culminated in the Méline Tariff of 1892.[196] A number of uncompetitive industries won government support; agriculture was sheltered to compensate for depressed produce prices and the shift to the gold standard.[197] The bargain between "iron and wheat" offered cover for both industry and agriculture, and was the centerpiece of the conservative-liberal response to the looming threat of socialism.[198]

French imperialism was the overseas complement of these domestic measures. A colonial movement gained momentum in the 1880s and formed itself into a party in 1892. The *parti colonial* was a loose collection of not always like-minded enthusiasts who nevertheless enjoyed considerable influence in parliament, which was broadly sympathetic to colonial causes.[199] The history of the party provoked a spirited debate in the 1960s between those who argued that it was trying to restore national prestige and those who held that its main motives were economic.[200] The passage of time and the benefits of additional research have refined these positions.[201] A quest for national renewal after the disaster of 1870 undoubtedly motivated many supporters of the colonial party, which included journalists, explorers, and former military officers in its ranks. The search for *la gloire*, they claimed, would build character and avert racial degeneration; once found, it would restore pride and energy at home and promote a *mission civilisatrice* abroad.[202] It is equally the case that business interests lobbied for support, whether for territorial expansion or for protective tariffs, in regions that had been acquired or were being claimed.[203] The Lyon silk industry was effective in pushing for control of Indo-China; merchants in Marseilles helped to draw the French government into Dahomey; the railway lobby lay behind French plans to expand in North and West Africa.[204] The Foreign Office and banks also worked closely together to safeguard French investments in regions where France had considerable informal influence, such as the Ottoman Empire.[205]

The political leaders of the time reflected this mélange of motives. Eugène Étienne, the long-serving deputy from Oran and principal figure in the colonial party, believed that French settlers in Algeria should be strengthened, that the colony should be developed and used as a base for expanding the French empire into Africa, and that overseas territories would restore French vitality and standing.[206] Jules Ferry, who was Prime Minister in 1880–1881, merged the French republican tradition of revolutionary progress with a belief that "higher races" had a mandate to rule others, while also claiming that colonies were economically advantageous.[207] On the other hand, Gabriel Hanotaux, who was Minister of Foreign Affairs for much of the 1890s, developed a concept of the civilizing mission that explicitly rejected economic motives for empire-building.[208] His position, in turn, contrasted with that of Maurice Rouvier, a businessman and banker from Marseilles who held a series of senior ministerial positions in the 1880s and 1890s and was prime minister in 1887 and 1905–1906. Rouvier was far more sympathetic than Hanotaux to the economic case for colonies, but he also knew enough about business to take a hard-headed view of the options put before him.

Evidently, it is harder to determine motives in the French case than it is with regard to either Britain or Italy. The work of Jacques Marseille, however, suggests how diverse and ambivalent motives can be combined.[209] Marseille showed that French capitalism was consistent with French imperialism during this period, even though most French trade and investment remained in Europe. The expanding export industries and import-processing activities connected to the empire typified the capitalism of the late nineteenth century, as did French shipping, commercial services, and banking. It should be unsurprising to find that such groups, which were well represented in parliament, were able to influence colonial policy. At the same time, these interests were sectional and regional, and were not synonymous with the national interest, which had to take account of the problems of the vast agricultural sector and the growing strength of Germany.

Looking beyond Marseille's study, it should also be apparent that the national crisis that confronted France after 1870 called for an expansive, morale-building response, which imperialism seemed to offer. If the French case is placed in a wider European perspective, commonalities become apparent. French leaders, like others, cast about for ways of managing the great transformation that threatened to overwhelm them. The domestic and imperial solutions they canvassed combined appeals to national solidarity with promises of relief from economic distress. The "alliance of iron and wheat" was specific to France, but variations on the formula were found among the other imperial powers, notably Germany, whose ultimate goal was to preserve property and privilege, and halt the advance of socialism.[210]

"THIS IS A NEW AGE; THE AGE OF SOCIAL ADVANCEMENT NOT OF FEUDAL SPORTS"[211]

Cobden superimposed his rhetoric about the "New Age" on a perceptive understanding of the social forces that contended for supremacy in nineteenth-century Europe. In the 1840s, when he made his assured assessment, the struggle was primarily between the landed aristocracy and the new, urban middle classes. Later in the century, following the expansion of industry, trade, and the franchise, the influence of the "middling sort" grew and the contest became more intense. It also became more complex. By then, a third element, consisting of urban and industrial wage-earners, had made its presence felt through labor organizations and strike action. The labor movement was influenced by a new, fortifying ideology—socialism—and voiced claims for political representation that challenged the existing distribution of power. An even more alarming phenomenon, anarchism, operating beyond constitutional limits, threatened to bring the established order to a sudden, violent end. To those who feared social change, Tocqueville's "democratic majority," tyrannical or not, had its foot in the door.

The transition to modern globalization lurched through a series of national crises. The apparatus of Britain's military-fiscal state was not dismantled until the close of the 1840s. Other European states followed during the second half of the century. As Britain grappled with Chartism and trade unions, so states on the continent negotiated their way through constitutional reform, revolution, and civil war. The outcome, though often presented as the "triumph of liberalism," was much clearer in John Stuart Mill's statement of principles than it was in the murky realities of political practice. Moreover, the rapidity of industrialization, combined with the compressed process of nation-building, stimulated thinking that departed from liberal norms. Joseph de Maistre's Catholic political philosophy continued to rally support for the union of Church and monarchy. Friedrich List's "national system" of political economy appealed to the autarkic ambitions of late-start industrializing states.[212] Karl Marx provided a political program for overthrowing the whole structure of bourgeois capitalism. Friedrich Nietzsche's invocation of a Godless, free-falling world opened avenues to both anarchism and autocracy. The world's first national-industrial polities arose from a bruising, brutal process of development. By 1914, they had either been hammered into new shapes to meet the needs of modern globalization or were about to be hammered into the ground for failing to do so.

Montesquieu had already observed how economic and territorial expansion created problems of political control that established institutions of government could solve only by lapsing into despotism. Benjamin Constant developed the insight by distinguishing between "ancient" and "modern" liberty. Constant saw that modern liberty, for all its merits, posed problems of scale, representation, and accountability that were absent from small states, where direct democracy was feasible. His hope, which Cobden shared, was that the outcome would be pacific. Richard Cobden and Norman Angel were not alone among liberals at discovering, to their distress, that international integration was compatible with international war.

The nation-state emerged as a mechanism for managing the tensions arising from rapid socioeconomic change, containing the resulting incompatibilities, and converting them into state power. New and revitalized nation-states spanned a wide range of possibilities. They included monarchies and republics, unitary and federal forms of government, and various degrees of electoral participation. Like their predecessors, they deployed the power of central government to expand the military capacity and fiscal reach of the state. Nation-states, however, were more efficient engines of taxation than their predecessors had been: they drew on extensive resources; they exercised a greater degree of central control; they spent far more on welfare to foster national identities and inculcate loyalty among their citizens.[213] Expenditure on welfare, however, did not inhibit political leaders from devising novel ways of waging larger and more devastating wars. Parliamentary oversight proved to be an uncertain check on irrational or aggressive policies.[214]

Although early-start and late-start modernizers had different priorities, they grappled with what they saw as the same basic issue: how to harness capitalism, and how then to save it from what increasingly appeared to be self-destruction. Urbanization, industrialization, and the threat of socialism transformed the "liberal project" in the second half of the century. Emerging realities tempered idealism. The romantic nationalism exemplified by Byron and Kossuth gave way to more realistic and more cautious approaches to political reform. Liberals and conservatives who thought they stood at the edge of political disaster responded with policies designed to ward off conflict between capital and labor, incorporate new social groups within the nation-state, and defend property rights. Nationalism trumped internationalism because it was better placed to deal with these divisive issues.

The imbalances arising from the uneven nature of the transformation to modernity made international conflict possible and, from the perspective of the powerful, even advantageous. While it is true that some of the leading European states did not engage one another in major wars after 1815, it is also the case that scarcely a year passed between 1815 and 1914 without a war being fought on some part of the continent in the interests of nation-building. A wider view reveals a world of expanding conflict. Nation-states and warfare were willing partners in competing ventures to reshape the planet. Imperial expansion increased hostilities across the globe. The catastrophe of 1914–1918 was the culmination of a long period of growing hostility among nation-states and their imperial extensions. The *Pax Britannica* was not a proxy for a pacific century.

Imperialism was a gross offshoot of these domestic roots. Unprecedented and pressing needs called for novel forms of international integration. Imperialism was a means of connecting the world in ways that, so its advocates claimed, would restore economic health and political stability, and avert racial decline at a moment when all three were at risk. After 1850, improvements in technology made commercial expansion and territorial occupation feasible and cost-effective. It was then that the concept of free trade expanded to embrace a proselytizing mission to spread "civilization" far beyond territorial boundaries. New imperialism was not the highest stage of either capitalism or nationalism; higher peaks (and deeper depths) lay ahead for both impulses. It was, however, the culmination of the transition to modern globalization in the Western world.

The distinction between early-start and late-start modernizers makes it possible to assign different motives for imperial expansion. Britain's global dominance set the parameters for other modernizing states, which had to respond to the penetrating influence of British capital and sponsorship of free trade and the gold standard. Late-start countries had to play catch-up. They were mostly new or newly reconstituted states that were preoccupied with nation-building. Late-starters lacked the means to match their aspirations. Fiscal unity remained incomplete;

manufacturing was still in its early stages; protective tariffs defended agriculture and supported industry. In these cases, imperialism was driven largely by the need to support nation-building at home. The return from risky military investments, when forthcoming, was primarily national unity and the psychic income derived from prestige. Weak states, by definition, could erect few defenses against British influence. Even strong states had to compromise. If they adopted protectionist tariffs, they also welcomed British capital, joined the gold standard, and exported to Britain's relatively open market. Foreign tariffs hindered exports of British manufactures, but generated the revenue needed to service loans issued by the City of London, which had become the powerhouse of the international economy.

The penetrative power and insistent demands of modern globalization put the institutions and values of the recipients under pressure to adapt and conform. Where the necessary degree of integration could be achieved with minimal disruption, as most obviously in colonies of white settlement, the process was relatively painless—except for the indigenous inhabitants. In such instances, expansion came as close to the ideals of Adam Smith and Richard Cobden as reality allowed. Where integration called for significant institutional adjustment, as typically happened in Asia, Africa, and the Middle East, expansion was more likely to turn into assertive imperialism. Conquest and occupation were rarely the results of the breakdown of informal empire, but rather the products of the stresses generated by attempts to create it. It was in these continents that the most dramatic and widespread evidence of a backlash against enforced globalization appeared. Military resistance, guerrilla warfare, emigration, and political opposition formed a sequence that extended throughout the colonial era. Some new colonies were brought under control speedily; others defied their Western rulers for decades. In some regions, opponents of colonial rule rallied in support of an ancien régime and customs that the West had outlawed, such as slavery. In other cases, resistance was a protest against the terms of the new demands and the speed with which they were imposed. The self-strengthening movement in China, like the Young Turks in the Ottoman Empire, recognized the need to adopt Western improvements but sought to do so in ways that would preserve the core values that held their societies together.

When viewed in an international perspective, the imperialism of the United States fits readily into a common pattern arising from the problems of transforming military-fiscal states into national-industrial states. During the first half of the nineteenth century, as chapter 4 showed, the

Republic became the most successful and most neglected example of Britain's informal influence. It was not until after the Civil War that the United States joined states on the continent of Europe in undergoing the transition to modern globalization and becoming an imperial power. The transformation, which is discussed in chapter 7, was the greatest and by far the most successful of all the "self-strengthening" movements that made their mark in the late nineteenth century. Nevertheless, it brought acute strains of the kind that threatened the stability and cohesion of states in Europe. It also prompted the United States to reach for the imperial option and to do so for motives that reflected its position on the scale of uneven development.

The year 1898, when imperial enthusiasts in the United States pocketed the remnants of the Spanish Empire, represented one of the peaks of new imperialism. Britain completed its acquisition of the Sudan and came close to war with France over Fashoda, an obscure village in central Africa, and in association with France, Russia, and Germany extracted territorial concessions from China. The year before, the British had occupied Benin, the Germans had claimed Rwanda, and the French had annexed Madagascar. The year after, the British became embroiled in the Anglo–South African War, the French consolidated their hold on Laos, and the Boxer risings broke out in China.

By 1914, what Adam Smith had called the "golden dream" had become a reality.[215] Collectively, Western powers ruled or controlled the greater part of the world. In 1880, Britain held about 90 percent of all areas and people colonized by Western states, and had attained a degree of dominance that "probably has no equal in history."[216] In 1913, the Union Jack flew over two-thirds of the total land under colonial rule and nearly three-quarters of all colonial subjects, despite forceful competition from rival imperial powers and a huge increase in the area under colonial control.[217] This was an impressive haul for a country conventionally supposed to be in decline. In contrast, the United States accounted for only 0.6 percent of the territory held by the colonial powers in 1913 and 1.8 percent of their inhabitants.[218] Nevertheless, the Republic had joined the imperial club and was shortly to acquire a large stake in preserving it.

Richard Cobden recognized, as few of his contemporaries did, the potential global influence of the United States. As early as 1835, he chided British statesmen for being "engrossed with the politics of petty states," while taking little notice of "the country that ought, beyond all others, to engage the attention, and even to excite the apprehension of this commercial nation."[219] Thirty years later, Whitman looked even further ahead:

Are all nations communing: is there going to be but one heart to the
   globe?
Is humanity forming *en-masse*? For lo, tyrants tremble, crowns grow
   dim,
The earth, restive, confronts a new era, perhaps a general divine war,
No one knows what will happen next, such portents fill the days and
   nights. [220]

CHAPTER 7

ACHIEVING EFFECTIVE INDEPENDENCE

"IN THE MIDST OF CONFUSION AND DISTRESS"[1]

Tocqueville, writing in the 1840s, could speak about the consequences of political upheaval with authority drawn from his own experience. "The country then assumes a dim and dubious shape in the eyes of its citizens," he wrote.[2] In such times, "they have neither the instinctive patriotism of a monarchy nor the reflecting patriotism of a republic; but they have stopped between the two in the midst of confusion and distress." The turmoil arising from the Civil War was not resolved in 1865. The Union was restored, but unity, long a prospective quality, remained elusive. What followed was a troubled, prolonged, but ultimately successful venture in building a stable nation-state.

Tocqueville's instinctive sense of the comparative survives today in specialized studies to a greater extent than it does in overviews of the late nineteenth century as a whole.[3] The most familiar approach divides the national story into segments that have become stepping-stones for crossing the years between the Civil War and World War I.[4] The resulting narrative begins with the hope and disappointment of postwar Reconstruction, continues through the successes and excesses of the Gilded Age, transmutes into the renewed idealism and reforms of the Progressive Era, and halts in 1914. The sequence has a predominantly political character that is supplemented, in varying degrees, by subthemes drawn from an evolving (and revolving) historiography. The literature on development is typically allocated a minor role or left to economists, who generally omit political considerations. Cultural history has received overdue attention, but also tends to remain in a compartment of its own construction. Each specialization has produced an innovative and a voluminous literature. The questions addressed in the present chapter, however, require a way of threading these different contributions together.

Tocqueville's perspective is illuminating in revealing the extent to which developments within the United States were localized illustrations of changes that were occurring simultaneously in Western Europe. The United States was one among other newly minted or newly resuscitated Western states that emerged from war in the 1860s and 1870s, engaged in similar programs of economic development and nation-building, and struggled to prevent the strains of transition from disrupting the process. Tocqueville, a prophet of transition, saw that "epochs sometimes occur in the life of a nation when the old customs of a people are changed."[5] The late nineteenth century was such an epoch. The outcome, in the case of the United States, was a state whose political contours remained fixed until the mid-twentieth century, when a new era of decolonization and civil rights reshaped what by then had become the old order. The United States was distinctive in being the first of Britain's former colonies to wrestle with these problems. It was not, however, unique. As chapter 6 showed, European states, such as Germany and Italy, had also been subjected to colonial rule. Like the United States, they engaged with the same problems for the same purpose, which was to build a robust and independent nation-state. In all these cases, the transition to modern globalization was a necessary condition of achieving effective decolonization.

At the outset of the period, political stability remained provisional. New conflicts scarred the peace settlement that followed the Civil War. An intense and often bitter struggle between Republicans and Democrats over the shape and direction of the Union reached its high point in the 1890s, when it threatened to subvert the polity. Rapid industrialization, immigration, and urbanization produced new opportunities but also brought new conflicts between capital and labor, and created attendant social problems. The strains of structural transformation intersected with cyclical fluctuations and a long period of deflation to produce agrarian unrest and militant strike action.[6] Regional, sectoral, ethnic, and class differences continued to hamper the creation of a counterculture that was an essential foundation of national unity.

Political leaders hurried to produce solutions to the divisions brought by socioeconomic change. Federal authorities countered direct threats to civil order by applying the force of law and the force of arms. The Republicans ended a series of desperate electoral contests in the 1890s by confirming the supremacy of the Northern program of national economic development they had begun to install during the Civil War. A rich endowment of natural resources made a high degree of self-sufficiency possible. Republicans and Democrats redoubled their efforts to inculcate a sense of national identity by applying a mixture of Anglo-Saxon ethnicity, Anglo-Protestant values, and occasional bursts of Anglophobia to override regional, ethnic, and class affiliations. Half a century after Emerson had delivered his declaration of literary independence, artistic expression had drawn on indigenous sources of inspiration to a depth that freed it from dependence on foreign influences. Taken as a whole, the process of nation-building was essentially an exercise in bonding white Americans. The unqualified, principally Native Americans and former slaves, played their part by serving as antonyms who helped to define the values and superiority of others.

By 1914, the United States had achieved as much autonomy as involvement in a globalized world allowed. Relations with Britain retained respect but had discarded deference. Tocqueville thought that the "confusion and distress" he observed in France were best overcome by combining patriotism and religion in one ethnie. As subsequent sections of this chapter will show, the United States adopted his recommendation in resolving its own perilous uncertainties after 1865.

"ALL HAS BEEN LOST, EXCEPT OFFICE OR THE HOPE OF IT"[7]

James Bryce saw himself as a realist rather than as a cynic, and his comment, made in the mid-1880s, derived from his belief that the Civil War had settled the great issues of principle that had troubled the Republic since independence. Office and interest were indeed prime concerns of both Republicans and Democrats. The use of the term "pork barrel," which is a familiar part of the language of politics in the United States today, dates from the 1870s. Nevertheless, preoccupation with the spoils of office was consistent with the pursuit of larger political goals that sought to consolidate the Union and determine its future. Old enmities did not dissolve either easily or speedily. New problems, arising from rapid economic development, exerted unprecedented pressures on the still fragile polity. Bryce passed these developments by. He deployed his immense industry and learning to endorse his belief that an educated elite should run the world as an Anglo-Saxon fiefdom. He saw consensus where there was discord. To invert Clausewitz's observation, the politics of the period can be thought of as civil war continued by other means.

The victorious North placed its mark on the peace settlement that followed the Civil War. In contrast to the prewar era, the Republican Party dominated the Senate and provided every president except one between 1861 and 1913. Northern states also supplied the majority of Supreme Court justices during this period, and most of the Speakers of the House of Representatives. Nevertheless, the victors did not have a monopoly of the spoils of office.[8] The South survived because the Union survived. The Constitution guaranteed that former slave states would continue to send representatives to Congress. The assurance enabled elements in the South to mount a counterrevolution aimed at minimizing the consequences of defeat and reasserting states' rights, though shorn of the right to own slaves.[9] The losers found a powerful common cause in resenting abolition, central power, and military occupation, and in defending what was left of Southern institutions and values. Southern voters increased their commitment to the Democratic Party and ensured that elections were closely contested. Control of the House of Representatives oscillated. Democrats had majorities there in 1875–81, 1883–89, and 1891–95; their nominee, Grover Cleveland, became president in 1885–89 and again in 1893–97. It was not until the election of 1896 that the Republicans won what turned out to be a decisive victory, which was confirmed in 1900 and extended to 1913, when Woodrow Wilson, a Democrat, became president.[10]

The intensity of the struggle between Republicans and Democrats after the Civil War was a measure of the difficulty of reconciling victors and vanquished. Confederate soldiers returned from the battlefield to find their home states under a form of colonial military occupation.[11] A Northern army of "liberation" was installed in the South to oversee the abolition of slavery and to engage in what, today, would be called nation-building. Initially, the occupation forces made considerable progress in ensuring that formal abolition produced a labor force that was genuinely free and could exercise the right to vote.[12] By the early 1870s, however, a number of Confederate units had regrouped as White League militias and had become, in the language of the present, insurgents employing terrorist methods. By then, too, other vigilante organizations, including the Ku Klux Klan, had come into existence to oppose Reconstruction.[13] Francis Nicholls, a former Confederate brigadier general who became governor of Louisiana in 1876, was one example of the resurgent South. He ruled with the aid of a militia that helped to consolidate support for the Democrats and crush labor protests on the state's sugar plantations.[14] Armed resistance to occupation merged with anti-black violence to frustrate abolitionists and others who hoped that the peace settlement would bring far-reaching reform to the South.

Changing attitudes in the North also impeded Reconstruction.[15] After the Civil War, there was a pressing need for cooperation to restore political stability and economic growth, and little enthusiasm for further military action against white compatriots.[16] Northern business interests were particularly keen to see the resumption of cotton supplies, which entered the textile factories of New England as well as those of Manchester.[17] New York bankers had a stake to defend: they held most of the mortgages on Southern plantations.[18] Republicans, projecting Northern priorities onto the Union as a whole, were keen to retain protective tariffs and return to the discipline of the gold standard, which had been suspended during the war. Their program called for political concessions to gain the support, or at least the acquiescence, of the South and to retain the Midwest. The abolition of slavery had ended fears in the Midwest that an extension of the plantation system would overwhelm the region's small farmers. In doing so, however, it had also freed voters there to support policies advocating free trade and soft money, which inclined them to look to the Democrats rather than to the Republicans.[19]

A compromise reached in 1877 satisfied both sections of the political elite by confirming their privileges and giving them a common interest in guarding legitimate property rights, maintaining low taxes, and limiting excessive government intervention. By then, the North had abandoned its initial hope of developing a labor force in the South that was free and efficient.[20] In the eyes of many Northern commentators, liberated slaves had become either "lazy" or, worse still, political activists who would add to the growing criticism of the capitalist system. Reform was desirable, but opposition generated ill will without winning votes. Republicans and Democrats struck a deal whereby the North ended federal control over state governments in the South in exchange for a guarantee of loyalty to the Union. Having abandoned the South, the Republicans were free to turn their attention to the expanding Midwest, which had to be held if the Northern vision of the Union was to be realized.[21] Nation-building, as the United States first discovered at home and was later to rediscover elsewhere, was a task that could overwhelm victors, even after they had become superpowers.

Reconstruction ended by producing a series of durable one-party states based on an ideology of white supremacy and militarism. Southern states, rather like the British dominions or the princely states of India, continued to manage their internal affairs in accordance with their own priorities. The shattered institutions of the postwar South enabled "Big Men" to establish or expand patrimonial systems of local government that dispensed personal favors in return for political loyalty.[22] Although the white rajahs of the South had a more distinctive profile than their Northern counterparts had, the North also extended policies of segregation after the Civil War and supported federal agencies as they set about subduing the remaining independent Native American states and clearing their land for white settlement.[23] These initiatives set international standards for the globalization of discrimination: the "white Australia" policy and South Africa's system of apartheid both drew on the legislative example provided by Southern states.[24] The political economy of large segments of the South came to resemble that of ex-colonial states in what later became known as the Third World.[25]

The spread of Anglo-Saxon racism during the last quarter of the century added an ideological justification to the material basis of reunion.[26] Legislation passed by Southern states codified segregation and removed voting rights from African Americans.[27] These measures, known collectively as the "Jim Crow" laws, made their appearance in the 1870s, though the most far-reaching were passed in the 1890s. At the same time, religious spokesmen in the North exerted their influence to shift attitudes from moral improvement through emancipation to national reconciliation through forgiveness.[28] Redemption replaced retribution; the ethnie prevailed over the demos. Changing attitudes toward the South merged with a growing concern in the North with disturbing and potentially destabilizing increases in immigration and urbanization. Globalization was making its influence felt; the "haves" were beginning to fear the rise of the "have-nots." Reconciliation with the South, though still a work in progress, offered the prospect of devising common solutions to common problems.[29] White property owners and employers in North and South alike bonded by caste to avert conflict by class.

The compromise reached in 1877 merged with a wider challenge that threatened to subvert the newly restored Union during the last quarter of the century. Structural economic change following industrial expansion, urban growth, and increased population produced new social problems in the United States, as they did in Europe.[30] The scramble to adjust political organizations and programs to meet novel challenges threw the postwar party system into disarray and cast political control into the air. Discordant voices made themselves heard.[31] Two splinter groups, the Republican "Mugwumps" and "Bourbon" Democrats, enjoyed moments of influence during the 1870s and 1880s. They had much in common, despite belonging to different parties. They were liberal elitists who looked back at least as much as they looked forward, and looked askance at populist agitation. They supported free trade, the gold standard, and fiscal discipline, and were alienated from party machines and the patronage they dispensed. They shared a Gladstonian preference for cosmopolitan internationalism over strident imperialism. Their moments, however, were few, and the third party they proposed never materialized. As in Europe, the pressures of the time and the need to capture expanding electorates caused the main political parties to become increasingly professional. In the United States, the future lay with "machine politics" managed by party "bosses" who distributed "spoils" from the substantial revenues accruing to the enlarged federal state, and in return accumulated political capital in the form of electoral loyalty.[32]

The Republican Party used its dominance of Congress during the Civil War to deliver a substantial segment of the Hamiltonian development program, which the party's spokesmen had long claimed to be the only truly national policy and assured means of delivering effective independence.[33] The Morrill Tariff (1861) won the support of manufacturers in the North, who gained from increased protection, and shipbuilders on the East and West coasts, who benefited from sizeable naval contracts.[34] The Homestead Act (1862) greatly increased the number of small farmers, especially in the Midwest. Government support enabled the first transcontinental railroad to join West and East coasts in 1869 and added to the number of citizens who had a stake in the success of the Union. With both eyes focused on the Midwest, the Republicans refrained from adopting an uncompromising protectionist policy.[35] Similarly, while negotiating a return to the gold standard, the party offered concessions to the Midwest by allowing silver to regain its status as legal tender in 1878, and by retaining the possibility of adopting bimetallism if an international agreement could be reached.[36] The compromise aimed at recovering the Union's creditworthiness in the City of London and its standing in the global economy, while mollifying opinion in the Midwest, which feared the deflationary consequences of "sound money."[37] It was an uneasy balance. When pressed, however, the Republicans placed gold before silver.[38]

Postbellum Democrats, heirs to the Jeffersonian tradition, favored free trade and decentralized government.[39] Protective tariffs had an adverse effect on a large number of Democratic voters. They inflated the price of farm machinery and consumer goods imported into the South and Midwest, drew capital into the North by increasing profit margins there, and encouraged foreign states to impose retaliatory tariffs on agricultural exports from the United States. The redistributive consequences of this artificial subsidy, so opponents of the tariff argued, further entrenched the already uneven regional development of the Union.[40] Accordingly,

Democrats pressed for controls on monopolistic practices, which rural voters resented because they raised railroad freight rates as well as prices of manufactured goods. Democrats also feared that additional income raised from tariff rates that were higher than basic revenue needs would be used to fund "big government," especially big Republican government, at the expense of the states. A segment of the Democratic Party came to sympathize with the case for bimetallism, too, and was prepared to take unilateral action, if necessary. Bimetallism appealed as a means of alleviating the effects of the depression on farming and mining interests. The "silverites," as they were loosely called, presented bimetallism as an emblem of political independence and the gold standard as a symbol of continuing subordination to foreign influences and their financial agents in the Northeast. The reintroduction of silver currency, they claimed, would increase the money supply, cause the dollar to depreciate, boost exports, and ease the burden of debt repayment.[41] In contrast, gold allied to deflation transferred wealth from debtors to creditors, which in practice meant largely from the South to the North.

The election of Grover Cleveland, a Democrat, to the presidency in 1884 gave the party its first significant chance since the Civil War of modifying Republican policies. Democrats were not yet converted to bimetallism, and Cleveland himself supported the gold standard, but they were united on the tariff question. Most of Cleveland's senior colleagues in government were members of the Cobden Club, which was founded in Britain in 1866 to spread the theory and practice of free trade.[42] The Republicans had imposed high tariffs after the Civil War mainly to redeem the substantial public debt incurred by the conflict. By the mid-1880s, however, the federal government had settled the debt and accumulated a surplus, which opened Republicans to the charge that high tariff rates were creating an overmighty government.[43] The Democrats saw an opening and pressed the case for reverting to a basic revenue tariff. Cleveland, however, struggled unsuccessfully amid accusations from Republicans that he and the Democrats were pawns moved by British interests. In the election campaign of 1888, which put the issue to the vote, the Republicans made a visceral appeal to national sentiment by accusing their opponents of lacking patriotism, or, as one congressman put it, of attempting to "supplant the star-spangled banner everywhere by the British union jack."[44] When Cleveland lost his bid for reelection, the *New York Times* attributed it partly to the false belief that he would "surrender to British influence."[45]

The Republicans, having resumed their control of Congress and the presidency, celebrated in 1890 by spending the surplus revenue and raising tariffs. Part of the accumulated revenue funded a modern navy, which was deployed against Spain in 1898. Another slice financed pensions for Civil War veterans. The Dependent Pension Act (1890) was designed on Bismarckian lines to be a vote-winning measure.[46] During the 1890s, the Pension Act accounted for an astounding 40 percent of all federal government expenditures and covered about one million citizens.[47] According to one contemporary analyst, it was "the most extravagant pension law ever enacted," though from a Republican viewpoint well worth the money.[48]

The McKinley Tariff raised import duties to unprecedented heights.[49] Its purpose was to strengthen protection for domestic manufacturers while also helping to reduce the revenue surplus. In response to criticisms of his bill, Congressman William McKinley inserted a clause that allowed free entry to imported sugar and compensated domestic sugar-beet producers by giving them a bounty on their output. The free entry of sugar simultaneously reduced the revenue derived from one of the most important sources while dangling the prospect of lower prices for domestic consumers. At the insistence of his colleague, James G. Blaine, the Secretary of State and an ardent expansionist, McKinley also provided for reciprocity agreements in a last-minute attempt to retain the votes of farmers in the Midwest. The agreements allowed molasses, coffee, tea, and hides, as well as sugar, free entry into United States in exchange for reciprocal concessions for U.S. exports. McKinley was reluctant to accept Blaine's amendment but did so in the interests of party unity. The final package preserved protection while offering Republican supporters a counter to the free-trade arguments advanced by the Democrats.

Predictably, the Cobden Club called the McKinley Tariff "an outrage on civilization" that would probably "destroy British trade" and "lead to the annexation of Canada." An agitated correspondent for the *Times* in Canada judged that the tariff amounted to an unprovoked virtual "war on the British Empire."[50] Gladstone rehearsed the case for free trade; Blaine responded by declaring that Britain wanted to perpetuate "the old colonial idea of the last century," whereby the United States would remain a producer of raw materials.[51] Protection, Blaine concluded, had produced an "auspicious and momentous result."[52] "Never before in the history of the world," he asserted, "has comfort been enjoyed, education acquired, and independence secured by so large a proportion of the total population as in the United States of America."[53]

McKinley responded to attacks on his bill by claiming that the Democrats were conspiring with Britain to impose free trade on the United States, arguing that "they are both fighting for the same unpatriotic cause, that they are engaged in the same crusade against our industries. They rejoice together over the same victory; theirs is a joint warfare against American labour and American wages, a plot against the industrial life of the nation, a blow struck at the American commonwealth."[54] He reaffirmed, with an implied reference to Henry Clay, that "the American System or policy of a protective tariff has been fully vindicated."[55] Democrats struck back by accusing their opponents of favoring large corporations, big government, and foreign financial interests and of sacrificing the interests of consumers. This time, the charge stuck: the decision to raise the general tariff was a political miscalculation that cost the Republicans their majority in the House of Representatives in 1890 and the presidency in 1892, when Grover Cleveland was voted into the White House for his second term.

Both parties also had to contend with the appearance of mass movements that lay outside their control. Economic development had created towns and industries in the Northeast and upper Midwest; international demand had increased the number of farmers exporting to world markets. The long deflation of the late nineteenth century interspersed with sporadic bouts of depression, which were especially severe in 1873–78, 1882–85, 1887–88, and 1893–94, reduced living standards and expectations.[56] An uncertain world had become even more precarious. Populism was a backlash against globalization that challenged the existing political order, as it did in Europe. "Mugwumps" and "Bourbons" were survivors from a disappearing world. Popular disaffection in both country and town pointed to the politics of the future, which obliged Republicans and Democrats to sharpen their differences in a bid to capture and contain dissent.

The Grange associations, which appeared in 1867, were the first agrarian movements of national standing to express the concerns of farmers throughout the Union.[57] The Grangers were multipurpose, self-help organizations that aimed to bring social and educational improvements to rural areas and to raise farmers' living standards. They reached their peak in the mid-1870s, when they were superseded by the Farmers' Alliance, which was founded in 1876.[58] The Alliance accepted the realities of the capitalist system and focused on improving the bargaining power of its members by forming cooperatives and pressing for government action to control railroad and other business monopolies. The Alliance helped to secure the passage of the Interstate Commerce Act of 1887, which gave the federal government authority to promote competition, though in practice the Act had the opposite effect of sheltering collusive agreements.[59] At the close of the 1880s, after publicity and lobbying had achieved only limited results, the Alliance entered the political arena directly with a far-reaching program that called for decentralized banking, restraints on corporate power, and the adoption of bimetallism.

The first important urban labor organization, the Knights of Labor, was formed in Philadelphia in 1869.[60] As their name suggests, the Knights shunned the plutocratic values of the Gilded Age and drew their initial inspiration from Jefferson's ideal world of sturdy, individual craftsmen.[61] The Knights, however, were also realists who attempted to reach out from their artisanal base to workers in the new industries. Their support grew after they won national prominence by organizing a major strike on the railroads in 1877. By the late 1880s they had attracted more than one million members.[62] Despite these successes, internal dissension over policy, organizational weaknesses, and opposition from employers limited their effectiveness. Although the Knights continued to break a lance or two, a new champion, the American Federation of Labor (AFL), superseded them in 1886.[63] The AFL adopted a pragmatic approach to labor issues: like the Farmers' Alliance, it accepted the permanence of the industrial order and sought to improve labor conditions within it.[64] "Wage slavery," as seen by the Knights, became "wage work" undertaken by those whose honest toil deserved, in the malleable phrase of the day, a "living wage."[65]

Other organizations established at this time represented unskilled workers in particular industries. New trade unions, such as the United Mine Workers (1890) and the American Railway Union (1893), though willing to cooperate with private enterprise, were also prepared to take militant action to defend jobs and wages. On the other hand, the Socialist Labour Party (SLP), which was founded in 1877, was wholly opposed to capitalism, while various anarchist associates and splinter groups advocated the use of force to overthrow the existing system of political economy. Although the SLP struggled throughout the 1880s, it gained members and momentum after Daniel deLeon took charge of its fortunes in 1890.[66] However, the trend faltered and then faded. Socialism made little headway in the United States. At the time, though, civil authorities and employers, lacking prophetic insight, saw only a mounting threat to the world they had rebuilt after the Civil War. Many of them were aware that the challenge they faced was one that confronted governments in Europe too. The crisis was international; to those of a nervous disposition, it was part of a global conspiracy as well.[67]

In 1892, a sizeable segment of the agrarian interest, combined with elements of the AFL and residues of the Knights of Labor, entered the political arena directly.[68] The result was the creation of the People's Party (also known as the Populists), which attempted to break the two-party system by spanning differences of occupation, race, and region.[69] Populism, minimally defined, refers to movements that stand outside established political parties, distrust elite rule and big business, and seek what they conceive to be economic justice for the "common man."[70] The populists were carrying forward the "green uprising" begun by Andrew Jackson's movement against policies espoused by East Coast elites, though their prehistory can be traced to demonstrations against colonial rule in the eighteenth century.[71] In the 1890s, their aim was not to restrain economic development but to shape it to their own needs.[72] Their appearance complemented similar protests expressed elsewhere at this time in countries of white settlement, in continental Europe, and in resistance movements throughout the colonial world. Globalization had tightened the bonds of integration. The structural and cyclical changes that wrenched the international economy during the last quarter of the century were felt from New Hampshire to New Zealand.

The Populists made a creditable showing in the presidential election of 1892 and used their new standing to ally with the Democratic Party on terms that endorsed most of their reform program.[73] Cleveland's reelection as president raised anxiety levels in Republican circles and brought renewed attacks on his alleged pro-British policies.[74] The sudden onset of the most serious economic crisis of the period, which struck in 1893 and persisted until 1897 (with a brief and partial remission in 1894–1895), encouraged the Populists to believe that major political change was in sight.[75] At this point, there seemed to be a real chance of reversing the policies pursued by the Republicans since the Civil War.

Recent events overseas confirmed that the financial system was vulnerable to sudden shocks. A boom in foreign lending to Latin America ended abruptly at the close of the 1880s, when the Bank of England raised its discount rate to restrain domestic demand. Countries that relied on British capital to fund their development programs felt the consequences immediately.[76] Argentina defaulted on its external debt in 1890; there was a comparable financial panic in Australia in the following year.[77] The financial crisis of 1893 concentrated minds and resolved residual uncertainties. Increasing numbers of Democrats endorsed unilateral bimetallism in the interest of their largely agrarian base. Republicans retained bimetallism as an option in their manifesto, providing it could be incorporated into an international agreement. Meanwhile, they continued to back the gold standard in response to their key supporters in banking and other businesses whose priority was to maintain the international creditworthiness of the United States.

The United States felt the international reverberations of these events almost immediately because it drew about 75 percent of its long-term foreign capital from the City of London and relied on capital inflows to settle the balance of payments.[78] Confidence remained fragile in 1893, when the Treasury's reserves dropped below the level needed to support the gold standard.[79] The New York Stock Exchange suffered heavy losses; country banks in the Midwest experienced a rash of failures.[80] As confidence collapsed, investors liquidated their holdings. The withdrawal of foreign investments obliged the Treasury to defend the value of the dollar by depleting its gold reserves. The loss of gold reduced the stock of money in circulation, depressed prices, curtailed demand, and further inhibited new investment. A run on the reserves raised the prospect that the United States would be obliged to devalue, thus abandoning the gold standard, downgrading the country's credit rating, and presenting creditors with the prospect of repudiation.[81]

President Cleveland, the unlucky office-holder in 1893, was a monetary conservative as well as a Democrat. Under his direction, Congress repealed the Silver Purchase Act, which the Republicans had passed in 1890 in an attempt to mollify small businesses and consumers and persuade silverite Republicans in the Senate to support the McKinley Tariff.[82] The Act authorized the Treasury to purchase silver with the aim of boosting its price and reflating the economy, while also winning votes in silver-mining states in the Midwest, six of which had joined the Union in 1889–1890. Repeal was essential because the continuing decline in the price of silver placed an increasing burden on the Treasury's diminishing gold reserves. To compensate pro-silver critics within the party, Cleveland undertook to lower the tariff levels imposed by the Republicans in 1890. The result, the Wilson-Gorman Act of 1894, achieved only modest reductions. Republicans denounced the measure in terms that drew on familiarity to add credibility: Cleveland was a pro-British agent; reduced duties on imports would undercut American manufactures.[83]

The banking crisis, combined with falling manufacturing output and agricultural prices, provoked militant responses that further alarmed investors at home and abroad. The sporadic acts of political violence that scarred the United States during this period underlined the seriousness of the challenge to authority and the anxiety felt among middle classes over the prospect of wider attacks on property.[84] The Great Railroad Strike of 1877 and the Haymarket Riots in Chicago in 1886 provided previews of the intense turbulence that was to come in the 1890s. In 1877, several weeks of confrontation involving strikers, police, militias, and federal troops ended with more than one hundred deaths and massive damage to property.[85] In 1886, a demonstration by urban workers organized by a German Marxist-anarchist immigrant started as a strike and ended with a bombing, a fatality, and a number of wounded.[86] News of the event quickly spread to Europe, where it provided further encouragement for similar dissident movements. The episode was not repeated, but its memory lived on and added to fears that the stability of the state was under threat.

The AFL proceeded to organize a series of major strikes and protests during the early 1890s, when rising unemployment carried the conflict between capital and labor to unprecedented levels.[87] In 1892, a strike at the Homestead plant in Pittsburgh, which ended in violence, the intervention of the state militia, and a number of deaths, broke the Amalgamated Association of Iron and Steel Workers, the largest union of the day, and retarded the development of the trade union movement as a whole.[88] The high, or low, point came in 1894, which saw a national strike of coal-miners and the best-known strike of the decade involving workers of the Pullman Palace Car Company in Chicago and their affiliates elsewhere in the Midwest and in California.[89] The federal government mobilized 20,000 troops to crush the strike. Eugene Debs, the leader of the American Railway Union, spent six months in prison, where he read Karl Marx and subsequently became the first serious socialist candidate for the presidency of the United States.

Commentators portrayed the conflict between capital and labor in military terms that conjured up memories of the Civil War and the threat to national unity.[90] Labor leaders "declared war" on employers, government, and society; the combatants "marched" into "battle"; heroic deeds were recorded; "victories" were claimed. The mainstream press presented the issues in dispute as tests of loyalty. As *Harper's Weekly*, a moderate journal, declared in the middle of the Pullman strike: "The nation is fighting for its own existence just as truly as in suppressing the great rebellion."[91] The press called on the public to choose between patriotism, the buttress of civil order, and anarchy, the source of disunion. True Americans were urged to rally to Uncle Sam and the flag to repel an alien invasion. Strikers were portrayed as being un-American, which indeed many of them were. As one reporter commented, none too subtly, the Republic was under attack from a "malodorous crowd of anarchistic foreign trash."[92] As the language of militarism became politicized, politics became increasingly polarized, and the space for reasoned disagreement narrowed. Propertied interests fell in behind "law and order" at home, as they did abroad. Support for Irish rebels, who had been seen to be struggling for liberty against colonial rule, ebbed. Thereafter, American foreign policy tended to distance itself from radical movements and instead buttressed the representatives of stability and security.[93]

The novel feature of the Republican campaign, however, was the assertion that class warfare, propelled by strike action and agrarian discontent, was about to tear the Union apart. Northern veterans' organizations, mindful of the welfare benefits financed by the tariff, added their considerable weight to the Republican cause. In their view, "anarchist rebels" were as much a threat to the Union in 1896 as "secessionist rebels" had been in 1861.[94] McKinley himself appealed to Confederate veterans to fall in behind the Union flag: "Let us remember now and in all the future," he declared in a phrase that sprinkled hope over reality, "that we are Americans, and what is good for Ohio is good for Virginia."[95] The influential Roman Catholic Archbishop of St. Paul added a widely publicized statement denouncing the Democrats and warning of the "war of class against class" and of the "reckless men" who "may light up the country in the lurid fires of a commune."[96]

The scene was set for a major, and in the event decisive, ideological confrontation between two visions of the future of American capitalism. Disillusioned Democrats and Populists nominated William Jennings Bryan, a committed reformer in matters of economic policy, as their presidential candidate in 1896. The nomination of Bryan brought radical politics in the United States as close to power as it was to reach. Bryan was no Marxist, but his pronouncements, which included aphorisms, such as "plutocracy is abhorrent in a republic," and "no one can earn a million dollars honestly," alarmed the defenders of sound government, sound money, and large bank balances, and galvanized them into action.[97] Under Bryan's leadership, the Populist program of unilateral bimetallism and the redistribution of wealth represented a backlash against globalization and the East Coast bankers and industrialists who were regarded as its malevolent agents.

The election of 1896, which pitted Bryan's prophetic radicalism against McKinley's sober conservatism, resolved the central political debates of the last quarter of the nineteenth century.[98] Bryan's nomination prompted business and banking interests to engage in organized politics on a far greater scale than before.[99] By the 1890s, the business world included a number of large industrial corporations with the power to influence policies affecting their interests.[100] The National Association of Manufacturers was formed in 1895 to support McKinley's program of tariffs and reciprocity.[101] The "sound-money men," as one of them called the corporate elite, raised an unprecedented sum to defend the tariff and the gold standard.[102] Standard Oil and J. P. Morgan alone contributed an amount to the Republicans that exceeded the whole of the Democratic Party's campaign fund.[103] The largest single donor in 1896, however, was the neglected figure of Henry Havemeyer, the head of the mighty Sugar Trust.[104]

In the months before the presidential election, when the Treasury's difficulties were "even greater" than in 1895, J. P. Morgan organized a posse of New York bankers and called in reinforcements from the City of London to support the dollar by buying government bonds and stemming the outflow of gold.[105] The financial community underwrote the fiscal position of the United States to ensure that borrowers had the means of servicing their debts in sound money.[106] Business interests had an additional ally in the form of the Supreme Court, which took a friendly view of the needs of private enterprise. As a result, the weight of the federal government bore down on the labor movement. The Anti-Trust Act was deployed not to reel in the mega-corporations but to attack the unions.[107]

Marcus Hanna, who was McKinley's election manager and a wealthy businessman in his own right, mounted a highly effective campaign based on the themes of reconciliation and national unity.[108] Both parties claimed to speak for the national interest and appealed explicitly to memories of the Civil War to validate their claims. Democrats invoked the Jeffersonian tradition to emphasize states' rights, and advocated bimetallism as a means of winning Southern and Western votes. In 1896, Ben Tillman, a prominent senator from South Carolina and a candidate for the Democratic presidential nomination, began his speech to the convention with the words: "I come from the South, from the home of secession," and went on to call for unity with producers in Midwestern states against the power of Northern corporations and finance.[109] Republicans responded not only by criticizing unilateral bimetallism, but also by claiming that the strategy of the Democrats constituted "as wicked a movement as that after which it was deliberately patterned, the Southern rebellion of 1861."[110] Newspapers and campaign material made repeated references to the Civil War in stressing the threat that renewed sectionalism, disguised as bimetallism, posed to political stability.

Urgent appeals for national unity in the face of claims that class conflict and anarchism were about to destroy the Union attracted enough voters to deliver a Republican victory. The Democrats failed to make sufficient headway in the Midwest, despite the appeal of bimetallism and free trade. The Republicans covered themselves by reaffirming their willingness to consider an international agreement on bimetallism, but remained exposed on the issue of protection. By the 1890s, however, agriculture was changing as well as beginning to shrink. Tractors were plowing the homesteads of Jefferson's yeomen; highly capitalized agribusinesses were on the horizon. Towns and industries had grown up in the northern part of the region and were becoming integrated into the capital and commodity markets of the northeast, giving voters a stake in the Northern development program. The West was won by guns, barbed wire, and lawyers; it was won over by commercial inducements that integrated it with the economic heartland of the country.

The Democrats, though defeated in 1896, did not surrender, and were soon able to re-enter the contest. To extend Benjamin Franklin's observation, nothing in the United States is certain except death, taxes, and frequent elections. The mid-term elections in 1898 gave the Populist-Democratic alliance another chance to dislodge the Republicans. Unlike Cleveland, however, McKinley had luck on his side: the economy began to revive.[111] Reflecting a decade later on the crisis of the early 1890s, a prominent banker settled on 1897 as "the year in which were recognized the first sure signs of the present cycle of prosperity."[112] Business failures fell; industrial production increased; farm prices rose; the balance of payments recovered; foreign investors, encouraged by McKinley's victory in 1896, returned; the pressure on the Treasury eased. Unemployment peaked in 1894 and began to fall in 1898.[113] Aggressive strike-breaking action had quelled labor militants; some of the edge had worn off agrarian discontent. In 1897, the celebratory Dingley Act rewarded manufacturers by raising import tariffs to the highest levels seen in the nineteenth century.

McKinley's decision to go to war with Spain settled the matter. Popular demand for military action trumped the waning appeal of the Populists. In contrast to the election of 1860, the elections of 1896 and 1898 showed that well-executed appeals to national unity could prevail over competing ties of region and class. The election of 1900 confirmed the dominance of the Republican Party. An appropriate juxtaposition of opposites marked the occasion: the United States formally adopted the gold standard; Bryan's second bid for the presidency, which advertised his committed anti-imperialist stance, was easily defeated.

President McKinley had little time to enjoy the triumph of his party: Leon Czolgosz assassinated him in 1901.[114] McKinley joined the list of European leaders whose lives were ended at this time by men whose frustrations persuaded them that they had no alternative. Czolgosz was an unemployed steelworker who had lost his job in the depression that struck in 1893. His desperate action expressed his disillusion with McKinley and the economic system he represented as well as his outrage at the conduct of the war in the Philippines that McKinley had authorized. McKinley had sheltered the steel industry behind protective tariffs in 1890; contributions from grateful steel barons saved him from personal bankruptcy in the following year. One of the magnates who helped to rescue the president also approved the strike-breaking measures that cost the job of the man who was to kill him.

The assignation that brought victim and assassin together captured, in miniature, the much larger national and international events that swirled around two individuals at opposite ends of the social order. The assassination was an act of despair, not a prelude to further domestic "terrorism," and it produced a reaction that helped to prepare the way for Theodore Roosevelt's brand of militant, reforming conservatism. Thereafter, the sun continued to shine upon the Republican program. The economic recovery that began in 1897, though interrupted briefly by the financial panic of 1907, lasted until 1913. Prosperity softened the edges of discontent in the United States, as it did elsewhere. For those who had hoped to replace the Republicans' national-industrial program with a radical alternative, the game was lost.

Dissent did not die with McKinley, but it ceased to pose a direct and potentially revolutionary threat to the established political order. The courts brought the radical movements of the 1890s within the compass of the law, which remained generally unsympathetic to their cause, and into conventional politics. Agrarian populism and organized labor gravitated toward the Democratic Party, which enlarged its brief to include restraints on big business and the introduction of industrial and welfare improvements.[115] Big business responded by increasing its support for the Republicans. The same trend wound through Europe, as did the amorphous movement known in the United States as the Progressives, which drew on Republicans as well as Democrats and included luminaries such as Theodore Roosevelt and Woodrow Wilson in its ranks.[116] The Progressives, like Christian Socialists and various brands of "new liberals" in Europe, aimed to introduce ameliorative reforms that would avert the threat of a radical redistribution of wealth.[117] Regulation at the federal level was one feature of the enlarged "national administrative state," which expressed the bonding of white nationalism with renewed moral purpose.[118] In the eyes of Roosevelt and Wilson, the purpose was no longer confined to the nation but impelled a crusading foreign policy that would uplift the fallen, manage their future, and demonstrate to a skeptical public at home the benefits that great leaders at the head of a powerful, benign state could confer.[119]

In 1901, Roosevelt's fortuitous accession to the presidency opened the way to reforming legislation. Although Roosevelt was the son of a wealthy businessman, he had no sympathy with the "malefactors of great wealth," and he regarded "the tyranny of a plutocracy" as the "least attractive and the most vulgar" of all forms of tyranny.[120] If the phrasing suggested that old money was looking down on new, it nevertheless provided a spur to action. Roosevelt formed the Department of Commerce and Labor in 1903 to oversee competition in business, and reactivated the almost dormant Sherman Anti-Trust Act of 1890.[121] Some big beasts were slain: the Northern Securities Trust, which controlled a large segment of the rail network, was broken up in 1904; Standard Oil and American Tobacco followed in 1911. Reforms that became law, however, were designed to preserve, not to dismantle, the prevailing system of political economy. In the aftermath of the overwhelming Republican electoral successes in 1896 and 1900, even the victors acknowledged that moderate concessions were a necessary insurance against future radical claims.

Tocqueville regarded the uneducated demos as being the main threat to democracy; Bryce thought that incorporation had produced tranquility; Roosevelt realized that Lincoln's "plain man" was being elbowed out of the way. Large firms, in his view, were a result of evolution and were the indispensable shock troops of modernization.[122] His aim was to preserve the substance of capitalism while curbing its excesses. If the people were not given a square deal, the result would be conflict between capital and labor on a scale that could again tear the nation apart. As chapter 8 will show, the war with Spain sealed national unity; moderate reform at home enabled the compact to endure.

Viewed from this perspective, the leaders of the Progressive movement can be seen as anticipating Eisenhower's vision of a "corporate commonwealth," and Johnson's "Great Society," whereby a combination of business and government paternalism would forestall social conflict at home and prevent it from developing abroad.[123] Leon Czolgosz played his part in the turn toward Progressivism. As Jane Addams reflected, shortly after the event that gave Czolgosz his moment of fame:

> As the details of the meager life of the President's assassin were disclosed, they were a challenge to the forces for social betterment in American cities. Was it not an indictment to all those whose business it is to interpret and solace the wretched, that a boy should have grown up in an American city so uncared for, so untouched

by higher issues, his wounds of life so unhealed by religion that the first talk he ever heard dealing with life's wrongs, although anarchistic and violent, should yet appear to point a way of relief?[124]

Addams, the daughter of a wealthy Republican banker and industrialist, and the most prominent social reformer of the period, symbolized the liberal response to the crises that shook the Western world in the late nineteenth century.[125] Toynbee Hall in London inspired her to found the Settlement House movement in the United States; John Dewey guided her in formulating a philosophy that emphasized duties rather than rights; Theodore Roosevelt won her support for his domestic reforms— though not for his fervent imperialism.

The reach and effectiveness of both federal and state governments greatly expanded in the decades following the Civil War. Expansion created opportunities of the kind Bryce had in mind when he referred to "office or the hope of it."[126] At the same time, reformers began the lengthy process of creating a professional, impersonal bureaucracy.[127] The armed services underwent comparable improvements after the Spanish-American War. By the 1890s, a semi-professional "promotional" state had emerged.[128] In this respect, as in many others, the experience of the United States paralleled that of contemporary Europe and drew on British experience in particular. The enlarged state was an essential building block in the construction of a modern, national polity with global potential. It put the United States on the same footing as European polities that had exchanged military fiscalism for elements that Weber defined as forming the modern state, and with it the ability to step outside the borders of the nation.[129]

"BEAUTIFUL CREDIT! THE FOUNDATION OF MODERN SOCIETY"[130]

The policies of economic nationalism that triumphed in the elections of 1896, 1898, and 1900 ensured that development stayed on the path mapped by the Republican Party until Franklin Delano Roosevelt entered the White House in 1933, despite the electoral success of the Democrats in 1912. By 1900, moreover, the United States had achieved a degree of effective economic independence that was substantially greater than had existed between 1783 and 1861. The result, recorded in 1889 in one of the first statistical assessments of its kind, was a level of development "that is in a single generation unparalleled in the history of nations."[131] Recent research has confirmed the accuracy of this judgment.[132] By 1914, the United States had also become an economic power in the world at large.

The Northern victory in the Civil War transformed the Republic's prospects. When Southern representatives withdrew from Congress at the start of the war, they left the way clear for the rapid passage of legislation that the North had long supported.[133] Congress allocated land in the Midwest and Far West to smallholders, sanctioned railroad subsidies, established a system of national banks, and reinstated protective tariffs.[134] The victory of the North removed uncertainty about the future of the Union, ensured that there would continue to be one national market, and installed policies of industrial development that helped to shift the economy from agriculture to manufacturing. Big government shaped economic opportunities as much as market forces did.[135] Federal initiatives encouraged immigration, opened additional tracts of appropriated land, and devised a regulatory regime that placed a relatively light hand on business while preventing individual states from erecting barriers to interstate commerce. These measures facilitated internal settlement, expanded the national market, and restored the confidence of foreign investors.[136] This is not to claim that the war brought about a "Second American Revolution," if the term is taken to mean a radical break with the past, because evidence now available shows that economic growth was under way well before the conflict broke out.[137] Nevertheless, the outcome of the war greatly accelerated the process of economic development because it facilitated structural change as well as quantitative growth.[138] It is in this sense that the "market revolution" occurred after the Civil War rather than before it.

The statistical evidence for the second half of the century is sufficiently robust to support reasonably accurate measurements of economic progress. From the perspective of the present study, the key development was the success of the United States in freeing itself from dependence on Britain. The share of agriculture in the Gross National Product (GNP) fell from 35 percent to 18 percent between 1860 and 1900; the share contributed by manufacturing rose from 22 percent to 31 percent during the same period, which was close to the highest point it would reach in the twentieth century.[139] Occupational change accompanied these trends: agriculture employed about three-quarters of the labor force in 1800 but little more than one-third in 1900. Natural increases and surges in immigration expanded the total population from 23 million in 1850 to 76 million in 1900 and to 92 million in 1910. Railroad construction, which stood at 30,000 miles in 1860, exceeded 350,000 miles in 1916. Locomotives, greatly improved from the early "steam wagons," carried the population westward, colonized the prairies, and set the scene for confrontations between farm and town that movies, known generically as "Westerns," later embedded in public mythology. The extension of banking, telegraph, and postal services (including mail-order facilities) helped to integrate the market.[140] Despite the large increase in population, productivity gains enabled consumption per head to more than double between 1834/44 and 1899/1903.[141] By 1913, the Gross Domestic Product (GDP) of the United States was more than twice that of Britain and was almost double that of Germany, while output per head in Europe as a whole had fallen to about half that of the United States.[142]

The domestic market was at the center of these developments.[143] The proportion of total output exported after the Civil War amounted to no more than 6 percent of total GNP at its peak between 1890 and 1913. The ratio of exports to output was generally low, even in the case of agriculture: only the old "colonial" staples of cotton and tobacco exceeded 50 percent. Exports of manufactured goods generally remained under 5 percent of total manufactures; only a small number of resource-oriented industries (such as those based on petroleum and coal) reached 10 percent. The share of imported manufactures in domestic consumption also fell sharply between 1869 and 1909, at which point they averaged less than 10 percent of the total. This impressive degree of self-sufficiency separated the United States from Europe and most other developing countries, and was in marked contrast to Britain in particular.

Regional disparities widened as economic development proceeded. The financial and industrial centers in the Northeast led the way; manufacturing spread in the upper Midwest; the boom in the Far West, which began with gold in the 1840s, continued with a series of other products. The South, however, languished, even though raw cotton remained the largest single export from the United States.[144] Slaveholders lost much of their investment; new capital was scarce.[145] Many large landowners, however, managed to remain sizeable producers.[146] Some transferred cotton production to tenant farmers, sharecroppers, and wage laborers; others resorted to forced labor.[147] Although elements of modernity appeared in the guise of improved communications, some urban growth, a few textile mills, and even signs of an African American middle class, economic development continued to bypass the region. The South became a low-wage enclave in an otherwise burgeoning national economy. By 1900, per capita incomes had fallen far below the national average and the region had subsided into a degree of poverty that lasted well into the twentieth century.[148] The "new South" was an aspiration that realities denied.[149] The opportunity to restructure the economy called for fundamental sociopolitical changes that those in power were unwilling to contemplate.

Foreign trade was nevertheless important because it created linkages with the domestic economy that the figures relating external trade to total output fail to capture. Exports as a whole doubled in value between 1877 and 1900.[150] Agricultural products, especially cotton, wheat, and corn, continued to dominate the export list, though they fell from about 80 percent of total exports by value in 1869–1878 to 53 percent in 1904–1913. Overseas demand stimulated the expansion of wheat and corn production in the Midwest and in doing so increased the market for farm machinery and transport, banking, and insurance services.[151] Cotton production boosted income from exports, drew in foreign exchange, increased the money supply, and kept interest rates low, and in these ways stimulated industrial output.[152] Exports of finished manufactures rose from about 15 percent of total exports in 1858–1888 to 28 percent in 1904–1913.[153] The fastest growth in exports of manufactures came after 1896, when output of iron and steel products surged.[154] By 1900, the United States had ceased to be a net importer of finished goods.[155]

External trade remained oriented toward Europe, which took 80 percent of U.S. exports between 1879 and 1898 and supplied 52 percent of its imports between 1889 and 1898.[156] Britain remained the Republic's leading trading partner, but the relationship with its ex-colony changed significantly after the Civil War. Britain's imports rose to the point where they accounted for about 50 percent of Europe's imports from the United States between 1879 and 1898, but its share of U.S. imports fell sharply, from 42 percent in 1849–1858 to 21 percent in 1889–1898. The change was a measure of Britain's relative decline as an exporter of manufactures and, more generally, of the growing ability of the United States to diversify its trading links and reduce its dependence on the former colonial power, as the dominions, India, and a number of other ex-colonies were to do in the twentieth century. The ex-colony was also striking back: in the 1880s and 1890s, agitated British commentators described imports of manufactured goods from the United States as an "invasion."[157] The penetration of Britain's open-door market, combined with the fact that the United States imposed the highest import duties in the industrial world, added a note of informed anxiety to the long-running debate in Britain about the merits of free trade and protection.[158]

The balance of payments reflected the trends in foreign trade.[159] The appearance of an export surplus during the last thirty years of the century reversed the long-standing deficit on merchandise trade. Interest payments, the other main item on the current account, were always in deficit and substantially so from the 1870s. Capital imports met the deficiency and ensured that the United States remained a net borrower. This position gave foreign investors a claim on the wealth of the United States, though the amount fell from a high point of about 13 percent of all domestic capital in the late eighteenth century to less than 2 percent of a much larger total in 1900. These percentages, like those relating foreign trade to domestic output, disguise the importance of capital imports for particular sectors and periods.[160] Before the Civil War, foreign investment played a vital role in state-building by funding federal and state institutions, railroads, utilities, and education. After the Civil War, and especially during the last quarter of the century, foreign investors shifted out of government-sponsored investments and into the private sector. Railroads continued to dominate portfolio investments; direct investment began to feature in industries such as chemicals, food, and drink.

Britain's supremacy in services and finance outlasted its faltering performance as an exporter of manufactured goods, and was a feature of the transition to becoming a mature creditor.[161] The country remained the principal source of foreign investment and retained its dominance of the trans-Atlantic shipping trade in both freight and passengers.[162] Foreign lending resumed after 1865 and quickly assumed massive proportions. Britain supplied more than three-quarters of long-term foreign investment placed in the United States at the end of the century and became, by default, the lender of last resort.[163] The New York Clearing House (1853) cooperated with the City of London in managing liquidity problems arising from Anglo-American financial relations.[164] Subsequently, the two financial centers acted in concert to defend the gold standard and oppose exchange controls.[165] In the 1870s, the federal government had to appeal to the City of London for assistance in repaying Civil War debts; in 1895, J. P. Morgan's syndicate called upon the City to provide about half the bullion needed to keep the United States on the gold standard.[166] Financial integration grew as the century advanced. Long-term interest rates moved in harmony, especially from the 1870s, when they began a downward trend to the end of the century, as did real returns to stocks and bonds; consumer prices followed suit.[167] Fluctuations in the exchange rate between the dollar and sterling also declined, especially from the 1870s, as did the spread between the rates.[168]

Republican reforms boosted financial integration and international confidence. The National Bank Acts of 1863–64 provided a uniform national currency, licensed banking throughout the Union, and encouraged the growth of an interbank payments network. In 1873, the Republicans demonetized silver coin and authorized the return to the gold standard, which was reinstated in 1879 at the prewar rate of exchange.[169] Although a central bank had not yet been established, the federal Treasury subjected national banks to controls that encouraged responsible lending.[170] The return to gold provided hard evidence that the Republicans intended to repudiate the soft-money policies that had prevailed during the Civil War.[171] The party retained an option on bimetallism, as we have seen, but in practice adhered to a policy of sound money throughout the turbulent years of the late nineteenth century. By 1900, fiscal unity and, with it, fiscal probity had been achieved.

The City of London traded a large proportion of U.S. company shares and funded risky ventures that local investors were reluctant to support, as well as steady stocks, such as railroads. City insurance companies and Scottish investment trusts also contributed substantial sums to North American development. Britain's considerable financial presence enabled it to influence the management of a selection of local firms, especially railroad companies.[172] However, there were political limits to Britain's financial penetration. Popular resentment of foreign control of U.S. resources rose to the point where, in 1887, the federal government placed legal restrictions on aliens wishing to own land and mines in federal territories. By 1900, thirty of the forty-five states of the Union had passed similar legislation.[173] These measures, like the "indigenization decrees" enacted by ex-colonial states after World War II, were aimed at preventing neocolonial control of basic resources. Like the later decrees, too, investors found ways of circumventing them where the demand for capital exceeded local supplies. Nevertheless, the federal government had signaled its willingness to limit foreign investment where it was judged to be contrary to national interests.

By the end of the century, Congress was able to assert itself because the U.S. financial sector had matured to the point where it dealt with the City of London on a basis of equality. The Civil War had revealed the potential of the domestic capital market, which succeeded in funding virtually the whole of the Northern war effort. In 1871, in a symbolic move that represented the rising confidence of the restored Union, Jay Cooke, an American banker, replaced Barings as the financial representative of the U.S. government in London.[174] In the 1890s, following further growth in the financial sector, J. P. Morgan promoted the consolidation and relocation of banks on Wall Street, which in turn encouraged the expansion of the New York Stock Exchange.[175] In a symbolic reversal of roles, J. P. Morgan's Bank of New York provided financial assistance to Britain during the

Anglo-South African War of 1899–1902.[176] In 1907, however, the Bank of England was obliged to support Morgan and a New York banking syndicate in extricating the U.S. Treasury from what one banker called "a situation fraught with the gravest danger."[177] Yet, the panic of 1907 did not repeat the panics of the early 1890s. As one banker explained, "in 1893 we were threatened with repudiation, whereas in 1907 the whole world has confidence in our ability to pay our obligations in gold."[178]

Despite these developments, U.S. overseas investment remained on a small scale, even though it experienced a fivefold increase between 1897 and 1914.[179] Geographical diversification was limited. U.S. investment in Europe, Canada, and Mexico accounted for 79 percent of the total in 1897 and 69 percent in 1914, by which time Latin America and Asia had joined the list of recipients. At this point, financial imperialism, like its manufacturing counterpart, was a matter for special interests rather than one of national survival.

By 1907, too, the federal budget was in good order, the balance of payments was healthier than it had been in the 1890s, and the uncertainty created by the debate over bimetallism had dissipated. The banking industry had become larger and stronger: total deposits increased threefold between 1896 and 1906, yet only twenty-one banks failed in 1907 compared to 160 in 1893.[180] Nevertheless, the House Banking and Currency Committee noted in 1912 that what it termed the "money trust" had concentrated banking and finance in a few hands and that dependence on a handful of private bankers to handle national issues left the state exposed to a recurrence of financial crises. Proposals for reform led in 1913 to the creation of the Federal Reserve Bank, which removed national responsibilities from private bankers and gave the new institution the task of maintaining a stable, yet flexible, financial system. The reform followed pressure from Democrats and Progressives, who wanted to achieve financial stability, but it also met the needs of New York bankers, who were keen to see the dollar assume a larger role in international trade and investment.[181] The foundation of the Fed, as it soon became known, symbolized the achievement of financial independence in a field long dominated by the City of London, and pointed toward the reign of the "almighty dollar" that was to follow later in the century.

In a further move, which put the seal on fiscal unity, Congress agreed in 1913 to introduce income tax.[182] In 1890, the tariff still supplied about 60 percent of federal revenues; by 1920, the figure had dropped to 5 percent.[183] The Democrats attempted to introduce an income tax in 1894, but the Supreme Court ruled that the measure was unconstitutional. Once Congress had approved the tax, the import tariff, which had generated most federal revenue in the nineteenth century and had proved to be highly politicized and divisive, faded from view. Progressive taxation replaced the regressive indirect taxes that were the legacy of the military-fiscal state and an underdeveloped economy. The transformation was conceptual as well as technical. It established the principle that taxation should be based on the ability to pay rather than on the ability to burden those with low incomes. As in Europe, the reform was part of a movement to reshape political systems to enable them to cope with the consequences of industrialization and the claims of enlarged electorates. Progressives in the United States, liberals in Britain, and conservatives in Germany all accepted that a revised social contract was a necessary counterweight to corporate power and, ultimately, as a means of preserving political stability.

By the close of the century, corporate power had created what contemporaries termed a "plutocracy."[184] With remarkable prescience, Lincoln had already foreseen that the "money power" might "destroy" the country.[185] Writing at the close of the century, William Graham Sumner, the noted social scientist, believed that plutocracy was "the great foe of democracy now and in the immediate future."[186] As a disciple of Herbert Spencer, Sumner endorsed the process by which the fittest firms survived and created great wealth for their owners. Like Spencer, however, Sumner also linked plutocracy to militarism, and militarism to imperialism, which he opposed.[187] Modern research has confirmed the broad accuracy of these impressions of the rise of "big business," even though control over the far-flung, diverse enterprises that the United States spawned was never fully centralized.[188] What Eisenhower was to call the "military-industrial complex" had its origins in the late nineteenth century.[189]

Spencer's weighty authority was needed to counter the surge of critical commentary on plutocracy that accompanied the political battles of the period. In 1873, Mark Twain and Dudley Warner gave the period its enduring title, *The Gilded Age*, and excoriated its striking excesses. In 1879, Henry George produced his highly influential analysis of *Progress and Poverty*, which sought to explain why economic development had sharpened the contrast between "the House of Wealth and the House of Want."[190] Thorstein Veblen complemented George's approach in 1899, when he produced his mordant analysis of the "leisure class" dominated by a "pecuniary elite," with its habit of compulsive "conspicuous consumption."[191] The defense drew its validating ideology from Spencer's reassuring law of progress. Large firms were a necessary consequence of freedom, so the argument went, because they realized economies of scale. The resulting efficiencies produced high wages, or at least the highest wages that enterprise could achieve, thereby undercutting the appeal of socialism.[192] The philosophy of plutocracy authorized action taken against what its advocates regarded as the excesses of democracy and the threat it presented to business freedoms and the existing distribution of wealth. The moral complement of this partisan ethos endorsed private philanthropy, which would remedy the grossest injustices of unregulated capitalism. In these ways, the operation of the market would promote social harmony and national unity.

The "robber barons" themselves came in varied shapes and sizes. They had some common characteristics, beyond the necessary degree of dedication and ruthlessness: they were nearly all northerners; they built their empires in the United States rather than overseas; their lifestyles conformed to the standards of the new international rich; they were, to varying degrees, philanthropists. Beyond these features, they diverged: some moved up from rags to riches, others had a generous head start; some were religious, others were not; most had Republican leanings but few had direct political ambitions; nearly all opened their purses to secure contracts, tariff concessions, and other privileges. John D. Rockefeller formed one of the largest firms, Standard Oil, in 1870, and became the richest man of the era.[193] Andrew Mellon made his money by investing in a range of new industries, including aluminium and coke, at the close of the century.[194] John Pierpont Morgan, the principal banker and key deal-maker of the time, put together some of the major railroad companies, helped to create General Electric in 1892, formed the United States Steel Corporation in 1901, and also consolidated the banking industry in New York.[195]

Andrew Carnegie, a pioneer of the iron and steel industry and the wealthiest entrepreneur of the Golden Age after John D. Rockefeller, added his own distinctive qualities to the list.[196] He was born in Dunfermline in 1835 to a family that knew rags rather than riches. His father, William, was a handloom-weaver whose livelihood was put at risk by the mechanization of the textile industry. In 1848, William and his family emigrated to the United States and settled in Pennsylvania, where he resumed work as a weaver. The Scottish community that had helped him find employment also gave Andrew a start. In 1853, he joined the Pennsylvania Railroad Company as a clerk, but soon rose to a senior managerial position, where he acquired the organizational skills and focus on cost-cutting that were features of his subsequent success. He then moved into finance before entering the steel business in the 1870s and acquiring a number of firms, which he brought together in Carnegie Brothers & Co. in 1881 and turned into the Carnegie Steel Company in 1892.[197] Carnegie made it clear from the outset that his managers had to attain high standards and be paid accordingly. His attitude toward workers evolved: his early inclinations toward benevolence hardened into the view that they were dispensable. He applied the principle in 1892, when the notorious Homestead strike at one of his steel plants deteriorated into armed conflict.[198]

Carnegie was at war with himself as well as with the unions. He was ruthless to the point of brutality but also carried with him discordant radical values inherited from his father's commitment to the cause of Chartism and his own experience of poverty as a child. The first characteristic drove him to make money; the second urged him to spend it. He did both on a grand scale. His philanthropy began in the 1880s, as his wealth accumulated, and occupied him fully after 1901, when he sold Carnegie Steel to J. P. Morgan. Between then and his death in 1919, Carnegie disposed of nearly the whole of his vast fortune. He was unusual among plutocrats in both being self-taught and having aspirations to become a commentator on public affairs.[199] He devised a philosophy, advertised as "The Gospel of Wealth," which proclaimed that "he who dies rich thus dies disgraced."[200] His aim was to achieve "the reconciliation of rich and poor"; his method was to bend "the universal tree of humanity a little" by exerting the strength of philanthropy.[201] Amelioration would improve opportunities, reduce discontent, and fend off socialism. Carnegie believed in the unity of the Anglo-Saxon "race" but judged that the road to success lay through American republicanism and democracy rather than through Britain's monarchical, class-based sociopolitical system.[202] The priority he gave to education ensured that academic institutions and libraries gained liberally from his generosity; his commitment to international amity and opposition to imperialism led him to found the Carnegie Endowment for International Peace in 1910. As a first-generation citizen, Carnegie kept in touch with his home town, Dunfermline, which he supported financially and visited almost annually. The Andrew Carnegie Birthplace Museum, opened in 1928 by his widow, Louise, remains a popular attraction for visitors to the town today.

As they put down strikers and dispensed charity, the plutocrats also presided over a process of development that widened and deepened the market and gave consumers a stake in a common enterprise. Large corporations expanded consumption by eliminating competition as well as through economies of scale.[203] New department stores and mail-order facilities provided efficient outlets. Advertisements, often linked to national symbols such as Uncle Sam and the flag, beguiled money from purses and pockets.[204] Christmas festivities, filtered through the nation after the Civil War, became a national consumer celebration in the 1870s, and helped to create a sense of commonality.[205] Trees, cards, and gifts signaled the arrival of the modern world of consumption and its harmonious, providential union with the Christian calendar. These developments taught citizens to think as consumers and to respond to market potential in ways that assisted the organization of mass production and distribution.[206] The spread of branded goods helped to create shared aspirations and a common identity.[207] The classical republican ideal that had inspired the Founding Fathers retreated further before the advancing world of technology, industry, and mass marketing.[208]

Corporate power allied to modern marketing techniques redefined the concept of civic duty by promoting the idea that unrestrained consumption was an "inalienable right" expressed through life, liberty, and the pursuit of happiness. The virtuous citizen had become a virtuous consumer, whose activities as a purchaser fulfilling individual desires contributed to the common good. Although Carnegie's hopes for world peace were about to be disappointed, his faith that consumer loyalty would prevail over class solidarity appeared to be justified. In 1903, when one commentator posed the question of what was to come after plutocracy, another provided the answer in the title of the book published in 1922: *Triumphant Plutocracy*.[209]

By 1914, the United States had achieved an unprecedented degree of self-sufficiency and affluence. The Republic had endured the economic crises of the late nineteenth century that had also blighted Western Europe, and had grappled with the political disaffection, class conflict, and subversive tendencies they generated. Material improvement was crucial to the cause of national unity, which is why the "great deflation" was so troubling and why the revival of prosperity at the turn of the century brought such relief. No other country possessed the resources of the United States; few could manage the transition to becoming modern, national-industrial states without even greater degrees of internal turmoil.

THE CULTURE OF COSMOPOLITAN NATIONALISM

The upheaval brought by the Civil War and the strident class conflict of the 1880s and 1890s shook the assumption that the United States had won exemption from the historical processes that marked the emerging nation-states of Europe.[210] Nevertheless, the belief that the Almighty had selected the Republic to undertake a preordained mission was too important to the still fragile sense of national unity to be abandoned, especially at a time when social divisions had opened the door to subversive political claims. Inherited ideological ingredients were remixed to accommodate the challenges of the Gilded Age.[211] White racism, resurgent Protestantism, and lingering Anglophobia came together to create a counterculture that offset residual colonial influences and shaped a unifying American nationalism that had been purged of sin.

The need to provide an updated, comprehensive, and comforting version of the founding myth was closely connected to the rapid development of the social sciences at the close of the century and their organization into professional bodies. A form of scientism pervaded intellectual thought and wrapped older verities in an impersonal and seemingly objective set of propositions that underpinned the status quo and developed reassuring strategies for controlling dissident views of the world. Anglo-Saxon race theory received "scientific" support that turned it into the towering wisdom of the day. Protestantism benefited from a renewed infusion of enthusiasm that carried Christian soldiers into battle with the abundant evils that threatened the purity of the "city upon a hill." Political parties drew on latent Anglophobia to demonize their opponents in an effort to demonstrate that they were the true custodians of the national interest. The notion of exceptionalism was successfully refashioned to become a durable principle that remains the touchstone of foreign policy today.

The issue of slavery had proved to be irredeemably divisive; the problems that arose in the late nineteenth century, challenging though they were, were more amenable to a national response. The rapid increase in immigration made assimilation into Anglo-Saxondom a necessary priority. As in Europe, the growth of industrial society and associated radical political demands united property owners behind conservative policies. Unemployment and urban distress inspired the Social Gospel movement. The secular and the spiritual achieved a degree of harmony that made them highly effective agents of national unity. Spencer's materialism undoubtedly challenged Christian theology and disconcerted evangelicals in particular. Nevertheless, the meeting of discordant minds, fashioned through a dialogue of opposites, produced a compelling synthesis of certainties. Creation produced evolution, and human evolution culminated in the messianic role of the United States—the nation selected by providence to redeem others.

The Anglo-Saxon, Protestant elite warmed to a theory of race that confirmed their own eminence. Public intellectuals presented the United States as being the youthful and energetic gladiator of the West charged with the task of felling barbarians and spreading civilization.[212] Hegel's influence, seemingly exemplified by the dazzling example of German unity, encouraged the belief that the United States should adopt a form of Teutonic corporatism and carry it to the rest of the world. This idea called for a strong state in the tradition of Hamilton and List accompanied by an assertive, unifying foreign policy.

Brooks Adams, one of the most prominent public intellectuals, exemplified the response of the influential Northeastern elite to the desperate difficulties of the time. He began as a liberal, turned right in reaction to the financial crisis of 1893, which eroded his family's fortune, and thereafter regarded bankers as a malign force whose activities were destined to bring about the collapse of civilized social institutions.[213] Two influential books followed. *The Gold Standard*, published in 1894, treated the shift to gold as the progenitor of deflation and the cause of social decay.[214] *The Law of Civilization and Decay*, published the following year, offered a sweeping historical analysis of current discontents, which held that all societies were subject to entropy, or the dissipation of energy.[215] The result was what one commentator called a theory of "cosmic dynamics."[216] Adams drew from Hegel the notion that power was migratory and judged that it was currently shifting from Britain to the United States. He used Spencer to show that social evolution progressed from militant to industrial societies. While Spencer approved the evolutionary sequence, Adams took the view that industrial societies lacked staying power; decline was a permanent threat. He deplored the spread of urban values, which he regarded as being timorous, sordid, and corrupting, and lamented the loss of martial qualities of courage, honor, and duty.[217] Although the United States had become the custodian of Anglo-Saxondom, there was no guarantee that its stores of energy would remain at the required level. Strong leadership accompanied by physical endeavor was needed to recharge the nation's batteries and restore society to health.

Religious inspiration and new scientism joined hands to preserve the purity of the Anglo-Saxon master race. Charles Davenport, a committed Protestant and eminent biologist, launched the eugenics movement in the 1890s and went on to found the influential Eugenics Record Office in 1910.[218] Davenport's authority, which linked the theories of Francis Galton and Karl Pearson to Mendelian genetics, claimed to offer a means of manipulating human reproduction to ensure the survival of the fittest and the elimination of the weakest.[219] Although eugenics provoked criticism, its scientific origins and congenial political message gave it a degree of credibility that lasted until World War II.[220]

During the last quarter of the century, the idea of an Anglo-Saxon ethnie helped to define the national identity of the United States, whereas
previously it had served to reinforce Britain's informal influence.[221]
The change in the relationship stemmed partly from an updated theory
of race, which authorized the United States to act as an independent
agent of Anglo-Saxondom, and partly from the development of material
resources that gave the ex-colony a sense of its power and worth. Anglophobia was still brandished for electoral purposes in the 1890s, and
President Cleveland deployed it to particularly dramatic effect in 1895,
when he won instant popularity for standing up to Britain in the dispute
over the boundary between Venezuela and British Guiana.[222] Nevertheless, polemical Anglophobia faded once the desperate competition for
votes in the crucial election of 1896 had produced a Republican victory.
A spirit of reconciliation resumed its place in the repertoire of attitudes
toward foreign countries, though residual strands of suspicion and hostility lingered well into the twentieth century. A growing sense of commonality and friendship was palpable and extended well beyond diplomatic and intellectual circles.[223] The British were attracted to the notion
of Anglo-Saxondom because it offered the prospect of linking their small
homeland to the wider, welcoming world populated by "Greater" Britons
overseas. In the United States, the cosmopolitan qualities of the Anglo-
Saxon idea mattered less than their value in instilling a sense of ethnic
nationalism among white citizens.[224] Anglophile sentiments were no longer signs of either deference or lack of patriotism, but open expressions
of a relationship that was conducted on an equal basis.

Immigration provided a critical test of Anglo-Saxon race theory. The
scale of immigration was such that by 1910 newcomers accounted for
almost one-third of the total population.[225] Immigrants were essential
additions to the labor force, but they posed problems of incorporation
that threatened the unity of the state and the dominance of its Anglo-
Saxon core. Moreover, increasing numbers of job-seekers pushed wages
down and created discontent among the existing labor force. About two-
thirds of immigrants between 1891 and 1920 came from southern, central, and eastern Europe; a much smaller number, though more alarming
in their novelty, came from Asia. According to racial theory, these origins
were either dubious or degraded, and they produced what one respected
theorist called in 1896 "beaten men from beaten races; representing the
worst failures in the struggle for existence."[226] Few of the new immigrants could speak English; many were Catholics and Jews; a high proportion settled in the great cities of the Northeast, adding to the region's

urban problems; those who moved elsewhere became detached from the political influence exercised by the Anglo-Saxon heartland.

The utopian vision of the United States as a "melting pot" that merged ethnic diversity into one amalgam has failed the test of historical research. Like most other nation-states, the United States was constructed by a process of assimilation into a dominant ethnic group.[227] Accordingly, the decision to allow virtually unrestricted immigration obliged policy-makers to devise policies of "Anglo-conformity" that would assimilate otherwise unqualified newcomers.[228] Assimilation provided a guarantee of ethnic superiority and offered an approved route to success. Public schools, outreach programs, and informal influences, such as churches, unions, and communal organizations, encouraged immigrants to Anglicize their names, to learn English, and to adopt Anglo-Saxon values and behavior.[229] The Civil War greatly influenced the model of white supremacy on offer by promoting forms of flag-waving nationalism in the North that were elaborated during the peace that followed.[230] Veterans' organizations, assisted by a corps of like-minded historians, infused the concept of nationalism with a strong dose of romantic militarism that sanitized the horrors of war and emphasized the values of duty, courage, and loyalty to the Republic.[231] The formula not only healed the wounds of battle, but also helped North and South, immigrants and established families, to fall in under one banner.[232]

The boundaries of white unity were partly set by excluding those who were judged incapable of being assimilated. Southern and eastern Europeans tested Anglo-Saxondom to the limit; Native Americans were relegated after a brief period of experimentation; African Americans lay beyond it. The Jim Crow laws passed after the end of Reconstruction entrenched segregation. Accounts of the Civil War written to foster white unity eliminated African Americans from the story. States' rights, not slavery, became the cause of war; combatants who engaged in acts of tragic heroism were all white. The Supreme Court's decision in *Plessy v. Ferguson* in 1896 drew on "scientific" racism, including craniometric evidence, to uphold the doctrine of separate but equal development.[233] Leading authorities argued that segregation was necessary to save Anglo-Saxons from the racial degeneration that would follow intermarriage. The decision bonded South and North in much the same way that Afrikaners and English settlers came together in 1902 at the conclusion of the Anglo-South African war. As a corollary, segregation confirmed the subordinate status of African Americans and ensured that they would form a permanent reservoir of cheap labor. The number of lynchings rose rapidly.[234]

The principle of white supremacy applied to Native Americans, too, though officials implemented policies in ways that reflected circumstances on the plains of the Midwest and West rather than on the former plantations of the South. In the second half of the century, settlers and miners in search of land and gold invaded the vast region west of the Mississippi known generically as Indian Country. In 1871, Congress determined that Native American tribes would no longer be treated as independent polities. The decision opened the way for the federal government to intervene in what previously had been the internal affairs of sovereign states. The conflict over resources that followed from the influx of white settlers led to measures that herded Native Americans into reservations, provoked a further bout of regional warfare, and ended with the defeat of the Sioux in 1876. The Dawes Act, which followed in 1887, reallocated tribal lands by creating small, individual plots and allowing the alienation of freeholds. The aim was to produce self-sufficient yeomen farmers and pace-setting, middle-class individualists.[235] Ostensibly, the program was part of the wider, nation-building project. The result, however, was a comprehensive failure in social engineering that undermined kinship systems and the extensive political economy of hunting, and instead created a set of poverty-stricken *Bantustans*.[236] Native Americans lost most of their land, were bypassed, and then forgotten.[237]

Official reports and press commentary concurred in portraying Native Americans as backward savages who did not deserve to remain in charge of the rich resources providence had entrusted to them. Once the "savages" had been tamed, however, enterprising promoters could display them in exhibitions, circuses, and Wild West shows as relics of a doomed species whose function was to prepare the way for the dashing representatives of modernity.[238] When William Cody (Buffalo Bill) brought his troupe to London in 1887 to participate in the celebrations of Queen Victoria's diamond jubilee, the performance was both a personal triumph and an exhibition of Anglo-Saxon unity and dominance.[239] On this occasion, the Queen was amused as well as impressed.[240]

The decision to allow unrestricted immigration provoked a nativist reaction among Anglo-Saxons who feared for their jobs, wages, and status. The Grange and Populist movements expressed the resentment of rural, white Anglos against newcomers. The Knights of Labor and the American Federation of Labor called for restrictions on immigration on racial as well as economic grounds.[241] The Immigration Restriction League, formed in 1894, campaigned for limits on immigrants who were considered racially inferior and likely to dilute the purity and strength of the Anglo-Saxon core. In 1911, the Dillingham Commission questioned the effectiveness of assimilation policies.[242] Both Republicans and Democrats, however, recognized that economic development would stall without cheap immigrant labor. Consequently, the only controls imposed before 1914 were those applied to Chinese and Japanese in 1883 and 1907 respectively. Asians were an easy target because their numbers were small and they lacked political influence.

A number of intellectuals dissented, too. The "American rebellion" of the 1890s aimed at breaking the cultural monopoly exercised by Anglo-Saxon Brahmins in the Northeast.[243] The movement criticized what George Santayana famously called the "genteel tradition," which allied Victorian morality with cultural nationalism and instead advocated a form of cosmopolitan modernism that would reflect the increasingly diverse population of the United States.[244] Santayana argued that elite, literary culture had ceased to represent the "new type" of American who arrived "not in the hope of founding a godly commonwealth, but only of prospering in an untrammelled one."[245] Official policy, however, recognized that assimilation served the cause of national unity, whereas pluralism threatened to undermine it. Santayana himself had no wish to lead a revolution. He distrusted democracy and regretted the transformation of society brought by industrialization. His attack on Anglo-American culture, though influential, remained within the ivory tower.[246]

Secular doctrines of race received spiritual support. The second half of the century witnessed a religious revival, known as the Third Great Awakening, which complemented the resurgence of faith in Protestant and Catholic Europe. The Third Awakening, like the Second, occurred during a period of considerable instability brought about by political upheaval and rapid economic development.[247] The Third Great Awakening drew its inspiration from post-millennial theology, which held that the Second Coming would occur only after mankind had reformed the world. Few doubted the need for reform or the importance of starting at home before taking on the world. Civil war, poor working conditions, widespread unemployment, poverty, alcoholism, and crime were all signs, for those who could read them, of man's failure to do God's work in preparation for His return. Healing the nation and dealing with the social problems arising from economic development called for a comprehensive program of moral rearmament.

The call was urgent; the response was wholehearted. Northern religious spokesmen led the way after the Civil War by adapting moral precepts that helped the two sides to come together. In 1865, it was more important to redeem the nation than to judge the South. Abolition achieved redemption. Thereafter, the sanctity of the Union stood above other claims. Protestant leaders gave their blessing to the Anglo-Saxon alliance, which endorsed racial discrimination and allowed the ideal of inclusive, civic nationalism to founder.[248] The Southern "Bible Belt" acquired greater definition and visibility.[249] Social issues came to the fore from the 1870s. The Protestant churches became increasingly aware that they were losing influence in the expanding towns both to impious materialism and to ultra-pious American Catholicism, which grew rapidly after 1865. Church leaders regarded these failings as indications of moral atrophy and potential racial decline. Both trends had to be reversed if, as Josiah Strong claimed in 1885, "America is to become God's right arm in His battle with the world's ignorance and oppression and sin"[250]

A clutch of popular evangelists appeared from the 1850s, each proclaiming messages of moral reform to counter the sins that modernity had scattered over society. In 1858, Dwight L. Moody (1837–1899) started a Sunday school movement that spread from Chicago to other parts of the country. Moody went on to become the first of the modern evangelists, drawing huge crowds to meetings in the United States and Britain in the 1870s and 1880s.[251] Mary Baker Eddy (1821–1910) advocated spiritual healing in the 1860s and founded the Christian Science Church in 1879. A bible-reading student movement, begun in the 1880s, developed into the organization that eventually became Jehovah's Witnesses. The Woman's Christian Temperance Union (WCTU), founded by Methodists in 1874, expanded its program in the 1880s and 1890s to include prison reform, cultural uplift, and the extension of the franchise. The organization also acquired an ideology of prejudice that included African Americans among those whose inherent inferiority threatened the strength of the nation.[252]

The Young Men's Christian Association (YMCA), the largest of the Anglo-Saxon organizations formed during the Third Great Awakening, has claims to being the first major international nongovernmental organization (INGO).[253] From its origins in the early nineteenth century, the YMCA had become sufficiently global by 1855 to agree upon a set of federal principles for its numerous affiliates. The London branch inspired an American visitor in 1851 to export the movement to Boston, from which point it spread across the United States and in the process stimulated a parallel movement—the Young Women's Christian Association (YWCA). The founding principle of health in mind, spirit, and body had wide appeal that also resonated with public figures, like Theodore Roosevelt, who wanted to develop a new generation of virile, muscular

Christians to prevent the "law of entropy" from debilitating the Anglo-Saxon race.[254]

The Social Gospel movement, which arose in the 1880s, spanned the interests of the smaller revivalist organizations and carried the reform program to the towns, to Congress, and into the ameliorative program advanced by the Progressives.[255] The movement sought to adapt the Christian message to meet the challenge of urbanization and immigration. As barbarians had overwhelmed Rome, so Lucifer's latest home-grown recruits were corrupting the people selected by God to spread His word across the globe. Reform was necessary to sustain national unity. A renewed commitment to Christian teaching would rejuvenate the morality that underpinned society. A revival that re-emphasized the role of Anglo-Saxons as the Chosen People sustained the Anglo-Protestant alliance and gave it a worthy purpose: the conversion and assimilation of less favored peoples. Social Gospelers criticized capitalism without seeking to subvert it. The movement promoted reform as the antidote to the social conflict of the 1880s and 1890s, and endorsed the consumer ethos that gave the nation a common purpose. The spiritual and the material acted in unison: where deprivation and decadence ruled, God's work could not flourish.

Josiah Strong, the General Secretary of the Evangelical Alliance between 1886 and 1898, was one of the most prominent leaders of the Social Gospel movement. His numerous publications and speeches gave him public eminence and friends, including Theodore Roosevelt, in high places. His popular book, *Our Country: Its Possible Future and Its Present Crisis*, published in 1885, captured the concerns of the times and rallied readers to the Christian reform program. Strong was a more complex figure than stereotypes of him as a gung-ho imperialist suggest. The greater part of *Our Country* was devoted to the numerous "perils" that beset Americans at home, and ended with a substantial appeal for the funds needed to counter the social decline that threatened to bring down the nation.[256] Strong's main concern was to promote missionary activity within the United States. Immigrants, like "Goths and Vandals," had taken over the towns of the Northeast and were destroying the Anglo-Saxon way of life; in the South and West, either Romanism was gaining ground or the Ten Commandments were largely unknown.[257]

Strong was part of a long-standing evangelical tradition of millennial redemption-theology, which he fused with Anglo-Saxon nationalism.[258] The opening and closing flourishes to his book had wide appeal because of their effectiveness in staging the drama of the time, which opposed the forces of darkness led by foreign invaders and "Papists," to the soldiers of light, headed by the energetic American branch of the Anglo-Saxon race.[259] Strong had reassuring news of the outcome: God and evolution had selected Anglo-Saxons to prevail—providing they remained united and proclaimed Christian values.[260] Strong revitalized the notion of "manifest destiny" and extended its field of endeavor. His observations on overseas expansion, though brief and incompletely considered, offered material for imperialists to fashion. The "final competition" of the races was at hand; the Anglo-Saxon "genius for colonizing" and the "peculiarly aggressive traits" of the United States would determine the outcome.[261] Expansion was "God's final and complete solution of the dark problem of heathenism among many inferior peoples."[262] Yet, the contest was not "one of arms, but of vitality and of civilization."[263] The task facing the American vanguard was to "dispossess many weaker races, assimilate others, and mould the remainder until . . . it has Anglo-Saxonised mankind."[264] Strong's spacious vision was commensurate with his confident understanding of God's purpose. Duty impelled the reform of the world; failure invited divine retribution.

The belief that the leadership of the Anglo-Saxon world had passed to the United States, combined with the conviction that God had selected Americans to redeem the world, generated a new sense of confidence that found expression in the cultural aspirations of the postwar era. Cosmopolitan influences remained, though less as atavisms than as responses to the increasing globalization of cultural exchange. American voices now had sufficient scope, as well as volume, to record their own tunes. This development can be seen in the high culture of the time, and particularly in the creation of an urban middle class with broadly similar tastes, habits, and values.[265] It fell to this class, and especially to its self-appointed agents in the towns of the Northeast, to point the way to assimilation by setting standards of "cultural uplift" for others to emulate. Social markers, proxies for the goals of life, were widely distributed, as a selection of examples, from marriage to fashions and from literature to sport, will illustrate.

"Gentility" embodied a set of cultural norms that enabled those who qualified to recognize others irrespective of their geographical location. Social interchange provided a route to intermarriage and a measure of the relationship between national and international cultures.[266] Henry Adams, in his satirical novel published in 1880, caught one of the cultural trends of the period: the desire of those who were gilded but not yet aged to add status to wealth by forging prestigious international alliances, notably with the British aristocracy:

Who do you think is engaged? Victoria Dare, to a coronet and peat bog, with Lord Dunbeg attached. Victoria says she is happier now than she ever was before in any of her other engagements, and she is sure this is the real one. She says she has thirty thousand a year derived from the poor of America, which may just as well go to relieve one of the poor in Ireland. You know her father was a claim agent, or some such thing, and is said to have made his money by cheating his clients out of their claims. She is perfectly wild to be a countess, and means to make Castle Dunbeg lovely by-and-by, and entertain us all there.[267]

By the 1870s, American observers of the social scene regarded marriage to foreign aristocrats as a measure of acceptance based on equality rather than as a betrayal of republican principles. The union of circumstance and pomp met the needs of both parties: wealthy Americans who craved social distinction were in a position to buy inherited status; impecunious aristocrats who needed to refinance their titles were glad to offer their main asset.[268] Britain, the country of choice, supplied the most spectacular examples, notably the marriage of Jennie Jerome to Lord Randolph Churchill in 1874, and that of Consuelo Vanderbilt to the Duke of Marlborough in 1895. Reporting on one such event in 1878, the *New York Times* noted the "wave of Anglo-mania which has swept over our fashionable society," and judged that it was likely to increase the "kindly feeling between the two countries which now so happily prevails."[269] The chronicler of the day, Henry James, made these alliances the subject of his novels in the 1870s and 1880s and infused them with his characteristic mix of restrained patriotism, Anglophile leanings, and distaste for what Matthew Arnold termed "Philistinism."[270] The combination produced affiliations that rose above the nation-state and into a commitment to the cause of Anglo-Saxondom.[271]

Trends in fashions were a further indication of Anglo-Saxon cultural convergence during this period. As prices and wages, a standard measure of integration, came into line in Europe and the Americas during the second half of the century, styles in men's dress and whiskers, an unfamiliar index of globalization, became synchronized too.[272] Matching changes of fashion advertized trans-Atlantic harmony. Beards grew, in every sense, in Britain during the Crimean War and in the United States during the Civil War, when they became symbols of Samsonite, masculine strength, political leadership, and professional competence. President Lincoln was at the forefront of the new style; Uncle Sam acquired a beard in 1869.[273] The fashion for beards peaked in both countries in the late 1880s and early 1890s; in due course, mustaches provided a disciplined, military substitute.

Flagrant deviations provoked cultural pressures that restored manly dress to its established boundaries. The success of Frances Hodgson Burnett's *Little Lord Fauntleroy*, published in 1886, started a craze among the affluent, trend-setting classes for dressing boys in Van Dyke revivalist costume, which symbolized a form of manliness associated with nobility of spirit and moral purity.[274] By 1898, however, the arbiters of style had decided that the junior version of civic virtue fostered the over-civilized effeminacy of male children, and they promoted alternatives that emphasized rugged, outdoor, militaristic values. Boy Scouts did not wear velvet.

Women's fashions converged similarly. The hooped skirt reached its high point of expansion in the 1860s, bustles in the 1870s and 1880s, and tight corsets after the turn of the century, though there were lags in the outer provinces: women in Texas were still struggling with crinolines in the 1890s. To be sure, the trans-Atlantic feminist movement challenged both foreign influences on fashion and the subordination they implied, and in doing so pointed toward future freedom in matters of dress.[275] In the late nineteenth century, however, orthodoxy dominated. In matters of style, as in matters of politics, powerful influences blunted the edges of dissent. The expansion of consumer culture drew all citizens toward conformity, and the allure of fashion beguiled even committed feminists, despite the fact that it underlined orthodox distinctions between the sexes.[276]

Trans-Atlantic trends in intermarriage and fashions were statements of values that revealed the extent to which the upper reaches of American and British societies shared similar patterns of behavior. In the early nineteenth century, elements of a common Anglo-American culture were expressions of continuing deference to the ex-colonial power. By the close of the nineteenth century, deference had turned into parity as Americans gained confidence from their postwar economic development and growing political unity. President Harrison's luxuriantly whiskered cabinet was not seeking the approval of Britain's cultural authorities but signaling their participation as equals in the cosmopolitan world of the civilized.

What was true of fashion held good for literature too.[277] As the noted British journalist William Stead observed in 1904, "The old, almost pathetic humility with which American writers listened to the criticisms of Europe has disappeared."[278] By then, the literature produced in the United States included celebrations of the country's distinctive qualities and its diverse social mix.[279] Henry James, long settled in London, measured the change in his novels, which began in the 1870s by portraying how Europeans outwitted untutored Americans and ended by demonstrating how formidable Americans were becoming in the new century.[280] The search for cultural independence inspired much of the genre, which anticipated perspectives that were to become prominent throughout the ex-colonial world in the twentieth century.

Walt Whitman's manifesto, *Democratic Vistas*, published shortly after the Civil War, was a plea for literary independence of the kind that Emerson had made, with very limited success, a generation earlier. Whitman observed:

> We see the sons and daughters of the New World, ignorant of its genius, not yet inaugurating the native, the universal and the near, still importing the distant, the partial and the dead. We see London, Paris, Italy—not original, superb, as where they belong—but second-hand here, where they do not belong. We see the shreds of Hebrews, Romans, Greeks; but where, on her own soil, do we see, in any faithful, highest, proud expression, America herself?[281]

Whitman had partly answered his own question in 1855, when he published the first of several editions of *Leaves of Grass*, a collection of poems that expressed, in subject and style, an independent American voice. Whitman rejected what he called the "feudal" literature of Scott, Tennyson, and Shakespeare, and responded vigorously to the attacks on American culture mounted by the British critics, Thomas Carlyle and Matthew Arnold, who viewed with horror what Arnold grandly called "the predominance of the common and ignoble."[282] Although Whitman shared some of Arnold's elitist reservations, his optimistic, Dickensian faith in the human spirit sustained his defense of American democracy and his belief in its potential.[283] At the same time, Whitman regarded the nation-state, not as the terminal point of political life, but as the preface to the emergence of a cosmopolitan, globalized world. Whitman's imagination extended well beyond the boundaries defined by the theme of Anglo-Saxon unity that absorbed Henry James.[284] The new order was to be the era of the "average man," whose "daring foot is on land and sea everywhere" with "consequences yet unknown."[285]

Emily Dickinson (1830–1880) also spoke with a distinctive voice, though in an introspective style that contrasted with Whitman's bluff extroversion.[286] Her poetry, like Whitman's, was distinctively American. The constraints that American democracy imposed on single women, the oppressive character of religious revivalism, and the effects of mass consumerism on individual values were all themes she took from the world around her. The first versions of her collected poems, which were published in the 1890s, unsettled the critics. "Miss Dickinson was evidently born to be the despair of reviewers," observed one commentator who was disconcerted by her idiosyncratic departures from convention.[287] Her imaginative use of half-rhyme, innovative meters, punctuation, and occasional colloquialisms displeased the guardians of good taste and led to an extended debate about the respective merits of content and style in her work.[288] Recognition eventually came in the twentieth century, when modernity caught up with her poetry, which became valued for its directness, succinctness, imagery, and depth.

Mark Twain provided a very different but still wholly American account of what Whitman called the "native, the universal and the near" in *Adventures of Tom Sawyer* (1876) and *The Adventures of Huckleberry Finn* (1884), which described a world far removed from that inhabited by East Coast elites, who wrote about themselves. Shakespeare used characters from society's underworld to offset his depiction of high politics. Twain selected characters from the underworld of childhood, losers, adventurers, and outcasts to show that the low politics of everyday life also dealt with universal moral dilemmas: the persistence of inequality; the shaping of identity; the basis of prejudice; the nature of justice. He put Whitman's "average" people in authentic local settings of rural poverty, minstrel shows, and racist social codes in the Midwest and South. He gave them the freedom to describe their world in their own vernacular, which many contemporary critics thought was unacceptably coarse and at points obscene.

Twain's voice was independent in every sense. *A Connecticut Yankee in King Arthur's Court* (1889) began as a satire on Britain's feudal past, a "place where brains were not needed," but ended by being equally critical of the version of modernity embraced by the United States, which the novel portrays as being destroyed by the misuse of its own advanced technology. Twain's disillusion with Republican government and its attendant corruption, which he had first pilloried in *The Gilded Age* (1873), grew as his observations of the political world accumulated. By the time he published *The Tragedy of Pudd'nhead Wilson* in 1894, his mood had darkened further and reflected both the hardening of white racism and the disruptive consequences of uncontrolled immigration.[289] Unsurprisingly, Twain's veracity penetrated to the point where those who preferred conventional views of the world made persistent attempts to ban his best-known books.[290] Twain, however, made the weak strong. His characters were American in locality and global in spirit. They embodied nationality but avoided nationalism and its extension, imperialism, which he drew his deadly pen to oppose.

Sport was also decolonized after the Civil War. Organized games became a powerful means of uniting regions that had been in conflict and of inculcating the 'manly" virtues that helped to shape a new image for white America. This development was especially important in the South, where sport helped to preserve regionalism within a framework of national unity, softened the impact of defeat, and made reunification more acceptable. Confederate veterans introduced baseball; Northern influences disseminated football. Southern progressives overcame the hostile attitude of evangelicals who held that sports elevated the body above the spirit, and blended the new games with older traditions of courage, honor, and civility. Football became especially popular in the South, where it appealed to the region's culture of martial values and blood sports, and created opportunities for reviving Southern pageantry.[291] Sporting victories restored Southern pride in much the same way that they boosted the morale of countries within the British Empire when (as increasingly happened) they defeated the "mother country." Sports also extended down the social order to parts of society that high culture did not reach. Baseball, for example, was the quintessential democratic sport: it required an open terrain and minimal equipment, and for this reason was the favorite game of the troops on both sides of the Civil War.[292]

The British made a number of unofficial efforts to counter the growing independence of the United States in matters of sport.[293] Baseball, which had its origins in cricket and rounders, was already popular before the Civil War and developed rapidly after the restoration of peace. In the 1860s, commentators referred to baseball as being America's national game; in 1876, the centennial year, promoters formed the first National League. Cricket enthusiasts in Britain responded by sponsoring tours of the United States in the hope of reclaiming the game. These ventures failed, partly because English immigrants dominated cricket in the United States and gave it a colonial, elitist image.[294] Supporters of baseball went on the offensive in 1888–1889, when Albert Spalding organized a world tour to advertise the merits of the game and to foster national pride in "home-grown" sports.[295] Cricket was "caught and bowled" by its imperial image, which was a poor match for America's new patriotism.[296]

American football grew out of existing college games that centered on English soccer and (at Harvard) rugby. The American game issued a declaration of independence in 1876, when its advocates agreed to new rules and formed a league to celebrate the centenary of the declaration of political independence.[297] British sporting enthusiasts attempted to keep the cause of soccer alive by sending touring teams to the United States, as sponsors of cricket had done. A formidable squad of amateurs, named, perhaps insensitively, the Pilgrims, toured the United States in 1905.[298] The Pilgrims represented more than a game: they advertised a set of values. The leaders of the tour claimed that soccer was a game for gentlemen rather than one that "develops the brute in man."[299] The team's muscular performance on the field did not always display the honesty, fairness, and respect for traditional authority its sponsors proclaimed. Nevertheless, the tour coincided with adverse publicity given to American football following a season of record-breaking deaths and injuries, and the British hoped that the public would view soccer as an attractive alternative. The U.S. authorities, backed by President Roosevelt, who was a keen football supporter, reformed the game instead.[300] Soccer's opportunity passed. By 1914, football had joined baseball as one of the two principal national sports, and neocolonial influences had faded. Football represented American sensibilities: it was a game for men rather than for gentlemen. It validated qualities of masculinity that expressed a degree of programmed ferocity beyond the needs of physical health. It far exceeded the random violence dispatched by the muscular and sometimes devious gentlemen of England, who "played the ball" more often than they "played the man."

The route to cultural independence was protracted and uneven. There were laggards as well as leaders. The preeminent American artists of the age, James McNeil Whistler and John Singer Sargent, spent the greater part of their lives in Europe. Classical music struggled to escape its European heritage.[301] Edward McDowall, the leading composer of the period, is virtually unknown today. In 1892, a group of wealthy New Yorkers felt obliged to import a European, Anton Dvorak, specifically to create an American school of music.[302] The Gothic revival of the late nineteenth century was a celebration of Anglo-Saxondom that prompted the United States to import elements of a feudal order, while in other fields it was self-consciously creating independent forms of artistic expression.[303] Yet, even as Gothic churches and universities were under construction, George A. Fuller was developing skyscrapers; shortly after the turn of the century Frank Lloyd Wright, the leader of the Prairie School, produced a striking new form of domestic architecture partly in reaction to imported medieval and classical styles.[304] Similarly, as McDowell struggled to shape local melodies in the style of Liszt and Wagner, countless forms of popular music flourished beneath the gaze of the advocates of high culture.[305] Those who stood outside the world of Anglo-Saxon culture were largely responsible for creating the Appalachian, folk, country, ragtime, and spiritual idioms that contributed to the popular music of today.[306] The struggle between uplift and downbeat that epitomized the tension between assimilation and pluralism continued into the twentieth century until jolted into resolution by the Civil Rights movement in the 1960s.

FROM "UNION" TO "AMERICA"

The United States was in an unequaled position by virtue of its huge size, large population, and plentiful resources to achieve a degree of effective independence far in excess of the levels attained by other ex-colonies, including Britain's dominions. Even with these advantages, however, it was not until the close of the century that the republic was able to mobilize its political, economic, and cultural resources to turn aspirations into reality.

The Civil War, though crucial in securing the Union, created a state rather than a nation-state. Unity founded on a shared sense of nationality remained a work in progress, as it did in Germany, Italy, and other new or newly reconstructed states. The political debates of the time represented a backlash against the strains imposed by the transition to modern globalization. The rival programs of the two main parties in the United States were, in effect, proposals to renegotiate the terms of international integration. The transformation that followed was tense and contested. Republicans and Democrats battled to shape the Union to conform to their contrasting visions of its future, while trying to settle the regional issues that arose with Reconstruction and grappling with the militant class conflict that marked the 1880s and 1890s. Agrarian populists resented their subordination to the rising power of industrial capitalism; urban workers disputed the terms of their incorporation into it; property owners searched for ways of maintaining civil order without destabilizing the state or derailing economic development.

The key issues were not resolved until the crucial federal elections of 1896 and 1900, which signaled the triumph of the Republican program. The Democrats were out-funded and out-maneuvered. They were handicapped by their support of free trade, which their opponents claimed would continue to subordinate the United States to what today would be called "neocolonialism" and its malign British agents. Tariff protection appealed to nationalist sentiments, as it did in continental Europe, and delivered the pensions, contracts, and votes that helped the Republicans to retain power. Hamilton's spirit oversaw the success; List's economic nationalism steered it. Powerful interests held on to the gold standard, despite the widespread appeal of soft money. Militant dissent was suppressed; radical alternatives lost credibility in national politics. The South devised ways of reaffirming its values and distinctiveness after 1865, but never again ventured to disrupt the Union. The victors, having saved capitalism from gilded excess, accepted that a measure of reform was needed to prevent a recurrence of the desperate conflicts of the 1890s. At the turn of the century, the Progressives in the United States, like their counterparts among new liberals and conservatives in Europe, turned to central governments to curb monopolistic behavior and institute welfare reforms. Even plutocrats saw that amelioration was preferable to revolution.

A growing sense of national independence found expression abroad as well as at home. In 1895, the first Venezuela Crisis demonstrated that the United States felt confident enough to defy Britain and add substance to the Monroe Doctrine. Three years later, the Republicans deployed the U.S. Navy to defeat Spanish forces in the Caribbean and Pacific. The war with Spain demonstrated that the United States had acquired the capacity to undertake assertive action at an international level and no longer depended on the Royal Navy for defense. The naval program, funded by the protective tariff, provided the Republicans with the means they needed. Progressives, like Roosevelt and Wilson, believed that the national purpose was no longer confined to national borders but validated a crusading foreign policy that would uplift the fallen, manage their future, and demonstrate to a skeptical public at home the benefits that great leaders at the head of a powerful, benign state could confer.

Economic development underpinned political nationalism. Quantitative evidence shows that the real "market revolution" occurred after the Civil War, rather than during the first half of the century. By about 1900, and certainly by 1914, the United States combined self-sufficiency and rising living standards to an unprecedented degree in what Alfred Marshall called "the largest Free Trade area in the world."[307] After 1865, the Republicans established high tariffs on imports while keeping the economy open to foreign capital and immigration. The tariff was vital because it contributed substantially to the revenues that underpinned the gold standard, which gave foreign creditors confidence that the restored Union would honor its debts. The return of peace, followed by the return to gold, attracted huge inflows of British capital and cemented a profitable business alliance with Northern and Midwestern banking, manufacturing, and railroad interests. American manufactures began to invade the British market; British manufactures experienced increasing difficulties in penetrating the United States. The deterioration in Britain's balance of trade with the United States helped to drive British exports into Asia and Africa, where political pressure opened new markets for its manufactured goods. By 1914, the United States had become the largest producer of goods and services in the world, and had finally broken free from the colonial inheritance that had characterized its foreign trade down to the Civil War.

Unlike British goods, British finance retained its importance in the development of the U.S. economy. Even so, the success of British investment helped the federal government to achieve fiscal unity and private enterprise to expand the domestic capital market. By the 1890s, the City of London and Wall Street were acting in unison; after 1900, they took it in turns to help each other out. The two parties reached parity mainly because the combined strength of the North and Midwest tilted the balance of power toward the United States. Meanwhile, the South remained a quasi-colonial subsidiary, supplying raw materials for the Northern region's expanding textile industry and for its long-standing trading partners in Manchester. Its diminished importance to the economy as a whole provided a measure of the relative decline of Britain's influence on the United States. In 1901, W. T. Stead anticipated the reversal of roles that would eventually follow the growth of U.S. investments in Britain: the "Old Country," he observed, "will become the new home of the American colonists."[308] "John Bull," he added, "will have to smarten up."[309]

Elements of a counterculture were present well before the Civil War, as Tocqueville noted in the 1840s in his comments on the evolving sense of American character, but fell short of creating a truly national identity.[310] The disaster of the Civil War, however, provided a compelling incentive to create bonds of unity that would prevent the Republic from tearing itself apart again. An ideology of national solidarity based on an inclusive, white, Anglo-Protestant citizenry served the purpose. Membership of the Anglo-Saxon union shed the deference that had accompanied it earlier in the century. Theorists refined racial doctrines that authorized the Republic to act as the most dynamic and independent branch of Anglo-Saxon ethnie. Religious leaders emphasized reconciliation rather than retribution and appealed to the faithful as a whole rather than to sectional interests. The Third Great Awakening carried the message into battle against the dark forces of immorality and divisiveness that sprang, unforeseen, from industrial capitalism. By 1900, evidence of maturing cultural independence had appeared not only in the high arts but also in social relations, public celebrations, intermarriage, and fashions, and in activities, such as sport, that reached across regions and appealed to all sections of white society. Earlier in the century, cultural similarities reflected American deference. At the close of the century, similarities were a measure of parity in an integrated world, while differences were marks of independence.

Changes in the language and symbols used to describe evolving identities provide indices of the progress made in nation-building. The national flag and anthem displaced rivals and gained popularity as a result of the Civil War.[311] Uncle Sam, who was invented during the War of 1812, replaced his competitors. By 1876, the year of the centennial, he had assumed his familiar lean, Lincoln-esque form as the undisputed symbol of the nation—and one that was distinctly white as well as assertively male.[312] By the 1880s, the term "Union," which had become synonymous with the loose, regional compromise that had failed so spectacularly in 1861, had fallen out of favor and was relegated to the lesser function of describing new labor organizations. "America" took its place in the 1890s and thereafter became the permanent referent.[313] The Pledge of Allegiance was composed in 1892 to celebrate Columbus Day on the 400th anniversary of the famous, and now controversial, landing.

In the 1890s, veterans' and other patriotic organizations, headed by the Grand Army of the Republic, the Sons of the American Revolution, the Daughters of the American Revolution, and the Flag Day Association, extended the flag and anthem to schools, public events, and private homes.[314] Thanksgiving, which was originally a "Yankee" custom, was on its way to becoming a national festival. By then, too, all the Northern states observed Decoration Day (now Memorial Day), though in the South it was still an occasion to reaffirm the values embodied in the Lost Cause. By 1913, however, fifty years after the Battle of Gettysburg, the event had assumed a national character.[315] Historians, the perennial acolytes of newly independent states, added their authority to the cause of national unity. Eminent scholars constructed a romantic "grand narrative" that validated the nation by enshrining its leaders, endorsing the ideals of liberty and democracy, and endowing the American past with a distinctiveness that became encoded as exceptionalism.[316] In 1901, Woodrow Wilson felt able to proclaim, uncontroversially, that "we have come to full maturity with this new century of our national existence and to full self-consciousness as a nation."[317] By the end of the period under review, national loyalties based on the enduring triumvirate of faith, family, and flag sat comfortably with regional and other affiliations.

The historical record fixes the United States firmly within the category of late-start countries that struggled to create national-industrial states in the second half of the nineteenth century.[318] The particulars differed, but the problems were essentially the same. This observation ought to be a commonplace, but has not yet received the full attention it merits. Late-starters were all engaged in negotiating a transition of historic proportions: the transfer of economic and political power from agriculture to industry. They all confronted, typically for the first time, issues arising from rapid urbanization and class conflict. They all struggled to create a sense of national identity that would draw diverse ethnic, regional, and religious loyalties under one banner. They were all sufficiently integrated to be jointly affected by disturbing oscillations in international trade and particularly by the combination of volatility and deflation that marked the last quarter of the century. The thinkers of the time, like the *philosophes* in the eighteenth century, developed and shared theories of cause, consequence, and cure. The challenging and often desperate confrontations of the period were all manifestations, as Montesquieu's insight suggests, of growing imbalances between economic growth and political control. Put another way, all these states were engaged in the transition to modern globalization and attempting to deal with the backlash it caused. This was "structural adjustment," as the World Bank would later call it, on a grand scale.

Effective independence prepared the United States for an international role that expressed its growing sense of power and confidence. In 1908, the Harvard historian, Albert Coolidge, judged that the newly united nation was one of the leading four "world powers," a term, he noted, that had come into use only during the last twenty years.[319] By 1910, Theodore Roosevelt could refer to "we, the great civilized nations," knowing that his audience would readily accept the assertion that the United States had joined other advanced countries in attaining the highest known stage of political and economic development.[320] This stage included bearing the burden of imperial responsibilities that fell unevenly upon "civilized" countries. During his European tour of that year, Roosevelt spoke with assurance of the "honorable privilege" this lofty status conferred, of the duties attached to the role, and of its global scope and permanent obligations. The United States had indeed come of age.[321]

CHAPTER 8

ACQUIRING AN UNEXCEPTIONAL EMPIRE

"OUR WORLD OPPORTUNITY, WORLD DUTY, AND WORLD GLORY"[1]

By 1898, the United States had become a formidable and fully independent state; in that year, too, the Republic's newfound strength was applied to invade Cuba, Puerto Rico, and the Philippines, and to annex Hawai'i.[2] Suddenly, and very visibly, the ex-colonial republic became an imperial power. With equal speed and publicity, these dramatic developments prompted a debate over causation that has lasted for more than a century. The interpretations currently on offer are illuminating, if also frequently conflicting. But they rarely place the United States in the international context shaped by the lengthening reach of globalization and the problems of integration it generated. The line of sight from the mainland captures the national story in immense and impressive detail. A wider angle of vision reveals that the United States participated with the European states in a common, if also competitive, venture to ensure that the Western powers remained in charge of the new world order that was emerging from the debris of the old.

The limited consideration given in studies of U.S. imperialism to the international context is apparent in the treatment of Spain, whose remaining possessions in the Caribbean and Pacific were annexed in 1898. Spain, having sunk without a trace for most of the century, suddenly resurfaces in the 1890s as a passive and declining power. In reality, Spain, like the United States, was engaged in a long-running and divisive effort to deal with the strains imposed by the challenge of creating a national-industrial state. The Spanish-American War of 1898 was a conflict between powers that were attempting to manage broadly similar problems of transition, albeit under different circumstances.

The history of the islands acquired by the United States also receives summary treatment in standard accounts, which generally limit themselves to the immediate antecedents of the wars with Spain and tend to represent the islanders as recipients of the actions of greater powers. Notable exceptions to this generalization can certainly be found, but for the most part they are confined to U.S. relations with one particular island. When viewed in a wider perspective, it is apparent that the Caribbean and Pacific islands were grappling with unprecedented problems of integration as globalizing influences washed over them in the nineteenth century. A full account of the causes of imperialism needs to identify and unravel the destabilizing ramifications of this attempted transformation, which will be given separate treatment in chapter 9.

The aim of the present discussion is to offer an explanation of U.S. imperialism that relates it to the desperate political struggle, analyzed in chapter 7, to control the Republic and shape its future. In retrospect, the presidential election of 1896 was decisive in installing the Republican Party's development program. At the time, however, uncertainty lasted into the mid-term elections of 1898 and was not entirely eliminated until the Democrats were crushed in 1900. War with Spain occurred in the middle of this fraught period. Scholars have assembled a list that includes both the immediate and the distant causes of the conflict. The devil no longer lies in the profuse details of the case but in the relationship between different parts of the argument. The basic, and familiar, problem is to make an effective connection between the general and the particular. The account offered here identifies the necessary causes in the progress of industrialization after the Civil War, expanded immigration and urbanization, growing regional and social divisions, and increasing civil disorder. These developments, however, are insufficient to explain the decision to create a territorial empire because they are consistent with other outcomes. Policy-makers provided the sufficient causes of action by judging that conflict with Spain would reinforce the dominance of the Republicans and thereby ensure that the Party's plans for dealing with the pressing domestic issues of the day would prevail. The territorial annexations that followed the decision to go to war celebrated electoral as well as military victories. The elections of 1898 and 1900 confirmed that the Republican vision of an independent United States would triumph. Successful wars in the Caribbean and the Pacific created a sense of national solidarity that the Civil War had made possible but had been unable to realize.

Political machinations in the United States were variations on a theme that was common to all the Western powers in the second half of the nineteenth century: the transformation of military-fiscal states based on agriculture into nation-states based on industry. The metamorphosis imposed wrenching demands that shook established hierarchies and endangered political stability. Imperialism was a partial solution that was tailored to the specific problems of individual states. Chapter 6 argued that the uneven character of the transformation ensured that diverse states had distinct priorities. The assessment that follows will suggest that, as a late-start country, the overt motives behind U.S. imperialism were mainly political. The war with Spain undoubtedly engaged particular economic interests, but its immediate purpose was to solidify national unity. The story, however, does not end at this point. The leading expansionists were convinced that the future of the nation, and of the capitalist system that underpinned it, were at stake, and they saw themselves as the providential agents of deliverance. The connection between foreign policy and the economy was indirect, being mediated by electoral imperatives, but was no less compelling for being so. These considerations stood behind Senator Albert Beveridge's rousing speech in 1898, when he urged the audience to grasp "world opportunity, world duty, and world glory." He was appealing to his compatriots, but his call, and its subtext, would have been readily understood in Europe, where expansionists of a similar stripe were using the same words for the same purpose.

THE BATTLE OVER THE WARS OF 1898

The generation of historians writing shortly after the conflict with Spain laid out the principal approaches to a controversy that remains alive today.[3] Scholars associated with the Progressive School argued that imperialism was the product of long-term economic causes stemming from the evolution of industrial capitalism. Dissenters insisted on the importance of the particular, the unforeseen, and the irrational, and consequently emphasized the unpredictable character of the events of 1898.[4] The debate that unfolded in the course of the twentieth century, though largely self-referencing, paralleled the evolution of the much larger literature on European imperialism.

The Progressive School has been castigated for alleged economic determinism, for its willingness to impose unquestioned assumptions on diverse, detailed evidence, and for failing to assign appropriate importance to causes that had other, often non-material, sources of inspiration. The dissenters have been criticized, in turn, for their insularity and for counting too many trees while seeing too little of the forest.[5] Some versions of this position held that the acquisitions made in 1898 were brief and uncharacteristic departures from the principal theme of American history, which centered on the steady spread of republican ideals and democratic values. According to this view, the United States was an exceptional nation, and the imperialism of 1898 was no more than a "great aberration."[6] Since similar "aberrations" were occurring elsewhere at exactly the same time, historians who wish to argue that the United States was, in this respect, exceptional have to discount commonalities among the imperialist powers that cannot plausibly be dismissed as being striking coincidences.

The Progressive tradition found a fresh voice in the 1960s and 1970s, when the New Left branch of the Wisconsin School revived the materialist standpoint and disputed the associated claim that the central theme of American history was one of consensus rather than of conflict.[7] The restatement held that imperialism was not a random interlude in a steadily unfolding story of progress, but a product of long-term economic developments culminating in a commercial depression in the 1890s that drove business interests to seek new markets abroad. A series of monographs added detailed studies and plausibility to the argument. The result was a bold and appealing interpretation that responded to the mood of the 1960s, which favored critics of capitalism, as it did in the 1890s.

The revitalized economic interpretation enjoyed considerable influence until the 1980s. By then, economic history was becoming a product without a market, and few new recruits came forward to respond to the increasing criticisms aimed at the New Left viewpoint. Conceptually, the literature was not always systematic in distinguishing between expansion and imperialism, with the result that evidence for one was sometimes taken to be proof of the other. While the terms may be, or may become, synonymous, the connection is neither necessary nor exclusive. There is a distinction to be drawn, for example, between business expansion that seeks to influence other parties who are relevant to the success of the enterprise, and business expansion that requires as a condition of its success the diminution of the sovereignty of the country in which it conducts operations.[8] The routine claim that business interests sought markets is evidence of commercial expansion; the more ambitious assertion that they were influential in curtailing the independence of the recipient country to attain this goal is evidence of imperialism. The intention can be achieved only by enlisting government support or by exerting a degree of informal influence far in excess of normal business operations.

A further conceptual difficulty is that the original interpretation appeared in two versions that were never fully integrated. One, outlined by William Appleman Williams in 1959, emphasized the need for overseas markets to boost sales of manufactured goods at a time of acute depression.[9] The other, which Williams developed a decade later, set out the case for a type of agrarian imperialism propelled by farmers in the Midwest who were suffering from hardships caused by falling prices for their output.[10] Since town and country did not form a natural, harmonious alliance, the question of which interest predominated is important both for understanding the balance of social forces in the United States in the late nineteenth century and for assigning motives to the aggressive imperialism of 1898. Williams himself did not fully reconcile his analysis of the problems faced by urban manufacturers with his Turnerian sense of empathy with the "dirt farmers" of the Midwest.[11] His notion of agrarian imperialism, though illuminating, remained undeveloped and is now neglected.

Most members of the New Left wing of the Wisconsin School gave their support to the industrial version of the thesis, which Walter LaFeber expanded in a notable study published in 1963.[12] LaFeber developed the argument that businesses seeking new markets at a time of depression pushed the government into war with Spain. He acknowledged that Spain's insular markets were undeveloped, but suggested that policymakers were influenced by perceptions, however exaggerated, of their potential value.[13] LaFeber also accepted that a large segment of business opinion had long opposed hostilities, which were likely to add to the commercial disruption inflicted by the continuing war between Spain and her rebellious subjects. Businessmen on the mainland changed their minds and exerted pressure only at the last moment and then chiefly to end the uncertainty generated by the crisis.[14] Nevertheless, LaFeber claimed that their intervention occurred at a critical point, and influenced Congress to declare war.[15] Subsequent research, however, has weakened confidence in the argument. Indeed, by 1991, one highly respected historian felt able to report that the "Wisconsin school view of the 1890s" had become "an artefact of the past."[16]

The interpretation associated with the Wisconsin School competed with an array of other possibilities, which emphasized the role of politics, personalities, and accidents, and what Richard Hofstadter called the "anxious irrationality" resulting from a collective "psychic crisis."[17] However, a broad alternative with wide appeal awaited the rise of cultural history, which added race, gender, and identity to the mix of explanations of late nineteenth-century imperialism.[18] Historians have long recognized the importance of racial stereotypes in shaping attitudes toward aliens at home and abroad, as the large literature on slavery, segregation, and

Anglo-Saxondom testifies.[19] Earlier work concentrated on the projection overseas of notions of racial superiority formed in the United States. Later research demonstrated that racial attitudes were not simply exported but were shaped by interactions with indigenous peoples on the frontiers of empire, and explored how that experience was recycled to influence aspects of American culture.[20]

Interest in gender has produced a clutch of related studies explaining how constructions of manliness and femininity affected attitudes and policies toward empire and how, in turn, expansion overseas influenced gender issues at home. Some studies have shown how virile, martial qualities became predominant influences on definitions of masculinity that then found expression in the wars of 1898; others have traced the connections between the new empire and the movement for women's rights in the United States.[21] The most directly relevant of these accounts has argued that the war with Spain was a display of militant masculinity, which was itself a reaction to the blows to male esteem delivered by occupational change, economic depression, and claims for women's rights.[22] The short and decisive conflict with Spain reasserted manly qualities; the long and grueling conflict in the Philippines threatened to destroy them. These contrasting experiences explain why jingoism fell as swiftly as it rose.

The presence of these ideas is not at issue: a strong sense of racial superiority and a desire to reinvigorate martial virtues of courage and honor were widespread in the publications and pronouncements of the time. These findings undoubtedly need to be built into any explanation of America's role in the era of new imperialism. Difficulties arise once the evidence presented to verify the hypothesis is subjected to what Descartes termed "the power of systematic doubt." Beliefs about racial superiority, for example, were indeed an important impulse toward expansion, but they competed with powerful alternative arguments that used race to oppose policies that might result in incorporating nonwhite peoples into the United States.[23]

A further problem surfaces in relating declamations to decisions.[24] The desire to advertise and reinforce particular notions of manliness, though undoubtedly present, has to be weighed against motives derived from other values. Gender is a constituent of identity, not its totality. Elements that enter into the making of identities, which in turn contribute to an understanding of actions, have other sources, such as social status, occupation, ethnicity, and religion, to name a few. Since policy-makers in 1898 were male, it is self-evident that they thought the way men of the time thought. Being men of the time, however, they also thought as business men, ministers, intellectuals, and politicians, as well as, or perhaps in preference to, thinking about the need to arrest their declining virility. Manliness, moreover, can take different forms and can include qualities such as judgment, steadiness, and restraint.[25] The leading advocates of war cast the national interest in different ways: McKinley countered jingoism with a policy of persistent and firm negotiation; Albert Beveridge stressed moral renewal rather than masculinity; Woodrow Wilson saw the war as an opportunity to regenerate politics; Theodore Roosevelt tied honor to duty.

It is still possible to claim, as chapter 5 suggested, that masculinity and violence were joint products that occupy a special place in the history of the United States.[26] Since war was a familiar and accepted solution to political problems, the upsurge of martial feelings in the 1890s was not a novelty. Accordingly, the increased volume of rhetoric about masculinity at that moment is to be understood, not as a free-standing expression, but as a response to promptings stemming from economic, social, and political causes. At this point, however, the cultural approach is limited by its own specialization, which rarely engages with the politics and economics of imperialism. Cultural historians have undoubtedly enlarged the subject, but they have not offered a new "master narrative"; nor could they do so without being accused of advocating a form of cultural determinism.

All attempts at understanding large events have their drawbacks. They also have merits that can be carried forward and incorporated into subsequent efforts to formulate a synthesis. The forces at work in the 1890s were distinctive in the sense that they had not appeared previously to the same degree and with the same effect. Foreign policy was made, not by reified entities, but by the personalities and politics of the moment.[27] Intervention overseas also raised novel questions of constitutional propriety and political purpose that could not be answered by applying precedents from continental experience. At the same time, American imperialism was not an "aberration," if the term is taken to mean a departure from an assumed norm. The fact that it appeared to be short-lived does not make it exceptional; rather, it casts doubt on the concept of normality in history. The movement was generic. The "new imperialism" of the United States rose and fell in concert with that of the European powers. It had common causes as well as distinctive features.

DON QUIXOTE'S LAST RIDE

The Spanish empire disappears from the view of non-specialist historians after the upheaval at the beginning of the nineteenth century, when the viceroyalties in South and Central America were divided into independent republics.[28] Occasional sightings preserve the image of a people whose declining energies were directed into religious zeal, and of a state that had lost its encounter with progress.[29] The history of the residues of the empire rarely enters general discussions of European imperialism and is left to specialists on Iberia, who tend to treat them as minor appendages of the turbulent and complex national story.[30] Of course, Spain's experience had distinctive features, but it was also representative in grappling with problems of nation-building and economic development that confronted all Western states in the nineteenth century.[31] More precisely, Spain provides an apt illustration of the wrenching strains arising from the transition from proto-globalization to modern globalization. The United States acquired an overseas empire to consolidate national unity in the aftermath of the Civil War and to calm the stresses caused by rapid urban and industrial development. Spain tried to use the resources of her once extensive empire to finance political ambitions on the Peninsula at a time when the struggle for power between conservative and liberal interests was still far from being resolved.

As shown in previous chapters, the French Wars damaged and in some cases destroyed military-fiscal states in Europe without replacing them with stable alternatives.[32] The period after 1815 witnessed a protracted contest between conservatives and reformers to determine the shape of the post-Napoleonic state. Spain's political oscillations had already been set in motion by the French occupation and the revolutions in the Americas. Instability continued during the nineteenth century through a series of revolts, coups, and civil wars, as monarchists and republicans competed for power in a rapidly changing world.[33] In 1814, the restored Bourbon dynasty in Spain, like the Habsburgs in Austro-Hungary, attempted to resurrect the military-fiscal state and impose absolutist rule. Opponents of this program were divided between those who wanted a constitutional monarchy and those who favored a republic. Liberal ideas, followed later by Marxism, surmounted the Pyrenees; Adam Smith and John Stuart Mill arrived by sea; nationalism drew inspiration from the Risorgimento, and from more distant developments in Ireland and India; anarchism was smuggled in from Italy in the closing decades of the century.[34] Democracy advanced and retreated. The right to vote, first granted to adult males in 1812, was rescinded and reissued on several occasions before becoming permanent in 1890.

Competing elites and their *caciques* networks presided over the lurching political fortunes of a society that was still predominantly agricultural.[35] Rule by oligarchy was the standard form of government, whether monarchists or republicans were in power. Nevertheless, bouts of reform, notably between 1869 and 1876, began to open up the political system during the second half of the century, as economic development altered the traditional basis of political power.[36] Despite persistent political uncertainties, agriculture, industry, and foreign trade all increased in volume and value. The pace of expansion was not spectacular, but it was robust enough to permit average living standards to keep up with population growth, which doubled between 1770 and 1910. The urban population doubled in a much shorter time: from 16 percent of the total population in 1857 to 32 percent in 1900.[37] The growth of manufacturing in the Basque Country and Catalonia created a new, progressive middle class and a complementary working class, both of which stood outside established political networks. Barcelona, in particular, developed global connections as a major conduit for shipping, commerce, and emigration.[38] Liberal thinking, which was also especially prominent in Catalonia, moved behind colonial reform, including the abolition of slavery, in the hope of preventing revolution and secession. Seen from Madrid's perspective, these claims were proxies for Catalonia's own desire to restore the independence it had lost in 1714.[39]

The Peninsula undoubtedly lagged behind the leaders in Europe, but there was no "great divergence" of principle in matters political and economic: Spain shared the same goals as other countries in trying to transform its military-fiscal state and create a modern economy in the second half of the century. Revisions to Spain's economic record contradict the stereotype of a country in which stagnation was punctuated by atypical and temporary bursts of growth.[40] Spain's relative economic backwardness was distinguished not by over-centralization and endemic conservatism, but by the strength of the provinces and a persisting sense of local priorities, which inhibited fiscal and market integration.[41]

Political parties adjusted their programs to meet these developments. All shades of opinion tied nationalism to the continuing imperial mission.[42] Conservatives, who presented themselves as guardians of the national interest, hoped to enlarge their base while conceding as little as possible to popular demands. Liberals, who advocated social reform and republican government, actively sought popular support. These broad positions were complicated, as they were in France, by conflicts between the center and the provinces, and between Catholics and secularists. The testing conditions of the 1880s and 1890s favored populist politics in Spain, as they did elsewhere in Europe and the United States. Radical republicanism made rapid progress with a campaign to replace the monarchical regime, which opponents portrayed as being decadent, and to restore Spain's standing as a world power.[43] The Cuban uprising in 1895, followed by the sinking of the *Maine* and the war of 1898, generated unprecedented expressions of popular nationalism in Spain, just as they did in the United States.[44] Conservatives were caught: the integrity of the homeland and the need to repel radical attacks obliged them to take a stand against the Cuban rebels and the United States. By amplifying nationalist rhetoric, however, they risked linking the imperial cause to popular demands for reform. Radicals, on the other hand, relished the chance to mobilize the wider public. They blamed conservatives for the deteriorating situation in the colonies, fused imperialism and nationalism, joined the people to the military, and used the crisis to discredit the restored monarchy, which had held power since 1876. In the 1890s, jingoism spanned many ideological frontiers.

These developments joined the Peninsula and the colonies in a marriage of inconvenience that eventually ended in divorce. The loss of her extensive possessions on the mainland of South America cost Spain much of her international prestige and about two-fifths of the revenues she had deployed to uphold her position as a great power. Mexico had provided crucial support for the revival of the Spanish empire after 1763, especially by financing Spain's wars with Britain and France. Increased taxation coupled with increasing indebtedness bankrupted first France and then Spain, generated widespread discontent, and helped to provoke the rebellion that led to Mexico's independence in 1821. The extensive monetary union based on the peso fell apart; the peso itself ceased to be accepted as the common standard of value and began a long decline that accelerated in the last quarter of the century.[45] Since debt service and the military continued to absorb a large proportion of Spain's national income, successive governments were under permanent pressure to extract as much revenue as possible from the remaining colonies to compensate for the independence they had reluctantly conceded to states in Central and South America.

Accordingly, the imperial dimension of the story should no longer be read as being one of unremitting decline, still less as one of official lassitude.[46] Fiscal imperatives and the need to retain her status as a world power ensured that Spain made a determined effort to revitalize the remnants of her empire after peace returned to Europe in 1815.[47] "Spain Overseas," though greatly reduced in size, was reorganized for the purpose of contributing to the resources of the homeland as it struggled to master the political forces unleashed by the French Revolution and the economic forces spread by Britain's industrial revolution. Initially, Madrid hoped to establish an extractive empire of the kind that Grenville had planned for the mainland colonies in the 1760s. Spain's star, however, was no longer ascendant. The refurbishment of the empire required foreign assistance, principally from Britain, and extractive policies provoked dissent that eventually swelled to revolutionary proportions. Moreover, Madrid failed to take advantage of emerging global opportunities. The Opium Wars and the opening of the Suez Canal transformed trade and politics in the China Sea and the Indian Ocean, but presented Spain with far more competition than she had faced during the golden age of the galleon trade and greatly reduced her prominence and prestige in these regions.

Following the loss of Mexico, Madrid gave governors-general in the remaining territories enlarged civil and military powers, which they used to increase taxation and suppress slave revolts and other subversive movements. Technically, the "empire" remained *La España Ultramar*; in practice, the empire of citizens increasingly became one of subjects, who were to be kept down rather than raised up. In 1837, the Spanish islands lost their representation in the Cortés. In 1863, Madrid established a new *Ministerio de Ultramar* to coordinate and centralize control of the colonies. Complementary policies encouraged emigration, especially to Cuba and Puerto Rico, with the aim of reducing poverty at home and fostering a new generation of colonial loyalists. The number of Spanish families with ties across the Atlantic grew as the century advanced. The reassertion of Madrid's authority put an end to the idea that equality could be achieved by assimilation or incorporation. Disenfranchisement at the imperial level stimulated the desire for greater local representation; infringements of established civil freedoms in the islands added impetus to embryonic nationalist movements.[48]

The slave trade and slavery, which Spain promoted from the close of the eighteenth century, formed the basis of a massive increase in exports from the Caribbean colonies.[49] Cuba, in particular, developed a dynamic capitalist economy based on slave labor and became the largest producer of sugar in the world by the middle of the century, as well as a leading supplier of high-quality tobacco.[50] The island replaced Mexico as the main source of colonial revenues, contributed significantly to Madrid's resources, and fed the appetite of the political class in the metropolis. Spain also developed nearby Puerto Rico as a producer of sugar and coffee, reoccupied Santo Domingo briefly (from 1861 to 1865), and extended her hitherto limited control over the distant Philippines, which also became an exporter of sugar and, subsequently, abaca (hemp).[51]

Mercantilist policies were too restrictive to promote colonial development, which was made possible by a shift to freer trade. Without access to other markets, the colonies would be unable to generate the income from foreign trade that produced revenue for Madrid. The underlying problem was Spain's own level of development: Spain's manufactured goods were uncompetitive and the domestic market was too small to absorb exports from the colonies. The slave trade was opened to other nations in 1789; Puerto Rico was allowed freer trade in 1815; Cuba in 1818; the Philippines (Manila) in 1835. Although commercial policy oscillated with political fortunes in Spain, the trend toward open trade was not checked until tariff preferences were applied to Cuba and Puerto Rico in the mid-1860s and to the Philippines in 1871. Discriminatory tariffs favored exports from Spain; reciprocal concessions were not offered to colonial exports.[52] Freer trade did not mean free trade: it increased the number of foreign commercial partners while discriminating in ways that created advantages for Spain.

Freer trade undoubtedly stimulated colonial exports, made an increasingly valuable contribution to Spain's balance of payments, and forged a new alliance with colonial elites, whose fortunes came to rely on the new, more open, trading system.[53] By the 1820s, Cuba was already part of a thriving international commercial network, though little of the empire's trade was conducted with the Peninsula.[54] To some extent, the move toward open trade recognized the reality of large-scale smuggling, which the British had promoted energetically after 1763.[55] Britain, the long-standing interloper, then took advantage of Madrid's needs to become a fully legitimate partner in Spain's international commerce. British merchants, shippers, and bankers expanded their share of Spain's imperial trade in the nineteenth century and formed joint ventures with Spanish companies to circumvent discriminatory tariffs.[56] The long-run effect of freer trade was to separate the economy from the polity. Export producers in the colonies, headed by *criollos* and *mestizos*, were keen to capitalize on opportunities outside the empire. Spain, on the other hand, needed to retain control of its colonies to ensure that tax revenues continued to flow to the Peninsula. These contradictory developments eventually became irreconcilable.

Despite the expansion of international trade, Spain's finances continued to deteriorate.[57] The accumulating cost of wars, civil and colonial, combined with the recycling of public revenues for unproductive purposes, placed increasing burdens on the budget and produced a series of financial crises from the 1860s onward. In the 1880s, the search for revenue prompted Spain to introduce a series of colonial tax reforms and to stiffen protectionist policies. To the extent that the reforms were effective, they increased the tax burdens on colonial subjects. To the extent that protection succeeded, it benefited Spain's exports far more than imports from the colonies. Both measures extended the reach of the colonial administration and were viewed by the recipients as an unwelcome form of recolonization.

The insular dimension of these trends is examined in chapter 9. Here, it is sufficient to note that Spain's colonies were snared in a trap of global proportions known to historians as the "crisis of transition."[58] International forces impelled structural economic changes that destabilized the social order and challenged political legitimacy. These pressures caused Spain's refurbished imperial system to buckle in the second half of the century. In the Caribbean, as in tropical Africa, the crisis of transition centered on the conversion of slave labor to free labor, following international restrictions on slave trading. In the Pacific, the upheaval involved large-scale immigration and access to land. Economic discontent and political disappointment turned protest into rebellion. The Ten Years' War in Cuba (1868–1878) foreshadowed what was to come in the 1890s, when large-scale revolts in Cuba and the Philippines brought the Spanish empire to an inglorious finale.[59]

The far-reaching structural adjustments involved in the transformation of export production in the Pacific and Caribbean islands intersected with the depression of the late nineteenth century to produce social discontent on a scale that undermined, and in some cases overturned, the established political order. The problem of oversupply in the face of constrained demand was a global one that overrode political boundaries. Farmers in the American Midwest and sugar producers in imperial Spain faced identical problems, even though they exported different commodities. Hawai'i, as chapter 9 will show, was affected in much the same way as Spain's colonial territories, particularly the Philippines.

Sugar prices fell more than prices of most other primary products: the wholesale price of cane sugar dropped by about 65 percent between 1885 and 1906.[60] Competition among producers intensified from the 1870s as beet sugar, which was grown mainly in Europe, cut into markets previously supplied by cane. The share of beet in the production of world sugar rose from 25 percent in 1864 to 65 percent in 1899. This trend had a devastating effect on exporters in the Caribbean. In 1870, Cuba, the largest producer of cane sugar, shipped 37 percent of its output to Europe; in 1890, the figure was less than 1 percent. Indebtedness increased; planters went out of business; banks closed.[61] Although the United States began to recover from depression in 1897, the sugar islands did not revive until the turn of the century, when expanding demand finally translated into higher produce prices.

In an era of deflation, the cost of manufactures dropped too, and freight rates declined as the steamship replaced sail.[62] The relationship between these variables and the terms of trade is complex and still imperfectly understood.[63] Current analysis suggests that secular trends in the terms of trade of primary producers during the last quarter of the nineteenth century mattered less than the volatility of externally induced price shocks and their variable effects, which were particularly marked on commodities such as sugar and coffee. There were also supply-side shocks, especially in the case of coffee, which was vulnerable to disease and sensitive to changes in the weather. Volatility was destabilizing because it created uncertainty, which drove farmers to find alternative exports, but also limited the capital investment needed to develop them. Questions about these trends and their consequences remain. It is evident, nevertheless, that a wide range of primary producers in the Spanish empire, as in the United States, believed that their standard of living and way of life were being threatened. Initially, they responded by making entrepreneurial adjustments; when these failed, they turned to political action.

Gains in productivity provided one means of retaining a margin of profit; another alternative was diversification. Improvements in productivity, however, were confined mainly to Cuba (and Hawai'i) and were incomplete when depression struck in the 1890s. Puerto Rico was more fortunate in adapting to coffee, which was the country's leading export by the 1890s. The world price of coffee declined between 1875 and 1886, but enjoyed a short boom between the late 1880s and the early 1890s before falling again between 1895 and 1900.[64] The expansion of coffee, however, had destabilizing consequences of its own: it reduced the land, incomes, and status of small farmers, created a rural proletariat, and encouraged estate owners to press Spain to adopt liberal economic policies.[65] The Philippines adapted by developing exports of abaca, but the price paid for this product also fell sharply toward the close of the century.

An additional consideration, the falling gold price of silver currency, needs to be introduced at this point.[66] Spain's persistent budgetary deficits prevented her from following other European countries when they joined the gold standard, and would have been even more serious without the contribution the colonies made to the balance of payments.[67] Spain adopted a bimetallic standard in 1868 but moved to a de facto silver standard in 1883. The peso lost more than 50 percent of its value against the gold-backed U.S. dollar between 1874 and 1898.[68] Inflows of foreign investment, which had supported public expenditure, fell sharply.[69]

Spain's exports gained from the depreciation of the peso: shipments to the colonies rose from 10 percent of total exports in 1882 to a peak of

29 percent in 1896.[70] The benefits, which were also a product of the reinforced protectionist system, accrued to Spanish manufacturers rather than to colonial consumers.[71] Moreover, most manufactured goods entering Spain's colonial markets became steadily more expensive relative to exports because they originated in the United States and Britain, and were priced in currencies backed by gold. The falling value of the peso may have helped colonial exporters retain a degree of competitiveness in world markets, but it did nothing to shield them from rivalry with other exporters, within and beyond the Spanish empire, whose currencies were also still based on silver.[72] Colonial debtors with obligations in stronger currencies had to work harder to meet their payments. Diminishing confidence in silver currencies raised the cost of credit and deterred foreign investment. Debts were re-priced when they fell due and shipping companies increased their rates to offset the decline in freight charges paid in pesos.[73]

As far as the import-dependent colonies were concerned, the disadvantages of retaining a silver standard appear to have outweighed the benefits.[74] By 1895, discontent in the Philippines and Puerto Rico had crystallized into a demand for currency reform and had stimulated a debate about the merits of gold and silver standards that echoed the controversy taking place in Europe and the United States. The Spanish government dithered in the face of complexity but was saved from decisiveness by the outbreak of rebellions in Cuba and the Philippines. The task of resolving the currency confusion was left to the United States.

The depression, combined with abrupt changes to the U.S. tariff on sugar imports, destroyed Spain's slim chances of holding her empire together and brought down the Hawaiian state at the same time. The territories "taken into care" by the United States at the close of the century fractured under pressure at points that joined the seams of government. Political elites fragmented. Mounting economic difficulties increased political friction and caused splits that produced new alliances between segments of the elite and foreign interests. At the same time, the "huddled masses" asserted claims of their own. Emancipation increased the fluidity of societies formerly marked by slavery; the continuing expansion of the sugar industry added to the diversity and size of the labor force. Proletarians, sharecroppers, and tenant farmers appeared; migrants from Asia made their way, not only to the Philippines and Hawai'i, but also to the Caribbean, where many of them later joined the struggle, first against Spain and then the United States. In the 1890s, elements of the elite and the lower orders came together, in different degrees in different places, to produce a popular front against foreign dominance. Rival factions advanced competing political programs: moderates in the Spanish empire campaigned for autonomy, or home rule, within the empire; radicals pressed for full independence.

Spain's rulers battled throughout the nineteenth century to contain the competing forces of conservatism and liberalism and the rise of militant regionalism represented in particular by the growing alienation of Catalonia.[75] Abrupt shifts between monarchical and republican governments, and between extractive and developmental colonial policies, greatly complicated the transition to modern globalization and unsettled the overseas territories. Ultimately, Spain lost control of her remaining colonies in the Caribbean and Pacific because she was unable to manage the transition from military fiscalism to a more open, liberal regime in an orderly manner. Economic reforms were too limited; political concessions were "too little and too late."[76] Both aroused expectations that increased rather than dissolved colonial discontent. Spain's failure in the 1890s provided opportunities for other Western powers to expand. The United States, the confident newcomer on the imperial block, was on hand to show that it was time for the Old World to take lessons from the New.

Byron thought that Cervantes had "smiled Spain's chivalry away."[77] A sense of honor and its companion, duty, however, survived satire and was refashioned in the nineteenth century to fit the needs of nationalism. Madrid had no option but to stand and hope for deliverance because the colonies, long a source of revenue, had also become central to Spain's identity and status as a great power. Don Quixote's last ride ended in 1898 in what became known as "*el desastre*," which initiated a period of prolonged and intense soul-searching. In 1918, Federico García Lorca saw few smiles on his journey through "warrior Spain," as he called Castille, where he recorded the "broken lances" and "leaden melancholy" of "silent forgotten cities."[78] The rise to power of General Francisco Franco in 1936 did not resolve the debate between conservatives and progressives, but it did bring it to an abrupt, if temporary, halt.[79] Members of the Falange assassinated Lorca in the same year.

MOBILIZING THE MEANS OF DESTRUCTION

The last quarter of the nineteenth century witnessed the start of the arms race that was to culminate in World War I. Germany began building a modern navy in the 1880s; Britain adopted the two-power standard in 1889. Steam replaced sail; steel supplanted wood; the submarine cable transformed communications across the oceans. Globalization was rapidly eliminating isolation. As one U.S. Army officer observed in 1898: "The genius of invention has changed all the essential conditions of a few years ago. Time and space are being rapidly annihilated."[80]

The union of patriotism, military experience, and martial values was one of the most important and enduring legacies of the Civil War.[81] Presidents themselves set the example. Every president of the United States between 1865 and 1898, except Grover Cleveland, had served in the Civil War, all at the rank of major or above.[82] Nevertheless, in the 1880s, the United States could not have fought a war with Spain, and still less have contemplated a war of choice rather than of necessity.[83] In 1898, the Regular Army remained capped at 28,000 men, and traditional fears of federal despotism blocked all efforts to increase it. Although some officers recognized the need for an expanded, professional force, there was no substantive increase until after the Spanish-American War.[84] The militia, though much larger, was designed for service at home, not overseas, and in any case had long been a declining force. Consequently, any engagement more demanding than the Indian Wars had to rely on the uncertain size and quality of a volunteer force.[85] The navy did not begin to replace wooden vessels with steel until 1882, had no battleships in commission even a decade later, and was short of modern ships in 1898. At the outbreak of war, the United States had still not developed Pearl Harbor in Hawai'i or Pago Pago in Samoa and had not laid a submarine cable in the Pacific, despite pressure to do so.[86] The Marine Corps lacked a sense of mission and suffered from low morale and poor discipline.

Although the merchant marine had been decimated during the Civil War, shipping interests failed to persuade Congress to subsidize the service, and the fleet languished thereafter.[87] In 1900, ships registered in the United States carried only 10 percent of the country's total foreign trade.[88] Supporting services were equally unimpressive. The Foreign Service was a reservoir of political patronage. Diplomats and consuls lacked expertise and experienced rapid turnover, which denied the benefits of continuity.[89] Business interests pressed for reform in the 1890s but failed to curb the spoils system. Change did not come until 1906, after the war with Spain, when Congress finally passed measures aimed at producing a professional consular service.[90]

The United States could contemplate war with Spain in 1898 only because the naval lobby, which did not have to combat fears that it harbored tyrannical ambitions on land, had achieved enough progress to make conflict at sea possible. A group of officers at the Naval War College, which opened in 1884, won sufficient support in Congress to fund the construction of modern fighting ships. By 1898, the United States possessed four first-class and two second-class battleships and a number of cruisers.[91] This was not a striking total in absolute terms, but it was just large enough to place the Republic among the major naval powers of the day.[92] Standard accounts of the period assign a leading role to Alfred Thayer Mahan, the naval strategist, in achieving this outcome. Mahan's celebrated study, *The Influence of Sea Power upon History* (1890), was undoubtedly influential and deserves the credit it has long received. Mahan favored close ties with Britain, was impressed by the achievements of the Royal Navy, and drew on that experience to shape American naval planning in the 1890s.[93] His ideas were not especially novel but they gained acceptance because they were expressed at a moment when men of influence were ready to listen to them. Theodore Roosevelt was a particularly well-placed member of the audience. He was a naval expert in his own right and politically influential even before he was appointed Assistant Secretary of the Navy in 1897. The two enthusiasts cooperated with other expansionists during the 1890s to create a modern navy.[94] They appealed to Congress by playing up the threat from Germany, and to the public by advertising the role of the navy as the valiant defender of liberty.

Naval expansionists owed their success to the fact that their aims fitted the Republican Party's development policy. Material considerations complemented Mahan's ideas on strategy. In the late 1880s and early 1890s, Democrats made much of the criticism that high import tariffs were allowing the federal government to accumulate reserves beyond revenue needs.[95] Republicans responded in ways that solidified their support. Generous pensions delivered the votes of veterans; an expansive naval program generated valuable contracts for businesses in the Northeast and Far West, stimulated employment, and expanded the party's list of donors.

The short-lived career of the *USS Maine*, the most famous of the new ships, is an apposite example of the program. The *Maine* was a second-class battleship of just under 7,000 tons, built in New York at a cost of $4.7 million, launched in 1890, commissioned in 1895, and sunk in 1898. On the West Coast, the port in California named after Henry Oxnard, the sugar beet magnate, benefited from naval contracts, while Oxnard's refinery there also gained from tariff protection. Proceeds from the tariff enabled the United States to fund the war with Spain without raising taxes or borrowing, and to outbid her after the loss of the *Maine*, when both countries scrambled to buy or lease the additional vessels they needed.[96]

In 1898, however, the United States was still ill-prepared for war. In July of that year, three months after the *Maine* had been sunk, Mahan, the leading strategist, expressed reservations about engaging in a war with Spain.[97] Nevertheless, all things being relative, if war came, the odds-on victory favored the United States. Spanish forces had failed to subdue Cuban nationalists and had suffered significant losses (albeit largely from disease) in the process. The war effort had increased Spain's indebtedness and had become increasingly unpopular on the Peninsula. The possibility of extending the conflict by involving the United States was a prospect that few in Madrid relished. War with the rising power in the region would place even greater demands on scarce resources and confront strategists with the formidable problem of managing long supply lines. Moreover, Spain was bereft of allies.[98] Monarchical Europe and even republican France simmered with anti-American sentiment and expressed sympathy for Spain, but were not prepared to act. Britain, the superpower of the day, supported the United States, though without issuing a formal declaration to that effect. Spain, though still a moving target, was no longer fleet of foot—or paddle.

Lack of preparation casts doubt on the idea that there was a carefully laid plan to dislodge Spain and occupy the islands by force. This conclusion, however, does not imply that the United States was a passive actor in the events leading to war, though it may help to explain why McKinley persisted with diplomatic initiatives. The chosen strategy was to use the navy to blockade Cuba and allow the insurgents there to harry the Spanish forces into defeat. The United States had sufficient means for this purpose without risking its poorly equipped and inadequately trained army in an extensive engagement on foreign terrain. The old navy might have been able to ferry troops to Cuba, though at great risk, but it fell far short of the requirements for action in the Philippines. The modern navy made it possible for Washington to contemplate war at sea. The new fleet, championed by eager, young officers, did not, however, bring about the war with Spain. The navy was the willing agent of the forward party in Congress, who saw, in overseas expansion, a national cause, which they believed would heal the divisions that threatened to destabilize the mainland in the 1890s.

"THE IRRESISTIBLE TENDENCY TO EXPANSION . . . SEEMS AGAIN IN OPERATION"[99]

Republican development policy rested on a form of corporate capitalism defended by a protective tariff and adherence to the gold standard.[100] The program was sectional in the sense that it served some interests, principally in the Northeast and Far West, much better than others, notably in the South and the Plains states. Successive Republican administrations therefore needed to present their approach as constituting a national policy, partly to mollify the South and, more importantly, to win the Midwest, which became a crucial battleground in the 1890s, when Congress was evenly divided between the two parties. Two strategies enabled the Republicans to achieve their aim. One involved manipulating the tariff to offer concessions to relevant constituencies without destroying its fundamental protective purpose. The other led the administration to embrace two of the most powerful cultural forces of the day, Anglo-Saxon racism and evangelical revivalism, to foster a sense of American nationalism that rose above sectional material interests.

Electoral success depended on converting the economic power of the Northeast into political capital that could be spent nationally.[101] The Northeast itself was in general strongly Republican because it gained heavily from industrial protection, the gold standard, which reassured Wall Street and foreign investors, and the pensions and contracts that federal revenues supported. Although these policies were highly unpopular in the South and the Plains states, where the costs were felt more than the benefits, political leaders there were unable to formulate a winning alternative, notwithstanding the appeal of free trade and bimetallism, and their electoral success in 1892. The political compromise that returned local power to Southern elites after the Civil War inhibited them from mounting a fundamental challenge to the Northern system of political economy, while the rise of rural populism presented a radical threat to "bossism," monopolies, and, ultimately, property rights that reinforced their conservative inclinations. Grover Cleveland, the Democratic president between 1893 and 1897, supported the gold standard and took care not to commit to free trade, even though he promised to reduce tariffs. The Midwest was the key swing region, and there Republicans were able to attract enough votes to secure crucial electoral successes in 1896 and 1900. The upper Midwest was becoming increasingly urbanized and integrated with the Northeast; the Far West (principally California) was attracted by substantial naval contracts. Segments of the agrarian West were won over by the prospect of new export markets that purportedly were to be opened by the reciprocity treaties touted by the Republicans.[102]

The trade depression gave the tariff a critical role in joining domestic politics and expansionist policies abroad.[103] High import tariffs, like the McKinley Tariff, created barriers to the expansion of exports because prospective trading partners had no incentive to give the United States free entry to their own markets. McKinley dealt with the problem by making concessions that kept the principle of protection in place. The reciprocity treaties envisaged by James Blaine offered free entry to specified products in exchange for equivalent concessions for American exports. The free entry of sugar and other food imports was designed to attract the votes of domestic consumers; the opening of new markets abroad appealed to hard-pressed producers at home. These concessions, like the tariff itself, were crafted with the aim of satisfying, appeasing, or neutralizing domestic pressure groups and voters in swing states. They took no account of the consequences for the countries overseas that were drawn into the arrangement.

Reciprocity agreements were not new: one had been signed with Canada in 1855, another with Hawai'i in 1876. Others had been advocated and blocked in the 1880s. Reciprocity became a key feature of the Republicans' international economic policy only in the 1890s, when the United States signed, or attempted to sign, a series of bilateral treaties principally with countries in Latin America and the Caribbean, and (during McKinley's presidency) with states in Europe. Most discussion of the reciprocity treaties has linked them to the need for manufacturers to secure new markets abroad.[104] This motive was undoubtedly present, but it is questionable whether it can carry the burden of causation conventionally attached to it. The United States signed reciprocity treaties either with poor countries whose immediate economic potential was limited, or with European states that confined the terms to a restricted range of generally minor products. Unsurprisingly, a decade of diplomatic endeavor produced only modest results. Some countries in Latin America and the Caribbean could be tempted or coerced into signing reciprocity agreements, but the trade that followed was far too small to have a noticeable effect on the nationwide scale of the depression in the United States. Lack of complementarity between the United States and such countries proved to be an insuperable obstacle. The idea that surplus wheat and beef from the United States could find markets in countries in Latin America that also produced large quantities of wheat and beef was never realistic; the notion that the Midwest could persuade China's millions to abandon rice for wheat was a pipe dream beyond even the most fanciful hopes for the China market.

The principal advocates of reciprocity were expansionists, like Blaine, whose trade as a politician and propagandist included the sale of elixirs of dubious quality.[105] The true test of the importance that business attached to the reciprocity treaties lay, not in the treaties that were signed, but in those that were not. The United States conducted more trade with Canada and Mexico than with any other countries, apart from those in Europe. By the late nineteenth century, too, earlier hopes of annexing both countries had given way to a clearer recognition of the insuperable nature of the obstacles and an acceptance of the need to expand trade rather than territory. Even so, negotiations in the last quarter of the nineteenth century, though earnest and protracted, failed to produce reciprocity treaties with either country.[106] None of the parties was prepared to make sufficient concessions, and the United States was unable to cajole Canada and Mexico in the way it could treat smaller countries.

Considered from another angle, it can be said that American businesses would have been willing to make greater concessions in negotiating trade agreements had they been convinced that reciprocity was crucial to their survival at a time of economic depression. The British adopted free trade in 1846, despite howls from major interest groups, because the Prime Minister, Robert Peel, could see no other way of dealing with the crisis that confronted the country. The United States, on the other hand, was unwilling to modify its tariff system sufficiently to give reciprocity a chance of boosting exports to Canada and Mexico, even though these countries had far greater market potential than islands such as Cuba and Hawai'i.

This assessment suggests that the purpose of the reciprocity agreements was to safeguard the protective tariffs that underpinned the power base of the Republican Party. Republicans defended the tariff by defusing the criticism that high taxes produced surplus revenues, and by promoting reciprocity treaties as a costless means of expanding markets. The treaties were designed to appeal particularly to voters in swing states in the agrarian Midwest, which needed new markets for their produce. Frank W. Taussig, the distinguished economist and close observer of the contemporary scene, noted that some of the changes introduced by the McKinley tariff "may fairly be said simply to try to throw dust in the farmers' eyes."[107] The strategy worked just well enough to beguile a sufficient number of voters, whose vision was temporarily impaired, into supporting the Republicans in the close-fought elections that culminated in their triumph in 1896.

All parties to the historical debate on the economic aspects of U.S. expansion agree that commerce with regions that were acquired or annexed formed a minuscule part of total traded output. The value of exports to Europe, by far the most important market, continued to expand, even during the 1890s; trade with the areas annexed in 1898 remained insignificant.[108] The proposition that a handful of poverty-stricken islands could end a depression of national importance is at first sight implausible. The chief response to this objection is that perceptions were more important than realities, and that policy-makers acted on their understanding, however exaggerated, of the potential value of the countries concerned.[109] The rejoinder, though cogent, does not dispose of the problem. Realities matter too. In Britain, where employment, profits, and incomes were heavily dependent on overseas trade and investment, policy-makers could reasonably claim that imperial policy and national policy were closely entwined. The evident disparity between the two in the United States challenges the credibility of the argument. Special interests were committed, as always, to advancing their particular concerns, but the wider business community remained skeptical of the vistas conjured up by the political advocates of empire.[110] This conclusion falls short of the evidence needed to show that the business lobby aimed for, and achieved, a policy that resulted in war with Spain. It is possible to meet this problem by arguing that recovery spurred expansion, but only at the cost of falling back on the more general and less helpful proposition that businesses seek to expand under a variety of circumstances.[111]

One of the few detailed assessments available has shown that large firms, which dominated the export trade in manufactures, adjusted to the depression through mergers, price agreements, and labor controls within the United States, and rarely called for government support in overseas markets.[112] Smaller firms formed the National Association of Manufacturers in 1895 to bring their interests before policy-makers, and gave strong backing to the Republican Party's policy of tariff protection. Small firms, however, rarely traded in overseas markets and, as far as is known, had no significant influence on the broader policies that produced America's overseas empire.[113] Potential investors remained skeptical of spacious invitations that seemed better suited to Swift's description of projects designed to extract sunbeams out of cucumbers. Leland Jenks's judgment, pronounced in 1928, that "business men interested in Cuba showed no war zeal" appears to have stood the test of time.[114]

Moreover, the depression began to lift in 1897, a year before the decision to declare war with Spain.[115] Trade with preferred markets recovered. By February 1898, the average price of leading U.S. stocks was close to its highest point in ten years.[116] Businesses were wary of jeopardizing the new prosperity; bankers were concerned that war might damage the dollar.[117] The evidence currently available indicates that substantial backing for a declaration of war had emerged well before sections of the business community belatedly added their support. The change of mind occurred partly because increasing uncertainty over Cuba's future was injuring commerce, and partly because U.S. firms trading with the island were persuaded that the prospective war was likely to be less hazardous than they had thought: the funding was in hand, the main European powers had indicated their neutrality, and the administration had given assurances about the military superiority of the United States.[118] Even so, the fact that business interests fell in behind the flag only after the sinking of the *Maine* suggests that they were not eager to develop an impoverished, war-torn market.[119]

This is not the end of the matter, however. The economic interpretation formulated by New Left members of the Wisconsin School focused on businesses producing goods for export. It had little to say about businesses involved in the import trade, even though raw sugar was the largest single import (by value) entering the United States in the late nineteenth century and the sugar tariff accounted for up to 20 percent of federal revenues.[120] Sugar refiners, unlike U.S. manufacturers, had a direct and sizeable interest in the islands that formed the American Empire in 1898.

Like other industrial companies, sugar refiners responded to the economic problems of the time by adjusting their business strategy within the United States. The squeeze on profits encouraged a process of consolidation that culminated in 1887 in the formation of the Sugar Trust under the dictatorial direction of the greatest of the sugar barons, Henry Osborne Havemeyer.[121] By 1892, the Sugar Trust accounted for more than 90 percent of refining capacity on the mainland, set domestic sugar prices, and dominated the home market for the next twenty years.[122] Besides controlling the Sugar Trust, Havemeyer was the largest single contributor to both political parties in 1892 and to the Republican Party in the crucial election of 1896.[123] Political philanthropy gave Havemeyer powerful connections: Elihu Root was his personal lawyer and the Sugar Trust's corporate attorney before becoming Secretary of War in 1899.[124] Nelson Aldrich, one of the most senior and influential Republican senators and a man with a formidable reputation as the master manipulator of tariff legislation, was Havemeyer's highly paid chief "fixer" in Congress.[125]

Havemeyer's investment in Congress paid dividends.[126] The McKinley Tariff, which was passed in 1890, helped to repay his substantial contribution to McKinley's election fund. At the same time, Havemeyer's financial support for Cleveland's election protected the Sugar Trust from action under new anti-trust legislation. His influence brought significant modifications to the Wilson-Gorman tariff in 1894 and dealt a damaging blow to the Democrats in the process. In 1896, Havemeyer abandoned his bipartisan policy, transferred his loyalty to the Republicans, and oiled the party machine that brought McKinley to power. His keen interest in tariff policy, however, did not translate readily into a zest for imperial acquisition. In 1893, he played a part in the decision not to annex Hawai'i because he judged that incorporation would have an adverse effect on his refining interests. His attitude toward Cuba was restrained because his principal agent on the island advised that the best course of action was to support the rebels' claim for autonomy within the Spanish empire.[127]

Havemeyer would not have been able to dictate imperial policy in 1898 even if he had set aside business calculations and entered into the "irrational exuberance" of the moment. In 1894, Havemeyer and Aldrich suffered a major defeat when they were unable to halt the passage of the Dingley Tariff, which raised rates on imported raw sugar and boosted the nascent beet industry.[128] Sugar beet was grown mainly in the swing states of the Midwest. It offered hope for depressed farming communities and brought a glow of optimism to the cheeks of equally depressed Democrats. By 1896, the new industry had spread across twenty states and had organized enough support in Congress to provide a counterweight to Havemeyer's influence.[129] Republicans had no alternative but to adjust to this development because they could not afford, in habitually close elections, to lose the Midwest.

The beet industry and mainland sugarcane producers (principally in Louisiana) opposed tariff concessions to foreign competitors and were generally hostile to imperial expansion, which they feared would open the door to incorporation and thereby place the sugar islands inside the tariff barriers erected to protect domestic suppliers. It was for this reason that the beet lobby campaigned vigorously against the Paris Peace Treaty, which transferred Spain's remaining islands to the United States. The treaty was ratified in 1899 only after Nelson Aldrich and his allies had opened the Republican war chest and distributed enough largesse to persuade members of the Senate to vote for the official cause of liberty and justice.[130] It was not until after the war that Havemeyer adapted his business strategy to take advantage of the new opportunities the insular empire presented. Once the federal government had given a guarantee of security at the expense of taxpayers rather than private enterprise, investment prospects brightened.[131] Havemeyer was not a keen imperialist but he was a good businessman, and he knew a safe bet when he saw one.

It is tempting to conclude that business interests played little part in the decisions that led the United States to acquire an overseas empire. The companies with most at stake were either ambivalent or opposed to overseas territorial acquisitions. Whether collusive or competing, the

parties concerned preferred to fight their battles in Congress and over
the tariff, and did not regard empire as a solution to their problems. This
conclusion, though accurate as far as it goes, needs extending. Big business was involved in important, though indirect, ways in the processes
that resulted in war and empire. Put starkly, the choice in the 1890s was
between two visions of capitalism: protection and the gold standard or
free trade and bimetallism. The large manufacturers, the principal sugar
refiners, and Wall Street backed the Republican program of development. When the Republicans faced the prospect of losing the mid-term
elections in 1898 if they failed to "liberate" Cuba, their wealthy backers
decided that it was better to have a small war, and possibly even a small
empire, than to allow free traders and silverites to run the country. Their
patriotism was no doubt sincere, but their imperialism was a political
calculation reached with long-term economic interests in mind.

"WE COME AS MINISTERING ANGELS, NOT AS DESPOTS"[132]

The leading advocates of an assertive foreign policy are well known
and guaranteed to appear in every account of the drama leading to the
Spanish-American War. Their careers, attitudes, attributes, and foibles
have been studied in great and often impressive detail.[133] Important
questions, such as how to measure the precise extent of their influence,
remain but are answerable only within the broadest of limits.[134] There is
room, however, for reappraising the historical context within which the
forward party operated.

The expansionists were members of the elite who came, for the most
part, from genteel, New England backgrounds. They owed their privileged positions to successful capitalist development, which, paradoxically,
they held at arm's length. Their mission was to save capitalism from its
many excesses, which had created social divisions, threatened civil order,
and jeopardized the political compromise that followed the Civil War. If
these developments were allowed to run their course, hopes of sustaining
their particular vision of the United States as an independent state and a
prospective world power would be lost. The expansionist impulse was a
means to a greater end, which was nothing less than the moral rearmament of the Republic. Seen from this standpoint, the expansionists were
political conservatives who wished to recreate a sense of organic unity,
which they located in a golden age before the Gilded Age. They looked
back to the early years of the Union, when great statesmen who were

"steeped in a thoughtful philosophy of politics," as Woodrow Wilson put it, managed the affairs of state in a spirit of educated wisdom that inspired the nation.[135] Overseas expansion and empire in particular were means of reasserting values once exemplified by the Founding Fathers but now corroded by party bosses, the spoils system, labor unrest, urban squalor, and anarchism. Across the Atlantic, European elites faced much the same dilemmas and devised similar programs to achieve comparable solutions.

The four leading figures, Theodore Roosevelt, Henry Cabot Lodge, Albert Beveridge, and Alfred Mahan, were all Republicans.[136] The first three were politicians; Mahan, the noted naval strategist, was connected to politics partly through them.[137] Roosevelt was Assistant Secretary of the Navy at a crucial moment in 1897–1898, when war was being debated and declared; Lodge was an influential senator; Beveridge had established himself as a national figure through his oratory, even before he joined the Senate in March 1899. None was in business or, as far as is known, in the pay of business interests. Their speeches and writings · frequently referred to the benefits of overseas commerce, but only in the broadest terms and with an eye to widening the appeal of their expansionist plans. Indeed, they recoiled from the unrestrained individualism that had produced, through rapid economic development, overcrowded towns and what they regarded as social decay.[138]

Roosevelt was a critic of corporatism and an active conservationist who promoted frontier qualities of fortitude, resilience, and resourcefulness, and who helped to preserve large slices of Turner's disappearing frontier.[139] Lodge typified the upper reaches of the Republican Party at the close of the century in wanting to control the unpredictable energies of the demos, limit immigration, and raise the standing of the United States in international affairs.[140] These aims called for a strong federal · state in the tradition of Hamilton and List, and an assertive, unifying foreign policy, which he helped to implement in 1898. Lodge's imperialism expressed the ideology of Anglo-Saxondom; his nationalism ensured that it was applied by the United States. Beveridge was a skilled demagogue who saw an opportunity to harness the restless populace to a cause that rose above immediate private and sectional interests.[141] His rhetoric linked the "march of the flag" and the "bugle call of liberty" to a conception of national greatness that assigned the United States the leading role as the divinely appointed agent of civilization.[142] Mahan was a prominent member of the Anglo-Saxon club and a committed Christian.[143] Like his associates, he based his thinking on a quasi-scientific belief in an "impulse to expansion" that was necessary to maintain the momentum of life. He, too, emphasized qualities of courage, loyalty, and service to the state, as his admiring biography of Nelson demonstrated.[144] He saw conflict looming, worried about the loss of martial spirit, and urged military preparations.

Other public figures stood just outside the inner circle but shared many of the same attributes. John Hay, to cite the most prominent example, was a diplomat who was unable to engage in open politics until he became Secretary of State in 1898, shortly after the end of the Spanish-American War.[145] Hay, who was strongly influenced by Lincoln, began his adult life as a reformer but became increasingly conservative after the militant railroad strikes of 1877 and increasingly nationalistic during the troubled 1890s. He combined a life of diplomacy with authorship. He published poetry, a vast biography of Lincoln, and a resentful anti-union novel, *The Bread-Winners: A Social Study*, in 1883. Hay was a plutocrat by marriage and donated generously to the Republican Party, which he saw as the last line of defense of capitalism and order. His commitment to McKinley in particular earned him appointment as Ambassador to Britain in 1897. Hay combined his developing sense of nationalism with admiration for the British Empire, which he used as a template for his own plans as Secretary of State.

The dapper, cultivated Hay was close to the Adams family and to Henry Brooks Adams, a plutocrat by inheritance and a literary lion by achievement, in particular.[146] However, it was Henry's brother, the prominent public intellectual, Peter Brooks Adams (known as Brooks Adams), who converted to imperialism in 1898. Brooks had not joined the march to war, but he warmed to the idea of empire once it had been acquired. In the 1890s, his pessimism about the present and nostalgia for the past were at odds with his confidence in the ability of the United States to shoulder the burdens of Western civilization.[147] He regarded Walter Scott as the icon of Europe's last heroic age, and Dickens as the spokesman of the new, unsettled, and fragile era. Dickens, Brooks Adams claimed, with a masculine, martial thrust of his own, appealed to an audience that was "largely feminine."[148] The Spanish-American War gave him a means of reconciling these divergent views.[149] An imperialist crusade, in alliance with the new corporations and guided by patrician intellectuals, would form an unbeatable coalition—at home and abroad. In Adams's imagination, if unavoidably not in person, Walter Scott rode with Roosevelt's Rough Riders in 1898.

The expansionists looked forward as well as back. They understood that the changes they deplored stemmed from industrialization and immigration, which were irreversible. Accordingly, they turned their attention to ways of harnessing the new power of the United States to the cause of national greatness. Their vision was of a United States that could achieve national unity and realize its potential as a world leader once its industrial might was placed under suitable political direction. Roosevelt, the man of action; Lodge, the man of influence; Beveridge, the man of words; Adams, the man of ideas; and Mahan, the man of strategy, were united in believing that the United States had a mission that was providential and therefore unquestionable. The divine purpose, to which they had unique access, was to carry Anglo-Saxon civilization across the world and to clear barbarism and savagery from its path. The act of spreading American values and influence abroad would also demonstrate and thereby reaffirm their importance at home. Manifest destiny, the phrase that validated continental expansion in the 1840s, was to be both globalized and relocalized to meet the needs of national regeneration.[150] War, if it came, would strengthen national solidarity; empire, if it emerged, would serve as a laboratory of good government. The two together would enhance the role of the executive and return to the president the power he had exercised in the days when the leaders of the Republic were great men. Last, but certainly not least, the intelligentsia would assume a vital role in guiding the United States into the new century and regain the status they had once enjoyed at the court of philosopher-presidents.

Outer circles of professionals, academics, and church leaders complemented the inner circle of well-placed expansionists. In the 1880s, the Naval War College began producing officers with knowledge of geopolitics as well as of strategy. By the close of the 1890s, officers in the U.S. Navy, like those in Britain and Germany, had adopted a view of sea power that extended beyond the limited needs of defense and encompassed broader strategies to advance the national interest.[151] Intermediaries like Mahan ensured that Congress was fully aware of the navy's increasingly visible profile and assertive stance.

Congress was also mindful of the attitude of the universities, the think tanks of the day, which had close ties both to the federal government and to big business. The most eminent of the learned societies all supported overseas expansion.[152] The American Historical Association (1884) held that empires were a force for progress and peace; the American Economic Association (1885) regarded empires as a form of corporate consolidation that would deliver the political equivalent of business efficiency; the American Academy of Political and Social Science (1889) gave its benediction to Social Darwinist teachings. Eminent individuals raised their voices in support. The historian, John Fiske, who counted himself a friend of Spencer's, was an Anglo-Saxon "race patriot" who portrayed the United States as being the youthful and energetic gladiator of the West charged with the task of felling barbarians and spreading civilization around the world.[153] John W. Burgess, also a noted historian and one of the founders of political science in the United States, made race the basis of the new science of politics.[154] Hegelian theory inspired him to believe that civilization had reached its destination in the United States. The example of nation-building in Germany led him to recommend that the United States should adopt a form of Teutonic corporatism and carry it to the rest of the world. There were dissenters, but also ways of dealing with them. The noted economist, John R. Commons, was dismissed from his post at Syracuse University in 1898 because his radical views, which included criticism of the connection between business and imperialism, hindered fund-raising.[155]

If business interests failed to rally to the flag until the last moment, Church leaders showed solidarity and commitment in helping to generate the momentum that carried the country to war. They were strongly in favor of intervention in Cuba on both spiritual and humanitarian grounds.[156] Divine guidance helped doubters to overcome their reservations. Protestant missionaries, who had long been excluded from Spain's possessions, seized a providential opportunity to mount their own assault on the islands. "The churchmen of our land," *The Advance* proclaimed, "should be prepared to invade Cuba as soon as the army and navy open the way."[157] Fractious Baptists, Episcopalians, Presbyterians, and Congregationalists came together as Christian soldiers to do their Protestant duty. Evangelicals viewed Catholics in the Spanish empire not as Christian brethren, but as challenges to Christian progress. As *The Christian and Missionary Alliance* put it, once the islands were freed from the "intolerable yoke of Spanish oppression," they would be opened to "the Gospel of the Lord Jesus Christ."[158]

Protestantism was "on the march" in a campaign to create a "world empire that has so long been waiting for it."[159] John R. Mott, one of the leading lay evangelists of his day, claimed that Hawai'i had a special place in the divine plan because God had "planted there a Christian nation which is at the same time a great lighthouse and a base of operations for the enterprise of universal evangelization."[160] Hawai'i was to be a staging post on the route to China, which had finally been forced to open its doors to the West and its numerous souls to Christianity. Providence had blessed the notion of manifest destiny and provided moral justification for imperialism. War purged sin and gave purified hands work to do. The cause, moreover, was now national and not sectional. Roman

Catholics on the mainland, though hesitant at first, joined the Protestant crusade.[161] Christianity bonded the nation in 1898 as it had fortified opposing sides during the Civil War. Christians were united where businessmen were divided. Surplus spiritual capital flowed to areas of greatest moral need; financial capital went to areas of greatest profit. Missionaries were enthusiastic about their prospects in the Pacific and East Asia; businessmen were reluctant to place their money in regions ruled by risk and uncertainty.

The advocates of imperialism met considerable resistance.[162] The Anti-Imperialist League, which was founded in 1898 to forestall the annexation of the Philippines, attracted an impressive list of supporters, including Grover Cleveland, the former president; William Jennings Bryan, the Populist leader; Andrew Carnegie, the industrial magnate; Samuel Gompers, the president of the American Federation of Labor; and, most famous of all, Mark Twain.[163] The League deployed a range of arguments that reflected the diverse sources of opposition to the new jingoism.[164] Cobdenite liberals adhered to a vision of a cosmopolitan, pacific world. Socialists such as the eccentric millionaire, H. Gaylord Wilshire, agreed with the British writer J. A. Hobson that imperialism was driven by large, new corporations that were searching for ways of disposing of surplus capital.[165] Labor leaders opposed imperialism because they feared that unrestricted immigration from Asia would cut domestic wage rates. Constitutionalists thought that imperialism would destroy the republican principle of government by consent and produce a federal despotism backed by a standing army. Intellectuals used the analogy with Rome to predict disaster.[166] Ultra-conservatives held that empire was inadmissible on racial grounds. As Senator Benjamin ("Pitchfork Ben") Tillman explained with his characteristic bluntness: "We of the South have never acknowledged that the negroes were our equals, or that they were fitted for or entitled to participate in government; therefore we are not inconsistent or hypocritical when we protest against the subjugation of the Filipinos and the establishment of a military government over them by force."[167]

Anti-imperialists looked back to historical precedent and republican ideals, and across to Europe, where common problems arising from industrialization, depression, and income inequality produced similar analyses.[168] Despite its star-spangled cast, however, the American League was no more successful than its counterparts in Europe were. Its elitist image limited its popularity; its cosmopolitan arguments appealed to an older generation; its racial claims resonated but were eventually accommodated. William James and John Dewey tried to reclaim patriotism by attaching it to civic virtues. By then, however, the alternative vision was too well established to be redirected. The image of war had been sanitized, romanticized, and accepted as being the most effective means of upholding the values of fortitude and duty that were essential ingredients of national identity and unity. The cerebral arguments of James and Dewey were no match for Theodore Roosevelt's visceral appeal to racial instinct and national destiny.[169] War, in his view, was necessary to avoid degeneration at home, to reinstall core principles of public duty, and to civilize savage peoples abroad. The anti-imperialists, he asserted, were "men of a by-gone age having to deal with the facts of the present."[170]

The momentum generated by the pro-imperialist lobbies enabled them to out-run the League and its less sprightly supporters. The imperial message found a receptive audience in Congress, where members also had to assess and calibrate the views of their constituents. Initially, public opinion was amorphous and not easily gauged. The press was divided on partisan lines: newspapers supporting the Democrats pushed for an assertive policy to liberate Cuba from colonial rule; those backing the Republicans advised restraint.[171] The balance of advantage was determined at the margin, where wavering Republicans were won over by local campaigns. On this view, party policy and organization shaped public opinion rather than the other way round. Popular feeling, however, was a developing force and not merely an element to be manipulated by puppet masters in Congress. After the loss of the *Maine* in February 1898, numerous demonstrations and petitions, which were endorsed by growing numbers of religious leaders, expressed patriotic sentiments and a desire for retribution.[172] At the beginning of April 1898, the French Ambassador in Washington summarized the mood of the moment by reporting to the Minister of Foreign Affairs in Paris that a "sort of a bellicose fury has seized the American nation."[173]

Both Houses contained voluble expansionists who pushed the president to take assertive action even before the *Maine* was sunk, who became excitable and vociferous after the event, and who were moved on the eve of the declaration of war to fill the corridors of the Capitol with patriotic songs.[174] The motives of members of Congress cannot be anatomized in the detail needed to produce certainty, and inferences can be mistaken.[175] An analysis of the background of members of both Houses shows that a substantial majority were lawyers, and that business and agriculture had very limited direct representation.[176] Irrespective of their occupations, members were in general well-educated and affluent men of property. The pattern of recruitment remained unchanged during the 1890s. There was no sudden infusion of new members with a particular commitment to empire-building. Foreign policy was generally given low priority even in the Senate, where the tariff was the most discussed issue. A very high proportion of members of both Houses had served as officers in the Civil War. While it is impossible to say whether this experience made them more or less likely to favor military action, it is reasonable to suppose that they were likely to respond positively to appeals to patriotism and the call of duty.

The evidence suggests that Congress supported the war for reasons of political advantage that could also double as being in the national interest.[177] Republicans had used the Cuban problem to embarrass President Cleveland; Democrats used the same issue to poke a sharp stick at President McKinley.[178] Although the election of 1896 had been a triumph for the Republicans, the Democrats were still influential in the Senate and hoped to make significant gains in the mid-term elections of 1898. In March and April, shortly before the declaration of war, it was their turn to bang the drum of liberty by accusing the Republicans of being more interested in making money than in promoting freedom. Republicans responded by urging McKinley to act rather than talk. Henry Cabot Lodge, the influential senator and advocate of empire, claimed that, unless the president declared war, the Democrats would win "a sweeping free-silver victory" in the forthcoming elections.[179] Russell A. Alger, the Secretary of War and a distinguished veteran, also criticized McKinley's continuing preference for diplomacy: "he is in danger of ruining himself and the Republican Party by standing in the way of the people's wishes."[180] Elihu Root, who was shortly to replace Alger, urged the president to lead the nation in a conflict that he thought had become inevitable or risk destroying the party and installing a "Silver Democracy."[181] Knute Nelson, a Republican senator and Civil War veteran, was even more explicit: "A popular war might do more than anything else to relieve the country from the night mare [sic] of the free silver question. The success of Bryanism, Populism, and free silver would inflict infinitely more damage on this country than a short, sharp war with Spain."[182]

The antique claim that the president was an irresolute leader who was driven to war by a sensation-seeking press can no longer be sustained.[183] Unlike Theodore Roosevelt, who was a much younger man, McKinley had no hawkish instincts. He had served in one horrific war, the Civil War, and did not wish to see another.[184] The notion that he was manipulated by Mark Hanna, businessman, fellow Ohioan, and *eminence grise*, can also be discounted.[185] McKinley knew his own mind, and it did not go round in circles. His priorities and expertise lay in domestic matters and not in international affairs. His goal, following the electoral triumph of 1896, was to consolidate the dominance of the Republican Party and, as far as possible, to make it synonymous with the national interest. He was well aware that foreign policy had a part to play in this strategy but equally aware that annexation was a divisive issue that required careful handling. He hoped to secure a pacific resolution to the Cuban problem, preferably by arbitration, and he adhered to this approach while under pressure from the various contending interests, including the expansionists in his own party.

McKinley had good reason for caution.[186] War was unpredictable. Hostilities could jeopardize the economic recovery that had just started. Military reverses would damage the party in power; defeat, though not seriously contemplated, would be disastrous in every respect. The enterprise could divide rather than unite the country and bring the Republicans down. Although the Republican manifesto of 1896 had declared the party's support for Cuban independence as well as advocating the annexation of Hawai'i and reaffirming the Monroe Doctrine, McKinley was aware that intervention remained controversial, even within his own ranks. After the loss of the *Maine*, however, the clamor for action became irresistible, and McKinley was obliged to alter course. In April, amid tears, scuffles, flag-waving, and astral rhetoric, Congress authorized the president to intervene and, if necessary, to use force. The euphoria of the moment concealed the fact that the adventure was launched with far more enthusiasm than forethought.

War fever took hold of the nation. The president called for 125,000 volunteers; at least one million men came forward.[187] North and South had a chance to demonstrate their sense of unity for the first time since the end of the Civil War. The war bonded the white nation. Politicians and the press passed over or minimized the achievements of the four regiments of African American soldiers that had been sent to "liberate" Cubans, who had just been given home rule and adult male suffrage.[188] The South responded enthusiastically to the opportunity to parade its suppressed martial values in a national cause. Thousands of Texans hastened to join the army, though only a handful of them saw action and many more died in disease-ridden camps in Florida.[189] Roosevelt took great care to ensure that his Rough Riders were recruited from all parts of the country and, within racial limits, from all walks of life.[190] McKinley shrewdly appointed four ex-Confederate generals, all aged over sixty, to equivalent positions in the expeditionary force, and placed one of them, Major-General Joseph Wheeler, in command of the cavalry division of the Volunteer Force.[191] The press depicted the war, not only as a victory over a decaying relic of the Old World, but also as a triumph of

FIGURE 8.1. The Union of North and South, 1898. *Source*: Library of Congress / LC-USZ62-63679

national solidarity: one striking official photograph depicted two former Union and Confederate officers clasping hands against a background filled by a light-skinned, blonde damsel (supposedly representing Cuba) being freed from her chains. The South had come in from the cold.

The peace treaty that settled the war settled the opposition too. Senator George F. Hoar was left to regret that the United States had become a "vulgar, commonplace empire founded upon physical force."[192] William Graham Sumner, the sociologist, concluded that Spain was the real victor because she had drawn the United States into the old European game of empire-building.[193] The British, too, were acting out of self-interest rather than altruism: "They are encouraging us to go into difficulties, first because our hands will be full and we will be unable to interfere elsewhere, and secondly because if we are in difficulties we shall need allies, and they think that they will be our first choice."[194] The Anti-Imperialist League had some sharpshooters but nevertheless lost the battle. The League was marginalized by World War I and wound up in 1921. Nationalism had trumped internationalism—and would do so again.

The "splendid little war," as Ambassador John Hay famously called it, was an unequaled opportunity to show that ploughshares could be beaten into swords to advance the national interest abroad while consolidating the peace at home.[195] Celebration followed victory. Popular plays, novels, poems, and songs commemorated the war and reinforced racial stereotypes for future use.[196] Authors of all kinds responded swiftly to the dramatic events of 1898.[197] Theodore Roosevelt published a typically racy account of his exploits in Cuba entitled *The Rough Riders*.[198] Henry Cabot Lodge cast the war as a crusade against bigotry and tyranny.[199] A clutch of novelists caught the mood of the moment. Elbridge S. Brooks, the leading author of juvenile imperial novels, produced tales of adventure set in sanitized versions of the wars with Spain and the Philippines.[200] Edward Stratemeyer, who started the first known fiction factory, employed teams of writers who included imperial themes in their vast output of pulp fiction.[201] Both authors, once popular and now long forgotten, played their part in justifying the conflict with Spain by placing it at the end of a line of heroic antecedents that included the Indian Wars and acquisitions from other former Spanish territories, notably Mexico.[202]

A chorus of composers tugged at patriotic and personal emotions.[203] None could match the popularity of Sousa's famous "Stars and Stripes Forever," but "Our Nation's Battle Cry" and "We'll Stand by the Flag" nevertheless captured the spirit of the moment. Although "My Sweetheart Went Down with the Maine" sank when the war ended, "There'll be a Hot Time in the Old Town Tonight," the favorite song of the Rough Riders, enjoyed a boisterous life after the war, while the sentimentality of "Goodbye, Dolly Gray" pulled at even more hearts during World War I. Union was now bound by unity.

Heavyweight commentators added the voice of authority. President McKinley was finally able to relax in the arms of victory: "Military service under a common flag and for a righteous cause," he intoned, "has strengthened the national spirit and served to cement more closely than ever the fraternal bonds between every section of the country."[204] In 1900, the president of the University of Illinois offered one of many warmly self-congratulatory pronouncements:

> One of the happy consequences of the war is the extent to which it developed a new spirit of union among the American people, as nothing else has done since the commencement of the bitter sectional

contest over slavery. When the call came for a warlike patriotism and an unbroken front against a foreign foe, the old differences between the North and the South seemed to disappear; men who had waged deadly battle against each other in the last generation fought side by side with enthusiastic, fraternal regard. In stopping oppression and in helping others towards freedom, they gained new attachments for each other and new devotion to their common country.[205]

In the same year, Albert Beveridge, in full Shakespearean flow, issued a challenge to the faint-hearts who contemplated trying to halt the march of progress:

> That flag has never paused in its onward march. Who dares halt it now—now, when history's largest events are carrying it forward; now, when we are at last one people, strong enough for any task, great enough for any glory destiny can bestow? How comes it that our first century closes with the process of consolidating the American people into a unit just accomplished, and quick upon the stroke of that great hour presses upon us our world opportunity, world duty, and world glory, which none but the people welded into an invisible nation can achieve or perform?[206]

The answer was as irrefutable as it was obvious: "Blind indeed is he who sees not the hand of God in events so vast."[207]

Woodrow Wilson, speaking at the 125th anniversary of the Battle of Trenton in 1901, made the same point about the achievement of national unity, though he expressed it in the formal academic style appropriate to one of Princeton's noted professors:

> No war ever transformed us quite as the war with Spain transformed us. No previous years ever ran with so swift a change as the years since 1898. We have witnessed a new revolution. We have seen the transformation of America completed. That little group of states, which one hundred and twenty-five years ago cast the sovereignty of Britain off, is now grown into a mighty power. That little confederation has now massed and organized its energies. A confederacy is transformed into a nation.[208]

"DESTINY, DIVINITY AND DOLLARS!"[209]

The foregoing discussion can now be recast to draw together the two main components of causation: structure and agency. Structure provides the context within which decisions are made and actions are taken; agency identifies the part played by different interests and individuals in producing outcomes. The motives of agents can be considered as reasons for actions and causes of actions. Reasons are not necessarily causes: public statements may be mistaken, misleading, or duplicitous. Causes, moreover, reach beyond reasons even when the two are in harmony, and encompass a cascade of possibilities ranging from those that set the parameters of actions to the actions themselves. The debate over American imperialism contains claims that appear irreconcilable partly because the protagonists have not always considered how one type of explanation relates to others of a different order. The contest between the role of individuals and the influence of implacable forces is, in principle, unnecessary. The interpretation advanced here attempts to unite reasons and causes by showing how McKinley the decision-maker complemented the wider system of political economy he so ably represented. Karl Marx expressed the relationship between the two in a well-known formulation: "Man makes his own history, but he does not make it out of the whole cloth; he does not make it out of conditions chosen by himself, but out of such as he finds close to hand."[210]

The conditions that lay close to hand arose from the profound upheaval caused by the twin processes of industrialization and nation-building that were the basic components of modern globalization. Contemporary commentators in the Anglo-Saxon world portrayed the conflict of 1898 as being between the Old World and the New. One was progressive, dynamic, and modern; the other was conservative, lethargic, and medieval. The perspective adopted here regards the United States and Spain as grappling with broadly similar problems of transition. Both were engaged in transforming agrarian societies into states that approximated Weber's notion of modernity; both faced consequential domestic strains in the late nineteenth century. Spain's incomplete transition from military fiscalism illustrates the longevity of the conflict in Europe between monarchs and republicans. The transition in the United States after 1865 was a case study in modern nation-building. The need to retain national unity at home committed Spain to defend her empire overseas, literally at all costs. A policy that appealed in Spain, however, aroused strident opposition in the colonies that challenged Madrid's authority and demanded liberal reform. The same imperative impelled the United States to wrench Spain's empire from her. The Caribbean colonies were taken to seal national unity and entrench the Republican Party. The New World defeated the Old, not because energy levels had drifted westward across the Atlantic, but because the United States managed the transition to modernity more successfully than Spain did. The islands were ground between two millstones. Far from basking in tropical indolence, they, too, were trying to adjust to the new, penetrative form of globalization that drew them into the international economy as export producers and into the cosmopolitan world as advocates of liberal aspirations.

The struggle to shape these gigantic processes found political expression in the United States in the contest between Republicans and Democrats. Although the Republican North won the war in 1865, an intense political conflict followed, as the two main parties fought for control of the national agenda. Both claimed to be custodians of the national interest and to possess policies that would safeguard independence and deliver prosperity. The struggle became inflamed in the 1880s and 1890s, when a combination of deflation and depression sharpened the antagonism between town and country and caused the representatives of capital and labor to confront each other with increasing hostility.

The development of the nation-state was predicated on expanding frontiers and unchecked immigration, which enlarged the economy and strengthened the polity, but also raised formidable problems of social unity and political control. Economic policy pitted Republicans, who favored manufacturing, protection, the gold standard, and a positive role for the federal government, against Democrats, who stood for agriculture, free trade, bimetallism, and decentralization. Republicans had to pay particular attention to voters in important swing states, where the gold standard and protective tariffs were deeply unpopular. The gold standard was non-negotiable as far as Republicans were concerned because the City of London was an important source of credit for both government and business. The tariff supported manufacturers and generated contracts and employment but hampered business expansion overseas by limiting the return trade in imports. Reciprocity was an ingenious device to overcome the handicap imposed by protection without destroying the system as a whole. Reciprocity agreements allowed particular countries and commodities privileged access to the United States; in return, the countries concerned opened their own markets to exports from the United States. The aim was to gain votes in specific manufacturing and agricultural constituencies that hoped to win export markets, while permitting entry to commodities that did not compete with domestic producers, and could therefore be shipped without also importing political costs.

The conflict taking place in the United States echoed that in Europe as the balance of economic and political power shifted from agriculture to industry, from country to town, and from one region to another.[211] In Europe, as in the United States, political parties with sectional bases had to devise programs that had national appeal if fragile, fractious states were to be held together. Tariff and monetary policies were everywhere weapons of choice as well as necessity because they had the power to turn economic resources into political capital. They were the principal means of raising revenue, protecting favored economic activities, redistributing income, and rewarding supporters. In France, an alliance of wheat and iron produced a conservative coalition that prevented the country from veering too far to the left. In Germany, the "marriage" of rye and iron achieved a comparable result.[212] In the United States, the Republicans brought together a similar coalition for the same purpose. Nevertheless, an economic platform consisting of the tariff and the gold standard was too narrow to achieve national appeal on its own. Whether to disguise sectional advantage or to make it palatable, political parties fused their economic principles with a wider set of beliefs that incorporated diverse interests into a developing sense of national identity.

In the United States, the Republicans stood behind the trinity of religiosity, ethnicity, and liberty. Religion and ethnicity were particularly effective instruments of group solidarity. They spanned large numbers of otherwise disparate regions and occupations, forged loyalties that could be attached to the state through the medium of patriotism, and enabled the nation's governing representatives to exercise a form of moral hegemony that muted alternative claims of region and class. Liberty was an even larger, all-encompassing principle. It became the official justification for the war with Spain, the subsequent conflict in the Philippines, and the annexation of Hawai'i. Cubans and Filipinos were to be freed from Spanish oppression; Hawaiians were to be freed from incompetence and corruption. Wars and territorial acquisitions were legitimate because they were undertaken for humanitarian reasons. Moral outrage at the alleged excesses of Spanish rule was sincere and powerful. Liberty, however, is a universal concept and acquires substance and meaning only when filled with specifics of time and place. In 1898, the brand was manufactured in the United States, and the model on offer was designed by the Republican Party.

Liberty was the embodiment of the nation and the justification for its existence. It was a capacious term that had the merit of appealing above party politics and across the nation. The Cuban crisis provided an opportunity for expansionists to focus public attention on a cause that was national rather than sectional. As with the case of the abolition of the Atlantic slave trade a century earlier, the reformers implemented their domestic program of moral rearmament by promoting a conception of liberty that linked it to oppression overseas. The Republicans, the ruling party, were able to capture the moral high ground by leading the nation in a crusade that could be presented as being selfless and Protestant.[213] Expansionists within the party looked abroad for a cause that would demonstrate the superiority of the values they wished to reaffirm and revitalize at home. Liberty meant upholding existing property rights, which were the creation of individual enterprise, defusing radicalism, which threatened to redistribute wealth, and limiting the potentially oppressive power of the state. The strategy enabled the Republicans to sweep the board: they disarmed the Democrats, united the nation in support of a noble ideal, and won backing for their program of political economy.

The expansionists cut their cloth from this particular bale of circumstances. They seized the moment, the means, and the rhetoric. Like the neoconservatives in the 1990s, they, too, had a dream.[214] Their big idea was to impress the world and the nation with a spectacular demonstration of the power of the United States. By doing so, they aimed to revitalize and solidify the nation at a time when centrifugal forces were again tugging at its center, and to reestablish themselves as the navigators on board the ship of state. The expansionists needed to find a dramatic and compelling opportunity. The colonial uprisings that submerged Spanish rule met requirements: events in the Caribbean were close enough to command attention but distant enough to insulate the mainland from unwelcome influences; the rebel cause could easily be worked into an argument for championing liberty against Spanish oppression; war, if it came, appeared to be winnable.

Ernest R. May's suggestive exploration of what he termed the "foreign policy elite" led him to conclude that a split among a key group of cosmopolitan "opinion leaders" in the 1890s allowed the imperialist wing to overcome isolationism and implement an expansionist policy.[215] William Graham Sumner, commenting in 1899, took a similar if also narrower view of the issue: "The original and prime cause of the war," he observed, "was that it was a move of partisan tactics in the strife of parties at Washington."[216] May listed a number of familiar reasons for the breakdown of consensus, but emphasized particularly the influence of Britain, a great power that possessed a mighty empire, and of British notions of world order and development. Older members of the foreign policy elite, whose outlook had been shaped by Cobden and Bright, tended to oppose foreign intervention; the younger generation was more impressed by the assertive positions staked out by Dilke and Chamberlain.[217] May probably overestimated the solidarity of the elite before it split in the 1890s and underestimated the extent to which prospects of expansion were already present in the minds of those who thought about foreign policy. Nevertheless, it is certainly the case that an increasing number of intellectuals and public commentators in the 1890s believed that great-power status and empires went together. The world of states, like the world of business, appeared to be moving toward consolidation. Britain, the imperial superpower of the day, provided seemingly conclusive proof of this proposition and of the benefits it appeared to confer. If the United States wanted to be recognized as a great power, Washington would have to equip the nation with an empire.

Charles A. Beard, an unlikely source, anticipated May's judgment. Beard will be forever stereotyped, and in some quarters forever casti-gated, for being an economic determinist.[218] It is certainly the case that Beard's general histories of the United States contained broad statements about overseas expansion that included the desirability of foreign mar-kets. However, Beard also took care to avoid merging expansion and im-perialism.[219] His detailed analysis of the causes of imperialism, especially the acquisitions that followed the war with Spain, is unexpected and has been neglected, even by specialists.[220] Beard rejected not only Marxist interpretations of imperialism, but also the proposition that American business interests lay behind the push for war and territorial annexation. On the contrary, he argued, imperialism was "worked up" by an element of the foreign policy elite who were "phrase-makers" and not "men of hard economic experience."[221] The wordsmiths included the naval strat-egist, Alfred Thayer Mahan, whose motives were "little more than the rationalized war passion of a frustrated swivel-chair officer who had no stomach for the hard work of navigation and fighting."[222] Although Beard expressed this particular claim with more commitment than objectivity, he phrased his main thesis in sober language: "Loyalty to the facts of historical record must ascribe the idea of imperialist expansion mainly to naval officers and politicians rather than to business men."[223]

Although May and Beard agreed on the question of agency, their as-sessment of structural considerations was very different. May held that the war of 1898 was an emotional reaction to events of the moment and had no larger, imperial purpose. The United States had "greatness thrust upon it" by forces that lay beyond its borders and its reach.[224] This argu-ment truncates the larger, domestic causes of imperialism and reduces foreign policy to a set of passive reactions to outside pressures.[225] The claim that the international order drove American policy is not easily substantiated. The United States was singularly free from external con-straints on its foreign policy in the late nineteenth century. Beard had a much larger view of causation.[226] He did not doubt that the United States was in charge of its own destiny, and his instinct led him to believe that domestic economic and political developments underlay the push for overseas expansion. He formulated the "Hamiltonian-Jeffersonian dialectic" of rival visions of the national interest, understood that protectionist policies implied assertive rather than pacific methods of expanding trade, and drew attention to the function of war in diverting attention from domestic problems.[227] Despite these insights, Beard never closed the gap between the broad causes he assigned to expansion and the narrower motives he attributed to the outburst of imperialism in 1898.

Research completed since May and Beard made their important contributions to the debate suggests that a junction between structure and agency can now be formed. It is apparent that the foreign policy elite was not an isolated group of prominent individuals, even though this is still how they are often presented, but drew support from a large number of sympathizers in Congress. The hawks, moreover, were adroit in turning the rifts among other interests to their advantage. Business was divided between advocates and opponents of expansion; racists were split between those who wished to carry the flag of Anglo-Saxondom to the ends of the earth and those who were determined to prevent "inferior peoples" from becoming citizens of the United States. The imperialists couched their general appeal in terms that rose above these differences, while simultaneously helping to devise detailed concessions that appeased opponents and skeptics. Protection was preserved: reciprocity agreements offered some prospects for new markets overseas without damaging important business interests at home. Opposition was neutered: antiimperialists became an isolated minority who lost the rhetorical battle to control public sentiment—not for the last time. Imperialism became a national cause. Opponents, though not yet deemed unpatriotic, were defending a principle that had already been abandoned: the idea of a republic based on classical, eighteenth-century beliefs in civic virtue and cosmopolitan values.

Party politics, in turn, were connected to still wider calculations in which the ultimate goal was to control the means of resolving the tension between pursuing economic development and maintaining political unity. The balance between the two was nearly lost in the late nineteenth century. The years of deflation and sporadic depression exacerbated problems of economic development by reducing farm prices and increasing urban unemployment; discontent translated into political protest on a scale that challenged the established order. Republicans and Democrats battled to control these forces and to channel them into support for their own competing sectional agendas. The Republican Party's program prevailed, and in doing so put its stamp upon the nation. Reciprocity agreements won votes at home at the cost, which at first was ignored, of helping to create havoc abroad. The link between the growth of capitalism in the United States and the war of 1898 is to be found, not by trying to connect business interests to imperialism, but by joining economic development to political imperatives.

In this respect, the United States was an exemplary member of the group of late-start empire-building states in Europe that placed political unity before economic advantage.[228] Britain, the first-start country, developed extensive economic commitments overseas that linked imperialism to the national interest. French economic interests, though regional and sectional, were sufficiently prominent to earn a place with the politics of "la gloire" in explaining the imperialism of the Third Republic. Italy, one of the laggards, remained largely undeveloped and participated in imperial expansion principally to promote national unity. The United States ranked with Italy in harboring predominantly political motives. Unlike Italy, the United States had a substantial manufacturing sector and powerful business lobbies, which were a familiar presence in the corridors of power. The direct influence of economic interests on foreign policy, however, was muted. The new economy offered far greater opportunities in the huge domestic market than were available overseas. At the same time, divisions within businesses committed to overseas trade limited the effectiveness of their advocacy. Consequently, representations of the national interest overseas took a predominantly political form, though they did so to preserve the route to economic development charted by the Republican Party.

In one important respect, however, overseas expressions of U.S. imperialism differed from those of Western Europe in pursuing, simultaneously, a policy of internal colonization. This experience, however, did not make the United States unique. Rather, as chapter 5 suggested, it complemented parallel movements in the Anglo-world and in parts of the French Empire, where the frontiers of white settlement were being rolled back, and rolled over, indigenous societies. The end of the Civil War gave renewed impetus to the westward movement of settlers. Native Americans ceased to be treated as citizens of independent states; resistance was crushed by armed force. At the same time, Congress granted Southern states a large measure of Home Rule to reconcile them to the Union, and allowed African Americans to be subjected to renewed legal and social discrimination. The process of nation-building in the United States was essentially an exercise in uniting white Americans. The unqualified played their part by serving as antonyms who helped to define the values and superiority of others.

The deteriorating situation in Cuba provided an opportunity, not to create new markets abroad, but to demonstrate the unity of the nation behind the Republican consensus. War with Spain entrenched a sectional, Northern agenda by giving it an appeal that reached far beyond the primary beneficiaries. Tariff protection and the gold standard were controversial; liberty was a cause that resonated nationally. McKinley linked liberty to duty, duty to patriotism, and patriotism to Protestantism. As a committed Methodist, he prayed with conviction before deciding formally on war with Spain.[229] As a committed politician, he had taken the necessary soundings before praying and believed that a decision to go to war had popular support and would benefit the Republican Party. In 1898, the United States joined the Anglo-Saxon army of crusaders "marching as to war" and "treading where the saints have trod" to bring Christianity and civilization to the world.[230]

The wars with Spain and with the liberation movement in the Philippines were wars of choice. The United States intervened deliberately in the affairs of other countries, even though none of its vital interests was at stake. Britain had signaled its benign neutrality and provided covert support. No other power challenged the United States in the Caribbean or could conceivably have done so. Cuba, the nearest of Spain's colonies, did not and could not endanger the United States. On the contrary, whether as an autonomous or an independent state, Cuba would have had strong incentives to cooperate with the United States because exports of sugar to the mainland were vital to the island's welfare. The Philippines, the most distant of Spain's colonies, was virtually off the map as far as U.S. policy-makers were concerned. U.S. interests there were minimal. Had Germany or Japan taken a larger stake in the islands, the United States would have lost nothing and saved lives and treasure. McKinley was genuinely reluctant to resort to war. Once committed, however, he warmed to the fire that others had stoked. Victory turned even his sober head. The Philippines had to be acquired because it had become available. Capacity rather than necessity determined strategy.

This explanation of U.S imperialism poses interesting questions of taxonomy. Theories that draw on the Marxist tradition hold that imperialism is an assertive expression of a particular stage of capitalism. An alternative tradition, stemming from Cobden and Spencer and formulated by Schumpeter, argues that capitalism is inherently pacific and that imperialism stems from atavistic elements in society. It is evident that the American contribution to new imperialism was not driven by a rising industrial bourgeoisie searching for new markets to solve problems of falling profits and surplus capital at home. On the other hand, it is hard to portray

American advocates of imperialism as representatives of atavistic forces. Ardent imperialists in the United States were neither remnants of a feudal order nor gentlemanly capitalists of the kind found in the City of London. Rather, they were scions of capitalism who had inherited, married, or made money and so had the good fortune, in every sense, to be able to distance themselves from it. Financial independence gave them the means of criticizing the world that had made them. They exemplified Veblen's theory of the leisure class; they also had the leisure of the theory class, which allowed them to ruminate on "present discontents" and their remedies. They looked back to an imagined era, when different sections of society were interlocked in organic unity under the enlightened leadership of philosopher presidents. Their aim, however, was not to escape capitalism, still less to destroy it. They were realistic enough to appreciate that they owed their own privileged lives to wealth created in manufacturing and finance. Accordingly, they looked forward to a world of reformed capitalism purged of the excesses of the Gilded Age and the menace of socialism.

Imperialism was a means to this end. It promised to reaffirm the centrality of the core values of duty, honor, and courage, to create a sense of national identity that rose above sectional and regional divisions, and to restore members of the educated elite, namely themselves, to the position they had once held, or thought they had held, as honorary, and honored, philosopher-guardians of the Republic.[231] By grafting some of the old world on to the new, they hoped to produce a hybrid that would surmount the challenges of modernity. They were not alone in this endeavor. "In this immense empire, created by ourselves, we will see the material symbol of that patriotic unity that is not yet in our hearts. We will direct toward the vast and fertile problems of colonization part of the activity that now renders our political quarrels irritating and sterile."[232] The American imperialists of 1898 would surely have recognized and endorsed these sentiments, which a Belgian lawyer expressed in 1904 in referring to King Leopold's Congo.

There was, however, an evident difference of scale. Belgium did not possess a navy worth the name; after the turn of the century, the United States ranked with the major powers. In 1907, President Roosevelt sent the new U.S. fleet around the globe. Sixteen battleships manned by 14,000 sailors called at twenty ports in the course of a cruise that lasted for more than one year.[233] Although the ships were heavily armed, they were painted in white, which was the navy's peacetime color. Nevertheless, the expedition signaled to the world that the United States had arrived as a power of the first rank.[234] Whether or not the president spoke softly, and he rarely did, there could be no doubt that he now carried a very big stick.

CHAPTER 9

INSULAR PERSPECTIVES ON AN INTRUSIVE WORLD

"THE WHEELS OF THE MODERN POLITICAL JUGGERNAUT"[1]

The rhetoric of the empire-builders, swollen with talk of liberty, civilization, and progress, warmed hearts on the mainland but had a chilling effect on those who were about to become the objects of the United States' first experiment in overseas development and nation-building. Writing shortly before his death in 1895, the Cuban patriot, José Martí, sounded an alarm that anticipated impending reality. In fighting for Cuba's independence, it was his "duty," he said, to prevent the United States "from spreading over the West Indies and falling, with that added weight, upon other lands of Our America."[2] Martí had spent nearly thirty years in the United States living, as he put it, "inside the monster," and claimed to "know its entrails."[3] Luis Muñoz Marín, the principal political figure in Puerto Rico, was more moderate, more circumspect, and initially more welcoming, but by 1904 even he felt compelled to express his disillusion. "In 1901," he observed, "only a few of us distrusted the United States. Today, all are beginning to realize that we have been deceived."[4]

Reactions in the Pacific expressed opposition and alienation even more explicitly. Filipinos took up arms against the United States as soon as it became clear that the liberators were going to deny them independence. A spokesman for Emilio Famy Aguinaldo, the leader of the resistance, advised an American audience in 1899 that the nationalists were "engaged in a struggle for liberty," even though, "for the time being we are crushed under the wheels of the modern political juggernaut."[5] "Be convinced," he continued, "the Philippines are for the Filipinos. . . . We have never assimilated with our former oppressors, and we are not likely to assimilate with you."[6] In 1897, "tens of thousands" of Hawaiians and part-Hawaiians petitioned McKinley to disallow the treaty of annexation, but were ignored.[7] In the following year, Rear-Admiral Lester Beardslee, recently retired from the U.S. Navy as Commander of the Pacific Station, recorded his observations of the ceremony marking the transfer of sovereignty.[8] Few besides government officials were present, he reported, and there was a notable lack of enthusiasm among the contingent of new colonial subjects who were assigned supporting roles in the ceremony.

> The band of Hawaiian damsels who were to have lowered for the last time the Hawaiian flag, as the government band played for the last time officially the *ponoi* [the Hawaiian national anthem], would not lower it. The band refused to play the *ponoi*, loud weeping was the only music contributed by the natives.[9]

The reactions of colonial subjects in the Caribbean and Pacific islands point to a perspective on imperialism that the view from Washington reveals either hazily or not at all. Historians of European imperialism have long recognized the important parts played by both indigenous societies and white settlers in resisting or assisting the occupation of their lands. It is now more than half a century since John Hargreaves set out an agenda for investigating the "missing element" in the partition of Africa: the "role of African states, their rulers and people."[10] Since then, historians of Africa, the Middle East, and Asia have produced work of extraordinary range and quality on this theme.[11] In recent years, scholarly contributions of the highest order have also been made to the history of the islands that fell under U.S. control. For the most part, however, the literature focuses on individual islands. Few insular studies attempt to cover the new American empire as a whole, and those that do rarely link their findings to the wider debates generated by the extensive historiography of European imperialism.[12] In making some of these connections, the present chapter also draws attention to ways of fitting together the specialized literature on the islands and advertising it to historians of the British and French empires who have yet to add it to their portfolios.[13]

The islands annexed by the United States following the war with Spain in 1898 are not easily categorized. They were divided between two different worlds in the Atlantic and the Pacific. Three islands had long been ruled by Spain; the fourth, Hawai'i, had long been independent. The Philippines was a sizeable, straggling archipelago; the other islands were small; some of the very smallest escaped the attention of cartographers until the nineteenth century.[14] For these reasons alone, it is understandable that the insular empire finds little place in standard histories of the United States, apart from its involvement in the Spanish-American War, and almost no place at all in broader histories of Western imperialism. There is, as they say, a gap to be filled. The story, moreover, is not merely a minor appendix to much grander events. Despite its modest size, the insular empire displayed a degree of diversity that made it a microcosm of the much larger British and French empires. It contained white settlers, allowed foreign concessions, and harnessed indigenous enterprise. The penetration of foreign influences raised questions of race relations, social adaptation, and political control that were replicated in other Western empires. The tightening bonds of global integration joined the American Empire to world developments, as they did elsewhere. As recipients of new foreign rulers, the islands gave the United States an exceptional opportunity to show whether the New World was not only different from, but also better than, the Old.

Given the current state of the historiography, it is necessary to emphasize that the imperialism of the United States, like that of the European powers, was the product of forces within the colonized societies themselves as well as of external influences. Had the view from the islands been allocated the space it merits, discussion of the acquisitions made by the United States at the end of the century would have taken greater account of the growing turmoil in the regions that fell under its control. The concepts of "informal empire," "sub-imperialism," and "collaboration" would have entered the historiography long ago, and the literature would now be bulging with debates on the respective merits of "metropolitan" and "peripheral" theories of causation and on the "excentric" thesis of empire-building.[15]

The assessment that follows will apply the argument developed in the previous chapter to understand the upheaval on frontiers where the American presence intersected with diverse societies overseas.[16] The decision that led to war with Spain and subsequent annexations was the product of the economic and political crisis that embroiled Europe and the United States, and reached its high point in the 1890s. This crisis, in turn, was rooted in the long and unsteady transition from agrarian military-fiscal states to what were becoming industrial nation-states. Its overseas complement was an incomplete transition to export agriculture and, in some cases, mining. Interactions between "home" and "abroad" in the late nineteenth century were expressed in deteriorating economic conditions and disappointed political expectations, which were amplified by Madrid's pressing need for revenue and Washington's abrupt changes in tariff policy. Opposition in the islands was widespread and often forceful, but ultimately futile. The crucial decisions were made in Washington, which gave the "civilizing mission," American-style, its first outing overseas. Imperialism, referred to here as "enforced globalization," was the assertive manifestation of this great transformation.

SUGARING THE PILL

American interests in the Caribbean and Pacific functioned within an international setting shaped by the lengthening reach of globalization and the problems of integration it generated.[17] The islands that fell under the control of the United States were engaged in a series of far-reaching changes that the World Bank would later call "structural adjustment." Their economies struggled to adapt to the demands of export development; their political systems became strained to the point of instability in making the attempt. The series of depressions that affected primary producers throughout the international economy in the late nineteenth century magnified these difficulties. By 1898, the countries that were shortly to fall under U.S. control were in various stages of disintegration. Expansionists saw an opportunity and grasped it: liberty was prescribed to cure disorder; armed intervention replaced informal relations.

Sugar, the "sweet malefactor," provided the common connection between the islands and the mainland.[18] Given that it was primarily a plantation crop grown for export, sugar attracted expatriates who could mobilize the necessary capital and marketing connections. Some U.S. entrepreneurs in what became the American Empire were settlers; the majority were absentees who employed local managers. On the eve of the War of 1898, American settlers were in short supply. Their main base was in Hawai'i, where their numbers rose swiftly from less than 2,000 in mid-century to about 29,000 in 1900, principally as a result of the expansion of the sugar industry after 1875.[19] U.S. settlers had a smaller presence in the western Pacific, where the "Manila Americans," as they were called, amounted to some 5,000 at the close of the century.[20] Cuba was the magnet in the Caribbean. Its accessibility to the mainland and rich endowment of land especially suited to cane sugar had long attracted foreign investors. Proximity and the steamship, however, encouraged mainlanders to be absentees or sojourners rather than permanent settlers in Cuba, as in Puerto Rico, and altered their attitude toward the long-term future of the islands they visited.[21]

The majority of white settlers in what became the American Empire were emigrants from Spain. The Spanish connection gave the insular possessions a distinctive character among the Western empires: no other

Western imperial power acquired a "ready-made" empire in this way. Moreover, the longevity of the Spanish Empire had turned the majority of settlers into locals, albeit with cosmopolitan connections.[22] The Spanish caste system in the empire evolved into a complex hierarchy of categories that looked precise but were mutable and, within limits, subjective. The principal distinctions attached identities to *peninsulares* and *criollos* (known collectively as *colonistas*), who were white, to *mestizos* and *mulatos*, who were of mixed blood, and to *indios*, *negritos*, and *negros*, who were either indigenous or treated as such by virtue of being nonwhite.[23] Peninsulares were born in Spain but lived in the Spanish colonies. They enjoyed high status and privileges, retained strong ties with their homeland, and were generally loyal to the Spanish cause. Criollos were children of peninsulares who ranked below them because they were born in the Americas. Many criollos were well educated and politically aware. They had strong affiliations with the land of their birth and became increasingly frustrated with restrictions that limited their opportunities for advancement. Predictably, criollos were in the forefront of the struggle for Latin American independence earlier in the nineteenth century, and they exerted a comparable influence on the movements for self-determination in the Caribbean at its close. Indios, negritos, and negros occupied places at the bottom of society but made their voices and their dissent heard in the struggles against slavery, Spain, and the United States.

These categories were distributed unevenly across the Spanish Empire. Spain's possessions in Central and South America were largely products of *conquistadores* and *colonistas*, who transplanted the social hierarchies of the Peninsula to the New World and adapted them to local conditions. The adaptation that transformed the Caribbean islands was the development of plantations through imported slave labor. Distinctions of caste in the Caribbean were qualified by differences between free and unfree, and between white and black. The Philippines, on the other hand, remained a frontier society centered on a major trading post, Manila, which attracted merchants rather than settlers.[24] Conquistadores and colonistas were few in number. Peninsulares remained at the top of the hierarchy but were inadequate substitutes. In the absence of a powerful settler oligarchy, the frontier was manned mainly by missionaries, known collectively as the Friars. Criollos were as politically unreliable in the Philippines as they were in Latin America, and in any case were outnumbered by a rising class of mestizos, most of whom were descended from Spanish and Chinese parents and had only tenuous ties with the Peninsula. These regional contrasts had important implications for the character of Spanish rule, the nature of colonial society, and the structure of the colonial economy.[25]

The assorted expatriate communities globalized themselves; their networks connected the scattered islands to the emerging world market for export crops. Recent scholarship has reacted against the predominance traditionally assigned to sugar and has emphasized the part played by other crops, such as tobacco, coffee, and abaca (hemp).[26] Nevertheless, it remains the case that sugar was the principal export from all four islands during the second half of the nineteenth century and was dislodged only briefly in the 1890s by coffee (in Puerto Rico) and abaca (in the Philippines). Accordingly, the traditional emphasis retains its relevance both as a proxy for the region's colonial export economies and as a central theme in the process of empire-building in the Pacific and Caribbean.

The consumption of sugar in the United States rose rapidly in the second half of the nineteenth century, as it did in Europe. By 1900, annual consumption had reached 2.66 million tons, which was a fivefold increase over the figure for 1866, and raw sugar accounted for 12 percent of all imports, which made it the largest single import into the United States.[27] Domestic production fell far short of demand, and in 1895 provided only about 19 percent of total consumption.[28] Cane sugar was confined to a small part of Louisiana; beet sugar did not expand until the turn of the century. Accordingly, imports of raw sugar met the greater part of home demand. As a corollary, the sugar islands came to rely on the U.S. market. The relationship, though mutual, was also unequal. Sugar consumption formed only a small part of total U.S. economic activity; sugar production was a very large part of the economies of the supplying countries.

Table 9.1 divides the major sources of sugar into three groups: overseas suppliers who gained from partial or total remission of duty at some point between 1870 and 1906; those who paid duty at the full rate; and domestic sources that were duty-free. Suppliers within each group are ranked by volume for the period 1870–1900, when the decisions leading to annexation or occupation were made. Supplies of sugar (which can be treated as a proxy for consumption) increased fivefold between 1870 and 1906. In 1895, Cuba alone supplied nearly half the sugar consumed in the United States. Other sources rose and fell in importance in response to changes in tariff levels enacted by Washington and political instability in the countries exporting sugar to the United States. Exports from Cuba and the Philippines suffered at the close of the century, when warfare interrupted production. These setbacks boosted exports from Java and Hawai'i, and stimulated domestic supplies from Louisiana.[29] European beet sugar made its mark in the 1890s, and was checked only after 1900,

TABLE 9.1. SUGAR SUPPLIES OF THE UNITED STATES, 1870–1906

(in millions of lbs: 15 = 15m. lbs)

Year	1870	1875	1880	1885	1890	1895	1900	1903	1906
OVERSEAS SOURCES (WITH TARIFF CONCESSIONS)									
Cuba	801	1090	1087	1115	1041	1845	705	2396	2782
Hawai'i	14	18	61	170	224	274	505	775	712
Philippines	59	119	133	179	260	69	49	19	69
Puerto Rico	131	110	84	160	77	56	72	226	410
OVERSEAS SOURCES (PAYING FULL DUTY)									
Europe (beet)				269	601	347	701	87	48
Java	15	74	23	7	112	280	1162	892	782
British West Indies	63	37	64	282	291	193	2001	91	37
Brazil	24	71	153	329	74	52	89	74	29
DOMESTIC SOURCES (DUTY-FREE)									
Louisiana	99	134	199	211	287	711	329	512	594
Beet sugar					10	45	163	437	672
Total	1206	1653	1804	2722	2977	3872	3975	5609	6135

Source: Adapted from F. W. Taussig, "Sugar: A Lesson on Reciprocity and the Tariff," *Atlantic Monthly*, 95 (1908), p. 334.

when the postwar settlement revived the Cuban industry and gave tariff concessions to Puerto Rico.

Cuba, Puerto Rico, the Philippines, and Hawai'i were not all ruled by Spain, but they were all ruled, in different degrees, by sugar. Tariff policy was the lever that gave the United States the power to influence states and economies in the Caribbean and Pacific. Wealth from sugar funded political parties in the islands during the period of American colonial rule. Reciprocity treaties were supplementary bilateral agreements that modified the general tariff. They had little influence on the volume and direction of U.S. commerce but were matters of life and death for the small countries affected by them. U.S. tariff policy was not designed to assist the long-run development of the sugar islands, but was the capricious outcome of domestic political rivalries. When the benign hand of political manipulation was turned toward them, producers suddenly gained access to a huge market on terms that gave them a considerable advantage over their competitors. They then scrambled to increase export production by applying as much capital and labor to farmland as they could. As a result, the affected export economies became heavily dependent on the artificial stimulus conferred by reciprocity agreements. When the concession was withdrawn or granted to rival producers, the original beneficiaries were plunged into economic depression that was quickly translated into political unrest. The market was distorted: prices were fixed by decisions made in Congress rather than by supply and demand. Tariff concessions diverted trade rather than created it, and mainly benefited offshore producers of raw sugar who received a subsidy from the U.S. Treasury; consumers won few benefits.[30]

At the close of the century, the difficulties arising from the unpredictability of the tariff were magnified by the slump in world markets and by the expansion of new sources of sugar. Insular exporters of sugarcane lost access to the large European market following the expansion of beet production and the adoption of protective tariffs on imports. The U.S. market became not just important but vital, and the struggle to secure shares in it grew increasingly brutal. These circumstances produced instability in the sugar-exporting countries and created political problems that the United States felt obliged to confront. Rivalry between Republicans and Democrats at home, projected abroad through tariff policy, helped to produce the conditions that resulted in the creation of the new American Empire. Hawai'i anticipated most of the issues and many of the arguments that arose later with the acquisition of the Spanish islands. Yet, the war with Spain in Cuba was the key event and one that ultimately also led to the formal annexation of Hawai'i. Accordingly, it is appropriate to begin in the Caribbean before crossing to the Pacific.

CUBA: "A LOT OF DEGENERATES ABSOLUTELY DEVOID OF HONOR AND GRATITUDE"[31]

By the middle of the century, Cuba had developed a vigorous capitalist economy, albeit based on slave labor, had established trade relations outside the crumbling mercantilist system, and had become the largest producer of sugar in the world, as well as being a leading supplier of high-quality tobacco.[32] The island exported coffee, too, but a series of hurricanes destroyed the crop in the 1840s and encouraged greater specialization in sugar, which further entrenched the plantation complex.[33] Nearly 600,000 slaves were shipped to the island between 1816 and 1867, which was more than reached the United States over the whole period of the Atlantic trade.[34] By 1846, slaves accounted for about 36 percent of the population and mulatos for a further 17 percent.[35] The wealth of the island in the mid-nineteenth century is often overlooked, as is its enhanced importance to Spain. Yet, Cuba was the first country in Latin America to erect steam-powered sugar mills (1817), to introduce steamship services to the United States (1836), to build railroads (1837), to install the telegraph (1844), and to lay a submarine cable (1867).[36] In the judgment of one authority: "Cuba may have been worth as much to Spain in the mid-nineteenth century as all her former mainland American colonies had been at the end of the eighteenth century."[37] Revenues derived from Cuba made a crucial contribution to Spain's budget and helped to fund Madrid's program of imperial revitalization.[38] Reciprocally, the crown established a "special relationship" with a cohesive elite of large sugar planters in the west of the island and defended their interests against other claimants, including tobacco farmers in the east, who were largely marginalized.[39]

Cuba's involvement in international trade, though long-standing, was limited until the late eighteenth century, when the Bourbon reforms stimulated the economy by opening the island to free trade and investing in its defenses.[40] Shortly afterward, sugar production in Cuba was boosted by the Haitian Revolution (1791–1804), which dislocated output from one of the world's leading exporters.[41] Cuba also gained from Britain's decision to end its involvement in the international slave trade in 1807 and to abolish the institution of slavery in its empire in 1833; France followed with similar measures in 1814 and 1848.[42] Cuba prospered because the demand for slave products continued to expand, the global slave trade flourished, and slavery on the island remained under Spanish protection. Under pressure from Britain, Spain signed treaties suppressing the slave trade in 1817 and 1835, but failed to implement them. Cuba's contribution to the Treasury was too important to be put at risk. Until the 1860s, Cuba, like the Southern states, was part of a flourishing economic system based on slave labor.

There was no gain, however, without strain. Cuba's economic success prompted Spain to increase the burden of taxation on the island, beginning with the loss of Mexico in 1825 and continuing down to 1867, when a new tax of 6 percent was imposed on property. The timing showed that Madrid had lost touch with colonial realities. The growing assertiveness of the abolitionist movement in the 1840s and 1850s, combined with increasing fear of slave revolts, prompted large planters in Cuba to anticipate the future by investing in mechanization and importing indentured laborers, principally from China.[43] In the 1860s, however, productivity gains were insufficient to offset the decline in the net barter and income terms trade.[44] Fresh tax demands threatened planters' welfare at a moment when it was already being squeezed. Political aspirations were also being frustrated: in 1837, Spain debarred the residual parts of the empire from representation in the Cortés. Loss of status encouraged claims for the devolution of power and greater local representation in exercising it.[45] The future arrived in 1867, when Spain finally agreed to ban the slave trade.[46] Lincoln's Emancipation Proclamation followed by the victory of the North in the Civil War raised the prospect of a slave revolt in Cuba. Madrid chose abolition to avoid the prospect of following the precedent set by Haiti and to hold on to the revenues the Treasury needed.

The end of the Cuban slave trade was followed in 1868 by Spain's "Glorious Revolution," which deposed Queen Isabella and encouraged liberals on the Peninsula and throughout the empire to hope that major reforms would follow. These events prompted a revolt in Cuba in 1868, which led to what became known as the Ten Years' War.[47] The uprising was instigated by a section of landowners under the leadership of a criollo, Carlos Manuel Céspedes, who liberated his slaves and promoted mulatos to muster support for a movement that aimed to bring independence to Cuba.[48] Céspedes was based in eastern Cuba, which grew more tobacco than sugar, had a limited number of plantations, and relatively few slaves. The east also lacked cost-cutting technology, which was located mainly in the west, and was particularly vulnerable to adverse movements in international economic conditions.[49] Opposition to the revolution was organized by groups of peninsulares in the central and western parts of the island, which remained dependent on slave-grown sugar.

Although the revolution failed in the short run, it had long-term consequences that contributed significantly to the revolt against Spain in 1895. The war began the transformation of the labor market.[50] Slaves in the eastern part of the island became *libertos*, though genuine freedom had to await the coming of new opportunities. Some slaves in the principal sugar-producing region in western and central Cuba were freed by the Moret Law in 1870, but the condition of the majority remained unchanged until the Spanish Cortés, cajoled by Britain, abolished slavery in 1886.[51] The resulting flexibility of the labor force benefited export development, but fell short of constituting an immediate social revolution. Most former slaves continued to work on the island's large estates as wage-laborers, and their opportunities for advancement were limited by a lack of alternative employment and low pay, which was held down by imports of indentured workers. The traffic in semi-free (or semi-slave) labor became a major feature of the international economy in the second half of the century and an apposite example of the globalizing forces of the time.[52] The British, acting either independently or in joint ventures with Spanish firms, dominated an extensive carrying trade, which transported increasing numbers of Chinese and other Asian laborers to the Pacific islands and beyond to the Caribbean.[53]

American expansionists kept an eye on Cuba throughout the nineteenth century.[54] Many Southerners, in particular, regarded the island as an extension of the mainland that had drifted out to sea and ought to be reclaimed. Annexation, if it could be achieved, would bring a new slave-state into the Republic and strengthen Southern power in Congress. This prospect was sufficiently alarming to mobilize opposition from other members of Congress who regarded Spain as being a relic of the Old World in unwanted proximity to the New, and had no wish to expand the Republic by adding Roman Catholics from the Latin states of Europe. In the end, successive U.S. administrations opted to deal with Spain by diplomacy rather than through confrontation, and the demise of slavery in the United States made annexation less appealing. Spain was left to manage her imperial affairs while her conduct neither threatened U.S. interests nor created opportunities that were sufficiently inviting for Washington to risk upsetting the status quo.

Consequently, the American presence in Cuba was confined to business affairs. The loss of production and the destruction of capital assets during the war of 1868–1878 brought indebtedness to many Cuban planters and enabled foreign investors with an appetite for risk to expand their stake in the economy. U.S. firms increased their share of the import and export trades, though without displacing their rivals. Tariff protection helped Spain to retain a prominent place in the island's external trade. The British took over many of the railroads previously owned by Cubans and supplied most of the finance during the last quarter of the century for utilities, such as gas, electricity, and water services.[55] A recent assessment concluded that "by 1898, the British probably had a stronger position within the Cuban economy than the Americans."[56]

The Ten Years' War provided opportunities for injections of foreign capital that enabled the sugar industry to adopt industrial methods of production.[57] The incentive, however, came from the growing competition of European beet sugar, which prompted Cuba to turn increasingly to the U.S. market from the 1870s. Industrialization based on central factories and power-driven mills cut production costs and improved quality. Estates grew larger and ownership became concentrated in fewer hands. A new generation of Cuban entrepreneurs contributed to these developments as owners and managers of estates, and as import and export merchants. The transformation, however, was incomplete. In Cuba, as in Africa during the era of "legitimate" commerce, the old and the new marched side by side. As a rural proletariat emerged from the debris of slavery, many slave owners continued to run their plantations with slave labor.[58]

Necessity obliged Spain to offer a number of political concessions at the end of the Ten Years' War, but their effect was to raise expectations rather than to satisfy them. The independence achieved by Spain's mainland colonies had focused the attention of Cuba's political class on three possible options: greater autonomy within the Spanish Empire, independence, and annexation to the United States. The war turned these aspirations into programs. As part of the peace settlement, Spain agreed to allow the formation of political parties and representation in the *Cortés* in Madrid.[59] In 1878, Spanish loyalists in Cuba formed the *Partido Unión Constitucional*, which was headed by peninsulares, most of whom wished to uphold the union with Spain. In 1883, a group of moderates came together in the *Partido Liberal Autonomista*, which was a broad-based nationalist party whose aim, citing the precedent of Canada, was home rule within the Spanish Empire.[60] Although the electoral system favored Cuba's conservative loyalists, the liberals commanded a greater degree of popular support. Spain was caught between the two: she could neither ignore demands for reform nor yield to them.[61]

Governments in Madrid steered an unsteady course between competing conservative and liberal factions, but in general supported the peninsulares, who identified most closely with Spain's national interest. Immediately after the Ten Years' War, the Spanish authorities in Cuba confiscated property to raise revenue and imposed prison sentences to discourage dissidents who might still contemplate autonomy or independence. These arbitrary and repressive actions fell disproportionately on criollos and the innocent.[62] Spanish agencies reinforced these measures by paying colonial officials to oppose or frustrate reform. This policy was widely resented. It added to the costs of imperial administration and installed a culture of corruption that lasted well beyond the period of Spanish rule.[63] One consequence was to interrupt postwar reconstruction; another was to encourage prospective reformers to emigrate to the American mainland, where many of them adopted radical solutions to

Cuba's problems. By backing the conservatives, Spain alienated the moderates and greatly diminished the prospects of securing an evolutionary transition from the creaking eighteenth-century system of political economy.

Emancipation in 1886 set in train a second important political development that the authorities were equally unable to control: the additional freedoms extended to mulatos following the abolition of slavery.[64] New voices could be heard, even in distant Madrid, and they called for radical change. The war had been fought by a multiracial army of liberation; it made officers of slaves and mulatos; it put guns into many hands—where they stayed. The assumed "right to bear arms" was fully exercised in political banditry, which became a feature of the landscape in western Cuba, where paramilitary units continued to oppose Spanish rule and fund the developing nationalist cause right down to the outbreak of the revolution in 1895.[65]

Spain reacted to these challenges by attempting to make race the deciding factor in political loyalties. Cuba, so the argument went, could either be Spanish or African but not a hybrid.[66] Madrid supported the policy by subsidizing emigration in the 1880s. By 1887, the racial mix had changed: the census of that year listed 150,000 peninsulares and 950,000 criollos out of a total population of 1.6 million.[67] Madrid hoped that, with nearly 70 percent of Cuba's population being either Spanish or closely affiliated by birth, the "Ever-Faithful Isle" would remain loyal to the imperial cause. The authorities miscalculated. Although most peninsulares continued to support official policy, they had become a small minority. Criollos, who formed the majority of whites, had accumulated sufficient numbers to express their resentment at the privileges peninsulares claimed by right of birth. Cuban nationalists responded to Madrid's appeal to "race patriotism" by making racial equality a key element in creating a distinct identity for the island's people. This was José Martí's theory and his practice too: his two closest associates in the struggle for independence, Juan Gualberto Gómez and José Antonio Maceó y Grajales, were both Afro-Cubans.[68]

Political developments intersected with the crisis in the international sugar market, which greatly increased the tension between colonial aspirations and imperial policy.[69] Cuba's contribution to the Spanish budget was too important for Spain to risk making radical concessions to the island. It seems likely that the modernization of the sugar industry, combined with the expanding volume of exports, enabled Cuba to counter the fall in the price of sugar, at least down to 1880.[70] In the 1880s, however, Cuba's economy deteriorated to the point where a serious situation became a desperate one. As Cuba lost the European market to competition from sugar beet, world sugar prices continued to slide. Bankruptcies increased; unemployment rose; the debt Spain had loaded on to Cuba after the Ten Years' War became even more onerous. In the 1890s, revenues derived from the sugar trade declined, and Spain's own fiscal problems grew.[71] Madrid responded in 1893 and again in 1895 by raising taxes in Cuba on land, manufactures, and consumption goods. Even death became more expensive: the cost of the licenses issued to undertakers increased between three and four times in the course of the decade.[72]

Powerful interests on the Peninsula stood behind protectionist policies, as they did in the United States.[73] In 1890, however, following the McKinley tariff, Cuban interests and American planters on the island petitioned Spain and the United States to conclude a reciprocity agreement.[74] The United States, with James Blaine as Secretary of State, was quick to respond. Spain gave way, reluctantly and despite metropolitan opposition, because there was no other means of keeping Cuba's sugar exports flowing. Spain herself could not absorb Cuba's sugar and in any case was developing beet as an alternative to cane. Meanwhile, the tariff imposed on foreign goods entering Cuba hampered the import trade. The outcome in 1891 was the Foster-Cánovas Treaty, which allowed raw sugar from Cuba free entry to the United States, permitted manufactures from the United States free entry into Cuba, and reduced the tariff on shipments of American wheat to Cuba.

The Foster-Cánovas Treaty gave an immediate and considerable boost to Cuba's sugar exports and a less dramatic but still manifest stimulus to U.S. exports.[75] The U.S. stake in Cuba soared; Cuba's dependence on the American market deepened. By 1894, the United States took about 90 percent of Cuba's exports and supplied about 40 percent of her imports.[76] In 1894, however, the politics of the U.S. tariff intervened once more. The Wilson-Gorman Tariff effectively rescinded reciprocity by imposing a substantial duty on imports from Cuba. Spain retaliated by canceling the Foster-Cánovas Treaty, and Cuba reverted to Spain's imperial tariff system. Reciprocity, which was as close to free trade as Cuba could reach, had produced prosperity; tariff protection under Spain's direction seemed guaranteed to send the island into bankruptcy. As the reciprocity treaty had taken the edge off political discontent, so its abrogation, combined with increased taxation, revived militancy. By 1895, the opponents of Spanish rule were better organized and financed than they were in 1868, and had reached the conclusion that Spain lacked the power either to solve Cuba's economic problems or to defend its position in the Caribbean effectively. Nationalists and sugar planters intensified the pressure

on the Spanish government to introduce free trade and renegotiate Cuba's external obligations; alienated taxpayers began direct action. The
rebellion that was to destroy much of Cuba's fragile economy and bring
down Spanish rule began in 1895.

Meanwhile, successive Spanish governments engaged in protracted
negotiations with Cuba's political parties in the hope either that "something would turn up" or that the problem could be handed over to future
administrations. In the event, Madrid was not blessed with Mr. Micawber's good fortune. What turned up was the *Partido Revolucionario Cubano* (1892) under the leadership of José Martí, the intellectual, poet,
journalist, and activist who was to become Cuba's national hero.[77] Martí
was born in Havana in 1853. As the son of Spanish immigrants, he was
a criollo and heir to a radical tradition, which he upheld with particular
distinction. Martí was arrested and jailed in 1869 at the age of sixteen for
supporting the revolt against Spanish rule that had begun in the previous year. He was released in 1871 and exiled to Spain, where he earned a
degree in law. From there, he went to France, where he met his literary
hero, Victor Hugo, whose political opinions had also taken him into exile.
Martí returned to Cuba briefly in 1878, at the end of the Ten Years' War,
but spent most of his time until 1895 in the Americas publicizing the
cause of independence, organizing Cuban *émigrés* in Florida and New
York, and raising money to support his political goal: *Cuba Libre*. Martí
was the mastermind behind the invasion of Cuba in 1895. His death in
battle shortly afterward at the age of forty-two cut short his contribution
to Cuba's future, but also made him a martyr and the island's anointed
"apostle of liberty."

Martí's politics were a fusion of cosmopolitan thought and local experience.[78] He applied radical ideas of national self-determination, drawn
partly from his travels in Europe, Latin America, and the United States,
to his experience of Cuba under Spanish rule. He concluded that Cuba's future lay, not in the compromise of home rule, but in full independence. To this end, he constructed an ideology of "raceless nationality"
to overcome the discriminatory caste system Spain had exploited during
the Ten Years' War, and to weld a popular and effective insurgent movement.[79] Since negotiations had failed to secure even modest goals, Martí
concluded that forceful means were needed to achieve ambitious ones.
He and other political exiles mobilized crucial support from Cuban emigrants who had settled in the United States after the Ten Years' War.[80]
A number of refugees had established tobacco factories in Florida to
avoid the high duties the United States imposed on imported cigars.[81]
In this indirect way, tariff manipulation in Washington had the wholly

FIGURE 9.1. José Martí, 1875. *Source*: Cuba Heritage http://www
.cubaheritage.org/subs.asp?sID=34

unanticipated consequence of creating an onshore industry staffed by
immigrants who helped to finance the revolt against Spain—a revolt that
the United States then decided to bring under control in 1898.[82] Tariffs
and U.S. imperialism were yoked together, even when they pulled in different directions.

Developments after Martí's death further polarized the contending parties. The uprising that began in 1895 squeezed moderate, centrist opinion and prompted conservatives to reaffirm their support for
continuing union with Spain. Home rule became more attractive to the
Spanish authorities at the moment it became less attainable by pacific
means. The armed struggle became more extreme as it became more
desperate. Governor-General Weyler won notoriety in 1896–1897 for in-

stituting a policy of repression that herded several hundred thousand Cubans into concentration camps. The insurgents retaliated by sponsoring the assassination of Spain's prime minister, Antonio Cánovas del Castillo, in August 1897.[83] The liberal government that replaced him recalled Weyler, and in November granted Cuba universal male suffrage and home rule as an overseas territory of Spain. Necessity rather than conviction inspired Madrid's newfound commitment to reform. The war had to be brought to an end; possible intervention by the United States had to be averted. Cuba's first autonomous government, though still provisional, took office in January 1898 and was endorsed by elections held in April. Belated though the action was, it seemed that Spain had decided, after all, to make Cuba her Canada in the tropics.

Cuba's status as a Spanish dominion did not long survive the controversial explosion that sank the *Maine* in Havana harbor on February 15, 1898.[84] The war that followed lasted less than three months and ended with the surrender of Spanish forces. More than 5,000 American troops lost their lives. Most died from disease; 379 were killed in battle.[85] The considerable publicity the war attracted at the time has been sustained subsequently by historians and the media, who were quick to incorporate Theodore Roosevelt's Rough Riders into the national legend. The much larger war, which has received far less attention, was between the Cuban Liberation Army and Spanish forces. Cubans sustained losses that were considerably greater than those incurred in the conflict between the United States and Spain. Approximately 300,000 of the island's inhabitants, mostly civilians affected by disease, died between 1895 and 1898 in the course of the Cuban-Spanish war.[86] Tens of thousands of Spanish troops also died—again mainly from disease. As the trail of destruction on Cuba came to an end, a small force under General Nelson A. Miles landed on Puerto Rico in July to secure the island for the United States.[87]

PUERTO RICO: "INTO HISTORY AS A PICNIC"[88]

Accounts of the acquisitions made by the United States in 1898 typically treat Puerto Rico as a minor appendage of Cuba. This bias results more from an abiding preoccupation with military drama than from a comparative assessment of the two islands on the eve of the Spanish-American War. The islands were linked by region and by Spanish rule; both depended on agricultural exports; both had populations of over one million at the start of the new century. Yet Puerto Rico, unlike Cuba, had no significant independence movement and no insurgency. More striking still, Puerto Ricans welcomed U.S. troops when they arrived in 1898. The explanation of the difference lies in the divergent paths taken by the two islands from the 1820s, as initial similarities turned into contrasts in the course of the nineteenth century.

Puerto Rico, like Cuba, was incorporated into Spain's plan for re-generating her empire after the loss of her mainland colonies. Madrid hoped that freer trade would promote the island's exports, raise incomes and revenues, and give Spanish rule a new lease on life.[89] Sugar planta-tions owned by peninsulares, criollos, and other white settlers increased in size and number; imports of slaves rose from the 1820s.[90] Sugar ex-ports, which mainly fed growing demand in the United States, prospered during the first half of the century.[91] Competition from Cuba was an in-creasingly visible consideration, but countervailing influences kept ex-ports buoyant: Britain's adoption of free trade in 1846 opened the UK market to foreign suppliers; the Civil War cut sugar production in the United States.[92]

From the 1870s, however, the growth of the sugar beet industry in Europe greatly increased supplies and precipitated a fall in the world price of raw sugar. This trend intersected with another: the abolition of slavery, which was formally ended in 1873. Slavery in Puerto Rico was more widespread and less lenient than was once believed.[93] Slave re-volts were common, punitive laws and forceful suppression were stan-dard reactions. Abolition had diverse outcomes.[94] Puerto Rico's planters were slow to promote the transformation of the workforce and to adopt central milling, even though they faced testing problems in adjusting to rising labor costs.[95] They were obliged to hire wage-laborers where they were unable to secure adequate supplies of low-paid, foreign, contract workers, or to extract forced labor from the luckless local peasantry.[96] At the same time, in some areas the *emancipados* lost access to land, were subjected to rigorous labor laws, and were obliged to become day labor-ers.[97] Moreover, opportunities were limited: land available for sugar was not only far less extensive than it was on Cuba, but also less fertile. Con-sequently, Puerto Rico's production costs were higher than Cuba's, and the island's exports of sugar quickly became uncompetitive. By the close of the 1870s, the sugar plantations were in serious difficulties. In 1878, the British Consul reported that "everyone" was talking about the "ruin" of the industry.[98] Sugar production fell by nearly 50 percent between 1871 and 1898; the value of sugar exports dropped from 69 percent of total exports in 1871 to 21 percent in 1896.[99] Cuba's sugar industry was shaken by the depression; Puerto Rico's was almost destroyed.

Puerto Rican entrepreneurs sought compensation in other fields. The tobacco industry was transformed in the second half of the century.[100] Small producers expanded production of a new strain of tobacco; factories relying on wage-labor produced cigars for export in competition with better-known Cuban varieties. The rapid growth of the coffee industry was an even more important development.[101] Coffee exports experienced a fivefold increase in volume between 1846 and 1897, at which point coffee accounted for about 75 percent of the value of all exports and for 65 percent of the revenue derived from exports.[102] The expansion of coffee shifted export production to Puerto Rico's central uplands, which were especially well suited to growing high-quality beans, and further enlarged the role of small farmers using household labor and supplementary wage-earners. The rise of coffee also influenced the direction of Puerto Rico's overseas trade. Whereas sugar was shipped to the United States, coffee went mainly to Spain and, to a lesser extent, Cuba. In the absence of a reciprocity treaty, the import trade also remained in Spanish and (by proxy) British hands.[103] By 1898, Cuba's economy was tied to the United States, whereas Puerto Rico remained, in every sense, a colony of Spain.

Economic differences had a powerful influence on political developments. The plantation sector on Puerto Rico was much smaller than it was on Cuba, and slaves, though more numerous than once thought, accounted for a smaller percentage of the total population. The process of emancipation changed labor relations but was less fraught than it was in Cuba.[104] The revolt in Cuba in 1868 that turned into the Ten Years' War had its parallel in Puerto Rico, but the uprising there involved only a few hundred activists and lasted for less than 24 hours.[105] Moreover, coffee prices held up much better than sugar prices in the late-nineteenth century and enjoyed additional protection from Spain's mercantilist tariff.[106] Since coffee farmers were dispersed in uplands that were far from the island's main urban centers, mass political organization of any kind was harder than it was in Cuba. Poverty on Puerto Rico was endemic, but the island appears to have escaped the progressive immiseration Cuba suffered in the late nineteenth century. A high proportion of Puerto Rico's landowners were recent immigrants whose commitment to the island was qualified.[107] National consciousness was correspondingly poorly developed—except for loyalty to Spain. Puerto Rico's conservative elites looked to Madrid to quell the development of radicalism; coffee farmers were keen to retain the privileged place they enjoyed in the Spanish market.[108]

Accordingly, economic motives for political action in Puerto Rico contrasted with those that drove Cuba to revolt. There was no shortage of discontent on the island arising from disparities of wealth, caste, class, and race, but it was not of the kind that would support a popular rising against Spain.[109] Sugar planters (drawn mainly from peninsulares and criollos) suffered during the economic depression just as their counterparts in Cuba did. Some of them, however, saw their salvation, not in independence, but in ties with the United States that might lead to incorporation, statehood, and improved prospects for sugar exports. From their perspective, the mainland was both their major market and the prime exemplar of progressive capitalism. They were ready to embrace a system that protected property rights and regarded social differentiation as a just outcome of the operation of competitive forces. They also assumed that their education, culture, and status as white Christians would qualify them for equal treatment with their peers in the United States. Their aspirations, however, were diluted by internal divisions. Racial solidarity was limited, and the representatives of capital were fractured. The majority of criollos remained vexed by legal restrictions that gave peninsulares preferential opportunities in the economy and administration.[110] These resentments had caused criollos to press for free trade earlier in the century; continuing frustration led to demonstrations and episodic violence in the 1880s and 1890s.

The concessions Spain made after the Ten Years' War were extended to Puerto Rico, where members of the elite began to define political programs and form parties. Essentially, high politics on the island became split between *autonomistas*, who wanted home rule and a form of dominion status approximating that of Canada, and loyalists, who wanted closer association with Spain. The *Partido Liberal Reformista*, founded in 1870, expressed the first claim, which its successors, the *Partidio Federal Reformista* (1873) and the *Partido Autonomista Puertorriqueño* (1887), carried forward. The autonomistas drew support from frustrated criollos, disaffected sugar planters, and urban workers who had lost their jobs following the collapse of the sugar market.[111] Conservatives responded in 1873 by forming the *Partido Incondicional Español* in 1880 to represent the interests of peninsulares, the military, the clergy, and some coffee producers.[112] A small segment of the political class favored incorporation into the United States; an equally small group of activists demanded full independence.

The career of Luis Muñoz Rivera, the leader of the *Partido Autonomista*, illustrates the ambitions and ambiguities of Puerto Rican politics during this period.[113] Muñoz Rivera was born in Puerto Rico in 1859. His grandfather was a peninsular; his parents were middle-class criollos. Muñoz Rivera's formal education was limited by financial constraints and the lack of opportunities on Puerto Rico, but his talents enabled him to become a successful poet, journalist, and politician. In this regard his credentials were similar to those of the *ilustrados* in the Philippines and the exceptionally gifted José Martí in Cuba. Although these representatives of Spain's colonial elites adopted different programs, they were all influenced by the national aspirations that took flight over Europe in the second half of the nineteenth century and subsequently winged their way across the world. Muñoz Rivera joined the Partidio Federal Reformista in 1883 and became leader of its successor, the Partido Autonomista, in 1887. In his judgment—which still resonates today—Puerto Rico lacked the viability needed for independence, even if it were desirable. Moreover, there was no mass movement on the island propelling, still less compelling, political change. Accordingly, Muñoz Rivera argued that progress could be achieved only through an alliance with liberals in Spain, and he pointed to the turmoil in Cuba in attempting to persuade Madrid that reform was preferable to revolt. His representations played a part in the decision of the Cortés in 1897 to grant Puerto Rico autonomy under a liberal constitution that gave the island's new parliament broad powers and its people universal suffrage. Having opposed political reform for so long, Spain concluded several centuries of colonial rule with a flurry of measures that put Puerto Rico ahead of Britain and France, the self-professed leaders of imperial progress.

The subtleties of developments within Puerto Rico fell beyond the purview of policy-makers in Washington. Understanding, however, was at a discount in 1898. A minor military campaign secured Puerto Rico in August 1898, partly to deprive Spain of a bargaining chip at the peace talks and partly to ensure that the island's strategic location came under U.S. control. Neither motive, however, was sufficiently compelling to explain a forcible and permanent change of sovereignty.[114] In July 1898, when General Miles landed with 3,000 U.S. troops and a mandate to liberate the island from Spanish tyranny, Puerto Rico had just installed its first democratically elected, autonomous government. Some decision-makers in Washington had doubts about invading Puerto Rico, but when the moment came they did not fear to tread.

THE PHILIPPINES: "LAND THAT I IDOLISE, SORROW OF MY SORROW"[115]

By the time General Miles began his trek across Puerto Rico, the battle for control of the Philippines, nearly 10,000 miles away, was well advanced. In May 1898, Admiral George Dewey destroyed the Spanish fleet in Manila Bay; by the end of June, American and Filipino forces had achieved superiority on land; Manila itself was captured in August, at which point the United States and Spain agreed to end hostilities. In December 1898, the United States acquired the Philippines under the terms of the Treaty of Paris in exchange for a payment of $20 million, which the Spanish government reluctantly accepted.[116] The first of the empires on which the sun was supposed never to set was eclipsed; a new imperial dawn arose for the United States. Washington's recently ignited enthusiasm for empire gave the United States responsibility for the whole archipelago, consisting of several thousand islands extending over 1,000 miles and containing more than seven million inhabitants, who were divided into numerous ethnic and linguistic groups.[117]

Although Spain had laid claim to the Philippines in 1521, it was not until the close of the eighteenth century that a serious effort was made to turn formal possession into effective control.[118] Until then, Spain regarded the Philippines as a staging post in the exchange of Mexican silver for Chinese silk and Southeast Asian spices. The entrepôt trade, centered on the "Manila Galleon," left most of the interior untouched.[119] As noted in chapter 8, there was little plantation development and too few Spanish settlers to provide a basis for colonial rule.[120] Potential collaborators among criollos and mestizos proved steadfast only in defending their own interests. Outside Manila, the Friars were the most visible Spanish presence. Although the religious orders acquired substantial land grants and the potential to develop *haciendas*, the "Friar lands," as they came to be called, produced subsistence and rents until the nineteenth century, when the demand for exports developed. The administration, such as it was, employed a form of indirect rule that treated the Friars as its principal agents and harnessed indigenous authorities to collect taxes and supply labor.[121] Limited though it was, Spanish rule was a sufficient burden on those it touched to provoke substantial resistance, which ranged from open rebellion to nativist rejection of foreign influences, and included selective adaptations and syncretic syntheses aimed at fusing elements of both worlds.[122] In an archipelago of abundant land, dense forest, and inaccessible uplands, there was also the option of escaping to regions that lay beyond the reach of Spanish officials.[123] All these expressions of protest, forged in the first two centuries of Spanish rule, were carried into the nineteenth and twentieth centuries, when, tempered by time, they provided steely opposition to foreign rule.

The archipelago the Spanish found and claimed in the sixteenth century was neither isolated nor static. Like the Portuguese in the Indian Ocean, the Spanish stumbled upon a diverse and dynamic world, which they fitted into as much as adapted.[124] The straggling islands were in-habited by an extraordinarily wide range of people and polities. The most recent estimate puts the population in 1565, on the eve of Spanish rule, at about 1.5 million.[125] This revision raises the previously accepted figure and strengthens confidence in judgments made about the adverse con-sequences of Spanish rule. Military operations and the spread of disease reduced the population by more than 36 percent by 1600 and by an addi-tional 20 percent by 1700.[126] The increased loss of life under this phase of Spanish rule exacerbated the state of underpopulation that already characterized the islands, as it did elsewhere in Southeast Asia. Under-population, in turn, reinforced the prevalence of subsistence and semi-subsistence cultivation, while scarcity of labor promoted slave-raiding and trading.[127]

There was no central government and no prospect of creating one, given the technological limits of the time. Instead, as Spain and the United States were to discover, and Filipino nationalists were to contend with, decentralization allowed strong provincial loyalties to develop and often to frustrate directions issued from the capital, Manila. A multiplic-ity of polities arose. These ranged from small-scale, dispersed societies to larger segmentary or pyramidal states, some of which conducted regional and international trade with countries in East Asia.[128] Immigrants from the Pacific and South Asia introduced Hindu and Muslim cultures and founded polities headed by rajahs and sultans. To Spaniards, seeking to extend the frontier of the counter-Reformation to Asia, as to Americans trying later to convert the region to evangelical Protestantism, this was a world of heathens and false gods and a challenge to test the survival of even the fittest representatives of self-identified superior civilizations.

The chief purpose of Spanish policy in the eighteenth century was to raise the revenue needed to protect the galleon trade and pay for the colonial government, and to secure the labor needed to support the ac-tivities of the administration, which included service in the army. The accumulation of colonial rivalries combined with the decline of the gal-leon trade at the close of the century raised the costs of protection and prompted a search for new ways of funding the colony. The loss of Mex-ico in 1821 made fiscal innovation imperative. Madrid extended existing state monopolies of tobacco and alcohol to capture taxes from consump-tion; the authorities in Manila launched a "big push" to expand colonial rule and encompass new taxpayers.[129] Revenue needs lay behind official efforts to develop cash crops and monetize the economy. Military ac-tivity accompanied all these endeavors.[130] The Sultanates in the south were pushed back; slave-trading was curtailed, though not eliminated;

a trail of latent resistance and open protest followed the advance of the military. Political battle lines were drawn too: the Muslim south thought of itself as being besieged by the Catholic north; "states' rights" became a cause that rallied the provinces against centralization—and still does.

Revenue needs led to a further policy change: the opening of imperial trade to foreign states.[131] Manila's overseas trade was liberalized in 1834; that of Visayas in 1855. Elements of mercantilism remained in place: state monopolies continued; tariffs were levied on imports into Spain; tariff preferences were retained to assist Spain's exports to the colonies. Freer trade was a progressive strategy put to a conservative political purpose—the defense of the Spanish Empire—and it rested on the assumption that the growth of trade with other nations would be consistent with the maintenance of Spanish rule. Spain, however, was not at the forefront of economic development in the nineteenth century.[132] Other states, especially Britain, had much greater potential to expand colonial trade by providing export markets, by supplying manufactured goods, and by shipping and financing the whole operation. Britain and its Asian possessions dominated the archipelago's external trade and foreign investment; Spain was in second place; the United States, third.[133] In 1883, the French Consul in Manila observed that "to all intents and purposes The Philippines are a British possession."[134]

The strategy succeeded in developing sugar, abaca (hemp), and coffee, which became staple exports in the course of the nineteenth century.[135] Growth occurred on the extensive margin, and was largely the result of indigenous initiatives within existing household structures.[136] Filipinos took up land in areas that were suited to export-crops and well placed for transport to the coast; a small number of Europeans and Americans joined them. The result was a set of separate moving frontiers—the ultimate Far West in the Pacific—which had its pioneers and wagon trains, and even its cowboys and rustlers.[137] The cultivation and marketing of these and other crops produced what has been termed a "proto-middle class," which competed successfully with Spanish companies, acquired Western education, and adopted some of the liberal aspirations that accompanied progressive thinking in the nineteenth century.[138] By the 1890s, too, modern technology was starting to connect the Philippines to the wider world through the telegraph (1872), steamship (1873), submarine cable (1879), telephone (1890), and railroad (1892). Spain's political control depended increasingly on globalizing forces that bypassed or overrode government authority and turned the Philippines in directions that lay beyond the reach of officials in both Madrid and Manila.

Domingo Roxas and Antonio de Ayala were among the most dynamic members of the emerging middle class.[139] They were criollos who took advantage of Spain's move toward open trade to form a partnership in 1834 that developed into the Ayala Corporation, the oldest and largest indigenous business in the Philippines.[140] The firm began by opening a distillery in Manila, and in the course of the century expanded into property, finance, construction, and utilities. The corporation bought swampland at Makati that later became Manila's central business district, participated in founding the country's first bank in 1851, built Manila's first steel bridge, and introduced tramcars and telephones to the islands.[141] The fortunes of *Casa Ayala* undulated with the turbulence of the times. Domingo Roxas was both a critic of government monopolies and a political liberal whose opposition to Spanish rule eventually led to him being committed to prison, where he died in 1843. His daughter, Margarita, took over the company and later married Antonio de Ayala.[142] Opportunities for women had opened just enough to allow Margarita to exercise her formidable business talents, which expanded the firm's activities into mining and agriculture, and further into real estate. During the critical decade of the 1890s, Margarita and Antonio's grandson, Fernando Antonio Zóbel de Ayala, was instrumental in persuading the family to support Aguinaldo and the nationalists against Spain; Fernando himself later joined the struggle against the United States.[143] Despite this risky start, the company negotiated its way successfully through the period of U.S. colonial rule and achieved new heights of prosperity after independence.

Mestizos were the most numerous of the proto-middle class, and the Chinese-Filipino element was especially prominent among them.[144] Chinese immigrants had settled in the Philippines before the arrival of the Spanish, but their numbers grew in the nineteenth century following the opening of trade opportunities and the removal of restrictions that had inhibited their activities. They were active in expanding the sugar industry and were at the forefront of the islands' political development. Sugar production in the Philippines was distinctive because it was based on a mix of estates and homesteads, which were worked by tenant farmers, local and imported wage-earners, and sharecroppers. [145] Accordingly, producers did not have to grapple with the problem of emancipating slaves and converting them to legitimate forms of labor. In the political sphere, mestizos were eager promoters of the concept of a Filipino identity that, through a process of ethnogenesis, eventually helped to create the Philippine nation.

Spain's attempt to encourage the development of the Philippines while continuing to maximize revenues from the colony ran into insurmountable problems during the last quarter of the nineteenth century. Part of the difficulty stemmed from continuing economic weaknesses and political fragility on the Peninsula. The collapse in the price of silver weakened the exchange rate with gold-based currencies and deterred the capital investment Madrid's colonial development policy needed.[146] Spain's chronic and worsening fiscal problems ensured pressures to extract revenue from the Philippines intensified. Madrid needed to bring the colony to the point where it could contribute to the Spanish treasury, even though the colonial budget was still in deficit. The colonial administration redoubled its efforts to extract more revenue from the production of tobacco, which remained a government monopoly.[147] As the tax burden increased, resistance grew and collection costs rose. By the close of the 1870s, the monopoly had become unproductive and unworkable.

In the 1880s, Madrid had no option but to implement far-reaching revenue reforms. The burden of domestic taxation shifted from the tribute system to assessments based on wealth, which in practice loaded the Chinese community with the highest rates.[148] The tobacco monopoly was dismantled in 1882, and its remaining assets privatized and transferred to a new organization, the *Compañia General de Tabacos de Filipinas*, which was founded in Barcelona in 1881.[149] The aim was to strengthen the empire by attracting new investment from the Peninsula. The result was the creation of a private conglomerate that allowed Spanish immigrants to invest in large tracts of land for the production of tobacco and sugar. Filipinos interpreted this development as further evidence that Spain was trying to devise a more effective way of strengthening her hold on the colony.[150] The firm grip increased revenues from taxation but also added opportunities for administrative corruption and arbitrary action.[151] By the close of the 1890s, the burdens placed on the Philippines had brought the colony close to fiscal self-sufficiency, though at the cost of provoking militant opposition to Spanish rule.[152]

Spain's fiscal problems intersected with the agrarian crisis that struck the Philippines in the late nineteenth century, as it did the colonial world as a whole. Falling prices for primary products reduced the returns to both sugar and abaca. Sugar production had long suffered from low yields and poor quality, and few producers had the capital to adopt cost-cutting improvements, such as central milling.[153] Sugar suffered an additional handicap because it was adversely affected by the reciprocity treaties that had stimulated the sugar industries of Hawai'i and Cuba. The Foster-Cánovas Treaty of 1891 was particularly bad news for the

Philippines because it boosted sugar exports from Cuba, which produced better-quality sugar and lay much closer to the main source of demand.

Diversification, where it was an option, was an imperfect remedy. Abaca expanded to reach just over 40 percent of exports from the Philippines in the 1890s.[154] After 1873, however, the price fell, apart from short booms in 1880–1882 and 1888–1889, and touched its lowest points between 1890 and 1897, when weakening demand in the United States and competition from sisal further depressed the market.[155]

International migration, a classic index of globalization, reinforced the effects of the decline in produce prices. Export growth in the Philippines attracted large numbers of immigrants, principally from China and Malaya, who rapidly became a major presence on the islands.[156] Immigration increased the demand for land that was suitable for export crops in areas where the cost of transport to the coast was low enough to make production profitable. Predictably, land reform became a central plank of the nationalist platform. The search for land also engaged the established population, which had recovered from the devastating effects of the Spanish conquest and increased rapidly until the late nineteenth century. In 1818, the total population was approximately two million; in 1903, it had risen to around seven million.[157] Lacking alternatives, and in the absence of gains in productivity, farmers tried to offset falling unit prices by expanding output, which meant increasing the acreage under cultivation. The outcome was mounting conflict between applicants for land and land holders, especially the Friars, who controlled vast swaths of the most fertile terrain.[158] Large land holdings expanded at the expense of household farms. Consequently, there was a shortage of basic foods, such as rice, which had to be imported from the 1870s.[159] The full ramifications of these trends have yet to be revealed. It is clear, however, that key sectors of the rural economy were in turmoil at the close of the century.

After a long upswing, population growth slowed markedly during the last quarter of the century, mainly as a result of the spread of disease, which in turn was linked to poor nutrition.[160] The authority on the subject has called the 1880s the "decade of death" throughout the Philippines; the northern island of Luzon, which was the region most closely involved in overseas trade, was particularly badly affected.[161] Subsequent work has shown that the "health crisis" extended through the 1890s and into the period of U.S. rule.[162] Malaria, cholera, beriberi, dysentery, and smallpox decimated the population; rinderpest, imported from Hong Kong and Indo-China, destroyed cattle stocks and contributed to the collapse of the rural economy. Evidence of stunted growth is compelling: the average height of adult males did not regain levels achieved in the

1870s until the 1940s.[163] Facilitated by the steamship and increased migration, globalization succeeded in linking vectors of disease even more efficiently than it linked markets.

Fiscal and agrarian problems were translated into political action in the 1890s, as they were elsewhere in the Spanish empire—and well beyond it. Warning signs, which the Spanish authorities ignored, had already appeared. A rebellion in Tayabas in 1841 was suppressed by force with considerable loss of life; a mutiny in Cavite in 1872 was followed by executions.[164] Both events took place in the key province of Luzon and did much to alienate Tagalog sentiment. The perceived inequalities of Spain's revenue-raising reforms added to growing resentment. Renewed attempts to extend the judicial and coercive power of the colonial state confirmed the impression that Madrid had no intention of offering the Philippines even a modest measure of devolution. Unlike Cubans and Puerto Ricans, Filipinos were considered to be insufficiently civilized to deserve any form of self-government. They were regarded as permanent subjects, not as potential citizens, Deprivation and disappointment stoked the resistance movements that led to the rupture with Spain in the 1890s.[165]

Chinese and Filipino mestizos, typically with Tagalog connections, formed the vanguard of the nationalist leadership in the Philippines.[166] Mestizos on Luzon were intimately connected to export production and trade, and strongly motivated by the desire for land reform, especially the redistribution of the Friar lands.[167] They resented the checks placed on their aspirations by peninsulares and criollos, who owed their superior positions to their ethnicity and place of birth.[168] Their ambitions, however, were larger than their economic interests.[169] In the second half of the century, they spawned an elite of self-styled ilustrados ("enlightened people"), who had been educated in Europe or had traveled there and had absorbed a range of political ideas, extending from liberal reform to anarchism.[170] Significant numbers of Filipino clergy also supported the nationalist movement. Some were ilustrados who were inspired by visions of a progressive future; others were close to the communities they served and identified with the plight of the rural and urban poor.[171] The ilustrados were the first to reconstruct an indigenous, pre-Hispanic culture and assert its superiority to Spanish values and customs.[172] A globalized network of contacts linked resistance movements in the Philippines to Cuba and the major European centers.[173] The result was a mix of often conflicting aspirations. Militant anarchism, which appealed in the face of Spanish obduracy, struggled with the attraction of middle-class values, which harmonized with pacific liberalism.

Differences among elites were complicated by popular movements that developed outside the ranks of privileged and wealthy minorities. Support came from a broad range of urban and rural workers, women as well as men, including laborers, sharecroppers, and small tenant farmers. Their vision of the future expressed a syncretic mix of Christian and indigenous beliefs; their aim was to improve, or at least ameliorate, the position of the mass of the population.[174] These were desperate groups in desperate times. Low incomes, liability for forced labor, land shortage, malnutrition, and a series of devastating epidemics in the 1880s and 1890s drove them toward desperate remedies.[175] As living conditions continued to deteriorate in the 1890s, political protest became vocal; banditry, smuggling, and cattle rustling proliferated. Coincidentally, the incidence of volcanic activity and earthquakes increased. When troops from the United States appeared, they were seen not as representatives of liberty, but as heralds of the Apocalypse. Established institutions lost credibility. Millenarian movements gained momentum.[176] The Philippine Independent Church was founded in 1902 after seceding from Rome. Like the African Church in Nigeria, which broke from Anglicanism in 1901, the Philippine Church was trying to preserve a space where cultural independence could survive at a time when economic distress and foreign invasion were redrawing the boundaries of social order.[177]

Regional diversity remained an additional obstacle to creating a sense of national consciousness among the inhabitants of the multiplicity of diverse and poorly connected islands. The rice producers of northern Luzon looked to Asia for their markets, while sugar exporters shipped an increasing proportion of their crop to the United States. Abaca producers in Bikol in southeast Luzon were joined mainly to the United States. Sugar planters of Visaya, further south still, exported their product to Asia, the United States, and Spain. These regions, and others, were characterized by different patterns of landownership and political authority, and were joined to the wider world by mercantile elites who invested in the development of ports in their own localities rather than in one central entrepôt.[178] Seen from a provincial perspective, national unity was a prospect that threatened to install Tagalog dominance. Regional autonomy was a more attractive and a more realistic ambition. Visayans did not recognize the First Philippine Republic when it was proclaimed in 1898. Mindanaoans, in the distant south, pursued their long-standing claim to be independent.

The evolution of this loose and shifting coalition of proto-nationalist forces can be seen in the sequential contributions made by the three leading figures in the movement: José Rizal, Andrés Bonifacio, and Emilio Aguinaldo, whose careers chart the evolution of nationalist policies as they moved from moderation to militancy. The historiography of early Philippine nationalism has followed the course taken by studies of other former colonial states. The tendency toward hagiography that marked early accounts of nationalist leaders has given way to more critical appraisals. Rizal's image was burnished during the period of American rule because it suited the administration to emphasize the restrained, constitutional character of his opposition to Spanish policy.[179] Bonifacio, whose standing was greatly enhanced by nationalist writers, now falls short, in some accounts, of the ambitious claims made for him.[180] Aguinaldo's seemingly contradictory decisions have long made him a controversial figure, and he has suffered, too, from critical reevaluations of his military and political leadership.[181] However, the transition from veneration to admonition does not disturb the general argument presented here that opposition to Spanish colonial rule emerged from social classes created by economic development, that the leaders aimed to join the modern world, not to escape from it, and that what was happening in the Philippines fits into a much wider comparative context, which is often missing from specialist accounts of nationalism in one country.

José Rizal (1861–1896), linguist, novelist, poet, and ophthalmologist, was the first of the eminent political moderates, though he also accepted that circumstances could justify the use of force.[182] Although Rizal's talents were exceptional, his situation typified elite opposition to Spanish policy. He came from a wealthy mestizo (Chinese-Tagalog) farming family, was widely traveled, and highly educated. His family had experienced the abuses practiced by Spain's secular and spiritual authorities. His mother had been jailed illegally for two and a half years in 1871; his family had been evicted and their home burned down in 1888 following a protest against rent increases imposed by their Dominican landlords. The firebrand on that occasion was none other than General Valeriano Weyler, who was to carry his scorched earth policy to Cuba with equally devastating and counterproductive results. Despite these provocations, the *Liga Filipina*, which Rizal founded in 1892, aimed to use peaceful means to achieve autonomy within the Spanish Empire. Rizal himself was strongly influenced by the mixture of liberal, anti-clerical, and Enlightenment thought he had absorbed when studying in Madrid in the early 1880s.[183] While he was in Spain, Rizal petitioned the government to promote assimilation and allow Filipinos representation in the Cortés. When his appeal was put aside, he concluded that progress would be made only when Filipinos themselves were mobilized. He returned home to turn thought into action.

Rizal's program, moderate though it was, nevertheless exceeded the limited tolerance of the Spanish authorities. In 1896, he was arrested, convicted of rebellion, sedition, and conspiracy, and executed.[184] The night before he faced the firing squad, Rizal composed his famous *Último Adiós*. The penultimate stanza stands as his unfading memorial:

> Land that I idolise, sorrow of my sorrow,
> Beloved Philippines, hear this last farewell.
> I give you now my all, my parents, all I have loved.
> I go where there are no slaves, no hangmen, no oppressors,
> Where faith does not slay, where he who reigns is God.

After Rizal's execution, the complete poem was smuggled out of prison, published, and circulated throughout the Hispanic world, where it gave further inspiration to the nationalist cause. Among the miscalculations of the authorities, few could match their failure to appreciate the full consequences of the education they had helped to provide or the spread of the print culture that sustained it.[185]

Armed rebellion against Spain started shortly before Rizal's death in 1896 and gained momentum after it.[186] By then, the moderate reformers had lost ground to a more radical group led by Andrés Bonifacio, whose secret organization, *Katipunan*, founded in 1892, endorsed violence as the means of overthrowing Spanish rule.[187] Bonifacio's purpose and methods matched those of his contemporary, José Martí, in Cuba, though Martí's background was closer to that of Rizal. Bonifacio was a mestizo who represented a different segment of the social order: he was a self-educated member of the urban, lower middle class and had less to lose from armed insurrection than did moderates whose property was at risk.[188] However, after a series of military reverses, Bonifacio lost support to the third of the great revolutionary leaders, Emilio Aguinaldo, who took charge of the movement in 1897 and had his rival executed for treason.

Aguinaldo, like Rizal, came from a wealthy Chinese-Tagalog mestizo family but, like Bonifacio, he endorsed the armed struggle when it became clear that Spain would not yield to moderate demands moderately expressed.[189] Aguinaldo is a nationalist hero who made some seemingly unheroic, or at least controversial, decisions.[190] In 1897, with the conflict deadlocked, he cut a deal with the Spanish authorities that took him into voluntary exile in Hong Kong, leaving others to continue the armed struggle. At that moment, the treaty ports were in ferment, anti-Manchu nationalists were gathering, and Japan had just emerged as a major power in East Asia. Japanese pan-Asian groups gave Aguinaldo moral, and possibly financial, support as he reorganized his supporters.[191] In May 1898, shortly after the outbreak of the Spanish-American War, Aguinaldo re-entered the fray with the encouragement of the United

FIGURE 9.2. General Emilio Aguinaldo, 1899.
Source: The Philippine Islands by John Foreman (1906)

States, whose senior representatives, he claimed, asked for his support against Spain and assured him that the United States had no imperial designs on the islands.[192] In June, Aguinaldo issued a declaration of independence and established a new government, the short-lived First Philippine Republic. Like his counterparts in Cuba, he was confident that he had the support of the United States. Like them, he too was to be disillusioned.

The liberation forces made rapid progress. By July, they had recovered much of the territory held by Spanish troops and were camped outside the capital, Manila. At this point, however, the United States ceased to cooperate with the nationalists. The declaration of independence remained unrecognized; the surrender of Manila was arranged between the United States and Spain without reference to Aguinaldo; the independent government was excluded from the Treaty of Paris, which authorized the sale of its territory to the United States. These provocations made enemies of former allies. In January 1899, in an act that reaffirmed his political purpose, Aguinaldo became President of the Philippine Republic.[193] In February, a conflict that was to prove prolonged and debilitating broke out between the United States and the new government.[194]

The wars to control the Philippines have only recently begun to attract the attention their scale and longevity demand.[195] Standard accounts of U.S. imperialism at this time concentrate on the conflict in Cuba. The *Maine* is easily remembered and often recalled; the battles of Manila, Quingua, Zapote Bridge, and Tirad Pass, like the brutal campaigns in Batangas and Samar, are barely known today—outside the Philippines. Yet, military operations in the Philippines were far more extensive than in Cuba and also lasted much longer.[196] After a few initial engagements, the war developed into one of guerrillas against regulars and spread far into the countryside, where the civilian population was subjected to strategies of "counter-insurgency." The United States began with 40,000 troops and increased the number to a peak of 74,000; the Liberation Army had between 80,000 and 100,000 men, though many were part-time combatants and all were poorly armed. The U.S. Army lost 379 men in the minor war with Spain and 4,234 in the major conflict with the Philippine Republic. The Liberation Army lost between 16,000 and 20,000 men; civilian losses are unknown with any degree of accuracy, but estimates range from a minimum of 200,000 to as many as one million. As in Cuba, the majority of civilian casualties resulted from disease, especially cholera and dysentery, which itself was largely a product of poor nutrition resulting from the devastation of the rural economy.[197] Military tactics covered the full range of possible brutalities.[198] The methods included torture, the collective punishment of civilians, a "scorched earth" policy, and concentration camps of the kind that the United States had condemned in Cuba as being prime examples of Spain's disregard of civilized values.[199]

Aguinaldo was captured in 1901 and issued a proclamation of formal surrender.[200] Fresh leaders, however, continued armed resistance after he had left the scene. His immediate successor, Miguel Malvar, conducted guerrilla operations until he, too, was forced to surrender in April 1902.[201] The issue was decided partly by American troops but also by divisions within the nationalist camp.[202] Moderates doubted the wisdom of pursuing an armed struggle against the United States, and worried about the radical consequences that might ensue if the militants prevailed.

Export producers could see the advantage of close ties with the U.S. market. National identity was scarcely formed; national unity was beyond reach. Aguinaldo had acknowledged the strength of provincialism by offering the prospect of autonomy within a federal system in the hope that the concession would be sufficient to attract the islands south of Luzon to the national cause. In July 1902, with Malvar removed, the United States declared victory—and then stayed on. The conflict, however, continued. The U.S. declaration pardoned participants but allowed the authorities to classify continuing resistance as banditry. In 1904, Macario Sakay formed a breakaway Tagalog Republic and contested American rule until he was betrayed and hanged as a bandit in 1907.[203] Armed resistance to American rule persisted in the less accessible southern islands of Mindanao until 1913.[204]

The Republican administration in the United States had not planned to assume responsibility for the whole archipelago. Admiral Dewey's action in the Pacific was designed first to help win the war in the Caribbean and then to secure deep-water ports to accommodate the new U.S. Navy. At the end of May 1898, McKinley's Secretary of State, William R. Day, was prepared to return the islands to Spain and retain rights of naval access only. In June, Senator Henry Cabot Lodge made a case for keeping at least the northern island of Luzon, which contained about half the total population, including the capital, Manila, on the grounds that it was unwise to surrender what had been gained because it would open the door for other powers, especially Germany and Japan.[205] In October, after sounding diplomatic opinion and testing the mood of the public, McKinley decided to retain the whole archipelago. In November, with the mid-term elections safely settled, he pressed the case at the Paris peace talks with added confidence.[206] Spain tried to salvage what she could, but her lack of bargaining power and the absence of diplomatic support from other powers ensured that her empire came to an end. Amid recriminations and talk of a "disaster," the Madrid stock market rose on the news.

The United States became a recognized imperial power in February 1899, when the Senate ratified the Treaty of Paris. Imperialists regarded the new status as the realization of divine will, a sign that the United States had come of age, and a mandate to proceed with the civilizing mission. Filipinos were left to contemplate what they saw as a catastrophe, which left them without independence and with the challenge instead of adjusting to a new set of foreign rulers who spoke, not Spanish, but English. After 1898, leading Filipino writers and artists faced the task of communicating in the language of the new rulers. Although their early efforts were unavoidably imitative, they nevertheless ensured that colonial forms conveyed patriotic sentiments—and a measure of irony too.[207]

> Ours not to rest till our banner wave,
> Lifting its folds on high,
> Greeting the flag of the stars and bars,
> The emblem of Liberty.

HAWAIʻI: "A PEOPLE FAST PASSING AWAY"[208]

Hawaiʻi, which signed a reciprocity treaty with the United States in 1875, was the first of the sugar islands to be drawn into a special relationship created by the tariff.[209] The treaty was the culmination of an extensive history of Western penetration, which began with the arrival of Captain James Cook in 1778.[210] The islands Cook came upon were mobile, creative, and open to the wider world. Migrants from Polynesia, who settled in Hawaiʻi in the thirteenth century, introduced belief systems, social hierarchies, domestic animals, and a variety of crops (notably taro, sweet potato, coconuts, and sugarcane).[211] By the late eighteenth century, rising population had led to agricultural innovation, market exchange, and social differentiation. Small polities increased in size and competed for territorial supremacy.[212] Canoe transport joined the islands; political rivalries divided them. The resulting states produced chiefs who ruled by divine right, networks of temples that gave secular power spiritual validation, and social hierarchies marked by relations of caste and class. A command economy extracted tribute and labor from commoners to support the conspicuous consumption of the chiefly elite. This was the dark side of the Hawaiian landscape that, later in the century, famous visitors, including Herman Melville, Robert Louis Stevenson, and Mark Twain, did not see. Their reports on the islands contributed unwittingly to the image of a tropical Eden; the tourist industry magnified the picture in the twentieth century.

British intervention in the late eighteenth century helped the most powerful chief, Kamehameha, to unite the islands by 1810. Independence, however, remained precarious: the British nearly annexed Hawaiʻi in 1843; the French raided the islands in 1849; the United States contemplated claiming them in 1853. Foreign missionaries began proselytizing in the 1820s, opened schools, applied their own moral standards to indigenous customs, and acquired sufficient political influence to turn the ruler into a constitutional monarch in 1840.[213] British and American traders developed exports of sandalwood early in the century, promoted the whaling industry from the 1820s, and won the right to buy land in 1850. Foreign settlers of all kinds became eligible to participate in the government of the islands under the constitution of 1852, and from then on regularly held ministerial positions. By the 1870s, Hawai'i had lost its effective independence to a coalition of foreign residents headed by U.S. citizens, who dominated the production of sugar, supplied much of the foreign investment, ran the missions and the education system, and held high positions in government. The ruling chief, though by then referred to as a king, had become a puppet managed by American settlers.

The encroachment of Western interests intersected with growing difficulties within Hawai'i's polities. The spread of novel diseases combined with the lack of immunity caused the population to fall precipitously. Estimates of the indigenous population of the islands suggest a total of about 500,000 in the late eighteenth century.[214] The figure had dropped to roughly 116,000 in 1840 and to about 40,000 in 1890. The decline in population obliged the chiefs to increase the burden of tribute and taxation, and load it onto a decreasing number of commoners. By the 1840s, the command economy was under considerable strain and encountering local resistance.[215] It was also failing to compete with agricultural systems introduced by foreign settlers. In these increasingly desperate circumstances, the monarch decided in 1848 to introduce a major land reform, known as the *Māhele* (division).[216] The aim was to preserve the rights of the ruler, the chiefs, and commoners by transforming the semi-feudal system of land tenure into forms of private ownership that advancing Westerners would recognize and respect. The outcome favored the king and the chiefs, and disadvantaged the majority of commoners. Two years later, however, land was made available to foreign buyers, who purchased or leased large tracts and turned them into sugar plantations in the second half of the century. By 1900, foreigners, principally Americans, owned or leased a large proportion of the total acreage of Hawai'i.[217] In that year, too, there were nearly 30,000 white settlers, and almost 90,000 immigrant workers from Asia and the Pacific. Hawaiians had become a minority in their own country. American settlers were able to dominate the islands far more easily than they could elsewhere in the insular empire, or in colonies such as Algeria, Kenya, and South Africa, where white immigrants were heavily outnumbered by the indigenous population.

By the 1870s, Hawai'i's economic viability as well as its political independence was in doubt. Sandalwood and whaling were in decline, and the small sugar industry, which had begun in the 1830s, suffered a relapse following a brief boom during the American Civil War. The consequent fall in revenues greatly increased the public debt.[218] These developments prompted American sugar producers and missionaries to form a coalition, led by Henry A. Peirce, the U.S. Resident Minister, to secure support from Washington.[219] Peirce's original plan was for a reciprocity treaty tied to the cession of Pearl Harbor, which the U.S. Navy was keen to obtain, but fierce local opposition caused the scheme to be abandoned. When King Kamehameha V died in 1872, however, the coalition maneuvered to elect a compliant successor, who was eventually installed in 1874, though only after a show of force had quelled opposition from nationalist groups.[220] In 1875, King Kalākaua duly signed the reciprocity treaty with the United States, and it became operational in the following year.[221]

Under the terms of the treaty, Hawai'i's sugar and rice entered the United States free of duty; in return, Hawai'i gave favorable treatment to goods imported from the mainland. Hawai'i retained Pearl Harbor but agreed not to cede or lease commercial or naval privileges to any other powers. As President Grant's Secretary of State, Hamilton Fish, put it, the treaty guaranteed "the interested friendship of a people fast passing away, but who occupy a fertile group of islands which neither the material nor political interests of this country could allow to become a waste, or a dependent of any other Power."[222]

The treaty with Hawai'i served a limited purpose at little cost. It secured the embryonic American settlement, preserved U.S. strategic interests in the Pacific, and helped to meet the expanding demand for sugar in the United States. Moreover, at this point the concession did not alarm domestic interests. Hawai'i's sugar exports were on a small scale; transport costs prevented sugar from Louisiana (which in any case was still in disarray after the Civil War) from being competitive on the West Coast, which was Hawai'i's main market.

The treaty produced the equivalent of a lucky strike for sugar producers in Hawai'i.[223] Exports of raw sugar grew from 18 million pounds in 1875 to 224 million pounds in 1887. Foreign investment in sugar estates rose from less than $2 million in 1875 to more than $33 million in 1890. Irrigation and steam-powered milling delivered all the productivity gains that the technology of the time allowed.[224] Approximately half of all foreign investment went into sugar production; about two-thirds of that came from the United States. American planters were responsible for nearly three-quarters of Hawai'i's output of sugar; the United States took virtually all Hawai'i's exports. Claus Spreckels, who was already the largest sugar refiner on the West Coast, became the most important sugar planter in Hawai'i too.[225] By the close of the 1880s, Spreckels, the "sugar king" of Hawai'i (known informally as His Royal Saccharinity), was responsible for more than half the sugar produced on the islands, and was also heavily invested in steamship services and banking. Expanded output required large inputs of labor, which came mainly from Japan and China. Jefferson's agrarian frontier had reached across the Pacific, but its character had changed. Peirce's ideal of an American settler economy based on large estates and cheap contract labor had taken the place of the imagined "sturdy yeomanry."[226]

The bonanza for planters turned Hawai'i's economy and society upside down by making the islands wholly dependent on the artificial market created for exports of sugar.[227] By the time the reciprocity treaty came up for renewal in 1883, the stakes on both sides were high: planters would suffer heavy losses if the treaty lapsed; Hawai'i's total subordination would be confirmed if it were renewed. The huge expansion of the island's sugar industry ensured that renewal would be highly controversial, not only in Hawai'i itself but also in the United States, where producers and refiners outside California had become concerned at the inroads Hawai'i's subsidized sugar imports were making into markets in the Midwest. Planters on the islands, on the other hand, were anxious to safeguard their swelling capital investment and to secure shelter from the depression in international trade.

Meanwhile, King Kalākaua had stiffened his resolve in response to popular feeling among native Hawaiians, and decided to oppose renewal.[228] For its part, Washington looked for further concessions from Hawai'i to compensate for lost tariff revenue. After protracted negotiations, the balance of forces settled on renewal, which the Senate finally approved in January 1887. Settler interests were prepared to cede more of the country's sovereignty in return for extending the tariff advantage that underpinned their investment. They were alarmed by demonstrations of proto-nationalist sentiment, and by Hawai'i's mounting fiscal problems. In 1886, the king had unwisely supported a loan of $1 million that had been floated in the City of London on disadvantageous terms.[229] The budget was already in deficit; the new loan placed an additional burden on government revenues and raised the prospect of increased British influence in the islands. The settlers triumphed because the growth of the sugar economy had weakened the nationalist cause. Some native Hawaiians had gained from the export economy; others had not. The losers were the main force behind the proto-nationalist reaction, as they were in other parts of the world. The settlers took full control of the kingdom's budget and willingly paid the price for renewing the reciprocity treaty:

they gave the United States exclusive rights over Pearl Harbor for the duration of the treaty.

The renewal of the treaty precipitated a crisis rather than resolved a dispute.[230] In 1887, when King Kalākaua refused to sign the new treaty, the settler alliance mounted a coup. The king was forced to accept a new cabinet and an amended constitution that limited both his power and the franchise. These modifications cleared the way for the election of a pro-American government, at which point the king signed the new reciprocity treaty. This seemingly conclusive event proved to be the prelude to the final act in the history of the decline and fall of the Hawaiian kingdom. The end of the drama, fittingly, was brought about by a further change in the United States tariff. In 1890, the McKinley tariff, while raising the general rate on imports, allowed raw sugar free entry and compensated domestic sugar producers with a bounty on their output. Congress was aware of the consequences for Hawai'i but decided that the island would have to take its chance on the open market.[231] From Hawai'i's viewpoint, this was a neat (and dastardly) "bait and switch" operation: the United States retained its Pearl Harbor concession without abrogating the reciprocity treaty, while effectively canceling the privileges sugar exporters thought they had locked in. The advantages were eliminated overnight: sugar prices fell dramatically; export values dropped; investments in the sugar industry were downgraded.[232]

In the ensuing turmoil, economic causes translated rapidly into political consequences. American settlers scrambled to secure a new treaty, while also setting their sights on annexation. Since they now controlled the government, they were in a position to grant rights to Pearl Harbor in perpetuity. Hawaiian opposition, already vociferous, gained an outspoken advocate in Queen Lili'uokalani, who succeeded King Kalākaua in 1891.[233] The queen rejected the proposed cession of Pearl Harbor and drew up a new constitution that aimed to return power to Hawaiians. In January 1893, the settler alliance, acting through a self-styled Committee of Safety, intervened for the second time. On this occasion, the Committee (which President Cleveland later said should have been called the Committee of Annexation) had the enthusiastic support of the resident U.S. Minister, John L. Stevens.[234] The Minister was a personal friend, political ally, and appointee of James G. Blaine, who was President Harrison's Secretary of State and an avid expansionist. The textbook operation that followed could well have been copied from the British manual of imperial practice. Stevens cited the classic justification in international law for foreign intervention, the need to "protect American lives and property," and called in the navy. A small force of U.S. Marines occupied key points; the Committee of Safety formed a provisional government; the queen surrendered.

The new government, backed by Stevens, immediately petitioned Washington to confirm the annexation of Hawaiʻi.[235] John W. Foster, who had succeeded Blaine as President Harrison's Secretary of State, prepared a treaty of incorporation, but it was held up in the Senate and then overtaken by the election of President Cleveland, who assumed office in 1893.[236] As an adherent of classical republican values, Cleveland was disinclined to support annexation by force rather than by consent; as an Anglo-Saxon, he shrank from the prospect of incorporating a large number of Asians into the Union; as a Democrat, he favored free trade and had little sympathy for the largely self-induced plight of the settlers.[237] Cleveland's reservations were reinforced by his Secretary of State, Walter Gresham, who was firmly against annexation on legal and moral grounds.[238] The treaty was set aside, Stevens was recalled, and Hawaiʻi was left in political limbo. The monarchy was not reinstated; the status of the provisional government remained uncertain.

Political ambivalence was partly resolved in 1894, when the leaders of the coup acted unilaterally to establish the Republic of Hawaiʻi (timed, evocatively, to take place on July 4) under the presidency of Sanford Dole. The new president embodied the forces that had brought the settlers to power. His family contained both Protestant missionaries who were influential in education and government, and entrepreneurs who were soon to make Hawaiʻi the world's primary exporter of canned pineapples.[239] The man who stood behind the republican throne, Lorrin A. Thurston, personified the Hawaiian saying that the missionaries "came to do good and stayed to do well." His parents were missionaries; he himself acquired extensive business interests in publishing and sugar.[240] Thurston was instrumental in transforming the loosely organized "missionary party" into the Reform Party in 1887 to reflect the increasing importance of local business interests. He appointed Dole to the presidency of the Republic, and was the leading figure in the struggle for annexation down to 1898, when he retired from politics. It was Thurston who advised Dole to turn to the Mississippi Constitutional Convention of 1891 for guidance on how to hold down large numbers of the population who were considered to be undesirable.[241] Dole himself sought direction from the eminent political scientist, John W. Burgess, who complemented Thurston's advice by recommending that the state should be run by sound men of Teutonic stock supported by a strong executive and judiciary and underpinned by a limited franchise.[242] This was congenial advice and Dole took it.

One month after the inauguration of the new republic, tariff reform in the United States again impinged on the political situation in Hawai'i. In August 1894, the Wilson-Gorman tariff modified the McKinley tariff by imposing an import duty on raw sugar.[243] This stroke of fortune placed Hawai'i's competitors, notably Cuba, at a considerable disadvantage, while allowing Hawai'i to regain the privileges guaranteed by reciprocity. Sugar production almost doubled between 1894 and 1900, the economy revived, and the new Republic suddenly regained the viability it had lost. As the political situation slipped away from them, opponents of the settler state made what turned out to be a final attempt to unseat the regime. In 1895, a group of nationalists—a coalition of royalists and republicans— launched an unsuccessful coup.[244] The queen was implicated, though on questionable evidence, and obliged formally to abdicate.

With this constitutional obstacle removed, President McKinley made preparations for a treaty of annexation in 1897.[245] As he did so, however, the ever-present and ever-contentious tariff issue intervened yet again. Hawai'i's privileges under the reciprocity treaty obtruded into negotiations over the proposed Dingley tariff, which was to replace (and largely reverse) the Wilson-Gorman tariff. The prospect that the reciprocity issue might wreck, or at least unacceptably delay, a much larger item on his political agenda caused McKinley to press ahead with annexation.[246] Opposition to the treaty remained persistent and powerful, but war with Spain the following year was decisive in enabling the proposal to succeed. Hostilities aroused nationalist feeling in the United States and directed attention to Hawai'i's strategic value, which the settler government exploited by placing the facilities of Honolulu harbor at the disposal of the United States.[247] Even so, the measure was unable to secure the necessary two-thirds majority in the Senate and it limped into law by meeting the easier test of a joint resolution of Congress.[248] The resolution served the purpose. The settlers won what they wanted most: security. The U.S. government assumed responsibility for Hawai'i's public debt; the price of shares in sugar plantations on the islands soared. The annexationists celebrated in an atmosphere of relief, delight, and self-congratulation. Hawaiians protested but were ignored.

The difficulty of securing annexation points to the near equilibrium between the contending parties. The leading planters clung to reciprocity because it was the foundation of their wealth. At the same time, they were wary of annexation because they feared that incorporation into the

FIGURE 9.3. Queen Lili'uokalani, c. 1877 (ruled 1891–1893).
Source: Hawai'i State Archives, Photograph Collection,
Lili'uokalani, Queen of Hawai'i, 1838–1917. Call number:
PP-98-11-005

United States would extend the Chinese Exclusion Act of 1886 to the
islands and end the practice of importing Asian contract workers. Without this source of cheap labor, sugar production in Hawai'i would have
become uncompetitive, even with the support of the reciprocity treaty.
There was no guarantee, however, that reciprocity would be renewed.
Meanwhile, the rapid expansion of beet sugar in California in the late
1890s posed a competitive threat that had the potential to obliterate Hawai'i's exports of sugarcane. The odds were nicely balanced until 1898,
when it seemed that reciprocity might be withdrawn.[249] In these circumstances, incorporation into the Union was a risk worth taking because
it would put Hawai'i inside the tariff wall and offer its main industry a

chance of surviving.[250] At the last moment, the planters made up their minds and threw their weight behind annexation.

The keenest annexationists in Hawai'i were settlers of some standing who were closely connected, directly or indirectly, to the sugar industry.[251] Foreign settlers in Hawai'i had long complained about administrative inefficiency and corruption, but their concerns multiplied from the late 1880s, when nativist reactions to the growth of foreign influences increased the likelihood of a populist government that would raise taxes and reappraise property rights. Queen Lili'uokalani's attempt to uphold local rights drew particular criticism. The prospect that President Cleveland might try to restore the queen to the throne in 1893 led the Protestant press, prompted by Hawai'i's missionary families, to denounce her as a "vicious, immoral, irresponsible woman surrounded by knavish advisers" who would remove "guarantees of protection to life, liberty and possessions."[252] There is no doubt that the Hawaiian government, especially under Kalākaua, failed to manage its financial affairs prudently and was guilty on several counts of corruption.[253] The fundamental problem, however, was the growing imbalance between economic power and political authority on the island. The sugar industry had eroded the authority of the monarchical government charged with guaranteeing the security of the expatriate community.[254] By vilifying the indigenous people and their representatives, the white minority made race prejudice a centerpiece of their appeal to their Anglo-Saxon compatriots in the United States.

The islands' annexationists faced opposition from powerful domestic interest groups who opposed reciprocity or annexation or both. Hawai'i's tariff advantage, combined with expanding demand in California, had produced a rapid and unforeseen growth in the islands' sugar exports in the 1880s and 1890s.[255] Refiners on the East Coast and cane growers in Louisiana reacted by banding together to prevent annexation and to lobby for the abolition of reciprocity, which, they claimed, had given importers on the West Coast an unfair advantage. Hawai'i's presence in the Union, they argued, would increase competition by allowing new overseas constituents to ship sugar duty-free and by encouraging investment in overseas refineries.

The resulting coalition trained some heavy guns on Washington. Havemeyer's Sugar Trust led the charge; Henry T. Oxnard, the West Coast sugar-beet magnate, mobilized funds and connections; the American Federation of Labor, which feared that low-wage Asian workers would flood the labor market, added its substantial weight to the campaign.[256] Spreckels had fought the Sugar Trust in the 1880s, but in 1890 the McKinley

Tariff, which opened Hawai'i to competing sugar suppliers, put his company in serious difficulties, and in 1894 the Sugar Trust bought the business and its owner. Meanwhile, Spreckels had invested in beet sugar in California, partly to escape the tariff uncertainties attending cane exports from Hawai'i, and this gave him an additional motive for opposing free entry for the islands' sugar. The coalition sank a considerable sum into lobbying to prevent annexation. Its members gained the support of the *Washington Post*, won over a number of senators, and found a powerful ally in Thomas B. Reed, the Speaker of the House of Representatives.[257] The formidable opposition generated by the unusual alliance of capital and labor explains why the administration had to resort to the "Texas precedent" to secure a joint resolution of Congress instead of a formal treaty.[258]

Nevertheless, Hawai'i's planters were able to prevail over the anti-annexationist coalition on the mainland because their cause joined others that were moving in the same direction. Annexationists banged a drum to alert Washington and the public to the alleged menace of foreign powers. Britain, the target of choice, served to refract sentiments that gave shape and impetus to American nationalism. The *Washington Star*'s rhetorical question, posed in 1893, allowed only an affirmative answer in 1898: "Shall we take Hawai'i and thereby prosper and magnify ourselves, or shall we let England take it, and thereby enfeeble and humiliate us?"[259] In fact, the British had given quiet assurances that they had no interest in acquiring Hawai'i. On the contrary, they viewed the expansion of the United States in the Pacific as being a useful counterweight to German and French ambitions and a means of drawing their former colony into the imperial club, and so compromising the republic's aversion to empire-building.[260] However, these diplomatic considerations were too subtle to counter the strident appeal of nationalism, which carried Hawai'i's annexationists much further than they could have traveled unaided.

Japan was a different proposition. Japan's armies had recently defeated China, and the land of the rising sun had become designated the new "yellow peril" of the East. Japanese workers were present in Hawai'i in force, and were vital to the sugar industry. Yet, their increasing numbers threatened to bring about, in the phrase of the day, the "Mongolization" of the islands and the liquidation of a valiant but vulnerable outpost of the Western world.[261] As the *Hawaiian Star* crisply put it in 1897: if "the Japanese ever got the franchise here, good bye to Western civilization."[262] Rising tension between Japan and the United States in Hawai'i during 1897 gave annexationists an opportunity to generate sensational rumors about the possibility of war and provided an extra incentive to push the treaty through Congress.[263]

At least one member of McKinley's administration reacted to the news by reaching for his hyperbole. Theodore Roosevelt, then Assistant Secretary of the Navy, wrote to the naval strategist, Alfred Mahan, in May 1897, expressing the frustration of a man whose time had almost come.

> If I had my way, we would annex those islands tomorrow. . . . I have been getting matters in shape on the Pacific Coast just as fast as I have been allowed. My own belief is that we should act instantly before the two new Japanese warships leave England. I would . . . hoist our flag over the island leaving all details for after action.[264]

At this point, the president tightened his grip on what he already held. The Yellow Peril was spreading across the Pacific. Action was needed. The United States could not stand by and "let those islands go to Japan."[265]

WARS OF CHOICE

The insular revolutions that produced the American Empire need to be understood in the broad context set by the transition from proto-globalization to modern globalization. The United States and Spain were both attempting to transform agricultural into industrial societies, while trying to consolidate political unity and promote a sense of national identity that would outweigh divisive forces of region and class. A form of enforced globalization, expressed as imperialism, carried the impulses of the transition into the Caribbean and Pacific. As a late-start modernizer, Spain's policy toward her remaining colonies reflected her persistent struggle with the legacy of military fiscalism. Extractive policies predominated, while the need to make concessions to freer trade directed commerce into British and American hands and eventually weakened Madrid's political control of her overseas territories. The United States, though also a late-start modernizer, had ceased to be hampered by the residues of the military-fiscal state and had made considerable progress toward creating an industrial nation-state. Nevertheless, both countries experienced a series of crises at the close of the nineteenth century, when incomplete structural changes intersected with adverse movements in the international economy. Spain's struggle to manage destabilizing forces at home and abroad led to the loss of her remaining colonies. The United States negotiated similar difficulties with greater success and was in a position to replace her. Spain, so imperialists argued, deserved a drubbing. Her Latin, Catholic roots and allegedly corrupt and cruel methods of government disqualified her from continuing to rule over an empire. "Spain and Turkey," Roosevelt declared in 1898, "are the two powers I would rather smash than any in the world."[266] No doubt there were sighs of relief elsewhere.

As this chapter has argued, no explanation of imperialism is complete unless it includes indigenous, and in this case insular, perspectives. Agricultural exports and their principal determinants, world prices for primary products and the prevailing tariff regime, formed the most important common link between the islands and the U.S. mainland throughout the nineteenth century. These causes are not exclusive; nor are they, on a priori grounds, necessarily paramount. In this case, however, the evidence places them at the center of explanations of late nineteenth-century imperialism. They provided the context within which political decision-making took place and often the immediate stimulus to action, too.

The link between economic adversity and political action emerges as the common theme in the four cases examined here. The commitment to export production followed by a decline in real incomes, and possibly in unreal expectations too, led to rising discontent. Colonial elites, inspired by a combination of pride in their culture and European liberal values, provided the leadership. In this regard, as in many others, the insular empire replicated movements that appeared elsewhere in the colonial and semi-colonial worlds at this time. General processes, however, need to be fitted to specific cases. The contrast between Cuba and Puerto Rico makes the point that common influences can have different outcomes. Cuba's sugar economy, which was fully exposed to world conditions and relied on the U.S. market and tariff policy, transmitted adversity directly to producers. Puerto Rico's coffee exports, on the other hand, were sheltered by imperial protection. Cubans were anxious to end Spanish rule; Puerto Ricans had material reasons for retaining it.

Differences based on economic considerations need refining to allow for other significant variables, such as the relative size of settler and indigenous populations, distinctions of caste, race, and class, and the political programs that characterized the various islands. These influences help to explain the ability of colonial societies to resist the demands made on them and their inclination to do so. Hawaiians were few in number and had already conceded effective control over their land. Filipinos, on the other hand, had the power of numbers and continued to manage the political networks that were key agencies of government. Hawaiians were overwhelmed; Filipino resistance lasted as long as the Iraq War of 2003–2011 did, and cost the lives of about the same number of U.S. troops. Attitudes and outcomes diverged in Cuba and Puerto Rico, despite some obvious similarities between them. This was partly because the islands related to the international economy in different ways, as we have seen, but also because Cuba's history nurtured assertive claims for independence, whereas Puerto Rico's inheritance produced cautious leaders who aimed for home rule, or even incorporation into the United States.

These observations leave the issue of the direction of causation open. Were impulses toward expansion transmitted primarily from the United States, or did they flow predominantly from sub-imperialist agents, whether American citizens abroad or local "collaborators"? One conclusion can be stated unambiguously. Only in Hawai'i was sovereignty compromised to the point where it could be said that the United States had established an informal empire in the period before the islands were annexed in 1898. A handful of large firms owned by white settlers from the mainland had long dominated Hawai'i's exports and oriented them toward the United States. The same group of settlers had taken over the government and penetrated Hawaiian culture through Christian missions, which spread Protestantism and Western education. Representatives of the settlers and U.S. government officials also had a voice in Washington, where they presented themselves as members of a gallant but precarious Anglo-Saxon community seeking to establish a new Jeffersonian frontier at the distant edge of Western civilization. The U.S. Minister in Hawai'i, John L. Stevens, was an enthusiastic expansionist who used his authority to assist his compatriots to remove Queen Lili'uokalani in 1893.

Nevertheless, the "men-on-the-spot" in Hawai'i succeeded only because their cause fitted the aims of expansionists in the United States.[267] The forward party appealed to Congress and through the press to sensibilities of kith and kin and to the obligation to spread Christianity and civilization, and they used their influence to provide the settlers with economic support through tariff concessions. Stevens himself qualifies as a sub-imperialist, as the literature on empire calls local expansionists. However, unlike Cecil Rhodes and Carl Peters, his more famous counterparts, Stevens was not acting independently but as the appointee of his powerful sponsor, the Secretary of State and ardent expansionist, James G. Blaine.[268] Even so, Hawai'i's imperialists made no progress once President Cleveland, who had little time for them, took office in 1893. As late as 1898, when conditions were at their most favorable, annexation squeezed through Congress only after a very close vote and because matters of national interest, notably the possible threat from Japan, tilted the balance. Hawai'i's settlers facilitated the solution they finally fixed upon, but they were able to do so because their interests were congruent with wider purposes.

Considered from another angle, the annexation of Hawai'i shows how the breakdown of collaboration opened the way to formal control. Informal influence, which in Hawai'i amounted to informal rule, depended on the continuing ability of the settlers to work with and through indigenous authorities. In the case of Hawai'i, the arrangement functioned well enough until the 1870s, when mounting economic problems led to the reciprocity treaty and the leasing of Pearl Harbor. The rapid and visible increase in American influence provoked a nationalist reaction. Public opinion obliged the previously pliable monarchy to stiffen its attitude toward the United States. When Queen Lili'uokalani acceded to the throne, collaboration ended. Formal rule then became the only alternative to leaving the settlers to fend for themselves. To have disowned the settlers would have been to abandon the blend of ethnicity and Protestantism that had become central to shaping the national identity of the United States. Support, on the other hand, came at a low cost and mainly in the disguised form of a tariff subsidy. Powerful sugar interests in the United States opposed the incorporation of Hawai'i, as they opposed similar claimants. In the end, however, Hawai'i gained admission as an exceptional case and was the only acquisition to be granted the status of an incorporated territory with the right eventually to seek statehood.

If the acquisition of Hawai'i was a matter of housekeeping, where existing informal relations needed to be rearranged, the Spanish islands were a clear case of housebreaking, where property was purloined. The United States had only limited influence on the Spanish Empire. Even in Cuba, where U.S. interests were more extensive than in Puerto Rico and the Philippines, it is hard to argue that informal expansion also translated into extensive informal influence, still less informal empire. Spain retained political control of the island until shortly before 1898, when it became clear that she was unlikely to quell the insurgency. The Spanish authorities, in conjunction with the Roman Catholic Church, obstructed Protestant missions and the educational facilities they sponsored, thus excluding the main alternative source of cultural influence. Protestantism made modest advances in Cuba during the last quarter of the century, partly as a result of the reforms Spain conceded after the Ten Years' War, and partly in sympathy with the anti-colonial movements.[269] Nevertheless, its influence was limited and its empire, culturally speaking, existed only as a distant vision of missionary enthusiasts.[270]

U.S. influences were felt mainly on the economy, and especially on the sugar trade, which the mainland refineries came to dominate during the second half of the century. Commercial interests, however, stemmed from competing business and political factions in the United States rather than from a coordinated effort by Washington to shape events on Cuba to a larger purpose. Moreover, Spain and Britain retained impor-

tant stakes in Cuba's overseas commerce as a whole, and Britain continued to be the leading foreign investor in the island. U.S. companies in
Cuba undoubtedly had privileged connections in Washington. Edward
Atkins, the most prominent of the American sugar planters on the island, had access to senior members of McKinley's administration, including the president himself.[271] However, Atkins consistently advised
Washington to support home rule for Cuba within the Spanish orbit,
which he thought was the best way of protecting American investments.
By the time he realized his miscalculation and advocated U.S. intervention, the decision to act had already been made. This is not to say that
the United States was devoid of influence in Cuba. The Foster-Cánovas
Treaty is a clear example of Washington's strength and Madrid's weakness, but it was indicative of a future that was to unfold after 1898 rather
than of relations that pertained before then. Had the United States and
Britain acted in concert, they might have been able to bend Spain to their
will, but the British were unwilling to take an initiative in the matter and
Spain was unwilling to bend, which is why a war was fought.

The U.S. Consul-General in Havana, Colonel Fitzhugh Lee, was a former Major-General in the Confederate army, a veteran of wars against
the Comanches, and an active agent in the final stages of the crisis.[272]
Like Stevens in Hawai'i, however, Lee was a sub-imperialist in the restricted sense of interpreting locally the intentions of his superiors in
Washington. In January 1898, when royalists staged demonstrations
in Havana against the newly elected autonomous government, Lee responded by requesting a naval presence to protect lives and property,
and the *Maine* arrived shortly afterward.[273] While it is possible that Lee's
action was intended to be a provocation rather than a precaution, the
leading authority on the subject does not draw this conclusion.[274] Lee
had little sympathy for the rebels and was wholly opposed to the autonomous government. Nevertheless, he cooperated with the insurgents,
whose representatives had asked for assistance in their continuing struggle against Spanish forces and had been assured that the United States
would back their bid for full independence.[275] Lee's attitude implies
that support for the insurgency would provide the United States with
a means of controlling Cuba that was preferable to home rule, which
promised to deliver a considerable degree of real political independence.
Lee was undoubtedly a colorful figure, but he was never as important as
he thought he was or hoped to become.[276]

Stewart L. Woodford, the other U.S. diplomat who was directly involved in processes that led to war, also had little influence on the final
decision.[277] Woodford was a Civil War veteran, a New York lawyer, and

a Republican who was appointed by McKinley to the post of Envoy Extraordinary and Minister Plenipotentiary to Spain in 1897. Woodford's performance did not match his impressive, if also fanciful, title. He had no diplomatic experience, did not speak Spanish, and arrived in Madrid when events were moving at a speed that even experienced observers had difficulty matching. Woodford carried out McKinley's instructions more or less as indicated. By March 1898, he had reached the conclusion that "early American ownership and occupation of the island" was the only solution to Cuba's problems.[278] This was not a novel thought; McKinley had long considered the possibility and understood that it was increasingly likely as his hopes for a noncombative solution to the issue faded.

At the point when the *Maine* was sunk, the political situation in Cuba was confused by the uncertainties of war. Some scholars hold that the insurgents were on the brink of defeating Spain, and that the United States intervened to prevent a rebel victory.[279] Others claim that the Liberation Army appealed to the United States for support because it was unable to make further progress by itself.[280] Whichever view is taken, it is evident that contemporaries were aware that Spain's era of rule in the New World was coming to an end. Madrid's inept response to the crisis, though an understandable product of Spain's political fragility, helped to drive the dispute from the negotiating table to the battlefield. The authorities had failed to put down the insurgency, and the financial and human costs of attempting to do so had sapped Spain's resources and threatened her own stability. She could survive as a colonial power only with outside assistance. No other state had an incentive to provide the degree of charity required.

McKinley explored various options. His preference was for a diplomatic solution to the Cuban "problem." As Seward bought Alaska from Russia in 1867, so McKinley offered to buy Cuba from Spain in 1897.[281] Although the Spanish government refused to sell the island, the president persisted with the idea until March 1898. Nevertheless, in 1897, long before the *Maine* steamed into Havana, McKinley had also prepared an ultimatum that would almost certainly have led to war had the political situation in Spain not been transformed by the assassination of the prime minister in August of that year.[282] By then, too, official and public attitudes in the United States had changed from sympathy toward the plight of Cubans to a feeling that perhaps they were not ready for independence after all. These increasingly uncompromising attitudes were consistent with McKinley's decision not to pursue another option, which was to support the newly elected Cuban government, even though it was led by liberal reformers who stood for home rule within the Spanish empire.

The war that followed encouraged the belief that Cubans were unprepared for self-government. Proximity shed darkness rather than light. American soldiers and officials found that their encounters with Cubans confirmed the prejudices they carried in their knapsacks. Major-General Samuel Young was sufficiently confident of his appraisal of the situation in 1898 to express himself without qualification: "the insurgents are a lot of degenerates, absolutely devoid of honor and gratitude. They are no more capable of self-government than the savages of Africa."[283] Even though the Cuban Liberation Army had assisted U.S. troops, its leaders were never treated as allies. They were excluded both from the formal ceremony marking the surrender of Spanish forces and from the peace negotiations, and then disbanded by U.S. military decree in 1899, when the war of liberation became an act of occupation.

The joint resolution of Congress in April proclaimed that Cuba should be free and independent. An amendment added by Senator Henry Teller, a keen expansionist, stated that the United States had no intention of exercising sovereignty over the island. However, the Teller Amendment was devised to appease the anti-annexationist lobby, and particularly to allay fears that the United States might be burdened with the Cuban national debt.[284] The measure carefully avoided recognizing the autonomous government, the Cuban Liberation Army, or the putative Cuban Republic. Accordingly, it did not commit the United States to hand power to any of the credible political organizations in Cuba, nor did it set a date for conferring sovereignty.[285] Some months later, Teller explained that the Amendment was not intended to be applied unconditionally or immediately, but only when Cubans had shown themselves capable of self-government.[286] Meanwhile, the Amendment offered reassurance to Cubans who had fought for independence, while satisfying President McKinley that he retained the right to exercise a measure of control over developments in Cuba. McKinley was willing to see Cubans press their claims against Spain, but he expected them to conform to U.S. demands once Spain had ceased to feature in the postwar settlement.[287]

U.S. influence in Puerto Rico was equally limited. Before 1898, political authority remained with Spain; the export economy was directed toward the Peninsula; Protestant missions had a very modest presence. Shortly before American troops landed, the U.S. Consul on the island reported that Puerto Ricans remained loyal to Spain and were satisfied to have been granted autonomy.[288] An alternative sense of national consciousness had scarcely developed. The island was occupied by U.S. troops not because of "turbulence on the frontier" but as a by-product of the war in Cuba. The invading forces met little resistance and, in some parts of the island, were welcomed. The islanders' reaction, however, was to an event that was already taking place and was not a cause of it. From their perspective, the United States stood for liberty and progress; it was not immediately apparent that the autonomy they had just won would be lost. Moreover, there was a prospect of reviving the depressed sugar trade by gaining access to the U.S. market. Muñoz Rivera reflected these changes of mood. Soon after the invasion, he shifted his support from home rule to incorporation. In 1898, he declared: "We must move rapidly toward our identity. The Liberal Party desires that Puerto Rico become a sort of California or Nebraska."[289] Disillusion followed as soon as it became apparent that the prospective collaborators, though predominantly white and wholly Christian, were judged to be unqualified for the task of self-government.[290]

The Philippines was as far removed from American influence as it was from the U.S. mainland. As in the cases of Cuba and Puerto Rico, Spanish rule was unchallenged by other major powers until the close of the century, when the anti-colonial movement on the island wounded the sitting tenant and created opportunities for hungry predators. The United States had only a modest commercial stake in the islands, and just a handful of "Manila Americans" to represent its interests there. Although Protestant churches in the United States were vociferous advocates of expansion in the Philippines, the Roman Catholic Church retained its monopoly of Christian truth, as it did elsewhere in the Spanish Empire.[291] The first Protestant missionaries did not arrive until the U.S. Army landed in 1898.[292] Washington's interest in the Philippines before 1898 can scarcely be underestimated.

Since the largest possession acquired by the United States resulted from the smallest degree of informal influence, the explanation must return to the metropolis. Military imperatives arising from the war in the Caribbean have become a substantial part of the explanation of the annexation of the Philippines. The navy, which was keen to secure bases in the Pacific, devised the plan to attack Spain's colonies there; the army, which arrived later, joined the navy in urging the administration to bid for the whole archipelago.[293] Yet, neither the navy nor the army carried Washington's policy-makers beyond their preferred limits, and their initiatives gained momentum only after the decision to declare war with Spain had been taken.

The idea of treating the Philippines as a stepping stone to East Asia had already entered hawkish rhetoric, but it was not until after the battle of Manila that the possibility entered American diplomacy.[294] The United States, like other foreign powers in East Asia, had great expectations of the China market.[295] In retrospect, however, it is evident that the

China market was more of a myth than a reality. U.S. trade with China increased in the 1890s but remained trivial. While mistaken perceptions can be causes of actions, in this case they did not lead very far.[296] U.S. companies took the opportunity to invest in the Philippines seriously only after McKinley had decided to annex the archipelago.[297] Furthermore, the United States had a very modest presence in China and lacked both the will and the capacity to increase it. Commitments in the Caribbean and Hawai'i, as well as the continuing war in the Philippines, prevented Washington from investing significant resources of men and money elsewhere. The facilities of the port of Manila, which expansionists claimed would become a "way station" to East Asia, were inadequate and were not upgraded until shortly before World War I.

The protective tariff and discrimination against Chinese immigrants were additional barriers to improving trade relations with China. American exporters claimed that free trade was the most promising strategy for increasing commerce with East Asia, and recommended that tariff levels in the Philippines be fixed for revenue purposes only. Washington could not follow this advice, at least while the Republicans were in power, because it threatened the protectionist system as a whole.[298] When John Hay, the Secretary of State, issued his famous (and greatly over-publicized) "Notes" in 1899 and 1900, he was not proclaiming a new policy. There could be no "open door" until the United States opened its own door. The "Notes" simply called upon foreign powers to uphold the territorial integrity of China and the principle of equality of treatment in matters of trade. They were flourishes to appease segments of American business that were unable to dent the protectionist system, and did no more than restate established British policy toward China. Since they were concocted with British assistance, this ought not to be surprising.[299]

On this occasion, the British well deserved the cooperation they received. They used their influence against Spain in Europe and played a key role, through their consuls in Spain's colonies, in negotiating the surrender of Spanish forces. Britain also provided practical support for the war effort by allowing the U.S. Navy to use Hong Kong as a base and by blocking the passage of a Spanish naval squadron through the Suez Canal.[300] In September 1898, Sir Charles Dilke, the eminent politician and colonial expert, thought that it would be "impossible" for the United States to "hand back" to Spain people who had just been "emancipated."[301] Ambition, however, marched heedlessly alongside victory. With Spain defeated and the remaining European powers silently consenting, McKinley took what had become his. To the victor went the spoils—and also the toils in the long reckoning that followed.

Assumptions of racial superiority, the staples of imperialist rhetoric, were used to deny recognition to the first Philippine Republic and to justify continuing the war against the nationalists.[302] In 1902, President Roosevelt defended the operations, and even the atrocities, as being necessary if civilization were to triumph over forces that "stand for the black chaos of savagery and barbarism."[303] Yet, as argued in chapter 8, racial impulses toward imperial expansion were strongly contested in the United States by those who held that annexing territories inhabited by nonwhite people would endanger the racial purity of the homeland. To the extent that the pro-imperial argument succeeded, it did so because race was part of a much wider conception of power, which included other character traits located in a developing sense of nationalism and burgeoning economic strength.

The wider considerations explain why McKinley rejected the option of supporting the highly educated mestizos who established the Philippine Republic and the criollos who led the opposition to Spain in Cuba and Puerto Rico, even though it was plausible to argue that they were well fitted to steer the unenlightened toward civilization. A similar contention can be applied to Hawai'i, where nativist aspirations were linked to a desire for Western education and to claims for equal political rights and economic opportunities. Insular reformers in the Caribbean and the Pacific were the counterparts of the Young Turks in the Ottoman Empire and the self-strengthening movement in China. Their modernizing ambitions were hampered by restrictive policies imposed by Spain and the United States, made wildly unpredictable by the reciprocity treaties, and significantly jeopardized by the depression of the late nineteenth century. They were not rejecting globalization but resisting the terms on which it was being imposed. The self-styled agents of civilization, on the other hand, were resolute in limiting the freedoms they claimed to be advancing.

What ensued were wars of choice in Cuba and the Philippines that rejected both independence and home rule, and aimed at achieving U.S. dominance. Expansionists in the United States, capitalizing on nationalist fervor, needed a highly visible triumph, which victory over an enfeebled Spain delivered. Beyond that success, leaders in Washington hankered for a permanent declaration of great-power status, which, according to the yardstick of the time, only the possession of an empire could certify. As the now muscular and self-confident Republic advanced into the new century carrying the export version of its civilizing mission with it, the recipients confronted the prospect of retreating into a disenfranchised past they thought they had left behind.

TARZAN'S MIRROR TO MODERNITY

Edgar Rice Burroughs (1875–1950) was the supremo of popular fiction during the first half of the twentieth century.[1] He published *Tarzan of the Apes* in 1912, extended the first set of adventures to a series of twenty-four novels, produced fifty other books, achieved sales in his lifetime estimated at between 30 and 60 million copies, and lived to see his hero become a major film star.[2] By 1923, he was already successful enough to found Edgar Rice Burroughs Inc., which continues to administer his affairs from its headquarters in what can only be called—and is—Tarzana, California.[3]

The popular impression of Tarzan, which pictures him swinging through trees while yodeling, derives from Hollywood's adaptations of the novels, which first appeared in the 1930s. The Tarzan movies, though highly popular, were insipid versions of the originals, and became increasingly distanced from them. The novels themselves, though set in Africa's "jungles," reveal nothing of interest about the continent, except that, in Burroughs's opinion, it was a very dark place about which, as he admitted, he was poorly informed. The plots creak with coincidence; the characters sit reassuringly within the security of caricature; the whole fantastic assemblage borders on self-parody. Burroughs himself had a refreshingly low estimation of his literary skills and readily acknowledged that he was writing escapist adventures at great speed for the mundane but pressing purpose of making enough money to support his family.

Unsurprisingly, Tarzan is not a man for all seasons. Nevertheless, he offers unexpected insights into the issues of the day. These relate, not to the state of Africa, as might be thought, but to the state of the Union. The success of the Tarzan novels rests not only on a degree of improbable exoticism that trumped the competition, but also on their ability to ring a carillon of bells in the heads of readers.[4] Burroughs had an instinct for identifying dilemmas that his readers faced in their everyday lives, a gift for presenting them in ways that were thrillingly removed from reality, and a talent for resolving them in a manner that provided reassurance, purpose, and even inspiration.

Burroughs himself was a proxy for his huge, predominantly white readership, which occupied the large social space between the lower working class and the lofty intelligentsia. He was proud of his Anglo-Saxon ancestry, which he traced (albeit with competition from numerous others) to the original Pilgrim voyagers. His sense of racial superiority drew on generalized versions of Social Darwinism and extended into eugenics.[5] His sense of social superiority derived from his middle-class origins, as did his anxiety that he might lose his status and his alarm at the menace militant workers posed to civil order. He came from a military family, sought a career in the army but was discharged on medical grounds, applied to join Roosevelt's Rough Riders in 1898, and volunteered to serve during World War I. He was a keen sportsman and advocate of physical exercise, which he regarded as a means of reviving the frontier spirit and countering the debilitating effects of urban living. Burroughs knew urban life at first hand. He grew up in Chicago and experienced failure in business there before making a success of himself. He lived in the city at a time when its unrestrained industrial development had prompted Upton Sinclair to label it, in 1906, *The Jungle*, and when the risk of contamination from European immigrants of dubious origin was a topical and contentious issue.[6]

The Tarzan novels present these realities as fantasy.[7] Tarzan, the infant son of Lord and Lady Greystoke, is brought up by apes after the death of his parents in Africa. The young Tarzan survives a series of compelling and generally savage encounters to become king of the apes and later chief of the Waziri, by which time he has fallen in with a set of American castaways, and fallen in love with one of their number, the eligible and desirable Jane Porter. The company is rescued and returns to the United States accompanied by Tarzan, who discovers, but nobly conceals, his true origins to avoid disturbing relations with his cousin, who has taken the title of Greystoke, and upsetting the impending marriage between a reprehensible businessman and Jane. Tarzan then leaves for Africa, determined to abandon the manifest complications of the modern world. The call of the wild, however, is unable to dispel the lure of civilization. After further adventures, all marked by the violence needed to produce strength of mind as well as of body, Tarzan again meets Jane who, fortuitously, is still unmarried and, improbably, has been cast once more upon the shores of Africa. Her business suitor has been shown the door and she is now engaged to none other than Tarzan's cousin, the pretender to the Greystoke title. Yet more escapades ensue, including the discovery of gold ingots in the lost city of Opar and the timely death of Tarzan's cousin, after which Tarzan can take his place at the apex of society as the rightful Lord Greystoke, and he and Jane are free to marry.

The Tarzan stories are variations on a central theme: the interplay of heredity and environment. Tarzan is the noblest member of the master race because his blood is the bluest, which is why Burroughs identifies him with ancient English stock. The purity and strength of his genetic inheritance enable him to defeat the forces of darkness and overcome the pull of the beastly world that nurtured him. Genetic inheritance is necessary but insufficient. Energy levels, like batteries, are discharged with the passage of time and need replenishing if the master race is to retain its supremacy. Environmental challenge reinvigorates flagging genes. Tarzan's resourcefulness is developed on exotic frontiers far from the debilitating influences of the city. His physical prowess, nurtured by deprivation and adversity, allows him to subdue primitive and dangerous people. His sky-high energy level, constantly topped up by stirring adventures in dangerous places, qualifies him to be the symbol and savior of Anglo-Saxon manhood. Not even Charles Atlas would dare to kick sand in his face.

The fittest not only survive: they triumph and do so deservedly. Tarzan's upward social mobility, from ape to chief and from chief to noble, symbolizes the unfolding evolutionary imperative. His marriage to Jane celebrates monogamy and puts paid to the dangers of miscegenation that lurk in the jungle. Their alliance personifies the Anglo-Saxon union and gives notice of the arrival of a new global superpower. Civilization, however, is complicated and expensive; even Tarzan needs more than blood and guts to maintain his exalted status. The gold from Opar provides a convenient solution. Tarzan's Waziri carry the ingots to the coast, where they can be shipped to the civilized world and put to productive use. Tarzan becomes an imperialist; Burroughs, his creator, becomes a plutocrat.

The other characters are even more blatant stereotypes of the values Burroughs wished to promote. Jane herself is the epitome of social orthodoxy. Although she later learns to swing through trees, she takes care to confine the activity to Africa. Her role is to reaffirm conservative values. Her decorative presence captivates Tarzan and gives him the incentive to redeem himself from barbarism. Thereafter, she stands by her man when she is not following him, and defers to his judgment to an extent that must have infuriated the suffragettes of the day. Tarzan's antonym is Professor Archimedes Porter, Jane's father, who is a weak, bumbling man given to ornate utterances that are irrelevant to the pressing issue of the moment, which in any case he is unable to grasp. Tarzan himself is the first of a line of strong, silent men whose later exponents include John Wayne and Clint Eastwood. Tarzan is the original "Pale Rider," who descends, destroys, and disappears.

The message is clear: actions speak louder than words; those who cannot act are inconsequential dreamers. By saying so little and achieving so much, Tarzan becomes an eloquent spokesman for the anti-intellectual strand in American culture. Tarzan's cousin, William Clayton, has inherited laudable qualities but they have atrophied because they have not been exposed to the regenerative infusion distilled from the many challenges of the frontier. Robert Canler, the only businessman in the cast, is several rungs short of gentlemanly status. His dastardly attempt to secure Jane's hand by exerting financial pressure on the gullible Professor Porter is throttled, literally, by Tarzan's ultra-powerful grip. The real scoundrels, however, are foreigners: a pair of Russians serves the purpose well, theirs being a land replete with rogues, spies, and anarchists. The lower orders are held at more than arm's length. Burroughs portrays Esmeralda, Jane's ever-loyal African American servant, as an infantile character whose actions are as inadequate as her few words. The largely anonymous workers, mostly crew members, exhibit a mixture of fecklessness and treachery that are transparent expressions of their inferior breeding.

Burroughs was the archetypal race patriot, a man of words who wanted to be a man of action and who greatly admired Theodore Roosevelt, who was both. Nevertheless, words alone were sufficient to serve Burroughs's purpose and to make him the most widely read American author during the first half of the twentieth century. His books reflected and reinforced qualities that shaped American character and identity. He achieved success by dispensing a brand of jungle juice that consumers who had never heard of the intellectual champions of Anglo-Saxondom found irresistible. Brooks Adams, Henry Cabot Lodge, Alfred Mahan, and Josiah Strong were close to power but remote from the people. Burroughs, on the other hand, knew Main Street, where Tarzan's battle cry was heard and repeated from town to town, if not from tree to tree. It was there that McKinley felt the pulse of the nation during the heady years of new imperialism, and found it to be beating to the rhythm of his own. Tarzan swung in Africa but resonated in the United States. Burroughs, unschooled and without academic ambition, was the master sociologist of his time.

PART III

EMPIRES

AND

INTERNATIONAL

DISORDER

1914-1959

CHAPTER 10

THE MODERN IMPERIAL SYSTEM

FROM CONQUEST TO COLLAPSE

THE "AMERICAN CENTURY"?

Henry Robinson Luce's identification of the "American Century" has become one of the most cited phrases in the study of twentieth-century international relations.[1] It is also one of the most frequently misused. Although specialists in the field are well aware of the context surrounding Luce's article, numerous other commentators have attached scope and meaning to the term that Luce did not have in mind. The American Century is frequently used in a broad sense to refer to the twentieth century as a whole, as if it were synonymous with American dominance. "The twentieth century," claims one widely read account, "belongs to the United States."[2] In fact, Luce regarded the first forty years of the century as being "a profound and tragic disappointment" because the United States had repeatedly failed to accept the duties of global leadership, even though the "Goddess of Democracy" was on hand to bless the endeavor. Luce, the proprietor of *Time*, *Fortune*, and *Life* magazines and the son of a missionary in China, applied Christian zeal to the secular task of spreading American ideas of freedom and democracy to the rest of the world. His famous editorial, published in February 1941 at a crucial moment in the rapidly unfolding world war, had the specific aim of persuading Congress to reject "the virus of isolationist sterility" and grasp the world leadership that, providentially, awaited the Republic. He was not commenting on an existing state of affairs but issuing a call "to create the first great American Century."

Luce's proclamation and the generous interpretations it has inspired provide an appropriate introduction to the story of the rise and fall of the Western empires in the twentieth century. Scholarly anticipations of future American greatness find a congenial complement in conventional interpretations of the decline of the rest of the West. The most familiar inherited orthodoxy treats World War I as a watershed: the century before 1914 was one of imperial expansion; the half century that followed was one of contraction. The band of experts who deal with the century between 1815 and 1914 retire from the field and leave the conflict to military historians. Fresh recruits, marching to different orders, arrive in 1918 to cover the postwar era. Attention shifts from the assertive initiatives of freebooters and pro-consuls to the rebellious activities of nationalist leaders as they gather momentum and eventually lead their countries to independence. As the long retreat began, the United States stepped forward to carry the banner of liberty across the world.

This chapter takes a different position. From the perspective of the present study, World War I marks an important stage in the history of globalization because it brought the long struggle between military-fiscal states and their rivals to a close. Dynastic, absolutist states, which had fought a sustained rearguard action to retain power in the second half of the nineteenth century, were felled by the war. Surviving monarchies either acquired or perpetuated constitutional checks on their freedom of action. Industrial nation-states became the predominant political force in Europe.

These states, however, remained committed to the imperial cause. Those with empires that had survived the war were resolute in defending them; those without empires were determined to acquire or repossess them. From an imperial standpoint, World War I signified the extension of the age of empires, not the beginning of its demise. Cataclysmic events can disguise long-term continuities and reinforce conservative tendencies, while retrospective knowledge can easily inflate elements of the past to suit the pressing (but also passing) needs of the present. In 1918, contemporaries did not assume that the age of great empires was at its close. On the contrary, the Western empires reached their greatest extent after World War I, when newly mandated territories swelled their holdings. The civilizing mission continued to inspire imperial policy. Belief in the supremacy of the white race remained the unwavering justification of colonial rule. The uneven development of industrial nation-states influenced international rivalries after 1918, as it had done before 1914. Modern globalization was to be prolonged, not replaced. Empires were to be preserved because they were functional to the process.

It is now apparent that older views linking the "hardening of the arteries" to Britain's loss of industrial supremacy in the late nineteenth century need revision.[3] The interpretation relies ultimately on the assumption that manufacturing output can be used as a proxy for national power. After 1850, however, Britain's world standing rested increasingly on its dominance of international finance and commercial services.[4] Consequently, conventional theories of decline need reordering to take account of Britain's global position as the first modern "mature credi-tor." In the 1920s, Britain, the new Rome, could still "quail and shape the orb" like "rattling thunder," despite losses sustained during the war.[5] On the eve of World War II, the European empires were still intact, and the zeal of their presiding emperors remained undiminished. Moreover, the imperial powers fought the war to preserve their empires, not to see them dismantled, and the allies planned the peace to consolidate their victory. Despite the huge losses caused by the global conflict, the victors revitalized the imperial mission and looked forward to extending their dominance indefinitely. A cooperative Commonwealth would keep the "Great" in Britain for the rest of the century, if not beyond it; a rebranded *Union française* would rescue France from a costly victory and maintain her status as a major power. Seen from this perspective, the era of mod-ern globalization and its imperial counterpart extended into the second half of the twentieth century, and the end of empire, when it came, was quite sudden.

The imperial continuities that characterized the first half of the twen-tieth century nevertheless included signposts that pointed toward the ultimate dissolution of the West's territorial empires. The upheaval brought by World War II is an obvious candidate. The emphasis in this chapter, however, will be on the crisis of the 1930s, which eroded the economic basis of imperial power and provoked unprecedented demonstrations of popular hostility to colonial rule. The war then added to the sense that a new world order was needed to keep the peace. Changes in the international economy altered the structures of integration the Western empires had created in the nineteenth cen-tury and perpetuated in the twentieth. Changes in international values undermined the moral authority of the West and erased its claims to imperial legitimacy. In the 1950s, the movement toward decoloniza-tion became swift and irreversible. The assumption of imperial per-manence was swept aside as if it had never been contemplated. The world, almost unknowingly, had entered a new era, that of postcolonial globalization.

After 1941, the United States accepted what Luce called its "manifest duty," and became fully engaged in international affairs. The purpose of the present chapter, however, is not to add another contribution to the mountain of available studies that trace the rise of the United States as a world power. It is rather to provide the broad context for understanding the history of the Republic's own territorial empire during the twentieth century. From this standpoint, the United States needs to be placed in the matrix formed by other Western empires, especially that of Britain, which was the largest, the most influential, and the one that caught Washington's eye.

ISOLATION OR INTEGRATION?

What Luce called "the virus of isolationist sterility" was once thought to characterize U.S. policy between the two world wars. The concern to avoid "foreign entanglements" originated with the Founding Fathers, who instilled in their successors an aversion to formal treaties involving long-term commitments to other powers.[6] Large signposts pointed in the direction of withdrawal after the experience of World War I: the United States did not ratify the Versailles Treaty, join the League of Nations, or participate in the Permanent Court of International Justice. The rapid demobilization of U.S. armed forces made it clear that Washington did not intend to engage with the world in a way that might involve substantial military action.[7] The obtrusive barriers erected by the Smoot-Hawley Tariff in 1930 confirmed the Republic's desire to "live of its own."[8] On the other hand, internationalist sentiment still had spokesmen in Congress, and informal expansion progressed rapidly during the war, when the European powers were otherwise engaged.[9] Historians associated (sometimes loosely) with the New Left have long regarded these tendencies as evidence of the continuous character of U.S. expansion since the nineteenth century and of the central role of business interests in seeking an "Open Door" throughout the world.[10]

These positions are not as opposed as they might seem. Both traditions were present during the interwar period, but the balance between them shifted. Examples of government initiatives in the 1920s included the Washington Agreements, which determined the distribution of global naval power, and the Dawes Plan, which provided loans to enable Germany to pay reparations.[11] It is evident, too, that informal expansion, which brought fewer political complications than formal colonial rule, continued during and after the war.[12] The strategic preoccupations of the European powers during the conflict gave the United States an opportunity to test its strength off the field of battle as well as on it. The struggle for supremacy in South America intensified, especially in Argentina and Brazil, where much was at stake and there were big prizes to be won. In East Asia, competition for influence in China increased, while in Japan the British suffered a reverse in 1922, when the United States succeeded in terminating the Anglo-Japanese alliance. The British reluctantly agreed not to renew their treaty with Japan in the hope, which was unfulfilled, of securing favorable terms from the United States for repaying their war debt.[13] After 1918, Americans undoubtedly flexed their muscles with new confidence. Coincidentally or not, it was in the 1920s that Tarzan and Charles Atlas first reached heights of popularity that they were to sustain until the 1970s, when the effective devaluation of the dollar signaled that peak muscularity had been reached.

In the 1920s, the United States was not only the world's leading producer of manufactured goods, but also its chief creditor and potential bailiff.[14] Trade with Latin America and Asia grew impressively; foreign direct investment doubled in the course of the decade. In 1929, Europe and Canada still received about 71 percent of U.S. exports and 44 percent of its direct investments, but Latin America and Asia combined provided 44 percent of U.S. imports and accounted for 38 percent of U.S. direct investment. By the close of the decade, the United States had ceased to import the bulk of its manufactured goods from Europe and had increased its imports of raw materials and foodstuffs from other parts of the world. The regional balance of trade had changed: the United States generated a surplus with Europe that helped to settle its deficit with the rest of the world. As U.S. commerce became globalized, multilateral trade ties became more complex and more important.

These expansive trends have to be placed in context. U.S. economic development remained predominantly homegrown. In 1929, Britain's share of foreign investment and world trade in manufactures still exceeded that of the United States, if only barely.[15] Between 1900 and 1929, foreign investment accounted for no more than about 6 percent of all U.S. investment, which was less than the increase in investment in California alone during the same period.[16] Moreover, business expansion needs to be distinguished from business imperialism, or "dollar diplomacy," as it has been called.[17] One arm of the policy, symbolized by Hay's Open Door "Note" of 1899, was intended to prevent foreign states from discriminating against U.S. goods and services.[18] The other, summarized in Theodore Roosevelt's Corollary to the Monroe Doctrine in 1904, proclaimed the right of the United States to intervene unilaterally in Latin America.[19] Hay hoped to keep the door open; Roosevelt intended to put his foot through it, by force if necessary, to support loans from private banks and to reform governments that were judged to fall short of "civilized" standards. Appropriately, the policy drew heavily on U.S. experience in Cuba, where the Platt Amendment appeared to offer a means of control without formal responsibilities.

A full assessment of what the literature on empire calls "informal imperialism" lies beyond the scope of this study.[20] Formal colonial acquisitions virtually ended in 1900, shortly after they had begun. By then, most eligible parts of the world that were within reach had been annexed, so there was little scope for adding new territory. Moreover, the imperialist lobby faced powerful opposition. Democrats berated the Republican Party for abandoning traditional republican teaching, which held that military expansion abroad would produce despotism at home. Domestic economic interests campaigned to limit U.S. investment in the colonies and prevent colonial competitors from gaining access to the mainland market on favorable terms. These concerns merged with visceral racial anxieties. If the colonial lobby was allowed a free hand, it might open the door to immigration from nonwhite sources. Although these explanations carry considerable weight, they were not exclusive to the United States. The decisive consideration, which limited further attempts to expand overseas, was one of scale. The United States occupied the richest half of a large continent. If the frontier seemed to be closing in the 1890s, it opened wide thereafter. Opportunities on the mainland dwarfed those that could be created abroad, at least before 1945. The most appealing form of colonization was that which took place at home.

Research into "dollar diplomacy" has provided a clear indication of the scale and effectiveness of U.S. influence beyond its borders during this period. The Dawes Plan, the most notable example of dollar diplomacy in Europe at this time, had some short-term success, but was replaced by the Young Plan in 1929, which in turn was aborted by the onset of the world slump. Aspirations were also more prominent than achievements in China, the fabled market that refused to materialize. Not much went through the Open Door mainly because U.S. banks were wary of investing in a country that had just introduced the term "warlord" to the world, but also because protectionist policies limited the prospects for exporters wishing to enter the U.S. market. The United States had greater influence in smaller states that were closer to home, particularly those in Central America. There is no doubt, too, that U.S. financial, commercial, and cultural influences penetrated South America in the 1920s, though they made little headway in the biggest prize: Argentina.

Important though they were, the Central American republics were scarcely weighty international powers, even with Mexico added to the scales. On the other hand, they were attractive precisely because, being independent, they did not arouse the degree of opposition that curtailed expatriate enterprise in the formal empire.[21] Once invested, however, U.S. companies invariably committed Washington to intervene when

business plans went awry. The United States took control of the Dominican Republic's finances in 1904 after a New York firm, the San Domingo Improvement Company, had "improved" the country to the point
where it faced bankruptcy.[22] Washington's decision to occupy Haiti in
1915 was motivated partly by apprehension that Germany and France
might secure naval bases there, but also by appeals from the National
City Bank of New York, which had invested heavily in the island and was
anxious to consolidate and reschedule the state's debts.[23] The United
Fruit Company (1899), which became the largest foreign employer of
labor in Central America in the 1920s, helped to draw in U.S. military
support for its operations in Costa Rico, Honduras, and Guatemala.[24]
The main beneficiaries of dollar diplomacy were a handful of U.S. banks
and a few large corporations and contractors.[25] Ironically, too, Washington's intervention, which was intended to establish U.S. paramountcy,
helped European (especially British) investors, who gained protection
without having to pay for it.[26] Short-term successes, however, proved
to be costly. The "banana republics" that arose from a combination of
foreign commercial dominance and military force were not as pliable as
their name suggests.[27] Widespread proto-nationalist reactions prompted
the withdrawal of U.S. troops from Cuba (1921), the Dominican Republic
(1924), Nicaragua (1933), and Haiti (1934).[28]

During the 1930s the United States drew back even from these limited
positions. At the close of the 1920s, President Herbert Hoover abandoned
the robust policies associated with Presidents Roosevelt, Taft, and Wilson,
and halted military incursions into Central America.[29] In 1934, President
Franklin D. Roosevelt confirmed the change of direction by introducing
the "Good Neighbor" policy, which set out to "make friends and influence
people" by means other than overt coercion. Anxiety in Washington about
the spread of communism and fascism in the 1930s reinforced the need
for policy toward the Southern Hemisphere to become more responsive
to local opinion. The world slump, however, greatly reduced material support for the new policy. The Smoot-Hawley Tariff inhibited trade.[30] Some
U.S. investment in the region was lost; more was repatriated as investors
lost their nerve. Mexico seized the opportunity to reclaim huge tracts of
land from U.S. companies and to nationalize the oil industry.[31] In the
1930s, the United States lacked both carrots and sticks.

To acknowledge that the United States increased its involvement with
the world beyond its borders during and after World War I is not to accept that it had become the "heir to empire."[32] Hay's Open Door "Note"
announced a new policy but did not deliver it.[33] Roosevelt's Corollary
claimed the right to "police" countries in Latin America "in the interest of

order and civilization," but policing guaranteed neither "order" nor "civilization."[34] Housebreaking opened a few doors; housekeeping proved to be a burdensome undertaking. A generous assessment might conclude that the United States had become a "regional hegemon," though one with limited influence in parts of South America. A wider informal empire had still to materialize. Henry Luce was right in 1941, when he claimed that the United States had failed to transform its potential power into a commitment to engage fully with the wider world. The beneficiary could not inherit the estate because the testator had yet to write a will. At that moment, there was still only one truly global power, and it was Great Britain.[35]

WORLD WAR I AND THE RETURN TO NORMALITY

In 1918, the victorious imperial powers set about returning to "normalcy," as Warren Harding called it during his presidential campaign in 1920.[36] The war had ruptured the colonial order. Britain and Germany fought in Africa for control of their colonies there; African troops from British and French colonies saw action in Europe for the first time.[37] India, the largest of Britain's overseas barracks, supplied nearly one million troops who served in Africa and the Middle East as well as in Europe. Commerce was disrupted: shipping and consumer goods were in short supply; price inflation, strikes, and protests followed. A new generation of nationalist leaders capitalized on mounting disaffection. This was the moment when Mohandas Gandhi, Mao Tse-tung, Ho Chi Minh, and Emir Khaled either absorbed radical views of colonial rule or began to act on them, and when Lenin set a spectacular example in applied thought by leading a revolution to overthrow Tzarist autocracy.[38]

The extent of the upheaval reinforced the conservative inclinations of the victors. Broadly speaking, returning to normality meant reconstructing the world as it was before 1914. Although the map had changed, policies and attitudes inherited from the past persisted. Established economic doctrines continued to hold sway. Racial prejudices remained unaltered. The British lit a celebratory bonfire of wartime controls, which burned brightly between 1918 and 1921.[39] In a move driven by official persistence rather than by popular enthusiasm, Britain returned to the prewar gold standard in 1925, followed by France in 1926.[40] Both powers devised ambitious plans to enable their colonies to help win the peace.[41] The colonial administration was reorganized; the civilizing mission was revitalized. The war had increased the visibility of both empires and demonstrated their value in supplying men and materials.[42] Imperial propaganda penetrated all levels of society; imperial history entered schools in Britain and France.[43] New technologies helped the imperial masters to run ahead of those trying to chase them down. Radio and film were powerful advocates for the imperial cause.[44] Enhanced information-gathering and policing, backed by air power, dealt with waverers and dissenters.[45] The Bolshevik Revolution, by challenging Western orthodoxies, provided an incentive for the "agents of freedom" to show doomsters that capitalism had a future and not just a past.[46]

The peace settlement in 1919 helped to make the world safe for the empires of the victors. The overseas possessions of Britain, France, Belgium, the Netherlands, Italy, Portugal, Japan, and the United States remained intact; the dynastic states of the defeated were taken down, and the German, Austro-Hungarian, and Ottoman Empires were carved into pieces. The aspirations of the leading powers extended well beyond self-preservation. Britain and France acquired large slices of the German and Ottoman Empires, which they managed through the newly instituted mandate system.[47] A total of fourteen mandated territories were held in trust by the League of Nations and administered by appointed trustees.[48] These colonies in camouflage were distributed among the victors and gave countries such as Australia, New Zealand, and South Africa their first experience of being imperial powers in their own right. The British, enthused by victory, even devised a plan for incorporating Abyssinia, which they thought had potential for white settlement.[49] As the *Chicago Tribune* commented in 1920, "The British mopped up." "This is the golden age of the British Empire, its Augustan age."[50]

Self-determination, the most publicized principle of the peace settlement, retained its pristine quality. It was an honored concept, but not one the colonial powers wished to implement immediately or indeed on any timescale other than the longest of long runs. Lenin and Trotsky were the first to propose that the peace settlement should be based on self-determination. Lloyd George adopted the phrase; Woodrow Wilson popularized it.[51] Wilson's idealism was matched by his concern to counter Bolshevik propaganda. Even so, Wilson did not intend principle to prevail over practicality: regional stability, in his view, came before nationalist aspirations.[52] Once in the public domain, however, the phrase spread across the world by means of the proto-internets of the day: the telegraph, telephone, and press services, and through the agency of the Committee on Public Information, a unit that Wilson himself had created to propagate the idea that the United States was the agent of freedom. Although Wilson rapidly retreated from the unforeseen consequences of his pronouncement, regret could not cancel his utterance.

Policy-makers adapted the existing formula for combining economic development with political stability. The economic plan applied a familiar orthodoxy: the standard import-export economies were to be expanded, not transformed. Necessity, however, extended the role of colonial governments to assist the development of agriculture and to improve transport facilities. Officials set about implementing the political doctrines that were to characterize the era. The British, turning pragmatism into faith, became missionaries for indirect rule; the French, turning faith into pragmatism, adopted the complementary policy of *association*.[53] Acculturation (or *assimilation*) was retained as an ideal and ultimate goal of French policy but was to be reached at a point so distant as to be incalculable. Indirect rule commissioned indigenous authorities to be agents of colonial governments. A new generation of experts supplied scholarly credibility for the policy. Enthnographers unraveled the intricacies of local customs and beliefs and showed how they formed coherent, stable structures. Lucien Lévy-Bruhl dug deeper still in searching for a distinct "primitive mentality."[54] Indirect rule had many attractions. It was conservative, and it was cheap. It deflected criticism from colonial rulers to the chiefs, *caids*, and others who were appointed to collect taxes and supply compulsory labor. It provided a counterweight to the "uppity" Westernized "oriental gentlemen" who displayed a disturbing ability to criticize colonialism in the language of the rulers.

The plans of the empire-builders depended on a sustained recovery of the world economy following the short-lived but severe slump after the brief boom at the end of the war. Directly or indirectly, colonial fortunes relied on external trade to generate the revenues that funded government projects for improving transport, utilities, education, and agriculture; raised the incomes needed to reward key intermediaries; and held living standards in the wider society above protest point. At the start of the 1920s, there appeared to be a chance that the gamble on international trade might succeed. The return of more stable conditions and a hint of prosperity took the edge off the sharpest expressions of discontent and dissolved many of the embryonic political organizations that had sprung up in the colonies during the war. Hindsight reveals signs of cracks in the imperial wall by the end of the decade. Yet, the imperialists of the time held a positive view of the world and their role as trustees with imperial responsibilities. Their task was to carry forward the civilizing mission by means of paternal tuition and resolute control, and they worked assiduously to implement the "dual mandate" that was intended to deliver benefits to rulers and ruled alike.[55]

Adaptations to changing circumstances were nothing new in the long history of empires. Inflexible empires became unresponsive; only the supple could hope for longevity. The managers of the British Empire reacted vigorously to two challenges in the 1920s: colonial nationalism and the rise of the United States. Some nationalists were put down; others were put up. Immediate threats to civil order were suppressed; moderate political organizations, if powerful enough, were promoted by being brought into the colonial system. Disappointment with the political consequences of the peace, stoked by continuing discontent, produced a series of revolts across the colonial world—from Egypt to Korea via India—that were put down by displays of considerable force. The Royal Air Force, on the point of being disbanded in 1918, created a role for itself as the new destroyer of colonial insurgencies.[56] Bombs dropped on the Sudan, Afghanistan, and the much-blitzed Kurds were scarcely missiles of precision, but they had a powerful effect in demonstrating that the white man, having wreaked havoc upon his fellows, had enhanced his power to cause mayhem for others too.

Not all insurgencies could be bombed into submission. White settlers, who were in the vanguard of colonial nationalism at this time, could not be bombed at all. They could, however, be disciplined. When a group of settlers led by a former Brigadier General attempted to seize power in Kenya in 1923, Whitehall reacted decisively.[57] The plot, which involved kidnapping the governor of Kenya and replacing him with Lord Hugh Delamere, the unofficial leader of the settlers, was a madcap scheme destined to be undone by its own improbabilities. Nevertheless, the Colonial Office quickly brought the rebels to heel and denied them the political control they sought. In Happy Valley they could roam free; in matters of high politics they had to play by the rules of the constitutional game. The Irish revolt, the prelude to the creation of the Irish Free State in 1922, was an altogether more serious affair and evinced a military response, though one that stopped short of aerial bombing of civilians. In its final stages, however, Irish resistance to the British gained strength, not from a perception of imperial weakness, but from the fear that Britain was set on reversing prewar trends toward devolution.[58] Even so, the Free State was not entirely free: it was granted the status of a dominion, not full independence, and its economic and strategic ties to Britain, though stretched, remained firmly in place.

Opposition within the political system had to be handled differently. In these cases, colonial rulers began to adapt by working with nationalists instead of against them. White nationalists continued to set the pace. Settlers in Southern Rhodesia were granted self-government in 1923 because (unlike the case of Kenya) devolution suited the British government.[59] The precedent had already been established by conferring dominion status on the most important settler colonies: Canada, Australia, New Zealand, and South Africa. The dominions capitalized on their contribution to the war effort by pressing their claims for greater autonomy. The British procrastinated until 1926, when the Balfour Report pronounced in terms of profound ambiguity that were not clarified until the Statute of Westminster was inscribed in 1931.[60] As a result, the dominions acquired almost complete legislative autonomy, though effective independence had yet to be achieved.

After World War I, Britain had to consider extending the principle of devolution to non-settler parts of the empire, too. Nationalists in India were elevated by being offered concessions aimed at deflecting them from pressing for independence. The Montagu-Chelmsford reforms, embodied in the Government of India Act of 1919, enlarged the franchise and inaugurated a degree of internal self-government.[61] The Indian case, however, was the exception rather than the norm. In the 1920s, few other colonies had developed political parties that also encompassed mass movements. Most nationalist organizations operating constitutionally remained elitist and urban-based, and posed only a limited threat to colonial rule.

Important though the concessions made to the dominions and India were, they did not point directly toward independence. Nationalism in the dominions was combined with a powerful sense of what, in the language of the day, was known as "race patriotism." This much-advertised concept held out the prospect of combining two sets of affiliations that were still thought to be compatible, and remained so even after World War II. With respect to India, the Montagu-Chelmsford reforms have been reinterpreted as measures taken to preserve the essence of British power rather than to give it away.[62] What mattered in relations with both the dominions and India, as Jeremy Bentham had observed of the continuing links between the United States and Britain, was not the formalities but the realities of power. In both cases, the "ties that bind" remained strong throughout the interwar period.[63]

The United States presented Britain with a challenge of a different order. The two countries had forged an informal Anglo-Saxon alliance in the late nineteenth century and had cooperated successfully during the Spanish-American War. The British assisted the subsequent installation of the United States as a new imperial power in the Pacific and the Caribbean; the United States reciprocated by helping the British diplomatically and financially during the Anglo-South African War. By the end of World War I, however, the United States had begun to make its weight felt. American troops and money were vital to the success of the allies in the closing stages of the conflict, by which time Britain was heavily in debt to its former colony. Assertiveness accompanied by Anglophobia cut across the harmonies that Andrew Carnegie and other commentators had idealized at the turn of the century.[64] American observers happily mixed stereotypes, prejudice, and a few grains of truth to produce a guiding image of Britain as a monarchial, aristocratic, decadent, class-ridden, and imperialistic nation. The British responded with an equal measure of bias to objectivity. Americans were brash, ignorant, aggressive blunderers who gave particular offense by being imperial-deniers. The last quality puzzled and frustrated the Foreign Office (and the Quai d'Orsay) throughout the colonial era. Seen from Whitehall's standpoint, the United States clearly had a tangible, territorial empire. Yet the Republic acted as if its providential purity had been unsullied by conquest either within or beyond its borders. British policy-makers found this contradiction, as they saw it, to be especially galling when the United States chose to lob unhelpful public comments into the cauldron of Irish and Indian nationalism.

In 1918, Britain tried to persuade the United States to join the feast of the victors by taking a mandate of its own.[65] This was an offer that President Wilson felt compelled to refuse. Wilson, a Democrat, led a party that was officially opposed to imperialism, and he did not intend to provoke disunity by acquiring high-profile colonies, especially if they entailed international obligations. The imperial mentality, however, remained intact.[66] The purchase of the Virgin Islands from Denmark in 1917 showed that Washington still thought that property and people could be bought and sold by powers holding an imperial license. Wilson also ensured that no hasty moves were made to speed progress toward independence in the insular empire, and he supported the imperial club by recognizing Japan's suzerainty over Korea in exchange for Japan's recognition of U.S. rule over the Philippines and Britain's protectorate in Egypt.[67]

The informal expansion of the United States presented a formidable challenge. British governments responded by making determined efforts to regain ground lost during the war. The 1920s witnessed an intense diplomatic and economic struggle for predominance in three key regions: South America, China, and parts of the Middle East that had escaped the annexationist ambitions of eager imperialists.[68] Although Britain was unable to keep pace with the United States in commerce with Latin America as a whole, by the end of the decade it was not far behind the United States in Argentina and Brazil, the two largest markets. In finance, however, Britain's position remained unchallenged. In 1929, its investments in Argentina and Brazil were three times greater than those of the United States.[69] Britain fared much better in China. Despite the enforced cessation of the alliance with Japan, the British had no intention, as Lloyd George put it, of letting the United States "walk all over them" in China or any other part of the quasi-imperial world.[70] The United States had built up a considerable cultural presence in education and missionary work, but had only a modest stake in trade and investment, and could not rival Britain's political influence.[71] Britain retained its place as the leading foreign power in the economic sphere, and successfully adjusted its diplomacy to cultivate allies among the nationalists as an alternative to shelling them. Britain's position in the Middle East was even stronger.[72] It gained mandates in Iraq, Trans-Jordan, and Palestine, and remained the dominant foreign power in Egypt, Saudi Arabia, and Iran. Inevitably, expansion brought problems of control, notably in Palestine, but it delivered compensation too—notably in the form of oil resources.[73] The United States, by contrast, still had only a limited presence in the region.

"ONE OF THE GREATEST ECONOMIC CATASTROPHES OF MODERN HISTORY"[74]

Things fell apart in 1929. The stock market crash of that year was followed by a financial crisis in 1931. Confidence collapsed; unemployment rose sharply; the gold standard was defended and then abandoned. World stock markets lost about two-thirds of their value between 1929 and 1935; foreign investment slowed and in some cases ceased.[75] The demand for colonial products dropped, taking prices down with them. Incomes shrank; colonial revenues fell. Colonial governments confronted acute difficulties in servicing the development debts they had contracted in more buoyant times.

The immediate causes of this transformative event lie beyond the scope of this chapter.[76] It is sufficient for present purposes to say that a combination of potentially disastrous elements emerged from World War I.

The peace settlement divided Europe over the issue of reparations and made it especially hard to solve international economic problems. In the late 1920s, excessive lending, errors in monetary policy, and lack of co-operation among central banks coalesced to create widespread panic.[77] As the system buckled, the inflexibility of the gold standard's regime of fixed exchange rates, which had facilitated the postwar recovery, com-pounded the difficulties of adjusting to the downturn. The deflationary consequences of adhering to fixed exchange rates were not eased until 1931, when Britain and Germany left the gold standard. Imperial states that remained in the gold bloc, notably the United States, France, Bel-gium, and the Netherlands, faced an even greater struggle to overcome deflation and unemployment.[78]

One longer-term development deserves emphasis here because it has a direct bearing on imperial relationships during the 1930s, as well as being a major precondition of the Depression itself. By the late 1920s, one of the principal dialectics driving imperialism had surfaced in the form of an oversupply of primary products, which was manifested in fall-ing prices even before 1929. Imperial expansion from the late nineteenth century onward had "opened up" underdeveloped regions and provided, in Adam Smith's terminology, a "vent" for their "surplus." Producers ev-erywhere responded rapidly to price incentives facilitated by railroads, steamships, and foreign investment, and poured colonial raw materials into Western markets. In this way, the success of imperialism in devel-oping the classic exchange of primary commodities for manufactured goods generated forces that had the potential to alienate producers from the system that had helped to reconcile them to colonial rule. After 1900, when the international economy revived, primary producers competed across borders in a global market that was more open than closed. After 1929, when world trade contracted, they were obliged to compete within imperial blocs that limited their access to other markets.

Increasing specialization made it hard for primary producers to re-spond to shifts in the market without cutting their living standards. Those who relied on tree crops, such as cocoa, coffee, palm oil, and co-conuts, had long-term fixed investments that could not be altered easily. Those who produced annual crops, such as groundnuts (*arachides*) and sugar, often had no alternative apart from subsistence farming, and even that could become problematic. This is not to claim that the effects of the Depression were uniform or uniformly disastrous. Revisionist research has drawn attention to the diverse consequences of the event in the colo-nial world.[79] A minority of producers, notably gold-mining companies, gained from the disruption that affected others. Nevertheless, as a broad generalization it remains the case that prices of most primary products slumped significantly after 1929, did not begin to recover until 1934, and failed even then to regain the levels achieved in the prewar period. Although prices of manufactured goods also fell, the terms of trade moved against primary producers, who compensated for declining unit returns by expanding the volume of exports, which reached peak levels in the late 1930s.[80] The response was an indication of the difficulty of making further productivity gains, as well as of a lack of alternatives. By the 1930s, most of the available improvements in productivity, whether through reduced transport costs or advances in agronomy, such as central milling, had been achieved. Producers found themselves deposited in a large elephant trap with little prospect of being set free.

The imperial powers responded to the Depression by retrenching. Protectionist sentiment overcame residual hopes, still lingering in Britain, of returning to a world of free trade. In 1930, the United States adopted the highly protectionist Smoot-Hawley tariff; in the following year, France increased the protectionist measures that already surrounded her empire; in 1932, Britain followed suit with the Ottawa Agreements, which established free trade within the empire and protection (through tariffs and quotas) against the rest of the world. The primary motive behind these measures was to defend economic interests at home: support for the colonies was a desirable but secondary consideration. Despite the advances made by manufacturing industries, agricultural employment remained significant in all the imperial states except Britain, where it accounted for only 6 percent of the labor force. About 42 percent of the labor force was employed in farming in France, and about 25 percent in the United States.[81] Consequently, the rural vote (which was much larger than the agricultural labor force itself) still exerted a powerful influence on domestic political fortunes. The British, however, had strong domestic incentives for introducing imperial protection because they needed to ensure that colonial producers had a means of continuing to service the considerable debts they had contracted with the City of London.[82]

The most visible consequence of neo-mercantilist policies was to direct an increasing share of trade and investment toward protected imperial commercial and monetary blocs.[83] This trend had the effect of strengthening imperial ties, even though it occurred in a declining world market. The French imperial connection reached unprecedented levels: in 1913, France sent about 13 percent of her exports to the overseas empire, which accounted for about 9 percent of imports into France; by 1939 the figures had jumped to 40 percent and 37 percent respectively.[84]

Britain took a parallel but smoother path: in 1909–1913, it shipped 35 percent of its exports to the empire, which in turn supplied about 27 percent of Britain's imports; in 1934–1938 the equivalent figures for exports and imports each stood at 41 percent.[85] Capital flows followed a similar course in both countries: the proportion of foreign investment directed to imperial destinations soared: in the case of France, from around 12 percent of the total in 1914 to around 40 percent in 1939; and in the case of Britain, from an average of 39 percent of the total in 1900–1914 to 86 percent in 1934–1938.[86] In both cases, signs of recovery in private investment in the 1920s were followed by a dramatic contraction in the 1930s. There was a corresponding shift from private to public capital as governments attempted to make up the shortfall, and in the case of France managed to do so.

The trend toward government funding was an early indication of the emergence of the subsidized and protected imperial economies that in different degrees were to characterize Britain and France for the remainder of the colonial period. The 1930s were again a point of transition. As Jacques Marseille has shown in his now classic study, the French empire provided a good fit with French capitalism down to 1914; thereafter, and especially from the 1930s, the two began to part company.[87] The empire served increasingly as a refuge for declining French industries whose exports were otherwise uncompetitive in world markets. It is unclear whether, and if so how well, this analysis applies to the British case, though some similarities are apparent. The empire provided a safe haven for Britain's old staple industries, which were becoming uncompetitive and were to decline further after the war. The Sterling Area also sheltered the City of London and the pound, but in this case it helped to nurse the patient back to reasonable health.

The severe economic contraction of the 1930s has led some economists to describe the period as being one of "deglobalization."[88] The characterization has merit if it is treated as a check on the assumption that the process of globalization was one of unbroken expansion from a starting point in the nineteenth century down to the present day. From another perspective, however, the description is narrow and overdramatic. Most of the industrial powers, apart from Britain, were already protectionist before the 1930s, and the tariff increases that occurred during that decade intensified rather than transformed existing flows of trade and finance.[89] Moreover, as this study has argued, the Western empires were themselves globalizing forces that had helped to integrate the world.[90] The imperial reach had limits and was further constrained by protectionism in the 1930s, but the renewed expansion that took place after World War II was also less than fully global. The attempt to achieve freer world trade was hampered by the Cold War, which created two hostile, sealed blocs that struggled for supremacy for more than forty years.

A more important qualification is that globalization encompasses a wider world than the one economists inhabit. Political and cultural forces that are regarded today as essential components of contemporary globalization emerged during the interwar era and were extended after World War II. Liberalism, communism, and fascism spread across the world.[91] The rise of mass nationalism in the colonies of the Western powers dates from the 1930s. The concepts of self-determination and human rights that helped to inspire these movements, and were later adopted by the United Nations, first became popular causes during this period.[92] Ideas had wings, as Francois-Rene de Chateaubriand had foretold in 1841. Personal experiences, whether in the trenches, through education, or in migrating for work, welded ideas to reality. Despite protectionism, people still moved readily within and across imperial borders. New technologies helped global connections to multiply. The development of the "flying machine" in the 1930s allowed regular passenger and commercial services to be established throughout the world and enabled ideas, such as self-determination, to take off. Radio, telephone, cinema, and motor vehicles helped to shrink the world. Reuters, founded in London in 1851, was on hand to harness new means of communication to its global news service.[93]

The conventional emphasis on the nation-state, whether as an ideal type or as a failed experiment that ended in conflict, has also obscured the development of supranational organizations during this period.[94] The much criticized and underestimated League of Nations played an important part in nurturing reformist ideas.[95] The League was the precursor of organizations that were to become the World Health Organization (WHO) and the United Nations Educational, Scientific and Cultural Organization (UNESCO). It reinvented itself in the 1930s to produce plans for economic and financial cooperation that were to influence both the United Nations and the Bretton Woods Agreements. The League's team of experts was the first to draw attention to issues of nutrition and global food security, and to formulate the idea of "basic needs," which development economists rediscovered and adopted as a universal measure of welfare after World War II.[96] British policy-makers advanced the idea of the Commonwealth as a set of diverse but freely associated states that would offer an alternative to the competing universal philosophy propagated by communism.[97] Official and private organizations and networks multiplied, spanned political borders, and achieved global agreements in matters ranging from maritime safety to labor rights, refugees, and environmental conservation.[98] These globalizing impulses did not simply spring out of the postwar order after 1945, but had their expansive origins at a time that is generally seen to be one of contraction.

Political and cultural influences became most potent when they joined forces in the nationalist movements that challenged the colonial order during the 1930s. The junction was effected through a further imperial irony, whereby the success of imperial globalization in integrating large segments of the world opened channels for flows of information that not only carried imperial propaganda but also transmitted ideas aimed at subverting the whole enterprise. Censorship endeavored to regulate information, just as exchange controls tried to check the movement of capital. In the end, however, ideas "knew no frontiers." They spread, as colonial governors saw it, "like the plague," infecting whole populations with radical, anti-imperial thoughts and supplying easily absorbed remedies for the ills of subject peoples. Mohandas Gandhi is a prime example of these trends.[99] Education drew him to London; opportunities within the imperial system took him to South Africa, where he spent twenty-one formative years from 1893 to 1914.[100] It was in South Africa that the young Gandhi experienced race prejudice, formulated ideas of nonviolent protest, founded his first political organization (the Natal Indian Congress) in 1894, and had his initial encounter with a colonial jail. It was there, too, that he pondered the cosmopolitan ideas that evolved into the political philosophy he was to practice in India. The fusion of Gujarati experience and Hindu beliefs with eclectic gleanings from Plato, Tolstoy, Thoreau, and Ruskin, among others, was testimony not only to his principled politics, but also to the influence of globalization on his intellectual formation.

The novel feature of colonial nationalism during the 1930s was the transformation of politics resulting from what Huntington referred to, in a different context, as the "green uprising."[101] Early colonial politics was largely urban-based, elitist, and reformist; the green uprising made the countryside a permanent feature of the political system, and altered its character by adding the voices of the rural majority. Although green shoots were present before the 1930s, rural activism tended to be sporadic and took place outside established political organizations. India was the exception that led the way in the 1920s because it had reached a relatively advanced stage of political and economic development. Elsewhere, it took the shock of the Depression to galvanize rural society, and access to modern communications to overcome barriers of distance and facilitate political mobilization on a national scale. Towns developed, too. Urban employment in government offices, public utilities, harbors, manufacturing, and business grew as export economies expanded. These conditions created the potential for what might be called a "brown uprising," when contraction followed expansion and urban discontent was harnessed to political purposes by trade unions and other organizations representing the interests of an expanding wage-labor force.

The world slump cracked the existing political order everywhere, and opened the way for new parties to mobilize the mass of the population.[102] Unemployment and hardship provoked repeated protests, strikes, and violence. Strong men on horseback arose in Europe, Latin America, and parts of Asia to guide their lost people out of chaos and into a new and supposedly better future.[103] Politics in the dependencies were transformed too, even though the only strong men allowed on horseback were government troops. Established elitist parties were fractured and had to reset their organizations and programs to keep pace with developments they had not anticipated. New radical groups—trade unions, youth movements, and branches of the Communist Party—arose to claim popular support. By the time World War II broke out, the shape of colonial politics in the postwar era could already be discerned.

The leading imperial powers had no intention of abandoning what some observers judged to be a sinking ship. Their initial response to the Depression was to apply to the colonies the orthodoxy that dominated policies at home. Austerity was the maxim; solvency was the objective. Governments cut expenditure; colonies continued to service their debts. Economic purity, however, incurred political costs. Job losses and increasingly efficient tax-gathering in the colonies added to the hardship brought by the economic downturn and delivered supporters to new, radical political parties. The authorities reacted to the challenge by clamping down on "extremists," "agitators," and violence of all kinds, except their own, while redoubling their efforts to identify and work with conservative and moderate leaders.[104] Concessions were made where they were unavoidable and providing they did not subvert imperial interests. The most prominent example was again India, which moved toward self-government once the British had reserved control of key aspects of policy and after it became clear that the Congress Party's financial backers had no intention of underwriting radical attacks on private property.

India, as we now know, showed the face of the future to the colonial world. In the 1930s, however, there were very few Indias and many far less compelling Gambias and Guinées, and their influence on policy was secondary to pressures exerted by intransigent South Africas and Algerias, whose settlers had powerful affiliations with "kith and kin" in the home country. Nevertheless, the decade should not be dismissed as one destined to mark time while awaiting the metamorphosis brought by World War II. The Depression prompted a fundamental reconsideration of the orthodoxies that were being applied at home and abroad. In 1930, John Maynard Keynes had already called the world slump "one of the greatest economic catastrophes of modern history" and advocated increased public investment to stimulate employment.[105] Subsequently, he expanded his famously innovative challenge to conventional wisdom, though his influence on policy before 1945 was greater in the United States than in Britain.[106] Amidst continuing depression, Arnold Toynbee produced several volumes of his widely publicized and monumentally pessimistic study of history, which confirmed (for any remaining doubters) that all civilizations, no matter how powerful, were destined to decay and crumble.[107] At the close of the decade, when the brittle peace had given way to a global war, even Joseph Schumpeter concluded that capitalism no longer had a future.[108]

Colonial policy-makers were less fatalistic than Toynbee and Schumpeter and more successful than Keynes in securing converts in Westminster and Whitehall, where it mattered.[109] Malcolm MacDonald, who became Secretary of State for the Colonies in 1935, was the first holder of the office to lead the way in shifting policy toward economic development and political reform.[110] The new direction received strong support in 1936 from William Macmillan's *Warning from the West Indies*, which shook any remaining complacency about the orthodoxies of colonial policy, and from Lord Hailey's weighty *An African Survey*, which was published in the same year.[111] Hailey's own warning drew on his extensive experience of India during Gandhi's rise to national prominence, and came with recommendations advising the government to step up its development effort, reconsider its commitment to indirect rule, and adopt a more accommodating attitude toward nationalist leaders. A generalized version of Keynesian ideas added endorsement to a long-standing belief in the British colonies that government intervention was part of the duty of paternal care in backward societies. In France, the *dirigiste* tradition was updated to fit the compelling needs of the decade.[112] Experts in both countries went further still in thinking the unthinkable and expressing it in tentative plans to encourage manufacturing in the colonies.

The problem as far as colonial policy was concerned was not the shortage of reforming ideas but the difficulty of implementing them. All proposals for colonial reform were costly, and hard-pressed Western governments were either unwilling or unable to produce the required funding. Reformers also faced opposition overseas, especially in colonies of settlement. Colonial manufacturing, which its advocates regarded as a step in the right direction if the European empires were to survive, was seen by opponents as a step too far that would undermine existing interests and, with them, the whole imperial project. These obstacles reduced the scope for change. Nevertheless, the British political system retained the flexibility to press ahead with reforms that did not have direct financial implications. Despite deep internal divisions, the National government negotiated a historic constitutional settlement in 1935, when the Government of India Act prepared the way for the "jewel in the crown" to become self-governing.[113]

In France, on the other hand, the Popular Front, which came to power in 1936, struggled unsuccessfully with a combination of constitutional rigidities, excessive optimism about colonial resources, and its own lack of resolve.[114] Moreover, there was little support, either in the French parliament or the country, for progressive policies, which conservatives could easily present as a master plan for defeat.[115] A modified version of the *mission civilisatrice* retained its prime place as a rhetorical proclamation; the *pacte colonial* and its associated vested interests remained the basis for action.[116] The colonies were too poor to rescue France, and France lacked the resources to rescue the colonies.

The Government of India Act opened a door for officials to reassess other previously non-negotiable tenets of imperial policy. Unrest resulting from the slump, which culminated in serious riots in Trinidad in 1937 and Jamaica in 1938, compelled change in the empire as a whole.[117] Disturbances that broke Britain's shop window in the Caribbean alarmed both the Colonial Office and the Foreign Office, which were concerned to avoid stoking anti-imperial feelings in the United States. Indirect rule, which had guided policy for a generation, was to be superseded by an ambitious plan to raise up a new generation of educated and, so it was hoped, cooperative colonial intermediaries. The hitherto timeless principle of self-sufficiency was to be abandoned and replaced by government-funded development.[118] This momentous change was embodied in the Colonial Development & Welfare Act, which was formulated before the outbreak of war, though not passed until 1940. The Treasury fought to retain Gladstonian principles but suffered one of its rare defeats. Contemplating what he saw as a future of guaranteed insolvency, a gloomy Treasury official commented that the measure would put the colonies "on the dole from henceforth and forever."[119] On the eve of World War II, postwar development policies of government-sponsored foreign aid and its subsequent complement, deficit financing, were already either in hand or in view.

THE WAR TO BREAK AND
RE-MAKE EMPIRES

Pressing colonial issues arose within a context of mounting international tensions that threatened to destroy the fragile peace inherited from 1919, and eventually did so. Historians commonly treat the events leading to World War II from the perspective of the international diplomacy of the great powers. This is, of course, an indispensable approach.[120] An alternative, but still complementary, way of viewing the period emphasizes the specific part played by imperialist rivalries in leading to the outbreak of war. Lenin's contention that World War I was an imperialist conflict generated a long-running debate about whether it was the efflorescence of the highest stage of capitalism or of the highest stage of nationalism.[121] If the revisionist claim that the imperialist dynamic retained its momentum after 1918 is accepted, without being shackled by Lenin's particular argument, it is logical to explore the possibility that continuing imperialist rivalries played an important part in the outbreak of World War II.

Economic distress and political instability spurred the newly saddled men on horseback and their equivalents to seek national solidarity and personal popularity in adventurous solutions beyond their borders. There followed what contemporary commentators categorized as a global struggle between the "haves" and the "have-nots."[122] The division was not, as might be thought, one that separated the rich from the poor, but one that distinguished countries that possessed colonies from those that did not. Colonies conferred international status. They boosted depressed national egos by providing evidence of the superiority of the colonizers. They were thought to offer remedies for the acute economic ailments of the time. The "haves" presided over empires and enjoyed access to protected markets, which they closed to others. The "have-nots" were those without colonies who had lost the peace by being defeated in war or by being denied the spoils of victory. The result was an increasingly belligerent diplomatic and commercial struggle as the "have-nots," principally Germany, Italy, and Japan, sought to gain territory or influence in countries that remained outside protected imperial blocs.[123]

The road to war was paved with bad intentions. German aggression, which brought conflict to Europe in 1939, is conventionally taken to mark the start of World War II. From an imperialist perspective, however, there is a case for claiming that world war began in East Asia in 1937, when Japan invaded China.[124] This episode followed others in the non-Western world that pointed in the same direction. Japan's annexation

of Manchuria in 1931 provided a precedent for land-grabbing that the
major powers either condoned or overlooked. Success in Manchuria encouraged Japan to make bolder moves that resulted in the Second Sino-
Japanese War, at which point the Western powers and the Soviet Union
had to make diplomatic and strategic dispositions with the prospect of
war in East Asia in mind.[125] Meanwhile, Italy's invasion of Abyssinia
in 1935 reverberated throughout the colonial world. Besides stirring the
spirit of the Italian nation at a time of general depression, revenge for
the defeat at Adowa in 1897 advertised the fact that imperial ambitions
remained a vibrant force in international affairs well after 1914.[126] The
other imperial powers allowed the event to pass unchecked, despite
statements of condemnation and attempts to impose sanctions.[127] Failure to control Italian aggression inflamed nationalist feelings in the British and French colonies and prompted demonstrations and riots in African American communities in the United States.[128] Italy gained a brief
and ultimately costly victory; the League of Nations lost its remaining
credibility; the "have" powers added to the bill they would be called on
to pay after the war.

Imperial commitments featured prominently in the controversial
policy of appeasement that the British and the French adopted to deal
with the imperialist claims of the "have-not" powers.[129] The empire had
long performed a reciprocal function in British strategy: its acquisition
greatly strengthened Britain's position in fending off larger, predatory
continental powers; its defense called for adroit diplomacy in maintaining a balance of power in Europe.[130] Diplomatic setbacks in peacetime,
like defeat in battle, damaged the prestige of the imperial powers and
loosened their grip on imperial and world events. In the 1930s, as Italy
moved closer to Germany, Britain abandoned its traditional balancing
policy and adopted a bilateral approach aimed at compensating the
"have-not" powers. The shift to the new policy, long known as "appeasement," occurred in 1937, when Neville Chamberlain, the new prime minister, took charge of foreign policy.[131]

Appeasement was an imperial form of crisis management.[132] The
imperial mentality had survived World War I unscathed, even though
the means of realizing imperial ambitions had diminished. Chamberlain
took it for granted that he had the right to act like Lord Salisbury in disposing of other people's territory for the purpose of safeguarding Britain
and its empire. After 1935, he explored various proposals advanced by
the Foreign Office for offering Germany colonies in Africa in the hope of
keeping peace in Europe.[133] He took care, nevertheless, not to surrender
British territory: his idea was to return parts of the former German col-

onies supplemented by segments of Africa assigned to Belgium and Portugal. Chamberlain's attitude and approach were widely shared. Leading imperialists were prepared to give ground in central Europe as the price of strengthening the empire.[134] The dominions were solidly behind the policy of appeasement and Britain needed their support in the event that war overtook negotiations to preserve peace. The City of London was anxious to keep the peace to safeguard its considerable financial interests in the have-not nations.[135]

Chamberlain also had his eye on compelling economic considerations. He bought time because he could not afford to buy arms. Although public opinion had become uneasy about Britain's defensive capacity by the mid-1930s, the level of anxiety had yet to reach taxing point.[136] The concern in political and official circles was that rapid rearmament might lead to instability by provoking inflation or burdensome taxation at a time of high unemployment, and damage the economy by widening the balance-of-payments deficit. The view from all angles was unattractive; the outcome, if pessimistic predictions were met, might be the collapse of Britain's position as head of a great empire.

The United States added its considerable weight to Chamberlain's already heavy burdens. As relations in continental Europe deteriorated, Britain was obliged to turn to the United States for diplomatic support in the hope of deterring Germany from further aggressive action. The United States was unresponsive. The Anglo-Saxon alliance had lost much of the harmony that had once accompanied international equality. Chamberlain, who was deeply suspicious of the United States, was not the man to mend the fence; Roosevelt, who regarded Chamberlain as a "slippery" politician "playing the usual game of the British, peace at any price," was not inclined to lend him a hammer and nails.[137]

Slanted opinions on both sides derived from substantial policy differences. Hostility toward Britain increased in the United States after the British adopted imperial protection and created a sterling bloc. As the largest foreign country trading with the British Empire, the United States suffered from imperial protection after 1932; as the leading protagonist of the gold standard, Washington wanted to draw Britain out of the sterling bloc and into gold at a fixed exchange rate. Britain could not make these concessions without damaging and perhaps even unraveling the empire. If appeasement succeeded, the British could preserve the empire without going cap in hand to the United States. If, on the other hand, territorial concessions failed to satisfy the have-nots, the British would be forced to appeal to the United States for material support, in which case Roosevelt would hold the hammer and might use it to break up the empire. Even this tempting prospect did not guarantee that the United States would rally to the cause of freedom in Europe if it meant supporting Britain. As late as February 1939, Roosevelt still thought that Britain's problem was a lack of will rather than of means. "What the British need today," he wrote, "is a good stiff grog, inducing not only the desire to save civilization but the continued belief that they can do it."[138] Chamberlain certainly needed the grog, if only to obliterate Roosevelt's breezy assertion that the problems facing the British could be overcome simply by exercising mind over matter.

The outbreak of war in Europe in September 1939 confirmed the failure of appeasement. With the fall of France in the following year, one of the two great European empires was disabled; the other was delivered into the hands of the United States. The leading authorities on the subject are on firm ground in concluding that 1940 rather than 1918 represents the point at which the United States, the heir apparent, began to acquire its onerous inheritance.[139] From an imperial perspective, however, December 7, 1941 is a more appropriate date. That was the day of "infamy," as Roosevelt called it, when Japan, one of the "have-not" powers with imperialist ambitions in East Asia and the Pacific, bombed Pearl Harbor.[140] This action caused the United States, one of the "have" powers, to end its isolation and declare war, initially to defend one of its own colonies, Hawai'i. Coincidentally, it was in 1941, too, that Dean Acheson joined the Department of State as an Assistant Secretary. He was present 'at the creation," not only of the postwar world, but also at the moment when his elevated office in the neighborhood of Foggy Bottom in Washington gave him a clear view of the end of isolation, the beginning of the transfer of power from Britain to the United States, and the first dramatic indications, in the heat of sudden battle, of the burdens that would shortly accompany great-power status.[141]

The story of World War II is a well-known and frequently told chronicle of the triumph of allied resources and resolve.[142] Amidst inevitable disputes over strategy and timing, the coalition for victory stayed the course. There is, however, an equally well attested but less publicized aspect of the conflict: a contest between Britain and the United States over the fate of the empire and the shape of the postwar order. After the failure of appeasement, the British entered the war knowing that they needed material support from the United States if they were to survive the imminent threat from the Axis powers and retain the empire as a viable enterprise. After the disaster at Pearl Harbor, the United States entered the war primarily to defeat the Axis powers, but also to dismantle imperial protection and the sterling bloc, and ultimately to place Britain's colonies under international control.[143]

Early negotiations between the two allies bridged these divergent positions without reconciling them.[144] In March 1941, Britain and the United States entered into a Lend-Lease Agreement that delivered ships, munitions, and food to Britain in exchange for allowing the United States access to bases in the British Empire, principally in the West Indies and Newfoundland.[145] The supplies were vital to the war effort; the concessions gave the United States a foothold in neighboring British colonies.[146] At this stage in the conflict, Roosevelt still hoped that material assistance to the countries resisting Germany would be sufficient to keep the United States out of the war. Churchill, however, continued to angle for a stronger, more direct declaration of support. In August, the two leaders produced the Atlantic Charter, which set out the principles that were to govern the peace settlement, even though the United States had yet to enter the war.[147] In return for drawing the United States toward combatant status, Churchill was forced to widen the breaches in the walls of Britain's imperial fortress. He endorsed the principle of self-determination and reduced restrictions on U.S. trade with the empire. Even so, it was not until December, when Pearl Harbor was bombed, that there was sufficient support in the United States for a declaration of war.

Heartening news was swiftly followed by dispiriting headlines: in February 1942, Singapore fell to the Japanese and opened the way for the invasion of Burma and India. Once again, it seemed that the British Empire was doomed. The only question remaining was whether the hands around its throat would be those of its current Atlantic ally or those of its former Asian ally. The assailants had inside help. Gandhi's "Quit India" movement brought turmoil in pursuit of its demand for immediate independence; Subhas Chandra Bose's Indian National Army undertook guerrilla operations as a prelude to assisting a Japanese-led invasion. Once again, however, Whitehall's escapologists astounded the audience, though this time they could only loosen the shackles rather than discard them. The Foreign Office could do little to modify the commercial undertaking given to the United States; as a result, Britain's external trade suffered for the rest of the war.[148] Churchill, however, displaying characteristic *chutzpah*, stamped a wholly British interpretation on the Atlantic Charter by announcing that self-determination meant self-government, not independence, and was applicable to states occupied by the Axis powers rather than to the British Empire. Shortly afterward, in answer to many fervent prayers, the fortunes of war turned in Britain's favor and boosted its bargaining position and morale: in November 1942, Lieutenant-General Bernard Montgomery defeated German and Italian forces in North Africa at the battle of El Alamein.

By this time, too, Roosevelt had accepted that more than a "stiff grog" was needed to hold the line against fascism, and that an assault on the British Empire, if pressed too hard, would weaken Britain's effectiveness as a wartime ally. In this matter, sentiment reinforced strategy. Despite the persistence of an assertive strain of Anglophobia in the United States, political leaders on both sides of the Atlantic shared an unquestioned belief in the innate superiority of the Anglo-Saxon "race."[149] Roosevelt and his Secretary of State, Cordell Hull, doubted that colonial subjects were ready for self-government.[150] Personal commitment and rhetorical necessity prompted Roosevelt in 1942 to express support for Indian protests against British rule; racial assumptions and exigent realities ensured that U.S. policy took an increasingly cautious, evolutionary approach to the demands of colonial nationalists.[151] Roosevelt's restraint gave the British a free hand in suppressing the Quit India movement, which they did by applying a well-seasoned combination of coercion and mass detentions. Meanwhile, the Indian National Army lost momentum in 1944, when the Japanese were defeated in Burma.[152] At the Yalta Conference held in February 1945, Roosevelt accepted Churchill's request that the Allies should be allowed to retain their colonies after the war.

THE SECOND COLONIAL OCCUPATION

At the end of the war, the United States emerged as the dominant economic and military power in the West and was finally in a position to act on its anti-imperial sentiments seemingly untrammeled by the need to bolster its wartime allies. Roosevelt's unexpected successor as president, Harry S. Truman, while sharing his predecessor's belief in the providential mission of the Anglo-Saxon "race," was also eager to establish the leadership of the American branch of the tribe. Britain, on the other hand, had suffered huge material and human losses. The country was heavily in debt to the United States and to the empire, which had contributed to the war effort in exchange for credits that were eligible for redemption once peace was restored. These credits, called sterling balances, were seven times larger in 1945 than Britain's gold and dollar reserves.[153] Since Britain's external trade had been reduced to less than one-third of its prewar value and the City of London was constrained by a shortage of funds, the prospect of meeting these obligations was remote.[154] France, which stood outside the Anglo-Saxon club, was in an even worse position, having been defeated, occupied, and despoiled, and having lost control of her most valuable colonies in Indochina and North Africa. Both countries, though victors in the war, were supplicants in the peace.

Britain's hope that wartime support would be extended was doused in August 1945, when Truman abruptly ended Lease-Lend, and instead offered a loan tied to conditions that first twisted and then knotted the lion's tail. William S. Clayton, the Vice-Chairman of the U.S. negotiating team, viewed the occasion as an opportunity "to force the British to give up the sterling area, abandon imperial preference and eliminate quotas and exchange controls."[155] The eventual agreement, reached despite Keynes's formidable negotiating skills, bound Britain to liberalize imperial trade and open the sterling area.[156] Leopold Amery, writing as a lifelong defender of the British lion, emitted a roar of protest: "the British Empire is the oyster which this loan is to prise open. Each part of it is to be swallowed separately, to become a field for American industrial exploitation, a tributary of American finance, and, in the end, an American dependency."[157] It was about time, he asserted, that the British government issued its own declaration of independence.

Britain's new Labor government felt Amery's pain but was not in a position to respond as he had urged. American influence—from GIs to canned spam, sliced bread, and "movies"—had become irresistible; American power—from the atomic bomb to the gold reserves in Fort Knox—had become unanswerable.[158] It was the pervasive presence of the United States after 1945, in Britain and throughout the world, that inspired Gallagher and Robinson to formulate their celebrated theory of informal empire, though their interest lay in applying it to British expansion in the nineteenth century rather than to the appearance of an American superpower in their own time.[159] If, to adopt their insight, empires end when the periphery takes over the center, the eager representatives of the former mainland colonies had arrived in the right place at the right time. Yet, this episode, too, had an unexpected ending: after 1945, the British Empire experienced what has been called a second colonial occupation.[160] Simultaneously, France engaged in a recolonization of her overseas territories. Sudden death at the hands of a coalition of the willing, led by American policy-makers and supported by colonial nationalists, was averted. Decolonization, when it came, arose from developments in the postwar world that had not yet revealed themselves fully in 1945, even to well-placed observers.

Part of the explanation of this unexpected turn of events lay in the determination of Britain and France to remain in charge of what they still regarded as their imperial mission. World War II, like its predecessor, had increased the visibility of the British Empire and underlined its value to the war effort. Even as bombs were falling on London, senior officials in Whitehall were planning, not whether to return to parts of the Asian empire lost to Japan, but when and on what terms Britain would do so.[161] The French Empire, on the other hand, had lost both visibility and value, but still remained a talisman without which national self-respect would be lost and the recovery of grandeur would be impossible. Both empires, once regained, were to be refurbished and given new leases on life. Reforming ideas that had come to the fore in the 1930s and been given structure, content, and impetus in Britain by Beveridge and Keynes were adapted for imperial purposes.[162] This time, there was to be no bonfire of controls. Instead, the machinery of government, much enlarged during the war, was to be redirected to create a brave new world of full employment and enhanced social welfare. Export versions were to become development policies for the colonies in the postwar era.

The concept of a reformed and refashioned colonial empire became operational because it had broad bipartisan support. The Labour government that came to power in Britain in 1945 held no brief for extravagant territorial ambitions. The existing empire was already a considerable challenge, not least because Britain, with American cooperation, had been able to recover its lost colonies in Asia and retain the former mandated territories in Africa and the Middle East.[163] Nevertheless, Clement Attlee and his colleagues accepted the duties of stewardship and saw in the empire an opportunity to demonstrate the universal applicability of their development ideals.[164] Sentiment played a part in the process. The imperial mentality shaped the minds of even Labor's policy-makers. Attlee, though scarcely a militarist, felt the pull of an empire that had been part of his own life. It was as natural for the new government to view the occupation of Germany as an exercise in colonial administration as it was self-evident that officials from India should be assigned the task of introducing a form of indirect rule that would carry the civilizing mission to the heart of darkness on the European mainland.[165] Imperial loyalties, enhanced by shared contributions and losses during the war, also percolated down the social scale and across the nation, forming bonds of unity that helped to ease the grind of digging for peace.[166] Sentiment and idealism had political underpinnings.[167] Influential figures, such as Jan Christian Smuts, argued that empires, unlike nation-states, had a proven capacity to protect the rights of minorities and therefore had a constructive role to play in the postwar order. Accordingly, the British carried forward, enlarged, and publicized the idea of the Commonwealth as a comprehensive supra-state organization.[168]

Public opinion clearly favored retaining the empire in France, too.[169] Even the Communist Party, which was part of the government in 1946–1947, placed the idea of "Greater France" before the principle of international solidarity of the working classes. In 1946, the French produced a complement to the British Commonwealth, the *Union française*, which allowed the colonies to exchange their subordinate status for the more dignified designation of "*territoires d'outre-mer.*"[170] The concept of *La Plus Grande France* had gained currency during the interwar period as a means of supplementing French security.[171] The overseas territories would add 60 million people to the 40 million in the metropole; supplies of food would help France to become self-sufficient.

These ideas lacked a coating of altruism and could not be implemented without additional funding. The Union française refurbished the concept of Greater France, inserted egalitarian principles, and offered substantial finance. If nation-states had incubated the aggression that had led to war, so the argument went, alternative political systems, which included empires, might be better fitted to keep the peace. Empires, however, had to become more inclusive. Reform was needed to forestall demands for independence. Subjects might even have to become citizens.[172] Citizens might then seek full equality, in which case assimilation would replace association, and centralization might overwhelm claims for devolution. In these ways, deliberations over the structures of the Commonwealth and the Union raised fundamental questions about the concept and composition of both nation-state and empire that were to become even more taxing in the coming decades.[173]

Britain and France needed their empires to help them recover from the depredations of war. Europe was devastated and offered no immediate solution to pressing economic problems. Both countries planned to use their colonies to earn the dollars needed to repay their debts to the United States and, in the British case, to creditors in the empire.[174] Protective tariffs were extended into the postwar era, as was the Sterling Area, which was joined by the Franc Zone in 1945.[175] Foodstuffs, raw materials, and minerals from imperial sources (and the wider sterling area), would help recovery at home, earn dollars in other markets, improve the balance of payments, and ultimately release Britain and France from dependence on the United States.[176] If these targets could be met, and if the empires could be turned into free associations in the guise of the Commonwealth and the Union française, Britain and France could re-establish themselves as credible forces in world affairs.[177] They could then hope to act on equal terms with the United States and the Soviet Union, and use their unrivaled experience to mediate and moderate relations between the two great rivals. Such were the ambitions that arose from the debris of war.

In 1948, these prospects were sufficiently promising to carry Britain's Foreign Secretary, Ernest Bevin, a step beyond realism: "if only we pushed on & developed Africa," he noted, "we could have the U.S. dependent on us, & eating out of our hand in four or five years."[178] Nevertheless, there were castles on the ground as well as in the air, and these were the bases for Britain's longer-term aim, which was to re-enter a free, or freer, trading world, where the potential for growth was almost unlimited and where the City of London in particular would be able to resume its former role as the chief financier of international trade. If the transition could be managed effectively, there was a chance that sterling could repel the dollar before it became almighty. In the short term, however, the ambition would remain in committee unless Britain continued to benefit from imperial preference, and the Sterling Area was retained to defend the value of the pound.

These ambitions were wholly contrary to declared U.S. policy. At the end of the war, and without pausing to reflect on its own long-standing commitment to protection, the United States planned to create an open and durable international economy to replace the closed and fragile systems that had disintegrated with such catastrophic consequences at the end of the 1930s. The Bretton Woods Agreements in 1944 established the key institutions (the International Monetary Fund and the World Bank) that were designed to oversee a stable international monetary system based on the dollar, which in turn was linked at a fixed rate to gold.[179] The aim of Washington's diplomacy was to use the financial resources of the United States as a crowbar to open protected trading regimes throughout the world, and especially major markets in Europe. However, once it became clear that neither the victors nor the vanquished in Europe were able to swim without armbands, diplomatic support for a new world of open trade had to be modified.

Britain provided confirmation of this emerging realization in 1947, when the attempt to make sterling freely convertible, in accordance with the conditions of the American loan granted in 1945, ended in disaster almost as soon as it began.[180] The demand for dollars was so great that Britain's reserves were drained within a few weeks, at which point the Labor government was forced to re-impose exchange controls. In the event, the Bretton Woods Agreements did not enable the dollar to supersede sterling as the numerator of the international monetary system.[181] Despite its vulnerability, sterling still accounted for about half of all international transactions in 1950.[182] The continued stability of the pound, as the United States came to appreciate, was vital to the operation of the Bretton Woods system, and gave Washington a compelling reason for helping to keep it afloat.

The nerve-racking convertibility crisis convinced even skeptical observers in Washington that the British were not, after all, bluffing when they claimed that imperial protection and the Sterling Area were vital to the country's postwar recovery. Britain's desperate economic situation called for measures that harmonized with President Truman's interventionist policy, adopted earlier in 1947, of providing material support for countries in Europe that were threatened by communism. At the same time, George Marshall, Truman's Secretary of State, announced complementary plans for supplying substantial financial aid to assist the recovery of the world economy. The greater part of the aid was disbursed under what became known in 1948 as the Marshall Plan, and was directed to Europe, though a significant proportion was then reassigned to the colonies of the imperial powers.[183] Britain, the largest single recipient, received more than 25 percent of the total funds distributed between 1948 and 1951.

The Marshall Plan, which in essence was a scheme for recycling America's huge surplus of dollars, had two aims. Its economic purpose was to boost Europe's recovery, thereby restoring the continent to its former position as the largest foreign market for American goods. Its political purpose was to protect what had become known as the "free world" from the spreading stain of communism. The military component of the new strategy was put in place in 1949 with the creation of the North Atlantic Treaty Organization (NATO), which, in the words of its first Secretary General, Lord Ismay, was designed to "keep the Russians out, the Americans in and the Germans down."[184] Ismay's crisp formulation drew on his extensive experience in managing allies and enemies in the empire. He began his career as an officer in the Indian Army, and was closely involved in the affairs of the subcontinent right down to the partition of India in 1947.[185]

These developments caused Washington to call off its pursuit of the wounded British lion. If Britain were to play a part as an effective ally in the new battle against communism, it had to be allowed to retain the empire.[186] The same argument applied to France. The communists were ejected from government in 1947 and were repressed, as far as possible, in the colonies.[187] France then engaged in colonial wars, which were largely funded by the United States, to reassert control over Indochina and Algeria.[188] Imperial protection, the Sterling Area, and the Franc Zone all survived. In exchange, the United States established a line of defense against communism in Europe and gained access to a string of ready-made military bases across the globe. In these ways, the set of largely unanticipated events that became known as the Cold War played their part in saving the European empires from the demise their American ally had planned for them. The advent of the Cold War also dissipated the Anglophobia that had vexed Anglo-American relations intermittently since 1783.[189] Washington remained suspicious of France because General Charles de Gaulle showed disconcerting signs of adopting an independent foreign policy. The British, however, fell into line, if not always with military precision. With Britain so clearly a cooperative junior partner in the "special relationship," the United States no longer had anything to fear from its former overlord.

The "second colonial occupation" that followed was launched with an extraordinary degree of enthusiasm and commitment. The British Empire was to be revived; the French Empire was to be raised from the dead. Revisionist accounts of this final burst of European imperial energies focus on the contribution made by colonies in Asia and sub-Saharan Africa. However, the imperialists of 1945 had a much wider vision, which included, in the British case, old colonies of white settlement, and in France the substantial and highly valued settlement in Algeria. Britain's dominions, however, had gained rights of self-government, whereas Algeria had been administered as an integral part of France since 1848. The brutal conflict to keep Algeria French is well known; the place of the old dominions in Britain's restored empire has long been underestimated or even omitted from standard histories of the period.[190] Most historians have taken the view that, by 1945, the story of the dominions was best told as one of new nation-states rather than of continuing components of empire.[191]

Yet, in 1945 the old dominions had yet to achieve effective independence. Unlike colonies, they could not be directed to serve British interests, but they had a keen self-interest in preserving the ties that bound them to what was still referred to as the 'mother country.' Cultural affinities sustained connections that were independent of legislation or imperial command. Bonds of "kith and kin" remained strong: in 1945, settlers in the dominions were still almost exclusively British in origin (with the partial exception of South Africa). After the war, successive British governments sought to nourish the relationship by sending forth, in Kipling's phrase, "the best ye breed," and subsidizing emigration to the dominions. The range of resources and the advanced state of development among members of Britain's wider Anglo-world offered attractive openings for investment; their commitment to the Sterling Area (with the exception of Canada), and abiding ties of overseas trade continued to orient them toward Britain. The British link survived even in matters of defense, which had prompted Australia and New Zealand in particular to turn to the United States during the darkest days of the war. In 1945, the dominions occupied a central place in Britain's grand plan for a harmonious Commonwealth of free nations whose instinct, whether through inheritance or training, would incline them to continue to defer to the home country. Such was the hope of the magicians who conjured life into the postwar empire. They were short on material assets but long on ambition: the revitalized empire was the designated means of bringing the two together.

The masses had spoken, too, in Britain and across Europe. Postwar governments everywhere scrambled to meet the pent-up demand for improved employment opportunities and welfare provision after long years of deprivation. The machinery of government, greatly enlarged during the war, was applied to the urgent needs of peace. Military language was mobilized for the task ahead: there was to be a "war" on want and a "battle" for food. Comprehensive, government-inspired plans were formulated to lift colonial export economies to new levels of output and productivity. Vast sums of public money were advanced for the purpose; expanded numbers of colonial administrators and technical personnel were trained and dispatched to oversee the creation of the new imperial order. A novel subject, development economics, made its appearance.[192] Political reform complemented economic planning. An updated "dual mandate" offered colonial subjects greater political participation and an explicit agreement that self-government was the ultimate goal of policy. After 1945, the future of the reinvigorated civilizing mission depended on the ability of the colonial powers to reconcile two imperatives that would otherwise collide: the determination to retain central control of enlarged political systems, and the need to make them more democratic. Imperial legitimacy had been enforced at gunpoint: could it also be achieved by consent?

Britain and France placed their bets on an affirmative answer and leapt into the political unknown. For nearly a decade after World War II, it appeared possible, at least in the eyes of policy-makers, to satisfy both parties to the new imperial contract. A "big push" for colonial development, which London and Paris still visualized as consisting of exports of raw materials, began as soon as the war ended. In 1945, Britain renewed and greatly enlarged the Colonial Development & Welfare Act of 1940. France devised an even more ambitious policy under the acronym

FIDES, which was responsible for investing more capital (in real terms) in French Africa between 1947 and 1959 than had been invested during the previous sixty-five years.[193] Loans and grants, assigned in large part to improve transport and agriculture, primed the pump. An immense flow of colonial exports flooded Western markets. The most valuable products included major dollar-earners—such as rubber, tin, bauxite, and copper—and dollar-savers—such as petroleum, timber, and a variety of foodstuffs, notably cocoa, palm-oil and kernels, and groundnuts. Supplementary mechanisms, particularly marketing boards (*caisses de stabilisation*), enabled Britain and France to buy colonial produce at submarket prices; the devaluation of the pound in 1949 gave a further boost to sterling-based exports.

By the start of the 1950s, the success of the export drive, combined with imperial protection and the adroit management of the sterling area, had closed Britain's dollar gap and helped to produce a surplus on the balance of payments. Economic recovery had reached the point where it was possible for Britain to plan on extending overseas trade and finance beyond the borders of imperial preference and the Sterling Area. The French record was far less encouraging.[194] Trade with the empire increased, but mainly because it was heavily subsidized by French taxpayers, who also funded the trade deficits incurred by the overseas territories. Neither settlers nor investors were attracted to the empire. Tourists came—and went; public loans, financed ultimately by taxpayers, supplied 80 percent of all capital flows to the empire between 1945 and 1958.[195] The franc zone became a burden; the dollar gap widened. The costs of empire contributed to France's own balance-of-payments deficits.

The big push on the economic front was intended to complement political reforms aimed at giving colonial subjects a stake in the new empire. The proposed transformation of empire into Commonwealth was partly presentational and designed to appease anti-colonial sentiment in Britain, France, and the United States, and in the colonies themselves, but it had substance, too, as a way of recognizing the progress made in applying egalitarian principles. After the war, the Colonial Secretary in the Labor government, Arthur Creech Jones, pressed ahead with policies designed to re-equip the colonies with political institutions based on the British model.[196] Representative government was to be extended to provincial and local government and, in time, which policy-makers thought they had, to central government. A large part of the welfare component of the funding made available after 1945 went into education. The reformed empire needed to produce professionals and technocrats who would be capable of running a modern state. The expectation in London was that the skilled elites who emerged from new universities and colleges would supply a new generation of political leaders whose self-interest would prompt them to cooperate with Britain within the Commonwealth. Self-government, as the Colonial Office saw it, was now inevitable; the future debate was about timing. Further ahead, which few policy-makers had time to ponder amidst the pressures of immediate events, independence was a possibility but not one placed high on the agenda.

France followed a broadly similar policy, beginning with the reforms announced by General de Gaulle at the Brazzaville Conference in 1944. The constitution of the Republic, however, presented conceptual and legal difficulties for any policy of devolution. The French Republic, like the United States, was designed to be "one and indivisible." Colonies were ill-fitting additions to the constitution. The term "empire" was not in official use before the 1940s, and it was not until 1946 that the Fourth Republic introduced a wider imperial vision into the new French Union.[197] "Decolonization," when used by the Ministry for Overseas France, referred not to independence, but to reform and modernization within the French Union. Ultimately, if sovereignty was indivisible, progress had to be defined as successful assimilation leading to incorporation. Assimilation, however, was a slow and costly process. Moreover, rights of citizenship did not appeal to many subjects, and when granted could be exercised in favor of independence. The idea of reform opened prospects that the reformers had no means of controlling.[198]

Lofty calculations made in sedate corridors of power also had to take account of the unruly forces of colonial nationalism. Manifestations of the green uprising that had first appeared in the 1930s multiplied after 1945.[199] India had led the way in the 1920s and 1930s; Southeast Asia, the Middle East, and Africa followed in the 1940s. Protest ceased to be confined to sporadic, single-issue politics attached to particular regions or occupations, and was directed instead into permanent parties with aspirations for independence. Imperial policy had to steer a course between subordinating the empire to the needs of the metropole and embracing enough reform to appease anti-imperialist feelings at home and in the United States, while also making concessions to colonial nationalists.

White settlers in Britain's dominions had won reforms and were beyond subordination; one million *colons* were determined to keep Algeria French. Political leaders in the dominions in the immediate postwar period were not militant separatists. They were still old-school "Greater Britons" who saw no contradiction between national and imperial loyalties.[200] Their attitude reflected the feelings of the majority of their electorates, who were in favor of upholding traditional ties with the "old country." Although dissenting voices could be heard, especially in South Africa and to some extent in Canada as well, white nationalists were unable to break free from the British connection. In 1948, South Africa demonstrated its independence in internal affairs by creating the formal structures of *apartheid*, but remained tied to Britain by its overseas trade, its need for foreign investment, and its membership of the Sterling Area.

The dependent empire presented a larger and more challenging problem. Some colonies were in revolt in 1945; others needed massive investment if they were to play their part in Europe's postwar recovery. The independence granted to India in 1947 (followed by Burma and Ceylon in 1948) was a dramatic development that brought nearly 200 years of British rule to a close.[201] Stalwart imperialists were shaken; a few were temporarily traumatized. Brigadier Enoch Powell, then a rising Conservative M.P. with an ambition to become Viceroy, was so shocked by the news of India's imminent independence that he spent a sleepless night pacing the streets of London.[202] Yet, the independence of India, momentous though it was, did not initiate a process of continuous decline that ended with the decolonization of the remaining African colonies in the 1960s. Withdrawal from empire occurred in two approximate phases: the first embraced India, Burma, and Palestine in 1947–1948; the second covered Malaya and the most important African countries between 1957 and 1963.

Although India had long been the centerpiece of the British Empire, her independence took a form that was broadly consistent with British interests. The upheaval caused by the war had made the subcontinent ungovernable and had destroyed the contrived legitimacy of colonial rule.[203] Yet, Enoch Powell's personal disappointment did not symbolize a wider imperial disaster. Independence reduced the pressure on Britain's defense budget, offered a concession to anti-colonial sentiment in Britain and the United States, and renewed the prospect of working with nationalists instead of against them. The opportunity was embraced like the renewal of an old friendship. When Jawaharlal Nehru, India's prime minister from 1947 to 1964, described himself as being "the last Englishman to rule in India," the tone of self-mockery contained a fundamental truth.[204] Nehru, like Robert Menzies in Australia, was the last of a generation of leaders in the old empire who venerated the system they sought to change. Nehru could not be manipulated, but in matters of geopolitics he could be trusted to pursue a style of cooperative neutrality that helped the West during the most difficult years of the Cold War. While he lived, so did the British connection. In 1955, the U.S. State Department ruefully observed of relations with India that "the British have a certain advantage over us in the form of Mr. Nehru's adoration of English civilization and individuals."[205]

Moreover, Britain's material losses from India's independence were minimal. The two great concerns at the end of the war were that India would stand aside from the Commonwealth, the organization that carried Britain's hopes for a new imperial compact, and would demand early repayment of her sterling credits.[206] Adroit negotiation settled both issues. A formula was agreed whereby India would become a republic within the Commonwealth and claim her sterling balances in an orderly manner that would not threaten Britain's reserves. By 1947, India's trade and investment ties with Britain had lost much of their historic significance. After the war, India made only a limited contribution to Britain's dollar-earning priority. By then, too, financial relations between the two countries had been transformed. Before the war, India's indebtedness to Britain had slowed her progress toward self-government; by 1945, India had become a major creditor. In 1947, Britain no longer worried about debts that India might not repay; any concerns were on India's side should Britain decide to renege on its obligations. The deal struck in 1947, notwithstanding the upheaval caused by partition, enabled the emollient guardians of empire to claim that they were acting in accordance with long-established principles of trusteeship. The rights attached to imperial rule were justified by duties, which involved a broad commitment to progress. What Canada achieved in 1867, India exceeded in 1947. As seen from London, it was all in the master plan.

The empire was not relinquished in 1947, but repositioned. Malaya, the Middle East, and Africa became the key components of the reformed empire-Commonwealth. The French Empire was repositioned too, but by force of arms. At the beginning of the 1950s, unheard voices in Paris, including that of François Mitterand, urged France to withdraw from Indo-China and consolidate her position in Africa. The war in Asia, however, was fought to defeat in 1954, at which point national prestige and the morale of the French Army determined that a stand had to be made in Algeria, where a further defeat left General de Gaulle with no choice but to concede independence in 1962.[207] This searing experience influenced the more conciliatory approach that de Gaulle took toward France's territories in sub-Saharan Africa, which followed a negotiated route to independence in 1960.[208]

Malaya, the Middle East, and Africa acquired enhanced importance as crucial dollar-earning and dollar-saving components of Britain's post-war recovery plan. Malaya produced rubber and tin; the Middle East had vast oil reserves; Africa supplied foodstuffs and minerals.[209] British policy in these regions aimed at pressing ahead with economic development in the hope that the benefits to the colonies would be sufficient to soften the demand for radical constitutional change and allow time for a new generation of amenable leaders to emerge. The strategy required a degree of calibration that colonial realities quickly made obsolete. The outbreak of guerrilla warfare in Malaya in 1948 obliged the colonial government to exchange political negotiation for full-scale military action. Strikes and protests across the tropical colonies, notably Nigeria's first general strike in 1945 and extensive riots in the Gold Coast in 1948, forced the Colonial Office to accelerate its preferred timetable for constitutional change. In the Middle East, Britain withdrew from the upheaval in Palestine in 1948 to preserve its more important relations with the wider Arab world, where support for the Middle East potentates who guarded vital reserves of oil was a priority.[210] The hope, soon to be disappointed, was that they would also be able to control the flow of support for nationalist elements that was beginning to make its appearance.

In all these regions and associated strategic points, such as Singapore, Aden, the Suez Canal, and Malta, the Labour government defended British interests with Churchillian determination, a policy that Churchill himself endorsed when he returned to office in 1951. Military force was applied in Malaya from 1948 to suppress a full-scale guerrilla uprising (misleadingly called an "emergency"); a huge garrison was maintained in Egypt down to 1954 to ensure the security of the Suez Canal; a large counter-insurgency operation was mounted in Kenya from 1952 to deal with the Mau Mau rebellion.[211] The military option was costly and produced unfavorable publicity elsewhere in the empire and in the United States. The pacific alternative, which was generally more feasible in colonies that were largely devoid of settlers, lay in negotiating progressive policies with nationalist leaders. The difficulty here was that the priority attached to Britain's own recovery pushed the needs of the colonies down the policy agenda. The Treasury's preoccupation with dollar-earning exports and dollar-saving imports trumped the Colonial Office's plans to develop colonial manufactures and increase welfare spending.[212] Exports of British manufactures were promoted; colonial imports of often cheaper foreign goods were restricted. By 1954, Sir Robert Hall, the government's chief economic adviser, could reflect on the success of the postwar arrangements with considerable satisfaction: "we could scarcely have done better," he commented, "if we had intended to exploit the Colonies."[213] Even as he wrote, however, the political costs of the exercise, which stoked resentment in the colonies, were rising to levels that would soon be beyond control.

LIBERATION—COLONIAL STYLE

In 1945, Britain's stars were more or less in alignment. Imperial policy reflected a bipartisan commitment to retain and develop the empire, which was considered vital to the country's postwar recovery. Colonial nationalism, though gathering speed, had still to reach the broad level of support needed to make it a compelling influence on imperial policy. Exceptions, when they arose, were dealt with by repressive policies in the expectation that "agitators" and "terrorists" could be tamed or eliminated. The United States fortuitously abandoned its long-standing anticolonial stance and gave its support to the European colonial powers in the interests of winning the Cold War. In the course of the 1950s, all three variables were reordered in ways that brought independence to the colonies. Exactly when this transformation occurred is a controversial matter that can be answered satisfactorily only from the records of the history of particular colonies.[214] There were leaders and laggards: the Netherlands pulled out of Indonesia in 1949; Portugal battled on until 1974 in a costly attempt to hold on to its large African colonies; various islands and enclaves remain colonies even today. Nevertheless, there is now a broad consensus that the turning point for Britain and France, the most important of the Western empires, came in the mid-1950s.[215] The defeat of France in Indo-China in 1954 was followed by independence for Morocco and Tunisia in 1956, French West Africa in 1960, and Algeria in 1962. Britain conceded independence to Malaya and the Gold Coast in 1957, and Nigeria in 1960. By 1964 the British flag had been replaced by new colors in nearly all the remaining African colonies, as well as in the West Indies.

Conservative governments, which were in power between 1951 and 1963, began by upholding Churchillian principles but ended by abandoning them.[216] The transition caused a great deal of soul-searching, much regret, and some defiance. Even today, unrealistic pretensions to great-power status live on in a ghostly revenge of history, which appears first to mesmerize and then to haunt governments in Britain and France, irrespective of party affiliations.[217] The power of illusion replaced the material bases of power in the empire and the Sterling Area, leaving only history and hope as fragile supports for future global ambitions. At the outset, the Conservatives sought to manage change by slowing the transition to self-government until the colonies had reached the point where, in the official language of the day, they were "viable" as independent states.[218] Viability was a term of portmanteau proportions: it could be filled with conditions that would always exceed the reach of nationalist leaders; it could also be emptied quickly if a rapid exit became necessary. By 1960, when the British Prime Minister, Harold Macmillan, delivered his famous "Wind of Change" speech in Cape Town, a gale was carrying the empire in unplanned directions. Macmillan's words were aimed at South Africa's system of apartheid, but Britain itself was running before the storm in search of shelter.

A gradual but profound change in the assessment of the costs and benefits of empire eroded the material support for imperial ambitions. By the mid-1950s, the empire had played its assigned, and heroic, part in rebuilding Britain after the war. Most colonial products were no longer in short supply; the dollar gap had been closed. With the end of the Korean War boom in 1953, prices paid for primary produce began a long decline that reduced purchasing power in the colonies and made them less valuable as importers of manufactures. Attitudes toward the wider Sterling Area underwent a similar evolution.[219] In the course of the 1950s, the credits held by members of the Sterling Area as claims on Britain had either been run down or were being phased out. The City of London wanted to lift exchange controls to take advantage of unrestricted global commercial opportunities. The Treasury, on the other hand, was keen to regulate capital movements to maintain the value of the pound and its status as a reserve currency, which reduced the government's borrowing costs. The struggle between these interests moved in favor of the City as the decade advanced, with the result that convertibility was restored in 1958. This outcome, however, exposed the fragility of Britain's economic base. It became increasingly clear that there were insufficient reserves to sustain sterling as a major world currency and that the cost of trying to do so outweighed the benefits. Defeat came in 1967, when sterling had to be devalued and several members of the Sterling Area chose not to follow Britain's lead.[220] In the course of the 1970s, the Area shrank, receded, and finally disappeared.

The underlying problem Britain faced, but never overcame, was its inability to generate the assets needed to support the pound as a reserve currency.[221] A wide-ranging review of policy commissioned by Anthony Eden, the Prime Minister, in 1956 concluded (even before the Suez crisis) that Britain had "ceased to be a first class power in material terms."[222] In the same year, Harold Macmillan, in his capacity as Chancellor of the

Exchequer, signaled his willingness to consider "shedding some of our burdens" within the empire.[223] The Suez crisis fully exposed Britain's pretensions to great-power status. The last veil dropped when the United States threatened to end its support for sterling unless Britain withdrew its troops; the scrambled retreat was a public humiliation observed throughout the empire.[224] In 1957, Macmillan, newly appointed as Prime Minister, commissioned a full audit of the empire, which showed that there were no longer compelling economic reasons for Britain to stay where it was unwelcome and that there were advantages to moving with the flow of events.[225] After 1945, British governments were committed to policies that would assure full employment and generous welfare provision. If a choice had to be made between domestic priorities and defending what was becoming seen as a lost cause, the empire would lose, and it did.

Nevertheless, Macmillan was determined to be, as he put it, the "remodeller" rather than the "liquidator" of the empire.[226] Accordingly, Britain pressed ahead with plans for self-government as a means of making friends and influencing people in the remaining imperial possessions. Despite the lack of material resources, Macmillan hoped that the British could still "exert our influence in other ways," especially by "living by our wits, as we had in earlier periods."[227] Neocolonialism was not planned in 1945 because decolonization was not then envisaged. The idea arose late in the day, when Britain lacked the substance that had stiffened its informal presence in the nineteenth century. By the 1960s, British "wits" were no longer able to supply the resources needed for exercising power in world affairs.[228]

Changes in material circumstances alone were insufficient to persuade the Conservative Party to favor decolonization. Visceral responses to the prospect, whether derived from ties of "kith and kin" or from a belief that "other races" were unfit for independence, held a substantial segment of the Party to its traditional commitment to the empire. Where kith and kin saw themselves as embattled minorities, as they did in Kenya, Southern Rhodesia, and Nyasaland, the home government felt obliged to support them. In South Africa, where ethnic ties were diluted by settlers of Afrikaner origin, economic and strategic considerations restrained Britain from supporting the black majority. White minorities were eventually removed from power after violent, costly, and increasingly unpopular struggles.[229] The costs, however, could no longer be borne at the level needed, as the defense "White Paper" indicated in 1957 and the decision in the following year to abandon the planned independent nuclear deterrent confirmed.[230] Moreover, the damaging publicity arising from military excesses during the various "emergencies" of the time alienated public support for colonial rule. By 1960, the "people's empire" that had emerged in 1945 from wartime solidarity had become the people's burden and an electoral liability rather than an asset.[231]

The options available to the imperial powers were increasingly constrained by the continuing development of colonial nationalism. In the 1940s, anti-colonial movements in the Middle East and Africa were unsure whether to focus on securing nationalism "in one country" or whether to direct their efforts toward designing larger pan-Islamic, pan-Arab, pan-African, or other forms of supranational unity. Kwame Nkrumah was the standard-bearer among those who sought to combine the two principles. Gandhi and Nehru, drawing on long experience, knew how difficult it was to hold even "mother India" together. As the 1950s advanced, political elites concentrated their energies on the more immediately practical goal of winning independence for existing countries, as defined by inherited colonial boundaries. They were well aware that they inhabited states, not nations, and that nation-building was a project for the future. Regions and localities had to be persuaded to acquire a larger loyalty; diaspora and other supranational religious and ethnic affiliations had to be attached to new reference points within the state. Accordingly, nationalist leaders shaped their opposition to colonial rule in ways calculated to foster domestic party loyalties and used their political organizations to eliminate local rivals. For the same reason, they opposed the efforts made by the colonial powers to perpetuate or create federal organizations because they threatened to weaken local bases, on which their political support depended.

The focus on securing independence within colonial borders increased the effectiveness of the resistance movements. Colonial policy indirectly assisted their progress. The development effort after World War II helped to integrate societies within individual colonies by creating a network of roads suitable for motor transport and by raising literacy levels. Improved communications enabled political parties to extend their reach; "spreading the word" made English and French part of the language of liberation. The revival of primary produce prices after the war also helped, despite the policy of the marketing boards in withholding a percentage of the price farmers would otherwise have received. Improved terms of trade put money in farmers' pockets and enabled them to contribute funds to local political parties and to buy, among other things, radios and newspapers that carried nationalist messages to the outer reaches of the colonies. By the late 1950s, too, a powerful demonstration effect was at work. As more colonies became independent, the remainder saw that what they thought was a remote possibility had become an immediate prospect. Some, indeed, even urged the Colonial Office to extend its timetable to enable them to be fully prepared for the responsibilities of independence. The Bandung Conference, held in 1955, was a particularly effective advertisement for the emerging global order. It was there that twenty-nine countries, representing half the world's population, came together in shared opposition to the continuing dominance of the "have" powers. The scale of the meeting and the sensitivity of the Free World to the needs of the Cold War ensured that, this time, the voices of "the underdogs of the human race," as one observer described them, would command attention.[232]

An equally important but far less publicized decolonization, so silent that historians have only recently recognized it, occurred elsewhere in the "white empire," as the old dominions began to look to themselves rather to the "mother country" for directions to their future.[233] The attempt after 1945 to restock the settler parts of the empire with emigrants from Britain achieved only limited success. The recipients confronted a dilemma: they could either maintain the British connection and the discriminatory racial legislation that accompanied it, or admit immigrants who were not British and perhaps not even white. Faced with a choice between maintaining racial purity at the expense of economic development with unlimited supplies of heterogeneous labor, the dominions chose the latter.

The decision was helped by a steady weakening of commercial ties with Britain and by the growth of regional connections: Canada's existing links with the United States strengthened in the postwar period; Australia and New Zealand developed new relationships with Japan and Southeast Asia.[234] The results were dramatic: in 1966 Asians accounted for 9 percent and 12 percent of all immigrants entering Australia and Canada respectively; in 1986, the figures were 43 percent and 42 percent.[235] A further regional development, the creation of the European Economic Community (EEC), accelerated these trends. Britain's decision to apply for membership of the EEC in 1961 gave the dominions an unexpected shock. The application failed, but the fact that it was made signaled Britain's intention of casting off from its imperial moorings and confirmed the need for the dominions to do the same.[236] By then, too, the last loyalist leaders had given way to a generation whose priorities reflected the new imperatives. Constitutional changes affecting citizenship and the monarchy completed the separation from the "old country." Cuts in Britain's defense budget obliged the dominions to provide their own security, often in association with the United States. Taken together, these developments shook established verities: the dominions could no longer be considered British, but had to develop distinct identities. What Australians referred to, memorably, as "cultural cringe" gave way to new expressions of creative autonomy.[237] Today, Australians cringe no more.

The third star in the imperial firmament, the United States, had also altered its position by the close of the 1950s.[238] By then, Washington had recognized that the European empires had served their purpose. European states, having recovered from the war, were strong enough to defend the Free World without imperial support, and strategic bases could be secured by negotiation or purchase without the need for extensive territorial commitments. More important still, the United States was becoming increasingly concerned at the failure of the European empires to contain militant nationalism. In 1945, the Allies anticipated that reformed, progressive empires would advertise the merits of the Western way of life. By the mid-1950s, amidst colonial wars, "emergencies," continuing unrest, and manifest poverty, the record had fallen far short of expectations. The shortfall mattered because the Cold War had entered a new phase of "competitive coexistence," which committed the Free World to demonstrate the superiority of Western systems of political economy. Greater progress was needed on all fronts if Soviet influence was to be kept at bay. Accordingly, in 1956, even before the Suez crisis, British and American officials agreed that the African colonies were to move "towards stable self-government or independence" as rapidly as possible, "in such a way that these governments are willing and able to preserve their economic and political ties with the West."[239] Fortunately for British policy, the view from Washington suited the new direction marked out by the Treasury's own assessment of Britain's future interests. As they changed places, sorcerer and apprentice combined in attempting to conjure a new relationship with the remaining constituents of empire.

France followed a similar course, but in reduced circumstances.[240] Like Britain, France hoped to harness colonial resources to serve the cause of postwar recovery in exchange for a package of reforms featuring increased development expenditure, greater political participation, and improved welfare programs. The policy had broad political support and was designed to strengthen the empire, not to dispose of it. The French Empire, however, was smaller and poorer than its British equivalent and became a burden rather than a benefit.[241] Even with financial help from the United States, the high cost of retaining the overseas territories weighed on the budget and helped to provoke the populist, anti-tax movement led by Pierre Poujade in the 1950s.[242] Britain's empire assisted its postwar recovery; France's empire delayed it. France contracted an awkward marriage of convenience with Germany partly because the imperial option lacked viability. Britain divorced the empire only after it had served its purpose, and so missed both the wedding and the party. Exit matched entry: the French Empire was a mixture of grandeur and commerce from the outset, whereas the "nation of shopkeepers" kept a sharp eye on the accounts.

Both countries met militant opposition with repression; both began by being supported by the United States before being pushed toward transferring power.[243] France had her own Suez crisis in 1958, when the United States exerted financial pressure on Paris to reduce her military commitment in Algeria. The political consequences were even greater in France than they were in Britain.[244] The British lost a prime minister; the French lost a government and a constitution. John Foster Dulles, the U.S. Secretary of State, was aware of the consequences of his action but preferred to deal with the independent-minded Charles de Gaulle rather than risk losing a country in North Africa that was considered vital to the outcome of the Cold War. Constitutional differences between the two leading imperial powers added to the turbulence of the exit. Britain could claim that the transition to self-government and independence was consistent with a tradition that reached back to the Canadian precedent of 1867. Evolution allowed for devolution. The French constitution, which assumed that evolution would lead to incorporation, made parting more difficult. Despite these differences, the presence of common features of motive, timing, and outcome suggest that both powers were driven by forces that rose above state borders. Since this sequence also applied to the United States, the ultimate causes need to incorporate developments that were global rather than national.

THE END OF THE AFFAIR

In 1950, two aging buildings in central London, both constructed after 1815 as Britain emerged as the leading global power, were demolished to make way for new, spacious accommodation for the Colonial Office, which needed extra room for increased staff and expanded duties. Even at this late date, after the Indian sun had set, the authorities in London were convinced that a new dawn was about to brighten the imperial sky. Disappointment overtook optimism in the course of the 1950s. The foundations of the building were laid, but work was halted in 1952. After 1960, little was left for the Colonial Office to administer and in 1966 it was merged with the Commonwealth Relations Office to form the Commonwealth Office. The history of an event that did not take place symbolizes the unexpected rapidity with which the colonial empire, having been resuscitated, reformed, and reintegrated after 1945, expired at the close of the 1950s.[245] A decade after the empires had been given infusions of money and purpose, they were beyond resuscitation. No new Romes were to be built; no new Romans were needed.

The rise of the United States as a global power remains central to an understanding of the twentieth century as a whole. From a global perspective, however, it is not the principal theme of the first half of the century. Before World War II, the United States commanded power that it did not exercise. The Republic did indeed enter the war, as Luce hoped it would, and after 1945 became, in his judgment, the "Good Samaritan of the entire world." [246] Nevertheless, as he also made clear, "the vision which will guide us to the authentic creation of the 20th Century—our Century," had only just begun to materialize, and it remained very much a work in progress.

It is as easy to exaggerate Britain's decline after World War I as it is to anticipate the entry of the "heir to empire." Power is relative and not just absolute, and by 1918 Britain's continental rivals had been put out of action for the foreseeable future. France had been flattened by the war; Germany was shackled by the peace; Russia was preoccupied with building "socialism in one country." Britain, on the other hand, had been spared invasion and devastation. Its resources had been depleted, but the country emerged from the conflict with its empire not only intact but also enlarged. The guardians were morally rearmed; the civilizing mission was renewed. The "Titan" may have been "weary" but was still strong enough to outpace its challengers.[247] In 1938, Britain controlled no less than 59 percent of the total area held by the Western empires and 69 percent of all colonial peoples, which represented almost 500 million subjects.[248] France, its nearest rival, was a long way behind. On the eve of World War II, Britain possessed the greatest empire of the modern era and enjoyed unmatched standing as a global power. 1914, the traditional turning point, anticipates events that only started to take shape in the embattled 1930s.

The 1930s emerge as the crucial decade, when developments that were to be decisive after World War II began to alter the colonial landscape.

The Western empires were undermined by forces they themselves had conjured into being: the over-production of primary products, which created widespread economic distress, and the over-selling of the rhetoric of freedom and democracy, which created hope among the disenfranchised. This cocktail stirred unrest into sustained political action and gave self-determination the vitality it had previously lacked. The failure of existing political and economic orthodoxies, combined with the challenge of colonial nationalism, obliged the imperial powers to rethink inherited attitudes and policies, and even to contemplate the idea of decolonization.[249] World War II undoubtedly moved these developments on, but it did not "shatter" a period of "colonial calm," either in Africa or Asia.[250] Colonial turbulence had its counterpart in gathering imperialist rivalries. National enmities within Europe were one very evident cause of hostilities; competition between "have" and "have-not" powers was another. It is the latter that entitles the conflict to be thought of as an imperialist war on a global scale.

Although the war began by tearing the European empires apart, it ended by reassembling them. Once the United States joined the Allies in 1941, the balance of world power began to change. The consequences, however, differed from predictions made at the outset of the conflict. Shortly after 1945, it became clear that the perceived threat to the Free World had shifted from fascism to communism. At that point, the United States adjusted its anti-colonial stance and assisted the recovery and reconstruction of Europe's colonial possessions. The United Nations, then dominated by the "big four" powers, fell into line by excluding independence from its agenda for the future global order.[251] The imperial powers responded enthusiastically to this endorsement by investing unprecedented levels of capital and personnel in a New Deal that was designed to extend colonial rule.

The victorious allies miscalculated. They underestimated the social and political upheaval the war had created in the colonies and the degree of discontent it had nourished.[252] The power of protest found full expression after 1945. Hardship during the war years and disappointed hopes after it merged in mass movements aimed at ending colonial rule. When Marx, who claimed that revolutions arose from increasing immiseration, joined hands with Tocqueville, who held that they resulted from checks to rising expectations, colonial policy ran out of options. Initially, the imperial powers, supported by the United States, sought to repress the "agitators" and "terrorists" who formed militant anti-colonial movements. Policy was modified from the mid-1950s, when Europe had recovered from the devastation brought by the war. As colonies lost some of their value and the cost of holding them against their will increased, the imperial powers found it necessary to work with nationalists instead of against them. The evolution of the Cold War reinforced these trends and obliged the United States to support moves toward independence. The defense of the Free World had begun by revitalizing the Western empires; it progressed by assisting their demise. Political euthanasia brought colonial rule to a quick if not entirely peaceful end, and relief to all the parties concerned.

When placed in the longest perspective, the final crisis of the modern imperial system was a symptom of a momentous shift that was taking place in the nature of global integration after World War II as modern globalization, in the shape of nation-states and industrial economies, began to adjust to new forms of incorporation, characterized here as postcolonial globalization. The outcome of this third crisis of globalization will be considered in chapter 15. The immediate question, which will be examined in the next four chapters, is whether the analysis of the European empires presented here fits the history of the United States. The first half of the twentieth century provides a unique opportunity to compare imperial principles and practices because it was the only time when the U.S. and British empires coexisted as territorial entities. The argument that follows suggests that commonalities far outweighed differences. In its role as an imperial power, the United States shared the same assumptions and methods of rule as Britain and France. It also followed a comparable trajectory. The insular empire was acquired at the high point of "new" imperialism in 1898 and was decolonized after World War II. In the intervening period, it experienced the same undulations of fortune as the other Western empires. This finding suggests that there is a common explanation for the rise and fall of the Western empires as a whole in the twentieth century. National characteristics, or exceptionalism, added particularities and distinctiveness, but neither diverted nor diluted the influence of supranational forces.

It is fitting that Henry Luce's own life spanned that of the U.S. insular empire. He was born in 1898, at the moment of acquisition; he died in 1967, shortly after its dissolution. In common with most of his contemporaries and many subsequent historians, Luce knew little about the Republic's possessions in the Caribbean and Pacific.[253] His appeal for the renewal of America's "manifest destiny" omitted any reference to the insular empire, even though it was already serving as a testing ground for the spread of the values of democracy and freedom he so cherished. His lofty conception of the "first great American Century" envisaged a world dominated by the United States, whose Christian soldiers would defeat communism abroad and create national consensus at home. Accordingly, there is room for an assessment of the first large-scale experiment the United States undertook to exert "upon the world the full impact of our influence for such purposes as we see fit and by such means as we see fit."[254] At the time of Luce's death, the United States was about to be defeated in Vietnam, and anti-war and civil rights activists were splitting the nation apart. It was by no means evident, even in 1967, that the "American Century" Luce cherished would be realized.

CHAPTER 11

RULING THE FORGOTTEN EMPIRE

BUYERS' REMORSE

We've taken up the white man's burden
Of ebony and brown;
Now will you tell us, Rudyard,
How may we put it down?[1]

Anti-imperialists produced numerous satirical versions of Rudyard Kipling's appeal to the United States to "Take up the white man's burden."[2] In 1899, when Kipling composed his famous poem, Cuba, Puerto Rico, Hawai'i, the Philippines, Guam, and Samoa had just fallen under the control of the United States. His invocation was aimed, not at persuading the United States to acquire more territory, but at encouraging Washington's imperial novices to manage well what they had just accumulated.[3] The task was formidable, which is why Kipling urged the Republic to "Send forth the best ye breed." The purpose was lofty: "To seek another's profit / And work another's gain." The method called for restraint rather than force: "To veil the threat of terror, / And check the show of pride." The immediate reward was ingratitude: "The blame of those ye better / The hate of those ye guard." Yet, the enterprise was a noble one, and dedication received a prize beyond price: the performance of duty, the realization of manhood, and "The judgment of your peers!"

Enthusiasm for the task ahead, however, evaporated almost as soon as the contract with empire had been sealed. By 1900, the acquisitions had already served their purpose. Success in the war against Spain had boosted national morale and helped to close the regional and social fissures that had opened up during the turbulent 1890s. The election in that year endorsed the Republican Party and ensured that its development program would be carried forward as a national project and not solely as a sectional one. The heavens smiled on the victors, too: the fortuitous recovery of the international economy took the edge off discontent, and the increased flow of gold supplies removed the fear that deflation would extend into the new century. William Jennings Bryan, the nominee of the Democrats and defeated presidential candidate in 1896 and 1900, was well aware that conditions had turned against him. "The Republican victory," he declared after the election of 1900, "was due to money, war, and better times."[4] The "most potent" of the three, he judged, was "the prosperity argument," which caused the electorate to reject radical change.

The newly acquired territories also failed to deliver the good news heralded by imperial enthusiasts in 1898. There were no lucky strikes of gold, oil, or other dollar-coining minerals; investment opportunities were limited and risky; the market for consumer goods turned out to be small and impoverished. The colonial subjects were restless and ungrateful and in the Philippines had taken up arms against their benefactors. Contrary to uninformed expectations, American troops had not been greeted as liberators. The long, brutal war in the Philippines was costly and unpopular. It damaged the image of the untainted Anglo-Saxon warrior at home and handed the Democrats a coupon that could be redeemed in future elections.[5]

As these realities registered, leading imperialists either faded from view, like Albert Beveridge, or displayed symptoms of buyers' remorse, like Theodore Roosevelt. In 1907, Andrew Carnegie reported that Roosevelt and Taft were both keen to leave the Philippines, but that duty compelled them to stay.[6] One aspect of the duty Carnegie referred to was the need to avoid sinking deeper into the first of many foreign quagmires that were to immobilize the United States in the century ahead. Another, which gave the administration a sinking feeling of a different kind, was the realization that the Philippines was a sprawling and vulnerable possession that was hard to defend and could fall prey to another rising power: Japan. Belatedly, Roosevelt abandoned the "large policy" that he had done so much to instigate. Commitments acquired speedily, however, could not be shed lightly. Rudyard could not tell Theodore how to put the burden down because the tasks of imperial government stretched into a very distant, and possibly unending, future.

As the zest for empire diminished, so the empire itself receded from the public mind. Its existence inspired no fresh bursts of composition to complement the popular novels, songs, and gung-ho commentary that had accompanied the war with Spain. Odes to colonial bureaucracy, if they were written, have yet to be recovered. Historians appear to have been as exhausted by the effort needed to understand the events of 1898 as contemporaries were in participating in them. The voluminous research on the wars with Spain and the Philippines ends abruptly with the

Peace of Paris. Thereafter, historians return to the national story, which they enlarge to include two World Wars and one Cold War. The American Empire, though acquired amidst dazzling international publicity and touted as a new species of "benevolent imperialism," is left to wither from scholarly neglect.

The disappearance of the insular empire after 1898 is an omission unparalleled in the historiography of modern empires.[7] Small though the American Empire was in relation to its British and French comparators, it nevertheless contained about 23 million subjects in 1940.[8] This number ought to be large enough not to be overlooked and more than sufficient to test bold claims made for the "civilizing mission." Yet, the agreement to bury the empire before its time, though unwritten and unspoken, is as effective as it is comprehensive: major syntheses of U.S. history, authoritative studies of foreign affairs, and college textbooks all adhere to the rule of silence. Ongoing manifestations of American imperialism, notably the freebooting expeditions and sporadic official interventions that took place in the Caribbean and Central America after 1898, continue to attract attention, as does their complement: "dollar diplomacy." In addition, there is a long-standing discussion, from the perspective of international relations, of the emergence of the United States as a world power. One set of specialists pursues what they take to be continuities in American imperialism; the other traces the stages of growth from chrysalis to Leviathan or Good Samaritan. Neither includes the story of imperial management within the formal empire.

A rare exception opens a window to a wider world. Half a century ago, Robin Winks produced an exploratory essay that, though long buried in obscurity, remains one of the most thoughtful of the very few attempts to relate the period of American colonial rule to the experience of other empires.[9] Winks recognized that modern empires had common features, but he also drew attention to the "significant differences" that distinguished the American variant.[10] The most important of these, he claimed, was the assumption among U.S. policy-makers that the empire they administered was transitory rather than permanent. This belief, Winks suggested, explains why administrators were concerned from the outset to prepare the dependencies for self-government; why, accordingly, they tried so earnestly to Americanize indigenous cultures; why, by extension, the "intensity of local nationalist movements" was lower in the American Empire than it was in the colonies held by the European powers; and why, finally, the empire was given up so readily after 1945.[11] The empire served no grand geopolitical purpose, was of marginal economic importance, and was a departure from republican principles, all of which explain why "the American imperial experience is comparable to that of other nations only briefly, somewhat incidentally, and then but half the time."[12] With this judgment, Winks laid out the elements of a discussion that has yet to take place.

A single chapter cannot fill the considerable gap in the literature. It can, however, plant some signposts to assist future work. The assessment presented here considers how far the history of the overseas territories ruled by the United States paralleled that of the European empires described in the previous chapter and how far it ran on a course of its own making. In doing so, the discussion offers an alternative account of the issues that Winks raised so perceptively. The American Empire undoubtedly possessed distinctive features, but so did the other Western empires. Since all imperial states consider themselves to be exceptional, the important question is whether the singularities outweigh the commonalities. The argument advanced here is that the degree of distinctiveness attached to the insular possessions was insufficient to launch them on an exceptional trajectory. Between acquisition and decolonization, the Western empires were driven by similar causes and developed in similar ways. Consequently, the evolution of the American Empire accompanied that of the European empires charted in the previous chapter. If the comparison can be substantiated, future studies of the Western empires in the twentieth century will be able to add the American case to the existing roster of illustrations.

"A GREATER ENGLAND WITH A NOBLER DESTINY"[13]

Senator Albert Beveridge was a patriot whose commitment to the national cause put him in the vanguard of those waving the flag in the 1890s.[14] Yet, even he could not conceive of the destiny of the United States without treating Britain (or, as he put it on this occasion, "England") as the accepted standard of measure for the rising powers of the day. The close relations between what one wit called the "saxophone countries," combined with Britain's long and widely publicized experience of empire-building, ensured that the United States looked across the Atlantic for guidance on imperial management.[15] The Schurman Commission undertook a thorough assessment of British colonial administration before reporting in 1900 on the options for governing the Philippines.[16] The commission was the prelude to a series of wider consultations with European imperial powers that covered detailed aspects of colonial rule in the tropics, including civil administration, military efficiency, conservation, and health policies. The U.S. Treasury's weighty report on *The Colonial Systems of the World* (1900) commended the British in particular for giving "wherever practicable, a large degree of self-government to the colonies."[17]

In this regard, the connection between the two countries was more than a matter of cultural affiliation cemented, on the American side, by temporary deference to a greater power. The problems of pacification and administration arising from the acquisition of the insular empire compelled imitation because they admitted only a limited range of solutions, and these had already been applied in the European empires. Moreover, the American Empire, far from being an insular oddity requiring unique analysis, contained all the diversity found in the larger European empires. As microcosms of the species of empire that arose or expanded at the close of the nineteenth century, the insular possessions of the United States are candidates for the comparative treatment they have yet to receive. The possibilities can be seen in the typologies of empires originally devised by European commentators, the familiar distinction between assimilation and association, and the widespread use of direct and indirect methods of rule.

The numerous dependencies of the European powers differed widely in their location, size, and resources, and occupied a variety of constitutional categories, which included dominions, colonies, territories, protectorates, condominiums, and mandates.[18] The need to comprehend the otherwise baffling diversity of colonial possessions stimulated considerable discussion in the late nineteenth century, when Western empires were being created and expanded at unprecedented speed. The classical concept of a "colony" reserved the term for new territories settled by (white) migrants.[19] This usage remained influential until the close of the nineteenth century. John Seeley, the acknowledged founder of imperial history as a subject of professional study, considered the legitimate empire to consist of regions settled by British emigrants.[20] India was, for him, a regrettable addition that could not now be abandoned but should not become a precedent for similar acquisitions. Seeley, however, was writing shortly before extensive annexations in Africa and Asia of the kind he deprecated compelled a change of language. The typology adopted (and adapted) here derives ultimately from the contemporary debate on "new imperialism" at the end of the nineteenth century.[21] The most influential classification of the time was made by the notable

French economist, Pierre Paul Leroy-Beaulieu, who distinguished between colonies of settlement (*colonies de peuplement*), where white settlement predominated, and colonies of concession (*colonies d'exploitation*), where foreign-owned plantations and mines led development.[22] W. K. Hancock later refined Leroy-Beaulieu's classification by adding a third category, called colonies of trade (*colonies de traite*).[23]

Although these categories appear to be exclusively economic in character, they had weighty political and social attachments. Colonies of settlement were populated by white immigrants who controlled the principal economic resources, held political power, and imposed racial segregation. In colonies of trade, on the other hand, the indigenous population was left in charge of production, including export crops; the white presence was confined to administration and wholesale trading; and racial distinctions tended to be less rigorously enforced. Colonies of concession occupied a midpoint, where expatriates either were absentee owners or were present as managers, administrators, and merchants, but not as settlers, and where foreign rule and associated racial distinctions were correspondingly less overt than in colonies of settlement but more apparent than in colonies of trade. Policy decisions early in the colonial period created or endorsed the distribution of the three types of dependency, determined the way colonies were governed, and influenced the manner of decolonization. The transfer of power, for example, was more likely to be negotiated in colonies of trade than in colonies of settlement, where confrontation and conflict were almost guaranteed.

This tripartite typology fits the U.S. case with no greater modification than it needs elsewhere. Hawai'i, at one end of the continuum, was predominantly a colony of settlement; the Philippines, at the other end, was predominantly a colony of trade. Puerto Rico and Cuba were hybrids: they were, in different degrees, colonies of concession and colonies of trade. Constitutionally, Cuba was not a colony at all but an independent state. In practical terms, however, its status was that of a protectorate lodged within the sphere of informal influence exercised by the United States. In addition, the United States possessed in Guam and Samoa complements to the deep-water ports and staging posts that the British established in Malta, Aden, and Singapore, and the French in their *points d'appui* on international sea-lanes.

The most interesting feature of the classification as far as the U.S. case is concerned is one that historians have generally overlooked: an ambitious plan devised at the outset of the colonial period to create an empire of white settlement. Initially, the United States, like Britain and

France, was uncertain of the form the colonial presence would take. Expansionists were keen to open new overseas frontiers of settlement in Hawai'i, Cuba, and even the distant Philippines, which would be stocked by emigrants from the mainland. Puerto Rico was excluded from consideration because the island was already densely populated and suitable land there was in short supply. By extending the frontier overseas, the imperial party hoped to revitalize the Jeffersonian spirit embodied in the concept of a sturdy yeomanry and use it as a counterweight to the industrial and urban forces that, in their view, were sapping the character of the nation at home. As it happened, new settlers' frontier failed to materialize, except to a very limited extent in Hawai'i. The agricultural lobby in Washington diminished the appeal of emigration by blocking plans for substantial land sales in the other islands, except in Cuba and, to a modest degree, Puerto Rico. Economic recovery reinforced political pressure. Once farm incomes revived after 1900 and the internal combustion engine arrived to speed the home frontier on its way, destiny's opportunities were attained more easily within the United States.

The distinction between assimilation and association was also one that French thinkers formulated with characteristic precision. The terms arose from the need to define the civilizing mission and to classify colonial subjects according to their potential for progressing to the highest stage of the social order, namely the one occupied by the colonial power itself. Trustees of the welfare of colonial subjects interpreted their mandate as an obligation either to promote the civilizing mission by undertaking a fundamental transformation of indigenous societies, or to preserve "native laws and customs," where they were consistent with principles of "natural justice." The progressive policy had at its goal *assimilation*, which was intended to turn subjects into citizens and colonies into outer provinces of the home country. The conservative alternative, which the French termed *association*, offered a slow route to "civilization." There is no evidence that French thinking on these matters had a direct influence on deliberations in Washington, though the formula was very similar to the one adopted by the United States. British policy recognized a similar distinction, though it remained characteristically imprecise.[24] The British thought of assimilation as an informal and individual cultural process. There was no expectation that the dependencies would evolve to become overseas provinces of Britain, and rights of citizenship remained nominal rather than substantive.[25] Enthusiasts made an ambitious attempt to integrate Britain and the white empire in the late nineteenth century by proposing to incorporate the settler colonies in an imperial federation, but by then diversity was too entrenched and the initiative withered.

Commentators in the United States already distinguished between assimilation and association at home and extended both concepts to the new empire after the Spanish-American War. American usage differentiated between, but sometimes also confused, assimilation and Americanization.[26] In principle, it was possible to be Americanized without being assimilated, but impossible to be assimilated without being Americanized. Acceptance of various features of the "American way of life" involved a measure of choice that was consistent with the maintenance of the core values of the recipient community. Assimilation, however, called for a wholesale approval of American values, which required the subordination, or even the abandonment, of previous norms. Some societies that were judged unsuitable for assimilation could nevertheless be Americanized to a greater or lesser degree; others were to be shielded from the unsettling process of acculturation.

At the outset of the new colonial era, expansionists banged the drum for what McKinley called "benevolent assimilation" to justify the "civilizing mission" and to demonstrate the superiority of the American model over what were held to be the crude forms of imperialism sponsored by the European powers. Policy-makers in Washington, and influential officials, like Governor Leonard Wood, assumed that assimilation would be the popular choice, especially in parts of the empire, such as Puerto Rico, where the majority of subjects were of European descent. Assimilation, however, met strong opposition from anti-imperialists, who feared that it would lead to the incorporation of insular territories as states of the Union. Americanization was acceptable, indeed desirable, but in their view no policy of assimilation could ever overcome inherent racial distinctions. Ultimately, the issue was decided by the failure of early hopes of creating a substantial new empire of white settlement in Hawai'i and Cuba, and by the reactions of the recipients of U.S. policy. By the 1930s, the policy of assimilation, benevolent and otherwise, had been scaled down or jettisoned. It had become evident by then, even to imperial enthusiasts, that Puerto Ricans, Cubans, Filipinos, and Hawaiians were unwilling to lose their cultural identities. Among the many freedoms advertised by the civilizing mission, the most cherished was the right exercised by colonial subjects not to surrender any more of their independence than they had been obliged to concede in 1898. Given even a limited choice, the overseas territories opted for an informal, gradual, and selective process of Americanization, which appeared to be consistent with maintaining their own values.[27]

The difficulties of assimilating very different societies had become apparent before 1898, though the lesson appears not to have registered with those in charge of the overseas territories. In 1887, the Dawes Act instituted a policy of assimilation that was intended to supersede the regime of separate development that had held Native Americans in reservations.[28] The implementation of the Act made possible the large-scale dispossession of Native American lands and the disruption of indigenous societies without providing compensating alternatives. The acquisition of the insular empire presented even greater problems in evaluating potential candidates for assimilation because policy-makers had little or no knowledge of the people they had undertaken to civilize. Ignorance led officials to act on presuppositions derived from race relations at home, which were turned into policy recommendations by leaders of the new social sciences and endorsed by public prejudices.[29] Racial stereotyping, updated to fit the changing needs of government, formed the basis of policy, as the evolution of official attitudes toward Spain's colonial legacy illustrates.

In the early colonial period, the Spanish legacy was denigrated to justify the war of 1898 and to emphasize the urgency and importance of the task the new rulers faced. At the same time, American capacities were generously overstated. In 1900, the Schurman Commission claimed that, with suitable guidance, Filipinos would become "more American than the Americans themselves."[30] Excessive optimism disappeared shortly afterward, when Filipinos had given militant evidence of their resistance to American rule. Governor Taft, who was well disposed toward his new colonial subjects, nevertheless described them in language that the British novelist, G. A. Henty, would have recognized as his own: they were "a vast mass of ignorant, superstitious people, well intentioned, light-hearted, temperate, and somewhat cruel, domestic and fond of their families, and deeply wedded to the Catholic Church."[31] It followed, in Taft's judgment, that Filipinos were not a people to be entrusted with self-government without a long period of preparation.

Later on, after the U.S. administration in the Philippines had adopted many of Spain's colonial institutions, and the desire for independence had fully registered, officials took a more generous view of their inheritance. In the 1930s, the Vice Governor-General of the Philippines, Joseph R. Hayden, reflected that Spanish rule had been "in many respects corrupt and demoralizing, yet in theory and profession the colonial system of Spain was fine and uplifting."[32] Moreover, "the long Spanish tutelage which the Filipinos received in political philosophy and procedures of the West has given them a great advantage over other Oriental peoples."[33] By then, too, Hayden had come to appreciate that "a people held by force in a position of political subordination . . . achieves its own ends through informal and extra-legal procedures" that twist legal constraints "into the shape of native desires."[34] Here was evidence that, with the passage of time, pupils could educate their masters.

The distinction between assimilation and association correlates very loosely with forms of colonial government, known as direct and indirect rule, which were present throughout the Western empires. Direct rule placed colonial administrators in charge of a central government and gave them key positions in the provincial bureaucracy. Indirect rule relied to a greater extent on the preservation, adaptation, and sometimes even the invention, of indigenous hierarchies. Although an older literature associated direct rule with France and indirect rule with Britain, historians now acknowledge that both forms of government were present in both empires, and that in practice the difference between the two was blurred.[35] Lord Lugard was the most famous exponent of indirect rule, which he derived from India and applied to Africa; his French counterpart, the celebrated Marshal Hubert Lyautey, introduced indirect rule into Morocco.[36] Colonies of settlement were well placed to obtain rights of direct rule over indigenous populations. Elsewhere, the chosen method of administration was determined partly by conditions on the ground and partly by the prevailing wisdom of the time. Although recent research has drawn attention to the limits of colonial rule, it remains the case that, directly or indirectly, the administrative capacity of the new rulers far exceeded that of most precolonial polities.[37] This Leviathan, moreover, did not age: the legacy of "big government" is one of the characteristic features of ex-colonial states today.

Elihu Root, who held the key offices of state when U.S. policy toward the insular possessions was being formulated, took particular note of the British example, which he applied in both the Pacific and the Caribbean.[38] Respect for Britain's colonial administration remained long after American rule had been established. Lord Lugard's teachings inspired John Collier, the Commissioner of Indian Affairs between 1933 and 1945, to abandon direct rule, which had failed (often disastrously) in the reservations, and to adopt indirect rule instead.[39] His initiative led to the Indian Reorganization Act of 1934, which substituted pluralism for assimilation. Collier aimed to manage Indian reservations in the United States in the way that Britain ruled the Gold Coast. Accordingly, he increased the number of Native Americans in the Indian Service and added a clutch of anthropologists to advise on "native laws and customs." By adopting Lugardian methods, Collier hoped to avoid the mistakes of his predecessors who, so he thought, had replicated the appalling conditions prevailing in the Belgian Congo.

The American Empire, like its European counterparts, adopted an eclectic mix of direct and indirect rule based on a combination of racial assumptions and related estimates of evolutionary potential.[40] American settlers in Hawai'i were in the vanguard of development; the *ilustrados* of the Philippines, Puerto Rico, and Cuba had potential; less advanced societies lacked the ability and energy of superior races and were scheduled for conservation. Accordingly, Hawai'i was designated an incorporated territory, and American settlers there were granted effective self-government, which gave them the power of direct rule over the islands. In Puerto Rico, where intervention was considered necessary to transform "this Island and its people into truly American types," the American governor ruled indirectly through competing groups of politicians who formed the "white chiefs" of the colony. Cuba was judged to have approximately the same potential as Puerto Rico, but could not be directed in the same way. Instead, the island was treated as an exercise in "moral suasion" of the kind that Britain applied in Egypt in the hope that informal influences would lead to the adoption of American values and ways of life.[41]

The Philippines was a more complicated case. There, the American governor interacted with an educated and ambitious ilustrado elite in much the same way as in Puerto Rico, but directed policy to different purposes. Policies of assimilation, adapted from the Dawes Act, were to be applied to the "wards" of the state held in "tutelage." Inhabitants who were deemed unfit or unready for assimilation were to be allowed to retain their "tribal customs."[42] Accordingly, in the northern island of Luzon, policy-makers set out to change "Hispano-Malayo" institutions and to "uproot or modify all impediments to democratic institutions."[43] Further south in Muslim Mindanao, indirect methods, borrowed from British rule in Fiji, were applied with the aim of protecting indigenous institutions and inhibiting change.[44] A similar policy of conservation was followed in Guam and Samoa.[45]

THE MODERNIZING MISSION

Colonial classifications and styles of rule formed part of a larger mission. The American Empire was the first venture in overseas development and nation-building the United States undertook in the twentieth century. Given that the experiment was followed by many others after World War II, specialists on development policy might gain from rediscovering it. Some of the most influential foundations of modern development thinking were laid in the late nineteenth century. They bore the deep imprint of British influences and had been absorbed into U.S. colonial policy by the time of the Spanish-American War. Sir Henry Maine, the distinguished British jurist and legal historian, enjoyed a position of authority among intellectuals and experts in policy-making circles in the United States that was matched only by Herbert Spencer.[46] Maine's historical studies, reinforced by service in India, led him to the proposition that societies evolved from relations of status to those of contract. This core idea was subsequently greatly elaborated in the United States as well as in Britain and elsewhere in Europe, notably by Max Weber. It reached the peak of its influence in the mid-twentieth century, when it formed the basis of what became known as modernization theory.[47]

Maine himself thought that "progress" was exceptional rather than normal and he defended traditional social structures and values in cases where change brought disruption without countervailing advantages. The Indian Mutiny in 1857 was a turning point for Maine, as it was for British policy. As he saw it, the great rebellion was a judgment on earlier policies that had harnessed government initiatives to the cause of progress and had envisaged British rule as a form of temporary trusteeship. In Maine's view, the Mutiny demonstrated that profound cultural differences were responsible for the failure of earlier policies. Progress remained a long-run possibility, but for the foreseeable future traditional societies needed continuing imperial supervision to guarantee their stability.[48] This conclusion completed the transition from the optimistic liberalism of the early Utilitarians that John Stuart Mill had already signaled, and grounded the justification of permanent colonial rule in a persuasive reading of history, custom, and principles of human behavior.[49] Liberty remained the goal, but it had to be "ordered liberty," a state that was reached by the deserving only after a very long apprenticeship.[50]

The spacious propositions advanced by Maine and Spencer allowed room for commentators and policy-makers to insert refinements that suited particular national interests. The champions of overseas expansion in the United States, like those elsewhere, grafted their own assumptions and experience onto these European imports. A combination of Maine and Spencer produced a satisfying intellectual justification for the "survival of the fittest," namely themselves, and of the emergence, through the process of evolution, of the large corporations that had come to dominate business and politics by the late nineteenth century. It followed, too, that the white Anglo-Saxons who were designated the "fittest" had valid claims to manage society and dominate others. Yet neither Maine nor Spencer settled the question of nature versus nurture. Phrenology provided supporting evidence of inherent genetic disparities; eugenics planned to manage the gene pool by eliminating poorly endowed members of society. On the other hand, Progressives and environmentalists believed that dominant states had both the duty and the power to improve the lot of the disadvantaged, as they had improved themselves.[51] The role of the helping hand was to assist the course of evolution, and to do so in a visible way through the agency of government.

The history of race relations within the United States, as interpreted by the dissenting parties, provided support for those who believed in the rule of nature as well as for those who placed their faith in the power of nurture. According to the conservative view, Native Americans had succumbed to superior competitors because they were a weaker race. This assumption underlay the policy of establishing reservations to isolate tribes from the destabilizing influences and allow the agents of civilization to colonize the land around them. African Americans, whose capacities were also judged to be irredeemably limited, suffered similarly through segregation and other forms of discrimination that raised racial boundaries as the century advanced.[52] Prevailing attitudes toward nonwhite Americans supplied powerful backing for the view that "inferior" racial groups in the new insular possessions should be kept firmly in their place. An influential element among white supremacists carried this position to the point where they opposed the acquisition of overseas territories precisely because they did not wish to invite contamination from abroad. Subsequent attempts to classify the "new caught, sullen peoples" according to their presumed capacities owed much to existing relations with Native Americans and African Americans, and produced a series of dilemmas that were to inform, and muddle, colonial policy for half a century.

Progressives shared the racial prejudices of the time and stopped well short of Rousseau's belief in mankind's capacity for improvement. Nevertheless, they were committed advocates of "efficiency" and "progress," and they treated the new empire as a laboratory for testing their faith in government-led development policies. Plans that had been frustrated at home could be applied abroad; once achieved, their success would illuminate the path to reform in the United States and advertise the superiority of American "know-how" and values to the world. A formidable triumvirate consisting of President Theodore Roosevelt, Elihu Root (Secretary of War and then of State) and William H. Taft (Civil Governor of the Philippines, Secretary of War, and then President) gave initial direction and impetus to colonial policy.[53] Lofty purpose inspired them; a new generation of "experts" bestowed validation; innocence amplified enthusiasm.[54] The three principals were joined later by Woodrow Wilson, a Democrat among Republicans who shared Progressive ideals but expressed them in his own idiom, which was one of bleak assurance: "Our almost accidental possession of the Philippines," he intoned in 1901, and the "new duties now thrust upon us," provide an opportunity to "teach them order as a condition precedent to liberty, self-control as a condition precedent to self-government."[55] Lord Curzon and Lord Cromer could not have put it better.[56]

The significance of the racial issue in domestic affairs guaranteed that it would have a powerful influence not only on the typology of the insular empire and the various styles of rule, but also on U.S. international policy in general.[57] Although different interpretations of racial qualities and their potential continued to infuse the debate on empire, the balance of opinion and policy remained firmly on the side of upholding white supremacy. This objective inspired the systematic study of international relations, which provided a defense of white dominance without denying others the prospect of development.[58] The Spanish-American War expanded the publicity given to the risk of racial pollution from non-European sources. Japan's victory over Russia in 1905 stimulated anti-Japanese sentiment in the United States and reinforced the bunker mentality.

World War I aroused fervent anti-German feelings, which then developed into a wider attack on ethnic diversity. White ethnic pluralism had already been eroded: although more Americans came from Germany than from any other part of continental Europe, there was little German-American ethnic consciousness even before World War I—and none after it.[59] Instead, the war reinforced a form of Anglo-conformity under WASP leadership that perpetuated segregation and denied efforts to legislate against the practice of lynching.[60] The Russian Revolution in 1917 reinforced these tendencies by raising fears that Bolshevism would not only challenge capitalism but also inspire a hostile union of nonwhite peoples. The defensive reaction to these developments in the United States culminated in the Immigration Act of 1924, which restricted incomers on grounds of race by favoring Northern over Southern Europeans and barring Asians.[61] The Act carried the policy of assimilation to its furthest extent by defining national identity in terms of an ideal segment of the white "race" to which all citizens were expected to conform. The famous "melting pot" had dissolved only white ingredients. It was not to add color to the mix until after the decolonization of the formal empire, when, in the 1960s, internal colonialism could no longer be sustained.

Imperial enthusiasts therefore had to surmount a wall of opposition, spiked with indifference, from the majority of their compatriots. Their response was to bid for the rhetorical high ground. The idea that the

United States had a providential mission to deliver the American version of progress to the rest of mankind was one that resonated even with anti-imperialists.[62] Advocates of expansion, led by Theodore Roosevelt, reinvigorated the notion of manifest destiny, which had validated westward expansion earlier in the century, to justify the burst of new activity beyond the borders of the mainland. Turner's frontier, if closed at all, was shut only briefly. The key to making the rhetoric of destiny manifest was to be found, according to the Progressives' handbook of development, in the scientific and technological advances that had propelled the United States to the forefront of the industrial world. In 1903, Brooks Adams, one of the most eminent of the Northeastern Brahmins, expressed the self-confidence that was beginning to attach itself to the emerging world power:

> American supremacy has been made possible only through applied science. The labors of successive generations of scientific men have established a control over nature which has enabled the United States to construct a new industrial mechanism, with processes surpassingly perfect. Nothing has ever equalled in economy and energy the administration of the great American corporations.[63]

This strongly technocratic approach to the civilizing mission stemmed partly from a long-standing reaction to the ideas of the *philosophes*, who were held responsible for inspiring the Godless revolution in France, and partly from practical experience in the United States, where mechanization was adopted in the nineteenth century to overcome labor shortages. Seen from this perspective, the imperial mission was primarily an exercise in social engineering. Advanced technology had unlocked the vast resources of the United States; the same formula would work its magic on the insular empire.[64] The policy of acculturation applied the principle that entry into the modern world depended on turning colonial subjects into Americans. Although experience revealed the manifold difficulties of achieving the required transformation, faith in the master plan revived after World War II, when U.S. dominance appeared boundless.

The technocratic approach reached its fullest formulation in modernization theory, which inspired development programs in the 1950s and 1960s and lingered long enough to be re-invented.[65] The theory codified strands of late nineteenth-century scientism and applied them to the task of modernizing what had become known as the Third World. The social scientists who supplied the intellectual support for policies designed to demonstrate the superiority of the Western model of development bypassed history. Practitioners were unaware that their key concepts, "traditional" and "modern," were solidified versions of Maine's more fluid distinction between status and contract. More surprisingly, the experts of the day did not refer to the insular territories to test the universal applicability of their theories, even though Operation Bootstrap in Puerto Rico was a nearby and highly publicized example of an attempted "great transformation." "Becoming modern" still involved turning "traditional" societies into the model exemplified by the United States.[66] The lessons of experience were left unlearned.[67]

OWNING AN EMPIRE:
CONGRESS AND THE CONSTITUTION

The rhetoric was strident, the plans were ambitious, the aim was uncompromising. To make them operational, however, the protagonists had to marshal the necessary political support and overcome formidable constitutional obstacles. The civilizing mission entailed a thorough-going, long-term commitment to promote assimilation, Americanization, and what today would be called nation-building. The political context within which these goals were placed, however, greatly reduced the chances of success. The checks and balances the Founding Fathers inserted into the federal constitution produced, in the course of the nineteenth century, a political system that could easily become deadlocked—and gave interest groups a prominent role in unblocking it. Rexford G. Tugwell, who became governor of Puerto Rico in 1941, thought that "our government is unsuited to colonial administration—the Congress always has and always will find itself so much at the mercy of interests adverse to offshore areas, that we should not be able to build up a Caribbean economy, as we ought to do."[68]

Britain, in contrast, had a unitary government, a parliamentary system based on the principle of majority rule, and an upper chamber that had very limited powers after the Parliament Act neutered the House of Lords in 1911. Furthermore, the executive branch in Britain was staffed by career civil servants, whereas key senior positions in the United States were subject to change following presidential elections, which were held every four years. In the absence of the necessary comparative research, the significance of these institutional differences to imperial policy must remain speculative, but there is a case for suggesting that the British system of government was better suited to maintaining continuity in imperial policy. This hypothesis does not, of course, imply that Britain's policies were superior to those of other imperial powers: continuity can entrench the bad as well as the good.

It is also clear that differences between national political institutions can explain only part of the variations in the formulation and application of imperial policies. The relevant comparison here is not the one most commonly made, with Britain, but the one largely ignored, with France. The French, like the United States, had a republican form of government, a *mission civilisatrice* that was as ambitious as that advertised by the United States, if not more so; a matching sense of the superiority of their own culture; and long-standing policies of *assimilation* and *association*. Admittedly, France had a unitary rather than a federal government, but it was one that, far from guaranteeing stability, was characterized by shifting coalitions and the influence of special interests. France, like the United States, also had an idealized conception of overseas territories as being extensions of the homeland, and a corresponding difficulty in defining the constitutional status of colonies that were judged to be unqualified for the privilege. The French, like Americans, referred to "overseas territories"; "empire" did not enter the official vocabulary until World War II. Assimilation, in the French lexicon, offered the prospect of incorporation into France just as, in the United States, it allowed territories to apply for statehood. In this respect, if no other, Algeria was Washington's Hawai'i.

Despite similarities between political institutions in the United States and France, both Britain and France were able to sustain bipartisan policies on imperial issues for virtually the whole of the colonial period, whereas political disagreements in the United States were translated into competing policies. Variations in the level of opposition to empire cannot account for the singularity of U.S. policy in this regard because left-wing parties in Britain and France were also prominent critics of imperialism. A more persuasive explanation lies in the relative importance of the overseas territories to their respective homelands. The United States occupied a vast land-space and had modest imperial attachments; Britain was a small country with a huge empire; France, though larger than Britain, stood in much the same relation to her empire.[69] One quantitative measure illustrates the general point: in 1913, about one-third of Britain's net national wealth was held overseas; between 1900 and 1929 only about 6 percent of all U.S. investment went abroad, and only a small proportion of that was placed in the formal empire, even if Cuba is added to the list.[70] The American Empire was of little national consequence, whether measured by trade, investment, or the level of awareness it enjoyed among the wider public. The empires of Britain and France, on the other hand, achieved considerable importance not only on these counts, but also because of their strong links with "kith and kin" overseas and the value attached to supplies of imperial troops and *materiel*.

The difference in relativities accounts for the greater commitment to empire in Britain and France. Hostility to imperialism, though articulate and persistent, was offset by the belief that the empire was a vital component of the national interest. In the United States, in contrast, the political system allowed competing interest groups far greater scope to shape policy because they did not have to adjust their claims to meet countervailing national concerns. As the Secretary of State, Elihu Root, observed in 1902:

> Philippine Questions are so interwoven in the political game that the most curious results follow combinations of influence. . . . Among a large part of the gentlemen who are actually discussing the subject, the question, "What will be good for the Philippines" plays a most insignificant part.[71]

More than a generation later, Governor Theodore Roosevelt, Jr., confirmed Root's judgment. Writing in the light of his experience in Puerto Rico and the Philippines, Roosevelt stated in 1937 that he could not "conceive of the United States having a consistent, long-range colonial policy" and that it would continue "to fit our policies in the islands to our own internal political opinions."[72]

The gentlemen who were "actually discussing the subject" had to impress their views on Congress if they were to influence policy. After 1898, when the national relish for war and empire had subsided, the direction of imperial policy was driven by the oscillating fortunes of the two main political parties, which were conduits for competing interest groups. Democrats, generally speaking, favored expansion but opposed imperialism. Their aim was to move the colonies toward self-government and, ultimately, to independence at a pace that was consistent with the principles of viability. Republicans, having acquired the empire, felt obliged to make it a success, though their enthusiasm cooled as the obstacles confronting them appeared as roadblocks to their progress. Their aim was to promote assimilation as a qualification for self-government within the American orbit; independence was a possibility but one that lay in the distant future. Republicans imposed an additional test: the achievement of democratic government as well as viability. Realities ensured that these goals, so clear in principle, became blurred in practice. As far as policy on the ground was concerned, the two parties were separated mainly by the different arrival times their schedules for colonial progress envisaged. Democrats were prepared to move forward; Republicans were inclined to hold back. The absence of bipartisan agreement gave policy toward the empire a capricious quality that greatly added to the uncertainties already facing officials, investors, and the colonial subjects who were the recipients of the civilizing mission.

When the Republicans dominated Congress, as they did between 1900 and 1913, the imperial party, led by Roosevelt, Taft, and Root, was able to embed the empire in the constitution, complete the process of occupation, and begin to promote assimilation and Americanization. Even so, the Democrats were sometimes able to express their opposition effectively, as they did, for example, in blocking ambitious development plans for the Philippines.[73] Between 1913 and 1921, power shifted to the Democrats, who took the opportunity to press ahead with measures designed to extend self-government and speed the transfer of power "as soon as a stable government can be established."[74] Republicans, who held office during the 1920s, set about reversing these initiatives by re-imposing controls over the direction and pace of change. Democrats, who returned to power in 1933 and remained there until shortly after World War II, reverted to their previous policy by preparing to shed the unwanted burdens of empire. John Wheeler-Bennett, a noted British specialist on international affairs with pro-American sympathies, observed these oscillations of policy even before the Democrats took office in 1933: "It is one of the gravest features of the Philippine problem," he wrote in 1929, "that it has been made a subject for American party politics. There is no American policy towards the Philippines."[75]

LOBBIES AND LIBERTIES

An array of pressure groups competing for votes in Congress stood behind party labels, though the research needed to assess their influence still awaits scholarly attention. The most prominent lobbies were those representing the interests of religion and commerce. God and Mammon had different priorities, but were united in one central belief: people of non-European stock were members of an inferior species. This assumption inspired the civilizing mission: it underpinned the idea that indigenous people needed spiritual uplift and firm, paternal guidance; it ensured that opposition to the prospect of nonwhites securing constitutional rights of free entry to the United States was resolute and persistent.

The crusading element in American imperialism was expressed primarily by Christian missions, which shared the prevailing notion of

white supremacy but coupled it with a commitment to bring enlightenment to the "underpeople." In this endeavor, the United States was part
of an international movement sponsored by white Christians and galvanized in the late nineteenth century by charismatic figures, such as David
Livingstone in Britain, Cardinal Charles Lavigerie in France, and Josiah
Strong in the United States.[76] Although Protestant missions were prominent advocates of imperial expansion in 1898, their subsequent influence
on colonial policy was limited. By the 1920s, the missionary impetus itself had begun to flag.[77] Conversion rates were depressingly low and the
results of the temperance campaign were disappointing. The material
attractions of Americanization, especially education, medical services,
sport, and consumer goods, proved more compelling than their spiritual
underpinning.[78] Organizations such as the YMCA and the Rotary Club,
which spread internationally in the twentieth century, also made their
mark through the material benefits they offered, but they, like the missions, worked within the colonial system and lacked both the inclination
and the power to change it.

The more important domestic influence on colonial policy was one
that historians have largely bypassed since the heyday of the New Left
in the 1960s: the economic links between the mainland and the overseas
territories. To be sure, policy by itself could not determine fate or fortune
because, as the previous chapter showed, the colonies were subject to
even larger influences transmitted by international forces, notably economic fluctuations and decisions leading to war or making for peace.
Nevertheless, the effect of economic policy on the American Empire was
far greater than any of the other pressures originating on the mainland.
Had the rhetoric about benevolent assimilation, the civilizing mission,
and uplifting fallen peoples been translated into effective action, policy
toward the empire would have been consistent and adequately financed.
The reality was quite the opposite: policy was dominated by what
Tugwell called the "slick sheen" of powerful economic interests whose
rivalry ensured that it was unpredictable and whose voices in Congress
helped to keep the colonies permanently underfunded.[79]

Henry Osborne Havemeyer, the monarch of the Sugar Trust, instigated the proceedings that determined the most vital issue of all: the
constitutional status of the insular possessions. The acquisitions of
1898 raised the urgent question of whether the constitution allowed the
United States to exercise authority in circumstances that did not entail incorporation, statehood, and citizenship.[80] The constitution recognized
progress through assimilation—the route taken by continental territories

that joined the Union in the course of the nineteenth century. However, the constitution did not deal with the possibility of permanent association, and legal precedents for governing areas that had not become states pointed, unhelpfully, in different directions.[81] Continuing uncertainty generated a prolific debate about the status of the islands in the years following the Treaty of Paris. Advocates of annexation argued that the United States could legitimately acquire territory without also offering the prospect of statehood. The precedent had been established, so they claimed, because the federal government already treated Native Americans as subjects rather than as citizens.[82] Anti-imperialists countered that the analogy was flawed because the new territories were located overseas and stood outside the constitution, which was intended to apply to the continental landmass. Imperialists responded that the constitution made no distinction between land and sea, and pointed out that improved communications made the Pacific islands more accessible from Washington in 1898 than California had been when it was annexed fifty years earlier.

A decision to grant the insular possessions the same status as continental territories, with the right ultimately to join the Union, would have had profound consequences. The newcomers would have enjoyed the benefit of free trade within the federal tariff regime, which is exactly what sugar refiners, like Havemeyer, and producers in the islands wanted. Producers on the mainland were alarmed at the prospect of increased competition; nativists were appalled at the thought of incorporating allegedly inferior races into the Anglo-Saxon heartland.[83] The tariff system, on which the Republican Party was founded and funded, would crumble; uncivilized aliens would claim citizenship; the end of the world, politically speaking, would be at hand. If, on the other hand, the United States retained the new territories, denied them rights of statehood, and designated them "colonies," all claims to the moral high ground would be surrendered. The principle of liberty, which was crucial to national ideology, would be abandoned. The Republic would then put itself on the same constitutional footing as the European empires, and in consequence damage its self-esteem and image as the exceptional exemplar of republican virtues. This outcome, as a former Democratic congressman pointedly described it, would need to be recognized formally: "the titular designation of our Executive shall be President of the United States of America, and Emperor of the Philippines."[84]

The conundrum called for expertise of the kind that could steer between rocks and hard places. Came the hour, came the men. With a display of juridical acrobatics made possible only by a lifetime of preparation and practice, the U.S. Supreme Court rose to Solomonic heights in the landmark Insular Cases, which were determined between 1901 and 1905.[85] In essence, the Court invented a distinction between incorporated and unincorporated territories. The former had the prospect of achieving statehood; the latter did not. Incorporated territories needed to be developed and acculturated so that they could join the United States on an equal footing with other states of the Union. Unincorporated territories could be treated as dependencies, regarded as foreign countries for purposes of tariff policy, and prepared for eventual self-government at speeds that fitted their circumstances. In effect, the Court amended the constitution to validate colonial acquisitions. It offered imperialists territory while calming the fears of their opponents. In doing so, the ruling also clarified the question of secession that had exercised Lincoln and remained a constant concern for a generation that retained personal memories of the Civil War. Unincorporated territories could be surrendered if they became burdensome or, if necessary, allowed independence without endangering the constitution.[86]

The Supreme Court's judgments in the Insular Cases enabled the United States to grade its overseas possessions according to estimates of their importance and desirability.[87] Hawai'i, a settler colony, was the only constituent of the new empire to be granted, in 1900, the status of an incorporated territory. Thereafter, the island adopted the form of territorial government found on the mainland in having an appointed governor, an elected legislature, and the prospect, however distant, of attaining statehood. The remaining insular possessions were designated unincorporated territories, which belonged to, but were not part of, the United States, and lacked rights of citizenship and statehood. Most of the unincorporated territories were administered by a governor appointed by the president and possessed some of the formal institutions of self-government. As operated in the Philippines, however, the constitutional provisions enabled governors to exercise powers that were colonial in character and far-reaching in effect. Puerto Rico's position was exceptionally complex because the interests there favoring and opposing incorporation were evenly balanced. The outcome was a constitutional jumble that has persisted to the present. At the outset, at least, Puerto Rico had fewer powers of self-government than an incorporated territory, less independence than a protectorate, and most closely approximated the status of a colony.

Cuba, which became formally independent in 1902, stood outside the Supreme Court's decisions. The island was recognized in international law as a separate, sovereign state and retained its autonomy in matters of internal policy. Nevertheless, Cuba was bound to the United States by treaty, which eliminated its independence in foreign policy, and in practice had to manage its domestic affairs to avoid offending its mighty neighbor. U.S. agencies referred to Cuba as an "insular area" to avoid any taint of colonialism; in reality, the island was a protectorate. In case the powers conferred by treaty were inadequate, the Roosevelt Corollary to the Monroe Doctrine, issued in 1904, asserted the right of the United States to act unilaterally anywhere in the Western Hemisphere if it judged that its interests, whether life, liberty, the pursuit of property, or debt collection, needed military support.

Protectionists succeeded in imposing controls over the extent to which land, franchises, and concessions could be allowed in the islands. Although these measures were not fully implemented, they nevertheless checked U.S. investment in the new empire and limited developments that might have threatened domestic interests. The contest between lobbies representing "home" and "abroad" then focused on the tariff, which determined the balance of advantage between the parties. Tariff policy tied the colonies into a neo-mercantilist system of controls that influenced the prices farmers received and, intermittently, the quantities they were permitted to ship to the United States. The tariff on sugar was especially important because sugar was the commodity that bound the insular territories to the United States and compelled them to compete among themselves for a share of the mainland market. Other agricultural products, notably abaca, pineapples, and coffee, had parts to play in the story, but sugar remained the most important single export from the overseas possessions throughout the colonial period. Raw sugar was also the leading import into the United States during the first half of the twentieth century and raised more revenue from the tariff than any other single item. More than 75 percent of the sugar consumed in the United States during the interwar years was supplied by Cuba and the insular territories, which shipped almost all of their output to the mainland (table 11.1). Domestic producers of beet and cane accounted for the residue; the tariff on imports of foreign sugar ensured that potential competitors were virtually excluded.

Sugar has another claim to distinction: from the slave trade to the present, the market for sugar has been the most rigged of all the world commodities—despite serious competition for the title from other protected products.[88] An array of tariffs, subsidies, and bounties has long distorted prices and ensured that massive investments of time and money have been devoted to influencing government policy. Adjust-

TABLE 11.1. TOTAL SUGAR DELIVERIES FOR U.S. CONSUMPTION BY COUNTRY OF ORIGIN (%), 1917–1939

Years	Total Sugar Deliveries ('ooos Short Tons)	U.S. Continental		Hawai'i	Puerto Rico	Philippines	Cuba	Others
		Beet	Cane					
1917	4,415.0	21.3	7.0	16.1	11.7	2.0	40.9	1.0
1918	4,189.0	15.1	6.5	12.3	9.5	1.3	53.8	1.5
1919	4,875.0	21.4	3.8	12.7	7.0	1.8	50.8	2.5
1920	4,895.0	11.1	2.0	9.6	8.2	2.8	52.1	14.2
1921	4,922.0	23.1	6.7	11.7	9.1	3.2	45.4	0.8
1922	6,103.0	17.6	5.4	9.1	6.1	4.2	56.7	0.9
1923	5,729.0	18.4	4.5	9.6	5.3	4.1	55.4	2.7
1924	5,818.0	15.3	1.7	10.4	7.1	5.5	58.2	1.8
1925	6,603.0	16.1	2.3	11.6	9.1	7.3	52.8	0.8
1926	6,797.0	15.4	1.3	10.9	8.1	5.5	58.0	0.8
1927	6,348.0	14.8	0.7	12.0	9.1	8.2	55.0	0.2
1928	6,643.0	18.7	2.1	12.3	10.5	8.6	47.10	0.8
1929	6,964.0	14.7	2.7	13.3	6.6	10.4	51.9	0.4
1930	6,710.0	17.0	2.9	12.0	11.6	12.0	43.9	0.6
1931	6,561.0	20.5	3.1	14.8	11.4	12.4	37.2	0.6
1932	6,249.0	21.1	2.6	16.4	14.5	16.7	28.2	0.5
1933	6,316.0	21.6	5.0	15.7	12.5	19.6	25.4	0.2
1934	6,154.0	25.1	4.2	14.4	13.6	18.0	24.6	0.1
1935	6,400.0	22.1	4.9	15.5	12.8	14.0	30.7	–
1936	6,617.0	22.1	6.7	14.0	13.2	14.0	29.8	0.2
1937	6,861.0	18.1	7.2	14.3	13.1	14.5	31.4	1.4
1938	6,619.0	21.9	6.8	13.7	12.3	14.8	29.3	1.2
1939	7,465.0	24.2	7.9	12.9	15.1	13.1	25.9	0.9

Source: Brian Pollitt, "The Cuban Sugar Economy and the Great Depression," *Bulletin of Latin American Research* 23 (1984), p. 8.

ments to the import tariff, though unable to affect world prices, were nevertheless crucial to the political economy of the empire. The results of intensive lobbying influenced the distribution of wealth and power on the mainland and reverberated throughout the colonies by altering the incentives given to producers, the profitability of different export crops, the social distribution of returns, and government revenues. These effects, in turn, had major consequences for social order and the character of colonial politics. Much was at stake: the struggle for market shares was correspondingly intense and, at times, desperate.

A full analysis of the politics of the sugar trade during this period must await future studies. In general terms, however, it can be said that Democrats favored a low import tariff on raw sugar to reward the loyalty of refiners on the West and East coasts, while Republicans supported high or discriminatory tariffs to shield beet producers in the Midwest and cane producers in Louisiana. The period of Republican dominance between 1900 and 1913 saw the introduction of trade and reciprocity agreements that established the terms on which the new possessions were integrated with the mainland. The process was completed in 1909, following a long tussle between rival pressure groups, when the Payne-Aldrich Tariff allowed sugar from the Philippines free entry into the United States, subject to a generous quota. The concession was made primarily to encourage trade that would benefit U.S. exporters. As a result of these measures, the value of trade between the United States and its colonies underwent a marked increase, as did the share of the United States in the trade of its empire. At the same time, the fortuitous recovery of primary produce prices boosted growth and helped the new rulers to stamp their authority on their new domains.

When the Democrats came to power in 1913, they immediately passed the Underwood Tariff, which brought about the first significant reduction in import duties since the Civil War. The principal consequence for the empire was to accelerate sugar exports, particularly from developing new regions in Cuba and the Philippines. World War I created a further boost to cane sugar in the colonies by destroying beet production in Europe. The end of the war saw an unprecedented boom in sugar prices that ended, inevitably, in a slump of matching proportions. The Republicans, who returned to office in 1922, pledged to safeguard the position of American farmers. The Fordney-McCumber Act, passed in the same year, raised sugar duties at a moment when farm prices were dropping and supplies, stimulated by favorable conditions before and during the war, were rising. Real wages in the islands fell and profit margins narrowed for all but the very largest sugar producers. By the close of the decade, and in the absence of a sustained recovery in the international economy, the demand in the United States for stronger defenses against competing imports reached critical voting point. The Republicans read the message and responded in 1930 by imposing the highly protectionist Smoot-Hawley Tariff.

The Smoot-Hawley Tariff helped to turn a serious situation into a disaster. The viability of the colonies was already in question; the hardship of the 1930s ravaged colonial producers, threatened political stability, and brought a raw form of populist democracy to bear on the pressing issues of the day. The Democrats, who returned to power in 1932, passed the Jones-Costigan Act, which attempted to stabilize the sugar market by allocating quotas to both insular and mainland producers. As table 11.1 shows, the Smoot-Hawley and Jones-Costigan Acts benefited domestic cane and beet producers, who had full voting rights, and gave modest support through the quota system to colonial producers. These gains were made at the expense of Cuba, which was treated as a foreign country and left to swing in the wind—which was blowing at gale force. In the 1920s, the island supplied 53 percent of all the sugar consumed in the United States; in the 1930s, the figure dropped to 30 percent. Protectionist measures imposed by other countries had closed all other markets.

The consequences were far-reaching. Cuba underwent an immediate upheaval; distant aftershocks were felt in the Revolution of 1959. Islands within the empire also faced radical challenges. The white oligarchs who ran the government of Hawai'i were so dismayed to find that the island was being treated as a colony for the purpose of determining quotas, rather than as an incorporated territory, that they decided, reluctantly, to give up its existing status and apply for statehood. The Philippines, an unloved and now unwanted competitor, had to adjust rapidly to President Roosevelt's decision to cut the islands loose as soon as possible. Independence, long wished for, was to be granted, or rather imposed, in circumstances that fell far short of the advertised criteria. By the close of the 1930s, even the rhetoric of the civilizing mission had evaporated. All that was left was a face-saving operation designed to suggest that Washington's pilots were steering the ship of empire into port, whereas in reality they were abandoning it as speedily as they could, having thrown overboard the burdensome ballast of "viability" and "democracy."

The history of the sugar lobbies remains as opaque as the dealings of the insiders who managed them. From what is currently known, the period between 1898 and 1941 can be divided into two overlapping phases. The first, which ran from the 1890s down to 1912, was dominated by the American Sugar Refining Company, known simply as the Sugar Trust, which was directed by the dictatorial and devious Henry Havemeyer until his death in 1907.[89] Havemeyer represented the type of corporate capitalism that developed during the Gilded Age; his distinction was to extend it to the new empire. By the time of the Spanish-American War, Havemeyer controlled the principal sugar refineries in the United States, and in 1902–1903 acquired the most important sugar beet interests on the mainland. After the war, his interests spread into sugar production in the overseas territories, especially Cuba. Havemeyer's strategy owed nothing to economies of scale and everything to the imperative of muting political opposition to his plans for controlling the sugar market. If the best of all monopoly profits is a quiet life, or at least a predictable one, by 1903 Havemeyer appeared to have a restful conclusion to his turbulent career in view. As it happened, his demise took the form of a Dickensian morality tale: his death in 1907, following an exceptionally hearty Thanksgiving dinner, was linked to the imminent exposure of massive fraud perpetrated by the Sugar Trust over several decades.[90]

Havemeyer's political influence during this critical period, when the spoils of empire were being divided, deserves much greater attention than it has received.[91] Besides being monarch of the Sugar Trust, Havemeyer was also the largest single contributor to Republican Party funds. Political philanthropy on the scale he supported opened doors to Congress and the White House. He had powerful allies in Congress: Elihu Root, who was successively Secretary of War and Secretary of State between 1899 and 1909, and Nelson Aldrich, one of the most senior and influential Republican senators, continued to smooth his path, as they had done in the 1890s.[92] It was Havemeyer's action in challenging the right of the U.S. government to levy taxes on Puerto Rico that ultimately led to the Supreme Court's celebrated judgment in the Insular Cases.[93] When the decision went against him, Havemeyer responded in 1902–1903 by acquiring the most important sugar beet interests in the United States. In buying the companies, he also bought their silence and disarmed their powerful lobby in Congress.[94] He was then able to use his connections in Congress to negotiate free trade for the island, thus ensuring that raw sugar could enter his refineries as cheaply as possible. Havemeyer was also the prime mover behind the reciprocity treaty that granted Cuba a tariff concession on its exports of sugar to the United States in 1903. Simultaneously, he accelerated his already vigorous policy of horizontal and vertical integration by establishing sugar plantations throughout the new insular empire in a bid to control competition from rival producers. In characteristic freebooting style, he circumvented the formal limits on land-holding in Puerto Rico and the Philippines to create large sugar estates there, and opened a new plantation frontier in eastern Cuba. Havemeyer was exceptionally adroit in turning Smith's invisible hand to his own advantage and in keeping its assistants well hidden.

After Havemeyer's death in 1907, the power of the Sugar Trust began to wane.[95] Action taken under anti-trust legislation in 1912 sapped the Trust's monopoly of refining; beet production expanded beyond its control. By 1921, the Sugar Trust controlled only about one-quarter of the refining capacity in the United States. By then, too, the beet industry was rooted in a large number of states and could again act as an independent influence on voices and votes in the House and Senate.[96] Thereafter, the lobbies representing domestic beet and cane sugar had the upper hand. Congressmen from the beet- and sugar-producing states steered the protective tariffs enacted in 1922 and 1930 through the House and Senate and ensured that they, and the quotas introduced in 1934, were tailored to fit the needs of their constituents. In the battle of interests, the colonial branch of American capitalism, though prominently represented by investments in sugar production in Cuba, lost to resurgent domestic interests. It is no wonder that Hawai'i decided to campaign for statehood to get inside the tariff, while the unincorporated territories were left out in the cold to ponder how to reconcile continuing economic dependence with aspirations for political independence.

"A COURSE OF TUITION UNDER A STRONG AND GUIDING HAND"[97]

It was left to officials in Washington and on the frontiers of empire to translate the rhetorical ambitions of expansionists into management policy and to turn the technology prized by Progressives into operational tools of development. Unfortunately, the assessment of their endeavors that follows must be provisional because the record of the colonial service is yet another neglected aspect of the history of the American Empire.[98] Two large initiatives, however, command attention: the first, taken by a Republican administration shortly after the end of the Spanish-American War, established colonial rule; the second, taken by Democrats amidst the international crises of the 1930s, prepared the way for its demise.

The acquisition of the American Empire was not accidental, but it was unplanned. The United States had neither a Colonial Office nor a colonial service. The federal bureaucracy was itself rudimentary and still riddled with products of the "spoils system." In 1901, Woodrow Wilson commented on the "dispersion of authority" that produced "untrained officials" and regretted the fact that "an expert civil service is almost unknown to us."[99] The British retained a small Gladstonian state, but civil service reforms had been under way since the mid-nineteenth century and Whitehall was able to attract recruits from Oxford and Cambridge and a number of private schools that specialized in producing candidates for public office. Colonial service offered a prestigious and reasonably prosperous career with opportunities for advancement through a well-established bureaucratic hierarchy. The English gentlemen who staffed the service were much admired, not least by Marshal Hubert Lyautey, who reformed the *École coloniale* (founded in 1888) after the turn of the century to raise administrative standards in the French colonies to the level found in the British Empire.[100] Tugwell, the governor of Puerto Rico, said that he "understood better" why the "colonial system had persisted" after he became acquainted with British colonial officers.[101] "All of them were different but all of them were somehow alike."[102] They shared "a vast dignity founded on an ancient tradition considered changeless and impregnable."[103] By "becoming identified with the person of the King," they themselves were invested "with more regality than ever seems quite natural or appropriate to an American. Long accustomedness," he concluded, "makes them marvelously at home in their roles, however, and they live their lives without ever unbending."

It fell to Elihu Root to assemble a colonial service speedily and from existing resources.[104] Urgency added momentum to the cause of civil service reform, which had struggled to overcome long-standing opposition to changes that threatened to augment the power and effectiveness of central government. By 1914, about two-thirds of federal civil servants were appointed by merit, and the bureaucracy had become a political force in its own right.[105] By then, too, Root had succeeded in the substantial task of reforming the army, whose lack of preparation had been exposed during the Spanish-American War. Public service abroad, however, lagged behind developments on the mainland. It was not until the Foreign Service Act of 1924 that consular and diplomatic services were amalgamated to create the U.S. Foreign Service.[106] Before then, appointments continued to be made largely through political connections, and recruits still needed private resources because Congress was unwilling to fund a fully professional foreign service. Thereafter, applicants were selected on merit, though women and "persons of color" were still effectively barred. The result was a dramatic, if also belated, transformation: in 1924, 73 percent of U.S. diplomats had been educated in private schools; by 1936, the figure had dropped to 25 percent. By the 1930s, the

rational-legal structures that Max Weber put at the center of his definition of the modern state were more or less in place—at the moment,
ironically, when the United States was planning its exit from empire.[107]

President McKinley had intended to create a department of colonial
affairs in the State Department to oversee the new overseas territories.[108] Congress, however, had spent its imperial passion and was unwilling to add to the power of the federal government. McKinley and
Roosevelt then proposed to place the overseas territories under one authority, preferably the War Department, but this idea, too, was defeated.
The outcome was a compromise: the Bureau of Insular Affairs, which
was created in 1902, was given jurisdiction over the Philippines and (in
1909) Puerto Rico; the Interior Department handled federal responsibilities for Hawai'i (and Alaska); the Navy took charge of smaller islands,
such as Guam and Samoa.[109] This arrangement honored the principle
of decentralization and satisfied critics who feared the extension of a tyrannical federal state. It also hampered the different authorities in charge
of the overseas territories from presenting a united front to Congress and
frustrated any attempt to coordinate policy for the empire as a whole.
The Bureau remained a minor entity within the War Department, which
was ill-equipped to deal with problems of postwar reconstruction and
the task of what later became known as "nation-building."[110]

The new Bureau absorbed the attitudes of the Bureau of Indian Affairs, on which it was modeled. In 1899, Root set the tone of policy, which
remained unchanged until the 1930s: "Before the people of Porto [sic]
Rico can be fully intrusted [sic] with self-government," he stated in 1899,
"they must first learn the lesson of self-control and respect for the principles of constitutional government, which require acceptance of its peaceful decisions. This lesson will necessarily be slowly learned." Otherwise:
"They would inevitably fail without a course of tuition under a strong
and guiding hand."[111] Principles thought to be appropriate for Puerto
Rico applied with even greater rigor to parts of the insular empire that
were considered to be less advanced. Until the 1930s, the Bureau's directors were U.S. Army generals who embraced Root's attitudes, viewed
government as an exercise in military command, and applied their experience of fighting Native Americans to the task of ruling alien peoples.
Its senior colonial officials had "a status very much like that of British
residents in the native states of India," and a matching paternal attitude
toward their charges.[112]

The Bureau acted as the intermediary, through the Secretary of War,
between Congress and the colonial administrations. Until the history of

the Bureau is written, it is difficult to say exactly how power was divided among these interests.[113] Nevertheless, the Bureau appears to have exercised considerable control over administrative decisions within the insular territories because Congress showed little interest in the empire it had urged into being with such emotional commitment, and because most colonial governors complied with the Bureau's instructions.

Governorships remained unreformed offices. Positions were filled by political appointees who knew little of the territories they administered. Roosevelt's first appointment as governor-general of the Philippines in 1933 was Frank Murphy, a prominent Democrat and mayor of Detroit, who was rewarded for political services.[114] The president repaid another Democratic supporter, Robert H. Gore, by appointing him governor of Puerto Rico, also in 1933, and disposed of a potential rival, Paul McNutt, by sending him to the Philippines as High Commissioner in 1937.[115] Murphy remained in the Philippines until 1935; Gore's missteps, which included a scheme to encourage tourism by legalizing cockfighting, led to his resignation after just over a year in his post; McNutt's presidential ambitions, which he hoped to polish in high office, were frustrated in 1940, when Roosevelt decided to run for an unprecedented third term.

Governors stayed too briefly to acquire the knowledge they needed for independent judgment. The fifteen U.S. governors of Puerto Rico between 1900 and 1946 each held their posts for an average of 3.1 years.[116] All came from the mainland; only one spoke Spanish fluently; most did not speak it all.[117] Their power was limited and much of their time was spent trying to tread a path between the Bureau's instructions and opposition from local nationalists. The Bureau supported governors against local critics while they followed official policy, but could dispose of them if they strayed beyond authorized bounds. In 1921, President Warren Harding appointed Emmet M. Reily, a Republican, to the governorship of Puerto Rico, partly to reward his loyalty and partly to remove him from Washington.[118] Once installed, Reily pushed ahead with an assertive program of Americanization that provoked popular protest and exposed the Bureau to awkward questions about its ability to control events on the ground. He was recalled after serving less than two years.

The history of the lower ranks of the colonial service remains obscure, in contrast to the British and French empires, which have been studied in some detail.[119] Current evidence suggests that the "best ye breed" did not respond to Kipling's call but preferred to stay at home. Colonial rule in the Philippines, for example, got off to a bad start: in 1902–1903, seventeen Americans, including five provincial treasurers, were imprisoned for fraud.[120] Colonial administration lacked the prestige it enjoyed in Britain and, to a lesser extent, France. The financial incentives were unattractive and career prospects were uncertain, given the absence of a bipartisan policy toward the empire and the Democrats' stated aim of bringing it to an end.[121] Governor Francis Harrison, a Democratic appointee, reduced the American component of the Philippines' colonial service substantially between 1913 and 1921 in an attempt to accelerate the process of decolonization.[122] His successor, a Republican, then tried to reverse Harrison's policy. Duty called, but in an uncertain voice. If the purpose of administration was to prepare the empire for a speedy transition to independence, prospects for a long career studded by successive promotions were dim. Meanwhile, the drudgery of administration in unknown but unappealing parts of the world was unlikely to attract recruits whose talents matched those Kipling had publicized. As Theodore D. Roosevelt, Jr., governor successively of Puerto Rico and the Philippines reflected in 1937: "we had no colonial service and we did not develop one"[123]

Elihu Root began his period in office hoping to fuse American democratic and republican principles to British colonial practice. In the event, he was more successful in creating the means of policy than in willing the ends. As the difficulties of the undertaking became clear, Root adopted a less ambitious strategy of delegating broad powers to executive officers in the hope that they would pursue policies that were independent of the unpredictable pressures stemming from American politics and nationalist demands. In this aim, too, he was disappointed.[124] As an imperial power, the United States found itself beholden to international forces, which it could not control, and constrained by its constitution, which gave competing interest groups considerable scope for influencing colonial policy.

Delegation handed authority to Washington's representatives in the colonies. The recipients, however, were few in number and had only a limited grasp of local cultures and languages. In these circumstances, indirect rule was a necessity. Colonial authorities governed through local Big Men whose networks extended into hinterlands that were beyond the official field of vision.[125] Colonial rule became a set of bargains between chains of intermediaries. Big Men undertook to deliver civil order in return for government contracts and associated privileges. Expatriate firms helped to finance local political organizations in exchange for assistance in securing access to land and managing the labor force. Governments stiffened their presence by forming police and paramilitary forces, creating intelligence services, and establishing networks of spies. These supports for the "civilizing mission" were found throughout the overseas territories, besides being a feature of dollar diplomacy.[126] In this matter, the United States followed established practice. Britain's imperial police originated with the East India Company and evolved to the point where British members of the Palestine Police considered themselves to be the equivalent of the French Foreign Legion.[127] French imperial policing derived from Napoleon's European conquests and built on institutions introduced after the French Revolution, notably the *Gendarmerie nationale* (1791).[128] Techniques of control developed in the colonies were exported to deal with dissidents in the home country.[129] Experience in the Philippines helped to control labor unrest in the United States in the 1920s; Britain's colonial police advised the metropolitan force about dealing with subversive activities in the 1960s.[130] Colonial governments pioneered techniques of control because their lack of legitimacy obliged them to devise innovative means of ensuring civil obedience. The security state that was handed on to independent governments was one of the universal legacies of colonial rule.

The economic crisis of the 1930s forced all colonial powers to reassess the orthodoxies that guided economic policy. None, however, did so quite as rapidly or as enthusiastically as the United States, where the very lack of bipartisanship opened the door to change. When Franklin D. Roosevelt entered the White House in 1933, he brought with him members of his Brains Trust and associated New Dealers who were eager to grasp the opportunity, denied in the 1920s, of applying Progressive ideas to reform capitalism at home and in the empire. Progressives who supported the acquisition of overseas possessions in 1898 did so because they saw in empire an opportunity to implement their ideas of social engineering and economic development. Their successors who came to prominence in the 1930s were, with some notable exceptions, Democrats who lacked the enthusiasm for empire that Republicans of an earlier generation had displayed. They coupled their reforming ethos with a keen awareness of the need to improve the disappointing colonial record they had inherited. As Democrats, they shouldered the burden of empire, not with the eagerness of imperialists, but with the commitment of trustees who sought improvement as a means of making independence a viable prospect.

Roosevelt's chief institutional reform was to create the Division of Territories and Island Possessions in the Interior Department in 1934, and to close the Bureau of Insular Affairs, which ceased operations in 1939. The Division was given jurisdiction over Hawai'i, Puerto Rico, Alaska, and the Virgin Islands in 1934, and the Philippines in 1939, and began what turned out to be a long process of centralizing the administration of the scattered island empire.[131] The Navy was left in charge of Guam and Samoa and a number of smaller islands for reasons of cost and not, as might be thought, for reasons of defense: in 1931, the Secretary of the Navy declared that neither island had strategic value.[132] The Division also gave priority to economic and social problems, which the Bureau had been criticized for neglecting.[133]

Yet, though the Bureau's military cast of mind was judged to be ill-equipped to deal with these issues, no plans were made for creating a professional colonial service. Moreover, the Division, like its predecessor, lacked weight in policy-making circles.[134] In the judgment of Tugwell, who governed Puerto Rico between 1941 and 1946, it remained "an organization whose personnel hardly reached beyond the level of clerks and secretaries, without specialists, without technicians—and naturally without any objectives beyond informational contacts with the territorial governments."[135] Policy was still determined by the sporadic actions of Congress, the persistent claims of pressure groups, and the occasional interventions of committed individuals.[136] The outbreak of World War II stalled even the modest institutional reforms that were taking place. Having adjusted policy to meet civilian priorities, the United States found that its paramount interest in the island empire during and after the war was strategic and, once again, military. The United States was no exception to the rule that empires have a habit of baffling their emperors' plans, whether or not they are well laid.

The important innovations of the time came from individual reformers who were elevated to positions of authority by President Roosevelt. The president's "new brooms" were the first to come almost exclusively from occupations outside politics or the military. They brought a fresh attitude toward colonial government, sympathized with the aspirations of colonial nationalists, and gave policy a new direction. Their plans for the empire were precursors of policies that were to be applied more widely in the Third World from the 1950s onward, and deserve a more prominent place in the history of theories of development than they have received. They drew upon Progressive ideas that had been prominent during their formative years, they aimed to rid capitalism of illegitimate accretions, especially monopolies, and they shared a belief in the merits of planning, whether through government intervention or communitarian action.

Three of Roosevelt's appointees, Harold L. Ickes, Ernest Gruening, and Rexford G. Tugwell, deserve to be discussed here, though several other figures should also be mentioned. One, Joseph R. Hayden, a professor of political science at the University of Michigan and a specialist on the Philippines, was Vice-Governor General of the colony between

1933 and 1935, and produced a major work on his experiences: *The Phil-ippines: A Study in National Development*.[137] Another, Theodore Roose-velt, Jr., a Progressive Republican like his father, had much in common with Ickes, Gruening, and Tugwell, but he and his cousin, Franklin, were political rivals. When the Democrats came to power in 1933, Theodore resigned from his position as Governor General of the Philippines.[138] Shortly afterward, he produced a survey of America's overseas posses-sions that was unreserved in its criticism of the lack of structure and system in the colonial administration.[139]

Harold Ickes was a politician, though an obscure one, who was picked by Franklin Roosevelt to be Secretary of the Interior in 1933.[140] The ap-pointment was made not as a reward for services rendered but in the hope of those to come, and more particularly to ensure that the Dem-ocrats included a progressive Republican in the cabinet. Whether in-spired or fortuitous, the office made of Ickes what he made of it: both occupied a central place in the formulation of U.S. domestic and colonial policy until 1946, when President Truman replaced him. By then, Ickes had become the longest-serving Secretary of the Interior in U.S. history. Ickes was a liberal who supported civil rights at home and colonial in-dependence abroad. At the start of his tenure, he was responsible for implementing much of the New Deal; at its close, he brought his anti-colonial stance to the founding conference of the United Nations, which he attended as an official delegate. Ickes outraged the conservative right. Clare Boothe Luce is said to have remarked that he had "the mind of a commissar and the soul of a meat axe."[141] Ickes, however, was well able to look after himself and rarely missed a chance to return an arrow for every stone thrown. Like Theodore Roosevelt, Jr., he was highly critical of America's colonial record. Writing in the 1930s, he deplored the "wide-spread misery and destitution" in Puerto Rico.[142] Shortly after resigning his post in 1946, he published a devastating critique of the history of Guam and Samoa under the rule of the Navy.[143]

Ickes created conditions that gave other like-minded officials oppor-tunities to mold colonial policy. Few had a career path as unorthodox as that of Ernest H. Gruening, who graduated from Harvard Univer-sity as a doctor, turned to journalism, became a convert to Roosevelt's New Deal policies, and was appointed the first Director of the new Di-vision of Territories and Island Possessions in 1934.[144] Gruening tried to shape colonial policy on progressive principles that would alleviate poverty and advance independence. Like others before him, he tested his ideas on Puerto Rico, which he hoped would serve as a shop window for the whole of Latin America. Conditions in the 1930s had demonstrated the inadequacy of existing policies but also made the success of alternatives problematic. Gruening encountered opposition in Puerto Rico, and failed to create a constructive relationship with the moderate nationalists. He eventually lost the support of Ickes, and finally fell out with Franklin Roosevelt over issues of international policy. He resigned in 1939 and was re-assigned as governor of Alaska, which was known as "the Siberia of the Interior Department."

At this point, however, Gruening's career began rather than ended. He remained Governor of Alaska until 1953, and became its first senator in 1959, when the territory became a state. Gruening viewed Alaska as a colony that needed development and emancipation, and he did much to achieve both.[145] In the process, he had a disagreement of the kind that was also taking place in India and Africa, when he clashed with John Collier, the Commissioner for Indian Affairs, over "native" policy. Gruening was keen to assimilate the Aleut and the Inuit; Collier, another reformer who owed his position to Ickes's influence, argued for indirect rule and conservation. Gruening was a man of principle who found compromise difficult. His final stand against the Vietnam War brought him unpopularity and, in some quarters, derision. As a prophet of what he saw to be the truth, Gruening was honored less by his country than by his own integrity, which remains part of the historical record.

Rexford G. Tugwell came to public prominence as a key member of Roosevelt's Brains Trust and as a major contributor to the ideas that went into the New Deal.[146] Tugwell was an economist at Columbia University, New York, and a former pupil of Scott Nearing, the prominent radical critic of capitalism and imperialism. He was an institutionalist in the tradition of Wesley Mitchell and John Commons with interests ranging from town planning to agricultural economics. As a member of Roosevelt's administration, he helped to create the Federal Emergency Relief Administration in 1933, and became Director of the Agricultural Adjustment Program and of the Resettlement Administration in 1935. It was in these capacities that he sponsored the offshoot programs that Gruening oversaw in Puerto Rico. Tugwell, like Gruening, aroused considerable opposition as he tried to put his plans into operation. His interventionist policies led him to be stigmatized as "Rex the Red"; his resignation in 1936 was greeted by critics as a lucky escape from Soviet collectivism. Tugwell, again like Gruening, was far from finished. In 1941, Roosevelt appointed him governor of Puerto Rico, and in this capacity he worked closely with the island's leading nationalists to craft a new development plan and to steer the country toward a greater degree of effective independence. The title of his major study, *The Stricken Land: The Story of Puerto Rico* (1947), pointed to the urgency of the island's predicament. In 1946, Tugwell helped to ensure that his successor was Puerto Rican and that future governors would be elected rather than appointed. Three years later, he was investigated by the House's Un-American Activities Committee.

"HARDLY A RIPPLE OF FAILURE UPON THE STREAM OF OUR SUCCESS"[147]

Theodore Roosevelt's confident assertion, made in 1909, referred to Puerto Rico, which was at peace. Undaunted, he made a similar claim about the Philippines, where a long war of resistance to American rule, though formally ended by administrative fiat, had yet to be concluded.

> I believe I am speaking with historic accuracy and impartiality when I say that the American treatment of and attitude toward the Filipino people, in its combination of disinterested ethical purpose and sound common sense, marks a new and long stride forward, in advance of all the steps that hitherto have been taken, along the path of wise and proper treatment of weaker by stronger races.[148]

The gap between rhetoric and reality is never larger than in imperial affairs, where distance and subordination combine to diminish accountability. Expansive claims are nevertheless worth investigating, particularly in the case of the United States, where assumptions about exceptionalism have a special place in the national psyche.

Winks's thoughtful assessment of U.S. imperialism, though far removed from naïve exceptionalism, nevertheless concluded that the American Empire differed from its European counterparts principally because the United States was itself an ex-colonial power with a republican tradition.[149] This combination of experience and principle produced a colonial system based on the assumption that "independence or statehood was the goal."[150] There was no grand design because there was no long-term purpose. Instead, there was a "brutally fast" process of Americanization to ensure that statehood or independence was reached in the shortest possible time. The transitory nature of colonial rule explains both the absence of a permanent overseas civil service and the "decreased intensity of local nationalist movements." For these reasons, the "American imperial experience is comparable to that of other nations only briefly, somewhat incidentally, and then but half the time."[151]

These stimulating, speculative conclusions need modifying to take account of the argument presented in this chapter. The fact that the United

States was a former colony did not prevent it from acquiring colonies of its own by deploying the standard tools of the trade: firearms and finance. In practice, if not in principle, republicanism was no barrier to empire-building; had that been the case, the French would not have established overseas territories in Africa, Asia, and the Pacific. In this respect, the United States stood with other colonial powers rather than against them. The United States had a well-organized and articulate anti-colonial movement, but so too did monarchical Britain and republican France. The anti-colonial tradition in the United States, though reputable and long-standing, had not prevented the seizure of Native American lands or the acquisition of territory from Mexico, and it was unable to halt the expansion of the insular empire in 1898.

The assumption that the purpose of colonial rule was to create the conditions that would lead to independence or statehood was not unique to the United States. Britain envisaged the prospect of independence through various stages of self-government; France shared with the United States the view that assimilation would culminate in constitutional equality though incorporation. The main difference among the colonial powers in this regard lay in the timing of the transition. Although the United States began by assuming that the transfer of power would be accomplished easily and speedily, experience soon defeated hope. Within about a year of taking office in 1901 as Civil Governor of the Philippines, William Taft was reckoning in terms of two or three generations, a forecast he repeated when he became Secretary of War in 1904. His prediction turned out to be accurate. Moreover, it is hard to sustain the argument that the United States led the way in preparing the insular territories for either incorporation or self-government. Hawai'i applied for statehood in the 1930s but was refused until 1959, though it had long met the entry requirements. The Philippines began the process of transition to formal independence in 1934 but did not complete it until 1946. The motive for decolonization owed almost nothing to republican traditions and everything to pressures of the moment. One inducement, which fell far short of republican ideals and Theodore Roosevelt's lofty claims, was the need to appease various domestic pressure groups by jettisoning what were thought to be the burdens of empire. Another, which appeared after World War II, was the need to realign colonial and domestic policies to meet the strategic and ideological demands of the Cold War. If civic virtue was in the mix, it was well hidden.

Contrary to Winks's suggestion, the United States did have a "grand design." The proclaimed goal was to spread the "civilizing mission" in the form of "benevolent assimilation," and to do so by novel and superior means. The American Empire was to be an exceptional empire because it would be benign rather than exploitative, promote freedom rather than suppress it, and lift the light hand of colonial rule with a degree of rapidity that other empires could not match, even if they wanted to. Once accomplished, the undertaking would demonstrate to the world, and particularly to the older colonial powers, that the United States had the insight and technical skills to succeed where they had failed.

These ambitions were less distinctive than their advocates thought. All Western colonial powers believed that they were benign rather than tyrannical and that their style of rule was superior to that of their comparators. This conclusion followed reassuringly from the premise of national virtue and virtuosity, and maintained its hold on truth by being consistently shielded from contrary evidence. In fact, the "brutally fast" process of Americanization turned out to be painfully slow. Congress was generally indifferent to the needs of the colonies but roused itself sporadically to prevent the expansion of government. It refused to vote the money to support policies it had formally approved and hobbled all efforts to produce the requisite personnel. Achievements in spreading education and medical services should be acknowledged. So, too, however, should the fact that policy toward education produced a reaction that reinforced Spanish culture and language and stimulated colonial nationalism throughout Spain's former overseas possessions. In the 1930s, Americanization lost its place at the center of colonial policy and was replaced, after a brief experiment with policies inspired by the New Deal, by the pragmatic principle that guided all colonial powers at that testing time: getting by.

Arguably, too, the absence of a Colonial Office was not the "clearest proof" that the American Empire was to be transient, but an illustration of congressional deadlock.[152] The lack of bipartisan agreement on the future of the insular territories enabled anti-imperialists to block efforts that would have promoted the civilizing mission more effectively. Abrupt changes in colonial policy following congressional elections truncated the continuity that was indispensable to the success of ambitious development plans. The policy void was filled by competing special interests whose concern lay first with themselves, and second, if at all, with the recipients of "benevolent assimilation." Britain and France, on the other hand, were able to maintain common policies toward their respective empires, despite multiple tensions and the presence of anti-colonial sentiment in high places. They also developed a permanent, professional colonial civil service that acquired and transmitted collective knowledge of the languages, social structures, and politics of countries they ruled. Of course, Britain and France also had special interests: chambers of commerce, bankers and, in France, the *parti colonial*, all tried to influence policy. In both cases, too, the funds available were never sufficient for the needs of policy. Nevertheless, the broad distinction stands, though its full effect on policy outcomes remains to be determined.

PROSPECTIVE

The insular empire exhibited distinctive features that Winks was unable to explore in the 1960s and that remain as opportunities for historians today. The legacy from Spain, which he mentioned briefly, is potentially the most important of these, though it has received little attention from a comparative perspective.[153] In the eighteenth century, the imperial powers exchanged islands as a matter of course, but in the nineteenth century the United States was unique in inheriting nearly all of its new empire from another Western power. Whereas the European imperial states governed through the agency of indigenous authorities and settlers from their own countries, the United States ruled three of its four major acquisitions through intermediaries whose origins lay in Spain. The new colonial power began by emphasizing its superiority over Spain and its determination to deliver a new, progressive program of development. The indications, however, are that continuities with the imperial past extended far into the twentieth century. In the Philippines, for instance, the inheritance from Spain had a considerable influence on the administrative structure, the legal system, racial attitudes, and habits of mind formed through education, language, and religion.[154] How far the legacy from Spain gave the United States a head start in promoting the "civilizing mission," and how far it constituted an obstacle to assimilation and Americanization, are questions that cannot be judged at present. It is clear, however, that, apart from Hawai'i, the American Empire was at least as much "a greater Spain" as it was a greater United States.

These considerations point to the importance of race as an ingredient of policy, a topic that Winks bypassed in his short essays. All the Western empires displayed the same racial prejudices, which were derived from similar intellectual and "scientific" sources and applied with similar effect in colonial policies. The United States, however, was the only one of the Western imperial powers to have a long-standing "race problem" at home rather than encountering (and creating) it abroad. Racial concerns were a particularly strong and sustained influence on the anti-colonial movement in the United States, which was stiffened by nativist opposition to both immigration and emancipation. Anti-colonial racists feared that Uncle Sam might open the door to nonwhite immigrants, and that progressive policies applied overseas might also be applied on the mainland. The fear was well founded, though it was not realized until the 1960s. Race prejudice expressed in policies toward the insular possessions fortified anti-colonial feelings in the American Empire, which included many subjects who not only were white but who also thought of themselves as representatives of European culture overseas. As in other regions of white settlement, the European heritage had been modified by local conditions but also in some respects strengthened to prevent the standard bearers from "going native." Former citizens of the Spanish Empire objected to the loss of electoral and other reforms they had wrung from the Spanish government before 1898. They resented becoming colonial subjects once again, and they resisted assimilation. In this way, policies that suited interests on the mainland alienated those who were supposed to benefit from the civilizing mission.

A further distinction, which Winks noted but did not explore, was the wholly insular character of the American Empire, which contrasted with the extensive territorial possessions of the British and French empires. It is unclear, however, how much significance to attach to this indisputable fact. The questions it raises about the relationship between the size of colonies and the nature of colonial rule are intriguing but, in the present state of knowledge, unanswerable. What can be said, in the case of the United States, is that the possession of islands appears to have had little or no influence on the formulation of colonial policy. As we have seen, the diversity of the islands ensured that they illustrated the full range of colonial categories—from direct and indirect rule to assimilation and association—found in the larger territorial empires. In this respect, the islands were microcosms of the much larger British and French empires rather than special, limited cases. Nor were the insular possessions, scattered though they were, isolated backwaters. They had multiple connections, apart from those with the American mainland. Filipino and Asian immigrants accounted for most of the labor force on the sugar plantations of Hawai'i; Chinese immigrants settled in the Philippines and, in smaller numbers, in Cuba; Puerto Ricans were distributed throughout the Caribbean as well as on the mainland. Progressive ideas, including self-determination, flowed around the Spanish-speaking islands in the Pacific and Caribbean, and gave the political opponents of colonial rule a sense of common purpose. Hawai'i spread Pentecostalism to Puerto Rico and Cuba, and exported capital to the Philippines. The islands were not merely minor recipients of globalization but active agents distributing its influence.

Some of the claimed differences between the American and European empires were unimportant or even illusory; others qualify as being distinctive. None of the distinctive characteristics, however, was powerful enough to give the American Empire a unique trajectory. The insular territories were acquired at the close of the nineteenth century, which was exactly when other "late-start" imperial powers, such as Germany, Italy, and Japan, were seeking overseas possessions, and when the established imperial powers were adding to their holdings. The empire ended in the 1940s and 1950s, which was precisely when the other Western imperial powers also abandoned colonial rule. In between, the fortunes of all the Western empires moved in unison. Exceptionalism was claimed; normality ruled.

In all cases, colonial rule became a gamble on the continuing success of international trade. The Western colonies in Asia, Africa, the Caribbean, and the Pacific relied on exports of primary products to generate the revenues and incomes that sustained standards of living above subsistence, funded government projects—such as transport, utilities, education, and agricultural improvements—and entered the coffers of governments. Producers in the American Empire operated within the same framework of constraints and opportunities as exporters of raw materials in and beyond the European empires. Their fortunes depended ultimately on world demand, as expressed in the prices paid for their produce, and immediately on colonial policies, especially those regulating tariffs. They were also obliged to compete with one another for market shares of identical or substitute products. Marked fluctuations in the international economy reverberated throughout the world during the colonial period, demonstrating that specialization delivered competitive advantages but also vulnerability to exogenous shifts in demand.

This dynamic was not the sole determinant of events in the colonial empires. Colonial policy and attitudes toward it drew on additional sources of inspiration. Nevertheless, the evidence indicates that economic considerations were instrumental in shaping policy and influencing the reactions of colonial subjects. It further suggests that the history of the insular empire fits the better-known history of the British and French empires because their fortunes were all driven by a common cause. Future research may modify these claims. For the present, however, they will serve as signposts to the case studies that follow in chapters 12 and 13. The main argument applies to both chapters, and is summarized here to avoid repetition there.

The period from 1900 to 1913 saw a recovery in export prices that boosted colonial economies everywhere and assisted new rulers to manage the transition from acquisition to occupation. Although militant resistance continued in the Philippines, as in parts of Africa and south Asia, the revival of revenues and incomes helped to fund fledgling administrations, expand export crops, and reconcile key interest groups to a new era of subordination. World War I disrupted markets and shipping, but also increased demand for most primary products. The resulting oscillations culminated in a postwar boom and slump. The first produced "mushroom gentlemen," as they were called in Nigeria; the second swallowed them. The disruption of the war years, the shortage of manufactured goods, and the loss of life of many colonial subjects also had marked political repercussions. Disillusion spread; popular protests and nationalist claims tested colonial rule throughout the Western empires. This was when Gandhi came to prominence, Mao Tse-tung began to make his mark, Quezon and Osmeña amplified their calls for independence for the Philippines, and a young Puerto Rican nationalist, Albizu Campos, turned to radical solutions to solve the colonial "problem." In Hawai'i, half the labor force on the sugar plantations struck for higher wages; in Cuba, political instability prompted the United States to re-occupy the island.

The 1920s marked the high tide of the American Empire, as arguably, for the European empires as well. Britain and France emerged from the conflict with their empires intact and with a renewed determination to reassert their grip on their possessions, which had demonstrated their value during a time of siege and need. The return of more stable economic conditions in the 1920s took the edge off the sharpest expressions of discontent and dissolved many of the embryonic political organizations that had sprung up during the war. British policy mixed repression with concession in India, shelved gunboat diplomacy in China, and began to work with important nationalists, such as Mahatma Gandhi and Chiang Kai-shek. The Republicans returned to power in the United States with the aim of reviving the civilizing mission. Radicals were taken out of the political system, where possible; moderates were given moderate encouragement. In the Philippines, Governor Wood held fast to a policy of firm tutelage while cooperating cautiously with moderates, like Quezon and Osmeña. In Cuba, the United States backed another moderate, President Gerardo Machado, in the hope that he would control the radical nationalists and deliver stability. In Puerto Rico, radical elements were too divided to present a serious challenge to the forces of moderation. In Hawai'i, white settlers felt secure enough to deal with sporadic strike action by repressing it. At this time, most colonial nationalists aimed for reform, not revolution, and had yet to encompass the wider populace. The Indian National Congress was an exception, but in the 1920s it was by no means clear that even movements with grass roots would grow strongly enough to produce a green uprising.

The global depression that marked the 1930s wrecked colonial economies, galvanized radical nationalism, and polarized the choices facing the ruling powers and their moderate colonial allies. The collapse of primary produce prices reduced living standards and increased unemployment. Colonial nationalism assumed a novel and more threatening character: a green (and brown) uprising brought peasants and urban workers into the political arena; a new generation of leaders, drawn from the so-called youth movements, arose to direct their energies. Colonial rulers scrambled to devise ways of maintaining political stability in the face of mass demonstrations, strikes, civic violence, and the claims of radical political parties. Despite assertions to the contrary, the "intensity of local nationalist movements" in the American Empire was no less than it was in the European empires.[155] In Hawai'i, newly organized, militant interracial unions cut into the power of the settler oligarchy. In the Philippines, mass discontent compounded by the radical Sakdalista movement drove moderate leaders toward independence at a much faster pace than their comfort dictated. In Puerto Rico, official violence in the name of law and order produced a backlash that led to the attempted assassination of the governor. In Cuba, widespread hardship culminated in a civil war that destroyed the old political system and installed Sergeant Batista as the new voice of the people.

By the close of the decade, colonial authorities everywhere had come to accept the need for change. Britain and France formulated policies for colonial development that involved an increased role for government and plans for producing a new generation of educated colonial intermediaries. Roosevelt's New Dealers set about applying similar ideas to the insular territories. Britain's reforms were devised to hold an empire that was worth retaining; Roosevelt's were a belated attempt to prepare the way for unloading an unpopular set of troublesome islands. As it became clear that the war on want was to be one of costly attrition with an uncertain outcome, scuttle was preferred to battle.

World War II, which was long considered to be decisive in cracking open the sealed containers of colonial rule, now appears as a disruptive event at the end of a process that saw the key elements of change assembled and mobilized during the 1930s. The war itself had a differential effect on the Western empires. Large segments of the European colonies in Asia and Africa were fought over and occupied; others, notably India and the dominions, were heavily involved in the conflict but did not become theaters of war. The same contrasts marked the American Empire: Hawai'i was bombed, Guam was invaded, the Philippines became a major battleground; Cuba and Puerto Rico, like the British West Indies, were left relatively undisturbed. The war jumbled fortunes everywhere: Hawai'i recovered faster from the disaster at Pearl Harbor than it did from the military rule that followed; the Philippines suffered immeasurably from the Japanese occupation and the guerrilla warfare that accompanied it; demand for their exports helped Puerto Rico and Cuba to recover from the trials of the 1930s. Despite these diverse experiences, in 1945 colonial subjects across the colonial world shared a determination not to return to the prewar order they had helped to undermine, and an ambition to put something different and better in its place. This time there was to be no restoration of the prewar order, no bonfire of controls, and no high-flying promises about self-determination that would be allowed to wing their way to oblivion.

CHAPTER 12

CARIBBEAN CARNIVAL

PLEASURE ISLANDS

It is remarkable that the Caribbean, so long a home to slavery, should have succeeded in acquiring an image of sunshine, carnivals, calypsos, and happy-go-lucky natives. The triumph of art over artifact was a feature of the twentieth century, as it was in the Pacific, and was primarily the work of the tourist industry, ably assisted by the music industry. At the turn of the century, however, the United States saw little sunshine in Cuba and Puerto Rico and few happy-go-lucky natives. In 1900, Major-General Leonard Wood, the military governor of Cuba, prepared for a long and demanding assignment: "We are dealing with a race that has steadily been going down for a hundred years, and into which we have to infuse new life, new principles and new methods of doing things."[1] Elihu Root, the Secretary of War, took a similar view of Puerto Rico. The fact that the majority of the population was white did not compensate for the island's Latin, Roman Catholic inheritance or for the debilitating influence of what Senator Albert Beveridge called "the weak, corrupt, cruel, and capricious rule of Spain."[2] As Root saw it, the United States was obliged to become the benign but firm guardian of the island's inhabitants, who required "a course of tuition under a strong and guiding hand."[3]

The transformation of Cuba's image dates from the 1920s, by which time the *Maine*, though still remembered, had ceased to stir warlike passions. Prohibition and proximity combined to make Havana an international center of high living, a "paradise of cocktails" that included gambling and prostitution.[4] The mainland's rediscovery of the island featured music, dance, and carnivals, which magnified Cuba's image as a site of perpetual indulgence. Popular manifestations of island culture were appropriated and adapted for mainland consumption, as images of the Philippines and Hawai'i were, too.[5] The Havana Casino Orchestra had its first big hit in 1930, when it took the song, *"El Manisero"* (The Peanut Vendor), to the United States. The lyrics were reassuringly banal:

If you haven't got bananas don't be blue
Peanuts in a little bag are calling you.[6]

Representations of Puerto Rico never reached the levels of extravagance associated with Cuba, partly because its status as an unincorporated territory imposed controls that did not apply to an independent country, and partly because it had escaped the extreme turbulence that had loosened the bonds of Cuban society in the late nineteenth century. Nevertheless, Puerto Rico acquired a "stylish mystique" from visiting celebrities, and had its own distinctive cultural expressions that contributed to its aura as a tropical haven.[7]

Beyond either the reach or the comprehension of foreign recipients and tourists, however, original idioms retained their independence and vigor in the Caribbean, as they did in the Pacific. What became known, generically, as "Latin American" dance conveyed messages that derived from distinctive local origins. Rumba and salsa enjoyed popularity in Puerto Rico and Cuba not only as statements of social engagement but also as expressions of liberation.[8] Puerto Rico perpetuated long-standing forms of musical expression in the *jíbaro*, which was originally "country" music, and the *plena*, which emerged early in the twentieth century as a form of "newspaper in song" serving the expanding urban labor force.[9] Jíbaro idealized, celebrated, and reaffirmed the simple virtues of rural life threatened by intrusive forces:

I know what love is
of one who was on the land
when love's joy is embraced
and works by the sweat of his brow.
because I know how to value it
and I know how to win and lose,
but I don't want to relapse
and I want you to be motivated
because in this *jíbaro* live
the customs of before.[10]

Cultural idioms responded creatively to the changes brought by colonial influences. The spirit of Cuba's national hero, José Martí, who died in the war against Spain in 1895, lived on in criticism of the United States and in continuing hopes for genuine independence. Martí himself was impressed by the material progress of the mainland but was appalled by what he saw as "the crude, uneven, and decadent character of the United States, and the continuous existence there of all the violence, discord, immorality, and disorder blamed upon the peoples of Spanish America."[11] Martí's hopes of stemming the spread of U.S. influence were frustrated, but the ideal of selfless patriotism he represented contributed indelibly to Cuba's evolving sense of national identity. His life, values, and verse inspired the lyrics of the island's most famous song, *Guantanamera*:

> With the poor people of the earth I cast my lot
> With the poor people of the earth I throw my fate
> For the brooks of the mountains please me more than the sea.[12]

Puerto Rico's sober, elitist image disguised a lively literary scene that included discussion of an enduring theme: how to combine the traditional with the modern. Emilio Delgado captured the unfolding story with a mixture of nostalgia and dissent in 1929:

> Today you are sad, Island
> The peasant sees you leave—resigned—
> In the smoke sent up by the *centrales*
> And in the bourgeois pipe of Uncle Sam.[13]

Colonizers and colonized viewed reality through mutually uncomprehending images. They were, in Longfellow's phrase, like ships that pass in the night with no more than a brief signal or a distant voice of recognition. Reality itself was shaped by larger forces that altered the context and hence the content of cultural expression. The context, as this chapter will show, was the product of interactions between global and local influences. Colonial politics was the result of mixing techniques of indirect rule and informal influence with the ambitions of political elites in Puerto Rico and Cuba. Colonial economies arose from decisions made about allocating land rights, opening overseas markets, and developing monocultures based on sugar. Colonial cultures emerged from attempts to deliver a civilizing mission to those who thought that they were already civilized. A shared heritage derived from Spanish rule, Spanish settlers, Roman Catholicism, and African slaves underlined these similarities.

Common features, however, were consistent with long-standing contrasts that were amplified in the nineteenth century and further complicated after 1898 by the intrusive and varied influence of the United States. Puerto Rico and Cuba differed in size, resources, and constitutional standing. Puerto Rico was small and overpopulated, lacked a rich natural endowment, and was an unincorporated territory under the jurisdiction of the United States. Cuba was much larger than Puerto Rico, had abundant fertile resources, and was formally independent.[14] Commonalities help to explain why the islands cohabited within a broad

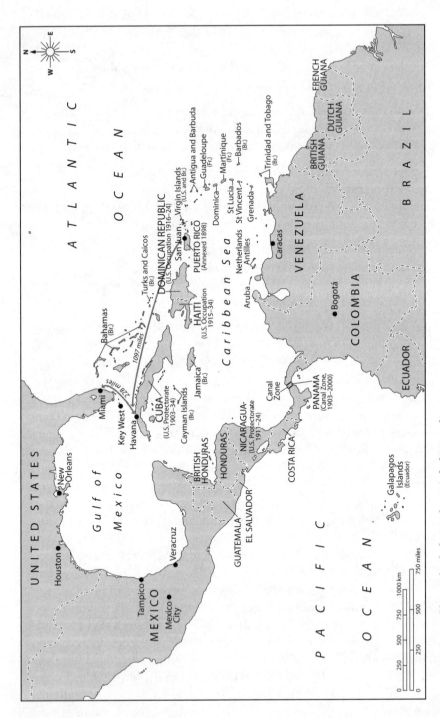

MAP 12.1. The Caribbean Islands during the Period of U.S. Rule.

imperial framework. Diversity helps to explain why they developed separate identities.

PUERTO RICO: "AN EXAMPLE OF THE BEST METHODS OF ADMINISTERING OUR INSULAR POSSESSIONS"[15]

"So excellent has been the administration of the island, so excellent the effect of the legislation concerning it, that their very excellence has caused most of us to forget all about it."[16] That was President Theodore Roosevelt's confident, if also premature, judgment delivered in 1902. A generation later, the president's son, arriving in Puerto Rico as governor in 1929, recorded a different impression: "Poverty was widespread and hunger, almost to the verge of starvation, common, and the island remained disease ridden."[17] The senior Roosevelt was impressed by the military thoroughness the ubiquitous and ever-energetic General Wood had applied to refurbishing the instruments of state after the rapid termination of Spanish rule. Theodore Roosevelt, Jr., on the other hand, was reflecting on three decades of civilian endeavor in attempting to turn the "civilizing mission" into reality. His impression, recorded before the effects of the depression were felt, was echoed by the Brookings Institution, which reported in 1930 that "the condition of the masses of the Island people remains deplorable."[18]

No case illustrates better than Puerto Rico the determination of the United States to join the ranks of Western empire-builders. The island had been acquired as a by-product of the Cuban war. It was neither a threat to the mainland nor a strategic necessity; its economic importance and potential were limited. Yet, Puerto Rico occupied a special place in the official mind of U.S. imperialism. Elihu Root, the Secretary of War, expressed a long-standing view in regarding the island as constituting a test case of the superiority of the American version of the civilizing mission and as a display window advertising the values of liberty and democracy to the whole of Latin America[19] The Philippines, beset by a rampant insurgency, had damaged the expansionists' cause at home. Fires had been lit in Luzon, but the intended beacon of civilization and progress had scarcely flickered there, still less illuminated the unknown depths of Southeast Asia. Puerto Rico, closer to home, smaller, and seemingly more easily controlled, was to provide the justification for empire that the Philippines had denied.

Despite the disparaging remarks made at the turn of the century, Washington's experts viewed the future with a measure of optimism.

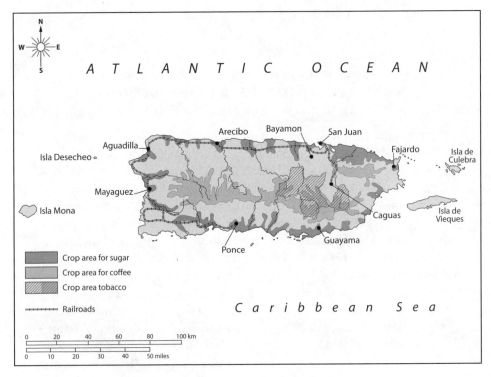

MAP 12.2. Puerto Rico: Export Crops, Railroads, and Towns, 1920.

Puerto Rico had developed a capacity for self-government that stood in comparison with Hawai'i, which had been registered as an incorporated territory. A substantial, and largely white, landowning class and an educated elite had grown up during the nineteenth century.[20] One segment of the elite (predominantly *criollos*) had arrived as political refugees from the upheavals on the mainland of South America; another (*peninsulares*) had emigrated from Spain in the second half of the century.[21] Both groups, broadly speaking, were conservative loyalists who, unlike Cubans, did not take up arms against the motherland. Most of them settled in the two principal towns. San Juan, the administrative and cultural center, was also a major port. Ponce was a thriving center of commerce and finance, with modern utilities (including electricity), an educated and prosperous middle class, and connections to the wider world provided by submarine cable. These attributes were insufficient to persuade Root to deviate from the policies he had devised for the other territories acquired from Spain in 1898. Whiteness alone was insufficient qualification for superior status, while to be semi-white was, so to speak, a black mark. The belief that the Latin "race" lacked Anglo-Saxon attributes weighed heavily in the minds of policy-makers, while Roman Catholicism was thought to add undesirable qualities that only Protestantism could expunge. Nevertheless, American know-how, energy, and direction could succeed where centuries of Spanish rule had failed.

The Foraker Act, passed in 1900, provided Puerto Rico with its first constitution as an unincorporated territory of the United States.[22] The legitimacy of the Act was then tested by the Supreme Court, which confirmed that the United States could exercise authority in ways that did not entail incorporation and citizenship.[23] The judgment left Puerto Rico in constitutional limbo until 1952, when the United States granted the island the full uncertainties of Commonwealth status.[24] In 1901, Luis Muñoz Rivera, Puerto Rico's leading political figure, summarized the ambivalence that was to characterize the island's standing throughout the century: "We are and we are not an integral part of the United States. We are and we are not a foreign country. We are and we are not citizens of the United States. The Constitution covers us and does not cover us."[25] Muñoz Rivera's own position reflected these ambiguities. In 1897, he stood for home rule; in 1898, following the arrival of American troops, he hoped that Puerto Rico would be incorporated into the United States; by 1901, he again advocated autonomy, though this time from the United States rather than from Spain.

In accord with the Foraker Act, and supported by the judgment of the Supreme Court, policy-makers installed institutions of government that combined elements of territorial administration, drawn from the mainland, with borrowings from the British colony of Trinidad, where levels of economic development, education, and health were considered to be far ahead of those found in Puerto Rico.[26] Accordingly, the island was assigned a governor, who was selected by the President, an appointed Executive Council, and a House of Delegates elected by a limited franchise. Legislative power, however, was subject to the approval of the governor and ultimately to the right of veto held by Congress in Washington. Key positions in the police force, the senior courts, government finance, and education were filled by American citizens. These provisions gave Puerto Ricans less power than territorial governments enjoyed on the mainland and offered little scope for the proposed training in self-government. The new constitution was also a step backward. Under Spanish rule, Puerto Rico had become a province of Spain and its inhabitants had been Spanish citizens who sent representatives to the Cortés.[27] Root's "strong and guiding hand" was present; the "course of tuition," assuming it was required, was largely absent.

Nevertheless, the guiding hand, no matter how strong, needed help from local agents. As in the Philippines, the United States found that government could function only by harnessing and rewarding members of the great; the good were an asset but not a necessity. As in the Philippines, too, collaborative arrangements were stiffened by covert policing operations that kept political activities under permanent surveillance.[28] For their part, political activists in Puerto Rico began by hoping that the United States would confirm their success in winning autonomy from Spain. Disillusion arrived by courier. By 1904, Muñoz Rivera and other political leaders no longer expected the U.S. presence to deliver liberty, equality, or autonomy. Like their counterparts in Cuba and the Philippines, they were compelled instead to edge their way between rocks and hard places. Some degree of cooperation with the United States was essential; full cooperation, however, would compromise even modest nationalist goals. The two main political parties adapted to the new colonial order. The *Partido Republicano* (1899) aimed at statehood; the *Partido Unión* (formed in 1904 from the *Partido Federal*) hoped for independence or, if that option proved to be unattainable, some form of autonomy.

Before long, however, it became apparent that the United States intended to offer neither statehood nor independence. Advocates of the Jones Act, which became law in 1917, presented it as a progressive measure that conferred American citizenship on Puerto Ricans and expanded the political process by creating an elected senate.[29] In reality, the Act was designed to ensure that the United States would control the island in perpetuity, which is why Muñoz Rivera and the House of Delegates opposed it.[30] Unsurprisingly, the Act had a limited effect on political realities. The extension of the franchise did nothing to disturb the power of veto, which the governor and Congress continued to deploy to stymie unacceptable proposals.[31] From this perspective, citizenship was an unwelcome consolation prize for the reluctance of the United States to grant either statehood or significantly greater autonomy. The Supreme Court endorsed the nationalists' assessment in 1922, when it confirmed that the island would remain an unincorporated territory. The Jones Act was also motivated by needs of the moment that were far removed from the lofty ideals of liberty and democracy: President Wilson hoped that citizenship would generate loyalty in case the United States was drawn into the European war. One of the first consequences of the privilege was to make Puerto Ricans eligible for service in the armed forces. By the end of the war, about 20,000 men had been conscripted.

Once the United States had excluded the key constitutional issues from serious consideration, political parties were obliged to concentrate their energies on the limited range of matters over which they had some influence. The spoils of peace, represented by expanded opportunities for patronage in an enlarged electoral system, became the focus of political rivalry. A self-imposed motive for limiting the range of political debate reinforced this trend. The two leading parties represented propertied interests. The Partido Republicano spoke for substantial sugar interests; the Partido Unión drew on a mixture of sugar and coffee producers and merchants.[32] Neither party was willing to risk espousing radical claims. Both were well aware that the "Isle of Enchantment," as Spain had named it, contained volatile elements that needed to be cooled down rather than brought to a boiling point. The rapid development of the export sector in the second half of the nineteenth century, the abolition of slavery, the persistence of rural poverty, the continuing incidence of brigandage, and the influx of peninsulares constituted a potentially explosive mixture.[33] Political progress was highly desirable; the defense of property more so. Warning signs appeared during World War I, when large-scale strikes and rural unrest demonstrated the extent of discontent with the new colonial order.

The Foraker Act raised economic as well as constitutional issues. McKinley and Root had originally planned to allow Puerto Rico's sugar free entry into the United States. The concession was a departure from Republican protectionist principles but was made in response to the island's urgent needs. The dislocation experienced as a result of the Spanish-American War had intensified in 1899, when a hurricane destroyed 80 percent of the coffee crop, which was then the leading export.[34] The new and still uncertain American administration in Puerto Rico sent an urgent call for remedial action. McKinley responded with a proposal to allow Puerto Rico's sugar and tobacco exports free entry into the United States. Coffee was already on the free list, but had difficulty competing with cheaper coffee from Brazil.[35] Powerful interests, led by the Sugar Trust, gave the proposal immediate and enthusiastic support.[36]

Havemeyer and the Sugar Trust were elated by McKinley's proposal. If Puerto Rico were treated as an incorporated territory for tariff purposes, raw sugar would enter the United States, and the Trust's refineries, free of duty.[37] Mainland producers of sugarcane, beet, and tobacco, and protectionists in general, on the other hand, were dismayed, even though the immediate competitive threat from the island was minimal. If tariff concessions were granted to Puerto Rico, the objectors argued, Cuba and the Philippines would demand similar treatment.[38] Faced with the prospect of immolation, McKinley dropped his original plan and substituted the compromise that emerged in the Foraker Act, which imposed a tariff of 15 percent of the prevailing rate on Puerto Rico's exports (principally, sugar, coffee, and tobacco). Even so, beet and cane interests in the United States remained concerned that the tariff would fail to curb Puerto Rico's sugar exports. In an adroit, last-minute maneuver aimed at preventing the development of large, efficient plantations on the island, lobbyists added a clause to the Foraker Bill limiting corporations to maximum holdings of 500 acres.[39] The episode established the vital principle that the United States could legislate for Puerto Rico, and by extension for other possessions, without incorporating them. It also confirmed that, even where economic and political circumstances were reasonably propitious, economic interests and nativist sentiment in the United States remained implacably opposed to giving insular territories, apart from Hawai'i, opportunities to become incorporated states of the Union.

This was not the end of the matter, however. In 1902, Congress granted Puerto Rico complete free trade with the United States. The concession was made chiefly to prop up the precarious Puerto Rican economy and to support the fledgling American administration there, but it was won largely by the actions of the Sugar Trust, which worked assiduously after 1900 to nullify protectionist interests by taking over the requisite number of sugar beet firms.[40] In the case of the American Empire, free trade was imperial preference under a benign name: it stimulated U.S. investment, buttressed corporate capitalism, and encouraged monopolistic tendencies. Additional support for American interests came from measures that confined shipping to and from the mainland to U.S. vessels, prevented Puerto Rico from negotiating commercial treaties and adjusting tariff levels, and replaced the peso with the dollar.[41]

In 1901, the South Porto Rico Sugar Company, one of the Sugar Trust's few significant if also temporary competitors, began to construct what became one of the world's largest milling complexes in the southern coastal town of Guánica.[42] The company built a sizable, self-sufficient complex around the spire of its huge cathedral-like sugar mill, called on agronomic expertise from Louisiana and Barbados, drew finance from New York, and hired labor from across the Caribbean.[43] Similarly, the Tobacco Trust expanded its presence on the island to control the processing and marketing of the crop, though production remained in the hands of small producers.[44] These developments were manifestations of the growing concentration of power among emerging transnational corporations. Former distinctions among contending parties became blurred as beet producers merged with refiners, as refiners turned themselves into overseas producers, as newly enlarged producers spread themselves over different islands in the Caribbean, and as the New York banks supplied an increasing share of the capital these costly developments required. The process of integration reached its highest point during the wartime sugar boom, when Horace Havemeyer, Henry's son, joined the board of the South Porto Rico Sugar Company in 1916.[45]

The arcane, back-room negotiations surrounding the Foraker Act changed the shape of Puerto Rico's future. In the 1890s, the United States had an increasing but still modest stake in Puerto Rico's economy. After 1898, the Republic, in line with trends in other Western empires, rose to a position of dominance. By 1930, Puerto Rico conducted nearly 95 percent of its overseas trade with the United States.[46] Coffee, which had accounted for about three-quarters of the island's exports in the 1890s, slumped to 7 percent in 1920, and dwindled further thereafter. Raw sugar took its place: in the 1890s, sugar accounted for about 21 percent of all Puerto Rico's exports; by 1920, the figure had risen to 72 percent.[47] The transformation illustrated what happened when the ideals of the civilizing mission passed through the sieve of special interests. The coffee industry languished once it was deprived of tariff support in the Spanish market and had to surmount U.S. tariffs, which an established lobby of importers and distributors of Brazilian coffee held firmly in place.[48] Sugar production boomed, despite continuing opposition from growers on the mainland, because it had the support of East Coast refiners and New York investors attracted by the possibility of circumventing the formal limits on the size of foreign holdings and establishing plantations. Trade followed the tariff as well as the flag, and the tariff was determined by bruising battles among special interests calibrated by considerations of domestic political advantage and the ever-pressing needs of the moment.

The substantial economic changes that occurred after 1898 should not be read as evidence that the United States brought capitalism to Puerto Rico. That process was already well under way before 1898 and was manifested in the growth of export crops, increasing rural differentiation leading to the concentration of land holdings, and an expanding pool of landless, rural laborers.[49] What the United States did was to wrench the export economy away from coffee, propel it into sugar production, and use its political leverage to enlarge opportunities for new investment. The result undoubtedly took Puerto Rico's economy into a new phase of capitalist expansion, but it did so, not by realizing the potential of comparative advantage, but by the artifice of tariff manipulation. The island's economy came to rest on a huge subsidy and thereby on the uncertain political inclinations of its foreign controller. By 1935, sugarcane occupied about one-third of all cultivated land on the island, and new, highly capitalized mills dotted the land. Economic and social differentiation had become marked: in the mid-1930s four U.S. companies, whose owners were absentees, held about one-quarter of all land under sugar and processed about half of the island's total sugar output; some 6,000 cane growers supplied them with cane; a floating force of 100,000–120,000 workers provided the necessary manual labor.[50] Wage rates, held down partly by population growth, remained low; unemployment remained high. Emigration to the mainland and beyond, even as far as Hawai'i, became an outlet for those seeking work.

Even so, it would be misleading to conclude that foreign firms destroyed local entrepreneurs. Recent research has begun to reveal a more complex understanding of the agrarian order during the early colonial period.[51] *Colonos* occupied about half the land under sugar and produced about one-third of the cane sent for milling; *centrales* (sugar mills) owned by Puerto Ricans processed about half of the sugar exported from the island. Small farmers, responding to market incentives, increased their numbers, even though the average size of holdings declined. Land shortage characterized the island's economy, but landlessness, though widespread, was not uniform. Consequently, in the absence of radical expropriation, development under U.S. rule built on and conformed to existing systems of land holding, as it did in the sugar-producing region of Luzon in the Philippines. Cuba, on the other hand, was similar in this respect to the island of Negros, where the frontier was more open and the problem was not availability of land but shortage of labor. Puerto Rico's pattern of development was sufficiently concentrated to give a few large firms, expatriate and domestic, absentee and local, a substantial stake in the system and an accompanying measure of visibility and political influence. At the same time, export production was sufficiently differentiated to include smaller farmers, whose representatives were capable of making their voices heard when the need arose. Tobacco farmers, for example, were principally owner-occupiers, who were well organized, maintained an active lobby in Washington, and extracted valuable concessions from the colonial authorities.[52]

Americanization, the cultural arm of U.S. imperialism, applied a set of universal principles that took little account of the diversity of the new empire. Education, the prime mediator of modernity, led the way toward acculturation. Officials began the new era of colonial rule with a major effort to improve literacy and introduce English into the curriculum. Literacy rates, though measured very imperfectly, rose from about 20 percent in 1899 to a claimed 65 percent in 1935.[53] This was a considerable achievement, even if the figures flattered reality, because the population of the island almost doubled between 1899 and 1935 to reach a total of 1,724,000. Nevertheless, the results fell far short of the declared aims of policy. A comprehensive survey completed at the close of the 1930s recorded that fewer than half of the children aged between five and 17 attended school, that facilities and equipment were seriously deficient, and that funding was held far below the level needed to secure improvement.[54]

Acculturation made little progress. The education program failed in its aim of making English a second language on a par with Spanish. In 1935, two-thirds of even the school-age population were unable to speak the second language. The increase in literacy related primarily to proficiency in Spanish. Worse still from the perspective of policy-makers, cultural assimilation had become counterproductive. School textbooks that promoted Anglo-Saxon values and relegated or ignored local culture provoked resentment, as did heavy-handed attempts to deal with resistance to the introduction of English.[55] The reaction of Puerto Ricans to the Americanization program helped to confirm Spanish as the language of national identity, and "Hispanism" as an alternative cultural reference.[56] Teachers, the appointed instruments of modernity, were among the most effective agents of the counterculture.[57]

Protestant missions, which in 1898 had been eager to secure new fields of endeavor overseas, found that their seed, too, fell on stony ground. Various Comity Agreements divided the island among competing denominations, which made a lasting impression on local communities by providing much-needed medical services and schools, as well as churches. Conversion rates, however, disappointed expectations. Roman Catholicism slowly adapted to the new colonial order and became an enduring point of reference for an emerging sense of national identity, if never exactly the agent of the oppressed. Ironically, Protestantism made visible progress only toward the close of the twentieth century, after most of the foreign missions had withdrawn, and then in a form, pentecostalism, that none of them had sponsored. The secular agents of moral regeneration also failed to achieve the results they had anticipated. Colonial officials encouraged civil marriage and its complement, divorce, in an attempt to reduce the number of consensual unions and the consequent incidence of illegitimacy.[58] Their efforts did little to increase the rate of marriage, but a good deal to stimulate the rate of divorce. In this way, policies that began with the aim of stabilizing society ended by promoting the liberation of women. Reforms affecting marriage added weight to a gathering feminist movement headed by tobacco workers, who wanted to join trade unions, and elite women, who wanted the right to vote. Both outcomes were far removed from the intentions of the males who had formulated the original policies.

These developments had profound consequences for the evolution of Puerto Ricans' sense of national identity.[59] The nineteenth-century movements for autonomy and independence had already provided evidence of a growing awareness of Puerto Rico's distinctiveness, albeit still within the context of Latin American culture. Annexation by the United States threw a complication into the mix. Thereafter, politicians and intellectuals struggled with the problem of how to define an emerging Puerto Rican identity without being overwhelmed by new influences from the mainland. Ambiguities were as numerous as they were inevitable. Some commentators traced the roots of Puerto Rico's society to a mythical golden age of Spanish culture; others censured Spain for perpetuating subordination and poverty. One line of thought, reinforced by notions of self-determination, the rise of Gandhi, and the Mexican and Russian Revolutions, criticized the United States for blocking progress toward independence. Another viewpoint, held by those who hoped to gain from opportunities presented by the link with the mainland, accepted the need to collaborate with the dominant colonial power. Race was an awkward element in all these perspectives. Few among elite commentators wished to include black Puerto Ricans in their version of the national story. One solution was to omit them; an alternative was to blur formal divisions of race so that the problem could be conjured out of sight, and, to a degree, out of existence.[60]

A sense of Puerto Rican identity slowly developed amidst these crosscurrents and contradictions. Self-respect drove claims for areas of independence within the framework of colonial rule. By the 1930s, too, the colonial administration had conceded that Americanization, in its pristine form, had failed. This was the time when the popular composite, *Ibero Pancho*, became a literary symbol of the melding of Spanish origins with local distinctiveness.[61] Political and economic subordination seemed, increasingly, to be inescapable, but cultural independence could be nurtured as a substitute and as a prelude to possible future achievements.

Material expressions of resentment nevertheless found expression, and in doing so strengthened the bonds of solidarity that cultural relations had helped to nurture. World War I had initiated a short but giddy boom, as the disruption of beet output in Europe created opportunities for sugar producers elsewhere. The postwar slump that followed brought bankruptcy for some and distress for many. The rest of the 1920s saw a partial and insecure recovery that was halted by the onset of a renewed and severe economic depression in 1929.[62] Radical movements, which had appeared during the war, lost momentum.[63] Their energy was sapped by internal dissension; their ideas were redirected into intellectual debate rather than political action.[64]

The 1930s resolved these uncertainties. The absolute level of overseas trade fell, foreign investment dried up, and the terms of trade turned against Puerto Rico, which imported nearly half of its food supply from the United States. Unlike Cuba, however, the island could not be abandoned because Puerto Ricans, being U.S. citizens, could migrate to the mainland.[65] Moreover, the sugar industry, again in contrast to Cuba, was integrated into the refining industry on the mainland and would suffer directly if Puerto Rico was left unprotected. Accordingly, the island's sugar industry was sheltered from the full force of the gale battering the world by being included in the U.S. free-trade area and by receiving a guaranteed quota under the terms of the Jones-Costigan Act of 1934, even though the allowance fell short of output for the remainder of the 1930s (apart from 1935). Most of the large sugar companies remained profitable, but unemployment increased and the standard of living of those who remained employed fell. Sugar could not carry the burden assigned to it; the coffee industry had been eliminated; tobacco was in steep decline; needlework, the island's main handicraft industry, suffered from falling demand. In 1929, Rafael Hernández Marín, Puerto's Rico's national composer, captured the desolation already prevailing in the countryside in his *Lamento Borincano*, which achieved unparalleled popularity:

> Everything,
> everything is deserted
> the town has died from neediness
> from neediness.
> We can hear the wailing
> everywhere
> in my God forsaken Borinquen.[66]

The situation deteriorated further as the 1930s advanced. In 1936, Harold L. Ickes, the Secretary of the Interior, observed in a private comment that: "There is today more widespread misery and destitution and far more unemployment in Puerto Rico than at any previous time in its history."[67] In 1940, the Work Projects Administration certified that 40 percent of families in Puerto Rico were "needy."[68]

Economic distress produced militant action, which in turn generated political change. Strike action across a variety of occupations increased sharply and became more violent.[69] In 1933, 7,000 tobacco workers, mostly women, went on strike; the needlework industry, which was also dominated by women, experienced a parallel series of strikes and protests. In 1934, there was a massive general strike of sugar workers and a further upsurge of violence in 1935, which culminated in the assassination of the Commissioner of Police in the following year.[70] In 1937, police broke up a nationalist demonstration with considerable violence: what became known as the "Ponce Massacre" resulted in twenty deaths and more than 200 casualties.[71] In 1938, a major dock strike halted international shipping for over a month. Later in the year, there was an attempt to assassinate the governor. In 1939, there were some forty-five strikes involving 31,000 workers. Long before then, it was evident that neither the magic of the "Enchanted Isle" nor "the best methods of administrating our insular possessions" were capable of preventing the transmission of international economic disorder.

These events linked the discussion of Puerto Rico's constitutional status to a debate over pressing material conditions. A green uprising of discontent brought rural voters as well as urban workers into the political arena. The elite parties that had dominated the political scene since 1898 were divided and reshaped. Elections in 1932 displaced the *Partido Liberal* (formerly the *Partido Unión*), brought a coalition of the *Partido Socialista* and *Partido Republicano* to office, and gave the *Partido Nacionalista* the national prominence it had lacked since its foundation in 1922. A large segment of the Liberals regrouped under the leadership of Luis Muñoz Marín (the son of Luis Muñoz Rivera), turned themselves into the *Partido Popular Democrático* in 1938, and thereafter dominated politics until the 1960s. The nationalists, who achieved more visibility than votes, increasingly resorted to militant action that led, through a dubious judicial process, to a long term of imprisonment for their leader, Pedro Albizu Campos.

Muñoz Marín (1898–1980) and Albizu Campos (1891–1965) were members of the first generation of Puerto Rican patriots to grow up under American rule.[72] Both came from well-connected families (in Muñoz Marín's case distinctively so); both received education in the United States; both wanted to see Puerto Rico become independent; both recognized the importance of incorporating the majority of the citizenry in the political process. At this point, the two leaders parted company. Muñoz Marín accepted the necessity of working within the constitutional framework established by the United States. In doing so, he joined nationalist leaders in the Philippines and in parts of the British and French Empires whose strategies of accommodation compromised their radical ambitions.[73] Albizu Campos held fast to the goal

FIGURE 12.1. Luis Muñoz Marín, c. 1957.
Source: http://batallante.blogspot.co.uk

FIGURE 12.2. Pedro Albizu Campos, 1936.
Source: Mary Evans Picture Library / Everett
Collection

of independence, carried his political activities beyond the limits of colonial tolerance, and refused to bend his principles. The two leaders achieved prominence on one small island, but the divergent routes they took qualified them to be globalized representatives of their colonial times.

Muñoz Marín was a pragmatist who learned his trade from his father's adept management of political networks and balances. His skill lay in turning anomalies into assets. His party, the Partido Popular Democrático, was predominantly secular, but made effective use of religious rhetoric; he appealed to rural voters, but pursued a policy of industrialization; he advertised independence, but aimed increasingly for autonomy. By straddling diversity, he made his party the sole intermediary between Puerto Rico and the United States. Albizu Campos, on the other hand, was an idealist who embraced the notion of self-determination with greater fervor than its progenitor, Woodrow Wilson, expected or wished. He had mixed with Eamon de Valera and Subhas Chandra Bose at Harvard, shared the hope that their generation would see the downfall of colonialism, and agreed with them that the end of colonial rule justified the means of securing it. Muñoz Marín, it is pertinent to add, was officially classified as white; Albizu Campos was an Afro-Puerto Rican who suffered discrimination while serving in the U.S. Army as a volunteer during World War I and later as a student at Harvard. The pragmatist became

Governor of Puerto Rico; the idealist spent most of the latter part of his life in jail.

The Democrats, who came to power in the United States in 1933, responded to the economic crisis by offering a mixture of repression and hope. President Franklin D. Roosevelt's appointment of General Blanton C. Winship as governor in 1934 was evidence of Washington's determination to regain control of the deteriorating situation on the island. Winship, a veteran of both the Spanish-American War and World War I, brought military methods to the tasks of government. His close associate, Colonel Francis E. Riggs, another veteran and newcomer to Puerto Rico, became Chief of Police. Winship and Riggs worked in overt and covert ways to control, and if possible prevent, strikes and demonstrations, and to discredit and ultimately destroy the radical nationalist movement. Their greatest success was the conviction and imprisonment of Albizu Campos. They failed, however, to defuse either discontent or militancy. Riggs was assassinated in 1936; Winship was recalled in 1938. Authoritarian rule had the unintended consequence of helping to unite the population in support of Muñoz Marín's Partido Popular Democrático, which won a decisive victory in the elections held in 1940.

Hope, accompanying repression, issued from the New Deal, which brought a fresh set of policy-makers and administrators to prominence and, briefly, to power. Their principles were universal; their focus was selective. Puerto Rico caught their attention. Its situation was especially grim and potentially calamitous, but its modest size suggested that its problems might be manageable with appropriate policies and matching resources. The proximity of the island to the mainland gave it visibility as well as a degree of familiarity that the Philippines, for example, lacked. The emigrant community on the East Coast ensured that the island's needs were well represented in political circles. Despite setbacks, Puerto Rico still retained the diplomatic attractions that Elihu Root had ascribed to it. Franklin Roosevelt took readily to the idea that the island had a special part to play in advertising the beneficial consequences of his Good Neighbor policy to the whole of Latin America.[74]

Two of the most influential of the newly elevated policy-makers, Ernest H. Gruening and Rexford G. Tugwell, held positions that enabled them to influence events in Puerto Rico during the 1930s.[75] Gruening managed the Puerto Rico Reconstruction Administration (PRRA) from 1935 to 1937; Tugwell was Under-Secretary in the U.S. Department of Agriculture from 1933 to 1936, and served as Governor of Puerto Rico between 1941 and 1946. Gruening and Tugwell were Progressives who hoped to introduce reforms that would improve the living standards of

Puerto Ricans. Gruening, however, lacked political subtlety, fell out with his superiors and with leading nationalists on the island, and resigned from the Reconstruction Administration after less than two years in office.[76] Tugwell, on the other hand, formed a constructive relationship with Puerto Rico's moderate nationalists, led by Luis Muñoz Marín, and cooperated with them in devising measures to restructure the island's economy.[77]

Gruening and Tugwell endorsed and amplified the radical plan drawn up by the distinguished agronomist, Carlos Chardón, in 1934, when he was head of the PRRA.[78] The innovative ideas advanced by the three officials reflected the desperation of the 1930s and the new thinking it inspired. A planned form of structural adjustment was formulated to fund public works, reform and diversify agriculture, increase the island's supply of basic foodstuffs, and encourage manufacturing. These goals were to be achieved by enforcing the limit on the amount of land corporations were entitled to hold, authorizing official purchases of corporate lands and mills, encouraging local refineries and small capitalist enterprises, and protecting infant industries.

The new colonial policy failed to transform the island's economy in the 1930s, though it did have an important influence subsequently.[79] Irrespective of their merits, the reforms ran into two obstacles: they were inadequately funded, and they provoked an aggrieved and resolute response from established interests.[80] Expatriate corporations and mainland sugar refiners denounced what they saw as attacks on private enterprise, and activated their allies in Congress to frustrate what they labeled as "socialist" measures. Faced with unbending opposition to his policies, Tugwell resigned from Roosevelt's administration in 1937.[81] The immediate outcome was political rather than economic. The conflict between the New Dealers and conservative interests coincided with the high point of the Nationalist Party's activities and the assassination of Police Commissioner Riggs in 1936. Uncertainty about the island's future and frustration with its apparently intractable problems created an opportunity for different parties to propose that Puerto Rico be granted independence.[82] Senator Millard Tydings, a fiscal conservative (and personal friend of Riggs), introduced a bill to this effect because he wanted to halt New Deal profligacy and immigration into the United States, and felt, as he felt about the Philippines, that it would "be better for us to be out of this place."[83]

The bill died of complications arising from opposition in Puerto Rico. Political leaders who had based their careers on the quest for independence rejected the measure because it proposed to withdraw, with little notice, the tariff and other concessions that kept the island afloat. The bill, impulsive in conception and potentially disastrous in its results, nevertheless concentrated minds on the realities of what Muñoz Marín called "threats of ruin and hunger."[84] The prospect of immediate independence suddenly became a hazard that pointed to the need for an alternative route to the future. It was then that Muñoz Marín and his party turned toward a form of association that eventually became the Commonwealth of Puerto Rico.

The alliance that emerged from this realignment of interests joined Muñoz Marín's determination to reshape the economy and make independence a practical, if now long-term, prospect to Roosevelt's need for reliable allies in the Caribbean.[85] Muñoz Marín's plans for reformed capitalism were far more acceptable in Democratic Washington than Albizu Campos's radical assault on it. Strategic concerns reinforced political calculations. Heightened tension in Europe at the close of the 1930s enhanced the importance of the island's port facilities. Independence ceased to be on the agenda. Roosevelt chose instead to support reforms that would strengthen the position of the moderate nationalists, even though, inevitably, his program ran into opposition from established U.S. business interests.

In this way, World War II enabled Muñoz Marín and the Partido Popular Democrático to begin a process of change that was to accelerate rapidly after 1945. The new policies were formulated and applied in cooperation with Rexford Tugwell, who returned to Puerto Rico as governor in 1941. An Industrial Development Company and a Development Bank offered facilities and funding for new manufacturing projects; a Land Law, passed in 1941, aimed to resettle landless families and turn them into industrial workers.[86] The industrial slant of the new economic policy helped the Partido Popular Democrático to win the support of the labor movement, which had increased in size and improved in organization following the series of militant strikes at the close of the 1930s. Unemployment was eased by increased migration to the mainland to meet the needs of war production and by recruitment into the armed services of some 65,000 volunteers and conscripts. These initiatives had mixed results.[87] Despite the sizable exit provided by emigration, serious poverty persisted and the threat of "ruin and hunger" still lay in wait. By 1940, the number of landless families and the extent of unemployment among the working population approached catastrophic proportions.[88]

The war itself touched Puerto Rico lightly. The construction of a military complex in Ceiba and on the nearby island of Vieques created what became one of the largest naval bases in the world and brought the spending power of the U.S. Navy and some local employment to the region.[89] The military also brought the assertive intrusiveness and accompanying racial prejudices of the dominant power. Nevertheless, the fortunes of war dealt far more leniently with Puerto Rico than with the Philippines and Hawaiʻi—with consequences that were to mark the paths they took in the postwar era.

CUBA: "THAT INFERNAL LITTLE REPUBLIC"[90]

Cuba, being highly visible and ruggedly independent, was Washington's principal insular irritant. The island had been the center of the Spanish Empire for most of the nineteenth century, and the main arena of combat between Spanish and American troops in 1898. Thereafter, Cuba ceased to be regarded as "Ever-Faithful" and became Eternally Exasperating instead. The island was neither fish nor fowl: neither formally annexed nor fully independent. Its status as an unacknowledged protectorate enabled the United States to intrude on the island's sovereignty but not to eliminate it. Powers that Washington regarded as limited, however, were judged in Havana to be excessive. Policies formulated in the spirit of "benevolent assimilation" created opportunities for collaboration, but also deeply offended nationalist sentiment in what was, in principle, a sovereign state. Constitutional uncertainties ensured that relations between the two countries were uncomprehending as well as unequal. President Roosevelt expressed his frustration with Cuba as early as 1906, when he proposed, in what was presumably a moment of irrational exuberance, to "wipe its people off the face of the earth."[91] Decades later, when assimilation had failed and benevolence had long fled, stereotypes arising from the repetition of differences had become unquestioned assumptions of policy. In 1946, Henry Norweb, the American ambassador, shook his head over the "unfortunate admixture and interpenetration of Spanish and Negro culture—laziness, cruelty, inconstancy, irresponsibility and inbred dishonesty."[92] This judgment was not the low point it might seem to be: relations between the United States and Cuba were to deteriorate even further in the years ahead.

Standard accounts of Cuba's history between 1898 and 1959 reflect familiar stereotypes in the historiography of modern colonialism.[93] The Cuban case, however, has special attributes because historical writing during the last half century has been strongly influenced—and sometimes seemingly mesmerized—by the Revolution of 1959. Official wisdom in the United States cast Cuba as the fearsome agent of the "Evil Empire," and tailored its history to fit a pre-cut, satanic design. U.S. policy, as seen from Washington, was benign and progressive; Cuban responses were truculent and ungrateful.[94] The island that had committed the irredeemable sin of rejecting American values deserved a history of self-willed intransigence that condemned it to authoritarianism and backwardness. Sins unrepented needed to be punished—and in the case of Cuba they certainly have been.

The Cuban viewpoint, neglected outside Cuba until relatively recently, portrayed the United States as being a new colonial power that substituted subordination for liberation in the interest of expropriating the island's resources. After 1959, Cuban nationalists intensified their condemnation of imperialists and their malign purposes, and held reified forces, typically referred to as world capitalism, responsible for reducing Cubans to the status of hapless victims. Cuba's history was rearranged so that the past could be judged according to whether it assisted or hindered the "long revolution" that culminated in 1959. By this measure, the First and Second Republics, which covered the years between 1902 and 1953, were run by collaborators who betrayed the Cuban people and the ideals of nineteenth-century nationalists.

Both perspectives, though far apart, share a deterministic view of Cuba's colonial past that points toward failure. For one account, it is the story of liberation offered and refused followed by descent into darkness; for the other, it is a tale of degradation inflicted by an unholy alliance of alien and domestic forces whose machinations could be halted only by revolutionary means. Much of the complexity of Cuba's history between 1898 and 1959 has been ground between these unyielding millstones. Recent work, however, has questioned formulaic interpretations of what might be called the "forgotten era" of Cuban history, and has begun to reveal the diversity that stereotypes conceal.[95] A revisionist perspective also makes it possible to fit the distinctive features of Cuba's history into a wider imperial setting. The two main influences on Cuba's fortunes were those that shaped the rest of the U.S. Empire: the character of the political settlement that followed the war of 1898, and the fortunes of the export crops that were the island's main sources of income and revenue.

The political settlement was shaped by four major legislative measures. The Cuban Constitution, which took effect in 1902, established a republican political system modeled on that of the United States and consisting of a bicameral Congress, an elected president, and an independent executive and judiciary.[96] Although these formalities laid the foundation for an autonomous government, they were shackled by three far-reaching qualifications: the Teller Amendment, which Congress passed in 1898; the Foraker Amendment, which followed in 1899; and the Platt Amendment, which sealed the deal in 1901. These congressional decisions show, in slow motion, how imperialist and anti-imperialist forces wrestled for the spoils of victory at the crucial moment the peace settlement was being determined.[97]

Senator Henry Teller's Amendment declared that the United States had no intention of exercising "sovereignty, jurisdiction, or control" over Cuba: "the government and control of the island" were to be left "to its people."[98] This unambiguous statement claimed the moral high ground for the United States. European imperial powers might grub for material gain, but in the matter of spreading progress and civilization, the United States would advance under the banner of idealism. Teller had taken the unusual step of transferring his allegiance from the Republicans to the Democrats. In accordance with the policy of his new party, he opposed annexation. In accordance with the needs of his constituency in Colorado, he supported the nascent sugar beet industry, which the state hoped would compensate for the collapse of wheat prices in the 1890s. The two interests were in happy alignment: if Cuba remained a foreign country, its exports to the United States would be obliged to pay import duties, thus providing a measure of protection for the beet industry.[99]

To prevent the incorporation of Cuba into the United States, Teller had to strike a compromise that would be accepted by different factions in Congress. Sugar producers on the mainland did not want Cuban sugar to have free access to the United States; Washington did not want to be burdened with the debts that Spain had loaded the island with and would be assigned to the United States if sovereignty were transferred.[100] Teller's formula retained independence as a prospect but refrained from committing the United States to handing power to any of the credible political organizations in Cuba, or from setting a date for conferring sovereignty.[101] Independence was to be granted only when Cubans had shown themselves to be capable of managing their own affairs.[102] The Amendment gave President McKinley and his administration an assurance that they retained the right to exercise a degree of control over developments in Cuba, while offering Cuban nationalists the hope that independence was still attainable.

The success of the United States in the short war against Spain, however, altered the tone of official announcements. In his annual message,

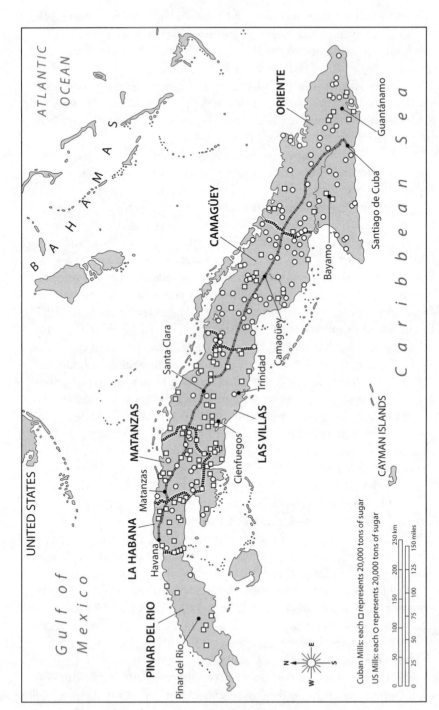

MAP 12.3. Cuba: Sugar Production (by Province), Towns, and Railroads, 1924.

delivered in December 1999, President McKinley stated that the United States had now assumed "a grave responsibility for the future good government of Cuba which needs to be bound to us by ties of singular intimacy and strength."[103] At the same time, McKinley had his eye on the fact that opposition to the occupation was growing, not only in Cuba but also in the United States. It was becoming hard to justify the U.S. presence either on grounds of cost or as a strategic imperative, since no foreign power had shown itself keen to shoulder this particular burden of empire. The president and his party remained determined to control events on the island, but they also needed a means of extricating themselves from a potential quagmire in the Caribbean of the kind that was sucking them into unknown depths in the Philippines.

McKinley's prospectus for controlling Cuba by informal means included a scheme for offering concessions to mainland investors.[104] Once the opponents of annexation became aware of the proposal, however, they blocked the move by passing the Foraker Amendment in 1899. The measure prohibited concessions, franchises, and grants of property on the grounds that substantial U.S. investment in Cuba would turn a temporary occupation into a permanent commitment. Although Foraker's initiative appeared to settle the matter, it produced an unexpected outcome. A group of wealthy East Coast investors, who had formed the Cuba Company in 1900 to secure concessions on the island, set about turning defeat into victory. They were ably assisted by the governor, Major General Wood, who was a keen annexationist, and they also won the cooperation of the *Partido Revolucionario Cubano*. By pushing for independence, the Cuba Company and its allies circumvented the Foraker Amendment, and Cuban nationalists were able to achieve their main aim. Sugar beet interests on the mainland welcomed the result.

The remaining problem, how to secure foreign investment in an independent state, was solved by the Platt Amendment, which transformed the ties of "intimacy and strength" into bonds of steel.[105] The Platt Amendment was devised in 1901, incorporated into the Cuban Constitution in 1902, and endorsed by the Cuban-American Treaty of 1903. It remained the chief determinant of relations between the two states until it was rescinded in 1934. The Amendment, which was presented to Congress by Senator Orville Platt but drafted by Elihu Root, the Secretary of War, ensured that Cuba's independence would be greatly circumscribed.[106] In formulating the terms of the Amendment, Root drew direct inspiration from the master craftsmen of imperial diplomacy: the British. After occupying Egypt in 1882, Britain had devised a covert plan that enabled it, in Root's words, to "retire and still maintain her moral control."[107] Platt's Amendment achieved a similar result. It prohibited Cuba from contracting treaties with other foreign powers that would impair its independence, and from incurring debts that could not be repaid from regular sources of revenue. At the same time, the Amendment gave the United States the right to intervene in Cuba's affairs for a variety of reasons relating to the "preservation of Cuban independence." Congress offered Cuba a face-saving concession, which restricted the amount of land foreign corporations were entitled to hold on the island. The Amendment was, in effect, an ultimatum, though it was presented as a matter for negotiation. The Cuban Convention opposed the measure but was obliged to accept it as the price of ending the military occupation, securing tariff concessions, and opening the way to a much-needed loan. This was Cuba's first, but by no mean last, experience of "dollar diplomacy." Thus constrained, and with nationalist aspirations quashed, the Cuban Republic hobbled into the first phase of its highly qualified independence.

The administration failed, however, to achieve its primary aim, which was to marry the Amendment to a reciprocity agreement. A bill was brought forward in 1901 but was killed in Congress by an alliance of orthodox protectionists and anti-imperialists.[108] Reciprocity was not achieved until December 1903, amidst unruly scenes in Congress, and by treaty rather than by a bill, which President Roosevelt knew would be shot down by the House of Representatives.[109] This belated success owed a great deal to Henry Havemeyer, the monarch of the Sugar Trust, who had a keen interest in enabling Cuba's sugar to enter the United States on advantageous terms.[110] The Reciprocity Treaty granted Cuba's sugar exports a reduction of 20 percent of the full tariff levied on imports into the United States; U.S. exports received a discount of between 20 and 40 percent on import duties levied by Cuba. Domestic beet and cane lobbies were defeated; refiners of raw sugar and Cuban producers gained from lower costs. Cuba needed the concession to support its postwar economic recovery, which underpinned political stability; sugar importers and refiners, in alliance with Elihu Root, the Secretary of War, worked toward the same end for their own purposes.

The "men-on-the-spot," to use a term employed by historians of empire, played an active part in these protracted negotiations. Major-General Wood, the Military Governor, put his considerable weight behind annexation. He had commanded the Rough Riders, and was well known, with Theodore Roosevelt, his friend and brother officer, to be an active member of the "war party." Tomás Estrada Palma, who became leader of the Partido Revolucionario Cubana after Martí's death, had weakened the political opposition to Wood's scheme by dissolving the party in 1898. Wood's predecessor, Major-General John Brooke, had eliminated potential military resistance by disarming and demobilizing the Cuban Liberation Army in 1899 in exchange for a cash payment of $3 million, and by installing military administrators in the island's seven provinces. Wood was then free to extend U.S. control, and in particular to create a white-dominated political economy of the kind that had emerged in the South after the Civil War.

Wood's political strategy aimed to promote what he called the "better classes" of Cubans, whose self-interest, he judged, would lead them to cooperate with the United States.[111] His optimism was misplaced: the majority of Cubans wanted neither to join the United States nor to be subordinated to it. Municipal elections held in 1900 were a success for the Cuban National Party; elections to the Cuban Constitutional Convention later that year returned, in Wood's words, "the worst political element in the island," even though the suffrage had been confined to about one-third of the adult male population in an effort to produce a favorable result.[112] Faced with the prospect of Cuba falling into the hands of "ignorant masses, unruly rabble and trouble-makers," Wood concluded that the island was not ready for independence. Accordingly, he put his weight behind the Platt Amendment and the Reciprocity Treaty, which produced control by imposition. Even so, Wood still hankered after annexation. "There is of course little independence left Cuba under the Platt Amendment," he wrote to Roosevelt in 1901. "The more sensible Cubans realize this and feel that the only consistent thing to do now is to seek annexation."[113] Wood's quest for annexation continued with his support for Tomás Estrada Palma as the first President of the Cuban Republic.[114] Estrada Palma, a pro-American exile and U.S. citizen living in New York, won an uncontested election in 1901 without leaving the mainland. He was carried into office on a wave of popular apathy after his opponent withdrew in protest against electoral manipulation. Wood's idea of democracy did indeed come from the United States, but it derived from the practices of Tammany Hall rather than the principles of the founding fathers.[115]

Wood also persisted with an ambitious scheme for long-term settlement in Cuba.[116] It is an almost forgotten fact that, at this time, Cuba was marked out as a potential settler colony that would realize a long-standing dream of extending the South into the Caribbean. Wood aimed to populate the frontier lands of eastern Cuba with farming families from the mainland. His idea was to fill the empty spaces with colonists who would then petition Congress to join the Union. Where diplomacy had failed, the democracy of the immigrants, carefully arranged, might succeed. Joseph Chamberlain had hatched a similar plan in the 1890s in the hope that rising numbers of *uitlanders* in the Transvaal would vote President Kruger out of office. Settlers from the mainland, however, were no more forthcoming in Cuba than they were elsewhere in the insular empire: in 1907, there were only 6,713 U.S. citizens in Cuba. Although the number had doubled by 1919, it fell sharply after the postwar slump of 1920 and never recovered.[117] Wood's policy failed, as did Chamberlain's. In Cuba, the settlers' frontier shriveled; in the Transvaal, it remained in the hands of Afrikaners.

Wood's strategy was to pack as many U.S. companies and as much foreign investment into Cuba as he could in the short time before he was obliged to hand power to an independent Cuban administration. When asked what constituted a stable government, he replied, with military crispness, "money at 6 per cent."[118] The formula, restated, was confidence plus opportunity. The Platt Amendment provided the former; the latter came with reciprocity. Wood moved energetically to make the legislation operational. Prospects in east Cuba (as in Negros in the Philippines) were highly promising. Large tracts of land suitable for growing sugarcane could be acquired there without difficulty, unlike in Puerto Rico and much of Luzon in the Philippines, where local farmers were well established, titles complex, and prices relatively high. With Wood's active support, and the cooperation of friendly Cuban political figures, two huge enterprises opened up the region by evading the legal restrictions on foreign corporations introduced by the Foraker Amendment. The Cuba Company, which became one of the leading expatriate firms in Cuba, also made the largest single investment in the island when it completed a 350-mile rail line linking Havana to Santiago in 1902.[119] Havemeyer's Sugar Trust, which had already purchased the greater part of a prime site, the offshore Isle of Pines, was the principal U.S. company among a group of more than fifty that acquired hundreds of thousands of acres at this time for sugar plantations, chiefly in the eastern region.[120] When the civil government replaced the military in 1902, it found itself committed to endorsing the legality of investments that had been made in defiance of the law.

The combination of opportunity and security that followed the settlement of 1898 produced a large increase in foreign investment in Cuba and a concomitant expansion of the island's external trade.[121] In 1894, U.S. capital invested in Cuba stood at $50 million; in 1906 it reached

$200 million; by 1929, it exceeded $1 billion. By the mid-1920s, U.S. investments in Cuba surpassed its total investments in Mexico and were not far short of its investments in Latin America as a whole. All the same, the United States was far from being a lone financial presence in Cuba. British investment in the island matched that of the United States down to 1914, and gave way only slowly thereafter.[122] Spanish investment, though smaller, also continued to make an important contribution. If investment from Cuban entrepreneurs, drawing on foreign as well as domestic sources, is added, a remarkable picture emerges of an island that, on a per capita basis, was one of the largest recipients of foreign capital in the non-industrial world during the first three decades of the twentieth century.

Foreign capital was attracted primarily by the island's unrivaled land reserves, which were exceptionally well suited to growing cane sugar. Accordingly, most foreign investment went into the export sector, principally in sugar plantations, mills, and associated enterprises, such as railroads and public utilities.[123] Sugar production, encouraged by generally favorable prices, rose from just under 1 million (short) tons in 1902 to a peak of nearly 6 million tons in 1929. Exports of sugar from Cuba consistently exceeded the combined output of the other leading constituents of the island empire (Hawai'i, Philippines, and Puerto Rico), and supplied about half the sugar consumed in the United States between 1900 and 1930. At its highest point, in 1919, sugar accounted for 90 percent of the island's exports and about 25 percent of world production. If, as has been claimed, Robert Louis Stevenson set *Treasure Island* in Cuba, he chose wisely, though the real wealth of the island arose from the development of sugar, which far exceeded the value of the cache of gold that Long John Silver and his piratical crew pursued with such avaricious intent.[124]

The development of the sugar industry after 1900 turned the export economy decisively toward the United States. In 1904, U.S. companies owned 12 percent of the centrales in Cuba and were responsible for producing 18 percent of total output. In 1913, the equivalent figures were 23 percent and 37 percent. In 1924, U.S. companies accounted for 60 percent of the sugar crop; in 1928, the figure rose to 76 percent. This trend was accompanied by increased concentration as mills became fewer in number but larger in capacity. In 1925, more than half the sugar crop was produced by twelve mills owned by companies controlled by banking, refining, and mercantile interests in the northeastern United States.

Evidence of increasing integration has long entered the debate over whether the consequences of export development are benign or malign. Recent research has uncovered complexities that suggest modifications to both positions. The consolidation of holdings and the shift to centralized mills were under way before 1898 and were not results of U.S. control. Even after 1898, the United States achieved dominance incrementally rather than immediately. The most striking advance came in the 1920s, after World War I had reduced competition from European rivals and the postwar slump had driven many Cuban producers into bankruptcy. It was only then, too, that U.S. banks began to predominate in the financial sector. A similar story can be told of the import trade. The United States supplied about half of Cuba's imports in 1909–1914, increased its share in the 1920s, but never achieved the degree of control it exerted over Cuba's exports. In this respect, the Reciprocity Treaty did not deliver the rapid boost to U.S. exports that some of its advocates claimed would be the case.[125] U.S. manufacturers were concerned more with protecting the large home market than with plans for opening Cuba to business, which is why they opposed the free-trade proposals made by the Cuban negotiators.

Although Cubans were greatly constrained by the terms of the peace settlement that followed the war of 1898, their strong tradition of innovation and enterprise ensured that they had a continuing role in the development of the island's economy. The recovery of the economy after the war of 1898 was the work of Cuban and Spanish enterprise as well as of American firms. In 1914, local farmers still produced more than 60 percent of Cuba's sugar, and it was not until the close of the 1920s that this figure was reduced to about 25 percent. Moreover, the conventional emphasis on the export trade has obscured important developments in the domestic economy, which not only expanded after 1900 but also altered its structure to include import-substituting manufactures. Demand for manufactured goods—from clothing to construction—increased as the export economy revived and as local entrepreneurs responded by investing in new types of business. Tariff policy assisted innovation. The Reciprocity Treaty did not prevent Cuba from altering its tariffs. In this respect, Cuba had a degree of independence that was denied to other members of the insular empire. In 1903, Cuba doubled its general import tariff. The aim was to raise revenue; the effect was to protect infant industries. The pattern is a familiar one in the history of economic development and can be traced to the eighteenth century, when Britain, another agricultural economy, increased tariffs for the same reason and with similar results.[126]

The fortunes of Cuban producers also varied according to place and time. Independent farmers survived in the western part of the island, where a well-established system of land tenure protected families from foreign investors seeking large estates.[127] The open lands in the east, on the other hand, favored the creation of a settlers' frontier.[128] Development there was so rapid that by the mid-1920s the island's two eastern provinces were responsible for more than 50 percent of all Cuba's sugar exports. The boom years down to 1920, and the dynamic growth of the eastern region in particular, attracted large numbers of immigrants, who by 1930 accounted for more than 20 percent of Cuba's population of four million. Most of the newcomers were from Spain and not, as Roosevelt and Wood had hoped, from the United States. The large, foreign-owned plantations relied heavily on seasonal labor from Puerto Rico and elsewhere in the Caribbean, especially Jamaica and Barbados. Even in the eastern region, however, there was still room for low-cost colonos, either as independent farmers or tenants, who produced a substantial proportion of the cane entering the large, foreign-owned mills.

Business enterprise was present in all levels of society. Politicians, to take the most prominent example, did indeed make money from politics, just as they did in the United States, but they also used politics to expand their existing business interests. These "capitalist *caudillos*," as they have been called, were often veterans with long histories of business activity as well as of military service.[129] Mario García Menocal, a war hero who was president of the Republic between 1913 and 1921, successfully combined the two activities. In 1899, before entering politics, he initiated the construction of the world's largest sugar mill in eastern Cuba. After he became president, he built a second large mill, which he sold to an American company shortly before the sugar market collapsed in 1920. One of Menocal's principal political opponents, Colonel Orestes Ferrara, was a wealthy businessman as well as a lawyer, a writer, and an exanarchist.[130] In association with another former president, General José Miguel Gómez, Ferrara founded the Vega Sugar Company, made a fortune, and by luck or judgment sold his business just before the postwar slump destroyed the sugar market. Gerardo Machado y Morales, another veteran general, had his first taste of business rustling cattle with his father, and progressed to the point where he owned a large sugar mill and a substantial stake in Havana's public utilities before becoming president in 1925.[131] Other less well-studied figures, civilians as well as veterans, took advantage of the boom years to enter banking, printing, publishing, real estate, and many other forms of business.

Manuel Rionda, the most famous Cuban merchant of his day, is an example of the cosmopolitan character of Cuban enterprise that was such a prominent feature of the quasi-colonial system.[132] Rionda was born in Spain in 1854 and migrated to Cuba at the age of fifteen to join his uncle's mercantile business. From there, he went to the United States for further education and to gain business experience. In 1891 he invested in a sugar mill in Cuba and five years later joined Czarnikow-MacDougall, the New York branch of the world's largest sugar brokerage firm, which was based in London. In 1909, he became president of the American company and moved to New York, at which point the firm was renamed Czarnikow-Rionda. Meanwhile, in 1899, he had taken advantage of the peace settlement to found the Francisco Sugar Company, which developed sugar production on newly available land in central Cuba. By 1914, Rionda's success and immense wealth encouraged him to expand even further, and in 1915 he formed the Cuba Cane Sugar Corporation, which became the leading sugar company in Cuba and, as far as can be judged, in the world too.[133] Within a few years, the new company controlled nearly one-quarter of Cuba's sugar output, while Czarnikow-Rionda sold about 40 percent of the island's total exports of sugar. The postwar slump, combined with the imposition of a highly protective tariff levied on sugar entering the United States, wrecked Rionda's business and that of others too. In 1929, when the next economic crisis struck, Rionda was seventy-five years old and his best years lay behind him. Cuba Cane struggled throughout the 1930s and was dissolved in 1938; at the same time, Czarnikow-Rionda lost its place as the leading sugar broker in the United States.[134]

Formally speaking, Czarnikow-Rionda was a U.S. firm. Rionda himself, however, had cosmopolitan affiliations that matched his wide-ranging business interests. He began life as a Spanish citizen, married an American, had a residence in New York, but considered himself to be Cuban. He owned houses in Cuba, knew the island intimately, and retained close family ties there. His brothers and nephews managed several of his companies, lived in Cuba, and identified themselves fully with the island's fortunes and future. The example of the Rionda family points to the difficulty of making unambiguous claims about ownership and national identity. It underlines, too, the vital part played by strategically placed islands as progenitors of globalization and not merely as its recipients.

Questions of identity also greatly concerned the United States. Although Washington did not possess the formal control over Cuba's domestic affairs that it exercised elsewhere in the insular empire, its agents, informal as well as official, were no less determined to Americanize the island.[135] The "tyranny of distance" did not rule in the Caribbean as it did in the Philippines, which was penetrated to a lesser extent, not least because it was more than 7,000 miles from the United States.[136] Proximity to the mainland, which was only about 100 miles away, ensured that American influences in Cuba became pervasive.

Cuba soon displayed many characteristic features of the American way of life. English became the medium of modernity.[137] Although English never replaced Spanish, it became a second language for a privileged minority, and was acknowledged to be one of the keys to advancement. Protestant missions were the single most important influence on the effort to draw the inhabitants into the Anglo-version of civilization prevailing on the mainland. In 1902, the rival denominations, following precedents in Puerto Rico and the Philippines, reached a Comity Agreement that effectively partitioned Cuba into non-competing regions. Thereafter, the missions were active in building churches and chapels and providing valuable medical and educational facilities. As their presence spread, so too did the English language. The large plantations and company towns became congenial partners in the work of the missions and frequently helped to fund them. The company culture, allied to the company store, was expressed in the company mentality, which placed a premium on forms of training that aimed to produce disciplined workers, responsive consumers, and upright, law-abiding citizens.

Department stores sprang up in the large towns, introduced new goods and styles, and acted as centers of emulation and diffusion. Tourism brought visitors from the mainland and exposed the island to new values, styles, and forms of behavior. Treasure Island became, for a privileged few, pleasure island.[138] It was in the 1920s, as we have seen, that Havana acquired particular notoriety as a center of delights that were not so readily available on the mainland.[139] Visitors who survived a "Hard Day's Night" dancing stylized versions of rumba in Havana could recuperate by watching or participating in one of several new sports that had taken root in the island. Baseball, which was introduced as early as the 1860s, became the national sport after 1900.[140] Leagues were formed; talent was developed; attendance soared. Large numbers of women, whose opportunities for public participation expanded after 1898, joined the crowds of supporters.

Cubans were to a degree Americanized but not assimilated. To be Cuban was to be involved in a rolling program of negotiation and selection. In this respect, the evolution of Cuba's own way of life resulted from choices that, in principle, applied to other colonial and quasi-colonial societies—from Nigeria to New Zealand. Initially, as in Puerto Rico,

Cubans hoped that the United States would open the door to modernity. Nationalist leaders had long concluded that Spain represented the past and the United States, the future. Cubans emulated the tastes and values of American consumers because they represented an enticing world of opportunity that was far beyond the range of Spain's conservative, mercantilist system. After 1898, Cuba began to replace Spanish symbols and images with Cuban American street names, holidays, and heroes.[141] Baseball was embraced because it was modern; bullfighting was rejected because it was primitive.[142]

Acculturation was not entirely a one-way process, however. Cuba influenced the United States in diverse ways. Cuban music, especially dance, spread throughout the United States in the 1920s and enjoyed numerous subsequent revivals. Afro-Cubans joined African Americans in creating a cosmopolitan diaspora without losing their own still developing sense of being Cuban.[143] Emigrants transformed Miami and helped to influence U.S. policy toward Cuba, especially after 1959. Cuba appeared, though not always to advantage, in numerous Hollywood films and television series. The movie *Guys and Dolls* represented Cuba about as well as *West Side Story* represented Puerto Rico. Fortunately for the image of both countries, the dissolute gambler in the one and the lawless gangs in the other have yet to be joined in one grand celluloid epic.

Uplift was accompanied by downshift. Once the gulf between rhetoric and reality began to emerge, Cubans, again like Puerto Ricans, adopted a more informed and discriminating view of the U.S. presence. Baseball appealed partly because it nurtured a degree of social solidarity that eventually became part of Cuba's national identity. Like cricket in the British Empire, baseball provided an opportunity, through sporting achievement, of winning parity with the dominant power. Victory over representatives of the master race was an event much savored and a memory that entered the national legend. As Spain receded as a symbol of colonialism and disillusion with the United States grew, Spanish reaffirmed its role as the language of nationalism. Spanish absorbed elements of English to the point where "el staff meeting" could be held over "el sandwich" to discuss "el know-how," but nevertheless remained the language of custom and choice.

Protestant missions were welcomed more for the material facilities they provided than for the spiritual sustenance they offered. Although the rate of conversion was higher in Cuba than it was elsewhere in Latin America, by the 1950s Protestants accounted for only about 7 percent of the population.[144] Theology remained welded to nationality. The missions shared the racial prejudices of their time, were reluctant to appoint

Cubans to senior positions, even though local pastors had pioneered and steered Protestantism on the island before 1898, and were hostile to radical nationalism.[145] American missions began to promote Cubans from the 1940s, but provoked resentment by continuing to pay them well below the rates their American counterparts received. Meanwhile, the Roman Catholic Church was still seen as an alien institution, even after Spain ceased to be the ruling colonial power. The Church persisted in appointing Spanish priests, as it had done for centuries, was slow to carry the Faith into the island's developing provinces, and had little sympathy with nationalist aspirations.[146]

These and similar perceptions caused Cubans to separate American representations of modernity from the realities of America's presence and power. The U.S. model of progress encouraged emulation; U.S. policy, however, appeared to block the aspiration. Prevailing notions of racial superiority frustrated attempts by Cubans to win respect and gain equality.[147] Viewed from a local perspective, Cuba's economic fortunes seemed to be manipulated by pressure groups in Washington that had little interest in the island's welfare. Discontent mounted; grievances accumulated. In the 1930s, the bypassed majority found their voices, and their growing sense of injustice was expressed in militant demands for political change.

The radicalism of the 1930s had both local and international sources.[148] The Platt Amendment and the Reciprocity Treaty prepared Cuba, not for independence, but for continued subordination and possible absorption. By holding the door open for intervention, the peace settlement enlarged and distorted Cuban politics. Cuba's David had to respond to Washington's Goliath by trying to devise ways of turning its all-powerful neighbor to local advantage. The challenge was made more difficult by the fact that the new Republic had yet to produce a unified political elite. Lack of political opportunities under Spanish rule, combined with a long history of armed struggle and social upheaval in the cause of *Cuba Libre*, had ensured that the embryonic political class remained fragmented. In these circumstances, the *caudillo* networks that emerged in the nineteenth century as a means of relating rural areas to the central institutions of government continued to function after 1898, but their affiliations remained primarily regional; wider concerns produced temporary alliances rather than truly national political parties. The closest imperial analogy is with the Philippines, whose regional *caciques* networks exhibited a similar degree of continuity. The distinctive feature of Cuban politics before the 1930s was the continuing prominence of veterans and the persistence of the old structures of command.[149] In the Philippines, the United States overcame armed resistance and executed, exiled, or otherwise neutered its leaders. In Puerto Rico, there were no caudillos because there was little or no armed resistance. In Cuba, the army was paid off rather than defeated and its organization survived well enough to form the basis of political mobilization after 1898. Caudillos enjoyed great prestige as representatives, and in some cases heroes, of the national cause. Whether as leaders, allies, or competitors, their influence added a measure of discipline to the fractious oligarchy that managed Cuban politics during the early decades of the twentieth century.

Conditions in postwar Cuba were scarcely conducive to settled civil government.[150] War had devastated the country. The destruction of estates and infrastructure had dislocated the economy. Loss of population, increased poverty, and continuing banditry impaired social cohesion. Fifty thousand demobilized war veterans restlessly awaited employment. Women suffered disproportionately, as did the next generation of Cubans—the children whose lives had been shaped by destruction and deprivation. Privilege did not guarantee immunity. Segments of the planter elite, whose fortunes had already been reduced by economic adversity during the 1890s, were obliged after the war to sell their estates to foreign creditors. In short, the whole of Cuban society was affected by what would later be called, in an era of advanced political euphemisms, "collateral damage." In these circumstances, Cuba had about as much chance of achieving political stability after 1898 as Iraq had after the invasion of 2003. Accordingly, the puzzle is not to explain why Cuba failed to become an exemplar of national self-determination, liberty, and democracy, but to wonder how the polity held together and performed as well as it did.

The political elite had to deal with these pressing issues within the framework set by the United States. In doing so, they redefined the concept of the national interest. José Martí's ideal nation of one people living in freedom was carried into the new era as a star to be followed, and the principle of racial equality remained embedded in nationalist rhetoric. However, the trans-racial alliance formed in the struggle against Spain had never been fully sealed, and the potential for disunity following the wars of the 1890s hovered over the polity. Immediate practicalities in a new and still uncertain era ensured that security headed the list of priorities. U.S. investors and Cuban property owners alike required protection from unruly and potentially destabilizing elements. This age-old concern acquired new-age validation. The notion of modernity, transmitted from the mainland and much discussed in Cuba after the turn of the century, took an evolutionary form that allowed for social differentiation according to levels of acculturation and gradations of class.[151] These distinctions cut into the ideal of racial unity, attached acceptability and status to those with education and training in Western ways, and tied the notion of equality to a long process of preparation. This development legitimated the superiority of Cuba's white elite and reassured the United States that the independent republic would not subject the ideal of racial equality to far-reaching tests of practicality.

This conception of progress was not exclusive to the United States: the British had long applied the precept of making haste slowly to their own empire. In this way, political thought and practice in Cuba, which are often considered to be inimitable, fell into line with developments in the colonial world at large, as well as in other parts of the insular empire. Political leaders in Cuba, Puerto Rico, and the Philippines lowered their expectations and raised their negotiating skills. Like true *compradors*, their survival and future success depended on their agility in balancing the demands of a major foreign power with the pressing needs of their domestic constituencies.

The residues of the nationalist movement regrouped to form two parties: the Conservatives, led by Tomás Estrada Palma, who favored autonomy, and the Liberals, led by José Miguel Gómez, who retained a commitment to independence.[152] Broadly speaking, the Conservatives attracted returning exiles and the more affluent white civilians, who had a strong presence in the bureaucracy, and cultivated connections with expatriate sugar companies. The Liberals drew on veterans, urban workers, and a predominantly rural constituency of farmers. Washington's policymakers viewed the two parties in the light of their own shifting priorities. After 1902, the banner of liberty was lowered and the less colorful flag of stability unfurled. The transition inclined the United States to favor the Conservatives, though their willingness to risk creating disorder to preserve party support made them uncertain and at times reckless allies.

The battle for power in Cuba was intense and often violent. Ideological differences between the parties, though wider in rhetoric than in reality, were the most visible cause of conflict. Behind the scenes, the struggle for office was directly related to the ability to command patronage, which produced jobs, contracts, and, so the patrons hoped, party loyalty.[153] The Cuban Constitution had raised the electoral stakes by providing for full adult male suffrage, irrespective of race.[154] The provision was a step ahead of the other insular territories, where the United States had the power to keep voting rights out of the hands of those Governor

Wood had called the "ignorant masses." Although some of Cuba's leaders shared his opinion, they adapted to the new quasi-democracy in a thoroughly modern manner: promises of employment opportunities grew to match the size of the expanded electorate; voting procedures were manipulated in an effort to achieve the desired result.

These developments found militant expression in the sporadic eruptions that marked the politics of the early colonial period. The first of these arose from a dispute over the validity of the results of the election held in 1905, which returned the Conservatives to power.[155] The vociferous objections of Liberals and allied veterans turned into a revolt, which prompted the United States to intervene in 1906 to "protect lives and property." This was not a moment the United States wanted to seize. President Roosevelt, his imperial enthusiasm spent, wished neither to provoke resistance of the kind that had frustrated the United States in the Philippines nor to provide the Democrats with free supplies of electoral ammunition.[156] The Conservatives in Cuba, however, reckoned that they could cross the line in dealing with the Liberals because they calculated, correctly, that the United States would be certain to support them should civil order break down. The episode illustrates a familiar theme in colonial history: how the external power became involved in local politics to an extent that was either unwitting or unwanted, and how the subordinate state bent its mentor to serve its own purposes.

The occupation of Cuba lasted until 1909, by which time U.S. representatives had introduced electoral reforms and authorized the creation of a Permanent Army to insure against possible future challenges to the political system.[157] Observers judged that the election held in that year was conducted fairly, though the new rules were probably less influential in this regard than the threat of continuing U.S. intervention.[158] José Miguel Gómez and the Liberals, who took office, made the most of their success by expanding public investment to create jobs for their supporters, who included many unemployed and disgruntled veterans. This strategy helped to produce a second crisis because it omitted Afro-Cubans, who suffered from the double disadvantage of high levels of unemployment and race prejudice.[159] As José Martí's dream of a united Cuba began to fade, Afro-Cubans began to organize. In 1908, they formed the *Partido Independiente de Color*, which the Liberals promptly banned, thus driving the Afro-Cuban movement out of civic politics and into armed revolt. The rebellion of 1912 was put down by the new Permanent Army at the cost of several thousand lives, but it set a precedent for extra-political action that was followed in the sporadic strikes and demonstrations that occurred in the years ahead.

Further disruptions characterized the war years and their immediate aftermath.[160] The outbreak of World War I devastated Europe's sugar beet fields, raised the demand for sugar, and boosted Cuba's main export. The boom in sugar prices replenished the Cuban treasury, enlarged the scope for patronage, and raised electoral stakes. The enhanced importance of sugar supplies prompted Washington to devise ways of exerting greater control over Cuba without also provoking a level of resistance that would endanger the flow of exports. A disputed presidential election in 1916 provoked a rebellion by Liberal dissidents who refused to accept that the ruling Conservative, Mario García Menocal, had won a second term.[161] Both sides gambled on securing U.S. support. The Conservatives prevailed: U.S. Marines landed in 1917; Menocal was installed; the Cuban army was purged of its influential Liberal officers.[162] The settlement compelled Cuba to accept controls on the price and shipment of sugar to ensure the return flow of foodstuffs, on which the island depended.

The war years created hardship as well as some highly publicized fortunes. Export regulations combined with the shortage and high price of imported goods provoked demonstrations and strike action. In 1919, President Woodrow Wilson, fearing further damage to U.S. interests, dispatched a personal representative, Major-General Enoch H. Crowder, with a mandate to prevent civil disorder during the presidential election of 1920 and avert the need for a further military occupation.[163] Crowder's principal aim, like Lord Cromer's in Egypt, was to preserve the interests of creditors by insisting on budgetary oversight and cuts in public-sector employment and wages in exchange for a loan to rescue the Cuban treasury and U.S. investors from prospective default. The deal exposed the limits of dollar diplomacy. The election of 1920, which installed Alfredo Zayas (Menocal's nominee) as president, was as fraudulent as its predecessors. Protests followed. Austerity, in association with the collapse of the sugar boom in 1920, generated discontent in the corridors of power as well as in the streets. Banks failed; fortunes were lost; creditors were unable to call in debts. The Cuban government itself was technically bankrupt.[164] The language of nationalism was revitalized; the Platt Amendment, the symbol of subordination, was vilified.[165] The reaction obliged the United States to step back. The marines left in 1922. Crowder stayed on as Ambassador, but his elevated status carried far less power than he had enjoyed when he held the informal and ambiguous title of Personal Representative. Self-determination had reached Cuba in a radical form that President Wilson had no wish to encourage; correcting it, however, was a task beyond Washington's reach.

Cuba's fortunes remained tied to sugar exports, which continued to depend on global demand and U.S. tariff policy. By 1922, world demand had recovered from the postwar slump. Prosperity returned to the export trade; government finances ceased to be on life support. Cuba also benefited from the low rates of the Underwood Tariff, which the Democrats had introduced when they took control of Congress in 1913. These favorable conditions enabled Cuba to increase its share of the U.S. market: in 1922, the island supplied about two-thirds of all the sugar consumed on the mainland.[166] Unfortunately for producers, the blue sky over the sugar plantations soon clouded. The election of 1920 gave the Republicans control of Congress and the White House. Two years later, the Fordney-McCumber Tariff raised the duty on imported raw sugar by about 75 percent with the aim of protecting domestic beet and cane producers.[167] Moreover, sugar prices began to drop after 1925, and by 1929 had fallen below the cost of production.[168] Producers in Cuba had little room to maneuver because they had become heavily dependent on the mainland market. By the 1920s, the island had created one of the most advanced agricultural industries in the tropical world.[169] The principal technological innovation in the production process, central milling, had been introduced in the late nineteenth century and was complete by the early 1920s. Unrestricted immigration held down labor costs. The transition from old-style latifundia to modern agribusiness was well advanced.

The expansion of the sugar industry generated structural changes that extended far beyond the agricultural sector. Cuba had long been the most advanced of the Caribbean islands and by the mid-1920s seemed "poised to become one of the wealthiest nations in the western hemisphere."[170] The long export boom had raised incomes, however unevenly, and stimulated investment in other activities, from import-substituting manufactures to real estate.[171] The public sector had expanded too: the number of official employees doubled between 1902 and 1924; the number of literate and articulate citizens also increased, if not commensurately.[172] Cuba possessed the first modern telephone system in Latin America, the first international airport, one of the first electric tramways, and more motor vehicles per head of population than most of its South American neighbors.[173] Economic change was beginning to transform the political scene as well.[174] A new generation of businessmen and professionals who had little or no direct connection to the wars of the 1890s appeared; so, too, did a growing urban labor force, which included increasing numbers of women.[175] These groups spoke with different voices but their claims, which ranged from protection for local manufactures to minimum wages for workers, collectively posed a challenge to the old landed oligarchy, which itself had lost ground to American sugar companies.

The controversial presidency of Gerardo Machado illustrates how a leading member of the old guard tried to come to grips with these divergent new forces. Machado was the last of the veteran generals to climb to the top of Cuba's political tree. He became the Liberal nominee for the presidency in 1924, and held the office from 1925 to 1933. Machado combined both military and business experience, and responded to the needs of the new order, prominently represented by U.S. corporations, while also presenting himself as championing the national interest.[176] In 1926, as sugar prices fell and resentment of U.S. protectionism rose, Machado's government passed the Verdeja Act, which restricted sugar output in the hope of raising prices, and introduced measures to protect the position of the colonos and other small farmers.[177] In the following year, as the domestic economy faltered and Cuban manufacturers clamored for support, the government passed a protective tariff, which increased duties on imported manufactures and reduced them on imported raw materials.[178] The Verdeja Act failed to deliver higher prices for exporters, and the protective tariff failed to produce immediate results. Nevertheless, both measures were significant indicators of an upsurge of economic nationalism that aimed at exerting greater control over agricultural exports and at diversifying the economy.[179]

The Cuban economy was already struggling when the global depression struck in 1929. The world price for raw sugar fell from $2.78 per pound in 1927 to $0.78 cents in 1932. It recovered to $1.00 in 1937, but did not regain the level achieved in 1927 until 1945.[180] Increasing protectionism in countries that were also major consumers of sugar damaged the market further. The Fordney-McCumber Tariff had already cut into the profit margins of Cuban exporters; the Smoot-Hawley Tariff, passed in 1930, delivered the industry a near-fatal blow.[181] The new tariff was not a consequence of the Depression, as is commonly thought: the Republicans had already declared their intention of raising tariffs during the election campaign of 1928.[182] Their strategy was a response to widespread distress among America's farmers, who were already suffering from falling produce prices. Legislators with both eyes fixed on reelection focused on winning the agricultural vote, and gave high priority to the domestic sugar industry in particular.[183] By the 1920s, sugar beet had spread well beyond the Midwest; sugarcane remained important in Louisiana and Florida. Once the election campaign was under way, the sugar lobby benefited from "log-rolling": as the prospect of enhanced protection moved up the political agenda, other interests, including manufacturers, added their support. The strategy succeeded: in 1929, Herbert Hoover entered the White House and the Republicans took control of Congress. Unfortunately for Cuba, tariff revision was an election pledge that Congress kept. Reed Smoot, the senator from Utah, steered the legislation through its contentious passage.[184] Smoot was a long-standing and committed protectionist whose commercial principles were buttressed by the need to safeguard the interests of the sugar beet farmers, who were an important part of his constituency. The tariff brought him short-term fame—and enduring notoriety.

The Smoot-Hawley Tariff, which took effect in 1930, was catastrophic for the Cuban economy. Although Congress knew that the consequences for Cuba would be dire, when faced with a choice between the interests of voters and non-voters, the legislature decided to allow the island a dubious form of freedom—the right to find its own way out of the problems the tariff had created.[185] The brief outburst of idealism associated with the imperialists of 1898 had long receded; the civilizing mission had ceased even to be rhetoric. The new tariff raised the duty on imported raw sugar to 2 cents per pound, which was higher in 1930 than the price paid in New York for the sugar itself.[186] Cuba was trapped. More than 80 percent of the island's exports consisted of sugar, of which more than 70 percent was destined for the United States.[187] The U.S. market had almost closed; European countries were either protectionist or moving swiftly in that direction; sugar beet had recovered from the destruction caused by World War I; competing sugarcane producers within and beyond the insular empire added to the glut on the world market.

Tropical export producers in the British and French empires responded to the fall in prices by expanding output. Cuba was denied this possibility. Had the sugar market been competitive, Cuba's position would have been unrivaled. Favorable growing conditions and a highly efficient agronomy ensured that the island's costs of production were 40–70 percent lower than those prevailing elsewhere in the U.S. empire and on the mainland itself.[188] The penalty imposed on Cuba, which lay outside the formal jurisdiction of the United States, was a windfall for Puerto Rico and the Philippines, both higher-cost producers, and enabled them to increase their share of the U.S. sugar market.

The figures speak for themselves with exceptional clarity.[189] Between 1929 and 1933, the value of Cuba's exports of sugar fell by 53 percent, export revenues by 83 percent, and sugar production from 5.4 to 2.1 million (short) tons. Viewed in a longer perspective, the total value of Cuba's exports between 1930 and 1934 was less in real terms than it was in 1904–1909. Import values dropped, too, and the economy as a whole contracted. Expatriates as well as Cubans were affected. Not even the powerful lobby representing American owners of Cuban sugar estates could tilt the political balance away from domestic sugar interests.[190] The Chairman of the failed Santa Cecilia Sugar Company, himself a U.S. citizen, summarized the situation, with evident bitterness, in 1933: "The blow that killed Cuba was the tariff and Smoot was the man who struck it; while President Hoover looked on and permitted it without a gesture of dissent or word of regret."[191] The effects were immediate, deep, and comprehensive. Santa Cecilia was just one of many companies that went out of business; profitability among the survivors was greatly reduced; foreign investment was withdrawn; public finances were severely pruned; unemployment rose sharply; the wages of those who remained employed were slashed by as much as 50 percent, and in the case of cane cutters, even more. By 1933, it was estimated that 60 percent of Cuba's population had "sub-marginal" incomes.[192]

The consequences of these trends provide an exemplary illustration of the direct influence of economic forces on political developments. Economic hardship produced outbursts of discontent that threatened civil order and eventually destroyed it. Machado's attempt to borrow his way out of trouble landed the government with repayment charges that could be met only by austerity measures that increased the burdens borne by Cuban citizens.[193] In November 1930, Harry Guggenheim, the U.S. Ambassador, reported on the "revolutionary movement" . . . born of the misery on the island" and "fathered by aspiring politicians."[194] The "basic cause," he confirmed a week later, "is poverty."[195] The inevitable manifested itself in a series of mass demonstrations, strikes, and rural protests.[196] The Communist Party gained support in the towns; a general strike in 1930 brought out some 200,000 protesters. Rural action came with drama and violence. The countryside was literally in flames: colonos set fire to their fields to force the mills to grind more sugar; farm laborers acted similarly in an attempt to improve their working conditions; lawlessness turned into banditry.[197] Cuba fell under virtual martial law in 1930, and descended into open warfare in the following year. President Machado's increasingly harried political trajectory reflected these developments. As the economy deteriorated and civil order disintegrated, Machado strengthened ties with the United States and aligned himself firmly with the forces of law and order, which applied heavy-handed measures to control Cuban dissidents. The reaction to Machado's policies produced a struggle for power between contending factions that lasted until 1933, when an army coup installed Sergeant Fulgencio Batista as chief of the armed services and the effective ruler of Cuba.[198]

The dramatic events leading to the fall of Machado and the rise of Batista have inspired a substantial literature.[199] For present purposes, however, an assessment of the episode can be confined to what it reveals about the evolution of the colonial order. Seen from this standpoint, Cuba becomes, not an exception, but a standard case. The history of the island during the 1930s marched in step with other parts of the American Empire and with trends in the larger British and French empires as well. Batista himself symbolized the emergence of a new, postwar generation of "men of the people." He came from a family of sugarcane workers, and was classified as being mulatto, though the term masked the rich diversity of his African, Chinese, and Amerindian ancestry. His rise to power marked the end of the dominance of the fractious oligarchy of sugar and military interests that lost credibility during the Depression, and the appearance of a new generation of nationalist populists who were to win support throughout the Western empires during the 1930s.[200] Urban and rural protest movements had sprung up during World War I, but they lacked permanent organizations, and government repression prevented them from developing further.[201] By 1930, however, the economic crisis had encouraged key interest groups to establish durable institutions in the form of trades unions, cooperatives, and self-help groups, and to broaden their base by appealing across racial divisions and by including large numbers of women.[202]

These developments, summarized here as the "green uprising" in politics, proved to be a turning point in Cuban and colonial history, though there were too many hands on the steering wheel for the turn to be made smoothly.[203] The army wanted order but was unsure whether to secure it by military or civilian means; the liberals wanted reform through the democratic process. Batista represented the army and the *sans-culottes*. Ramón Grau San Martin, the leader of the liberals, acted for Cuba's new professional class; appropriately, he came from a family of rich tobacco farmers and had qualified as a doctor before entering politics.[204] In the turmoil of the time, Grau emerged to hold the presidency briefly in 1933–1934.[205] His provisional government entered office with a manifesto that proclaimed "Cuba for the Cubans," and a set of proposals to match: the dissolution of established political parties, votes for women, a minimum wage, immigration controls to preserve employment for Cubans, and the abolition of the reviled Platt Amendment. Radical nationalists regarded Grau's program as being too timid; conservatives saw it as being

FIGURE 12.3. Fulgencio Batista and Ramón Grau San Martín, 1933. *Source*: Mary Evans Picture Library/ SZ Photo / Scherl

too extreme. The army, which had hoisted the provisional government into office, pulled it down shortly afterward. Grau's temporary associate, Sergeant Batista, engineered the president's resignation in 1934, took effective control of the government, and promptly promoted himself to the rank of colonel.[206]

The United States struggled to keep up with these rapid changes. Rival groups in Cuba both feared and invited U.S. intervention; the United States wavered uncertainly between the two options.[207] Washington began by offering cautious support for Machado's reforms in the late 1920s, and backed his strong-arm tactics when civil unrest threatened to destabilize the island. By then, old-style intervention had lost favor. Crowder's presence had been counterproductive in stimulating nationalist resentment; Roosevelt's election in 1933 confirmed that the United States would not wield its big stick in Cuba. The Democrats had long adopted an anti-imperialist stance while pursing expansionist policies, and their election platform in 1928 had included a pledge to give the Philippines immediate independence. Their aim after 1933 was to promote "Good Neighbor" policies by winning hearts and minds in Latin America. The good neighbor, being also a big neighbor, remained free to meddle in the internal affairs of other states. Ambassador Sumner Welles provided an apposite example in helping to overthrow first Machado, after he had lost the confidence of key interests, and then Grau, believing that he was set on nationalizing U.S. investments on the island.[208] Welles acted by stirring disaffection among the president's supporters and threatening the use of force, but without intending to call in the marines. Machado left in spectacular haste with "five revolvers, seven bags of gold, and five friends in pyjamas" in a plane "riddled with bullets" to reflect, first in Nassau and then in Miami, on a life lived to the fullest, if not always well.[209] Thereafter, the United States supported the government in Cuba that was consistent with its interests, which favored stability, and kept the advertised causes of freedom and democracy for future use.

The role of corporate interests in these events is either missing or unexplored. The actions of the American & Foreign Power Company (AFP), however, provide a rare insight into relations between business and politics during this exceptionally turbulent period.[210] The AFP was established in 1923 as a subsidiary of General Electric (1892) to develop electrical power facilities throughout the world. The company was an early manifestation of the global spread of the second industrial revolution through large corporate entities, which provided finance for colonial development that Congress was unwilling to sanction. By 1932, AFP had invested more than $100 million in generating and transmitting electricity in Cuba and selling electrical products. The company was also heavily invested in politics: it contributed $500,000 to Machado's presidential campaign in 1924 and gave financial support to other high-level political figures. In return, successive Cuban governments helped to embed the company in the economy by encouraging foreign investment, by opening the door to contract workers, principally from Jamaica and Haiti, and by introducing repressive labor regulations.[211]

AFP's operations produced a backlash. Modern management techniques, including mechanization, cost jobs; land purchases in eastern Cuba displaced small farmers; high electricity rates, which were needed to pay huge political subsidies, alienated consumers. Protests against AFP, including a nationwide boycott in 1930–1931, contributed to the gathering discontent caused by the deteriorating economic situation at the close of the 1920s. Between 1929 and 1933, the company halved its workforce and imposed pay cuts on remaining employees. Further boycotts obliged President Grau to impose a drastic reduction in electricity rates in 1933, and to authorize the labor unions to take over AFP in the following year. After Carlos Mendieta replaced Ramón Grau, the company regained control of its operations in return for accepting union demands for improved working conditions. Normal business, however, was not resumed: it took AFP several decades to recover from the slump in world trade, at which point its plant and property were expropriated after the Cuban Revolution.[212] Corporate reformers who aimed to change the world by making it American found, at least in Cuba, that the world was inclined to change them.

Batista ruled with U.S. approval and the support of the Cuban army from 1934 to 1940, when he became president. The army had become a highly visible and an effective force. It had grown from 10,000 personnel in 1910 to 30,000 in 1930 and was both mentor and adjunct to civilian rule.[213] It was fully capable of suppressing opposition, and did so comprehensively in 1935, when a series of demonstrations and strikes in 1933 and 1934 culminated in a general strike involving an estimated half a million participants.[214] Since the strikers' aims included an uncompromising demand to bring the military under civilian control, the army reacted with predictable and disproportionate force. The fortunate went into exile; the unlucky went to jail; the doomed joined the ranks of the disappeared.

Nevertheless, Batista should not be written off as just another of Latin America's petty dictators ruling with the connivance of the Good Neighbor. His regime marked neither a reversion to old-style oligarchy nor unqualified subservience to the United States. Batista was astute enough to recognize the limits of rule by rifle and he grasped the political possibilities of incorporating new social forces into a Cuban form of nationalist populism, which long survived his departure.[215] The United States also realized that the rules of the game had changed and that some concessions to nationalism were essential to keep the island both stable and open for business. Accordingly, Washington backed Batista in preference to competitors, such as Grau, whose reforming liberalism had the potential to threaten U.S. interests in Cuba. Batista himself complemented military rule with a policy of state-led improvement that began with the abrogation of the Platt Amendment (in cooperation with the United States) in 1934, and continued with reforms to agriculture, health, welfare, education, and political practice, notably by extending voting rights to women.[216]

By 1940, Batista felt secure enough to permit free elections. Three-quarters of Cuba's electorate voted to make him president and to give his Democratic Socialist Coalition a majority in the Senate; they also installed the opposition coalition under Ramón Grau as the majority party in the House of Representatives.[217] Both parties cooperated in producing a new constitution, which was enacted in the same year. This "post–New Deal document" codified many of the earlier social reforms proposed by Grau's liberal nationalists but set them in the context of the enabling, guardian state.[218] Insofar as Batista had a political philosophy, it was one that envisaged a period of authoritarian discipline and paternal tutelage leading eventually to a form of organic democracy that relied on ties of nationality to offset divisions of class and region. The former was a legacy of Spanish and American rule; the latter drew upon contemporary experiments with government intervention, which ranged from Soviet planning to National Socialism and included, in between, Roosevelt's New Deal.

Batista also attempted to lift Cuba's vital sugar industry out of its deep depression. Experiments with controlling output through the Verdeja Act and the Chadbourne Plan had demonstrated that world prices were beyond the influence of even a major producer like Cuba.[219] Accordingly, Batista reverted to Cuba's established policy of seeking improved terms in the U.S. market. His initiative intersected with Roosevelt's New Deal, which included a package of trade reforms aimed at stabilizing agricultural prices. Roosevelt was prepared to modify the Smoot-Hawley Tariff, not because it had devastated the Cuban economy, but because it had disappointed domestic interests and voters.[220] Although the tariff had protected mainland sugar producers from Cuban competition, it had failed to raise farm prices and had stimulated imports from the Philippines and Puerto Rico, which enjoyed tariff privileges in the U.S. market. The aim of the Jones-Costigan Act (1934) was to give mainland producers greater protection by imposing quotas on overseas suppliers. Cuba suffered disproportionately because the quota for the island reflected years when the Verdeja Act and Chadbourne Plan had limited output. Nevertheless, in the harsh conditions of the time, the Cuban government judged that the predictability the Act conferred was preferable to wayward fluctuations in the U.S. tariff. To sweeten the medicine, Roosevelt reduced the tariff imposed by Smoot-Hawley in 1930, though he also extracted tariff concessions from Cuba that benefited U.S. exporters.[221]

The Jones-Costigan Act achieved its purpose. Mainland producers increased their share of the mainland market appreciably: sugar beet accounted for 16 percent of the market in 1925–1929 and 22 percent in 1935–1939; sugarcane rose from less than 2 percent of the market to almost 7 percent in the same period.[222] The insular territories also improved their positions. Cuban interests were sacrificed to make these gains possible. The quota was just sufficient to permit Cuba to climb above the lowest point, reached in 1934, but too restrictive to allow the island to approach its years of unequaled dominance in the U.S. market. American investments in Cuba suffered from the priority given to interests on the mainland. The reduction in the rate of duty levied by the Smoot-Hawley Tariff, though intended to help U.S. sugar companies in Cuba, was insufficient to repair the damage already done. U.S. firms, having achieved a leading position in sugar production and exporting, began to withdraw; many of those that remained struggled to survive.[223]

The corollary, which has received less attention in the literature than it merits, was the beginning of the repatriation of the Cuban sugar industry.[224] As Americans divested, Cubans invested. Cuban-owned mills, which had ground 37 percent of the sugar crop in 1929, increased their share to 43 percent in 1939. Following the revolution of 1933, the colonos formed an effective lobby, the Cuban Cane-Growers Association, to present their grievances and remedies. Batista, who greatly preferred to have the colonos as allies rather than as cane-burning rebels, welcomed them as electoral assets. The colonos became Cuba's officially approved sturdy yeomanry, bulwarks of stability at home who also stood in the front line of the national struggle against foreign and imperialist interests. In this struggle they received support from a battery of measures that were codified in the Sugar Coordination Law of 1937.[225]

If the colonos and the military were the main beneficiaries of the revolution of 1933, labor gained too from legislation protecting trade unions, improving welfare provision, increasing wage rates, and limiting hours of work. U.S. protectionism, imposed for domestic purposes, was largely responsible for stimulating its Cuban counterpart. In doing so, Washington contributed unwittingly to the formation of a level of nationalist resistance that was to perplex successive administrations in the years ahead. Batista did not need to fix his election as president in 1940: by then he had succeeded in incorporating key interest groups and winning their support. As a capitalist caudillo, Batista was an authentic representative of the harsh conditions of the 1930s that fostered nationalist populism and authoritarian rule across the world.

Cuba, like Puerto Rico, had a relatively a "good" war.[226] As happened during World War I, the disruption of sugar supplies from other parts of the world greatly improved Cuba's commercial prospects. After the United States suspended sugar quotas, Cuba's output nearly doubled between 1941 and 1944, and the value of sugar exports almost tripled. However, there was no "dance of the millions" as there had been during World War I. Cuba was obliged to sell its sugar on terms fixed by the United States and was unable to benefit from the full market price. The deal was not entirely one-sided. The United States agreed, in exchange, to improve the position of Cuba's sugar in the mainland market once the war ended. Despite fixed prices for sugar, the export boom delivered gains that greatly eased the strains of the 1930s and helped to keep Batista and his key supporters in power. There were some shortages of imported manufactures and foodstuffs, but in general the United States was able to provide the shipping and goods that kept the sugar trade flowing. In diplomatic as well as commercial terms, the war tightened the ties between the two countries. Cuba provided two large air bases for the U.S. Air Force; the United States greatly expanded its naval base at Guantánamo Bay.[227]

"NOW, NO LONGER CAN WE BE UNMOVED"[228]

President William McKinley considered the creation of an overseas empire to be "a natural and inevitable consummation" of trends that placed the United States in the vanguard of world progress.[229] Prevailing images of the Caribbean islands supported his judgment by depicting the islanders as being in need of civilizing influences that only a superior power could bestow. Experience disillusioned both rulers and ruled, and produced harsher stereotypes. The lyrics composed for "*La Borinqueña*" by Lola Rodríguez de Tío in 1868 acquired a new relevance that reflected the confrontational politics of the late colonial period:

> Now, no longer
> can we be unmoved
> Now we do not want timidly
> to let them subjugate us.

In principle, the United States exercised direct rule over Puerto Rico and informal influence in Cuba. In practice, these distinctions were narrowed, though not eliminated, by political realities—as they were in the other Western empires. In Puerto Rico, the slender U.S. colonial administration was obliged to cooperate with the island's ruling oligarchy, whose networks and supporting patronage were the indispensable means of implementing policy. As direct rule became indirect in Puerto Rico, so it came closer to the informal collaboration that regulated relations between the United States and the caudillos who governed Cuba. In both cases, U.S. policy became a compromise between what was sought and what was possible. The system of management operated more effectively in Puerto Rico than in Cuba, where military opposition to foreign intrusion was a feasible option. Similarities can nevertheless be discerned at critical moments. Militant anti-colonial protests appeared in both islands during World War I, and reappeared during the 1930s, when they transformed politics. The political arena expanded, not only to include increasing numbers of small farmers but also to encompass the emerging middle class and the burgeoning urban labor force. This development marked the demise, or at least the metamorphosis, of the old oligarchies and the appearance of the populist nationalism that was to characterize the postwar era.

The "men on the spot" in both Puerto Rico and Cuba had only limited influence on the direction of policy, and were mainly conduits for decisions made in Washington. The principal exception, Major General Wood, exercised authority as military governor at a moment of exceptional fluidity. At the highest levels of policy-making, the constitutional distinction between the two islands allowed for different outcomes. The experimental development policies that President Roosevelt's "New Dealers" applied to Puerto Rico in the 1930s were possible only because Washington had the power to authorize them. Nevertheless, this was a rare initiative and the product of desperate circumstances. For the most part, Congress took little sustained interest in either Puerto Rico or Cuba. Colonial policy, to the extent that it existed, lurched unpredictably from one alternative to another according to fluctuations in the electoral fortunes of the two mainland political parties. Congress was consistent, however, in ensuring that neither the Bureau of Insular Affairs nor its successor, the Division of Territories and Insular Possessions, had the funds or staff needed to implement the expansive claims broadcast by imperialists in 1898.[230]

Limits to official authority allowed scope for private interests to influence, and even to shape, policy. This was nowhere more apparent than in the decisions made in Washington determining tariff levels on imports from the islands. The tariff was a tool for converting economic interests into political capital. At the outset of the colonial period, the main battle was between refiners on the East Coast, who wanted low tariffs on imports of raw sugar, and sugar beet growers in the Midwest, who lobbied for protection. The 1920s and 1930s saw a realignment of these interests: by then, mergers had produced a degree of collusion among mainland refiners and beet growers, and left producers in the islands as the main champions of low tariffs. When the economic crisis struck in the 1930s, domestic agriculture won protection at the expense of overseas producers. As an unincorporated territory, Puerto Rico gained some support but not enough to ameliorate the hardship that engulfed the island. The sugar industry had been brought into being by tariff concessions, was never competitive in international markets, and had little scope for improvements in productivity. Cuba, being formally independent, was cut adrift and left to fend for itself. The island's sugar industry led the world in productivity but was shut out of all major markets by protective tariffs. The proceeds from sugar exports were vital to the welfare of both islands. Economic adversity eroded political stability in Puerto Rico and Cuba, heightened nationalist resentment, and created conditions that first reshaped colonial rule and then contributed to its downfall. Colonial policy in the Caribbean, as in the Pacific, exemplified the adage that all politics is local, the localities in this case being constituencies on the mainland, where voters resided, rather than on the islands, which had no voice in congressional deliberations.

Capitalism was already established in the Caribbean islands when the United States arrived in 1898. Informal influences from the mainland, though present, were limited and expanded only after the war with Spain had made the islands safe for foreign investment. In this instance, trade followed rather than preceded the flag. The United States then introduced a brand of neo-mercantilist capitalism that inhibited the free market. The irony of colonial development was that Cubans wanted free trade and access to the United States while upholding their political independence, whereas the United States wanted to retain tariff protection while continuing to exert political control over the island. Puerto Rico, on the other hand, was driven into sugar production by tariff manipulation, and depended thereafter on protection and quotas for its welfare. From a strictly economic viewpoint, the island was a loss-making acquisition that produced profits only for those engaged in the sugar industry, which explains why proposals for shedding the burdens of empire circulated in Washington in the 1930s. By then, too, the civilizing mission had been effectively abandoned. "Americanization" needed funding that was not forthcoming and energy that had been dissipated. Brooks Adams's "law of entropy" applied to the new colonizers in ways that neither he, nor they, had envisaged.

These developments entered the cultural commentaries of the time. Foreigners continued to adopt and adapt indigenous forms of cultural expression. What was colonized, however, was not lost to its progenitors. Local idioms not only lived on, but were also revitalized by the need to create a counterculture that would contribute to a sense of national identity.[231] Export versions of these idioms bonded the Caribbean diaspora as it spread further into the mainland.[232] Extended networks instilled a sense of belonging that periodically summoned emigrants home, like pilgrims, to reaffirm their ties to the islands.[233] In these ways, islanders strengthened their own sense of nationality even as they appropriated elements of U.S. culture.

Laments for a past being lost to progress reminded listeners of the need to preserve the essence of what remained:

Today, while I sing, I'll tell you,
I feel an emptiness in my soul,
Because they've changed my hut
For a house made of cement. [234]

Protests at the economic burdens that weighed so heavily on the islands in the 1930s provided the stimulus for devising an alternative future:

The black man
in the cane field
The Yankee
on the cane field
The earth
beneath the cane field
Our blood drains
out of us! [235]

The evidence relating to the Caribbean islands bears out the argument advanced in chapter 11, which identified the 1930s as being the decade when widespread, organized opposition to colonial rule challenged all the Western empires. On the eve of World War II, as the next chapter will show, the American Empire in the Pacific was also in disarray. "The awkward squad of the rejected," as Byron called them, was on the march. [236] The mission, unaccomplished, was on the brink of being abandoned.

CHAPTER 13

PARADISE IN THE PACIFIC

"WHERE SKIES OF BLUE ARE CALLING ME"[1]

The appearance of the United States as a new imperial power added a fresh layer of impressions to the rich inheritance of myths and facts about the Pacific that had long circulated in the West. The image of Hawai'i that became established in the United States took shape in the 1890s and was updated but not significantly revised thereafter.[2] The main island and its indigenous population were small enough to fit the Western idea of a tropical Eden. Foreign observers soon agreed on an image of Hawaiians as simple primitives who lacked the skills to develop their abundant resources. The tourist industry developed this theme in the twentieth century, but slanted it to suit the interests of business rather than of government. The imagery shifted to the natural environment; the inhabitants were typecast and allocated sentimental, stereotyped parts in the island story. The "Song of Hawai'i," adapted from indigenous sources, became popular on the mainland during World War I, and endured long enough to inspire, in 1942, the title of a musical comedy starring Betty Grable wearing, inevitably, a grass skirt. The lyrics were attuned to the purpose:[3]

> Islands of Hawai'i
> Where skies of blue are calling me
> Where balmy air and golden moonlight
> Caress the waving palms of Wai Kiki

The Philippines, at the western edge of the Pacific, could not be categorized so easily. The archipelago consisted of more than 7,000 islands stretched over 1,100 miles, and in 1903 had an estimated population that exceeded seven million. Governor William H. Taft initially described Filipinos as our "little brown brothers" who needed several generations of firm paternal direction before they could be sure of assimilating the Anglo-Saxon qualities needed for success in the modern world. This indulgent but condescending image changed when the nationalists took up arms against United States. Long years of paternal control became even more necessary, but the implied family relationship was dropped. Filipinos became savage rather than sentimental primitives and their evolutionary potential was called into question. In 1900, Senator Albert Beveridge doubted the capacity of "a race of Malay children of barbarism, schooled in Spanish methods and ideas" and wondered "what alchemy will change the Oriental quality of their blood and set the self-governing currents of the American pouring through their Malay veins?"[4] The blood never became blue, or even Anglo-Saxon; nor did the sand become gold.[5] The Philippines was too distant from the United States to acquire the glittering embellishments of a major tourist industry. Necessity, however, improved the image of Filipinos once resistance had been crushed. American officials found that they could not govern without the cooperation of key Filipino intermediaries and associates, whose status, by association, improved markedly, not least because they were often better educated than their rulers.[6]

Scholarly criticism of these stereotypes is now as familiar as the stereotypes themselves. In recent years, cultural historians have added substantially to the existing stock of knowledge on this subject by unmasking the false representations of African and Asian societies fabricated during the period of colonial rule. A more difficult task, which has attracted a correspondingly smaller number of historians, is to reveal the subtle ways in which colonial societies "struck back," once militant resistance had ended, to preserve their own traditions and self-respect. The Hawaiian *hula*, to take one example, though appropriated, was not obliterated.[7] Although hula was separated from its origins, shredded, and repackaged for tourist consumption, the original conception of the art form as poetry in motion lived on; so did its accompanying chants, which continued to bond Hawaiians to their land and values:[8]

> Hold fast to and refuse to part with your traditions, oh child of the
>   land
> Defend and protect your way of life
> Keep them precious for one day your traditions
>   will be taken

The Philippines had already developed formidable forms of cultural resistance in the course of the long struggle against Spanish rule, and these were redeployed after 1898 to deal with the new colonialism imposed by the United States.[9] Popular Tagalog poetic songs and metrical romances, known as *awit* and *corrido*, survived and adapted. Some forms persisted with little change to their content because one of their

central themes, liberty (*kalayaan*), could be preserved and celebrated as
an ideal, irrespective of the nationality of the colonizing power.[10]

> The bygone days of joy
> The future that is hoped
> When the slaves will be freemen
> Where can this be found but in one's native land?

These binary oppositions capture, in literary form, the fundamental divide between imperial and nationalist viewpoints that forms the core
of the historiography of the modern colonial period. The analysis that
follows attempts to draw the two together and attach them to the general argument advanced in chapter 11. Admittedly, the connections between imperial and indigenous history suggested here are provisional,
and serve partly to advertise themes that require further investigation.[11]
It is possible, nevertheless, to identify some of the realities behind the
grand rhetoric of the civilizing mission and the fanciful Western images
of the Pacific. The record of U.S. colonial rule fell far short of the ambitious claims of its advocates: its performance was, at best, no better than
that of the other Western imperial powers. An indifferent and often wayward Congress was consistent only in its failure to fund development and
welfare projects. Colonial subjects, the objects of policy, harnessed, harassed, and bypassed alien rule when they could, as they did in the other
Western empires. International economic and political relations were
far more influential in shaping the fortunes of the Pacific empire than
were either colonial consuls or colonial subjects. The crisis that struck in
the 1930s shook the Pacific islands as it did Puerto Rico, Cuba, and the
rest of the colonial world. Both parties to the contract "rode the tiger" of
modern globalization; neither was able to tame it.

"HAWAI'I: A WORLD OF HAPPINESS IN AN ISLAND OF PEACE"[12]

Hawai'i takes primacy of place in this treatment of the American Empire
in the Pacific, even though it was far smaller in size and population than
any of the three other islands considered in this study, and the value
of its overseas trade, though close to the level achieved by Puerto Rico,
fell far short of that of the Philippines and Cuba. Hawai'i, however, can
claim priority on both constitutional and substantive grounds. As a settler colony, it was the only one of the insular possessions to be granted
the privileged status of an incorporated territory. Hawai'i also set a material precedent as the first of the insular possessions to be integrated

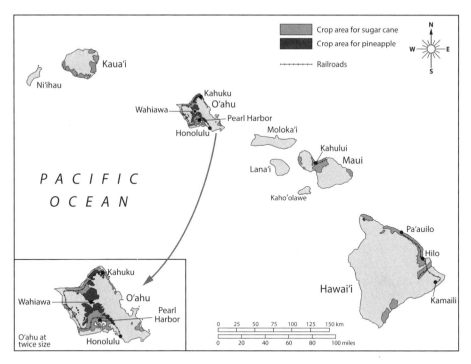

MAP 13.1. Hawai'i: Export Crops and Towns in the Interwar Period.

effectively, if not formally, with the mainland following the Reciprocity Treaty of 1875. Expansionists made the Hawaiian precedent a prominent part of their ambitious claims in the 1890s; their opponents cited it as an example of a foreign policy that had taken the wrong turn. The "skies of blue" beckoned commentators of all persuasions.

Hawai'i stands apart from the rest of the American Empire as well as from the American mainland. The separation is partly geographical: the islands are 2,500 miles from California, 5,500 miles from the Philippines, and farther still from the Caribbean. The cultural distance is even greater. Unlike the rest of the American Empire, Hawai'i was not bought or appropriated from Spain: Spanish was not the language of the elite; Catholicism was not the adopted version of Christianity.[13] The pattern of specialization followed by historians of the American Empire reflects these idiosyncrasies. The bulk of the literature concentrates on the former Spanish territories: one branch deals with the Pacific; the other with the Caribbean. The Pacific agency, however, is fully occupied with the large and complex Philippine archipelago and rarely encompasses Hawai'i, while specialists on the Caribbean feel, perhaps understandably, no obligation to do so. This arrangement leaves historians of Hawai'i to record specific features of the islands almost single-handedly; it also ensures that Hawai'i's place in the wider empire is understated, and sometimes not stated at all.[14]

Yet, the literature on imperialism ought to recognize and include Hawai'i as an unqualified example of a settler colony, even though it was far removed in size and population from large-scale polities such as Canada, Australia, South Africa, and Algeria. Hawai'i was an overseas extension of the original settlements that formed the core of the United States. The agrarian ideal promoted by Jefferson and championed by Jackson, though increasingly overtaken on the mainland by the growth of modern manufactures, was revitalized in Hawai'i, which utopian expansionists envisaged as an island Arcadia far removed from the influences that were eroding the rural order at home. Arcadia or not, Hawai'i was ruled by a white oligarchy who controlled the most valuable land, managed substantial plantations, regulated a subordinate labor force, and manipulated racial divisions to preserve its power. Seen from this angle, the acquisition of Hawai'i was both a Southern victory after military defeat in the Civil War and a Northern concession made to seal the unity of the Republic.

Small though it was, Hawai'i was distinctive among settler colonies because of the extent to which the American settlers restocked and refashioned the islands' population. Other settler colonies consisted of white minorities who either ruled often sizeable indigenous populations, as in South Africa, Kenya, and Algeria, or eventually outnumbered them after successive infusions of white immigrants, as happened in the United States, Canada, Australia, and Latin America. In Hawai'i, white settlers remained a minority; the indigenous population (*Kanaka Maoli*) formed a small and diminishing proportion of the total; the bulk of the remainder consisted of imported laborers from Asia and other parts of the Pacific.

In 1900, the total population was only 154,000, of which 27,000 (18 percent) were white, 40,000 (26 percent) were Hawaiian or part-Hawaiian, and 87,000 (56 percent) were immigrants from Asia and the Pacific.[15] In 1950, after half a century of colonial rule, the total population had risen to 500,000, the white population had increased to 115,000 (23 percent), Hawaiians and part-Hawaiians amounted to 86,000 (17 percent), and those originating in Asia and the Pacific numbered 278,000 (56 percent). The share of the white segment of the population had increased slightly, while that of the Hawaiian element had diminished. The striking feature of the data, however, is the fact that immigrants from Asia and other parts of the Pacific accounted for more than half the population throughout the period under review. The composition of the population, as defined by the authorities, was central to the structure and operation of the colonial enterprise: it determined the size and character of the labor force, established the rules governing race relations, and defined the basis of the political system for much of the colonial period.

Hawai'i was incorporated as a self-governing territory in 1900 and was the only one of the acquisitions of 1898 to have the prospect of obtaining statehood.[16] Congress granted this exclusive privilege because Hawai'i was categorized as a settler colony that was analogous to the continental territories of the United States, even though it was separated by a wide stretch of ocean. Incorporation confirmed the existing order in Hawai'i represented by the settler-dominated government and conferred the legitimacy needed to underpin its authority. The islands adopted the standard form of territorial administration in having a governor directly appointed by Washington and an elected legislature consisting of a Senate and a House of Representatives. A provision in the constitution requiring that the office of governor be held by a citizen of Hawai'i ensured that a member of the white elite would continue to preside over the administration.[17] However, there were no risky experiments with democracy: liberty was defined by the ruling oligarchy, which controlled the political arena, the labor market, the legal system, and education. Behind the formalities, the patrimonial system of government inherited from Hawai'i's monarchs survived and was adapted to serve the interests of the new rulers.[18] These arrangements delivered a large measure of self-government, though the United States retained control of immigration, tariffs, and defense, as well as foreign policy.[19] Hawai'i's constitutional status as an incorporated territory made it rather more than a colony but rather less than a dominion.

Initially, the franchise was confined to a small minority of adult males who were literate in either English or Hawaiian; the large number of Asian and Pacific contract workers, the majority of the population, were disqualified from voting. These provisions restricted the number of eligible voters to less than 8 percent of the total population and kept power in the hands of the white settlers (*haole*), who dominated the legislature though the agency of the Republican Party from 1903 to 1954. The newly formed Home Rule Party made a brief showing by mobilizing the Hawaiian vote and winning the first elections held in 1900. The party mismanaged its success, however, crumbled before the financial and organizational power of the local Republican machine, and was disbanded in 1912. Its short history was symbolized by the career of Prince Jonah

Kūhiō Kalanianaʻole, who was an active nationalist and one of the leading advocates of home rule. He abandoned the party in 1902, joined the
Republicans, and became their (nonvoting) representative in Congress
from 1903 until his death in 1922.[20] His leadership and connections were
influential in directing the Hawaiian vote to the Republican Party.[21] The
Democratic Party, formed in 1900, had even less success than the Home
Rule Party: it was unable to establish an electoral base and was marginalized until the close of the colonial era.

In political terms, Hawaiians became bystanders in what had been
their own country. In being relegated, they also became part of the distinctive underclass that arose where settler societies overwhelmed indigenous societies, whether by numbers or firepower. In the twentieth century, native Hawaiians joined the list of ethnic casualties that included
Native Americans in the United States, Inuit and Innu in Canada, Aborigines in Australia, Maori in New Zealand, Sami in the Arctic, and
many others. These groups suffered from a high incidence of economic
deprivation, incarceration, alcoholism, and ill-health, and low levels of
education and correspondingly poor employment prospects.[22]

Despite these setbacks, Hawaiians continued to defend their sense of
identity. Indigenous customs lived on in the royal household and in some
of the smaller islands.[23] Strenuous efforts were made to keep Hawaiian
and creole languages alive, despite official policy, which promoted the
use of English.[24] At the same time, Hawaiians turned the Americanization of the islands to their own advantage in the hope that the selective
acceptance of foreign customs would be consistent with the preservation
of indigenous values. High rates of literacy supported a lively press that
kept questions of sovereignty before the public. Conversion to Christianity was in part a means of winning respect and gaining bargaining
power in dealings with the United States. The experience of subordination, and the efforts made to prevent it from submerging Hawaiian
society, formed the underside of the islands' history as an incorporated
territory. They had no place in the historiography of colonial rule and
they did nothing to darken the sunny image of the tourists' paradise. It
was not until the second half of the twentieth century that Native Hawaiians, like other First Peoples, increased in numbers, found a voice, and
gained an audience.

Incorporation generated confidence in the colony, attracted investment, and stimulated economic expansion. Like other constituents of the
American Empire, Hawaiʻi depended on agricultural exports, especially
sugar, for its development and welfare, and on the home government for
tariff concessions and a political guarantee of its viability. Hawaiʻi, like

Alaska, automatically became part of the United States for tariff purposes and was granted equality of trade with other states of the Union. Sugar exports responded immediately to this long-awaited encouragement. Production grew from 290,000 (short) tons in 1900 to a peak of 1,057,000 tons in 1932 before falling slightly to 961,000 tons in 1950.[25] At its peak in the 1930s, production was concentrated on the island of Hawai'i, which accounted for nearly 45 percent of the acreage under sugar; most of the remainder was divided more or less equally between Kaua'i, Maui, and O'ahu.[26] The number of plantation employees rose from 36,050 in 1900 to a high point of 56,630 in 1928 before dropping to 19,340 in 1950 (principally as a result of improved productivity).[27] Sugar remained the leading export and the single most important employer throughout the colonial period, followed by pineapples, which expanded rapidly after World War I.[28] In 1939, the sugar industry accounted for 36 percent of total personal incomes in Hawai'i and the pineapple industry, for 21 percent.[29]

This huge expansion was overseen by a small group of firms known as the Big Five.[30] These firms originated in the nineteenth century, pressed for annexation at the close of the 1890s, and were well placed to gain from the opportunities incorporation offered. After 1900, the Big Five became even bigger: contemporaries regarded their increasing size as a further illustration of the law of evolution exemplified by the rise of corporatism at home. The firms extended their reach horizontally by acquiring and consolidating additional land (including plantations formerly owned by Claus Spreckels) with the result that by the 1930s they controlled about 95 percent of Hawai'i's sugar output.[31] Simultaneously, they expanded vertically by moving into banking, processing, and shipping. Members of the group owned, singly or jointly, the Bank of Hawai'i (1893); a refinery in California (purchased in 1905), which became one of the largest in the world; and the Matson Shipping Line, which by the 1930s had achieved a monopoly of routes to the West Coast.[32] These developments produced a typically colonial outcome in further strengthening ties between Hawai'i and the United States, which soon accounted for more than 90 percent of the islands' import and export trade during the colonial era.[33]

The pineapple industry initially developed outside the orbit of the Big Five, though the founder, James D. Dole, came from one of the leading settler families: his cousin, Sanford B. Dole, was President of the Republic of Hawai'i (1894–1898) and the first governor of the new Territory (1900–1903).[34] Hawai'i's favorable tariff status protected entrepreneurs from potential foreign competitors and encouraged Dole to apply his technical insight to the development of the canning industry. The Hawaiian

Pineapple Company, which he founded in 1901, achieved almost total control of the U.S. market by the 1920s, at which point it had also become the world's largest producer.[35] The firm reached its highest stage of development on the small island of Lana'i, where Dole established a plantation of 14,000 acres in 1922. Imperial overstretch, however, affects companies as well as governments. Heavy investment left Dole ill-prepared for the economic crisis that struck in 1929; an unwise attempt to break the monopoly of the Matson Navigation Line compounded his problems. In 1932, the Big Five stepped in, displaced Dole, and took over his company, which they renamed the Pineapple Producers' Corporation.[36] Thereafter, production shifted principally to O'ahu and Maui, which accounted for about 55 percent and 31 percent respectively of the total acreage under pineapples by the late 1930s.[37]

With the acquisition of the Hawaiian Pineapple Company, the Big Five reached the peak of their influence over the economy of the islands. Their success depended on their ability to control three essential ingredients: land, labor, and the franchise; capital came from reinvesting past profits.[38] A high proportion of the land occupied by the settlers was held on low-cost leases obtained originally from the Hawaiian monarchy. The political settlement following 1898 confirmed leaseholders in their existing holdings but also sought to control their expansionist ambitions. Federal policy aimed to make the "mountains and valleys the home of a million good American citizens," or, as President Theodore Roosevelt put it, in characteristically robust style, to keep the islands for "small, white landowners" and to discourage planters from "bringing in every kind of Asiatic to help them to make fortunes for a moment and to ensure the extinguishment of their blood in the future."[39]

From the standpoint of the existing settlers, these were disturbing prospects that threatened the foundation of their prosperity while also promising to install independent, yeomen-style farmers who might bring an unwanted degree of practical democracy to the islands. Accordingly, the territorial government set about blocking the proposals. It halted land reform, fended off the federal government's attempts to diversify agriculture, and circumvented the limit of 1,000 acres on land holdings, which was imposed in 1900 and repealed in 1921.[40] By 1908, the federal Department of Agriculture had given up its attempt to attract white immigrants by making family farms accessible. The federal government then fell back on a scheme to turn native Hawaiians into substitute homesteaders. However, the Hawaiian Homes Commission Act of 1921, which aimed to set aside public lands for this purpose, benefited the settlers more than the indigenous inhabitants.[41] The settlers succeeded in reserving the best public land for continued sugar production, made it difficult for native Hawaiians to establish their entitlement, and pushed those who qualified onto marginal lands. Roosevelt's formulation of Jefferson's vision failed in Hawai'i, as it was to do in the Philippines and Cuba.

By 1921, the idealism that had inspired imperialists such as Roosevelt, Root, and Taft, had broken on the rocks of colonial realities. In principle, Congress was prepared to sanction a degree of social engineering and had a broad faith that technical solutions could produce, in the favorite term of the day, "efficiency." At the same time, Congress was profoundly suspicious of "socialistic" measures, and was also reluctant to spend money on overseas possessions that lacked federal voting rights.[42] Lack of political will, however, was only part of the story. Conditions of production in Hawai'i encouraged capital-intensive techniques, which required considerable investment in milling, irrigation, fertilizers, and research, and favored a high degree of integration.[43] Unit costs were much higher in Hawai'i than in Cuba, and the Pacific islands remained competitive only because they were able to achieve remarkably high yields and operate within the shelter of the U.S. tariff.[44] Pineapples had proved to be the only successful alternative to sugar and they, too, were a plantation crop.

Labor supply was the other key issue facing the planters. Given the small size of the indigenous population and the reluctance of mainland Americans to move to Hawai'i at the prevailing wage rates, the only solution was to promote immigration from sources outside the United States. Contract labor, however, ran into constitutional objections, while nativist feelings on the mainland, stoked by fears of competition from cheap labor, halted Chinese and Japanese immigration in 1886 and 1907 respectively, and prohibited it entirely in 1924.[45] The Territorial authorities adapted by negotiating concessions where they could, evading restrictions where enforcement was difficult, and complying where they had no choice. Following a brief period of uncertainty immediately after 1900, the inflow of labor resumed. Planters wanted a steady supply and a stable workforce, but also a degree of ethnic diversity that would impede labor solidarity and prevent Asians from dominating the polity.[46]

What they received in large numbers were Japanese immigrants, who were already the largest ethnic group in 1900 and remained predominant throughout the colonial period. By 1924, when further immigration was prohibited, the Japanese community in Hawai'i numbered 180,000 and had become indispensable to the islands' export industries.[47] What is known in business circles today as "burn and churn" applied in Hawai'i a century ago. There was a high rate of turnover. Some immigrants went home; others left the plantations for different occupations in Hawai'i.[48]

Those who remained on the plantations lived under the jurisdiction of an encompassing paternalism, which provided accommodation in crowded barracks and a measure of social welfare.[49] Although wages on the sugar plantations in Hawai'i were higher than they were in America's other sugar islands, they were not high enough to prevent discontent or to mitigate the resentment caused by persistent racial discrimination.[50]

World War I touched the islands but did not scar them. Hawai'i continued to export sugar, though it was sold by arrangement with the U.S. Food Administration rather than on the open market. The only victory worth recording was bloodless: property owned by German companies was confiscated and sold at half its value to the Big Five, who thereby strengthened their grip on the islands' economy.[51] U.S. troops arrived and bases were built, but the principal consequence of their presence was social rather than military. American soldiers of all shades of color experienced a novel form of race relations. Whiteness and supremacy still went together on Hawai'i, but the sheer number and variety of non-white faces on the islands ensured a greater degree of fluidity than was found on the mainland. The troops also became, in unforeseen ways, pioneer tourists who returned home carrying impressions of Hawai'i that were to become big business after World War II. By then, Hawai'i's image had been fixed so firmly in the public imagination that it survived not only the grim conditions of the interwar period, when "blue skies" and "balmy air" were poor compensation for material hardship, but also the war itself.[52]

The dark side of the "island paradise" was revealed in a series of strikes over conditions of work, wages, and discrimination that marked the history of the colonial period. The first major strike on the sugar plantations occurred in 1909, when 7,000 Japanese workers struck for four months in support of higher wages.[53] The Hawaiian Sugar Planters' Association, the employers' union, broke the strike and succeeded in having its leaders imprisoned on charges of conspiracy. They also conceded some of the strikers' demands, while simultaneously arranging to hire cheaper, more pliant labor from the Philippines. The next large stoppage took place in 1920, when almost half the labor force on the sugar plantations struck for increased wages to compensate for price inflation after World War I.[54] The strike was again led by Japanese workers, though this time with Filipino participation, and lasted more than six months. The strike was broken, as it had been in 1909, by determined brutality, otherwise known as the full force of the law, but the employers also made concessions, as they had done in 1909, and renewed their search for cheaper and more docile workers. This time they set their sights on what British colonial officials called "the industrious and shifty Chinaman" to replace the increasingly defiant and politically involved Japanese. Congress, however, deferred to representations from a broad-based anti-immigrant coalition on the mainland that included labor unions and veterans' organizations, and proceeded to pass the restrictive Immigration Act of 1924.[55] The planters then turned to inter-imperial transfers to bridge the labor gap. Additional imports of Filipino workers, however, created new problems: in 1924, the Filipinos, who stocked the lowest levels of the labor market, struck in protest against their meager wages and poor conditions.[56] Several thousand workers came out in a stoppage that lasted for eight months, but they were defeated, amidst considerable bloodshed, and their leaders imprisoned.[57] Having broken the strike, the planters applied their previous strategy of initiating reforms that were intended to avert future labor disputes.[58]

Asian immigrants, especially the large Japanese community, presented the settler oligarchy with a more serious challenge. The first generation of Japanese immigrants (*Issei*) did not have voting rights, but the second generation (*Nisei*), who were born in Hawai'i, were included in the franchise under the provisions governing territorial incorporation. Democracy, however, arrived by default rather than by design. The intention at the time of annexation was to populate the islands with white smallholders from the mainland. When they did not materialize, the resident settlers had to adapt to the prospect of living with a potentially unfriendly electorate. President Dole had anticipated the problem in 1902 by initiating a policy of assimilation.[59] The aim, however, was not to merge the races but to turn Asian immigrants into Americans by putting them through an English-based schooling system. There followed a protracted struggle over Japanese-language schools, Buddhist temples, and the issue of dual citizenship, all of which turned on the question of how far immigrants were required to abandon their own cultures to meet the standards required by assimilation.[60] An inherent contradiction flawed the policy: assimilation presumed equality, but the white settlers, echoing sentiments expressed on the mainland, regarded Asians as inferior beings.[61] The "island paradise" in Hawai'i was a judiciously constructed fiction, just as it was in Bali.[62]

During the 1920s, Hawai'i struggled, like the rest of the world, to return to normality after the upheaval of World War I. Events in the 1930s, however, unsettled the precarious equilibrium established after 1900. The international economic crisis, which began in 1929 and lasted through much of the 1930s, reduced the profitability of Hawai'i's exports and stoked discontent among plantation and urban workers. A series of protests culminated in two major strikes. In 1937, Filipino employees of the sugar plantations on the island of Maui stopped work for three months. Their claims included a call to "Make this a Workers' Paradise," which in effect meant subverting the settler order.[63] In the following year, dock workers in Hilo on the island of Hawai'i went on strike for seven months; their protest was broken only after the use of considerable force.[64]

The strike on Maui in 1937 was the last major event of its kind supported by a single racial group. The Hilo strike that followed was planned by well-organized trade unions and backed by a variety of workers, irrespective of race or ethnicity.[65] This episode was the first clear indication that racial divisions, which the Big Five had encouraged as a means of perpetuating their dominance, were being overcome. Although trade unions had appeared in Hawai'i during the 1920s, they were transformed by the longshoremen's strike in California in 1934. Strikers on the mainland formed a new union, the International Longshore & Warehouse Union (ILWU), which exported its principles and organization to Hawai'i in 1937.[66] By the close of the 1930s, the new labor movement was becoming a formidable force.

Adverse developments stemming from the mainland exacerbated the internal difficulties confronting the Big Five. In 1933, Roosevelt's new administration cast a critical eye over Hawai'i.[67] The Secretary of the Interior, Harold L. Ickes, was ready to bring the territorial government under closer control by appointing nonresidents to senior positions in Hawai'i. In 1935, Congress passed the Wagner Act, which legalized the right to join trade unions. The administration in Hawai'i managed to ward off the constitutional challenge, and benefited from a concession that excluded agricultural workers from the provisions of the Wagner Act. Nevertheless, the writing, if not yet on the wall, was present in draft form.

The message arrived in 1934 in the form of the Jones-Costigan Act, which reduced the volume of raw and refined sugar Hawai'i was permitted to export to the United States.[68] The purpose of the Act was to protect mainland producers at a time of depression by limiting imports from offshore and foreign suppliers. The shock to Hawai'i arose not only from the loss of almost 10 percent of its sugar exports to the United States, but also from being treated, with Puerto Rico and the Philippines, as an unincorporated territory.[69] Before 1934, the Big Five had opposed statehood because territorial status gave them access to the U.S. market on favorable terms while preserving local autonomy. After 1934, they reversed their position and pressed Hawai'i's case for becoming a new state of the Union. As an incorporated state, Hawai'i would have irrevocable rights guaranteeing equality of trade with other states of the Union and the ability to represent its interests through voting members of Congress. On the other hand, statehood would confer equal voting rights on Hawai'i's citizens and increase the difficulty of managing the electorate. By the 1930s, second-generation Asian immigrants constituted a sizable proportion of those entitled to vote; statehood would give nonwhites a majority and a governor elected by popular vote.

A desperate situation, however, required a matching remedy. The Big Five opted for statehood, that is to say an end to colonial status, not because they were keen to realize the ideals of liberty and democracy, but because they judged it to be their only chance of preserving the privileged position they had won after annexation. Although the congressional committee of inquiry was impressed by the case for statehood, the application was turned down in 1935 because of concerns about Japan's ambitions in the Pacific and its influence in Hawai'i.[70] Relations between the United States and Japan had deteriorated in the 1930s and had exposed the vulnerability of both Hawai'i and the Philippines. Congress was unwilling to confer statehood on a territory containing a large Japanese population whose loyalties were thought to be divided. Negotiations over statehood were suspended and left unresolved until 1959.

War came suddenly to Hawai'i in 1941, when Japan attacked Pearl Harbor. Overnight, the islands lost the invisibility that had shielded them from serious scrutiny from the mainland and they were immediately assigned a prominent role in the war effort.[71] Washington had already decided that the Philippines was indefensible and that Pearl Harbor would serve as the base of the Pacific Fleet. Annexation to the United States, as the inhabitants abruptly realized, gave Hawai'i a wholly unexpected exposure to foreign aggression. The islands were immediately placed under martial law.[72] The military administration, "the generals," as they were called, instituted an authoritarian regime that was unprecedented in the history of the United States in the twentieth century. The new administration suspended habeus corpus, established military courts, authorized "preventive detention," imposed censorship, restricted movement, and covered the islands with blackout. A new command economy sprang into being as the generals took control of production, prices, and overseas trade and shipping, overrode labor legislation, and froze wages.

These measures delivered a series of contrasting shocks.[73] The expansion of the military created an economic boom. The population of the islands doubled between 1940 and 1944, following successive infusions of military personnel and civilian auxiliaries. About 400,000 American soldiers, including some 30,000 African Americans, observed the fluidity of race relations in Hawai'i, and took the message home.[74] The demand for labor, particularly for construction, reduced unemployment to zero and drew large numbers of women and children into the workforce. The two main exports, sugar and pineapples, were classified as priority foods. Fortuitously, the rapid increase in the number of local consumers provided a substantial local market for products that otherwise would have been cut off from the mainland because of the shortage of civilian shipping. Consequently, the chief agricultural products escaped the difficulties of market access that many other colonial exporting countries faced: in 1945, production of sugar and pineapples in Hawai'i was not far short of what it had been in 1941.

On the other hand, the controls imposed by the military government aroused widespread discontent, especially after the defeat of the Japanese navy at Midway in 1942, when numerous military restrictions were relaxed on the mainland but held in place in Hawai'i until 1944.[75] Plantation workers resented the fact that their wages and mobility were frozen at a time when the shortage of labor had increased opportunities and earnings in other occupations. The trade unions, headed by the ILWU, had pledged not to strike during the war, but they campaigned energetically and successfully to raise membership in the interim. Moreover, they no longer appealed only to unskilled and illiterate workers but to the new generation of Nisei, who by 1941 represented three-quarters of the Japanese community.[76] This generation had acquired education and articulate representatives who were well equipped to express their aspirations. Their claims were greatly helped by the outstanding war record of the Japanese community in Hawai'i, which erased all doubts about its loyalty. Internment had been considered for Hawai'i but was ruled out as being impractical, though it was implemented on the mainland.[77] Japanese volunteers came forward in large numbers and served with distinction: the 442nd Regimental Combat Team and its 100th Battalion became the most decorated units (in relation to their size) in the history of the U.S. Army.[78] By 1945, the new generation had made its mark and signaled its determination to put an end to second-class citizenship.

By contrast, the settler oligarchy suffered an immediate loss of power and status after the military took control of all important economic and political activities, notwithstanding the buoyant market for plantation crops, fixed wage rates, and the absence of strike action. The elite suddenly became commoners and could no longer command the deference that had long helped to underpin their authority. Elite housewives also lost status: lacking servants, they even had to do their own housework.[79] The balance of power on Hawai'i had shifted; where it was to settle would not become clear until after the war.

THE PHILIPPINES: "SUBSTITUTING THE MILD SWAY OF JUSTICE AND RIGHT FOR ARBITRARY RULE"[80]

The generals of the U.S. Army who helped to expel Spain from the Philippines, and then suppressed the nationalist movement, shared with the civilian authorities who followed them an almost complete ignorance of the tasks they faced.[81] President McKinley, so it was said, could not locate the islands on the map; his first representatives there knew nothing of the extensive, straggling archipelago and its numerous, diverse inhabitants. Reports and recommendations appeared with the rapidity demanded by the needs of the moment. The Schurman Commission investigated, assessed, and pronounced in 1899; a second commission recommended a form of government in 1900; the first civil governor, William H. Taft, was appointed in 1901; a census of the islands was completed in 1905.[82]

Knowledge of a kind filled blank spaces and shaped the principles that were to guide the new colonial government. Filipinos were divided into two categories: "civilized" and "wild."[83] Fortunately or not, the great majority of the population was declared to be "civilized," though, as the Schurman Commission concluded, still "wholly unprepared" for self-government and in need of considerable further tutelage. Spain, the Commission judged, had begun the process of spreading Western civilization but was a power long in decline and therefore incapable of completing its assignment. The baton had now passed to a younger, more virile nation that would carry the mission to completion. The Philippines was allotted a place in world history: its role was to realize the destiny of the West, as interpreted by the United States, and in due course to become a beacon of liberty and democracy shining a light on darkest Asia.

Armed with these propositions, colonial officials proceeded to distinguish between those of their colonial subjects who would propel the cause of progress and those who were likely to obstruct it. The ilustrados, or elements among them, recommended themselves as being the most qualified agents of modernity.[84] They were, by definition, already educated in Western ways. Some of them spoke English, which made them literally intelligible to American officials, who knew little if any Spanish and had no grasp of any of the numerous indigenous languages.[85] Many ilustrados were mestizos, which lodged them high up the racial hierarchy and gave them a head start in the new game of seeking American approval. The new game was an adaptation of the old one. Having disparaged Spanish rule, the United States entered the Philippines with the idea

MAP 13.2. The Philippines under U.S. Rule.

of "beginning the world anew," but quickly realized that existing institutions were not only durable but also had considerable administrative value.[86] The new rulers adopted the social and racial hierarchy introduced by Spain and carried forward the legal system that upheld it. The Catholic Church reached an accommodation with the colonial authorities, preserved a good deal of its traditional authority, despite being disestablished, and continued to serve as a bulwark of social stability.[87] The Big Men who survived the turmoil at the turn of the century found that they had more opportunities under the enlarged U.S. administration than they had enjoyed previously. The changing of the guard came with some striking continuities.

The opposition was harder to categorize. The mass of the population was neither easily reached nor readily understood. Although they were not benighted, they were self-evidently so far from the American way of life as to need firm paternal direction. "Benevolent assimilation," in McKinley's famous phrase, aimed to spread cultural uplift, inculcate American values, and defuse opposition to colonial rule. The truly "uncivilized" were few in number and politically unimportant. The Muslims in Mindanao, however, presented a problem that could not be ignored, even though their southern location was far from the main island of Luzon. They qualified for inclusion among the "civilized" colonial subjects because they had developed well-organized polities and espoused a form of religion, Islam, that placed them several cuts above paganism. On the other hand, their sense of political identity nurtured an obtuse belief in their independence, while their religion did not lend itself readily to assimilation to Western concepts of spirituality.

The policy of benevolent assimilation had three strands: training in democracy; economic development; and acculturation. The colonial rulers assumed that democracy, a generic concept, could be equated with the species *Americanus*. The Schurman Commission had looked favorably on Britain's methods of colonial government, which combined the authority of an appointed governor with "the promise and potency of genuine home rule."[88] In the end, however, the Commission recommended the American territorial system, which was in accord with the U.S. Constitution, distanced the administration of the Philippines from more overt forms of colonial rule, and was more effective, so it was assumed, than the British system in delivering self-government. The British, for their part, viewed the emphasis on the rapid achievement of self-government as evading a responsibility rather than as implementing a principle.[89] Yet querulous criticism from Britain did nothing to halt "the march of the flag." The Philippines was quickly provided with institutions imported from the United States that were judged to be appropriate for an unincorporated territory: a governor nominated by Washington and a form of Congress consisting of an Assembly with an appointed upper house and an elected lower house, which began to function in 1907. The governor retained the power of veto in case unwanted measures managed to reach his office. The electorate was restricted to less than 3 percent of the population, and excluded Muslims and other non-Christians.

While some of these provisions were consistent with American constitutional principles, they were also a necessary means of reconciling Filipinos to a further installment of foreign rule. Policy-makers in the United States had not anticipated either the extent or the tenacity of the opposition they encountered. Although the capture of Emilio Aguinaldo in 1901 had removed the leading opposition figure, the war against the nationalists continued after 1902, when the United States declared that it had ended. The declaration pardoned participants while allowing the authorities to classify continuing resistance as banditry. In 1904, Macario Sakay formed a breakaway Tagalog Republic and contested American rule until 1907, when he was betrayed and hanged as a "bandit."[90] Armed resistance to American rule persisted in the less accessible southern island of Mindanao until 1913.[91]

The protracted, costly, embarrassing, and paradoxical struggle to liberate nationalists had far-reaching consequences for American policy. It brought disillusion to Washington's imperialists, including Theodore Roosevelt, and donated a set of arguments to the Democrats for use against the Republican Party's foreign policy. The intensity of opposition to colonial rule, and the prospect that it might recur, influenced policy on the ground, too. Officials realized that they needed to win at least the most important "hearts and minds" if they were to succeed in connecting the new machinery of government to the population at large. Accordingly, they moved swiftly to strike a political deal that detached key interests from the independence movement and established collaborative ties with their principal representatives.[92] Compromise was not part of the rhetoric of the civilizing mission, but it quickly became an axiom of colonial rule in the Philippines, as it had long been in the European empires.

The administration's search for solutions included the possibility of importing techniques of indirect rule from British Malaya.[93] The idea was abandoned because rajahs and sultans were in short supply except in the far south, where the two ancient Sultanates of Maguindanao and Sulu presented both obstacles and opportunities. In this region, which became Moro Province in 1903, the United States replayed, largely unwittingly, a script that was familiar in other Western empires whose rul-

ers had already debated the merits of direct and indirect rule and the degree to which "native laws and customs" were consistent with imported
versions of civilization.

Where inexperience met novelty, the outcome was inconsistency. In
1899, Brigadier General John C. Bates struck a deal whereby the Sultanates acknowledged U.S. sovereignty in exchange for a place on the payroll
and acceptance of "native customs," which included slavery and polyg-
amy.[94] In 1904, the United States disowned the Bates "Treaty," and authorized the new governor of the province, Major General Leonard Wood,
to introduce direct rule. Wood and his successors extended martial law,
crushed opposition, often with great brutality, and introduced civilizing
reforms. Studies of military affairs have long overshadowed the civil component of this policy, which Wood saw as an opportunity to demonstrate
to the world the superiority of American values and methods. Wood, like
his friend Theodore Roosevelt, was an "armed Progressive."[95] His qualifications as an exponent of force were impeccable: he had fought in the
"Indian" Wars and commanded the Rough Riders in Cuba. He regarded
Moro Province as an opportunity to wipe the slate clean and institute
a form of assimilation that, if lacking benevolence, would nevertheless
produce a civilized society. Wood deprived the Sultans of their secular
power, promoted economic development, confronted slavery, and introduced American-style education. Islam was to be tolerated but tamed so
that it would eventually merge, in some unspecified way, with Western
civilization. The resulting social upheaval eventually produced a new
group of collaborators, drawn primarily from the nobility (*datus*), who
saw in American rule an opportunity to win protection from their traditional enemies in the Christian north.

In Luzon and, at the periphery of its reach, Visayas, the colonial government turned to two sources of support: key figures among the ilustrados and an overlapping group, the caciques, or local Big Men, who
exerted influence in the provinces.[96] The ilustrados had come to prominence in the nineteenth century under Spanish rule, but their eminence
resulted more from their economic and cultural achievements than from
their political services, which did not extend, as American officials supposed, to effortless control of the unheard, though far from silent, majority.[97] The caciques had enhanced their positions during the military
phase of the revolution but had seen political authority snatched from
them by the United States just as it seemed to be within their grasp.
Spain had depended heavily on the Friars to supplement its understaffed
administration, but the U.S. authorities had deprived them of their
quasi-political functions. Accordingly, the new colonial government had

to act speedily to find alternative agents. The ilustrados were on hand and they presented themselves, as Manuel Quezon, one of their leading spokesmen, put it in 1908, as "the directing class."[98] Simultaneously, the creation of an elected Assembly held out the prospect of access to resources and patronage. At this point, the ilustrados and their associates were in sight of adding political power to their other sources of influence.

The administration had no alternative but to strike a deal with these groups. The new rulers were not so much harnessing tradition as inventing it: in a grand bargain of collaboration that lasted throughout the colonial era, Governor Taft and his successors endowed the ilustrados with a degree of political authority and hence legitimacy that they had not enjoyed under Spanish rule. The accord, moreover, was negotiated rather than imposed: the United States was ruler of its subjects but a prisoner of its colony. The anti-government tradition in the United States prevented the creation of a strong central authority, and Jeffersonian ideals positively encouraged decentralization.[99] Elihu Root, the Secretary of State, was soon forced to recognize the impossibility of founding colonial policy on either central direction or democratic principles, and had to fall back on the idea of delegating broad powers to the executive in the Philippines.[100] Political realities limited this strategy as well. In 1908, the former chief of the executive and newly elected President, William H. Taft, offered a highly qualified view of the ability of the executive to deliver popular self-government and feared that policy might descend into a compromise that would merely "await the organization of a Philippine oligarchy or aristocracy competent to administer government and then turn the islands over to them."[101] Taft was not a dedicated imperialist but he was an instinctive paternalist who thought that external supervision was needed if civilization was to advance.[102]

Representatives of the United States were deficient in numbers as well as in knowledge. An effort was made to install a bureaucracy based on merit and to turn the debate over the justification for colonial rule from questions of morality to matters of technology.[103] However, the optimism of Progressive reformers who hoped to use the new overseas colonies to demonstrate the superiority of their plans for enlightened and efficient government soon waned.[104] Difficulties in recruiting capable civil servants from the United States appeared at the outset of the undertaking and were never overcome. Incentives for joining the colonial service were inadequate; doubts about the duration of colonial rule discouraged recruitment; turnover was rapid. Consequently, policy-makers were unable to construct a strong, permanent central bureaucracy and were compelled to fill the administration with Filipino recruits at a much earlier stage than they had originally planned. This trend accelerated rapidly under the governorship of Francis Harrison, a Democratic appointee, who reduced the American contingent in the Philippine colonial service from 2,632 in 1913 to 614 in 1921, and increased Filipino representation from 6,363 to 13,240.[105] The change enlarged the scope for ilustrados and regional caciques to reward their followers and enabled the provinces to colonize the center, which was the reverse of what had been intended. Taft had begun by hoping to implant an alternative to the "spoils system" that still prevailed in the United States; he ended by re-creating this well-oiled domestic machinery in the Philippines, where it became the chief source of political accumulation in the twentieth century.

The embryonic oligarchy accepted the franchise of the patrimony with enthusiasm.[106] Political parties, which had begun to organize under Spanish rule, quickly adjusted to the second colonial occupation. Governor Taft gave the process a helping hand by encouraging the formation of the *Federalistas*, who were pro-American advocates of assimilation and statehood. In 1907, however, the *Nacionalistas* emerged to campaign for independence "under the protectorate of the United States." The contest, which was less about different programs than about contrasting styles of collaboration, ended with the triumph of the Nacionalistas in the elections held for the new Assembly. The Americans took the result in their stride. The political influence of the Federalistas was limited to Manila. The Nacionalistas were a more promising prospect. Their leader, Sergio Osmeña, who was married to a wealthy Chinese mestizo, had a power base in Cebu Province as well as in Manila.[107] No wonder that William C. Forbes, a senior official and future Governor-General, recorded in his diary how pleased he was at the success of "his very good friend," as it would give him "great power with the Assembly."[108] Evidently, the two sides had reached an accommodation that bridged the distance between their public positions, which were diametrically opposed.

The accommodation was the product of mutual interests that were, literally, policed by innovative techniques of surveillance and control.[109] As Taft was declaring his commitment to establishing democracy in the Philippines, he was also putting in place an intelligence network designed to disarm and, if necessary, destroy dissident elements. The pleasure Forbes expressed at the success of "his very good friend" can be understood fully only in the light of evidence that Osmeña had been drawn into the system Taft had instituted. Forbes knew this better than anyone because, as Commissioner of the Philippine Constabulary, he had created the network of spies, informers, and rumor-mongers who provided the

FIGURE 13.1. Sergio Osmeña, Governor Francis Harrison, and Manuel Quezon, 1918. *Source*: Photo, "Sergio Osmeña, Govr. Francis Harrison, and Manuel Quezón" (1918) as reprinted in Kasaysayan, *The Story of the Filipino People* ed. by Henry S. Totanes, Asia Publishing Company Ltd. (1998)

means of control. This was not an isolated case. Quezon was an undercover operative during the early stage of his political career; in return, the police suppressed information that could have halted the progress of the Philippines' most famous nationalist leader.[110] Forbes, whose prejudices were not always concealed, later referred to Quezon, infelicitously, as "the most responsive little organism to outside influences that I know."[111]

Forbes's handiwork endured. Quezon adopted his network of controls, presumably with considerable satisfaction, when the Commonwealth was formed in 1934. It was later deployed on a large scale to help defeat the

Huk Rebellion in the 1950s, and reached full maturity under President Ferdinand Marcos. The export model did well too. Forbes's system was adopted in the United States, where it was used to crush strikers and dissidents in the 1920s. By then, police surveillance in the Philippines had become an important service industry and had developed links with criminal elements that fueled corruption. No doubt Taft had good intentions, but the road he chose eroded the democracy he wished to see established and pointed instead in the direction of a police state.

The alliance between colonial rulers and members of the political elite was confirmed in 1916, when the Jones Act gave the Filipino oligarchy an opportunity to increase the scale of its political activities.[112] The Act enlarged the franchise, opened the Senate to election, and promised independence "as soon as a stable government can be established."[113] Here, on the face of it, was an example of an enlightened power exceeding expectations and doing so in record time. The reality was rather different. In the United States, the Democrats, who had pledged to end the imperial venture, unseated the Republicans in 1912, when Woodrow Wilson was elected president, and dominated Congress until 1920. Even so, the Act passed through Congress only after a long struggle. Taft and the Republicans opposed the bill, as did American business interests in the Philippines and the Roman Catholic Church, which feared that the islands would descend into a state of "barbarous infidelity."[114] Taft was concerned with principle as well as with timing: in his view it would take another generation or two before the Philippines could support a popular democracy capable of resisting rule by an "oligarchy or aristocracy."[115] Theodore Roosevelt, once the arch-imperialist, favored withdrawal on the grounds that the islands were a military liability.[116] Sugar producers in the United States supported independence because they hoped it would eliminate the favorable tariffs the Philippines enjoyed. Osmeña and Quezon wanted independence but also guarantees of U.S. support against possible Japanese aggression.[117] Wilson, the prophet of self-determination, dragged his feet. Elections held in 1916 installed Osmeña as head of the majority party in the lower chamber, Quezon as leader of the Senate, and gave the Nacionalistas almost permanent dominance in what became, effectively, a one-party state.

"Civilization" had not conquered "barbarism" by 1916, nor had democracy triumphed. "Native laws and customs" deemed unacceptable had not been eradicated. In 1922, the enlarged electorate encompassed only 7 percent of the population, and election fraud and fixing were commonplace. The Jones Act redeemed a pledge that had been an ingredient of party politics since 1898 and emerged as a practical possibility from the electoral cycle in 1912. The reference to "stable" government was the key phrase in the Act: viability had become the goal; democracy lay in an unspecified future. By 1916, politicians of both mainland parties had become weary of the cost and conflict that the burdens of empire had brought. Those who were once eager to shoulder the load were now keen to shed it. The sequence of groundless optimism followed by well-founded despair was to be repeated elsewhere in the course of the new century—and beyond.

Economic policy underwrote the political compact between colonial officials and the ilustrado-cacique elites, and ensured, as far as possible, the stability of the new state. The colony was expected to pay its way without directly billing Congress and American taxpayers. At the same time, officials were inhibited from imposing appropriate levels of taxation on wealthy property-owners in the Philippines whose support was essential to the survival of colonial rule. Governor Taft had hoped to deal with the funding problem by attracting private investment from the United States and immigrants from Asia. Congress, however, imposed strict limits on foreign corporations that wished to acquire natural resources in the Philippines, restricted the colonial government's ability to raise development loans in case rising levels of debt breached the principle of self-sufficiency, and only rarely supplemented colonial revenues with federal grants.[118]

By default, government revenues depended on customs duties and a mixture of head taxes and excises.[119] This formula combined practices inherited from Spain (including compulsory labor) with principles borrowed from Britain, where "self-sufficiency" had long been an accepted maxim of colonial government. After 1909, however, when free trade was established between the Philippines and the United States, the colonial government could levy duties only on commerce with foreign countries. From then on, trade with the mainland affected revenues indirectly by raising or lowering domestic purchasing power, thereby influencing taxes on consumption.[120] As the United States increased its share of foreign trade with the Philippines, the tariff base contracted. The colony's revenues came under pressure; development plans were constrained. The government in Manila was forced to increase domestic taxes to compensate, and thus courted unpopularity at times of economic difficulty.

Expenditure also conformed to the characteristic priorities of colonial rule, which allocated funds mainly to military and administrative services, and left little scope for financing development from colonial sources.[121] The modest residue was assigned, as in the British and French colonies, to infrastructure and public utilities, which extended Spanish policies, and to measures designed to improve agriculture and conserve forests, which drew on Britain's colonial experiments (and also exhibited some of their ambiguous results).[122] Colonial policy, however, did score a largely unheralded success in raising agricultural productivity to the point where, by the 1920s, the Philippines became self-sufficient in rice, which had long been a major import.[123] Unfortunately, the initiative faltered from the mid-1920s for lack of money and trained personnel, and rice yields began a slow decline that lasted for half a century. In 1931, Governor-General Dwight Davis should not have been as shocked as he was to discover, on a tour of Southeast Asia, that per capita revenue and expenditure in the Philippines were below levels found in Dutch Indonesia and Siam, and eight times lower than in the Federal Malay States.[124]

The success of the development strategy rested on the performance of the international economy, which lay beyond the control of colonial policy. Nevertheless, policy played an important part in the process by converting the monetary system to the gold standard and linking the Philippine peso to what was, in effect, a dollar-exchange standard, and securing tariff concessions from Washington. The peso gained strength and stability by being linked to the dollar, and gave foreign investors confidence in the economy and the state.[125] Tariff preferences were crucial to maintaining the viability of sugar and coconut exports, and to a limited extent, abaca.[126] All three products, however, were subject to the whims of Congress, which reflected the capriciousness of electoral politics in the United States. In effect, development policy was a gamble that export earnings would continue to generate revenues for the state, income for key interest groups, and employment for the impoverished and unenfranchised majority.

Governor Taft pressed for tariff reductions to assist economic recovery after the war and as a means of detaching sugar planters from the nationalists. Initially, however, the beet lobby on the mainland was powerful enough to counter his efforts. In 1902, the Philippines won a discount of 25 percent off the regular tariff, but it was not until 1909, after the Sugar Trust had taken over the major beet firms, that the way was clear for the Payne-Aldrich Tariff to establish free trade between the two countries, subject to generous quotas.[127] Finally, in 1913, the Underwood Tariff, in reducing the general tariff, also abolished quotas on imports from the Philippines.[128] In this case, protectionists had to concede to a higher interest: the survival of the new colonial empire. Tariff concessions were in effect subsidies made by taxpayers in the United States for the privilege of having an empire. The main beneficiaries were large-scale sugar planters and millers, whose increasing wealth funded their generous lifestyle and political ambitions, and ultimately enabled them to compete with the colonial government for control of the state.[129]

Exports experienced a long boom during the first two decades of the new century.[130] Primary produce prices recovered from the late nineteenth-century slump, and imperial preference gave the Philippines privileged access to the vast U.S. market.[131] The volume of sugar, coconuts, and abaca, the three major exports, grew substantially; export values experienced a threefold increase between 1908–1912 and 1933–1937. The three leading products accounted for a steady 85 percent of all exports between 1900 and 1940, though the contribution of each changed during the period: sugar came to dominate the export list; coconuts held their place; abaca declined in the face of foreign competition. In 1934, a peak year, sugar exports generated an estimated 40 percent of government revenues and 30 percent of national income.

Trade followed the flag in the Philippines, as elsewhere in the insular empire. Before 1898, Britain, Hong Kong, Singapore, and Spain dominated the export trade. Annexation enabled the United States to overtake its competitors. The proportion of Philippine exports shipped to the United States rose from 30–40 percent in the 1900s to 50–60 percent in the 1910s and to 70–80 percent in the 1920s and 1930s. Imports from the United States followed a parallel path, increasing from 10 percent in the 1900s to 40–60 percent in the 1910s and to 60–65 per cent in the 1920s and 1930s. The Philippines, helped by broadly favorable terms of trade, also maintained a persistent and substantial balance-of-trade surplus, which was returned to the United States through shipping, interest, and dividend payments. This pattern of exchange characterized a number of other colonies, notably India, which for this reason occupied a central position in Britain's balance of payments.

In the terminology adopted here, the Philippines became a "colony of trade" rather than of (white) settlement.[132] As late as 1939, there were only about 8,000 U.S. citizens on the islands. The majority were in the administration or the military; about half resided in Manila.[133] The "Manila Americans," as U.S. business interests were known, fell far short of the Big Five who ran Hawai'i.[134] Although they spoke with one voice, especially in favor of continuing colonial rule, they were barely heard in Washington. The Spanish presence fell sharply immediately after the war but rose slowly following the peace settlement to reach a total of about 5,000 in 1939.[135] Spanish trade and investment in the Philippines grew after 1898. Initially, the representatives of the former colonial power were helped by a condition of the Treaty of Paris guaranteeing that Spain could trade for 10 years on the same terms as U.S. firms enjoyed.[136] After

1908, Spain's commerce with the Philippines continued to expand, even as the export economy was reoriented toward the United States.[137] Spanish businesses operated successfully within the U.S. protectionist system while losing the stigma of being the direct agents of colonial rule. French interests, though informal rather than formal, benefited similarly after Britain occupied Egypt in 1882.

The Philippines was in general unattractive to mainland investors, despite the reassurance provided by American rule. Although the United States supplied about half the private investment in the Philippines in 1937, this figure accounted for only about 1 percent of all U.S. capital invested abroad. Direct investment, principally in public-service enterprises, predominated; portfolio investment was placed mainly in government bonds. Attempts to displace the British from their dominant position in finance failed. In 1938, U.S. capital controlled less than 10 percent of the islands' banking resources. The Philippine National Bank, which was founded in 1916 partly to promote American interests, quickly became a tool of the local sugar barons who had initiated it.[138] The wartime boom encouraged excessive lending; the slump that followed led to business failures and put the Bank into serious difficulties. The blame was attributed to mismanagement and corruption among the Filipino staff; the bank's president, Venancio Concepción, was convicted of fraud.[139] The real cause, however, lay with U.S. officials, who misused the bank's currency reserves and committed a number of other financial irregularities.[140]

Colonial land policy was the major obstacle to extensive foreign investment.[141] Governor Taft, searching for revenue and allies, wanted to open the natural resources of the islands to private enterprise by making the "Friar lands" available to large foreign corporations and by encouraging the entry of Chinese laborers.[142] His plans met resistance from the U.S. beet industry, which feared the prospective competition, and from nativists in the United States, who were opposed to any scheme that might allow nonwhites entry to the mainland. After a long wrangle, Congress passed the Public Land Act in 1902, which limited the holdings of foreign corporations to approximately 2,500 acres. The restriction deterred prospective planters because it was insufficient to deliver significant economies of scale. Instead, the U.S. government purchased about 445,000 acres of prime land from the Roman Catholic Friars and sold it to sitting tenants and wealthy local investors.[143] Henry Havemeyer, the sugar magnate, managed to skirt the law in 1909, when he bought some 44,000 acres on the island of Mindoro, but the Philippine legislature acted to halt further sales on this scale. In 1926, when Harvey S. Firestone applied to start large-scale rubber plantations in the Philippines, he was turned away.[144] A handful of Americans established cattle ranches in Mindanao, but their efforts were unsuccessful.[145] The British followed a similar policy in West Africa after the turn of the century, when the Colonial Office refused W. H. Lever, the soap magnate, permission to establish palm oil plantations in British possessions there.[146] Firestone departed for Liberia, where he received a warmer welcome; Lever transferred his proposal to the Belgian Congo, where the colonial government took a more indulgent view of expatriate entrepreneurs seeking very large places in the tropical sun.

Countervailing influences caused the United States, the powerhouse of twentieth-century capitalism, to frustrate the demands of some of its mightiest representatives. The hope of encouraging homesteading, however unrealistic, weighed against Firestone and others promoting grand projects. Representations from the sugar beet and sugarcane lobbies, which were suspicious of all plans for large-scale agricultural development in the overseas territories, counted against him too. Political considerations, however, were an even more important determinant of land policy. In the decade after 1898, the United States was desperate to win over ilustrados, caciques, and their followers. Land policy that favored local interests was an ideal means of encouraging collaboration. Accordingly, export production remained in the hands of local farmers. Smallholders predominated, but some sizable estates developed too, as rural entrepreneurs used the opportunities created by annexation to the United States to expand activities they had initiated during the period of Spanish rule.

Pampagna and Negros, the two largest sugar-producing regions, illustrate the diversity of production structures, and parallel in particular the difference between western and eastern Cuba.[147] In Pampagna, on the northern island of Luzon, settlement, land-tenure arrangements, and patron-client relationships were long established. Sugar production was dominated by tenants, who worked scattered farms that in 1910 averaged no more than about 90 acres.[148] Land holders, principally mestizos, supplied credit and undertook the processing of the crop. Farther south in the remote island of Negros, on the other hand, settlement was sparse, land readily acquired, and existing titles unrecognized. Frontier development there was reminiscent of the American West and South. Migrants from other parts of the Philippines displaced indios and small farmers, and either seized land or bought it very cheaply. It was here that the large-scale enterprise usually associated with sugar production arose in the second half of the nineteenth century. By 1896, shortly before the advent of U.S. rule, twelve families controlled nearly one-third of the 130,000 acres under sugar, and self-contained haciendas employing local and imported wage labor had become part of the landscape.[149] Despite differences in structures of production and location, Pampagna and Negros nurtured sugar elites who formed social and political ties between the two regions. The sugar barons, as they were known, accumulated great wealth, invested in high politics and high living, and mortgaged their future to the American connection and the tariff advantages it brought.[150] They were well represented in the new Assembly when it opened in 1907, and they retained their predominance throughout the period of American rule.

The coconut industry, unlike sugar, still awaits the attention of historians, despite the fact that the Philippines became the world's largest producer and exporter of the commodity.[151] The industry developed under Spanish rule and expanded rapidly after 1898, when the Philippines gained access to the huge American market. Coconuts did not benefit from tariff concessions to the same degree as sugar but nevertheless received a boost in 1922, when the United States granted coconut oil advantageous terms of entry. The effect was immediate: oil became the most important of the coconut exports; copra (coconut "meat"), which had predominated previously, fell into second place.[152] The expansion of the industry was the result of indigenous enterprise responding to price incentives in much the same way (and at much the same time) as farmers in tropical West Africa reacted to new opportunities in producing groundnuts, cocoa, and palm oil and kernels. Coconuts were predominantly a smallholder crop: there were few economies of scale in production, and the initial stages of processing also remained decentralized. In the 1960s, long after independence, the size of the average coconut farm was still only about 10 acres, and farms of 100 acres or more accounted for only 10 percent of the land devoted to the crop.[153] The majority of coconut farms were worked by their owners, though holdings were sufficiently diverse to allow for tenants and wage laborers too. Coconuts grew readily in many parts of the Philippines, but the story of how they spread remains to be told. For present purposes, the point to be made is that the export industry drew an increasing amount of land and a growing number of Filipinos into dependence on the export market opened up by colonial rule.

The third main export, abaca (also known as Manila hemp), had an equally long history of export production.[154] Abaca, a member of the banana family, was indigenous to the Philippines and was found throughout the islands. Kabikolan in southeast Luzon produced more than half the exports of abaca from the Philippines down to 1916. Thereafter, Visayas and Mindanao became the leading centers of production, and by the 1930s Kabikolan's share had fallen to 25 percent.[155] Abaca, like coconut, was grown mainly by smallholders, who used family labor, wage labor, and sharecroppers. Although the Philippines was the world's leading producer, abaca faced increasing difficulty in the twentieth century as the development of alternative means of manufacturing cordage and paper exerted downward pressures on producer prices. Filipino producers also competed among themselves, as well as in the world market. Kabikolan suffered particularly from the development of abaca plantations on Mindanao, where settlers drove the frontier forward and created a number of relatively large holdings.[156] Japanese colonists were especially prominent in establishing estates growing both abaca and coconuts. These enterprises had sufficient capital to increase productivity, improve quality, and employ a sizable wage-labor force. Davao, Mindanao's main port, expanded rapidly from the beginning of the century and soon acquired a cosmopolitan character that set Japanese and Christian influences in a predominantly Muslim context. Successful Japanese estate owners gradually made their way into the emerging national elite founded on sugar. They, too, understood the importance of the politics of influence in protecting property, profits, and, when the international situation deteriorated at the close of the 1930s, themselves.

The cultural branch of the civilizing mission was devoted to applying policies of assimilation.[157] If subject peoples were inferior, as racial assumptions held, the task of government was to uplift them. Improvement, however, was retarded by intractable dilemmas. Failure would destroy the justification for empire; success would make it redundant. Furthermore, success could not culminate in statehood, a possibility held open for Hawai'i, but could have only one outcome: independence. Filipinos thus had to be trained to become Americans but also taught to be liberated from them. Unsurprisingly, the timetable for delivery became a matter of contention. If the trainees were inclined to be impatient, American tutors were inclined to make haste slowly to ensure that their vision of the future was not dimmed before it was realized. Moreover, given the fact that the Philippines was effectively under indirect rule, policy at the point of delivery was largely in the hands of Filipinos, who interpreted and applied the civilizing mission in ways that, as far as possible, suited their own purposes. Assimilation policies resulted in a series of imperfect compromises in which American ideals, filtered through Philippine realities, emerged in unanticipated forms of hybridity.

The Philippines was a laboratory for reforms that Progressives advocated, with limited success, in the United States. The reform program was not only consistent with continuing racial discrimination, but also depended upon it.[158] While the war against the nationalists was being fought, Filipinos were portrayed in homogeneous terms as being a degenerate and barbaric enemy. When peace was established, the United States needed to reorder the racial hierarchy to distinguish between collaborating elites and those who were less promising. Hispanic or part-Hispanic Christians qualified as being rational and recognizable; others fell into place according to their distance from the ideal. Ethnographic surveys provided the "science" supporting racial classification and reinforced an enduring set of stereotypes. The Kalanguya, who inhabited the mountains of northern Luzon, were judged to be insufficiently advanced to be classified officially, and consequently had difficulty accessing government resources; women in the region were categorized as "domestics" and were deprived of entitlements to property.[159] The Tiv in the uplands of central Nigeria were among many groups who suffered similarly in other Western empires.[160]

Missionary enterprise, which was intended to aid assimilation by converting Filipinos to Protestantism, made only modest progress. Shortly after annexation, the Protestant missions undertook their own partition of the archipelago. The Methodists were assigned the populous region of northern Luzon and Manila, the Presbyterians acquired southern Luzon and western Visayas, the Baptists took central and eastern Visayas, and the Congregationalists were left with the greatest challenge of all: Muslim Mindanao. Most of the Philippines was already formally Christian, apart from Mindanao (which included Sulu), but the Protestant missions viewed Roman Catholicism as a type of civilized heathenism that presented a special challenge to the true faith, even though that, too, came in several competing varieties. The Roman Catholic Church was not easily outbid by its Protestant rivals, who shared the racial prejudices of their compatriots in the colonial government, even while criticizing them for falling short of their proclaimed ideals.[161]

Charles Briggs, the first Baptist missionary to reach the islands in 1898, spoke for the majority, who were shortly to follow him, in regarding Filipinos as being like gullible children in supporting the insurgents against the U.S. Army. For good measure, Briggs also gave spiritual approval to water torture (known today as water-boarding), which he regarded as being "humane, just and effective."[162] He was convinced that the United States was executing a divine responsibility, and that the rebels stood in the way of the great majority of their compatriots, who were keen, so it was assumed, to be Americanized.[163] After a century of missionary endeavor, fewer than 10 percent of Filipinos could be counted as Protestant converts at the close of the twentieth century.[164]

Progressive reformers had some successes. They were instrumental in suppressing, or at least in diverting, the opium trade, and they supported measures to abolish slavery.[165] Abolition, however, created difficulties of its own. The long struggle against domestic slavery, for example, not only involved a protracted and disruptive military campaign against the Moros, but also strengthened anti-imperial forces in the United States and eased the path toward the Jones Act, which began the process of emancipating the United States from its troublesome colony.[166]

Education was the principal means of transmitting cultural uplift, and its agent in the Philippines was the government rather than the missions. The Bureau of Education oversaw a massive campaign to bring education to the people.[167] An impressive network of primary and secondary schools arose; institutions of higher education were established; the University of the Philippines was founded in 1908. School enrollments increased; literacy rates improved markedly.[168] These achievements, however, were qualified. The colonial government put English on course to become the primary language, but failed to displace Spanish, which benefited from being the language of resistance to U.S. rule.[169]

A thorough investigation of public education, undertaken in 1925, criticized the quality of teaching, the high dropout rate, the inappropriate content of the school syllabus, and the lack of funds.[170] Some programs were either misconceived or misdirected. Educationalists brought assumptions to their duties that were inherited from previous, largely unsuccessful attempts to civilize and assimilate Native Americans.[171] Indigenous cultures, the message read, were primitive; the route to progress was through the adoption of American values.[172] As the British delivered Wordsworth's flowering "Daffodils" to the tropics, where they were unknown, so the Americans introduced Longfellow's "Hiawatha" to the Philippines, where (we may guess) the recipients were equally perplexed. A vast effort at industrial education, devised to put "primitive" people on the first step of the ladder to progress, accompanied these alien innovations.[173] One initiative led to a campaign to grow corn where it was unsuited and unwanted; another yielded a mountain of woven baskets for which there was no demand. Informal influences, notably the introduction of popular American sports, complemented official policy, but, where successful, became an expression of resistance rather than assimilation, as they did in Cuba.[174]

World War I left the Philippines unscathed. Japan, considered to be the main potential threat, joined the allies at the start of the conflict and remained for the duration; Germany had only a limited naval presence in the region. Demand for the leading export crops remained buoyant, though shortages of shipping prevented the Philippines from joining Cuba's exuberant "dance of the millions." The principal struggle was political rather than military. The Democrats finally had a chance to act on their long-expressed opposition to the occupation of the Philippines when they took control of Congress and the White House in 1912. Debate centered on the Jones Act and the controversy over Governor Harrison's radical plan for transferring posts in the civil service to Filipinos.[175] The war had an important, if indirect, effect on these developments. President Wilson's highly publicized proclamation of the principle of self-determination reverberated around the world in ways he had not anticipated and could not control. Quezon and Osmeña responded by amplifying their calls for independence. A developing national consciousness added popular voices to the demand, which was expressed far beyond the political arena in a variety of ways—from the movies of José Nepomuceno to the spread of Tagalog as the language of independence.[176]

The Republicans, who returned to power in 1921 and dominated Congress for the rest of the decade, set about reversing these trends.[177] The newly elected Republican administration took advantage of the crisis afflicting the Philippine National Bank to halt the Democrats' policy of promoting Filipinos. President Warren Harding installed the robustly conservative General Leonard Wood as governor-general in 1921, with a mandate to restore the policies formulated by Root and Taft, who envisaged a long period of tutelage before independence could become a practical proposition. Wood crafted an informal alliance with the moderate nationalist Sergio Osmeña, blocked declarations of future independence, and prevented a plebiscite on the issue.[178] Harding's policy was followed by his successor, Calvin Coolidge, who stated that independence was a possibility "in time," but in 1924 took the view that "it is not felt that that time has come."[179] Wood died in 1927, while still in office, and was replaced as governor-general by Henry L. Stimson, who pursued the same policies, though with more tact. As in the British and French empires, the 1920s were a time when colonial controls were tightened, not loosened.

Developments in the export sector complemented these trends. The favorable tariff for sugar, achieved in 1913, combined with rising demand prompted first by World War I and then by postwar reconstruction, boosted exports and enhanced the reliance of the Philippines on the U.S. market. Export expansion had internal repercussions, though these have yet to be fully incorporated into the political history of the period. Belatedly, the sugar industry followed Hawai'i and Cuba in adopting centralized milling, increasing productivity, and improving quality.[180] Unrefined muscovado sugar, which was previously exported in quantity to China, gave way to white sugar, which was in demand in the United States, but required greater processing. Economic power became increasingly concentrated as the industry became more capital-intensive. By the mid-1930s, seven Filipino (mostly mestizo) families controlled between one-half and two-thirds of the output of central mills; the remainder was in the hands of American and Spanish firms.[181] Lines of potential conflict were drawn between the new "super millers" and planters who had lost the capacity to mill their own sugar, on the one hand, and between small farmers, who were struggling to manage the transition from muscovado to white sugar, and the millers and planters who stood above them, on the other. The colonos in Cuba grappled with similar developments after World War I.

Conflicting U.S. policies and mounting tensions within the Philippines reached the snapping point in the 1930s, when the economic crisis that began in 1929 compelled a fundamental revision of colonial policy. Rising unemployment in the United States galvanized calls for protection. Beet and cane sugar producers in over half the states of the Union came together to demand revisions to the tariff concessions that had enabled the Philippines to increase its share of U.S. sugar imports from 8 percent in 1921 to 24 percent in 1933.[182] Cotton and dairy interests added their weight because coconut oil competed with cottonseed oil in the manufacture of soap, and was also an ingredient in the production of margarine, which competed with butter.[183] The American Federation of Labor stepped up its campaign to exclude Filipino migrants from the United States on the grounds that they were taking unskilled jobs from American citizens. As colonial subjects, Filipinos had a right to travel to the United States and for this reason had been excluded from the restrictive Immigration Act of 1924.[184] Economic imperatives, however, generated a vociferous campaign to remove their rights of entry. Although the campaign was unsuccessful in the short run, it added momentum to the movement in the United States to give the territory independence, created resentment in the Philippines, and increased the uncertainty felt by all parties about the direction of U.S. policy.

Complementary motives strengthened the pressure exerted by economic interests. Racist agitation lent popular support to the exclusionist cause; the eugenics movement gave it pseudo-scientific respectability.[185] Jobs were at stake; so too, commentators claimed, were racial purity and vitality. Strategic considerations also came to the fore in the early 1930s, when policy-makers became increasingly alarmed by Japan's expansion-ist ambitions. Soon after the war with Spain, Theodore Roosevelt real-ized that the acquisition of the Philippines had created an inner weakness rather than an outer defense; in the 1930s, strategists concurred. Theo-dore Roosevelt, Jr., who was Governor-General of the Philippines in 1932–1933, commented that "one of the most influential motives" prompting the move toward independence was the desire to shed "a responsibility that might entail a war."[186] It was difficult, if not impossible, to defend the Philippines against outside attack and costly to make the attempt. Con-gress had failed to spend money on the islands' defenses before the onset of the economic crisis and was indisposed to do so after it had struck.

These disparate forces converged on a single conclusion: the burden of empire was such that the interest of the United States lay in unloading it as soon as possible.[187] Viability and democracy, the official measures of the success of colonial policy, were set aside. The Philippines was to have the independence its leaders had clamored for in public but disowned in private.[188] Congress made the case even before Franklin D. Roosevelt took office as president in 1933. The Hare-Hawes-Cutting Act, passed in 1932, offered the Philippines independence after a transitional period of ten years. President Hoover, who judged the measure to be premature, vetoed the Act, but Congress reaffirmed it in 1933, and it was the Philip-pine Senate that declined to accept it.[189] Two key provisions of the Act expressed the triumph of domestic lobbies over the opposition, which was represented mainly by the "Manila Americans," who lacked influence in Washington, and U.S. investors, who had been hobbled by restrictions placed on opportunities in the Philippines.[190] One provision progres-sively eliminated the tariff advantages Philippine exports enjoyed in the U.S. market, while ensuring that imports from the United States were admitted to the Philippines free from customs duties; the other prevented prospective Filipino immigrants from entering the United States.[191] Ex-ports to other Asian countries also suffered because the Philippine peso, being tied to the U.S. dollar at a fixed rate, was effectively overvalued, while currencies elsewhere in the region depreciated or were devalued.[192]

Roosevelt, helped by his party's control of Congress, moved swiftly to resurrect legislation that would deliver independence. "Let's get rid of the Philippines," he declared in a private meeting with congressio-nal leaders in 1934, "that's the important thing."[193] Expedience joined Democratic policy in a happy union and was soon consummated in the Tydings-McDuffie Act, which passed Congress in March 1934 and was ratified in the Philippines the following year. The Tydings-McDuffie Act was substantially the same as the Hare-Hawes-Cutting Act passed in 1932. The new Act established a transitional entity, called the Commonwealth of the Philippines, to oversee the final stage of home rule before independence, which was scheduled for 4 July 1946. Emigration to the United States was virtually halted; in exchange, the United States abandoned its previous insistence on retaining military bases in the islands. In May 1934, Congress approved a complementary measure, the Jones-Costigan Act, which established quotas on imported sugar and phased out free trade for the Philippines in stages between 1940 and 1946.[194]

Political leaders in the Philippines were reluctant to drink such a sour brew. They hoped for effective autonomy while maintaining advantageous links with the United States. Full independence, as they realized, might convert a paper triumph into a material disaster. Yet, independence was a talisman displayed to rally political support and to conjure a better future out of a depressed present. Quezon and Osmeña pressed forward because they could not turn back. Popular discontent held them to their self-appointed task; internal political rivalries ensured that they reached the highest stage of brinkmanship in the race to be the first to claim the prize. Muñoz Marín, faced with a similarly unappealing offer in 1936, chose instead to adopt policies aimed at giving Puerto Rico a sound material basis for establishing effective independence.

The period was one of political ferment arising from economic hardship. Trade unions were organized in Manila and other towns of Luzon.[195] The Communist Party was formed in 1930, declared illegal in the following year, and transferred its influence to the Socialist Party, which was founded in 1932. Strikes, unrest, and violence continued throughout the decade and reached a peak in 1939–1941.[196] Some rural areas were able to react to economic decline by retreating into subsistence farming, as happened in parts of India and tropical Africa too.[197] Elsewhere, millenarian and peasant movements grew in size and stridency.[198] The Sakdalistas, formed in 1933 under the banner "no master but the people," demanded radical land and tax reforms.[199] In 1935, the movement mobilized 60,000 peasants in a rebellion against the Filipino oligarchy and the newly agreed terms of independence. Although the rebellion was put down by force and with loss of life, it shook the political establishment and obliged the ilustrado-cacique elites to ponder how to bring popular movements into the established political arena without conceding their radical demands. For their part, the leaders of these movements decided that they were now strong enough to work successfully within constitutional limits.[200]

The presidential election of 1935 also witnessed a sizable protest vote. General Emilio Famy Aguinaldo, without an effective political organization but with the support of his veterans, came out of retirement to stand for office. Bishop Gregorio Aglipay, veteran, dissident, and head of the Philippine Independent Church, stood on behalf of his 1.5 million members. Quezon was able to enlist the Philippine Constabulary in his cause for the first time. Elections were subjected to interference; unrest was suppressed.[201] As expected, the election confirmed Quezon as president of the new Commonwealth. The two dissenting candidates, who had attracted nearly one-third of the vote between them, protested; episodes of violence followed. Rumors of a plot to assassinate Quezon circulated; Quezon responded by investigating the possibility of dispatching Aguinaldo. The outcome remained within the bounds of the constitution.[202] It was nevertheless a dramatic symbol of the changing of the guard, as the old nationalists of 1898 gave way, finally, to the new forces formed by collaboration and patronage.

The prize went to Quezon because his risky strategy for achieving independence was rewarded by good luck and skillful management, as well as by friendly agents of the state. Quezon and Osmeña were friends but also rivals who could carry rivalry deep into acrimony. They fell out in 1922, reconciled two years later by forming the Partido Nacionalista Consolidado, split again in 1934, and came together in the following year, when Osmeña was elected Vice President.[203] Quezon had opposed the Hare-Hawes-Cutting Act in 1932 partly in the hope of securing better terms and partly to prevent Osmeña from claiming the credit. Two years later, he supported the Tydings-McDuffie Act, even though it offered no significant concessions, because he realized that the United States had no intention of improving its offer, and that acceptance would enable him, rather than Osmeña, to present the prize to the Filipino people in time for the elections held in 1935.

Once elected president, Quezon set about strengthening the weak position the United States had imposed upon him. He first needed to reassure wealthy elements in the sugar industry and big businesses in Manila that were his principal supporters.[204] These groups were wary of independence and some opposed it, whereas small farmers, who resented the ascendancy of the centrales, hoped that independence would restore some of their former dominance. In steering a course that would appeal to both sets of interests, Quezon tried to reassure his followers without retreating from the goal of independence, which he presented as being inevitable as well as desirable. Negotiations through the agency of the Philippine Sugar Association held the sugar quota at a reasonable level; existing tariff concessions, though set to be phased out, nevertheless enabled the Philippines to sell its sugar above world prices.

These achievements could scarcely be counted as triumphs, but in the circumstances they "probably staved off the demise of the export sugar industry."[205] The new conditions set a course for the future by providing means of rewarding followers and penalizing dissent. As president, Quezon assumed a key role in tariff negotiations, in allocating quotas among sugar growers, and in distributing the resources of the Philippine National Bank. He also used his executive authority on behalf of sugar interests to repress strikes and postpone reforms in working conditions.

Concerns about defense matched anxieties over the economy. The threat from Japan grew, even as the United States limited its commitment to defend its colony. Quezon responded by exploring alternative means of guaranteeing the security of the islands. His most serious proposal, extraordinary though it now seems, was to join the British Commonwealth with dominion status.[206] This idea, which was discussed between 1935 and 1937, appealed because it offered, in principle, two benefits: a better guarantee of defense than the United States was willing to supply, and greater political independence than the Tydings-McDuffie Act provided. Under the terms of the Act, the United States retained sovereignty over the Philippines until the end of the transitional period in 1946. The Act, however, also permitted the United States to reject measures that were thought undesirable on financial grounds or in their effect on foreign relations.[207] Quezon, with the Canadian example in mind, judged that dominion status would confer a greater degree of effective independence than the designation "Commonwealth" allowed. Although the proposal died, Paul McNutt, the High Commissioner, shared Quezon's concerns without supporting his proposed remedy.[208] McNutt, a Democrat with some strikingly Republican ideas, wanted to retain the Philippines, notwithstanding the Tydings-McDuffie Act, and urged the United States to guarantee the defense of the islands.

This was independence of a punitive kind. The Philippines was to be cast adrift not merely on a sea of troubles but in the path of a cyclone. The country was effectively defenseless against the militant expansionism of Japan. The export economy was called upon to adapt, without adequate preparation, to the imminent amputation of its major market. In 1934, Filipinos were reclassified as aliens and excluded from opportunities in the United States.[209] They suffered the injury of increased unemployment at home and the insult of racial prejudice abroad. One respected American commentator felt obliged to conclude, with evident regret, that "the law thrusting independence upon the Philippines showed little statesmanship and no generosity."[210] The civilizing mission had scarcely reached the foothills. Viability, as measured by fiscal health, was achieved only by dubious accounting devices.[211] Democracy, as measured by the extension of the franchise, had reached only about 14 percent of the potential electorate, even after the formation of the Commonwealth in 1934.[212] This proportion was smaller than the equivalent figure for India following the Government of India Act in 1935. Independence had been promised but not yet bestowed. As Quezon and McNutt searched for alternatives, world events threatened to destroy the road to decolonization.

Japan attacked the Philippines just hours after bombing Pearl Harbor in December 1941. Hawai'i, however, escaped invasion, whereas the Philippines suffered a devastating land war followed by three and a half years of Japanese rule. Japan's economic interests in the Philippines had grown since World War I and had become especially prominent in shipping and the production of abaca. After 1934, when the United States signaled its intention of withdrawing from the archipelago, Japan took steps to increase its informal presence in the islands.[213] This was also the moment, however, when Japan's foreign policy was shifting from pacific to assertive forms of expansion.[214] Unfortunately for the Philippines, no one read the signals in time. As late as September 1940, one informed reporter stated: "a good many people believe" that "there is no threat to the security of the Commonwealth within the immediate future."[215] Decades of political indifference accompanied by systematic underfunding and uncertainty within the armed services about their respective roles rendered the Philippines defenseless.

American and Filipino forces were defeated in 1942.[216] Quezon escaped to the United States, where he formed a government-in-exile.[217] Filipinos, meanwhile, acquired a third colonial power in the span of fifty years at the point when they were once again planning their independence. The Japanese sponsored a new entity, the Philippine Republic, staffed by members of the Filipino elite, to act as a cover for their military presence. Popular resistance to the occupying force, however, limited the effectiveness of the proxy regime. An estimated 250,000 Filipinos became actively engaged in guerrilla operations that tied down Japanese troops and frustrated Japan's plans to harness the islands' resources.[218] This remarkable commitment, like the invasion itself, carried a high cost: widespread destruction, acute food shortages, and appalling loss of life. Between half a million and one million Filipino troops and civilians died in the course of the occupation. The battle for survival had a profound influence on the independence movement. Common suffering and united resistance strengthened the emerging sense of national unity. After the experience of World War II, there was no turning back; not even a master manipulator like Quezon could seriously think of alternatives to full independence on the date already fixed.[219] The war also left a darker legacy: a society that had become armed and, perforce, lawless. In 1945, on the eve of independence, the Philippines, it seemed, had to make yet another new start, as it had tried to do under Aguinaldo fifty years earlier.

Little of the Filipino side of the war entered public consciousness in the United States; even today, the story is told in specialized studies rather than in broader syntheses. The war was reported in ways that were designed to reaffirm American values and stiffen public resolve. Hollywood films from *Texas to Bataan* (1942) to *Back to Bataan* (1945) via *They Were Expendable* (1945) were transposed Westerns.[220] They conveyed a familiar message of continuing white racial supremacy, dedication, and technological wizardry, but set the "Indians" in a distant and unthreatening location. Filipinos were still depicted as children who needed paternal direction or as savages who had to be brought under control. *The Real Glory*, released in 1939 but set in 1906, had already demonstrated how resourceful U.S. Army officers (played by Gary Cooper and David Niven) trained raw Filipino recruits to protect villages against the fearsome Moros and their diabolical leader. The quality of the recruits was unpromising, but the quality of the American officers ensured that the training program succeeded.[221] Hollywood continued to give the impression that troops from the United States did all the fighting. Filipinos were assigned inferior, nonspeaking roles, despite the visibility and scale of the resistance movement in the Philippines.

Back to Bataan (1945) was a purposeful exception. John Wayne assumed his familiar leading role, but on this occasion a Filipino was given a prominent part.[222] The part, however, was played not by a Filipino but by Anthony Quinn, who appeared as Captain Andrés Bonifacio, the grandson of the nationalist hero. Unfortunately, the ancestral blood had thinned in the course of time. This scion of the family was demoralized and uncertain; it was American leadership that inspired him to rejoin the resistance. In 1945, when the flag of the United States was again hoisted in Manila, liberation was firmly joined to independence.

"OURS NOT TO REST TILL OUR BANNER WAVE"[223]

The "waving palms of Wai Kiki" provided a congenial backdrop to Hawaiian hula; the "little brown brothers" of Taft's imagination performed traditional romances in the tropical warmth of the Philippines. "Primitive" people, once conquered, were transformed into child-like innocents who, according to circumstance, were sometimes treated as custodians of eternal verities, and sometimes portrayed as being misled by their lack of guile into opposing the march of civilization. Either way, they needed paternal guidance. Art forms that became emblems justifying colonial rule were also continuing expressions, reaffirmed by performance, of the core values of the colonized society. Images that colonial authorities interpreted as validating their dominance were, from an indigenous standpoint, statements of independence in conditions of enveloping subordination. Different readings of common cultural idioms summarize the experience of colonial rule as a non-meeting of minds in proximity.

Hawai'i gave the United States its first firm foothold in the Pacific. Giant steps could be taken from there to the Philippines and beyond to China. The frontier of settlement could extend elsewhere in the Pacific and incorporate the people of the region into the modern world. However, a "Greater America," anchored by settlers from the mainland, never materialized. Economies of scale in sugar production made it difficult for the disappearing and no longer "sturdy" yeomen to stage a revival in the new possessions overseas. Concerted opposition from interest groups in the United States, who feared competition from low-cost homesteaders, ensured that the potential threat never developed. An acute shortage of labor on the islands obliged the settler minority to import contract workers from Asia and elsewhere in the Pacific, and thereafter to gamble on their continuing ability to control the political and social consequences of their enterprise. The experiment in creating a novel society gave Hawai'i a special place in the history of globalization. Other settler societies dominated larger or smaller indigenous populations. Hawai'i was one of the very few examples of a settler society that created a population of imported workers greatly in excess of the number of white immigrants. In doing so, Hawai'i became the progenitor of a cosmopolitan society that was to "show the face of the future" to the mainland. The initiative first laid the foundations of the wealth of the ruling oligarchy and then brought about the reversal of its fortunes, as the disenfranchised acquired rights that enabled them to challenge the legitimacy of the unrepresentative minority. In 1900, Hawai'i was an extension of the South; in 2000, following the demise of colonial rule, there was a possibility that the South might one day become an extension of Hawai'i.

The distinctiveness of the Philippines lay in its sprawling size, its numerous and diverse societies, and its long-standing connections with the rest of Asia. The archipelago had acted as the turnstile of the Pacific for centuries before representatives of the United States arrived with a mission to open it to the modern world. The new frontier of American settlement envisaged by expansionists on the mainland proved to be abortive. Yeomen were not forthcoming; mainland lobbies blocked the development of large, American-owned plantations. In the terminology adopted here, the Philippines was primarily a colony of trade, not of Anglo-settlement, and had no prospect of securing statehood. Settlers were present, though originally they came from Asia and Spain. The majority were no longer first-generation newcomers but had become indigenized through custom, intermarriage, and the elapse of time. They were key figures on the main island of Luzon and in developing southern regions, such as Negros, in promoting an export economy and in helping to manage the new colonial polity. From a colonial point of view, they served as intermediaries or, in the now rather dated language of imperial specialists, "collaborators." From an indigenous perspective, however, they were the established local Big Men who grew to national importance during the colonial period, as the United States came to depend on their networks, experience, and goodwill. The focus on elites has yet to bond with a history from below.[224] A full understanding of the relationship joining ilustrados, caciques, and distant voices in the villages and towns is likely to lead to a more representative appraisal of the period.

It is clear, nevertheless, that the indigenous inhabitants of the islands endeavored to hold on to their own values, despite the misfortunes that afflicted them in the name of progress. Vindications of the past sustained the present; hopes for the future eased the humiliation of colonial subordination. Language was attuned to give popular voice to meanings that were inaccessible to the rulers. In Hawai'i, the song-form of hula (*hula-ku'i*) was used to express lyrics of resistance:[225]

> Famous are the children of Hawai'i
> Ever loyal to the land,
> When the evil-hearted messenger comes
> With his greedy document of extortion.

Composers in the Philippines adapted the traditional Tagalog romantic song (*kundiman*) in the early twentieth century to produce a hybrid genre of patriotic music that incorporated Western compositional formalities [226] In the 1930s, "Bayan Ko" (My Country), a semi-disguised serenade to patriotism, became the unofficial national anthem:[227]

> My dear country, the Philippines,
> Land of gold and flowers.
> Love is in her palms
> Offering beauty and splendour.

And to her refinement and beauty,
Foreigners were enticed.
My Dear Country, you were enslaved,
Mired in suffering.

And the chorus responded:

My Philippines that I treasure,
Cradle of my tears and suffering,
My aspiration is,
To see you truly free!

THE INSULAR EMPIRE IN RETROSPECT

Despite their evident diversity, the four islands considered here and in the previous chapter can be divided into two groups. The Philippines and Cuba had similar attitudes toward the colonial power, even though their constitutional status was very different. Filipinos and Cubans had fought against Spain and the United States; neither island experienced substantial Western settlement; both had populations with the capacity to check Americanization and the resources needed to support successful independence movements. Hawai'i and Puerto Rico, on the other hand, were in much weaker positions. Hawai'i's resistance to foreign penetration was limited by its small and diminishing population, by the presence of white settlers who controlled both the government and the export economy, and by complexities arising from large-scale immigration from Asia. Puerto Rico lacked the militant tradition that characterized the Philippines and Cuba, was too small and too poor to fend off the United States, and was unable to make independence a viable option.

The two groups nevertheless shared a wider context that transcended the differences between them. They were bound together by a common fortune and fate: they were the objects of the first of the development plans the United States launched on the overseas world in the twentieth century. The significance of this early experiment in structural adjustment, social engineering, and nation-building has been lost to later generations of practitioners, and the "lessons of history," assuming they can be discerned, have long disappeared into a limbo of discarded knowledge. Yet, the insular territories offer development specialists long-term case studies of two of the most common types of colonial development: one based on plantation enclaves, and the other on a mixture of household and estate agriculture.[228] Structural differences, however, were subordinated to a common driving force: international demand for primary products filtered through the sieve of tariff policy. These determinants explain the trajectory of both sets of islands during the first half of the twentieth century: the oscillations in their economic fortunes, the extent of social unrest, and the shift toward the form of nationalist populism that challenged old-style colonial rule.

In all these respects, the insular possessions provide specific illustrations of the general argument advanced in chapter 11, which in turn fits into the broader story of the rise and demise of Western empires outlined in chapter 10. The trends influencing the course of the American Empire were the same as those shaping the other Western empires in the twentieth century. If this interpretation finds support, the islands that are currently either bypassed or treated with utmost brevity by specialists on the history of the United States deserve to be incorporated into the history of Western colonial rule and allocated places in the larger study of modern globalization.

A full analysis of the U.S. development program, known at the time as the civilizing mission, requires separate treatment and an allocation of space commensurate with its importance. The observations made here are confined to the issue under review, namely whether, as a number of commentators have suggested, the record of the United States was superior in this respect to that of the other Western imperial powers.[229] The contest is not between Western exponents of imperial rhetoric, which attained stratospheric levels in all cases; nor does it require an estimate of varying levels of sincerity among those who sounded the call to empire. It is outcomes that matter, and present evidence makes it hard to argue that the brand of colonial rule exercised by the United States differed significantly from the other Western colonial powers. The related claim that any failings can be attributed to the recipients and not to the plan rests on a stereotype of "traditional" societies that historians of the British and French colonies have long rejected.[230] This conclusion, however, like the arguments it contests, needs to be treated with caution. The costs and benefits of colonial rule are not easily researched, and in the case of the American Empire the subject has scarcely been raised, let alone fully investigated.[231]

The evidence presented here supports three observations on this issue. In the first place, it should be clear that the United States did not introduce capitalism to the islands that fell under its control. Various types of capitalist enterprise were present through the agency of Spain, the initiatives of settlers in Hawai'i, and the enterprise of indigenous peoples long before the onrush of imperialism at the close of the nineteenth century. From this standpoint, it can be said that trade came before the flag. As far as commerce with the United States is concerned, however, trade largely followed the flag. Before 1898, the United States had a limited share of the foreign trade and investment of the islands it came to control. It was only after 1898 that the Republic came to occupy a dominant position, and even this belated success was not established firmly until the 1920s. Even so, it was not free-market capitalism that triumphed but a form of neo-mercantilism, which guaranteed investors, planters, and traders political security backed by military force and economic subsidies supported by tariff concessions. If there was a lesson that colonial subjects could draw from their experience of American enterprise, it was one that emphasized the importance of mobilizing political connections in the cause of market management rather than one that demonstrated the advantages of price incentives, competition, and efficiency.

The economic element in the civilizing mission was built on a paradox: producers in the colonies wanted open access to the United States; agricultural and manufacturing interests on the mainland stood solidly for protection. The contest was one-sided: success went to those with electoral weight and the ability to lobby Congress. The chief disadvantage the colonies faced was not export dependence, for this was a state that most countries experienced in the course of their development, but the terms on which exports were marketed. Prices were set partly by world conditions, which were beyond national control, and partly by tariffs, which were determined by Congress. Tariffs were raised and lowered, not according to the needs of colonial development, but to reward or appease domestic lobbies. Uncertainty penalized investment; variations in tariff levels opened and closed the mainland market in unpredictable ways. The adverse consequences of domestic protection were particularly marked in the 1930s, when reduced living standards and rising unemployment produced the discontent that fueled anti-colonial nationalism.

The second observation is that the political component of the colonial mission also fell far short of expectations. The advertised program of training in self-government was compromised from the outset. Effective political independence was incompatible with continuing economic dependence. The paradox appears not to have been recognized in Washington, except toward the close of the colonial period, and then only by a minority of those charged with reconciling incompatible forces. The need to cooperate with local Big Men, irrespective of their democratic credentials, ensured that the United States adapted its presence to local circumstances more than it was able to adapt local circumstances to its blueprint for self-government. The circumstances included the colonial legacy from Spain, which the United States adopted and adapted to maintain administrative order. Colonial governors had the power to limit the decisions made by elected representatives to those that met official approval. Consequently, until events in the 1930s shook the colonial system, political debate was directed away from issues of long-term national importance and into matters, such as patronage, which became a central feature of party rivalries.

The final comment concerns the policies of Americanization and assimilation, which were intended to assist progress toward self-government. These, too, disappointed their advocates and by the 1930s had been largely abandoned. By then, the idealism and optimism that had energized the imperialists of Theodore Roosevelt's generation had long faded. Most members of Congress preferred not to think about the insular possessions; when they did, it was invariably in connection with the import tariff, which they related to the interests of their mainland constituents. When the United States offered the Philippines independence in 1934, the colony was neither viable nor democratic. The aim, in the midst of the world slump, was to cast off an economic and political liability, and thus to free the Republic from burdensome military and financial obligations. Motives of this order were not confined to the United States. Nevertheless, the decision was scarcely a mark of a mission successfully accomplished, still less a triumph for the spread of Western values and institutions.

World War II compelled the United States to strengthen its commitment to its insular dependencies, which had suddenly acquired strategic significance. With the return of peace in 1945, Washington faced a dilemma: whether to retain its newfound interest in its overseas possessions, or whether to press on with its long-standing undertaking to deliver independence to subject peoples. At that point, international developments prompted policy-makers to consider crafting a compromise that ceded formal sovereignty but retained effective control. If speculation became policy, John Wayne might still have a part to play in shaping the postwar order, providing he could "speak softly" as well as carry a gun.

CHAPTER 14

"THE TWILIGHT OF CONFUSED COLONIALISM"[1]

"SURRENDERING AUTHORITY AND RETAINING RESPONSIBILITY"[2]

Rexford Tugwell's impression of Puerto Rico provides an epitaph for the final years of the territorial empire. "The occupiers," he concluded, "were defeated by their own bungling and by the everlasting self-interest and intimate knowledge of the occupied. The shell of authority was empty."[3] Tugwell was one of a rare species: as Governor of Puerto Rico from 1941 to 1946, he had an exceptional understanding of colonial issues; as an anti-imperialist, he was determined to bring the island to independence in a condition that would enable it to survive without U.S. support. Theodore Roosevelt, Jr., an authority of equal standing but less radical opinions, agreed that confusion had swamped aspiration. Commenting in 1934 on the decision to grant independence to the Philippines in 1946, he observed that "we have committed the crowning government atrocity of surrendering authority and retaining responsibility."[4]

By the time World War II struck, the "occupiers" were in trouble throughout the insular possessions. Democracy had yet to be delivered; development remained heavily dependent on imperial subsidies through tariff preferences. The United States was eager to liberate itself from its colonies; Taft's "little brown brothers" had demonstrated their keen desire to help the process. Puerto Rico, impoverished and militant, had witnessed the assassination of the Chief of Police and an attempt on the life of the Governor; Cuba had been sacrificed to help the insular territories survive the worst consequences of the world depression. By the end of the war, Hawai'i had been first bombed and then turned into a fortress; the Philippines had been overrun by Japanese forces. Logic suggested that the United States, the self-proclaimed leading anti-imperial power, would move rapidly to shed the burdens of empire after World War II. By

1946, however, calculations of the national interest had changed. A new set of circumstances encouraged the United States to retain control over its colonies and, where possible, to extend its influence beyond them.

Chapter 10 viewed postwar developments from the perspective of the victorious European powers, which reaffirmed their commitment to the imperial mission in the hope of reconciling colonial subjects to a new era of colonial rule. The period of extended colonialism lasted for about a decade and was dominated by efforts to suppress radicals who could not be tamed and to conjure moderate opponents into conformity. From about the mid-1950s, progressive influences began to redirect imperial policy, and colonial nationalists increased their influence and impetus. There followed a rush for the exit that ended in the termination of formal colonial rule. By the mid-1960s, most colonial states had become independent, though, like the United States before them, ties of dependence remained a feature of the new international order. By the 1970s, territorial empires had become either impractical or irrelevant to the emerging world order. Modern globalization had given way to what is referred to here as postcolonial globalization.

The present chapter offers a revisionist account of U.S. policy during this period by piecing together the virtually untold story of the end of the U.S. insular empire and fitting it into the trajectory of decolonization described by the major Western empires. Historians have generally followed the lead of policy-makers in Washington in viewing geopolitical events after 1945 primarily in terms of the Cold War. Attention has focused on the intricacies of high politics and, to a lesser extent, on the consequences of what were often low policies. Interactions at the grassroots level remain understudied. Prevailing approaches focus on postwar Europe and are inclined to regard the rest of the world as an extension of Western problems. Questions of empire are generally treated as being derivative rather than primary and are hitched to the juggernaut of Cold War studies only where they appear to be particularly relevant to that theme. Although this formula has many merits, it nevertheless echoes the earlier story of Rise of the West (and the Fall of the Rest) under a revised title that suits the circumstances of the postwar era: the Recuperation of the West (and the Manipulation of the Rest).

This chapter advances a case for rebalancing these priorities. Instead of fitting decolonization into the Cold War, the Cold War needs to be fitted into decolonization, which in turn needs to be placed in the even wider context of the global transformation of power, interests, and values in the postwar era.[5] Conventional studies of decolonization concentrate on the dramatic changes that transformed the Western empires in Africa and Asia. Movements to assert or reassert national sovereignty, however, spread far beyond even this spacious canvas. An enlarged conception of decolonization encompasses a range of countries—from China to Australia—that are currently omitted from consideration, and includes unambiguous cases of internal colonialism, of which the United States serves as the prime exemplar.

The claim that decolonization was a global process that extended well beyond formal colonies requires an equally expansive explanation. The argument made here is that decolonization was the product of the third major crisis identified by this study: the shift from modern to postcolonial globalization. From a point in the mid-century, the conditions that underpinned the great Western territorial empires began to unravel. The "classic" colonial exchange of manufactured goods for raw materials lost the central place it had long held in the international economy; economic integration based on inter-industry trade drew the advanced economies together. At the same time, the belief in white supremacy that had justified imperialism and facilitated colonial rule began to falter. Self-confidence accompanied self-determination; the ex-empire began to "strike back" in novel ways; multiethnic societies posed challenges that the old order was slow to recognize and manage. The twenty-first century was at hand.

THE GLOBAL SETTING

The international contest between the United States and the Soviet Union was not between the benign and the malevolent, as oversimplified claims long held, but between two competing visions of modernity, both derived ultimately from the Enlightenment, both claiming universal applicability, and both seeking to convert the world to their particular version of globalization.[6] Weighty structural similarities underlay these ideological contrasts. Both states had long histories of continental expansion accompanied by a keen sense of destiny made manifest on distant frontiers. Both devised civilizing missions based on assumptions of their own racial superiority.[7] Both had an unquestioned belief in their providential exceptionalism, which they demonstrated to their own satisfaction by self-referencing allusions. Both possessed territorial empires while denying that they were imperial powers.[8] Both were adept at manipulating imperial policies to suit changing geopolitical considerations, while asserting their commitment to different conceptions of liberty.

The story of postwar decolonization usually begins with the independence of India in 1947, but might well start with the upheaval in East Asia during and after World War II, following China's long struggle to free itself from subordination to foreign powers.[9] With the defeat of the Japanese Empire in 1945 and the success of the Chinese Revolution in 1949, the nationalist revolt against colonial and neocolonial influences and the political factions allied to them emerged triumphant. The fateful involvement of the United States in trying to control a related nationalist revolt in Indo-China was a reaction to the fear that Chinese expansion would inject the region with the poison of communism while also damaging France's prospects of becoming an effective ally in Europe.[10] A parallel situation arose in Korea, where the expulsion of the Japanese and the heavy-handed division of the country both aroused and frustrated nationalist sentiments. Similar considerations drew Washington into first supporting and then supplanting the Dutch in Indonesia and into cooperating with Britain in "holding the line" in Malaya.[11]

The struggle for paramountcy in the Middle East, though linked to the increasing importance of petroleum resources, needs to be understood in the broader context of the collapse of the Ottoman Empire during World War I and subsequent attempts to assemble client states from the debris. The resulting fabricated and unsteady polities were characterized by a mixture of vibrant and often competing national, pan-Arab, and Pan-Islamic loyalties and by an incomplete sense of unity that nevertheless drew strength from a gathering resentment of foreign interference.[12] These states were neither fully colonized nor fully independent. They were, however, programmed for instability, which foreign powers tried to manage by supporting conservative, and often authoritarian, political elements.

In Africa, the United States fell in behind Britain and France in supporting their plans to rejuvenate the colonial mission, even though the "green uprising" had reached the continent, and political parties with mass bases were aiming, not just for reform, but for independence. Latin America also fits into this larger story. There, too, the struggle to achieve effective independence long antedates World War II. The global slump radicalized nationalist movements in the 1930s and produced the vociferous populism of Juan Perón in 1946. These developments alarmed the United States and prompted Washington to intervene in the Latin American republics to support like-minded, conservative clients, and to do so long before the Cuban Revolution provoked outright panic in 1959.[13]

These well-known events are summarized here to illustrate the general point that the Cold War was part of a much broader theme: the attempted restoration and eventual unraveling of the Western empires after World War II.[14] Although the shifting elements of this story took time to settle, some astute contemporaries foresaw the future before it was unrolled. In 1948, the CIA had already placed the crumbling colonial world at the center of its analysis:

> The US, therefore, is faced with a serious dilemma. On the one hand US encouragement of colonial self-determination and economic development may itself incur the charge of US imperialism and run the risk of alienating the colonial powers. On the other hand, the US may be unable to afford to let its policy on colonial issues be swayed by the colonial powers if such support of its allies tends to alienate the dependent peoples and other non-European countries, lay the groundwork for future disruption, and in the long run weaken the power balance of both the US and the Western European nations vis-à-vis the USSR.[15]

The quandary identified by the CIA preoccupied successive administrations, which found themselves riding a tiger with a will of its own. Impelled by conviction and bereft of alternatives, they nevertheless clung on. As Harry Truman remarked of the presidency, "a man has to keep on riding or be swallowed."[16]

The oddity about the imperial setting, as reflected in the current literature, is the omission of the American Empire itself. Admirable studies of the United States and decolonization are available, but they refer almost exclusively to Washington's policy toward the British and French empires.[17] There is an obvious justification for this emphasis: the British and French empires were large and of unquestioned geopolitical and economic importance; the American Empire was small and had a minor place in grand geopolitical calculations. However, the role taken by the insular possessions in the story of decolonization was much greater than their size suggests. Cuba, for example, was no bigger than Tennessee, but its proximity and independence magnified its significance in the eyes of U.S. policy-makers to the point where it assumed almost continental proportions.

HOLDING ON

After 1945, the "have" powers had to be helped to their feet; the "have-nots" needed to be resurrected. To this end, big government, in the guise of the security state and the armed forces, was retained after the war and expanded to a degree that prompted President Dwight D. Eisenhower in 1961 to voice his concern about the power of the military-industrial complex. President Harry S. Truman's mailed fist was felt in the policy of containment, which included a commitment to strengthen Britain and France in Europe by helping them to rebuild their overseas empires. Germany and Japan had to be reconstructed, though with their wings clipped, to ward off the Soviet Union and halt the spread of Chinese influence. Although policy-makers were preoccupied in 1945 with European issues, the global manifestations of what, in effect, was a long struggle for independence quickly compelled attention.

Conservative interests treated victory as a mandate to reinforce the sociopolitical order that had survived World War II. Britain and France aimed to reassert control over their extensive empires to assist their economic recovery and to restore their battered prestige as great powers. The United States had a similar purpose but different motives. Policy-makers in Washington had two main priorities: to consolidate the outer defenses of the United States in locations that met the new conditions of long-distance warfare, and to shield the mainland from the far-reaching and unsettling ideological challenges presented by Soviet communism and, later, colonial nationalism. The insular territories were of minor importance to the economy of the mainland, even though they mattered to the prosperity of specific interest groups, and they added little to the prestige of the new superpower, which rested on the strength of its domestic economy and the might of its military machine. Strategic considerations, however, overrode the attitudes of indifference and even rejection that had prevailed before the war, elevated the importance of the islands in the eyes of Washington's policy-makers, and became the paramount motive for holding on rather than moving on. The fundamental assumption that drove policy toward the colonial world has survived attempts to dislodge it: policy-makers unerringly mistook popular nationalism for communism, which they attributed, in turn, to the machinations of Moscow.[18]

The Cold War also served to consolidate national unity at a time when radical criticism of the established order, stirred by the Depression of the 1930s and shaken by the disruption caused by the World War, had found expression in political claims.[19] If patriotism could be linked to the defense of the established order, dissident elements could be categorized as being subversive and hence unpatriotic. Freedom could be identified with conformity; democracy could be redefined as a strategy for keeping change within acceptably narrow bounds. Religion, specifically Protestantism, could be mobilized against Soviet atheism, thereby reaffirming the values and virtues of American culture.[20] Evil could be put to the sword; civilization could be saved. It followed that colonial nationalism, which was readily equated with communism, was regarded as a threat to political order that had to be contained and, if possible, defused.

The war in the Pacific had finally jolted Congress into funding the outer fortresses that had been one of the declared reasons for annexing Hawai'i and the Philippines in 1898. At the close of World War II, the interests of defense prompted Washington to extend the insular empire in the Pacific. The United States occupied and controlled Okinawa and the numerous small islands of Micronesia, which became Trust Territories (updated mandates) under the authority of the United Nations.[21] The Caribbean had escaped the direct consequences of the war, but was judged to be too close to the mainland to be left unsupervised. The United States had spread its influence throughout the region after 1940, while Britain was otherwise preoccupied, and had no intention of pulling back, especially because the nearby British colonies were becoming restive.[22] If Plan A was to help Britain revive its imperial mission, Plan B was to act on its behalf if restoration faltered or became impossible.

Studies of the domestic implications of policy toward the insular empire have yet to travel beyond a specialized subset of the literature on international relations during this period, and accordingly need to be underlined here. President Harry Truman, a Democrat, and his successor, Dwight D. Eisenhower, a Republican, followed broadly similar policies at home and abroad. Their inclinations were in tune with Congress on most issues, though ahead of it where geopolitical considerations claimed priority. The legacy of the New Deal survived; civil rights were noted but not asserted, though the cause engaged Truman rather more than it did Eisenhower. The Democratic Party dominated Congress between 1945 and 1961, apart from 1947–1949 and 1953–1955. The Democratic vote was anchored in the South, which remained committed to policies that enforced segregation and perpetuated inequalities of opportunity. "Separate development" had as much empty aspiration and as little practical achievement in the United States as it had in South Africa, which explains its enduring appeal to its advocates. Republicans were less intransigent than Democrats on the race question but fully committed to anti-communism. When the two issues were brought together, Congress formed an immovable bloc.

The insular territories were a potential threat to the sociopolitical order on the mainland, particularly in the South, because popular nationalism had made headway in the empire since the 1930s with an agenda that gave prominence to the goals of political liberty and social equality. After 1945, African American troops returned from the islands, particularly from Hawai'i, in considerable numbers, having become aware that discrimination was neither a universal nor an eternal condition of mankind. All things being relative, the degree of discrimination practiced on Hawai'i was less overt and less rigid than it was on the mainland.[23] One solution to this potentially volatile issue was to grant the insular territories independence, thereby also winning the approval of sugar beet and sugarcane producers in the United States. This idea had been touted in the 1930s, and was favored after World War II by a considerable body of opinion in the Southern states. By then, however, the insular territories could not be abandoned because they had acquired compelling strategic significance. Accordingly, nationalist movements had to be controlled and, if necessary, suppressed. Containment applied to the insular territories, and indeed to the mainland too, and not just to the Soviet Union.

International developments after 1945 gave reformers hope—but also curtailed their expectations. The Western powers acknowledged that appropriate gestures had to be made to meet promises issued during the war and, increasingly, to counter Soviet propaganda. The United Nations (UN), which was established in 1945, provided a forum for discussing world affairs. The Nuremberg trials, which began in the same year, paved the way for international cooperation on matters affecting human rights.[24] The Universal Declaration of Human Rights followed in 1948; the Genocide Convention was adopted in 1948 and applied from 1951; the European Convention on Human Rights, drafted in 1950, became effective in 1953. These measures became foundational statements of principle that eventually helped to validate the claims of anti-colonial movements throughout the world. In the short run, however, they lacked political heft. They were declarations of ideals, not blueprints for action.

The "have" powers took care to secure their core interests and particularly to prevent interference in their own internal affairs.[25] In the minds of policy-makers in what was becoming known as the Free World, the purpose of the United Nations, like the League before it, was to protect the interests of the West.[26] The guiding hand of Jan Christian Smuts drew a line of continuity that joined both organizations, though in contrast to 1919, the inclusion of the United States in 1945 added substance to conservative interests. Consequently, the charter of the UN publicized long-term goals of development and internal self-government but avoided a commitment to decolonization and human rights.[27] Eleanor Roosevelt, who led the commission that produced the Universal Declaration, ensured that no binding obligations were included in the final document.[28] Similarly, the British took credit for helping to produce the European Convention, but made sure that it did not apply to their own colonies.[29] This was just as well, because the overt and covert means employed to prosecute the Cold War greatly increased violations of human rights.[30] Real equality would sink empires; symbolic equality helped to keep them afloat.[31]

Domestic pressures for reform also became more insistent after 1945. If the "negro problem," as Gunner Myrdal called it in his classic study, is reconceptualized as an example of what has been termed "internal colonialism," the analogy with the anti-colonial movements in the other Western empires becomes apparent.[32] The oldest African American political organization, the National Association for the Advancement of Colored Peoples (NAACP), founded in 1909, began as a middle-class, predominantly urban reformist movement that operated within the constitution and mainly through the courts. In these respects, the NAACP was very similar to the early anti-colonial movements in India and Africa. In the 1930s, again like colonial liberation organizations elsewhere, the NAACP reached out to urban workers and increased its political activism. In the 1940s, the organization extended its platform beyond civil rights in an attempt to make human rights, a much broader concept, the standard for equality of treatment.[33] By the middle of the decade, the NAACP had acquired a mass base of nearly 500,000 members and had established an international presence.[34] In 1947, it submitted a petition to the UN on the issue of racial discrimination in the United States, and went on to play an important part in halting South Africa's plan to annex South-West Africa and in supporting movements for self-determination elsewhere in Africa.[35]

The NAACP hoped that moderate means would be sufficient to achieve its enlarged goals. However, its failure to transform the politics of discrimination opened the way in 1946 for a more radical organization, the Civil Rights Congress (CRC), which had communist sympathies. The CRC challenged the basis of capitalist democracy in the United States and publicized its case internationally with a degree of assertiveness that alarmed the authorities in Washington. In 1951, for example, the CRC caused a stir in Europe and consternation in the United States by appealing to the UN on grounds that linked racial discrimination to genocide.[36]

The reaction in Washington to these developments was to concede as little as possible while trying to discredit and disarm radical critics. Truman, though sharing the racist assumptions of his generation, realized that action was needed to improve the image of the United States in the eyes of foreign governments.[37] In 1948, with wartime promises still fresh, he issued executive orders ending segregation in the armed forces and discrimination in the federal civil service.[38] The Senate, however, consistently blocked all attempts at instituting reforms affecting society as a whole and steadfastly refused either to control the resurgent Ku Klux

Klan or to make lynching illegal. Although Truman needed the black vote, he needed the white South even more. Once elected in 1948, his commitment to the uphill struggle to reform human rights waned in the face of congressional intransigence.[39] Internationally, the United States, like Britain, had few misgivings about supporting South Africa's apartheid system after 1948, approving its militant anti-communist stance, and buying its uranium.[40]

As the Red Scare reached obsessive levels in the early 1950s, even modest progress on civil rights came to a halt. Defeating communism became more important than ending racism. Southern Democrats took the lead in accusing civil rights organizations of conspiring to promote communism. The Federal Bureau of Investigation (FBI), under the zealous leadership of J. Edgar Hoover, crushed all challenges to the established order. The FBI harassed the CRC, arrested its leaders, and hastened its liquidation in 1955.[41] The NAACP's attested record of moderation was insufficient to protect it from the inquisitorial eye of the House Un-American Activities Committee, and the organization was effectively shut down until the McCarthy era came to an end.[42] Forces working for change in the United States were present and active, but in the decade after the war they were defeated by the apparatus of the state. W. E. B. Du Bois's perceptive comment, made in 1947, had to wait for its fulfillment: "It is not Russia that threatens the United States so much as Mississippi."[43] Meanwhile, the lynchings continued.

American Indians, like other First Peoples with a long history of protest against government intrusions, were also encouraged by the international approval civil and human rights received after 1945.[44] Their particular concerns arose from the policy known as "termination," which was introduced in the late 1940s and formally adopted by Congress in 1953. In the 1930s, Lord Lugard's example in the British Empire had inspired John Collier, the Commissioner of Indian Affairs between 1933 and 1945, to replace assimilation with indirect rule.[45] Termination rejected cultural pluralism and reinstated assimilation, even though its record was one of failure. The intention, however, was not to achieve full integration, which would have approved the principle of inter-marriage, for example, but rather to apply the concept of "separate but equal" development to American Indians.[46] The policy aimed to impose social conformity by halting the development of separate communities that, given the mood of the time, could readily be presented as being proto-communist. If successful, termination would also remove evidence of continuing inequality and deprivation, which was highly visible in the reservations, and eliminate a potential source of international criticism. Development was to be accelerated by opening tribal lands to private enterprise, which had the added advantage of allowing the federal government to reduce public expenditure in the reservations.

American Indians reacted in 1944 by forming the National Congress of American Indians (NCAI), which aimed at representing all the numerous, diverse, and scattered tribes.[47] The NCAI proceeded cautiously. It lobbied Congress, stayed within the law, and steered clear of public demonstrations. It laid the organizational basis for future pan-Indian political action, but lacked the influence needed to achieve significant reform. Given that American Indians accounted for less than 0.5 percent of the electorate and were spread over numerous states, Congress was able to apply the new policy without having to make concessions to the recipients. Americanization, though abandoned in the colonies, would have its final triumph imposed at home.

PROTECTION IN THE PACIFIC

Most surveys of U.S. international relations after 1945 look outward from Washington. The view from the periphery receives less attention; the view from the islands is usually overlooked. The conventional focus needs adjusting to enlarge the contribution the insular possessions made to their own fortunes, and to relate the analysis of U.S. policy to studies of decolonization in the other Western empires, where research has long incorporated indigenous perspectives.[48] The account that follows, though necessarily preliminary, suggests that the character of the independence movements in the islands was similar to that found in the British and French colonies, and that the reaction of U.S. policy-makers also followed a comparable, and hence familiar, pattern.

Hawai'i, though small and distant, caught the eye of Congress after the war because it was an incorporated territory with a claim to statehood. Since 1898, settlers from the mainland had controlled the economy of Hawai'i through the Big Five firms and the territorial government through the Republican Party. In 1933, the government of Hawai'i began to campaign for statehood to secure free entry for the islands' sugar exports to the United States. The onset of World War II postponed consideration of the application; it also changed the terms of the debate. After 1945, the pressure on Washington to grant full incorporation increased. The islands' experience of military authoritarianism was decisive in mobilizing public support for a measure that its sponsors hoped would protect civil rights.[49] The rise of organized labor, building on foundations laid during the desperate years of the 1930s, gave prominence to a new and powerful advocate of statehood.

By 1945, the International Longshore and Warehouse Union (ILWU), which had spread to Hawai'i from the West Coast, had overcome racial divisions and united the islands' workers in the sugar and pineapple industries and the docks to create Hawai'i's first mass, interracial, working-class movement.[50] Union membership expanded rapidly in the immediate postwar years, when the economy suffered from the withdrawal of the military and the sluggish growth of the main export industries. The ILWU advertised its new power by mounting a series of major strikes that dealt the Big Five their first significant defeat of the century.[51] The strike that paralyzed the sugar industry in 1946 was a crucial moment of transition: it turned economic grievances into political action and led to the revival of the island's nearly moribund Democratic Party. Militant action continued and reached a peak in 1949, when a major dock strike, which lasted for six months, reduced the islands almost to a state of siege. Although the ILWU's campaign focused on conventional union issues of pay and conditions, it also included an explicit demand that racial discrimination be made illegal. Observers on the mainland viewed this claim as a Trojan horse, which, if allowed entry, would trample on the discriminatory practices that underpinned privilege and power in the Southern states.

Not all segments of Hawai'i's population were enthusiastic about the prospect of statehood. Some members of the white community feared that the oversight exercised by the federal government would diminish their own power, boost the Democratic Party, and add to its representation in Congress. Native Hawaiians felt that statehood would increase the number of newcomers from the mainland and further depress their already reduced circumstances. The large Japanese community, on the other hand, was strongly in favor of the application. The original immigrants had labored in the sugar fields; the second and third generations were educated and ambitious, and viewed statehood as a means of attaining full equality as citizens of the United States.[52] The most powerful white interests were also convinced that statehood was the islands' best option. It would give the main industry, sugar, the support it needed to stay in business; it would also encourage new investment, which was essential if the islands were to diversify into more promising alternatives.[53] Although the sugar industry was highly efficient, it could not match low-cost producers in Asia and Cuba. The scope for increasing output was limited; profit margins narrowed in the 1950s; additional productivity gains were achieved through mechanization, which reduced employment opportunities for Hawai'i's growing population.[54] The pineapple industry experienced similar problems: in 1945, it accounted for 75 percent of world production; by 1958 the figure had dropped to 57 percent.[55]

A coalition of supporters on Hawai'i and the mainland developed a powerful case for conferring statehood. The islands already met formal tests for full incorporation, which included population size, income levels, fiscal responsibility, and majority support for the proposal. After 1945, advocates supplemented these qualifications with arguments tailored to postwar conditions. Statehood, they claimed, would be immeasurably valuable to the United States in prosecuting the Cold War. By admitting Hawai'i to the Republic, Washington would demonstrate its support for racial equality, win elusive hearts and minds, and increase its influence in Asia.[56] These arguments had considerable appeal. They converted Presidents Truman and Eisenhower, who were embarrassed by Hawai'i's semi-colonial status, which placed it on the UN's highly visible list of non-self-governing territories.[57] The pro-statehood lobby also gained supporters in the House of Representatives and among the population at large. In 1946, 60 percent of mainlanders were already persuaded of the merits of the case; by 1953, the figure exceeded 70 percent.[58]

Nevertheless, the opponents of statehood in the Senate were able to block approval of Hawai'i's application by combining visceral appeals of the kind Oscar Wilde referred to as "hitting below the intellect" with adroit manipulation of congressional procedures. The most persuasive argument, which resonated particularly among Southern Democrats, rallied electoral troops to uphold the integrity and superiority of the white race. The more Hawai'i's supporters extolled the success of its multiracial society and its increasing number of mixed marriages, the more determinedly the opponents of statehood sharpened their swords in defense of the purity of the Republic. Drew L. Smith's *The Menace of Hawaiian Statehood* (1957) was one of many publications that offered exaggerated summaries of long-standing beliefs about the inherent superiority of white Protestant males and their special gifts for democratic rule.[59] Southern Democrats saw that a vote for Hawai'i would also be a vote for civil rights. Statehood would entitle Hawai'i to two seats in the Senate that would almost certainly be filled by representatives who were hostile to Southern values.[60] Since the Democrats were not guaranteed a majority in the Senate, they had to maneuver, bargain, and fix to attract the necessary Republican support. It was in this spirit that they linked Hawai'i's entry to that of Alaska, which they judged would be more sympathetic to their cause.

Anti-communism tapped independent sources of motivation. Christian soldiers were ready to march "as to war," if necessary; capitalists could be counted on to defend the free market, if less directly. Racial supremacists joined the legion too. In their view, inferior peoples were inclined to degeneracy, which was only a short step from deviance and from there to disloyalty and subversion—culminating in communism.[61] Accordingly, the appeal of anti-communism was broad-based, which helps to explain why Southern Democrats were able to attach a sufficient number of Republicans to their cause.[62] Policy-makers with a conspiratorial turn of mind had long imagined that communist doctrines would help to fuse a union of the "colored" races, who would then seek to overthrow the Anglo-Saxon world order.[63] This suspicion tainted the Japanese community in Hawai'i before the war, and was used to postpone consideration of the statehood question. It was deployed again after 1945 to delay statehood, despite the fact that Japanese-Hawaiian troops had shown unfailing loyalty and extraordinary bravery during the war. The ILWU provided an easier target because solidarity among the islands' workers, very visibly expressed in strike action, could readily be presented as being communist in inspiration.[64] Opponents of statehood fastened upon the alleged connection and built it into a towering threat. The Big Five firms, though favoring statehood, also used the Red Scare to try to weaken the labor union. The assertions lacked substance, but in the early postwar years they were sufficiently alarming to help swing the Senate vote against statehood.

Washington faced different and more challenging problems in the Western Pacific. In 1945, the American Historical Association prepared a pamphlet for the War Department entitled, "What Lies Ahead for the Philippines?"[65] The answer, predictably, was uncertainty. Even then, however, it was evident that the United States was preparing to face the unknown by providing substantial military protection for the devastated state.[66] According to the pamphlet, the United States still had "responsibilities" in the Philippines, and Americans had a reputation there for "keeping their word."[67] The obligation, so the pamphlet claimed, arose from the need to safeguard the independence that enlightened rule had promised and was about to deliver. The pamphlet made no mention of the inadequate preparation for independence, the widespread popular discontent with American rule expressed in the 1930s, the real motives for allowing the Philippines to "go it alone," or the extent to which the war had destroyed the prospects of a smooth transition. By 1946, myth had surpassed fact: the legend that the decision to confer independence was the culmination of a carefully laid plan to foster democracy and viability was firmly in place. It lives on today in the speeches of U.S. presidents and in commentary about America's exceptional role in the world.

The Historical Association's pamphlet also missed the great irony that inaugurated Philippine independence in 1946: the United States, having done its best to cast off the colony in the 1930s, was by the end of the war scrambling to hold on to it. Formal recolonization was out of the question. The Filipino people had fought not only against the Japanese but also for their independence. They considered the matter settled, even if their leaders quavered in the face of the difficulties that lay ahead. Meanwhile, the new priority assigned to strategic considerations had given U.S. policy toward the Philippines a fresh sense of purpose. Washington's aim was to create a military base in the western Pacific to serve its geopolitical needs in East Asia. Although competing political interests and rival departments of state debated the issues involved, Congress was never as divided about the future of the Philippines as it was about Hawai'i. There was no substantial body of white settlers to mobilize kith and kin on the mainland, and no debate over statehood, which was never an option. Other parties, especially the business lobby, had a voice in the discussion, but it was neither loud enough nor sufficiently harmonious to affect the strategic considerations that drove U.S. policy.[68]

The degree of influence the United States retained after World War II has led historians to classify the Philippines as a prime example of neocolonialism.[69] The islands appeared to have no means of correcting the long-standing political imbalance between the two countries. They were in a desperate state after years of warfare. Approximately one million Filipinos had died, innumerable farms had been destroyed, Manila had been obliterated, mass starvation was imminent, and civil order had broken down. These urgent realities moved one member of the Philippine Congress to declare his support for the package of measures put forward by the United States in 1946: "I vote yes because we are flat broke, hungry, homeless, and destitute."[70] If the structures of power were fixed, however, relations within them were open to manipulation.[71] It soon became apparent that neocolonialism served interests that the United States had not anticipated when it set out to control its ex-colony in 1946.

The postwar settlement was accepted only after considerable arm-twisting, some dubious deals, and widespread electoral malpractice.[72] The U.S.-Philippine Trade Act (the Bell Act), passed in 1946, rescued the Philippines' export industries by offering duty-free entry to the United States and guaranteed quotas on sugar and abaca until 1954, thus extending the colonial concessions that were scheduled to expire at independence. In return, the Act provided a degree of security for U.S. capital by granting American firms equal rights with Filipinos in acquiring natural resources in the islands, and by fixing the exchange rate between the Philippine peso and the US dollar. The Philippine Rehabilitation Act, passed in the same year, provided compensation for war damage to private property and funds to restore public utilities. The Defense Agreements signed in 1947 were the sting in the tail. The newly independent Philippine government was obliged to accept military assistance, not for service abroad, but to ensure civil order at home, and to make provision for sizable military and naval bases, which in the case of the largest, Clark Air Base, occupied an excessively expansive 250 square miles north of Manila.

The measures approved in 1946–1947 established the Philippines as the outer bastion of the United States in the Pacific. The base, though bristling with armaments, remained vulnerable to domestic political instability. Accordingly, Washington tried to restore the collaborative relations that had existed during the colonial period by installing allies who would be capable of guaranteeing civil order.[73] It was in this spirit that the United States provided strong backing to Manuel Acuña Roxas in the election held in 1946 to mark the transition from Commonwealth to Republic. Manuel Luis Quezon, president in exile, had died in 1944 and had been succeeded by his vice president, Sergio Osmeña, who returned to the Philippines with General Douglas MacArthur in the same year. Although Osmeña was the heir apparent of the Nacionalistas, the party's political monopoly had been destroyed by the war. By then, too, the candidate himself had lost his youthful energy. Moreover, Roxas was MacArthur's choice and also that of Paul McNutt, the High Commissioner.

Predictably, Osmeña lost the election after a campaign that was notable, among many others, for its violence and corruption. The backing he received from a new party, the Democratic Alliance, which represented small farmers and urban workers, may also have hindered more than it helped. The Alliance's program of radical reform drove undecided landowners into the newly formed Liberal Party and confirmed Washington's support for its leader, Manuel Roxas, who duly became the first president of the independent Republic. Ideological differences between the Nacionalistas and the Liberals were marginal, where they could be discerned at all. Both parties represented elite interests; both opted for continued dependence through bilateral ties with the United States; both avoided the daunting issues of reducing economic inequality and achieving effective political independence.

Roxas's success draws attention to an under-emphasized feature of colonial and neocolonial management in the American Empire: the ex-

tent to which senior figures in the U.S. administration were embedded
in the politics of the territories they governed. This is not to say that
they had become "Asian despots," as critics claimed had happened to the
British in India, still less that they had abandoned Western ways and
"gone native." Nevertheless, both MacArthur and McNutt accumulated
commitments beyond their professional obligations to an extent that affected their conduct and counsel.[74] MacArthur had developed a close
personal friendship with Roxas during the war and strongly favored him
as the candidate to manage the peace. Roxas had served in the resistance,
and been captured by the Japanese before reappearing as a member of
the wartime, collaborationist government. Roosevelt had instructed officials to treat collaboration as a criminal offense; MacArthur ensured
that Roxas escaped all charges. His intervention led in 1948 to a general
amnesty that freed other wealthy members of the elite, who also had
personal and financial ties to senior officers in the U.S. Army, including
MacArthur himself.[75] McNutt's civilian connections with the political
class produced a number of lucrative business opportunities in the Philippines after he retired as ambassador in 1947. It is evident that Washington's agents were not simply representatives of the United States.
They also acted as compradors interpreting official policy to local elites,
who in turn stood at the head of networks that reached into the archipelago's distant regions. The scope for manipulation, mutual advantage, and
misunderstanding was infinite.

On one issue at least there was no misunderstanding and full cooperation: the need to destroy the radical movement gathered under
the name Hukbalahap, popularly known as the Huks.[76] The tumultu-
ous 1930s had stimulated radical nationalism throughout the Western
empires. In the Philippines, rural populism found expression in the
Sakdalista movement, which in turn contributed to the Huks, who came
together in 1942 to fight the Japanese. Huk leaders were undoubtedly
influenced by Marxist ideology and communist forms of organization,
but treated them as agencies serving much broader goals.[77] The Huks
were nationalists who wanted to rescue their country from foreign control of all kinds, radicals who wanted fundamental land reform, and
partisans who wanted a share of the compensation for war damage authorized by the Rehabilitation Act.[78] From their base in the rural center of Luzon, the Huks established links with labor organizations in
nearby towns, notably Manila, and advanced the principle of equality
by incorporating women, some of whom commanded guerrilla units,
into their ranks.[79] Estimates of the numbers involved in the movement,
though subject to wide variation, suggest that membership of the Huks

peaked in 1950, when there were about 20,000 guerrillas and 100,000 active supporters.

The Huks represented a frontal challenge to the landowning elite and to Washington's plan of restoring the prewar system of collaborative rule.[80] That system, already strained in the 1930s, fell apart during the war, when a combination of necessity and opportunity led the Huks to abolish rents, redistribute land, and establish local governments in areas under their control. The outcome was a series of major strikes in 1946, and an unprecedented attack on the landed order that resulted in civil war in central Luzon. These events revealed how tenuous patron-client relations had become. The causes of the breakdown reached back to the nineteenth century, when the expansion of agricultural exports started to alter relations on the land. The Huk rebellion showed that the political system was no longer contained within familial bounds, but extended into impersonal relations of class and violence. Concessions to the Huks would have transformed the basis of wealth and power in the Philippines. Roxas had no intention of being the turkey who voted for Christmas, or even the Robert Peel who voted for free trade. The first response of the inappropriately named Liberal Party was to deploy unconstitutional measures to block the Huks' attempt to advance their program through the Democratic Alliance. At that point, the Huks returned to the hills and resumed guerrilla warfare.

Roxas and his allies then applied military force to suppress the rebels. The long and debilitating struggle that followed culminated in 1950, when a major offensive carried the Huks to the gates of Manila. By then, the Philippines was nearly bankrupt and, as Dean Acheson warned Truman, in danger of "total collapse."[81] At this point, the United States stepped in with an additional package of economic aid and military assistance. Experience since the war had made Washington reluctant to distribute costly food parcels on demand, but in 1950 the hand that fed did not need to be forced. The Chinese Revolution, the opening of the Korean War, France's deteriorating position in Indo-China, and Britain's developing guerrilla war in Malaya were setbacks that sent shivers through the Truman administration. These events enhanced the strategic importance of the Philippines, which, geopolitically, had become too big to fail.[82] The Huks were eventually turned back by a combination of armed force, large promises, and small concessions, and by 1954 had ceased to pose a threat to central authority. Nevertheless, "normal service" was not resumed. Traditional patron-client relations were not easily restored, and democracy lay far off in what seemed to be a receding future.

COERCION AND COLLABORATION
IN THE CARIBBEAN

At the end of the war, Governor Rexford Tugwell reflected that, though Puerto Rico was now "completely out of danger," the island was "also completely at a loss in both the political and economic senses; neither Statehood nor Independence nor even Commonwealth is on the immediate horizon."[83] The United States had considered giving Puerto Rico independence in 1936, not because the civilizing mission had been completed, but because, as Senator Millard E. Tydings put it, "it would be better for us if we were out of this place."[84] The proposal was revived in 1945, but quickly discarded. Puerto Rico's leaders wanted independence with continued economic support; the United States could see no gain and much pain in such a one-sided deal. Without external support, however, the economy would struggle to provide even subsistence for its growing population, which was already suffering from high unemployment, low wages, and a chronic shortage of skills. Overseas trade was tied almost exclusively to the United States. The export economy remained heavily reliant on tariff concessions given to sugar; imports contained a high proportion of essential foodstuffs. In 1945, only about half of Puerto Ricans between the ages of six and eighteen attended school.[85] Real incomes, similarly, were only about half the level attained in Mississippi, which was the poorest state on the North American mainland.[86] After nearly a half century of endeavor, it was evident that the "civilizing mission" was still in its preparatory phase.

Aspirations for political independence and awareness of economic dependence interacted after the war to alter the dilemmas Tugwell observed, but not to resolve them.[87] The United States was obliged to adjust its policy toward Puerto Rico, as elsewhere in the island empire, to take account of the gathering strength of colonial nationalism while also devising a strategy that complemented the emerging needs of the Cold War. By 1945, Puerto Rico possessed in Culebra and Vieques one of the largest naval complexes in the world. The island could no longer be uncoupled from the United States in case it fell into the hands of hostile forces. The goal of imperial policy was to retain control while simultaneously trying to win hearts and minds. Nationalists who were classified as "extremists" were to be suppressed; cooperative elements advancing moderate programs were to be given limited encouragement.

The decision to withhold independence had the predictable effect of galvanizing the militant nationalists led by Pedro Albizu Campos, the President of the *Partido Nacionalista de Puerto Rico* (PNPR), which had come to prominence during the distressed conditions of the 1930s. The PNPR survived the war years and became the uncompromising voice of the independence movement after 1945. Albizu Campos was all that a militant political figure should be: single-minded, courageous, committed to the point of obstinacy, and motivated by unrealistic expectations.[88] In 1947, he reappeared after nearly a decade in prison to organize the campaign to secure independence. The Puerto Rican authorities responded in 1948 by passing Law 53, known informally as the Gag Law, which prohibited all expressions of nationalist sentiment, including talk of independence. The measure gave the FBI and the island's secret police the power to hunt down anyone who exhibited dissident tendencies.[89] It also hardened the resolve of the militants. In 1950, the PNPR launched armed uprisings in five major towns, including an attempted coup in the capital, San Juan, and ordered the assassinations of President Truman and Muñoz Marín, the leader of the *Partido Popular Democrático* (PPD), the island's principal political party. The coup failed, as did the attempted assassinations, but twenty-eight people were killed, including the Mayor of San Juan, and forty-nine were wounded. Albizu Campos returned to prison. The nationalists were not quite finished, however. In 1954, four Puerto Ricans sprayed bullets around the House of Representatives in Washington, DC, wounding five congressmen. Albizu Campos was not directly implicated, though he had been pardoned and was out of prison when the shootings took place. Nevertheless, the authorities made the most of the opportunity: he was arrested and again sent to prison, where he died in 1965.

The fundamental problem the radical nationalists faced was not official repression but lack of popular support. The PNPR's program had broad appeal: it attacked plutocrats at home and abroad, advocated land reforms, and recommended improved conditions for wage-earners, but stopped short of proposing socialist solutions; its social policies took their cue from Roman Catholic teachings. These policies were very similar to those of the PPD—apart, of course, from the fundamental divide over the question of independence. Yet the PNPR failed to secure a sizable share of the vote, even in the depressed 1930s, and was unable to gain strength from the successes of anti-colonial movements elsewhere after 1945. The main obstacle, which the party was never able to remove, was the widespread perception among voters that political independence would be economically disastrous.[90] Muñoz Marín and the PPD wrestled with this issue in the 1930s and early 1940s before concluding in 1946 that independence would have to be a long-term goal rather than an immediate one.[91] In the different circumstances of the Gold Coast,

Kwame Nkrumah formulated his celebrated adaptation of the biblical injunction, "seek ye first the political kingdom," with the expectation that "all things shall be added unto you." Muñoz Marín reversed the principle: his big idea was to begin by creating the economic conditions that would eventually enable political independence to become practical politics.

Washington cooperated with Muñoz Marín's vision of reformed and diversified capitalism for the same reason that it backed Manuel Roxas in the Philippines: both leaders pledged to allow the United States to use military bases in their countries, to pursue anti-communist policies, and to oppose radical nationalist movements. In the case of Puerto Rico, U.S. policy steered the PPD away from independence and toward Home Rule.[92] For his part, Muñoz Marín opted for a form of negotiated autonomy, which he hoped would eventually lead to independence, as it had done in the Philippines. Albizu Campos and the PNPR served a purpose they had not intended: by pushing the United States into making concessions to Muñoz Marín and the PPD, they drained support from their own militant program. The PPD attracted nearly two-thirds of the vote in elections held in 1944 and almost as much in 1948, when Muñoz Marín became the first Puerto Rican to be elected governor. Superior organization and an ability to appeal to urban labor unions, rural colonos, and farm workers, while reassuring big business, put the PPD ahead of its rivals. The controversial issue of land reform was resolved in ways that left most of the plantations run by expatriate companies undisturbed, while distributing enough land for family housing to win votes for the party.[93] Meanwhile, the PPD acquired a role as the gatekeeper of new foreign investment in manufacturing, and with it a rich source of patronage that reinforced its political dominance.

The election of Muñoz Marín as governor was one step forward; the decision of the authorities to abandon the failing program of Americanization in 1949 was another. The two events were linked: Muñoz Marín and the PPD needed to sever the historic bond between nationality and status if they were to turn the electorate toward Home Rule instead of independence. Washington's acceptance of the reality of Spanish as the language of education, as well as of the people, helped the PPD to promote a sense of Puerto Rican identity that was distinct from the island's constitutional standing.[94] The settlement that turned Puerto Rico into a Commonwealth was the big prize that followed in 1952. The precise meaning of the term "Commonwealth" was unclear at the time and remains uncertain today.[95] Essentially, however, the island secured internal self-government while retaining its association with the United States as an unincorporated territory. Partial sovereignty lodged Puerto

Rico somewhere between a colony and a dominion, which meant that it lacked autonomy in a number of areas, notably foreign affairs, defense policy, and tariff arrangements with the United States.[96] Congress also removed a section of the proposed constitution that would have incorporated elements of the UN Declaration of Human Rights relating to living standards, education, health insurance, and child welfare. The leader of the House Republicans offered his colleagues an option they were eager to refuse: "If you vote for some of these things, you had better get ready to vote for them back home, or you had better get ready to answer questions as to why you voted for them."[97] The message did not need to be repeated.

Cuba was the only island to escape without permission.[98] As we have seen, Cubans had a long tradition of militant resistance to foreign dominance and had never been brought fully under U.S. control. The independent republic, though effectively a protectorate and strongly influenced by the United States, exercised a greater degree of self-government than was available to the unincorporated territories, and was better placed to give political expression to national sentiments. Despite these differences, the underlying causes of political change were similar to those found elsewhere in the insular empire, even though the outcome was distinctive in being revolutionary rather than evolutionary. Admittedly, the influential historiography that arose after the Revolution of 1959 was distinctive in asserting that previous decades were devoid of either economic or political progress. Recent scholarship, however, suggests revisions to the story that make it possible to reshape the history of the years preceding the Revolution and to point toward ways of reappraising the Revolution itself.

Cuba's well-being remained tied to exports of sugar throughout the century. When Cuba lost its tariff advantages in the U.S. market in the 1930s, the consequences were comprehensive and devastating.[99] Although the island received a quota instead, the level was fixed well below Cuba's potential output. Quotas were suspended during World War II, when the disruption of world supplies raised the demand for sugar and returned Cuba's export trade to prosperity. The shift of export production away from U.S. firms continued: by 1955, Cuban planters were responsible for about 55 percent of the island's sugar production.[100] By then too, an economic boom had placed average per capita incomes in Cuba close to the top of the Latin American rankings; levels of consumption, measured by numbers of radios, television sets, and motor vehicles per head, put Cuba at the head of the list; infant mortality levels were much lower than elsewhere in Latin America; life expectancy was much higher.[101] Simple averages necessarily disguise the fact that the distribution of gains was manifestly unequal, and they say nothing of the continuing racial discrimination suffered by the Afro-Cuban population. Nevertheless, the record makes it clear that, when sugar exports were doing well, so was Cuba.

The revival of the economy provided conditions that favored the democratic principles advertised in the 1930s. It was President Batista, then a young reformer, who had convened the assembly that inscribed the new, progressive Constitution in 1940. The elections held in 1944 and 1948 were generally free and fair, and reporting was uncensored. Batista retired from the presidency in 1944, though with the hope of continuing to influence Cuban politics. The election of 1944, however, gave the presidency to his long-time rival, Ramón Grau San Martín, the reformer of 1933 and leader of the *Partido Auténtico* (PA). The next election, held in 1948, was won by Grau's successor, Carlos Prío Socarrás, who extended the period of PA rule to 1952, when Batista returned to power, this time following a military coup.

Between them, the two PA leaders mustered some good intentions: they made attempts to implement the reform program of 1933, which proposed to reduce the size of the large sugar estates, devolve land to small farmers, and diversify the economy.[102] Their version of democratic liberalism, however, faced problems that turned out to be insurmountable. By the end of the 1940s, wartime demand for sugar had been replaced by a global surplus; the Truman administration was unwilling to support Cuba's government-led plan of economic diversification; and at that point in the Cold War the island did not rank as a high priority.[103] Moreover, the young radicals of the 1930s turned either soft or hard with the passage of time. Grau San Martín and Prío Socarrás went soft; Batista compensated by becoming an authoritarian of granite consistency. The two liberals quailed in the face of opposition, and were unable to control the military and its private enterprise associate, known locally as "gangsterism." Instead, Grau San Martín and Prío Socarrás resorted to governing by purchasing favors, which included lavish payments to themselves.[104] State agencies, founded in the 1930s and retained thereafter, greatly enlarged the potential for patronage and corruption.[105]

By the close of the 1940s, the period of PA rule was beginning to sink beneath the weight of self-induced excess and accumulated inefficiencies. It was submerged, finally, by Cuba's historic nemesis: the market for sugar. In 1948, the PA took the blame for failing to secure an increase in the sugar quota: when the quota was cut in 1951, discontent spilled into the breakdown of civil order. The party's remaining supporters looked for new saviors: business interests wanted efficiency; the army wanted strong government. Both groups received some of what they wished for when Fulgencio Batista, aided by a group of young army officers, short-circuited the electoral process and took power in 1952.

The coup was unexpected and occurred when public support lay dormant. Disillusion with the present rather than enthusiasm for the alternative helped Batista to regain the presidency. Nevertheless, at the outset Batista had the backing of key interests in the army, business, and trade unions. The middle class fell in with events; the Church hierarchy, though ambivalent, rallied to his side.[106] Overt opposition came mainly from students in Havana, who displayed the spontaneous courage of youthful idealists in confronting their new ruler.[107] Washington had kept an eye on Cuba in case nationalist rhetoric should turn into socialism but was also prepared to support reforms that reduced the likelihood of political instability and helped to safeguard U.S. interests. Batista promised stability and fiscal probity, and re-advertised his long record of hostility to communism. Washington moved swiftly to recognize the new regime in the hope that change would bring improvement.

Batista's second coming fell far short of being miraculous. His years of voluntary exile in the United States, where he divided his time between New York and Florida, had given him a taste for the good life, which he upgraded to prodigality. On his return to Cuba, it soon became apparent that he was a changed man: the enthusiastic, young reformer had metamorphosed into a dedicated, middle-aged kleptocrat. He suspended the progressive Constitution of 1940, reduced civil liberties, imposed censorship, expanded the secret police, and developed close and profitable ties with the *mafia*. The tropical Reign of Terror that followed enabled Batista to amass a personal fortune and bestow proportionate rewards on his principal supporters. For a while, too, the Cuban authorities were able to keep a heavy hand on the lid of discontent.

MOVING ON

By about the mid-1950s, the most militant expressions of postwar colonial radicalism had been either tamed or suppressed. The challenge to internal colonialism appeared to have been contained; Hawai'i's application for statehood had been blocked; the Huks had been defeated in the Philippines; the most assertive nationalists in Puerto Rico were in disarray or in prison; eternally "troublesome" Cuba was under Fulgencio Batista's lock and key. The underlying forces nurturing discontent and dissent, however, retained their vitality. The political situation at home and in the overseas territories remained fluid. It was also beginning to move in directions that Washington could not predict and at a pace that it could not control.

Unforeseen international developments had unsettling consequences for U.S. policy. After Joseph Stalin's death in 1953, Moscow adapted its foreign policy to produce a strategy, later termed "peaceful coexistence," which increased the Soviet Union's potential for influencing countries in the Third World through trade, aid, and propaganda. The countries identified as forming a potentially receptive audience for the Kremlin's Pied Pipers included those in the Caribbean and Latin America that the United States had long considered to fall within its own orbit.[108] By the mid-1950s, too, the United States was wading into several quagmires in East Asia.[109] The Chinese Revolution in 1949 had already marked a major setback for U.S. policy in the region. By 1950, President Truman had decided to support France in Indo-China; after the defeat of French troops at Dien Bien Phu in 1954, his successor, President Eisenhower, felt obliged to expand the U.S. commitment to what would soon become the lost cause of French colonialism. The rise of China also required the United States to reinforce the defenses of its main ally in the region, Japan, which had been prohibited from rearming after World War II.

The Korean War, which began in 1950 and was fought to a draw in 1953, strengthened the Chinese government and lured the United States into the dead end of supporting Chiang Kai-shek and the offshore island of Taiwan. The Korean War pointed to future developments in less dramatic but equally telling ways: the 100,000 African American troops who served in Korea were integrated into the U.S. Army for the first time; the Armistice signed in 1953 was brokered by an ex-colony, India. Although the defeat of the United States itself still lay in what was to become the ruins of Vietnam's future, by the close of the 1950s it was evident that the Free World had lost a good deal of ground, influence, and prestige in East Asia.

India and China also featured prominently in the Bandung Conference of non-aligned states held in 1955.[110] The proliferation of governmental (and nongovernmental) international organizations was a marked characteristic of the globalizing world after 1945.[111] Usually, however, the "have" powers took the initiative. The meeting at Bandung was a novel development because it was sponsored by ex-colonies and other "have-not" states. Richard Wright, the African American activist who attended the conference, referred to the members as "the despised, the insulted, the hurt, the dispossessed—in short, the underdogs of the human race."[112] "This meeting of the rejected," he concluded, "was itself a kind of judgment upon the Western world!"[113] The publicity and diplomatic initiatives that followed gave the principles of self-determination, racial equality, and non-alignment new voices on the international stage. By the mid-1950s, too, a number of former colonies had become members of the United Nations; an additional fifty new states joined the organization between 1955 and 1965. The founders of the UN could now be outvoted in the General Assembly, though they retained control of the Security Council. Democracy, which had begun to transform the politics of Western nation-states in the nineteenth century, was now beginning to transform the world's international organizations.

Although the practical effects of the resulting multiplicity of resolutions and declarations escape precise measurement, it is clear that the appearance of the Bandung states on the international scene put the "have" powers on the defensive. The increasing number and diversity of the countries constituting what came to be called, with misleading uniformity, the Third World, frustrated attempts by the two superpowers to create solid blocs of support, while the effort required forced them to make concessions to potential allies, even those earmarked as satellites.[114] The additional publicity given to self-determination, Woodrow Wilson's troublesome legacy, obliged the United States to look afresh at the status of its own territorial possessions. The heightened awareness of racial discrimination personified by the emergence on the world stage (and sometimes fresh from prison) of leading figures, such as Kwame Nkrumah, Jawaharlal Nehru, and Gamal Abdel Nasser, presented a direct challenge to established assumptions about the God-given superiority of Anglo-Saxons and their heritage.[115]

The battle for "hearts and minds" was fundamentally a conflict over the legitimacy of Western dominance. Legitimacy bestowed prestige, which allowed the "have" powers to command the high ground of moral certitude and cast a spell of acceptability on those who classified themselves as followers or were categorized as inferiors. From the perspective of the ex-colonial states, however, the devil had played the best tunes for far too long. By the 1950s, the once captive audience was able to relay its own compositions across the world. Some, advertising the creativity and flexibility of indigenous cultures, were original; others, emphasizing principles of liberty and equality, played back at maximum volume the sounds of the West to the West.[116] By then, too, much of the technology of communication had been democratized. The "have" powers no longer held a tight grip on the international media: newspapers, radios, telephones, and film had slipped into other hands and told other stories.

Events once obscure, or obscured, could be brought into the daylight; colonial linen could be washed in public.

The "have" powers were unable to escape the consequences of these far-reaching developments. The greater the power, the more that was at stake; the larger its world role, the more exposed it was to adverse commentary. The United States, the self-proclaimed herald of liberty and democracy, had no choice but to address its own colonial problems—at home as well as overseas. The resulting literature has established a convention that divides internal colonialism into two self-contained parts. One treats African Americans and equates their struggle with the Civil Rights movement; the other deals with the history of American Indians without integrating it into the battle for self-determination beyond the borders of the United States. The convention undoubtedly has the weight of numbers on its side: in the 1960s there were about 20 million African Americans in the United States and only about 400,000 American Indians. From the perspective of decolonization, however, much can be gained from viewing the Civil Rights movement within the United States as a whole and joining it to the global trends that brought the Western empires to a close.

The Supreme Court's decision in 1954 to outlaw segregation in education has been regarded, routinely but also rightly, as a "landmark" in the progress of civil rights. Nevertheless, successive presidents, with their eyes on the Southern vote, kept their distance from the Court's decision, which was not applied effectively until the 1970s.[117] In the short run, moreover, the decision inspired segregationists as well as their opponents, and increased the incidence of racial violence.[118] In 1955, Emmett Till, a fourteen-year-old African American boy, was lynched in a desolate small town in the Mississippi Delta, inappropriately named Money, in circumstances that were exceptionally horrific.[119] "Strange Fruit," the anthem of the anti-lynching movement, rapidly gained a new and expanded audience:[120]

> Southern trees bear a strange fruit,
> Blood on the leaves and blood at the root,
> Black bodies swinging in the Southern breeze,
> Strange fruit hanging from the poplar trees.

Bob Dylan was inspired to add a memorial and make an appeal:[121]

> If you can't speak out against this kind of thing, a crime
> that's so unjust,

Your eyes are filled with dead men's dirt, your mind is
filled with dust.
Your arms and legs they must be in shackles and chains, and
your blood it must cease to flow,
For you let this human race fall down so God-awful low!

The human race, however, still had some way to go. In 1957, Governor
Orval Faubus mobilized the National Guard to halt integration in Little
Rock, Arkansas. President Eisenhower was compelled to dispatch federal
paratroops to reestablish peace. The resulting confrontation captured the
attention of the media in the United States and across the world. Similar
events, enacted subsequently, ensured that persistent racial problems in
the Land of the Free remained headline news and a deep embarrassment to U.S. diplomacy. The crisis at Little Rock prompted John Foster
Dulles, the Secretary of State, to send President Eisenhower an urgent
and unvarnished message: "this situation is ruining our foreign policy."
The effect in Asia and Africa, he added, "will be worse for us than Hungary was for the Russians."[122] Both superpowers, it seemed, could scrape
the bottom of the barrel far more easily than they could reach the heights
of political excellence they advertised with such assurance.

Eisenhower was an unenthusiastic observer of the Civil Rights movement, but the need to reassert federal control internally and the pressure
to regain credibility internationally meant that he could not let matters
pass him by.[123] As yet, there was no "wind of change" at his back, though
a few straws were blowing in that direction. The Civil Rights movement
had been largely detached from its broader agenda of human rights and
confined to a more limited range of domestic options. These aims were
still ambitious and were guaranteed formidable opposition, but they offered some prospect of reform, whereas wild talk of rights to housing,
health, and employment could readily be condemned as schemes to destroy American liberties and impose socialism. There were signs, too,
that the postwar generation of American citizens was becoming more
flexible in its attitudes toward race. The favorable opinion of the public
toward the admission of Hawai'i as a state was one indication; shifting
voting behavior, especially in the North and Far West, was another. By
the late 1950s, the intransigence of the Southern Democrats was losing
the party valuable support. The Republicans began to capitalize cautiously on the electoral possibilities by incorporating elements of civil
rights into their program.[124] Lyndon Johnson, who became Senate Majority Leader in 1954, realized that the Democrats needed to catch the
tide or be beached. Under his wily and forceful direction, the party re-

luctantly accepted a modest civil rights bill as the price of avoiding more radical reform, though with the hope that its practical consequences could be diluted or diverted. The master manipulator had stolen the Republicans' new clothes and logged a considerable propaganda victory in the ideological contest with the Soviet Union.

The Civil Rights Act of 1957, the first reform of its kind since Reconstruction, was the beginning of a process that had a protracted ending. During the 1960s, the contending parties fought in Congress, in the courts, and in the streets. The level of popular participation increased; the degree of publicity at home and abroad grew commensurately. It was a decade of violence that brought death to the mighty as well as to the meek. President Kennedy was assassinated in 1963; his brother, Robert, met the same fate in 1968, as did Martin Luther King, also in 1968. With an eye on the Southern vote, President Kennedy's instinct was to make haste slowly. However, the scale of the demonstrations and the extent of the challenge to law and order forced his hand, while the prospect of winning the black vote was an electoral reward worth nurturing. In 1963, shortly before his assassination, Kennedy sponsored a new and more comprehensive Civil Rights Bill, which his successor, Lyndon Johnson, saw through Congress in 1964. The Voting Rights Act followed in 1965; a series of complementary decisions by the Supreme Court in the mid-1960s extended public rights to justice and provided protection from misapplications of the law.

The extension of civil rights was a large step toward dismantling the discriminatory laws and practices that upheld the structure of internal colonialism. Advocates who hoped that the Act of 1964 was a prologue to legislation covering wider issues of human rights, however, were disappointed.[125] The reform movement split at the close of the 1960s. A younger generation of radicals, led by Malcolm X, Stokely Carmichael, and the Black Panthers, spoke in fiery language and advocated sweeping socioeconomic changes. Moderates, such as Whitney Young, who spoke softly and in committee, lost credibility.[126] Martin Luther King was greatly influenced by Mahatma Gandhi's philosophy of passive resistance. The Black Panthers drew inspiration from Frantz Fanon's doctrine of violent revolution, though they shared with King the belief that problems of race and inequality in the United States were common to colonial societies everywhere.

Attempts to generalize the struggle, however, proved to be counterproductive. The wider public judged that the new legislation reduced the need for further reform and were alarmed by radical claims that could easily be presented as opening the door to communism. Popular support ebbed; before long, the radicals were either suppressed or marginalized.[127] At the same time, growing opposition to the Vietnam War diverted attention from domestic reform. President Johnson's Great Society program, which Whitney Young had influenced, attempted to tackle the larger issues of poverty, health, and education, but the increasing commitment in Vietnam drained energy and money, and the conservative reaction in the 1970s began to reduce the role of government in these areas.[128] Change was confined to civil rights, and activists concentrated on seeing that legislation in this more restricted area was implemented.

By the 1960s, claims for self-determination and the recovery of land rights advanced by American Indians were also engaging Washington's attention. A long history of protest against government intrusions gained impetus after World War II, as they did throughout the world.[129] Indigenous peoples—from Maori to Inuit—became more insistent in demanding the civil and human rights that had secured international approval after 1945. American Indians, like other First Peoples, drew inspiration from this development. They, too, saw themselves as part of a global decolonizing movement that aimed to recover sovereignty, achieve economic independence, and revitalize their cultures.[130] Like African Americans, they argued that the battle to win hearts and minds in the Cold War ought to begin at home. The policy of "termination" applied after 1953 had far-reaching consequences. Between 1953 and 1964, about 100 tribes lost the sovereignty attached to the reservations, rights over protected land were rescinded, funding for health and education was reduced, and American Indians were persuaded to migrate to towns.

These developments provoked a determined response that overtook the restrained approach of the National Congress of American Indians. A more radical organization, the National Indian Youth Council, broke away in 1961 to spur opposition to termination, and in 1968 the American Indian Movement (AIM) was formed to coordinate the resistance movement and raise its visibility. A series of well-publicized demonstrations followed. In 1969–1971, protesters occupied the deserted penitentiary of Alcatraz, once American Indian land, for nineteen months.[131] In 1972, a large caravan of vehicles made its way from the West Coast to Washington on what later became known as the Trail of Broken Treaties. On arrival, a small group of demonstrators occupied (and took apart) the headquarters of the unpopular Bureau of Indian Affairs. In the following year, the town of Wounded Knee, the site of the massacre of the Lakota in 1890, was seized and occupied for two months. These events, and numerous others, received national and international publicity, while also attracting support for AIM's campaign.

Washington's initial response, as in the case of the movement for African American rights, was to classify AIM as an "extremist" organization and apply counter-insurgency measures to suppress radical dissent.[132] Repression, however, soon gave way to conciliation. Policy toward American Indians had already begun to change from the mid-1960s as a result of President Johnson's "war on poverty," which directed new funds and new ideas to the reservations.[133] Although the program had shortcomings, it succeeded in raising expectations among the recipients and helped to boost the campaign for self-determination. In 1968, Johnson announced that termination would itself be terminated, and Congress passed the Indian Civil Rights Act later in the year. The adverse publicity accompanying the occupation of Alcatraz pushed President Nixon further along the path Johnson had signaled, and in 1975 Congress passed the Indian Self-Determination and Education Act. This measure was itself the prelude to further negotiation and extensive litigation, which is still continuing.[134] From the perspective of the present study, the Act marked the end of a long period of colonial tutelage that had striking similarities with the experience of other colonial powers. Congress approved indirect rule in the 1930s, when Lord Lugard's policy was at the height of its influence, and exchanged it for assimilation in the 1950s, when Britain and France were also searching for new ways of managing subject peoples. The United States then opted for self-determination for American Indians at the same time as the old European empires were converting colonial rule to independence.

PROGRESS IN THE PACIFIC?

The reluctant and partial accommodation with reform at home interacted with complementary developments in the Pacific. Two considerations guided U.S. policy toward its Far-Western frontier: the increasingly desperate situation in East Asia, which raised the strategic and political importance of Hawai'i and the Philippines; and the need, once the militants had been controlled, to ensure that cooperative and reliable allies remained in power.

As we have seen, Congress blocked Hawai'i's application for statehood until the late 1950s, when the balance of interests tilted toward admission.[135] The final decision, however, was not just a response to political trading in Congress. Developments in Hawai'i moved events forward decisively. In 1954, the revived Democratic Party won a historic election: the Republicans were ousted from office for the first time since 1898; their successors were to hold power for the next forty years. The triumph of the Democrats was more than a shift from one party to the other: it was a victory for a new form of progressive populism as well as a defeat for the Big Five firms and the conservative, white elements they represented. Numbers counted: by 1945 more than 85 percent of Hawai'i's population, overwhelmingly children of the first generation of Asian immigrants born in Hawai'i, were U.S. citizens and had voting rights in territorial elections.[136] The Democratic Party in Hawai'i, like the concept of democracy itself, bore little relation to its counterpart in the United States. The islands' Democrats represented Hawai'i's multicultural character and expressed the aspirations of the nonwhite majority. Democrats on the mainland, on the other hand, blocked statehood for Hawai'i to preserve states' rights and segregation.

Given the constitutional framework of the American Empire, the option open to Hawai'i was not independence but equality, and the goal of colonial nationalism, accordingly, was statehood, which the islands' Democrats advocated with skill and determination. The economic arguments underpinning their strategy had become more insistent by the late 1950s. Statehood would entitle Hawai'i to representatives in Congress, who would greatly improve the islands' ability to safeguard the interests of the troubled sugar industry and attract the new investment needed to diversify the economy. Meanwhile, Hawai'i contributed more than many other states to federal revenues. The cry of "no taxation without representation" struck home, as it had in the eighteenth century. On the mainland, doubts about the loyalty of Japanese Hawaiians lost credibility in the face of consistent evidence, manifested in successive plebiscites and territorial elections, of their desire for statehood. The alleged communist menace, though floated and flaunted, ceased to have credibility, despite the fact that policy-makers in the United States continued to see little else in the wider world. Moreover, Hawai'i was an increasingly important military base in the Pacific: the number of U.S. troops on the islands, having been reduced in 1945, surged again in the 1950s. The decision to expand Hawai'i's strategic role was a vote of confidence in the islands that dissolved the smoke screen of doubt about their loyalty and communist leanings. Positive arguments also began to enter the debate: forward-looking commentators realized that Hawai'i's multiracial society could be an asset for the United States in its efforts to counter Soviet propaganda.[137]

The bill conferring statehood was passed in 1959, twenty-two years after a Congressional Committee had reported that Hawai'i met all the requirements. Simultaneously, as part of a complex deal, Alaska was admitted to the Union as the forty-ninth state; Hawai'i became the fiftieth. UN Resolution 742 (1953) enjoined member states to allow dependencies a free choice, including independence, at the point where their status changed.[138] Although Hawaiians undoubtedly preferred to become a state rather than to remain a territory, the United States presented no other option and simply notified the UN that statehood had been conferred. The episode illustrated Washington's increasing distance from the UN, which had begun to show that it had a mind of its own.

The Republicans had supported statehood partly to have a stick to beat the Democrats with, though Eisenhower was personally in favor of full incorporation because he knew and respected Hawai'i's significant contribution during World War II. The Civil Rights Act of 1957 opened the door, but the islands' application for statehood was a cause and not just a consequence of Johnson's adroit maneuvers in Congress. Daniel K. Inouye, who entered Congress as a representative in 1959 and became Hawai'i's first senator in 1963, later observed that the proposed statehood legislation was "a pure and simple civil rights bill," and that the opposition was entirely racist: "as one senator said: 'how would you like to be sitting next to a fellow named Yamamoto?' "[139] The Act approved in 1957 was a modest measure that opponents of civil rights hoped to be able to manage to their advantage. The admission of Hawai'i in 1959 created an irreparable hole in the wall enclosing segregation on the mainland. The succeeding Civil Rights Act, passed in 1964, took down the defenses, even if the rearguard action that followed was bitter and prolonged.

It was appropriate that Daniel Inouye was in the forefront of the battle for statehood. He was a second-generation (*nisei*) son of Japanese immigrants to Hawai'i. He had served with the famous 442nd Regimental Combat Team of Japanese Hawaiians during World War II with such distinction that he was later awarded the Medal of Honor. Inouye represented more than a constituency in Congress: he symbolized the emergence of a new world order after 1945 that would bring to an end the era of colonial rule based on doctrines of racial supremacy.

The mid-1950s also saw the beginnings of a major shift in U.S.-Philippine relations.[140] The continuing precariousness of the economic situation in the Philippines, combined with Washington's enhanced estimate of the country's strategic significance, strengthened the bargaining power of the Philippine government. The political elite in Manila was committed to extracting as much money from the U.S. government as possible; the United States was prepared to pay handsomely to ensure that the Philippines remained a loyal and stable ally. President Manuel Roxas and his successor, Elpidio Rivera Quirino, had already persuaded the United States to soften some of the conditions attached to its trade and aid package. Ramón del Fierro Magsaysay, who replaced Quirino as president in 1953 and remained in office until 1957, went further. Magsaysay was Washington's favored candidate for the presidency. Like Roxas, he had won MacArthur's approval during the war. His subsequent action in suppressing the Huks had demonstrated his militant pro-American stance and earned him the support of the CIA, which backed his election campaign by deploying the dark arts of money-laundering, arson, and blackmail.[141] After his election, *Time* paid Magsaysay the demeaning compliment of calling him "America's Boy."[142]

Yet, things were not entirely what they seemed. Magsaysay, like his predecessors, pursued a dual agenda. He was demonstrably anxious to satisfy the United States, but keener still to cement his own power base, which depended on striking bargains with such varied groups as sugar producers, coconut farmers, manufacturers, and the Roman Catholic Church. Political success depended on securing aid and other concessions from the United States and turning them into contracts, subsidies, and slices of "pork" that could be distributed to supporters. In effect, the Big Men in the Philippines had solved a neocolonial variation of Marx's transformation problem: how to create surplus value and convert it into political capital at an exchange rate that was a fair reward for loyalty. Successful political leaders performed a high-wire act without a safety net: they acted as sturdy Cold War allies upholding the lease of military bases while also appealing to the wider public, whose latent anti-American sentiments were easily aroused.

Although the defeat of the Huks eliminated the most radical form of political dissent, militant opposition to the central government remained a threat. The roots of discontent were deeply embedded, and popular politics had become a permanent and an expanding feature of the political scene.[143] In 1959, the electorate was three and a half times larger than it had been in 1940. Political parties had to reach beyond elite networks to win support from peasants and urban workers across the country. Since existing patron-client relations did not stretch that far, the power brokers in Manila had to cut deals with caciques in distant localities. Magsaysay added to the developing program of political outreach by using modern communications to appeal directly to the populace. The resulting quasi-national political system was characterized by sets of unstable coalitions that formed what has been called "cacique democracy."[144]

Magsaysay was a trapeze artist and an illusionist whose career suited his name, which in Tagalog means "to tell a story."[145] Far from being simply "America's Boy," Magsaysay held the balance between competing interests while giving each the sense that he was committed to their cause above all others. His inclination, like his grasp, did not extend to land reform, taxing the rich, or recovering bases leased to the United States. However, his manipulative skills enabled him to transform latent anti-American sentiment into hostility toward the substantial Chinese community, thus satisfying ethnic prejudices without offending the country's chief paymaster. Magsaysay's constructive successes greatly enlarged the concessions won by his predecessors. When Eisenhower cut aid to the Philippines in 1954, Magsaysay banged the nationalist drum and boosted his popularity by refusing to sign a new agreement extending the leases on military bases. This action brought the United States to heel. In 1955, Magsaysay negotiated a new agreement that extended the privileges granted to sugar exporters shipping to the United States, gave the Philippines the right to impose high tariffs on imports from the United States, and confirmed the country's independence in fiscal and monetary affairs.[146] Powerful lobbies in the United States opposed these concessions, but were defeated.[147]

Magsaysay's most important initiative was to begin to diversify the colonial export economy by promoting modern industry.[148] Manufacturing in the Philippines was not the creation of a rising urban bourgeoisie, but a means of perpetuating established interests in a conservative political system. The landed oligarchy initiated the policy, which it saw as a way of preserving its wealth and political power.[149] Long-standing concern about the future of sugar, coconuts, and abaca was one motive; worry about providing employment for a rapidly increasing population was another. Manufacturing, if suitably protected, had the additional advantages of enabling the existing elite to stay ahead of competitors in the Chinese community and of preventing large U.S. firms from taking control of the local market. The United States, departing from the stereotype of a neocolonial power, fully supported the new development plan. Washington reasoned that successful development would raise living standards, diminish discontent, and increase local sources of revenue, thus easing the burden of aid that an increasingly reluctant Congress felt obliged to authorize. In return, Magsaysay provided an array of import and exchange controls, tax holidays, and government investment. The initial focus was on import-substituting consumer goods, though joint ventures with U.S. firms added more complex products, such as pharmaceuticals and motor vehicles. The liberal reforms that the United States hoped would be implemented in return for its continued backing were unacceptable to the ruling oligarchy and were put aside.

Magsaysay, who died in 1957, set a pattern that his successors gratefully followed.[150] President Carlos Polístico García and the Nacionalistas, who gained power in the same year, adopted an even more assertive attitude toward the United States. As the Philippines began to sink under mounting deficits at the close of the 1950s, the Nacionalistas ramped up their demands on the United States. García's Filipino First movement, launched in 1958, was a protection racket with nationalist appeal. It expanded Magsaysay's industrial program, kept Chinese competitors out of the sector, and forced American companies to choose among unpalatable options: joint ventures, disguised nationalization, and expatriation. A new agreement on leasing military bases was concluded in 1959 only after Washington had undertaken to increase the sugar quota and provide additional financial support. U.S. companies protested, but Washington turned a tin ear to their complaints.

The CIA continued its clandestine efforts to fix "democratic" elections, but to no material effect. The political machine, engorged by U.S. subsidies and oiled by extensive patronage, ground on, encompassing the archipelago and reaching its apogée in the flamboyant authoritarianism of Ferdinand Marcos, who began his long reign as president in 1965. The phenomenon that development specialists refer to as "crony capitalism" was not, in this case, the illegitimate offspring of a purer American version, but the freakish accompanist of the Cold War, which confirmed and deepened relationships that had emerged during the period of colonial rule.[151] In these ways, the cause of anti-communism constrained the power of the mighty and exalted that of their clients.

CONTRASTS IN THE CARIBBEAN

The Caribbean also had an important place in U.S. strategic thinking, but its role was very different from that assigned to the Philippines and Hawai'i. Distance allowed the Pacific possessions to act as bases for extended American interests in Asia. Proximity ensured that the United States had a permanent interest in guaranteeing the stability and cooperation of the islands in the Caribbean, which Washington had long considered to fall "naturally" within its orbit.

The creation of the Commonwealth of Puerto Rico in 1952, and the defeat of the militants, enabled the PPD to retain power until 1968. Three-quarters of the electorate approved the constitutional change, though the level of support reflected the fact that the only alternative was to maintain the island's colonial status, since neither statehood nor independence was on offer. The constitutional settlement also enabled the United States to polish its image as the leader of the free world by allowing the United Nations to remove the island from its list of non-self-governing territories in 1953.[152] In doing so, however, the UN showed that it had begun to outgrow its progenitor. Although twenty-six members voted in favor of the proposal, sixteen were against, including several that lay outside the Soviet bloc. The dissenters also ensured that the UN, rather than the colonial power, retained the right to judge when self-determination had been achieved. The outcome was not the unqualified endorsement the United States had anticipated.

Thereafter, the United States and Puerto Rico concentrated on a cooperative venture that was designed to achieve a "peaceful revolution" and demonstrate to Latin America and the wider world how the "American way" could be transplanted successfully. Muñoz Marín's economic strategy, originally launched in 1948 under the code name Operation Bootstrap, was the centerpiece of the program and complemented the political bargain struck in 1952.[153] The policy originated in the adverse conditions of the 1930s and drew upon ideas formulated by Roosevelt's New Dealers, including Rexford Tugwell, who was Governor of Puerto Rico between 1941 and 1946.[154] The aim was to diversify the economy and develop manufacturing, thereby creating employment and raising living standards. Puerto Rico's main export, sugar, was suffering from overproduction on a global scale; the island's principal manufacture, needlework, was itself an outgrowth of poverty. Neither activity had the potential to deal with the rapid increase in the island's population, which rose from 986,000 in 1900 to 2,218,000 in 1950, largely as a result of declining infant mortality. Attempts to promote state-run industries and implement land reforms in the early 1940s had met opposition from Congress and the large sugar interests, and had limited success.[155] In 1948, however, Muñoz Marín was able to use his authority as the first elected governor of the island to promote a modified form of the original policy.

The White House and the State Department endorsed Operation Bootstrap, which they regarded as an asset in the Cold War. Congress concurred because the revised plan shifted the initiative away from government and toward the private sector. Rex ("the Red") Tugwell had argued for public enterprise and against colonial management by "the sporadic whimsies of Congressional Committees," which, he thought, led to "a regime of unplanned interferences."[156] He admired Britain's Colonial

Development & Welfare Act (1940), which "compared distressingly with our own lethargy and indifference."[157] Muñoz Marín and his close associate, José Teodoro Moscoso, on the other hand, were willing to give domestic and foreign firms a starring role in their development plans, which centered on export-led industrialization.[158] The strategy was chosen because it enabled Puerto Rican exporters to take advantage of tariff concessions in the U.S. market. Import substitution, an alternative starting point, was less attractive because Puerto Rico (unlike Cuba) lacked the authority to raise tariffs on goods imported from the mainland.[159]

A "big push" to eliminate poverty in Puerto Rico followed in the 1950s.[160] A forest of tariff concessions, tax holidays, and subsidies, bolstered by a low-wage economy and reassured by the constitutional settlement, attracted large inflows of foreign capital, principally from the United States, and mainly in the form of direct investment. Generous incentives led to the development of a wide range of local manufactures, beginning with food and clothing, and advancing to capital-intensive activities, such as pharmaceuticals, chemicals, machinery, and electronics. Tourism, assisted by cheap air travel, also took off: in the late 1950s, 250,000 U.S. tourists visited Puerto Rico annually; by 1970, the figure had reached one million.[161] The result was a massive transformation of the colonial economy: in 1956, manufacturing generated more income than agriculture for the first time in Puerto Rico's history; by 1965, employment in non-agricultural occupations was five times greater than in agriculture.[162] Unemployment came down; average living standards went up. Per capita real incomes increased by 75 percent between 1940 and 1953 and by an additional 30 percent in the short period between 1950 and 1956.[163] Public investment associated with Operation Bootstrap greatly improved health provision and led to a dramatic increase in life expectancy at birth, which rose from forty-six years in 1940 to seventy-three in 1980.[164] Literacy levels, though hard to quantify accurately, advanced from 69 percent in 1940 to 91 percent in 1980.

Operation Bootstrap achieved widespread and favorable publicity in its time, and became a model for development elsewhere in the evolving world of late colonialism.[165] Washington and the press marked out the island as a beacon of liberal capitalist progress that would shine a light on the rest of Central and South America. Visiting experts, undeterred by previous failures, applied the principles of modernization theory and had them confirmed. Leading figures of the day, from President Eisenhower (who played golf there) to President Kennedy (who was received with a motorcade) visited the island to testify to its ongoing "peaceful revolution" and to contrast it with the wild upheaval taking place neighboring Cuba.[166]

The impressive achievements of Operation Bootstrap, however, were short-lived. Puerto Rico's "Caribbean miracle" did not lead to the "self-sustained take-off" that the gurus of the day had envisaged.[167] Far from creating the basis for effective independence, Operation Bootstrap tied Puerto Rico even more closely to the United States, entrenched large foreign corporations in the economy, and obliged the government in San Juan to extend tax and tariff concessions beyond their intended span to ensure that foreign firms kept their capital on the island. Even so, new employment in manufacturing was unable to compensate for the loss of jobs in the sugar and needlework industries. The fall in the level of unemployment to a low point of 11 percent in 1964 was accounted for partly by emigration, principally to the mainland, which reached a peak in the 1950s, when nearly half a million Puerto Ricans left the island.[168] Although average per capita incomes rose, living standards remained low and large pools of poverty persisted in both town and country. Puerto Rico's experiment in what, today, would be called "outsourcing" depended not only cheap labor but also on large subsidies. The global oil crisis, which struck in 1973, retarded the whole enterprise. As the U.S. economy faltered, so Puerto Rico wilted. Deficits in trade and services became persistent, unemployment rose, strike action intensified, poverty increased. Congress wriggled but could not escape. Ultimately, Puerto Rico had to be sustained to preserve the credibility of the United States throughout Latin America. It is no wonder that former Governor Tugwell, writing in 1958, rated Muñoz Marín's achievement so highly: "he ended by exploiting the exploiter, and making Congress like it."[169]

Batista's authoritarian regime kept the peace in nearby Cuba until the mid-1950s, though with mounting difficulty. The excesses of arbitrary rule provoked a series of reactions across the island. Large-scale student demonstrations were held in 1955; a strike of half a million sugar workers was threatened at the end of that year; dissident army officers attempted a coup in 1956; the presidential palace was attacked in 1957; a general strike was declared in 1958. The Church was progressively alienated by the regime's incursions into its property rights and freedom of worship. The long-standing belief that the Revolution was almost exclusively the work of a handful of guerrillas who struck out from inaccessible bases in the Sierra Maestra has now been modified.[170] In its initial stages, the opposition to Batista was led by urban-based, middle-class professionals and supported by exiles who supplied arms and money. Batista, however, refused to negotiate with moderate reformers.[171] After the failure of the general strike in April 1958, the initiative shifted to the mountains. Even so, Fidel Alejandro Castro Ruz remained one of several leaders and his dominance was confirmed by the Revolution rather than before it. The rural guerrillas began operations in 1956; by the time they had taken the initiative in 1958, resistance had turned into civil war. By the close of that year, the rebels had defeated government forces and succeeded in driving Batista and most of his money into exile in Portugal by way of Dominica.[172] After a short interregnum, Fidel Castro became Prime Minister in 1959 and assumed the additional office of President of the Republic in 1976.

The Revolution was a colonial revolt by proxy. Batista came to be seen as the collaborator-in-chief of American imperialism and, as such, the personification of the evils that had fallen upon Cuba. Fidel Castro was his antonym: the agent of deliverance.[173] Castro appealed to secular authority; his supporters endowed him with a form of divine right to revolutionary action. He drew on socialist axioms to predict the future but took spiritual inspiration from the ideals and example of José Martí, Cuba's greatest hero. Castro's ideology floated before it settled. His closest associates, his brother Raúl and Ernesto "Che" Guevara, were committed communists while Fidel was still assembling a coherent political philosophy, which remained a "work in progress" until after the Revolution. Nevertheless, Fidel Castro took his bearings from certain fixed points: he was a Cuban nationalist, an enemy of imperialism, and an activist who believed that tyrannical rule justified revolution. These sentiments resonated with Cubans. They appealed across social boundaries, explained discontents, and offered remedies. They resuscitated enthusiasms that had been crushed by experience but kept alive by hopes for a better future. They were not far removed from those that had inspired the revolutionaries of 1776.

The popularity of the Revolution of 1959, though well attested, can be further illustrated from an unlikely source: Julio Lobo y Olavarría, the "sugar king" of Havana.[174] Julio Lobo was born in Venezuela in 1898 but moved to Cuba with his parents when he was a child. He grew up in Havana at a time when U.S. interference in the island's affairs was very visible, and he acquired a commitment to nationalist aspirations that remained throughout his life. After studying in the United States, Lobo entered the family sugar business and progressed to the point where his sugar plantations and refineries produced as much as half of Cuba's total annual output. According to stereotype, Lobo ought to have acted as a

loyal bourgeois supporter of the political establishment. The bourgeoisie, however, "played a most revolutionary part," in ways that Marx and
Engels did not always anticipate. Lobo supported Batista's coup because
he thought it would be an improvement on the corrupt administration of
Carlos Prío Socarrás. He deserted Batista when the president departed
from the ideals incorporated in the Constitution of 1940. Lobo's nationalism derived from José Martí; his sense of the potential for revolutionary action came from his admiration of Napoleon Bonaparte, which he
shared with Fidel Castro. He matched his sentiments with financial support for the opposition to Batista.

At the same time, Lobo remained an active and successful businessman. Although sugar was his central concern, by the 1950s he had diversified into banking and tourism, and had acquired a large stake in the
Cuban economy as a whole. He backed Batista partly because he judged
that the president would safeguard the sugar industry; he opposed him
when that appeared no longer to be the case. His big mistake came later,
when Fidel Castro took power. It is unclear whether Lobo's patriotism
caused his heart to rule his head, whether he thought that the United
States would act to forestall the revolution, or whether he believed that
he could influence the course of events sufficiently to safeguard his business interests. In 1960, Che Guevara offered to appoint Lobo to a new,
salaried post as director of Cuba's sugar industry in exchange for nationalizing his sugar refineries and estates.

Lobo was too shocked to answer immediately, but decided to leave
the island shortly afterward. He abandoned his estates, his mansions, his
fine collection of artwork, and his archive of Napoleon's papers and relics,
and left, so it is said, with a small suitcase and a toothbrush. Although
Cuba's richest man lost his fortune, his memories remained intact. In
his prime, Lobo had dated famous movie stars, such as Joan Fontaine
and Bette Davis, and is said to have filled one of his swimming pools
with scent as a gesture of welcome to Esther Williams, the Hollywood
swimming star. Presumably, she kept her eyes shut. With these glories
behind him, Lobo lived modestly in Madrid. When he died, in 1983, his
body was wrapped in a Cuban flag, as he had requested. Like Timon of
Athens, he had few mourners.

Julio Lobo's career hints at the complexity of the causes of the Cuban
Revolution. Any attempt to go beyond an initial set of undemanding
explanations—that Batista was increasingly unpopular and the rebels
attracted widespread support—runs into controversy. Most scholars have
set economic arguments to one side because, by and large, sugar exports

were doing well in the late 1950s.[175] By extension, it has also been suggested that revolutionary movements in Cuba before 1959 took place during periods of prosperity.[176] Other scholars have qualified standard political arguments by claiming that Cuban nationalism was not strongly anti-American at this time.[177] An amplification of this argument has tried to distinguish between anti-imperialism and anti-Americanism.[178] These analyses are valuable not only in themselves but also for obliging future commentators to be wary of standard formulations when explaining the turmoil of 1959.

The indices of economic performance conventionally cited in this connection refer to the volume and price of sugar exports. Export volumes in the late 1950s were higher than in the 1930s and 1940s, but no higher than in the second half of the 1920s. Similarly, the world price for raw sugar was higher in the 1950s than it had been in the 1930s and 1940s, but did not scale the peaks of the boom years between 1915 and 1921. As they stand, however, these figures are inadequate measures of prosperity. Without knowing more about the terms of trade, productivity, and the distribution of gains among factors of production, it is unwise to assume that increased volumes and prices were translated into rising prosperity. What can be said is that the volume of exports in the 1950s was stuck at about half of Cuba's potential, that there were few productivity gains in the sugar industry at this time, and that the distribution of rewards benefited large sugar producers and exporters more than their workers, whose wages were held down by imported labor from other parts of the Caribbean. Moreover, Cuba's population had grown dramatically in the course of the century, and had doubled since 1930 to reach a total of seven million in 1960.

These facts may not have been fully known to ordinary cane cutters, but they were a cause of concern for large firms and their investors. Well-placed observers also realized that much of the buoyancy of the sugar market in the 1950s was sustained by fortuitous events, notably the Korean War boom and the Suez Crisis. The underlying trends, however, were a cause of pessimism. Population increase had created demands for employment and welfare that could not be met from current export earnings. The reappearance of rival producers after the war raised the prospect of a global surplus of sugar and cast doubt on the long-term future of the industry. Cuba was in an especially precarious position because it depended so heavily on the U.S. market and on the unpredictable actions of Congress in adjusting sugar tariffs and quotas.

These fears were raised in the late 1940s and realized in the 1950s.[179] The principal sugar interests had backed Batista's coup in 1952 because they believed that he would create conditions that favored business.[180] Their immediate concern was that output in 1953 would greatly exceed the quota limit and push down sugar prices.[181] In the short run, their judgment was correct. Once installed, Batista repaid his backers by withdrawing nearly two million tons of sugar from the market. His action stopped prices from collapsing, though the overhang of stocks had a depressing effect until 1955, when prices improved for the rest of the decade.

By then, however, a far more serious problem had emerged: a rise in protectionist sentiment in the United States expressed in revisions to the quota that determined Cuba's share of the mainland market. When quotas were reinstated after the war, Cuba found itself caught between the State Department, which feared that economic hardship would again create "chaos" and "strengthen the hand of 25,000 active communists" who were supposed to be on the island, and the Department of Agriculture, which acted in the interests of mainland producers of beet and cane.[182] The domestic lobby prevailed when the Democrats gained control of Congress in 1955 and implemented a pledge to give more support to mainland producers. Cuba's quota had been held down in 1951 but was cut significantly in 1956. The prospect of finding alternative markets was minimal. The island was the lowest-cost producer of high-quality sugar in the world, but national governments and large sugar interests combined to rig the market while proclaiming themselves to be champions of free-enterprise capitalism. The International Sugar Agreement, signed in 1953, extended the quota system to all sugar producers. Cuba was trapped.

The reduction of Cuba's sugar quota had far-reaching consequences. The projected loss of nearly two million tons a year amounted to almost one-third of the existing quota. Cuba was unable to sell enough sugar after 1956 to maintain the living standards achieved in 1947. One projection estimated that the new quota would cut Cuba's GDP in 1960 by about 6 percent.[183] These prospects checked the profitability of U.S. capital in Cuba, reduced the incentives for new investment, and limited the money available to fund diversification and welfare. The price of stock in sugar companies connected to Cuba started to fall as early as 1954, as investors anticipated that the review of the quota would greatly increase the risks of trading with the island; after 1956, when their fears were confirmed, stock prices fell further. Batista's business supporters, who were tied into the sugar complex, began to search for alternative leaders and policies. Meanwhile, they urged the State Department to persuade the Cuban government of the need for major political and economic reform.[184] In the course of 1958, however, U.S. business interests in Cuba decided that the regime no longer had a future. The military, which had financial links to sugar interests, had already begun to withdraw its support.[185] The short-term improvement of the economy in 1958 came too late to save the President: Batista disappeared as swiftly as he had reappeared in 1952.

The political consequences of these developments extended well beyond the narrow limits of regime change. Cubans had adopted Americanization selectively, first as an expression of anti-colonialism directed against Spain, and then as a path to modernization.[186] By the 1950s, disillusion had long replaced optimism. Material aspirations derived from the mainland remained highly prized, but U.S. support for Batista's corrupt authoritarianism showed Cubans that Washington was willing to exchange its proclaimed ideals of liberty and democracy for less elevated geopolitical considerations. In taking this decision, U.S. policy-makers were also expressing their low estimation of Cuban abilities. In the 1950s, the attitude of the United States toward Cuba was still that of a superior power with "natural" rights of control.[187] Policy-makers in Washington continued to regard Cubans as exotic inferiors who were "half devil and half child," and lacking the qualities needed for the higher reaches of political life.[188] Although the Revolution did not begin as "a volcanic Cuban cultural explosion against U.S. penetration of the Cuban soul," it was founded, nevertheless, on a dispute over political and economic relations that went to the heart of Cuba's sovereignty.[189] It is in this sense that the Revolution was a national event and Fidel Castro, the caudillo and romantic, was Cuba's Garibaldi.

Fidel Castro was self-propelled, but he was also driven along by U.S. policy.[190] Washington's attitude toward Cuba was never likely to produce a meeting of minds. When Castro visited the United States shortly after the Revolution, Eisenhower ignored him, while Nixon patronized him. At that moment, the United States had both motive and opportunity to strike a deal with Cuba. The motive arose from the need to counter Moscow's new strategy of peaceful coexistence; the opportunity appeared because the USSR had yet to establish a foothold in Cuba.[191] Washington reacted, as it had in Vietnam, by adopting a hostile attitude toward anti-colonial nationalism. Early in 1959, the State Department declined to make the obvious concession of increasing Cuba's sugar quota.[192] In May, Castro pushed ahead with proposals to redistribute sugar estates owned by U.S. investors. Washington reacted by encouraging anti-Castro elements on the mainland to overturn the Revolution by force. Despite these provocations, by the close of the year the CIA remained confident that Cuba was still not aligned with the Soviet Union, and Washington had yet to decide on taking direct action to remove Castro.[193] At this stage, the chief aim of policy was to pressure the Cuban government to abandon land reforms that damaged U.S. interests. In 1960, however, relations deteriorated rapidly. Castro proceeded with land reform, reached an agreement with the Soviet Union over sales of sugar, and nationalized foreign companies. Eisenhower retaliated by canceling Cuba's sugar quota and imposing a trade embargo on the island.[194] By the middle of the year, the point of no return had been reached.

Castro, like Ho Chi Minh, was a radical nationalist before he became a communist. Ho joined the Communist Party to advance the cause of independence; Castro turned to communism to consolidate a revolution that had already taken place. Geopolitical and ideological motives drew the United States into Vietnam. The same motives, heightened by proximity, were present in Cuba. The difference was that, in Cuba, U.S. investments were also at risk. Revolutions freed Cuba and Vietnam from the United States; survival made them dependent on allies that were hostile to the Land of the Free.[195]

CONCLUSION: "A SHINING EXAMPLE OF THE AMERICAN WAY FOR THE ENTIRE EARTH"[196]

The distance between rhetoric and reality was just as great at the end of the colonial era as it was at its beginning. Theodore Roosevelt's declarations about America's civilizing mission carried hyperbole to new levels of excess; Dwight Eisenhower's "shining example," displayed to support Hawai'i's application for statehood, was a close second. The issue is not the sincerity of these and similar pronouncements but their value as guides to the past. Hawai'i's application for full incorporation was less a "shining example" of progress than a cause of it. Statehood for Hawai'i's cosmopolitan society undoubtedly opened doors on the mainland, but acceptance of multiculturalism across "the entire earth" was the result of many other influences that had independent sources of origin. The rhetoric was unexceptional. The European colonial powers made similarly spacious claims that had the merit of appealing to audiences at home without being called to account in the colonies, where subjects and citizens alike lacked the power to influence elections in the home country.

The reality was equally familiar. The assumptions underlying policy in the American Empire were in general terms identical to those prevailing in the European empires. The trajectory of the American Empire closely followed that of the European empires throughout the period of colonial rule. The results of policy are not measurable with the accuracy needed to support precise comparison, and for that reason (among others) require separate study. From the information presented here, however, the record appears to have been little different from that of the European imperial powers.

Policy in all the Western empires drew on shared intellectual foundations of racial superiority. American rule was distinctive to the extent that it was particularly marked by the influence of segregation on colonial policy. Racial discrimination on the mainland carried enough political weight to prevent the insular territories from becoming incorporated states, apart from Hawai'i, where white settlers were regarded as "kith and kin." Even so, the fact that the white minority there oversaw a mixed race of Asian Hawaiians was sufficient to block the islands' application for statehood until 1959, when a combination of colonial populism, Cold War imperatives, and competition between Democrats and Republicans on the mainland eventually pushed Congress to act. The European empires shared with the United States acute difficulties in bringing colonial rule to an end wherever white settlers were involved. In this respect, ending segregation in the United States and bringing down white rule in Algeria, South Africa, and elsewhere were chapters of the same story, even though the literature tends to assign them to different books.[197] The same could be said of the export model of Southern segregation, which contributed to the formation of apartheid in South Africa and to the "White Australia" policy.[198]

The trajectory of the American Empire confirms that what was distinctive was not exceptional. Wars intensify the contest between conservative and progressive forces. After 1945, as after 1918, the victorious imperial powers made determined efforts to hold on to their empires while reformers and dissenters redoubled their demands for change. Britain and France regained control of the territories they had lost during the conflict and undertook a "second colonial occupation." Militant nationalists were suppressed; concessions were packaged to support moderate leaders and to retain their allegiance to what was becoming known as the Free World. The United States acted similarly in subduing radicals at home, putting down the Huks in the Philippines and the revolutionary nationalists in Puerto Rico, and attempting to discredit the labor unions in Hawai'i. The return of prosperity during and after the war limited the force of Cuba's militants, but also created the circumstances that allowed Fulgencio Batista to seize power in 1952.

From the mid-1950s onward, colonial policy had to make a further adaptation: holding on no longer sufficed; moving on was unavoidable. Self-determination linked to broad claims about human rights had become a global and not just a local issue; peaceful but competitive coexistence made further progress imperative. The colonial powers redoubled their efforts to win hearts and minds. The United States, having approved Commonwealth status for Puerto Rico in 1952, increased its support for Muñoz Marín and the PPD. Lavish subsidies helped Ramón Magsaysay to retain control in the Philippines. Hawai'i achieved statehood in 1959. Batista was backed to the hilt and to the last moment in Cuba. Lincoln's first priority was to save the Union rather than to abolish slavery; Kennedy's was to save the United States from Southern intransigence rather than to complete the process of emancipation that Lincoln had begun. Both presidents ended by achieving more than they had anticipated.

This analysis suggests a fresh way of looking at the relationship between decolonization and the Cold War. The argument advanced in this chapter is that the context of the discussion needs to be greatly enlarged to overcome the European focus that has set the course of research since the subject first entered the study of international relations. Long-standing debates on the motives of U.S. foreign policy and the chronology of the Cold War remain valid.[199] The European bias of the literature, however, does a disservice to developments elsewhere in the world. The term itself is wholly inappropriate to countries like Korea and Vietnam, which endured wars that were hot enough to scald everyone they touched, as well as to the many regions, from China to Africa, that suffered devastating civil wars between the 1940s and the 1970s. The case made here is not only that decolonization needs to be built into the existing literature, but also that the study of the demise of the Western empires is itself a theme that needs to be joined to the process of globalization. Seen from this perspective, the final decades of the insular empire suggest a periodization that fits the Cold War to decolonization, and decolonization to the transition that saw one phase of globalization give way to another.

The economic crisis of the 1930s brought distress; world war brought devastation. The combination destroyed the legitimacy of the once "modern" empires of the West and revealed the limits of the colonial order that was the product of national-industrial states. The consequent loss of authority over large parts of the world combined with the disturbing appearance of new, mass nationalist movements drew in the two contending superpowers, carried the Cold War beyond Europe, and turned it into a global event. The ensuing rivalry between the United States and the Soviet Union then led to attempts to control change at home, as well as in satellites and colonies. At this point, the prosecution of the Cold War retarded decolonization. From the mid-1950s, however, the battle for hearts and minds obliged the "have" powers to make concessions that accommodated, in varying degrees, the aspirations of the "underdogs of the human race," as Richard Wright called them.[200] Concepts of racial supremacy, which had validated colonial rule, were eroded; demands for self-determination, which turned self-respect into political claims, mounted; pressure for a new economic deal, which carried ambition beyond the colonial system, intensified. The imperial powers, recognizing realities, prepared the way for moral disarmament by publicizing the term "decolonization" and presenting themselves as its prime mover.[201] The course of history could no longer be changed, but it was still possible to be on the right side of the future. At this point, the Cold War acted to spur progressive change, which ended in decolonization.

The shifting relationship between decolonization and the Cold War also helps to explain the malleable character of neocolonialism. It is now apparent that nationalist leaders used their leverage to extract concessions from the United States, just as they did from the other colonial powers. The United States was not the first imperial state to be trapped by its own actions into subsidizing a satellite to a degree that far exceeded its expectations or wishes. Equally, Puerto Rico and the Philippines were not alone among ex-colonial states in deciding that dependence with subsidies was preferable to independence with poverty.[202] Today, Puerto Rico has achieved a greater degree of integration with the United States than it had during the colonial period: more of its citizens are on the mainland than are on the island; New York is known as Puerto Rico's largest city.

Cuba was the exception. The island's experience indicates that constitutional standing mattered. Its status as a protectorate limited its ties with Washington and was consistent with a strong tradition of independence. The fact that the United States exercised greater control over its colonies than it did over protectorates and independent states suggests that the distinction between formal and informal empire should not be erased too readily. Once its privileges in the U.S. market had been whittled away to support mainland and other insular producers, Cuba had little to gain from cooperating with Washington's priorities. In return, the United States ensured that Cuba paid a high price for upholding its sovereignty.

"It has been observed," John Quincy Adams noted in 1793, "that the nations the most highly favored with freedom have not always been the most friendly to the freedom of others."[203] Adams was referring to Britain's attempt to coerce the mainland colonies into submission, but the aphorism applied to the United States, too, once it had risen to heights where fear of falling produced exaggerated assessments of threats posed by other states in the global order, including some of the most insignificant and others that would have preferred cooperation to confrontation.

PART IV

THE OUTCOME: POSTCOLONIAL GLOBALIZATION

CHAPTER 15

DOMINANCE AND DECLINE IN THE POSTCOLONIAL AGE

"THE ONE DUTY WE OWE TO HISTORY IS TO REWRITE IT"[1]

Oscar Wilde's characteristically confident directive applies to master craftsmen, like himself, rather than to journeymen and apprentices. Nevertheless, all historians aim to achieve a degree of novelty in their work. Given the assumption adopted here, namely, that historical studies advance through changes of emphasis rather than through revelation, it follows that the interpretation offered in this study has been aligned to relatively modest possibilities. The principal adjustment places the history of the United States in an international context. This perspective is scarcely unknown, but it often appears in a stereotyped or episodic form, at least before the twentieth century. The three substantial chapters of this study dealing with Western Europe, with an emphasis on Britain, update and amplify this dimension of the story and provide a fresh line of sight on familiar themes in the history of the United States. The argument derived from this position links key developments in the United States to those that were also shaping events in Europe. The Republic was undoubtedly distinctive in many respects, but it was not "exceptional" in the popular, providential sense of the term. The aim of the book, however, has not been to put the United States down, but rather to put it in—to the mainstream of Western history. In doing so, the wider context outlined here has also revealed examples of distinctiveness that have been overlooked or underplayed.

The present chapter begins by summarizing historical developments down to the mid-twentieth century, when the imperial branch of modern globalization encountered the forces of decolonization in what was to be its final crisis. The summary leads to a consideration of the outcome, which is characterized here as postcolonial globalization. This phase, which began after World War II and continues today, cannot be investigated in detail in the present study, but enough can be said to indicate the changing character of global power and some of its consequences for the United States and its former colonial territories.

After World War II, the United States exercised influence and exerted military force in conditions that allowed a measure of hegemony but denied the possibility of establishing an empire of the type that had existed in previous centuries. The position of the United States as a world power therefore differs markedly from that of its European imperial predecessors. Even at the height of its influence, between 1945 and 1975, the United States struggled to match its immense power and considerable effort to successful outcomes. During the last quarter of the century, Washington's global ambitions faced increasing obstacles, which were masked in the 1990s by the unexpected collapse of the Soviet Empire. None of these trends suggests that the United States has ceased to be a great power. They do, however, pose the question of what it means to "make America great again" in a world that is unsuited to empires, and raise the prospect of defining greatness to signify something other than the external projection of military and economic power.

GLOBALIZATION AND EMPIRES

What is clear to authors often remains obscure to readers. Authors have been locked up with their chosen subject for so long that what they once saw as novelty needing lucid exposition has been absorbed to the point where it is taken for granted. Spacious works of synthesis, such as this one, pose particular problems of organization and presentation. It is all too easy to overwhelm the interpretation by adding elaborations and qualifications that will satisfy different sets of specialists but bemuse or bore other readers. If the evidence is curtailed, on the other hand, the argument becomes highly visible but specialists are likely to find the presentation too thin to be convincing, while scholars wishing to introduce the subject to a new generation of students and researchers may lack the information they need. Evidently, a balance is needed. Equally evidently, no balance can satisfy all readers, who will bring different expectations and intellectual resources to bear on the text. The balance struck at this point errs on the side of caution in taking little for granted. Readers who have been able to carry the argument of the book forward to this chapter may find the summary remarks that follow reassuring or even over-familiar. Those who feel that they have been abandoned in a textual jungle may gain the clarity they deserve, even though at the last moment.

The interpretation presented in this study rests on three propositions: that the history of globalization can be divided into different analytical phases; that the transition from one phase of globalization
to another stemmed from a dialectical process; and that territorial
empires were the most powerful agents of globalization between the
eighteenth century and the mid-twentieth century.[2] The international
setting described here draws on the experience of Western Europe, and
Britain in particular, to reassess the history of the United States since
the eighteenth century. The argument has tried to show that both regions passed through three broad phases during this period, each corresponding to changes in the character of globalization, and each ending
in a transformative crisis.

The eighteenth-century military-fiscal state marked the high point
of proto-globalization. The period culminated in a series of major revolutions and was followed in the nineteenth century by a sustained and
often violent struggle between conservatives, who tried to reverse the
radical consequences of the revolutionary upheaval, and progressives,
who aimed to reaffirm them. Montesquieu's perception of the relationship between the size and structure of states provides an insight into the
dynamic process that converted one phase of globalization into another.
Britain's advanced military-fiscal state extended its reach into North
America and Asia and created a thriving relationship with the Caribbean
islands and the mainland colonies. The successful colonization of the
mainland encouraged the expansion of settlement, increased living standards, and raised expectations. The British government, however, was
unable to manage the growth it had helped to stimulate. The technology
of the time set limits to central control. Accessible land drew settlers
away from the coast and beyond British oversight.

The American Revolution was a reluctant act of secession initiated by
colonists who felt that their enterprise in developing "open" lands and
their largely conservative political aspirations were frustrated by the
home government. The scope for compromise, however, was constrained
by the revenue needs of the British government and its onerous commitments, which included substantial expenditure on public goods. Uncontrolled expansion across the North American continent would carry
settlers beyond the reach of the colonial tax-gathering machinery and increase the likelihood of costly wars with Native Americans and other European powers. Fiscal imperatives, which were felt across Europe, were
non-negotiable. They were vital to maintaining the stability of the state
and the dominance of the ruling agrarian elite. Expansion had outpaced
structure. Development enabled the outer provinces to assert themselves;

distance presented the home government with problems of control that exceeded its capacity. The result in the mainland colonies was matched by a succession of revolutions elsewhere in Europe and the New World.

The crisis of the military-fiscal state that brought Britain's American empire to an end inaugurated the independent Republic of the United States. The independence won in 1783, however, was formal, not effective. A perspective from the standpoint of imperial history suggests an alternative to the swelling national story that dominates accounts of the Republic thereafter. Liberty and democracy, the principal themes in conventional interpretations, need to be scaled down to make room for imperatives that propel all newly independent states: the quest for stability and development. The attempt to marry the two failed spectacularly in 1861, when the fragile state collapsed into civil war, a fate that many other ex-colonial states were to share in the twentieth century. By then, continental expansion, supported by Britain, had created a moving frontier of settlement in the United States that anticipated similar developments in other neo-European dependencies.[3] Territorial acquisition led to hostilities with indigenous people everywhere. In the United States, it also engendered conflict among rival settler interests. Internal rivalries destabilized the polity and ended in civil war. This catastrophe nevertheless created the conditions that eventually enabled the Republic to promote national unity.

Standard accounts of the period following independence pay only limited attention to the role of external relations. Far from being self-contained, however, the United States felt the effects of Britain's expanding informal influence after 1783 in economic development, political choice, and forms of cultural expression. For much of the nineteenth century, the United States was an ex-colonial state in which competing interests with different approaches to achieving substantive independence struggled to control the polity. The contest played out in North America was far from being unique. The fundamental issues were those expressed in the contemporary battle between conservatives and progressives in Europe. The real distinctiveness of the United States in this period lay in the hitherto unexplored way it anticipated dilemmas that were to face other ex-colonial states as they tried to make formal independence effective. The new Republic provided the first important example of a former colonial power exercising its informal influence. In 1783, Britain's American empire changed its form more than its substance.

The second phase, modern globalization, was marked by "nation-building," the growth of power-driven machinery, mass production, financial services, and the expansion of towns, all of which began to transform states and societies in the course of the nineteenth century. The period as a whole was one of uneven development that accelerated in the second half of the century. Military-fiscal states persisted far into the century, despite shocks transmitted by revolutions and war. Agrarian and manufacturing interests competed for control of the apparatus of state; new social forces representing the interests of capital and labor struggled for supremacy in the workplace. The next crisis of globalization, which occurred at the close of the century, was a manifestation of a historic shift of power from rural to urban centers that existing state structures were unable to contain. The incomplete resolution of these challenges was channeled through the nation-state and evoked a range of reactions, including assertive imperialism. New, refurbished, or expanded nation-states entered a competition to partition the world. This analysis provides a formula for relating the uneven character of development in Europe and the United States to the different contributions economic and political causes made to "new" imperialism.

Nation-building in the United States after 1865 joined a process that was under way simultaneously in continental Europe. In the United States, as in Europe, industrialization challenged the traditional power of the land, created problems of urbanization and unemployment, and threatened the stability of the state. "New" imperialism was a dramatic response to a crisis of welfare and order that affected the United States as it did the other Western powers. War with Spain in 1898, at the high point of "new" imperialism, expressed a novel sense of national unity, power, and purpose. The acquisition of colonies made the Republic a member of the imperial club; in doing so, it also celebrated the achievement of national unity and national sovereignty.

Modern globalization, as projected by territorial empires, was consolidated after 1900 by colonial rule before entering a long crisis from which it never fully recovered. The consequences of the wholesale redistribution of territory were challenged by developed states that lacked colonies and by subject peoples who wished to overthrow them. The collapse of commodity prices in the 1930s and the disruption caused by World War II destroyed the fragile, collaborative basis of colonial power and set the scene for militant confrontations between rulers and subjects. Aspirations derived from Western liberalism and absorbed by urban elites led to demands for a new deal for the colonial world that the imperial powers could neither accommodate nor eliminate. Existing structures were again unable to control the expansive tendencies they had incubated. The crisis of modern globalization culminated in decolonization, which swept the territorial empires away after World War II. The outcome, which was part-cause and part-consequence, was a new phase: postcolonial globalization.

After 1898, the literature on the United States experiences an extraordinary change. The war itself is the subject of innumerable studies; the period of colonial rule that followed has no place in standard texts. Yet, the empire created in 1898, though undeniably small, was a diverse territorial empire of the kind that can be compared to other Western empires of the time. The comparison undertaken here shows that successive administrations in the United States, far from being exceptional, approached colonial rule with the same assumptions and employed the same techniques of management as were applied in the European empires, and borrowed from Britain in particular. The U.S. Empire experienced the same oscillations of fortune during two world wars and the world slump, and adopted similar policies toward nationalist "agitators" during and after the 1930s. Decolonization came after World War II at the same time and for the same reasons as it did in the case of the European empires. Yet, it was not until the formal empire was dissolved that the label "empire" was attached to the United States to describe its status as a superpower. As argued here, the designation is a misnomer. After 1945, the conditions that had sustained territorial empires ceased to apply. The United States, though a great power, was an aspiring hegemon operating in a postcolonial world. Commentators who seek historical guidance in shaping U.S. policy toward the ex-colonial world would do well to exchange Greece and Rome for the Philippines, Hawai'i, Puerto Rico, and Cuba.

POSTCOLONIAL GLOBALIZATION

Postcolonial globalization, the third and still current phase, began to make its presence felt in the 1950s. The international order changed in ways that altered established patterns of commerce and regional integration, questioned the sovereignty of the nation-state, and turned world opinion against imperial domination. Territorial empires became either redundant or unworkable. The term "postcolonial globalization" is applied here to the period after the end of formal colonial rule.[4] "Postimperial" is a possible alternative but one that might suggest that all forms of imperialism had been eliminated. This assertion would preclude a consideration of neocolonialism, the term commonly used to refer to the persistence of informal influence in the era following the decolonization of the Western territorial empires. "Post-industrial" is another possibility that undoubtedly reflects emerging trends in some developed economies, but misrepresents the character of the transition after World War II. The label is typically attached to the rise of finance and commercial services, but it fits neither Britain—where investment, distribution, and insurance had long been linked to empire, nor the United States—which was the world's principal exporter of manufactured goods at this time. The colonies, moreover, aspired to imitate their mentors: they wanted to install nation-states and shift their economies from agriculture to industry. "Postcolonial" suffers from the imperfections that attend all holistic terms, but nevertheless serves the purpose of the present discussion.

Elements of the new postcolonial order that appeared in chapters 10 and 14 can now be combined and extended. The decade after World War II witnessed the revival of the old colonial economies, as the imperial powers gave priority to securing raw materials and restoring their manufacturing capacity. The recovery of Europe and Japan, however, was unexpectedly rapid. By the late 1950s, a postwar reconstruction boom had transformed prospects for the international economy. Markets that had been reduced to rubble in 1945 presented new opportunities a decade later. Europe's "dollar gap," which was a legacy of wartime indebtedness, had been greatly reduced, and in the case of Britain closed. The market for petroleum and strategic minerals remained strong, but prices eased for a broad range of other primary products as demand slackened and the adoption of synthetic substitutes provided alternatives to commodities such as cotton and rubber. These developments, in turn, reduced import-purchasing power in the colonies and diminished their attraction as markets for Europe's traditional manufactured exports. The trend did not provide the imperial powers with sufficient grounds for abandoning their colonies, but it nevertheless reduced the barriers to decolonization and allowed other considerations to come to the fore.[5]

These considerations multiplied as the 1950s progressed. The cost of maintaining colonial rule in the face of nationalist opposition burdened the budgets of the major imperial powers. Britain and France were caught between conflicting commitments: on the one hand, the promise to improve welfare provision at home after World War II; on the other, the need to increase military expenditure to defend the imperial heritage. Fiscal imperatives obliged both countries to cut overseas defense spending. In Britain, rising costs and adverse publicity following news of atrocities committed in Kenya and other colonies eroded public support for empire. In France, militant anti-colonial radicalism combined with anti-tax populism obliged successive governments to offload the burdens of empire in Asia to a formidably proxy, the United States, while trying to hold the line in Algeria, the land that was to be forever French. Developments in the Cold War influenced these geopolitical decisions. By the close of the 1950s, the United States judged that the Western empires had ceased to be bulwarks of the Free World and were becoming aids to Soviet propaganda. The United Nations, which had been founded in 1945 primarily to represent the interests of the victorious Allies, was becoming stocked with ex-colonial states. At the Bandung Conference in 1955, a new group of non-aligned countries, headed by China and India, issued a declaration of independence in matters of foreign policy. The battle for hearts and minds turned strategic thinking toward decolonization. The imperial powers began to plan a postcolonial future that involved working with nationalists instead of against them.

The colonies viewed the same issues from a different angle. After World War II, nationalist leaders made the promotion of manufacturing a key element in their popular appeal. Manufacturing had greater potential than agriculture for adding value to the economy, reducing unemployment, and raising living standards. Modern industry became the talisman of the time. It symbolized a "new deal" that could be implemented once decolonization had been achieved. It was the route to full independence and the good life that colonial rule had advertised but failed to deliver. Direction of the new, diversified economy was to remain in the hands of governments. The difficulties of the 1930s had encouraged official intervention; the war years had produced command economies. These institutions and assumptions supporting them were carried into the postwar period. Weak states, a term applied to many of the Asian and African colonies, needed strengthening if the "war" on poverty was to be successful.[6] Only the strong state, which in practice became the big state, would have the necessary resources and authority to plan a new future for its liberated people. Utopian visions raised expectations to levels that exceeded pragmatic possibilities. Not for the first time, the rhetoric needed to galvanize independence movements was paired with the disillusion that followed the achievement.

Nationalist leaders couched these ambitions in the language of self-determination and, selectively, human rights.[7] In one sense, this was an old vocabulary. Self-determination was a cause brandished in the nineteenth century before receiving global publicity at the close of World War I. Human rights stemmed from the Enlightenment and found political expression in the French and American revolutions and in pacific reform movements, such as the abolition of slavery. The novelty after World War II was that these ideas were adopted and applied globally.[8] An influential network of international commentators endorsed principles of human rights and declared them to be universal; the leading international organization, the United Nations, translated them into policy. Large sections of humanity that had been excluded from human and civil rights on grounds of race, creed, gender, or poverty were accorded equality. Empires could no longer be defended by exercising a form of moral hegemony based on assumptions of racial supremacy. Of course, there was still a wide gap between principle and practice, but the debate placed a sharp sword in the hands of nationalist leaders who could attack colonial rule by citing the liberal ideals that the rulers themselves proclaimed as the justification for their imperial mission.

The colonial powers found that their room for maneuver was increasingly circumscribed. If they accepted that the values they stood for were applicable to their colonies, they were signing up to decolonization. If they denied these values, they risked provoking further outbursts of militant nationalism and driving their subjects into the welcoming arms of the Soviet Union. The dilemma produced different outcomes. In colonies of settlement, the political appeal of "kith and kin" compelled imperial governments to persist with policies of repression, even as the prospects of success diminished. Elsewhere, the colonial powers put their support behind "moderate" nationalists who were likely to be cooperative partners after independence. Neocolonialism was a belated thought that aspired to become a strategy. A new, informal empire was not planned in 1945 because the principal imperial powers had yet to put decolonization on the agenda.

The insular empire, as argued in chapter 14, should be included in this postwar story. There were, of course, differences between the experiences of the European imperial powers and that of the United States. The insular empire was small and made an insignificant contribution to the U.S. economy; management costs were equally trivial in relation to the huge resources at the command of the United States. With so little at stake, the United States was willing to allow the Philippines to become independent in 1946 in accord with the agreement made in 1934, and to contemplate offering independence to Puerto Rico too. Policy changed, not because the islands were vital to the needs of capitalism but because they acquired geopolitical and ideological significance in the emerging Cold War. Thereafter, the United States followed the same course as the European imperial powers in first suppressing radical nationalist movements of the type represented by the Huks in the Philippines and Albizu

Campos in Puerto Rico, and then supporting leaders like Ramón Magsaysay, Muñoz Marín, and Fulgencio Batista, whom those in Washington considered to be reliable allies in the Cold War.

Neocolonial intentions, however, rarely produced the anticipated results. Tiny though they were, the inhabitants of Lilliput were able to pin down Gulliver and use his strength to their advantage. Leaders in the Philippines charged a high price for enlisting in the Cold War. Puerto Rico secured funding from U.S. sources for Operation Bootstrap, which was one of the most ambitious (and now one of the most neglected) colonial development plans of the early postwar period. The insular empire was brought down by a mixture of economic discontent, frustrated expectations, and the ideological deficit incurred by the methods used to uphold the doctrine of racial supremacy. The brutality dispensed in Kenya and Algeria found an echo in Little Rock, which was especially embarrassing because it occurred at home. The political reaction that followed allowed Hawai'i to become an incorporated state. Cuba, the protectorate that could not be bludgeoned or bought, was cast into outer darkness.

The assessment offered so far is broadly consistent with the notion of imperial overstretch, which posits a causal relationship between rising expenditure and the subsequent decline of great empires.[9] The basic idea takes the form of a cost-benefit analysis drawn from principles of accounting, but can be expanded to include, for example, the psychic or moral considerations noted here. These, too, have credits and deficits. Great states benefit from occupying the "moral high ground" and lose credibility when they are overtaken by the changing tenor of the times. The United States was a minor imperial power with huge resources, but it was compelled to join the European states in terminating colonial rule in the insular empire and ending racial discrimination within its own borders to deal with the increasing moral deficit incurred as a result of the Cold War. Considerations of cost entered the accounts later on, as the attempt to achieve global hegemony became increasingly burdensome. The addition of the United States to the conventional list of decolonizing powers underlines the need to ensure that assessments of the end of the Western empires are fully global in scope. Decolonization was not confined to formal empires in Asia and Africa, but involved semi-colonies, such as China, and dominions, such as Canada, Australia, and New Zealand, which also achieved a great degree of effective independence at this time.[10] Similarly, the Cold War was not a separate episode in the history of the period, though this is how it is usually studied, but part of the wider process of decolonization suggested here.[11] The transition from modern to postcolonial globalization is a theme capacious enough to include both subjects.

Notwithstanding the merits of the idea of "overstretch," an analysis confined to adjusting the balance of accounts has its limits. In particular, it fails to capture crucial structural transmutations of the kind identified by Montesquieu, which have been central to the analysis presented in this study. The changes that occurred after World War II were not just oscillations within a given structure, but manifestations of novel forces that were to transform it. These developments can be discerned in the 1950s, as the foregoing discussion has indicated, though their full extent only became evident as the rest of the century unfolded. Nevertheless, by 1964 the noted economist, Gotfried Haberler, could describe "the third wave of world-wide integration and growth" that had begun after World War II, using language that today would be phrased in terms of globalization.[12]

The principal commercial developments are best summarized as long-run orders of magnitude to avoid the classificatory and allied problems that are inherent in the data.[13] Global trade grew at an unprecedented rate in the second half of the century, despite checks following the oil crises of 1973–1974 and 1979–1980. Increases in merchandise trade were complemented by the rapid expansion in the value of world trade in services, which rose nearly threefold between 1980 and 1995.[14] The "great expansion" brought the first major change in the composition of trade for more than a century as demand shifted from agricultural exports and raw materials (apart from petroleum) to manufactures. The share of exports of foodstuffs and raw materials in total exports of world merchandise fell from 57 percent in 1950 to 26 percent in 1995, while the share of manufactures rose from 43 percent to 74 percent during the same period.[15] The indications are that the (net barter) terms of trade also moved against a number of important agricultural exports, beginning in the 1960s and accelerating from the 1970s onward.[16]

The aggregate data conceal the full significance of these trends. One notable development from the 1950s was the growth of inter-industry and intra-regional trade among the leading economies. Advanced technology, increasing specialization, and rising incomes drew the economies of Western Europe, North America, and Japan closer together in what became known as the "triad" of rich regions. An associated development, the growth of transnational corporations, made its mark from the 1970s. Large corporations first took advantage of the recovery in Europe, where they could realize economies of scale and apply strategies of vertical and horizontal integration. Subsequently, they spread to the former colonial and semicolonial countries, as newly independent governments removed imperial restrictions and diversified their foreign trading partners. Foreign

direct investment grew rapidly, especially in Asia, typically to participate in new manufacturing ventures. The composition of trade within
the triad altered as traditional consumer goods gave way to capital goods
(especially engineering products) and intermediate goods that contributed to complex final products, such as motor vehicles. The "Buy British"
campaign launched in 1968 collapsed soon after it began, when its supporters surprised themselves by discovering that few of the staple manufactures they wished to protect were produced entirely at home, even at
that date. The campaign's T-shirts, it turned out, were made in Portugal.

A further departure was the growth of exports of manufactures from
former colonies and semi-colonies, particularly those in Asia, which increased after 1960 and doubled in (current) value between 1980 and 2011.
By 2015, with the addition of China's weighty contribution, Asia as a
whole accounted for almost one-third of the world's visible trade. By then,
too, the triad had been joined by the BRICS, an acronym for a group of
late-start (or, in the case of Russia, re-start) countries that traded with
the triad but were independent of it.[17] Diversification, improved communications, and rising demand for labor produced a dramatic reversal of
migration flows. The main direction of international migration from the
mid-nineteenth century had been from Europe to various neo-Europes
around the world. This pattern continued immediately after World War II.
From about 1960, however, the current ran the other way: from the former colonies and semi-colonies to Europe and the United States. Whether
permanent or temporary, legal or illegal, the presence of newcomers has
influenced host communities in ways that were rarely anticipated and became apparent only after they became established. The empire came back
long before it began to strike back.

These developments have had important consequences for the global
balance of payments. By the close of the twentieth century, Asia and the
Middle East had positive balances on their visible trading accounts; the
United States had a large and growing deficit. The advanced economies
continued to dominate invisible trade (principally commercial services
and income from foreign investments), and most, with the considerable
exception of the United States, accumulated surpluses on this account.
Capital markets, however, grew rapidly in the leading developing countries, and capital exports followed. In 2015, the BRICS formed the New
Development Bank with headquarters in Shanghai. What the Bandung
Conference signified for world politics half a century previously, the new
bank signified for world economic development in the twenty-first century.

Economic changes interacted with far-reaching political developments.
The most notable innovation affecting the character of globalization

was the rapid growth of international and regional institutions. The origins of contemporary governmental and nongovernmental international organizations can be traced to the nineteenth century, if not earlier, but it was only after World War II that they increased markedly in number and size, and acquired permanence, visibility, and influence.[18] The leading institution, the United Nations, created a multiplicity of substantial subsidiaries, all of which had the potential to intrude on national sovereignty. The Commonwealth and the Union française attempted to update and bring a measure of equality to old imperial structures. The institutions arising from the Bretton Woods conference aimed to restore order to the world economy after the disasters that had accompanied two world wars and an intervening world slump. The International Monetary Fund (IMF) underwrote temporary imbalances in payments among participants in the postwar monetary system, which fixed exchange rates in relation to gold backed by the U.S. dollar. The International Bank for Reconstruction and Development (IBRD), which became part of the World Bank, supplied loans for development, initially to help the recovery of Western Europe and subsequently to provide foreign aid on an unprecedented scale.

Numerous regional organizations appeared in response to the changing needs of the postwar order. The largest and most ambitious of these, known today as the European Union (EU), began in 1952 primarily as an agency for encouraging economic integration. By 2015, the six founding states had been joined by twenty-two others, and the aims of the organization had expanded to include closer political union. In addition to encouraging the free movement of commerce, people, and capital, the EU spawned a European Parliament, a European Commission, a European Court, a European Central Bank, a common currency, and European citizenship. It is the first, and so far the only, regional institution that comes close to fitting the idea of a postmodern state.

Other regional organizations, though more limited, were nevertheless departures from previous conceptions of national sovereignty. The Association of Southeast Asian Nations (ASEAN), which was formed in 1967, started with an agenda that covered regional security as well as economic integration. The ten member states have now endorsed free-trade agreements with China, Korea, Japan, Australia, and New Zealand, and have begun a campaign to promote a sense of regional identity. On the other hand, the North American Free Trade Agreement (NAFTA), which was signed in 1994, has remained faithful to its limited mandate, which was to reduce barriers to trade and investment among its three members: the United States, Canada, and Mexico. Nevertheless, cross-border commercial agreements have implications for national sovereignty. As the experience of NAFTA shows, transnational corporations may challenge national regulations, such as those protecting the environment or providing public services, on the grounds that they increase costs and unfairly impede trade.[19]

The presence of international organizations, transnational corporations, and immigrants from different cultures has confused the concept of the nationality and placed a question mark over the paramountcy of the founding ethnie. In some cases, sections of the local population have reasserted provincial loyalties as a means of defense against foreign influences that national governments have either encouraged or failed to control.[20] The trends, however, are not just in one direction.[21] Regional organizations can also promote the national interests of the leading members, as has happened, arguably, in the case of the EU. Transnational organizations can work harmoniously with and bolster the power of national governments, as has been suggested with respect to the United States. Anxieties about the loss of sovereignty can stimulate a revival of nationalism, as is also evident in the United States, as well as in many countries in Western Europe. The nation-state is not dead and may not be dying. What can be said is that, whereas in the nineteenth century globalization and the nation-state were mutually supportive, today postcolonial globalization presents a challenge to sovereignty that will change the concept of nationality, redefine the national interest, and in these ways alter the character of the state itself.

These trends have had a profound effect on the former colonial states. Leaders of anti-colonial movements aspired to create their own nation-states, and for the most part did so within the borders they inherited. The partition of India and the subsequent division of Pakistan were sizable exceptions, but the greatest obstacles to national unity arose from internal regional and ethnic divisions, which acquired greater prominence after the departure of the colonial power. Alternative affiliations, such as pan-Arabism and pan-Islamism, further complicated the task of nation-building within borders that were often arbitrary and contested. Consequently, new states had great difficulty creating a public sphere that was accepted and respected. Government itself became a resource that produced contracts and employment; politics became the art of capturing sources of redistribution monopolized by the center. Inevitably, too, heightened expectations fell precipitously as problems previously attributed to colonial rule persisted after independence and in some cases intensified. Countries that depended on agricultural exports faced particular difficulties as their terms of trade deteriorated and their products met tariff barriers in the developed world.[22]

The presence of transnational corporations was an additional complication. Diversification invariably required inputs of foreign capital and skills. The activities of foreign companies, however, proved to be controversial. Some critics pointed to the opportunities for corruption arising from joint ventures associated with policies of "indigenization." Others accused transnational corporations of exploiting the local labor force and encouraging a new "drain" of wealth from poor countries by repatriating profits to parts of the world that were already rich. Seen from this angle, political independence had perpetuated economic dependence, which commentators referred to as "neocolonialism."

Governments in the new states responded by applying firm measures to assert central authority. In some cases, civilian authorities were closely associated with the military; in others, they were ousted from office at gunpoint. The result was a drift toward autocratic control in much of the ex-colonial world. The tradition of John Locke, which held that human rights were primarily individual, took a different contractual turn, whereby the state became the custodian and arbiter of the rights its citizens could exercise. After independence, the former imperial powers, having jettisoned the opprobrium attached to empire, began to call their former dependencies to account for failing to uphold the liberal, democratic values they had once proclaimed. The irony manifested itself in new forms of Western intrusion, often referred to as "liberal imperialism."[23] Recipients who opposed intervention claimed that such actions were merely a cover for neocolonialism. The conundrum was left dangling: if there were universal values (though not all parties subscribed to the proposition), how far were foreign powers and international organizations justified in intervening in the affairs of sovereign states to ensure that they were upheld?

The economic, political, and cultural developments sketched here evolved in a staggered and uneven fashion, as the history of the once ubiquitous label, "Third World," illustrates. The term was invented during the Cold War to describe countries that were not affiliated with either the United States or the Soviet Union, and was later adapted to refer to underdeveloped or developing countries. Today, it has ceased to be a useful descriptor of the diversity that is one of the chief characteristics of the developing world, and is being withdrawn from circulation.[24] Parts of Asia, for example, are several rungs up the development ladder, whereas much of Africa has had difficulty establishing a foothold, which is why development economists have focused increasingly on the continent's "bottom billion."[25]

The differences between the imperial era and the postcolonial world that succeeded it should now be apparent. The "classic" exchange of colonial raw materials for basic consumer goods has ceased to dominate world trade.[26] Manufacturing has spread to parts of the former colonial world; new financial centers have appeared beyond Europe and the United States. Regional integration has replaced colonial ties that bound dependencies to imperial centers. Migration has brought settlers from the former colonies and semi-colonies to the old imperial homelands. Self-determination has validated new nation-states; advocates of human rights have established principles of equality. Doctrines of racial supremacy have ceased to provide legitimacy for imperial and other forms of political domination. The complex ties that integrate the world in the twenty-first century are increasingly managed by international governmental organizations, which are no longer exclusively Western in membership, and by transnational corporations, which may originate outside Europe and the United States.

The result has been a remarkable transformation of the global order. The leading Western powers have become reliant on inflows of overseas capital, particularly from Asia, and especially from China. In effect, if not in intent, credit supplied by China has become a major support of U.S. global leadership and, indirectly, of the military interventions associated with it. Britain, once the greatest of the territorial empires, has experienced a particularly dramatic loss of independence as former colonies and semi-colonies have practiced their own version of informal influence, beginning after World War II with the United States and continuing today with China and India.

The projected closure in 2016 of one of the largest steelworks in Europe, located in the Welsh town of Port Talbot, provides a parable of the decline and fall of empires. The Tata Group, the owners of the plant, was founded in Mumbai in 1868 by members of a Parsi family who had prospered under the auspices of the British Raj. By 2015, the group had branches all over the world, had diversified into a wide range of manufacturing activities, and had become one of the largest global producers of steel. Profits, however, turned into losses in the face of declining world demand and competition from China, which in 2015 produced no less than half the world's output of steel. In the mid-nineteenth century, Britain, then the largest producer of manufactured goods, forced China to open its doors to "free trade." A century and a half later, it was the British government's turn to complain vociferously about the "unfair dumping" of Chinese steel, which cost the jobs of many thousands of workers employed by an Indian company located in Wales.[27]

Both Adam Smith and Karl Marx could claim accuracy for their forecasts, even though they would almost certainly attribute the outcome to different causes. For Smith, international specialization was the key to increasing productivity. For Marx, the dynamic of capitalism, expressed through imperialism, would first trample over backward societies and then bring progress. Montesquieu could now add a chapter to his own work showing how the globalization of economic life has put current political structures under strain. The nation-state has struggled to adapt; new global and regional institutions are still works in progress. All three luminaries might agree, though this is a guess beyond literary license, that by the beginning of the twenty-first century a long transformation was under way and a great convergence was in prospect. Hegel, writing in the 1820s, equated modernity with what he called "world spirit," which he thought traveled from the Orient to the West, where it hovered over the "Germanic nations."[28] At the end of the nineteenth century, commentators in the United States, who were strongly influenced by German intellectual traditions, believed that the spirit of progress had migrated across the Atlantic. Today, it appears to be completing its circumnavigation of the globe and has reached what early admirers called Cathay. If so, the "mandate from heaven" has not been lost, but has just been awaiting renewal.

THE UNITED STATES:
THE ASPIRING HEGEMON

Contemporary observers are inclined to enlarge the importance of their own times and to compress the events of history. Commentators who have been understandably impressed by the global reach and formidable power of the United States exemplify this tendency by naming the twentieth century the "American century." As we have seen, however, the "century" did not begin until World War II, and no one can tell whether the United States will be more or less dominant in 2050 than it was in 1950.[29] It is possible, however, to venture a judgment about the extent to which the United States succeeded in exercising hegemonic authority during the second half of the twentieth century. Most specialists on the period are agreed that the United States reached "peak power" relative to its rivals during the thirty years after 1945, and it is principally this period that will be considered here. A full account would need to examine the role of the World Bank and its affiliates, assess the consequences of applying modernization theory, and inspect the record of the trans-national corporations.[30] These subjects are indeed relevant, but they also encompass broader questions of economic development that are beyond the remit of the present study.[31] The omission of these disputed examples of informal imperialism, however, does not diminish the case for concentrating on the period before rather than after the mid-1970s, when developments at home and abroad made it harder for the United States to achieve its foreign policy objectives.

World War II caused widespread devastation and huge loss of life. Most of Europe was flat on its back; large parts of the Middle East and Asia had suffered from war or hardship, or both; Japan had been singled out for special treatment delivered by nuclear bombs. The United States had made a crucial contribution to the success of the Allies, while also escaping invasion. As the world's leading military power, principal cred-itor, and largest producer of manufactured goods, the United States was exceptionally well placed to become the preeminent Western power in the postwar era.[32] U.S. agencies moved swiftly to establish the means of turning the vision into reality. Troop deployments in bases throughout the world provided visible reminders of U.S. military power; prohibitions on treaties that were judged to be potentially hostile placed a check on the foreign policies of sovereign states.[33] The institutions formed after the agreement at Bretton Woods in 1944 provided a secure base for cur-rencies linked to the dollar. The General Agreement on Trade and Tariffs (GAAT), signed in 1947, began the long process of liberalizing trade. The Marshall Plan dispensed financial assistance between 1948 and 1952. In 1949, the North Atlantic Treaty Organization (NATO) brought twelve countries together under the leadership of the United States to provide collective security against possible Soviet aggression. The World Bank and its affiliates provided financial aid in return for policy adjustments in the recipient countries.

Yet, even during this period, the gap between potential and effective power remained stubbornly wide. Washington's concept of a new Eu-rope that would be integrated but open to the world, develop a com-plementary export economy, and become sufficiently Americanized to produce loyal consumers instead of political dissidents was never fully realized. The resulting supranational structure was very different from the one the United States had in mind at the end of the war. States on the continent moved cautiously toward integration and made only limited concessions of sovereignty to the new supranational organizations. Their aim was not to satisfy the United States, but to resuscitate and fortify the nation-state.[34] By helping Western Europe to recover, the United States was able to recycle its huge stockpile of dollars and create a market for its exports. Before long, however, recovery gave Europe its own political voice and enabled its refurbished industries to penetrate the U.S. market. Washington's power, though theoretically overwhelming, was muted by the overriding need to secure reliable and effective allies in the Cold War.[35]

The British, though seen in Washington as loyalists among a clutch of uncertain allies, provided the first disappointment. Britain declined to take the lead, as the United States had hoped it would, in creating a new, integrated Europe because its ambitions remained with the empire and sterling.[36] Subsequently, Britain dismantled the Singapore naval base and refused to send troops to Vietnam, a decision that the United States regarded as being "negative, defeatist, and hypocritical."[37]

Washington was forced to compromise even in Germany, where U.S. power was exercised with little or no resistance. Initial plans for reducing Germany's industrial capacity and turning the country into a pastoral economy had to be jettisoned in favor of a major program of reconstruction.[38] "Non-fraternization" decrees and punitive "denazification" measures were abandoned; Nazi sympathizers were restored to positions of influence. Alfred Krupp, who had been convicted of war crimes and sentenced to imprisonment for twelve years, was released in 1951 and reinstated as head of his huge family conglomerate.

France acted with a degree of assertiveness that belied the fragility of her position in the immediate postwar years.[39] Under General de Gaulle's leadership, the French frequently stood in the way of Washington's plans for Western Europe. De Gaulle had no intention of contributing to a supranational Euro-state. Dante, Goethe, and Chateaubriand, the president observed dismissively, "would not have served Europe very well if they had been stateless, or if they had thought and written in some kind of integrated Esperanto or Volupük."[40] The British, de Gaulle thought, lacked the true European spirit and were likely to act as a proxy for the United States, which was a good reason for keeping them at bay. The sharp accuracy of this insight confirmed de Gaulle's unpopularity in London.

De Gaulle's ambition was for France to manage Europe in association with Germany, which would act as a redeemed but decidedly junior partner. Under the Monnet Plan, which General de Gaulle adopted in 1946, France captured a large slice of the steel and coal resources of the Ruhr and made the Saar region a protectorate, even though the Plan was partly funded by the United States and the loss of Saar conflicted with Washington's development program for Germany.[41] In 1954, France vetoed the proposed European Defense Community, which the United States had backed in the hope of reducing the cost of keeping its troops on the continent. Continuing concern over the influence of the U.S. military prompted France to withdraw its forces from NATO in stages between 1959 and 1966, to reach an accord with Germany on matters of defense, and to develop its own independent nuclear deterrent, which was first tested in 1960. France also rejected Britain's applications to join the European Economic Community (EEC) in 1963 and 1967, thereby frustrating Washington's long-standing hope of ensuring that Britain took a leading role in Europe.[42] Subsequently, the Community began to formulate an independent foreign policy, which helped to thaw the Cold War by fostering relations with countries in the socialist bloc.[43]

Other initiatives taken by the United States after 1945 were also diluted or qualified. The Marshall Plan was less effective in stimulating economic recovery than was once thought, and had consequences that were as varied as the countries it encompassed.[44] The recipients set a trend, which was to be followed by ex-colonial states in Africa and Asia, of diverting a proportion of the aid they received to fund purposes other than those Washington had specified.[45] The GAAT's efforts to liberalize trade stalled after the initial cuts in 1947, which were made mainly by the United States.[46] The next important reductions came with the Kennedy Round in the 1960s, though by then the EEC was strong enough to negotiate on behalf of all its members and won further concessions from the United States.[47] By the 1960s, too, initiatives within the EEC had already reduced trade barriers among members and added impetus to the economic recovery. In 1960, Britain, France, and West Germany between them accounted for 38 percent of the value of the world's visible exports, while the United States represented 28 percent.[48] The U.S. share of world exports of manufactures had fallen from 29 percent in 1953 to 13 percent in 1976. Western Europe also dominated world trade in commercial services, which in 1980 amounted to five times the value of the services attributed to the United States.[49]

In the face of economic trends and continuing political obstacles, the United States retreated from its initial ideal for a redesigned Europe.[50] The "Year of Europe," as Henry Kissinger, the Secretary of State, called 1973, when Britain finally joined the EEC, converted hope into disenchantment.[51] The EEC, led by France, resisted U.S. demands that Europe should meet an increased proportion of NATO's defense costs.[52] International tensions arising from the fourth Arab-Israeli War and the oil embargo imposed by OPEC increased the differences between Europe and the United States. Britain chose to enhance its "special relationship" by supporting the United States. Continental Europe pursued its own path to progress by promoting the "Rhenish" version of capitalism in preference to the "Anglo" version, which followed the U.S. model in seeking to minimize the role of the state. [53] Even after joining Europe in 1973, the British found it much harder to bridge the Channel than to cross the Atlantic.

While wrestling with the unfamiliar intricacies of European politics, Washington became enmeshed in the even more inscrutable ways of East Asia. China's Long March from semicolonial subordination to effective independence in 1949 transformed Washington's geopolitical calculations throughout the region. Following the unexpected success of the Chinese Revolution and the hasty exodus of the nationalists to Taiwan, the United States scrambled to halt the further spread of communist influence throughout the region.[54]

These developments confirmed Japan's new role as the bulwark of the West. Japan, like Germany, had been flattened, had lost the means of basic subsistence, and had no choice but to comply with the demands of the large U.S. occupying force.[55] The United States initiated a series of political innovations: a new constitution, which came into effect in 1947, retained the emperor but made him subject to parliament, abolished the hereditary aristocracy, granted women the vote, and committed Japan to a pacific foreign policy. Complementary policies introduced Western liberal principles into education and promoted Christianity.[56] Economic strategy began by proposing to reduce Japan's industrial capacity, but by 1948 had reversed course, as it had in Germany, and embraced a program of development. Without development, Japan would continue to need costly food aid, would be unable to deal with its considerable trade deficit, and could not serve as a sturdy ally in the Cold War.[57] The onset of the Korean War in 1950 accelerated the process of rehabilitation. Reparations were virtually eliminated. A new industrial policy encouraged coal-mining, steel production, petrochemicals, electrical power, and shipping.[58] Radical land reform aimed to raise output by dividing large estates and creating a multiplicity of smallholders, who became owners rather than tenants. In 1952, when the U.S. occupation ended, Japan's recovery was under way and the economic "miracle" that was to follow was already in sight.

These were considerable achievements. They were made possible, however, by rebuilding and adapting existing state institutions and with the cooperation of key Japanese interest groups.[59] An informal conservative alliance, headed by the emperor, was installed to keep both right-wing militarists and left-wing communists at bay. Large family-owned cartels (known as *zaibatsu*), which had been scheduled for dissolution at the beginning of the occupation, were assigned the task of leading the new development policy. The zaibatsu, in turn, ran the Liberal Democratic Party (LDP), which held power for the rest of the century. Despite its name, the LDP represented the interests of a conservative oligarchy that drew electoral strength from big business, company workers, and the new generation of smallholders. As in the Philippines, the leadership was adroit at using the fear of communism to extract political subsidies from the United States.[60] Japanese governments agreed to a program of domestic rearmament in the 1950s in exchange for further financial support, and negotiated access to the U.S. market while retaining restrictions on imports into Japan. Having blocked trade with China, the United States had to open its own door to support Japan's export-led development plan.[61] Elements of American consumer culture were willingly absorbed, but core values were retained and strengthened. Traditional social customs were reaffirmed; Christianity made little progress. Corporate capitalism, Japan's version of Rhenish capitalism, prevailed over American individualism. The Constitution of 1947 was sufficiently un-American to include rights to education, welfare, and work.

After a chaotic start, Japan's former colony, Korea, was reshaped in similar ways.[62] Decolonization, which resulted from the defeat of Japan, was followed by civil war between nationalists with differing views on rebuilding the unity that had characterized the country for more than a thousand years. The Allies' response was to divide Korea into two military zones in 1945 and place it under trusteeship. The loss of unity and independence provoked mass protests against military rule, but failed to prevent the formal partition of the country into North and South in 1948. Partition was accompanied in the South by a purge of radical elements and the installation in 1948 of a strongly conservative president, Syngman Rhee, who was also the head of the Liberal Party. The Korean War reinforced Rhee's authoritarian instincts. The *chaebols* were restored to prominence in South Korea, as the zaibatsu were in Japan. These family-owned monopolies cooperated closely with South Korea's governing party, which in turn had close links with Washington.[63] The Party's name was a misnomer of Orwellian stature: Rhee ruled by oppression punctuated by culls of dissidents, which secured his own position while also meeting Washington's Cold War priorities. In return, Rhee received massive U.S. aid, which he deployed to reinforce a version of authoritarian rule that substituted economic growth for democracy.[64]

When Rhee was overthrown in 1960, the generals who succeeded him applied the same techniques in governing the country between 1961 and

1988. Trade concessions in the U.S. market encouraged exports. When Washington began to restrict the entry of Korean and Japanese textiles in 1969–1971, Korea responded by developing heavy industries.[65] The "Miracle on the Han River," built largely on indigenous institutions and including a strong element of central planning, followed the route taken by Germany and Japan.[66]

Elsewhere, the United States exerted influence but obtained mixed results. As detailed in chapters 10 and 14, one of the most important concessions the United States made to its principal allies at the end of World War II was to support the reconstruction of their empires. This was not a war aim, but it became a peace necessity. To their surprise and relief, after 1945 British and French governments found that they no longer had to devise fresh ways of defending the imperial mission. The priority of building an alliance of states in the Free World to combat the expansion of the Soviet Union took precedence over the ideals of liberation and self-determination. The imperatives of the Cold War ensured that imperial preferences and the Sterling Area were allowed to continue, contrary to U.S. wartime intentions. The protectionist arrangements France had established with its overseas territories were rehabilitated and extended, and a new Franc Zone was created to help rebuild the economy and conserve scarce hard currency.

The Netherlands, too, benefited from U.S. support in seeking to reestablish control of Indonesia. However, when it became clear that Dutch troops were likely to be defeated by nationalist forces, Washington threatened to impose financial sanctions if The Hague did not agree to relinquish power.[67] The Netherlands ended its long history of colonial rule shortly after being reinstated. The Republic of Indonesia was established as an independent state in 1949 under the presidency of Sukarno, its most famous nationalist.

Sukarno began by presiding over a fragile form of representative government, which was restricted to what became known, ominously, as "guided democracy" in 1957. This development did not trouble the United States, but Sukarno's increasingly outspoken anti-imperialism and drift toward the Communist Party to counterbalance the military, and to the Soviet Union and China to solicit aid, caused growing concern in Washington, while his "nationalization spree" in 1964 prompted Congress to call for action.[68] The CIA sponsored rebellions in 1957 and 1958, and in 1965 successfully goaded the Communist Party and the Army into a conflict that ended with a massacre of communist supporters and the effective removal of Sukarno in the following year.[69] Sukarno's successor, General Suharto, was firm both in his hostility to communism and in his opposition to parliamentary democracy. Under his rigid command, military modernization entrenched the military more successfully than it modernized the country.[70]

The French Empire was the scene of the most substantial intervention of the Cold War, when the United States decided to prop up French rule in Indo-China.[71] The Korean War took containment to Asia; the Vietnam War carried it to the point of self-destruction. After World War II, the United States chose to back French ambitions to regain Indo-China in preference to supporting Ho Chi Minh, a nationalist whose main aim at that stage was self-determination and democratic reform. Ho turned to the Soviet Union and China to win the backing he needed; the United States responded by raising its stake in the contest to quagmire levels. Following the defeat of France in 1954, successive presidents went "all in." At its peak in 1969, the United States had more than half a million troops in Vietnam; by 1975, the U.S. Air Force had dropped 10 million bombs on the country.[72] Nearly 60,000 U.S. troops were killed in the course of the war; many more were wounded. Almost 3.5 million Vietnamese civilians and soldiers died; countless more were disabled and displaced.

By 1973, the United States had been defeated; two years later, South Vietnam surrendered to the North. Washington spent an estimated $1.5 billion fighting a war that neither advanced the cause of capitalism nor defended a strategic base of any importance. The war was a massive investment in the principle of national security, which married a long-standing fear of foreign influences to a newfound ambition to control them at their source.[73] Far-reaching though they were, the consequences of the war did not extend to the creation of a U.S. empire in South Asia; nor did they deliver the hegemonic influence Washington hoped for.

When pro-imperial policies ceased to be an asset in the Cold War, the United States faced the prospect of stabilizing an array of colonies and satellites that were seething with anti-imperial sentiment or in various stages of upheaval—or a combination of the two. Examples drawn from the Middle East, Africa, Latin America, and its own former colonies show that "holding the line" was the best outcome that could be anticipated. Triumphs, once confidently anticipated, had ceased to be realistic ambitions.

The Middle East joined the ranks of unwilling participants in the Cold War when the two major protagonists entered the region in the 1950s. The United States marked its arrival with a dramatic formal intervention in 1953, when the CIA organized the removal of Mohammad Mossaddegh, the democratically elected prime minister of Iran, who had just increased his local popularity by nationalizing the oil industry.[74] The coup benefited U.S. oil interests, whose informal influence had grown with the rise of the Arabian American Oil Company (ARAMCO).[75] With Washington's support, ARAMCO was able to reduce Britain's dominance of the region's oil reserves.[76]

This example, though striking, sent a misleading signal: as it turned out, the United States was not on its way to predominance in the Middle East. Washington's influence was confined mainly to Iran and Saudi Arabia and was far from complete in those countries. Iran, though first identified as a compliant agent of U.S. policy, soon became a problem. The Shah, Mohammad Reza Pahlavi, who took control of the government after Mossaddegh had been ousted, was an ambitious nationalist who used oil revenues to modernize his country.[77] When the United States supported Israel during the Arab-Israeli War of 1973, OPEC reacted by raising prices, just as the United States was becoming a large-scale importer of oil for the first time.[78] Increased oil prices were consistent with Washington's strategic aims to the extent that they enabled Iran to equip a large modern army.[79] The problem was that buoyant prices were even more of a bonus for the Shah because they increased his scope for independent action. In 1977, Washington turned in frustration to Saudi Arabia, after the Shah had rejected an appeal to reduce the price of oil. The Saudis, who welcomed the opportunity to wound their main rival in the region, engineered a fall in prices that contributed to the removal of the Shah in 1979.[80] The upshot of U.S. policy was to help install a hostile government in Iran while obliging Washington to ally with a regime in Saudi Arabia that could scarcely be advertised as an example of liberty and democracy. The CIA first used the term "blowback" in 1954 to describe the possible consequences of the removal of Mossaddegh.[81] Washington evidently thought that "next time it would be different."

Elsewhere in the region, U.S. influence was either limited or subject to countervailing forces. However principled it was, the decision to recognize the state of Israel, followed by overt support after the Six-Day War in 1967, alienated the Arab world. Thereafter, the United States had no chance of winning hearts and minds in the region.[82] Instead, Washington had to appeal to wallets and to the hope that calculations of local advantage would deliver a measure of qualified collaboration. From the late 1960s, too, Big Oil had to adjust to the rise of OPEC and to differences with Washington over priorities.[83] The effective nationalization of the oil industry in the 1970s obliged foreign companies to work with regional governments. The preoccupation with winning the Cold War placed strategy above economics and weakened the link between the U.S. government and business interests. Washington's need for support in the region also led policy-makers to encourage Britain to stay on rather than move on. The invitation suited Britain's reduced but continuing ambitions, which were repositioned to concentrate on the Gulf states.[84] The assumption that the two powers had shared interests, however, was only partly correct. They differed over support for Israel and over Saudi policy toward the coastal states on the Saudi peninsula.[85] Meanwhile, Washington poured money into both Israel and Egypt without being able to control the foreign policies of either state. The U.S. presence in the Middle East fell far short of being hegemonic, even when it was at its most extensive.

The United States and the Soviet Union arrived late on the African scene.[86] The United States made its presence felt with a signature statement: in 1960, the CIA organized the overthrow and subsequent murder of Patrice Lumumba, the democratically elected prime minister of the Congo, shortly after the country gained independence from Belgium.[87] Lumumba's successor, Mobutu Sese Seko, installed a military dictatorship and fashioned a close alliance with the United States that lasted until 1997, when he was forced into exile. Despite growing reservations, Washington also felt obliged to provide financial support for French efforts to retain control over Algeria to preserve the stability of its ally in Europe.[88] The policy changed shortly before Algeria won independence in 1962, but by then Algerian sympathies lay with Moscow rather than Washington.[89] Other interventions, clandestine and overt, followed. The most extensive was the backing given to pro-Western parties in Angola during the 1970s. The decision alienated other nationalist groups, which turned to the Soviet Union, China, and Cuba for support.[90] Military assistance from both sides brought turmoil to the country and death to many of its inhabitants. U.S. policy failed: Washington's favored candidates were defeated and Congress halted further military backing in 1975. Assertive policies were no more successful elsewhere. An exercise that began as humanitarian intervention in Somalia in 1992, ended in political entanglements and the withdrawal of U.S. troops in the following year.[91]

U.S. policy toward Africa lacked coherence. Republicans and Democrats had different attitudes toward the continent; presidential views oscillated as the occupants of the White House changed places.[92] Given its extensive commitments in Asia, Washington was obliged to allow Britain and France scope to manage the affairs of the Free World in Africa.[93] The franchise suited both imperial powers, which had continuing plans for the continent. The Suez Crisis in 1956 did not confirm the paramountcy of the United States, as is often thought. France resented the exposure and humiliation, and reacted by strengthening its position in sub-Saharan Africa.[94] Britain responded similarly by devising new ways of perpetuating her influence and by attempting to manipulate U.S. policy toward the continent.[95] Manipulation was not always needed. The two powers had shared interests and attitudes that brought them together on some major issues, including the largest of them all: South Africa. A sense of racial affinity, a common desire to protect huge investments (especially in minerals), and joint hostility to communism ensured that Britain and the United States supported the apartheid regime almost to the last moment. Congress finally passed the Comprehensive Anti-Apartheid Act in 1986; Britain made its own way to the same conclusion.[96] By leading from behind, however, both powers had forfeited goodwill in Africa and had to devise new ways of making friends and influencing people in the postcolonial world.

The case of Latin America was distinctive to the extent that the United States had long claimed special rights in what ethnocentric commentators called their "backyard."[97] Unlike the position in Asia and Africa, policy-makers in Washington found diplomatic cover for their actions in Theodore Roosevelt's Corollary to the Monroe Doctrine.[98] Dramatic events in Cuba galvanized U.S. policy. The success of the Revolution in 1959 alarmed Washington and inspired radical movements throughout Latin America. In 1961, President John F. Kennedy responded by launching the Alliance for Progress, which aimed to bring development and democracy to the region through a combination of financial aid and American know-how. This alternative to the Cuban vision drew on Operation Bootstrap, the development program in Puerto Rico that was Latin American in spirit and capitalist in substance. The pacific character of the Alliance was strengthened by overt and covert political and military involvement in the affairs of the Latin American republics. In Central America and the Caribbean, the United States reinvigorated a tradition of "filibustering" that went back to the 1850s. What became the Reagan Doctrine of direct foreign intervention on behalf of political parties that favored the United States produced numerous instances of military involvement between the 1950s and the 1980s, when smaller republics, such as Nicaragua, El Salvador, and Guatemala, experienced the destructive consequences of great power rivalry.[99] Military action in the larger republics of South America, though more limited, was expressed in clandestine support from the CIA, which helped to depose the left-wing president of Brazil, João Goulart, in 1963, and remove the democratically elected Marxist president of Chile, Salvador Allende, in 1973.[100]

The Alliance for Progress had few achievements and became defunct in 1973.[101] The scale and complexity of the development problems facing

Latin America far exceeded the aid available, which mainly benefited large U.S. corporations. American "know-how" was no more equal to the task of nation-building than it had been in the insular empire earlier in the century. The various military interventions succeeded in removing a series of governments that Washington considered to be unfriendly, but also generated unforeseen adverse consequences.[102] Military aid was used by local political interests to install authoritarian governments, which provided a congenial environment for large foreign firms but had no interest in advancing democracy.[103] This development eventually produced a nationalist reaction that fueled anti-American sentiment, strengthened the advocates of human rights, and helped to subvert military rule.[104] At the turn of the twenty-first century, some commentators noted that a number of Latin American states were distancing themselves from policies advocated by the United States, the World Bank, and the IMF.[105] Others wondered if the United States was "losing" Latin America.[106] Introspection and globalization do not go well together.

The United States also had to align its own former colonial territories with the needs of the Cold War. As noted in the previous chapter, the four principal islands compelled Washington's attention after 1945 because they were all important military bases. Hawai'i, the home of the U.S. Pacific Fleet, was secured by being incorporated as a state of the Union. As Hawai'i was pulled in, Cuba was pushed out and, as far as possible, isolated, though the United States retained its controversial lease on the naval base in Guantánamo Bay. Puerto Rico received Commonwealth status and lavish financial support in exchange for continuing loyalty and the use of bases on the islands of Culebra and Vieques. At the same time, the proximity of Puerto Rico to Cuba heightened Washington's nervousness about the spread of communism and led the FBI to mount an extensive campaign against the island's nationalists. The Philippines, which acquired unexpected strategic prominence following the Chinese Revolution in 1949, provided the site for the vast Clark Air Field in exchange for commercial and financial concessions.

With the end of the Cold War, and after considerable pressure from local activists, the bombing site on the island of Kaho'olawe in Hawai'i in 1990 was closed and turned into a nature reserve. The island of Vieques in Puerto Rico followed the same course in 2003, and the nearby U.S. naval base at Ceiba was transferred to Florida in 2004.[107] Clark Air Field ceased to be a U.S. base in 1991, when the Philippine government refused to renew the lease.[108] The movements that led to these closures were local expressions of nationalist sentiment, and were especially notable in Hawai'i, where the indigenous community gained inspiration from the progress made by First Peoples elsewhere.[109] The Hawaiian Renaissance, which began in the 1970s by reasserting indigenous forms of cultural expression, developed by the close of the century into a movement to secure political autonomy within the United States.[110]

In other matters, the islands reflected both the shared features and the diversity of the West's former colonies elsewhere. The most important commonality was the falling price and profitability of primary exports, and of sugar in particular, which affected the export earnings of all the islands from the 1970s onward.[111] Other major crops, such as pineapples and abaca, were similarly affected. As importers of petroleum, the islands also had to grapple with the rapid increase in prices from the 1970s. The principal difference lay in their varying responses. In 1959, Hawai'i's stars were in the ascendant. Incorporation as a state provided the political security investors needed. Economic opportunity appeared at the same time in the form of cheap air transport, which transformed the island's prospects. The result was the foundation of the great industry of the postcolonial age: tourism.[112] As Hawai'i diversified, it also became a secondary financial center, supplying funds to businesses elsewhere in the Pacific.

The Philippines, on the other hand, struggled to adapt to the postcolonial world. The political fragility of the islands at the point of independence in 1946 was further tested by militant secessionist movements in the Muslim south, which reacted against the assimilationist character of the nation-building program introduced by the central government in the Christian north.[113] Martial law, which followed in 1972, spurred the insurgents to greater endeavor. Economic diversification had only limited success; population increase fed into high unemployment, which Filipinos dealt with by migrating internationally, as well as to other regions in the Pacific, including Hawai'i.[114] The spacious confidence with which Roosevelt and Taft proclaimed the "civilizing mission" that was to transform the Philippines had long evaporated. Modest achievements were offset by other features of the colonial legacy: the expansion of an authoritarian state, the perpetuation of the politics of oligarchy, and the descent into kleptocratic indulgence under the rule of Ferdinand Marcos.

Cuba's fortunes were determined largely by the Revolution of 1959. Cuba already had a promising tourist industry, but it was eliminated after the Revolution, when the United States placed an embargo on trade with the island. Thereafter, the sugar industry survived on subsidies from the Soviet Union, which ceased in the 1990s, and help from Venezuela, which was cut, with the price of oil, in 2015. Despite these adverse conditions, Cuba set standards of education, welfare, and medical provision that enabled exports of these services to make a major contribution to the country's balance of payments.[115] The authoritarian political system that accompanied these developments was less oppressive than Sukarno's "guided democracy" but also no more successful than Puerto Rico's semi-free market in solving endemic economic problems. Cuba's economic prospects would brighten if the United States restored commercial relations, but the sentence imposed in 1959 has still to run its course and efforts to secure remission have so far been unsuccessful.[116]

Cuba's neighbor, Puerto Rico, also diversified into tourism, but continued to suffer from chronic unemployment and endemic poverty. The island is kept afloat by remittances from Puerto Ricans working in the United States and massive subsidies from the federal government. In 2016, however, the boat sank: Puerto Rico defaulted on nearly $1 billion of its public debt.[117] The plight of the island, which is in marked contrast to Hawai'i's prosperity, prevents Puerto Rico from becoming an incorporated state and confines support for full independence to a small minority of political activists.

There is no doubt that the United States was the single most influential world power during this period. There are abundant examples of military intervention, of the exercise of economic pressure, and of the spread of cultural influence. A long tradition of policy studies that begins in Washington, and often stays there, has emphasized the enveloping quality of the U.S. presence throughout the globe. An equally formidable anti-imperial tradition has attributed postcolonial ills to outside intervention. Both positions have merit, but need adjusting to take account of qualifications to the aims and outcomes of policy.

Washington's priority was to procure a series of security pacts that would keep the Soviet Union at bay. Rhetorical declarations of support for self-determination, democracy, and development, though often well-intentioned, were subordinated to the ideological commitment to defeat communism. To this end, the United States fought wars, arranged revolts, and mounted a campaign of cultural conversion after World War II. Victories were elusive; political intervention typically scored only short-term successes; the cultural crusade produced limited results.[118] In exercising informal influence, the United States had to make substantial concessions to retain the loyalty of its allies. Research on the history of the recipients of U.S. policies has revealed how the weak manipulated the strong: in exchange for military bases and compliant foreign policies, Washington was obliged to provide financial largesse and trade concessions, which the recipients used to bolster their political positions. The resulting pattern of assisted development went hand-in-hand with authoritarian rule. The priority of "military modernization" was stability, not democracy. Concessions made to friends, combined with the cost of defeating enemies, became a drain on U.S. resources that eventually sapped its authority.

It is important to remember, too, that large parts of the world were never candidates for subordination to the United States. If a map of the U.S. "empire" after 1945 were to be produced, it would have to omit Western Europe, the Soviet Union, the Eastern bloc, China, and India, to cite only the largest of the most unproblematic cases, and to place large question marks over other regions, where influence was limited and control elusive. The judgment that, at the end of the Cold War, "the United States enjoyed a degree of hegemony beyond George Washington's most extravagant dreams," stretches credibility.[119] The demise of a rival, however considerable, does not automatically convert the victor into an effective hegemon. The United States remained a superpower, but its hegemony was restricted in time and space. If dominance is limited, then decline is less precipitous. Put another way, unipolarity in international relations is rare, even assuming that it has existed for more than brief periods. Accordingly, judgments about the dominance and decline of great powers call for assessments of degrees of multipolarity, which in turn require that a balance is struck among relationships that are governed more by relativities than by absolutes.

CAPTAIN AMERICA: TO BE CONTINUED?

Captain America, the patriotic hero who fought the Axis powers in the 1940s, lives on.[120] He started life as a scrawny arts student in New York, applied to join the U.S. Army in 1941 but was rejected on medical grounds. Unlike Tarzan, whose genetic superiority assured his eventual success, or Charles Atlas, whose superhuman physique was built in the gym, Captain America was the product of scientific progress: an experimental serum, supplemented by "Vita-ray" treatment, turned him into a "super-soldier." Victory in World War II was followed by further exploits, as Captain America and his "Avengers" adjusted to the complexities of the postwar order. "The Captain," as he became known, rose above party politics.[121] His role, approved by the president, was to defend the fundamental American values of liberty and democracy against an array of enemies, including exceptionally alarming "cosmic entities." He tackled the job by deploying stunning military force across the world and inflicting widespread destruction in the cause of global freedom. This is mythology with a message: the United States continues to have a special mission to save the world; the pristine qualities of American values are threatened by evil conspiracies; war is the unavoidable cost of preserving freedom.

From the 1970s, the United States operated in a world that had changed greatly since 1945.[122] The recovery of Europe and Japan diminished their dependence on the United States and increased their competitiveness in international trade. Costly wars in Korea and Vietnam and an ambitious program of foreign aid weighed on the U.S. Treasury. The rapid growth in the number of independent ex-colonial states in the 1960s and 1970s compelled Washington to abandon the idea that containment could be enforced at source throughout the world. As détente with the USSR and China followed, commercial competition became more important than military confrontation. The United States became increasingly dependent on foreign trade. In 1970, imports and exports of goods and services accounted for just under 11 percent of GDP; in 2000, the figure had risen to 26 percent.[123] At the same time, the United States lost the competitive advantages it had enjoyed in 1945.[124] In 1971, Washington was obliged to abandon the system of fixed exchange rates inaugurated at Bretton Woods and to devalue the dollar. The move, however, did little to boost exports. The U.S. share of the world trade in manufactures declined; foreign goods penetrated the domestic market; large imports of petroleum began to feature in the balance of trade for the first time. The growth in productivity was too slow to arrest these trends. From the 1970s, the United States incurred a current account deficit that persisted for the remainder of the century and was met by borrowing from abroad.[125]

The consequences of these developments are debated and in any case need to be kept in proportion. To some extent, the gap between the United States and other powers was bound to narrow as they recovered from the destruction brought by war. Equally, the balance-of-payments deficit was not a pressing problem because the dollar retained its status as the leading reserve currency, despite the devaluation that occurred in 1971. The demand for dollars to settle global payments drew in foreign capital and provided the means for Washington to spend beyond the limits set by taxation and other recurring revenues. Consequently, the United States was able to meet potential balance-of-payments' crises by printing dollars to satisfy external demand. This "exorbitant privilege" helped to fund Washington's geopolitical strategy, including its massive military presence throughout the world.[126]

Nevertheless, perceptions matter in estimates of global standing, and from the 1970s onward commentators began to worry that the United

States was losing ground to resurgent foreign rivals. The 1980s saw a flurry of pessimistic comments about how and why the presumed hegemon had become a faltering giant. Astrologers read the signs: the United States was burdened by an industrial structure that had become conservative and inflexible; the national debt weighed heavily on taxpayers and weakened the hand of government at a time when the Cold War required it to be strong and resilient; high unemployment, widespread poverty, and racial discrimination spawned demoralizing and intractable social problems. Theorists of international relations pondered the irony that the altruism of the hegemon in supplying costly public goods, principally in the form of military protection, was leading to its downfall. As the sun set in the West, so it rose in the East. Japan was identified as the problem of the day and the power of the future: cheap Japanese imports alarmed producers in the United States; the inflow of Japanese investment was thought to undermine the independence of business and government alike. Commentators with an apocalyptic turn of mind claimed that doom was imminent: historical forces, it seemed, made a precipitous fall inevitable.[127] The American Century was about to be abruptly foreshortened; a new Pacific Century was in view.[128]

The prediction that the United States would fall from grace, or at least from preeminence, was falsified almost overnight by two wholly unforeseen developments: the crisis and stagnation of the Japanese economy, and the collapse of the Soviet Empire. When Japan subsided, the Pacific Century receded. When the Berlin Wall crumbled, the United States arose from the rubble as the lone superpower. In the course of the 1990s, base metal was transmuted into forms of silicon that carried the Dow Jones index to record levels. "Declinism," as it became known, was swiftly replaced by euphoria. Influential opinion in the United States was captivated by the claim that the victory of the Free World in the ideological battle that had been at the center of the Cold War signaled the "end of history."[129] Commentators elevated the United States to a new and higher status, that of a hyperpower. The term, though never precisely defined, was generally accepted to mean that the United States had become so dominant that it could act unilaterally. Cooperation with international organizations, such as the UN, was no longer necessary. The nation-state, personified by the United States, could project itself globally, as it had done in the days of the great Western empires. [130] A triumphalist literature promoted policies that aimed to make the "unipolar moment" permanent. The Project for the New American Century (1997–2006) advanced plans to consolidate U.S. military dominance and install Western versions of freedom and democracy in the Middle East.[131]

The mood of triumphalism lasted for little more than a decade. The destruction of the Twin Towers on September 11, 2001 demolished the illusion of effortless supremacy, but also presented an opportunity to demonstrate the power of military force to reorder the world, and to do so by "preemptive strikes," if necessary.[132] The spacious purpose, announced as a "war on terror," received a correspondingly capacious justification, which contrasted the forces of darkness with those of light. The ambitions of martial diplomacy, first expressed in the invasion of Iraq in 2003, died as casualties mounted. The U.S. Army toiled through the same sequence as its forgotten predecessors had done in the Philippines a century earlier. Confrontation with reality presented unexpected complications and revealed, veil by veil, the impossibility of the task the military had been ordered to undertake. After years of effort, widespread destruction, death, and misery, which also extended to Afghanistan, the United States reduced its aspirations, declared victory, and withdrew.[133] The mission unaccomplished left deep incisions that infected both regions with a degree of political turmoil that shows no signs of ending. "Irrational exuberance" is even more dangerous in foreign policy than it is in banking.

Commentators were right to feel a little of the "shock and awe" visited upon Iraq. The decision to invade Iraq produced an animated debate on the question of whether the United States was, or was becoming, an empire, and, if so, whether the assertion of paramountcy was an expression of the providential mission to bring liberty and democracy to the world, or an anachronistic imposition of the worst features of Western imperialism. The word "empire" became obligatory in the titles of the books that speedily appeared on the subject. Few writers, however, were aware that the debate that began in 2003 rehearsed arguments that had been advanced with equal fervor in 1898. Then, as a century later, a small group of Republican conservatives pumped up the pressure that led to war. Then, too, they were able to capitalize on a nationalist reaction to a crisis linked to foreign agency. The sinking of the *Maine* was to the Spanish-American War what the destruction of the Twin Towers was to the invasion of Iraq. In both cases, the forward party was able to draw support from domestic discontent and uncertainty about the future. Populism, conflicts between capital and labor, and unemployment made the 1890s a fraught decade. Foreign purchases of national assets, inflows of migrants from Central America, the loss of jobs caused by outsourcing, and of security and benefits for those who remained in employment, were among the anxieties that marked the 1990s.[134] On both occasions, too, the populace rallied behind the patriotic triumvirate of flag, faith, and family.

There was a decisive difference between the two cases, however: the global context had been transformed in the course of the twentieth century. The imperialism of the late nineteenth century expressed the trauma of transition from agricultural states to industrial nation-states. The protagonists were trying to save an emerging order from what they thought was immolation. Distant lands were acquired to assist the transition, whether by strengthening an incomplete sense of nationality or by serving economic purposes. Western empires, moreover, were dynamic agents of modern globalization. By 2003, on the other hand, industrial capitalism and the nation-state, though well established, were being challenged by the forces summarized here as postcolonial globalization. An imperial solution had ceased to be either appropriate or feasible. The reaction in Washington to the events of 9/11 showed that policy-makers had failed to understand that the age of territorial empires lay behind them and that neither democracy nor development could be delivered at gunpoint. Once again, *nemesis* followed *hubris*, though the tragedy that unfolded departed from Greek custom in visiting the consequences on the recipients rather than on the instigators.

As death, destruction, and debt mounted, the American public turned against the occupation of Iraq. By 2004, a majority thought that the venture had been a mistake; by 2007, the mood favored withdrawal; by 2011, U.S. troops had left. As the realities of a failing foreign policy began to imprint themselves, a mighty financial tsunami swamped the world in 2008. In the United States, as in Europe, the authorities lost control of a borrowing bonanza they had helped to initiate. Economies slowed; unemployment accelerated. These depressing events were joined by a third novelty: the rapid rise of China as an economic superpower with global political influence. As Chinese manufactures flooded the U.S. market, China's purchases of U.S. government debt averted a balance-of-payments crisis. The outlook changed further in 2015, when the BRICS consortium led by China and India founded the New Development Bank. The event caused consternation in Washington.[135] The new Bank aimed to bypass the IMF and the World Bank by offering financial support to developing countries. The prospect that the dollar might cease to be the reserve currency of choice came a little closer. Economists became increasingly preoccupied with the size of the federal debt and with Washington's ability to finance the U.S. balance-of-payments deficit by continuing to attract funds from abroad.[136]

These developments astonished the world, alarmed commentators and politicians in the United States, and raised doubts about whether the "American century" would run its full course. The immediate reaction to these novelties was the revival of "declinism," which reappeared with the economic crisis in 2008 and has continued to preoccupy commentators and policy-makers.[137] The arguments are familiar and need only be mentioned here. Optimists point out that the United States possesses a huge economy that is growing in absolute terms, if not relative to late-start rivals. It remains the world's leading military power, has considerable reserves of what has been termed "soft" power, and benefits from an open, inventive society.[138] Pessimists hold that China will soon match the United States in economic power. It is expanding its military power, extending its soft power, and founds its success on commercial dynamism that long antedates the rise of the West.[139] As they ponder the outlook, Washington's policy-makers are also aware that China's command capitalism advertises an alternative to the version prevailing in the United States. Cathay capitalism, Rhenish capitalism, and Muslim fundamentalist anti-capitalism between them ensure that the "end of ideology" has yet to take place and may have to be postponed once more—and perhaps indefinitely.[140]

The financial crisis accelerated two trends that had their origins in the late twentieth century: increasing inequality of incomes, and a reaction against globalization. Detailed research has shown that average pretax earnings of the bottom 50 percent of wage-earners in the United States scarcely improved between 1974 and 2014, whereas the top 10 percent enjoyed a rise of 231 percent.[141] As the American Dream faded; the politics of resentment made their appearance. Globalization became a threat rather than a promise. Foreign immigrants, foreign capital, and foreign goods were seen as destroying jobs and eroding values in the host society. Since pessimism in politics lacks stamina, the changing mood inspired a new message of hope. Donald J. Trump was elected president in 2016 on a nationalist platform and with a pledge to "make America great again."

The presidential election provided a dramatic illustration of the main theme of this study. What happened in the United States was distinctive but not unique: the same forces were at work in Europe. The economic crisis that struck in 2008 was a manifestation of the postcolonial world order, where finance rather than industry was the principal influence driving the world economy. Britain's decision to leave the EU in 2016 arose from the same causes that carried Donald Trump to the White House. Both events were populist reactions against neoliberal economic policies and the elites who were seen to have benefited from them. BREXIT can be translated as a plea to make Britain great again.[142] Both powers hope that restoring past glories, real and imagined, will erase unwanted features of the present.[143] The United States carries forward an image of its status that exaggerates the extent of its former dominance. It also harbors an ambition to recover a state of "splendid isolation" that is at variance with the seemingly irreversible degree of integration that binds the country to the rest of the world. Britain cherishes illusions that far exceed its shrinking power base. The "Special Relationship" melts hearts in London but leaves them unmoved in Washington. More than half a century ago, Harold Macmillan knew that the game was up. Following the failure of the Paris Summit in 1960, he realized that "Britain counted for nothing."[144] BREXIT implies that Britain's reliance on the United States will increase rather than diminish. Nostalgia for hegemony is itself an expression of the hegemony of nostalgia.

When history meets the present, social scientists are expected to make predictions, and historians are tempted to join them. At this point, however, it is worth recalling that Dante reserved the Fourth Chasm in the Eighth Circle of the Fraudulent for "augurers, diviners, astrologers, and prophets," who were "forced to walk backwards" for eternity with "their faces twisted around," as a punishment for trying to see a future that was unforeseeable.[145] Regrettably, all such forecasts are likely to be flawed or facile.[146] Social scientists generally extrapolate from points selected from the recent past that reflect the transient mood of the moment. Historians take a much longer view of the present but in doing so offer a range of possibilities that depart from the "parsimony of explanation" social scientists aim for and politicians need. Despite its abysmal record, fortune-telling continues to thrive. The need for certainty in an uncertain world is so compelling that it allows even unwelcome prophecies to gain credence. The fact that the forecasts of today are frequently confounded by the events of tomorrow means only that soothsayers resolve to try harder in the future. As fresh predictions are announced, with all the assurance that accompanies simple theories of a complex world, it is as well to remember that elixirs come in many different bottles, and that we have yet to find a way of walking on water.[147]

Although history is ill-suited to prophecy, historians can nevertheless use the past to offer a view of the present. Montesquieu's observations about scale and structure that appeared at the outset of this study remain relevant at its conclusion. When placed in the longest perspective, the large issues of the early twenty-first century can be seen to derive from the continuing transition to postcolonial globalization. Advances in technology combined with various forms of deregulation have integrated the world to an unprecedented degree. Global flows of trade, investment, people, and ideas have outstripped the reach of existing political institutions. Not even a hyperpower, as we have discovered, can impose its will on a postcolonial world. The nation-states that outlasted the demise of empires, or were founded in the course of their rise and fall, have yet to create coordinating institutions that can deal effectively with supranational problems. The European Union, which is currently the most advanced postmodern state system, was insufficiently developed to respond effectively to the economic crisis that struck in 2008, or to solve the problem of resettling refugees that followed the civil war in Syria. It remains to be seen whether the EU can develop as a cohesive political force following Britain's decision in 2016 to cancel its membership after forty-three years of ambiguous endeavor.

The United States remains resolutely national in its outlook and wary of international organizations, including the United Nations. Yet, it too struggles to manage incoming global influences, whether these are "insurgents" and "terrorists," illegal immigrants, foreign investment, or the consequences of climate change. The bipartisan presumption that the United States is, in Madeleine Albright's now famous phrase, "the indispensable nation," whose unmatched power serves a unique and providential purpose, is not well suited to supranational thinking.[148] The belief that American values, expressed in a generalized and partisan notion of liberalism, are global values that need to be universally recognized remains an orthodoxy among policy-makers and their academic advisors.[149] The attitude summarized in 1937 by Theodore Roosevelt, Jr., a former Governor of Puerto Rico and Governor-General of the Philippines, still resonates: "We have one besetting sin in common with many other peoples, including the British. We think we are better than other people. Anyone who does things in different fashion from us is either comic or stupid. We regard being a foreigner in the nature of a defective moral attribute."[150] Encounters with value systems outside the United States continue to produce reactions of incomprehension, anxiety, and hostility.[151] The response reinforces the national mythology rather more than it advances international understanding, and increases the likelihood that other states will be cast as instigators of problems that are global in cause and scope.

Captain America Civil War (2016), the latest movie in the series, opens with the controversial proposition that the United Nations should regulate the Avengers to control the mayhem they have caused throughout the world. The prospect of subordination to an international organization is so offensive that it provokes civil war among the formerly united team. Captain America upholds the principle of individual enterprise against state control; Iron Man favors regulation. Battle is joined; the war continues. Will Captain America persist with military force to advance freedom and democracy, or will he adopt a form of smart diplomacy informed by an understanding of the root causes of global discontents and an awareness that there are different ways of achieving the good life? The Avengers and Washington face the same question. Captain America's answer may be given when the next installment of the saga is issued. No one, however, can foretell if Washington's response will correspond with fiction or conform to reality.

LESSONS OF LIBERATION

IRAQ, 2003-2011

The ghosts of American soldiers
wander the streets of Balad by night,
unsure of their way home, exhausted,
the desert wind blowing trash
down the narrow valley as a voice
sounds from the minaret, a soulful call
reminding them how alone they are,
how lost. And the Iraqi dead,
they watch in silence from the rooftops
as date palms line the shore in silhouette,
leaning toward Mecca when the dawn wind blows.

—*Brian Turner, "Ashbah"*[1]

We are a free people. We don't accept anyone to come
and control us. The US should leave by themselves.
They came to occupy us, and we have never accepted
that. They want to be an empire, but we don't see it that
way. They are a new country with little culture and a
big military. To use your might to fight small countries
is not being an empire, it is just being a bully.[2]

—*Omar Darwish, known as Mukhtar Omar
(town leader, Kut, whose father fought in the siege
of Kut in 1916), speaking in November 2003*

We cannot be certain, but it is unlikely that Corporal Mark Evnin had
heard of Major General Charles Townshend. Even if he had, it seems safe
to assume that Evnin was not thinking of Townshend as he steered his
Humvee into Kut on the morning of April 3, 2003.[3] Evnin was a member
of a sniper unit of the Third Battalion of the U.S. Fourth Marine Regiment. Concentration and precision were his watchwords. The approach
to Kut was full of uncertainties, not least being the novelty of the experience. Evnin had wanted a military career since he was a boy growing
up in Burlington, Vermont.[4] His family supported his ambitions without
pushing him in that direction. Mark was particularly close to his mother,

Mindy, a physiotherapist, and his grandfather, Max Wall, a prominent rabbi who had been a chaplain during World War II. Mark was an engaging, popular student who was known for his outgoing personality and generous spirit. He was keen on sports and adept at technical matters, especially computing. In 2000, shortly after graduating from high school, he joined the Marines, less to see the world than to find himself. His letters to his family trace his progress in settling on a long-term purpose for his life. The invasion of Iraq, which had begun just two weeks before he drove into Kut, was his first experience of combat. Operation Iraqi Freedom had begun. "Shock and awe" were about to descend on what Townshend knew as Mesopotamia.

By the time Evnin and the Third Battalion reached Kut, the fog of war had already enveloped planners and troops alike. Expectations that the army of liberation would be greeted with enthusiasm were jolted at Nasiriya, a town on the Euphrates about 100 miles southwest of Kut, where the battalion ran into fierce opposition and suffered its first casualties. It had become apparent, too, that Iraqi combatants were often indistinguishable from civilians. Families leaving targeted towns clogged the roads and jeopardized the blitzkrieg strategy that was designed to carry the invasion force to the gates of Baghdad in record time. Contradictory purposes ensured that Iraqis suffered what official briefings referred to, with increasing frequency, as "collateral damage."[5] No wonder Colonel Joseph D. Dowdy, the Regimental Commander of the First Marine Division, had doubts about advancing too swiftly into the unknown.[6] Townshend would have understood his reservations. Dowdy's superior, General James ("Mad Dog") Mattis, who had overall command of the Division, took a different view, and ordered Dowdy to maintain the momentum of the advance.[7] Accordingly, Dowdy took the regiment through Nasiriyah on the night of March 25. When he emerged the next day, he found himself engaged in a "running gunfight through the Mesopotamian mud" and had to battle his way toward Kut.[8] This, too, was not in the invasion plan.

There were other troubling uncertainties. Kut, which had become a large town of about 375,000 people, was on Highway 7 to Baghdad and also controlled a nearby air base. Intelligence reports indicated that the town was defended by the formidable Baghdad Division of the Iraqi Army, which had chemical weapons and was prepared to use them. On March 27, Dowdy halted, this time with the approval of his seniors, about 50 miles from Kut. The plan at this point was for the regiment to act as a decoy, holding Iraqi troops in place while other units of the Expeditionary Force moved swiftly toward Baghdad.[9] General Mattis, however, amended the order. Information that villagers in the area had welcomed the Marines encouraged him to think that resistance was waning. Dowdy was instructed to advance to Kut to see if the regiment could save time in reaching Baghdad by moving directly through the town. On arrival, Dowdy judged that the likelihood of opposition made it unwise to make the attempt and recommended a detour instead. General Mattis overruled him. On April 3, two of Dowdy's battalions began the assault on Kut.[10] It was eighty-eight years since Townshend's Sixth Division had first occupied the town.

The Third Battalion of the Fourth Marines swung into action. The Battalion Commander, Lieutenant Colonel Bryan P. McCoy, fully accepted the need for speed and its corollary: action. His aim was to demonstrate that there were "new alpha males" in Iraq by establishing what he termed "violent supremacy."[11] The Battalion's 1,500 troops were trained in desert warfare, equipped with thirty Abrams tanks and sixty armored assault vehicles, and backed by artillery and aircraft. The engagement that followed was intense but one-sided.[12] Beyond what Donald Rumsfeld, the Secretary of Defense, called the "known unknowns," there were knowns (beliefs) that were mistaken.[13] U.S. military intelligence thought that the Baghdad Division of the Republican Guard was still in Kut, whereas it had been withdrawn a few days earlier.[14] Several thousand Iraqi troops were overtaken and captured in the next few days as the Marines made rapid progress toward Baghdad. Other members of the Republican Guard opted for flight; some lived to fight another day. Those who resisted the U.S. Army in Kut had limited and inferior equipment, which ensured that much of the fighting was at close quarters.[15] John Koopman, an embedded reporter and himself a former Marine, described the scene:

> At dawn, 155-mm howitzers shake the earth. They're launching high-explosive rounds into the outskirts of Kut. The Battalion moves toward the city, following a path taken by another regiment. Death and destruction are everywhere. Bodies lie on the side of the road, jackets covering faces. Iraqi military vehicles are smoking ruins. A herd of sheep lies silent, mowed down by machine-gun fire. . . . For a long time, I see no live Iraqis. Armored vehicles, tanks and artillery pieces are on the road and in nearby fields. Marine tanks blew holes in everything. Just in case.[16]

At this point, Evnin's Humvee was following a tank in a column that was approaching the town center.[17] Most of the column had passed without serious resistance. The tail end, however, which also included

Colonel McCoy, was caught in an ambush. Evnin and his comrades suddenly found themselves at the wrong end of machine-gun fire and rocket-propelled grenades, which came from a small palm grove close to the road. The Marines returned fire and called for support. Koopman recorded the deafening eruption of noise: "The grove is filled with gun smoke. You can hardly see. The last two tanks in the column are still close enough to fire. They shoot their high-explosive rounds directly into the groves. The blasts cut palm trees in half. All I can think is: God help anyone underneath those blasts."[18] Evnin took shelter behind the Amtrac that was just ahead of the Humvee, grabbed his grenade-launcher, fired into the palm grove, and stepped back to reload.[19] When he stepped out again, he was hit by machine-gun fire. Two bullets penetrated his upper thigh and abdomen just below his body armor. Koopman was at the scene: "It doesn't look bad. Not a lot of blood. I look away from the wounds. Evnin is awake and alert. The corpsman tries to work on him. A Humvee roars to a halt on the road next to them. [Sergeant Major David] Howell looks down at Mark and smiles. 'Hey, Evnin. Look at the bright side. You won't have to ride with me anymore.'"[20]

The Humvee raced to the medical station at the outskirts of Kut, where, by chance, another reporter, Peter Maass, was on hand to take up the story.[21] "A marine, whose body was rag-doll floppy, was pulled out and put on a stretcher. A marine doctor and medics surrounded him. His clothes were stripped off and needles and monitors placed on and into his body, and the dialogue of battlefield medicine began among the team, all of whom had slung their M-16s over their backs as they tried to save their comrade's life." The dialogue continued, this time with the patient: "Keep talking to us. Where are you from?' 'Remon,' he mumbled. "Where? Where are you from? Verrrmon." Evnin was struggling. The battalion chaplain, Bob Grove, started to read the 23rd Psalm, at which point Evnin said, "Chaplain, I'm not going to die." A Chinook landed 50 yards away. "Evnin's stretcher was lifted from the asphalt and rushed to the chopper. Shortly after he was airborne, Evnin went into shock and died." He was just short of his twenty-second birthday.

Once through Kut, the Third Battalion sped north on Highway 6, reaching the outskirts of Baghdad on April 5.[22] The advance was held up at Diyala Bridge, which commanded one of the main routes into the city, but the Battalion fought its way across and thereafter met only sporadic resistance.[23] The anticipated blood bath never materialized. On April 9, the Battalion entered Paradise Square and helped to pull down the massive statue of Saddam Hussein in what became an "Iwo Jima moment" that was beamed across the world.[24] As the statue fell, so did the regime. As the United Nations Ambassador, who was still in the city, remarked: "the game is over."[25] It was just three weeks since the invasion had begun.

The mission, however, was far from accomplished. Within days, the Marines were assigned the task of dealing with the misery that had descended on Iraqi civilians. "This is a huge departure for them," Koopman observed: "they're more comfortable smashing and bashing and destroying things. There's no way to sugarcoat it. They fight, they kill. Now they're told to make nice and help the civilians."[26] The "smashing and bashing" had destroyed roads, airports, and hospitals, and disrupted supplies of electricity, water, and oil.[27] The administration had broken down. Food was in short supply. Banks, museums, libraries, and offices had been ransacked. Schools had been disrupted. Colonel McCoy foretold what would happen: "We will go from hero liberators to despised occupiers."[28] This prediction, at least, was correct. What General Maude had called, in 1917, "the tyranny of strangers" was about to be revisited on Iraq.[29]

Other confident assertions were wholly mistaken. There were no weapons of mass destruction. There was no postwar plan, either. The Pentagon had assumed, wrongly, that Iraqis would welcome their liberators and that the removal of Saddam Hussein would be sufficient to turn Iraq toward its prescribed democratic destination. Yet, the second anniversary of the destruction of Saddam Hussein's statue saw a massive demonstration in Baghdad against the U.S. occupation.[30] The "insurgency" was under way. By the time the United States withdrew its troops in 2011, 4,488 soldiers had been killed and 32,000 wounded. The cost of the operation was heading toward US$3 trillion. Well over 100,000 Iraqis had lost their lives, countless more had been injured, and even larger numbers turned into refugees. Stability had fled; democracy had yet to arrive.[31] In the words of the Iraqi poet, Fadhil al-Azzawi, "Every morning the war gets up from sleep."[32]

* * *

There are obvious parallels between the siege of Kut that began in 1915 and the invasion that passed through it in 2003.[33] Most famously, Britain and the United States both declared that they came as liberators and not as occupiers.[34] Both proceeded to install themselves in a manner that precluded an early exit. The invaders had an unquestioned belief in the superiority of their own values and a limited knowledge of the people they were to conquer and control. Military success was accompanied by inadequate planning for the postwar order. Occupation provoked resistance that was misunderstood and mishandled. Neither army was trained to deal with "insurgents."[35] Communication between civil and military authorities was often poor and sometimes dysfunctional. Neither power had an exit strategy; both were strongly motivated by fear of losing face. Unsurprisingly, great powers approve of themselves and feel superior to others. Assertiveness driven by a mixture of confidence and ignorance produced defective planning, as Townshend and Evnin, in their different ways, found out. Warfare confuses even the best plans. Predicted short wars turn readily into quagmires. Destruction is easy and immediate; construction is laborious, complicated, and costly.[36] Indigenous societies are far more complex than the stereotypes drawn of them allow. These facts are rediscovered as novelties every time an invasion takes place.

Commentators have cited these and other similarities to support large claims about the place of Britain and the United States in world history. The United States has been regarded as the "heir to empire"; both powers have been compared to Rome. A sweeping sequence of Western empires has been tied to predictive purposes. Previous empires eventually declined; some fell abruptly. What Britain learned from Rome, the United States might learn from Britain. By joining the analysis of history to the expertise of today, policy-makers might be able to avert decay and consolidate dominance.

At this point, however, it is wise to pause. Comparisons of this order require a sufficient degree of similarity for particular differences to be identified. Ibn Khaldun, one of the first and most famous practitioners of comparative history, understood the need for care in drawing lines of connection between different objects of study. His remarkable work, *The Muqaddimah*, written in 1377, presented history as the systematic study of the interaction of economic and political forces and their influence on the rise and decline of societies and states.[37] He saw that comparisons had the merit of identifying differences as well as resemblances. He was aware, too, that the exercise could be warped by ideological intent and misdirected by methodological errors that could result in faulty analogies and disastrous policies. Ibn Khaldun's precepts underline the hazards of looking for similarities where differences may be more significant.

Britain and the United States were both major powers, and they exhibited a number of common features, some of which have just been enumerated. Many of the similarities, however, were not only true but also truisms, and apply to a range of states other than the two chosen for comparison. Furthermore, it is misleading to argue that these shared characteristics justify the claim that Britain and the United States were both empires, unless the term is used in a very general sense to refer to all states that controlled regions beyond their ethnic core. Such a reference, however, sheds darkness rather than light. What Rome, Venice, and the United States had in common may be less significant than what separated them.

The comparison fails even in the case of Britain and the United States, which were contemporaneous industrial nation-states with a shared inheritance and an acknowledged role as world powers. As has been argued throughout this book, Britain and the United States operated in a global context that altered significantly in the course of three centuries. The Pax Britannica was exercised in an era that either favored or required territorial control; the Pax Americana was applied in an age when annexations were either impracticable or unnecessary. The potential for comparison existed during the first half of the twentieth century, when the United States acquired and managed a territorial empire, but the possibility has been ignored because scholars have long consigned the insular possessions to a limbo of obscurity. Paradoxically, comparisons proliferated during the second half of the twentieth century, when the United States became a world power and an aspiring hegemon, despite the fact that the global context had been transformed, the insular empire dissolved, and the basis of comparison profoundly altered.

Britain was dominant at a time when empires were not only a familiar part of the international scene but were also regarded as a measure of international stature. The United States functions in a postcolonial era that is hostile to imperialism and empires. For most of its history, the British Empire dealt with proto-nationalist protests rather than with fully formed and well-organized mass movements. The United States has to find its way in a world of independent states founded on principles of self-determination. The invasion of Iraq in 1915 was part of a war among nation-states, which Britain could pursue by mobilizing the Indian Army to defend imperial territories. The United States is engaged in hostilities with movements that are supranational, and relies on a volunteer force of national citizens. The British encountered resistance that was unable to strike beyond its locality. The United States faces the prospect that weapons of mass destruction can arrive from any part of the globe. Postcolonial development has democratized the means of destruction faster than it has democratized the standard of living.

Dubious arguments gain credibility if changes in the historical context are ignored or underestimated. Economic strength and military might are routinely compared as if time can be discounted. On this reckoning, the United States emerges as a superpower, even a "super-empire," when ranked against previous great powers. Absolute measures, however, ignore the fact that power in international relations is also relative. The appropriate comparison is one that relates the power of a state to the problems it faces. On this measure, the United States possesses colossal military might that is inappropriate and frequently counterproductive when applied to movements labeled as insurgencies. Moreover, the events of 9/11 showed that a small-scale operation could produce large-scale results. There is no advantage in being Goliath if David can fell you with a sling and a stone.

The problem is not so much collective forgetfulness as selective remembrance. Like other great states, the *United States of Amnesia*, as it has been called, carries forward elements of the past that are congenial to those in power, while discarding alternatives that might challenge the dominant orthodoxy.[38] As a result, the "lessons of liberation" are often unknown or ignored. Hubris then works its way toward nemesis, which may result from overstretch, as in the case of Britain, or overconfidence, as in the case of the United States. There is no easy solution to this problem. Indeed, there may be no solution at all. Great powers may be incapable of overcoming the constraints imposed by their past successes. Alternative policies begin to commend themselves only in retrospect, which is too late for effective action.[39] As General Stanley McChrystal, the commander of coalition forces in Afghanistan in 2009–2010, admitted: "We didn't know enough and we still don't know enough. Most of us—me included—had a very superficial understanding of the situation and history, and we had a frighteningly simplistic view of recent history, the last 50 years."[40] These remarks were representative, if also exceptionally honest. They were made in 2011, after McChrystal had already served in both Gulf Wars. Yet the knowledge he lacked was available before the invasion of Iraq in 2003. Specialists on colonial rule and decolonization were aware that it would all end in tears. The tears are still falling.

As an eminent jurist who was close to the Egyptian government, Ibn Khaldun was obliged to accompany a military campaign led by the Mamluk Sultan, al-Nasir Faraj, in 1401.[41] The expedition was undertaken against Ibn Khaldun's advice, was poorly planned, and was irredeemably compromised when the bulk of the Egyptian force was withdrawn from the field. At this point, Ibn Khaldun found himself, at the age of sixty-nine, besieged in Damascus by the fearsome conqueror, Tamerlane. Unlike Major-General Townshend, moreover, he had no prospect of receiving reinforcements. A desperate situation required a desperate remedy: Ibn Khaldun arranged for himself to be lowered by ropes from the city walls so that he could negotiate with the enemy. In the course of seven weeks, he so impressed Tamerlane with his erudition that he was able to secure a safe conduct for himself and his associates, though he had to submit a substantial intelligence report on North Africa to his captor to seal the deal.[42]

The quagmire in Iraq, quick to entice and slow to submerge, reaffirms the wisdom of Ibn Khaldun's belief that history is, or should be, a practical art needed for the "acquisition of excellence in ruling."[43] Although the "lessons of history" are contested, their merits and defects can still be debated to ensure, minimally, that policies are formulated in the light of the evidence and not in the face of it. Today, historians are not obliged to place themselves in physical danger on behalf of their national governments, not least because, unlike Ibn Khaldun, they are now far removed from the corridors of power. Given the relationship between defective knowledge and defective policies, however, the profession still needs to be prepared to lower its representatives by ropes from the city walls, if necessary, to ensure that its voice is heard in the tents of the mighty.

NOTES

PROLOGUE: LESSONS OF LIBERATION: IRAQ, 1915–1921

1. The first four of the six stanzas of Kipling's poem, published simultaneously in the *Morning Post* (London) and the *New York Times* on July 11, 1917, expressed his frustration and fury at the conduct of the war, with particular reference to the siege of Kut. Originally, Kipling had been a keen advocate of the war and had used his influence to ensure that his son, John (who had defective eyesight), joined the army. John was killed at the battle of Loos in September 1915, six weeks after his eighteenth birthday. Kipling never forgave himself.

2. Arnold Talbot Wilson, *Mesopotamia, 1917–20: A Clash of Loyalties* (London, 1931), p. 254. Wilson (1884–1940) spent his career in India before becoming Deputy Civil Commissioner for Mesopotamia in 1917 and Acting Civil Commissioner, 1918–1920. He was recalled in 1920, following the uprising provoked by the British occupation. He volunteered for service with the RAF in 1939 and served with distinction before being killed in action in 1940 at the age of fifty-six. There is a well-documented biography by John Marlowe, *Late Victorian: The Life of Sir Arnold Wilson* (London, 1967).

3. George Townshend (1724–1807), Viscount (by inheritance, 1764), Marquis (1787), was Charles Townshend's great-great-grandfather. Charles was a product of Cranleigh public school and the Royal Military College, Sandhurst.

4. N. S. Nash, *Chitrál Charlie: the Rise and Fall of Major General Charles Townshend* (Barnsley, 2010), deals with the Mesopotamian campaign in chs. 12–14.

5. This theme is well covered by James Renton, "Changing Languages of Empire and the Orient: Britain and the Invention of the Middle East, 1917–1918," *Historical Journal*, 50 (2007), pp. 645–67.

6. Sir John Eccles Nixon (1857–1921) spent his career in the Indian Army and became Senior Commander in 1915.

7. See Wilson's candid comment in *Loyalties*, pp. 226–7. The War Office assigned a purely defensive role to Mesopotamia and had no wish to tie down troops in a region that was peripheral to the main war effort.

8. Studies of the Mesopotamia campaign have been reinvigorated since 2003. See especially Charles Townshend (no relation), *Desert Hell: The British Invasion of Mesopotamia* (Cambridge, MA, 2011). The starting point is A. J. Barker, *The Neglected War: The Mesopotamian Campaign, 1915–1918* (London, 1967). See also Paul K. Davis, *Ends and Means: The British Mesopotamian Campaign and Commission* (Rutherford, 1994), which should be read with Paul Rich's review at www.h-net.org/reviews/showrev.cgi?path (January 1995).

9. This is the direct distance; the driving distance given today is about 250 miles. Townshend's supply line was already fully stretched. At the time of the siege, the civilian population of Kut was estimated at about 6,000. Kut (also Al Kut or Kut-el-Amara) derives from the Hindi *kot* (fortress).

10. In this case, the direct and traveling distances (principally by river) were similar. Nixon fell ill and was replaced in January 1916 by General Sir Percy Lake (1855–1940). The Mesopotamia Commission's *Report* (1917) criticized Nixon's conduct and brought his career to an end.

11. Major-General Sir Charles V. F. Townshend, *My Campaign in Mesopotamia* (London, 1920), pp. 168–9.

12. Field Marshall Wilhelm Leopold Colmar, Baron von der Goltz (1843–1916) played an important part in modernizing the Turkish army before World War I. He died of typhus on April 19, ten days before Townshend surrendered. Townshend regarded him as "the leading strategist in Europe" (*My Campaign*, p. 246).

13. Jan Morris, *Farewell the Trumpets* (Harmondsworth, 1979), calls it "the most abject capitulation," p. 171. Singapore, however, trumped all predecessors. For varying assessments (in addition to those given in notes 4 and 7) see Patrick Crowley, *Kut 1916: Courage and Failure in Iraq* (Stroud, 2009); and Nikolas Gardner, *The Siege of Kut-al-Amara: At War in Mesopotamia, 1915–1916* (Bloomington, 2014). Also Robert F. Jones, "Kut," *Quarterly Journal of Military History*, 4 (1992), pp. 58–68; Edwin Latter, "The Indian Army in Mesopotamia, 1914–18," *Journal of the Society for Army Historical Research*, 72 (1994), pp. 92–102 and 160–79.

14. Although Kut on the Tigris was joined to Nasiriyah on the Euphrates by the Shatt-al-Hayy river-canal, the channel was dry for six months of the year and a long stretch of it was "lost in marshes and irrigation canals" and was of little value to enemy troops. See Wilson, *Loyalties*, pp. 51, 79, 192.

15. David French, "The Dardanelles, Mecca and Kut: Prestige as a Factor in British Eastern Strategy," *War & Society*, 5 (1987), pp. 45–61.

16. Townshend, *My Campaign*, p. 216, and for his earlier plan, pp. 219–21. The plan was a measure of Townshend's desperation because Kut stood on a bend so tight that it was almost an island with limited access and egress.

17. Nikolas Gardner, "British Prestige and the Mesopotamian Campaign, 1914–1916," *Historian*, 77 (2015), pp. 269–89.

18. Scurvy, arising from malnutrition, was a particular problem: Mark Harrison, "The Fight Against Disease in the Mesopotamia Campaign," in Hugh Cecil and Peter Liddle, eds., *Facing Armageddon: The First World War Experienced* (London, 1996), pp. 475–89.

19. This quotation and the one that follows are taken from Robert Palmer, "Letters for Mesopotamia," Project Gutenberg Book No. 17584, released January 23, 2006 at www .informotions.com/etexts/gutenberg/dirs/1/7/5/8/17584/htm. Project Gutenberg asks that the following acknowledgment be made: "This eBook is for the use of anyone anywhere at no cost and with almost no restrictions whatsoever. You may copy it, give it away or re-use it under the terms of the Project Gutenberg License included with this eBook or online at www.gutenberg.org."

20. Hon. Robert Stafford Arthur Palmer (1888–1916), the second son of William Waldegrave Palmer, the second Earl of Selborne (1859–1942), First Lord of the Admiralty (1900–1905), High Commissioner for South Africa (1905–1910).

21. Townshend's own account is in *My Campaign*, chs. 12–18. There are several other first-hand accounts, e.g., Major E.W.C. Sandes, *In Kut and Captivity with the Sixth Indian Division* (London, 1919), chs. 9–15. Wilson, *Loyalties*, summarizes some of the criticisms of Townshend that emerged after the war, notably failures of management during the siege and exaggerated claims made at the time and in his published memoir.

22. Sandes, *In Kut*, p. 162.

23. The significance of the refusal of Indian troops to eat horsemeat is explored by Nikolas Gardner, "Sepoys and the Siege of Kut-al-Amara, December 1915–April 1916," *War in History*, 11 (2004), pp. 307–26.

24. Townshend, *My Campaign*, p. 245, and the communiqué he issued to his soldiers on January 26 containing some unwise disclosures, as he himself admitted: pp. 264–6.

25. Khalil Pasha (1864–1923) was governor of Baghdad province and also commander of the Turkish Sixth Army.

26. Reeva Spector Simon and Eleanor H. Tejirian, eds., *The Creation of Iraq, 1914–1921* (New York, 2004), p. 11. Estimates vary according to the source consulted. The figures given here and in the following sentence are approximate. The apparent discrepancy between the number of troops (9,000) in Kut at the time of the siege and the number sent into captivity (13,000) is explained by the addition of auxiliaries to the second figure.

27. The disaster at Kut led to a parliamentary enquiry and numerous subsequent appraisals. See "Report of the Commission to Enquire into the Operations of War in Mesopotamia," Cd. 8610 (1917). The two individuals most criticized were Lord Hardinge, the Viceroy of India, and General Sir John Nixon. See Douglas Goold, "Lord Hardinge and the Mesopotamia Expedition and Inquiry," *Historical Journal*, 19 (1976), pp. 919–45. The administrative failings are recounted by John S. Galbraith, "No Man's Child: The Campaign in Mesopotamia, 1914–16," *International History Review*, 6 (1984), pp. 358–85.

28. Townshend was a courageous and skilled officer, but his career was "marred by his arrogance, egotism, ambition, and intense dislike of routine soldiering." T. R. Moreman, "Sir Charles Vere Townshend," *Oxford Dictionary of National Biography*, at www.oxforddnb .com. In this case, however, Townshend had been put in an impossible position by his superiors, who, following a long tradition, greatly underestimated the difficulties facing the expeditionary force.

29. Sir (Frederick) Stanley Maude (1864–1917), like Townshend, came from a military family with a long and distinguished history of service in and beyond the British Empire. His father won the Victoria Cross during the Crimean War. The figures given for the number of troops at Maude's disposal vary markedly. I have followed Wilson, *Loyalties*, p. 209.

30. V. H. Rothwell, "Mesopotamia in British War Aims," *Historical Journal*, 13 (1970), pp. 273–94, charts the expansion of Britain's ambitions in the region.

31. Sir William Raine Marshall (1865–1939) had participated in the recapture of Kut and the capture, subsequently, of Baghdad.

32. James D. Scudieri, "Iraq, 2003–04 and Mesopotamia, 1914–18: A Comparative Analysis in Ends and Means," in Williamson Murray, ed., *A Nation at War in an Era of Strategic Change* (Carlisle Barracks, 2004), p. 101. This figure was close to the numbers General Eric Shinseki, Chief of Staff of the U.S. Army, 1999–2003, suggested were needed in Iraq in 2003. His comments caused him to lose favor with the Secretary of Defense, Donald Rumsfeld. See Matthew Engel, "Scorned General's Tactics Proved Right," *Guardian*, March 29, 2003.

33. The full text is reproduced in Wilson, *Loyalties*, pp. 237–8.

34. Marlowe, *Late Victorian*, ch. 9, provides a thorough and balanced account of the criticism directed at Wilson's policies.

35. Ian Rutledge, *Enemy on the Euphrates: The British Occupation of Iraq and the Great Arab Revolt, 1914–1921* (London, 2014), chs. 21–34. Also Charles Tripp, *A History of Iraq* (Cambridge, 2nd ed. 2000), pp. 40–45; Simon and Tejirian, *Creation of Iraq*, especially chs. 1–3; Marlowe, *Late Victorian*, ch. 11.

36. Arnold Wilson gave a full account of the events in *Loyalties*; also Marlowe, *Late Victorian*, ch. 12.

37. T. E. Lawrence, "A Report on Mesopotamia," *Sunday Times*, August 22, 1920. Also Timothy J. Paris, "British Middle East Policy-Making after the First World War: The Lawrentian and Wilsonian Schools," *Historical Journal*, 41 (1998), pp. 773–93.

38. King Faisal I (1885–1933). Even though promoting devolution, the British were not fully in charge. See Efraim Karsh, "Reactive Imperialism: Britain, the Hashemites, and the Creation of Modern Iraq," *Journal of Imperial and Commonwealth History*, 30 (2002), pp. 55–70; and the discussion of formal independence in Susan Pedersen, "Getting Out of Iraq in 1932: The League of Nations and the Road to Normative Statehood," *American Historical Review*, 115 (2010), pp. 975–1000.

39. Wilson, *Loyalties*, pp. 237–8.
40. Vico, and before him Ibn Khaldun, should also be credited with the perception that each age was full of surprises that made prediction an art rather than a science. On Toynbee, see Cornelia Navari, "Arnold Toynbee (1889–1975): Prophecy and Civilization," *Review of International Studies*, 26 (2000), pp. 289–307.
41. J. A. Hobson, *Imperialism: A Study* (3rd ed., London, 1938), p. 9.
42. Francis Fukuyama, *The End of History and the Last Man* (London, 1992). The title is an indirect guide to the argument, which claimed that the fall of the Soviet Empire marked the end of the great ideological divisions in the world and the triumph of Western liberal democracy.
43. Kenneth Burke, *Permanence and Change* (Berkeley and Los Angeles, 1984), pp. 7–11, discusses what the French call, rather more elegantly, "*la déformation professionelle.*"
44. Odysseus also had help from Athena, the goddess of wisdom and war.

CHAPTER 1: THREE CRISES AND AN OUTCOME

1. Peter Winch, *The Idea of a Social Science and Its Relation to Philosophy* (London, 1958; 1990), is a remarkably lucid and now neglected study.
2. Introductions to different features of what is now a huge literature include: Kevin H. O'Rourke and Jeffrey G. Williamson, *Globalization and History: The Evolution of a Nineteenth-Century Atlantic Economy* (Cambridge, MA, 1999); A. G. Hopkins, ed., *Globalisation in World History* (London and New York, 2002); Jürgen Osterhammel and Niels P. Petersson, *Globalization: A Short History* (Princeton, NJ, 2003): Patrick Manning, *Navigating World History: Historians Create a Global Past* (New York, 2003); Patrick Manning, ed., *World History: Global and Local Interactions* (Princeton, NJ, 2005); A. G. Hopkins, ed., *Global History: Interactions Between the Universal and the Local* (Basingstoke, Hants, 2006), suggests how localities react to and reshape global impulses; Laurent Testot, ed., *Histoire globale: Un autre regard sur le monde* (Auxerre, 2008), provides a concise but wide-ranging overview; Philippe Beaujard et al., eds., *Histoire globale: mondialisations et capitalisme* (Paris, 2009) offer twelve wide-ranging essays; Pierre-Yves Saunier, *Transnational History* (New York, 2013), deals with supranational connections beyond those considered here; Jürgen Osterhammel, *The Transformation of the World: A Global History of the Nineteenth Century* (Princeton, NJ, 2014), is the fullest account of the changes that took place in the nineteenth century; Dominic Saschsenmaier, *Global Perspectives on Global History: Theoriesand Approaches in a Connected World* (Cambridge, 2011), traces the evolution of the subject in the United States, Germany, and China; James Belich, John Darwin, Margret Frenz, and Chris Wickham, eds., *The Prospect of Global History* (Oxford, 2016), is particularly valuable for paying attention to the neglected early phases of globalization.
3. Paul Kramer, "Power and Connection: Imperial Histories of the United States in the World," *American Historical Review*, 116 (2011), pp. 1348–91, provides a full and accessible guide to recent literature.
4. Oscar Wilde, "The Decay of Lying," *Intentions* (London, 1891), p. 44.
5. Christopher Bayly, "History and World History," in Ulinka Rublack, ed., *A Concise Companion to History* (Oxford, 2001), ch. 1.
6. Accordingly, great credit should be given to scholars who have explored these possibilities from different perspectives, and in doing so have opened new routes into the past. An incomplete list of contributions would have to include: Frank Ninkovich, *The United States and Empire* (Oxford, 2001); Thomas Bender, ed., *Rethinking American History in a Global Age* (Berkeley, 2002); Niall Ferguson, *Colossus: The Rise and Fall of the American Empire* (London, 2004); Thomas Bender, *A Nation among Nations: America's*

Place in World History (New York, 2006); Charles Maier, *Among Empires: American Ascendancy and its Predecessors* (Cambridge, MA, 2006); Ian Tyrrell, *Transnational Nation: United States in Global Perspective since 1789* (New York, 2007); Michael Hunt, *The American Ascendancy: How the United States Gained and Wielded Global Dominance* (Chapel Hill, 2007); Kathleen Burke, *Old World, New World: Great Britain and America from the Beginning* (New York, 2007); Julian Go, *Patterns of Empire: The British and American Empires, 1688 to the Present* (Cambridge, 2011). Nicolas Barreyre, Michael Heale, Stephen Tuck, and Cécile Vidal, eds., *Historians Across Borders: Writing American History in a Global Age* (Berkeley and Los Angeles, 2014).

7. Louis A. Pérez, Jr., "We Are the World: Internationalizing the National, Nationalizing the International," *Journal of American History*, 89 (2010), pp. 558–66, provides a thoughtful reflection on these themes.

8. For one agenda of possible junctions between history and the other social sciences, see Hopkins, *Globalisation in World History*, ch. 1.

9. For a recent indication of changes in the scholarly mood, see Kenneth Lipartito, "Reassembling the Economic: New Departures in Historical Materialism," *American Historical Review*, 121 (2016), pp. 101–39.

10. This perception draws on my own involvement with Area Studies since the 1960s.

11. See, for example, Sujit Sivasundaram, *Islanded: Britain, Sri Lanka and the Bounds of an Indian Ocean Colony* (Chicago, 2013).

12. Pérez, "We are the World," makes the point that internationalizing national history can "signify an act of appropriation," pp. 65–66. Jay Sexton, "The Global View of the United States," *Historical Journal*, 48 (2005), pp. 261–76, observes that "transnational history has often served to reinforce the distinctiveness of the United States" (p. 275). Accordingly, Ian Tyrrell (the leading Australian historian of the United States) deserves particular credit for his distinctive study, *Transnational Nation* (referred to in n. 6).

13. Daniel Immerwahr, "The Greater United States: Territory and Empire in U.S. History," *Diplomatic History*, 40 (2016), pp. 373–91, at p. 377. Dr. Immerwahr is among a small group of historians who recognize the importance of this neglected subject.

14. Dorothy Ross, *The Origins of American Social Science* (Cambridge, 1991), p. xiv. I have gained far more from this learned and deeply considered study than appears from this brief reference.

15. Readers who are unfamiliar with the discussion of this concept (which could fill many large volumes) should find the following helpful: Ian Tyrrell, "American Exceptionalism in an Age of International History," *American Historical Review*, 96 (1991), pp. 1031–55; Michael Kammen, "The Problem of American Exceptionalism: A Reconsideration," *American Quarterly*, 45 (1993), pp. 1–43; Deborah L. Madsen, *American Exceptionalism* (Jackson, 1998); Donald E. Pease, "Anglo-American Exceptionalisms," *American Quarterly*, 60 (2014), pp. 197–209. For the promotion of the term as a "state fantasy" after 1945, see Donald E. Pease, *The New American Exceptionalism* (Minneapolis, 2009). Elizabeth Glaser and Hermann Wellenreuther, eds., provide some international views in *Bridging the Atlantic: The Question of American Exceptionalism in Perspective* (Cambridge, 2002), even if the bridge does not quite reach the shore.

16. As Michael Kammen put it in 2003: "Major and outstanding books written by comparative practitioners trained as historians of the United States can be counted on the fingers of one hand": "Clio, Columbia, and the Cosmopolitans: Beyond American Exceptionalism and the Nation-State," *History & Theory*, 42 (2003), p. 106.

17. Originally published in 1928. Translated from French and published as "Toward a Comparative History of European Societies," in Frederick C. Lane and Jelle C. Riemersma, eds., *Enterprise and Secular Change: Readings in Economic History* (Homewood, 1953), pp. 494–521. The best analysis remains William H. Sewell, "Marc Bloch and the Logic of Comparative History," *History & Theory*, 6 (1967), pp. 208–18. Additional difficulties and possibilities are reviewed by Raymond Grew, "The Case for Comparing Histories,"

American Historical Review, 85 (1980), pp. 763–78; and Chris Lorenz, "Comparative Historiography: Problems and Perspectives," *History & Theory*, 38 (1999), pp. 25–39.

18. For a recent discussion, see Vladimir Putin, "A Plea for Caution from Russia," *New York Times*, September 11, 2013, and the flurry of exceptionalist refutations that followed. "The Divine Purposes of America and Russia," *Economist*, February 27, 2015, attempted to strike a balance.

19. Oscar A. Haac, "La Révolution comme religion: Jules Michelet," *Romanticisme*, 15 (1985), pp. 75–82.

20. Jacques Lafon, "Langue et pouvoir: aux origines de l'exception culturelle française," *Revue Historique*, 292 (1994), pp. 393–419; Dino Costantini, *Mission civilisatrice: la rôle de l'histoire coloniale dans la construction de l'identité politique française* (Paris, 2008).

21. As late as 2002, a number of prominent French businessmen scandalized their compatriots by declaring the end of *"l'exception française."* See Jean-Pierre Dormois, *The French Economy in the Twentieth Century* (Cambridge, 2004), ch. 1.

22. Peter Bergmann, "American Exceptionalism and Germany: *Sonderweg* in Tandem," *International History Review*, 23 (2001), pp. 505–34.

23. I have been unable to find a source for this quotation, which suggests, unfortunately, that it may not be authentic—even though it deserves to be.

24. Thomas Bender, in particular, made a bold start in *A Nation Among Nations*. See also Bender, ed., *Rethinking American History*, and the references in n. 6 above. Contributions to the sub-branches are noted, where relevant, in the chapters that follow.

25. On the "consensus school," see Michael Kazin's illuminating essay: "Hofstadter Lives: Political Culture and Temperament in the Work of an American Historian," *Reviews in American History*, 27 (1999), pp. 334–48. Kazin brings out the subversive elements in Richard Hofstadter's work and reminds readers that he reached an audience well beyond academia, as did Louis Hertz and Charles Beard. Hofstadter's longest book, *Anti-Intellectualism in American Life* (New York, 1963), provides an unsurpassed insight into one of the distinctive features of U.S. society.

26. The key text is William Appleman Williams, *The Tragedy of American Diplomacy* (New York, 1959). See also Lloyd C. Gardner, ed., *Redefining the Past: Essays in Diplomatic History in Honor of William Appleman Williams* (New York, 1986); and special issues of *Diplomatic History* devoted to Williams, 25, 2 (2001) and Walter LaFeber, 28, 5 (2004). James G. Morgan, *Into New Territory: American Historians and the Concept of US Imperialism* (Madison, 2014), offers a recent guide.

27. Richard Van Alstyne took an independent and hard-headed position that traced U.S. expansion to the eighteenth century, but he also believed that the period after 1898 was one of "consolidation": *The Rising American Empire* (New York, 1960; 2nd ed. 1974).

28. Howard Zinn, *A People's History of the United States* (New York, 1980, 2005). See also Robert Cohen, "The Second Worst History Book in Print? Rethinking a People's History of the United States," *Reviews in American History*, 42 (2014), pp. 197–206.

29. "The national culture of the United States will always include a semiofficial national narrative, no matter what historians do or do not do in relation to it." David Hollinger, "National Culture and Communities of Descent," *Reviews in American History*, 26 (1998), p. 326.

30. Charles McLean Andrews, "Present-Day Thoughts on the American Revolution," *Bulletin of the University of Georgia*, 19 (1919), p. 4.

31. David Waldstreicher, "Founders' Chic as Culture War," *Radical History Review*, 84 (2002), pp. 191–2; H. W. Brands, "Founders Chic," *Atlantic Monthly* (September, 2003), pp. 101–10.

32. Thomas Carlyle, *On Heroes, Hero-Worship, and the Heroic in History* (London, 1841). Carlyle's huge illustrative study, *The History of Friedrich II of Prussia, Known as Frederick the Great*, appeared subsequently in six volumes (1858–65).

33. Notably, Geir Lundestad, *The American "Empire"* (Oxford, 1990); and variations on this theme; "'Empire by Invitation' in the American Century," *Diplomatic History*, 23 (1999), pp. 189–217; *"Empire" by Integration: The United States and European Integration, 1945–1997* (New York, 1998); *The Rise and Decline of the American "Empire": Power and Its Limits in Comparative Perspective* (Oxford, 2012).

34. George Liska, *Career of Empire: America and Imperial Expansion over Land and Sea* (Baltimore, 1978); for Liska's recent views, see *Twilight of Hegemony: The Late Career of Imperial America* (Dallas, 2003).

35. On offensive realism see John J. Mearsheimer, *The Tragedy of Great Power Politics* (New York, 2001).

36. Emily S. Rosenberg, "'The Empire' Strikes Back: Three Faces of Imperialism," *Reviews in American History*, 16 (1988), p. 586.

37. The concept of effective independence is discussed in chapter 4 of this text.

38. This is the phrase made famous by Samuel Flagg Bemis, *A Diplomatic History of the United States* (New York, 1936), ch. 26: "The Great Aberration of 1898."

39. Julian Go deserves credit for his work linking the Philippines and Puerto Rico (listed in his *Patterns of Empire* and cited here in chapters 11 and 12).

40. Readers who sense exaggeration in these statements can find assurance in the commentary of an acknowledged authority: Emily S. Rosenberg, "World War I, Wilsonianism, and Challenges to the U.S. Empire," *Diplomatic History*, 38 (2014), pp. 853–63.

41. The quotations are from Whitney T. Perkins, *Denial of Empire: The United States and Its Dependencies* (Leyden, 1962), p. 10. On the redemption thesis, see Stanley Karnow, *In Our Image: America's Empire in the Philippines* (New York, 1989), which won a Pulitzer Prize in 1990, and is the only general work on the American Empire (albeit one confined to the Philippines) to achieve popularity beyond a narrow range of specialists. Its sin-to-salvation sequence has an incisive critic in Michael Salman, "In Our Orientalist Imagination: Historiography and the Culture of Colonialism in the United States," *Radical History Review*, 50 (1991), pp. 221–32; and Reynaldo C. Ileto, *Knowing America's Colony: A Hundred Years from the Philippine War* (Manoa, 1999), pp. 41–65.

42. Ian Tyrrell shows how cosmopolitan themes gave way to national preoccupation in "Making Nations/Making States: American Historians in the Context of Empire," *Journal of American History*, 86 (1999), pp. 1015–1044.

43. *Imperialism and World Politics* (New York, 1926), pp. 525, 396–7, 422, 561.

44. Julius W. Pratt, *America's Colonial Experiment: How the United States Gained, Governed, and in Part Gave Away a Colonial Empire* (New York, 1951), p. 3.

45. Perkins, *Denial of Empire*. The book was not helped by being published abroad (in the Netherlands). Perhaps as a result, it contained a number of misprints that caught the eyes of the few reviewers who commented on it.

46. Scott Nearing and Joseph Freeman, *Dollar Diplomacy: A Study in American Imperialism* (New York, 1925). Nearing (1883–1983), radical economist (Ph.D. 1909); dismissed from the Wharton School, University of Pennsylvania in 1915 for social activism (decision reversed, 1973, when Nearing was 90); pacifist, joined Socialist Party, 1917, Communist Party, 1927. His related studies are scarcely known today: *The American Empire* (New York, 1921); *The Twilight of Empire: An Economic Interpretation of Imperial Cycles* (New York, 1930); *The Tragedy of Empire* (New York, 1945). The most recent biography is John A. Saltmarsh, *Scott Nearing: An Intellectual Biography* (Philadelphia, 1991). Emily S. Rosenberg expands Nearing's materialist position in "Revisiting Dollar Diplomacy," *Diplomatic History*, 22 (1998), pp. 155–76, by introducing postmodernism and gender.

47. Nearing, *Dollar Diplomacy*, p. 220.

48. Leland H. Jenks's *Our Cuban Colony: A Study in Sugar* (New York, 1928).

49. Jenks, *Our Cuban Colony*, p. 6.

50. For one of many examples, see Eliot A. Cohen, "History and the Hyperpower," *Foreign Affairs*, 83 (2004), p. 62.

51. I am indebted here to Huw V. Bowen, "British Conceptions of Global Empire," *Journal of Imperial and Commonwealth History*, 26 (1998), pp. 1–27; and Brian P. Levack, "Britain's First Global Century: England, Scotland and Empire, 1603–1707," *Britain and the World*, 6 (2013), pp. 101–18.

52. Levack, "Britain's First Global Century," pp. 115–16.

53. John Gallagher and Ronald Robinson, "The Imperialism of Free Trade," *Economic History Review*, 2nd series, 6 (1953), pp. 1–15.

54. Further references to the debate are given in P. J. Cain and A. G. Hopkins, *British Imperialism, 1688–2015* (London, 3rd ed. 2016), p. 66, n. 8.

55. James Kurth, "Migration and the Dynamics of Empire," *National Interest*, 71 (2003), p. 5.

56. Philip Zelikow, "The Transformation of National Security," *National Interest*, 71 (2003), p. 19.

57. Snyder, "Imperial Temptations," *National Interest*, 71 (2003), pp. 29–40; Rosen, "An Empire, If You Can Keep It," *National Interest*, 71 (2003), pp. 51–61.

58. Or with key references to the historiography. Despite the importance of ideology in the thinking of neoconservatives, few commentators cited the seminal studies of Michael H. Hunt and Anders Stephanson, and it was left to Andrew J. Bacevich to re-introduce the work of William Appleman Williams. See Hunt, *Ideology and American Foreign Policy* (New Haven, 1987); Stephanson, *Manifest Destiny: American Expansion and the Empire of Right* (New York, 1995); Bacevich, *American Empire: The Realities and Consequences of U.S. Diplomacy* (Cambridge, MA, 2002).

59. Niall Ferguson, *Colossus: The Price of America's Empire* (New York, 2004); Ferguson, "The Unconscious Colossus: Limits of (& Alternatives to) American Empire," *Daedalus* 134 (2005), pp. 18–33; Bernard Porter, *Empire and Superempire: Britain, America, and the World* (New Haven, 2006).

60. Porter, *Empire*, p. 162.

61. John Lewis Gaddis, *We Now Know: Rethinking Cold War History* (Oxford, 2001), p. 27.

62. Emily Eakin, "It Takes an Empire," *New York Times*, April 2, 2002; Paul Kennedy, "The Greatest Superpower Ever," *New Perspectives Quarterly*, 19 (2002); Kennedy, "Mission Impossible," *New York Review of Books*, 51 (2004).

63. Arthur Schlesinger, "The American Empire? Not So Fast," *World Policy Journal*, 22 (2005), p. 45, quoting political scientist John Ikenberry.

64. Anthony Pagden, "Imperialism, Liberalism, and the Quest for Perpetual Peace," *Daedalus*, 134 (2005), pp. 46–57.

65. Hunt, *The American Ascendancy*, pp. 308–24; Hunt, "Empire, Hegemony, and the U.S. Policy Mess," *History News Network*, May 21, 2007, p. 4, makes rather more use of the term "empire."

66. Charles S. Maier, *American Ascendancy and Its Predecessors* (Cambridge, MA, 2006), p. 3. See also pp. 7, 31, 109.

67. Dane Kennedy, "On the American Empire from a British Imperial Perspective," *International History Review*, 29 (2007), pp. 84–108.

68. Evelyn Baring, First Earl of Cromer, *Ancient and Modern Imperialism* (London, 1910); C. A. Hagerman, *Britain's Imperial Muse: The Classics, Imperialism, and the Indian Empire, 1783–1914* (Basingstoke, Hants, 2013).

69. Duncan Bell, *The Idea of Greater Britain: Empire and the Future of World Order, 1860–1900* (Princeton, NJ, 2007), ch. 8. Bell also shows that the analogy eventually became unsatisfactory because the decline of Greece and Rome jarred with the Victorian idea of progress. A new and more promising candidate, the United States, became the analogue. I am indebted to Dr. Bell for valuable discussions on this and allied subjects. See also Daniel Deudney, "Greater Britain or Greater Synthesis? Seeley, Mackinder and Wells on Britain in the Global Industrial Era," *Review of International Studies*, 27 (2001), pp. 187–208.

70. Maine's Rede Lecture of 1875, republished in his *Village Communities* (London, 4th ed. 1881), p. 238.

71. Sohui Lee, "Manifest Empire: Anglo-American Rivalry and the Shaping of U.S. Manifest Destiny," in Jeffrey Cass and Larry Parr, eds., *Romantic Border Crossings* (Aldershot, 2008), ch. 14.

72. For a compilation of fits and misfits, see Cullen Murphy, *Are We Rome? The Fall of an Empire and the Fate of America* (New York, 2007).

73. One of many examples is Robert Kaplan, *Warrior Politics: Why Leadership Demands a Pagan Ethos* (New York, 2002).

74. Comparisons made in the literature on empires rarely take note of this scholarship. Accessible introductions include Richard Hingley, *Globalizing Roman Culture* (London, 2005); Barbara Goff, ed., *Classics and Colonialism* (London, 2005); and Henry Hurst and Sara Owen, eds., *Ancient Colonizations: Analogy, Similarity and Difference* (London, 2005).

75. Anthony Pagden, *Lords of All the World: Ideologies of Empire in Spain, Britain and France, c. 1500–c. 1800* (New Haven, 1995), ch. 1; Pagden, "Fellow Citizens and Imperial Subjects: Conquest and Sovereignty in Europe's Overseas Empires," *History & Theory*, 44 (2005), pp. 28–46, shows how diversity can be recognized but also organized to produce a coherent typology. See also James Muldoon's wide-ranging and thoughtful *Empire and Order: The Concept of Empire, 800–1800* (New York, 1999).

76. J. A. Hobson, *Imperialism: A Study* (3rd ed., London, 1938), pp. 207–8.

77. Helpful discussions can be found in Michael W. Doyle, *Empires* (Ithaca, 1986), pp. 12, 20–21, 30–40, 81; and Herfried Münckler, *Empires: The Logic of World Domination from Ancient Rome to the United States* (Cambridge, 2007), pp. 4–8.

78. See the references in n. 2 of this chapter.

79. David Held, Antony McGrew, David Globlatt, and Jonathan Perraton, *Global Transformations: Politics, Economics and Culture* (Cambridge, 1999); Held et al., *Globalisation: Key Concepts* (London, 1999), provides a full introduction.

80. Kevin H. O'Rourke and Jeffrey G. Williamson, "When Did Globalisation Begin?" *European Review of Economic History*, 6 (2002), pp. 23–50. Jan de Vries offers a fascinating comment on a much earlier period: "The Limits of Globalisation in the Early Modern Period," *Economic History Review*, 63 (2010), pp. 710–33.

81. Michael Lang, "Globalization and Its History," *Journal of Modern History*, 78 (2006), pp. 899–931.

82. Not all authors see, or accept, this distinction. For a different position see, for example, Jeanne Morefield, *Empires Without Imperialism: Anglo-American Decline and the Politics of Deflection* (New York, 2014).

83. This is not, of course, to claim that national states eliminated multicultural and regional ties. The twin themes of integration and diversity run through the contributions to Susan E. Alcock, Terence N. D'Altroy, Kathleen D. Morrison, and Carla M. Sinopoli, eds., *Empires: Perspectives from Archaeology and History* (Cambridge, 2001).

84. George Steinmetz, "Return to Empire: The New U.S. Imperialism in Comparative Perspective," *Sociological Theory*, 23 (2005), pp. 339–67, has helped me to clarify this claim.

85. M. I. Finlay, "Colonies—An Attempt at a Typology," *Transactions of the Royal Historical Society*, 26 (1976), pp. 167–88.

86. Valuable discussions include Robert Keohane, *After Hegemony*; "The United States and the Postwar Order: Empire or Hegemony?" *Journal of Peace Research*, 28 (1991), pp. 435–9; Michael Walzer, "Is There an American Empire?" *Dissent*, Fall (2003), pp. 27–31; G. John Ikenberry, "Illusions of Empire: Defining the New American Order," *Foreign Affairs*, 83 (2004), pp. 144–54; Alexander J. Motyl, "Empire Falls," *Foreign Affairs*, 85 (2006), pp. 190–94; Doyle, *Empire*, 12–13, 40–44, 81; Münckler, *Empires*, pp. 6–7, 40–46; Patrick Karl O'Brien and Armand Clesse, eds., *Two Hegemonies: Britain, 1846–1914 and the United States, 1941–2001* (Aldershot, Hants, 2002). Michael Cox provides a balanced

but firm defense of the term "hegemon" in "September 11th and US Hegemony," *International Studies Perspective*, 3 (2002), pp. 63–7; Joseph Nye offers a more qualified view in *The Paradox of American Power* (Oxford, 2002), pp. 12–16. John A. Thompson, *A Sense of Power: The Roots of America's Global Role* (Ithaca, 2015), pp. 1–24, provides an accessible summary of the relevant literature.

87. The concept of hegemony originated with the distinguished economic historian, Charles Kindleberger, who explained the instability of the 1930s by referring to the breakdown of the "primacy" exercised by Britain. See *The World in Depression, 1929–1939* (Berkeley, 1973). O'Brien, *Two Hegemonies*, provides an excellent introduction, pp. 1–56. But note also the different ways the contributors apply the term. John Agnew, *Hegemony: The New Shape of Global Power* (Philadelphia, 2005), provides a perspective from the standpoint of historical geography.

88. The leading advocate of hegemonic stability theory is Robert Gilpin, *U.S. Power and the Multinational Corporation: The Political Economy of Foreign Direct Investment* (New York, 1975). See also Gilpin, *War and Change in the International System* (Cambridge, 1981); Gilpin, *The Political Economy of International Relations* (Princeton, NJ, 1987).

89. Arthur A. Stein, "The Hegemon's Dilemma: Great Britain, the United States and the International Economic Order," *International Organization*, 38 (1984), pp. 355–86.

90. I am indebted here to the discussion in Doyle, *Empires*, pp. 26–30, 125–7, 233–4.

91. Critics of realism and neorealism who have made a case for the role of institutions, agency, and preferences include Keohane, *After Hegemony*; Ronald Rogowski, *Commerce and Coalitions* (Princeton, NJ, 1989); Robert O. Keohane and Helen V. Milner, eds., *Internationalization and Domestic Politics* Cambridge, 1996); Helen Milner, *Interest, Institutions and Information: Domestic Politics and International Relations* (Princeton, NJ, 1997); Jack Snyder, *Myths of Empire: Domestic Politics and International Ambition* (Ithaca, 1991); Simon Reich and Richard Ned Lebow, *Good-Bye Hegemony! Power and Influence in the Global System* (Princeton, NJ, 2014).

92. See particularly, Daniel Garst, "Thucydides and Neorealism," *International Studies Quarterly*, 33 (1989), pp. 3–27; David Bedford and Thom Workman, "The Tragic Reading of the Thucydidean Tragedy," *Review of International Studies*, 27 (2001), pp. 51–67; Richard Ned Lebow and Robert Kelly, "Thucydides and Hegemony: Athens and the United States," *Review of International Studies*, 27 (2001), pp. 593–609; Lebow and Kelly, *The Tragic Vision of Politics: Ethics, Interests and Orders* (Cambridge, 2003), chs. 3–4.

93. See Helen Milner, "The Assumption of Anarchy in International Relations," *Review of International Studies*, 17 (1991), pp. 67–85; Robert Powell, "Anarchy in International Relations," *International Organization*, 48 (1994), pp. 329–34. Also theorists of the "English School": Andrew Linklater and Hidemi Suganami, *The English School of International Relations* (Cambridge, 2006).

94. The best comparative assessment is O'Brien and Clesse, *Two Hegemonies*.

95. John M. Hobson, "Two Hegemonies or One? A Historical-Sociological Critique of Hegemonic Stability Theory," in O'Brien and Clesse, *Two Hegemonies*, ch. 15.

96. Mearsheimer, *The Tragedy of Great Power Politics*; Richard N. Rosecrance, "War and Peace," *World Politics*, 55 (2002), pp. 137–66.

97. Isabelle Grunberg's devastating analysis has revealed the ancient metaphors implicit in the theory: "Exploring the 'Myth' of Hegemonic Stability Theory," *International Organization*, 44 (1990), pp. 431–77.

98. Susan Strange, *States and Markets* (London, 1988; 2nd ed. 1994), ch. 2, on the distinction between structural and relational power. A. G. Hopkins, "Informal Empire in Argentina: An Alternative View," *Journal of Latin American Studies*, 26 (1994), pp. 469–84, applies the distinction to a particular case.

99. I have gained here from the discussion in Doyle, *Empires*, pp. 12–13, 40, 129–30.

100. I am in accord here with, among others, Yale H. Ferguson, "Approaches to Defining 'Empire' and Characterizing United States Influence in the Contemporary World," *Interna-*

tional Studies Perspectives, 9 (2008), pp. 272–80; Hendrick Spruyt, "'American Empire' as an Analytical Question or a Rhetorical Move?" *International Studies Perspectives* 9 (2008), pp. 290–99; Daniel H. Nexon, "What's This, Then? 'Romanes Eunt Domus'?" *International Studies Perspectives* 9 (2008), pp. 300–308; Paul K. MacDonald, "Those Who Forget Historiography Are Doomed to Republish It: Empire Imperialism and Contemporary Debates about American Power," *Review of International Studies*, 35 (2009), pp. 45–67.

101. Hopkins, *Globalisation in World History*; Hopkins, *Global History*, and the sources given in n. 2 above.

102. Hopkins, *Globalisation in World History*, chs. 1–2. Cain and Hopkins, *British Imperialism, 1688–2015* (3rd ed. London, 2016), pp. 706–25, provide a substantial illustration of the British case.

103. Charles-Louis de Secondat, Baron de la Brède et de Montesquieu (1689–1755). David W. Carrithers, Michael A. Mosher, and Paul A. Rahe, eds., *Montesquieu's Science of Politics: Essays on the Science of the Laws* (Lanham, MD, 2001), contains a wide-ranging set of essays. Werner Stark, *Montesquieu: Pioneer of the Sociology of Knowledge* (London, 1960) retains its value. For the present discussion see especially chs. 3, 7, 15; Jacob T. Levy, "Beyond Publius: Montesquieu, Liberal Republicanism and the Small-Republic Thesis," *History of Political Thought*, 27 (2006), pp. 50–90.

104. Michael A. Mosher, "Montesquieu on Empire and Enlightenment," in Sankar Muthu, ed., *Empire and Modern Political Thought* (Cambridge, 2012), ch. 5. Daniel Deudney, *Bounding Power: Republican Security Theory from the Polis to the Global Village* (Princeton, NJ, 2007), joins Montesquieu's thought to a revisionist view of the realist perspective on international relations.

105. Robert Howse, "Montesquieu on Commerce, Conquest, War, and Peace," *Brooklyn Journal of International Law*, 31 (2006), pp. 1–16. The need for brevity has obliged me to pass over some of the ambiguities in Montesquieu's formulation.

106. Anne M. Cohler, *Montesquieu's Comparative Politics and the Spirit of American Constitutionalism* (Lawrence, 1988); Daniel Walker Howe, "Why the Scottish Enlightenment Was Useful to the Framers of the American Constitution," *Comparative Studies in Society & History*, 31 (1989), pp. 572–87.

107. Stephen J. Rowe, "Commerce, Power and Justice: Montesquieu on International Politics," *Review of Politics*, 46 (1984), pp. 346–66.

108. Manjeet Kauer Ramgotra, "Republic and Empire in Montesquieu's Spirit of the Laws," *Millennium*, 42 (2014), pp. 790–816. There are extensive discussions of these issues in the Federalist Papers: Terence Hall, ed., *Alexander Hamilton, James Madison, and John Jay, The Federalist with Letters of "Brutus"* (Cambridge, 2003).

109. Catherine Larrère, "Montesquieu on Economics and Commerce," in Carrithers, Mosher, and Rahe, *Montesquieu's Science of Politics*, pp. 335–73.

110. Terminology is a sensitive (and shifting) matter, as it was in the case of the European colonies at the time of independence. I have applied the term "Native American" in chapters 1–14 because it is widely used by historians who work on the period before World War II. Specialists on the period after 1945, however, prefer the term "American Indian," which appears in chapter 15.

111. I use the term "postcolonial" in the sense that is familiar to historians of imperialism and empire to refer to the period following the end of formal colonial rule. The postmodernist adaptation of the term to refer to the colonial experience from its inception elides "colonial" and "postcolonial" in ways that, for the purposes of the present study, are unhelpful.

112. Alexander Pope, "An Essay on Criticism" (1711), extracted from the longer citation reproduced with the preliminary matter above.

113. The numerous citations that accompany each chapter are intended to convey my considerable debt to the scholars who have made this book possible.

CHAPTER 2: THE ADVANCE AND RETREAT
OF THE MILITARY-FISCAL STATE

1. A notable exception, and one that proves the rule, is P. J. Marshall, *Remaking the British Atlantic: The United States and the British Empire after American Independence* (Oxford, 2012), though his study ends in 1790.

2. This is the point to pay an overdue tribute to Frank Thistlethwaite, whose pioneering study, *The Anglo-American Connection in the Early Nineteenth Century* (Philadelphia, 1959), anticipated much that is only now being rediscovered following the recent interest in globalization.

3. Jeremy Adelman, "An Age of Imperial Revolutions," *American Historical Review*, 113 (2008), pp. 319–40; David Armitage and Sanjay Subrahmanyam, eds., *The Age of Revolutions in Global Context, c. 1760–1840* (Basingstoke, Hants, 2010); Richard Bessel, Nicholas Guyatt, and Jane Rendall, eds., *War, Empire and Slavery, 1770–1830* (Basingstoke, 2010).

4. John Stuart Mill, *Principles of Political Economy* (London, 1848; 1909), vol. 3, ch. 25, para. 17. Mill's point was that external trade within the empire was not foreign trade but trade between town and country carried on at a distance.

5. In the present context, see Geoffrey Parker, *The Military Revolution: Military Innovation and the Rise of the West, 1500–1800* (Cambridge, 1988). The key work applying the term to Britain in the eighteenth century is John W. Brewer, *The Sinews of Power: War, Money and the English State (1688–1783)* (Cambridge, 1989). Christopher Storrs, "Introduction: The Fiscal-Military State in the 'Long' Eighteenth Century," in Storrs, ed., *The Fiscal-Military State in Eighteenth-Century Europe: Essays in Honour of P. G. M. Dickson* (Farnham, 2008), provides an admirable survey of recent work.

6. Miguel de Cervantes, *The Ingenious Gentleman Don Quixote of La Mancha* (Madrid, 1605; Newark, 2007), ch. 38.

7. Edward Gibbon, *The Decline and Fall of the Roman Empire*, Vol. 1, David Womersley, ed. (London, 1776; 1994), p. 68.

8. Guides include Richard Bonney, ed., *The Rise of the Fiscal State in Europe, c. 1200–1815* (Oxford, 1999); Mark Ormrod, Margaret Bonney, and Richard Bonney, eds., *Crises, Revolutions and Self-Sustained Growth: Essays in European Fiscal History, 1130–1830* (Donington, 2000); Storrs, *The Fiscal-Military State in Eighteenth-Century Europe*. See also Jan Glete, *War and the State in Early Modern Europe: Spain, the Dutch Republic and Sweden as Fiscal-Military States* (Hoboken, 2002).

9. Examples of new, global approaches include C. A. Bayly, *The Birth of the Modern World, 1780–1914: Global Connections and Comparisons* (Oxford, 2004); Armitage and Subrahmanyam, eds., *The Age of Revolutions*; Bessell, Guyatt, and Rendall, eds., *War, Empire and Slavery*; Dominic Sachsenmaier, *Global Perspectives on Global History: Theories and Approaches in a Connected World* (Cambridge, 2011); Bartolomé Yun-Casalilla and Patrick K. O'Brien, eds., *The Rise of Fiscal States: A Global History, 1500–1914* (Cambridge, 2012). Historians of the mainland colonies are now looking beyond the Atlantic and across the Pacific. See Peter A. Coclanis, "Atlantic World or Atlantic/World?" *William & Mary Quarterly*, 63 (2006), pp. 725–42; and Eliga H. Gould, "Entangled Histories, Entangled Worlds: The English-Speaking Atlantic as a Spanish Periphery," *American Historical Review*, 112 (2007), pp. 764–86; Trevor Burnard, "Placing British Settlements in the Americas in Comparative Perspective," in H. V. Bowen, Elizabeth Mancke, and John G. Reid, eds., *Britain's Oceanic Empire: Atlantic and Indian Ocean Worlds, 1550–1850* (Cambridge, 2012), ch. 15.

10. Dennis O. Flynn and Arturo Giráldez, *China and the Birth of Globalisation in the Sixteenth Century* (Farnham, 2010); Matt K. Matsuda, *Pacific Worlds: A History of Seas, Peoples, and Cultures* (Cambridge, 2012); A. G. Hopkins, ed., *Globalization in World History* (New York, 2002).

11. Victor Lieberman, *Strange Parallels: Southeast Asia in Global Context, c. 800–1830*, vol. 2: *Mainland Mirrors, Europe, China, South Asia and the Islands* (Cambridge, 2009). Some scholars have argued, controversially, that parity between Europe and Asia extended to economic welfare, scientific knowledge, and comparable institutions. See, for example, Prasannan Parthasarathi, *Why Europe Grew Rich and Asia Did Not: Global Economic Divergence, 1600–1850* (Cambridge, 2011).

12. Jack A. Goldstone, *Revolution and Rebellion in the Early Modern World* (Berkeley, 1991).

13. Bayly, *The Birth of the Modern World*.

14. Armitage and Subrahmanyam, *The Age of Revolutions*, p. xxiii.

15. The substantial literature on this subject can be followed through Kenneth Pomeranz, *The Great Divergence: China, Europe, and the Making of the Modern World Economy* (Princeton, NJ, 2000), and the subsequent discussion of his work, especially the riposte by Ricardo Duchesne, *The Uniqueness of Western Civilisation* (Leiden, 2011); and Peer Vries, *State, Economy and the Great Divergence: Great Britain and China, 1680s to 1850s* (London, 2015).

16. Jack A. Goldstone, "Efflorescences and Economic Growth in World History: Rethinking the 'Rise of the West' and the Industrial Revolution," *Journal of World History*, 13 (2002), pp. 323–89; Goldstone, *Why Europe? The Rise of the West in World History, 1500–1850* (New York, 2008). On the importance of energy sources, see E. A. Wrigley, *Continuity, Chance, and Change: The Character of the Industrial Revolution in England* (Cambridge, 1988).

17. See Randolph Starn's engaging commentary: "The Early Modern Muddle," *Journal of Early Modern History*, 6 (2002), pp. 296–307.

18. Paolo Malanima, "Energy Crisis and Growth, 1650–1850: The European Deviation in a Comparative Perspective," *Journal of Global History*, 1 (2006), pp. 101–21. The ecological argument relies heavily on Wrigley, *Continuity, Chance, and Change.*

19. For this see Pomeranz, *The Great Divergence*.

20. Specialists will recognize that my position on this subject is very close to that of Peer H. H. Vries, "Governing Growth: A Comparative Analysis of the Role of the State in the Rise of the West," *Journal of World History*, 13 (2002), pp. 67–138; Vries, "The California School and Beyond: How to Study the Great Divergence?" *History Compass*, 8 (2010), pp. 730–51; Vries, *Escaping Poverty: The Origins of Modern Economic Growth* (Vienna, 2013); Vries, *State, Economy and the Great Divergence.* Vries's emphasis on the importance of a strong developmental state is a theme echoed here.

21. Vries, *State, Economy and the Great Divergence*, is the definitive study. Wenkai He, *Paths Toward the Modern Fiscal State: England, Japan, and China* (Cambridge, MA, 2013), reaches a similar conclusion.

22. Stephen R. Halsey, "Money, Power, and the State: The Origin of the Military-Fiscal State in Modern China," *Journal of the Economic & Social History of the Orient*, 56 (2013), p. 393, n.2. For distant antecedents, see William Guanglin Liu, "The Making of a Fiscal State in Song China, 960–1279," *Economic History Review*, 68 (2015), pp. 48–78.

23. Halsey, "Money, Power, and the State."

24. For reasons explained by Steven Wilkinson, *Army and Nation: The Military and Indian Democracy since Independence* (Cambridge, MA, 2015).

25. For one of many criticisms, see Kelly de Vries, "Gunpowder Weaponry and the Rise of the Modern State," *War in History*, 5 (1998), pp. 127–45.

26. Richard Bonney, "Absolutism: What's in a Name?" *French History*, 1 (1987), pp. 93–117.

27. Rafael Torres Sánchez, ed., *War, State and Development: Fiscal-Military States in the Eighteenth Century* (Pamplona, 2007); Stephen Conway and Raphael Torres Sánchez, eds., *The Spending of States: Military Expenditure during the Long Eighteenth Century* (Saarbrucken, 2011); Yun-Casalilla and O'Brien, eds., *The Rise of Fiscal States*.

28. Glete, *War and the State in Early Modern Europe*.

29. Richard Bonney, "France and the First European Paper Money Experiment," *French History*, 15 (2001), pp. 254–72. Claude C. Sturgill, "Considerations sur le budget de la guerre, 1720–1729," *Revue Historique des Armées*, 1 (1986), pp. 99–108, estimates that about 40 percent of the royal budget was devoted to the army during this period.

30. Javier Cuenca-Esteban, "Statistics of Spain's Colonial Trade, 1747–1820: New Estimates and Comparisons with Great Britain," *Revista de Historia Económica*, 26 (2008), pp. 324–54; Regina Grafe, *Distant Tyranny: Markets, Power, and Backwardness in Spain, 1650–1800* (Princeton, NJ, 2012); Rafael Torres Sánchez, *Constructing a Fiscal-Military State in Eighteenth-Century Spain* (London, 2015).

31. Michael Kwas, *Privilege and the Politics of Taxation in Eighteenth-Century France: Liberté, Egalité, Fiscalité* (Cambridge, 2000). For the debate on public debt in France, see Michael Senescher, *Before the Deluge: Public Debt, Inequality and the Intellectual Origins of the French Revolution* (Princeton, NJ, 2007).

32. On the Bourbon reforms, see John H. Elliott, *Empires of the Atlantic World: Britain and Spain in America, 1492–1830* (New Haven, 2007), chs. 10–12.

33. There are now admirable correctives to stereotypes of Spain as a backward state, even if the revisionists disagree among themselves about some of the revisions they propose. See Carlos Marichal, *Bankruptcy of Empire: Mexican Silver and the Wars between Spain, Britain, France, 1760–1810* (Cambridge, 2007); Regina Grafe and Maria Alejandra Irigoin, "A Stakeholder Empire: The Political Economy of Spanish Imperial Rule in America," *Economic History Review*, 65 (2012), pp. 609–51.

34. José Jurado Sánchez, "Military Expenditure, Spending Capacity and Budget Constraints in Eighteenth-Century Spain and Britain," *Revista de Historia Económica*, 27 (2009), pp. 141–74, contrasts Spain's inferior financial institutions with those of Britain.

35. The role of France in supporting the American colonists is well known; the contributions made by Spain and the Netherlands are commonly underestimated.

36. Elements of the argument that follows can be found in P. J. Cain and A. G. Hopkins, *British Imperialism, 1688–2000* (London, 1993; 3rd ed. 2016), chs. 1–2.

37. The key work is Brewer, *The Sinews of Power*. This is an opportunity, however, to pay tribute to E. James Ferguson, whose contribution has not always been acknowledged: *The Power of the Purse: A History of American Public Finance, 1776–1790* (Durham, 1965); "The Nationalists of 1781–1783 and the Economic Interpretation of the Constitution," *Journal of American History*, 56 (1969), pp. 241–61; "Political Economy, Public Liberty, and the Formation of the Constitution," *William & Mary Quarterly*, 40 (1983), pp. 389–412.

38. In addition to Vries (notes 15 and 20 above), see the series of powerful restatements by Patrick Karl O'Brien cited in the next section of this chapter. In his most recent work, Jack A. Goldstone appears to be moving toward the "traditional" standpoint, though he remains concerned to defend his position as a champion of the great divergence. See "Divergence in Cultural Trajectories: The Power of the Traditional in the Early Modern," in David Porter, ed., *Comparative Early Modernities, 1100–1800* (Basingstoke, 2012), pp. 165–94.

39. As argued by David Stasavage, *States of Credit: Size, Power and the Development of European Polities* (Princeton, NJ, 2011).

40. Richard Bonney, "The Rise of the Fiscal State in France, 1500–1914," in Yun-Casalilla and O'Brien, *The Rise of Fiscal States*, ch. 4.

41. François Marie Arouet de Voltaire, *Lettres sur les Anglais* (Rouen, 1731; London, 1933), 8, "On the Parliament."

42. Quoted in J.H.M. Salmon, "Liberty by Degrees: Raynal and Diderot on the British Constitution," *History of Political Economy*, 20 (1999), p. 101.

43. Quoted in Julian Hoppit, "The Nation, the State, and the First Industrial Revolution," *Journal of British Studies*, 50 (2011), p. 300. See also the complimentary remarks of Carl Philip Moritz, *Journeys of a German in England* (London, 1783; 1965), p. 57.

44. A valuable assessment of these issues, and a fitting tribute to the outstanding contribution to scholarship made by Patrick O'Brien, is Leandro Prados de la Escosura, ed., *Exceptionalism and Industrialisation: Britain and Its European Rivals, 1688-1815* (Cambridge, 2004).

45. Stephen Broadberry, Bruce M. S. Campbell, and Bas van Leeuwen, "When Did Britain Industrialise? The Sectoral Distribution of the Labor Force and Labor Productivity in Britain, 1381-1851," *Explorations in Economic History*, 50 (2013), pp. 20, 22-23.

46. N.A.M. Rodger, "From the 'Military Revolution' to the 'Fiscal-Naval State,'" *Journal for Maritime Research*, 12 (2011), pp. 119-28. Also Rodger, "War as an Economic Activity in the 'Long' Eighteenth Century." *International Journal of Maritime History*, 22 (2010), pp. 1-18.

47. On this and allied naval matters see N.A.M. Rodger, *The Command of the Ocean: A Naval History of Britain, 2, 1649-1815* (London, 2004); Daniel Baugh, *The Global Seven Years' War* (Harlow, 2011). Patrick Karl O'Brien and Xavier Duran, "Total Factor Productivity for the Royal Navy from Victory at Toxal (1653) to Triumph at Trafalgar (1805)," in Richard W. Ungar, ed., *Shipping and Economic Growth, 1350-1850* (Leiden, 2010), ch. 12.

48. Roger Morriss, *The Foundations of British Maritime Supremacy: Resources, Logistics, and the State, 1755-1815* (Cambridge, 2011), explores the Royal Navy's extensive relations with the mercantile marine, private merchants, contractors, and victuallers, as well as with the burgeoning government bureaucracy.

49. John R. Hale, *Lords of the Sea: The Epic Story of the Athenian Navy and the Birth of Democracy* (New York, 2009).

50. For a full account that rehabilitates some older views, see Tim Harris, *The Great Crisis of the British Monarchy, 1685-1720* (London, 2006).

51. J.C.D. Clark, *English Society, 1660-1832: Religion, Politics and Society During the Ancien Régime* (2nd ed., Cambridge, 2000); and the commentary by Joanna Innes, "Social History and England's 'Ancien Régime,'" *Past & Present*, 115 (1987), pp. 295-311.

52. Largely inspired by the work of J.G.A. Pocock, notably in *The Machiavellian Moment: Florentine Political Thought and the Atlantic Republican Tradition* (Princeton, NJ, 1975; 2003). For a concise survey of the present state of the voluminous discussion Pocock's work has stimulated, see William Walker, "J.G.A. Pocock and the History of British Political Thought: Assessing the State of the Art," *Eighteenth-Century Life*, 33 (2009), pp. 83-96.

53. Research since Dickson's study was published has shown that fiscal reforms were under way well before 1688. Henry Roseveare, *The Financial Revolution, 1660-1760* (London, 1991); Anne L Murphy, *The Origins of English Financial Markets: Investment and Speculation before the South Sea Bubble* (Cambridge, 2009).

54. Steve Pincus, *1688: The First Modern Revolution* (New Haven, 2009). *British Scholar*, 2 (2010), pp. 295-338, provides representative examples of the discussion this book has provoked.

55. Paul W. Schroeder, *The Transformation of European Politics, 1763-1848* (Oxford, 1994), p. vii, suggests that there were more deaths on European battlefields in the eighteenth century than in the nineteenth century. For a discussion of whether the period witnessed the introduction of "total war," see Roger Chickering and Stig Förster, eds., *War in an Age of Revolution, 1775-1815* (Cambridge, 2010).

56. Rodger, "War as an Economic Activity."

57. Andrew Jackson O'Shaughnessy, "'If Others Will Not Be Active, I Must Drive': George III and the American Revolution," *Early American Studies*, 2 (2004), pp. 1-47.

58. For an authoritative overview see Patrick K. O'Brien, "Inseparable Connections: Trade, Economy, Fiscal State, and the Expansion of Empire, 1688-1815," in P. J. Marshall, ed., *Oxford History of the British Empire*, vol. 2 (Oxford, 1998), ch. 3.

59. Ralph Davis, "The Rise of Protection in England, 1689-1786," *Economic History Review* 19 (1966), pp. 306-17; and D. C. Coleman, "Mercantilism Revisited," *Historical Journal*, 23 (1980), pp. 773-91, remain important points of departure from (even) older studies.

The seventeenth-century context for the chapter is provided by Robert Brenner, *Merchants and Revolution: Commercial Change, Political Conflict, and London's Overseas Traders 1550-1653* (Princeton, NJ, 1993), chs. 12, 13, and postscript.

60. Robert B. Ekelund and Robert D. Tollison, *Mercantilism as a Rent-Seeking Society: Economic Regulation in Historical Perspective* (Austin, 1981).

61. A. W. Coats, "Adam Smith and the Mercantile System," in Andrew S. Skinner and Thomas Wilson, eds., *Essays on Adam Smith* (Oxford, 1975), pp. 218-36.

62. S. D. Smith, "Prices and Value of English Exports in the Eighteenth Century: Evidence from the North American Colonial Trade," *Economic History Review*, 48 (1995), pp. 575-90.

63. The data in this paragraph are drawn mainly from R. P. Thomas and D. N. McCloskey, "Overseas Trade and Empire, 1700-1820," in Roderick Floud and D. N. McCloskey, eds., *Cambridge Economic History of Modern Britain*, Vol. 1 (Cambridge, 1981), ch. 4; C. Knick Harley, "Trade, Discovery, Mercantilism and Technology," in Roderick Floud and Paul Johnson, eds., *Cambridge Economic History of Modern Britain*, Vol. 1 (Cambridge, 2004), ch. 5.

64. Jacob M. Price, "The Imperial Economy, 1700-1776," in P. J. Marshall, ed., *The Oxford History of the British Empire*, Vol. 2 (Oxford, 1998), p.101.

65. O'Brien and Duran, "Total Factor Productivity for the Royal Navy."

66. Patrick K. O'Brien and Philip A. Hunt, "England, 1485-1815," in Bonney, *The Rise of the Fiscal State in Europe*, pp. 53-100.

67. Patrick Karl O'Brien, "The Triumph and Denouement of the British Fiscal State: Taxation for the Wars Against Revolutionary and Napoleonic France, 1793-1815," in Storrs, *The Fiscal-Military State*, pp. 162-200; O'Brien, "The Nature and Historical Evolution of the Exceptional Fiscal State and Its Significance for the Precocious Commercialisation and Industrialisation of the British Economy from Cromwell to Nelson," *Economic History Review*, 64 (2011), pp. 428-31.

68. Richard Cooper, "William Pitt, Taxation, and the Needs of War," *Journal of British Studies*, 22 (1982), pp. 94-103. On the imposition of income tax in 1799, see S. J. Thompson, "The First Income Tax, Political Arithmetic, and the Measurement of Economic Growth," *Economic History Review*, 66 (2013), pp. 873-94.

69. Quoted in O'Brien, "The Triumph and Denouement of the British Fiscal State," p. 174.

70. Cain and Hopkins, *British Imperialism*, ch. 1.

71. This gargantuan concept is full of ambiguities and is readily annexed to ideological purposes. Unfortunately, an untainted substitute has yet to appear. In standard usage, the term refers to the growth of constitutional government, the formation of nation-states, the development of power-driven manufacturing processes, and a degree of individual freedom sufficient to encourage innovation, whether in commerce, scientific inquiry, or political discourse. A conception of British "exceptionalism" that equated it with modernization provided ready support for a heroic view of the process and its subsequent diffusion. It endowed Britain with qualities of leadership and superiority that could be deployed to justify empire-building, and it allowed colonial rule to be presented as a necessary and beneficial stage in what became known as the "civilizing mission."

72. Two authorities on the period have taken this position recently. See Joel Mokyr, *The Enlightened Economy: An Economic History of Britain, 1700-1850* (New Haven, 2009); Patrick O'Brien, "Historical Foundations for a Global Perspective on the Emergence of a Western European Regime for the Discovery, Development, and Diffusion of Useful and Reliable Knowledge," *Journal of Global History*, 8 (2013), pp. 1-24.

73. Jan de Vries and Ad van der Woude, *The First Modern Economy: Success, Failure, and Perseverance of the Dutch Economy, 1500-1815* (Cambridge, 1997). The decline of the Dutch Republic was relative, not absolute. In the course of the century, the Republic abandoned its ambitions to be a major power but developed a successful fiscal-financial complex before the 1790s, when the French Wars ruined the economy.

74. See especially Joseph M. Bryant, "The West and the Rest Revisited: Debating Capitalist Origins, European Colonialism, and the Advent of Modernity," *Canadian Journal of Sociology*, 31 (2006), pp. 403–44, and the discussion in *Canadian Journal of Sociology*, 33 (2008), issue 1; Bryant, "A New Sociology for a New History? Further Critical Thoughts on the Eurasian Similarity and Great Divergence Theses," *Canadian Journal of Sociology*, 31 (2008), pp. 149–67.

75. Such claims can plausibly be made: O'Brien, "The Nature and Historical Evolution of the Exceptional Fiscal State."

76. S. D. Smith, "British Exports to Colonial North America and the Mercantilist Fallacy," *Business History*, 37 (1995), pp. 45–63.

77. India became particularly important in this regard during the last twenty years of the century: Javier Cuenca-Estaban, "The British Balance of Payments, 1772–1820: Indian Transfers and War Finance," *Economic History Review*, 54 (2001), pp. 58–86; Cuenca-Estaban, "Comparative Patterns of Colonial Trade: Britain and Its Rivals," in Leandro Prados de la Escosura, ed., *Exceptionalism and Industrialisation: Britain and Its Industrial Rivals, 1688–1815* (Cambridge, 2004), ch. 2; Cuenca-Estaban, "India's Contribution to the British Balance of Payments, 1757–1812," *Explorations in Economic History*, 44 (2007), pp. 154–76.

78. Jeremy Black, *The Continental Commitment: Britain, Hanover and Interventionism, 1714–1793* (Abingdon, 2005), provides an accessible survey; Stephen Conway, *Britain, Ireland, and Continental Europe in the Eighteenth Century: Similarities, Connections, Identities* (Oxford, 2011), moves beyond high politics to emphasize the strength of the European connection.

79. These wider considerations are discussed in Tim Harris and Stephen Taylor, eds., *The Final Crisis of the Scottish Monarchy: The Revolutions of 1688–91 in Their British, Atlantic, and European Contexts* (Woodbridge, 2013).

80. The fundamental work remains P.G.M. Dickson, *The Financial Revolution in England: A Study in the Development of Public Credit, 1688–1756* (London, 1967). These claims stand, even though some consequences of institutional change took time to appear. See Yishay Yafeh, "Institutional Reforms, Financial Development, and Sovereign Debt: Britain, 1690–1790," *Journal of Economic History*, 66 (2006), pp. 906–35.

81. On London's relations with its closest rival see, Larry Neal, "Amsterdam and London as Financial Centres in the Eighteenth Century," *Financial History Review*, 18 (2011), pp. 21–46.

82. Paul Langford, *A Polite and Commercial People: England, 1727–1783* (Oxford, 1989), ch. 1, provides a judicious account of the title.

83. Nicholas Rogers, *Whigs and Cities: Popular Politics in the Age of Walpole and Pitt* (Oxford, 1989); Rogers, *Crowds, Culture and Politics in Georgian Britain* (Oxford, 1998); Rogers, *Mayhem: Post-War Crime and Violence in Britain, 1748–53* (New Haven, 2012); Bob Harris, *Politics and the Nation: Britain in the Mid-Eighteenth Century* (Oxford, 2002); Adrian Randall, *Riotous Assemblies: Popular Protest in Hanoverian England* (Oxford, 2006), provide representative accounts of newer views.

84. Brewer, *The Sinews of Power*.

85. Daniel Carey and Christopher J. Finlay, eds., *The Empire of Credit: The Financial Revolution in the British Atlantic World, 1688–1815* (Dublin, 2011). Hoppit, "The Nation, the State, and the First Industrial Revolution," shows that the military-fiscal state was an English device that was less popular in the outer provinces than in the Home Counties.

86. Hamish Scott, "The Seven Years' War and Europe's Ancien Régime," *War in History*, 18 (2011), pp. 319–55; Jan Eloranta and Jeremy Land, "Hollow Victory? Britain's Public Debt and the Seven Year's War," *Essays in Economic & Business History*, 29 (2011), pp. 101–18.

87. Julian Hoppit, *Risk and Failure in English Business, 1700–1800* (Cambridge, 1987), traces this development in detail; Hoppit, "Attitudes to Credit in Britain, 1680–1790," *Historical Journal*, 33 (1990), pp. 305–22.

88. Alexander Dick, "New Work on Money," *Eighteenth-Century Life*, 34 (2010), pp. 105–13.

89. John Brewer, *Party Ideology and Popular Politics at the Accession of George III* (Cambridge, 1976).

90. As Linda Colley has shown for the Tory Party during the years of Whig ascendancy: *In Defiance of Oligarchy: The Tory Party, 1714–60* (Cambridge, 1982). J.C.D. Clark provides a clear guide to what, for non-specialists, is nevertheless a baffling kaleidoscope of shifting alignments: "A General Theory of Party, Opposition and Government, 1688–1832," *Historical Journal*, 23 (1980), pp. 295–325.

91. Henry Horwitz, "The East India Trade, the Politicians, and the Constitution, 1889–1702," *Journal of British Studies*, 17 (1978), pp. 1–18.

92. For confirmation of the Whig-City link, see David Stasavage, "Partisan Politics and Public Debt: The Importance of the Whig Supremacy for Britain's Financial Revolution," *European Review of Economic History*, 11 (2007), pp. 123–53.

93. Søren Mentz, *The English Gentleman Merchant at Work: Madras and the City of London, 1660–1740* (Copenhagen, 2005).

94. Colin Lees, "What Is the Problem About Corruption?" *Journal of Modern African Studies*, 3 (1965), pp. 215–30. What commentators call corruption characterizes all underdeveloped countries and a good many developed ones, too, and can contribute to development despite its many acknowledged deficiencies. The morality of corruption, and of rent-seeking generally, is of course a separate matter.

95. 1678–1751. The pioneering study is Caroline Robbins, *The Eighteenth-Century Commonwealth Men* (1959; 2004). See also Isaac Kramnick, *Bolingbroke and His Circle: The Politics of Nostalgia in the Age of Walpole* (Ithaca, 1992).

96. David Armitage, "A Patriot for Whom? The Afterlives of Bolingbroke's Patriot King," *Journal of British Studies*, 36 (1997), pp. 397–418.

97. Paul Langford, *The Excise Crisis: Society and Politics in the Age of Walpole* (Oxford, 1975).

98. Daniel Carey and Christopher J. Finlay, eds., *The Empire of Credit: The Financial Revolution in the British Atlantic World, 1688–1815* (Dublin, 2011).

99. Hoppit, *Risk and Failure in English Business*, traces this development in detail; Hoppit, "Attitudes to Credit in Britain, 1680–1790," *Historical Journal*, 33 (1990), pp. 305–22.

100. Richard Harding, *The Emergence of Britain's Global Supremacy: The War of 1739-1748* (Woodbridge, Suffolk, 2010).

101. P. J. Marshall and Glyndwr Williams, *The Great Map of Mankind: Perceptions of New Worlds in the Age of Enlightenment* (Cambridge, MA, 1982); Armitage and Subrahmanyam, *The Age of Revolutions*.

102. Including topographic images, which became more numerous after 1750: J. E. Crowley, *Imperial Landscapes: Britain's Global Visual Culture, 1745–1820* (New Haven, 2011).

103. Anthony Pagden, *Enlightenment: And Why It Matters* (Oxford, 2013); Caroline Winterer, *American Enlightenments: Pursuing Happiness in the Age of Reason* (New Haven, 2017).

104. Peter Lake and Steve Pincus, "Rethinking the Public Sphere in Early Modern England," *Journal of British Studies*, 45 (2006), pp. 270–92; James Van Horne Melton's *The Rise of the Public in Enlightenment Europe* (Cambridge, 2001), provides a valuable comparative study of England, France, and Germany that emphasizes the role of private initiatives.

105. David Hancock, *Citizens of the World: London Merchants and the Integration of the British Atlantic Community, 1735–65* (Cambridge, 1995); Huw Bowen, *Elites, Enterprise, and the Making of the British Overseas Empire, 1688–1775* (London, 1996), ch. 7.

106. Bowen, "Perceptions from the Periphery," pp. 295–6.

107. Hancock, *Citizens of the World*; Sheryllynne Haggerty, *The British-Atlantic Trading Community, 1760–1810: Men, Women and the Distribution of Goods* (Leiden, 2006), draws attention to the important role women played in private overseas networks.

108. David Armitage, "Globalizing Jeremy Bentham," *History of Political Thought*, 32 (2011), pp. 63–82.

109. Emma Rothschild is characteristically illuminating on this subject: "Global Commerce and the Question of Sovereignty in the Eighteenth-Century Provinces," *Modern Intellectual History*, 1 (2004), pp. 3–25.

110. Huw V. Bowen, "British Conceptions of Global Empire," *Journal of Imperial and Commonwealth History*, 26 (1998), pp. 1–27; Brian P. Levack, "Britain's First Global Century: England, Scotland and Empire, 1603–1707," *Britain and the World*, 6 (2013), pp. 101–18.

111. Explored by Lauren Benton, *A Search for Sovereignty: Law and Geography in European Empires, 1400–1900* (Cambridge, 2010). Anthony Pagden, "Fellow Citizens and Imperial Subjects: Conquest and Sovereignty in Europe's Overseas Empires," *History & Theory*, 44 (2005), provides a succinct and wide-ranging assessment.

112. Alison L. LaCroix, *The Ideological Origins of the American Federalism* (Cambridge, MA, 2010).

113. This subject has been an abiding theme of Jack P. Greene's work. See particularly *Peripheries and Center: Constitutional Development in the Extended Polities of the British Empire and the United States, 1607–1788* (Athens, 1986); Greene, *Negotiated Authorities: Essays in Colonial and Constitutional History* (Charlottesville, 1994).

114. On this, and much more, see Stewart J. Brown, ed., *William Robertson and the Expansion of Empire* (Cambridge, 1997).

115. Sankar Muthu, *Enlightenment against Empire* (Princeton, NJ, 2003).

116. Although recent interest in multiculturalism has given prominence to this theme, credit should be given to a previous generation of scholars whose work is now largely unread. See, for example, Lawrence Henry Gipson, *The British Empire before the Revolution*, Vol. 1 (Caldwell, 1936).

117. The definitive study is Richard Bourke, *Empire and Revolution: The Political Life of Edmund Burke* (Princeton, 2015). For discussions of Ireland's status, see John Gibney, "Early Modern Ireland: A British Atlantic Colony?" *History Compass*, 6 (2008), pp. 172–82; Stephen Howe, "Questioning the (Bad) Question: Was Ireland a Colony?" *Irish Historical Studies*, 36 (2008), pp. 138–52.

118. David Armitage, "Making the Empire British: Scotland in the Atlantic World, 1542–1707," *Past & Present*, 155 (1997), pp. 34–63. Limitations of space prevent a consideration of the neglected case of Wales, on which see the pioneering study edited by Huw Bowen, *Wales and the British Overseas Empire: Interactions and Influences, 1650–1830* (Manchester, 2012).

119. For a little-known feature of these exported influences, see Myron C. Noonkester, "The Third British Empire: Transplanting the English Shire to Wales, Scotland, Ireland and America," *Journal of British Studies*, 36 (1997), pp. 251–85.

120. Michael Fry, *The Scottish Empire* (Edinburgh, 2001); T. M. Devine, *Scotland's Empire, 1600–1815* (London, 2003); Devine, *To the Ends of the Earth: Scotland's Global Diaspora, 1750–2010* (London, 2012); John M. MacKenzie, "Irish, Scottish, Welsh and English Worlds? A Four-Nation Approach to the History of the British Empire," *History Compass*, 6 (2008), pp. 1244–63; John M. MacKenzie and T. M. Devine, eds., *Scotland and the British Empire* (Oxford, 2011).

121. For different views of the health of the Scottish economy on the eve of Union, see Christopher A. Whatley with Derek J. Patrick, *The Scots and the Union* (Edinburgh, 2006); and Alan J. Macinnes, *Union and Empire: The Making of the United Kingdom in 1707* (Cambridge, 2007). See also Bob Harris, "The Anglo-Scottish Treaty of Union, 1707 in 2007: Defending the Revolution, Defeating the Jacobites," *Journal of British Studies*, 49 (2010), pp. 28–46; Alvin Jackson, *The Two Unions: Ireland, Scotland, and the Survival of the United Kingdom, 1707–2007* (Oxford, 2011).

122. G. E. Bannerman, "The Nabob of the North: Sir Lawrence Dundas as Government Contractor," *Historical Research*, 83 (2010), pp. 102–23. Lawrence Dundas and Henry Dundas were unrelated.

123. Andrew Mackillop, "A Union for Empire? Scotland, the East India Company, and the British Union," *Scottish Historical Review*, 87 (2008), Supplement, pp. 116–34; George K. McGilvany, *East India Company Patronage and the British State: The Scottish Elite and Politics in the Eighteenth Century* (London, 2008).

124. John M. Mackenzie, "Empire and National Identities: The Case of Scotland," *Transactions of the Royal Historical Society*, 8 (1998), pp. 215–31.

125. Bob Harris and Christopher Whatley, "'To Solemnize His Majesty's Birthday': New Perspectives on Loyalism in George II's Britain," *History*, 83 (1998), pp. 397–420.

126. John M. MacKenzie, "Essay and Reflection: On Scotland and the Empire," *International History Review*, 15 (1993), pp. 714–39.

127. Initially amidst controversy in Scotland: Matthew P. Dziennik, "Hierarchy, Authority and Jurisdiction in the Mid-Eighteenth-Century Recruitment of the Highland Regiments," *Historical Research*, 85 (2012), pp. 89–104.

128. Andrew Mackillop, "The Political Culture of the Scottish Highlands from Culloden to Waterloo," *Historical Journal*, 46 (2003), pp. 511–32, charts the development of a mutually supportive relationship between 1746 and 1815.

129. I owe this illustration to Emma Rothschild's skillful reconstruction: *The Inner Life of Empires: An Eighteenth-Century History* (Princeton, NJ, 2011).

130. Rothschild, *The Inner Life of Empires*, p. 15.

131. "Nabob," a corruption of "nawab" (the name for a provincial governor of the Mughal Empire), was used from the late seventeenth century to describe wealthy Britons who had made their money in India (and later in the empire generally). Nabob, in turn, gave rise to the contraction "nob."

132. *Theory of Moral Sentiments*, pp. 183–4. Quoted in Rothschild, *Inner Life of Empires*, p. 13.

133. Their story of success should be read with that of the losers. See Linda Colley, *Captives: Britain, Empire and the World, 1600–1850* (London, 2002).

134. On antecedents, see James Scott Walker, *Cromwell in Ireland* (New York, 1999); Micheal Ó. Siochrú, "Atrocity, Codes of Conduct, and the Irish in the British Civil Wars, 1641–1653," *Past & Present*, 195 (2007), pp. 55–86; more generally, Nicholas Canny, *Making Ireland British, 1580–1650* (Oxford, 2001); and Kevin Kenny, ed., *Ireland and the British Empire* (Oxford, 2004), chs. 2–3.

135. On the subsequent accord, see Oliver P. Rafferty, "The Catholic Church, Ireland, and the British Empire, 1800–1921," *Historical Research*, 84 (2011), pp. 288–309.

136. Patrick A. Walsh, *The Making of the Irish Protestant Ascendancy: The Life of William Conolly, 1662–1729* (Woodstock, 2010). See also n. 122 above.

137. Patrick A. Walsh, "The Fiscal State in Ireland, 1691–1769," *Historical Journal*, 56 (2013), pp. 629–56. About 12,000 troops before 1769; about 15,000 thereafter. Ibid., p. 633.

138. Alvin Jackson, *Home Rule: An Irish History, 1800–2000* (Oxford, 2003), provides an excellent guide to the later period, as does his study of Scotland (n. 122).

139. Jackson, *The Two Unions*.

140. This is not, of course, to deny that the Irish, too, had imperial networks of their own: Craig Bailey, "Metropole and Colony: Irish Networks and Patronage in the Eighteenth-Century Empire," *Immigrants & Minorities*, 23 (2005), pp. 161–81.

141. This is a generalization with important exceptions, notably the work of Michael R. Broers, *Europe under Napoleon, 1799–1815* (London, 1996); and the further references in Michael Broers, Peter Hicks, and Agustín Guimerá, eds., *The Napoleonic Empire and the New European Political Culture* (New York, 2012). I have also gained from Stuart Woolf, *Napoleon's Integration of Europe* (London, 1991); Woolf, "Napoleon and Europe Revisited," *Modern & Contemporary France*, 8 (2004), pp. 469–78; Philip G. Dwyer, ed., *Napoleon and Europe* (London, 2001); Philip G. Dwyer and Alan Forest, eds., *Napoleon and His Empire: Europe, 1804–1814* (Basingstoke, Hants, 2007).

142. Stephen A. Kippur, *Jules Michelet: A Study of Mind and Sensibility* (New York, 1981), ch. 12. On different characterizations of British and French expansion, see Emma Rothschild, "Language and Empire, c. 1800," *Historical Research*, 78 (2005), pp. 208–29.

143. Michael Broers, "Cultural Imperialism in a European Context? Political Culture and Cultural Politics in Napoleonic Italy," *Past & Present*, 170 (2001), pp. 152–80.

144. Napoleon's imperial policing system derived from institutions established by the French Revolution. The *Gendarmerie Nationale* was formed in 1791. The term "insurgent" spread from France to other parts of Europe in the second half of the eighteenth century.

145. Suzanne Dean, Lynn Hunt, and William Max Nelson, eds., *The French Revolution in Global Perspective* (Ithaca, 2013).

146. T.C.W. Blanning, *The French Revolution in Germany: Occupation and Resistance in the Rhineland, 1792–1802* (New York, 1983).

147. Byron, "The Isles of Greece," in *Don Juan* (1819), Canto 3.

148. Percy Bysshe Shelley (1792–1822), "Ode to Liberty" (1820).

149. Enrico Dal Lago, *William Lloyd Garrison and Giuseppe Mazzini: Abolition, Democracy, and Radical Reform* (Baton Rouge, 2013).

150. Garrison (1805–79) was a reformer in the spirit of Byron, Lafayette, and Cobden, and, like them, was a cosmopolitan who was nevertheless anchored in his own country. See W. Caleb McDaniel, *The Problem of Democracy in the Age of Slavery: Garrisonian Abolitionists and Transatlantic Reform* (Baton Rouge, 2013).

151. Yonatan Eyal, *The Young America Movement and the Transformation of the Democratic Party, 1828–1861* (Cambridge, 2012), pp. 107–10. Kossuth (1802–94) was lionized during his visit to the United States at the close of 1851 and early 1852. The mania had ebbed by the time Kossuth left the United States, and he never received the official support he sought.

152. Richard Carwardine and Jay Sexton, eds., *The Global Lincoln* (Oxford, 2011).

153. Victor Hugo, *Les Misérables* (Paris, 1862; Adelaide, 2014), vol. 2, book 1, ch. 17.

154. Author's "Introduction" (written in 1842) to *La Comédie humaine* (Paris, 1855), pp. 23–4.

155. Brendan Simms, "Reform in Britain and Prussia, 1797–1815: (Confessional) Military-Fiscal State and Military-Agrarian Complex," *Proceedings of the British Academy*, 85 (1999), pp. 79–100.

156. Although the Catalan Revolt extended into 1848, its broadly conservative character excluded it from the revolutionary movements north of the Pyrenees.

157. R.J.W. Evans and Harmut Pogge von Strandmann, eds., *The Revolutions in Europe, 1848–1849: From Reform to Reaction* (Oxford, 2000).

158. Dieter Dowe, Heinz-Gerhard Haupt, Dieter Langewiesche, and Jonathan Sperber, eds., *Europe in 1848: Revolution and Reform* (New York, 2001).

159. See Miles Taylor's illuminating article, "The 1848 Revolutions and the British Empire," *Past & Present*, 166 (2000), pp. 146–80.

160. Taylor, "The 1848 Revolutions"; C. A. Bayly, "The First Age of Global Imperialism, c. 1760–1830," *Journal of Imperial and Commonwealth History*, 26 (1998), pp. 28–47.

161. Timothy Mason Roberts, *Distant Revolutions: 1848 and the Challenge of American Exceptionalism* (Charlottesville, 2009).

162. Andre M. Fleche, *The Revolution of 1861: The American Civil War in the Age of Nationalist Conflict* (Chapel Hill, 2012).

163. Roberts, *Distant Revolutions*, p. 185, suggests that this concern contributed to the formation of the Republican Party.

164. Betsy Erkkila, "Lincoln in International Memory," in Shirley Samuels, ed., *The Cambridge Companion to Abraham Lincoln* (Cambridge, 2012), pp. 157–9.

165. Edmund Burke, quoted in Daniel E. Ritchie, *Edmund Burke: Appraisals and Applications* (London, 1990), p. 247.

166. Canning to Hookham Frere, January 8, 1825. Quoted in E. M. Lloyd, "Canning and Spanish America," *Transactions of the Royal Historical Society*, 18 (1904), p. 77. The specific context was the independence of Mexico, which Canning saw as an opportunity for Britain to "slip between" the two parties.

167. Joseph Eaton, *The Anglo-American Paper War: Debates About the New Republic, 1800–1825* (Basingstoke, Hants, 2012), pp. 49, 103, 106, 114, 121–2.

168. Beatrice de Graaf, "Second Tier Diplomacy: Hans von Gagern and William I in their Quest for an Alternative European Order, 1813–1818," *Journal of Modern European History*, 12 (2014), pp. 546–66; de Graaf, "Bringing Sense and Sensibility to the Continent—Vienna, 1815 Revisited," *Modern European History*, 13 (2015), pp. 447–57.

169. Kim Oosterlinck, Loredana Ureche-Rangau, and Jacques-Marie Vaslin, "Baring, Wellington, and the Resurrection of French Public Finances Following Waterloo," *Journal of Economic History*, 74 (2014), pp. 1072–1102. I am grateful to Dr. David Todd, King's College, London, for alerting me to this episode.

170. Robert Banks Jenkinson (1770–1827), 2nd Lord Liverpool. Foreign Secretary, 1801–04; Home Secretary, 1804–05, 1807–09; Secretary of State for War, 1809–12; Britain's longest serving prime minister, 1812–27.

171. The quotation is from Peter Mandler, *Aristocratic Government in the Age of Reform: Whigs and Liberals, 1830–1852* (Oxford, 1990), p. 28.

172. David Todd, *L'identité économique de la France: libre-échange et protectionnisme, 1814–1851* (Paris, 2008); Alain Clément, "Libéralisme et anti-colonialisme: La pensée économique française et l'effondrement du premier empire colonial (1789–1830)," *Revue Économique*, 63 (2012), pp. 5–26, adds the voices of Say and Sismondi.

173. Boyd Hilton, *The Age of Atonement: The Influence of Evangelicals on Social and Economic Thought, 1785–1865* (Oxford, 1986); and more generally, idem, *A Mad, Bad, and Dangerous People? England, 1783–1846* (Oxford, 2006).

174. Herbert Schlossberg, *The Silent Revolution and the Making of Victorian England* (Columbus, 2000). British and American evangelicals remained in close touch. See Thistlethwaite, *The Anglo-American Connection*), ch. 3.

175. David W. Bebbington, *Evangelicalism in Modern Britain: A History from the 1730s to the 1980s* (London, 1989), pp. 107–9.

176. Victor G. Kiernan, *Poets, Politics, and the People* (London, 1989), p. 65.

177. Hilton, *The Age of Atonement*, p. 6.

178. The quotations are from Robert Browning, "The Lost Leader," written in 1843 in criticism of Wordsworth's growing conservatism.

179. Guides include Arthur Burns and Joanna Innes, eds., *Rethinking the Age of Reform: Britain, 1780–1850* (Cambridge, 2003); and for a comparative perspective Joanna Innes and Mark Philp, eds., *Re-Imagining Democracy in the Age of Revolution: America, France, Britain, Ireland 1750–1850* (New York, 2013).

180. J. E. Cookson, *The British Armed Nation, 1793–1815* (Oxford, 1997); Jennifer Mori, "Languages of Loyalism: Patriotism, Nationhood and the State in the 1790s," *English Historical Review*, 118 (2003), pp. 33–58; Mark Philp, *Resisting Napoleon: the British Response to the Threat of Invasion, 1797–1815* (Ashgate, 2006).

181. As Katrina Navickas has demonstrated in her subtle and illuminating study: *Loyalism and Radicalism in Lancashire 1798–1915* (Oxford, 2009). In a complementary work, Nicholas Rogers has shown how support for the monarchy contrasted with food riots and protests against impressment: "Burning Tom Paine: Loyalism and Counter-Revolution Britain, 1792–1793," *Social History*, 32 (1999), pp. 139–71.

182. Robert Saunders, "God and the Great Reform Act: Preaching against Reform," *Journal of British Studies*, 52 (2014), pp. 378–99.

183. Miles Taylor, "Empire and Parliamentary Reform: The 1832 Reform Act Revisited," in Arthur Burns and Joanna Innes, eds., *Rethinking the Age of Reform, 1780–1850* (Cambridge, 2003), ch. 13.

184. Nicholas Draper, *The Price of Emancipation: Slave-Ownership, Compensation, and British Society at the End of Slavery* (Cambridge, 2010). Approximately 46,000 claims were submitted, about 25 percent by women.

185. Duke of Wellington to Croker, March 6, 1833. Quoted in John A. Phillips and Charles Wetherell, "The Great Reform Act of 1832 and the Political Modernization of England," *American Historical Review*, 100 (1995), p. 434.

186. David F. Krein, "The Great Landowners in the House of Commons, 1833–85," *Parliamentary History*, 32 (2013), pp. 460–76, shows that the important change came with the Reform Act of 1867.

187. Current scholarship is inclined to give more weight to the "Great" Reform Act than has been the case for some time. See Bruce Morrison, "Channeling the Restless Spirit of Innovation: Elite Concessions and Institutional Change in the British Reform Act of 1832," *World Politics*, 63 (2011), pp. 678–710; Phillips and Wetherell, "The Great Reform Act."

188. Arthur Burns and Joanna Innes, eds., *Rethinking the Age of Reform, 1780–1850* (London, 2003); Joanna Innes and François-Joseph Ruggiu, "La réforme dans la vie publique anglaise: les fortunes d'un mot," *Annales*, 24 (2005), pp. 63–88.

189. Miles Taylor, *The Decline of British Radicalism, 1847–1860* (Oxford, 1995); Krein, "The Great Landowners in the House of Commons."

190. Peter J. Stanlis, ed., *Edmund Burke, Selected Writings and Speeches* (New York, 1963; New Brunswick, 2009), p. 263. The quotations are representative of Burke's views, though they are taken from a more specific context.

191. This paragraph follows the main lines of the argument in Cain and Hopkins, *British Imperialism*, ch. 3, updated where relevant.

192. O'Brien, "The Nature and Historical Evolution of the Exceptional Fiscal State," p. 430.

193. Giovanni Federico, "The Corn Laws in Continental Perspective," *European Review of Economic History*, 16 (2012), pp. 166–87, shows that other European countries took similar action to support established landed interests.

194. Paul Sharp, "1846 and All That: The Rise and Fall of British Wheat Protection in the Nineteenth Century," *Agricultural History Review*, 58 (2010), pp. 76–94, evaluates the effective degree of protection after 1815.

195. C. R. Fay, a remarkable and underestimated historian, remains an indispensable source: *Huskisson and His Age* (London, 1951).

196. Starting points for entering the considerable literature on this subject include: Hilton, *The Age of Atonement*; Anthony Howe, *Free Trade and Liberal England, 1846–1946* (New York, 1997); Anna Gambles, *Protection and Politics: Conservative Economic Discourse, 1815–1852* (Woodbridge, 1999); Cheryl Schonhardt-Bailey, *From the Corn Laws to Free Trade: Interests, Ideas and Institutions in Historical Perspective* (Cambridge, MA, 2006). On the Navigation Acts, see Sara Palmer, *Politics, Shipping and the Repeal of the Navigation Laws* (Manchester, 1990). Gambles, *Protection and Politics*.

197. Cain and Hopkins, *British Imperialism*, pp. 80–87.

198. Gareth Steadman Jones, Daniel Argeles, and Philippe Minard, "Repenser le Chartisme," *Revue d'Histoire Moderne et Contemporaine*, 54 (2007), pp. 7–68.

199. Cain and Hopkins, *British Imperialism*, pp. 612–13.

200. Boyd Hilton, "Peel: A Reappraisal," *Historical Journal*, 22 (1979), pp. 601–2.

201. Paul A. Pickering and Alex Tyrrell, *The People's Bread: A History of the Anti-Corn Law League* (Leicester, 2000). For a recent guide to "Cobden Studies," see Anthony Howe and Simon Morgan, eds., *Rethinking Nineteenth-Century Liberalism: Richard Cobden Bicentenary Essays* (Aldershot, 2006).

202. Danilo Raponi, "An 'Anti-Catholicism of Free Trade?' Religion and the Anglo-Italian Negotiations of 1863," *European History Quarterly*, 39 (2009), pp. 633–52, provides a fascinating example of an attempt to carry Protestantism into the Catholic heartland. Frank Trentmann, *Free Trade Nation: Commerce, Consumption, and Civil Society in Modern Britain* (Oxford, 2008), traces the sanctification of business.

203. Palmer, *Politics, Shipping and the Repeal of the Navigation Laws*.

204. Michael J. Turner, *Independent Radicalism in Early Victorian Britain* (Westport, 2004), pp. 64–73.

205. Simon Morgan, "The Anti-Corn Law League and British Anti-Slavery in Trans-Atlantic Perspective, 1838–1846," *Historical Journal*, 52 (2009), pp. 87–107.

206. Schonhardt-Bailey, *From the Corn Laws to Free Trade*, provides full details. Kevin H. O'Rourke, "British Trade Policy in the Nineteenth Century: A Review Article," *European Journal of Political Economy*, 16 (2000), pp. 829–42, presents a lucid review of the literature, which tends to neglect the consequences of free trade for foreign investment.

207. Henry Miller, "Popular Petitioning and the Corn Laws, 1823–46," *English Historical Review*, 127 (2012), pp. 882–919. Cobden used the term, and variations of it, on innumerable occasions.

208. Schonhardt-Bailey, *From the Corn Laws to Free Trade*, p. 228.

209. Philip Harling and Peter Mandler, "From 'Fiscal-Military' State to Laissez-Faire State, 1760–1850," *Journal of British Studies*, 32 (1993), pp. 44–70; Philip Harling, *The Waning of "Old Corruption": The Politics of Economical Reform in Britain, 1779–1846* (New York, 1996); David Cannadine, "The Context, Performance and Meaning of Ritual: The British Monarchy and the 'Invention of Tradition,'" in Eric Hobsbawm and Terence Ranger, eds., *The Invention of Tradition* (Cambridge, 1983), pp. 101–64; Duncan Bell, "The Idea of a Patriot Queen? The Monarchy, the Constitution, and the Iconographic Order of Greater Britain, 1860–1900," *Journal of Imperial & Commonwealth History*, 34 (2006), pp. 3–21.

210. Peter Mandler, *The English National Character* (New Haven, 2007), notes how reformers promoted a sense of common nationality as a means of establishing equal rights.

211. Anthony Webster, *The Twilight of the East India Company: The Evolution of Anglo-Asian Commerce and Politics, 1790–1860* (Woodbridge, 2009), ch. 3. The company lost its governmental functions in 1858 and was dissolved in 1874.

212. Richard Huzzey, *Freedom Burning: Anti-Slavery and Empire in Victorian Britain* (Ithaca, 2012), traces the history of abolitionist sentiment after 1833.

213. Quoted in Brendan Simms, "The Connection Between Foreign Policy and Domestic Politics in Eighteenth-Century Britain," *Historical Journal*, 49 (2006), pp. 605–25, at p. 620. The phrase, which had classical origins, was borrowed from contemporary Spanish usage. Macartney (1st Earl, 1737–1806), diplomat and colonial administrator: Governor of the British West Indies, 1775, Madras, 1781–1785, Cape Colony, 1796; Envoy to China, 1792.

214. Simms, "The Connection Between Foreign Policy and Domestic Politics," at p. 620.

215. O'Brien and Duran, "Total Factor Productivity for the Royal Navy." David Killingray, Margarette Lincoln, and Nigel Rigby, eds., *Maritime Empires: Britain's Imperial Maritime Trade in the Nineteenth Century* (Woodbridge, 2004), is a wide-ranging account of a neglected subject; Barry Gough, *Pax Britannica: Ruling the Waves and Keeping the Peace Before Armageddon* (London, 2014) provides an authoritative survey.

216. Schroeder, *The Transformation of European Politics*; and the further discussion in the *International History Review*, 16 (1994), issue 2; and Peter Kruger and Paul W. Schroeder, eds., *The Transformation of European Politics, 1763–1848: Episode or Model in Modern History?* (Munster, 2002).

217. Todd Shepard, *The Invention of Decolonization: The Algerian War and the Remaking of France* (Ithaca, 2006), ch. 1.

218. Having declared independence in 1822.

219. Adam Smith, *The Wealth of Nations* (New York, 1937), pp. 781–2.

220. See the authoritative judgment of François Crouzet, "Mercantilism, War and the Rise of British Power," in Patrick Karl O'Brien and Armand Clesse, eds., *Two Hegemonies: Britain, 1846–1914 and the United States, 1941–2001* (Aldershot, 2002), pp. 80–81.

221. I follow here the general argument advanced by Marshall, *Remaking the British Atlantic*.

222. Kevin O'Rourke, "The Worldwide Economic Impact of the French Revolutionary and Napoleonic Wars, 1793–1815," *Journal of Global History*, 1 (2006), pp. 123–49.

223. Ibid., pp. 148–9.

224. Karl Patrick O'Brien, "The Contributions of Warfare with Revolutionary and Napoleonic France to the Consolidation and Progress of the British Industrial Revolution," *LSE Working Paper*, no. 150/11 (2011). I am grateful to Professor O'Brien for allowing me to cite this paper.

225. A. G. Hopkins, "The 'New International Order' in the Nineteenth Century: Britain's First Development Plan for Africa," in Robin Law, ed., *From Slave Trade to Legitimate Commerce: The Commercial Transition in Nineteenth-Century West Africa* (Cambridge, 1995), pp. 240–64.

226. Quoted in James R. Fichter, *So Great a Proffit: How the East Indies Trade Transformed Anglo-American Capitalism* (Cambridge, MA, 2010), pp. 56, 67, 73. Henry Dundas (1742–1811), 1st Viscount Melville, Secretary of State for War, 1794–1801.

227. See, generally, James Belich, *Replenishing the Earth: The Settler Revolution and the Rise of the Anglo-World, 1783–1939* (Oxford, 2009). Albert Schrauwers has shown how a financial oligarchy in Upper Canada shaped the economy and polity before the Rebellion of 1837 in ways that complemented the activities of their counterparts in Britain: "The Gentlemanly Order and the Politics of Production in the Transition to Capitalism in the Home District, Upper Canada," *Labour/Le Travail*, 65 (2010), pp. 9–45.

228. Anthony Webster, *The Twilight of the East India Company: The Evolution of Anglo-Asian Commerce and Politics, 1790–1860* (Woodbridge, 2009), ch. 3.

229. Fichter, *So Great a Proffit*, pp. 74–6.

230. Bernard Semmel, *The Liberal Ideal and the Demons of Empire* (Baltimore, 1993), pp. 27–33. For a skeptical view of Wakefield's schemes, see Ged Martin, *Edward Gibbon Wakefield: Abductor and Mystagogue* (Edinburgh, 1997).

231. Quoted in Semmel, *The Liberal Ideal*, p. 29.

232. Thomas Babington Macaulay (1800–1859). This quotation and those that follow are from "The Government of India," Speech to the House of Commons, July 10, 1833, in Thomas Babington Macaulay, *Miscellaneous Writings and Speeches*, vol. 4 (London, 1889), at http://www.gutenberg.org/etext/2170.

233. Herman Merivale (1806–74), *Lectures on Colonisation and Colonies* (London, 1841; New York, 1967). Merivale, Professor of Political Economy at Oxford University (1837–42), Permanent Under-Secretary at the Colonial Office (1848–60), is now an under-studied figure.

234. Merivale, *Lectures*, p. vi.

235. Ibid., p. 159.

236. Quoted in Semmel, *The Liberal Ideal*, p. 72.

237. Seymour Drescher, *Abolition: A History of Slavery and Anti-Slavery* (Cambridge, 2009); Drescher, "Capitalism and Abolitionism," *History & Theory*, 32 (1993), pp. 311–29. The relationship was often fraught: Morgan, "The Anti-Corn Law League."

238. Scholars should salute the originality of Christopher L. Brown's *Moral Capital: Foundations of British Abolitionism* (Chapel Hill, 2006). Young Hwi Yoon, "The Rise of Abolitionism during the Revolutionary Period, 1770–1800," *East Asian Journal of British History*, 3 (2013), pp. 1–25, provides a valuable supplement.

239. Philip Harling, "Robert Southey and the Language of Social Discipline," *Albion*, 30 (1998), pp. 630–55, shows how Southey abandoned his radicalism for Tory paternalism.

240. Richard R. Follett, "After Emancipation: Thomas Fowell Buxton and Evangelical Politics in the 1830s," *Parliamentary History*, 27 (2008), pp. 119–29.

241. Clare Midgley, *Women Against Slavery: The British Campaigns, 1780–1870* (London, 1992); Seymour Drescher, "Whose Abolition? Popular Pressure and the Ending of the British Slave Trade," *Past & Present*, 143 (1994), pp. 136–65; J. R. Oldfield, *Popular*

Politics and British Anti-Slavery: The Mobilisation of Public Opinion against the Slave Trade, 1787–1807 (London, 1998).

242. Christer Petly, " 'Devoted Islands' and 'That Madman Wilberforce': British Proslavery Patriotism during the Age of Abolition," *Journal of Imperial & Commonwealth History*, 39 (2011), pp. 393–415.

243. W. Caleb McDaniel, *The Problem of Democracy in the Age of Slavery: Garrisonian Abolitionists and Transatlantic Reform* (Baton Rouge, 2013); Thistlethwaite, *The Anglo-American Connection*, chs. 3–4.

244. On the complex relationship between the anti-slavery movement and the campaign to repeal the Corn Laws, see Morgan, "The Anti-Corn Law League," pp. 87–107.

245. Rowan Strong has established the longevity of the Anglican commitment to empire and the consistency of its views on the subject in *Anglicanism and the British Empire, c. 1700–1850* (Oxford, 2007).

246. Quoted in Allan McPhee, *The Economic Revolution in British West Africa* (London, 1926; 1971), p. 31.

247. (1792–1872); polymath, M.P., diplomat, and committed free-trader. See David Todd, "Sir John Bowring and the Global Dissemination of Free Trade," *Historical Journal*, 51 (2008), pp. 373–97.

248. See now Gough, *Pax Britannica*, especially chs. 7, 10, 11.

249. Douglas M. Peers, *Between Mars and Mammon: Colonial Armies and the Garrison State in India, 1819–1835* (London, 1995), underlines the importance of the military element in British colonial rule, while drawing attention to the part army officers played in gathering and communicating information about largely unknown territories. In this way, they contributed to the debate between Enlightenment principles and what were perceived to be unenlightened societies.

250. Muthu, *Enlightenment Against Empire*.

251. Jennifer Pitts, *A Turn to Empire: The Rise of Liberal Imperialism in Britain and France* (Princeton, 2005).

252. Eileen P. Sullivan, "Liberalism and Imperialism: J. S. Mill's Defence of the British Empire," *Journal of the History of Ideas*, 44 (1983), pp. 5, 99–617; Lynn Zastoupil, *John Stuart Mill and India* (Stanford, 1994); Beate Jahn, "Barbarian Thoughts: Imperialism in the Philosophy of John Stuart Mill," *Review of International Studies*, 31 (2005), pp. 599–618. John Stuart Mill, *On Liberty* (1859), ch. 1.

253. Ibid.

254. Jennifer Pitts, ed., *Alexis de Tocqueville, Writings on Slavery and Empire* (Baltimore, 2001). On the liberal cosmopolitanism of Benjamin Constant (1767–1830), see Helena Rosenblatt, "Why Constant? A Critical Overview of the Constant Revival," *Modern Intellectual History*, 1 (2004), pp. 439–54.

255. Smith, *Wealth of Nations*, p. 899.

256. Ibid., p. 900.

257. Samuel Taylor Coleridge, quoted in Harold Bloom, ed., *Samuel Taylor Coleridge* (New York 2010), p. 117. Coleridge (1772–1834), along with Wordsworth, was one of the founders of the Romantic Movement, and drew in particular on Southey, Burke, and Kantian idealism.

258. R. R. Palmer, *The Age of Democratic Revolution* (Princeton, NJ, 1969); Eric Hobsbawm, *Industry and Empire: From 1750 to the Present Day* (London, 1968; 1999).

259. Edmund Burke, "Reflections on the Revolution in France," in *Works*, vol. 3 (Boston, 1904), p. 315.

260. The reference is to Geoffrey Blainey's now classic *Tyranny of Distance: How Distance Shaped Australian History* (1966; 1982).

261. Antonio Pablo Pebrer, *Taxation, Revenue, Expenditure, Power, Statistics, and Debt of the Whole British Empire* (London, 1833), p. v. Pebrer also commended Britain's fiscal institutions to the Queen of Spain.

CHAPTER 3: FROM REVOLUTION
TO CONSTITUTION

1. The story that follows has been made possible by the exceptional research of Cassandra Pybus, "Washington's Revolution," *Atlantic Studies*, 3 (2006), pp. 183–99; Pybus, *Black Founders: The Unknown Story of Australia's First Black Settlers* (Sydney, 2006), which deserves to be known well beyond the limits set by specialized studies of the eighteenth century.

2. John Murray, 4th Earl of Dunmore (1730–1809), was Governor of New York (1770–1771), Virginia (1771–1776), and the Bahamas (1787–1796).

3. Sir Guy Carlton (1724–1808), a career soldier from an Anglo-Irish Protestant family; Commander-in-Chief of British forces in North America (1782–1783); 1st Baron Dorchester (1786); Governor-General, British North America (1786–1796).

4. Cassandra Pybus, "Jefferson's Faulty Math: The Question of Slave Defections in the American Revolution," *William & Mary Quarterly*, 62 (2005), pp. 243–64, is the most thorough attempt to estimate the numbers.

5. For a broad, accessible account see Simon Schama, *Rough Crossings: Britain, the Slaves, and the American Revolution* (New York, 2006).

6. The most recent treatment is Maya Jasanoff, *Liberty's Exiles: American Loyalists in the Revolutionary World* (New York, 2011).

7. Clarkson's younger brother, John (1764–1828), a lieutenant in the Royal Navy who had served in the West Indies, took the lead in organizing the contingent from Nova Scotia and became the first governor of the settlement.

8. Bruce Mouser, "Rebellion, Marronage and *Jihad*: Strategies of Resistance to Slavery on the Sierra Leone Coast, c. 1783–1796," *Journal of African History*, 48 (2007), pp. 27–44. I am grateful to Dr. Mouser for resolving some of my uncertainties about Macaulay's attitude.

9. The best corrective for this period is Alan Taylor's notable *American Colonies: The Settling of North America* (New York, 2001), and his expanded account in *American Revolutions: A Continental History, 1750–1804* (New York, 2016). Bernard Bailyn has produced the most impressive, refined, and influential of the "national" interpretations. For full references to his work see James A. Henretta, Michael Kammen, and Stanley N. Katz, eds., *The Transformation of Early American History* (New York, 1991). For a concise and penetrating appraisal see Alan Taylor, "The Exceptionalist," *New Republic*, June 9, 2001, pp. 33–7.

10. As chapter 1 made clear, this study does not attempt to comprehend the totality of U.S. history.

11. Diverse examples include: Jeremy Adelman, "An Age of Imperial Revolutions," *American Historical Review*, 113 (2008), pp. 319–40; Peter A. Coclanis, "Atlantic World or Atlantic/World?" *William & Mary Quarterly*, 63 (2006), pp. 725–42; and Eliga H. Gould, "Entangled Histories, Entangled Worlds: The English-Speaking Atlantic as a Spanish Periphery," *American Historical Review*, 112 (2007), pp. 764–86; Trevor Burnard, "Placing British Settlements in the Americas in Comparative Perspective," in H. V. Bowen, Elizabeth Mancke, and John G. Reid, eds., *Britain's Oceanic Empire: Atlantic and Indian Ocean Worlds, 1550–1850* (Cambridge, 2012), ch. 15; David Armitage, *The Declaration of Independence: A Global History* (Cambridge, MA, 2008); Linda Colley, "Empires of Writing: Britain, America, and Constitutions, 1776–1848," *Law & History Review*, 32 (2014), pp. 237–66.

12. Carlos Marichal, *Bankruptcy of Empire: Mexican Silver and the Wars between Spain, Britain, France, 1760–1810* (Cambridge, 2007), pp. 100, 152.

13. Mouser, "Rebellion, Marronage and *Jihad*," p. 41. Zachary Macaulay (1768–1838), abolitionist, evangelical, and father of Thomas Macaulay, was a Council Member of the Sierra Leone Company in 1792–1793 and governor of Freetown in 1794–1795 and 1796–1799.

Iain Whyte's welcome biography corrects a number of long-standing stereotypes: *Zachary Macaulay, 1768–1838: The Steadfast Scot in the British Anti-Slavery Movement* (Liverpool, 2011).

14. "The first glimmerings of the new colony-system dawned under Mr. Grenville." Edmund Burke, Speech in Parliament, April 19, 1774.

15. This paragraph connects with the discussion in chapter 2 of this text and extends it into a consideration of the domestic and imperial consequences of the mid-century wars.

16. (London, 1764): now available online.

17. Richard Harding, *The Emergence of Britain's Global Supremacy: The War of 1739–1748* (Woodbridge, Suffolk, 2010).

18. Fred Anderson, *Crucible of War: The Seven Years' War and the Fate of Empire in British North America, 1754–1766* (New York, 2000).

19. James M. Vaughn, *The Politics of Empire at the Accession of George III: The East India Company and the Crisis and Transformation of Britain's Imperial State* (New Haven, 2018), ch. 1. I am greatly indebted to Dr. Vaughn for allowing me to read and use the longer manuscript on which his book is based; Bob Harris, "'American Idols': War and the Middling Ranks in Mid-Eighteenth-Century Britain," *Past & Present*, 150 (1996), pp. 111–42; Marie Peters, "Early Hanoverian Consciousness of Empire or Europe?" *English Historical Review*, 122 (2007), pp. 632–88.

20. Harris, "American Idols"; Peters, "Early Hanoverian Consciousness of Empire."

21. J. E. Cookson, "Britain's Domestication of the Soldiery, 1750–1850: The Edinburgh Manifestations," *War & Society*, 28 (2009), pp. 1–28.

22. Miles Taylor, "John Bull and the Iconography of Public Opinion in England, c. 1712–1929," *Past & Present*, 134 (1992), pp. 93–128.

23. Harris, "American Idols."

24. Marie Peters, *Pitt and Popularity: The Patriot Minister and Popular Opinion During the Seven Years' War* (New York, 1981).

25. Marie Peters, "The Myth of William Pitt, Earl of Chatham, Great Imperialist: Part One, Pitt and Imperial Expansion, 1738–1763," *Journal of Imperial & Commonwealth History*, 21 (1993), pp. 31–74.

26. Vaughn, *The Politics of Empire*, ch. 2.

27. On this phase of Pitt's career see Marie Peters, "The Myth of William Pitt, Earl of Chatham, Great Imperialist: Part Two, Chatham and Imperial Reorganization, 1763–78," *Journal of Imperial & Commonwealth History*, 22 (1994), pp. 393–432.

28. Brewer, *Sinews of Power*, p. 114; Jan Eloranta and Jeremy Land, "Britain's Public Debt and the Seven Years' War," *Essays in Economic & Business History*, 29 (2011), pp. 101–18.

29. Eliga H. Gould, *The Persistence of Empire: British Political Culture in the Age of the American Revolution* (Chapel Hill, 2000), p. 108.

30. John J. McCusker, "British Mercantilist Policies and the American Colonies," in Stanley L. Engerman and Robert E. Gallman, eds., *The Cambridge Economic History of the United States*, Vol. 1 (Cambridge, 1996), pp. 358–62.

31. Arthur H. Cash, *John Wilkes: The Scandalous Father of Civil Liberty* (New Haven, 2006), provides a sober political biography; John Sainsbury, "John Wilkes, Debt, and Patriotism," *Journal of British Studies*, 34 (1995), pp. 165–95, adds a financial dimension.

32. Franklin to Priestley, June 7, 1782, quoted in Verner W. Crane, "The Club of Honest Whigs: Friends, Science and Liberty," *William & Mary Quarterly*, 23 (1966), pp. 210–33, at p. 233.

33. Miles Taylor, "The 1848 Revolutions and the British Empire," *Past & Present*, 166 (2000), pp. 146–80.

34. I am immensely grateful to Dr. Justin DuRivage for his generosity in allowing me to read his important dissertation, "Taxing Empire: Political Economy and the Ideological Origins of the American Revolution, 1747–1776" (Ph.D., dissertation, Yale University, 2013). On taxation, see pp. 4–5, 129–33. The vast literature on colonial taxation has been

assembled by Alvin Rabushka, *Taxation in Colonial America* (Princeton, NJ, 2008), who confirms the established view of the burden borne by the colonists. On this subject generally, see Fred Anderson, *Crucible of War: The Seven Years' War and the Fate of Empire in British North America, 1754-1766* (New York, 2000).

35. See n. 14.

36. DuRivage, "Taxing Empire," ch. 4.

37. Henry Seymour Conway (1721–1795), a career soldier and an MP; joined the Rockingham Whigs; vehement in opposing Grenville's reforms, the Townshend Duties, and the use of force against the colonists; Commander-in-Chief of British forces, 1782–93.

38. James E. Bradley, *Popular Politics and the American Revolution in England: Petitions, the Crown, and Public Opinion* (Macon, 1986), shows that the war that followed was unpopular in England.

39. Nicholas Phillipson, "Providence and Progress: An Introduction to the Historical Thought of William Robertson," in Stewart J. Brown, ed., *William Robertson and the Expansion of Empire* (Cambridge, 1997), p. 73.

40. William E. Todd, ed. David Hume, *History of England* (1778 edition; Indianapolis, 1983), vol. 5, pp. 146–8.

41. Quoted in Nicholas Capaldi and Donald W. Livingston, eds., *Liberty in Hume's History of England* (Dordrecht, 1990), p. 113.

42. Quoted in John Y. T. Grieg, ed., David Hume, *The Letters of David Hume* (Oxford, 1932; 2011), vol. 2, p. 510.

43. Ibid.

44. Volume 1 was published in 1776; volumes 2 and 3 in 1781; 4, 5, and 6 in 1788–1789. See Eran Shalev, *Rome Reborn on Western Shores: Historical Imagination and the Creation of the American Republic* (Charlottesville, 2009); P. J. Marshall, "Empire and Authority in the Later Eighteenth Century," *Journal of Imperial & Commonwealth History*, 15 (1987), pp. 105–22.

45. William Playfair (1759–1823), *An Inquiry into the Permanent Causes of the Decline and Fall of Powerful and Wealthy Nations Designed to Shew how the Prosperity of the British Empire may be Prolonged* (London, 1805), now available online.

46. Francis Hutcheson, *A System of Moral Philosophy* (1755), II, book 3. Quoted in Caroline Robbins, "'When it is that Colonies may Turn Independent': An Analysis of the Environment and Politics of Francis Hutcheson (1694-1746)," in Robbins, *Absolute Liberty* (Hamden, 1982), pp. 133–67.

47. Nigel Leask, "Thomas Muir and the Telegraph: Radical Cosmopolitanism in 1790s Scotland," *History Workshop*, 63 (2007), pp. 48–69. In 1793, Muir was transported to Australia, where he made reform an international cause. He was convicted by a hard-line Tory judge, who served in a Scottish legal system that had been protected by the Act of Union in 1707.

48. The colloquial name for the East India Company originated in the nineteenth century and was adopted by Holden Furber in his pioneering account, *John Company at Work: A Study of European Expansion in the Late Eighteenth Century* (Cambridge, MA, 1948).

49. Tirthankar Roy, "Rethinking the Origins of British India: State-Formation and Military-Fiscal Undertakings in an Eighteenth-Century World Region," *Modern Asian Studies*, 47 (2013), pp. 1125–56.

50. Philip J. Stern, *The Company State: Corporate Sovereignty and the Early Modern Foundations of the British Empire in India* (Oxford, 2011).

51. Robert Travers, "Ideology and British Expansion in Bengal, 1757-72," *Journal of Commonwealth & Imperial History*, 33 (2005), pp. 7–27.

52. Guido Abbattista, "Empire, Liberty and the Rule of Difference: European Debates on British Colonialism in Asia at the End of the Eighteenth Century," *European Review of History*, 13 (2006), pp. 473–96.

53. Sanjay Subrahmanyam has provided an admirable case study showing how the East India Company's demands increased the fiscal and political difficulties of an Indian State: "The Politics of Fiscal Decline: A Reconsideration of Maratha Tanjavur," *Indian Economic & Social History Review*, 32 (1995), pp. 177–217.

54. For characteristically learned and balanced accounts, see P. J. Marshall, "The Rise of British Power in Eighteenth-Century India," *Journal of South Asian Studies*, 19 (1996), pp. 71–6; Marshall, "Britain and the World in the Eighteenth Century. III, Britain and India," *Transactions of the Royal Historical Society*, 10 (2000), pp. 1–16; Roy, "Rethinking the Origins of British India."

55. Vaughn, *The Politics of Empire*, ch. 3.

56. James W. Frey, "The Indian Saltpetre Trade, the Military Revolution, and the Rise of Britain as a Global Superpower," *Historian*, 71 (2009), pp. 507–54.

57. Spencer A. Leonard, "'A Theatre of Disputes': The East India Company Election of 1764 as the Founding of British India," *Journal of Imperial & Commonwealth History*, 42 (2014), pp. 593–624.

58. P. J. Marshall, "British Society in India under the East India Company," *Modern Asian Studies*, 31 (1997), p. 91.

59. John Adolphus, *The History of England from the Accession of George III to the Conclusion of the Peace in the Year 1783*, vol. 1 (London, 1801), p. 342.

60. Travers, "Ideology and British Expansion," pp. 15–16.

61. Hartley, *The Budget*, and others had exposed what they regarded as dubious accounting methods.

62. Quoted in James C. Davies, ed., *When Men Revolt and Why* (New Brunswick, NJ, 1971; 1997), p. 96.

63. Ibid.

64. James C. Davies, "Toward a Theory of Revolution," *American Sociological Review*, 27 (1962), pp. 5–19.

65. Tocqueville, quoted in Davies, *When Men Revolt*, p. 96.

66. Drew R. McCoy, *The Elusive Republic: Political Economy in Jeffersonian America* (Chapel Hill, 1980).

67. James L. Huston, "The American Revolutionaries, the Political Economy of Aristocracy, and the American Concept of the Distribution of Wealth, 1765–1900," *American Historical Review*, 98 (1994), pp. 1079–1105; Lee J. Alston and Morton Owen Schapiro, "Inheritance Laws across Colonies: Causes and Consequences," *Journal of Economic History*, 44 (1984), pp. 277–87.

68. Jon Butler, "Enthusiasm Described and Decried: The Great Awakening as Interpretive Fiction," *Journal of American History*, 69 (1982), pp. 305–25.

69. Frank Lambert, *"Pedlar in Divinity": George Whitefield and the Transatlantic Revivals* (Princeton, NJ, 1994), emphasizes marketing techniques associated with expanding consumption; W. R. Ward, *The Protestant Evangelical Awakening* (Cambridge, 1992), treats the Awakening as an extension of a European-based movement; Thomas S. Kidd, *The Great Awakening: The Roots of Evangelical Christianity in Colonial America* (New Haven, 2007), sees it as inspiring evangelicalism.

70. Frank Lambert, *The Founding Fathers and the Place of Religion in America* (Princeton, 2003). For a stronger case than the one advanced here, see Thomas S. Kidd, *Religion and the American Revolution* (New York, 2010).

71. James P. Byrd, *Sacred Scripture, Sacred War: The Bible and the American Revolution* (Oxford, 2013).

72. I am indebted here to John Murrin's perceptive contribution: "No Awakening, No Revolution?" *Reviews in American History*, 11 (1983), pp. 161–71.

73. I owe this point to Nicholas Guyatt, *Providence and the Invention of the United States, 1607–1876* (Cambridge, 2007).

74. Particular mention should be made of the pioneering work of John J. McCusker and Russell R. Menard, *The Economy of British America, 1607-1789* (Chapel Hill, 1985), on which see the sprightly essay by Peter A. Coclanis, "In Retrospect: McCusker and Menard's *Economy of British America*, *Reviews in American History*, 30 (2002), pp. 183-97. Coclanis points the way forward but also observes that there are too few economic historians left to take it. See also Ronald Hoffman, ed., *The Economy of Early America: The Revolutionary Period, 1763-1790* (Charlottesville, 1988); Marc Egnal, *New World Economies: The Growth of the Thirteen Colonies and Early Canada* (New York, 1998); Stanley L. Engerman and Robert E. Gallman, eds., *The Cambridge Economic History of the United States*, Vol. 1 (Cambridge, 1996); John J. McCusker and Kenneth Morgan, eds., *The Early Modern Atlantic Economy* (Cambridge, 2000); Cathy Matson, ed., *The Economy of Early America: Historical Perspectives and New Directions* (University Park, 2006).

75. David W. Galenson, "The Settlement and Growth of the Colonies," in Engerman and Gallman, *Cambridge Economic History*, pp. 170-73. The black population rose from 137,000 to 890,000 during the same period.

76. On this subject, all authorities are agreed: McCusker and Menard, *Economy of British America*; Gallman, "Settlement and Growth of Population."

77. Jacob M. Price, "The Imperial Economy, 1700-1776," in P. J. Marshall, ed., *Oxford History of the British Empire*, Vol. 2 (Oxford, 1998), p. 103.

78. Edwin Cannan, ed., Adam Smith, *The Wealth of Nations* (1776; 1937), p. 393.

79. Ibid.

80. Ibid., p. 540.

81. Gallman, "Settlement and Growth of the Colonies," pp. 190-93.

82. Peter H. Lindert and Jeffrey G. Williamson, *Unequal Gains: American Growth and Inequality Since 1700* (Princeton, NJ, 2016), pp. 39-42.

83. John Komlos, "On the Biological Standard of Living of Eighteenth-Century Americans: Taller, Richer, Healthier," *Research in Economic History*, 20 (2001), pp. 223-48.

84. Cary Carson, Ronald Hoffman, and Peter J. Albert, eds., *Of Consumer Interests: The Style of Life in the Eighteenth Century* (Charlottesville, 1994); T. H. Breen, *The Market Place of Revolution: How Consumer Politics Shaped American Independence* (New York, 2004).

85. Eric P. Kaufmann, *The Rise and Fall of Anglo-America* (Cambridge, MA, 2004), p. 13. By their nature, these figures are no more than approximations; other sources give somewhat different percentages.

86. Bernard Bailyn, *The Peopling of British North America: An Introduction* (London, 1986).

87. On (varying) commitment to the market, see Allan Kulikoff, *The Agrarian Origins of American Capitalism* (Charlottesville, 1992); Kulikoff, *From British Peasants to Colonial American Farmers* (Chapel Hill, 2000). On the distribution of wealth, see the definitive studies by Alice H. Jones, *Wealth of a Nation to Be: The American Colonies on the Eve of the Revolution* (New York, 1980); Lee Soltow, *The Distribution of Wealth in the United States in 1798* (Pittsburgh, 1989).

88. Julie M. Flavell, "The 'School for Modesty and Humility': Colonial American Youth in London and their Parents, 1755-1775," *Historical Journal*, 42 (1999), pp. 377-403; John E. Crowley, *The Pursuit of Comfort: The Modern and the Material in the Early Modern British Atlantic World* (Baltimore, 2001).

89. Quoted in James Belich, *Replenishing the Earth: The Settler Revolution and the Rise of the Anglo-World*, 1783-1939 (Oxford, 2009), p. 147.

90. John Grenier, *The First Way of War: American War-Making on the Frontier, 1607-1814* (Cambridge, 2005).

91. Lindert and Williamson, *Unequal Gains*, ch. 2; Christopher Clark, "Reshaping Society: American Social History from Revolution to Reconstruction," in Melvyn Stokes, ed., *The State of US History* (New York, 2002), p. 48.

92. Quoted in R. A. Burchell, "The Role of the Upper Class in the Formation of American Culture, 1780–1840," in Burchell, ed., *The End of Anglo-America: Historical Essays in the Study of Cultural Divergence* (Manchester, 1991), p. 196.

93. Malcolm Gaskill, *Between Two Worlds: How the English Became Americans* (Oxford, 2014), covers the seventeenth century admirably in showing (despite his title) how the English in the mainland colonies were slow to become Americans. See also Richard L. Bushman, *The Refinement of America: Persons, Houses, Cities* (New York, 1992); Cornelia D. Hughes, *Women before the Bar: Gender Law and Society in Connecticut, 1639–1789* (Chapel Hill, 1995).

94. Quoted in Carl Louis Becker, *The Eve of the Revolution* (New Haven, 1918), p. 11.

95. 3 January 1760. Quoted in H. V. Bowen, "Perceptions from the Periphery: Colonial American Views of Britain's Asiatic Empire, 1756–1783," in Christine Daniels and Michael V. Kennedy, eds., *Negotiated Empires: Centers and Peripheries in the Americas, 1500–1820* (London, 2002), pp. 283–300 at p. 285.

96. Richard S. Dunn, "The Glorious Revolution and America," in Nicholas Canny, ed., *The Oxford History of the British Empire*, Vol. 1 (Oxford, 1998), ch. 20.

97. Quoted in Paul Langford, *A Polite and Commercial People: England, 1727-1783* (Oxford, 1989), p. 172.

98. Edmund Burke, *Works*, Vol. 1 (London, 1834), p. 186.

99. James A. Henretta, *"Salutary Neglect": Colonial Administration under the Duke of Newcastle* (Princeton, NJ, 1972); Alison G. Olson, *Making the Empire Work: London and American Interest Groups, 1690-1790* (Cambridge, MA, 1992).

100. T. H. Breen, "Ideology and Nationalism on the Eve of the American Revolution: Revisions Once More in Need of Revising," *Journal of American History*, 84 (1997), pp. 13–39.

101. As expressed in the Olive Branch Petition, July 8, 1775: www.ahpgatec.edu/olive _branch_1775.html.

102. Larry Sawyers, "The Navigation Acts Revisited," *Economic History Review*, 45 (1992), pp. 262–84, assesses the costs and benefits and emphasizes the former.

103. John W. Tyler, *Smugglers and Patriots: Boston Merchants and the Advent of the American Revolution* (Boston, 1986); Benjamin L. Carp, *Defiance of the Patriots: The Boston Tea Party and the Making of America* (New Haven, 2010); Carp, "Did Dutch Smuggling Provoke the Boston Tea Party?" *Early American Studies*, 10 (2012), pp. 335–69.

104. I am drawing a line here between John E. Crowley, *The Privileges of Independence: Neomercantilism and the American Revolution* (Baltimore, 1993); and Margaret Ellen Newell, *From Dependency to Independence: Economic Revolution in Colonial New England* (Ithaca, 1998).

105. On the evolution of public morality under the influence of commercial expansion, see Bruce H. Mann, *Republic of Debtors: Bankruptcy in the Age of American Independence* (Cambridge, MA, 2003).

106. Quoted in Breen, *The Market Place of Revolution*, p. 117. Hancock (1737-1793), president of the 2nd Continental Congress (1775-1777); first signatory of the Declaration of Independence (1776); 1st and 3rd governor of Massachusetts (1780-1785, 1787-1793). There is a long-standing discussion of Hancock's role in Boston's smuggling activities, on which see his latest biographer, Harlow Giles Unger, *John Hancock: Merchant King and American Patriot* (New York, 2000), p. 114.

107. Tyler, *Smugglers and Patriots*.

108. T. H. Breen, *The Market Place Revolution*.

109. Jill Lepore, *The Whites of their Eyes: The Boston Tea Party's Revolution and the Battle over American History* (Princeton, NJ, 2010), stresses the internal conflicts that underlie the popular "national" interpretation of the episode.

110. Merrill Jensen, *The Founding of a Nation: A History of the American Revolution, 1763–1776* (New York, 1968), ch. 14, remains a valuable source for this subject.

111. Gary Nash, *The Urban Crucible: Political Consciousness and the Origins of the American Revolution* (Cambridge, 1979); Alfred F. Young, *The Shoemaker and the Tea Party: Memory and the American Revolution* (Boston, 1999).

112. Breen, "Ideology and Nationalism on the Eve of the American Revolution," is persuasive on this point.

113. Jacob M. Price, *Capital and Credit in British Overseas Trade: The View from the Chesapeake, 1770–1776* (Cambridge, MA, 1980); T. H. Breen, *Tobacco Culture: The Mentality of the Great Tidewater Planters on the Eve of the Revolution* (Princeton, NJ, 1985); Alan Kulikoff, *Tobacco and Slaves: The Development of Southern Cultures in the Chesapeake, 1680–1800* (Chapel Hill, 1986).

114. In the authoritative judgment of Lorena S. Walsh, *Motives of Honor, Pleasure, and Profit: Plantation Management in the Colonial Chesapeake, 1607–1763* (Chapel Hill, 2010), p. 6.

115. Adolphus, *The History of England*, Vol. 3 (London, 1802; 3rd ed. 1810), p. 136. Adolphus included Maryland and South Carolina in his comment.

116. I have gained here particularly from Bruce A. Ragsdale, *A Planter's Republic: The Search for Economic Independence in Revolutionary Virginia* (Madison, 1996); and Walsh, *Motives of Honor.*

117. T. M. Devine, *The Tobacco Lords: A Study of the Tobacco Merchants of Glasgow and their Trading Activities, c. 1740–1790* (Edinburgh, 1975). Part of their enterprise lay in developing a reexport trade in tobacco to meet increasing demand in France.

118. Richard B. Sheridan, "The British Credit Crisis of 1772 and the American Colonies," *Journal of Economic History*, 20 (1960), pp. 161–86.

119. Joseph A. Ernst, *Money and Politics in America, 1755–1775: A Study in the Currency Act of 1774 and the Political Economy of the Revolution* (Chapel Hill, 1973). But see, too, Jacob M. Price, "The Money Question?" *Reviews in American History*, 2 (1974), pp. 364–73.

120. Woody Holton, *Forced Founders: Indians, Debtors, Slaves and the Making of the American Revolution in Virginia* (Chapel Hill, 1999).

121. Ben Baack, "British Versus American Interests in Land and the War of American Independence," *Journal of European Economic History*, 117 (2004), pp. 519–54.

122. Gregory Evans Dowd, *War under Heaven: Pontiac, the Indian Nations and the British Empire* (Baltimore, 2002); Dowd, *A Spirited Resistance: The North American Indian Struggle for Unity, 1745–1815* (Baltimore, 1992).

123. Holton, "The Ohio Indians," reaffirms the importance of the Line as a contributory cause of the Revolution.

124. On developing border conflicts during and after the Seven Years' War, see Patrick Griffin, *American Leviathan: Empire, Nation, and Revolutionary Frontier* (New York, 2007).

125. Gage (1719–1787), a career soldier with considerable experience of war in North America, was Commander-in-Chief from 1763 to 1775.

126. It would be injudicious for this study to attempt to adjudicate the claim made by neo-Progressive historians, such as McDonnell, *The Politics of War*, and Holton, *Forced Founders*, that these expressions of dissent can be classified as divisions of class. It is sufficient here to refer to differences of interest.

127. Holton, *Forced Founders*, ch. 5; Robert A. Olwell, "Domestick Enemies: Slavery and Political Independence in South Carolina, May 1775–March 1776," *Journal of Southern History*, 55 (1989), pp. 21–48.

128. Michael A. McDonnell and Woody Holton, "Patriot vs Patriot: Social Conflict in Virginia and the Origins of the American Revolution," *Journal of American Studies*, 34 (2000), pp. 231–56.

129. Stephen Conway, *The War of American Independence* (London, 1995).

130. Maya Jasanoff, *Liberty's Exiles*, "Appendix: Measuring the Exodus," pp. 351–8.

131. Ruma Chopra, *Unnatural Rebellion: Loyalists in New York City during the Rebellion* (Charlottesville, 2011). William Franklin (1730–1814), qualified as a lawyer and owed his appointment as governor of New Jersey (1763–1776) to his father's political influence in London. Father and son were never reconciled.

132. John C. Weaver, *The Great Land Rush and the Making of the Modern World* (Montreal, 2006).

133. Andrew Jackson O'Shaughnessy, *An Empire Divided: The American Revolution and the British Caribbean* (Philadelphia, 2000).

134. As pieced together by Simon D. Smith's exceptionally diligent research: *Slavery, Family and Gentry Capitalism in the British Atlantic: The World of the Lascelles, 1648–1834* (Cambridge, 2006).

135. Trevor Burnard, "Harvest Years? Reconfigurations of Empire in Jamaica, 1756–1807," *Journal of Imperial & Commonwealth History*, 49 (2012), pp. 533–55.

136. The Rockingham Whigs, who continued to oppose the war, were the principal exceptions in parliament. See also P. J. Marshall, "Empire and Authority in the Later Eighteenth Century."

137. Bernard Donoughue, *British Politics and the American Revolution: The Path to War, 1773–75* (London, 1964), pp. 151–6, 289.

138. For the Petition, see www.ahpgatec.edu/olive_branch_1775.html.

139. July 20, 1776. Quoted in DuRivage, "Taxing Empire," p. 378. On Franklin's conversion, see Sheila Skemp, *The Making of a Patriot: Benjamin Franklin at the Cockpit* (New York, 2013), though her argument seems to exaggerate the importance of the episode she describes.

140. George Washington, "Circular Letter to the Governors of the States," June 8, 1783, in John C. Fitzpatrick, ed., *The Writings of George Washington from the Original Manuscript Sources*, Vol. 26 (Washington, DC, 1938), pp. 484–5. I owe this reference to Dr. George Forgie, University of Texas at Austin.

141. The destruction caused by the war is detailed by Richard Buel, *In Irons: Britain's Naval Supremacy and the American Revolutionary Economy* (New Haven, 1998).

142. Holton, *Unruly Americans*, pp. 29, 131.

143. Lindert and Williamson, *Unequal Gains*, ch. 4.

144. On Shays's Rebellion, 1786–1787, see Leonard L. Richards, *Shays's Rebellion: The American Revolution's Final Battle* (Philadelphia, 2002); Woody Holton, "'From the Labors of Others': The War Bonds Controversy and the Origins of the Constitution in New England," *William & Mary Quarterly*, 61 (2004), pp. 271–316.

145. Carl L. Becker, *The History of Political Parties in the Province of New York, 1760–1776* (Madison, 1909), p. 22. This book was Becker's dissertation, completed in 1907 under the direction of Frederick Jackson Turner. If all Ph.D. dissertations had to reach this standard today, the number of doctorates completed in history would fall rapidly. An illuminating discussion of the issues formulated by Becker can be found in a special issue of the *William & Mary Quarterly*, 64 (2007).

146. Becker, *The History of Political Parties*, p. 276.

147. All thirteen states had signed by 1790. For a detailed account of the process of compromise, see David Robertson, *The Original Compromise: What the Constitution's Framers Were Really Thinking* (Oxford, 2013). Pauline Maier, *Ratification: The People Debate the Constitution* (New York, 2010), and the complementary work by Akhil Reed Amar, *America's Constitution: A Biography* (New York, 2005), explore the degree of public participation in the deliberations.

148. And has generated a huge literature, some of which is cited in subsequent notes. I have drawn here particularly on David Hendrickson, *Peace Pact: The Lost World of the American Founding* (Lawrence, 2003); Max M. Edling, *A Revolution in Favor of Government: Origins of the U.S. Constitution and the Making of the American State* (New York, 2003). Gary J. Kornblith and John M. Murrin provide an admirable synthesis in "The Dilemmas

of Ruling Elites in Revolutionary America," in Steve Fraser and Gary Gerstle, eds., *Ruling America: A History of Wealth and Power in a Democracy* (Cambridge, MA, 2005), ch. 1.

149. Proposals made by British governors for coordinating the administration of the mainland colonies, which may have been informed by their knowledge of the Iroquois Confederacy, may also have had an influence. See Drew R. McCoy, *The Elusive Republic: Political Economy in Jeffersonian America* (Chapel Hill, 1980); Alison, E. LaCroix, *The Ideological Origins of American Federalism* (Cambridge, MA, 2010).

150. See also John Jay's use of the phrase in "Federalist Paper No. 5," November 10, 1787, in Terence Ball, ed., James Madison, Alexander Hamilton, and John Jay, *The Federalist, With the Letters of "Brutus"* (Cambridge, 2003), p. 16.

151. Anne M. Cohler, *Montesquieu's Comparative Politics and the Spirit of American Constitutionalism* (Lawrence, 1988); Daniel Walker Howe, "Why the Scottish Enlightenment Was Useful to the Framers of the American Constitution," *Comparative Studies in Society & History*, 31 (1989), pp. 572–87.

152. Robert Howse, "Montesquieu on Commerce, Conquest, War, and Peace," *Brooklyn Journal of International Law*, 31 (2006), pp. 1–16. The need for brevity has obliged me to ignore some of the ambiguities in Montesquieu's formulation.

153. Madison, "Federalist," No. 10, in Ball, ed., *Hamilton, Madison, and Jay*, pp. 40–46.

154. For two contrasting views, see Gordon S. Wood, *The Radicalism of the American Revolution* (New York, 1992); Wood, *Empire of Liberty*; and Holton, *Unruly Americans*.

155. Hendrickson, *Peace Pact* (Lawrence, 2003). See also the discussion in Tom Cutterham, "The International Dimension of the Federal Constitution," *Journal of American Studies*, 48 (2014), pp. 501–15.

156. Carroll Smith-Rosenberg, *This Violent Empire: The Birth of an American Identity* (Chapel Hill, 2010).

157. Roger H. Brown, *Redeeming the Republic: Federalists, Taxation, and the Origins of the Constitution* (Baltimore, 1993).

158. Holton, *Unruly Americans*, attaches great weight to this cause.

159. The fullest and most recent statement is Max M. Edling, *A Revolution in Favor of Government: Origins of the U.S. Constitution and the Making of the American State* (New York, 2003). Credit should also be given to an older literature, notably William Appleman Williams, "The Age of Mercantilism: An Interpretation of the American Political Economy, 1763–1828," *William & Mary Quarterly*, 15 (1958), pp. 419–37; and especially E. James Ferguson, *The Power of the Purse: A History of American Public Finance, 1776–1790* (Durham, 1965); Ferguson, "The Nationalists of 1781–1783 and the Economic Interpretation of the Constitution," *Journal of American History*, 56 (1969), pp. 241–61; Ferguson, "Political Economy, Public Liberty, and the Formation of the Constitution," *William & Mary Quarterly*, 40 (1983), pp. 389–412.

160. Quoted in Peter James Stanlis, *Edmund Burke: The Enlightenment and Revolution* (London, 1991), p. 233.

161. The U.S. Bill of Rights is a collective term for ten amendments to the Constitution that were passed by Congress to allay the fears of anti-federalists, and came into effect in 1791.

162. Mark G. Spencer, "Hume and Madison on Faction," *William & Mary Quarterly*, 59 (2002), pp. 869–96.

163. J.G.A. Pocock, "Virtue and Commerce in the Eighteenth Century," *Journal of Interdisciplinary History*, 3 (1972), pp. 119–34; David Armitage, "A Patriot King for Whom? The Afterlives of Bolingbroke's Patriot King," *Journal of British Studies*, 36 (1997), pp. 397–418.

164. In practice no president served more than two terms, though several made the attempt, until Franklin Roosevelt in 1940. A formal limit of two terms was approved in 1951.

165. Simon Newman, "Principles or Men? George Washington and the Political Culture of National Leadership," *Journal of the Early Republic*, 12 (1994), pp. 477–507; Frank

Prochaska, *The Eagle and the Crown: Americans and the British Monarchy* (New Haven, 2008).

166. Zelinsky, *Nation into State*, pp. 56–62, attributes the phrase to Douglas Brinkley.

167. Quoted in Alan Houston, *Benjamin Franklin and the Politics of Improvement* (New Haven, 2008), p. 189. The Marquis de Condorcet (1743–1794), eminent Enlightenment mathematician and philosopher.

168. Lawrence D. Cress, *Citizens in Arms: The Army and Militia in American Society to the War of 1812* (Chapel Hill, 1982).

169. Max Edling, *A Hercules in the Cradle: War, Money and the American State, 1783–1867* (Chicago, 2014), p. 237.

170. Ibid. p. 13.

171. Ibid. chs. 1–3. At this stage, the bank did not have a monopoly of note issue, and its control over state banks was limited. Nevertheless, it marked an important step toward coordinating national fiscal and monetary policy.

172. Thomas P. Slaughter, *The Whiskey Rebellion: Frontier Epilogue to the Revolution* (New York, 1986).

173. Robin L. Einhorn, *American Taxation, American Slavery* (Chicago, 2006).

174. Peter Zavodnyik, *The Age of Strict Construction: A History of the Growth of Federal Power, 1789–1861* (Washington, DC, 2007), has a full discussion of the issue.

175. When "almost every state in the Union in turn declared its own sovereignty." Arthur Meier Schlesinger, "The State Rights Fetish," in Schlesinger, *New Viewpoints in American History* (New York, 1922), p. 222.

176. Kornblith and Murrin, "Dilemmas of Ruling Elites," p. 43. I am aware of an anachronism in referring to "the South" at a time when the diversity of all the ex-colonies exceeded their sense of commonality. The closer the focus, however, the harder it is to generalize about Southern (or Northern) unity even today. Here the term is used to apply to the colonies south of Maryland (with Maryland included or excluded according to the particularities of the comparison being made).

177. But see Earl M. Maltz, "The Idea of the Proslavery Constitution," *Journal of the Early Republic*, 17 (1997), pp. 37–59, which challenges the argument that the Constitution favored the South. The extended slave trade had to be conducted in foreign ships, though the formal restriction proved not to reduce the number of arrivals.

178. James Madison, in Hamilton, Madison, and Jay, *The Federalist Papers*, No. 10, p. 44.

179. Max M. Edling and Mark D. Kaplanoff, "Alexander Hamilton's Fiscal Reform: Transforming the Structure of Taxation in the Early Republic," *William & Mary Quarterly*, 61 (2004), p. 743.

180. Paul Douglas Newman, *Fries's Rebellion: the Enduring Struggle for the American Revolution* (Philadelphia, 2004).

181. Seth Cotlar, *Tom Paine's America: The Rise and Fall of Transatlantic Radicalism in the Early Republic* (Charlottesville, 2011), treats the informal politics of the period. Andrew Shankman, *Crucible of American Democracy: The Struggle to Fuse Egalitarianism and Capitalism in Jeffersonian Pennsylvania* (Lawrence, 2004), provides a case study exploring the link between capitalism and democracy.

182. Quoted in Ferguson, "Political Economy, Public Liberty," p. 389.

183. Beard's position on this subject, as on many others, evolved in the course of a long career and over a large number of publications. Clyde W. Barrow provides an illuminating guide in *More than a Historian: The Political and Economic Thought of Charles Austin Beard* (New Brunswick, 2000).

184. Karl-Friedrich Walling, *Republican Empire: Alexander Hamilton on War and Free Government* (Lawrence, 1999).

185. Hamilton was one of Washington's leading advisors before becoming Secretary of the Treasury, 1789–1795. The fullest biography is Ron Chernow, *Alexander Hamilton* (New York, 2004).

186. Ferguson, "Political Economy, Public Liberty"; Peter L. Rousseau and Richard Sylla, "Emerging Financial Markets and Early US Growth," *Explorations in Economic History*, 42 (2005), pp. 1–26; Richard Sylla, "The Transition to a Monetary Union in the United States, 1787–1795," *Financial History Review*, 13 (2006), pp. 73–95; Robert E. Wright's accessible summary goes a step further in according Hamilton heroic status: *One Nation under Debt: Hamilton, Jefferson and the History of What We Owe* (New York, 2008); Douglas A. Irwin and Richard Sylla, eds., *Founding Choices: American Economic Policy in the 1790s* (Chicago, 2011). Other financial services followed: Sharon A. Murphy, *Investing in Life: Insurance in Antebellum America* (Baltimore, 2010). Hamilton built on the remarkable contribution of Robert Morris (1734–1806), who did more than anyone else to finance and supply the American Revolution, and who laid out plans that Hamilton developed and applied. See Ferguson, "The Nationalists of 1781–1783"; Charles Rappeleye, *Robert Morris, Financier of the American Revolution* (New York, 2010). Morris, however, gained little from his contribution. His investments in real estate failed; he was declared bankrupt in 1797, imprisoned for debt in 1798–1801, and died a pauper. The Spanish dollar was the most common currency circulating in the thirteen colonies; accounts continued to be kept in pounds, shillings, and pence for some time into the nineteenth century.

187. Douglas A. Irwin, "The Aftermath of Hamilton's 'Report on Manufactures,'" *Journal of Economic History*, 64 (2004), pp. 800–821.

188. Quoted in Ferguson, "Political Economy, Public Liberty," p. 411. John Taylor (1753–1824), popularly known as Taylor of Caroline (County, Virginia), was a powerful advocate of states' rights and contributed notably to the libertarian tradition. See Robert E. Shalhope, *John Taylor of Caroline: Pastoral Republican* (Columbia, 1980).

189. Brian Schoen, "Calculating the Price of Union: Republican Economic Nationalism and the Origins of Southern Sectionalism, 1790–1818," *Journal of the Early Republic*, 23 (2003), pp. 173–208. In the early days, the party was known as the Democratic-Republicans or Jeffersonian Republicans.

190. Henry St. John (1678–1751), 1st Viscount Bolingbroke. See Isaac Kramnick, *Bolingbroke and His Circle: The Politics of Nostalgia in the Age of Walpole* (Cambridge, MA, 1968; 2nd ed. 1992); Michael Durey, *Transatlantic Radicals and the Early Republic* (Lawrence, 1997); and the discussion in chapter 2 of this text.

191. Both positions allowed room for considerable diversity. See, for example, Saul Cornell, *The Other Founders: Anti-Federalists and the Dissenting Tradition in America, 1788–1828* (Chapel Hill, 1999).

192. Drew R. McCoy, *The Elusive Republic: Political Economy in Jeffersonian America* (Chapel Hill, 1980).

193. John Murrin, "The Jeffersonian Triumph and American Exceptionalism," *Journal of the Early Republic*, 20 (2000), pp. 1–25.

194. Drew R. McCoy, *The Last of the Fathers: James Madison and the Republican Legacy* (New York, 1989), pp. 173–92; Andrew Shankman, "'A New Thing on Earth': Alexander Hamilton, Pro-Manufacturing Republicans, and the Democratization of the American Political Economy," *Journal of the Early Republic*, 23 (2003), pp. 323–52.

195. Colleen A. Sheehan, *James Madison and the Spirit of Republican Self-Government* (Cambridge, 2009).

196. See especially Donald Ratcliffe's important new research, "The Right to Vote and the Rise of Democracy, 1787–1828," *Journal of the Early Republic*, 3 (2013), pp. 230, 232; Jeffrey L. Pasley, *The First Presidential Contest: 1796 and the Founding of American Democracy* (Lawrence, 2013).

197. Ratcliffe, "The Right to Vote," p. 221.

198. Albert O. Hirschman, *Exit, Voice, and Loyalty: Reponses to Decline in Firms, Organizations, and States* (Cambridge, MA, 1970).

199. Stanley L. Engerman and Kenneth L. Sokoloff, "The Evolution of Suffrage Institutions in the New World," *Journal of Economic History*, 65 (2005), pp. 891–921; Peter Temin,

"Free Land and Federalism: A Synoptic View of American Economic History," *Journal of Interdisciplinary History*, 21 (1991), pp. 371–89, applies a similar argument to the period after the Civil War.

200. Engerman and Sokoloff, "The Evolution of Suffrage Institutions," pp. 898, 901–5, 907–8, 916.

201. David Waldstreicher, *In the Midst of Perpetual Fetes: The Making of American Nationalism, 1776–1820* (Chapel Hill, 1997); Simon P. Newman, *Parades and the Politics of the Street: Festive Culture in Early American Republic* (Philadelphia, 1997); Jeffrey L. Pasley, Andrew W. Robertson, and David Waldstreicher, eds., *Beyond the Founders: New Approaches to the Political History of the Early United States* (Chapel Hill, 2004). Gary B. Nash, *The Urban Crucible: Social Change, Political Consciousness, and the Origins of the American Revolution* (Cambridge, MA, 1979); Joyce Appleby, *Capitalism and a New Social Order: The Republican Vision of the 1790s* (New York, 1984), argues that the decade saw a break with the past. Peter S. Onuf sees a synthesis of classical concepts of virtue and newer libertarian ideals emerging: *Jefferson's Empire: The Language of American Nationhood* (Charlottesville, 2000).

202. Ronald P. Formisano, *Reform and Reaction: For the People: American Populist Movements from the Revolution to the 1850s* (Chapel Hill, 2007); Michael Kazin, *The Populist Persuasion: An American History* (New York, 1995). On the anti-elite character of populism see Margaret Canovan, *Populism* (London, 1981).

203. As Linda Colley notes, constitutions were controlling as well as liberating documents: "Writing Constitutions and Writing World History," in James Belich, John Darwin, Margret Frenz, and Chris Wickham, eds., *The Prospect of Global History* (Oxford, 2016), p. 170.

204. Madison, "Federalist No. 14," in Hamilton, Madison, and Jay, *The Federalist*, p. 69. See also Federalist No. 10.

205. J.G.A. Pocock, "The Classical Theory of Deference," *American Historical Review*, 81 (1976), pp. 516–23. Jefferson's solution was, for John Adams, a problem. He accepted the emergence of a natural aristocracy but thought it needed to be controlled.

206. Quoted in Lloyd S. Kramer, "The French Revolution and the Creation of American Political Culture," in Joseph Klaits and Michael H. Haltzel, eds., *The Global Ramifications of the French Revolution* (Cambridge, 1994), p. 32.

207. Ibid., p. 31.

208. Paul Langford, "Old Whigs, Old Tories and the American Revolution," in Peter Marshall and Glyn Williams, eds., *The British Atlantic Empire Before the American Revolution* (London, 1980), pp. 106–30; Thomas Philip Schofield, "Conservative Political Thought in Britain in Response to the French Revolution," *Historical Journal*, 29, 1986, pp. 601–22; Seth Cotlar, "The Federalists' Transatlantic Cultural Offensive of 1798 and the Moderation of American Democratic Discourse," in Pasley, Robertson, and Waldstreicher, *Beyond the Founders*, pp. 274–99; Terry Bouton, *Taming Democracy: "The People," the Founders, and the Troubled Ending of the American Revolution* (New York, 2004).

209. The Marquis de Condorcet, known as Nicolas de Condorcet (1743–1794). Condorcet's own (moderate) views did not commend him to the extremists who took power in France in 1793. He was declared a traitor and died in prison in the following year. See Max M. Mintz, "Condorcet's Reconsideration of America as a Model for Europe," *Journal of the Early Republic*, 11 (1991), pp. 493–506; and more generally David Williams, *Condorcet and Modernity* (Cambridge, 2004).

210. William Cobbett returned to England with Paine's bones in 1819 but never managed to give them a decent burial. See David A. Wilson, *Paine and Cobbett: The Transatlantic Connection* (Kingston and Montreal, 1998). Paine's deism compounded his political radicalism. He had no public memorial in the United States until 1850, when a monument to him was finally erected in New York.

211. Young, *The Shoemaker and the Tea Party*.

212. Adam Smith, *Wealth of Nations*, p. 899.

213. Ibid.

214. Ibid., p. 900. This is the final sentence of Smith's book.

215. Smith's preferred solution was to add the mainland colonies to the United Kingdom, grant them representation in parliament, and thus give taxation an agreed constitutional basis.

216. For one relevant lament see James L. Huston, "Economic Landscapes Yet to Be Discovered," *Journal of the Early Republic*, 24 (2004), pp. 219–31.

217. Anne M. Cohler et al., eds., *Montesquieu: The Spirit of the Laws* (Cambridge, 1989), pp. 224–5.

218. Pitt also warned that it would be impossible to conquer North America. However, when negotiations broke down and hostilities began, he opposed independence on patriotic grounds.

219. Matthew, 6:33.

220. Jack P. Greene, *Peripheries and Center*, pp. 162–3, is authoritative on this point. For a seminal criticism of the "revolution still to come," see John M. Murrin, "The Myths of Colonial Democracy and Royal Decline in Eighteenth-Century America: A Review Essay," *Cithara*, 5 (1965), pp. 53–69.

221. On the popular base see Nash, *The Unknown American Revolution*; and T. H. Breen, *American Insurgents, American Patriots: The Revolution of the People* (New York, 2010).

222. Michael McDonnell, "National Identity and the American War for Independence Reconsidered," *Australasian Journal of American Studies*, 20 (2001), pp. 3–17; John M. Murrin and David S. Silverman, "The Quest for America: Reflections on Distinctiveness, Pluralism and Public Life," *Journal of Interdisciplinary Studies*, 33 (2002), pp. 235–46; Michael Zuckerman, "Regionalism," in Daniel Vickers, ed., *A Companion to Colonial America* (Oxford, 2003), ch. 13; Jack D. Greene, "Early Southeastern North America and the Broader Atlantic and American Worlds," *Journal of Southern History*, 73 (2007), pp. 1–14.

223. Formally, the Republic of the Seven United Netherlands. See J. W. Schulte Nordholt, "The Example of the Dutch Republic for American Federalism," *Low Countries Historical Review*, 94 (1979), pp. 437–49.

224. French Canadians, though not reconciled to the British Empire and monarchy, were unable to escape, and eventually reached an accommodation with both.

225. The term appears in *Common Sense* (Philadelphia, 1776) and elsewhere in his numerous other works.

226. Specialists on nineteenth- and twentieth-century imperialism will recognize my (speculative) application of Robinson's notion of collaboration to an earlier period: Ronald Robinson, "Non-European Foundations of European Imperialism: Sketch for a Theory of Collaboration," in E.R.J. Owen and R. B. Sutcliffe, eds., *Studies in the Theory of Imperialism* (London, 1972), ch. 5.

227. Burke, Speech in Parliament, February 27, 1775.

228. Ibid.

CHAPTER 4: THE STRUGGLE FOR INDEPENDENCE

1. Salman Rushdie, *Midnight's Children* (London, 1980), follows the fortunes of Saleem Sinai, who was born at the moment of India's independence.

2. Nehru (1889–1964), "Speech on the Granting of Independence" August 14, 1947, *Internet Modern History Sourcebook*, www.fordham.edu/halsall/mod/1947nehru1.html. Nehru was Prime Minister of India, 1947–1964.

3. John Quincy Adams (1767–1848), "Oration," on the anniversary of American independence, July 4, 1793, Collection of 4 July Speeches; Special Collections, Ellish Library,

University of Missouri, Columbia. Adams was Secretary of State, 1817–1825, and President, 1825–1829.

4. This is true of the otherwise impressive volumes in the Oxford History of the United States, and also of Charles Sellers, *The Market Revolution: Jacksonian America, 1815–1846* (New York, 1991).

5. Kathleen Burk, *Old World, New World: Great Britain and America from the Beginning* (London, 2007), ch. 5, deserves particular mention among the other exceptions to this generalization, which are noted in the citations that follow.

6. Susan Strange, *States and Markets* (London, 1988; 2nd ed. 1994), ch. 2, on the distinction between structural and relational power. See also A. G. Hopkins, "Informal Empire in Argentina: An Alternative View," *Journal of Latin American Studies*, 26 (1994), pp. 469–84.

7. Ephraim Kleiman, "Trade and the Decline of Colonialism," *Economic Journal*, 86 (1976), pp. 459–80; Lance Davis, "The Late Nineteenth-Century Imperialist: Specification, Quantification and Controlled Conjectures," in Raymond E. Dumett, ed., *Gentlemanly Capitalism and British Imperialism: The New Debate on Empire* (Harlow, 1999), pp. 82–4. I am grateful to Dr. Davis for making me think harder about these issues. See P. J. Cain and A. G. Hopkins, "The Theory and Practice of British Imperialism," in Dumett, *Gentlemanly Capitalism*, pp. 202–10.

8. Strange, *States and Markets*, ch. 2.

9. Senator William L. Marcy produced the phrase in 1828 to describe the electoral success of the Jackson Democrats.

10. Sellers, *The Market Revolution*.

11. The term appears in a variety of contexts. It is used here in the way applied by Anthony D. Smith, one of the leading authorities on nationalism. See especially *Theories of Nationalism* (1983); *Nationalism* (2nd ed., Cambridge, 2010).

12. *New York Times*, February 10, 1853. Quoted in Stuart Ward, "The European Provenance of Decolonization," *Past & Present*, 230 (2016), pp. 227–60, at p. 232.

13. Matthew, 6:33.

14. A fuller statement of these positions is given in chapter 3 of this text.

15. Peter S. Onuf, " 'The Strongest Government on Earth': Jefferson's Republicanism, the Expansion of the Union, and the New Nation's Destiny," in Sanford Levinson and Bartholomew H. Sparrow, eds., *The Louisiana Purchase and American Expansion, 1803–1898* (Lanham, 2005), ch. 2.

16. As Max M. Edling has clearly demonstrated in his important study: *A Hercules in the Cradle: War, Money, and the American State, 1783–1867* (Chicago, 2014).

17. I am indebted in what follows to William J. Novak, "The Myth of the 'Weak' American State," *American Historical Review*, 113 (2008), pp. 752–72, and the discussion in *American Historical Review* 115 (2010); Richard R. John, *Spreading the News: The American Postal System from Franklin to Morse* (Cambridge, MA, 1995); John Lauritz Larson, *Internal Improvement: National Public Works and the Promise of Popular Government in the Early United States* (Chapel Hill, 2001); Peter Zavodnyik, *The Age of Strict Construction: A History of the Growth of Federal Power, 1789–1861* (Washington, DC, 2007); Brian Balogh, *A Government Out of Sight: The Mystery of National Authority in Nineteenth-Century America* (Cambridge, 2009); Edling, *Hercules in the Cradle*.

18. John C. Weaver, *The Great Land Rush and the Making of the Modern World, 1650–1900* (Montreal, 2003), p. 191, and chs. 5–7 as a whole for an excellent exposition of this huge subject.

19. Don E. Fehrenbacher with Ward M. McAfee, *The Slaveholding Republic: An Account of the U.S. Government's Relations to Slavery* (Oxford, 2001).

20. Fehrenbacher, *The Slaveholding Republic*, p. 111; David Ericson, *Slavery in the American Republic: Developing the Federal Government, 1791–1861* (Lawrence, 2011).

21. I am indebted here to Gary Gerstle, *Liberty and Coercion: The Paradox of American Government from the Founding to the Present* (Princeton, NJ, 2015), chs. 1–2; and John Joseph Wallis, whose work is cited in notes 22 and 23 below.

22. Richard Sylla, John B. Legler, and John J. Wallis, "Banks and Public Finance in the New Republic: The United States, 1790–1860," *Journal of Economic History*, 47 (1987), pp. 391–403; John Joseph Wallis, "The Property Tax as a Coordinating Device: Financing Indiana's Mammoth Internal Improvement System, 1835–1842," *Explorations in Economic History*, 40 (2003), pp. 223–50; Wallis, "Constitutions, Corporations, and Corruption: American States and Constitutional Change, 1842–1852," *Journal of Economic History*, 65 (2005), pp. 211–56; John Joseph Wallis and Barry R. Weingast, "Equilibrium Impotence: Why the States and Not the American National Government Financed Economic Development in the Antebellum Era," NBER *Working Paper*, 11397 (2005).

23. John Joseph Wallis, "The Other Foundings: Federalism and the Constitutional Structure of American Governmet," in Douglas A. Irwin and Richard Sylla, eds., *Founding Choices: American Economic Policy in the 1790s* (Chicago, 2011), pp. 177–213; Edling, "'A Mongrel Kind of Government': The U.S. Constitution, the Federal Union, and the Origins of the American State," in Peter S. Onuf and Peter Thompson, eds., *State and Citizen: British America and the Early United States* (Charlottesville, 2013), pp. 150–77.

24. Jefferson's attitude toward expansion evolved. In the 1780s he was more inclined to limit the size of the government: Reginald Horsman, "Thomas Jefferson and the Ordinance of 1784," *Illinois Historical Journal*, 79 (1986), pp. 99–112.

25. Onuf, "'The Strongest Government on Earth,'" pp. 43–8.

26. The phrase was put into circulation by Samuel P. Huntington, *Political Order in Changing Societies* (New Haven, 1968), ch. 7.

27. All historians are indebted here to an outstanding study: Leonard L. Richards, *The Slave Power: The Free North and Southern Domination, 1780–1860* (Baton Rouge, 2000). Philip H. Burch, *Elites in American History*, Vol. 1 (New York, 1981), shows that Southerners were disproportionately represented in cabinet and diplomatic posts down to 1861.

28. James McPherson, *The War that Forged a Nation: Why the Civil War Still Matters* (Oxford, 2015), p. 7.

29. For an interesting discussion of this theme, see James Oakes, "The Ages of Jackson and the Rise of American Democracies," *Journal of the Historical Society*, 6 (2006), pp. 491–500; and for a wider view, Joanna Innes and Mark Philp, eds., *Re-Imagining Democracy in the Age of Revolutions: America, France, Britain, and Ireland, 1850–1950* (Oxford, 2013).

30. See chapter 3 in this text.

31. Alexander Keyssar, *The Right to Vote: The Contested History of Democracy in the United States* (New York, 2000; 2009), chs. 1–3.

32. John Ashworth, *"Agrarians" and "Aristocrats": Party Political Ideology in the United States, 1837–1846* (New York, 1987); Harry L. Watson, *Liberty and Power: The Politics of Jacksonian America* (New York, 1990).

33. Richards, *The Slave Power*, p. 49.

34. On the election of 1800, see Jeffrey L. Pasley, "Politics and the Misadventures of Thomas Jefferson's Modern Reputation: A Review Essay," *Journal of Southern History*, 72 (2006), pp. 871–908.

35. Robert P. Forbes, *The Missouri Compromise and Its Aftermath: Slavery and the Meaning of America* (Chapel Hill, 2007); Matthew H. Crocker, "The Missouri Compromise, the Monroe Doctrine, and the Southern Strategy," *Journal of the West*, 43 (2004), pp. 45–52; Adam Rothman, "Slavery and National Expansion in the United States," *OAH Magazine of History*, 23 (2009), pp. 23–9.

36. Levinson and Sparrow, *The Louisiana Purchase*, pp. 3, 6–7.

37. For different approaches to the issue see, among many possible examples, Joyce Appleby, *Capitalism and a New Social Order: The Republican Vision of the 1790s* (New York, 1984); Gordon Wood, *The Radicalism of the American Revolution* (New York, 1992); Pasley, "1800 as a Revolution in Political Culture."

38. Jefferson (1743–1826) was the Republic's third president (1801–09).

39. Edling, *Hercules in the Cradle*, ch. 4.

40. Forrest McDonald, *The Presidency of Thomas Jefferson* (Lawrence, 1976), pp. 79, 115–17, 163.

41. Jefferson's ambivalent attitude toward commerce is discussed by Doron S. Ben-Atar, *The Origins of Jeffersonian Commercial Policy and Diplomacy* (New York, 1993).

42. Burton Spivak, *Jefferson's English Crisis: Commerce, Embargo, and the Republican Revolution* (Charlottesville, 1979).

43. The wider aspects of the war are discussed in chapter 5 of this text.

44. James Madison (1751–1836), fourth president, 1809–17. On this topic, see Edling, *Hercules in the Cradle*, ch. 4.

45. Edling, *Hercules in the Cradle*, ch. 4.

46. John Quincy Adams (1767–1848), the son of John Adams (second president), was the sixth president (1825–29). See Leonard L. Richards, *The Life and Times of Congressman John Quincy Adams* (New York, 1986); William Earl Weeks, *John Quincy Adams and American Global Empire* (Lexington, 1992).

47. Weeks, *John Quincy Adams*, traces the contradictions in his long career.

48. Jackson (1767–1845) has been the subject of innumerable biographies. H. W. Brands, *Andrew Jackson: His Life and Times* (New York, 2005), is a full and accessible example.

49. Donald J. Ratcliffe, "Popular Preferences in the Presidential Election of 1824," *Journal of the Early Republic*, 34 (2014), pp. 45–77, has revised standard interpretations of the election; Joel H. Sibley, *Martin Van Buren and the Emergence of American Popular Politics* (Lanham, 2002), covers his life (1782–1862) and time as the eighth president (1837–41).

50. Herbert E. Sloan, *Principle and Interest: Thomas Jefferson and the Problem of Debt* (New York, 1995).

51. Ashworth, *"Agrarians" and "Aristocrats"*; Harry L. Watson, *Liberty and Power: The Politics of Jacksonian America* (New York, 1990); Christopher Clark, *Social Change in America: From the French Revolution Through the Civil War* (Chicago, 2006).

52. Notable accounts of these contrasting interpretations, which are over-simplified here, can be found in: Sellers, *The Market Revolution*; Sean Wilentz, *The Rise of American Democracy: Jefferson to Lincoln* (New York, 2005); and Daniel Walker Howe, *What Hath God Wrought: The Transformation of America, 1815–1848* (Oxford, 2007).

53. Donald J. Ratcliffe is convincing on this point: "The Right to Vote and the Rise of Democracy, 1787–1828," *Journal of the Early Republic*, 33 (2013), pp. 219–54. See also John L. Brooke, " 'King George has Issued too Many Patents for Us': Property and Democracy in Jeffersonian New York," *Journal of the Early Republic*, 33 (2013), pp. 187–217, though Brooke was unable to take account of Ratcliffe's revision, which traces electoral expansion to the 1790s and even earlier.

54. John Lynch, *Argentine Caudillo: Juan Manuel de Rosas* (Oxford, 1981; 2001); Lynch, *Caudillos in Spanish America, 1800–1850* (Oxford, 1992). Rosas (1793–1877) was the effective ruler of the emerging federation of Argentina, 1829–32, 1835–52; Paez (1790–1873) was president of Venezuela, 1830–35, 1839–42, 1861–63. It goes almost without saying that there were also important contrasts between the United States and Latin America, as Weaver astutely observes: *The Great Land Rush*, pp. 12–18. Nevertheless, the comparative possibilities are understudied. For a stimulating exception, see Charles A. Jones, *American Civilization* (London, 2007).

55. On the *code duello*, see Bertram Wyatt-Brown, "Andrew Jackson's Honor," *Journal of the Early Republic*, 17 (1997), pp. 1–36.

56. Harvey M. Watterson to William Brent, *Charge d'Affaires*, Buenos Aires, April 22, 1844. Quoted in William Dusenberry, "Juan Manuel de Rosas as Viewed by Contemporary American Diplomats," *Hispanic American Historical Review*, 41 (1961), p. 500. I am indebted to Dr. Jay Sexton for this reference.

57. Eugene R. Sheridan, "Thomas Jefferson and the American Presidency: From Patriot King to Popular Leader," *Amerikastudien*, 41 (1996), pp. 17–31.

58. Richard E. Ellis, *The Union at Risk: Jacksonian Democracy, States' Rights and the Nullification Crisis* (New York, 1987), provides a detailed account. Donald J. Ratcliffe, "The Nullification Crisis, Southern Discontents and the American Political Process," *American Nineteenth-Century History*, 1 (2000), pp. 1–30, offers a persuasive revisionist interpretation.

59. Irwin, "Antebellum Tariff Politics: Coalitions and Shifting Economic Interests," *Journal of Law and Politics*, 51 (2008), p. 723. This is an appropriate point to record my debt to Dr. Irwin's invaluable work on nineteenth-century tariffs. Additional citations are made elsewhere in this chapter.

60. Ratcliffe, "The Nullification Crisis"; Howe, *What Hath God Wrought*, pp. 395–410.

61. Ellis, *The Union at Risk*, argues, against the standard view, that the outcome was not a triumph for federal power, despite Jackson's robust defense of central authority.

62. Irwin, "Antebellum Tariff Politics."

63. Alfred Marshall, *Industry and Trade* (New York, 1919; 3rd ed. 1920), p. 486.

64. Larson, *Internal Improvement*, p. 111.

65. Howe, *What Hath God Wrought*, pp. 357–61; Pamela L. Baker, "The Washington National Road Bill and the Struggle to Adopt a Federal System of Internal Improvement," *Journal of the Early Republic*, 22 (2002), pp. 437–64.

66. C. Knick Harley, "The Antebellum American Tariff: Food Exports and Manufacturing," *Explorations in Economic History*, 29 (1992), pp. 375–400; Irwin, "Antebellum Tariff Politics," p. 716.

67. Howe, *What Hath God Wrought*, pp. 359–61.

68. Jane Knodell, "Rethinking the Jacksonian Economy: The Impact of the 1832 Bank Veto on Commercial Banking," *Journal of Economic History*, 66 (2003), pp. 541–74.

69. Howe, *What Hath God Wrought*, pp. 373–83, also draws out the highly personal element in Jackson's attitude and his hostility toward Henry Clay (tariffs) and Nicholas Biddle (president of the Second Bank) in particular.

70. Edward J. Green, "Economic Perspective on the Political History of the Second Bank of the United States," *Federal Reserve Bank of Chicago Economic Perspectives*, 27 (2003), pp. 59–67. Green acknowledges that his argument remains tentative, pending further historical research.

71. For a stronger version of this argument, see Larry Schweinart, "Jacksonian Ideology, Currency Control and Central Banking: A Reappraisal," *Historian*, 51 (1988), pp. 87–102.

72. J. Lawrence Broz, "The Origins of Central Banking: Solutions to the Free-Rider Problem," *International Organization*, 52 (1998), pp. 234–68, has been neglected in this context.

73. Jane Knodell, "The Demise of Central Banking and the Domestic Exchanges: Evidence from Antebellum Ohio," *Journal of Economic History*, 58 (1998), pp. 714–31; Knodell, "Rethinking the Jacksonian Economy"; Wilson, "The 'Country' versus the 'Court.'"

74. The panic of 1837 prompted President Van Buren to press for an independent means of holding government funds. The Independent Treasury Act was passed in 1837, repealed in 1841, and reinstated by President Polk in 1846.

75. Irwin, "Antebellum Tariff Politics," p. 739.

76. Sven Beckert, "Merchants and Manufacturers in the Antebellum North," in Steve Fraser and Gary Gerstle, eds., *Ruling America: A History of Wealth and Power in a Democracy* (Cambridge, MA, 2005), ch. 3.

77. Sean Wilentz, "Jeffersonian Democracy and the Origins of Political Anti-Slavery in the United States: The Missouri Compromise Revisited," *Journal of the Historical Society*, 4 (2004), pp. 375–401.

78. James L. Huston, *The British Gentry, The Southern Planter, and the Northern Family Farmer: Agriculture and Sectional Antagonism in North America* (Baton Rouge, 2015).

79. The Whigs carried forward one of the names attached to American patriots in the 1770s, who in turn took it from the reform wing of the party in Britain: Howe, *What Hath God Wrought*, p. 390; Major L. Wilson, "The 'Country' Versus the 'Court': A Republican Consensus and Party Debate in the Bank War," *Journal of the Early Republic*, 15 (1995), pp. 619–47.

80. The point of departure is William E. Gienapp, *The Origins of the Republican Party, 1852–1856* (New York, 1987); also Michael F. Holt, *The Rise and Fall of the American Whig Party: Jacksonian Politics and the Onset of the Civil War* (New York, 1999).

81. Historians now credit the Free Soilers for their commitment to reform. See Jonathan Halperin Earle, *Jacksonian Anti-Slavery and the Politics of Free Soil, 1824–1854* (Chapel Hill, 2004); Richard S. Newman, *The Transformation of American Abolitionism: Fighting Slavery in the Early Republic* (Chapel Hill, 2002).

82. Thomas Brown, "The Southern Whigs and Economic Development," *Southern Studies*, 20 (1981), pp. 20–38; Edward L. Widmer, *Young America: The Flowering of Democracy in New York* (New York, 1998).

83. Yonatan Eyal, *The Young America Movement and the Transformation of the Democratic Party, 1828–1861* (Cambridge, 2007), is illuminating on this point.

84. See, for example, the *Cambridge Economic History of the United States*, Vols. 1 and 2 (Cambridge, 1996; 2000).

85. For the significance of the 1790s in setting the course of the new state, see Douglas Irwin and Richard Sylla, eds., *Founding Choices: American Economic Policy in the 1790s* (Chicago, 2011); also Edling, *A Hercules in the Cradle*, chs. 1–3.

86. William Appleman Williams, "The Age of Mercantilism: An Interpretation of the American Political Economy, 1763–1828," *William & Mary Quarterly*, 15 (1958), pp. 420–37, emphasizes the role of Madison rather than of Hamilton.

87. Hamilton's ideas merit comparison with those of Johann Gottlieb Fichte, who is a greatly neglected figure in the history of economic development. Fichte's views, formulated from the early 1790s, were assembled in a rarely cited work, *The Closed Commercial State* (1800). For some exceptions, see Stan Standaert, "Fichte as a Development Economist," *Cultures et développement*, 14 (1982), pp. 681–94; Richard T. Gray, "Economic Romanticism: Monetary Nationalism in Johann Gottlieb Fichte and Adam Muller," *Eighteenth-Century Studies*, 36 (2003), pp. 535–57.

88. Reprinted (Washington, 1913). See also Peter McNamara, *Political Economy and Statesmanship: Smith, Hamilton and the Foundation of the Commercial Republic* (DeKalb, 1998); Douglas A. Irwin, "The Aftermath of Hamilton's 'Report on Manufactures,'" *Journal of Economic History*, 64 (2004), pp. 800–821, shows that, contrary to conventional opinion, Hamilton's tariff proposals (but not his proposed subsidies) were adopted by Congress in 1792. List (1789–1846), still an underrated figure, lived in the United States between 1825 and 1831, wrote *Outlines of American Political Economy* in 1827 (New York, 1996), promoted Clay's "American System," and produced his most important work, *The National System of Political Economy*, in 1841. His support for Jackson in the election of 1828 remains a mystery. See also Andreas Etges, "Discovering and Promoting Economic Nationalism: Friedrich List in the United States," *Yearbook of German-American Studies*, 32 (1997), pp. 63–71.

89. Hamilton, *Report on Manufactures*, p. 3.

90. Ibid., p. 35.

91. Ibid., pp. 34–5.

92. Ibid., p. 33.

93. George C. Herring, *From Colony to Superpower: U.S. Foreign Relations since 1776* (Oxford, 2008), pp. 73–81.

94. Todd Estes, *The Jay Treaty Debate: Public Opinion and the Evolution of Early American Political Culture* (Amherst, 2006), lists additional references. The treaty was controversial in Britain too.

95. Quoted in Peter J. Cain, "Bentham and the Development of the British Critique of Colonialism," *Utilitas*, 23 (2011), p. 8.

96. Bradford Perkins, *The Cambridge History of American Foreign Relations*, Vol. 1 (Cambridge, 1993), pp. 203–4; Barry Gough, *Pax Britannica: Ruling the Waves and Keeping the Peace before Armageddon* (Basingstoke, 2014), ch. 5, explores Anglo-U.S. naval rivalry within the framework of Britain's dominance of the seas (exercised in North America from bases in Newfoundland and the West Indies, notably Bermuda).

97. Quoted in David C. Hendrickson, *Union, Nation, or Empire: The American Debate over International Relations, 1789–1941* (Lawrence, 2009), p. 86.

98. Clay (1777–1852); member of the House of Representatives (almost continuously, 1811–25); of the Senate (1806–07, 1810–11, 1831–42, 1849–52); Secretary of State (1825–29); founder of the Whig Party; presidential candidate (1824, 1832, 1844). The literature on Clay is immense. I have found the following particularly helpful: Maurice G. Baxter, *Henry Clay and the American System* (Lexington, 1995); John R. VanAtta, "Western Lands and the Political Economy of Henry Clay's American System, 1819–1832," *Journal of the Early Republic*, 21 (2001), pp. 633–65; Stephen Minicucci, "The 'Cement of Interest': Interest-Based Models of Nation-Building in the Early Republic," *Social Science History*, 25 (2001), pp. 247–74. Bernard Semmel's under-cited work, *The Liberal Ideal and the Demons of Empire* (Baltimore, 1993), pp. 73–83, also deserves to be mentioned.

99. Lawrence A. Peskin, *Manufacturing Revolution: The Intellectual Origins of Early American Industry* (Baltimore, 2004).

100. Kinley Brauer, "The United States and British Imperial Expansion, 1815–60," *Diplomatic History*, 12 (1988), p. 24. Brauer's innovative article was ahead of its time and still awaits both appreciation and pursuit.

101. Henry Clay, *In Defence of the American System: Against the British Colonial System* (Washington, DC, 1832).

102. Ibid., p. 11.

103. Mathew Carey (1760–1839). See Stephen Meardon, "A Reciprocity of Advantages: Carey, Hamilton, and the American Protective Doctrine," *Early American Studies*, 11 (2013), pp. 431–54.

104. Henry Charles Carey (1793–1879). See Rodney J. Morrison, *Henry C. Carey and American Economic Development* (Philadelphia, 1986); Stephen Meardon, "Reciprocity and Henry C. Carey's Traverses on the Road to Perfect Freedom of Trade," *Journal of the History of Economic Thought*, 33 (2011), pp. 307–33.

105. Henry C. Carey, *The Way to Outdo England Without Fighting Her* (Philadelphia, 1865), pp. 24, 27.

106. Ibid., p. 77.

107. Ibid., pp. 32, 65.

108. Ibid., p. 49.

109. Ibid., p. 125.

110. William D. Grampp, "On Manufacturing and Development," *Economic Development & Cultural Change*, 18 (1970), pp. 451–63. On the close connection between slavery and industry on Jefferson's own plantation, see Stephen B. Hodin, "The Mechanisms of Monticello: Saving Labor in Jefferson's America," *Journal of the Early Republic*, 26 (2006), pp. 377–418.

111. Jefferson's connection with physiocracy is traced by Manuela Albertone, "John de Crèvecoeur's Agrarian Myth," *History of European Ideas*, 32 (2006), pp. 28–57; and his

agrarian capitalism by Joyce Appleby, "Commercial Farming and the 'Agrarian Myth' in the Early Republic," *Journal of American History*, 68 (1982), pp. 833–49.

112. Drew R. McCoy, *The Last of the Fathers: James Madison and the Republican Legacy* (New York, 1989), pp. 173–92. Jefferson's personal indebtedness influenced his hostility toward banking and credit facilities. See Herbert E. Sloan, *Principle and Interest: Thomas Jefferson and the Problem of Debt* (New York, 1995).

113. Quoted in Andrew Shankman, "'A New Thing on Earth': Alexander Hamilton, Pro-Manufacturing Republicans, and the Democratization of American Political Economy," *Journal of the Early Republic*, 23 (2003), pp. 323–52, at p. 338. The *Aurora* was an anti-Federalist newspaper. Shankman refutes the widespread view that Jeffersonians opposed all forms of manufacturing.

114. Quoted in Irwin, "The Aftermath of Hamilton's 'Report on Manufactures,'" pp. 819–20.

115. The political crisis arising from Southern opposition to the tariff of 1828 is covered by Howe, *What Hath God Wrought*, pp. 395–410.

116. Joseph J. Persky, *The Burden of Dependency: Colonial Themes in Southern Economic Thought* (Baltimore, 1992).

117. Irwin, "Antebellum Tariff Politics." Nevertheless, the tariff helped the competitiveness of the U.S. cotton industry. See C. Knick Harley, "International Competitiveness of the Antebellum American Cotton Textile Industry," *Journal of Economic History*, 52 (1992), pp. 559–84.

118. Douglas A. Irwin, "New Estimates of the Average Tariff of the United States, 1790–1820," *Journal of Economic History*, 63 (2002), pp. 506–13; an illuminating case study is Carl E. Prince and Seth Taylor, "Daniel Webster, the Boston Associates, and the U.S. Government's Role in the Industrialising Process, 1815–1830," *Journal of the Early Republic*, 2 (1982), pp. 283–99. The controversy is reviewed by Robert E. Lipsey, "U.S. Foreign Trade and the Balance of Payments, 1800–1913," in Engerman and Gallman, *Cambridge Economic History*, pp. 725–6.

119. The authoritative study is now Edling, *A Hercules in the Cradle*, pp. 13, 242. Revenue from land sales was the third item.

120. Gene Dattel, *Cotton and Race in the Making of America: The Human Costs of Economic Power* (Chicago, 2009). The international setting is covered authoritatively by Sven Beckert, *Empire of Cotton: A New History of Global Capitalism* (London, 2014).

121. Douglas A. Irwin, "The Optimal Tax on Antebellum Cotton Exports," *Journal of International Economics*, 60 (2003), pp. 275–91, at p. 277.

122. Quoted in Irwin, "Antebellum Tariff Politics," p. 734.

123. Brauer, "The United States and British Imperial Expansion," pp. 25–9.

124. Ibid., p. 28. Robert Stewart (1769–1822), Lord Castlereagh and 2nd Marquess of Londonderry (1821), Secretary of State for Foreign Affairs (1812–22).

125. Lipsey, "U.S. Foreign Trade and the Balance of Payments," pp. 712–14, 722–3.

126. Memorial of the Boston Board of Trade addressed to Congress (on behalf of the American Shipping Company). Quoted in *North American Review*, 205 (October 1864), p. 484.

127. Kenneth Morgan, "Business Networks in the British Export Trade to North America, 1750–1800," in John J. McCusker and Kenneth Morgan, eds., *The Early Modern Atlantic Economy* (Cambridge, 2000), pp. 52–3, 61–2.

128. Edwin J. Perkins, *Financing Anglo-American Trade: The House of Brown, 1800–1880* (Cambridge, MA, 1975), remains the authoritative study.

129. See section titled "A Revolution of Declining Expectations" in chapter 3 of this text.

130. Cain and Hopkins, *British Imperialism*, chs. 5, 8. See, for a recent example, Andrew Smith, *British Businessmen and Canadian Confederation* (Montreal, 2008).

131. Howard Bodenhorn, *A History of Banking in Antebellum America: Financial Markets and Economic Development in an Era of Nation-Building* (New York, 2000), ch. 5; Robert E. Wright, *The Wealth of Nations Rediscovered: Integration and Expansion in American Financial Markets, 1780–1850* (Cambridge, 2002).

132. Jay Sexton, "Anglophobia in Nineteenth-Century Elections, Politics and Diplomacy," in Gareth Davies and Julian E. Zelizer, eds., *America at the Ballot Box: Elections and Political History* (Philadelphia, 2015), pp. 98–117, shows that British power was still feared at this time. Later, when anxieties faded, Anglophobia remained an element in electoral politics but became detached from other features of Anglo-American relations, which became increasingly cordial.

133. The main sources for this paragraph are: Lipsey, "U.S. Foreign Trade and the Balance of Payments"; Davis and Cull, "International Capital Movements"; and Mira Wilkins, *The History of Foreign Investment in the United States to 1914* (Cambridge, MA, 1989).

134. Limits of space preclude a consideration of venture capital, but Lance E. Davis and Robert J. Cull have shown that the City of London was more willing to invest in small, speculative businesses in the Far West than New York was: *International Capital Markets and American Economic Growth, 1820–1914* (New York, 1994).

135. Foreign holdings of the national debt peaked in 1803, when 56 percent of all federal debt was held abroad, mostly in Britain. Lance E. Davis and Robert E. Cull, "International Capital Movements, Domestic Capital Markets, and American Economic Growth, 1820–1914," in Engerman and Gallman, *Cambridge Economic History*, pp. 741, 745.

136. Ralph W. Hidy, *The House of Baring in American Trade and Finance* (Cambridge, MA, 1949), has lasted the course. Francis's father, John, was an immigrant from Bremen who became a successful merchant in Exeter. See also Jay Sexton, *Debtor Diplomacy: Finance and American Foreign Relations in the Civil War Era, 1837–1873* (Oxford, 2005), ch. 1.

137. On the Asian branch, see James R. Fichter, *So Great a Proffit: How the East Indies Trade Transformed Anglo-American Capitalism* (Cambridge, MA, 2010), pp. 141–8.

138. Levinson and Sparrow, *The Louisiana Purchase*, provide an unusually spacious view of the acquisition.

139. Sexton, *Debtor Diplomacy*, pp. 53–61.

140. Washington's "Farewell Address," 1796; Jefferson's "Inaugural Address," 1801.

141. Irwin, "The Optimal Tax on Antebellum U.S. Cotton Exports." As Irwin points out, there was no guarantee that the benefits of an export tax would have been passed on to producers.

142. For a rare exception (which failed), see Dattel, *Cotton and Race*, pp. 67–69.

143. Mette Ejrnaes, Karl Gunnar Persson, and Søren Rich, "Feeding the British: Convergence and Market Efficiency in the Nineteenth-Century Grain Trade," International Economics, University of Copenhagen, *Discussion Paper*, 28 (2004).

144. Kariann Akemi Yokota, *Unbecoming British: How Revolutionary America Became a Postcolonial Nation* (Oxford, 2011), pp. 102–5. This meticulous study contains a wide range of evidence on this theme.

145. Robert E. Gallman and John Joseph Willis, eds., *American Economic Growth and Standards of Living Before the Civil War* (Chicago, 1992), provide relevant indices for this period.

146. Kevin H. O'Rourke, "The Worldwide Economic Impact of the French Revolutionary and Napoleonic Wars, 1793–1815," *Journal of Global History*, 1 (2006), pp. 123–49.

147. Ibid., p. 147.

148. Clyde A. Haulman, *Virginia and the Panic of 1819: America's First Great Depression and the Commonwealth* (London, 2008), goes beyond Virginia in chs. 1, 2, and 7. See also Murray Rothbard, *The Panic of 1819: Reactions and Policies* (New York, 1962), ch. 1. The term "panic" was often applied in the nineteenth century to describe financial crises.

149. Jay Sexton, *Debtor Diplomacy*; Alasdair Roberts, *America's First Great Depression: Economic Crisis and Political Disorder after the Panic of 1837* (Ithaca, 2012). Jessica M. Lepler, *The Many Panics of 1837: People, Politics, and the Creation of a Transatlantic Financial Crisis* (Cambridge, 2013), underlines the international and personal aspects of the crisis. Namsuk Kim and John J. Wallis offer a different view in "The Market for

American State Bonds in Britain and the United States, 1830–43," *Economic History Review*, 58 (2005), pp. 736–64. Wallis also identified differences between 1837 and 1839, though there is still a case for linking the two: "What Caused the Crisis of 1839," NBER *Historical Working Paper*, 133 (2001); John J. Wallis, Richard E. Sylla, and Arthur Grinath, "Sovereign Debt and Repudiation: The Emerging Market Debt Crisis in the U.S. States, 1839–1843," NBER Working Paper, 10753 (2004).

150. *The National System of Political Economy* (1844; New York, 1966), p. 365.

151. Harrison (1773–1841), a Virginian and a hero of the War of 1812, had a long political career in Ohio, where he settled. He was the Whig presidential candidate in 1836 as well as in 1840.

152. Edward P. Crapol, *John Tyler: The Accidental President* (Chapel Hill, 2006). Tyler (1790–1862) was a Virginian who began as a Democrat, but fell out with Jackson and adopted the Whig program in 1840. He was expelled from the party in 1841, and reappeared as a Jeffersonian expansionist.

153. Clay approved the measure because he thought it would have protectionist consequences.

154. The Mexican-American War is discussed in the section titled "America Knows How to Crush as Well As How to Expand" in chapter 5 of this text.

155. Sexton, *Debtor Diplomacy*, pp. 40–45.

156. Mira Wilkins, "Foreign Investment in the U.S. Economy before 1914," *Annals of the American Academy of Political and Social Science*, 516 (1991), pp. 18–19.

157. Scott C. James and David H. Lake, "The American Walker Tariff of 1846," *International Organization*, 43 (1989), pp. 1–29; Irwin, "Antebellum Tariff Politics."

158. James L. Huston, *The Panic of 1857 and the Coming of the Civil War* (Baton Rouge, 1987). Charles W. Calomiris and Larry Schweikart, "The Panic of 1857: Origins, Transmission, and Containment," *Journal of Economic History*, 51 (1991), pp. 807–34, offer an explanation (noted in chapter 5) based on internal causes.

159. Sellers, *The Market Revolution*; Melvyn Stokes and Stephen Conway, eds., *The Market Revolution in America: Social, Political and Religious Expressions, 1800–1880* (Charlottesville, 1996). The best guide is now John Lauritz Larson, *The Market Revolution in America: Liberty, Ambition, and the Eclipse of the Common Good* (Cambridge, 2010).

160. Robert E. Gallman and John Joseph Wallas, eds., *American Economic Growth and Standards of Living before the Civil War* (Chicago, 1992); Stanley L. Engerman and Robert E. Gallman, eds., *The Cambridge Economic History of the United States*, Vol. 2 (Cambridge, 2000), pp. 7–9, 21–3, 49, 369, 373–6, 377, 379. Peter H. Lindert and Jeffrey G. Williamson, "America's Revolution: Economic Disaster, Development, and Equality," *Vox EU*, July 15, 2011; Lindert and Williamson, *Unequal Gains: American Growth and Inequality Since 1700* (Princeton, NJ, 2016), ch. 5.

161. Lindert and Williamson, *Unequal Gains*, p. 103.

162. John Komlos, "A Three-Decade History of the Antebellum Puzzle: Explaining the Shrinking of the U.S. Population at the Onset of Modern Economic Growth," *Journal of the Historical Society*, 12 (2012), pp. 395–445.

163. Criticism of Sellers, *Market Revolution*, has centered on his interpretation of Jackson's attitudes and policies. See, for example, Larsen, *The Market Revolution*; William E. Gienapp, "The Myth of Class in Jacksonian America," *Journal of Policy History*, 6 (1994), pp. 232–59.

164. Christopher Clark, *The Roots of Rural Capitalism: Western Massachusetts, 1780–1860* (Ithaca, 1990); Clark, *Social Change in America: From the French Revolution Through the Civil War* (Chicago, 2006); Alan Kulikoff, *The Agrarian Origins of American Capitalism* (Charlottesville, 1992); Kulikoff, *From British Peasants to Colonial American Farmers* (Chapel Hill, 2000); Winfred B. Rothenberg, *From Market Place to a Market Economy: The Transformation of Rural Massachusetts, 1750–1850* (Chicago, 1992); James Henretta, *The Origins of American Capitalism: Collected Essays* (Boston, 1991). It

need hardly be said that these authors have different concepts of markets and exchange, and advocate different dates for the transition to capitalism.

165. In 1860, about 80 percent of the population of the United States still lived in rural areas. The average was almost 75 percent, even in Northern states. Huston, *The British Gentry*, tables 4.1 and 4.2, pp. 76–7. See also Huston, *Securing the Fruits of Labor: The American Concept of Wealth Distribution, 1765–1900* (Baton Rouge, 1998). It is appropriate at this point to pay tribute to the exceptional contribution Dr. Huston has made to the history of agriculture in the United States in the course of the last thirty years. See also Adam Wesley Dean, *An Agrarian Republic: Farming, Anti-Slavery Politics, and Nature Parks in the Civil War Era* (Chapel Hill, 2015).

166. This is the claim made with respect to central New Jersey by Pierre Gervais: *Les origins de la révolution industrielle aux États-Unis: entre économie marchande et capitalisme industriel, 1800–1850* (Paris, 2004).

167. Howard Bodenhorn, *State Banking in Early America: A New Economic History* (Oxford, 2003).

168. Engerman and Gallman, *Cambridge Economic History*, p. 380; also pp. 21–3, 49–50; Robert J. Gordon, *The Rise and Fall of American Growth: The U.S. Standard of Living since the Civil War* (Princeton, NJ, 2016), pp. 1–2 and ch. 1.

169. Smith, *Theories of Nationalism* (1983); *Nationalism* (2nd ed.; Cambridge, 2010).

170. David M. Smith, "The American Melting Pot: A National Myth in Public and Popular Discourse," *National Identities*, 14 (2012), pp. 387–402. Curiously, it was a French immigrant, Hector St. John de Crèvecoeur, who in 1782 gave currency to the notion that immigrants were speedily melded into a new people. This perception has been incorporated into the national saga. Crèvecoeur's opposition to the Revolution and subsequent escape to England and then France have been correspondingly neglected. See Alan Taylor, "The American Beginning," *New Republic*, July 18, 2013.

171. An important reassessment, prompted by Jon Butler's *Becoming America* (2001), is John M. Murrin and David S. Silverman, "The Quest for America: Reflections on Distinctiveness, Pluralism and Public Life," *Journal of Interdisciplinary History*, 33 (2002), pp. 235–46. See, too, the full account in Malcolm Gaskill, *Between Two Worlds: How the English Became Americans* (Oxford, 2014).

172. Jack P. Greene, "Early Modern Southeastern North America and the Broader Atlantic and American Worlds," *Journal of Southern History*, 73 (2007), pp. 525–38; Armitage and Braddick, *British Atlantic World*; James D. Drake, "Appropriating a Continent: Geographical Categories, Scientific Metaphors, and the Construction of Nationalism in British North America and Mexico," *Journal of World History*, 15 (2004), pp. 323–57; Gregory E. Dowd, *War Under Heaven: Pontiac, the Indian Nations, and the British Empire* (Baltimore, 2002).

173. Nicholas Onuf and Peter Onuf, *Nations, Markets and War: Modern History and the American Civil War* (Charlottesville, 2006), ch. 7.

174. Eric Kaufman, "American Exceptionalism Reconsidered: Anglo-Saxon Ethnogenesis in the 'Universal' Nation, 1776–1850," *Journal of American Studies*, 33 (1999), pp. 437–53; Kaufman, "Ethnic or Civic Nation? Theorizing the American Case," *Canadian Review of Studies in Nationalism*, 27 (2000), pp. 133–54.

175. Anthony D. Smith, *The Ethnic Origins of Nationalism* (Oxford, 1986). I should also like to record my debt to: Reginald Horsman, *Race and Manifest Destiny: The Origins of American Racial Anglo-Saxonism* (Cambridge, MA, 1981); Rogers M. Smith, *Civic Ideals: Conflicting Visions of Citizenship in U.S. History* (New Haven, 1997); Eric Kaufmann, *The Rise and Fall of Anglo-America* (Cambridge, MA, 2004).

176. Kaufmann, "Ethnic or Civic Nation?" p. 440.

177. Jill Lapore, *The Name of War: King Philip's War and the Origins of American Identity* (New York, 1999) traces the process to the war between the colonists and the Algonquians in 1675.

178. François Furstenberg, *In the Name of the Father: Washington's Legacy, Slavery and the Making of a Nation* (New York, 2007).

179. And in Scotland, Wales, and Ireland too. Vivian Beckford-Smith, "Revisiting Anglicisation in the Nineteenth-Century Cape Colony," *Journal of Imperial & Commonwealth History*, 31 (2003), pp. 82–95, reviews the subject in the light of a pioneering article written by James Sturgis in 1982.

180. Nell Irvin Painter, "Ralph Waldo Emerson's Saxons," *Journal of American History*, (2009), pp. 977–85.

181. Frederic Cople Jaher, *The Urban Establishment: Upper Class Status in Boston, New York, Charleston, Chicago and Los Angeles* (Urbana, 1982).

182. Kaufman, *Rise and Fall of Anglo-America*, pp. 16–19.

183. Ritchie Devon Watson, *Normans and Saxons: Southern Race Mythology and the Intellectual History of the American Civil War* (Baton Rouge, 2008); Christopher Hanlon, "'The Old Race Are All Gone': Transatlantic Bloodlines and 'English Traits,'" *American Literary History*, 18 (2007), pp. 800–823.

184. James M. McPherson, "'Two Irreconcilable Peoples': Ethnic Nationalism in the Confederacy," in David T. Gleeson and Simon Lewis, eds., *The Civil War as Global Conflict* (Columbia, 2014), pp. 85–97, differs from the present work in positing a clear distinction between Northern (civic) and Southern (ethnic) nationalism.

185. A lucid starting point is Andrew Preston, "Bridging the Gap between the Sacred and the Secular in the History of American Foreign Relations," *Diplomatic History*, 30 (2006), pp. 783–812.

186. Frank Lambert, *Inventing the "Great Awakening"* (Princeton, NJ, 1999).

187. Nathan O. Hatch, *The Democratization of American Christianity* (New Haven, 1989), p. 3.

188. Laurence R. Iannaccone, "Introduction to the Economics of Religion," *Journal of Economic Literature*, 36 (1998), 1465–98. It should be acknowledged that qualifications for church membership were higher in the colonial period than in the nineteenth and twentieth centuries.

189. Michael P. Young, "Confessional Protests: The Religious Birth of US National Social Movements," *American Sociological Review*, 67 (2002), pp. 660–95. But see also Thistlethwaite, *The Anglo-American Connection*, chs. 3–5.

190. Nicholas Guyatt, *Providence and the Invention of the United States, 1607–1876* (Cambridge, 2007). I have gained far more from Guyatt's capacious and illuminating study than I am able to express here.

191. Ruth Miller Elson, *Guardians of Tradition: American Schoolbooks of the Nineteenth Century* (Lincoln, 1964).

192. Joyce Appleby, *Inheriting the Revolution: The First Generation of Americans* (Cambridge, MA, 2000), p. 199.

193. Jeffrey L. Pasley, Andrew W. Robertson, and David Waldstreicher, eds., *Beyond the Founders: New Approaches to the Political History of the Early United States* (Chapel Hill, 2004), are illuminating on this subject.

194. Michael O'Brien, *Conjectures of Order: Intellectual Life and the American South, 1810–1860*, 2 vols. (Chapel Hill, 2004) establishes the diversity and creativity of intellectual thought in the South during this period, and the extent to which it drew on conservative traditions associated with Burke in particular, but also Carlyle, whose romanticism, espousal of German idealism, and defense of slavery sounded melodious chords.

195. See, notably, the differences between Sellers, *Market Revolution*, and Howe, *What Hath God Wrought*.

196. Lloyd S. Kramer, "The French Revolution and the Creation of American Political Culture," in Joseph Klaits and Michael H. Haltzel, eds., *The Global Ramifications of the French Revolution* (Cambridge, 1994), pp. 26–54, is exceptionally illuminating on this subject.

197. Quoted in Kramer, "The French Revolution," p. 51. Robert Goodloe Harper (1765–1825) represented South Carolina in the House between 1795 and 1801.

198. Seth Cotlar, *Tom Paine's America: The Rise and Fall of Transatlantic Radicalism in the Early Republic* (Charlottesville, 2011).

199. Joyce Appleby, *Inheriting the Revolution*, pp. 250–59; Mark Noll, *America's God: From Jonathan Edwards to Abraham Lincoln* (New York, 2002).

200. Andrew Shankman, *Crucible of American Democracy: The Struggle to Fuse Egalitarianism and Capitalism in Jeffersonian Pennsylvania* (Lawrence, 2004).

201. Paul E. Johnson, *A Shopkeeper's Millennium: Society and Revivals in Rochester, New York, 1815–1837* (New York, 1978), shows how religious revivals helped the northern middle class to cohere and provided opportunities for wage-earners to improve their status.

202. This, at least, is the argument made by Sellers in *The Market Revolution*.

203. Elisa Tamarkin, *Anglophilia: Deference, Devotion, and Antebellum America* (Chicago, 2008).

204. Ibid., p. 30.

205. Ian Radforth, *Royal Spectacle: The 1830 Visit of the Prince of Wales to Canada and the United States* (Toronto, 2004).

206. *The Times*, April 27, 1865.

207. Ralph Waldo Emerson, *Essays and English Traits* (Danbury, 1909; 1980), p. 332.

208. Yokota, *Unbecoming British*, pp. 264–5.

209. Tamarkin, *Anglophilia*, ch. 4.

210. The notion of "uplift" survives today in discussions among African Americans of "racial uplift," and in science fiction. "Biological uplift" is the invention of the remarkable Cordwainer Smith (1913–1966), who applied it in *The Underpeople* (New York, 1966), as the means whereby an advanced civilization can improve another species.

211. Lawrence Levine, *Highbrow/Lowbrow: The Emergence of Cultural Hierarchy in America* (Cambridge, MA, 1988).

212. Caroline Winterer, *The Culture of Classicism: Ancient Greece and Rome in American Intellectual Life, 1780–1910* (Baltimore, 2002).

213. C. Dallett Hemphill, *Bowing to Necessities: A History of Manners in America, 1620–1860* (New York, 1999). R. A. Burchell, "The Role of the Upper Class in the Formation of American Culture," in Burchell, ed., *The End of Anglo-America: Historical Essays in the Study of Cultural Divergence* (Manchester, 1991), pp. 184–212. This revises the pioneering work of Stow Parsons, *The Decline of American Gentility* (New York, 1973); Richard L. Bushman, *The Refinement of America: Persons, Houses, Cities* (New York, 1992). In a rare comparative study, Linda Young draws attention to the rise of a middle class throughout the Anglo-world: *Middle Class Culture in the Nineteenth Century: America, Australia, and Britain* (New York, 2003).

214. Webster was an uncompromising Federalist whose desire to create an American identity was married to a respect for hierarchy and a suspicion of democracy. See Jill Lepore, *The Story of America: Essays on Origins* (Princeton, NJ, 2012), ch. 7.

215. Noah Webster (1758–1843), schoolmaster, lawyer, journalist, and lexicographer, born in Connecticut, where he spent most of his life. There are numerous popular and accessible biographies. See, for example, Joshua Kendall, *The Forgotten Founding Father: Noah Webster's Obsession and the Creation of American Culture* (New York, 2011).

216. Richard M. Rollins, *The Long Journey of Noah Webster* (Philadelphia, 1980); Kenneth Cmiel, "'A Broad Fluid Language of Democracy': Discovering the American Idiom," *Journal of American History*, 79 (1992), pp. 913–36.

217. Tamarkin, *Anglophilia*, pp. 290–91. Webster's *Dictionary* did not match the competition until 1864, when it appeared in a new and greatly expanded edition.

218. Ralph Waldo Emerson (1803–1882). Leonard Tennenhouse, *The Importance of Feeling English: American Literature and the British Diaspora, 1750–1850* (Princeton, NJ,

2007), makes the general point with a wealth of learning and a refreshing selection of literary illustrations.

219. Ralph Waldo Emerson, "The American Scholar" (Cambridge, MA, 1837), at http://www .emersoncentral.com/amscholar.htm.

220. Emerson's original was amended by his friend, Oliver Wendell Holmes, Sr., who gave it the ambitious title by which it is known.

221. Alexis de Tocqueville, *Democracy in America*, ed. J. P. Mayer (New York, 1969), Vol. 2, p. 477.

222. James Russell Lowell (1819–1891) transcribed authentic dialects in the 1840s and had an influence on Mark Twain, but was not an advocate of a new national literature.

223. Martin Griffin, "Emerson's Crossing: English Traits and the Politics of 'Politics,'" *Modern Intellectual History*, 5 (2008), 271–3.

224. Andrew H. Debanco, *Melville: His World and Work* (New York, 2005); Andrew Lawson, "Moby Dick and the American Empire," *Comparative American Studies*, 10 (2012), pp. 45–62. Nathaniel Hawthorne's work, published in the 1850s, was more accessible and had greater popularity.

225. Alan Taylor, "Fennimore Cooper's America," *History Today*, 46 (1996), pp. 21–7; Taylor, *William Cooper's Town: Power and Persuasion on the Frontier of the Early American Republic* (New York, 1995), which provides a reminder that the Revolution was about land speculation as well as ideology.

226. On the family origins of this belief, see Taylor, *William Cooper's Town*.

227. Barrett Wendell, *A Literary History of America* (New York, 1901), p. 187.

228. Alan Trachtenberg, *Shades of Hiawatha: Staging Indians, Making Americans, 1880–1930* (New York, 2004), ch. 1; Robert A. Ferguson, "Longfellow's Political Fears: Civic Authority and the Role of the Artist in 'Hiawatha': and 'Miles Standish,'" *American Literature*, 50 (1978), pp. 187–215. Whitman overlooked Longfellow's ambition, which anticipated Emerson, of helping to create a genuine American literature.

229. Tamara Plakins Thornton, *Cultivating Gentlemen: The Meaning of Country Life Among the Boston Elite, 1785–1860* (New Haven, 1989).

230. There is no adequate treatment of Benjamin that deals with the subjects touched on here. Kenneth Hafertepe and James F. O'Gorman, eds., *American Architects and Their Books* (Boston, 2001), provide some contextual information.

231. Alexander O. Boulton, "From the Greek," *American Heritage*, 41 (1990), pp. 80–87.

232. Wilbur Zelinsky, "Classical Town Names in the United States: The Historical Geography of an American Idea," *Geographical Review*, 57 (1967), pp. 463–95; Zelinsky, *Nation into State*, pp. 119–43, 208–13.

233. Kelley N. Seay, "Jousting and the Evolution of Southernness in Maryland," *Maryland Historical Magazine*, 99 (2004), pp. 50–79. Maryland, a border state, was split by the Civil War and perpetuated jousting as a means of reinforcing Southern values.

234. Robert C. Toll, *Blacking Up: The Minstrel Show in Nineteenth-Century America* (New York, 1974).

235. I am indebted to my former colleague, Dr. Karl Miller, for instruction on this subject.

236. Karl Hagstrom Miller, "The Sound of Antebellum Reform," *Reviews in American History*, 36 (2008), pp. 374–81.

237. Alexis de Tocqueville, *Democracy in America*, ed. Isaac Kramnick (London, 2003), pp. 11, 622–3.

238. The sentiments quoted in the rest of this paragraph are scattered throughout Tocqueville, *Democracy in America*, ed. J. P. Mayer, Vol. 2. See especially pt. 1, chs. 2, 11; pt. 2, chs. 10, 11, pt. 3, ch.16.

239. Lloyd S. Kramer develops this theme in *Nationalism: Political Cultures in Europe and America, 1775–1865* (New York, 2011).

240. Thistlethwaite, *The Anglo-American Connection*.

241. School textbooks presented the British in a favorable light because they were committed to portraying Americans as their descendants. Elson, *Guardians of Tradition*.

242. Nathan O. Hatch, *The Democratization of American Christianity* (New Haven, 1989).

243. William R. Hutchison, *Religious Pluralism in America: The Contentious History of a Founding Ideal* (New Haven, 2003).

244. Support for the Southern version of capitalism grew from the 1830s: John Patrick Daly, *When Slavery Was Called Freedom: Evangelicalism, Proslavery, and the Causes of the Civil War* (Lexington, 2002).

245. Rogers M. Smith, *Civic Ideals: Conflicting Visions of Citizenship in U.S. History* (New Haven, 1997), pp. 72–86.

246. Kaufmann's view on this matter (in *The Rise and Fall of Anglo-America*) is more sanguine than the one taken here.

247. Michael R. Haines, "The Population of the United States, 1790–1920," in Engerman and Gallman, eds., *Cambridge Economic History of the United States*, pp. 153–4.

248. O'Brien, *Conjectures of Order*, I, pp. 286–7.

249. Ibid., ch. 2; Bruce Levine, "Conservatism, Nativism, and Slavery: Thomas R. Whitney and the Origins of the Know-Nothing Party," *Journal of American History*, 88 (2001), pp. 455–88. The party had several names and finally settled on the "American Party" in 1855. By then, however, the popular name, Know Nothing (which was derived from the secrecy of the party's procedures), had stuck.

250. Bonner, *Mastering America*, citing David Potter's insight, p. xvii.

251. Samuel F. B. Morse (1791–1872), *Letters and Journals*, II (New York, 1914), p. 85.

252. Henry David Thoreau (1817–62), *Walden* (Boston, 1854), www.thoreau.eserver.org /walden00.html, ch. 1, section D 9.

253. John Adams, "Oration," on the tenth anniversary of American independence, July 4, 1793, Collection of 4 July Speeches; Special Collections, Ellish Library, University of Missouri, Columbia.

254. Howe, *What Hath God Wrought*, provides a capacious and lucid account of the years between 1815 and 1848.

255. Credit should go to Williams ("The Age of Mercantilism"), who saw that the new Republic aimed at establishing an independent mercantilist state. Williams judged that the experiment ended in 1828 with the rise of free trade and Jacksonian individualism.

256. Sam W. Haynes, *Unfinished Revolution: The Early American Republic in a British World* (Charlottesville, 2010); Joseph Eaton, *The Anglo-American Paper War: Debates about the New Republic, 1800–1825* (Basingstoke, Hants, 2012).

257. Ambrose G. Bierce, *The Devil's Dictionary* (New York, 1906; 2000), a collection of essays written after 1881.

258. James Belich, *Replenishing the Earth: The Settler Revolution and the Rise of the Anglo-World* (Oxford, 2009), is a notable exception. See also chapter 5 in this text.

259. Craig Calhoun, *The Roots of Radicalism: Tradition, the Public Sphere, and Early Nineteenth-Century Social Movements* (Chicago, 2012), ch. 9.

260. Mark W. Summers, *The Plundering Generation: Corruption and the Crisis of the Union, 1849–1861* (Oxford, 1987).

261. A preliminary statement of the argument of this chapter is in A. G. Hopkins, "The United States, 1783–1861: Britain's Honorary Dominion?" *Britain and the World*, 4 (2011), pp. 232–46.

262. Although the Address is regularly cited for Washington's advice on avoiding "foreign entanglements," taken as a whole it reads as an extended statement of the many possible causes of the failure of the Union.

263. As Alexis de Tocqueville, writing in 1856, observed of France in *The Old Regime and the Revolution* (New York, 1955); and Edward Hallett Carr, of Russia, in *The Bolshevik Revolution, 1917–1923*, 3 vols. (New York, 1951–53).

CHAPTER 5: WARS OF INCORPORATION

1. John L. O'Sullivan, "The Great Nation of Futurity," *United States Democratic Review*, 6 (1839), pp. 426–430.
2. The phrase is generally attributed to O'Sullivan, who popularized it in 1845. Robert D. Sampson, *John L. O'Sullivan and His Times* (Kent, 2004) reveals cosmopolitan and progressive aspects of a man who has become as stereotyped as his famous phrase. Linda S. Hudson claims that the author was Jane McManus, a southern expansionist, land speculator, and journalist: *Mistress of Manifest Destiny: A Biography of Jane McManus Storm Cazneau* (Austin, 2001), pp. 60–62.
3. This claim has been supported by scholars writing from very different perspectives. See, for example, Fred Anderson and Andrew Cayton, *The Dominance of War: Empire and Liberty in North America, 1500–2000* (New York, 2005); Robert Kagan, *Dangerous Nation: America and the World, 1600–1898* (London, 2006); Thomas R. Hietala, *Manifest Design: American Exceptionalism and Empire* (Ithaca, 1985; 2003).
4. Readers who suppose that this is a throw-away line might like to consult Andrew J. Bacevich, *The New American Militarism* (Oxford, 2005), which shows how civilians, not soldiers, made military strength the true measure of national greatness after the Vietnam War.
5. Current trends are well covered by William Earl Weeks, "New Directions in the Study of Early American Foreign Relations," in Michael J. Hogan, ed., *Paths to Power: The Historiography of American Foreign Relations to 1941* (Cambridge, 2000), ch. 2; Kinley Brauer, "The Great American Desert Revisited: Recent Literature and Prospects for the Study of American Foreign Relations, 1815–1861," in Hogan, ch. 3; Jay Sexton, "Towards a Synthesis of Foreign Relations in the Civil War Era, 1848–77," *American Nineteenth-Century History*, 5 (2004), pp. 50–73.
6. See chapter 3 of this text. Brauer, "The Great American Desert"; Michael J. Hogan, "Introduction, in Hogan, *Paths to Power*, p. 2, quoting a phrase borrowed from Jonathan Dull.
7. For different emphases, see Felix Gilbert, *To the Farewell Address: Ideas of Early American Foreign Policy* (Princeton, 1961); and James H. Hutson, *John Adams and the Diplomacy of the American Revolution* (Lexington, 1980).
8. George Washington, "Farewell Address," 1796. Hamilton's amendments to the draft inserted greater realism into the document.
9. This suggested sequence, here cryptically stated, owes much to Reginald Horsman, "The Dimension of an 'Empire of Liberty': Expansion and Republicanism, 1775–1825," *Journal of the Early Republic*, 9 (1989), pp. 1–20; and John M. Murrin, "The Jeffersonian Triumph and American Exceptionalism," *Journal of the Early Republic*, 20 (2000), pp. 1–25.
10. David C. Hendrickson, *Peace Pact: The Lost World of the American Founding* (Lawrence, 2003); Hendrickson, *Union, Nation, or Empire: The American Debate over International Relations, 1789–1941* (Lawrence, 2009).
11. John C. Weaver, *The Great Land Rush and the Making of the Modern World, 1650–1900* (Montreal, 2003); and James Belich, *Replenishing the Earth: The Settler Revolution and the Rise of the Anglo-World* (Oxford, 2009), are major contributions to our understanding of this subject.
12. I refer in this chapter to the self-governing settler states as dominions, even though the designation in some cases anticipates their formal status. The anachronism avoids constitutional distinctions that, in the present context, would be cumbersome and otiose.
13. The pioneering work on this theme has been undertaken by historians from the "old dominions": Donald Denoon, *Settler Capitalism: The Dynamics of Development in the Southern Hemisphere* (Oxford, 1983); Weaver, *The Great Land Rush*; Ian Tyrrell, *Transnational Nation: United States History since 1789* (Basingstoke, 2007); Belich, *Replen-*

ishing the Earth. One of the three editors (Christopher Lloyd, Jacob Metzer, and Richard Sutch) of *Settler Economies in World History* (Leiden, 2013), is from the United States. A U.S. historian, Walter L. Hixson, includes some brief historical comparisons: *American Settler Colonialism: A History* (New York, 2013), pp. 7–13.

14. Ambrose Bierce, *The Devil's Dictionary* (New York, 1906; 2000). Bierce (1842–c. 1914) grew up in the Midwest, fought on the Union side during the Civil War, and thereafter became a journalist and critic, notably in San Francisco, where he was one of William R. Hearst's most outspoken employees.

15. The feeling was mutual: David C. Hendrickson, *Union, Nation, or Empire*, pp. 86–9.

16. See Peter J. Cain, "Bentham and the Development of the British Critique of Colonialism," *Utilitas*, 23 (2011), pp. 1–24.

17. J. Hector St. John Crèvecoeur, *Letters from an American Farmer* (London, 1782). Quoted in Alan Taylor, "The American Beginning," *New Republic*, July 18, 2013. The subhead, as well as the quotations in the paragraph that follows, are from the same source. Taylor's article provides an admirable corrective to stereotypes of Crèvecoeur.

18. Turner's essay is readily available in several reprinted forms. John Mack Faragher, ed., *Re-Reading Frederick Jackson Turner* (New Haven, 1994), ch. 2, also reprints a number of Turner's other, mostly neglected, essays, including two interesting pieces on "Sections and Nation."

19. Such comparisons are harder to find today. Dane Kennedy provides a rare example in "The Frontier in South African History," *Journal of the West*, 34 (1995), pp. 23–31.

20. The phrase is Alfred W. Crosby's: *Ecological Imperialism: The Biological Expansion of Europe, 900–1900* (Cambridge, 1986). I am indebted to Belich, *Replenishing the Earth*, who treats westward expansion and state-building in far greater detail than is possible here.

21. Marilyn Lake, "The White Man Under Siege: New Histories of Race in the Nineteenth Century and the Advent of White Australia," *History Workshop Journal*, 58 (2004), pp. 41–62; Matthew Guterl and Christine Skwiot, "Atlantic and Pacific Crossings: Race, Empire, and the Labour Problem in the Late Nineteenth Century," *Radical History Review*, 91 (2005), pp. 40–61.

22. For the original formulation see Russell Ward, *The Australian Legend* (Melbourne, 1958); Richard Waterhouse, "Australian Legends: Representations of the Bush, 1813–1913," *Australian Historical Studies*, 31 (2000), pp. 201–21, provides a review.

23. *To a New World or Among the Gold Fields of Australia* (Philadelphia, 1893). Wilkins Micawber, it need hardly be said, retains his place as one of Charles Dickens's most famous characters (*David Copperfield*, 1850).

24. *The Call of the Wild* (New York, 1903). London had the imaginative idea of casting a dog, Buck, as his hero and transporting him from an easy life in California to the challenging wilderness of the far north. The central point becomes even more vivid: conflict produces character. The comparison with Tarzan (see the "Intermission" below) is illuminating.

25. See, for example, Marilyn Lake, "The Inviolable Woman: Feminist Conceptions of Citizenship in Australia, 1900–1945," *Gender & History*, 8 (1996), pp. 197–211.

26. I am indebted here to John Markoff, "Where and When Was Democracy Invented?" *Comparative Studies in Society & History*, 41 (1999), pp. 660–90; Markoff, *The Great Waves of Democracy in Historical Perspective* (Ithaca, 1994).

27. Donald J. Ratcliffe, "The Right to Vote and the Rise of Democracy, 1787–1828," *Journal of the Early Republic*, 33 (2013), p. 248.

28. Richard F. Bensel, *The American Ballot Box in the Mid-Nineteenth Century* (Cambridge, 2004).

29. The Indian Citizenship Act also provided for dual citizenship: Native Americans were not obliged to surrender tribal affiliations to become citizens of the United States.

30. Patricia Grimshaw, "Settler Anxieties, Indigenous Peoples and Women's Suffrage in the Colonies of Australia, New Zealand and Hawai'i, 1888–1902," *Pacific Historical Review*, 69 (2000), pp. 553–72.

31. David Goodman, "Gold Fields/Golden Fields: The Language of Agrarianism and the Victorian Gold Rush," *Australian Historical Studies*, 23 (1988), pp. 19–41, shows how the agrarian ideal was compromised by the gold rush of the 1850s.

32. Weaver, *The Great Land Rush*, explores the diversity of old and new property rights, and the important shift from land grants to market and other forms of distribution in chs. 5–7.

33. Bruce Buchan, "Traffick of Empire: Trade, Treaty and 'Terra Nullius' in Australia and North America, 1750–1800," *History Compass*, 5 (2007), pp. 386–405; Merete Borch, "Rethinking the Origins of 'Terra Nullius,'" *Australian Historical Studies*, 32 (2001), pp. 222–39.

34. Edward R. Kittrell, "Wakefield's Scheme of Systematic Colonization and Classical Economics" *American Journal of Economics & Sociology*, 32 (1973), pp. 87–111.

35. Edward Gibbon Wakefield, *England and America*, Vol. 2 (London, 1833), pp. 1–46; John R. VanAtta, "Western Lands and the Political Economy of Henry Clay's American System," *Journal of the Early Republic*, 21 (2004), pp. 633–65.

36. Macdonald (1815–91), "Father of the Confederation" and Canada's first prime minister (1867–73; 1878–91).

37. Devon A. Mihesuah, ed., *Natives and Academics: Researching and Writing about American Indians* (1998). Richard White's *The Middle Ground: Indians, Empires and Republics in the Great Lakes Region, 1650–1815* (New York, 1991), is acknowledged to be the ground-breaking work. Credit should be given to Victor G. Kiernan, *America: the New Imperialism: From White Settlement to World Hegemony* (London, 1978), pt. 1, ch. 3, pt. 2, ch. 4, and pt. 3, ch. 1, for introducing this theme before other historians of empire did.

38. Timothy J. Shannon, *Iroquois Diplomacy on the Early American Frontier* (New York, 2008); Pekka Hamalainen, *The Comanche Empire* (New Haven, 2008). The Iroquois Confederation or League has also been referred to as an empire.

39. See, for example, Brian DeLay, *War of a Thousand Deserts: Indian Raids and the U.S.-Mexican War* (New Haven, 2008); and for a different perspective, Ned Blackhawk's account of relations among the Utes, Paiute, and Western Shoshone: *Violence Over the Land: Indians and Empires in the Early American West* (Cambridge, MA, 2007). See also Gary C. Anderson, *Sitting Bull and the Paradox of Lakota Nationhood* (New York, 2nd ed. 2007).

40. Ivor Wilks, *Asante in the Nineteenth Century: The Structure and Evolution of a Political Order* (Cambridge, 1975); and R.C.C. Law, *The Oyo Empire, c. 1600–1836* (London, 1977), remain model studies of the highest quality.

41. The demographic debate is fraught with uncertainties and infused with powerful beliefs. David Henige, *Numbers from Nowhere: The American Indian Contact Population Debate* (Norman, 1998), erects warning signs that some scholars still manage to elude.

42. For one of many possible examples, see Hixson, *American Settler Colonialism*, citing Charles C. Mann's popular study, *1491: New Revelations on the Americas* (New York, 2005), p. 23.

43. On the United States, see White, *The Middle Ground*; Jane T. Merritt, *At the Crossroads: Indians and Empires on a Mid-Atlantic Frontier, 1700–1763* (Chapel Hill, 2003), chs. 3–4.

44. Katherine Ellinghaus, "Strategies of Elimination: Exempted Aborigines, Competent Indians, and Twentieth-Century Assimilation Policies in Australia and the United States," *Journal of the Canadian Historical Association*, 18 (2007), pp. 202–25.

45. South Africa is a partial exception. Dutch settlement in Cape Town had antiquity (having been founded in 1652), but expansion inland did not gather momentum until the 1830s.

46. By 1800, this was already an old story. See Alan Taylor, *American Colonies: The Settling of North America* (New York, 2001).

47. Gregory Evans Dowd, *A Spirited Resistance: The North American Indian Struggle for Unity, 1745–1815* (Baltimore, 1992).

48. On the predominance of violence, see James H. Merrell, *Into the American Woods: Negotiators and the Pennsylvania Frontier* (New York, 1999), pp. 221, 250; Patrick Griffin, *American Leviathan: Empire, Nation, and Revolutionary Frontier* (New York, 2007), pp. 97, 178.

49. François Furstenberg, "The Significance of the Trans-Appalachian Frontier in Atlantic History," *American Historical Review*, 113 (2008), pp. 647–77.

50. William S. Belko, ed., *America's Hundred Years' War: U.S. Expansion to the Gulf Coast and the Fate of the Seminole, 1763–1858* (Gainesville, 2011), represents recent trends in emphasizing developments in the southeast.

51. On Jefferson's determination to secure land for white settlement (and his ambivalent attitude toward Native Americans), see Anthony F. C. Wallace, *Jefferson and the Indians: The Tragic Fate of the First Americans* (Cambridge, MA, 1999).

52. Weaver, *The Great Land Rush*, p. 190. The Cherokee, Creek, Shawnee, and the majority of the Iroquois were the most prominent of Britain's allies.

53. Estimates of the numbers transported range from 15,000–20,000, with 4,000–5,000 deaths. These figures (and all others) need to be treated as very approximate orders of magnitude. The most systematic account of the consequences is Matthew T. Gregg and David M. Wishart, "The Price of Cherokee Removal," *Explorations in Economic History*, 49 (2012), pp. 423–42.

54. Bruce Vandervort, *Indian Wars of Canada, Mexico, and the United States, 1812–1900* (New York, 2006).

55. The recipient was Private Oscar R. Burkard (1877–1950), who was in the Hospital Corps and won the medal for showing exceptional courage during the Battle of Sugar Point in 1898.

56. Joseph M. Prince and Richard H. Steckel, "Nutritional Success on the Great Plains: Nineteenth-Century Equestrian Nomads," *Journal of Interdisciplinary History*, 33 (2003), pp. 353–84.

57. Hendrickson, *Union, Nation, or Empire*, pp. 252–3.

58. This provision of the Amendment confirmed the Civil Rights Act of 1866.

59. The extension of legal powers was completed in 1903, when Congress acquired comprehensive rights over Native American lands, law, and government: Blue Clark, *Lone Wolf v Hitchcock: Treaty Rights and Indian Law at the End of the Nineteenth Century* (Lincoln, 1995).

60. Rose Stremlau, "To Domesticate and Civilise Wild Indians: Allotment and the Campaign to Reform Indian Families, 1875–1887," *Journal of Family History*, 30 (2005), pp. 265–86.

61. Leonard A. Carlson, *Indians, Bureaucrats and Land: The Dawes Act and the Decline of Indian Farming* (Westport, 1981); Frederick E. Hoxie, *A Final Promise: The Campaign to Assimilate the Indians, 1880–1922* (Lincoln, 1984; 2001). For one of many detailed examples see William T. Hagan, *Taking Indian Lands: The Cherokee (Jerome) Commission, 1889–1893* (Norman, 2003).

62. Nancy Shoemaker, *American Indian Population Recovery in the Twentieth Century* (Albuquerque, 1999). The "Vanishing Indian" became the "Recovering Indian" in the twentieth century. By 2000, those identifying as "Native Americans" numbered about 2 million.

63. Peter J. Stanlis, ed., *Edmund Burke: Selected Writings and Speeches* (New Brunswick, 1963; 2009), p. 197.

64. On federal support on the frontier, see William H. Bergmann, *The American National State and the Early West* (Cambridge, 2012), which covers the Ohio Valley and Great Lakes region between 1775 and 1815.

65. It need hardly be said that the interpretation of the Second Amendment remains controversial. Written constitutions, though appealing, have drawbacks, as some of the founders recognized. Saul Cornell, *A Well-Regulated Militia: The Founding Fathers and the Origins of Gun Control in America* (New York, 2006), provides a scholarly guide.

66. Amy S. Greenberg, *Manifest Manhood and the Antebellum American Empire* (Cambridge, 2005), ch.1.

67. Quoted in Walter L. Williams, "United States Indian Policy and the Debate over Philippine Annexation: Implications for the Origins of American Imperialism," *Journal of American History*, 66 (1980), pp. 815–16.

68. "The Revenge of Rain-in-the-Face," in *Birds of Passage: Flight the Fifth* (New York, 1878).

69. Robert W. Rydell, *All the World's a Fair: Visions of Empire at American International Expositions, 1876–1916* (Chicago, 1985); also the alternative perspective of L. G. Moses, *Wild West Shows and the Images of American Indians, 1883–1933* (Albuquerque, 1996); Janet M. Davis, "Instruct the Minds of all Classes: Celebrations of Empire at the American Circus, 1898–1910," *European Contributions to American Studies*, 51 (2004), pp. 58–68.

70. Stephen G. Hyslop, "How the West Was Spun," *American History*, 43 (2008), pp. 26–33; Louis S. Warren, *Buffalo Bill's America: William Cody and the Wild West Show* (New York, 2005). See also Robert M. Utley, *The Lance and the Shield: The Life and Times of Sitting Bull* (New York, 1993).

71. Brian W. Dippie, *Custer's Last Stand: The Anatomy of an American Myth* (Lincoln, 1976; 1997), is a valuable guide. Many heroic figures, such as Kit Carson, have been cut down to size. Among his exploits, Carson directed a scorched earth policy that drove the Navajo from their homeland to a death camp at Bosque Redondo (in what became New Mexico) in 1863–1864. Carson (1809–1868) has moved from hero to villain and is currently poised in an intermediate position. See Tom Dunlay, *Kit Carson and the Indians* (Lincoln, 2000).

72. "From Far Dakota's Canyons" (1876).

73. Henry Cabot Lodge and Theodore Roosevelt, *Hero Tales from American History* (New York, 1895), p. ix.

74. Hollywood produced numerous versions of Custer's story, beginning in 1912.

75. Anthony Quinn (1915–2001), the son of an Irish-Mexican father and a Mexican-Aztec mother, fitted the specifications perfectly. He was sufficiently alien to be different but not so alien as to be alarming. He played every type of foreigner known to Hollywood, and ranged from Inuit to Arab and from Filipino to Hawaiian.

76. Frederick J. Turner, "The Significance of the Frontier in American History," in John M. Faragher, ed., *Rereading Frederick Jackson Turner* (New Haven, 1994), ch. 2. Richard Slotkin, *The Fatal Environment: The Myth of the Frontier in the Age of Industrialization, 1800–1890* (New York, 1985), provides an antidote.

77. David, M. Wrobel, *The End of American Exceptionalism: Frontier Anxiety From the Old West to the New Deal* (Lawrence, 1993), ch. 2. Wrobel's book must be counted as one of the most perceptive in the vast library of studies of the frontier.

78. Wroble, *The End of American Exceptionalism*, ch. 3.

79. See chapters 8–9 of this text.

80. Robert E. May, *Manifest Destiny's Underworld: Filibustering in Antebellum America* (Chapel Hill, 2002); Greenberg, *Manifest Manhood*, ch. 4.

81. Russell Roth, *Muddy Glory: America's "Indian" Wars in the Philippines, 1899–1935* (West Hanover, 1981).

82. Williams, "United States Indian Policy," p. 828.

83. Ibid., p. 826.

84. Ibid., p. 827.

85. Theodore Roosevelt, 1899, quoted in ibid., p. 826.

86. One stimulating study comparing the United States and Canada has suggested that variations in economic development can be attributed in part to differences between hierarchical and open societies. Studies of other societies, however, have shown that economic development is compatible with hierarchical structures. If this were not the

case, Britain would have been unable to create the first industrial revolution. See Marc Egnal, *Divergent Paths: How Culture and Institutions Have Shaped North American Growth* (New York, 1996).

87. Gavin Wright, "The Origins of American Industrial Success," *American Economic Review*, 80 (1990), pp. 651–68. David M. Potter's original formulation in *People of Plenty: Economic Abundance and the American Character* (New York, 1954) links resources to political attributes, such as democracy and equality, in ways that now seem unconvincing.

88. Robert E. Gallman, "Economic Growth and Structural Change in the Long Nineteenth Century," in Engerman and Gallman, *Cambridge Economic History of the United States*, II, pp. 4, 19.

89. Mary Ellen Rowe, *Bulwark of the Republic: The American Militia in the Antebellum West* (Westport, 2003).

90. Walter A. McDougall, *Promised Land, Crusader State: The American Encounter with the World since 1776* (Boston, 1977). McDougall argues that the Promised Land antedated the crusader state; there is a case for saying that they went hand in hand.

91. John A. Moses, "The Rise and Decline of Christian Militarism in Prussia-Germany from Hegel to Bonhoeffer: The End Effect of the Fallacy of Sacred Violence," *War & Society*, 23 (2005), pp. 21–40.

92. On the relatively peaceful advance of the frontier in Canada, see Weaver, *The Great Land Rush*, pp. 250–56. A rare comparative study is Hanna Samek, *The Blackfoot Confederacy, 1880–1920: A Comparative Study of Canadian and U.S. Indian Policy* (Albuquerque, 1987).

93. David B. Kopel, *The Samurai, the Mounties, and the Cowboy: Should America Adopt the Gun Controls of Other Democracies?* (1992), chs. 4, 9. Kopel cites two other comparators, Japan and Switzerland, to make the point that social and cultural controls, rather than laws, are the key determinants of the extent to which guns are used. Kopel, chs. 2, 8. It should also be noted, however, that both countries have long had strict laws controlling guns.

94. The contrast stands, though, as Kopel points out, the wildness of the West is easily exaggerated: *The Samurai, the Mounties*, ch. 9.

95. Craig Wilcox, "Did Australia Sustain an Armed Citizenry? Graeme Davison and the Gun Debate," *Australian Historical Studies*, 31 (2000), pp. 331–4.

96. Christopher Adamson, "God's Continent Divided: Politics and Religion in Upper Canada and the Northern and Western United States, 1775–1841," *Comparative Studies in Society & History*, 36 (1994), pp. 417–46; Stephen A. Chavara and Ian Tregenza, "A Political History of the Secular in Australia, 1788–1945," in Tim Stanley, ed., *Religion after Secularization in Australia* (New York, 2015), ch. 1.

97. As Howe reports: *What Hath God Wrought*, p. 71; and George C. Herring, *From Colony to Superpower: U.S. Foreign Relations since 1776* (Oxford, 2008), pp. 131–3. On this subject and associated patriotic slogans and images, see Donald R. Hickey, ed., *The War of 1812: Writings from America's Second War of Independence* (New York, 2013).

98. The bicentennial stimulated production. An authoritative guide is J.C.A. Stagg, *The War of 1812: Conflict for a Continent* (Cambridge, 2012); Alan Taylor, *The Civil War of 1812: American Citizens, British Subjects, Irish Rebels and Indian Allies* (New York, 2010), extends beyond military history to cover all the parties involved in what he sees as a sprawling civil war.

99. Troy Bickham, *The Weight of Vengeance: The United States, the British Empire, and the War of 1812* (New York, 2012), p. 276.

100. Richard W. Maass, " 'Difficult to Relinquish Territory which Had Been Conquered': Expansionism and the War of 1812," *Diplomatic History*, 39 (2015), pp. 90–92.

101. Richard Buel emphasizes the role of domestic politics in leading to war but places most weight on the machinations of the Federalists: *America on the Brink: How the Political Struggle over the War of 1812 Almost Destroyed the Young Republic* (New York, 2005).

102. Burton Spivak, *Jefferson's English Crisis: Commerce, Embargo, and the Republican Revolution* (Charlottesville, 1979).
103. Maass, "Difficult to Relinquish Territory which Had Been Conquered."
104. Lawrence A. Peskin, "Conspiratorial Anglophobia and the War of 1812," *Journal of American History*, 98 (2011), pp. 647–69; Joseph Eaton, *The Anglo-American Paper War: Debates about the New Republic, 1880–1825* (Basingstoke, Hants, 2012).
105. See, for example, Donald R. Hickey, *An American Perspective on the War of 1812: A Forgotten Conflict* (Urbana, 1989; 2012); Bickham, *The Weight of Vengeance*.
106. See Andrew Lambert, *The Challenge: Britain against America in the Naval War of 1812* (London, 2012).
107. See especially, Taylor, *The Civil War of 1812*, ch. 15.
108. Perkins, *Cambridge History of Foreign Relations*, pp. 207–8.
109. This issue is fully covered by Sexton, *Debtor Diplomacy*, ch. 1. On Barings see chapter 4 of this text.
110. If also disorganized. See Howard Jones, *To the Webster-Ashburton Treaty: A Study in Anglo-American Relatons, 1783–1843* (Chapel Hill, 1977).
111. Michael Golay, *The Tide of Empire: America's March to the Pacific* (New York, 2003).
112. Paul F. Sharp, "When Our West Moved North," *American Historical Review*, 55 (1950), pp. 286–300, provides an admirable illustration of the continuing fluidity of the western frontier, even after diplomats had placed it on the map.
113. See chapter 4 of this text. Also Eaton, *The Anglo-American Paper War*; Samuel W. Hayes, *Unfinished Revolution: The Early American Republic in a British World* (Charlottesville, 2010).
114. Hendrickson, *Union, Nation or Empire*, pp. 87–8, citing Alexander H. Everett's book (1827) and Canning's fulsome statement of the new special relationship between the two powers.
115. Anthony F. C. Wallace, *Jefferson and the Indians: The Tragic Fate of the First Americans* (Cambridge, MA, 1999); J.C.A. Stagg, *Borderlines in Borderlands: James Madison and the Spanish-American Frontier, 1776–1821* (Cambridge, 2009).
116. Alan Taylor traces this process in his study of Robert ("King") Carter's estate in Virginia: *The Internal Enemy: Slavery and War in Virginia, 1772–1832* (New York, 2013). See also Gene Allen Smith, *The Slaves' Gamble: Choosing Sides in the War of 1812* (New York, 2013).
117. Nicole Eustace, *1812: War and the Passions of Patriotism* (Philadelphia, 2012), p. 218.
118. The American Colonization Society was founded in 1817 by a coalition of white leaders (including Henry Clay) to resettle free blacks and ex-slaves in what became (in 1847) Liberia. The Society survived until 1964. See Amos J. Beyan, *The American Colonization Society and the Creation of the Liberian State: A Historical Perspective, 1822–1900* (Lanham, 1991); Marie Tyler-McGraw, *An African Republic: Black and White Virginians in the Making of Liberia* (Chapel Hill, 2007). Nicholas Guyatt provides a subtle reinterpretation in *Bind Us Apart: How Enlightened Americans Invented Racial Segregation* (New York, 2016).
119. Brian Shoen, "Calculating the Price of Union: Republican Economic Nationalism and the Origins of Southern Sectionalism, 1790–1828," *Journal of the Early Republic*, 23 (2003), pp. 173–206. Buel emphasizes the role of domestic politics in leading to war: *America on the Brink*; Lipsey, "U.S. Foreign Trade," pp. 724–6.
120. Lipsey, "U.S. Foreign Trade," in Stanley L. Engerman and Robert E. Gallman, *Cambridge Economic History of the United States*, 2 (Cambridge, 2000), pp. 724–6.
121. "Goldwyn Smith," *North American Review*, 99 (1864), p. 523. I owe this reference to Dr. George Forgie, University of Texas at Austin.
122. Ibid.
123. Ibid. Also Thomas W. Higginson, *The New World and the New Book* (New York, 1891), p. 63.

124. Herring, *From Colony to Superpower*, p. 156. The statement did not become known as a "Doctrine" until later in the century. The best guide is Jay Sexton, *The Monroe Doctrine: Empire and Nation in Nineteenth-Century America* (New York, 2011).

125. "Transcript of the Monroe Doctrine (1823)," available online at http://www.ourdocu ments.gov/doc.php?doc=23&page=transcript.

126. Herring, *From Colony to Superpower*, p. 151.

127. Bradford Perkins, *The Cambridge History of American Foreign Relations*, Vol. 1 (Cambridge, 1993), pp. 165–9; Sexton, *The Monroe Doctrine*, pp. 243–7.

128. Quoted in Hendrickson, *Union, Nation, or Empire*, p. 85.

129. Kinley Brauer, "The United States and British Imperial Expansion, 1815–60," *Diplomatic History*, 12 (1988), pp. 19–20, 23–5, 31. Britain (and the United States) recognized five new states in Latin America in 1822.

130. James E. Lewis, *The American Union and the Problem of Neighborhood: The United States and the Collapse of the Spanish Empire, 1783–1829* (Chapel Hill, 1998).

131. David M. Pletcher, *The Diplomacy of Annexation: Texas, Oregon, and the Mexican War* (Columbia, 1973), shows how these issues were related and how the continental expansion of the United States was obliged to take account of the interests of foreign powers, especially those of Britain. The point is confirmed by Howard Jones and Donald A. Rakestraw, *Prologue to Manifest Destiny: Anglo-American Relations in the 1840s* (Wilmington, 1997).

132. Matthew H. Crocker, "The Missouri Compromise, the Monroe Doctrine, and the Southern Strategy," *Journal of the West*, 43 (2004), pp. 45–52.

133. Walt Whitman, *Brooklyn Eagle*, May 11, 1846. Quoted in Archie P. McDonald, ed., *The Mexican War: Crisis for American Democracy* (Lexington, 1969), p. 47.

134. Quoted in Matthew Arnold, *Civilization in the United States* (Boston, 1888), p. 15. Different versions of this quotation can be found.

135. Ibid.

136. Specialists will be aware that I am placing an emphasis on sectionalism that some notable historians have questioned. See, for example, Joel H. Silbey, *Storm over Texas: The Annexation Controversy and the Road to War* (New York, 2005), who argues that party rather than section dominated politics until 1844. To some extent, the disagreement is a matter of perspective and emphasis. Subsequent references will show, I hope, that the view taken here also has the support of recent research.

137. Adam Rothman, *Slave Country: American Expansion and the Origins of the Deep South* (Cambridge, MA, 2005), covers the early stages.

138. The abolitionist cause gained popularity in the 1830s, when the internal slave trade ceased to benefit from unambiguous legal protection. See David L. Lightner, *Slavery and the Commerce Power: How the Struggle Against the Interstate Slave Trade Led to the Civil War* (New Haven, 2006).

139. James Oakes, *Freedom National: The Destruction of Slavery in the United States, 1861–1865* (New York, 2013).

140. Robert E. May, *Slavery, Race and Conquest in the Tropics: Lincoln, Douglas, and the Future of Latin America* (Cambridge, 2013); Hietala, *Manifest Design*, ch. 4; Matthew Karp, *The Vast Southern Empire: Slaveholders at the Helm of American Foreign Policy* (Cambridge, MA, 2016), also emphasizes the expansionist urge but regards it as being defensive rather than assertive.

141. The intricate politics of the issues are fully explored by Silby, *Storm over Texas*; and Michael A. Morrison, "Westward the Curse of Empire: Texas Annexation and the American Whig Party," *Journal of the Early Republic*, 10 (1990), pp. 221–49.

142. Ron Hunka, "The Financial Folly of the Republic of Texas," *Financial History*, 95 (2009), pp. 32–5.

143. E.g., Silbey, *Storm over Texas*.

144. Edward B. Rugemer, *The Problem of Emancipation: The Caribbean Roots of the American Civil War* (Baton Rouge, 2008).

145. Morrison, "Westward the Curse of Empire," pp. 221–49.

146. Lelia M. Roeckell, "British Opposition to the Annexation of Texas," *Journal of the Early Republic*, 19 (1999), pp. 257–78, is essential reading on this subject.

147. Norman A. Graebner, "The Mexican War: A Study in Causation," *Pacific Historical Review*, 49 (1980), pp. 405–26.

148. Quoted in Roeckell, "British Opposition," p. 257.

149. Ibid., pp. 264–5.

150. James Hamilton to Aberdeen, "Memorandum," Autumn 1841, FO 75/2, ff. 41–70. I owe this reference to Graham Earles, whose Cambridge Ph.D. dissertation, "The Role of International Law in the Relationship between the Governments of Britain and the United States, 1837–1856" (forthcoming) will further illuminate these issues.

151. Richard C. K. Burdekin, "Bondholder Gains from the Annexation of Texas and Implications of the U.S. Bailout," *Explorations in Economic History*, 43 (2006), pp. 646–66.

152. The final payment was about 77 cents for every dollar compared to a low of about 3 cents in 1845. Burdekin, "Bondholder Gains."

153. Sexton, *Debtor Diplomacy*, pp. 45–7.

154. Polk's concern to avoid a prospective war on two fronts moved him to reach a compromise with Britain on the disputed north-west border. The Oregon Treaty was signed in June 1846, one month after the United States declared war on Mexico. See Herring, *From Colony to Superpower*, pp. 188–94. For a full account see David M. Pletcher, *The Diplomacy of Annexation: Texas, Oregon, and the Mexican War* (Columbia, 1973), which is confirmed by Howard Jones and Donald A. Rakestraw, *Prologue to Manifest Destiny: Anglo-American Relations in the 1840s* (Wilmington, 1997).

155. Robert W. Merry, *A Country of Vast Designs: James K. Polk, the Mexican War and the Conquest of the American Continent* (New York, 2009), provides a vigorous defense of Polk, arguing that he was a man of vision who pursued the national interest in the face of a corrupt dictatorship in Mexico. Amy S. Greenberg, *A Wicked War: Polk, Clay, Lincoln, and the 1846 Invasion of Mexico* (New York, 2012), provides an equally vigorous set of criticisms. For a flavor of the debate, compare Merry's review of Greenberg in the *Wall Street Journal*, November 2, 2014, with McPherson's review in the *New York Review of Books*, February 7, 2013.

156. Allan Peskin, *Winfield Scott and the Profession of Arms* (Kent, 2003). Scott (1786–1866) was a veteran of the War of 1812 and subsequent "Indian" Wars. Although he was a Virginian, he developed a strong attachment to the Union and was the nominated Whig candidate for the presidency in 1852.

157. DeLay, *War of a Thousand Deserts*.

158. Paul Foos, *A Short, Offhand Killing Affair: Soldiers and Social Conflict during the Mexican-American War* (Chapel Hill, 2002), has the merit of telling the story "from below" instead of, as is conventional, "from above."

159. William Henry Seward, Speech in Rochester, New York, October 25, 1858. Quoted in Eric H. Walther, *The Shattering of the Union: America in the 1850s* (Wilmington, 2003), p. 158. Seward (1801–1872), a prominent Republican, was governor of New York (1839–1842), senator (1849–1861), and secretary of state (1861–1869).

160. Aaron Sheehan-Dean has produced what is now the indispensable guide: *A Companion to the U.S. Civil War*, 2 Vols. (Chichester, Sussex, 2014). The standard work is James McPherson, *Battle Cry of Freedom: The Civil War Era* (Oxford, 1988; 2003 with an Afterword). A recent, clear account is Adam I. P. Smith, *The American Civil War* (New York, 2007).

161. Walt Whitman, *Leaves of Grass* (New York, 4th ed., 1867). Whitman served as a volunteer nurse in army hospitals. He emphasized the transformative effect of the Civil War on his poetry in *November Boughs* (New York, 1888).

162. Oscar Wilde, 1882. Quoted in Kathryn Stelmach Artuso, *Transatlantic Renaissances: Literature of Ireland and the American South* (Newark, 2013), p. xvi. The recent flurry of

interest in international approaches includes: Andre M. Fleche, *The Revolution of 1861: The American Civil War in the Age of Nationalist Conflict* (Chapel Hill, 2012); Don H. Doyle, *The Cause of All Nations: An International History of the Civil War* (New York, 2013); Richard Carwardine and Jay Sexton, eds., *The Global Lincoln* (Oxford, 2011); David T. Gleeson and Simon Lewis, eds., *The Civil War as Global Conflict* (Columbia, 2014). Earlier generations did not need to be reminded of the broader features of the conflict: see David M. Potter, "The Civil War in the History of the Modern World: A Comparative View," in Potter, *The South and the Sectional Conflict* (Baton Rouge, 1968), ch. 11; also the extensive correspondence of Karl Marx and Friedrich Engels in Richard Enmale, ed., *The Civil War in the United States* (New York, 1937).

163. Timothy Mason Roberts, *Distant Revolutions: 1848 and the Challenge of American Exceptionalism* (Charlottesville, 2009), suggests that the failure of most of the revolutions of 1848 confirmed the belief that the United States was set on an "exceptionalist" path. The British thought the same of their own reform movement.

164. Lacy K. Ford, *Deliver Us from Evil: The Slavery Question in the Old South* (New York, 2009).

165. Robert E. Bonner, *Mastering America: Southern Slave-Holders and the Crisis of American Nationhood* (Cambridge, 2009).

166. Ritchie Devon Watson, *Normans and Saxons: Southern Race Mythology and the Intellectual History of the American Civil War* (Baton Rouge, 2008). Also Christopher Hanlon, "'The Old Race Are All Gone': Transatlantic Bloodlines and 'English Traits,'" *American Literary History*, 18 (2007), pp. 800–823; James M. McPherson, "'Two Irreconcilable Peoples': Ethnic Nationalism in the Confederacy," in David T. Gleeson and Simon Lewis, eds., *The Civil War as Global Conflict* (Columbia, 2014), pp. 85–97, which differs from the analysis in this chapter and in chapter 4 in positing a clear distinction between Northern (civic) and Southern (ethnic) nationalism.

167. George C. Rable, *Damn Yankees: Demonization and Defiance in the Confederate South* (Baton Rouge, 2015).

168. The alarmists included Samuel F. B. Morse, whose book, *Foreign Conspiracy against the Liberties of the United States* (New York, 1835), expressed a virulent anti-Catholicism inspired by his committed Calvinism.

169. Manisha Sinha, *The Slave's Cause: A History of Abolition* (New Haven, 2016).

170. George C. Rable, *God's Almost Chosen People: A Religious History of the American Civil War* (Chapel Hill, 2010).

171. Rable, *Damn Yankees*.

172. Hendrickson, *Union, Nation, or Empire*, chs. 13–15, provides numerous telling illustrations of this point.

173. Calhoun (1782–1850) held a series of senior positions either as a senator or as a member of the cabinet between 1817 and 1850. Among numerous biographies, John Niven, *John C. Calhoun and the Price of Union: A Biography* (Baton Rouge, 1988), holds its value.

174. Quoted in Samuel P. Huntingdon, *Who Are We? The Challenges to America's National Identity* (New York, 2004), p. 114.

175. Dorothy Ross, "Lincoln and the Ethics of Emancipation: Universalism, Nationalism, Exceptionalism," *Journal of American History*, 96 (2009), pp. 379–99; Rable, *God's Chosen People*.

176. Bruce Laurie, *Beyond Garrison: Anti-Slavery and Social Reform* (Cambridge, 2005). Frank Thistlethwaite, *The Anglo-American Connection in the Early Nineteenth Century* (Philadelphia, 1959), remains the starting point.

177. Richard Carwardine, "Lincoln's Horizons: The Nationalist as Universalist," in Carwardine and Sexton, *The Global Lincoln*, p. 38.

178. Richard Carwardine, *Lincoln: A Life of Purpose and Power* (London, 2003).

179. Susan-Mary Grant, *North over South: Northern Nationalism and American Identity in the Antebellum Era* (Lawrence, 2000).

180. As characterized in the classic parody of the English Civil War: W. C. Sellar and R. J. Yeatman, *1066 and All That* (London, 1930), p. 75.

181. Sven Beckert's exhaustive research has now placed the Southern cotton industry in its international setting: *Empire of Cotton: A New History of Global Capitalism* (London, 2014). David Ericson draws attention to the ways that federal government defended slavery in *Slavery in the American Republic: Developing the Federal Government, 1791–1861* (Lawrence, 2011).

182. James Oakes, "Capitalism and Slavery and the Civil War," *International Labour and Working Class History*, 89 (2016), pp. 195–220, emphasizes the continuing strength of the Southern economy.

183. On the diversity of slaveholding, see James Oakes, *The Ruling Race: A History of American Slaveholders* (New York, 1982).

184. Joseph P. Reidy, *From Slavery to Agrarian Capitalism in the Cotton South: Central Georgia, 1800–1880* (Chapel Hill, 1992), pp. 56–7.

185. Matthew Karp, "King Cotton, Emperor Slavery: Antebellum Slave-holders and the World Economy," in Gleeson and Lewis, *The Civil War as Global Conflict*, pp. 36–55.

186. Edward B. Rugemer, "Why Civil War? The Politics of Slavery in Comparative Perspective: The United States, Cuba, and Brazil," in Gleeson and Lewis, *The Civil War as a Global Conflict*, pp. 21–23. Enrico dal Lago, *American Slavery, Atlantic Slavery and Beyond: The U.S. "Peculiar Institution" in International Perspective* (Boulder, 2012), makes an even broader case for an era of "second slavery" in the nineteenth century, though the argument runs the risk of merging different forms of slave and unfree labor.

187. May, *Slavery, Race, and Conquest*.

188. Dal Lago, *American Slavery*.

189. Bonner, *Mastering America*.

190. To cite a recent example, Brian Schoen's otherwise admirable account comes close to equating markets with modernity: *The Fragile Fabric of the Union: Cotton, Federal Politics and the Global Origins of the Civil War* (Baltimore, 2009), while Nicholas Onuf and Peter Onuf hold that "there would have been no war had the North and South not been modern nations." *Nations, Markets, and War: Modern History and the American Civil War* (Charlottesville, 2006), p. 18.

191. Marc Egnal, *Clash of Extremes: The Economic Origins of the Civil War* (New York, 2009), provides valuable evidence in support of the view originally advanced by Charles and Mary Beard. See also John Ashworth, "Towards a Bourgeois Revolution: Explaining the American Civil War," *Historical Materialism*, 19 (2011), 193–205, and the further references given there, especially to his own substantial work. This is not to deny that examples of the "market revolution" can be found in the South. See, for example, Tom Downey's study of two districts in South Carolina: *Planting a Capitalist South: Masters, Merchants, and Manufactures in the Southern Interior, 1790–1860* (Baton Rouge, 2006).

192. This point was made with characteristic clarity by Hla Myint in *Economic Theory and the Underdeveloped Countries* (Oxford, 1971), with reference to plantation economies in the twentieth century employing low-wage migrant labor.

193. Peter H. Conclanis neatly summarizes the longer term causes of the economic differences between North and South in "Tracking the Economic Divergence of the North and the South," *Southern Cultures*, 6 (2000), pp. 82–103.

194. Susanna Delfino and Michele Gillespie, eds., *Technology, Innovation and Southern Industrialization* (Columbia, 2008).

195. As argued in the section titled "Dilemmas of Dependent Development" in chapter 4 of this text.

196. For a reaffirmation of the essentially agrarian character of the North at this time, see James L. Huston, *The British Gentry, The Southern Planter, and the Northern Farmer: Agriculture and Sectional Antagonism in North America* (Baton Rouge, 2015).

197. Edward E. Baptist, *The Half Has Never Been Told: Slavery and the Making of American Capitalism* (New York, 2014).

198. This is the key argument in Huston, *The British Gentry*, which builds on the basic insight in Roger L. Ransom, *Conflict and Compromise: The Political Economy of Slavery, Emancipation and the American Civil War* (Cambridge, 1989).

199. On this, and much more, see Elizabeth R. Varon, *Disunion! The Coming of the American Civil War* (Chapel Hill, 2010).

200. Don E. Fehrenbacher with Ward M. McAfee, *The Slaveholding Republic: An Account of the U.S. Government's Relations to Slavery* (Oxford, 2001); Ericson, *Slavery in the American Republic*.

201. On the evolution of Lincoln's attitude toward slavery, see Eric Foner, *The Fiery Trial: Abraham Lincoln and American Slavery* (New York, 2010).

202. See the section titled "Dilemmas of Dependent Development" in chapter 4 of this text for the main economic developments of the period.

203. I am greatly indebted in what follows to Ransom, *Conflict and Compromise*; Roger Ransom and Richard Sutch, "Conflicting Visions: The Civil War as a Revolutionary Event," *Research in Economic History*, 20 (2001), pp. 249–301; and James L. Huston, *Calculating the Value of the Union: Slavery, Property Rights, and the Economic Origins of the Civil War* (Chapel Hill, 2003). McPherson, *Battle Cry of Freedom*, ch. 6, adds valuable details.

204. James L. Huston, *The Panic of 1857 and the Coming of the Civil War* (Baton Rouge, 1987).

205. Charles W. Calomiris and Larry Schweikart, "The Panic of 1857: Origins, Transmission, and Containment," *Journal of Economic History*, 51 (1991), pp. 807–34.

206. Huston, *The British Gentry*, ch. 9.

207. Buchanan (1791–1868; president 1856–1860) was a Northern Democrat (from Pennsylvania) with sympathies for the South and slavery.

208. The 37th Congress, which followed elections in 1860, did not meet until 1861. Democrats supported a rail link to the Far West, but opposed a route that would tie the North and Midwest more closely together.

209. Leonard L. Richards, *The California Gold Rush and the Coming of the Civil War* (New York, 2007).

210. Fehrenbacher, *The Slaveholding Republic*, pp. 292–4.

211. May, *Slavery, Race and Conquest in the Tropics*, emphasizes the importance of this ambitious "southern" strategy.

212. Lightner, *Slavery and Commerce Power*; Steven Doyle, *Carry Me Back: The Domestic Slave Trade in American Life* (Oxford, 2005).

213. The response included the imposition of "gag rules," which stopped the presentation of abolitionist petitions in the House of Representatives between 1836 and 1844.

214. James L. Huston, "How the Secession Movement of 1850–51 Made Secession in 1861 Inevitable," forthcoming in Frank Towers, ed., *Secessions: From the Revolution to the Civil War* (Morgantown, forthcoming). I am most grateful to Dr. Huston for allowing me to cite his essay before publication.

215. Earl M. Maltz, *Dred Scott and the Politics of Slavery* (Lawrence, 2007), provides a clear guide to the generally accepted opinion that the case was wrongly decided.

216. California became a "free" state in 1850, Minnesota in 1858, Oregon in 1859, and Kansas in 1861.

217. Varon, *Disunion*, ch. 8, covers the episode known as "Bleeding Kansas."

218. See chapter 4 of this text.

219. Tyler Anbinder, *The Northern Know Nothings and the Politics of the 1850s* (New York, 1992), questions the revisionist view that the split was brought about by immigration and cultural issues, and reaffirms the traditional emphasis on the problem of slavery.

220. James Oakes, *The Scorpion's Sting: Anti-Slavery and the Coming of the Civil War* (New York, 2014).

221. This election, and the presidential election that followed in 1860, also opened the prospect of the extension of federal influence and patronage into the Southern states. See Peter Zavodnyik, *The Age of Strict Construction: A History of the Growth of Federal Power, 1789–1861* (Washington, DC, 2007), ch. 5.

222. A. James Fuller, ed., *The Election of 1860 Reconsidered* (Kent, 2013).

223. Eric H. Walther, *The Shattering of the Union: America in the 1850s* (Wilmington, 2003); Walther, "The Fire-Eaters and Seward Lincoln," *Journal of the Abraham Lincoln Association*, 32 (2011), pp. 18–32.

224. For an appropriate emphasis on contingency, see Michael F. Holt, *The Political Crisis of the 1850s* (New York, 1978); Holt, *Political Parties and American Political Development from the Age of Jackson to the Age of Lincoln* (Baton Rouge, 1992); and the shorter, sharper account in Holt, *The Fate of Their Country: Politicians, Slavery Extension, and the Coming of the Civil War* (New York, 2005).

225. Henry Timrod, "Ethnogenesis" (1861). Timrod (1829–1867) was born in Charleston of German descent. His father was an army officer who fought in the Seminole Wars but died of tuberculosis in 1838, leaving his family impoverished. Henry made his way through the University of Georgia with the help of a benefactor and became a writer and tutor. He enlisted in 1862 but was discharged on health grounds (having contracted tuberculosis himself), and died in poverty.

226. See chapter 2 of this text.

227. As J. David Hacker has shown in a major contribution: "A Census-Based Count of Civil War Dead," *Civil War History*, 57 (2011), pp. 307–48. See also Stig Föster and Jörg Nadler, eds., *On the Road to Total War: The American Civil War and the German Wars of Unification, 1861–1871* (Cambridge, 1997).

228. Hacker, "A Census-Based Count," makes it clear that this figure is a midpoint between estimates that may vary by 20 percent either way.

229. Ibid., p. 348.

230. I summarize here what I take to be the consensus among specialists on these subjects. This judgment is not to deny the brilliance of individuals, such as Robert E. Lee. Abraham Lincoln is regarded as being superior to Jefferson Finis Davis (1808–1889). Davis was a cotton planter and slave owner from Kentucky, who settled in Mississippi and represented the state in Congress in both the House and the Senate. He was a keen expansionist who supported Polk and the Mexican War, and hoped to annex Cuba.

231. James M. McPherson, *For Cause and Comrades: Why Men Fought in the Civil War* (New York, 1997). Gary W. Gallagher, *The Union War* (Cambridge, MA, 2012), confirms other recent judgments on this issue.

232. Douglas B. Ball, *Financial Failure and Confederate Defeat* (Urbana, 1991), emphasizes the incompetence of those in charge of the Confederacy's finances.

233. The Erlanger Loan was marketed in March 1863 but with limited success: Richard I. Lester, "An Aspect of Confederate Finance During the American Civil War: The Erlanger Loan and the Plan of 1864," *Business History*, 16 (1974), pp. 130–44.

234. Marc Weidenmier, "Gunboats, Reputation, and Sovereign Repayment: Lessons from the Southern Confederacy," *NBER Working Paper* 10960 (2004). Before the war, Jefferson Davis, the president of the Confederacy, had advocated that the states should repudiate their debts.

235. David G. Surdam, *Northern Naval Supremacy and the Economics of the American Civil War* (Columbia, 2001).

236. A full account of the evolution of the Southern ethnie is Paul Quigley, *Shifting Grounds: Nationalism and the American South, 1848–65* (New York, 2011).

237. Walter Johnson, *River of Dark Dreams: Slavery and Empire in the Cotton Kingdom* (Cambridge, MA, 2013) on what he terms the Lower Mississippi. The "Lower South"

had become the most important center of cotton and sugar. On the commercial elite, see Vicki Vaughn Johnson, *The Men and the Vision of the Southern Commercial Conventions, 1845–1871* (London, 1992).

238. W. Steven Deyle, *Carry Me Back: The Domestic Slave Trade in American Life* (Oxford, 2005), p. 14. See also William Kaufman Scarborough, *Masters of the Big House: Elite Slaveholders of the Mid-Nineteenth Century* (Baton Rouge, 2003).

239. Stephanie McCurry, *Confederate Reckoning*.

240. James Oakes, "From Republicanism to Liberalism: Ideological Change and the Crisis of the Old South," *American Quarterly*, 37 (1985), pp. 551–71.

241. Deyle, *Carry Me Back*.

242. McCurry, *Confederate Reckoning*, p. 136. See also Victoria E. Bynum, *The Long Shadow of the Civil War: Southern Dissent and Its Legacies* (Chapel Hill, 2010), which deals with North Carolina, Mississippi, and East Texas. R. Douglas Hurt, *Agriculture and the Confederacy: Policy, Productivity, and Power in the Civil War* (Chapel Hill, 2015), traces the declining output and rising prices of food supplies.

243. McCurry, *Confederate Reckoning*. An allied argument suggests that the South was compelled to keep fighting by the fear of slave revolts.

244. Steven Hahn, *A Nation Under Our Feet: Black Political Struggles in the Rural South from Slavery to the Great Migration* (Cambridge, MA, 2003).

245. Gary Pecquet, George Davis, and Bryce Kanago, "The Emancipation Proclamation, Confederate Expectations, and the Price of Southern Banknotes," *Southern Economic Journal*, 70 (2004), pp. 616–30; Lester, "An Aspect of Confederate Finance," p. 139. More precisely, the trend began in November 1862, when the result of the congressional elections ensured that the Proclamation would become law.

246. Marc D. Weidenmier and Kim Oosterlinck, "Victory or Repudiation? The Probability of the Southern Confederacy Winning the Civil War," NBER Working Paper, 13567 (2007). The figures are derived from the ingenious use of data relating to the gold bond market in Amsterdam.

247. Gary Gallagher, *The Confederate War: How Popular Will, Nationalism, and Military Strategy Could Not Stave off Defeat* (Cambridge, MA, 1997); McPherson, *For Cause and Comrades*, provides eloquent testimony to the commitment of troops on both sides of the war.

248. Lord John Russell, Speech in House of Commons, May 2, 1861. The quotation, and others from the same speech in the paragraph that follows, are taken from Richard Dean Burns, Joseph M. Siracusa, and Jason C. Flanagan, eds., *American Foreign Relations Since Independence* (Santa Barbara, 2013), p. 75. Russell (1792–1878), 1st Earl Russell (1861), Whig and (after 1868) Liberal politician. Prime Minister (1846–1852, 1865–1866); Foreign Secretary (1859–1865). As the younger son of the Duke of Bedford, Russell had a courtesy title and was not allowed to sit in the House of Lords until he was ennobled in 1861. Before then, he attended the House of Commons as the Member for the City of London.

249. Howard Jones, *Blue and Gray: A History of Union and Confederate Foreign Relations* (Chapel Hill, 2010), ch. 3.

250. This an opportunity to pay tribute to Howard Jones, and in particular to his three indispensable volumes on this subject: *Union in Peril: The Crisis over British Intervention in the Civil War* (Chapel Hill, 1992); *Abraham Lincoln and a New Birth of Freedom: The Union and Slavery in the Diplomacy of the Civil War* (Lincoln, 1999); *Blue and Gray Diplomacy*. Specialists will note a difference of emphasis here at two points: Palmerston's commitment to abolition, and the unlikely chance of war between Britain and the United States.

251. Donald Bellows, "A Study of British Conservative Reaction to the American Civil War," *Journal of Southern History*, 51 (1985), pp. 505–26.

252. On this much discussed topic, see now Beckert, *Empire of Cotton*, ch. 9.

253. Marc-William Palen, "The Civil War's Forgotten Transatlantic Tariff Debate and the Confederacy's Diplomacy of Free Trade," *Journal of the Civil War Era*, 3 (2013), pp. 35–61.

254. This was certainly Palmerston's view in 1861: Jasper Ridley, *Lord Palmerston* (London, 1970), p. 552.
255. This episode is well covered by Doyle, *The Cause of All Nations*, chs. 1, 9.
256. Surdam, *Northern Naval Superiority*. The blockade was imposed in July 1861.
257. It was at this point that Garibaldi wrote appreciatively to Lincoln, praising him as the "great emancipator."
258. The Amendment was ratified by the required number of states in December 1865.
259. Jones, *Union in Peril*, pp. 179–80, 225–6.
260. Ibid., pp. 2–9. Lewis (1806–1863), Secretary of State at the Home Office (1859–1861), War Office (1861–1863), philologist, social theorist, and a friend of Tocqueville, among other luminaries, was a formidable figure, though also one who has been understudied and underappreciated.
261. Richard Little, "Intervention and Non-Intervention in International Society: Britain's Responses to the American and Spanish Civil Wars," *Review of International Studies* (2013), pp. 111–29.
262. European volunteers also joined the Confederate Army, but on a much smaller scale.
263. "Therefore I say that it is a narrow policy to suppose that this country or that is to be marked out as the eternal ally or the perpetual enemy of England. We have no eternal allies, and we have no perpetual enemies. Our interests are eternal and perpetual, and those interests it is our duty to follow." Speech in the House of Commons, March 1, 1848, *Hansard, HC Debates*, 97, cc. 66–123. It is impossible to read the whole speech without wondering how many foreign ministers today could match Palmerston's grasp of international affairs.
264. Lawrence Goldman, "'A Total Misrepresentation': Lincoln, the Civil War and the British," in Carwardine and Sexton, *The Global Lincoln*, ch. 6.
265. Stephen Meardon, "Richard Cobden's American Quandary: Negotiating Peace, Free Trade and Anti-Slavery," in Anthony Howe and Simon Morgan, eds., *Rethinking Nineteenth-Century Liberalism: Richard Cobden Bicentenary Essays* (Aldershot, 2006), ch. 12.
266. Hugh Dubrulle, "We Are Threatened with Anarchy and Ruin: Fear of Americanization and the Emergence of an Anglo-Saxon Confederacy in England during the American Civil War," *Albion*, 33 (2001), pp. 583–613.
267. The standard work is R.J.M. Blackett, *Divided Hearts: Britain and the American Civil War* (Baton Rouge, 2001). For confirmation, of the complexity of the issue, if needed, see Mark Bennett, "Confederate Supporters in the West Riding, 1861–1865: Cranks of the Worst English Species," *Northern History*, 51 (2014), pp. 211–29.
268. Thomas E. Schneider, "J. S. Mill and Fitzjames Stephen on the American Civil War," *History of Political Thought*, 28 (2007), pp. 290–304.
269. T. Peter Park, "John Stuart Mill, Thomas Carlyle, and the U.S. Civil War," *Historian*, 54 (1991), pp. 93–106; quotation (1866) at p. 104.
270. On this subject, see the work of Douglas Farnie, a true scholar's scholar who was also underestimated in his time: D. A. Farnie, *The English Cotton Industry and the World Market, 1815–1896* (Oxford, 1979), pp. 144–67.
271. Jay Sexton's admirable study, *Debtor Diplomacy: Finance and American Foreign Relations in the Civil War Era, 1837–1873* (Oxford, 2005), is the starting point that should encourage further work on this subject. British investment was divided in unknown proportions between the North, the Midwest, and the South. Barings was among the City banks with substantial commitments in the South.
272. Niels Eichhorn, "North Atlantic Trade in the Mid-Nineteenth Century," *Civil War History*, 61 (2015), pp. 138–72. I am grateful to Dr. Eichhorn for his helpful correspondence on this subject.
273. On the improvement in Anglo-American relations, see Phillip E. Myers, *Caution and Cooperation: The American Civil War in British-American Relations* (Kent, 2008).
274. Brian Holden Reid, "Power, Sovereignty, and the Great Republic: Anglo-American Diplomatic Relations in the Era of the Civil War," *Diplomacy & Statecraft*, 14 (2003), pp. 45–

76; Niels Eichhorn, "The Intervention Crisis of 1862: A British Diplomatic Dilemma?" *American Nineteenth-Century History*, 15 (2014), pp. 287–310.

275. On the Mexican conservatives, see Brian Hamnett, "Mexican Conservatives, Clericals and Soldiers: The 'Traitor' Tomás Mejía Through Reform and Empire, 1855–67," *Bulletin of Latin American Research*, 20 (2001), pp. 187–110; Erika Pani, "Dreaming of a Mexican Empire: The Political Projects of the *Imperialistas*," *Hispanic American Historical Review*, 82 (2002), pp. 1–31.

276. Cobden to Gladstone, January 1, 1864, in Anthony Howe and Simon Morgan, eds., *The Letters of Richard Cobden, Vol. 4, 1860–1865* (Oxford, 2015), p. 456.

277. Cobden to Mallet, December 6, 1863, in Howe and Morgan, *Letters of Richard Cobden*, p. 438.

278. See, for example, Don H. Doyle, "How the Civil War Changed the World," *New York Times*, May 19, 2015, which summarizes the relevant section of his otherwise admirable book, *The Cause of All Nations*; and Brent E. Kinser, *The American Civil War and the Shaping of British Democracy* (Burlington, 2011).

279. The two leading authorities are agreed on this point: Robert Saunders, *Democracy and the Vote in British Politics, 1848–1867: The Making of the Second Reform Act* (Burlington, 2011); Michael J. Turner, *Liberty and Liberticide: The Role of America in Nineteenth-Century British Radicalism* (Lanham, 2014).

280. John Stuart Mill, *On Liberty* (London, 1859; 1985), chs. 3, 13. Mill's concern, which he shared with his friend, Alexis de Tocqueville, was that society was jeopardizing liberty by encouraging people, as he put it, to behave like sheep, even though (he hoped) they were not sheep.

281. James Madison, "The Utility of the Union as a Safeguard Against Domestic Faction and Insurrection," Federalist 10, *Daily Advertiser*, November 22, 1787.

282. Mark G. Spencer, "Hume and Madison on Faction," *William & Mary Quarterly*, 59 (2002), pp. 869–96.

283. This point stands irrespective of the controversy over Michael A. Bellesiles, *Arming America: The Origins of a National Gun Culture* (New York, 2000; 2nd ed. 2003 with a new Introduction). See, e.g., Alexander DeConda, *Gun Violence in America: The Struggle for Control* (Boston, 2003), ch. 6; Saul Cornell, *A Well Regulated Militia: The Founding Fathers and the Origins of Gun Control in America* (New York, 2006), ch. 6.

284. Paul S. Holbo even argues (though perhaps with some exaggeration) that public reaction to the allegations of corruption surrounding the purchase damaged the plans of expansionists to acquire Cuba, Hawai'i, and Samoa: *Tarnished Expansion: The Alaska Scandal, the Press, and Congress, 1867–1871* (Knoxville, 1983).

285. George Feifer, *Breaking Open Japan: Commodore Perry, Lord Abe, and American Imperialism in 1853* (New York, 2006).

286. The quotation is taken from the title of ch. 1 of LaFeber's *New Empire*, p. 1.

287. Henry C. Carey, *The Way to Outdo England Without Fighting Her* (Philadelphia, 1865), p. 53.

288. Victor Hugo, *Les Misérables* (Paris, 1862), vol. 5, book 1, ch. 20.

CHAPTER 6: UNEVEN DEVELOPMENT AND IMPERIAL EXPANSION

1. Walt Whitman (1819–1892), "Years of the Modern," in *Leaves of Grass* (New York, 1855–1891; 1900). The relevant section of the poem appears at the end of this chapter. *Leaves of Grass* went through numerous editions, and many of the poems appear in slightly different versions.

2. The literature on Whitman is immense. Ed Folsom, "Talking Back to Walt Whitman," in Jim Perrlman, Ed Folsom, and Dan Campion, eds., *Walt Whitman: The Measure of His Song* (Duluth, 2nd ed., 1998), ch. 1, provides a valuable introduction.

3. These terms are discussed in chapter 1 of this text.

4. Specialists will recognize that this distinction is derived (very loosely) from Alexander Gerschenkron, *Economic Backwardness in Historical Perspective* (Cambridge, MA, 1962), chs. 1–3; also A. G. Hopkins, "Afterword: Towards a Cosmopolitan History of Imperialism," in Olivier Pétré-Grenouilleau, ed., *From Slave Trade to Empire: Europe and the Colonisation of Black Africa, 1780–1880s* (London, 2004), pp. 231–43.

5. Charles Pierre Baudelaire, "The Painter of Modern Life," in Baudelaire, *Selected Writings on Arts and Artists*, translated and edited by P. E. Charvet (London, 1972), p. 403. The term "modernité" is commonly attributed to Baudelaire.

6. Whitman, "Years of the Modern," in *Leaves of Grass*. The poem was written and first published in 1865, though it drew on notes dating from 1856 and did not acquire its final title until 1871. I am immensely grateful to Professor Ed Folsom for clarifying this matter for me.

7. Mark Twain and Charles Dudley Warner, *The Gilded Age: A Tale of Today* (New York, 1873), ch. 7. The phrase is taken from Ben Johnson's satire, *The Staple of News* (1625), which had as its central character the sought-after Lady Aurelia Pecunia, who symbolized what was then thought of as the new spirit of capitalism.

8. Quoted in Emma Rothschild, "Globalization and the Return of History," *Foreign Policy* (Summer 1999), p. 107. Chateaubriand (1768–1848), politician, diplomat, author, royalist, and romantic, was writing in 1841.

9. See especially Timothy J. Hatton and Jeffrey G. Williamson, *The Age of Mass Migration: Causes and Economic Impact* (New York, 1998); Kevin O'Rourke and Jeffrey G. Williamson, *Globalization and History: the Evolution of a Nineteenth-Century Atlantic Economy* (Cambridge, MA, 1999).

10. Simon J. Potter, *News and the British World: The Emergence of an Imperial Press System, 1876–1922* (Oxford, 2003).

11. Historians have yet to give this development, which is expanded later in this chapter, the full consideration it deserves in marking the demise of the military-fiscal state. I am particularly indebted to Mark Dincecco, *Political Transformations and Public Finances: Europe, 1650–1913* (Cambridge, 2013); Dincecco, "The Rise of Effective States in Europe," *Journal of Economic History*, 75 (2015), pp. 901–18; Dincecco and Gabriel Katz, "State Capacity and Long-Run Economic Performance," *Economic Journal*, 126 (2016), pp. 189–218.

12. Akira Iriye, *Global Community: The Role of International Organizations in the Making of the Contemporary World* (Berkeley, 2002), ch. 1.

13. Daniel R. Headrick has provided accessible guides to this literature: *The Tools of Empire: Technology and European Imperialism in the Nineteenth Century* (Oxford, 1981); *The Tentacles of Progress: Technology Transfer in the Age of Imperialism, 1850–1940* (Oxford, 1988); *The Invisible Weapon: Telecommunications and International Politics, 1851–1945* (Oxford, 1991). Michael Adas deals specifically with the United States in *Dominance by Design: Technological Imperatives and America's Civilizing Mission* (Cambridge, MA, 2006).

14. Extracts from "Ode to the Opening of the International Exhibition, 1862," in David Rogers, ed., *The Collected Poems of Alfred Lord Tennyson* (Ware, Hertfordshire, 1994), p. 556.

15. Wolfram Kaiser, "Cultural Transfer of Free Trade at the World Exhibitions, 1851–1862," *Journal of Modern History*, 77 (2005), pp. 563–90.

16. Paul Greenhalgh, *Ephemeral Vistas: The Expositions Universelles, Great Exhibitions and World's Fairs, 1851–1939* (Manchester, 1988).

17. *Erewhon*, an anagram of *Nowhere*.

18. Anthony Howe, *Free Trade and Liberal England, 1846–1846* (Oxford, 1998). Specialists have debated the distinctiveness of British policy. John V. C. Nye has advanced a stimulating counterargument that, unsurprisingly, has been contested: *War, Wine and Taxes: The Political Economy of Anglo-French Trade, 1689–1900* (Princeton, 2007). See Douglas A.

Irwin, "Free Trade and Protection in Nineteenth-Century Britain and France Revisited: A Comment on Nye," *Journal of Economic History*, 53 (1993), pp. 146–52.

19. Marc-William Palen, *The "Conspiracy" of Free Trade: The Anglo-American Struggle over Empire and Economic Globalisation 1846–1896* (Cambridge, 2016), ch. 1.

20. Alfred Marshall, *Industry and Trade* (London, 1919; 3rd ed. 1920), appendix E. Marshall, like J. S. Mill, saw that there was a theoretical case for protective tariffs, but judged that, in practice, they would lead to rent-seeking and other market distortions. See also Douglas A. Irwin, "Challenges to Free Trade," *Journal of Economic Perspectives*, 5 (1991), pp. 201–8.

21. On global tariffs see Antonio Tena-Junguito, Markus Lampe, and Felipe Tâmega Fernandes, "How Much Trade Liberalization Was There in the World Before and After Cobden-Chevalier?" *Journal of Economic History*, 72 (2012), pp. 708–40.

22. Marcus Lampe, "Explaining Nineteenth-Century Bilateralism: Economic and Political Determinants of the Cobden-Chevalier Network," *Economic History Review*, 64 (2011), p. 645.

23. David Todd, "A French Imperial Meridian, 1814–70," *Past & Present*, 210 (2011), pp. 155–86, traces the resurgence of support for free trade in France. Ironically, Cobden's "triumph" was followed soon after by the revival of protectionism. See Olivier Accominotti and Marc Flandreau, "Bilateral Treaties and the Most-Favoured-Nation Clause: The Myth of Trade Liberalization in the Nineteenth Century," *World Politics*, 60 (2008), pp. 147–88.

24. Louis Menand, *The Metaphysical Club* (New York, 2001); Gerlach Murney, *British Liberalism and the United States: Political and Social Thought in the Late Victorian Age* (New York, 2001); Leslie Butler, *Critical Americans: Victorian Intellectuals and Transatlantic Liberal Reform* (Chapel Hill, 2007), chs. 4, 5, 6; Tamara Plakins Thornton, "New Perspectives, Liberally Applied," *Reviews in American History*, 36 (2008), pp. 60–67.

25. Albert Carreras and Camilla Josephson, "Aggregate Growth, 1870–1914: Growing at the Production Frontier," in Stephen Broadberry and Kevin H. O'Rourke, eds., *Cambridge Economic History of Modern Europe*, Vol. 2. *1870 to the Present* (Cambridge, 2010), ch. 2, and p. 34.

26. For a discussion of the starting point see Kevin O'Rourke and Jeffrey G. Williamson, "When Did Globalization Begin?" *European Review of Economic History*, 6 (2002), pp. 23–50.

27. Ivan T. Berend, *History Derailed: Central and Eastern Europe in the Long Nineteenth Century* (Berkeley, 2003), deals with the two most neglected regions.

28. Denmark provides a (rare) corrective example.

29. Stephen Broadberry, Giovanni Federico, and Alexander Klein, "Sectoral Developments, 1870–1914," in Broadberry and O'Rourke, *Cambridge Economic History*, p. 61.

30. Quoted in David D. Hall, "The Victorian Connection," *American Quarterly*, 27 (1975), pp. 568–9.

31. Coincidentally or not, the Ouija board was patented in 1890.

32. Giuseppe Mazzini, "Speech to Workers," Milan, July 25, 1848. Quoted in Martin Collier, *Italian Unification, 1820–71* (Oxford, 2003), p. 103.

33. In a famous lecture that still reads as if it were written recently: "The Liberty of the Ancients Compared to that of the Moderns" (Paris, 1819). See also Lloyd S. Kramer's perceptive study, *Nationalism in Europe and America: Politics, Cultures and Identities since 1775* (Chapel Hill, 2011).

34. A. J. Marcham, "Educating Our Masters: Political Parties and Elementary Education, 1867 to 1870," *British Journal of Educational Studies*, 21 (1973), pp. 180–91.

35. Jose Harris, "Political Thought and the Welfare State, 1870–1940: An Intellectual Framework for British Social Policy," *Past & Present*, 135 (1992), pp. 116–41; James T. Kloppenberg, *Uncertain Victory: Social Democracy and Progressivism in European and American Thought, 1870–1920* (Oxford, 1986), deals with Dilthey, Green, Sidgwick, Fouillée, Dewey, and James.

36. Neville Kirk, "Peculiarities Versus Exceptions: The Shaping of the American Federation of Labor's Politics during the 1890s and 1900s," *International Review of Social History*, 45 (2000), pp. 25–50; Howell Harris, "Between Convergence and Exceptionalism: Americans and the British Model of Labor Relations, 1867–1920," *Labor History*, 48 (2007), pp. 141–73. David Brian Robertson argues persuasively that the history of the American labor force was not "exceptional" in the late nineteenth century but became so subsequently: *Capital, Labor, and the State: The Battle for American Labor Markets from the Civil War to the New Deal* (Lanham, 2000).

37. Richard B. Jensen, *The Battle against Anarchist Terrorism: An International History, 1878–1934* (Cambridge, 2014), contrasts the attempts to coordinate a response in Europe with the unilateral action taken by the United States. See also David Peal, "The Politics of Populism: Germany and the American South in the 1890s," *Comparative Studies in Society & History*, 31 (1989), pp. 340–62; Richard B. Bach, "Dagger, Rifles and Dynamite: Anarchist Terrorism in Nineteenth-Century Europe," *Terrorism & Political Violence*, 16 (2004), pp. 116–53; Davide Turcato, "Italian Anarchism as a Transnational Movement, 1885–1915," *International Review of Social History*, 52 (2007), pp. 407–44; Pietro DiPaola, "The Spies Who Came in from the Heat: The International Surveillance of the Anarchists in London," *European History Quarterly*, 37 (2007), pp. 189–215, deals with the period 1870–1914.

38. As Robert David Whitaker has shown in his admirable dissertation: "Policing Globalization: The Imperial Origins of International Police Co-operation," Ph.D. dissertation, University of Texas at Austin (2014), ch. 1.

39. Thomas Adam, "Transatlantic Trading: The Transfer of Philanthropic Models between European and North American Cities during the Nineteenth and Early Twentieth Centuries," *Journal of Urban History*, 28 (2002), pp. 328–52; Seth Koven and Sonya Michel, "Womanly Duties: Politics and the Origins of Welfare States in France, Germany, Great Britain, and the United States, 1880–1920," *American Historical Review*, 95 (1990), pp. 1076–1109.

40. Peter J. Coleman, *Progressivism and the World of Reform: New Zealand and the Origins of the American Welfare State* (Lawrence, 1987); Daniel T. Rodgers, *Atlantic Crossings: Social Politics in a Progressive Age* (Cambridge, 1998); Larry Frohman, "The Break-Up of the Poor Laws—German Style: Progressivism and the Origins of the Welfare State, 1900–1918," *Comparative Studies in Society & History*, 50 (2008), pp. 981–1009, deals with German Progressives.

41. E. P. Hennock's rare and valuable comparison draws attention to differences in motives: *The Origins of the Welfare State in England and Germany, 1850–1914: Social Policies Compared* (Cambridge, 2007).

42. The case of Germany has also been well studied: Richard Weikart, "The Origins of Social Darwinism in Germany" *Journal of the History of Ideas*, 54 (1993), pp. 469–88; Weikart, "Progress Through Racial Extermination: Darwinism, Eugenics and Pacifism in Germany, 1860–1918," *German Studies Review*, 26 (2003), pp. 273–94. European racial theories also spread to Asia: see Cemil Aydin, *The Politics of Anti-Westernism in Asia: Visions of World Order in Pan-Islamic and Pan-Asian Thought* (New York, 2007).

43. Paul Crook, *Darwinism, War and History: The Debate over the Biology of War from the "Origin of Species" to the First World War* (Cambridge, 1994); Crook, "Social Darwinism: The Concept," *History of European Ideas*, 22 (1996), pp. 261–74; Crook, "Historical Monkey Business: The Myth of a Darwinised British Imperial Discourse," *History*, 843 (1999), pp. 633–57; Joseph-Arthur de Gobineau was a creationist, not an evolutionist: *Essai sur l'inégalité des races humaines*, 4 vols. (Paris, 1853–55).

44. Duncan Bell and Caspar Sylvest, "International Society in Victorian Political Thought: T. H. Green, Herbert Spencer, and Henry Sidgwick," *Modern Intellectual History*, 3 (2006), pp. 22–7.

45. Frank Prochaska, *Eminent Victorians on American Democracy* (New York, 2012), explores the relationship between ideas of Anglo-Saxon unity and the intellectual divergence between advocates and critics of democracy.

46. Katherine A. Bradshaw, "The Misunderstood Public Opinion of James Bryce," *Journalism History*, 28 (2002), pp. 16–25.

47. Bryce (1838–1922) is now an understudied figure, though we are fortunate to have Hugh Tulloch's study, *James Bryce's American Commonwealth: The Anglo-American Background* (Woodbridge, 1988).

48. H. A. Tulloch, "Changing British Attitudes Towards the United States in the 1880s," *Historical Journal*, 20 (1977), p. 828.

49. Peter Brooks Adams, *The Law of Civilization and Decay: An Essay on History* (London, 1895; 1896).

50. Tulloch, "Changing British Attitudes," p. 835.

51. Paul J. Wolf, "Special Relationships: Anglo-American Love Affairs, Courtships and Marriages in Fiction, 1821–1914," Ph.D. thesis, University of Birmingham (2007), p. 277.

52. Daniel Pick, *Faces of Degeneration: A European Disorder, 1848–1918* (Cambridge, 1989).

53. The Italian criminologist, Cesare Lombroso (1835–1909), achieved international influence in the late nineteenth century by advancing theories that claimed to identify the inherited physical features associated with criminal behavior. See Peter D'Agostino, "Craniums, Criminals and the 'Cursed Race': Italian Anthropology in American Racial Thought, 1861–1824," *Comparative Studies in Society & History*, 44 (2002), pp. 319–43.

54. The phrase is from F. H. Giddings, *Studies in the Theory of Human Society* (New York, 1922), quoted in Charles A. Beard, "Introduction" to Brooks Adams, *The Law of Civilization and Decay* (New York, 1896; 1943), p. 50.

55. On Kidd (1858–1916), see *Social Evolution* (London, 1894); D. P. Crook, *Benjamin Kidd: Portrait of a Social Darwinist* (New York, 1984).

56. Charles H. Pearson, *National Life and Character: A Forecast* (London, 1894); Marilyn Lake, "The White Man under Siege: New Histories of Race in the Nineteenth Century and the Advent of White Australia," *History Workshop Journal*, 58 (2004), pp. 41–62; Peter Cain, "Democracy, Globalization and the Decline of Empire: A View from the 1890s," in Falola and Brownell, *Africa, Empire and Globalization*, ch. 23.

57. Robert A. Nye, "The Rise and Fall of the Eugenics Empire: Recent Perspectives on the Impact of Biomedical Thoughts in Modern Society," *Historical Journal*, 36 (1993), pp. 687–700.

58. Edwin Black, *War Against the Weak: Eugenics and America's Campaign to Create a Master Race* (New York, 2003). Paul A. Lombardo provides further details of the campaign that sterilized more than 60,000 "mentally ill" people and continued, astonishingly, until the 1970s: *A Century of Eugenics in America: From the Indiana Experiment to the Human Genome Era* (Bloomington, 2010).

59. Verdi to Piave, April 21, 1848. Quoted in Scott L. Balthazar, ed., *The Cambridge Companion to Verdi* (Cambridge, 2004), p. 32.

60. Jean-François Drolet, "Nietzsche, Kant, the Democratic State, and War," *Review of International Studies*, 39 (2013), pp. 25–47.

61. Norman Angell, *The Great Illusion: A Study of the Relation of Military Power in Nations to their Economic and Social Advantage* (New York, 1910). Angell (1872–1967) was a prolific and influential journalist, author, and public figure. He was a Labor M.P. (1929–31), received a knighthood (1931), and was awarded the Nobel Peace Prize (1933). Martin Ceadel, *Living the Great Illusion: Sir Norman Angell 1872–1967* (Oxford, 2009), provides the definitive, and corrective, biography. See also J.D.B. Miller, *Norman Angell and the Futility of War* (1986).

62. Thomas Hardy (1840–1928), "The Breaking of Nations," in John Wain, ed., *The Oxford Library of English Poetry*, Vol. 3 (Oxford, 1986), p. 224.

63. Spengler (1880–1936) began his work shortly before the war and published a second volume in 1922.

64. H. G. Wells, *Outline of History* (London, 1920), p. 1290; Wells, *The Salvaging of Civilization* (London, 1921), which also records his disillusion with President Wilson and the League of Nations.

65. Marc Flandreau, *The Glitter of Gold: France, Bimetallism, and the Emergence of the International Gold Standard, 1848–1873* (New York, 2004), ch. 8 and pp. 212–13, advances a powerful case suggesting that bimetallism had supported a viable international monetary system between 1848 and 1873, but that Franco-German cooperation was destroyed by the Franco-Prussian War in 1870. On this view, France's decision to adopt the gold standard, and Germany's ability to do so, were products of political events rather than outcomes of purely economic forces.

66. There is a large literature on the difference between theory and reality. See Tamin Bayoumi, Barry J. Eichengreen, and Mark P. Taylor, eds., *Modern Perspectives on the Gold Standard* (Cambridge, 1996); Barry J. Eichengreen and Marc Flandreau, eds., *The Gold Standard in Theory and History* (New York, 1997); Marc Flandreau and Frederic Zumer, *The Making of Global Finance, 1880–1913* (Paris, 2004). The managerial function at this time was largely political. The Bank of England did not hold sufficient gold reserves to act as a lender of last resort. Nevertheless, Britain managed the system and it worked reasonably well. See Michael D. Bordo and Ronald MacDonald, "Interest Rate Interactions in the Classical Gold Standard, 1880–1914: Was There Any Monetary Independence?" *Journal of Monetary Economics*, 52 (2005), pp. 307–27; Maurice Obstfeld and Alan M. Taylor, "Sovereign Risk, Credibility and the Gold Standard, 1870–1913, Versus 1925–31," *Economic Journal*, 113 (2007), pp. 241–75.

67. Following S. B. Saul, *The Myth of the Great Depression* (London, 1969). I am grateful to my former colleague, Mark Metzler, for his advice on this subject. His much-needed restatement of the Great Depression of the late nineteenth century will be a major contribution to the international history of the period.

68. A recent, authoritative economic history of the period after 1870 has no discussion of what was once called the "Great Depression" of 1873–1896, and hardly any references to it: Broadberry and O'Rourke, *Cambridge Economic History*, pp. 64, 88.

69. Forrest Capie and Geoffrey Wood, *Money Over Two Centuries: Selected Topics in Monetary History* (Oxford, 2012), reprints a number of valuable papers on the subject. W. Arthur Lewis, *Growth and Fluctuations, 1870–1913* (London, 1978) remains an important and now a rather neglected source.

70. Economists are immune from this charge, but their analyses tend to fly above the needs of historians. Lewis, *Growth and Fluctuations*, chs. 7–8, offers an insightful typology of the options facing "late-start" countries.

71. I am indebted here to Scott Reynolds Nelson, "A Storm of Cheap Goods: New American Commodities and the Panic of 1873," *Journal of the Gilded Age & Progressive Era*, 10 (2011), pp. 447–53, and other articles in the special issue of the journal. See also Nelson, *A Nation of Deadbeats: An Uncommon History of America's Financial Disasters* (New York, 2012), which manages to be both illuminating and entertaining.

72. See chapter 4 of this text.

73. Forrest Capie and Geoffrey Wood, "Deflation in the British Economy, 1870–1939," *Journal of European Economic History*, 32 (2003), pp. 277–305. Michael D. Bordo, John Landon-Lane, and Angela Redish, "Good Versus Bad Deflation: Lessons from the Gold Standard Era," in David E. Altig and Ed Nosal, eds., *Monetary Policy in Low-Inflation Economies* (Cambridge, 2009), pp. 127–74; Altig and Nosal, "Deflation, Productivity Shocks and Gold: Evidence from the 1880–1914 Period," *Open Economy Review*, 21 (2010), pp. 515–46.

74. Bordo et al., "Good Versus Bad Deflation," compare the United States, the UK, and Germany.

75. Real wages for non-farm workers in the United States fell for periods in the last quarter of the century, partly because immigration increased the labor supply: Robert A. Margo, "The Labor Force in the Nineteenth Century," in Stanley L. Engerman and Robert E. Gallman, *Cambridge Economic History of the United States*, II (Cambridge, 2000), p. 223. See, too, Robert A. McGuire's study of sixteen Northern U.S. states: "Economic Causes of Late Nineteenth-Century Unrest: New Evidence," *Journal of Economic History*, 41 (1981), pp. 835–52 (and subsequent discussion); Ayers, *The Promise of the New South*, ch. 10, shows that populism in the South was bound up not only with racism, but also with conflicts arising out of postwar socioeconomic change.

76. It should be added that Angus Maddison's pioneering work, which is widely cited in this context, has to make some heroic estimates of the growth of per capita incomes between 1879 and 1896: *Monitoring the World Economy* (Paris, 1995).

77. See, for example, the complexities discussed by Jeremy Atack, Fred Bateman, and William N. Parker, "The Farm, the Farmer and the Market," in Engerman and Gallman, *Cambridge Economic History*, II, pp. 280–82.

78. Carreras and Josephson, "Aggregate Growth, 1870–1914," pp. 37–8.

79. Michael D. Bordo and Chris M. Meissner, "Foreign Capital, Financial Crises and Incomes in the First Era of Globalization," *European Review of Economic History*, 15 (2011), pp. 61–91.

80. Larry Neal and Marc D. Weidenmier, "Crises in the Global Economy from Tulips to Today: Contagion and Consequences," in Michael D. Bordo, Alan M. Taylor, and Jeffrey Williamson, eds., *Globalization in Historical Perspective* (Chicago, 2003), pp. 473–514.

81. Michael D. Bordo and Joseph G. Haubrich, "Credit Crises, Money and Contractions: An Historical View," *Journal of Monetary Economics*, 57 (2010), pp. 1–18.

82. Christian Suter and Hanspeter Stamm, "Coping with Global Debt Crises: Debt Settlements, 1820–1986," *Comparative Studies in Society & History*, 34 (1992), p. 645.

83. Marc Flandreau, "Sovereign States, Bondholders' Committees and the London Stock Exchange in the Nineteenth Century (1827–1868): New Facts and Old Fictions," *Oxford Review of Economic Policy*, 29 (2013), pp. 668–96, traces the prehistory of this development through initiatives taken by the London Stock Exchange before 1868.

84. And did their work effectively: Kris James Mitchener and Marc D. Weidenmier, "Supersanctions and Sovereign Debt Repayment," *Journal of International Money and Finance*, 29 (2010), pp. 19–36.

85. On the first see A. G. Hopkins, "The Victorians and Egypt: A Reconsideration of the Occupation of Egypt, 1882," *Journal of African History*, 27 (1986), pp. 363–91; on the second, essentially the work of J. A. Hobson, see the authoritative study by P. J. Cain, *Hobson and Imperialism: Radicalism, New Liberalism, and Finance, 1887–1938* (Oxford, 2002).

86. Matthew P. Fitzpatrick, *Liberal Imperialism in Germany: Expansion and Nationalism, 1848–1884* (New York, 2008), pp. 5–7.

87. Eric Grimmer-Solem, "The Professor's Africa: Economists, the Elections of 1907, and the Legitimation of German Imperialism," *German History*, 25 (2007), pp. 313–47.

88. Alain Clément, "L'analyse économique de la question coloniale en France (1870–1914)," *Review d'Économie Politique*, 123 (2013), pp. 51–82.

89. Charles A. Conant, "The Economic Basis of Imperialism," *North American Review* (September 1898), p. 326.

90. Guillaume Daudin, Matthias Morys, and Kevin H. O'Rourke, "Globalization, 1870–1914," in Broadberry and O'Rourke, *Cambridge Economic History*, 2, pp. 26–29.

91. On the differential consequences of free trade (in Britain) and protection (in continental Europe), see Kevin H. O'Rourke, "The European Grain Invasion, 1870–1913," *Journal of Economic History*, 57 (1997), pp. 775–801.

92. Principally the Netherlands, Denmark, and Belgium.

93. Christopher M. Meissner, "A New World Order: Explaining the International Diffusion of the Gold Standard, 1870–1913," *Journal of International Economics*, 66 (2006), pp. 385–406, notes the importance of low borrowing costs for developing countries.

94. For two different accounts, see Angela Redish, *Bimetallism: An Economic and Historical Analysis* (Cambridge, 2000); and Ted Wilson, *Battles for the Standard: Bimetallism and the Spread of the Gold Standard in the Nineteenth Century* (Aldershot, 2001), ch. 6. Flandreau, *The Glitter of Gold*, shows that the system was viable.

95. The terms were given currency in the critical U.S. election of 1896.

96. For two of many recent case studies see Gregory A. Barton and Brett M. Bennett, "A Case Study in the Environmental History of Gentlemanly Capitalism: The Battle between Gentlemen Teak Merchants and State Foresters in Burma and Siam, 1827–1901," in Falola and Brownell, *Africa, Empire and Decolonization*, ch. 16; Mark Metzler, "Revisiting the General Crisis of the Late Nineteenth Century: West Africa and the World Depression," in Falola and Brownell, *Africa, Empire and Decolonization*, ch. 16.

97. A. G. Hopkins, "Back to the Future: From National History to Imperial History," *Past & Present*, 164 (1999), pp. 198–243.

98. Adam Smith, *The Wealth of Nations* (New York, 1937), pp. 781–2.

99. Quoted in Todd Shepard, *The Invention of Decolonization: The Algerian War and the Remaking of France* (Ithaca, 2006), p. 20.

100. Richard Koebner and Helmut Schmidt, *Imperialism: The Story and Significance of a Political Word* (Cambridge, 1964); Mark F. Proudman, "Words for Scholars: The Semantics of 'Imperialism,'" *Journal of the Historical Society*, 8 (2008), pp. 395–433.

101. Shepard, *Invention of Decolonization*, ch. 2.

102. J. Gallagher and R. E. Robinson, "The Imperialism of Free Trade," *Economic History Review*, 2nd ser., 6 (1953), pp. 1–15.

103. Sir John Seeley (1834–1895), Regius Professor of History, University of Cambridge, 1869–95. His best-known work, *The Expansion of England* (1883), regretted the acquisition of India but held, nevertheless, that British rule there was a benign, progressive influence.

104. On this matter and much more see Duncan Bell, *The Idea of Greater Britain: Empire and the Future of World Order, 1860–1900* (Princeton, 2007), ch. 7.

105. These debates are reviewed by Roger Owen and Bob Sutcliffe, eds., *Studies in the Theory of Imperialism* (London, 1972); Wm. Roger Louis, ed., *Imperialism: The Gallagher and Robinson Controversy* (New York, 1976); Gregory A. Barton, *Informal Empire and the Rise of One World Culture* (Basingstoke, 2014); Anthony Webster, *The Debate on the Rise of the British Empire* (Manchester, 2006).

106. The best study of anti-imperialism in Britain during this period remains Bernard Porter, *Critics of Empire: British Radical Attitudes to Colonialism in Africa, 1895–1914* (London, 1968); John W. Crangle, "The Economics of British Anti-Imperialism: Victorian Dissent Against India," *Studies in History & Society*, 6 (1975), pp. 60–76, emphasizes objections made on grounds of cost, monopoly power, and loss of life. Jonathan Parry, *The Politics of Patriotism: English Liberalism, National Identity and Europe, 1830–1886* (Cambridge, 2004), shows how political developments in continental Europe led to concern among Britain's political leaders that foreign influences might have an adverse effect on British values and character.

107. Henri Brunschwig, "Vigné d'Octon and Anti-Colonialism under the Third Republic," *Journal of Imperial & Commonwealth History*, 3 (1974), pp. 140–72.

108. See chapter 7 of this text.

109. John M. MacKenzie, *Propaganda and Empire* (Manchester, 1984); John M. MacKenzie, ed., *Imperialism and Popular Culture* (Manchester, 1986); William H. Schneider, *An Empire for the Masses: The French Popular Image of Africa, 1870–1900* (Westport, 1982). Although Bernard Porter has challenged the view that imperial images and information pervaded British society, he allows that this was the case in the late nineteenth century:

Absent-Minded Imperialists: What the British Really Thought about Empire (Oxford, 2005).

110. It is unfortunate that national traditions have limited cross-country comparisons. Loti (1850–1923), whose real name was Julien Viaud, was a prolific writer but of a quality that secured his admission to the *Académie française* in 1892. The recent trend in "Loti studies" has reduced his role as a colonial novelist and increased his standing as a perceptive explorer of personal, sexual relationships.

111. Robert Irvine has drawn attention to the imperial context of R. M. Ballantyne's novels, the best known of which, *The Coral Island*, was published in 1857: "Separate Accounts: Class and Colonization in the Early Stories of R. M. Ballantyne," *Journal of Victorian Culture*, 12 (2007), pp. 238–61. Ballantyne (1825–1894) wrote tales of character forged through trial in distant places that anticipated many of the themes of later novelists. His admirers included Robert Louis Stevenson, who paid generous tribute to the influence of his novels.

112. Patrick A. Dunae, "Boys' Literature and the Idea of Empire, 1870–1914," *Victorian Studies*, 24 (1980), pp. 105–21.

113. Guy Arnold, *Held Fast for England: G. A. Henty, Imperialist Boys' Writer* (London, 1980) provides an accessible and concise guide to the substantial literature on Henty. More generally, see also MacKenzie, *Propaganda and Empire*; Jeffrey Richards, ed., *Imperialism and Juvenile Literature* (Manchester, 1989); Laurence Kitzan, *Victorian Writers and the Image of Empire: The Rose-Colored Vision* (Westport, 2001).

114. Henty's stories were well known in the United States, where they survived even longer than they did in Britain (Arnold, *Held Fast for England*, p. 19).

115. Trumbull White, *Our New Possessions: Four Books in One* (Philadelphia, 1898); James C. Fernald, *The Imperial Republic* (New York, 1899); see also chapter 7 of this text.

116. For a set of comparative studies, see Mark A. Noll, David W. Bebbington, and George A. Rawlyk, eds., *Evangelicalism: Comparative Studies of Popular Protestantism in North America, the British Isles, and Beyond, 1700–1900* (New York, 1994).

117. Quoted in Hopkins, "The Victorians and Africa," p. 384.

118. Pamela Walker, *Pulling the Devil's Kingdom Down: The Salvation Army in Victorian Britain* (Berkeley, 2001); Harald Fischer-Tine, "Global Civil Society and the Forces of Empire: The Salvation Army, British Imperialism, and the Prehistory of NGOs (ca. 1880–1920)"; in Sebastian Conrad and Dominic Sachsenmaier, eds., *Competing Visions of World Order: Global Moments and Movements, 1880s–1930s* (New York, 2007), pp. 29–67.

119. Rudyard Kipling, "Mandalay." On this subject, see P. J. Cain, "Empire and the Languages of Character and Virtue in Later Victorian and Edwardian Britain," *Modern Intellectual History*, 4 (2007), pp. 249–73.

120. There is now a considerable literature on the relationship between team games, Christianity, chivalry, and empire. See particularly, J. A. Mangan, *The Games Ethic and Imperialism: Aspects of the Diffusion of an Ideal* (New York, 1986), and for recent work, the series of articles by J. A. Mangan and Callum McKenzie in a special issue of the *International Journal of the History of Sport*, 25 (2008), pp. 1080–1273. D. L. LeMahieu offers a comparative perspective in "The History of British and American Sport: A Review Article," *Comparative Studies in Society & History*, 32 (1990), pp. 838–44.

121. Douglas H. Johnson, "The Death of Gordon: A Victorian Myth," *Journal of Imperial & Commonwealth History*, 10 (1982), pp. 285–310. Olive Anderson, "The Growth of Christian Militarism in Mid-Victorian England," *English Historical Review*, 86 (1971), pp. 46–72, traces the origins of the "saintly soldier" to the Crimean War and the Indian Mutiny.

122. Berny Sèbe, *Heroic Imperialists in Africa: The Promotion of British and French Colonial Heroes, 1870–1939* (Manchester, 2013), ch. 6. The comparative dimension of Sèbe's excellent study is especially valuable.

123. See also chapter 5 of this text.

124. Andrew C. Ross, *David Livingstone: Mission and Empire* (London, 2002), ch. 15.

125. François Renault, *Le Cardinal Lavigerie, 1825–1892: L'Eglise, l'Afrique, et la France* (Paris, 1992), is the standard work. Lavigerie, Archbishop of Carthage and Algiers, was made a cardinal in 1882.

126. Daniel Laqua, "The Tensions of Internationalism: Transnational Anti-Slavery in the 1880s and 1890s," *International History Review*, 33 (2011), pp. 705–26.

127. J. P. Daughton, *An Empire Divided: Religion, Republicanism, and the Making of French Colonialism, 1880–1914* (Oxford, 2007).

128. Andrew Porter, *Religion Versus Empire? British Protestant Missionaries and Overseas Expansion, 1700–1914* (Manchester, 2004), details important nuances in the relationship between missions and empire that cannot be dealt with in the present summary. See also the diverse case studies in Norman Etherington, ed., *Missions and Empire* (Oxford, 2007).

129. David Bebbington, *Victorian Nonconformity* (Lutterworth, 2011).

130. David Bebbington, "Atonement, Sin and Empire, 1880–1914," in Andrew Porter, ed., *The Imperial Horizons of British Protestant Missions* (Grand Rapids, 2003), pp. 14–31; Richard Huzzey, *Freedom Burning: Anti-Slavery and Empire in Victorian Britain* (Ithaca, 2012).

131. On the continuing religious commitment in Britain, see Hugh McLeod, *Religion and Society in Nineteenth-Century England, 1850–1914* (New York, 1996).

132. Tyrrell, *Transnational Nation*, p. 103, provides one estimate: Britain, 5,393; United States, 3,478.

133. Far less attention has been paid to a precursor, the Boys' Brigade, which was founded in 1883. See John Springhall, Brian Fraser, and Michael Hoare, eds., *Sure and Steadfast: A History of the Boys' Brigade, 1883–1983* (London, 1983).

134. Tammy M. Proctor, *Scouting for Girls: A Century of Girl Guides and Girl Scouts* (Santa Barbara, 2009), provides an outline.

135. Agnes Baden-Powell and Robert Baden-Powell produced a manual for the Guides in 1912 entitled, *The Handbook for Girl Guides or How Girls Can Help Build Up the Empire*. See also Richard A. Voltz, "The Antidote to 'Khaki Fever': The Expansion of the British Girl Guides During the First World War," *Journal of Contemporary History*, 27 (1992), pp. 627–38.

136. Cain, "Empire and Languages of Character and Virtue."

137. Sam Pryke, "The Popularity of Nationalism in the Early British Boy Scout Movement," *Social History*, 23 (1998), pp. 309–24. There has been a debate about the degree of militarism in the Boy Scout movement, on which see John Springhall, "Baden-Powell and the Scout Movement before 1920: Citizen Training or Soldiers of the Future," *English Historical Review*, 102 (1987), pp. 934–42, and the further references given there.

138. James Belich, *Replenishing the Earth: The Settler Revolution and the Rise of the Anglo-World, 1783–1939* (Oxford, 2009); Gary Magee and Andrew Thompson, *Empire and Globalisation: Networks of People, Goods and Capital in the British World, c. 1850–1914* (Cambridge, 2010).

139. David Day, *Antarctica: A Biography* (Oxford, 2013), chs. 5–8.

140. William Gervase Clarence-Smith, "The Imperialism of the Jackals: Economic Dynamics Driving Less Developed Powers in the Nineteenth and Twentieth Centuries," paper presented to the Global Economic History Conference, Istanbul, 2005. I am grateful to Prof. Clarence-Smith for allowing me to cite his paper and for his valuable comments on the issues it raises.

141. Clarence-Smith, "The Imperialism of the Jackals." The original citation is from V. I. Lenin, *Kommunist*, 1–2 (1915).

142. For some preliminary thoughts on this theme, see Hopkins, "Towards a Cosmopolitan History of Imperialism."

143. The "ragamuffins," as Giuseppe Maione called them with reference to Italy in the 1930s: *L'imperialismo straccione* (Bologna, 1979).

144. Lars Magnussen, *Nation, State, and the Industrial Revolution: The Visible Hand* (London, 2009), offers a categorization that links the development of modern state structures to industrialization.

145. Dincecco, *Political Transformations and Public Finances*. See also the references in n. 11 above.

146. See Jose Luis Cardosa and Pedro Lains, eds., *Paying for the Liberal State: The Rise of Public Finance in Nineteenth-Century Europe* (Cambridge, 2010).

147. The comparative point, emphasizing the role of war, has been well made by Michael Geyer and Charles Bright in an essay that itself has few comparators: "Global Violence and Nationalising Wars in Eurasia and America: The Geopolitics of War in the Mid-Nineteenth Century," *Comparative Studies in Society & History*, 38 (1996), pp. 619–57.

148. Pablo-Martín Aneña, Elena Martínez-Ruiz, and Pilar Nogues-Marco, "Floating Against the Tide: Spanish Monetary Policy, 1870–1931," *Working Papers in Economic History*, Universidad Carlos III de Madrid, WP 11–10 (2011).

149. Pedro Lains, "The Power of Peripheral Government: Coping with the 1891 Financial Crisis in Portugal," *Historical Research*, 81 (2008), pp. 485–506.

150. For a discussion of the latter, see Joel Mokyr, "The Industrial Revolution and the Netherlands: Why Did It Not Happen?" *De Economist*, 148 (2000), pp. 503–20.

151. Albert Schrauwers, "'Regenten' (Gentlemanly) Capitalism: Saint-Simonian Technocracy and the Emergence of the 'Industrialist Great Club' in the Mid-Nineteenth Century Netherlands," *Enterprise & Society*, 11 (2010), pp. 753–83.

152. Maarten Kuitenbrouwer, "Capitalism and Imperialism: Britain and the Netherlands," *Itinerario*, 18 (1994), pp. 105–16; Kuitenbrouwer, *The Netherlands and the Rise of Modern Capitalism: Colonies and Foreign Policy 1870–1902* (Oxford, 1991).

153. Marc Flandreau, "The Logic of Compromise: Monetary Bargaining in Austria-Hungary, 1867–1913," *European Review of Economic History*, 10 (2006), pp. 3–33.

154. Quoted in Rodney P. Carlisle and Joe H. Kirchberger, *World War I* (New York, 2009), p. 1. There are several versions of this quotation.

155. I follow the accepted attribution, though similar phrasing may have been circulating before 1914. The attitude in Vienna toward the problems the Austro-Hungarian Empire faced might well have prompted others to comment on the government's inability to recognize realities.

156. The Farmers' Alliance, founded in 1879, had lost what little influence it possessed in Britain by 1885.

157. George Joachim Goschen (1831–1907), First Lord of the Admiralty (1895–1900), created First Viscount Goschen (1900), coined the phrase in 1896. Britain entered an *Entente* with France in 1904.

158. The ever-inventive J. A. Hobson offered a pioneering analysis in *The Psychology of Jingoism* (London, 1901).

159. Miles Taylor, "John Bull and the Iconography of Public Opinion in England, c. 1712–1929," *Past & Present*, 134 (1992), pp. 93–128; Taylor, "Imperium et Libertas? Rethinking the Radical Critique of Imperialism during the Nineteenth Century," *Journal of Imperial & Commonwealth History*, 19 (1991), pp. 1–23, shows how the radical critique of imperialism derived from a concern with its constitutional and wider domestic consequences.

160. Linda Colley, *Britons: Forging a Nation, 1707–1837* (New Haven, 1992); Stephen Conway, "War and National Identity in the Mid-Eighteenth-Century British Isles," *English Historical Review*, 116 (2001), pp. 863–93.

161. On the qualities of Englishness, as seen by foreign observers, see Paul Langford, *Englishness Identified: Manners and Character, 1650–1850* (Oxford, 2000); Paul Readman, "The Place of the Past in English Culture, 1890–1914," *Past & Present*, 186 (2005), pp. 147–99. Overseas associations expressed and reinforced regional affiliations. See, for example,

Tanja Buelltmann and Donald M. MacRaild, "Globalizing St. George: English Associations in the Anglo-World to the 1930s," *Journal of Global History*, 7 (2012), pp. 79–105.

162. Paul Ward, *Britishness since 1870* (London, 2004), is an accessible guide.

163. On Britishness and the Anglo-World, see Carl Bridge and Kent Fedorowich, eds., *The British World: Diaspora, Culture, and Identity* (London, 2003); Belich, *Replenishing the Earth*; Kent Fedorowich and Andrew S. Thompson, eds., *Empire, Migration and Identity in the British World* (Manchester, 2013).

164. This move followed the failure of Overend, Gurney & Co., the leading discounting house of the time, which was heavily involved in international transactions. See Marc Flandreau and Stefan Ugolini, "Where It All Began: Lending of Last Resort and the Bank of England during the Overend Gurney Panic of 1866," *C.P.E.R. Discussion Paper*, 8362 (2011). "Gladstonian finance" ensured that tax revenues and public expenditure declined as a proportion of GDP until the last quarter of the century, but GDP itself increased and tax compliance remained high.

165. Robert Gilpin uses the term "mature creditor" to develop a different argument in *U.S. Power and the Multinational Corporation: The Political Economy of Foreign Direct Investment* (New York, 1975), p. 53.

166. On the first point, see Broadberry et al., "Sectoral Developments," p. 72. On Britain's financial supremacy, see Cain and Hopkins, *British Imperialism*, chs. 5–6.

167. The position taken here is explained at greater length in Cain and Hopkins, *British Imperialism*, pp. 137–45.

168. Edmund Rogers, "The United States and the Fiscal Debate in Britain, 1873–1913," *Historical Journal*, 50 (2007), pp. 593–622, shows how protection in the United States, combined with the expansion of U.S. exports to Britain, boosted support in the UK for imperial preference. Marc-William Palen provides a case study: "Protection, Federation and Union: The Global Impact of the McKinley Tariff upon the British Empire, 1890–94," *Journal of Imperial & Commonwealth History*, 38 (2010), pp. 395–418.

169. Sir Charles Dilke, *Greater Britain* (London, 1868), was an important influence on the thinking of the time.

170. Cain and Hopkins, *British Imperialism*, ch. 7; Andrew S. Thompson, "Tariff Reform: An Imperial Strategy, 1903–1913," *Historical Journal*, 40 (1997), pp. 1033–54; Roger Mason, "Robert Giffen and the Tariff Reform Campaign, 1865–1910," *Journal of European Economic History*, 25 (1996), pp. 171–88.

171. However, the political model was to be borrowed from the United States rather than from Rome. See Duncan Bell, "From Ancient to Modern in Victorian Thought," *Historical Journal*, 49 (2006), pp. 735–59; and, on this theme generally, Bell, *The Idea of Greater Britain*.

172. This is a major theme of Cain and Hopkins, *British Imperialism*. Other consequences of free trade are discussed by Kevin O'Rourke, "British Trade Policy in the Nineteenth Century: A Review Article," *Journal of Political Economy*, 16 (2000), pp. 829–42.

173. Daudin, Morys, and O'Rourke, "Globalization, 1870–1914," pp. 9–13.

174. William N. Goertzman and Urdrey D. Ukhor, "British Investment Overseas, 1870–1913: A Modern Portfolio Theory Approach," *NBER Working Paper*, 11266 (2005), p. 12 and table 3, p. 40. The figures refer to publicly invested capital.

175. But had been formulated earlier by émigrés following the collapse of Napoleonic rule. See Maurizio Isabella, *Risorgimento in Exile: Italian Émigrés and the Liberal International in the Post–Napoleonic Era* (Oxford, 2009).

176. Mariella Rigotti Colin, "L'idée de Rome et l'idéologie impérialiste dans l'Italie libérale de 1870 à 1900," *Mondiales et Conflits Contemporains*, 41 (1991), pp. 3–19.

177. This paragraph attempts to amalgamate and summarize material from two valuable studies: Vera Zamagni, *The Economic History of Italy, 1860–1990* (Oxford, 1993); and Stefano Fenoaltea, *The Reinterpretation of Italy's Economic History: From Unification to the Great War* (Cambridge, 2011).

178. On the important part foreign trade played in Italy's economic development, see Giovanni Federico and Nikolaus Wolf, "Italy's Comparative Advantage: A Comparative Perspective," C.E.P.R. Discussion Paper, 8758 (2012).

179. Simon Sarlin, "The Anti-Risorgimento as a Transnational Experience," *Modern Italy*, 18 (2014), pp. 81–92.

180. Enrico Dal Lago, *Agrarian Elites: American Slaveholders and Southern Italian Landowners, 1815-1861* (Baton Rouge, 2005).

181. Mark Dincecco, Giovanni Federico, and Andrea Vindigni, "Warfare, Taxation and Political Change: Evidence from the Italian Risorgimento," *Journal of Economic History*, 71 (2011), pp. 887–914. Camillo Benso, Count of Cavour (1810–61), Prime Minister of Piedmont-Sardinia (1852–61), Prime Minister of Italy (1861).

182. In 1870, less than 3 percent of Italians had the right to vote in elections to the lower chamber of parliament. Adult suffrage (for males only) was not introduced until 1913.

183. Maurizio Isabella, "Rethinking Italy's Nation-Building 150 Years Afterwards: The New *Risorgimento* Historiography," *Past & Present*, 217 (2012), pp. 247–68.

184. Mark Choate, *Emigrant Nation: The Making of Italy Abroad* (Cambridge, 2008).

185. Catherine Brice, *Monarchie et identité nationale en Italie (1861-1900)* (Paris, 2010); Brice, "Monarchy and Nation at the End of the Nineteenth Century: A Unique Form of Politicisation?" *European History Quarterly*, 43 (2013), pp. 53–72.

186. Crispi (1818–1901), was prime minister from 1887 to 1891 and from 1893 to 1896. See Christopher Duggan, *Francesco Crispi, 1818-1901: From Nation to Nationalism* (Oxford, 2002).

187. Christopher Duggan, "Francesco Crispi and Italy's Pursuit of War Against France, 1887–9," *Australian Journal of Politics and History*, 50 (2004), pp. 315–29.

188. Mark Choate, "From Territorial to Ethnographic Colonies and Back Again: The Politics of Italian Expansion, 1890–1912," *Modern Italy*, 8 (2003), pp. 65–75; Christopher Duggan, "Francesco Crispi's Relationship with Britain: From Colonisation to Disillusionment," *Modern Italy*, 16 (2011), pp. 427–36.

189. See, for example, Romain H. Romero's study of the Benadir Company in "An Imperialism with no Economic Basis: The Case of Italy, 1869–1939," in Pétré-Grenouilleau, *From Slave Trade to Empire*, pp. 91–6. On Richard A. Webster's attempt to promote the activities of a military-industrial complex in *Industrial Imperialism in Italy, 1890-1915* (Los Angeles, 1975), see Clive Trebilcock's incisive essay, "Economic Backwardness and Military Forwardness," *Historical Journal*, 20 (1977), pp. 751–60.

190. The loss of Alsace-Lorraine to Germany in 1870 excised a region that contained major manufacturing centers.

191. The data presented in this paragraph and the next are drawn primarily from Broadberry and O'Rourke, *Cambridge Economic History*, pp. 35–36, 44, 61, 72, 82–3.

192. René Girault, *Emprunts russes et investissements français en Russie, 1887-1914* (Paris, 1973).

193. I am particularly indebted to Dr. Stephen W. Sawyer, American University of Paris, for permission to cite his important work on this subject, some of which is now available: "A Fiscal Revolution: Statecraft in France's Early Third Republic," *American Historical Review*, 121 (2016), pp. 1141–66.

194. Marc Flandreau, "The Economics and Politics of Monetary Unions: A Reassessment of the Latin Monetary Union, 1865–71," *Financial History Review*, 7 (2000), pp. 25–43. The members of the Union were France, Belgium, Switzerland, and Italy.

195. Herman Lebovics, *The Alliance of Iron and Wheat in the Third French Republic, 1860-1914: Origins of the New Conservatism* (Baton Rouge, 1988); David M. Gordon, *Liberalism and Social Reform: Industrial Growth and "Progressiste" Politics in France, 1880-1914* (Westport, 1996). Gordon stresses the role of successful industrialists in pressing for a compromise that would offer a welfare estate as an alternative to socialism.

196. Michael S. Smith, *Tariff Reform in France, 1860–1900: the Politics of Economic Interest* (Ithaca, 1980); Smith, "The Méline Tariff as Social Protection: Rhetoric or Reality?" *International Review of Social History*, 37 (1992), pp. 230–43; Rita Aldenhoff-Hübinger, "Deux pays, deux politiques agricoles? Le protectionnisme en France et Allemagne (1880–1914)," *Histoire Sociales et Rurales*, 23 (2005), pp. 65–87.

197. Jonathan J. Liebowitz, "Rural Support for Protection: Evidence from the Parliamentary Enquiry of 1884," *French History*, 7 (1993), pp. 163–82; O'Rourke, "The European Grain Invasion," pp. 783, 786, 798.

198. Lebovics, *The Alliance of Iron and Wheat*.

199. Stuart M. Persell, *The French Colonial Lobby, 1889–1938* (Stanford, 1983), ch. 4.

200. The following is a selection from a substantial literature: Henri Brunschwig, *Mythes et réalités de l'impérialisme colonial français* (Paris, 1960); C. M. Andrew and A. S. Kanya-Forstner, "The French 'Colonial Party': Its Composition, Aims and Influence, 1885–1914," *Historical Journal*, 14 (1971), pp. 99–128; L. Abrams and D. J. Miller, "Who Were the French Colonialists? A Reassessment of the *Parti Colonial*, 1890–1914," *Historical Journal*, 19 (1976), pp. 685–725; Persell, *The French Colonial Lobby*.

201. Persell, *The French Colonial Lobby*.

202. Alice, L. Conklin, *A Mission to Civilize: The Republican Idea of Empire in France and West Africa, 1895–1930* (Stanford, 1997), shows how the mission developed, as conquest gave way to control.

203. Hubert Bonin, Catherine Hodir, and Jean-François Klein, eds., *L'esprit économique impérial (1830–1970): Groupes de pression et réseaux du patronat colonial en France et dans l'empire* (Paris, 2008), present a huge collection of studies that display a variety of motives and outcomes.

204. John F. Laffey, "Municipal Imperialism in Nineteenth-Century France," *Historical Reflections*, 1 (1974), pp. 81–114; Jean-François Klein, "Réseaux d'influences et stratégie coloniale: le cas des marchands de soie Lyonnais en mer de Chine, 1843–1906," *Outre-Mers*, 93 (2005), pp. 221–56; Xavier Daumalin, "Commercial Presence, Colonial Penetration: Marseille Traders in West Africa in the Nineteenth Century," in Pétré-Grenouilleau, *From Slave Trade to Empire*, ch. 11; T. W. Roberts, "The Trans-Saharan Railway and the Politics of Imperial Expansion, 1890–1900," *Journal of Imperial & Commonwealth History*, 43 (2015), pp. 438–62.

205. Jacques Thobie, *Intérêts et impérialisme français dans l'Empire ottoman, 1895–1914* (Paris, 1977).

206. Stuart M. Persell, "The Parliamentary Career of Eugène Étienne, 1881–1914," *Proceedings of the Annual Meeting of the Western Society for French History*, 4 (1976), pp. 402–9.

207. François Manchuelle, "Origines républicaines de la politique d'expansion coloniale de Jules Ferry (1838–1865)," *Revue Française d'Histoire d'Outre-Mer*, 75 (1988), pp. 185–206.

208. Peter Grupp, "Gabriel Hanotaux: Le personage et ses idées sur l'expansion coloniale," *Revue Française d'Histoire d'Outre-Mer*, 58 (1971), pp. 383–405.

209. Jacques Marseille, *Empire colonial et capitalisme français: histoire d'un divorce* (Paris, 1984). The author achieved the rare feat of alienating critics on both the left and right of the political spectrum. Given that his book is one of the most important studies of the French Empire produced in the twentieth century, if not the most important, it is lamentable that it has never been translated into English.

210. "Iron and Rye" in the case of Germany. See Cornelius Torp, "The Coalition of 'Iron and Rye' under the Pressure of Globalization: A Reinterpretation of Germany's Political Economy before 1914," *Central European History*, 43 (2010), pp. 401–27. Germany has been excluded from consideration here simply for reasons of space. The point of departure from the older literature on the *Sonderweg* is David Blackbourn and Geoff Eley, *The Peculiarities of German History: Bourgeois Society and Politics in Nineteenth-Century Germany* (Oxford, 1984).

211. Richard Cobden, Speech, March 13, 1845. Quoted in Michael Lusztig, *Risking Free Trade: The Politics of Trade in Britain, Canada, Mexico and the United States* (Pittsburgh, 1996), p. 38.

212. Palen, *The "Conspiracy" of Free Trade*, pp. 149–52, 172–9, 221–2 for its influence on Canada, the United States, and Australia. For an illuminating case study, see Mark Metzler, "The Cosmopolitanism of National Economics: Friedrich List in a Japanese Mirror," in Hopkins, *Global History*, ch. 4.

213. Peter H. Lindert, "The Rise of Social Spending," *Explorations in Economic History*, 31 (1994), pp. 1–37.

214. Dincecco, *Political Transformations and Public Finances*, takes a more optimistic view of parliamentary supervision than, arguably, the historical record warrants.

215. Smith, *Wealth of Nations*, p. 900.

216. Bouda Etemad, *Possessing the World: Taking the Measurements of Colonisation from the Eighteenth to the Twentieth Century* (New York, 2007), p. 130.

217. Etemad, *Possessing the World*, pp. 130–32, 165. The proportion of land under colonial rule increased by about 45 percent between 1880 and 1913. Britain's nearest rival, France, held about 18 percent of the total in 1913, but ruled only about 9 percent of all colonial subjects.

218. Etemad, *Possessing the World*, p. 131.

219. Richard Cobden, *England, Ireland and America* (2nd ed. 1835), p. 101.

220. Whitman, "Years of the Modern." See n. 1.

CHAPTER 7: ACHIEVING EFFECTIVE INDEPENDENCE

1. Alexis de Tocqueville, *Democracy in America*, ed. Phillips Bradley (New York, 1947), Book 1, ch. 14, p. 252.

2. Ibid.

3. This perception prompted Byron Shafer and Anthony Badger to produce a volume of essays that endeavor to overcome the problem: *Contesting Democracy: Substance and Structure in American Political History, 1775-2000* (Lawrence, 2001). Richard F. Bensel's three volumes: *Sectionalism and American Political Development, 1880-1980* (Madison, 1984); *Yankee Leviathan: The Origins of Central State Authority in America, 1859-1877* (New York, 1991); *The Political Economy of American Industrialization, 1877-1900* (New York, 2000), should be mentioned here because historians have yet to give his considerable contributions the full credit they merit. Among many possible specialized examples, see Heather Cox Richardson's study of the rise of a middle class in *West From Appomattox: The Reconstruction of America after the Civil War* (New Haven, 2007).

4. Each with its own subcategories. See, for example, Richard Schneirov, "Thoughts on Periodizing the Gilded Age: Capital Accumulation, Society and Politics, 1873–1898," *Journal of the Gilded Age & Progressive Era*, 5 (2003), pp. 189–224. Rebecca Edwards, *New Spirits: Americans in the Gilded Age, 1865-1905* (New York, 2006), offers an imaginative thematic treatment that cuts across conventional chronological divisions but in doing so also makes it hard to see the coherence of the period as a whole, notwithstanding her suggested "long Progressive Era," p. 7.

5. As outlined in chapter 6 of this text.

6. Deflation, which was an international phenomenon, is discussed in the subsection of chapter 6 of this text titled "The Great Deflation."

7. James Bryce, *The American Commonwealth*, 2 (London, 1888; 1941 ed.), p. 699.

8. Bensel, *Political Economy*, pp. 357–66, provides more details.

9. Gary Gerstle, *Liberty and Coercion: The Paradox of American Government* (Princeton, 2015), chs. 3–5.

10. Eric Rauchway, "William McKinley and Us," *Journal of the Gilded Age & Progressive Era*, 4 (2005), pp. 234–53, discusses the extent to which the election of 1896 brought about an enduring Republican realignment.

11. Gregory P. Downs, *After Appomattox: Military Occupation and the Ends of War* (Cambridge, MA, 2015), provides the most systematic account that also stresses the protracted nature of the transition from war to peace.

12. Heather Cox, *The Death of Reconstruction: Race, Labour and Politics in the Post-Civil War North, 1865–1901* (Cambridge, MA, 2001), emphasizes the importance of free labor in Northern attitudes and policies.

13. The Klan was founded by Confederate veterans in Tennessee in 1865. Elaine Frantz Parsons explores its theatricality in "Midnight Rangers: Costume and Performance in the Reconstruction-Era Ku Klux Klan," *Journal of American History*, 92 (2005), pp. 811–36.

14. James C. Hogue, *Uncivil War: Five New Orleans Street Battles and the Rise and Fall of Reconstruction* (Baton Rouge, 2006). Nicholls (1834–1912) was governor in 1876–80 and 1888–92.

15. The standard treatment is Eric Foner, *Reconstruction: America's Unfinished Revolution, 1863–1877* (New York, 1989).

16. Vincent P. de Santis, "Rutherford B. Hayes and the Removal of the Troops and the End of Reconstruction," in Morgan Kousser and James McPherson, eds., *Region, Race, and Reconstruction* (New York, 1982), pp. 417–50.

17. On the Northern stake in Southern cotton, see Harold D. Woodman, *King Cotton and His Retainers: Financing and Marketing the Cotton Crop of the South, 1800–1925* (Columbia, 1990); Gene Dattel, *Cotton and Race in the Making of America: The Human Costs of Economic Power* (Chicago, 2009), ch. 23.

18. Elizabeth Lee Thompson shows how the Bankruptcy Act of 1867 helped to stabilize Southern business interests and thus to hamper reform in the region: *The Reconstruction of Southern Debtors: Bankruptcy after the Civil War* (Athens, 2004).

19. I am indebted here to Nicolas Barreyre, *Gold and Reconstruction: The Political Economy of Reconstruction* (Charlottesville, 2016).

20. Richardson, *West from Appomattox*.

21. This is one of the principal themes of Barreyre's stimulating study, *Gold and Reconstruction*.

22. Gregory P. Downs, *Declarations of Dependence: The Long Reconstruction of Popular Politics in the South, 1861–1908* (Chapel Hill, 2011). Downs uses the term "patronalism" and draws his evidence from North Carolina. The anthropological term Big Men, originally put into circulation by Marshall Sahlins, is an alternative worth pursuing in this context.

23. Desmond King and Stephen Tuck, "De-Centering the South: America's Nationwide White Supremacist Order after Reconstruction," *Past & Present*, 194 (2007), pp. 213–52.

24. Credit should go to John Cell for his pioneering comparative study, *The Highest Stage of White Supremacy: The Origins of Segregation in South Africa and the American South* (Cambridge, 1982).

25. Hogue, *Uncivil War*, compares the South to the republics of Latin America.

26. Frank Ninkovich has drawn attention to the extent to which elites in the Northeast were attuned to the outside world and drew on liberal assumptions: *Global Dawn: The Cultural Foundations of American Internationalism, 1865–1890* (Cambridge, MA, 2009). Nevertheless, liberals could also be racists, and the racial component in Anglo-Saxon thinking remained dominant.

27. Edward L. Ayers, *The Promise of the New South: Life After Reconstruction* (New York, 1992), shows that segregation in the South was constructed in the 1880s and 1890s and not simply inherited from the prewar era.

28. Edward J. Blum, *Reforging the White Republic: Race, Religion, and American Nationalism, 1865–1898* (Baton Rouge, 2005).

29. Nina Silber, *The Romance of Reunion: Northerners and the South, 1865–1900* (Chapel Hill, 1993); David Blight, *Race and Reunion: The Civil War in American Memory* (Cambridge, MA, 2001); Caroline E. Janney, *Remembering the Civil War: Reunion and the Limits of Reconstruction* (Chapel Hill, 2013).

30. As discussed in chapter 6 of this text. Douglas Steeples and David O. Whitten, *Democracy in Desperation: The Depression of 1893* (Westport, 1999), provides a guide to the relevant literature on the United States.

31. Marc-William Palen, *The "Conspiracy" of Free Trade: The Anglo-American Struggle over Empire and Economic Globalisation, 1846–1896* (Cambridge, 2016), ch. 4. I should like to record a wider debt to Palen's work, which clarified important features of the politics of bimetallism and the issue of the tariff that had eluded me.

32. Bryce, *American Commonwealth*, 2, has extensive information on these subjects in chs. 53–75.

33. *The "Conspiracy" of Free Trade*, chs. 4–5.

34. Peter Trubowitz, *Defining the National Interest: Conflict and Change in American Foreign Policy* (Chicago, 1998), is especially illuminating on this subject. See also Bensel, *Political Economy*, chs. 3, 7. Marc-William Palen, "The Civil War's Forgotten Transatlantic Tariff Debate and the Confederacy's Diplomacy of Free Trade," *Journal of the Civil War Era*, 3 (2013), pp. 35–61, explores the diplomatic consequences of the tariff.

35. The Republicans also had a Cobdenite lobby and were not fully converted to protection until the 1880s. Palen, *The "Conspiracy" of Free Trade*, chs. 3–4.

36. Under the Bland-Alison Act (1878), the Treasury was obliged to buy silver and turn it into coin. The Act may have won votes but it became a "cross of silver" that burdened the federal budget.

37. Elmus Wicker, *Banking Panics of the Gilded Age* (Cambridge, 2000), ch. 2.

38. As during the crisis of 1873, when the demonetization of silver, combined with a major banking crisis, caused silver prices to fall and the decline in farm prices to accelerate. The Greenback Party urged the federal government to safeguard the interests of debtors and workers, but received an imperfect response in the Bland-Alison Act. Matthew Hild, *Greenbackers, Knights of Labor, and Populists: Farmer-Labor Insurgency in the Late-Nineteenth-Century South* (Athens, 2007), emphasizes the considerable degree of cooperation between farmers and laborers in Alabama, Arkansas, and Texas.

39. Palen, *The "Conspiracy" of Free Trade*. Support for free trade among Democrats hardened after the election of 1888: Joanne Reitano, *The Tariff Question in the Gilded Age: The Great Debate of 1888* (University Park, 1994).

40. Bensel, *Political Economy*, pp. 191–2.

41. Gretchen Ritter, *Goldbugs and Greenbacks: The Antimonopoly Tradition and the Politics of Finance in America, 1865–1896* (New York, 1997), ch. 5, emphasizes the strength of the bimetallist case. Jeffrey A. Frieden argues that the main aim of the "silverites" was to raise output prices by devaluing the currency rather than to secure debt relief: "Monetary Populism in Nineteenth-Century America: An Open Economy Interpretation," *Journal of Economic History*, 57 (1997), pp. 367–95.

42. Palen, *The "Conspiracy" of Free Trade*, ch. 5, and numerous index references.

43. Ibid., chs. 7–8. On the theory that a high tariff would reduce imports, see Douglas A. Irwin, "Higher Tariffs, Lower Revenues? Analyzing the Fiscal Aspects of the Great Tariff Debate of 1888," *Journal of Economic History*, 58 (1998), pp. 59–72. The surplus also created technical complexities in administering the bond market and managing the money supply. See Taussig, "The McKinley Tariff," p. 344.

44. William McAdoo, an Irish-born New Jersey Congressman: *Washington Post*, May 9, 1888. Quoted in Marc-William Palen, "Foreign Relations in the Gilded Age: A British Free-Trade Conspiracy?" *Diplomatic History*, 37 (2013), p. 236. Joanne Reitano traces the ideological issues of the 1888 campaign in *The Tariff Debate*.

45. Palen, "Foreign Relations in the Gilded Age," p. 239.

46. The Democrats had refused to introduce a similar proposal in 1887. Patrick J. Kelly, *Creating a National Home: Building the Veterans' Welfare State, 1860–1900* (Cambridge, MA, 1997), provides a fascinating account of a subject that military historians are inclined to overlook: the hazards that faced veterans after the war ended.

47. William H. Glasson, "The National Pension System as Applied to the Civil War and the War with Spain," *Annals of the American Academic of Political and Social Science*, 19 (1902), pp. 204–26.

48. Ibid., p. 214. In defending free trade, John Bright alleged that protection, by producing a "large surplus revenue," had promoted "a system of corruption unequalled in any other country." Quoted in *New York Times*, May 15, 1887.

49. See F. W. Taussig, "The McKinley Tariff Act," *Economic Journal*, 1 (1891), p. 326; Thomas E. Terrill, *The Tariff, Politics, and American Foreign Policy, 1874–1901* (Westport, 1973); Edward P. Crapol, *America for Americans: Economic Nationalism and Anglophobia in the Late Nineteenth Century* (Westport, 1973); and the penetrating review by Lewis L. Gould, "Tariffs and Markets in the Gilded Age," *Reviews in American History*, 2 (1974), pp. 266–71. Also Paul Wolman, *Most Favored Nation: The Republican Revisionists and U.S. Tariff Policy, 1897–1912* (Chapel Hill, 1992).

50. Palen, *The "Conspiracy" of Free Trade*, p. 213.

51. W. E. Gladstone et al., *Both Sides of the Tariff Question by the World's Leading Men* (New York, 1890), pp. 64, 72.

52. Ibid.

53. Ibid.

54. *Times*, February 14, 1891.

55. A speech delivered in 1891: William McKinley, *Speeches and Addresses* (New York, 1893), p. 562.

56. The international dimensions of the long deflation are dealt with in the section of chapter 6 of this text titled "The Great Deflation." The effect on living standards is complicated. See Jeremy Atack, Fred Bateman, and William N. Parker, "The Farm, the Farmer and the Market," in Engerman and Gallman, *Cambridge Economic History*, 2, pp. 280–82. Real wages for non-farm workers fell for periods in the last quarter of the century, partly because immigration increased the labor supply: Robert A. Margo, "The Labor Force in the Nineteenth Century," in Engerman and Gallman, *Cambridge Economic History*, 2, p. 223. See also Robert A. McGuire's study of 16 Northern states: "Economic Causes of Late Nineteenth-Century Unrest: New Evidence," *Journal of Economic History*, 41 (1981), pp. 835–52 (and the subsequent discussion); Ayers, *The Promise of the New South*, ch. 10, shows that populism in the South was bound up not only with racism, but also with conflicts arising out of postwar socioeconomic change.

57. There has been little sustained research on this subject since the 1960s. Thomas A. Wood, *Knights of the Plow: Oliver H. Kelley and the Origins of the Grange in Republican Ideology* (Ames, 1991), leaves room for a synthesis of the material aspects of the movement, which are broadly covered by Robert C. McMath, *American Populism: A Social History, 1877–1898* (New York, 1993).

58. Robert C. McMath, *Populist Vanguard: A History of the Southern Farmers' Alliance* (Chapel Hill, 1975); McMath, *American Populism*, chs. 1–4.

59. George W. Hilton, "The Consistency of the Interstate Commerce Act," *Journal of Law & Economics*, 9 (1966), pp. 87–113.

60. Kim Voss, *The Making of American Exceptionalism: The Knights of Labor and Class Formation in the Nineteenth Century* (Ithaca, 1994).

61. Robert E. Weir, *Beyond Labor's Veil: The Culture of the Knights of Labor* (University Park, 1996), examines the ideological and cultural features of the "fraternal lodges."

62. Daniel R. Ernst, "Free Labor, the Consumer Interest, and the Law of Industrial Disputes, 1885–1900," *American Journal of Legal History*, 36 (1992), pp. 19–37; Voss, *The Making*

of American Exceptionalism; Jason Kaufman, "Rise and Fall of a Nation of Joiners: The Knights of Labor Revisited," *Journal of Interdisciplinary History*, 31 (2001), pp. 553–79.

63. Julie Green, *Pure and Simple Politics: The American Federation of Labor and Political Activism, 1881–1914* (New York, 1998).

64. Victoria C. Hattam, *Labor Visions and State Power: The Origins of Business Unionism in the United States* (Princeton, NJ, 1993). The central point was made by Gerald N. Grob, "The Knights of Labor and the Trade Unions, 1878–1886," *Journal of Economic History*, 18 (1958), pp. 176–92.

65. Helga Kristin Hallgrimsdottir and Cecilia Benoit, "From Wage Slaves to Wage Workers: Cultural Opportunity Structures and the Evolution of Wage Demands of the Knights of Labor and the American Federation of Labor, 1880–1900," *Social Forces*, 85 (2007), pp. 1393–1411.

66. L. Glen Seretan, *Daniel DeLeon: The Odyssey of an American Marxist* (Cambridge, MA, 1979), retains its value, though bearing the mark of the psycho-history of the time.

67. The labor organizations had strong, visible international connections: Neville Kirk, "Peculiarities and Exceptions: The Shaping of the American Federation of Labor's Politics during the 1880s and 1890s," *International Review of Social History*, 45 (2000), pp. 25–50; Steven Parfitt, "Brotherhood from a Distance: Americanization and the Internationalism of the Knights of Labor," *International Review of Social History*, 58 (2013), pp. 463–91.

68. Samuel Gompers, the leader of the AFL, was unwilling to subordinate the labor movement to a political party; leaders of the important mining and railway unions took a different view.

69. McMath, *American Populism*; Joseph Gerteis, *Class and the Color Line: Interracial Class Coalition in the Knights of Labor and the Populist Movement* (Durham, 2007); Charles Postel, *The Populist Vision* (New York, 2007), stresses the diversity of support, which drew on towns as well as rural areas, and featured women in particular.

70. I have amalgamated, with apologies, the illuminating but rather different approaches of: Margaret Canovan, *Populism* (New York, 1981); Paul Taggart, *Populism* (Buckingham, 2000); Yves Meny and Yves Suri, eds., *Democracies and the Populist Challenge* (New York, 2001); Cas Mudde, "The Populist Zeitgeist," *Government and Opposition*, 39 (2004), pp. 542–63.

71. As Ronald P. Formisano, almost single-handedly, has argued: *For the People: American Populist Movements from the Revolution to the 1850s* (Chapel Hill, 2007). On the "green revolution," see chapter 4 of this text.

72. Postel, *The Populist Vision*, draws together the literature correcting Hofstadter's claim that the Populists were hankering after a golden age of rural harmony.

73. Elizabeth Sanders, *Roots of Reform: Farmers, Workers, and the American State, 1877–1917* (Chicago, 1999).

74. Steeples and Whitten, *Democracy in Desperation*, pp. 445, 59–60. See, for one example, P. Cudmore's outspoken indictment, *Cleveland's Administration: Free Trade, Protection and Reciprocity* (New York, 1896).

75. The fullest and most recent survey is Steeples and Whitten, *Democracy in Desperation*; also Hugh Rokoff, "Banking and Finance," in Engerman and Gallman, *Cambridge Economic History*, 2, ch. 14; Clifford F. Thies relates political events to the bond market in "Gold Bonds and Silver Agitation," *Quarterly Journal of Austrian Economics*, 8 (2005), pp. 67–86.

76. Michael D. Bordo, "Sudden Stops, Financial Crises and Original Sin in Emerging Countries: Deja Vu?" Paper prepared for the Conference on Global Imbalances and Risk Management (Madrid, 2006); Luis Catao, "Sudden Stops and Currency Drops: A Historical Look," in Sebastian Edwards et al., *The Decline of Latin America: Economies, Institutions and Crises* (Chicago, 2007), pp. 243–90.

77. P. J. Cain and A. G. Hopkins, *British Imperialism, 1688–2015* (London, 3rd ed., 2016), pp. 125–6, 139–41, 145–8, 216–28. The Argentine crisis also spread to Brazil: Gail D. Triner and Kirsten Wandschneider, "The Baring Crisis and the Brazilian *Encilhamento*, 1889–1891," *Financial History Review*, 12 (2005), pp. 199–225.

78. Robert E. Lipsey, "U.S. Foreign Trade and the Balance of Payments, 1800–1913," in Engerman and Gallman, *Cambridge Economic History*, 2, p. 698.

79. The McKinley Tariff had succeeded in reducing revenues; the Sherman Silver Act (1890) had committed the Treasury to buying even more silver than under the Bland-Allison Act (1878) as a means of securing the loyalty of five "silver states" that had just joined the Union. See François R. Velde, "Following the Yellow Brick Road: How the United States Adopted the Gold Standard," *Federal Reserve Bank of Chicago Economic Perspectives*, (April, 2002), pp. 42–58.

80. The links between these events, which I am obliged to run together, are carefully worked out by Wicker, *Banking Panics*, ch. 4.

81. Steeples and Whitten, *Democracy in Desperation*, ch. 4. No fewer than 160 banks had failed by the end of 1893. Charles W. Calomiris, "Greenback Resumption and Silver Risk: The Economics and Politics of Monetary Regime Change in the United States, 1862–1900," NBER Working Paper, 4166 (1992), emphasizes the concern about short-run convertibility rather than the risk of an immediate switch from gold to silver.

82. Lawrence H. Officer, "The Remarkable Efficiency of the Dollar-Sterling Gold Standard, 1890–1906," *Journal of Economic History*, 49 (1989), pp. 24–5.

83. Palen, "Foreign Relations in the Gilden Age," pp. 240–41.

84. The assassination of President James Garfield in 1881 is not included here because he was shot by a disappointed office-seeker, not by an agent of political revolution.

85. Troy Rondinone, "'History Repeats Itself': The Civil War and the Meaning of Labor Conflict in the Late Nineteenth Century," *American Quarterly*, 59 (2007), pp. 397–419. For a more extended account of this subject, see Rondinone, *The Great Industrial War: Framing Class Conflict in the Media, 1865–1950* (New Brunswick, 2010).

86. James Green, "The Globalization of a Memory: The Enduring Remembrance of the Haymarket Martyrs Around the World," *Labor: Studies in the Working Class History of the Americas*, 2 (2005), pp. 11–23.

87. Susan B. Carter, Richard Sutch, and Stanley Lebergott, "The Great Depression of the 1890s: New Suggestive Estimates of the Unemployment Rate, 1890–1905," *Research in Economic History*, 14 (1992), pp. 347–76.

88. Paul Krause, *The Battle for Homestead, 1880–1892* (Pittsburgh, 1992).

89. The starting point is now Richard Schneirov, Shelton Stromquist, and Nick Salvatore, eds., *The Pullman Strike and the Crisis of the 1890s: Essays on Labor and Politics* (Chicago, 1999).

90. This paragraph rests on Rondinone, "History Repeats Itself"; Rondinone, "Guarding the Switch: Cultivating Nationalism during the Pullman Strike," *Journal of the Gilded Age and Progressive Era*, 8 (2009), pp. 83–109; Rondinone, *The Great Industrial War*.

91. Quoted in Rondinone, "Guarding the Switch," p. 108.

92. *Harper's Weekly*, quoted in ibid., p. 87.

93. M. J. Sewell, "Rebels or Revolutionaries? Irish-American Nationalism and American Diplomacy, 1865–1885," *Historical Journal*, 29 (1986), pp. 723–33.

94. Rondinone, "Guarding the Switch," p. 271.

95. Ibid., p. 265.

96. Ibid., p. 269. The reference, for those who recognized it, was to the Paris commune of 1871.

97. The quotations are from Michael McGerr, *A Fierce Discontent: The Rise and Fall of the Progressive Movement in America, 1870–1920* (New York, 2003), p. 176; and William Jennings Bryan and Mary Baird Bryan, *Speeches of William Jennings Bryan* (New York, 1909), vol. 2, p. 342. Bryan had no conception of class struggle. He was a Victorian indi-

vidualist who believed in the uplifting power of religion and the political efficacy of what he termed "The Democracy." See Michael Kazin, *A Godly Hero: The Life of William Jennings Bryan* (New York, 2006); and Richard F. Bensel, *Passion and Preference: William Jennings Bryan and the 1896 Democratic National Convention* (Cambridge, 2008).

98. The status of the election of 1896 as a turning point has been questioned, but on narrow grounds that do not disturb the broad argument stated here. The references are given in Rauchway, "William McKinley and Us," pp. 234–53, notes 31, 32.

99. David Nasaw, "Gilded Age Gospels," in Steve Fraser and Gary Gerstle, eds., *Ruling America: A History of Wealth and Power in a Democracy* (Cambridge, MA, 2005), pp. 146–8; Alan Dawley, "The Abortive Rule of Big Money," in Fraser and Gerstle, *Ruling America*, pp. 149–58; Howell John Harris, "The Making of a 'Business Community,' 1880–1930: Definitions and Ingredients of a Collective Identity," *European Contributions to American Studies*, 47 (2000), pp. 123–39.

100. Anti-trust legislation prevented the development of cartels of the kind found, for example, in Germany, but in doing so encouraged firms in the United States to consolidate, thus assisting the rise of large corporations. David Brian Roberston, *Capital, Labor and State: The Battle for American Labor Markets from the Civil War to the New Deal* (Lanham, 2000), emphasizes the power and success of corporations in dealing with the labor movement in the early 1900s.

101. The NAM is an understudied organization. There is one dated book: Albert K. Steigerwalt, *The National Association of Manufacturers, 1895–1914: A Study in Business Leadership* (East Lansing, 1964). See also Philip H. Burch, "The NAM as an Interest Group," *Politics and Society*, 4 (1973), pp. 97–30; Cathie Jo Martin, "Sectional Parties, Divided Business," *Studies in American Political Development*, 20 (2006), pp. 160–84.

102. James J. Hill, a railroad magnate and Democrat who supported Cleveland's pro-gold policy. See Patrick J. Kelly, "The Election of 1896 and the Restructuring of Civil War Memory," *Civil War History*, 49 (2003), pp. 260–61, Chandler D. Aaron, "A Short Note on the Expenditures of the McKinley Campaign of 1898," *Presidential Studies Quarterly*, 28 (1998), pp. 88–91.

103. Kelly, "Election of 1896," p. 261.

104. Luzviminda B. Francisco and Jonathan S. Fast, *Conspiracy for Empire: Big Business, Corruption, and the Politics of Imperialism in America, 1876–1907* (Quezon City, 1985), pp. 67, 151. It is telling that Havemeyer, who was the largest single donor to both major parties in 1892, gave all his support to the Republicans in 1896.

105. Matthew Simon, "The Hot Money Movement and the Private Exchange Pool Proposal of 1896," *Journal of Economic History*, 20 (1960), pp. 31–50, quoting the *New York Herald*, June 27, 1896, pp. 47–8; Bensel, *Political Economy*, ch. 6. Barry Eichengreen shows that informal cooperation among American and European banks was vital to the working of the gold standard at this time: "Central Bank Co-operation and Exchange Rate Commitments: The Classical and Interwar Gold Standards Compared," *Financial History Review*, 2 (1995), pp. 99–117.

106. As it did in the dominions too: Cain and Hopkins, *British Imperialism*, ch. 8.

107. Harvey Gresham Hudspeth, "The Rise and Fall of the 'Greene' Doctrine: The Sherman Act, Howell Jackson, and the Interpretation of 'Interstate Commerce,' 1890–1941," *Essays in Economic & Business History*, 20 (2002), pp. 97–112; Hattam, *Labor Visions and State Power*, shows how judges used the concept of criminal conspiracy to prevent trade unions from expanding their power. In Britain, the law provided greater protection for trade unions. The legal complexities of the Act and subsequent judicial rulings defy easy generalization. See Peter C. Carstensen, "Dubious Dichotomies and Blurred Vistas: The Corporate Reconstruction of American Capitalism," *Reviews in American History*, 17 (1989), pp. 404–11.

108. The following two paragraphs owe a great deal to Kelly's important article: "The Election of 1896." There is no full, modern study of Hanna (1837–1904). A recent account

cautions against overestimating his influence during this period. See the extensive index entries in Richard F. Hamilton, *President McKinley, War and Empire*, 2 vols. (New Brunswick, 2006, 2007). Hanna's role in the election of 1896 is dealt with in ibid., vol. 1, ch. 2.

109. Kelly, "Election of 1896," p. 259, and pp. 260–61.

110. Ibid. p. 255, quoting Republican Senator William Chandler.

111. Steeples and Whitten, *Democracy in Desperation*, ch. 5.

112. Myron T. Herrick, "The Panic of 1907 and Some of Its Lessons," *Annals of the American Academy of Political and Social Science*, 31 (1908), p. 11. Herrick was Chairman of the Board Society for Savings, Cleveland, Ohio.

113. Susan B. Carter and Richard Sutch, "The Great Depression of the 1890s: New Suggestive Estimates of the Unemployment Rate, 1890–1905," *Research in Economic History*, 14 (1992), pp. 347–76.

114. Eric Rauchway, *Murdering McKinley: The Making of Theodore Roosevelt's America* (New York, 2003). Czolgosz, the son of Polish-Russian immigrants, was inspired partly by Gaetano Bresci, an Italian immigrant who returned to Italy in 1900 to assassinate the ultra-conservative King Umberto I.

115. Julie Greene, *Pure and Simple Politics: The American Federation of Labor and Political Activism, 1881–1917* (New York, 1998); Elizabeth Sanders, *Roots of Reform: Farmers, Workers, and the American State, 1877–1917* (Chicago, 1999).

116. Progressives included intellectuals and artisans, yeomen and townsmen, and secular and spiritual sources of inspiration. See Rodgers, *Atlantic Crossings;* Elizabeth Sanders, *Peasants, Pitchforks, and the (Found) Promise of Progressivism* (Chicago, 1999); Robert D. Johnston, *The Radical Middle Class: Populist Democracy and the Question of Capitalism in Progressive Era Portland, Oregon* (Princeton, NJ, 2003).

117. James T. Kloppenberg, *Uncertain Victory: Social Democracy and Progressivism in European and American Political Thought* (Oxford, 1986); Michael McGerr, *A Fierce Discontent: The Rise and Fall of the Progressive Movement in America, 1870–1920* (New York, 2003); Thomas F. Jorsch, "Modernized Republicanism: The Radical Agenda of Socialists in Manitowoc, Wisconsin, 1905–1917," *Historian*, 70 (2008), pp. 716–31, places the battle between the representatives of capital and labor in the context of the debate over classical republicanism.

118. Jerry M. Mashaw, "Federal Administration and Administrative Law in the Golden Age," *Yale Law Journal*, 119 (2010), pp. 1362–72; Eldon J. Eisenach, *The Lost Promise of Progressivism* (Lawrence, 1994).

119. The messianic element in Progressivism is brought out by Alan Dawley, *Changing the World: American Progressives in War and Revolution* (Princeton, NJ, 2003).

120. Quoted in Matthew Josephson, *The Robber Barons: The Great American Capitalists, 1861–1901* (New Brunswick, 1934; 2011), p. 448.

121. The principal arm of the department was the Bureau of Corporations, which joined the Federal Trade Commission in 1915: William Murphey, "Theodore Roosevelt and the Bureau of Corporations: Executive-Corporate Cooperation and the Advancement of the Regulatory State," *American Nineteenth-Century History*, 14 (2013), pp. 73–111; Jonathan Chausovsky, "From Bureau to Trade Commission: Agency Reputation in the State-Building Enterprise," *Journal of the Gilded Age and Progressive Era*, 12 (2013), pp. 343–78.

122. See also Bruce Bringhurst, *Antitrust and the Oil Monopoly: The Standard Oil Cases, 1890–1911* (Westport, 1979); Richard Sylla, "Experimental Federalism: The Economics of American Government, 1789–1914," in Engerman and Gallman, *Cambridge Economic History*, 2, p. 540.

123. Robert Griffith, "Dwight D. Eisenhower and the Corporate Commonwealth," *American Historical Review*, 87 (1982), pp. 87–122.

124. Jane Addams, *Twenty Years at Hull House* (New York, 1910; 1938), pp. 409–10. Toynbee Hall, named after the historian, was founded in 1884, and Hull House in Chicago in 1889.

125. Among several biographies, see Louise W. Knight, *Citizen: Jane Addams and the Struggle for Democracy* (Chicago, 2005); Knight, *Jane Addams: Spirit in Action* (New York, 2005).

126. Bryce, *The American Commonwealth*, 2, p. 699.

127. Ari Hoogenboom, *Outlawing the Spoils: A History of the Civil Service Reform Movement, 1865–1883* (Urbana, 1961); Ronald N. Johnson and Gary D. Libecap, *The Federal Civil Service System and the Problem of Bureaucracy: The Economics and Politics of Institutional Change* (Chicago, 1994); Daniel P. Carpenter, *The Forging of Bureaucratic Autonomy: Networks, Reputations, and Policy Innovation in Executive Agencies, 1862–1928* (Princeton, 2001); Sean M. Theriault, "Patronage, the Pendleton Act, and the Power of the People," *Journal of Politics*, 65 (2003), pp. 50–68, emphasizes the impact of public pressure in passing the Act in 1883.

128. Emily Rosenberg, *Spreading the American Dream: American Economic and Cultural Expansion, 1890–1945* (New York, 1982), ch. 3.

129. Stephen Skowronek, *Building a New American State: The Expansion of National Administrative Capacities, 1877–1920* (New York, 1982); Bensel, *Yankee Leviathan*; Brian Balogh, *A Government Out of Sight: The Mystery of National Authority in Nineteenth-Century America* (Cambridge, 2009), chs. 7–8; Morton Keller, *Regulating a New Economy: Public Policy and Economic Change in America, 1900–1933* (Cambridge, MA, 1990).

130. Twain and Warner, *The Gilded Age*, p. 193.

131. Michael G. Mulhall, "The Growth of American Industries and Wealth," in Josiah Strong, *The United States and the Future of the Anglo-Saxon Race* (London, 1889), p. 57.

132. Peter H. Lindert and Jeffrey Williamson, *Unequal Gains: American Growth and Inequality Since 1700* (Princeton, NJ, 2016), ch. 7.

133. Heather Cox Richardson provides a lucid account in *The Greatest Nation on Earth: Republican Economic Policies during the Civil War* (Cambridge, MA, 1997).

134. The Homestead Act (1862) had symbolic as well as practical importance in demonstrating the supremacy of the "Northern System" of free, wage-labor over slavery. The Act had far-reaching consequences for the pattern of development in the Western states: by 1900 more than 80 million acres had been given away to about 600,000 households.

135. Richard R. John, "Ruling Passions: Political Economy in Nineteenth-Century America," *Journal of Policy History*, 18 (2006), pp. 2, 10.

136. Generally speaking, foreign investors had kept clear of the United States during the Civil War. The French firm of Emile Erlanger raised one small foreign loan (for the Confederacy) in 1863. Sexton, *Debtor Diplomacy*, pp. 164–74.

137. The controversy over the interpretation advanced by the "Progressive" historians, Charles and Mary Beard, is summarized and assessed by Roger L. Ransom, "Fact and Counterfact: The 'Second American Revolution' Revisited," *Civil War History*, 45 (1999), pp. 28–60.

138. As Roger L. Ransom and Richard Sutch argue persuasively in "Conflicting Visions: The American Civil War as a Revolutionary Event," *Research in Economic History*, 20 (2001), pp. 249–301.

139. Gallman, "Economic Growth and Structural Change," pp. 21–3, 30–33, 49–50. GDP measures incomes within a country; GNP adds net income from foreign sources.

140. Richard B. Duboff, "The Telegraph and the Structure of Markets in the United States, 1845–1890," *Research in Economic History*, 8 (1982), pp. 253–77; David M. Henkin, *The Postal Age: The Emergence of Modern Communications in Nineteenth-Century America* (Chicago, 2006).

141. Stephen Broadberry and Kevin O'Rourke, eds., *The Cambridge Economic History of Europe*, 2 (Cambridge, 2010), pp. 23, 30–33.

142. Ibid., pp. 33, 39.

143. This paragraph, like many others in this section, rests heavily on Engerman and Gallman's indispensable *Economic History of the United States*, especially Lipsey, "U.S. Foreign Trade"; Gallman, "Economic Growth and Structural Change."

144. Gene Dattel, *Cotton and Race in the Making of America* (Chicago, 2009), chs. 17–19; Bensel, *Political Economy*, ch. 2.

145. Heather Cox Richardson, "A Marshall Plan for the South? The Failure of Republican and Democrat Ideology during Reconstruction," *Civil War History*, 51 (2005), pp. 378–87.

146. Joseph P. Reidy, *From Slavery to Agrarian Capitalism in the Cotton South: Central Georgia, 1800–1880* (Chapel Hill, 1992).

147. David L. Carlton and Peter A. Coclanis, *The South, the Nation, and the World: Perspectives on Southern Development* (Charlottesville, 2003); Douglas A. Blackmon, *Slavery by Another Name: The Enslavement of Black Americans from the Civil War to World War II* (New York, 2008), deals mainly with Georgia and Alabama but shows that U.S. Steel also used convict labor.

148. Gallman, "Economic Growth and Structural Change," p. 54; Lindert and Williamson, *Unequal Gains*, p. 147.

149. Gavin Wright, *Old South, New South: Revolutions in the Southern Economy since the Civil War* (New York, 1986); Carlton and Coclanis, *The South, the Nation and the World*.

150. Lipsey, "U.S. Foreign Trade."

151. The high price-elasticity of demand in Europe also meant that output could expand without causing a reduction in the prices paid to producers.

152. Joseph H. Davis, Christopher Hanes, and Paul W. Rhode, "Harvest and Business Cycles in Nineteenth-Century America," National Bureau of Economic Research, *Working Paper*, 14686 (2009), explain why these effects were linked to cotton in particular rather than to wheat or corn.

153. Stanley Engerman and Kenneth Sokoloff, "Technology and Industrialization, 1790–1914," in Engerman and Gallman, *Economic History*, p. 381.

154. Lewis, *Growth and Fluctuations*, p. 60; Douglas A. Irwin, "Explaining America's Surge in Manufactured Exports, 1880–1913," *Review of Economics and Statistics*, 85 (2003), pp. 364–76, confirms Gavin Wright's argument that the impressive performance can be attributed primarily to an abundance of natural resources.

155. Lipsey, "U. S. Foreign Trade," p. 703.

156. Ibid.

157. David E. Novack and Matthew Simon, "Commercial Responses to the American Import Invasion, 1871–1914: An Essay in Attitudinal History," *Explorations in Entrepreneurial History*, 3 (1966), pp. 121–47.

158. Engerman and Sokoloff, "Technology and Industrialization," p. 399; Edmund Rogers, "The United States and the Fiscal Debate in Britain, 1873–1913," *Historical Journal*, 50 (2007), pp. 593–622.

159. Rockoff, "Banking and Finance"; Lipsey, "U.S. Foreign Trade"; Davis and Cull, "International Capital Movements."

160. Lance E. Davis and Robert J. Cull, *International Capital Markets and American Economic Growth, 1820–1914* (New York, 1994).

161. Davis, "Late Nineteenth-Century British Imperialism," pp. 86–8.

162. As had been the case since the rise of the steamship in the 1840s. See "Ocean Steam Navigation," *North American Review*, 99 (1864), pp. 483–523.

163. The long-run trend, however, was for Britain's share to fall. The country supplied 90 percent of all foreign capital in the 1860s, 75 percent in the 1890s, and 60 percent by 1914. Davis and Gull, "International Capital Movements," pp. 746–8.

164. For different views of the success of this quasi-central bank, See Wicker, *Banking Panics*; John A. James and David F. Weiman, "The National Banking Acts and the Transformation of New York City Banking during the Civil War Era," *Journal of Economic History*, 71 (2011), pp. 338–62; John R. Moen and Ellis W. Tallman, "Liquidity Creation without a Central Bank: Clearing House Loan Certificates in the Banking Panic of 1907," *Journal of Financial Stability*, 8 (2012), pp. 277–91.

165. Bensel, *Political Economy*, p. 77; Cain and Hopkins, *British Imperialism*, chs. 3–7.

166. Morgan's syndicate provided a total of $65 million in gold to back a bond issue and restore the Treasury's reserve to the level needed to meet the requirements of the gold standard.

167. Jeremy J. Siegel, "The Real Rate of Interest from 1800–1990: A Study of the U.S. and the UK," *Journal of Monetary Economics*, 29 (1992), pp. 227–52, especially figs. 1–5. A standard of living (consumer price) index is available for the period after 1850.

168. Lawrence Officer, *Between the Dollar-Sterling Gold Points: Rates, Parity, and Market Behaviour* (Cambridge, 1996).

169. The United States was effectively on a bimetallic standard between 1792 and 1862, when an inconvertible fiat currency (Greenbacks) was issued during the Civil War and withdrawn in 1879. Velde, "Following the Yellow Brick Road," provides a succinct account.

170. J. Lawrence Broz, "The Origins of the Federal Reserve System: International Incentives and the Domestic Free-Rider Problem," *International Organization*, 53 (1999), pp. 39–70.

171. Michael D. Bordo and Hugh Rockoff, "The Gold Standard as a 'Good Housekeeping Seal of Approval,'" *Journal of Economic History*, 56 (1996), pp. 389–428. President Harrison, however, favored bimetallism, which remained an official option for Republicans until 1892.

172. Bensel, *Political Economy*, pp. 85–6; Davis and Cull, "International Capital Movements," pp. 750–55, list examples of British influence.

173. This issue is discussed by Davis and Cull, *International Capital Markets*, ch. 3.

174. Jay Sexton, *Debtor Diplomacy: Finance and American Diplomacy in the Civil War Era, 1848-1877* (Oxford, 2005), pp. 251–2.

175. Charles Dow founded the *Wall Street Journal* in 1889 to cater to the growing needs of the financial community and devised the Dow-Jones index shortly afterward.

176. Kathleen Burk, "Finance, Foreign Policy and the Anglo-American Bank: The House of Morgan, 1900–31," *Historical Research*, 61 (1988), pp. 199–211.

177. Herrick, "The Panic of 1907," p. 9; Wicker, *Banking Panics*, ch. 5.

178. Herrick, "The Panic of 1907," pp. 13.

179. Davis and Cull, "International Capital Movements," pp. 787–8.

180. Herrick, "The Panic of 1907," pp. 10, 12–16.

181. Broz, "The Origins of the Federal Reserve System," pp. 56–7; Gyung-Ho Jeong, Gary J. Miller, and Andrew C. Sobel provide a precise analysis of the compromise reached by the interested parties: "Political Compromise and Bureaucratic Structure: The Political Origins of the Federal Reserve System," *Journal of Law, Economics and Organization*, 25 (2008), pp. 472–98. Elmus Wicker, *The Great Debate on Banking Reform: Nelson Aldrich and the Origins of the Fed* (Columbus, 2005), evaluates the available interpretations.

182. Ajay K. Mehrotra, *Making the Modern American Fiscal State: Law, Politics, and the Rise of Progressive Taxation, 1877-1929* (Cambridge, 2013).

183. Ibid., p. 7.

184. See, for example, Thomas M. Norwood, *Plutocracy or American White Slavery* (New York, 1888); Milford W. Howard, *The American Plutocracy* (New York, 1895); John C. Reed, *The New Plutocracy* (New York, 1903).

185. Quoted in Howard, *The American Plutocracy*, pp. 8–9.

186. William Graham Sumner, *The Conquest of the United States by Spain* (Boston, 1899), p. 25.

187. Sven Beckert, *The Monied Metropolis: New York City and the Consolidation of the American Bourgeoisie, 1850–1896* (New York, 2001); Thomas Kessner, *Capital City: New York City and the Men Behind America's Rise to Dominance, 1860–1900* (New York, 2003); Dawley, "The Abortive Rule of Big Money."

188. Anthony P. O'Brien, "Factory Size, Economies of Scale, and the Great Merger Wave of 1898–1902," *Journal of Economic History*, 48 (1988), pp. 639–49, shows that most of the increase in the size of manufacturing firms that occurred between 1869 and 1929 had already taken place by 1889. For broader trends, see Beckert, "Merchants and Manufacturers"; Dawley, "The Abortive Rule of Big Money"; Nasaw, "Gilded Age Gospels," p. 140. A pioneering work is Martin J. Sklar, *The Corporate Reconstruction of American Capitalism, 1890–1916: The Market, the Law, and Politics* (New York, 1988).

189. B. Franklin Cooling, *Gray Steel and Blue Water Navy: The Formative Years of the Military-Industrial Complex, 1881–1917* (New York, 1979); Ben Baack and Edward J. Ray, "Special Interests and the Nineteenth-Century Roots of the U.S. Military-Industrial Complex," *Research in Economic History*, 11 (1988), pp. 153–69; Kurt Hackemer, *The U.S. Navy and the Origins of the Military-Industrial Complex, 1847–1883* (Annapolis, 2001), explores the antecedents.

190. Henry George, *Progress and Poverty: An Inquiry into the Cause of Industrial Depressions and of Increase of Want with Increase of Wealth* (New York, 1879; 1912), p. 10.

191. Thorstein Veblen, *The Theory of the Leisure Class* (Chicago, 1899); Veblen, *The Theory of Business Enterprise* (New Brunswick, 1904), ch. 10. Stephen Edgell, *Veblen in Perspective: His Life and Thought* (Armonk, 2001), corrects widespread misconceptions about Veblen's personality and its presumed effect on his work.

192. Richard J. Jensen, "Democracy, Republicanism and Efficiency: The Values of American Politics, 1885–1930," in Shafer and Badger, *Contesting Democracy: Substance and Structure in American Political History, 1775–2000*, ch. 6.

193. Ron Chernow, *Titan: The Life of John D. Rockefeller, Sr.* (New York, 1998); Grant Segall, *John D. Rockefeller: Anointed with Oil* (Oxford, 2001).

194. David Cannadine, *Mellon: An American Life* (New York, 2006).

195. Vincent P. Carosso, *The Morgans: Private International Bankers, 1854–1913* (Cambridge, MA, 1987); Jean Strouse, *Morgan: American Financier* (New York, 1999).

196. David Nasaw, *Andrew Carnegie* (New York, 2006), is the most recent biography; Joseph Frazier Wall, *Andrew Carnegie* (New York, 1970; 1989) retains its value.

197. Harold C. Livesay, *Andrew Carnegie and the Rise of Big Business* (Boston, 1975).

198. See the subsection of this chapter titled "Beautiful Credit!"

199. Carnegie drew inspiration from Spencer's teaching and sought his approval for his own publications, though in this regard he was disappointed.

200. Andrew Carnegie, *The Gospel of Wealth* (1889), p. 18.

201. Ibid., pp. 12, 18.

202. Elaborated in Andrew Carnegie, *Triumphant Democracy: Or 50 Years' March of the Republic* (London, 1886); on which see A. S. Eisenstadt, *Carnegie's Model Republic: Triumphant Democracy and the British American Relationship* (Albany, 2007). Carnegie's vision of a union of the two countries was quickly relegated to what one critic called "dreamland." H. A. Tulloch, "Changing British Attitudes Towards the United States in the 1880s," *Historical Journal*, 20 (1977), p. 835.

203. As O'Brien emphasizes: "Factory Size, Economies of Scale, and the Great Merger Wave."

204. William Leach, *Land of Desire: Merchants, Power and the Rise of a New American Culture* (New York, 1993); Charles F. McGovern, *Sold American: Consumption and Citizenship, 1889–1945* (Chapel Hill, 2006).

205. Penne L. Restad, *Christmas in America: A History* (New York, 1995).

206. Alan Trachtenberg, *The Incorporation of America* (New York, 1982), and the discussion in the special issue of *American Literary History*, 15, 4 (2003).

207. Gary Cross, *An All-Consuming Country: Why Consumerism Won in Modern America* (New York, 2000), argues that this provided reassurance at a time of rapid change.

208. Carl J. Richard, *The Golden Age of the Classics in America: Greece, Rome and the Antebellum United States* (Cambridge, MA, 2009), pp. 204–11.

209. Reed, *The New Plutocracy*, book 3, ch. 10; Richard Franklin Pettigrew, *Triumphant Plutocracy: The Story of American Public Life from 1870 to 1920* (New York, 1921; 2010).

210. The theorists of the time had great difficulty devising models of society that incorporated its emerging multiracial character: Dorothy Ross, "Are We a Nation? The Conjuncture of Nationhood and Race in the United States, 1850–1876," *Modern Intellectual History*, 2 (2005), pp. 327–60.

211. The indispensable guide is Dorothy Ross, *The Origins of American Social Science* (Cambridge, 1991).

212. Bluford Adams, "World Conquerors or a Dying People? Racial Theory, Regional Anxiety, and the Brahmin Anglo-Saxonists," *Journal of the Gilded Age & Progressive Era*, 8 (2009), pp. 189–215.

213. Brooks Adams, *The New Empire* (New York, 1902); LeFeber, *The New Empire*, pp. 80–85. Adams and his brother, Henry, had speculated in Western lands and were caught out when the boom suddenly collapsed.

214. *A Historical Study* (Boston, 1894).

215. Brooks Adams, *The Law of Civilization and Decay* (New York, 1896; 1943). The edition published in 1943 has a substantial introduction by Charles A. Beard that illuminates the thinking of both authors. It is easy to confuse Peter Chardon Brooks Adams (1848–1927), known as Brooks Adams, with his brother, Henry Brooks Adams (1838–1918), known as Henry Adams, because each drew on the work of the other. Brooks Adams expressed elements of what Henry was later to elevate to a law of entropy derived (very loosely) from the Second Law of Thermodynamics. Keith R. Burich, "Henry Adams, the Second Law of Thermodynamics, and the Course of History," *Journal of the History of Ideas*, 48 (1987), pp. 467–82. The brothers had patrician pedigrees as great-grandsons of the second president, John Adams (1735–1826). On the history of the family, see Richard Brookliser, *America's First Dynasty: The Adamses, 1735–1918* (New York, 2002).

216. F. H. Giddings, *Studies in the Theory of Human Society* (New York, 1922), quoted in Charles A. Beard, "Introduction" to Adams, *Law of Civilization*, p. 50.

217. Brooks Adams, *Law of Civilization*, pp. 347–51, on the losses sustained by "yeomen" at the hands of "usurers."

218. Charles Benedict Davenport (1866–1944). Jan A. Witowski and John R. Inglis, eds., *Davenport's Dream: 21st Century Reflections on Heredity and Eugenics* (New York, 2008), provides a rather restricted view of the legacy.

219. Garland E. Allen, "The Misuse of Biological Hierarchies: The American Eugenics Movement, 1900–1940," *History & Philosophy of the Life Sciences*, 5 (1983), pp. 105–28; Jonathan P. Spiro, *Defending the Master Race: Conservation, Eugenics and the Legacy of Madison Grant* (Lebanon, 2009). Mendel's research, conducted in the 1860s, was rediscovered in 1900.

220. And into the 1950s in the case of school and college textbooks. See Steven Selden, *Inheriting Shame: The Story of Eugenics and Racism in America* (New York, 1999).

221. As discussed in chapter 4 of this text.

222. See the discussion of the election campaigns of the 1890s in the subsection of this chapter titled "All Has Been Lost Except Office or the Hope of It." Stephen Tuffnell has reexamined the subject in "Uncle Sam Is to Be Sacrificed: Anglophobia in Late Nineteenth-Century Politics and Culture," *American Nineteenth-Century History*, 12 (2011), pp. 77–99. On the Venezuela crisis, see George C. Herring, *From Colony to Superpower: U.S. Foreign Relations since 1776* (Oxford, 2008), pp. 307–8.

223. Frank Prochaska, *Eminent Victorians on American Democracy* (New York, 2012), ch. 6.

224. Nina Silber, *The Romance of Reunion: Northerners and the South, 1865–1900* (Chapel Hill, 1993); Cecilia Elizabeth O'Leary, *To Die For: The Paradox of American Patriotism* (Princeton, 1999); David Blight, *Race and Reunion: the Civil War in American Memory* (Cambridge, MA, 2001).

225. Michael Haines, "The Population of the United States, 1790–1920," in Engerman and Gallman, eds., *Cambridge Economic History of the United States*, 2, pp. 154–203; Herbert S. Klein, *A Population History of the United States* (Cambridge, 2004), pp. 127–30.

226. Quoted in Bluford Adams, "World Conquerors or a Dying People? Racial Theory, Regional Anxiety, and the Brahmin Anglo-Saxonists," *Journal of the Gilded Age & Progressive Era*, 8 (2009), p. 209.

227. Rogers M. Smith, *Civic Ideals: Conflicting Visions of Citizenship in U.S. History* (New Haven, 1997); Eric P. Kaufmann, *The Rise and Fall of Anglo-America* (Cambridge, 2004). Matthew F. Jacobson's trilogy explores the function of popular culture, imperial wars, and foreigners in the process: *Special Sorrows: The Diasporic Imagination of Irish, Polish, and Jewish Immigrants in the United States* (1995); *Whiteness of a Different Color: European Immigrants and the Alchemy of Race* (1998); *Barbarian Virtues: The United States Encounters Foreign Peoples at Home and Abroad, 1876–1917* (New York, 2000).

228. The phrase derives from Milton M. Gordon, *Assimilation in American Life: The Role of Race, Religion and National Origins* (New York, 1965), p. 85.

229. Jeffrey E. Mirel, *Patriotic Pluralism: Americanization, Education and European Immigrants* (London, 2010); James R. Barrett, "Americanization from the Bottom Up: Immigration and the Remaking of the Working Class in the United States, 1880–1930," *Journal of American History*, 79 (1992), pp. 996–1020.

230. Melinda Lawson, *Patriot Fires: Forging a New American Nationalism in the Civil War North* (Lawrence, 2002).

231. O'Leary, *To Die For*.

232. Blight, *Race and Reunion*.

233. Charles A. Lofgren, *The Plessy Case: A Legal-Historical Interpretation* (New York, 1987).

234. The (imperfect) records for 12 Southern states show that there were about 4,000 lynchings between 1877 and 1950. Arkansas, Louisiana, and Mississippi headed the list, which reached a peak in the 1880s and 1890s. *Report of the Equal Justice Initiative* (Montgomery, 2015), quoted in the *New York Times*, February 9, 2015.

235. Rose Stremlau, "To Domesticate and Civilise Wild Indians: Allotment and the Campaign to Reform Indian Families, 1875–1887," *Journal of Family History*, 30 (2005), pp. 265–86.

236. James O. Gump offers a rare comparison in *The Dust Rose Like Smoke: The Subjugation of the Zulu and the Sioux* (Lincoln, 1994).

237. Frederick E. Hoxie, *A Final Promise: The Campaign to Assimilate the Indians, 1880–1922* (Lincoln, 1984; 2001). For one of many detailed examples see William T. Hagan, *Taking Indian Lands: The Cherokee (Jerome) Commission, 1889–1893* (Norman, 2003).

238. Robert W. Rydell, *All the World's a Fair: Visions of Empire at American International Expositions, 1876–1916* (Chicago, 1895); see also the alternative perspective of L. G. Moses, *Wild West Shows and the Images of American Indians, 1883–1933* (Albuquerque, 1996); Janet M. Davis, "Instruct the Minds of All Classes: Celebrations of Empire at the American Circus, 1898–1910," *European Contributions to American Studies*, 51 (2004), pp. 58–68.

239. Robert R. Rydell and Rob Kroes, *Buffalo Bill in Bologna: The Americanization of the World, 1869–1922* (Chicago, 2005); Louis S. Warren, *Buffalo Bill's America: William Cody and the Wild West Show* (New York, 2005); Stephen G. Hyslop, "How the West Was Spun," *American History*, 43 (2008), pp. 26–33.

240. *New York Times*, June 25, 1887.

241. Catherine Camp, "Unions, Civics, and National Identity: Organized Labor's Reaction to Immigration, 1881–1897," *Labor History*, 29 (1998), pp. 450–74.

242. The commission's 41 volumes await detailed historical scrutiny. At present, there is only one brief study: Robert F. Zeidel, *Immigrants, Progressives, and Exclusion Politics: The Dillingham Commission, 1900–1927* (DeKalb, 2004).

243. Kaufmann, *The Rise and Fall of Anglo-America*.

244. Robert Davidoff, *The Genteel Tradition and the Sacred Rage: High Culture vs. Democracy in Adams, James and Santayana* (Chapel Hill, 1992).

245. Quoted in Shira Wolosky, "Santayana and Harvard Formalism," *Raritan*, 18 (1999), p. 66.

246. Santayana's multiculturalism stemmed from his own Spanish origins and American upbringing. He is considered to be an American author but he never became an American citizen and spent the second half of his long life (1863–1952) in Europe. See John McCormick, *George Santayana: A Biography* (New York, 1988).

247. The difficulty of defining these "Awakenings" is well known. It is extraordinary, nevertheless, that the revivalism of the second half of the nineteenth century has been overlooked to the extent of being omitted from many standard texts on the period. Josiah Strong, who was especially well informed on the subject, identified the Third Awakening in the course of calling for the Fourth: *The Next Great Awakening* (New York, 1902), ch. 2. Robert W. Fogel offers a schematic account that recognizes the Third Awakening but dates it from the 1890s: *The Fourth Great Awakening and the Future of Egalitarianism* (Chicago, 2000).

248. Edward J. Blum, *Reforging the White Republic: Race, Religion and American Nationalism, 1865–1898* (Baton Rouge, 2005).

249. Gaines M. Foster, *Moral Reconstruction: Christian Lobbyists and the Federal Legislation of Morality, 1865–1920* (Chapel Hill, 2002).

250. *Our Country: Its Possible Future and Its Present Crisis* (New York, 1885; 1891), p. 263.

251. Bruce J. Evanson, *God's Man for the Great Awakening: D. L. Moody and the Rise of Modern Mass Evangelism* (Oxford, 2003).

252. Alison M. Parker, *Purifying America: Women, Cultural Reform, and Pro-Censorship Activism, 1873–1933* (Champaign, 1997); Francesca Morgan, *Women and Patriotism in Jim Crow America* (Chapel Hill, 2005). The WCTU diluted its pro-white bias by also treating recent immigrants and Roman Catholics as dangers to the state.

253. David I. Macleod, *Building Character in the American Boy: The Boy Scouts, YMCA, and their Forerunners, 1870–1920* (Madison, 1983); Thomas Winter, *Making Men, Making Class: The YMCA and Workingmen, 1877–1920* (Chicago, 2002).

254. Clifford Putney, *Muscular Christianity: Manhood and Sports in Protestant America, 1880–1920* (Cambridge, MA, 2001).

255. Susan Curtis, *A Consuming Faith: The Social Gospel and Modern American Culture* (Baltimore, 1991).

256. Strong, *Our Country*, chs. 4–11 (inclusive) deal with the perils (from immigration to the city); ch. 15 addresses the need to raise money in the service of God.

257. Strong, *Our Country*, pp. 45, 89–91. Strong was a Midwesterner who began his career as a missionary in "Indian country."

258. Ernest L. Tuveson, *Redeemer Nation: The Idea of America's Millennial Role* (Chicago, 1968); Anders Stephanson, *Manifest Destiny and the Empire of Right* (New York, 1995), pp. 79–80.

259. Strong presented data to show that the American branch was fitter than its English cousins: *Our Country*, pp. 217–20. His later publications struck a less confident note.

260. Stephanson, *Manifest Destiny*, pp. 79–80.

261. Strong, *Our Country*, pp. 221–2.

262. Ibid., p. 80.

263. Ibid., p. 223.

264. Josiah Strong, *The United States and the Future of the Anglo-Saxon Race* (London, 1889), p. 53.

265. Harvey Levenstein, *Revolution at the Table: The Transformation of the American Diet* (Oxford, 1988); Christopher Mulvey, *Transatlantic Manners: Social Patterns in Nineteenth-Century Anglo-American Travel Literature* (Cambridge, 1990); John F. Kasson, *Rudeness and Civility: Manners in Nineteenth-Century Urban America* (New York, 1990); Linda Young, *Middle Class Culture in the Nineteenth Century: America, Australia, and Britain* (New York, 2003).

266. Kathleen Burk, *Old World, New World: Great Britain and America from the Beginning* (London, 2007), ch. 7, provides a wealth of information on this subject.

267. Henry Adams, *Democracy: An American Novel* (New York, 1880; 1981), pp. 245–6. Adams began the book in 1867. It was published anonymously and his authorship was not revealed until after his death in 1918.

268. Burk, *Old World, New World*, pp. 529–48. About 450 American women married European aristocrats between 1870 and 1914: Woolf, "Special Relationships," p. 160. Gail MacColl and Carol McD. Wallace provide a lighter look at the subject in *To Marry an English Lord or How Anglomania Really Got Started* (New York, 1989).

269. *New York Times*, July 30, 1878.

270. Ironically, Matthew Arnold's daughter, Lucy, married a New Yorker she had met during one of her father's lecture tours in the United States.

271. Sara Blair, *Henry James and the Writing of Race and Nation* (Cambridge, 1996).

272. Dwight E. Robinson, "Fashions in Shaving and Trimming of the Beard: The Men of the 'Illustrated London News,' 1842–1972," *American Journal of Sociology*, 81 (1976), pp. 1133–41; Christopher Oldstone-Martin, "The Beard Movement in Victorian Britain," *Victorian Studies*, 48 (2005), pp. 7–34; Gerald Carson, "Hair Today, Gone Tomorrow," *American Heritage*, 17 (1966), pp. 42–7; James Hughes, "Those Who Passed Through: Unusual Visits to Unlikely Places," *New York History*, 87 (2006), pp. 378–82; Lucinda Hawksley, *Moustaches, Whiskers and Beards* (London, 2014).

273. The first picture of Uncle Sam with whiskers appeared in *Harper's Weekly*, February 6, 1869.

274. Katherine L. Carlson, "Little Lord Fauntleroy and the Evolution of American Boyhood," *Journal of the History of Childhood and Youth*, 3 (2010), pp. 39–64.

275. William R. Leach, *True Love and Perfect Union: The Feminist Reform of Sex and Society* (New York, 1980), ch. 9.

276. William R. Leach, *Land of Desire: Merchants, Power, and the Rise of a New American Culture* (New York, 1994).

277. Robert Weisbuch traces the emergence of American literature as postcolonial literature in *Atlantic Double-Cross: American Literature and British Influence in the Age of Emerson* (Chicago, 1987).

278. William T. Stead, *The Americanization of the World* (London, 1901), p. 277.

279. Ben Railton, *Contesting the Past, Reconstructing the Nation: American Literature and Culture in the Gilded Age* (Tuscaloon, 2007).

280. Priscilla Roberts, "Henry James and British Power," in Wm. Roger Louis, ed., *Resurgent Adventures with Britannia* (New York, 2011), ch. 4.

281. Walt Whitman, *Democratic Vistas and Other Papers* (London, 1888), p. 63. (*Democratic Vistas* was first published in 1870, though the imprint gives 1871, which has now become the accepted date.)

282. Matthew Arnold, *Civilization in the United States: First and Last Impressions of America* (Boston, 1888), p. 191.

283. Walt Whitman, "For You, O Democracy," in *Leaves of Grass* (1855); Jason Frank, "Aesthetic Democracy: Walt Whitman and the Poetry of the People," *Review of Politics*, 69 (2007), pp. 402–30.

284. It should be added that Henry James's last novels are now considered modernist before their time.

285. Whitman, "Years of the Modern," in *Leaves of Grass*.

286. Emily Dickinson, *Collected Poems* (New York, 1924; 1993). It was not until 1955 that all of her poems were published, and it was only in 1998 that they appeared with the original punctuation and spelling restored.

287. Quoted in Marietta Messmer, "The Politics of Dickinson's Critical Reception During the 1890s," *American Studies*, 45 (2000), p. 372.

288. Christanne Miller, *Reading in Time: Emily Dickinson in the Nineteenth Century* (Amherst, 2012), places Dickinson in the American lyrical tradition while also emphasizing her innovative qualities.

289. Christopher Gair, "Whitewashed Exteriors: Mark Twain's Imitation Whites," *Journal of American Studies*, 39 (2005), pp. 187–205. As Stephen Railton suggests, Twain was uneasy about his treatment of racial problems: "The Tragedy of Mark Twain, by Pudd'nhead Wilson," *Nineteenth-Century Literature*, 56 (2002), pp. 518–44.

290. Herbert N. Foerstel, *Banned in the U.S.A.: A Reference Guide to Book Censorship in Schools and Public Libraries* (2nd ed., Westport, 2002).

291. Patrick B. Miller, ed., *The Sporting World of the Modern South* (Urbana, 2002).

292. George B. Kirsch, *Baseball in Blue and Grey: The National Pastime during the Civil War* (Princeton, NJ, 2003).

293. On the role of sport in Britain and her empire, see Patrick F. McDevitt, *May the Best Man Win: Sport, Masculinity, and Nationalism in Great Britain and the Empire, 1880–1935* (London, 2004).

294. George B. Kirsch, *The Creation of American Team Sports: Baseball and Cricket, 1838–72* (Urbana, 1989).

295. Thomas W. Zeiler, *Ambassadors in Pinstripes: The Spalding World Tour and the Birth of the American Empire* (Lanham, 2006).

296. Boria Majumdar and Sean Brown, "Why Baseball, Why Cricket? Differing Nationalisms, Differing Challenges," *International Journal of the History of Sport*, 24 (2007), pp. 139–56.

297. Sam Whitsitt, "Soccer: The Game America Refuses to Play," *Raritan*, 14 (1994), pp. 58–69.

298. Ying Wu, "The Pilgrims Come to America: A Failed Mission of British Cultural Imperialism," *Sport History Review*, 29 (1998), pp. 212–24.

299. Sir Ernest Cochrane, the British sponsor of the tour, quoted in ibid., p. 217.

300. Tony Collins, "Unexceptional Exceptionalism: The Origins of American Football in a Transnational Context," *Journal of Global History*, 8 (2013), pp. 209–30.

301. Richard Cranford, *America's Musical Life: A History* (New York, 2001), ch. 19.

302. Michael B. Beckerman, *New Worlds of Dvorak: Searching in America for the Composer's Inner Life* (New York, 2003), stresses the influence of Longfellow's "Hiawatha" (chs. 2–5, 12) and of "negro melodies" (ch. 9).

303. Michael D. Clark, "Ralph Adams Cram and the Americanization of the Middle Ages," *Journal of American Studies*, 23 (1989), pp. 195–213.

304. H. Allen Brooks, *The Prairie School* (New York, 2006).

305. McDowell (1860–1908), who studied in Europe, never visited Native American societies and had little regard for African American music.

306. On the origins of blues, jazz, and gospel music in the South, see Ayers, *Promise of the New South*, ch. 14.

307. Quoted in Rogers, "The United States and the Fiscal Debate in Britain," p. 605.

308. Stead, *Americanisation of the World*, p. 358.

309. Ibid., p. 359.

310. The concept of a counterculture is discussed in the section titled "Cultural Continuities" in chapter 4 of this text.

311. Zelinski, *Nation into State*, pp. 172–3, 202.

312. Alton Ketchum, "The Search for Uncle Sam," *History Today*, 40 (1990), pp. 20–26.

313. Rogan Kersh, *Dreams of a More Perfect Union* (Ithaca, 2001), ch. 6. See also Thomas Bender, "What Is Americanism?" *Reviews in American History*, 35 (2007), p. 2.

314. Scott M. Guenther, *The American Flag, 1777–1924* (London, 1990), ch. 5; Marc Leepson, *Flag: An American Biography* (New York, 2005). The U.S. Navy recognized the anthem for official use in 1889.

315. David W. Blight, "Decoration Days: The Origins of Memorial Day in North and South," in Alice Fahs and Joan Waugh, eds., *The Memory of the Civil War in American Culture* (Chapel Hill, 2004), pp. 94–129.

316. Dorothy Ross, "Grand Narrative in American Historical Writing: From Romance to Uncertainty," *American Historical Review*, 100 (1995), pp. 651–6.

317. Woodrow Wilson, "The Ideals of America," *Atlantic Monthly*, 90 (1902), pp. 721–34.

318. As detailed in chapter 6 of this text.

319. Albert C. Coolidge, *The United States as a World Power* (New York, 1908; 1923), ch. 1.

320. Theodore Roosevelt, "Biological Analogies in History," in Roosevelt, *African and European Addresses* (New York, 1910).

321. Ibid.

CHAPTER 8: ACQUIRING AN UNEXCEPTIONAL EMPIRE

1. "In Support of an American Empire," Speech to the Senate, *Record*, vol. 33, 56th Congress, 1st Session, January 1900, pp. 704–12.

2. There were additional minor territorial acquisitions: Guam (ceded by Spain in 1898); the smaller, eastern part of Samoa (divided with Germany in 1899); the Panama Canal Zone (1903); and the Virgin Islands (purchased from Denmark in 1917).

3. John Offner provides concise and judicious overviews in "United States Politics and the 1898 War over Cuba," in Angel Smith and Emma Davila-Cox, eds., *The Crisis of 1898: Colonial Redistribution and Nationalist Mobilization* (New York, 1999), ch. 2; and "McKinley and the Spanish-American War," *Presidential Studies Quarterly*, 34 (2004), pp. 50–61.

4. Richard Hofstadter, *The Paranoid Style in American Politics* (New York, 1964), referred to the phenomenon as "anxious irrationality" resulting from a "psychic crisis."

5. Louis A. Pérez, Jr., *The War of 1898: The United States and Cuba in History and Historiography* (Chapel Hill, 1998), ch. 2, provides a devastating criticism of views that have stood unchallenged for far too long.

6. This is the celebrated phrase of Samuel Flagg Bemis, *A Diplomatic History of the United States* (New York, 5th ed., 1965), p. 463. It should be noted that Bemis was referring to what he called the "adolescent irresponsibility" of the United States in acquiring the Philippines. His well-known phrase "the great aberration" was subsequently generalized.

7. The "Wisconsin School" is often treated as if it were synonymous with New Left thinking, which is not the case. See James G. Morgan, *Into New Territory: American Historians and the Concept of U.S. Imperialism* (Madison, 2014), chs. 2–3. It remains true, however, that the New Left group was particularly influential. See Lloyd C. Gardner, ed., *Redefining the Past: Essays in Honor of William Appleman Williams* (Corvallis, 1986); Lloyd C. Gardner and Thomas J. McCormick, "Walter LaFeber: The Making of a Wisconsin School Revisionist," *Diplomatic History*, 28 (2004), pp. 613–24; William A. Williams, *The Tragedy of American Diplomacy* (1959, 1972; New York, 2009) with contributions by Lloyd C. Gardner, Andrew Bacevich, and Bradford Perkins; William A. Williams, *The Roots of Modern American Empire* (New York, 1969). Binoy Kampmark provides a refreshing, independent survey in "Historiographical Review: William A. Williams's *Tragedy* Fifty Years On," *Historical Journal*, 53 (2010), pp. 783–94.

8. D.C.M. Platt, ed., *Business Imperialism, 1840–1930: An Inquiry Based on British Experience in Latin America* (Oxford, 1977).

9. Williams, *Tragedy*; Walter LaFeber, *The New Empire: An Interpretation of American Expansion, 1860–1898* (Ithaca, 1963; 1998); LaFeber, *Cambridge History of American*

Foreign Relations: II. *The American Search for Opportunity, 1865–1913* (Cambridge, 1993).

10. Williams, *Roots*.

11. Ibid., pp. xx–xxiii. Williams himself came from Iowa.

12. LaFeber, *New Empire*. Thirty years later, LaFeber presented a restatement that, broadly speaking, reaffirmed his original argument. La Feber, *The American Search for Opportunity*, pp. 79, 93.

13. LaFeber, *New Empire*, pp. xxvii–xxviii.

14. Ibid. pp. 385–92; LaFeber, *American Search for Opportunity*, pp. 141–5; here in agreement with Julius W. Pratt, *Expansionists of 1898: The Acquisition of Hawai'i and the Spanish Islands* (Baltimore, 1936), p. 246.

15. LaFeber, *New Empire*, pp. 384–417.

16. Ernest R. May, *American Imperialism: A Speculative Essay* (Chicago, 1967; 2nd ed. 1991), p. xxxi.

17. Hofstadter, *The Paranoid Style*.

18. See Ann Laura Stoler, "Tense and Tender Ties: The Politics of Comparison in North American History and (Post) Colonial Studies," *Journal of American History*, 88 (2001), pp. 829–65; and the astute commentary by Robert J. McMahon, "Cultures of Empire," *Journal of American History*, 88 (2001), pp. 888–92.

19. An interesting example is Gary H. Darden, "The New Empire in the 'New South': Jim Crow in the Global Frontier of High Imperialism and Decolonization," *Southern Quarterly*, 46 (2009), pp. 8–25.

20. See, among numerous studies, Paul A. Kramer, *The Blood of Government: Race, Empire, the United States, and the Philippines* (Chapel Hill, 2006); Amy Kaplan and Donald Pease, eds., *Cultures of United States Imperialism* (Durham, 1993); Laura Wexler, *Tender Violence: Domestic Visions in an Age of U.S. Imperialism* (Chapel Hill, 2000); Matthew F. Jacobson, *Barbarian Virtues: The United States Encounters Foreign Peoples at Home and Abroad, 1876–1917* (New York, 2000); Ann Laura Stoler, *Haunted by Empire: Geographies of Intimacy in North American History* (Durham, 2006); McMahon, "Cultures of Empire," pp. 888–92.

21. For example: Gail Bederman, *Manliness and Civilization: A Cultural History of the United States, 1880–1917* (Chicago, 1995); John Pettigrew, *Brutes in Suits: Male Sensibility in America, 1890–1920* (Baltimore, 2007); Allison L. Sneider, *Suffragists in an Imperial Age: U.S. Expansion and the Woman Question, 1870–1929* (New York, 2008).

22. Kristin L. Hoganson, *Fighting for American Manhood: How Gender Politics Provoked the Spanish-American and Philippine-American Wars* (New Haven, 1998).

23. Eric T. Love, *Race over Empire: Racism and U.S. Imperialism, 1865–1900* (Chapel Hill, 2004), is a contribution of first importance in this regard.

24. As Hoganson readily acknowledges: *Fighting for American Manhood*, p. 3. But see also the perceptive essay by Frank Ninkovich, "Cuba, the Philippines, and the Hundred Years' War," *Reviews in American History*, 27 (1999), pp. 444–51.

25. As Amy Greenberg has pointed out in *Manifest Manhood and the Antebellum American Empire* (New York, 2005).

26. And an enduring theme, too: see Andrew J. Bacevich, *The New American Militarism: How Americans Are Seduced by War* (New York, 2013).

27. See, among many excellent studies, Lewis L. Gould, *The Presidency of William McKinley* (Lawrence, 1980); John Offner, *An Unwanted War: The Diplomacy of the United States and Spain* (Chapel Hill, 1992). The most recent assessment is Richard F. Hamilton, *President McKinley, War and Empire*, 2 vols. (New Brunswick, 2006, 2007).

28. Gabriel Paquette, "Historiographical Reviews: The Dissolution of the Spanish Atlantic Monarchy," *Historical Journal*, 52 (2009), pp. 175–212, provides a concise survey.

29. Richard L. Kagan, "Prescott's Paradigm: American Historical Scholarship and the Decline of Spain," *American Historical Review*, 101 (1996), pp. 423–46; Kagan, ed., *Spain in*

America: The Origins of Hispanism in the United States (Urbana and Chicago, 2002), ch. 1, esp. pp. 9–10. See also Christopher Schmidt-Nowara, *The Conquest of History: Spanish Colonialism and National Histories in the Nineteenth Century* (Pittsburgh, 2006).

30. Mónica Burguera and Christopher Schmidt-Nowara, "Backwardness and Its Discontents," *Social History* 29 (2004), p. 282: "the impact of colonial warfare, decolonization and efforts to defend and expand the remnants of empire in the modern period are poorly understood." Their article (pp. 279–83) introduces a special issue on this subject. See also Christopher Schmidt-Nowara, "A History of Disasters: Spanish Colonialism in the Age of Empire," *History Compass*, 5 (2007), pp. 943–54.

31. See chapter 6 of this text.

32. See chapters 2 and 6 of this text.

33. Florencia Peyrou, "A Great Family of Sovereign Men: Democratic Discourse in Nineteenth-Century Spain," *European History Quarterly*, 43 (2013), pp. 235–56.

34. For example, Robert Sidney Smith, "English Economic Thought in Spain, 1776–1848," *South Atlantic Quarterly*, 67 (1968), pp. 306–37; Jose-Luis Ramos, "John Stuart Mill and Nineteenth-Century Spain," *Journal of the History of Economic Thought*, 33 (2011), pp. 507–26; Julian Casanova, "Terror and Violence: The Dark Face of Spanish Anarchism," *International Labor & Working-Class History*, 67 (2005), pp. 79–99; and, more generally, Guy Thomson, *The Birth of Modern Politics in Spain: Democracy, Association and Revolution, 1854–1875* (Basingstoke, 2009).

35. Angel Smith, "The People and the Nation: Nationalist Mobilization and the Crisis of 1895–98 in Spain," in Angel Smith and Emma Davila-Cox, eds., *The Crisis of 1898: Colonial Redistribution and Nationalist Mobilization* (London, 1999), pp. 152–79. The Spanish applied the word *"cacique,"* which was derived from pre-Columbian Taino in the Caribbean, to refer to local leaders or Big Men and their networks throughout the Spanish empire, and later to political bosses in Spain, too. For the "system" in the Philippines, see Juan Antonio Inarejos Muñoz, "Reclutar caciques: la selección de las elites coloniales filipinas a finales del siglo XIX," *Hispania: Revista Española de Historia*, 71 (2011), pp. 741–61.

36. On the decline of the nobility, see Isabel Burdiel, "Myths of Failure, Myths of Success: Perspectives on Nineteenth-Century Spanish Liberalism," *Journal of Modern History*, 70 (1998), pp. 892–912; Gabriel Paquette, "Liberalism in the Early Nineteenth-Century Iberian World," *History of European Ideas*, 41 (2015), pp. 153–65, which introduces other essays on this theme in the same issue.

37. Smith, "The People and the Nation," p. 158.

38. César Yáñez, "Los negocios ultramarinos de una burguesía cosmopolita. Los catalanes en las primeras fases de la globalización, 1750–1914," *Revista de Indias*, 66 (2006), pp. 679–710.

39. Josep María Fradera, *Cultura nacional en una sociedad dividida: Cataluña 1838–1868* (Madrid, 2002).

40. Gabriel Tortella, *The Development of Modern Spain: An Economic History of the Nineteenth and Twentieth Centuries* (Cambridge, 1994; 2000), offers a less positive assessment.

41. David Ringrose, *Spain, Europe and the "Spanish Miracle," 1700–1900* (Cambridge, 1996); Regina Graf, *Distant Tyranny: Markets, Power and Backwardness in Spain, 1650–1800* (Princeton, NJ, 2012).

42. Christopher Schmidt-Nowara, "La España Ultramarina: Colonialism and Nation-Building in Nineteenth-Century Spain" *European History Quarterly*, 34 (2004), pp. 191–214.

43. On the wayward character of the monarchy, see Isabel Burdiel, "The Queen, the Woman, and the Middle Class: The Symbolic Failure of Isabel II of Spain," *Social History*, 29 (2004), pp. 301–19.

44. Smith, "The People and the Nation," pp. 163–73.

45. Maria Alejandra Irigoin, "Gresham on Horseback: The Monetary Roots of Spanish American Political Fragmentation in the Nineteenth Century," *Economic History Review*, 62 (2009), pp. 551–75; and the discussion of these matters in *Hispanic American Historical Review*, 88 (2008), issue 2.

46. Matthew Restall provides an astute evaluation in "The Decline and Fall of the Spanish Empire?" *William & Mary Quarterly*, 64 (2007), pp. 1–8, following Henry Kamen's pioneering revisionism: "The Decline of Spain: A Myth?" *Past & Present*, 81 (1978), pp. 24–50.

47. The authoritative study is Josep M. Fradera, *Colonias para después de un imperio* (Barcelona, 2005); also Francisco A. Scarano, "Liberal Pacts and Hierarchies of Rule: Approaching the Imperial Transition in Cuba and Puerto Rico," *Hispanic American Historical Review*, 78 (1998), pp. 583–601.

48. Vanessa M. Ziegler, "The Revolt of the 'Ever-Faithful Isle': The Ten Years War in Cuba, 1868–1878," Ph.D. dissertation, University of California (2007), pp. 8–10.

49. Elena Schneider, "African Slavery and Spanish Empire," *Journal of Early American History*, 5 (2015), pp. 8–29.

50. W. G. Clarence-Smith, "The Economic Dynamics of Spanish Colonialism in the Nineteenth and Twentieth Centuries," *Itinerario*, 15 (1991), p. 72. See also Christopher Schmid-Nowara and Josep M. Fradera, eds., *Slavery and Anti-Slavery in Spain's Atlantic Empire* (New York, 2013).

51. Clarence-Smith, "The Economic Dynamics," pp. 74–5, gives further examples of Spanish expansionist ambitions. Manila hemp (abaca) was used chiefly for cordage at this time but also gave its name to high-quality paper.

52. Clarence-Smith, "Spain, Europe and the 'Spanish Miracle,'" pp. 76–9.

53. Ibid.; Scarano, "Liberal Pacts and Hierarchies of Rule."

54. Jonathan Curry-Machado, *Cuban Sugar Industry: Transnational Networks and Engineering Migrants in Mid-Nineteenth-Century Cuba* (New York, 2011), pp. 1–23; Ringrose, *Spain, Europe, and the Spanish "Miracle,"* ch. 6.

55. Adrian J. Pearce, *British Trade and Spanish America, 1763–1808* (Liverpool, 2007).

56. For one example, see Jesús M. Valdaliso, "Trade, Colonies and Navigation Laws: The Flag, Differential Duty and the International Competitiveness of Spanish Shipping in the Nineteenth Century," *International Journal of Maritime History*, 17 (2005), pp. 31–60.

57. Pablo Martin-Acena, Angeles Pons, and María Concepción Betrán, "Financial Crises and Financial Reforms in Spain: What Have We Learned?" Universidad Carlos III de Madrid, *Working Papers in Economic History*, WP 10-01 (2010).

58. The debate originated in assessments of tropical Africa. For the most recent statement, see Toyin Falola and Emily Brownell, eds., *Africa, Empire, and Globalization: Essays in Honor of A. G. Hopkins* (Durham, 2011), chs. 2–7; A. G. Hopkins, "Asante and the Historians: Transition and Partition on the Gold Coast," in Roy Bridges, ed., *Imperialism, Decolonisation and Africa: Historical Essays in Honour of John Hargreaves* (Macmillan, 2000), pp. 25–64.

59. Louis A. Pérez, Jr., *Cuba: Between Reform and Revolution* (New York, 1988; 3rd ed. Oxford, 2006). This subject is treated in chapter 9 of this text.

60. Albert and Graves, *Crisis and Change*, pp. 1–3; John A. Larkin, *Sugar and the Origins of Modern Philippine Society* (Berkeley, 1993), pp. 49–50, 52; Benito J. Legarda, *After the Galleons: Foreign Trade, Economic Change and Entrepreneurship in the Nineteenth-Century Philippines* (Madison, 1999), pp. 120–23; Roy A. Ballinger provides a concise survey of the industry at this time: "A History of Sugar Marketing Through 1874," *U.S. Department of Agriculture Economic Report*, AER 382 (Washington, DC, 1978).

61. Pérez, *Cuba: Between Reform and Revolution*, pp. 98–100.

62. Saif I. Shah Mohammed and Jeffrey Williamson, "Freight Rates and Productivity Gains in the British Tramp Shipping, 1869-1950," *Explorations in Economic History*, 41 (2004), pp. 172–203.

63. The most thorough assessment is by Christopher Blattman, Jason Hwang, and Jeffrey Williamson, "Winners and Losers in the Commodity Lottery: The Impact of Terms of Trade Growth and Volatility in the Periphery, 1870–1939," *Journal of Development Economics*, 82 (2007), pp. 156–79; Yael S. Hadass and Jeffrey G. Williamson, "Terms of Trade Shocks and Economic Performance, 1870–1940: Prebisch and Singer Revisited," *Economic Development & Cultural Change*, 51 (2003), pp. 629–56 ; Jeffrey Williamson, "Globalization and the Great Divergence: Terms of Trade Booms, Volatility and the Poor Periphery, 1782–1913," *European Review of Economic History*, 12 (2008), pp. 355–91.

64. Complexities in measuring prices mean that the dates given in different sources are not identical: Bergquist, *Coffee and Conflict*, pp. 21–3; William Gervase Clarence-Smith, "The Coffee Crisis in Asia, Africa, and the Pacific, 1870–1914," in Clarence-Smith and Steven Topik, eds., *The Global Coffee Economy in Africa, Asia, and Latin America, 1500–1989* (Cambridge, 2003), p. 101.

65. Laird W. Bergad, *Coffee and the Growth of Agrarian Capitalism in Nineteenth-Century Puerto Rico* (Princeton, NJ, 1983); César J. Ayala and Rafael Bernabe, *Puerto Rico in the American Century* (Chapel Hill, 2007), pp. 18–20, 45–6.

66. What follows is a speculative treatment of a subject that remains to be fully understood. For three exploratory essays, see Maria Serena I. Diokno, "The Political Aspect of the Monetary Crisis in the 1880s," *Philippine Journal of Third World Studies*, 14 (1998), pp. 21–36; David J. St. Clair, "American Trade Dollars in Nineteenth-Century China," in Dennis O. Flynn, Lionel Frost, and A.J.H. Latham, eds., *Pacific Centuries: Pacific and Pacific Rim Economic History since the Sixteenth Century* (London, 1998), ch. 7; Allan E. S. Lumba, "Philippine Colonial Money and the Futures of the Spanish Empire," in Chia Yin Hsu, Thomas M. Luckett, and Erika Vause, eds., *The Cultural History of Money and Credit: A Global Perspective* (Lanham, 2016), ch. 7.

67. Marcela Sabaté, María Dolores Gadea, and Regina Escario, "Does Fiscal Policy Influence Monetary Policy? The Case of Spain, 1874–1935," *Explorations in Economic History*, 43 (2006), pp. 309–31.

68. Onofre D. Corpuz, *An Economic History of the Philippines* (Quezon City, 1997), pp. 180–82.

69. Pablo Martín-Aceña, "Spain during the Classical Gold Standard Years," in Michael D. Bordo and Forrest Capie, eds., *Monetary Regimes in Transition* (Cambridge, 1993), pp. 135–72.

70. Clarence-Smith, "Economic Dynamics of Spanish Colonialism," pp. 78–9.

71. Ibid.

72. In the case of the Philippines at least, exports were affected less by exchange rates during this period than by exogenous factors, such as the opening of the Suez Canal in 1869: Corpuz, *Economic History*, p. 184; Legarda, *After the Galleons*, pp. 335–6.

73. Diokno, "Political Aspect of the Monetary Crisis," p. 28.

74. This conclusion is in line with the wider analysis of Kris James Mitchener and Hans-Joachim Voth, "Trading Silver for Gold: Nineteenth-Century Asian Exports and the Political Economy of Currency Unions," in Robert J. Barro and Jong-Wha Lee, eds., *Costs and Benefits of Economic Integration in Asia* (New York, 2011), pp. 126–56. However, the conclusion must remain provisional until detailed accounts of the fortunes of different economic sectors and ethnic groups are available.

75. Angel Smith, *The Origins of Catalan Nationalism, 1770–1898* (Basingstoke, 2014), shows how the region's compatibility with Spain was lost during the last quarter of the century.

76. Rafael E. Tarragó, "Too Late? Social, Economic and Political Reform in Spanish Cuba, 1878–1898," *Colonial Latin American Review*, 5 (1996), pp. 299–314, offers a fresh view of this subject, as does the complementary study by María Dolores Elizalde Pérez-Grueso, "Emilio Terrero y Perinat, un reformista al frente del gobierno general de Filipinas (1885–1888)," *Hispanoamericana*, 6 (2016), digital publication online.

77. Byron, *Don Juan*, Canto 13, Stanza 11:
    > Cervantes smiled Spain's chivalry away;
    > A single laugh demolished the right arm
    > Of his own country;—seldom since that day
    > Has Spain had heroes.

78. Federico García Lorca, "Meditation," in *Impresiones y paisajes* (Granada, 1918; trans. Peter Bush, *Sketches of Spain: Impressions and Landscapes* (London, 2013). Lorca had a point to make: his "impressions" were those of a progressive.

79. Sebastian Balfour, *The End of the Spanish Empire, 1898–1923* (New York, 1997).

80. Quoted in Edward Coffman, "The Duality of the American Military Tradition: A Commentary," *Journal of Military History*, 64 (2000), p. 976.

81. I am indebted here particularly to Cecilia E. O'Leary, *To Die For: The Paradox of American Patriotism* (Princeton, 1999); Jonathan M. Hansen, *The Lost Promise of Patriotism: Debating American Identity, 1890–1920* (Chicago, 2003); and the perceptive essay by Claire B. Potter, "Nation and Reunification," *Reviews in American History*, 28 (2000), pp. 55–62.

82. Cleveland (president 1885–89 and 1893–97) paid a substitute $150 to serve in his place; Andrew Johnson (president 1865–69) served as military governor of Tennessee with the rank of brigadier general. McKinley held the rank of major; the remaining presidents ended the war with a rank of brigadier general or higher, reaching (with Ulysses S. Grant) the position of general-in-chief.

83. Mark R. Shulman, *Navalism and the Emergence of American Sea Power, 1882–1893* (Annapolis, 1995).

84. Coffman, "The Duality of the American Military Tradition," pp. 975–7.

85. Ibid., pp. 976–80; and the longer account in Coffman, *The Old Army: A Portrait of the American Army in Peacetime, 1784–1898* (New York, 1986).

86. James A. Field, "American Imperialism: The Worst Chapter in Almost any Book," *American Historical Review*, 83 (1987), pp. 658–9, 662–3.

87. Paul S. Holbo, "Economics, Emotion, and Expansion: An Emerging Foreign Policy," in H. Wayne Morgan, ed., *The Golden Age* (Syracuse, 1963), pp. 199–21, 211–12; Field, "American Imperialism," pp. 654–7.

88. Holbo, "Economics, Emotion, and Expansion," p. 211. Elihu Root, Secretary for War between 1899 and 1904, introduced the principal reforms.

89. Thomas G. Peterson, "American Businessmen and Consular Reform, 1890s to 1906," *Business History Review*, 40 (1966), pp. 91–4; Richard H. Werking, *The Master Architects: Building the United States Foreign Service, 1890–1913* (Lexington, 1977).

90. Werking, *The Master Architects*, argues that reform, when it came, was promoted by bureaucrats rather than by businessmen. See also Charles S. Kennedy, *The American Consul: A History of the United States Consular Service, 1776–1914* (Westport, 1990).

91. Joseph Smith, *The Spanish-American War: Conflict in the Caribbean and the Pacific* (London, 1994), ch. 3, provides an excellent account of the preparedness of the two powers.

92. By 1914, the U.S. Navy had expanded to the point where it was second in size only to the Royal Navy, though most of the growth occurred after 1898.

93. Dirk Bonker, "Admiration, Enmity, and Cooperation: U.S. Navalism and the British and German Empires before the Great War," *Journal of Colonialism & Colonial History*, 2 (2001), n.p.

94. Peter Karsten, "The Nature of 'Influence': Roosevelt, Mahan and the Concept of Sea Power," *American Quarterly*, 23 (1971), pp. 585–600. The more serious disagreements between the two arose after 1900: Richard W. Turk, *The Ambiguous Relationship: Theodore Roosevelt and Alfred Thayer Mahan* (New York, 1987).

95. Peter Trubowitz, *Defining the National Interest: Conflict and Change in American Foreign Policy* (Chicago, 1998), pp. 37–48. See also chapter 7 in this text.

96. Offner, *An Unwanted War*, pp. 129–30.

97. David L. T. Knudson, "A Note on Walter LaFeber, Captain Mahan, and the Use of Historical Sources," *Pacific Historical Review*, 40 (1971), pp. 520–21.

98. The starting point remains Ernest R. May, *Imperial Democracy: The Emergence of America as a Great Power* (New York, 1961), chs. 14–15. See also Sylvia L. Hilton and Steve J. S. Ickringill, eds., *European Perceptions of the Spanish-American War of 1898* (Berne, 1999).

99. Charles A. Conant, "The Economic Basis of Imperialism," *North American Review*, 167 (1898), p. 326. Conant (1861–1915) was a financial journalist who gained prominence in the 1890s and advised the government on financial reform in the Philippines. He believed that imperialism would provide an outlet for "surplus" capital and bring civilization to "decadent" peoples.

100. Marc William Palen, *The "Conspiracy" of Free Trade: The Anglo-American Struggle over Empire and Economic Globalisation, 1846–1896* (Cambridge, 2016), has disposed of any lingering assumptions that the Gilded Age was one of laissez-faire.

101. The discussion that follows deals with the international aspects of issues treated in their domestic context in chapter 7, though, inevitably, there is some overlap between the two.

102. As discussed in chapter 5 of this text. The key sources are Richard F. Bensel, *Sectionalism and American Political Development, 1880–1980* (Cambridge, 1984); Bensel, *Yankee Leviathan: The Origins of Central State Authority in America, 1859–1877* (Cambridge, 1991); Bensel, *The Political Economy of American Industrialization, 1877–1900* (Cambridge, 2000); Trubowitz, *Defining the National Interest.* See also Marc-William Palen, "The Imperialism of Economic Nationalism, 1890–1913," *Diplomatic History*, 39 (2015), pp. 157–85.

103. The domestic political consequences of the tariff are discussed in chapter 6 of this text. The best general statement of the international context is David M. Pletcher, *The Diplomacy of Trade and Investment: American Economic Expansion in the Hemisphere, 1865–1900* (Columbia, 1998).

104. LaFeber, *New Empire*, pp. 176–85.

105. David M. Pletcher's full and careful assessments have established this point beyond reasonable doubt: *The Diplomacy of Involvement: American Economic Expansion Across the Pacific, 1784–1900* (Columbia, 2001), p. 315; Pletcher, *Diplomacy of Trade and Investment.*

106. Pletcher, *Diplomacy of Trade and Investment*, chs. 2–3.

107. F. W. Taussig, "The McKinley Tariff Act," *Economic Journal*, 1 (1891), p. 347.

108. The "invasion" of Europe during this period was greatly helped by Britain's dogged commitment to free trade. See Mathew Simon and David E. Novack, "Some Dimensions of the American Commercial Invasion of Europe, 1871–1914: An Introductory Essay," *Journal of Economic History*, 24 (1964), pp. 591–605.

109. LaFeber, *New Empire*, pp. xxvii–xxviii.

110. It is extraordinary that the *locus classicus* of the subject is still Pratt, *Expansionists of 1898*. While this is a tribute to Pratt (who deserves far more credit as a historian than he has received), it is also a comment on the declining interest in economic history. Similarly, the difficulty of generalizing about the diverse business community remains, even though Robert H. Wiebe drew attention to the subject half a century ago in *Businessmen and Reform: A Study of the Progressive Movement* (Cambridge, 1962).

111. Williams, *Roots*, pp. 42, 413–6; LaFeber, *New Empire*, pp. 370–74; LaFeber, *American Search for Opportunity*, pp. 141, 236.

112. William H. Becker, *The Dynamics of Business-Government Relations: Industry and Exports, 1893–1921* (Chicago, 1982). In 1913, 67 of the largest firms supplied nearly 80 percent of U.S. manufactured exports.

113. Albert K. Steigerwalt, *The National Association of Manufacturers, 1895–1914: A Study in Business Leadership* (Ann Arbor, 1964). See also Offner, "United States Politics,"

p. 27; and Cathie Jo Martin, "Sectional Parties, Divided Business," *Studies in American Political Development*, 20 (2006), pp. 160–84. This is another subject that needs a full reappraisal.

114. Leland H. Jenks, *Our Cuban Colony: A Study in Sugar* (New York, 1928), p. 55.

115. Pratt, *Expansionists of 1898*, pp. 237–9, was characteristically astute in making this point, which later historians have tended to overlook. Thomas Schoonover blurs the distinction by stating that the "third trough" of the depression ran "from 1893 to 1898": *Uncle Sam's War of 1898 and the Origins of Globalization* (Lexington, 2003), p. 5; also p. 65.

116. Pratt, *Expansionists of 1898*, pp. 237–43.

117. See also the discussion of the recovery in chapter 5 of this text. LaFeber, *New Empire*, p. 390, notes this point but does not dispose of it.

118. LaFeber, *New Empire*, pp. 400–406.

119. Though it should be noted that Lewis L. Gould has shown that the Reick telegram, which assured McKinley of the support of the "big corporations" in March 1898, does not deserve the importance long attached to it: "The Reick Telegram and the Spanish-American War: A Reappraisal," *Diplomatic History*, 3 (1979), pp. 193–200.

120. Francisco and Shephard, *Conspiracy for Empire*, pp. 2, 15–16, 232. LaFeber, *New Empire*, does not index the Sugar Trust or its controller, Henry Havemeyer. Both are given further consideration in chapter 11 of this text.

121. (1847–1907). Richard O. Zerbe, "The American Sugar Refinery Company, 1887–1914: The Story of a Monopoly," *Journal of Law & Economics*, 12 (1969), pp. 339–75. Francisco and Shephard, *Conspiracy for Empire*, pp. 16–17, 29–32.The new company turned itself into the American Sugar Refining Company in 1891 but continued to be known as the Sugar Trust.

122. Francisco and Shephard, *Conspiracy for Empire*, p. 50.

123. Ibid., pp. 67, 151.

124. Ibid., pp. 207–9.

125. Jerome L. Sternstein, "Corruption in the Gilded Age: Nelson W. Aldrich and the Sugar Trust," *Capitol Studies*, 6 (1978), pp. 13–37.

126. Francisco and Shephard, *Conspiracy for Empire*, pp. 45, 68, 73–6, 83, 91.

127. Christopher Harris, "Edwin F. Atkins and the Evolution of United States Cuba Policy, 1894–1902," *New England Quarterly*, 78 (2005), pp. 202–31.

128. Francisco and Shephard, *Conspiracy for Empire*, ch. 13.

129. Ibid., pp. 110–16.

130. Ibid., ch. 20.

131. Richard C. K. Burdekin and Leroy O. Lancy, "Financial Market Reactions to the Overthrow and Annexation of the Hawaiian Kingdom: Evidence from London, Honolulu and New York," *Cliometrica*, 2 (2008), pp. 120–21, 127, 137.

132. Senator Knute Nelson, speaking in support of the Treaty of Paris, which was signed in 1899. Quoted in Stephen W. Stathis, ed., *Landmark Debates in Congress: From the Declaration of Independence to the War in Iraq* (Washington, DC, 2009), p. 234.

133. A representative study is Warren Zimmermann, *First Great Triumph: How Five Americans Made Their Country a World Power* (New York, 2002). Frank Ninkovich, *Global Dawn: The Cultural Foundations of American Internationalism, 1865–1890* (Cambridge, 2009), provides a valuable account of how liberal elites drew on cosmopolitan sources to formulate and debate the idea of a global civilization.

134. For a statement of the skeptical position and references to the opposite view, see Hamilton, *President McKinley*, vol. 2, ch. 2.

135. Woodrow Wilson, "The Ideals of America," *Atlantic Monthly*, 90 (1902), pp. 733–4.

136. See also chapter 7 of this text.

137. The list could be extended. Warren Zimmerman omits Beveridge but includes John Hay and Elihu Root: *First Great Triumph*. This list reflects his interests, which extend

beyond 1898. Hay was Secretary of State from September 1898 to 1905; Root succeeded him, 1905–1909.

138. Mahan, Lodge, and Roosevelt came from affluent families; Beveridge alone was a "self-made man," who qualified as a lawyer before entering politics.

139. Gary Gerstle explores other complexities of this over-stereotyped character in "Theodore Roosevelt and the Divided Character of American Nationalism," *Journal of American History*, 86 (1999), pp. 1280–1307.

140. William C. Widenor, *Henry Cabot Lodge and the Search for an American Foreign Policy* (Berkeley, 1980).

141. John Braeman, *Albert Beveridge: American Nationalist* (Chicago, 1971).

142. Albert J. Beveridge, *The Meaning of the Times and Other Speeches* (Indianapolis, 1908). His two most famous speeches are readily available: "The March of the Flag" (1898) at http://www.historytools.org/sources/beveridge.html; and "In Support of an American Empire" (1900), at http://www.mtholyoke.edu/acad/intrel/ajb72.htm.

143. Paul Kramer, "Empires, Exceptions, and Anglo-Saxons: Race and Rule between the British and United States Empires, 1880–1910," *Journal of American History*, 88 (2002), pp. 1315–53.

144. *Life of Nelson: The Embodiment of the Sea Power of Great Britain* (Boston, 1897). On the difficulties of simplifying the complexities of Mahan's thinking, see Robert Seager, *Alfred Thayer Mahan: The Man and His Letters* (Annapolis, 1977), p. xi. Much the same could be said of the other expansionists.

145. Kenton J. Clymer, *John Hay: The Gentleman as Diplomat* (Ann Arbor, 1975); a recent study is John Taliaferro, *All the Great Prizes: The Life of John Hay, From Lincoln to Roosevelt* (New York, 2013).

146. Gary Wills, *Henry Adams and the Making of America* (New York, 2005), provides a favorable assessment of Adams as a historian.

147. Brooks Adams and his brother, Henry, shared many characteristics, including a gloomy outlook on the world.

148. Brooks Adams, *America's Economic Supremacy* (London, 1900), compared the two authors in a chapter entitled "Natural Selection in Literature," pp. 86–141. The quotation is on p. 135.

149. Gary Marotta, "The Economics of American Empire: The View of Brooks Adams and Charles Arthur Conant," *American Economist*, 19 (1975), pp. 34–7, is illuminating on this point, as is Robert Vitalis, "The Noble American Science of Imperial Relations and Its Laws of Race Development," *Comparative Studies in Society & History*, 52 (2010), pp. 909–38.

150. Paul T. McCartney, *Power and Progress: American National Identity, the War of 1898, and the Rise of American Imperialism* (Baton Rouge, 2006), pp. 191–8.

151. Rolf Hobson, *Imperialism at Sea: Naval Strategic Thought, the Ideology of Sea Power, and the Tirpitz Plan, 18975–1914* (Boston, 2002); Jan Ruger, *The Great Naval Game: Britain and Germany in the Age of Empire* (Cambridge, 2007); Bonker, "Admiration, Enmity, and Cooperation."

152. Gary Marotta, "The Academic Mind and the Rise of U.S. Imperialism," *American Journal of Economics & Sociology*, 42 (1983), pp. 217–34. This valuable article has been unjustly neglected.

153. Bluford Adams, "World Conquerors or a Dying People? Racial Theory, Regional Anxiety, and the Brahmin Anglo-Saxonists," *Journal of the Gilded Age & Progressive Era*, 8 (2009), pp. 189–215.

154. Wilfred M. McClay, "John W. Burgess and the Search for Cohesion in American Political Thought," *Polity*, 26 (1993), pp. 51–73; Vitalis, "The Noble American Science," pp. 917–25, traces the evolution of Burgess's thinking on empire.

155. Marotta, "The Academic Mind," p. 225.

156. Pratt, *Expansionists of 1898*, ch. 8.

157. Quoted in ibid., p. 300. The *Advance* was a Congregationalist publication.

158. Quoted in ibid., p. 287.

159. Quoted in ibid., p. 281. Chapter 8, "The Imperialism of Righteousness," in Pratt's work remains the standard treatment of the subject.

160. Pratt, *Expansionists of 1898*, p. 282, quoting Mott in 1897. John Mott (1865-1955) founded the World Student Christian Federation in 1895 and served as General Secretary of the YMCA.

161. Ibid., p. 312. Quakers and Unitarians stood out against war. Benjamin Wetzel, "A Church Divided: Roman Catholicism, Americanization, and the Spanish-American War," *Journal of the Gilded Age & Progressive Era*, 14 (2015), pp. 348-66, also deals with Catholics who opposed the war.

162. Michael P. Cullinane, *Liberty and American Anti-Imperialism, 1898-1909* (New York, 2012), has rescued the League from a long period of neglect.

163. Other well-known supporters included Jane Addams, John Dewey, Henry James, William James, Thomas B. Reed, and William Graham Sumner.

164. Carl P. Parrini and Martin J. Sklar, "New Thinking about the Market, 1896-1904: Some American Economists on Investment and the Theory of Surplus Capital," *Journal of Economic History*, 43 (1983), pp. 559-78; Peter J. Cain, "Hobson, Wilshire, and the Capitalist Theory of Capitalist Imperialism," *History of Political Economy*, 17 (1985), pp. 455-60. Wilshire was exceptional in also being a millionaire, but he lost his fortune and joined the masses in being destitute when he died.

165. Charles A. Conant accepted the analysis but drew a different conclusion. See Conant, "The Economic Basis of Imperialism," *North American Review*, 167 (September 1898), pp. 326-40; also Carl Parrini, "Charles A. Conant, "Economic Crises and Foreign Policy, 1896-1903," in Thomas J. McCormick and Walter LaFeber, eds., *Behind the Throne: Servants of Power to Imperial Presidents, 1898-1968* (Madison, 1993), pp. 21-52.

166. Kristofer Allerfeldt, "Rome, Race, and the Republic: Progressive America and the Fall of the Roman Empire, 1890-1920," *Journal of the Gilded Age & Progressive Era*, 7 (2008), pp. 297-323.

167. "Causes of Southern Opposition to Imperialism," *North American Review*, 171 (1900), pp. 439-46 at p. 445. Tillman (1847-1918) was governor of South Carolina (1890-1894), senator (1895-1918), and a noted white supremacist and demagogue.

168. Cullinane, *Liberty and American Anti-Imperialism*, ch. 4.

169. Gerstle, "Theodore Roosevelt," on the tensions between nationalism based on civil liberties and nationalism based on racial distinctions.

170. Quoted in Stuart Creighton Miller, *Benevolent Assimilation: The American Conquest of the Philippines, 1899-1903* (New Haven, 1982), p. 117.

171. The fullest assessment of research on the press is Hamilton, *President McKinley*, vol. 2, chs. 5, 6, 7.

172. McCartney, *Power and Progress*, pp. 87, 99, 149-50; May, *Imperial Democracy*, pp. 139-47.

173. Jules-Martin Cambon to Gabriel Hanotaux, April 1, 1898. Quoted in May, *Imperial Democracy*, p. 143.

174. Offner, *An Unwanted War*, p. 190.

175. Howard W. Allen and Roger Slagter, "Congress in Crisis: Changes in Personnel and the Legislative Agenda in the U.S. Congress in the 1890s," *Social Science History*, 16 (1992), pp. 401-20. This article has yet to feature in the debate on the decision to declare war in 1898. See also Hamilton, *President McKinley*, vol. 1, ch. 7.

176. It is scarcely unprecedented for lawyers to be influenced by businessmen, but the connection needs to be demonstrated and not just assumed.

177. Offner, *An Unwanted War*. A definitive statement of the nature and extent of business influence must await a renewal of interest in the subject, given that the last full investigation, valuable though it still is, was published nearly 50 years ago: LaFeber, *The New*

Empire. David M. Pletcher provides a balanced summary of the literature as it stood in 1998 in *Diplomacy of Trade and Investment*, ch. 1.

178. Offner, *An Unwanted War*, pp. 231–3.

179. Ibid., p. 153.

180. Quoted in ibid. Alger, who took much of the blame for the lack of military preparation, defended himself ably in *The Spanish-American War* (New York, 1901).

181. Ibid.

182. Ibid.

183. As Lewis L. Gould's definitive study has made clear: *The Spanish-American War and President McKinley* (Lawrence, 1982). On the press, see W. Joseph Campbell, *Yellow Journalism: Puncturing the Myths, Defining the Legacies* (Westport, 2001); Hamilton, *President McKinley*, vol. 1, chs. 5–6; John Maxwell Hamilton, et al., "An Enabling Environment: A Reconsideration of the Press and the Spanish-American War," *Journalism Studies*, 7 (2006), pp. 78–93, show that the extensive coverage and anti-Spanish attitudes of the press facilitated a decision that was made on other grounds.

184. Nick Kapur, "William McKinley's Values and the Origins of the Spanish-American War: A Reinterpretation," *Presidential Studies Quarterly*, 41 (2011), p. 26.

185. Hamilton, *President McKinley*, vol. 2, pp. 46–7, 50–8, 94–5, 226–7. William T. Horner, *Ohio's Kingmaker: Mark Hanna, Man, and Myth* (Athens, 2010) tells a similar story.

186. The matters discussed in this paragraph are fully covered by Gould, *President McKinley*; Offner, *An Unwanted War*; Paul S. Holbo, "Presidential Leadership in Foreign Affairs: William McKinley and the Turpie-Foraker Amendment," *American Historical Review*, 72 (1967), pp. 1321–35.

187. Smith, *The Spanish-American War*, pp. 100–102.

188. Willard B. Gatewood, *Black Arms and the White Man's Burden, 1898–1903* (Urbana-Champagne, 1975), pp. 23–9. Booker T. Washington urged black Americans to enlist because he believed that a demonstration of loyalty would be rewarded by improved civil rights. Hope springs eternal partly because it has to recover from so many disappointments. U.S. sources also underplayed the vital contribution made by Cuban insurgents in assisting U.S. forces. See Pérez, *The War of 1898*, p. 86.

189. John L. Leffler, "The Paradox of Patriotism: Texans in the Spanish-American War," *Hayes Historical Journal*, 8 (1989), pp. 24–48; Scott Marshall, "East Texas and the Coming of the Spanish-American War: An Examination of Regional Values," *East Texas Historical Journal*, 37 (1999), pp. 44–52; James M. McCaffrey, "Texans in the Spanish-American War," *Southwestern Historical Quarterly*, 106 (2002), pp. 254–79.

190. Theodore Roosevelt, "The Reunited People," in Roosevelt, *American Problems* (New York, 1926), p. 27.

191. The others were Mathew G. Butler (1836–1909), Thomas L. Rosser (1836–1910), and Fitzhugh Lee (1835–1905), who was the U.S. Consul in Havana at the time.

192. Quoted in Beisner, *Twelve Against Empire*, p. 152. Hoar (1826–1904) was a Massachusetts senator, 1872–1904, a liberal Republican, and an outspoken critic of imperialism and racial discrimination.

193. William Graham Sumner, *The Conquest of the United States by Spain* (Boston, 1899).

194. Ibid., p. 27. It would appear that he was right: Geoffrey Seed, "British Views of American Policy in the Philippines Reflected in Journals of Opinion, 1898–1907," *Journal of American Studies*, 2 (1968), pp. 49–64.

195. John Hay to Theodore Roosevelt, July 27, 1898, in William R. Taylor, *The Life and Letters of John Hay*, vol. 2 (Boston, 1915), p. 337.

196. McCartney, *Power and Progress*, pp. 163–73.

197. Trumbull White, *Our New Possessions: Four Books in One* (Philadelphia, 1898); James C. Fernald, *The Imperial Republic* (New York, 1899).

198. Theodore Roosevelt, *The Rough Riders* (New York, 1899).

199. Henry Cabot Lodge, *The War with Spain* (New York, 1899).

200. *In Defense of the Flag: A Boy's Adventures in Spain and the West Indies during the Battle Year of Our War with Spain* (Boston, 1900); *With Lawton and Roberts: A Boy's Adventures in the Philippines and the Transvaal* (Boston, 1900).

201. *Under Dewey at Manila, or the War Fortunes of a Castaway* (Boston, 1898); *Under Otis in the Philippines, or a Young Officer in the Tropics* (Boston, 1899); *A Young Volunteer in Cuba, or Fighting for the Single Star* (1900); *Under MacArthur in Luzon or Last Battles in the Philippines* (Boston, 1904). See also Carol Bellman, *The Secret of the Stratemeyer Syndicate: Mary Drew, the Hardy Boys, and the Million Dollar Fiction Factory* (New York, 1986). At the time of his death in 1930, Stratemeyer had published more than 700 titles and had sold some 300 million copies of his books.

202. Jesse Aleman and Shelley Streeby, eds., *Empire and the Literature of Sensation* (New Brunswick, 2007); Andrew Hebard, "Romantic Sovereignty: Popular Romances and the American Imperial State in the Philippines," *American Quarterly*, 57 (2005), pp. 805–30.

203. Robert W. Rydell, "Soundtracks of Empire: The 'White Man's Burden,' the War in the Philippines, the 'Ideals of America,' and Tin Pan Alley," *European Journal of American Studies*, 7 (2012), pp. 1–14.

204. President William McKinley, "State of the Union Address," December 5, 1898.

205. Andrew S. Draper, *The Rescue of Cuba: An Episode in the Growth of Free Government* (New York, 1899), p. 177.

206. "In Support of an American Empire," Speech to the Senate, *Record*, vol. 33, 56th Congress, 1st Session, January 1900, pp. 704–12.

207. Ibid.

208. "The Ideals of America," *Atlantic Monthly*, 90 (1902), pp. 721–34.

209. William Jennings Bryan is responsible for the alliteration, which he devised as a heading for his own explanation of the Republicans' new "colonial policy" in the Philippines: "The Election of 1900," *North American Review*, 171 (1900), p. 795.

210. Karl Marx, *The Eighteenth Brumaire of Louis Bonaparte* (New York, 1897; 1913), p. 9.

211. As discussed in chapter 5 of this text. Particular acknowledgment should be made here of Peter Gourevitch's pioneering article, "International Trade, Domestic Coalitions, and Liberty: Comparative Responses to the Crisis of 1873–1896," *Journal of Interdisciplinary History*, 8 (1977), pp. 281–313, and the amplification in his important book, *Politics in Hard Times: Comparative Responses to International Crises* (Ithaca, 1986), ch. 3.

212. Cornelius Trop, "The Coalition of Rye and Iron under the Pressure of Globalisation: A Reinterpretation of Germany's Political Economy before 1914," *Central European History*, 43 (2010), pp. 401–27.

213. For invocations of the Almighty, see McCartney, *Power and Progress*, pp. 99–106.

214. For one view of developments leading to the invasion of Iraq in 2003, see A. G. Hopkins, "Capitalism, Nationalism and the New American Empire," *Journal of Imperial & Commonwealth History*, 35 (2007), pp. 95–117.

215. Ernest R. May, *American Imperialism: A Speculative Essay* (Chicago, 1967; 1991). The edition published in 1991 contains an illuminating new Introduction (pp. v–xxxii). See also Alan Dawley, *Changing the World: American Progressives in War and Peace* (Princeton, NJ, 2003); and Priscilla Roberts, "The Transatlantic American Foreign Policy Elite: Its Evolution in Generational Perspective," *Journal of Transatlantic Studies*, 7 (2009), pp. 163–83. Ninkovich, *Global Dawn*.

216. *The Conquest of the United States by Spain* (Boston, 1899), p. 4. This position is also taken by Offner in his authoritative account: *An Unwanted War*, pp. ix, 234.

217. The average age of the senior figures in the Anti-Imperial League was well over sixty. The leading imperialists, apart from Mahan, were in their forties: Goran Rystad, *Ambiguous Imperialism: American Foreign Policy and Domestic Politics at the Turn of the Century* (Stockholm, 1975), p. 56.

218. Clyde W. Barrow, *More than a Historian: The Political and Economic Thought of Charles A. Beard* (New Brunswick, 2000), ch. 6, provides an admirable introduction. I am grateful to Prof. Barrow for his patient responses to my questions on this subject.

219. Charles and Mary Beard, *The Rise of American Civilization* (New York, 1937), pp. 370, 374, 480, 491–5.

220. Charles A. Beard, *The Idea of National Interest* (New York, 1934); pp. 60–84; Beard, *Giddy Minds and Foreign Quarrels* (New York, 1939); Beard, *A Foreign Policy for America* (New York, 1940).

221. Beard, *Giddy Minds*, p. 16.

222. Beard, *A Foreign Policy*, p. 47.

223. Ibid., p. 72.

224. Ernest R. May, *Imperial Democracy: The Emergence of America as a Great Power* (New York, 1961), p. 270.

225. Brooks Adams took the same view in "The Spanish War and the Equilibrium of the World," *The Forum* (August, 1898), p. 650: "It is in vain that men talk of keeping free from entanglements. Nature is omnipotent; and nations must float with the tide."

226. William Appleman Williams, "A Note on Charles Austin Beard's Search for a General Theory of Causation," *American Historical Review*, 62 (1956), pp. 59–80, remains the most penetrating account.

227. Barrow, *More than a Historian*, p. 195.

228. The classification of motives is set out in chapter 6.

229. There is no reason to doubt the sincerity of McKinley's piety: Andrew Preston, *Sword of the Spirit, Shield of the Faith: Religion in American War and Diplomacy* (New York, 2012), pp. 156–7.

230. The Reverend Sabine Baring-Gould wrote the words of the hymn, "Onward, Christian Soldiers," in 1865; his compatriot (Sir) Arthur Sullivan, composed the music in 1871.

231. No one expressed the core values better than Theodore Roosevelt in *American Ideals, the Strenuous Life, Realizable Ideals* (New York, 1926).

232. Maurice Duvivier, quoted in Vincent Viaene, "King Leopold's Imperialism and the Origins of the Belgian Colonial Party, 1860–1905," *Journal of Modern History*, 80 (2008), p. 778.

233. James R. Reckner, *Teddy Roosevelt's Great White Fleet: The World Cruise of the American Battlefleet, 1907–1909* (Annapolis, 1988).

234. Barry Gough, the authority on the subject, sees 1898 as the turning point in the naval balance of power: by 1907, the new direction was becoming clear. See *Pax Britannica: Ruling the Waves and Keeping the Peace before Armageddon* (Basingstoke, 2014), ch. 13.

CHAPTER 9: INSULAR PERSPECTIVES ON AN INTRUSIVE WORLD

1. A Filipino, "Aguinaldo's Case against the United States," *North American Review*, September 1899, p. 427.

2. Martí to Manuel Mercado, 18 May 1895. Quoted in the frontispiece to Philip S. Foner, ed., *Political Parties and Elections in the United States* (Philadelphia, 1988).

3. Ibid. For Martí's commentary on the United States, see Philip S. Foner, ed., *Inside the Monster* (New York, 1975).

4. Quoted in James L. Dietz, *Economic History of Puerto Rico: Institutional Change and Capitalist Development* (Princeton, 1986), p. 94.

5. A Filipino, "Aguinaldo's Case," p. 427.

6. Ibid., p. 432.

7. Maia Lichtenstein, "The Paradox of Hawaiian National Identity and Resistance to United States Annexation," *Penn History Review*, 16 (2008), pp. 50–51.

8. On 12 August. Lester A. Beardsley, "Pilikias," *North American Review*, 167 (1898), pp. 473–80.

9. Ibid., p. 475. "Hawai'i Pono'i" (composed by Captain Henri Berger, the government's bandmaster, to words by King Kalākaua) was first performed in 1874 and became the official state anthem in 1967.

10. John D. Hargreaves, "Towards a History of the Partition of Africa," *Journal of African History*, 1 (1960), p. 7.

11. Beginning with the pioneering study by Ronald Robinson and John Gallagher with Alice Denny, *Africa and the Victorians: The Official Mind of Imperialism* (London, 1961; 2nd ed. 1981).

12. Alfred W. McCoy and Francisco A. Scarano, eds., *Colonial Crucible: Empire in the Making of the Modern American State* (Madison, 2009), is a large and valuable collection (with the rarity of a substantial index) that sets out an agenda for future research. Credit should also be given to Julian Go, writing in "the tradition of macro-comparative historical sociology," for his contribution: *Patterns of Empire: The British and American Empires, 1688 to the Present* (Cambridge, 2011).

13. Walter LaFeber, *The New Empire: An Interpretation of American Expansion, 1860–1898* (Ithaca, 1963; 2nd ed. 1998), p. xxix.

14. It is appropriate here to restate that the present study covers the Philippines, Hawai'i, Cuba, and Puerto Rico only. It omits Guam and American Samoa, which merit studies in their own right, instead of being tacked on to longer passages on the larger islands, and the numerous atolls in the Pacific that the navy gathered in the course of the nineteenth century.

15. The literature on these themes is too vast to be referred to here. Introductions include Robin W. Winks, ed., *The Oxford History of the British Empire*, Vol. 5, *Historiography* (Oxford, 1999); P. J. Cain and A. G. Hopkins, *British Imperialism, 1688–2000* (London, 3rd ed. 2016), ch. 1. See, too, the now classic studies by John Gallagher and Ronald Robinson, "The Imperialism of Free Trade," *Economic History Review*, 2nd ser. 6 (1953), pp. 1–15; Ronald Robinson, "Non-European Foundations of European Imperialism: Sketch for a Theory of Collaboration," in Roger Owen and Bob Sutcliffe, eds., *Studies in the Theory of Imperialism* (London, 1972), pp. 117–42.

16. The foundational source is John S. Galbraith, "The 'Turbulent Frontier' as a Factor in British Expansion," *Comparative Studies in Society & History*, 2 (1960), pp. 150–68.

17. As discussed in chapter 6 of this text.

18. Wallace R. Aykroyd, *Sweet Malefactor: Sugar, Slavery and Human Society* (London, 1967).

19. Eleanor C. Nordyke, *The Peopling of Hawai'i* (Honolulu, 2nd ed. 1989), table 3.4, pp. 178–81. I am indebted to Prof. David A. Swanson, University of California, Riverside, for this reference and for valuable additional information on Hawai'i's demographic history.

20. Lewis E. Gleeck, *The Manila Americans, 1901–1964* (Manila, 1975), pp. 39, 136.

21. The term "sojourner" has entered the literature primarily through work on Asia. See, for example, Anthony Reid, ed., *Sojourners and Settlers: Histories of Southeast Asia and the Chinese* (Honolulu, 2001).

22. Spanish and mestizo women may have adapted to the locality more readily than men, who were more concerned about the prospect of "going native." See Christine Doran, "Spanish and Mestizo Women of Manila," *Philippine Studies*, 41 (1993), pp. 269–86.

23. Mestizos (principally Europeans + Native South Americans, or Tagalog + Chinese in the Philippines); mulatos (principally Europeans + Africans in the Caribbean); Indios (principally indigenous inhabitants of South America); negritos (principally aboriginals in the Philippines); negros (principally African slaves in the Caribbean).

24. "Friars" is a collective name used in Philippine studies to refer principally to the Dominican, Augustinian, Franciscan, Recollect, and Carmelite religious orders.

25. Juan Antonio Inarejos Muñoz, "Caciques con sotana: control social e injerencia electoral de los eclesiásticos en las Filipinas españolas," *Historia Social*, 75 (2013), pp. 23–40, explores the complex relationship between the Friars and other political interests.

26. William A. Morgan, "Cuban Tobacco Slavery: Life, Labor and Freedom in Pinar del Río," Ph.D. dissertation, University of Texas at Austin (2013), reviews the literature on the "sugar-centric" thesis in ch. 1. I am grateful to Dr. Morgan not only for allowing me to read and cite his important dissertation, but also for his generous response to my wider questions about Cuban history in the nineteenth century.

27. Luzviminda Bartolome Francisco and Jonathan Shepard Fast, *Conspiracy for Empire: Big Business, Corruption and the Politics of Imperialism in America, 1876–1907* (Quezon City, 1985), p. 232.

28. Calculated from F. W. Taussig, "Sugar: A Lesson in Reciprocity," *Atlantic Monthly*, 95 (1908), p. 334. Roy A. Ballinger, *A History of Sugar Marketing* (Washington, DC, 1971), p. 10, gives a figure of 14 percent for 1896.

29. Java became one of the most efficient industries in the world in the 1880s: Willem G. Wolters, "Sugar Production in Java and in the Philippines during the Nineteenth Century," *Philippine Studies*, 40 (1992), pp. 411–34, at p. 413.

30. Taussig, "Sugar," p. 336, argued that consumers did not benefit. Sumner LaCroix and Christopher Grandy have confirmed his claim: "The Political Instability of Reciprocal Trade and the Overthrow of the Hawaiian Kingdom," *Journal of Economic History*, 57 (1997), pp. 170–72. See also F. W. Taussig, *Some Aspects of the Tariff Question* (Cambridge, MA, 1915), ch. 5; and Richard O. Zerbe, "The American Sugar Refinery Company, 1887–1914: The Story of a Monopoly," *Journal of Law & Economics*, 12 (1969), pp. 339–75.

31. General Samuel B. M. Young, 1898. Quoted in Louis A. Pérez, Jr., *Cuba in the American Imagination: Metaphor and the Imperial Ethos* (Chapel Hill, 2008), p. 179.

32. Exports of sugar increased 6.5 times between 1840 and 1868, at which point Cuba accounted for 30 percent of world output. See Vanessa M. Ziegler, "The Revolt of the 'Ever-Faithful Isle': The Ten Years' War in Cuba, 1868–1878," Ph.D. dissertation, University of California (2007), p. 5. Also W. G. Clarence Smith, "The Economic Dynamics of Spanish Colonialism in the Nineteenth and Twentieth Centuries," *Itinerario*, 15 (1991), p. 72. On tobacco, see Morgan, "Cuban Tobacco Slavery." Credit should be given here to Franklin W. Knight's pioneering study, *Slave Society in Cuba during the Nineteenth Century* (Madison, 1970).

33. Louis A. Pérez, Jr., *Winds of Change: Hurricanes and the Transformation of Nineteenth-Century Cuba* (Chapel Hill, 2001), adds a novel dimension to standard historical treatments. See also William C. Van Norman, *Shade-Grown Slavery: The Lives of Slaves on Coffee Plantations in Cuba* (Nashville, 2012).

34. Ada Ferrer, *Insurgent Cuba: Race, Nation, and Revolution, 1868–1898* (Chapel Hill, 1999), p. 2.

35. Ziegler, "The Revolt of the 'Ever-Faithful Isle.'"

36. Jonathan Curry-Machado, "'Rich Flames and Hired Tears': Sugar, Sub-Imperial Agents, and the Cuban Phoenix of Empire," *Journal of Global History*, 4 (2009), pp. 33–56.

37. Clarence Smith, "Economic Dynamics, p. 72.

38. Inés Roldán de Montaud, "España y Cuba: Cien años de relaciones financieras," *Studia Historica: Historia Contemopránea*, 15 (1997), pp. 35–69.

39. Dominique Concalvès, *Le planteur et le roi: L'aristocratie havanise et la couronne d'Espagne (1763–1838)* (Madrid, 2008).

40. Sherry Johnson, *The Social Transformation of Eighteenth-Century Cuba* (Gainesville, 2001).

41. Ada Ferrer, *Freedom's Mirror: Cuba and Haiti in the Age of Revolution* (New York, 2015). Cuba's planters even imported slaves and machinery from Haiti following the disruption of production there.

42. The agreement made in 1814 became operative in 1819, though France gave it only unenthusiastic support.

43. Manuel Moreno Fraginals, *The Sugarmill: The Socioeconomic Complex of Sugar in Cuba, 1760–1860* (New York, 1978); Rebecca J. Scott, *Slave Emancipation in Cuba: The Transi-*

tion to Free Labor, 1860-1899 (Princeton, 1986); Christian Schnakenbourg, "From Sugar Estate to Central Factory: The Industrial Revolution in the Caribbean (1840-1905)," in Bill Albert and Adrian Graves, eds., *Crisis and Change in the International Sugar Economy, 1860-1914* (Norwich, 1984), pp. 83-91, provides a concise overview. César J. Ayala, "Social and Economic Aspects of Sugar Production in Cuba, 1880-1930," *Latin American Research Review*, 30 (1995), pp. 95-124; Christopher Nowara-Schmidt, "The End of Slavery and the End of Empire: Slave Emancipation in Cuba and Puerto Rico," *Slavery & Abolition*, 21 (2000), pp. 188-207. On slave revolts, see Manuel Barcia, *Seeds of Insurrection: Domination and Resistance in Western Cuba, 1808-1848* (Baton Rouge, 2008); Barcia, *The Great African Slave Revolt of 1825: Cuba and the Fight for Freedom in Matanzas* (Baton Rouge, 2012). Lisa Yun, *The Coolie Speaks: Chinese Indentured Laborers and African Slaves in Cuba* (Philadelphia, 2008); and Kathleen López, *Chinese Cubans: A Transnational History* (Chapel Hill, 2013), provide admirable accounts set in an appropriately global context.

44. The data on Cuba are exceptionally good. See Linda K Salucci and Richard J. Salucci, "Cuba and the Latin American Terms of Trade: Old Theories, New Evidence," *Journal of Interdisciplinary History*, 31 (2000), pp. 202-6; Ziegler, "The Revolt of the 'Ever-Faithful Isle,'" pp. 13, 252-3.

45. Julia Solla Sastre, "Cuando las provincias de allende los mares sean llamadas por la Constitución (acerca del estatus constitucional de Cuba, Puerto Rico y Filipinas, 1837-1898)," *Giornale di Storia Costituzionale*, 25 (2013), pp. 61-78.

46. David R. Murray, *Odious Commerce: Britain, Spain, and the Abolition of the Cuban Slave Trade* (Cambridge, 1981), provides a full account; Murray, "The Slave Trade, Slavery, and Cuban Independence," *Slavery & Abolition*, 20 (1999), pp. 106-26, refers to subsequent studies.

47. Louis A. Pérez, Jr., *Cuba: Between Reform and Revolution* (New York, 1988; 3rd ed. Oxford, 2006).

48. Céspedes del Castillo (1819-1874) was killed during the war.

49. Ziegler, "The Revolt of the 'Ever-Faithful Isle,'" pp. 14, 22.

50. Scott, *Slave Emancipation in Cuba*; César J. Ayala, *American Sugar Kingdom: The Plantation Economy of the Spanish Caribbean, 1898-1934* (Chapel Hill, 1999), pp. 153-6; Nowara-Schmidt, "The End of Slavery and the End of Empire."

51. Scott, *Slave Emancipation in Cuba*, chs. 2-3.

52. Yun, *The Coolie Speaks*; López, *Chinese Cubans*.

53. Lisa Yun and Ricardo Rene Laremont, "Chinese Coolies and African Slaves in Cuba, 1847-74," *Journal of Asian American Studies*, 4 (2001), pp. 99-122; Jesús M. Valdaliso, "Trade, Colonies and Navigation Laws: The Flag, Differential Duty, and the International Competitiveness of Spanish Shipping in the Nineteenth Century," *International Journal of Maritime History*, 167 (2005), pp. 31-60.

54. Luis Fernández-Martínez, *Torn Between Empires: Economy, Society, and Patterns of Political Thought in the Hispanic Caribbean, 1840-1878* (Athens, 1994), places this theme in the context of Cuba, Puerto Rico, and the Dominican Republic.

55. Oscar Zanetti and Alejandro Garcia, *Sugar and Railroads: A Cuban History, 1837-1959* (Chapel Hill, 1998), provide a full account of the subject.

56. B.J.C. McKercher and S. Enjamio, "'Brighter Futures and Better Times': Britain, the Empire, and Anglo-American Economic Competition in Cuba, 1898-1920," *Diplomacy & Statecraft*, 18 (2007), p. 668.

57. Fraginals, *The Sugarmill*; Schnakenbourg, "From Sugar Estate to Central Factory"; César J. Ayala, "Social and Economic Aspects of Sugar Production in Cuba, 1880-1930," *Latin American Research Review*, 30 (1995), pp. 95-124.

58. Scott, *Slave Emancipation in Cuba*, pp. 26, 166-72.

59. Rafael E. Tarragó, "Too Late? Social, Economic and Political Reform in Spanish Cuba, 1878-1898," *Colonial Latin American Review*, 5 (1996), pp. 301-5; Susan J. Fernandez,

Encumbered Cuba: Capital Markets and Revolt, 1878-1895 (Gainesville, 2009), identifies the socioeconomic basis of party support.

60. J.C.M. Ogelsby, "The Cuban Autonomista Movement's Perception of Canada, 1865-1898," *The Americas*, 48 (1992), pp. 445-61.

61. Schmidt-Nowara, *Empire and Slavery*, covers these themes authoritatively.

62. Alfonso W. Quiroz, "Loyalist Overkill: The Socio-Economic Costs of 'Repressing' the Separatist Insurrection in Cuba," *Hispanic American Historical Review*, 78 (1998), pp. 295-6, 300, 303-5.

63. Alfonso W. Quiroz, "Implicit Costs of Empire: Bureaucratic Corruption in Nineteenth-Century Cuba," *Journal of Latin American Studies*, 35 (2003), pp. 473-511.

64. Karen Robert, "Slavery and Freedom in the Ten Years' War: Cuba, 1868-1878," *Slavery & Abolition*, 13 (1992), pp. 184-200.

65. Rosalie Schwartz, *Lawless Liberators: Political Banditry and Cuban Independence* (Durham, 1989). Louis A. Pérez, Jr., *Lords of the Mountain: Social Banditry and Peasant Protest in Cuba, 1878-1918* (Pittsburgh, 1989) offers a different perspective.

66. This is a leading theme in Ferrer, *Insurgent Cuba*.

67. Joseph Smith, *The Spanish-American War: Conflict in the Caribbean and the Pacific, 1895-1902* (London, 1994), pp. 2-3.

68. Gómez (1854-1933); Maceó (1845-1897).

69. Louis A. Pérez, Jr., "Towards Dependency and Revolution: The Political Economy of Cuba between Wars, 1878-1895," *Latin American Research Review*, 18 (1983), pp. 127-42; Ogelsby, "The Cuban Autonomista Movement's Perception of Canada," pp. 449-50.

70. Linda K. Salvucci and Richard J. Salvucci, "Cuba and Latin American Terms of Trade: Old Theories, New Evidence," *Journal of Interdisciplinary History*, 31 (2000), pp. 201-12, 217.

71. Fernandez, *Encumbered Cuba*, pp. 144-5. I am immensely grateful to Dr. Fernandez for taking the time to explain aspects of this complicated subject that had eluded me. Spain's increasingly desperate fiscal state is dealt with by Inés Roldán de Montaud, "Guerra y finanzas en la crisis de fin de siglo: 1895-1899," *Hispania: Revista Española de Historia*, 57 (1997), pp. 611-65. Antonio Santamaría García, "Precios y salarios reales en Cuba, 1872-1914," *Revista de Historia Económica*, 18 (2000), pp. 339-76, provides suggestive evidence to show that real incomes declined after 1883.

72. Fernandez, *Encumbered Cuba*, pp. 152-3.

73. See, for example, Inés Roldán de Montaud, "Spanish Fiscal Policies and Cuban Tobacco during the Nineteenth Century," *Cuban Studies*, 33 (2002), pp. 48-70.

74. Christopher Harris, "Edwin F. Atkins and the Evolution of United States Cuba Policy, 1894-1902," *New England Quarterly*, 78 (2005), pp. 207-8; Tarragó, "Too Late? Social, Economic and Political Reform in Spanish Cuba," pp. 301-3.

75. Louis A. Pérez, *Cuba between Empires, 1878-1902* (Pittsburg, 1983), pp. 30-31; David M. Pletcher, *The Diplomacy of Trade and Investment: American Economic Expansion in the Hemisphere, 1865-1900* (Columbia, 1998), pp. 265-6.

76. Pérez, "Towards Dependency and Revolution," p. 136; Ayala, *American Sugar Kingdom*, pp. 57-8.

77. The literature on Martí is extensive. Christopher Abel and Nissa Torrents, eds., *José Martí: Revolutionary Democrat* (London, 1986), is a useful collection of essays; Lillian Guerra, *The Myth of José Martí: Conflicting Nationalism in Early Twentieth-Century Cuba* (Chapel Hill, 2005), traces his evolution as a nationalist icon; Amando García de la Torre. *José Martí and the Global Origins of Cuban Independence* (Kingston, Jamaica, 2015), examines the cosmopolitan character of his thinking, which included Hindu and Pan-African sources.

78. Armando García de la Torre, "The Contradictions of Late Nineteenth-Century Nationalist Doctrines: Three Keys to the 'Globalism' of José Martí's Nationalism," *Journal of Global History*, 3 (2008), pp. 67-88.

79. The phrase is used by Ferrer, *Insurgent Cuba*. For a survey of the controversy over the concept, see Alejandro de la Fuente, "Myths of Racial Democracy: Cuba 1900–1912," *Latin American Research Review*, 34 (1999), pp. 39–73; also Rebecca J. Scott, "Race, Labor, and Citizenship in Cuba: A View from the Sugar District of Cienfuegos, 1886–1909," *Hispanic American Historical Review*, 78 (1998), pp. 687–729.

80. Louis A. Pérez, Jr., *Cuba and the United States: Ties of Singular Intimacy* (Athens, Georgia, 1990; 3rd ed. 2003), pp. 55–81.

81. Harris, "Edward F. Atkins," p. 210; Louis A. Pérez, Jr., ed., *José Martí in the United States: The Florida Experience* (Tempe, 1995).

82. The Cigar Makers' Union was a key source of support: LaFeber, *The New Empire*, pp. 286–7.

83. Antonio Cánovas del Castillo (1828–1897) was a committed monarchist who applied repressive measures of the most extreme kind in Spain as well as in Cuba. He appointed General Valeriano Weyler y Nicolau (1838–1930), Marquis of Tenerife, as governor general of Cuba in 1896. Weyler observed General William Sherman's "scorched earth" policy during the Civil War while he was acting as a military attaché in Washington and applied the technique when he was Captain-General of the Philippines, 1888–1892.

84. This famous episode has long been the subject of much study and speculation, though a good deal of it is repetitive. The cause of the explosion remains unknown. Different views are represented by Hyman G. Rickover, *How the Battleship* Maine *Was Destroyed* (Washington, DC, 1976); and Peggy Samuels and Harold Samuels, *Remember the Maine* (Washington, DC, 1995). See also Hugh Thomas's incisive comment on Admiral Rickover's report (*Cuba*, pp. 1039–40).

85. Yellow fever was a particular concern—and on the mainland too. See Mariola Espinosa, "The Threat from Havana: Southern Public Health, Yellow Fever, and the U.S. Intervention in the Cuban Struggle for Independence," *Journal of Southern History*, 72 (2006), pp. 541–68.

86. Matthew Smallman-Raynor and Andrew D. Cliff, "The Spatial Dynamics of Epidemic Diseases in War and Peace: Cuba and the Insurrection against Spain, 1895–98," *Transactions of the Institute of British Geographers*, 24 (1999), p. 332.

87. Miles (1839–1925); Union volunteer, 1861; Indian Wars, 1874–90; Commanding General U.S. Army, 1895–1903. Robert Wooster, *Nelson A. Miles and the Twilight of the Frontier Army* (Lincoln, 1993), and Peter R. DeMontravel, *A Hero to His Fighting Men: Nelson A. Miles, 1839–1925* (Kent, 1998), agree that he was a formidable soldier but a poor politician.

88. Richard H. Davis, *The Cuban and Puerto Rican Campaigns* (New York, 1898), pp. 296–300. Quoted in Davila-Cox, "Puerto Rico in the Hispanic-Cuban-American War," p. 98.

89. Dietz, *Economic History of Puerto Rico*, pp. 16–20.

90. Joseph C. Dorsey, *Slave Traffic in the Age of Abolition: Puerto Rico, West Africa, and the Non-Hispanic Caribbean, 1815–1859* (Gainesville, 2003), shows that Puerto Rico's slave trade was much larger than has been thought.

91. Luis A. Figueroa, *Sugar, Slavery and Freedom in Nineteenth-Century Puerto Rico* (Chapel Hill, 2005), provides a case study of the municipality of Guayama; Ricardo R. Camuñas Madera, *Hacendados y comerciantes en Puerto Rico en torno a la década revolucionaria de 1860* (Mayagüez, Puerto Rico, 1993), traces developments in western Cuba affecting Catalan and French settlers in the 1860s.

92. On British trade, see Emma Aurora Davila-Cox, *This Immense Commerce: The Trade Between Puerto Rico and Great Britain, 1844–1898* (San Juan, 1993).

93. Guillermo A. Baralt, *Slave Revolts in Puerto Rico: Conspiracies and Uprisings, 1795–1873* (San Juan, 1981; trans. Princeton, NJ, 2007).

94. And has stimulated controversy: See Tom Brass, "Free and Unfree Labour in Puerto Rico during the Nineteenth Century," *Journal of Latin American Studies*, 18 (1986), pp. 181–93.

95. Christopher Schmidt-Nowara, *Empire and Slavery: Spain, Cuba, and Puerto Rico, 1833–1874* (Pittsburgh, 1999), pp. 169–73; Andrés Ramos Mattei, Luz Arrieta-Longworth, and Patrick Bryan, "The Plantations of the Southern Coast of Puerto Rico, 1880 to 1910," *Social & Economic Studies*, 37 (1988), pp. 365–404.

96. Laird W. Bergad, *Coffee and the Growth of Agrarian Capitalism in Nineteenth-Century Puerto Rico* (Princeton, 1983), traces the rise of wage labor in the coffee industry.

97. Figueroa, *Sugar, Slavery and Freedom*, ch. 5; Rosa E. Carrasquillo, *Our Landless Patria: Marginal Citizenship in Caguas, Puerto Rico, 1880–1910* (Lincoln, 2006).

98. Quoted in Emma Davila-Cox, "Puerto Rico in the Hispanic-Cuban-American War: Reassessing the 'Picnic,'" in Angel Smith and Emma Davila-Cox, eds., *The Crisis of 1898: Colonial Redistribution and Nationalist Mobilization* (London, 1999), p. 108.

99. Dietz, *Economic History of Puerto Rico*, pp. 25–8; Davila-Cox, "Puerto Rico in the Hispanic-Cuban-American War," p. 109.

100. Juan José Baldrich, "From Handcrafted Tobacco to Machine-Made Cigarettes: The Transformation and Americanization of Puerto Rican Tobacco, 1847–1903," *Centro Journal*, 17 (2005), pp. 144–69.

101. Bergad, *Coffee and the Growth of Agrarian Capitalism*, is the principal source.

102. Dietz, *Economic History of Puerto Rico*, pp. 25–8; Davila-Cox, "Puerto Rico in the Hispanic-Cuban-American War," p. 109; Bergad, *Coffee and the Growth of Agrarian Capitalism*, p. 86, gives a figure of 70 percent for the value of coffee exports in 1897.

103. Davila-Cox, "Puerto Rico in the Hispanic-Cuban-American War," p. 110.

104. Luis Martínez-Fernández, *Frontiers, Plantations and Walled Cities* (Princeton, NJ, 2010), pp. 31–2; Dietz, *Economic History*, pp. 35–40.

105. Olga Jiménez de Wagenheim, *Puerto Rico's Revolt for Independence: El Grito de Lares* (Boulder, 1985).

106. Davila-Cox, "Puerto Rico in the Hispanic-Cuban-American War," pp. 116–18.

107. Luis Martínez-Fernández, *Frontiers, Plantations and Walled Cities*, p. 28.

108. Astrid Cubano, "El café y la política colonial en Puerto Rico a fines del siglo XIX. Dominación mercantil en el Puerto de Arecibo," *Revista de Historia Económica*, 8 (1990), 95–103.

109. On the myth of racial equality, see Jay Kinsbruner, *Free People of Color and Racial Prejudice in Nineteenth-Century Puerto Rico* (Durham, 1996).

110. Dietz, *Economic History of Puerto Rico*, pp. 53–9, 63–6.

111. Astrid Cubano Iguina, "Política radical y autonomismo en Puerto Rico: Conflictos de intereses en la formación del Partido Autonomista Puertorriqueño (1887)," *Anuario de Estudios Americanos*, 51 (1994), pp. 155–73; Cubano Iguina, "Political Culture and Male Mass Party Formation in Late Nineteenth-Century Puerto Rico," *Hispanic American Historical Review*, 78 (1998), pp. 631–63; Bergad, *Coffee and the Growth of Agrarian Capitalism*, traces the relations between coffee and politics during this period.

112. José Trías Monge, *Puerto Rico: The Trials of the Oldest Colony in the World* (New Haven, 1997), pp. 10–13.

113. César J. Ayala and Rafael Bernabe, *Puerto Rico in the American Century* (Chapel Hill, 2007).

114. Davila-Cox, "Puerto Rico in the Hispanic-Cuban-American War," pp. 102–3.

115. The first line of José Rizal's famous *Último Adiós*. See p. 412 of this text.

116. By then, Spain was also prepared to sell Cuba, but the Teller Amendment ruled out annexation.

117. The census of 1903 recorded 7.6 million inhabitants.

118. Fortunately, historians can take advantage of two valuable overviews of the subject: John A. Larkin, "Philippine Social History Reconsidered: A Socioeconomic Perspective," *American Historical Review*, 87 (1982), pp. 595–628; Josep M. Fradera, "The Historical Origins of the Philippine Economy: A Survey of Recent Research of the Spanish Colonial Era," *Australian Economic History Review*, 44 (2004), pp. 307–20. I should like to

record my appreciation of Dr. Fradera's work, which has been especially helpful in this chapter and in chapter 13 of this text.

119. Benito J. Legarda, *After the Galleons: Foreign Trade, Economic Change and Entrepreneurship in the Nineteenth-Century Philippines* (Madison, 1999), ch. 2.

120. I am particularly indebted here to Josep M. Fradera, "Reform or Leave: A Re-Reading of the So-Called 'Secret Report' by Sinibald de Mars About the Philippines," *Bulletin of Portuguese-Japanese Studies*, 16 (2008), pp. 83–99.

121. Greg Bankoff, "Big Fish in Small Ponds: The Exercise of Power in a Nineteenth-Century Philippine Municipality," *Modern Asian Studies*, 26 (1992), pp. 679–700; Juan Antonio Inarejos Muñoz, *Los (últimos) caciques de Filipinas: Las elites coloniales antes del 98* (Granada, 2015), chs. 1, 4, 5, traces the part played by the Filipino clergy in linking the friars, the administration, and taxation.

122. The fundamental work is Reynaldo Ileto, *Pasyon and Revolution: Popular Movements in the Philippines, 1840–1910* (Quezon City, 1979). See also Bruce Cruikshank, "Gaming the System: The Tribute System in the Spanish Philippines, 1565–1884," academia.edu at https://sites.google.com/site/dbcresearchinstitute/ (2014). Unpublished paper cited with the author's permission; Damon L. Woods, "Counting Time and Marking Time from the Precolonial to the Contemporary Tagalog World," *Philippine Studies*, 59 (2011), pp. 337–65, should be credited with opening a new line of thought on this subject. On the Tagalog Revolt of 1745, see Larkin, "Philippine Social History," pp. 609–10.

123. Larkin, "Philippine Social History," pp. 603–6.

124. Katherine Bjork, "The Link that Kept the Philippines Spanish: Mexican Merchant Interests and the Manila Trade, 1571–1815," *Journal of World History*, 9 (1998), pp. 25–50.

125. See Linda A. Newson's remarkable study, *Conquest and Pestilence in the Early Spanish Philippines* (Honolulu, 2009).

126. As did the response: Francisco Mallari, "Muslim Raids in Bicol, 1580–1792," *Philippine Studies*, 34 (1986), pp. 257–86.

127. James Francis Warren, "The Structure of Slavery in the Sulu Zone in the Late Eighteenth and Nineteenth Centuries," *Slavery & Abolition*, 24 (2003), pp. 111–28; Warren, "Saltwater Slavers and Captives in the Sulu Zone, 1768–1878," *Slavery & Abolition*, 31 (2010), pp. 429–49; Henry M. Schwalbenberg, "The Economics of Pre-Hispanic Visayan Slave-Raiding," *Philippine Studies*, 42 (1994), pp. 376–84. The Portuguese contributed by importing slaves from South Asia: Tatiana Seijas, "The Portuguese Slave Trade to Spanish Manila, 1580–1640," *Itinerario*, 32 (2008), pp. 19–38.

128. Specialists will appreciate that I am using these terms primarily to refer to the diversity of state systems. The definition of pre-Spanish states in the Philippines is a matter of controversy, as it is in Africa and Asia. I am grateful to Dr. Eduardo Ugarte for alerting me to the need to "proceed with caution" in this matter.

129. Larkin, "Philippine Social History," pp. 610–12; Fradera, "Historical Origins of the Philippine Economy," pp. 308–9.

130. Josep M. Fradera, "De la periferia al centro (Cuba, Puerto Rico y Filipinas en la crisis del Imperio español)," *Anuario de Estudios Americanos*, 61 (2004), pp. 161–99, emphasizes the role of the military in retaining the islands in the nineteenth century.

131. See the section titled "Don Quixote's Last Ride" in chapter 8 of this text. Also Larkin, "Philippine Social History," pp. 611–17.

132. As outlined in chapters 2 and 6 of this text.

133. Maria Dolores Elizalde, "1898: The Coordinates of the Spanish Crisis in the Pacific," in Angel Smith and Emma Davila-Cox, eds., *The Crisis of 1898: Colonial Redistribution and Nationalist Mobilization* (New York, 1999), pp. 136–7; Norman G. Owen, "Abaca in Kabikolan: Prosperity without Progress," in Alfred W. McCoy and Edilberto C. de Jesus, eds., *Global Trade and Local Transformation* (Quezon City, 1982), p. 197; Ifor B. Powell, "The Nineteenth Century and the Years of Transition: The Origins of the Firms," *Bulletin of the American Historical Collection*, 9 (1981), pp. 7–25; Powell, "The

Banks, *Bulletin of the American Historical Collection*, 9 (1981), pp. 39–52; Powell, "The Brokers," *Bulletin of the American Historical Collection*, 10 (1982), pp. 60–81.

134. Norman G. Owen, *Prosperity Without Progress: Manila Hemp and Material Life in the Colonial Philippines* (Berkeley and Los Angeles, 1984), p. 69.

135. Legarda, *After the Galleons*, chs. 4, 5, 6; John A. Larkin, *Sugar and the Origins of Modern Philippine Society*, chs. 2–3.

136. Owen, *Prosperity without Progress*.

137. Larkin, "Philippine Social History," pp. 615–17. Larkin, *Sugar and the Origins of Modern Philippine Society*, ch. 3, charts the opening of the sugar frontier on Negros.

138. Larkin, "Philippine Social History," pp. 617–20; Fradera, "Historical Origins of the Philippine Economy," p. 311.

139. Domingo Roxas y Ureta (1782–1843); Antonio de Ayala (1804–76). Roxas' family originally came from Andalusia but emigrated to Mexico before arriving in the Philippines; Ayala's family came from the Basque country.

140. Eduardo Lachica, *Ayala: The Philippines' Oldest Business House* (Makati, Philippines, 1984). Valuable though Lachica's book is, there is room for a fresh study of the Ayala Corporation, given its exceptional longevity and the considerable scale of its activities.

141. The bank was established by the Spanish governor under the name *El Banco Español-Filipino de Isabel II*, and became the Bank of the Philippine Islands in 1912.

142. 1826–69.

143. Marciano R. de Borja, *Basques in the Philippines* (Reno, 2005), pp. 124–7.

144. The pioneering work is Edgar Wickberg, *Chinese in Philippine Life, 1850–1898* (New Haven, 1965). See also Andrew Wilson, *Ambition and Identity: Chinese Merchant Elites in Colonial Manila, 1880–1916* (Honolulu, 2004); Richard Chu, *Chinese and Chinese Mestizos of Manila: Family, Identity and Culture, 1860s–1930s* (Leiden, 2010).

145. Larkin, *Sugar and the Origins of Modern Philippine Society*, ch. 3; Wickberg, *Chinese in Philippine Life*.

146. Allan E. S. Lumba, "Philippine Colonial Money and the Future of the Spanish Empire," in Chia Yin Hsu, Thomas M. Luckett, and Erika Vause, eds., *The Cultural History of Money and Credit: A Global Perspective* (Lanham, 2016), ch. 7.

147. Edilberto C. de Jesús, *The Tobacco Monopoly in the Philippines: Bureaucratic Enterprise and Social Change, 1766–1880* (Quezon City, 1980). Originally, the monopoly applied to all of Spain's colonies in the New World. See Susan Deans-Smith, *Bureaucrats, Planters and Workers in the Making of the Tobacco Monopoly in Bourbon Mexico* (Cambridge, 1992).

148. Legarda, *After the Galleons*, pp. 193–206.

149. Fradera, "Historical Origins," pp. 314–15.

150. The *Compañia General de Tabacos de Filipinas* adapted readily to the arrival of new colonial rulers in 1898 and remained a major operation throughout the colonial period.

151. Greg Bankoff, *Crime, Society & the State in the Nineteenth-Century Philippines* (Manila, 1995), is definitive on this subject.

152. Bankoff, *Crime, Society & the State*; Elizalde, "1898: The Coordinates of the Spanish Crisis in the Pacific," pp. 132–3.

153. Larkin, *Sugar and the Origins of Modern Philippine Society*, pp. 53–6. Low-grade sugar continued to be shipped to China, the traditional export market, but the surge in sugar production in the second half of the century was a response to expanding demand in Europe and the United States, which required high-grade sugar. Consequently, the China market was unable to insulate the Philippines from the effects of the fall in the world price of sugarcane at the close of the century.

154. Larkin, *Sugar and the Origins of Modern Philippine Society*, pp. 49–50.

155. Norman G. Owen, *Prosperity without Progress*, pp. 52–62.

156. Fradera, "The Historical Origins of the Philippine Economy," pp. 314–17.

157. Larkin, "Philippine Social History," p. 620.

158. María Dolores Elizalde and Xavier Huetz de Lemps, "Poder, religión y control en Filipinas. Colaboración y conflicto entre el Estado y las órdenes religiosas, 1868–1898," *Ayer: Revista de Historia Contemporánea*, 100 (2015), pp. 151–76. The Friars owned about 400,000 acres, of which 250,000 was in the desirable region around Manila. See Fradera, "Historical Origins of the Philippines Economy," pp. 314–17.

159. Legarda, *After the Galleons*, pp. 156–7.

160. The pioneering study is Peter C. Smith, "Crisis Mortality in the Nineteenth-Century Philippines: Data from Parish Records," *Journal of Asian Studies*, 38 (1978), pp. 51–76. See also Ken De Bevoise, *Agents of Apocalypse: Epidemic Disease in the Colonial Philippines* (Princeton, NJ, 1995), pp. 8–12.

161. Smith, "Crisis Mortality," p. 68.

162. De Bevoise uses the phrase as the central theme of *Agents of Apocalypse*.

163. Jean-Pascal Bassino, Marion Dovis, and John Komlos, "Biological Well-Being in Late Nineteenth-Century Philippines," National Bureau of Economic Research, *Working Paper*, 21410 (2015).

164. David Sweet, "John N. Schumacher, The Cavite Mutiny: Towards a Definitive History," *Philippine Studies*, 59 (2011), pp. 55–81.

165. Ibid., pp. 78–9.

166. John N. Schumacher, *The Making of a Nation: Essays on Nineteenth-Century Filipino Nationalism* (Quezon City, 1991); Reynaldo C. Ileto, *Filipinos and Their Revolution: Event, Discourse and History* (Quezon City, 1998), are admirable points of entry.

167. At this date, the term "Filipino" referred to Spaniards living in the Philippines and to Spanish mestizos born there. The term "Filipino" spread in the twentieth century and eventually applied to the whole population irrespective of origins.

168. Christine Doran underlines the social significance of these demarcations: "Spanish and Mestizo Women of Manila," *Philippine Studies*, 41 (1993), pp. 269–86, and emphasizes the contribution made by women to active service. See also Owen, *Prosperity and Progress*, pp. 192–7.

169. Fradera, "Historical Origins of the Philippine Economy," pp. 314–17.

170. Caroline Sy Hau, "'*Patria é intereses*': Reflections on the Origins and Changing Meanings of *Ilustrado*," *Philippine Studies*, 59 (2011), pp. 3–54.

171. John N. Schumacher, *Revolutionary Clergy: The Filipino Clergy and the Nationalist Movement, 1850–1905* (Quezon City, 1981), also estimates that in 1903 about 60 percent of the Filipino clergy opposed U.S. rule (p. 275).

172. Megan C. Thomas, *Orientalists, Propagandists and Ilustrados: Filipino Scholarship and the End of Spanish Colonialism* (Minneapolis, 2012).

173. Benedict Anderson, *Under Three Flags: Anarchism and the Anti-Colonial Imagination* (London, 2005), focuses on José Rizal, Mariano Ponce, and Isabelo de los Reyes. Armando García de la Torre, "The Contradictions of Late Nineteenth-Century Nationalist Doctrines."

174. Ileto, *Pasyon and Revolution*, develops this theme with particular reference to different interpretations of the meaning of *katipunan*.

175. Bankoff, *Crime, Society, and the State*.

176. Larkin, "Philippine Social History," pp. 621–3.

177. The first head of the Independent Church, Bishop Gregorio Aglipay Cruz y Labayan (1860–1940), was an assistant priest in the Catholic Church and a guerrilla leader.

178. Examples include: Violetta Lopez-Gonzaga, "The Roots of Agrarian Unrest in Negros, 1850–90," *Philippine Studies*, 36 (1988), pp. 151–65; Violetta Lopez-Gonzaga and Michelle Decena, "Negros in Transition, 1899–1905," *Philippine Studies*, 38 (1990), pp. 103–14; Volker Schult, "Revolution and War in Mindoro, 1898–1903," *Philippine Studies*, 41 (1993), pp. 76–90; Josélito N. Fornier, "Economic Developments in Antique Province, 1850–1900," *Philippine Studies*, 47 (1999), pp. 147–80.

179. There are numerous biographies. See, for example, Léon M. Guerrero, *The First Fili-pino: A Biography of José Rizal* (Manila, 1963). Floro C. Quibuyen, *A Nation Aborted: Rizal, American Hegemony, and Philippine Nationalism* (Quezon City, 1999), offers a revisionist account. The contribution of Rizal's older brother, Paciano (1851–1930), is generally overlooked in non-specialist accounts. Paciano was an active reformer who influenced José's political views and helped fund his studies. After his brother's execution, Paciano joined Aguinaldo as a senior commander and fought against both Spain and the United States. He was captured in 1900 but released shortly afterward and returned to farming.

180. Glen A. May, *Inventing a Hero: The Posthumous Re-Creation of Andrés Bonifacio* (Madison, 1996), deserves credit for initiating the scholarly reevaluation of mythology. The *Katipunan* website contains a discussion of this and allied matters: http://kasaysayan-kkk.info/.

181. Glen A. May, "Why the United States Won the Philippine-American War, 1899–1902," *Pacific Historical Review*, 52 (1983), pp. 353–77; René Escalante, "Collapse of the Malolos Republic," *Philippine Studies*, 46 (1998), pp. 452–76, catalogues a series of failings.

182. Manuel Sarkisyanz, *Rizal and Republican Spain and Other Rizalist Essays* (Manila, 1995), is relevant for present purposes.

183. Raul Bonoan, "The Enlightenment, Deism, and Rizal," *Philippine Studies*, 40 (1992), pp. 53–67.

184. Miguel A. Bernad, "The Trial of Rizal," *Philippine Studies*, 46 (1998), pp. 46–72.

185. Smita Lahiri, "Rhetorical *Indios*: Propagandists and Their Publics in the Spanish Philippines," *Comparative Studies in Society & History*, 49 (2007), pp. 243–75.

186. Milagros Guerrero and John N. Schumacher, *Kasaysayan: The Story of the Filipino People*, Vol. 5: *Reform and Revolution* (Hong Kong, 1998); Angel Velasco Shaw and Luis H. Francia, eds., *Vestiges of War: The Philippine-American War and the Aftermath of an Imperial Dream, 1899–1999* (New York, 2002), gives prominence to the long-term consequences of the war.

187. Bonifacio (1863–96) was one of the founders of *Katipunan*. The name derives from a Tagalog word meaning association or gathering. See especially May, *Inventing a Hero*; and the commentary by José S. Arcilla, "Who Is Andrés Bonifacio?" *Philippine Studies*, 45 (1997), pp. 570–77.

188. May, *Inventing a Hero*.

189. The collection of essays in the special issue of *Historical Bulletin*, 3 (1959), remains valuable.

190. The most controversial being his decision to cooperate with the Japanese occupying force during World War II.

191. Sven Saaler and Christopher W. A. Szpilman, eds., *Pan-Asianism*, I (Lanham, 2012), p. 24.

192. Emilio Aguinaldo, *True Version of the Philippine Revolution* (Tarlak, Philippines, 1899). The U.S. Consul in Hong Kong encouraged Aguinaldo to re-enter the battle against Spain; Aguinaldo himself claimed that Admiral George Dewey had assured him that the United States had no intention of annexing the islands. The episode has attracted different interpretations. For contemporary American support for Aguinaldo's interpretation, see Perry Belmont (1851–1947), Democratic Congressman for New York (1881–1889), who served in the Spanish-American War: "The President and the Philippines," *North American Review*, 169 (1899), pp. 894–911.

193. Also known as the First Philippine Republic or the Malolos Republic after the town (some 25 miles north of Manila) that served as the capital.

194. Benito J. Lagarda, *The Hills of Sampaloc: The Opening Actions of the Philippine-American War* (Makati City, 2001), evaluates the controversy over the responsibility for starting the war.

195. Matthew F. Jacobson, "Imperial Amnesia: Teddy Roosevelt, the Philippines, and the Modern Art of Forgetting," *Radical History Review*, 73 (1999), pp. 116–27. The long-term significance of the war is emphasized by Shaw and Francia, *Vestiges of War*. The leading contributors to the debate on this subject are Stuart C. Miller, who is highly critical of the record of the U.S. Army, and John M. Gates and Brian M. Linn, who write in its defense. See, especially, Miller, *Benevolent Assimilation: The American Conquest of the Philippines, 1899–1903* (New Haven, 1982); Linn, *The U.S. Army and Counterinsurgency in the Philippine War, 1899–1902* (Chapel Hill, 1989); Linn, *The Philippine War, 1899–1902* (Lawrence, 2000). Gates has placed his major contributions online, where they can be updated: http://www3.wooster.edu/history/jgates/book-contents.html. A balanced assessment of the issues is Kenton J. Clymer, "Not So Benevolent Assimilation: The Philippine-American War," *Reviews in American History*, 11 (1983), pp. 547–52.

196. Linn, *The U.S. Army and Counter-Insurgency*; Linn, *The Philippine War, 1899–1902*, provides the details; John M. Gates, "War-Related Deaths in the Philippines, 1899–1902," *Pacific Historical Review*, 53 (1984), pp. 367–78, surveys the problems of data; David J. Sibley, *A War of Frontier and Empire: The Philippine-American War, 1899–1902* (New York, 2007), offers an up-to-date account aimed at the substantial market for military history. These studies treat the subject from an American viewpoint; Filipino perspectives, though present, are understated.

197. According to De Bevoise, the American-Philippine War contributed "directly and indirectly" to the loss of more than one million people in a base population of seven million: *Apocalypse*, p. 13.

198. For one example, see Volker Schult, "Revolution and War in Mindoro, 1898–1903," *Philippine Studies*, 41 (1993), pp. 76–90.

199. Frank Schumacher, "'Marked Severities': The Debate over Torture during America's Conquest of the Philippines, 1899–1902," *Amerikastudien*, 51 (2006), pp. 475–98. Iain R. Smith and Andreas Stucki analyze the meaning of the term "concentration camp" in "The Colonial Development of Concentration Camps (1868–1902)," *Journal of Imperial & Commonwealth History*, 39 (2011), pp. 417–37; as does Jonathan Hyslop, "The Invention of the Concentration Camp: Cuba, Southern Africa, and the Philippines," *South African Historical Journal*, 63 (2011), pp. 251–76.

200. Aguinaldo (1869–1964) was released from prison and lived long enough to observe independence in 1946 and the activities of the first generation of postcolonial leaders.

201. On Malvar (1865–1911), see Glenn A. May, *Battle for Batangas: A Philippine Province at War* (New Haven, 1991).

202. May, "Why the United States Won the Philippine-American War," pp. 353–77; Escalante, "The Collapse of the Malolos Republic'; Larkin, *Sugar and the Origins of Modern Philippine Society*, pp. 116–21.

203. Macario Sakay y de León (1870–1907), an understudied leader, was a close associate of Andrés Bonifacio. The republic was proclaimed in 1902 but not effectively organized until 1904.

204. Andrew Bacevich, "Disagreeable Work: Pacifying the Moros, 1903–1906," *Military Review*, 62 (1982), pp. 49–61; Joshua Gedacht, "'Mohammedan Religion Made It Necessary to Fire': Massacres on the American Imperial Frontier from South Dakota to the Southern Philippines," in McCoy and Scarano, eds., *Colonial Crucible*, pp. 397–409.

205. Richard H. Werking, "Senator Henry Cabot Lodge and the Philippines: A Note on American Territorial Expansion," *Pacific Historical Review*, 42 (1973), pp. 234–40. The situation was sufficiently uncertain for King Leopold II, ever the opportunist, to consider applying for a charter to rule the islands on behalf of his Belgian Africa Company.

206. John L. Offner, "Imperialism by International Consensus: The United States and the Philippine Islands," in Daniele Rossini, *From Theodore Roosevelt to FDR: Internationalism and Isolationism in American Foreign Policy* (Edinburgh, 1995), pp. 45–54. The Republicans

lost seats in the House of Representatives, as often happens to the president's party in the first mid-term election after his own election, but remained the dominant party.

207. Santiago Sevilla, "My Dream" (1911), quoted in Gémino H. Abad, *Our Scene So Far: Filipino Poetry in English, 1905 to 1955* (Quezón City, 2008), p. 48.

208. Hamilton Fish, Secretary of State, 20 March 1875. Quoted in Rigby, "American Expansion in Hawai'i," p. 363.

209. Hawai'i consisted of a complex of islands, the six largest being (in order of size) Hawai'i, O'ahu, Maui, Kaua'i, Moloka'i, and Lana'i. The capital, Honolulu, and the chief port, Pearl Harbor, are located on O'ahu.

210. Cook was killed in Hawai'i in 1779 following a minor dispute that rose to the point where it involved the principal chief on O'ahu.

211. Special acknowledgment should be given here (and in notes 212, 214, and 215) to the pioneering contribution made by Patrick V. Kirch, *How Chiefs Became Kings: Divine Kinship and the Rise of Archaic States in Ancient Hawai'i* (Berkeley, 2010). On "archaic" states, see also A. G. Hopkins, ed., *Globalization in World History* (New York, 2002), chs. 1–3. Taro, a root vegetable, was a major staple until it was almost eliminated by the expansion of sugarcane in the nineteenth and twentieth centuries. Today, it is enjoying a revival.

212. Patrick V. Kirch, *How Chiefs Became Kings*; Kirch, *A Shark Going Inland Is My Chief: The Inland Civilization of Ancient Hawai'i* (Berkeley, 2012); also Mark D. McCoy and Michael W. Graves, "The Role of Agricultural Innovation on Pacific Islands: A Case Study from Hawai'i Island," *World Archaeology*, 42 (2010), pp. 90–107.

213. Carol A. MacLennan, *Sovereign Sugar: Industry and Environment in Hawai'i* (Honolulu, 2014), ch. 3. All scholars will be grateful to Dr. MacLennan for delivering the history of Hawai'i's major industry that has long been needed. See also Noenoe K. Silva, "He Kanawai Ho'opau i na Hula Kuolo Hawai'i: The Political Economy of Banning the Hula," *Hawaiian Journal of History*, 34 (2000), pp. 29–48; Jennifer Fish Kashay, "Agents of Imperialism: Missionaries and Merchants in Early-Nineteenth-Century Hawai'i," *New England Quarterly*, 80 (2007), pp. 280–98.

214. Patrick V. Kirch and Jean-Louis Rallu, eds., *The Growth and Collapse of Pacific Island Societies* (Honolulu, 2007), especially chs. 1, 4–7, 16; Seth Archer, "Remedial Agents: Missionary Physicians and the Depopulation of Hawai'i," *Pacific Historical Review*, 79 (2010), pp. 513–44, provides a subtle case study. I am also indebted to Prof. David A. Swanson, University of California, Riverside, for permission to cite his unpublished paper, "A New Estimate of the Hawaiian Population for 1778, the Year of First European Contact," and for further help well "beyond the call of duty" in subsequent correspondence.

215. There is a wealth of information on these matters in Marshall Sahlins, *Anahulu: The Anthropology of History in the Kingdom of Hawai'i*, Vol. 1 (Chicago, 1992); and Patrick V. Kirch and Marshall Sahlins, *Anahulu*: Vol. 2 (Chicago, 1992).

216. MacLennan, *Sovereign Sugar*, pp. 46–47; and, more generally, Stuart Banner, *Possessing the Pacific: Land, Settlers, and Indigenous People from Australia to Alaska* (Cambridge, MA, 2007).

217. Richard Hawkins, "The Impact of Sugar Cane Cultivation on the Economy and Society of Hawai'i, 1835–1900," *Iles i Imperis*, 9 (2006), pp. 59–77; Barry Rigby, "American Expansion in Hawai'i: The Contribution of Henry A. Peirce," *Diplomatic History*, 4 (1980), p. 355.

218. Rigby, "American Expansion in Hawai'i," p. 363.

219. Peirce (1808–85) had substantial investments in sugar estates.

220. Kamehameha V (1830–1872); reigned 1863–1872.

221. Kalākaua (1836–1891); reigned 1874–1891.

222. 20 March 1875. Quoted in Rigby, "American Expansion in Hawai'i," p. 365.

223. LaCroix and Grandy, "Political Instability of Reciprocal Trade"; Hawkins, "The Impact of Sugar Cane Cultivation"; Carol A. MacLennan, "Hawai'i Turns to Sugar: The Rise of Plantation Centers, 1860–1880," *Hawaiian Journal of History*, 31 (1997), pp. 97–125.

224. MacLennan, *Sovereign Sugar*, chs. 6–7.

225. Francisco and Fast, *Conspiracy for Empire*, pp. 2–6, 38–9, 74–5; Richard D. Weigle, "Sugar and the Hawaiian Revolution," *Pacific Historical Review*, 16 (1947), pp. 48–9; Richard P. Tucker, *Insatiable Appetite: The United States and the Ecological Degradation of the World* (Berkeley, 2000), pp. 79–82. The standard work remains Jacob Adler, *Claus Spreckels: The Sugar King in Hawai'i* (Honolulu, 1966).

226. Peirce himself came from Boston. His successor, John L. Stevens, came from Maine, which had an exceptional religious and commercial influence on Hawai'i. See Paul T. Burlin, *Imperial Maine and Hawai'i: Interpretive Essays in the History of Nineteenth-Century American Expansion* (Lanham, 2006).

227. These events have been covered extensively by other historians. The summary given here draws particularly on LaCroix and Grandy, "Political Instability of Reciprocal Trade"; Hawkins, "The Impact of Sugar Cane Cultivation"; Alfred L. Castle, "U.S. Commercial Policy and Hawai'i, 1890–1894," *Hawaiian Journal of History*, 33 (1999), pp. 69–82; and MacLennan, *Sovereign Sugar*, ch. 10.

228. The starting point is now the admirable study by Jonathan K. K. Osorio, *Dismembering Lahui: A History of the Hawaiian Nation to 1887* (Honolulu, 2002). Resistance and collaboration are now controversial subjects. See Noenoe K. Silva, *Aloha Betrayed: Native Hawaiian Resistance to American Colonialism* (Durham, 2004), and Kenneth R. Conklin's fierce criticism: "Noenoe Silva, *Aloha Betrayed: Native Hawaiian Resistance to American Colonialism*," at http://www.angelfire.com/hi2/Hawaiiansovereignty/noen oealhoabetrayed.html (2005).

229. Richard C. K. Burdekin and Leroy O. Lancy, "Financial Market Reactions to the Overthrow and Annexation of the Hawaiian Kingdom: Evidence from London, Honolulu and New York," *Cliometrica*, 2 (2008), pp. 123–5.

230. The events that follow are among the best documented and most discussed in Hawai'i's history. The standard work is Ralph S. Kuykendall, *The Hawaiian Kingdom, 1874–1893: The Kalākaua Dynasty* (Honolulu, 1967). Specialized studies include Pratt, *Hawaiian Revolution*; Sylvester K. Stevens, *American Expansion in Hawai'i, 1842–1898* (Harrisburg, 1945); Merze Tate, *Hawai'i: Reciprocity of Annexation* (East Lansing, 1968); William A. Russ, *The Hawaiian Revolution, 1893–4* (Selinsgrove, 1959); Russ, *The Hawaiian Republic, 1893–98* (Selinsgrove, 1961); These studies are reminders of the high standards of presentation and research attained by a previous generation of scholars.

231. LaCroix and Grandy, "Political Instability of Reciprocal Trade," pp. 182–3.

232. Hawkins, "Impact of Sugar Cane," p. 71, cautions against exaggerating the effects of the McKinley Tariff on Hawai'i.

233. Lili'uokalani (1838–1917); reigned 1891–1893.

234. President Grover Cleveland, "Message to the Senate and House of Representatives," 18 December 1893, at http://www.Hawai'i-nation.org/cleveland.html.

235. President Harrison, following the lead of his Secretary of State, James Blaine, had tried to secure a protectorate in 1890 but the negotiations had broken down: hence the shift to annexation.

236. Michael J. Devine, *John W. Foster: Politics and Diplomacy in the Imperial Era, 1873–1917* (Athens, 1981). Foster (1836–1917), who replaced the ailing Blaine in June 1892, shared his predecessor's views on expansion. Indeed, he is said to have overcome "certain inconvenient scruples" of President Harrison, who was inclined to seek popular approval for the proposed treaty of annexation. Julius W. Pratt, *Expansionists of 1898: The Acquisition of Hawai'i and the Spanish Islands* (Baltimore, 1936), pp. 19–20.

237. On the racial component of Cleveland's attitude toward Hawai'i, see Eric T. L. Love, *Race over Empire: Racism and U.S. Imperialism, 1865–1900* (Chapel Hill, 2004), pp. 113–14.

238. Charles W. Calhoun, "Morality, and Spite: Walter Q. Gresham and U.S. Relations with Hawai'i," *Pacific Historical Review*, 53 (1983), pp. 292–311; Alfred L. Castle, "Tentative Empire: Walter Q. Gresham, U.S. Foreign Policy, and Hawai'i, 1893–1895," *Hawaiian*

Journal of History, 29 (1995), pp. 83–96. Gresham (1832–95) was an ex-Republican who had a strong personal antipathy toward Harrison and his policies.

239. MacLennan, *Sovereign Sugar*, ch. 4, provides an excellent account of the early planters.

240. For information on Thurston (1858–1931) see the full index of entries in Russ, *Hawaiian Revolution*, and Russ, *Hawaiian Republic.*

241. William A. Russ, "The Role of Sugar in Hawaiian Annexation," *Pacific Historical Review*, 12 (1943), p. 349.

242. Alfred L. Castle, "Advice for Hawai'i: The Dole-Burgess Letters," *Hawaiian Journal of History*, 15 (1981), pp. 24–30. Burgess (1844–1931) studied in Germany under Wilhelm Roscher and Theodor Mommsen and became one of the founders of political science in the United States.

243. Arthur Pue Gorman (1839–1906), senator from Maryland (1881–1889; 1903–1906), was motivated at least partly by a concern to protect his state's sugar refineries, which included some of his own investments. Castle, "U.S. Commercial Policy," p. 79.

244. Russ, *Hawaiian Republic*, ch. 2. The leading independent nationalist was Robert William Kalanihiapo Wilcox (1855–1903), who organized several rebellions against the settler takeover of Hawai'i, but who criticized the monarchy too. See Ernest Andrade, *Unconquerable Rebel: Robert W. Wilcox and Hawaiian Politics, 1880–1903* (Boulder, 1996). Wilcox was part Hawaiian and to this extent represented the *hapa haole*, the mestizos of the islands, whose role needs further research.

245. On these final events see the judicious summary in Pletcher, *The Diplomacy of Involvement*, pp. 272–5.

246. Stevens, *American Expansion in Hawai'i*, pp. 284–6.

247. Julius W. Pratt, *America's Colonial Experiment* (New York, 1950), pp. 74–6. Paul S. Holbo's argument that Hawai'i had greater strategic value than the Aleutians remains persuasive: "Anti-Imperialism, Allegations, and the Aleutians: Debates over the Annexation of Hawai'i," *Reviews in American History*, 10 (1982), 377–8.

248. Russ, *Hawaiian Republic*, chs. 9–10 provide a full account.

249. This point was established by Pratt, *Expansionists of 1898*, confirmed by Weigle, "Sugar and the Hawaiian Revolution," and accepted by most subsequent scholars.

250. Tate, *Hawai'i*, pp. 251–2.

251. Weigle, "Sugar and the Hawaiian Revolution," pp. 48–50, 57, argues that their motives did not stem directly from sugar production or trade. Francisco and Fast, *Conspiracy for Empire*, ch. 9 and p. 346, n. 51, criticize this position. MacLennan, *Sovereign Sugar*, pp. 235–8, provides a judicious assessment.

252. *The Congregationalist*, cited in Stevens, *American Expansion*, p. 254.

253. Colin Newbury, "Patronage and Bureaucracy in the Hawaiian Kingdom, 1840–1893," *Pacific Studies*, 24 (2001), pp. 1–38.

254. Stevens, *American Expansion*, pp. 148–53; Tate, *Hawai'i*, pp. 242–5.

255. On the (underestimated) development of the West Coast at this time, see David Igler, "The Industrial Far West in the Late Nineteenth Century," *Pacific Historical Review*, 69 (2000), pp. 159–93.

256. Francisco and Fast, *Conspiracy for Empire*, pp. 72–5; LaFeber, *New Empire*, p. 363; *New York Times*, 17 June 1911. Oxnard began in New York, where he owned a sugar refinery, and then moved to California, where he invested in beets and gave his name to the port of Oxnard. He also acquired interests in the production of sugarcane in Louisiana.

257. Tate, *Hawai'i*, pp. 251–4. Reed (1839–1902), though a friend of Theodore Roosevelt and Henry Cabot Lodge, opposed the war with Spain and disagreed with McKinley when he changed his mind on the issue.

258. The joint resolution, which required a simple majority, embodied the terms of the annexation treaty and specified the conditions that were to operate until "Congress shall provide for the government of such islands." Tate, *Hawai'i*, p. 254; Pratt, *Expansionists of 1898*, ch. 9.

The Hawaiian nationalist movement now claims that annexation was illegal because the "Texas precedent" ought not to have applied to the compulsory acquisition of a foreign state.

259. 1 February 1893. Quoted in Stevens, *American Expansion*, p. 232.

260. As Sumner perceptively noted: *The Conquest of the United States by Spain*, p. 27; Merze Tate, "Great Britain and the Sovereignty of Hawai'i," *Pacific Historical Review*, 31 (1962), pp. 327–48; LaFeber, *New Empire*, p. 207.

261. Russ, *Hawaiian Republic*, pp. 375–6; Weigle, "Sugar and the Hawaiian Revolution," pp. 42–4, gives precision to Russ's argument by showing that fear of Asian labor arose after, and not before, the revolution of 1893.

262. Quoted in Russ, *Hawaiian Republic*, p. 376.

263. Pratt, *Expansionists of 1898*, pp. 217–18; Stevens, *American Expansion in Hawai'i*, pp. 282, 286–8.

264. Quoted in Pratt, *Expansionists of 1898*, p. 218. The fullest account is William M. Morgan, *Hawai'i in U.S. Strategy and Politics* (Annapolis, 2011).

265. Quoted in Eric Love, "White Is the Color of Empire: The Annexation of Hawai'i in 1898," in James T. Campbell, Matthew Pratt Gould, and Robert G. Lee, eds., *Race, Nation, and Empire in American History* (Chapel Hill, 2007), pp. 96–7.

266. Quoted in Joseph L. Grabill, *Protestant Diplomacy and the Near East: Missionary Influence on American Policy, 1810–1927* (Minneapolis, 1971), p. 45.

267. Rigby, "The Origins of American Expansion," pp. 234–7, strikes an appropriate balance.

268. Edward P. Crapol, *James G. Blaine: Architect of Empire* (Wilmington, 2000), provides a short introduction.

269. Luis Martínez-Fernández, *Protestantism and Political Conflict in the Nineteenth-Century Hispanic Caribbean* (New Brunswick, 2002).

270. Thomas O. Ott, "The Corbitts, the HAHR, and United States-Cuban Intellectual Relations," *Hispanic American Historical Review*, 59 (1979), pp. 108–9.

271. Harris, "Edwin F. Atkins and the Evolution of United States Cuba Policy," pp. 202–31; on his plantations see Rebecca J. Scott, "A Cuban Connection: Edwin F. Atkins, Charles Francis Adams, Jr., and the Former Slaves of Soledad Plantation," *Massachusetts Historical Review*, 9 (2007), pp. 7–34; Jason M. Colby, "Race, Empire and New England Capital in the Caribbean, 1890–1930," *Massachusetts Historical Review*, 11 (2009), pp. 1–25. Atkins (1850–1926) wrote a full memoir that suggests he had a limited understanding of the insurgency: *My Sixty Years in Cuba* (Cambridge, MA, 1926).

272. Fitzhugh Lee (1835–1905) was a nephew of Robert E. Lee, an ex-governor of Virginia (1866–1890) and a bimetallist Republican who became a Democrat. He was appointed to the post in Havana by President Cleveland in 1896.

273. Rafael E. Tarragó, "Cuba and Cubans through the Pages of the *New York Times* in 1898," *Jahbuch für Geschichte Lateinamerikas*, 39 (2002), pp. 356–9, 368–9.

274. John L. Offner, *An Unwanted War: The Diplomacy of the United States and Spain Over Cuba, 1895–1898* (Chapel Hill, 1992), pp. 94–100.

275. Tarragó, "Cuba and Cubans," pp. 347–8.

276. Gerald G. Eggert, "Our Man in Havana: Fitzhugh Lee," *American Historical Review*, 47 (1967), pp. 463–85.

277. Woodford (1835–1913) left Spain in 1898, when war was declared.

278. Quoted in Offner, *An Unwanted War*, p. 171.

279. Pérez, *Cuba Between Empires*, pp. 135, 175; Pérez, *The War of 1898*, p. 10.

280. John Lawrence Tone, *War and Genocide in Cuba, 1895–1898* (Chapel Hill, 2006), presents a carefully argued case against the conventional nationalist viewpoint. See also Tarragó, "Cuba and Cubans," pp. 347–8.

281. Pérez, *Cuba Between Empires*, pp. 172–3.

282. John L. Offner, "McKinley and the Spanish-American War," *Presidential Studies Quarterly*, 34 (2004), pp. 54–5.

283. Quoted in Tarragó, "Cuba and Cubans," p. 362.

284. Paul S. Holbo, "The Convergence of Moods and the Cuban-Bond 'Conspiracy' of 1898," *Journal of American History*, 55 (1968), p. 69.
285. Pérez, *Cuba Between Empires*, p. 187; Tarragó, "Cuba and Cubans," pp. 353–4.
286. Pratt, *Expansionists of 1898*, p. 354.
287. Offner, *An Unwanted War*, p. 234.
288. Davila-Cox, "Puerto Rico in the Hispanic-Cuban-American War," pp. 116–17.
289. Quoted in Martínez-Fernández, *Frontiers, Plantations, and Walled Cities*, p. 118.
290. Dietz, *Economic History of Puerto Rico*, p. 93.
291. Santiago Petchen, "The Training and Background of the Spanish Hierarchy in the Nineteenth Century," *Philippine Studies*, 22 (1974), pp. 93–116, stresses the conservatism of the hierarchy and its associated interest in retaining existing property rights.
292. Kenton J. Clymer, *Protestant Missionaries in the Philippines, 1898–1916: An Inquiry into the American Colonial Mentality* (Urbana, 1986), remains the best study.
293. John A. S. Grenville, "Diplomacy and War Plans in the United States, 1890–1917," *Transactions of the Royal Historical Society*, 8 (1961), p. 4.
294. Ibid., pp. 1–21.
295. Thomas J. McCormick, *The China Market: America's Quest for Informal Empire, 1893–1901* (Chicago, 1967); James J. Lorence, "Organized Business and the Myth of the China Market: The American Asiatic Association, 1898–1937," *Transactions of the American Philosophical Society*, 71 (1981), pp. 5–30.
296. Marilyn B. Young, *The Rhetoric of Empire: American China Policy, 1895–1901* (Cambridge, MA, 1958); Paul A. Varg, *The Making of a Myth: The United States and China, 1879–1912* (East Lansing, 1968); David Healy, *U.S. Expansionism: The Imperialist Urge in the 1890s* (Madison, 1970).
297. Elizalde, "1898: The Coordinates of the Spanish Crisis," p. 138.
298. Pletcher, *The Diplomacy of Involvement*, pp. 276–83; Lorence, *Organized Business*, pp. 20–21.
299. For more on this subject, see Michael H. Hunt, *The Making of a Special Relationship: The United States and China to 1914* (New York, 1983), pp. 143–68; Pletcher, *The Diplomacy of Involvement*, pp. 293–301; Cain and Hopkins, *British Imperialism*, ch. 13; George C. Herring, *From Colony to Superpower: U.S. Foreign Relations since 1776* (Oxford, 2008), pp. 329–35.
300. D. A Farnie, *East and West of Suez: The Suez Canal in History, 1854–1956* (Oxford, 1969), pp. 458–61; Wojciech, Rojek, "The Suez Theme in the 1898 Spanish-American War," *American Studies*, 16 (1998), pp. 67–77.
301. Sir Charles W. Dilke, "The Problem of the Philippines," *North American Review*, 167 (1898), p. 17.
302. Kramer, "Race-Making and Colonial Violence," p. 178. The full account is Paul A. Kramer, *The Blood of Government: Race, Empire, the United States, and the Philippines* (Chapel Hill, 2006).
303. Speaking on 4 May 1902. Quoted in Paul A. Kramer, "Race-Making and Colonial Violence," p. 169.

INTERMISSION: TARZAN'S MIRROR TO MODERNITY

1. The vast literature on Tarzan can be approached through John Taliaferro, *Tarzan Forever: The Life of Edgar Rice Burroughs* (New York, 1999); John F. Kasson, *Houdini, Tarzan, and the Perfect Man: The White Male Body and the Challenge of Modernity in America* (New York, 2001).
2. Taliaferro, *Tarzan Forever*, p. 13. Another estimate puts the total sales of all Burroughs' novels at over 100 million. See Bruce Watson, "Tarzan the Eternal," *Smithsonian*, 31 (2001), p. 62.

3. Though now in a modest way because most of the rights have been sold to the Walt Disney Company. See Jeffrey Gentleman, "Tarzan Swings Without Tarzana," *Los Angeles Times*, 4 June 1999.

4. Unsurprisingly, Burroughs also wrote science fiction.

5. William Gleason has suggested that Tarzan's oscillation between civilized and primitive life provides an example of recapitulation theory (a subsidiary of evolution theory promoted by Spencer): "Of Sequels and Sons: Tarzan and the Problem of Paternity," *Journal of American & Comparative Cultures*, 23 (2000), pp. 41–52.

6. Sinclair was concerned, not with the threat posed by immigrants, but with their exploitation at the hands of capitalists. On this theme see Catherine Jurca, "Tarzan, Lord of the Suburbs," *Modern Language Quarterly*, 57 (1996), pp. 479–504; and James R. Barrett, "Remembering the Jungle (1906)," *Labor: Studies in Working Class History of the Americas*, 3 (2006), pp. 7–12.

7. The interpretation presented here is based principally on the first two, formative novels: *Tarzan of the Apes* (1912; London, 2008) and the *Return of Tarzan* (1913; London, 2008). Gail Bederman, *Manliness and Civilization: A Cultural History of Gender and Race in the United States, 1880–1917* (Chicago, 1995), provides an admirable assessment of masculinity as it appears in the first Tarzan novel (pp. 217–32).

CHAPTER 10: THE MODERN IMPERIAL SYSTEM: FROM CONQUEST TO COLLAPSE

1. Henry R. Luce, "The American Century," *Life*, 17 February 1941, reprinted in Michael J. Hogan, ed., *The Ambiguous Century: U.S. Foreign Relations in the "American Century"* (Cambridge, 1999), pp. 11–28. Luce (1898–1967) remained proprietor and editor-in-chief of his influential magazines until 1964.The best of numerous biographies is by Alan Brinkley, *The Publisher: Henry Luce and His American Century* (New York, 2010), who brings out the many complexities in Luce's view of the world, which is too easily stereotyped. Andrew J. Bacevich, ed., *The Short American Century: A Postmortem* (Cambridge, MA, 2012), considers the extended consequences of Luce's dream.

2. Harold Evans, *The American Century* (New York, 1998), p. xiv. The quotation concludes: "because of the triumph of its faith in its founding idea of political and economic freedom." This well-received and highly popular work is, in this respect, typical of numerous others.

3. John Darwin, "Imperialism in Decline? Tendencies in British Imperial Policy between the Wars," *Historical Journal*, 23 (1980), pp. 657–79, advanced this argument and placed it in a broader context. John Gallagher (ed. Anil Seal), *The Decline, Revival and Fall of the British Empire* (Cambridge, 1982), put the case with reference to India in particular. P. J. Cain and A. G. Hopkins, *British Imperialism, 1688–2015* (London, 3rd. ed. 2016), extend the analysis further.

4. The phrase and the sentiment are from Ronald Robinson and John Gallagher, *Africa and the Victorians: The Official Mind of Imperialism* (London, 1962; 1982).

5. Cleopatra, speaking of Mark Antony, *Antony and Cleopatra*, Act 5, Scene 2.

6. For the immediate antecedents see Christopher McKnight Nichols, *Promise and Peril: America at the Dawn of a Global Age* (Cambridge, MA, 2011).

7. After World War I, Congress reduced the size of the regular army to 140,000 men and held the navy at parity with Britain: George C. Herring, *From Colony to Superpower: U.S. Foreign Relations since 1776* (Oxford, 2008), p. 439.

8. John M. Cooper, *Breaking the Heart of the World: Woodrow Wilson and the Fight for the League of Nations* (New York, 2001); Thomas N. Guinsberg, *The Pursuit of Isolationism in the United States from Versailles to Pearl Harbor* (New York, 1982).

9. Warren F. Kuehl and Lynne K Dunn, *Keeping the Covenant: Internationalists and the League of Nations, 1920–1939* (Kent, 1997); Cooper, *Breaking the Heart of the World*; Herring, *From Colony to Superpower*, pp. 427–35.

10. The classic statement, much elaborated since, is William Appleman Williams, "The Legend of Isolationism in the 1920s," *Science & Society*, 18 (1954), pp. 1–20. However, the line of thought began earlier with the Progressive historians and radicals, such as the prolific and highly individual Scott Nearing: *Dollar Diplomacy: A Study in American Imperialism* (New York, 1925), written with Joseph Freeman. Nearing's views led to his dismissal from the Wharton School, University of Pennsylvania in 1915. He was reinstated, more than half a century later, in 1973.

11. Frank Costigliola, *Awkward Dominion: American Political, Economic, and Cultural Relations with Europe, 1919–1933* (London, 1984), remains valuable.

12. Herring, *From Colony to Superpower*, pp. 427–35; Emily S. Rosenberg, *Financial Missionaries to the World: The Politics and Culture of Dollar Diplomacy, 1900–1930* (Cambridge, MA, 1999), provides a full account.

13. Cain and Hopkins, *British Imperialism*, pp. 453, 601, and the further references given there.

14. Statistical data are taken from CQ Research Online, "Foreign Trade of the United States," November 1, 1930, at library.cqpress.com; and Alfred E. Eckes, Jr. and Thomas W. Zeiler, *Globalization and the American Century* (Cambridge, 2003), chs. 3–4, and the tables on pp. 261–69. It should be said that the figures vary between different sources. Nevertheless, the data can be treated as indicating the main trends.

15. Roderick Floud and Paul Johnson, eds., *Cambridge Economic History of Modern Britain*, Vol. 2 (Cambridge, 2003), table 4.7, p. 83; Cain and Hopkins, *British Imperialism*, p. 440.

16. Stanley Lebergott, "The Returns to U.S. Imperialism, 1890–1929," *Journal of Economic History*, 40 (1980), pp. 230–31. Lebergott's neglected essay raises important issues that are overdue for further investigation.

17. As argued in chapter 8 of this text. Emily S. Rosenberg merits more than this compressed tribute to her pioneering work on this subject: *Spreading the American Dream: American Economic and Cultural Expansion, 1890–1945* (New York, 1982); Rosenberg, *Financial Missionaries*. Adam Tooze, *The Deluge: The Great War, America, and the Remaking of the Global Order, 1916–1931* (New York, 1914), explores the financial theme in detail with particular focus on 1916–1925, and takes a more positive view of the rise of the United States as a world power than the one offered here.

18. Yoneyuki Sugita, "The Rise of an American Principle in China: A Reinterpretation of the First Open Door Notes Towards China," in Richard Jensen, Jon Davidson, and Yoneyuki Sugita, eds., *Trans-Pacific Relations: America, Europe, and Asia in the Twentieth Century* (Westport, 2003), ch. 1.

19. Jay Sexton, *The Monroe Doctrine: Empire and Nation in Nineteenth-Century America* (New York, 2011), pp. 228–39. On the immediate causes (stemming from the Venezuelan Crisis), see Matthias Maass, "Catalyst for the Roosevelt Corollary: Arbitrating the 1902–1903 Venezuela Crisis and Its Impact on the Development of the Roosevelt Corollary to the Monroe Doctrine," *Diplomacy & Statecraft*, 20 (2009), pp. 383–402.

20. Noel Maurer's contribution to this subject is of utmost importance: *The Empire Trap: The Rise and Fall of U.S. Intervention to Protect American Property Rights Overseas, 1893–2013* (Princeton, NJ, 2013).

21. This is one of Maurer's central arguments in *The Empire Trap*.

22. Cyrus Veeser, *A World Safe for Capitalism: Dollar Diplomacy and America's Rise to Global Power* (New York, 2002).

23. Peter James Hudson, "The National City Bank of New York, and Haiti, 1909–1922," *Radical History Review*, 115 (2013), pp. 91–114.

24. Jason M. Colby, *The Business of Empire: United Fruit, Race, and U.S. Expansion in Central America* (Ithaca, 2011).

25. Chris James Mitchener and Marc Weidenmier, "Empire, Public Goods and the Roosevelt Corollary," *Journal of Economic History*, 65 (2005), pp. 658–92, show that the con-

fidence of investors and the price of government debt rose after intervention, though their view of the wider consequences is, arguably, too sanguine.

26. And also released the over-extended Royal Navy for duties elsewhere: Sexton, *Monroe Doctrine*, pp. 237–38.

27. The term "banana republic" was coined by O. Henry and first appeared in *Cabbages and Kings* (1904), which was based on his experience in Honduras in 1896–1897.

28. Alan McPherson, *The Invaded: How Latin Americans and Their Allies Fought and Ended U.S. Occupations* (New York, 2014), emphasizes the importance of local and regional claims for autonomy from increasingly centralized states and the lack of coordination among U.S. diplomats and military.

29. Herbert Hoover (1874–1964), president 1929–1933, following the Clarke Memorandum on the Monroe Doctrine (1928). Alan McPherson, "Herbert Hoover, Occupation Withdrawal, and the Good Neighbor Policy," *Presidential Studies Quarterly*, 44 (2014), pp. 623–39.

30. Paul A. Varg, "The Economic Side of the Good Neighbor Policy: The Reciprocal Trade Program and South America," *Pacific Historical Review*, 45 (1976), pp. 47–71, explains the failure of the Program. Also, more broadly, Cain and Hopkins, *British Imperialism*, ch. 22. On China and the Open Door, see chapter 9 of this text.

31. John J. Dwyer, *The Agrarian Dispute: The Expropriation of American-Owned Rural Land in Postrevolutionary Mexico* (Durham, 2008).

32. Carl P. Parrini, *Heir to Empire: United States Economic Diplomacy, 1916–1923* (Pittsburgh, 1969); see also Margaret Macmillan, *Paris 1919: Six Months that Changed the World* (New York, 2003), pp. 15–16.

33. For more on this subject, see Michael H. Hunt, *The Making of a Special Relationship: The United States and China to 1914* (New York, 1983), pp. 143–68; David M. Pletcher, *The Diplomacy of Involvement: American Economic Expansion Across the Pacific, 1784–1900* (Columbia, 2001), pp. 293–301. Gregory Moore, *Defining and Defending the Open Door Policy: Theodore Roosevelt and China, 1901–1909* (Lanham, 2015), confirms that the "Notes" were assurances that fell short of being commitments. Cain and Hopkins, *British Imperialism*, ch.13; Herring, *From Colony to Superpower*, pp. 329–35.

34. Sexton, *The Monroe Doctrine* pp. 228–39. The quotation is on p. 230.

35. B.J.C. McKercher, *Transition of Power: Britain's Loss of Global Pre-Eminence to the United States, 1930–1945* (Cambridge, 1999), pp. 339–43; John Darwin, *The Empire Project: The Rise and Fall of the British World System, 1830–1970* (Cambridge, 2009), pp. 474–6.

36. Warren G. Harding, "Return to Normalcy," Boston, 14 May 1920.

37. Edward Paice, *World War I: The African Front* (New York, 2008); DeWitt C. Ellinwood and S. D. Pradhan, eds., *India and World War I* (Columbia, 1978); Roy Kaushik, ed., *The Indian Army in Two World Wars* (Leiden, 2011).

38. Michael Adas, "Assault on the Civilizing Mission Ideology," *Journal of World History*, 15 (2004), pp. 31–63.

39. R. H. Tawney, "The Abolition of Economic Controls, 1918–21," *Economic History Review*, 13 (1940), pp. 7–17. In France, however, wartime controls were extended into the peace.

40. The wider issues are discussed in the context of Anglo-American rivalry in Cain and Hopkins, *British Imperialism*, ch. 19; also W. Max Corden, *Too Sensational: On the Choice of Exchange Rate Regimes*, (Cambridge, MA, 2004), pp. 12–13.

41. Martin Thomas, "Albert Sarraut, French Colonial Development, and the Communist Threat, 1919–1930," *Journal of Modern History*, 77 (2005), pp. 917–55.

42. Marc Michel, *L'appel à l'Afrique: contributions et réactions à l'effort de guerre en AOF, 1914–1919* (Paris, 1982); and the wider study by Richard S. Fogarty, *Race and War in France: Colonial Subjects in the French Army, 1914–1918* (Baltimore, 2008); Paice, *World War I: The African Front*.

43. This is an opportunity to say that no scholar has done more to develop the cultural history of modern empires than John M. MacKenzie. See *Propaganda and Empire: Manipulation of British Public Opinion, 1880–1956* (Manchester, 1986); "Passion or Indifference? Popular Imperialism in Britain: Continuities and Discontinuities over Two Centuries," in MacKenzie, ed., *European Empires and the People: Popular Responses to Imperialism in France, Britain, The Netherlands, Belgium, Germany and Italy* (Manchester, 2011), pp. 57–89. Also Berny Sèbe, "Existing Imperial Grandeur: the French Empire and Its Metropolitan Public," in MacKenzie, ed., *European Empires and the People*, pp. 35–42. Martin Thomas, *The French Empire Between the Wars: Imperialism, Politics and Society* (Manchester, 2005), ch. 6, takes a more cautious view.

44. Philip M. Taylor, *The Projection of Britain: British Overseas Publicity and Propaganda, 1919–1939* (Cambridge, 1981); Jeffrey Richards, "Patriotism with Profit: British Imperial Cinema in the 1930s," in James Curran and Victor Porter, eds., *British Cinema History* (1983), pp. 245–56.

45. Martin Thomas, *Empires of Intelligence: Security Services and Colonial Disorder after 1914* (Berkeley and Los Angeles, 2008).

46. Notably Oswald Spengler, *The Decline of the West* (Vols. 1 and 2, first published in German in 1918 and 1923, and in English in 1926 and 1928).

47. There is now a full study: Susan Pedersen, *The Guardians: The League of Nations and the Crisis of Empire* (Oxford, 2015).

48. On the effect of accountability on colonial administration, see Véronique Dimier, "L'internationalisation du debat colonial: rivalités Franco-Britanniques autour de la Commission Permanente des Mandats," *Outre-Mers: Revue d'Histoire*, 89 (2002), pp. 333–60.

49. Peter J. Yearwood, "Great Britain and the Repartition of Africa, 1914–19," *Journal of Imperial & Commonwealth History*, 18 (1990), pp. 316–41.

50. 4 January 1920. Quoted in Scott Nearing, *The American Empire* (New York, 1921), p. 200.

51. Erez Manela, *The Wilsonian Moment: Self-Determination and the International Origins of Anticolonial Nationalism (Oxford, 2007)*, pp. 6, 215, 218–19. The literature on Wilsonian foreign policy is vast. For an insightful overview, see David Steigerwald, "The Reclamation of Woodrow Wilson," in Michael J. Hogan, ed., *Paths to Power: The Historiography of American Foreign Relations to 1941* (Cambridge, 2000), pp. 148–75; and for a longer view, Frank Ninkovich, *The Wilsonian Century: U.S. Foreign Policy since 1900* (Chicago, 1999).

52. Allen Lynch, "Woodrow Wilson and the Principle of 'National Self-Determination': A Reconsideration," *Review of International Studies*, 28 (2002), pp. 419–36; Emily S. Rosenberg, "World War I, Wilsonianism, and Challenges to the U.S. Empire," *Diplomatic History*, 38 (2014), pp. 853–63. On the ambiguities of the term, see Brad Simpson, "The United States and the Curious History of Self-Determination," *Diplomatic History*, 36 (2012), pp. 175–94.

53. John W. Cell, "Colonial Rule," in Judith M. Brown and Wm. Roger Louis, eds., *The Oxford History of the British Empire*, Vol. 4 (Oxford, 1999), ch. 10; Alice Conklin, *A Mission to Civilize: The Republican Idea in France and West Africa, 1895–1930* (Stanford, 1997); on the intellectual basis of these principles in France, see Eric Savarese, *L'Ordre colonial et sa légitimation en France métropolitaine* (Paris, 1998).

54. Lévy-Bruhl (1857–1939), a pioneering anthropologist, became well known for *Les fonctions mentales dans les sociétés inférieures* (Paris, 1910; translated as *How Natives Think*, 1926), and *La mentalité primitive* (Paris, 1922; translated as *Primitive Mentality*, 1923). This is not to argue that anthropologists were simply agents of colonialism. On this issue see Adam Kuper, *Anthropology and Anthropologists: The Modern British School* (London, 1983).

55. The mission statement of the era was Frederick John Dealtry Lugard, *The Dual Mandate in British Tropical Africa* (London, 1922).

56. Jaffna L. Cox, "A Splendid Training Ground: The Importance to the Royal Air Force of Its Role in Iraq, 1919–32," *Journal of Imperial & Commonwealth History*, 13 (1985), pp. 157–84; Michael Paris, "Air Power and Imperial Defence, 1880–1919," *Journal of Contemporary History*, 24 (1989), pp. 209–25; and, more generally, David Omissi, *Air Power and Colonial Control* (Manchester, 1990).

57. C.J.D. Duder, "The Settler Response to the Indian Crisis of 1923 in Kenya: Brigadier General Philip Wheatley and Direct Action," *Journal of Imperial & Commonwealth History*, 17 (1989), pp. 349–73.

58. Darwin, *The Empire Project*, p. 357.

59. Ian Phimister, *An Economic and Social History of Zimbabwe, 1890–1948* (London, 1988), chs. 2–3.

60. Darwin, *The Empire Project*, pp. 443–5.

61. Philip Woods, *Roots of Parliamentary Democracy in India: Montagu Chelmsford Reforms, 1917–1923* (Delhi, 1996).

62. The considerable research on this subject is summarized by Judith M. Brown, "India," in Judith M. Brown and Wm. Roger Louis, eds., *The Oxford History of the British Empire* (Oxford, 1999), p. 430.

63. Peter J. Cain, "Bentham and the Development of the British Critique of Colonialism," *Utilitas*, 23 (2011), pp. 1–24.

64. John E. Moser, *Twisting the Lion's Tail: Anglophobia and the United States, 1921–48* (Basingstoke, Hants., 1999).

65. Wm. Roger Louis, "The United States and the African Peace Settlement of 1919: The Pilgrimage of George Louis Beer," *Journal of African History*, 4 (1963), pp. 413–33, deals with the diplomatic maneuvers of the time.

66. Emily S. Rosenberg, "World War I, Wilsonianism, and Challenges to U.S. Empire," *Diplomatic History*, 38 (2014), pp. 852–63.

67. Ibid., p. 860.

68. Cain and Hopkins, *British Imperialism*, chs. 22, 25.

69. 3.5 times in the case of Argentina. Cain and Hopkins, *British Imperialism*, ch. 22; Alan Knight, "Latin America," in Brown and Louis, *Oxford History of the British Empire*, Vol. 4, ch. 27. Knight takes a less sanguine view than Cain and Hopkins mainly because he emphasizes the role of visible trade rather than investments.

70. Lloyd George, 1921. Quoted in Cain and Hopkins, *British Imperialism*, p. 601.

71. Cain and Hopkins, *British Imperialism*, ch. 25; Jürgen Osterhammel, "China," in Brown and Louis, *Oxford History of the British Empire*, Vol. 4, pp. 643–4, 653–4. The cultural features of expansion are emphasized by Akira Iriye, *Cambridge History of American Foreign Relations*, Vol. 3 (Cambridge, 1993), ch. 7.

72. John Darwin, "An Undeclared Empire: The British in the Middle East, 1918–39," *Journal of Imperial & Commonwealth History*, 27 (1999), pp. 159–76.

73. Darwin, *The Empire Project*, pp. 375–85, 469–74.

74. John Maynard Keynes, "The Great Slump of 1930," *The Nation & Atheneum*, 20 December 1930, p. 1, reproduced as a Project Gutenberg Canada e-book, No. 197.

75. James Foreman-Peck, *A History of the World Economy: International Economic Relations since 1850* (Totowa, 1983), p. 215 (measured in gold dollars).

76. The starting point for entering the vast literature on this subject is Barry Eichengreen, *Golden Fetters: The Gold Standard and the Great Depression, 1919–1939* (Oxford, 1992). For a wider perspective see Charles P. Kindleberger, *Manias, Panics and Crashes* (Basingstoke, Hants, 2001); and Marc Flandreau, Carl-Ludwig Holtfrerich, and Harold James, eds., *International Financial History in the Twentieth Century: System and Anarchy* (Cambridge, 2003).

77. This summary reflects the emphasis given in the recent literature to the monetary aspects of the crisis. A fuller account would need to integrate political considerations, as argued by Kenneth Moure, *The Gold Standard Illusion: France, the Bank of France, and*

the International Gold Standard, 1914–1939 (Oxford, 2002). See also Barry Eichengreen and Kris Mitchener, "The Great Depression as a Credit Boom Gone Wrong," *Research in Economic History*, 22 (2004), pp. 183–237; Barry Eichengreen and Douglas A. Irwin, "The Slide to Protectionism in the Great Depression: Who Succumbed and Why?" *Journal of Economic History*, 70 (2010), pp. 871–97.

78. Moure, *The Gold Standard Illusion*, provides an admirable account linking economics and politics. France, in particular, persisted with the gold standard until 1936, and then found that devaluation did not bring the expected benefits.

79. See the pioneering essays edited by Ian Brown, *The Economies of Africa and Asia in the Inter-war Depression* (London, 1989). Also Dietmar Rothermund, *The Global Impact of the Great Depression, 1929–1939* (London, 1996).

80. Foreman-Peck, *A History of the World Economy*, pp. 198–204.

81. Harold James, *The End of Globalization: Lessons from the Great Depression* (Cambridge, MA, 2001), p. 111.

82. Cain and Hopkins, *British Imperialism*, chs. 17–20. The difficulty was that the British market was limited and re-exports were hampered by protectionist measures elsewhere.

83. My phrasing reflects the point made by Barry Eichengreen and Douglas A. Irwin that protected trade was built on existing informal links: "Trade Blocs, Currency Blocs and the Reorientation of World Trade in the 1930s," *Journal of International History*, 38 (1995), pp. 1–24.

84. Thomas, *The French Empire Between the Wars*, pp. 102–4. The fundamental work on this subject is Jacques Marseille, *Empire colonial et capitalism français: l' histoire d'un divorce* (Paris, 1984).

85. Cain and Hopkins, *British Imperialism*, pp. 431–3.

86. Marseille, *Empire colonial*, pp. 95–119; Cain and Hopkins, *British Imperialism*, pp. 437–40.

87. Marseille, *Empire colonial*.

88. Ronald Findlay and Kevin H. O'Rourke, *Power and Plenty: Trade, War and the World Economy in the Second Millennium* (Princeton, NJ, 2007); James, *The End of Globalization*.

89. Even Britain had begun to apply selective protectionist measures after 1914.

90. See also Hopkins, "Back to the Future."

91. See, for example, Federico Finchelstein, *Transatlantic Fascism: Ideology, Violence, and the Sacred in Italy and Argentina* (Durham, 2010).

92. Bruno Cabanes, *The Great War and the Origins of Humanitarianism, 1918–24* (New York, 2014), though the "origins" predate 1918–24 by a long way.

93. Tomoko Akami, *Japan's News Propaganda and Reuter's New Empire in Asia, 1870–1914* (Dordrecht, 2012), explores the competition between Reuters and Japanese news services.

94. Great credit should go to Akira Iriye for pioneering the study of this subject: *Global Community: The Role of International Organizations in the Making of the Contemporary World* (Berkeley, 2003), chs. 1–2.

95. Patricia Clavin, *Securing the World Economy: The Reinvention of the League of Nations, 1919–1946* (Oxford, 2013), provides a full account of these developments.

96. Sunil Amrith and Patricia Clavin, "Feeding the World: Connecting Europe and Asia, 1930–1945," *Past & Present*, Supplement (2013), pp. 29–50. Credit should go to Douglas Rimmer, who pioneered this subject: " 'Basic Needs' and the Origins of the Development Ethos," *Journal of Developing Areas*, 15 (1981), pp. 215–38.

97. Daniel Wold, "The Commonwealth: Internationalism and Imperialism, 1919–1939," University of Texas, Ph.D. dissertation (2012).

98. Cabanes, *The Great War*.

99. An accessible and up-to-date guide to the literature on Gandhi (1869–1948) is Judith M. Brown and Anthony Parel, eds., *The Cambridge Companion to Gandhi* (Cambridge, 2011).

100. Surendra Bhana and Goolam Vahed, *The Making of a Political Reformer: Gandhi in South Africa, 1893-1914* (New Delhi, 2005); also the perceptive review by Bill Freund in *Transformations*, 59 (2005), pp. 122-3.

101. Samuel P. Huntington, *Political Order in Changing Societies* (New Haven, 1968), pp. 74-8. See chapter 4 of this text for the application of the concept to the "Age of Jackson."

102. Alan de Bromhead, Barry Eichengreen, and Kevin H. O'Rourke, "Right-Wing Political Extremism in the Great Depression," *NBER Working Paper*, 178781 (2012).

103. The classic study is Samuel E. Finer, *The Man on Horseback: The Role of the Military in Politics* (Boulder, 1966). Hitler preferred motor cars.

104. Martin Thomas, *Violence and Political Order: Police, Workers and Protest in the European Colonial Empires, 1918-1940* (New York, 2012).

105. John Maynard Keynes, "The Great Slump of 1930," *The Nation & Atheneum*, December 20, 1930, p. 1, reproduced as a Project Gutenberg Canada e-book, No. 197; Robert Skidelsky, *John Maynard Keynes: The Economist as Saviour, 1920-1937* (London, 1994), is the authoritative account.

106. Patricia Clavin, "Reparations in the Long Run," *Diplomacy & Statecraft*, 16 (2005), pp. 515-30.

107. Arnold J. Toynbee, *A Study of History*, 12 vols. (London, 1934-61).

108. Joseph A. Schumpeter, *Capitalism, Socialism, and Democracy* (New York, 1942).

109. R. D. Pearce, *The Turning Point in Africa: British Colonial Policy, 1938-48* (London, 1982), carries this theme through the war years.

110. Clyde Sanger, *Malcolm MacDonald: Bringing an End to Empire* (New York, 1995). Malcolm John MacDonald (1901-81), son of Ramsey MacDonald, Prime Minister in the Labour government, 1929-31 and the National government, 1931-35, was Secretary of State for the Colonies, 1935, Secretary of State for Dominion Affairs, 1935-38, and of the combined offices, 1938-40. He then became High Commissioner for Canada, 1941-46, Governor of Malaya, 1947-48, High Commissioner for India, 1955-60, and Governor of Kenya, 1963-64.

111. *Warning from the West Indies: A Tract for Africa and the Empire* (London, 1936). The book is commonly cited without its subtitle, which makes it clear that Macmillan was using the West Indies to promote reform in Africa and the (tropical) empire as a whole. There is a fascinating memoir by Mona Macmillan: "The Making of Warning from the West Indies," *Journal of Imperial & Commonwealth History*, 18 (1980), pp. 207-19; William Malcolm Hailey, *An African Survey: A Study of Problems Arising in Africa South of the Sahara* (London, 1939; 1957). Hailey (1872-1969), 1st Baron Hailey (1936), Governor of the Punjab, 1924-28, United Provinces, 1928-34; John W. Cell, *Hailey: A Study in British Imperialism, 1872-1969* (Cambridge, 1992).

112. Martin Thomas, "French Empire Elites and the Politics of Economic Obligation in the Interwar Years," *Historical Journal*, 52 (2009), pp. 1-28, shows how the Sarraut Plan of 1921 was updated and then rejected, largely as a result of settler opposition.

113. Darwin, *The Empire Project*, pp. 445-9, 462-9.

114. Thomas, *The French Empire Between the Wars*, ch. 9; Thomas, "French Empire Elites"; Tony Chafer and Amanda Sackur, eds., *French Colonial Empire and the Popular Front: Hope and Disillusion* (London, 1990).

115. Thomas, *The French Empire Between the Wars*, ch. 9.

116. Alice Conklin, *A Mission to Civilize: The Republican Idea of Empire in France and West Africa 1895-1930* (Stanford, 1997), chs. 6-7.

117. Howard Johnson, "Oil, Imperial Policy and the Trinidad Disturbances, 1937," *Journal of Imperial and Commonwealth History*, 4 (1975), pp. 29-54; Johnson, "The Political Uses of Commissions of Enquiry (1): The Imperial Colonial West Indies Context, the Foster and Moyne Commissions," *Social & Economic Studies*, 27 (1978), pp. 256-83; Sahadeo Basdeo, "The 'Radical' Movement Towards Decolonization in the British Caribbean in

the Thirties," *Canadian Journal of Latin American & Caribbean Studies*, 44 (1997), pp. 127–46.

118. Cain and Hopkins, *British Imperialism*, pp. 588–90.

119. Quoted Jane H. Bowden, "Development and Control in British Colonial Policy with Reference to Nigeria and the Gold Coast," Ph.D. dissertation, University of Birmingham, 1981, p. 103.

120. The essential assessment is McKercher, *Transition of Power*. Older psycho-sociological accounts, for example, attributed the missteps of statesmen to weak leadership and failed to recognize that, had strong men been in charge, they would still have had to play the same poor set of cards. A post-revisionist school, however, has argued that Chamberlain could and should have pursued alternatives to appeasement. See especially R.A.C. Parker, *Chamberlain and Appeasement: British Policy and the Coming of the Second World War* (London, 1993); Parker, *Churchill and Appeasement* (London, 2000).

121. On the latter see Christopher M. Andrew and A. S. Kanya-Forstner, *France Overseas: The Great War and the Climax of French Imperial Expansion* (London, 1981). On the debates of the time see P. J. Cain, "Capitalism, Aristocracy and Empire: Some 'Classical' Theories of Imperialism Revisited," *Journal of Imperial & Commonwealth History*, 35 (2007), pp. 25–47.

122. Douglas Rimmer, "Have-Not Nations: The Prototype," *Economic Development & Cultural Change*, 27 (1979), pp. 307–25. For a popular contemporary statement see Norman Angell, *This Have and Have Not Business: Political Fantasy and Economic Fact* (London, 1936).

123. Antony Best, "Economic Appeasement or Economic Nationalism? A Political Perspective on the British Empire, Japan and the Rise of Intra-Asian Trade, 1933–37," *Journal of Imperial & Commonwealth History*, 30 (2002), pp. 77–101, details the conflict between British and Japanese exporters of textiles over control of unassigned markets in Asia.

124. Rana Mitter, *China's War with Japan, 1937–45: The Struggle for Survival* (London, 2013); Florentino Rodao explores the links between conflicts in the West and the East: "Japan and the Axis, 1937–38: Recognition of the Franco Regime and Manchukuo," *Journal of Contemporary History*, 44 (2009), pp. 431–47.

125. Rana Mitter and Aaron W. Moore, "China in World War II, 1937–1945: Experience, Memory and Legacy," *Modern Asian Studies*, 45 (2011), pp. 225–40; Sandra Wilson, "Containing the Crisis: Japan's Diplomatic Offensive in the West, 1931–33," *Modern Asian Studies*, 29 (1995), pp. 337–72; Tae Jin Park, "Guiding Public Opinion on the Far Eastern Crisis, 1931–1941," *Diplomacy & Statecraft*, 22 (2011), pp. 388–407.

126. Paul Corner, "Italian Fascism: Organization, Enthusiasm, Opinion," *Journal of Modern Italian Studies*, 15 (2010), pp. 378–89; Alexander de Grand, "Mussolini's Follies: Fascism in Its Imperial and Racist Phase, 1935–1940," *Contemporary European History*, 13 (2004), pp. 127–47.

127. Bruce G. Strang, " 'The Worst of All Worlds': Oil Sanctions and Italy's Invasion of Abyssinia, 1935–1936," *Diplomacy & Statecraft*, 19 (2008), pp. 210–35.

128. S.K.B. Asante, "The Italo-Ethiopian Conflict: A Case Study in British West African Responses to Crisis Diplomacy in the 1930s," *Journal of African History*, 15 (1974), pp. 291–302.

129. The tangled and often discordant relations between the two powers are traced by Martin Thomas, *Britain, France, and Appeasement: Anglo-French Relations in the Popular Front Era* (Oxford, 1996); Thomas, "Appeasement in the Late Third Republic," *Diplomacy & Statecraft*, 19 (2008), pp. 566–607; and Richard Davis, "Le débat sur l'appeasement britannique et français dans les années 1930: les crises d'Éthiopie et de Rhénanie," *Revue d'histoire moderne et contemporaine*, 45 (1998), pp. 822–36.

130. B.J.C. McKercher, "National Security and Imperial Defence: British Grand Strategy and Appeasement, 1930–1939," *Diplomacy & Statecraft*, 19 (2008), pp. 391–442.

131. B.J.C. McKercher, "Austen Chamberlain and the Continental Balance of Power: Strategy, Stability, and the League of Nations, 1924–29," *Diplomacy & Statecraft*, 14 (2003), pp. 207–36; McKercher, "The Last Old Diplomat: Sir Robert Vansittart and the Verities of British Foreign Policy, 1903–30," *Diplomacy & Statecraft*, 6 (1995), pp. 1–38; McKercher, "The Foreign Office, 1930–39: Strategy, Permanent Interests and National Security," *Contemporary British History*, 18 (2004), pp. 87–109.

132. See Cain and Hopkins, *British Imperialism*, pp. 479–83, 486–7, and the further references given there.

133. Andrew J. Crozier, *Appeasement and Germany's Last Bid for Colonies* (Basingstoke, 1988); Chantal Metzger, "D'une puissance coloniale à un pays sans colonies: L'Allemagne et la question coloniale, 1914–1945," *Revue d'Allemagne*, 38 (2006), pp. 555–69, presents a German perspective.

134. Richard S. Grayson, "Leo Amery's Imperialist Alternative to Appeasement in the 1930s," *Twentieth-Century British History*, 17 (2006), pp. 489–515.

135. Scott Newton, "The 'Anglo-German Connection' and the Political Economy of Appeasement," *Diplomacy & Statecraft*, 2 (1991), pp. 178–207.

136. Catherine Krull and B.J.C. McKercher, "Public Opinion, Arms Limitation, and Government Policy in Britain, 1932–34: Some Preliminary Considerations," *Diplomacy & Statecraft*, 13 (2002), pp. 103–37.

137. Quoted in Moser, *Twisting the Lion's Tail*, p. 112.

138. Quoted in ibid., p. 115.

139. McKercher, *Transition of Power*, pp. 339–43; Darwin, *The Empire Project*, pp. 511–13.

140. Emily S. Rosenberg, *A Day Which Will Live: Pearl Harbor in American Memory* (Durham, 2003), traces the enduring myths and some of the realities of the event.

141. Dean Acheson, *Present at the Creation: My Years in the State Department* (New York, 1969). Acheson (1893–1971) was Secretary of State, 1949–1953. Although the greater part of Acheson's huge book deals with the period after 1945, he begins in 1941 with sections in ch. 1 on "The Asian Civil War" and "American Notions about China." Robert J. McMahon, *Dean Acheson and the Creation of an American World Order* (Washington, DC, 2009), provides an authoritative account of how Acheson constructed a new strategy of liberal, interventionist internationalism.

142. For a full account of the involvement of the empire, see Ashley Jackson, *The British Empire and the Second World War* (London, 2006).

143. Warren F. Kimbell, "Lend-Lease and the Open Door: The Temptation of British Opulence, 1937–1942," *Political Science Quarterly*, 86 (1971), pp. 232–59.

144. The period is well covered by David Reynolds, *The Creation of the Anglo-American Alliance, 1937–1941: A Study in Competitive Co-operation* (London, 1981).

145. Britain was the major recipient but substantial aid went to the USSR and France, and smaller contributions to China, Latin America, and Saudi Arabia. See Warren F. Kimball, *The Most Unsordid Act: Lend-Lease, 1939–1941* (Baltimore, 1969); Alan P. Dobson, *U.S. Wartime Aid to Britain, 1940–1946* (London, 1986); Dobson, *The Politics of the Anglo-American Economic Special Relationship* (Brighton, 1988).

146. For some of the implications see Charlie Whitham, "On Dealing with Gangsters: The Limits of British 'Generosity' in the Leasing of Bases to the United States, 1940–41," *Diplomacy & Statecraft*, 7 (1996), pp. 589–630; Steven High, "The Racial Politics of Criminal Jurisdiction in the Aftermath of the Anglo-American 'Destroyers-for-Bases' Deal, 1940–50," *Journal of Imperial & Commonwealth History*, 32 (2004), pp. 77–105.

147. Douglas G. Brinkley and David R. Facey-Crowther, eds., *The Atlantic Charter* (New York, 1994).

148. Alan P. Dobson, "The Export White Paper, 10 September 1941," *Economic History Review*, 39 (1986), pp. 59–76.

149. Moser, *Twisting the Lion's Tail*, pp. 148, 169–70.

150. Cordell Hull (1871–1955), Democrat, free-trader, Spanish-American War veteran, and one of the principal architects of the United Nations. Member of Congress for Tennessee in the House of Representatives, 1907–1921, 1923–1931; Senator, 1930–1933, Secretary of State, 1933–1944.

151. Eric D. Pullin, "'Noise and Flatter': American Propaganda Strategy and Operation in India during World War II," *Diplomatic History*, 34 (2010), pp. 275–98; and more generally Kenton J. Clymer, *Quest for Freedom: The United States and India's Independence* (New York, 1995).

152. Peter W. Fay, *The Forgotten Army: India's Armed Struggle for Independence, 1942–1945* (Ann Arbor, 1993).

153. Cain and Hopkins, *British Imperialism*, p. 623.

154. Darwin, *Empire Project*, p. 518 and p. 765, n.5, quoting W. K. Hancock and M. Gowing, *British War Economy* (London, 1949), p. 354.

155. Quoted in Alan Bullock, *The Life and Times of Ernest Bevin*, Vol. 3 (London, 1983), p. 122. William ("Will") Clayton (1897–1966), Under-Secretary of State for Economic Affairs, 1945–1947.

156. Robert Skidelski, *John Maynard Keynes*, Vol. 3 (New York, 2000), deals with Keynes's formidable efforts as a wartime negotiator.

157. Quoted in Inderjeet Parmar, *Special Interests, the State and the Anglo-American Alliance, 1939–1945* (London, 1995), p. 171. Amery was writing in 1950. See also Wm. Roger Louis, *"In the Name of God, Go!" Leo Amery and the British Empire in the Age of Churchill* (New York, 1992).

158. Richard Pells, *Not Like Us: How Europeans Have Loved, Hated and Transformed American Culture since World War II* (New York, 1997).

159. John Gallagher and Ronald Robinson, "The Imperialism of Free Trade," *Economic History Review*, 2nd ser., 6 (1953), pp. 1–25.

160. D. A. Low and John Lonsdale, "Introduction: Towards the New Order, 1945–1963," in D. A. Low and Alison Smith, eds., *Oxford History of East Africa*, 3 (Oxford, 1976), p. 13.

161. A. J. Stockwell, "Colonial Planning during World War II: The Case of Malaya," *Journal of Imperial & Commonwealth History*, 2 (1974), pp. 333–51.

162. J. M. Lee and Martin Petter, *The Colonial Office, War and Development Policy: Organisation and the Planning of a Metropolitan Initiative, 1939–1945* (London, 1982); L. J. Butler, "Reconstruction, Development and the Entrepreneurial State: The British Colonial Model, 1939–51," *Contemporary British History*, 13 (1999), pp. 29–55.

163. Wm. Roger Louis, *Imperialism at Bay, 1941–1945: The United States and the Decolonization of the British Empire (Oxford, 1977)* , pp. 212, 464. Churchill wanted to add territory by annexing Siam. When this scheme failed, he turned to an alternative and extended Britain's control over Libya, which became a Trust Territory under the authority of the United Nations. Ibid., pp. 555–62.

164. D. K. Fieldhouse, "The Labour Governments and the Empire-Commonwealth, 1945–51," in Ritchie Ovendale, ed., *The Foreign Policies of the British Labour Governments, 1945–1951* (Leicester, 1984), pp. 83–120; R. M. Douglass, *The Labour Party, Nationalism and Internationalism, 1939–2004* (London, 2004), chs. 4–6; and more generally Stephen Howe, *Anticolonialism in British Politics: The Left and the End of Empire, 1918–1964* (Oxford, 1993).

165. Noel Annan provides a firsthand account in *Changing Enemies: The Defeat and Regeneration of Germany* (London, 1995), ch. 8, "Britain's New Colony."

166. Wendy Webster, *Englishness and Empire, 1939–1965* (Oxford, 2005); on civilian life see David Kynaston, *Austerity Britain, 1945–51* (London, 2007).

167. Scott Newton, "Britain, the Sterling Area and European Integration, 1945–50," *Journal of Imperial & Commonwealth History*, 13 (1985), pp. 163–82.

168. This is an opportunity to pay tribute to W. David McIntyre, who almost single-handedly kept the study of the constitutional history of the British Empire alive for decades while

other historians (including the present writer) passed it by. See, in this context, "The Admission of Small States to the Commonwealth," *Journal of Imperial & Commonwealth History*, 24 (1996), pp. 244–77; "The Strange Death of Dominion Status," *Journal of Imperial & Commonwealth History*, 27 (1999), pp. 193–212; "The Unofficial Commonwealth Relations Conferences, 1933–59: Precursors of the Tri-Sector Commonwealth," *Journal of Imperial & Commonwealth History*, 36 (2008), pp. 591–614.

169. Robert Aldrich, *Greater France: A History of French Overseas Expansion* (Houndmills, 1996), p. 283.

170. Bernard Droz, "L'evolution de l'Union française," *Historiens et géographes*, 89 (1998), pp. 259–70.

171. Gary Wilder, *The French Imperial Nation-State: Negritude and Colonial Humanism between the Two World Wars* (Chicago, 2005). The phrase was coined by Henri Vast, in *La Plus Grande France: Bilan de la France colonial* (Paris, 1909). See Kate Marsh, *Narratives of the French Empire: Fiction, Nostalgia, and Imperial Rivalries from 1784 to the Present* (Lanham, 2013), p. 17, n. 46.

172. Jonathan K. Gosnell, *The Politics of Frenchness in Colonial Algeria, 1930–1954* (Rochester, 2002), provides an excellent illustration of the conceptual ambiguities and the political animosities that followed.

173. Frederick Cooper, *Citizenship between Empire and Nation: Remaking France and French Africa, 1945–1960* (Princeton, NJ, 2014), presents a full discussion of these issues. Gary Wilder, *Freedom Time: Negritude, Decolonization, and the Future of the World* (Durham, 2015), illustrates the point with reference to Aimé Césaire and Léopold Sédar Senghor. See also Michael Collins, "Decolonisation and the Federal Moment," *Diplomacy & Statecraft*, 24 (2013), pp. 21–40; Véronique Dimier, "For a Republic 'Diverse and Indivisible'? France's Experience from the Colonial Past," *Contemporary European History*, 13 (2004), pp. 45–66.

174. Gerold Krozewski, *Money and the End of Empire: British International Policy and the Colonies, 1947–58* (London, 2001); and Allister Hinds, *Britain's Sterling Colonial Policy and Decolonization, 1939–1958* (London, 2001), provide complementary assessments.

175. The Franc Zone was much smaller than the Sterling Area and was confined mainly to francophone territories in West and Central Africa. Its initial aim was to limit the damage to the colonies from the devaluation of the French franc at the end of the war.

176. Cain and Hopkins, *British Imperialism*, ch. 26, provides one of numerous accounts.

177. Geoffrey Warner, "The Anglo-American Special Relationship," *Diplomatic History*, 13 (1989), pp. 479–99.

178. Quoted in R. D. Pearce, *The Turning Point in Africa: British Colonial Policy, 1938–1948* (London, 1982), pp. 95–6.

179. These institutions are discussed further in chapter 15 of this text.

180. Michael J. Hogan, *The Marshall Plan: America, Britain and the Reconstruction of Western Europe, 1947–1952* (Cambridge, 1987), ch. 6.

181. Catherine R. Schenk, *The Decline of Sterling: Managing the Retreat of an International Currency, 1945–1992* (Cambridge, 2010), ch. 1. On the relative standing of the dollar and sterling at the close of the 1930s, see Livia Chitu, Barry Eichengreen, and Arnaud Mehl, "When Did the Dollar Overtake Sterling as the Leading International Currency? Evidence from the Bond Markets," *European Central Bank Working Paper*, 1433 (2012).

182. Judd Polk, *Sterling: Its Meaning in World Finance* (London, 1956), p. 3.

183. The literature on this subject is now vast. Three key texts offering different interpretations remain essential reading: Hogan, *The Marshall Plan*; Alan S. Milward, *The Reconstruction of Western Europe, 1945–51* (London, 1984; 2006); Milward, *European Rescue of the Nation-State* (Berkeley, 1992).

184. There are several versions of this quotation. I follow here David Reynolds, ed., *The Origins of the Cold War in Europe: International Perspectives* (New Haven, 1994), p. 13.

185. General Hastings L. Ismay (1887–1965), 1st Baron Ismay, chief military assistant to Winston Churchill during World War II, Secretary General of Nato, 1952–1957.

186. David Ryan provides an accessible summary of the literature in "By Way of Introduction: The United States, Decolonization and the World System," in David Ryan and Victor Pungong, eds., *The United States and Decolonization* (Basingstoke, 2000), pp. 1–23.

187. Alexander Keese, "A Culture of Panic: 'Communist' Scapegoats and Decolonization in French West Africa and French Polynesia, 1945–1957," *French Colonial History*, 9 (2008), pp. 131–45.

188. See Elizabeth Schmidt, *Cold War and Decolonization in Guinea, 1946–1958* (Athens, 2007), ch. 1; Irwin Wall, "France in the Cold War," *Journal of European Studies*, 38 (2008), pp. 121–39. The Netherlands resumed control of Indonesia but was forced out in 1949. For a recent summary, see Nicholas J. White, "Reconstructing Europe through Rejuvenating Empire: The British, French, and Dutch Experiences Compared," *Past & Present*, Supplement 6 (2011), pp. 211–36.

189. Moser, *Twisting the Lion's Tail*, p. 188.

190. On Algeria see, among many studies, Todd Shepard, *The Invention of Decolonization: The Algerian War and the Remaking of France* (Ithaca, 2006), chs. 1–3.

191. What follows is drawn from A. G. Hopkins, "Rethinking Decolonisation," *Past & Present*, 200 (2008), pp. 211–47. See also Cain and Hopkins, *British Imperialism*, chs. 21, 26. The term "dominion" fell out of use in the 1950s. I use it here to refer to subsequent periods as a convenient short-hand reference to Commonwealth countries commonly designated as being of "white settlement" and to exclude new dominions such as India.

192. First summarized by one of the pioneers, W. Arthur Lewis, *The Theory of Economic Growth* (London, 1955), with a degree of clarity that continues to set standards. Appropriately, Lewis (1915–1991) was himself a colonial subject (from the West Indies) who was a disturbingly innovative advisor to the Colonial Office in the 1940s and later economic advisor to Kwame Nkrumah in Ghana. Robert L. Tignor has provided an admirable biography: *W. Arthur Lewis and the Beginning of Development Economics* (Princeton, NJ, 2006).

193. Fonds d'investissement pour le développement économique et social. Marseille, *Empire colonial et capitalisme français*, pp. 103–6, 128–49; François Pacquement, "Le système d'aide au développement de la France et du Royaume-Uni," *Revue Internationale de Politique et Développement*, 1 (2010), pp. 55–80, provides a valuable long-run comparison.

194. Jean-Pierre Dormais, *The French Economy in the Twentieth Century* (Cambridge, 2004), pp. 36–39.

195. Ibid., p. 37; and for a case study, see Martin René Atangana, "Mythes et réalités de l'investissement privé en Afrique noire française: le case du Cameroun dan les années 1940 et 1950," *Canadian Journal of African Studies*, 35 (2001), pp. 1–31.

196. Arthur Creech Jones (1891–1964), Under-Secretary of State for the Colonies, 1945–1946, Secretary of State, 1946–1950; John W. Cell, "On the Eve of Decolonisation: The Colonial Office's Plans for the Transfer of Power in Africa, 1947," *Journal of Imperial & Commonwealth History*, 8 (1980), pp. 235–57; Pearce, *The Turning Point in Africa*, ch. 5.

197. See the illuminating contribution made by Emmanuelle Saada, *Empire's Children: Race, Filiation, and Citizenship in the French Colonies* (Chicago, 2007).

198. This question is fully covered by Cooper, *Citizenship between Empire and Nation*.

199. The "green uprising" is discussed in connection with Andrew Jackson in the first two subsections of chapter 4, and with reference to India in the 1920s and 1930s, in the subsection titled "One of the Greatest Economic Catastrophes of Modern History" in this chapter.

200. Hopkins, "Rethinking Decolonisation," puts a case for incorporating the "old dominions" into the study of decolonization after World War II.

201. The coming of Indian independence is the subject of a vast literature; that of Burma has been relatively neglected. On the former, see R. J. Moore, *Escape from Empire: The*

Attlee Government and the Indian Problem (Oxford, 1983); and the more recent references in Judith Brown and Wm. Roger Louis, eds., *The Oxford History of the British Empire*, Vol. 4 (Oxford, 1999), ch. 18; Robin W. Winks and Alaine Low, eds., *The Oxford History of the British Empire*, Vol. 5 (Oxford, 1999); Douglas M. Peers and Nandini Gosptu, eds., *India and the British Empire* (Oxford, 2012), ch. 3. On Burma, see Balwant Singh, *Independence and Democracy in Burma, 1945–52: The Turbulent Years* (Ann Arbor, 1993); Ian Brown, "British Firms and the End of Empire in Burma," *Asian Affairs*, 40 (2009), pp. 15–33, shows that Britain's withdrawal from Burma was prompted largely by the unprofitable results of efforts to reconstruct the country in the aftermath of the Japanese occupation.

202. Robert Shepherd, *Enoch Powell: A Biography* (London, 1997), p. 308.

203. Christopher Bayly and Tim Harper, *Forgotten Wars: The End of Britain's Asian Empire* (London, 2007).

204. Quoted in Paul M. McGarr, "After Nehru, What? Britain, the United States, and the Other Transfer of Power in India, 1960–64," *International History Review*, 33 (2011), p. 117.

205. Ibid., p.124. Moreover, British influence survived into the 1960s, at least. Ibid., p. 138, n. 79.

206. B. R. Tomlinson, "Indo-British Relations in the Post-colonial Era: The Sterling Balances Negotiations, 1947–49," *Journal of Imperial & Commonwealth History*, 13 (1985), pp. 142–62. The role of the sterling balances in Britain's foreign and imperial policies has been thoroughly assessed by Krozewski, *Money and the End of Empire*; Hinds, *Britain's Sterling Colonial Policy*; Schenk, *The Decline of Sterling*.

207. Geoffrey Barei, "The Algerian War of Independence and the Coming to Power of General Charles de Gaulle: British Reactions," *Maghreb Review*, 37 (2012), pp. 259–83.

208. Berny Sèbe, "In the Shadow of the Algerian War: The United States and the Common Organisation of Saharan Regions (OCRS), 1957–62," *Journal of Imperial & Commonwealth History*, 38 (2010), pp. 202–22.

209. Discoveries of cobalt and uranium greatly enhanced Africa's importance in the new atomic age. See Raymond E. Dumett, *Imperialism, Economic Development and Social Change in West Africa* (Durham, 2013), ch. 20.

210. Steven G. Galpern, *Money, Oil and Empire in the Middle East: Sterling and Postwar Imperialism* (Cambridge, 2008), makes the point that exports and re-exports of oil boosted sterling's reserves. Ellen Jenny Ravndal, "Exit Britain: British Withdrawal from the Palestine Mandate in the Early Cold War, 1947–1948," *Diplomacy & Statecraft*, 21 (2010), pp. 416–33, argues (against the standard view) that withdrawal was not a symptom of Britain's decline as an imperial power.

211. Richard Stubbs, *Hearts and Minds in Guerrilla Warfare: The Malayan Emergency, 1948–1960* (Singapore, 1989); David Anderson, *Histories of the Hanged: The Dirty War in Kenya and the End of Empire* (New York, 2005); Daniel Branch, *Defeating Mau Mau, Creating Kenya: Counterinsurgency, Civil War and Decolonization* (Cambridge, 2009); Wm. Roger Louis, *The British Empire in the Middle East, 1945–1961* (Oxford, 1984). The Malayan "Emergency" was so named because, had it been called a "war," British plantation and mining assets would have lost their insurance cover.

212. On these themes see L. J. Butler, *Industrialisation and the British Colonial State: West Africa, 1939–1951* (London, 1997).

213. Minute, 12 November 1954, quoted in Morgan, *A Reassessment of British Aid*, p. 57. A biography by Kit Jones reproduces a number of Hall's perceptive memos: *An Economist among Mandarins: A Biography of Robert Hall, 1901–88* (Cambridge, 1994).

214. Ronald Hyam provides a full narrative account of the process in *Britain's Declining Empire: The Road to Decolonisation, 1918–68* (Cambridge, 2006).

215. See the detailed studies in Martin Lynn, ed., *The British Empire in the 1950s: Retreat or Revival?* (London, 2005). Also David Goldsworthy, "Keeping Change within Bounds: Aspects of Colonial Policy during the Churchill and Eden Governments, 1951–57,"

Journal of Imperial & Commonwealth History, 18 (1990), pp. 81–108; Marseille, *Empire colonial et capitalisme français*; Tony Chafer, *The End of Empire in French West Africa: France's Successful Decolonisation* (London, 2002).

216. The authoritative study is Philip Murphy, *Party Politics and Decolonisation: The Conservative Party and British Colonial Policy in Tropical Africa, 1951–1964* (Oxford, 1995).

217. Ashley Jackson, "Empire and Beyond: The Pursuit of Overseas National Interests in the Late Twentieth Century," *English Historical Review*, 122 (2007), pp. 1350–66; and the lively debate stimulated by Daniel Lefeuvre, *Pour en finir avec la repentance coloniale* (Paris, 2006); Catherine Coquery-Vidrovitch, "Colonisation, racisme, et roman national en France," *Canadian Journal of African Studies*, 45 (2011), pp. 17–44.

218. Goldsworthy, "Keeping Change within Bounds."

219. Krozewski, *Money and the End of Empire*; Hinds, *Britain's Sterling Colonial Policy*; Schenk, *The Decline of Sterling*. I hope the summary given here is consistent with the differences among these authors.

220. Scott Newton, "The Sterling Devaluation of 1967, the International Economy and Post-War Democracy," *English Historical Review*, 125 (2010), pp. 912–45.

221. The debate about Britain's economic performance during this period is covered by Jim Tomlinson, "Inventing 'Decline': The Falling Behind of the British Economy in the Postwar Years," *Economic History Review*, 49 (1996), pp. 731–57; Tomlinson, "The British 'Productivity Problem' in the 1960s," *Past & Present*, 175 (2002), pp. 188–210.

222. David Goldsworthy, ed., *Conservative Government and the End of Empire, 1951–1957* (London, 1994), part 1, p. 78.

223. Quoted in Morgan, *Guidance Towards Self-Government*, p. 90.

224. Guides to the large literature on the Suez crisis include: Wm. Roger Louis and Roger Owen, eds., *Suez 1956: The Crisis and Its Consequences* (Oxford, 1989); Simon C. Smith, ed., *Reassessing Suez, 1956: New Perspectives on the Crisis and Its Aftermath* (Aldershot, 2008); Wm. Roger Louis, *Ends of British Imperialism: The Scramble for Empire, Suez, and Decolonization* (London, 2006). The economic dimension is well covered by Diane Kunz, *The Economic Diplomacy of the Suez Crisis* (Chapel Hill, 1991).

225. A. G. Hopkins, "Macmillan's Audit of Empire, 1957," in Peter Clarke and Clive Trebilcock, eds., *Understanding Decline. Perceptions and Realities: Essays in Honour of Barry Supple* (Cambridge, 1997), pp. 234–60.

226. Harold Macmillan, *Riding the Storm, 1956–1959* (London, 1971), p. 200.

227. Ibid.

228. Minute, 12 November 1954, quoted in Morgan, *A Reassessment of British Aid*, p. 57. The Treasury remained convinced that "the Area and the system have in general brought us great advantages." Sir Leslie Rowan, Minute 31 December 1957, BoE, OV 44/65.

229. R. F. Holland, ed., *Emergencies and Disorders in the Euro-Empires after 1945* (London, 1994); Richard Stubbs, *Hearts and Minds in Guerilla Warfare: The Malayan Emergency, 1948–1960* (Singapore, 2004); Philip Murphy, "A Police State? The Nyasaland Emergency and Colonial Intelligence," *Journal of Southern African Studies*, 36 (2010), pp. 765–80.

230. Wyn Rees, "The 1957 Sandys White Paper: New Priorities in Britain's Defence Policy," *Journal of Strategic Studies*, 12 (1989), pp. 215–29.

231. Wendy Webster, *Englishness and Empire, 1939–1965* (Oxford, 2005).

232. Richard Wright, an African-American activist, quoted in Martin Evans, "Whatever Happened to the Non-Aligned Movement?" *History Today*, 57 (2007), p. 49.

233. Hopkins, "Rethinking Decolonisation." The pioneering research, however, should be attributed to Stuart Ward, especially *Australia and the British Embrace: The Demise of the Imperial Idea* (Melbourne, 2001); and Philip Buckner, ed., *Canada and the British Empire* (Oxford, 2008).

234. Hopkins, "Rethinking Decolonisation," summarizes the data and provides further references.

235. The trend has continued. The figures for New Zealand are especially striking: in 2013, Asians (mainly from China and India) accounted for about one-third of the population born overseas, or about 12 percent of the total population.

236. Britain did not gain membership until 1973. Andrea Benvenuti, *Anglo-Australian Relations and the "Turn to Europe," 1961–1972* (Woodbridge, UK, 2008), follows the process to completion.

237. For an assessment of the history of the term written by its author, see A. A. Phillips, *A. A. Phillips on the Cultural Cringe* (Melbourne, 2006).

238. Wm. Roger Louis and Ronald Robinson, "The Imperialism of Decolonization," *Journal of Imperial & Commonwealth History*, 22 (1994), pp. 462–511, makes an argument for U.S. influence that is stronger than the one advanced here, though the difference is one of emphasis. See also Martin Thomas, "France's North African Crisis, 1945–1955: Cold War and Colonial Imperatives," *History*, 92 (2007), pp. 207–34; Thomas, "Innocent Abroad? Decolonisation and U.S. Engagement with French West Africa, 1945–56," *Journal of Imperial & Commonwealth History*, 36 (2008), pp. 47–73.

239. Agreed U.S.-U.K. Paper, "Means of Combatting Communist Influence in Tropical Africa," 13 March 1957, *Foreign Relations of the United States, 1955–57*, 27; quoted in Louis and Robinson, "Imperialism of Decolonisation," p. 487.

240. Despite long-standing scholarly appeals, the difficulty of comparative studies has inhibited their development. R. F. Holland's pioneering work should be acknowledged: *European Decolonization, 1918–1981: An Introductory Survey* (London, 1985). Welcome additions to the limited literature available include: Martin Shipway, *Decolonisation and Its Impact: A Comparative Approach to the End of Colonial Empires* (Oxford, 2008); Martin Thomas, Bob Moore, and L. J. Butler, eds., *Crises of Empire: Decolonisation and Europe's Imperial States, 1918–1975* (London, 2008); Miguel Bandeira Jerónimo and António Costa Pinto, eds., *The Ends of European Colonial Empires: Cases and Comparisons* (Houndmills, 2015).

241. As Daniel Lefeuvre argues in *Chère Algérie: La France et sa colonie, 1930–1962* (Paris, 2005).

242. Poujade (1920–2003), a spokesman for provincial, rural, conservative France supported the empire. At the same time, the influential commentator, Raymond Cartier (1904–1975), advanced anti-colonial arguments (summarized as *Cartiérisme*), claiming that the overseas territories were a drain on the metropole.

243. Marseille, *L'Empire colonial français*. On the evolving influence of the Cold War, see Martin Thomas, "France's North African Crisis, 1945–1955: Cold War and Colonial Imperatives," *History*, 92 (2007), pp. 207–34; Thomas, "Innocent Abroad?"

244. Matthew Connelly, "The French-American Conflict over North Africa and the Fall of the Fourth Republic," *Revue française d'histoire d'outre-mer*, 84 (1997), pp. 9–27; Irwin M. Wall, *France, the United States, and the Algerian War* (Berkeley, 2001).

245. This decision had its symbolic counterpart in Paris. The Ministry of Overseas France, established in 1946 to manage relations with the new *Union*, was abolished in 1958. The *École Nationale de la France d'Outre-Mer*, the principal training academy for colonial administrators, was closed in 1956. Armelle Enders, "L'École National de la France d'Outre-Mer et la formation des administrateurs coloniaux," *Revue d'histoire moderne et contemporaine*, 40 (1993), pp. 272–88.

246. Luce, "American Century," in Hogan, *The Ambiguous Century*, p. 28.

247. Aaron L. Friedberg, *The Weary Titan: Britain and the Experience of Relative Decline, 1895–1905* (Princeton, NJ, 1988), presents a valuable account of the debate over the perception and measurement of decline, but may have been overly influenced by the similar debate in the United States in the 1980s. Only great powers worry about falling because only they have reached a great height. Phillips O'Brien, "The Titan Refreshed: Imperial Overstretch and the British Navy before the First World War," *Past & Present*, 172 (2001), pp. 146–69, provides a corrective. A revisionist argument suggests that Britain's global role extended even beyond decolonization: Jackson, "Empire and Beyond."

248. Bouda Etemad, *Possessing the World: Taking the Measurements of Colonisation from the 18th to the 20th Century* (New York, 2007), pp. 167, 186, 222, 225–6.

249. Stuart Ward, "The European Provenance of Decolonization," *Past & Present*, 230 (2016), pp. 227–60.

250. As Michael Crowder suggested: "The Second World War: Prelude to Decolonisation in Africa," in Crowder, ed., *The Cambridge History of Africa*, Vol. 8 (Cambridge, 1984), p. 20.

251. Mark Mazower, *No Enchanted Palace: The End of Empire and the Ideological Origins of the United Nations* (Princeton, NJ, 2009).

252. As Christopher Bayly and Tim Harper make clear in *Forgotten Armies: The Fall of British Asia, 1941–1945* (London, 2004); and *Forgotten Wars: The End of Britain's Asian Empire* (London, 2007).

253. On Luce's particular obsession with China, see Michael H. Hunt, "East Asia in Henry Luce's 'American Century,'" in Hogan, *The Ambiguous Legacy*, ch. 7.

254. Luce, "The American Century."

CHAPTER 11: RULING THE FORGOTTEN EMPIRE

1. Anonymous, published in the *New York World*, 15 July 1899. Quoted in H. Wayne Morgan, *America's Road to Empire: The War with Spain and Overseas Expansion* (New York, 1965), p. 111.

2. Commentary on Kipling is as voluminous as the repetition of stereotypes portraying him as a crude imperialist. Denis Judd, "Diamonds Are Forever? Kipling's Imperialism," *History Today*, 47 (1987), pp. 37–44, offers a concise corrective. See also Susan K. Harris, *God's Arbiters: Americans and the Philippines, 1898–1902* (Oxford, 2011), ch. 5. Thomas Pinney provides an admirable sketch of Kipling's affection for and hostility toward the United States in "Rudyard Kipling and America," in Wm. Roger Louis, ed., *Resurgent Adventures with Britannia* (New York, 2011), ch. 2. The suggestion that Kipling intended the poem to be satirical has not found favor with the majority of literary critics.

3. More precisely, the poem was published simultaneously in three newspapers in the United States in February 1899 to encourage the Senate to ratify the Treaty of Paris. Its subtitle, "The United States and the Philippine Islands," is rarely cited. On the mentoring element in Kipling's poem, see Susan K. Harris, "Kipling's 'The White Man's Burden' and the British Newspaper Context, 1898–1899," *Comparative American Studies*, 5 (2005), pp. 243–63.

4. William Jennings Bryan, "The Election of 1900," *North American Review*, 171, (1900), pp. 789, 790, 798, 801.

5. As Kristin L. Hoganson has argued: *Fighting for American Manhood: How Gender Politics Provoked the Spanish-American and Philippine-American Wars* (New Haven, 1998).

6. Whitney T. Perkins, *Denial of Empire: The United States and Its Dependencies* (Leiden, 1962), p. 207; David Traxel, *1898: The Birth of the American Century* (New York, 1998), pp. 315–17.

7. The historiography is set out in chapter 1 of this text.

8. Including Cuba as a protectorate. Daniel Immerwahr, "The Greater United States: Territory and Empire in U.S. History," *Diplomatic History*, 40 (2016), p. 377; Bouda Etemad, *Possessing the World: Taking the Measurements of Colonisation from the 18th to the 20th Century* (New York, 2007), p. 184.

9. Robin W. Winks, "Imperialism," in C. Vann Woodward, ed., *The Comparative Approach to American History* (New York, 1968), ch. 18. See also the thoughtful historiographical reflections in Winks, "The American Struggle with 'Imperialism': How Words Frighten," in Rob Kroes, ed., *The American Identity: Fusion and Fragmentation* (Amsterdam, 1980), ch. 7.

10. Winks, "Imperialism," p. 258. I have summarized and ordered these in a way that I hope is faithful to Winks's intentions, but omitted some of what I judge to be the less important or more complex differences he listed.

11. Winks, "Imperialism," p. 258.

12. Ibid., p. 268.

13. Speech delivered by Senator Albert Beveridge, 16 September 1898, at www.historytools .org/sources/beveridge.html.

14. Beveridge and other members of the forward party are treated in chapter 8 of this text.

15. Frank Schumacher, "Lessons of Empire: The United States, the Quest for Colonial Expertise and the British Example, 1898–1917," in Ursula Lehmkuhl and Gustav Schmidt, eds., *Anglo-American Relations in the 19th and 20th Centuries* (Augsburg, 2005), pp. 71–98; Schumacher, "The American Way of Empire: The United States and the Search for Colonial Order in the Philippines," *Journal of Global History and Comparative Social Studies*, 19 (2009), pp. 53–70.

16. Also known as the First Philippine Commission, and named after the Chair, Dr. Jacob G. Schurman (1854–1942), President of Cornell University.

17. Quoted in Frank Schumacher, "On the Frontier of Civilization: Deliberations of Exceptionalism and Environmental Determinism in the Creation of America's Tropical Empire, 1890–1910," in Sylvia Hilton and Cornelis van Minnen, eds., *Frontiers and Boundaries in U.S. History* (Amsterdam, 2004), p. 13.

18. Condominium is a term in international law that refers to territories ruled jointly and equally by two or more powers. Examples include: Oregon, 1810–1846 (Britain and the United States), Samoa, 1889–1899 (Britain, United States, Germany), Sudan, 1899–1956 (Britain and Egypt), and New Hebrides, 1906–1980 (Britain and France).

19. Moses I. Finley, "Colonies: An Attempt at a Typology," *Transactions of the Royal Historical Society*, 26 (1976), pp. 167–88. On the misuse of classical analogies, see the excellent essays in Henry Hurst and Sara Owen, eds., *Ancient Colonizations: Analogy, Similarity, and Difference* (London, 2005).

20. Sir John Seeley (1834–1895) appointed Regius Professor of Modern History at Cambridge University in 1869, and best known for *The Expansion of England: Two Courses of Lectures* (London, 1883). See Peter Burroughs, "John Robert Seeley and British Imperial History," *Journal of Imperial & Commonwealth History*, 1 (1973), pp. 191–211; and Deborah Wormell, *Sir John Seeley and the Uses of History* (Cambridge, 1980).

21. Norbert Dodille, *Introduction au discours coloniaux* (Paris, 2011).

22. Pierre Paul Leroy-Beaulieu, *De la colonisation chez les peuples modernes* (Paris, 1874), developed his typology and his enthusiasm for imperial expansion fully in the second edition of his book, which was published in 1882. *Exploitation* translates as "development" rather than as "concession," but the latter fits the activities Leroy-Beaulieu referred to. Leroy-Beaulieu (1843–1916) was a member of a distinguished family: his brother, Henri Jean (1842–1912), was a well-known specialist on Russian history; his son, Pierre (1871–1915), was a prolific writer on world affairs.

23. In his monumental *Survey of British Commonwealth Affairs, 1918–1939*, Vol. 2, Part 1 (Oxford, 1942), ch. 1. See especially pp. 19–20.

24. Daniel Gorman, *Imperial Citizenship: Empire and the Question of Belonging* (Manchester, 2006).

25. Rieko Karatani, *Defining British Citizenship: Empire, Commonwealth and Modern Britain* (London, 2003), shows how complex the notions of "citizen" and "subject" were in Britain, and how they remained poorly defined until the British Nationality Act of 1981.

26. There is a vast literature on both terms. See Russell A. Kazal, *Becoming Old Stock: The Paradox of German-American Identity* (Princeton, NJ, 2004); Kazal, "Revisiting Assimilation: The Rise, Fall and Reappraisal of a Concept in American Ethnic History," *American Historical Review*, 95 (1995), pp. 437–71; Rob Kroes, "Americanisation: What Are We Talking About?" *European Contributions to American Studies*, 25 (1993), pp. 302–18; Richard Kuisel, "Americanization for Historians," *Diplomatic History*, 24 (2000), pp. 509–16; Volker R. Berghahn, "The Debate on 'Americanization' among Economic and Cultural Historians," *Cold War History*, 10 (2010), pp. 107–30.

27. This process was not of course confined to the insular territories. See Robert W. Rydell and Rob Kroes, *Buffalo Bill in Bologna: The Americanization of the World, 1896–1922* (Chicago, 2005).

28. Janet A. McDonnell, *The Dispossession of the American Indian, 1887–1934* (Bloomington, 1991). See also chapter 5 of this text.

29. Robert Vitalis, "The Noble American Science of Imperial Relations and Its Laws of Race Relations," *Comparative Studies in Society & History*, 52 (2010), pp. 909–38.

30. *Report of the Philippine Commission*, 1, p. 184. Quoted in Perkins, *Denial of Empire*, p. 200.

31. Henry F. Pringle, *The Life and Times of William Howard Taft* (New York, 1939), Vol. 1, p. 173. Quoted in Perkins, *Denial of Empire*, p. 202.

32. Joseph R. Hayden, *The Philippines: A Study in National Development* (New York, 1945), p. 29.

33. Ibid., p. 30.

34. Ibid., pp. 34–5.

35. Véronique Dimier, a political scientist, re-examines the debate in *Le gouvernement des colonies: regards croisés franco-britanniques* (Brussels, 2004), which compares the two, principally from the 1930s.

36. Sir (later Lord) Frederick J. D. Lugard expounded his philosophy of trusteeship and indirect rule in *The Dual Mandate in British Tropical Africa* (London, 1922). The authoritative work on Lyautey is Daniel Rivet, *Lyautey et l'institution du protectorat français au Maroc 1912–1925*, 3 vols. (Paris, 1988).

37. Ronald Hyam, "The British Empire in the Edwardian Era," in Wm. Roger Louis, ed., *Oxford History of the British Empire*, Vol. 4 (Oxford, 1999), pp. 58–61.

38. Elihu Root (1845–1937), Secretary of War, 1899–1904, and of State, 1905–1909.

39. Kenneth R. Philp, *John Collier's Crusade for Indian Reform, 1920–1954* (Tucson, 1977); Laurence M. Hauptman, "Africa View: John Collier, the British Colonial Service, and American Indian Policy, 1933–1945," *Historian*, 48 (1986), pp. 559–74.

40. Lanny Thompson's incisive essay, "The Imperial Republic: A Comparison of the Insular Territories under U.S. Dominion after 1898," *Pacific Historical Review*, 71 (2002), pp. 535–74, shows how U.S. policy recognized the considerable differences that existed among its subject peoples (and in doing so criticizes Said's notion of a homogenized "other"). See now the expanded version of his argument in *Imperial Archipelago: Representation and Rule in the Insular Territories under Dominion after 1898* (Honolulu, 2010).

41. Louis A. Pérez, *Cuba under the Platt Amendment, 1902–1934* (Pittsburgh, 1987), p. 46.

42. Walter L. Williams, "United States Indian Policy and the Debate over Philippine Annexation: Implications for the Origins of American Imperialism," *Journal of American History*, 66 (1980), pp. 810–31 at p. 830.

43. Quotations from contemporary sources cited by Julian Go, "The Provinciality of American Empire: 'Liberal Exceptionalism' and U.S. Colonial Rule, 1898–1912," *Comparative Studies in Society and History*, 49 (2007), pp. 80, 83.

44. Ibid., p. 100.

45. Ibid., pp. 83–5.

46. Sir Henry James Sumner Maine (1822–88). See especially *Ancient Law: Its Connection with the Early History of Society and Its Relation to Modern Ideas* (London, 1861). The most recent of numerous studies is Karuna Mantena, *Alibis of Empire: Sir Henry Maine and the Ends of Liberalism* (Princeton, NJ, 2010). On the spread of Maine's ideas in the United States, see David M. Raban, "From Maine to Maitland via America," *Cambridge Law Journal*, 68 (2009), pp. 410–35.

47. David Ekbladh, *The Great American Mission: Modernization and the Construction of an American World Order* (Princeton, 2010), deals with the pre-history in chs. 1–2.

48. For a recent account of this evolution see Theodore Koditschek, *Liberalism, Imperialism, and the Historical Imagination: Nineteenth-Century Visions of a Greater Britain* (Cambridge, 2011).

49. On Mill, see Eileen P. Sullivan, "Liberalism and Imperialism: J. S. Mill's Defence of the British Empire," *Journal of the History of Ideas*, 44 (1983), pp. 599–617; Lynn Zastoupil, *John Stuart Mill and India* (Stanford, 1994); Beate Jahn, "Barbarian Thoughts: Imperialism in the Philosophy of John Stuart Mill," *Review of International Studies*, 31 (2005), pp. 599–618.

50. As Peter J. Cain has clearly shown: "Character, 'Ordered Liberty,' and the Mission to Civilise: British Moral Justification of Empire, 1870–1914," *Journal of Imperial & Commonwealth History*, 40 (2012), pp. 557–78.

51. Cain, "Character, 'Ordered Liberty,' and the Mission to Civilise."

52. See chapter 7 of this text.

53. Roosevelt (1858–1919), President, 1901–1909; Root (1845–1937), Secretary of War, 1899–1904, and of State, 1905–1909; Taft (1857–1930), Civil Governor of the Philippines, 1901–1903, Secretary of War, 1904–1908, President, 1909–1913.

54. Vitalis, "The Noble American Science of Imperial Relations."

55. Woodrow Wilson, "Democracy and Efficiency," *Atlantic Monthly*, 87 (1901), pp. 292, 298.

56. On Cromer and Curzon in this context, see Cain, "Character, 'Ordered Liberty,' and the Mission to Civilise," pp. 559, 568.

57. Gerald Horne, "Race from Power: U.S. Foreign Policy and the General Crisis of 'White Supremacy,'" *Diplomatic History*, 23 (1999), pp. 437–62.

58. Robert Vitalis, *White World Order, Black Power Politics: The Birth of American International Relations* (Ithaca, 2015).

59. Kazal, *Becoming Old Stock*, p. 1.

60. Desmond King, *Making Americans: Immigration, Race, and the Origins of the Diverse Democracy* (Cambridge, MA, 2000), pp. 153, 158, 163, 224; Kazal, *Becoming Old Stock*, p. 261. WASP (White Anglo-Saxon Protestant) was a term that gained currency in the 1950s to describe the long-standing dominance of an elite with these characteristics.

61. Matthew Frye Jacobson, *Whiteness of a Different Color: European Immigrants and the Alchemy of Race* (Cambridge, MA, 1998); Gary Gerstle, *American Crucible: Race and Nation in the Twentieth Century* (Princeton, NJ, 2001).

62. Michael Hawkins, "Imperial Historicism and American Military Rule in the Philippines' Muslim South," *Journal of Southeast Asian Studies*, 39 (2008), pp. 411–29. The modest title of this article disguises its wider import.

63. Brooks Adams, *The New Empire* (New York, 1903), p. xi.

64. Michael Adas, *Machines as the Measure of Men: Science, Technology and Ideologies of Western Dominance* (Ithaca, 1989).

65. Michael E. Latham, *Modernization as Ideology: American Social Science and "Nation Building" in the Kennedy Era* (Chapel Hill, 2000); and its complement, Latham, *The Right Kind of Revolution: Modernization, Development and United States Foreign Policy from the Cold War to the Present* (Ithaca, 2011). Ekbladh, *The Great American Mission*.

66. Alex Inkeles, *Becoming Modern: Individual Change in Six Developing Countries* (Cambridge, MA, 1974).

67. Some of the long-term consequences are explored in Nick Cullather's remarkable study, *The Hungry World: America's Cold War Battle against Poverty in Asia* (Cambridge, MA, 2010).

68. Tugwell, *Stricken Land*, p. 112.

69. Etemad, *Possessing the World*, pp. 219–27.

70. Michael Edelstein, "Foreign Investment, Accumulation, and Empire, 1860–1914," in Roderick Floud and Paul Johnson, eds., *The Cambridge Economic History of Modern*

Britain, Vol. 3 (Cambridge, 2004), p. 193; Stanley Lebergott, "The Returns to U.S. Imperialism, 1890–1929," *Journal of Economic History*, 40 (1980), pp. 230, 251.

71. Quoted in Perkins, *Denial of Empire*, p. 204.

72. Theodore Roosevelt, Jr., *Colonial Policies of the United States* (New York, 1937), pp. 195–7.

73. Frank H. Golay, "The Search for Revenues," in Peter W. Stanley, ed., *Reappraising an Empire: New Perspectives on Philippine-American History* (Cambridge, MA, 1984), pp. 236–9.

74. Woodrow Wilson, "Policy Statement," November 1912. Quoted in J. W. Wheeler-Bennett, "Thirty Years of American-Filipino Relations, 1899–1929," *Journal of the Royal Institute of International Affairs*, 8 (1929), p. 507.

75. J. W. Wheeler-Bennett, "Thirty Years of American-Filipino Relations," pp. 507–8.

76. Recent work has drawn attention to the important part female missionaries played. See Barbara Reeves-Ellington, Kathryn Kish Sklar, and Connie A. Shemo, eds., *Competing Kingdoms: Women, Mission, Nation, and the American Protestant Empire, 1812–1960* (Durham, 2010). Unfortunately (for the needs of this book), only one chapter (on the Philippines, 1902–30) deals with the U.S. Empire.

77. Ian Tyrrell, *Reforming the World: The Creation of America's Moral Empire* (Princeton, 2010), especially pp. 1–10, 229, 235, 227–9. Tyrrell deserves particular credit for carrying this story into the twentieth century.

78. Gerald R. Gems, *The Athletic Crusade: Sport and American Cultural Imperialism* (Lincoln, 2006).

79. Tugwell, *Stricken Land*, p. 236; also p. 343.

80. There is a substantial literature on this question. Important starting points include: Christina Duffy Burnett and Burke Marshall, eds., *Foreign in a Domestic Sense: Puerto Rico, American Expansion, and the Constitution* (Durham, 2001); and Bartholomew H. Sparrow, *The Insular Cases and the Emergence of American Empire* (Lawrence, 2006).

81. Perkins, *Denial of Empire*, ch. 1.

82. Kazal, *Becoming Old Stock*, pp. 817–21.

83. April Merleaux provides a case study of the link between race and protection, as seen through the eyes of Southern Senator Francis G. Newlands, in "The Political Culture of Sugar Tariffs: Immigration, Race, and Empire, 1898–1930," *International Labor and Working Class History*, 81 (2012), pp. 28–48.

84. Perry Belmont, "Congress, the President and the Philippines," *North American Review*, 169 (1899), p. 901. Belmont (1851–1947), a lawyer, was congressman for New York, 1881–89, and ambassador to Spain, 1889.

85. Sparrow, *The Insular Cases*.

86. Julius W. Pratt, *America's Colonial Experiment* (New York, 1951), pp. 161–4.

87. The constitutional features of colonial rule summarized here are surveyed at greater length in Pratt, *America's Colonial Experiment*, chs. 5–6, and even more fully in Perkins, *Denial of Empire*, chs. 3–8; Go, "Provinciality of American Empire," pp. 74–108; Julian Go, *American Empire and the Politics of Meaning* (Durham, 2008). Go provides a rare comparative assessment, from a predominantly cultural perspective, of the different outcomes of U.S. policy.

88. See Jose Alvarez and Leo C. Polopolus, "History of U.S. Sugar Protection," *University of Florida IFAS Extension Publication*, SC 019 (2002).

89. On Havemeyer, see also chapter 8 of this text.

90. Luzviminda Bartolome Francisco and Jonathan Shepard Fast, *Conspiracy for Empire: Big Business, Corruption and the Politics of Imperialism in America, 1876–1907* (Quezon City, 1985), pp. 273–9.

91. The principal source for what follows is Francisco and Fast, *Conspiracy for Empire*, chs. 27, 28, 30.

92. See chapter 8 of this text.

93. Francisco and Fast, *Conspiracy for Empire*, pp. 213, 242–3.

94. Ibid., ch. 27, and pp. 227–8.

95. A full analysis will need to take account of the degree to which battle lines were crossed by vertical and horizontal integration, as some refiners moved into cane production overseas and others into the beet industry on the mainland.

96. Kathleen Mapes, *Sweet Tyranny: Migrant Labour, Industrial Agriculture, and Imperial Politics* (Urbana, 2009), provides a valuable account of the beet industry in Michigan; ch. 8 deals with the industry's imperial connections.

97. Elihu Root, Secretary of War, quoted in Truman R. Clark, " 'Educating the Natives in Self-Government': Puerto Rico and the United States, 1900–1933," *Pacific Historical Review*, 42 (1973), p. 220.

98. A rare (and necessarily incomplete) exception is Cathleen Cahill, *Federal Fathers and Mothers: A Social History of the United States Indian Service, 1869–1933* (Chapel Hill, 2011).

99. Woodrow Wilson, "Democracy and Efficiency," *Atlantic Monthly*, 87 (1901), p. 296.

100. Armelle Enders, "L'École nationale de la France d'Outre-Mer et la formation des administrateurs coloniaux," *Revue d'Histoire Moderne et Contemporaine*, 40 (1993), pp. 272–88.

101. Tugwell, *Stricken Land*, p. 114.

102. Ibid., pp. 114–15.

103. This quotation and those that follow in this paragraph are from ibid., p. 115.

104. Richard H. Werking, *The Master Architects: Building the United States Foreign Service, 1890–1913* (Lexington, 1977).

105. Daniel P. Carpenter, *The Forging of Bureaucratic Autonomy: Reputations, Networks, and Policy Innovation in Executive Agencies, 1862–1928* (Princeton, 2001).

106. Robert D. Schulzinger, *The Making of the Diplomatic Mind: The Training, Outlook and Style of the United States Foreign Service Officers, 1908–1931* (Middletown, 1975).

107. Max (Maximilian Carl Emil) Weber, *Economy and Society* (Berlin, 1922; Los Angeles, 1978). Weber (1864–1920) had a distinctly unorthodox "trajectory" that would make him a dubious candidate for tenure today: his first book was not published until he was 40; much of his other work was compiled from lectures and articles and published posthumously.

108. Earl S. Pomeroy, "The American Colonial Office," *Mississippi Valley Historical Review*, 30 (1944), p. 524. It is a measure of the state of knowledge that it is necessary to go back to 1944 for the "latest" research on this subject.

109. See Perkins, *Denial of Empire*, pp. 205, 349.

110. Nadia Schadlow, "Root's Rules: Lessons from America's Colonial Office," *American Interest*, 2 (2007), pp. 92–102.

111. Quoted in Clark, "Educating the Natives in Self-Government," p. 220.

112. Albert Bushnell Hart in 1899, quoted in Williams, "United States Indian Policy," p. 830. Hart was a notable historian as well as a classmate and lifelong friend of Theodore Roosevelt.

113. Louis A. Pérez, Jr. drew attention to the importance and potential of this subject over 30 years ago, but the gap remains, despite the example he has set in using the Bureau's archive in his research on Cuba: "Cuba Materials in the Bureau of Insular Affairs Library," *Latin American Research Review*, 13, (1978), pp. 182–8. Peter C. Stuart, *Planting the American Flag: Twelve Men who Expanded the U.S. Overseas* (Jefferson, 2007), is a welcome start, though his emphasis is on those who acquired rather than administered the empire.

114. The senior colonial administrator in the Philippines had the title of civil governor from 1901 to 1906, but reverted to the Spanish title, governor general, from 1906 to 1935.

115. A much-needed biography has now appeared, though its focus (understandably) is mainly on McNutt's activities in the United States: Dean J. Kotlowski, *Paul V. McNutt and the Age of FDR* (Bloomington, 2015).

116. Truman R. Clark, *Puerto Rico and the United States, 1917–1975* (Pittsburgh, 1975), pp. 167–73.

117. The exception was James R. Beverley (1894–1967), a Texas lawyer who practiced in Puerto Rico and who (just) qualifies by being acting governor, 1932–33. Theodore Roosevelt, Jr. (governor of Puerto Rico, 1929–1932) was the first governor who attempted to speak the language on some formal occasions.

118. Clark, "Educating the Natives in Self-Government," pp. 232–3.

119. The literature on Africa alone is considerable: the numerous joint works of Louis H. Gann and Peter Duignan cover Britain, France, Germany, and Belgium between 1870 and 1914; Anthony Kirk-Greene, *Britain's Imperial Administrators, 1858–1966* (Basingstoke, Hants, 2000). See also William B. Cohen, *Rulers of Empire: French Colonial Services in Africa* (Stanford, 1971).

120. Paul D. Hutchcroft, "Colonial Masters, National Politicos, and Provincial Lords: Central Authority and Local Autonomy in the American Philippines, 1900–1913," *Journal of Asian Studies*, 59 (2000), p. 293.

121. Ibid., p. 289.

122. These events, and much else, are recorded in Francis Burton Harrison's memoir: *The Corner-Stone of Philippine Independence: A Narrative of Seven Years* (New York, 1922).

123. Roosevelt, *Colonial Policies of the United States*, p. 99.

124. Perkins, *Denial of Empire*, p. 202.

125. In the case of Hawai'i, the Big Men were settlers who also constructed a security state, primarily to control labor unrest.

126. Ellen D. Tillman, "Militarizing Dollar Diplomacy in the Early Twentieth-Century Dominican Republic: Centralization and Resistance," *Hispanic American Historical Review*, 95 (2015), pp. 269–97.

127. Two pioneering studies are David M. Anderson and David Killingray, eds., *Policing the Empire: Government, Authority, and Control, 1830–1940* (Manchester, 1991); Anderson and Killingray, *Policing and Decolonisation: Nationalism, Politics and the Police, 1917–65* (Manchester, 1992); Matthew Hughes, "A British Foreign Legion? The British Police in Mandate Palestine," *Middle Eastern Studies*, 49 (2013), pp. 696–711.

128. Michael Broers, "The Police and the *Padroni*: Italian *Notabili*, French Gendarmes and the Origins of the Centralised State in Napoleonic Italy" *European History Quarterly*, 26 (1996), pp. 331–53; Martin Thomas, "The Gendarmerie, Information Collection, and Colonial Violence in French North Africa Between the Wars," *Historical Reflections*, 36 (2010), pp. 76–96.

129. See Clive Emsley, who is one of the pioneers of this subject: "Policing the Empire, Policing the Metropole: Some Thoughts on Models and Types," *Crime, histoire et sociétés*, 18 (2014), pp. 5–25.

130. See Alfred W. McCoy's remarkable study, *Policing America's Empire: The United States, the Philippines, and the Rise of the Surveillance State* (Madison, 2009). Also Georgina Sinclair and Chris A. Williams, "Home and Away: The Cross-Fertilization between 'Colonial' and 'British' Policing, 1921–85," *Journal of Imperial & Commonwealth History*, 35 (2007), pp. 221–38.

131. The Division was renamed the Office of Territories in 1950, abolished in 1971, and reconstructed as the Office of Territorial Affairs in 1973. See Ruth G. van Cleve, *The Office of Territorial Affairs* (New York, 1973).

132. Pomeroy, "The American Colonial Office," p. 528.

133. Ibid., p. 527.

134. Ibid., pp. 530–31.

135. Tugwell, *Stricken Land*, p. 71.

136. Perkins, *Denial of Empire*, p. 132.

137. New York, 1942. Hayden's (1897–1945) numerous publications are informative not only about the Philippines but also about the evolution of his own understanding of the is-

lands and their people. He performed a great scholarly service in collecting documents dealing with the Philippines during the first half of the twentieth century and depositing them with the University of Michigan. See also Ronald K. Edgerton, "Joseph Ralston Hayden: The Education of a Colonialist," in Owen, *Compadre Colonialism*, pp. 195–226.

138. Theodore Roosevelt's eldest son (1887–1944). His political career on the mainland stalled in the 1920s; he then served as Governor of Puerto Rico, 1929–32, and Governor-General of the Philippines, 1932–33. He had a distinguished record in both world wars.

139. Roosevelt, *Colonial Policies of the United States.*

140. (1874–1952). See Graham White and John Maze, *Harold Ickes of the New Deal: Private Life and Public Career* (Cambridge, MA, 1985); Jeanne N. Clarke, *Roosevelt's Warrior: Harold L. Ickes and the New Deal* (Baltimore, 1996); T. H. Watkins, *Righteous Pilgrim: The Life and Times of Harold L. Ickes, 1874–1952* (New York, 1990) presents a mountain of information, but still leaves room for a study of Ickes's role in overseeing the colonies.

141. Ruth Sarles, *A Story of America First* (Westport, 2003), p. 108. The quotation appears in various forms. Clare Boothe Luce (1903–87) was a journalist, playwright, and noted wit, who also had a distinguished political career as conservative Republican. She was married to the publisher, Henry Robinson Luce.

142. Quoted in Thomas Mathews, *Puerto Rican Politics and the New Deal* (New York, 1976), p. 215.

143. "The Navy at Its Worst," *Collier's Magazine*, 31 August 1946, pp. 22–3.

144. Unlike most U.S. colonial officials, Ernest Henry Gruening (1887–1974) has been the subject of a full and admirable study: Robert D. Johnson, *Ernest Gruening and the Dissenting Tradition* (Cambridge, MA, 1998). See also Johnson, "Anti-Imperialism and the Good Neighbor Policy: Ernest Gruening and Puerto Rican Affairs, 1934–1939," *Journal of Latin American Studies*, 29 (1997), pp. 89–110.

145. Ernest Gruening, "Colonialism in Alaska," *Current History*, 29 (1955), pp. 349–55.

146. Tugwell (1891–1979) lacks a biography to match Johnson's *Ernest Gruening*. Michael V. Namorato, *Rexford G. Tugwell: A Biography* (New York, 1988), provides a sketch; Bernard Sternsher, *Rexford Tugwell and the New Deal* (New Brunswick, 1964), deals, understandably, mainly with domestic issues. Tugwell's own numerous publications remain valuable sources.

147. Theodore Roosevelt, "The Expansion of the White Races," Address, 18 January 1909, in Roosevelt, *American Problems* (New York, 1926), p. 271.

148. Ibid., p. 264.

149. Winks, "Imperialism," pp. 257–8.

150. Ibid., p. 258.

151. Ibid., p. 268.

152. Ibid., p. 259.

153. This subject has been explored recently in two exceptionally valuable sets of essays: Alfred W. McCoy and Francisco A. Scarano, eds., *Colonial Crucible: Empire in the Making of the Modern American State* (Madison, 2009); María Dolores Elizalde y Josep M. Delgado, eds., *Filipinas: un país entre dos imperios* (Barcelona, 2011).

154. I am indebted here to Paul Kramer's important contribution, "Historias transimperiales: Raíces españolas del estado colonial estadounidense en Filipinas," in Elizalde and Delgado, *Filipinas*, ch. 5.

155. Winks, "Imperialism," p. 258.

CHAPTER 12: CARIBBEAN CARNIVAL

1. Quoted in Louis A. Pérez, Jr., *On Becoming Cuban: Identity, Nationality, and Culture* (New York, 1999), p. 159. This is an opportunity to acknowledge the exceptional contribution made by Professor Pérez, whose authoritative publications, produced over many decades, are indispensable to all students of Cuba's history.

2. Albert J. Beveridge, "In Support of an American Empire," *Record*, 56 Congress, I Session, p. 707.

3. Quoted in Truman R. Clark, "'Educating the Natives in Self-Government': Puerto Rico and the United States, 1900–1933," *Pacific Historical Review*, 42 (1973), p. 220.

4. Rosalie Schwartz, *Pleasure Island: Tourism and Temptation in Cuba* (Lincoln, 1997); Peter Maruzzi, *Havana Before Castro: When Cuba Was a Tropical Playground* (Layton, 2008).

5. A rare comparative study is Christine Skwiot, *The Purposes of Paradise: U.S. Tourism and Empire in Cuba and Hawai'i* (Philadelphia, 2010).

6. First recorded in 1927. Various versions are available on YouTube.

7. Alyssa Abkowitz, "A Land Rush in Puerto Rico," *Wall Street Journal*, 4 October 2012. In the 1950s, the celebrities included Ava Gardner, Elizabeth Taylor, and John F. Kennedy. Puerto Rico has one large annual carnival (in Ponce).

8. Marisol Berrios-Miranda, "Salsa Music as Expressive Liberation," *Centro Journal*, 16 (2004), pp. 157–73.

9. Pedro Malavet, "Puerto Rico: Cultural Nation, American Colony," *Michigan Journal of Race and Law*, 6 (2000), pp. 2–106, is the authoritative source. See also Frances R. Aparicio, *Listening to Salsa: Gender, Latin American Popular Music and Puerto Rican Cultures* (Middletown, 1998), ch. 2. More generally on this subject (and on *plena*) see Juan Flores, *Divided Border: Essays on Puerto Rican Identity* (Houston, 1993).

10. Quoted in Joan Gross, "*Defendiendo la (Agri)Cultura*: Reterritorializing Culture in the Puerto Rican *Décima*," *Oral Tradition*, 23 (2008), p. 229.

11. José Martí, in Philip S. Foner, ed., *Inside the Monster: Writings on the United States and American Imperialism* (New York, 1975), p. 54.

12. Numerous versions of both melody and lyrics have been composed since its first performance in 1929.

13. Quoted in César J. Ayala and Rafael Bernabe, *Puerto Rico in the American Century: A History Since 1898* (Chapel Hill, 2007), p. 90.

14. Curiously, estimates of the relative size of the islands vary. The median figure taken from those commonly quoted suggests that Cuba was nine times the size of Puerto Rico.

15. Theodore Roosevelt, "The Administration of the Island Possessions," in Roosevelt, *Works of Theodore Roosevelt*, Vol. 18 (New York, 1925), p. 356.

16. Ibid.

17. Theodore Roosevelt, Jr., *Colonial Policies of the United States* (New York, 1937), p. 108.

18. Quoted in James L. Dietz, *Economic History of Puerto Rico: Institutional Change and Capitalist Development* (Princeton, 1986), p. 127. All scholars are indebted to Dr. Dietz for his pioneering work on this subject.

19. Courtney Johnson, "Understanding the American Empire: Colonialism, Latin Americanism, and Professional Social Science, 1898–1920," in Alfred W. McCoy and Francisco A. Scarano, *Colonial Crucible: Empire in the Making of the Modern American State* (Madison, 2009), pp. 175–90; Kyle T. Evered, "Fostering Puerto Rico: Representations of Empire and Orphaned Territories during the Spanish-American War," *Historical Geography*, 34 (2006), pp. 109–36.

20. Subjective though racial classifications were (and are), the last Spanish census in 1897 recorded that about two-thirds of the population was white. See Francisco A. Scarano, "Censuses in the Transition to Modern Colonialism: Spain and the United States in Puerto Rico," in McCoy and Scarano, *Colonial Crucible*, pp. 216–17.

21. An explanation of these terms is given in the subsection titled "Sugaring the Pill" in chapter 9 of this text.

22. Clark, "Educating the Natives in Self-Government."

23. The broad implications of the ruling are discussed in the subsection titled "Lobbies and Liberties," in chapter 11 of this text.

24. David A. Rezvani, "The Basis of Puerto Rico's Constitutional Status: Colony, Compact, or Federacy?" *Political Science Quarterly*, 122 (2007), pp. 115–40.

25. *San Juan News*, 29 May 1901. Quoted in Dietz, *Economic History*, p. 88.

26. Whitney T. Perkins, *Denial of Empire: The United States and Its Dependencies* (Leiden, 1962), p. 117.

27. Julius W. Pratt, *America's Colonial Experiment: How the United States Gained, Governed, and in Part Gave Away a Colonial Empire* (New York, 1951), pp. 187–8.

28. Kelvin Santiago-Valles, "American Penal Reforms and Colonial Spanish Custodial-Regulatory Practices in Fin de Siècle Puerto Rico," in McCoy and Scarano, *Colonial Crucible*, pp. 87–94.

29. Clark, "Educating the Natives in Self-Government," pp. 226–7; Perkins, *Denial of Empire*, pp. 129–30; Ayala and Bernabe, *Puerto Rico in the American Century*, pp. 55–9.

30. Frank Ninkovich, *The United States and Imperialism* (Malden, 2001), pp. 124–5.

31. Clark, "Educating the Natives in Self-Government," pp. 227–8; Clark, "President Taft and the Puerto Rican Appropriation Crisis of 1909," *Americas*, 26 (1969), pp. 152–70.

32. The material basis of the two parties was less distinct than used to be thought when the Unión was characterized as the party of declining coffee growers. See Ayala and Bernabe, *Puerto Rico in the American Century*, pp. 59–61.

33. Fernando Pico, *Puerto Rico, 1898: The War after the War* (Princeton, 2004).

34. Stuart B. Schwartz, "The Hurricane of San Ciriaco: Disaster, Politics and Society in Puerto Rico, 1899–1901," *Hispanic American Historical Review*, 72 (1992), pp. 303–35.

35. There were no coffee producers in the United States to oppose imports from Puerto Rico; cheaper coffee from Brazil, which had shaped the tastes of consumers in the United States, was defended by powerful, well-established interests.

36. Luzviminda Bartolome Francisco and Jonathan Shepard Fast, *Conspiracy for Empire: Big Business, Corruption and the Poliltics of Imperialism in America, 1876–1907* (Quezon City, 1985), ch. 23, argue that the advertised motives for assisting the island were a cover for business interests and for Havemeyer in particular. The evidence available makes it hard to offer a definitive judgment on this suggestive claim.

37. Ibid.

38. Perkins, *Denial of Empire*, p. 119.

39. In fact, the condition remained unenforced until 1940: Ayala and Bernabe, *Puerto Rico in the American Century*, pp. 36–7, 142–4.

40. See the subsection titled "Lobbies and Liberties," in chapter 11 of this text.

41. Dietz, *Economic History of Puerto Rico*, pp. 86–92.

42. "Porto" was the name given by the United States and used for official purposes between 1898 and 1935.

43. Humberto García Muñiz, *Sugar and Power in the Caribbean: The South Porto Rico Sugar Company in Puerto Rico and the Dominican Republic, 1900–1921* (Kingston, Jamaica, 2010).

44. Ayala and Bernabe, *Puerto Rico in the American Century*, pp. 41–5.

45. César J. Ayala, *American Sugar Kingdom: The Plantation Economy of the Spanish Caribbean, 1898–1934* (Chapel Hill, 1999), pp. 114–19, 225–6.

46. Dietz, *Economic History of Puerto Rico*, p. 119.

47. Ayala, *American Sugar Kingdom*, pp. 66–73, 197–8. The comparative features of this study are particularly valuable.

48. Dietz, *Economic History of Puerto Rico*, pp. 99–103; Luis Alberto Amador, "Amargo negocio: el café puertorriqueño y su comercialización (1898–1918)," *Revista de Centro de Investigaciones Históricas*, 16 (2005), 253–85.

49. Laird W. Bergad, "Agrarian History of Puerto Rico, 1870–1930," *Latin American Research Review*, 13 (1978), pp. 63–94.

50. Dietz, *Economic History*, pp. 104–13; Ayala and Bernabe, *Puerto Rico in the American Century*, pp. 38–9, 48–9. Where there are discrepancies in the figures, I have used Ayala and Bernabe, the later source. Thomas Pepinski, "Trade Competition and American

Decolonization," *World Politics*, 67 (2015), pp. 405–6, suggests that U.S. firms accounted for a higher proportion of sugar output, but does not cite the sources given here.

51. See especially the revisionist work of César J. Ayala and Laird W. Bergad, "Rural Puerto Rico in the Early Twentieth Century Reconsidered: Land and Society, 1899–1915," *Latin American Research Review*, 37 (2002), pp. 65–97; and José O. Solá, "Colonialism, Planters, Sugarcane, and the Agrarian Economy of Caguas, Puerto Rico, between the 1890s and 1930," *Agricultural History*, 85 (2011), pp. 349–72. Also Ayala and Bernabe, *Puerto Rico in the American Century*, pp. 38–9, 48–50; Dietz, *Economic History*, pp. 104–13.

52. Teresita A. Levy, *Puerto Ricans in the Empire: Tobacco Growers and U.S. Colonialism* (New Brunswick, 2015).

53. Charles F. Reid, *Education in the Territories and Outlying Territories of the United States* (New York, 1941), pp. 217–19.

54. Ibid., ch. 4.

55. José-Manuel Navarro, *Creating Tropical Yankees: Social Science Textbooks and U.S. Ideological Control in Puerto Rico, 1898–1908* (New York, 2002); Solsiree del Moral, *Negotiating Empire: The Cultural Politics of Schools in Puerto Rico, 1898–1952* (Madison, 2013), p. 7, confirms the opposition to creating "tropical Yankees."

56. Christopher Schmidt-Nowara, "Spanish Origins of American Empire: Hispanism, History, and Commemoration, 1898–1915," *International History Review*, 30 (2008), pp. 32–51.

57. Solsiree del Moral, "Negotiating Colonialism: 'Race,' Class, and Education in Early Twentieth-Century Puerto Rico," in McCoy and Scarano, *Colonial Crucible*, pp. 135–44; Pablo Navarro-Rivera, "The Imperial Enterprise and Educational Policies in Colonial Puerto Rico," in McCoy and Scarano, *Colonial Crucible*, pp. 163–74.

58. Eileen J. Findlay, *Imposing Decency: The Politics of Sexuality and Race in Puerto Rico, 1870–1930* (Durham, 1999), deals mainly with Ponce; complementary studies are needed.

59. Ayala and Bernabe, *Puerto Rico in the American Century*, chs. 4, 6.

60. On the shifting and subjective quality of racial categories see Mara Loveman and Jeronimo O. Muniz, "How Puerto Rico Became White: Boundary Dynamics and Intercensus Racial Reclassification," *American Sociological Review*, 72 (2007), pp. 915–39; Gabriel Haslip-Vera, "Changed Identities: A Racial Portrait of Two Extended Families, 1900–Present," *Centro Journal*, 21 (2009), pp. 36–51.

61. Iris M. Zavela and Rafael Rodíriguez, eds., *The Intellectual Roots of Independence: An Anthology of Puerto Rican Political Essays* (New York, 1980). "*Ibero Pancho*" was a generic representation of Spanish America.

62. This paragraph draws on Dietz, *Economic History of Puerto Rico*, pp. 100–101, 110–12, 116–24, 135, 137–43, 158–60, 176.

63. José O. Solá, "Partisanship, Power Contenders, and Colonial Politics in Puerto Rico, 1920s," *Caribbean Studies*, 38 (2010), pp. 3–35, provides a case study of Caguas.

64. Intellectual and artistic developments during this period are discussed in Ayala and Barnabe, *Puerto Rico in the American Century*, ch. 4.

65. Noel Maurer, *The Empire Trap: The Rise and Fall of U.S. Intervention to Protect American Property Overseas, 1893–2013* (Princeton, NJ, 2013), pp. 256–7.

66. Hernández (1892–1965); *Borincano* derives from *Borinquen*, the pre-Columbian name for Puerto Rico.

67. Quoted in Thomas Matthews, *Puerto Rican Politics and the New Deal* (New York, 1976), p. 50. Ismael García Colón, *Land Reform in Puerto Rico: Modernizing the Colonial State, 1941–1969* (Gainesville, 2009), describes the desperate state of the municipality of Cidra at the close of the 1930s.

68. Quoted in Harvey S. Perloff, "Transforming the Economy," *Annals of the American Academy of Political & Social Science*, 285 (1953), p. 50. The Work Projects Administration (1935–1943) was the largest agency of the New Deal.

69. Dietz, *Economic History of Puerto Rico*, pp. 147, 163–7, 169, 221; Ayala and Bernabe, *Puerto Rico in the American Century*, ch. 5.

70. Riggs was a U.S. Army veteran; the two assassins were shot by police while in custody.

71. Sources vary: reports of the number killed range from 17 to 21.

72. Matthews, *Puerto Rican Politics*; Gabriel Villaronga, *Towards a Discourse of Consent: Mass Mobilization and Colonial Politics in Puerto Rico, 1932–1948* (Westport, 2004).

73. Carlos R. Zapata Oliveras, *De independentista a autonomista: la transformación del pensamiento político de Luis Muñoz Marín (1931–1949)* (San Juan, 2003), covers the transition in detail.

74. Kiran Klaus Patel, *The New Deal: A Global History* (Princeton, NJ, 2015), pp. 160–67.

75. On Gruening (1887–1974) and Tugwell (1891–1979) see the subsection titled "A Course of Tuition under a Strong and Guiding Hand," in chapter 11 of this text.

76. Robert David Johnson, "Anti-Imperialism and the Good Neighbour Policy: Ernest Gruening and Puerto Rican Affairs, 1934–1939," *Journal of Latin American Studies*, 29 (1997), pp. 89–110. For Tugwell's critical assessment of Gruening, see Rexford Guy Tugwell, *The Stricken Land: The Story of Puerto Rico* (New York, 1946), pp. 5–11, 74.

77. Dietz, *Economic History of Puerto Rico*, pp. 143–7, 149–54; Ayala and Bernabe, *Puerto Rico in the American Century*, pp. 100–104.

78. Stuart McCook, "Promoting the 'Practical': Science and Agricultural Modernization in Puerto Rico and Colombia, 1920–1940," *Agricultural History Review*, 75 (2001), pp. 52–82.

79. On the afterlife of the reforms, see Perkins, *Denial of Empire*, pp. 137–41; Pratt, *America's Colonial Experiment*, pp. 271–4. The Puerto Rican Emergency Relief Administration (1933–1935) offered short-term food aid and made progress with road building and malaria control, but was short of funds and encountered official opposition. See Manuel R. Rodríguez, *A New Deal for the Tropics: Puerto Rico during the Depression Era, 1932–1935* (Princeton, NJ, 2010).

80. See Tugwell's full account in *Stricken Land*.

81. Tugwell's relations with Muñoz Marín had also become strained. See Tugwell, *Stricken Land*, p. 343.

82. Frank O. Gatell, "Independence Rejected: Puerto Rico and the Tydings' Bill of 1936," *Hispanic American Historical Review*, 38 (1958), pp. 25–44.

83. Quoted in Perkins, *Denial of Empire*, p. 140. Gruening supported the measure, even though he judged it to be impractical, because he believed that it would advertise the progressive character of U.S. colonial policy.

84. Quoted in Gatell, "Independence Rejected," p. 37. Tydings was alone in believing, even twenty years later, that the separation his bill envisaged would have worked out successfully. Ibid., p. 37, n. 72.

85. Matthews, *Puerto Rican Politics*; Ayala and Bernabe, *Puerto Rico in the American Century*, provide a conspectus of the views on this period.

86. Ismael García-Colón, *Land Reforms in Puerto Rico: Modernizing the Colonial State, 1941–1969* (Gainesville, 2009).

87. For contrasting views see, Perloff, "Transforming the Economy"; and Ismael García-Colón, "Playing and Eating Democracy: The Case of Puerto Rico's Land Distribution Program, 1940s–1960s," *Centro Journal*, 18 (2006), pp. 166–89.

88. García-Colón, *Land Reforms in Puerto Rico*, pp. 30, 43.

89. César J. Ayala, "From Sugar Plantations to Military Bases: The U.S. Navy's Expropriations in Vieques, Puerto Rico, 1940–45," *Centro Journal*, 13 (2001), pp. 22–43; Humberto García-Muniz and Judith Escalona, "Goliath against David: The Battle for Vieques as the Last Crossroad?" *Centro Journal*, 13 (2001), pp. 126–43.

90. Theodore Roosevelt to Henry L. White, 13 September 1906. Quoted in Louis A. Pérez, Jr., *Cuba under the Platt Amendment, 1902–34* (Pittsburgh, 1986), p. 9. The complete

sentence reads: "At the moment, I am so angry with that infernal little Cuban republic that I would like to wipe its people off the face of the earth."

91. See n. 1 of this chapter.

92. Norweb to Secretary of State, 14 January 1946. Quoted in Lars Schoultz, *Beneath the United States: A History of U.S. Policy Toward Latin America* (Cambridge, MA, 1998), p. 14. R. Henry Norweb (1895–1983), a career diplomat, was ambassador to Cuba from 1945 to 1947.

93. Louis A. Pérez Jr., *Essays on Cuban History: Historiography and Research* (Gainesville, 1995), is the authoritative guide.

94. For U.S. perceptions of Cuba, see the penetrating analysis by Louis A. Pérez, Jr., *Cuba in the American Imagination: Metaphor and Imperial Ethos* (Chapel Hill, 2009).

95. Louis A. Pérez, Jr., is the pioneer of the "indigenous point of view." See especially *Cuba Between Empires, 1878–1902* (Pittsburgh, 1983), which brings the Cuban side of the story into focus; *The War of 1898: The United States and Cuba in History and Historiography* (Chapel Hill, 1998) recounts Cuban viewpoints long neglected outside Cuba; also see the further references given there and elsewhere in this chapter. Vanni Pettinà, *Cuba y estados unidos, 1933–1959: del compromiso nacionalista al conflicto* (Madrid, 2011), provides a balanced account of the "lost decades" that characterizes Batista as a military modernizer. Among other recent examples, see Ayala's criticism of the "plantation school" in *American Sugar Kingdom*; and the articles by Mary Speck cited in n. 121. I am particularly grateful to Dr. Speck for allowing me to use her unpublished paper, "Democracy in Cuba: Principles and Practice, 1902–1952" (2011), and for correspondence on this subject generally.

96. Pratt, *America's Colonial Experiment*, pp. 120–23, provides a characteristically concise, lucid summary.

97. Credit should be given here to two older studies that saw the main point and expressed it with the clarity of their time: David F. Healy, *The United States in Cuba, 1898–1902* (Madison, 1963), pp. 194–206; Jules R. Benjamin, *The United States and Cuba: Hegemony and Dependent Development, 1880–1934* (Pittsburgh, 1974), chs. 1–2.

98. Healy, *The United States in Cuba*, p. 53. Henry M. Teller (1830–1914), the leader of the so-called silver Republicans in the 1890s, transferred his allegiance to the Democrats after the election of 1896.

99. Francisco and Fast, *Conspiracy for Empire*, pp. 154–6.

100. Paul S. Holbo, "The Convergence of Moods and the Cuban-Bond 'Conspiracy' of 1898," *Journal of American History*, 55 (1968), p. 69. I am immensely grateful to Dr. Susan Fernandez for guidance on this issue. Much later, the courts decided that the United States was not liable for Cuba's debt, but this was unclear at the time.

101. Pérez, *Cuba Between Empires*, p. 187; Tarrago, "Cuba and Cubans," pp. 353–4.

102. Pratt, *Expansionists of 1898*, p. 354.

103. Ibid., p. 119.

104. I am indebted here to Maurer, *The Empire Trap*, pp. 52–5.

105. The standard work is Pérez, *Cuba under the Platt Amendment*.

106. Francisco and Fast, *Conspiracy for Empire*, ch. 26. Orville H. Platt (1827–1905) was an influential and long-serving senator from Connecticut.

107. Quoted in Pérez, *Cuba under the Platt Amendment*, p. 46. Nominally, Egypt remained a part of the Ottoman Empire after 1882; in practice, it was under the effective control of Britain's Consul-General, Lord Cromer (1883–1907). Egypt did not become a formal protectorate until 1914 and achieved (formal) independence in 1923. British were less able and less willing to "retire" than Root thought.

108. Ibid., ch. 28.

109. Ibid., chs. 28, 30. Even so, the bill passed by just three votes, and only after dissident Republicans had been purged.

110. See the subsection titled "Lobbies and Liberties" in chapter 11 of this text.

111. Pérez, *Cuba under the Platt Amendment*, ch. 2, provides a full account of Wood's attitude.

112. Quoted in Pérez, *Cuba under the Platt Amendment*, p. 40; see also pp. 37–42.

113. Wood to Roosevelt, 28 October 1901. Quoted in Carmen Diana Deere, "Here Come the Yankees! The Rise and Decline of United States Colonies in Cuba, 1898–1930," *Hispanic American Historical Review*, 78 (1998), p. 734.

114. Pérez, *Cuba Between Empires*, pp. 370–73. Estrada Palma (1832/5–1908) had a distinguished record as a nationalist: he fought in the Ten Years' War, was a close associate of José Martí, and became leader of the Cuban Revolutionary Party after Martí's death. By 1901, however, his years as a revolutionary were behind him.

115. Tammany Hall was established even as the Founding Fathers were debating the Constitution. Shrewd minds were already working out how to bring formality into line with their perception of reality.

116. Leland Hamilton Jenks, *Our Cuban Colony: A Study in Sugar* (New York, 1928), ch. 9; Deere, "Here Come the Yankees!" pp. 729–65.

117. Deere, "Here Come the Yankees!" pp. 743–4.

118. Quoted in Pérez, *Cuba under the Platt Amendment*, p. 44.

119. Juan Carlos Santamarina, "The Cuba Company and the Expansion of American Business in Cuba, 1898–1915," *Business History Review*, 74 (2000), pp. 41–83 (also pp. 78–9, 81–2, and n. 12 on Cuban involvement); Santamarina, "The Cuba Company and the Creation of Informal Business Networks: Historiography and Archival Sources," *Cuban Studies*, 35 (2005), pp. 62–86.

120. Ayala, *American Sugar Kingdom*, pp. 80–85; Francisco and Fast, *Conspiracy for Empire*, pp. 233–4, 329–30, n. 33.

121. The data presented in this paragraph and the next four paragraphs are drawn from: Jenks, *Our Cuban Colony*; Ayala, *American Sugar Kingdom*; César J. Ayala, "Social and Economic Aspects of Sugar Production in Cuba, 1880–1930," *Latin American Research Review*, 30 (1995), pp. 95–124; Alan Dye, *Cuban Sugar in the Age of Mass Production: Technology and the Economics of Sugar Central, 1899–1929* (Stanford, 1998); Oscar Zanetti Lecuona and Aljezandro García Alvarez, *Sugar and Railroads: A Cuban History, 1837–1959* (Chapel Hill, 1998); Mary Speck, "Prosperity, Progress, and Wealth: Cuban Enterprise during the Early Republic, 1902–1927," *Cuban Studies*, 36 (2005), pp. 50–86; Speck, "Closed Door Imperialism: The Politics of Cuban-U.S. Trade, 1902–1933," *Hispanic American Historical Review*, 85 (2005), pp. 449–83; B.J.C. McKercher and S. Enjamiio, "'Brighter Future, Better Times': Britain, the Empire, and Anglo-American Competition in Cuba, 1898–1920," *Diplomacy & Statecraft*, 18 (2007), pp. 663–87.

122. British diplomats ably defended Britain's commercial stake in Cuba while taking care not to challenge the political dominance of the United States: Christopher Hull, *British Diplomacy and U.S. Hegemony in Cuba, 1898–1964* (Houndsmill, 2013).

123. Antonio Santamaría García, "Cambios y ajustes tecnológicos en la agro-manufactura azucarera cubana, 1898–1913," *Historia Agraria*, 66 (2015), pp. 105–45.

124. There are other claimants. The exact location remains unknown.

125. Speck, "Closed Door Imperialism," pp. 455–65, 467–70.

126. Ralph Davis, "The Rise of Protection in England, 1689–1786," *Economic History Review*, 19 (1966), pp. 306–17.

127. Ayala, *American Sugar Kingdom*, p. 245.

128. Pérez, *On Becoming Cuban*, pp. 105–15; and an urban frontier too: ibid., pp. 125–36.

129. Speck, "Prosperity, Progress, and Wealth," pp. 69–73. Specialists on Cuba prefer caudillo to cacique, though some authors use both terms: see Robert Whitney, *State and Revolution in Cuba: Mass Mobilization and Political Change, 1920–1940* (Chapel Hill, 2001), pp. 17–20. Pérez, *Cuba under the Platt Amendment*, ch. 3. Muriel McAvoy, *Sugar Baron: Manuel Rionda and the Fortunes of Pre-Castro Cuba* (Gainesville, 2003), p. 5.

130. Ferrara y Marino (1876–1972).

131. Gerardo Machado y Morales (1871–1939), president 1925–1933.

132. McAvoy, *Sugar Baron.*

133. Ayala, *American Sugar Kingdom*, pp. 87–9.

134. The company revived after World War II, survived the revolution of 1959 (despite its plantations being nationalized), and in the 1990s was the third largest sugar broker in the world before going into liquidation in 1999.

135. The principal source for this subject is Pérez, *On Becoming Cuban.*

136. Geoffrey Blainey, *The Tyranny of Distance: How Distance Shaped Australia's History* (Melbourne, 1966).

137. Pérez, *On Becoming Cuban*, pp. 148–57.

138. Schwartz, *Pleasure Island.*

139. Pérez, *On Becoming Cuban*, pp. 184, 468–72.

140. Roberto G. Echeverria, *The Pride of Havana: A History of Cuban Baseball* (Oxford, 2001); Pérez, *On Becoming Cuban*, pp. 75–83, 255–78.

141. Marial Iglesias Utset, "Decolonizing Cuba: Public Culture and Nationalism in the Years 'Between Empires,' 1898–1902," *Journal of Caribbean History*, 37 (2003), pp. 22–44.

142. Pérez, *On Becoming Cuban*, pp. 79–82.

143. Frank A. Guridy, *Forging Diaspora: Afro-Cubans and African-Americans in a World of Empire and Jim Crow* (Chapel Hill, 2010).

144. In 1953, Cuba's population was estimated to be 5,829,000. Figures for religious affiliation are informed guesses. I have used the highest number I could find: 400,000.

145. Jason M. Yarenko, *U.S. Protestant Missions in Cuba: From Independence to Castro* (Gainesville, 2000). Yarenko studied the developing provinces of eastern Cuba; the position might have been different elsewhere. Harold Greer discovered friendlier and more flexible attitudes among Baptists in the western part of the island: "Baptists in Western Cuba: From the Wars of Independence to the Revolution," *Cuban Studies*, 19 (1989), pp. 61–77.

146. Pérez, *On Becoming Cuban*, pp. 255, 466–7.

147. The complexities of race are dealt with by Alejandro de la Fuente, *A Nation for All: Race, Inequality, and Politics in Twentieth-Century Cuba* (Chapel Hill, 2001); Alejandra Bronfman, *Measures of Equality: Social Science, Citizenship, and Race in Cuba, 1902–1940* (Chapel Hill, 2005).

148. See chapter 10 of this text.

149. Whitney gives particular emphasis to this theme in *State and Revolution in Cuba.*

150. Pérez, *On Becoming Cuban*, provides a graphic account, pp. 97–104.

151. Ada Ferrer, *Insurgent Cuba: Race, Nation, and Revolution, 1868–1898* (Chapel Hill, 1999), ch. 7.

152. Pérez, *Cuba Between Reform and Revolution*, pp. 168–9.

153. Ibid., pp. 162–3, 166.

154. Alejandro de la Fuente and Matthew Casey, "Race and the Suffrage Controversy in Cuba, 1898–1901," in McCoy and Scarano, *Colonial Crucible*, pp. 220–29.

155. Pérez, *Cuba under the Platt Amendment*, pp. 91–104.

156. Christopher A. Abel, "Controlling the Big Stick: Theodore Roosevelt and the Cuban Crisis of 1906," *Naval War College Review*, 40 (1987), pp. 88–98.

157. Pérez, *Army Politics in Cuba*; Pérez, *Cuba between Reform and Revolution*, pp. 157–61, 167–8.

158. Pérez, *Cuba under the Platt Amendment*, pp. 105–7, 123–39, 146–7, 149–50.

159. Aline Helg, *Our Rightful Share: The Afro-Cuban Struggle for Equality, 1886–1912* (Chapel Hill, 1995).

160. Jenks, *Our Cuban Colony*, chs. 10–13, provides a full account of events in 1917–1920; also Pérez, *Cuba under the Platt Amendment*, pp. 167–96.

161. Menocal (1866–1941) was educated in the United States, joined the armed struggle against Spain, and was general manager of the Cuban-American Sugar Company before becoming a career politician and twice president (in 1912 and 1916).

162. Pérez, *Army Politics in Cuba*, ch. 4.

163. Crowder (1859–1932), a veteran of the Indian and Spanish-American Wars, was familiar with Cuban affairs, having been involved in the previous U.S. occupation of 1906–1909.

164. The price paid for Cuban sugar in New York peaked at 22.5 cents per pound in May 1920 and fell to 3.75 cents in December.

165. Pérez, *Cuba under the Platt Amendment*, pp. 269–71.

166. Dye, *Cuban Sugar in the Age of Mass Production*, p. 5. For the larger picture see Ayala, *American Sugar Kingdom*, pp. 66–73.

167. Alan Dye and Richard Sicotte, "The Inter-War Shocks to U.S.-Cuban Trade Relations: A View through Sugar Company Stock Price Data," in Jeremy Atack and Larry Neal, eds., *The Origins and Development of Financial Markets and Institutions* (Cambridge, 2009), pp. 360–61.

168. Speck, "Closed Door Imperialism," p. 479.

169. Dye, *Cuban Sugar in the Age of Mass Production*, is the authoritative study.

170. Speck, "Prosperity, Progress, and Wealth," p. 51.

171. Speck, "Closed Door Imperialism," pp. 473–7.

172. Alan McPherson, "Dollars, Diplomacy and the Missing Link: A Socio-Economic Perspective on Cuban-American Relations, 1900–1934," *Ex Post Facto*, 4 (1995), unpaginated.

173. Speck, "Prosperity, Progress and Wealth," p. 51.

174. McPherson, "Dollars, Diplomacy and the Missing Link"; Pérez, *Cuba under the Platt Amendment*, pp. 269–71.

175. Whitney, *State and Revolution in Cuba*, ch. 2.

176. Pérez, *Cuba between Reform and Revolution*, pp. 187–9.

177. Brian Pollitt, "The Cuban Sugar Economy and the Great Depression," *Bulletin of Latin American Research*, 23 (1984), pp. 12–13.

178. Speck, "Closed Door Imperialism," pp. 478–9.

179. Pérez, *Cuba between Reform and Revolution*, pp. 188–9.

180. Richard P. Tucker, *Insatiable Appetite: The United States and the Ecological Degradation of the World* (Berkeley, 2000), p. 46; Ayala, *American Sugar Kingdom*, pp. 234–5.

181. Douglas A. Irwin, *Peddling Protectionism: Smoot-Hawley and the Great Depression* (Princeton, NJ, 2011), provides an admirable account of this controversial measure.

182. The credit for this important finding and the assessment in the rest of this paragraph goes to Dye and Sicotte, "The Inter-War Shocks to U.S.-Cuban Trade Relations," pp. 345–87; Dye and Sicotte, "The Political Economy of Exporting Economic Instability: The U.S. Sugar Tariff and the Cuban Revolution of 1933" (unpublished paper, 1998). I am grateful to Dr. Dye for allowing me to read and cite this paper.

183. Maurer, *The Empire Trap*, pp. 210–16.

184. Reed Smoot (1862–1941) represented Utah in the Senate from 1903 to 1932 and was Chair of the powerful Finance Committee between 1923 and 1933, when he and Hawley both lost their seats in Congress.

185. Dye and Sicotte, "The Political Economy of Exporting Economic Instability," p. 34.

186. Speck, "Closed Door Imperialism," p. 480.

187. Ibid.

188. Dye and Sicotte, "The Inter-War Shocks to U.S.-Cuban Trade Relations," pp. 377–8.

189. The data in this paragraph are drawn mainly from Dye and Sicotte, "The Political Economy of Exporting Instability"; and Speck, "Closed Door Imperialism."

190. Maurer, *The Empire Trap*, pp. 216–19.

191. Montgomery H. Lewis to I. Howard Lehman, 1 December 1933. Quoted in Dye and Sicotte, "The Inter-War Shocks to U.S.-Cuban Trade Relations," p. 379.

192. Dye and Sicotte, "The Interwar Shocks to U.S.-Cuban Trade Relations," p. 5.

193. Maurer, *The Empire Trap*, pp. 220–34.

194. Quoted in Dye and Sicotte, "The Political Economy of Exporting Economic Instability," p. 12.

195. Ibid.
196. Pérez, *Between Reform and Revolution*, pp. 192–4.
197. Gillian McGillivray, *Blazing Cane: Sugar Communities, Class and State Formation in Cuba, 1868–1959* (Durham, 2009).
198. Fulgencio Batista y Zaldivar (1901–73; president, 1940–44, 1952–59). Frank Argote-Freyre, *Fulgencio Batista: From Revolutionary to Strongman* (New Brunswick, 2006), chs. 4–7, provides a full account of these years.
199. Pérez provides a concise but authoritative summary in *Between Reform and Revolution*, pp. 194–209.
200. These developments are well covered in Whitney, *State and Revolution in Cuba*.
201. Pérez, *Cuba under the Platt Amendment*, pp. 152–65.
202. Karen E. Morrison, "Civilization and Citizenship through the Eyes of Afro-Cuban Intellectuals during the First Constitutional Era, 1902–1940," *Cuban Studies*, 30 (1999), pp. 76–99, shows that inclusiveness encompassed Afro-Cubans too.
203. See chapter 4 of this text, where the term is first used to refer to President Andrew Jackson.
204. (1881–1969), president, 1933–34, 1944–48; founder of the Partido Auténtico (1934).
205. Pérez, *Between Reform and Revolution*, pp. 202–4, and passim for further details.
206. Batista ruled through a nominee, Carlos Mendieta y Montefur (1873–1960), who acted as provisional president, 1934–1935.
207. Marcin Kula, "United States Policy vis à vis the Cuban Revolution of 1933," *Hemispheres*, 3 (1986), pp. 97–115.
208. Philip Dur and Christopher Gilcrease, "U.S. Diplomacy and the Downfall of a Cuban Dictator: Machado in 1933," *Journal of Latin American Studies*, 43 (2002), pp. 255–82; Thomas F. O'Brien, "The Revolutionary Mission: American Enterprise in Cuba," *American Historical Review*, 98 (1993), p. 782 of pp. 765–85.
209. Hugh Thomas, *Cuba: A History* (London, 1971; 2010), p. 382.
210. Thanks to the diligent research of O'Brien, "The Revolutionary Mission."
211. By the close of the 1920s, immigrants accounted for about one-third of the labor force in the sugar fields. O'Brien, "The Revolutionary Mission," p. 770.
212. William J. Hausman and John L. Neufeld, "The Strange Case of American and Foreign Power," *Electricity Journal*, 10 (1997), pp. 46–53.
213. On the role of the army, see Louis A. Pérez, *Army Politics in Cuba, 1898–1958* (Pittsburgh, 1976).
214. Pérez, *Between Reform and Revolution*, pp. 210–12; Ayala, *American Sugar Kingdom*, pp. 236–8.
215. Whitney, *State and Revolution in Cuba*, chs. 6–7.
216. For further details see Dye and Sicotte, "The Political Economy of Exporting Economic Instability."
217. (1881–1969). Thomas, *Cuba*, pp. 717–20; Pérez, *Army Politics in Cuba*, pp. 168–71.
218. Thomas, *Cuba*, p. 720.
219. Pollitt, "The Cuban Sugar Economy," pp. 10–15. On the Chadbourne Plan see Fritz Georg Graevenitz, "Changing Visions of the World Sugar Market in the Great Depression," *European History Review*, 15 (2009), pp. 727–47.
220. Alan D. Dye, "Cuba and the Origins of the US Sugar Quota," *Revista de Indias*, 65 (2005), pp. 195–207.
221. Pollitt, "The Cuban Sugar Economy," pp. 17–18.
222. Calculated from ibid., p. 8.
223. Dye, "Cuba and the Origins of the Sugar Quota," pp. 209–10, 216.
224. Juan C. Santamarina, "The Cuba Company and Eastern Cuba's Economic Development, 1900–1959," *Essays in Business & Economic History*, 19 (2001), pp. 84–5; Pollitt, "The Cuban Sugar Economy."
225. Ayala, *American Sugar Kingdom*, pp. 240–41.

226. Philip W. Bonsal, *Cuba, Castro and the United States* (Pittsburgh, 1972), pp. 269–70; Thomas, *Cuba*, pp. 469–70. It should be said, however, that World War II is a neglected period in Cuba's history.

227. Guantánamo Bay had been leased to the United States in perpetuity in 1903. When the Platt Amendment was revoked in 1934, the United States and Cuba reaffirmed the lease and the United States agreed to double the rent from $2,000 p.a. to $4,000 p.a.

228. Taken from the original lyrics of "La Borinqueña," written in 1868 by Lola Rodríguez de Tió (1843–1924), the noted poet, patriot, and reformer. After Puerto Rico was annexed by the United States, the lyrics were judged to be subversive, and anodyne substitutions were made in 1903 to what eventually became Puerto Rico's national anthem.

229. President William McKinley, "State of the Union Address, 1899."

230. See chapter 11 of this text.

231. Carnivals in Cuba became statements of opposition to white dominance, autocracy, and corruption that led successive governments to try to suppress them in the 1920s and 1930s. See Robin D. Moore, *Nationalizing Blackness: Afrocubanismo and Artistic Revolution in Havana, 1920–1940* (Pittsburgh, 1997).

232. On this theme generally, see Philip W. Scher, *Carnival and the Formation of a Caribbean Transnation* (Gainesville, 2003); Susan Campbell, "Carnival, Calypso, and Class Struggle in Nineteenth-Century Trinidad," *History Workshop*, 26 (1988), pp. 1–27. Ernest D. Brown, "Carnival, Calypso, and Steelband in Trinidad," *The Black Perspective in Music*, 18 (1990), pp. 81–100; Guridy, *Forging Diaspora*.

233. See, for example, Peter Manuel, *Caribbean Currents: Caribbean Music from Rumba to Reggae* (Philadelphia, 1995), pp. 64–70.

234. Quoted in Peter L. Manuel with Kenneth Bilby and Michael Largey, *Caribbean Currents: Caribbean Music from Rumba and Reggae* (Philadelphia, 2nd ed., 2006), pp. 70–72. See also Francisco A. Scarano, "The *Jíbaro* Masquerade and the Subaltern Politics of Creole Identity Formation in Puerto Rico, 1745–1823," *American Historical Review*, 101 (1996), pp. 1398–1431; Nathaniel Cordova, "In His Likeness: The Puerto Rican *Jíbaro* as Political Icon," *Centro Journal*, 17 (2005), pp. 170–91.

235. Nicolás Guillén, Cuba's national poet, "The Cane Field" (1931). I am grateful to my former colleague, Dr. Frank Guridy, for this reference.

236. *Don Juan*, Canto 12, xxxvi.

CHAPTER 13: PARADISE IN THE PACIFIC

1. See n. 3.

2. A rare comparative study is Christine Skwiot, *The Purposes of Paradise: U.S. Tourism and Empire in Cuba and Hawai'i* (Philadelphia, 2010).

3. *Song of the Islands* also starred Victor Mature. The song itself spawned numerous versions. The popular image of Hawai'i was given its first outing on Broadway in 1912 with *Bird of Paradise*; a long series of shows and movies followed, reaching a high point in 1961 with *Blue Hawai'i* starring Elvis Presley. See Brian Ireland, *The US Military in Hawai'i: Colonialism, Resistance and Memory* (Basingstoke, Hants, 2011), ch. 4.

4. Albert Beveridge, "In Support of an American Empire," 9 January 1900. Speech to Congress in *Record*, 56th Congress, Session 1, pp. 704–12.

5. Reynaldo C. Ileto, *Knowing America's Colony: A Hundred Years from the Philippines War* (Manoa, Hawai'i, 1999), provides an illuminating account of how refined versions of these prejudices entered historical scholarship

6. Norberto Barreto Velázquez, *La amenaza colonial. El imperialismo norteamericano y las Filipinas, 1900–1934* (Seville, 2010), covers the spectrum of official opinion on Filipinos and the purposes of colonial rule.

7. Noenoe K. Silva, *Aloha Betrayed: Native Hawaiian Resistance to American Colonialism* (Durham, 2004), ch. 3.

8. Quoted in Momiala Kamahele, "Ilioʻulaokalani: Defending Native Hawaiian Culture," in Candace Fujikane and Jonathan Y. Okamura, eds., *Asian Settler Colonialism* (Honolulu, 2008), p. 76 and p. 96, n. 1. The presentation of hula to American audiences is covered by Adria L. Imada, *Aloha America: Hula Circuits Through the U.S. Empire* (Durham, 2012).

9. For a detailed analysis, including the importance of translations, see Vicente L. Rafael, *White Love and Other Events in Filipino History* (Durham, 2000); Rafael, *The Promise of the Foreign: Nationalism and the Technics of Translation in the Spanish Philippines* (Durham, 2005).

10. Andrés Bonifacio, "Love for the Country of One's Roots," quoted in translation from Tagalog by Reynaldo Clemeña Ileto, *Filipinos and their Revolution: Event, Discourse, and Historiography* (Quezon City, 1998), p. 24. On *kalayaan* see Ileto, *Pasyon and Revolution: Popular Movements in the Philippines, 1840–1910* (Quezon City, 1979). For the genre as a whole see Damiana L. Eugenio, *Awit and Corridoo: Philippine Metrical Romances* (Quezon City, 1987).

11. I am aware that the term "indigenous" is controversial and begs many questions, but considerations of space oblige me to use short-hand on this occasion.

12. Advertising slogan devised in 1940: Alexander McDonald, *Revolt in Paradise: The Social Revolution in Hawaiʻi after Pearl Harbor* (New York, 1944), p. 231.

13. Samoa stands outside this generalization.

14. Richard Lightner, *Hawaiian History: An Annotated Bibliography* (Westport, 2004) is helpful in listing a number of otherwise unknown dissertations; the *Hawaiian Journal of History*, first published in 1967, is the leading research outlet for specialists. Recent developments include an interest in linking the study of the islands to the American West: Aaron Steven Wilson, " 'West of the West': The Territory of Hawaiʻi, the American West, and American Colonialism in the Twentieth Century," Unpublished doctoral dissertation (University of Nebraska, 2008); Matthew Kester, "Hawaiʻi and the American West: A Reassessment," *Pacific Studies*, 32 (2009), pp. 467–84.

15. Susan Carter et al., eds., *Historical Statistics of the United States* (Washington, DC, 2006), table Ef 24–35. I have rounded the figures to avoid spurious accuracy and shown only the major groups, which explains why the figures for 1950 do not add up to 100 percent. Indeed, the arbitrary nature of the classifications casts doubt on the exercise; racial categories have become even more blurred since 1950. The figures given in www .census.gov/population/www/documentation/twps0056/tab26.pdf vary slightly. As Paul Schor points out, the census racialized differences by adopting "standard" categories (and inventing new ones): "Compter et classer par race: Hawaiʻi, les Îsles Vierges et le recensement américain, 1900–1940," *Histoire et Mesure*, 13 (1998), pp. 113–34.

16. The constitutional features of colonial rule summarized here are surveyed at greater length in Julius W. Pratt, *America's Colonial Experiment: How the United States Gained, Governed, and in Part Gave Away a Colonial Empire* (New York, 1951), chs. 5–6, and even more fully in Whitney T. Perkins, *Denial of Empire: The United States and Its Dependencies* (Leiden, 1962), chs. 3–8.

17. As well as, of course, being a citizen of the United States. Perkins, *Denial of Empire*, pp. 67–77; Noel J. Kent, *Hawaiʻi: Islands Under the Influence* (Honolulu, 1993), pp. 72–4.

18. Colin Newbury, "Patronage and Bureaucracy in the Hawaiian Kingdom, 1840–1893," *Pacific Studies*, 24 (2001), pp. 1–38.

19. Roger Bell, *Last Among Equals: Hawaiian Statehood and American Politics* (Honolulu, 1984), pp. 41–3.

20. Ibid., pp. 46–7. The prince remains a controversial figure in nationalist historiography: he is praised for his part in the rebellion of 1895 and the year he spent in prison subsequently, but criticized for collaborating with the settler regime thereafter.

21. Kent, *Hawaiʻi: Islands under the Influence*, p. 75.

22. The data are summarized by Brian Ireland, *The US Military in Hawaiʻi: Colonialism, Memory and Resistance* (Basingstoke, Hants, 2011), pp. xv–xvi.

23. Davianna P. McGregor, "Waipʻo Valley: A Cultural Kipuka in Early Twentieth-Century Hawaiʻi," *Journal of Pacific History*, 30 (1995), pp. 194–210.

24. Eileen H. Tamura, "Power, Status and Hawaiʻi Creole English: An Example of Linguistic Intolerance in American History," *Pacific Historical Review*, 65 (1996), pp. 431–55; Noenoe K. Silva, "I Kuu Mau: How Kanaka Maoli Tried to Sustain National Identity within the United States Political System," *American Studies*, 45 (2004), pp. 9–31.

25. Robert C. Schmitt, *Historical Statistics of Hawaiʻi* (Honolulu, 1977), pp. 418–19. Acreage under sugar increased from 63,816 tons in 1900 to a peak of 139,744 tons in 1932 before falling to 109,405 tons in 1950 (pp. 359–60).

26. Carol A. MacLennan, *Sovereign Sugar: Industry and Environment in Hawaiʻi* (Honolulu, 2014), ch. 9.

27. Schmitt, *Historical Statistics of Hawaiʻi*, pp. 359–60.

28. Ibid., pp. 546–7.

29. Thomas K. Hitch, *Islands in Transition: The Past, Present and Future of Hawaiʻi's Economy* (Honolulu, 1992), p. 133.

30. MacLennan, *Sovereign Sugar*, ch. 5. Also Hitch, *Islands in Transition*, pp. 89–90, 96–7; Kent, *Hawaiʻi: Islands Under the Influence*, pp. 70–75.

31. Richard P. Tucker, *Insatiable Appetite: The United States and the Ecological Degradation of the Tropical World* (Berkeley, 2000), pp. 83–4.

32. Tucker, *Insatiable Appetite*, p. 85.

33. Schmitt, *Historical Statistics*, pp. 542–8.

34. Hitch, *Islands in Transition*, pp. 99–109. A full history of the pineapple industry has yet to be written. Henry H. White, *James D. Dole: Industrial Pioneer of the Pacific* (New York, 1957), is a slim account; Jan K. Ten Bruggencate, *Hawaiʻi's Pineapple Century: A History of the Crowned Fruit in the Hawaiian Islands* (Honolulu, 2004), has some notable photographs.

35. The industry experienced extraordinary growth: 8,000 tons were harvested in 1900; 924,000 tons in 1950. Recovery was greatly helped by the development of canned juice in the 1930s.

36. Richard A. Hawkins, "James D. Dole and the 1932 Failure of the Hawaiian Pineapple Company," *Hawaiian Journal of History*, 41 (2007), pp. 149–70.

37. MacLennan, *Sovereign Sugar*, ch. 9.

38. Hitch, *Islands in Transition*, pp. 93–5.

39. Quoted in Perkins, *Denial of Empire*, pp. 71, 81. See also pp. 72, 75, 79–81.

40. Ibid., p. 75; Richard A. Overfield, "The Agricultural Experiment Station and Americanization: The Hawaiian Experiment, 1900–1910," *Agricultural History*, 60 (1986), pp. 256–66.

41. Jon M. Van Dyke, *Who Owns the Crown Lands of Hawaiʻi?* (Honolulu, 2008), ch. 22; also J. Kehaulani Kauanui, *Hawaiian Blood: Colonialism and the Policy of Sovereignty and Indigeneity* (Durham, 2008).

42. Perkins, *Denial of Empire*, p. 85.

43. This point has been demonstrated conclusively by Alan Dye in an exceptional comparative study: "Factor Endowments and Contract Choice: Why Were Sugar Cane Supply Contracts Different in Cuba and Hawaiʻi, 1900–1929?" in Kyle D. Kauffman, ed., *New Frontiers in Agricultural History* (Stamford, 2000), pp. 127–76. See also Tucker, *Insatiable Appetite*, pp. 88–93.

44. Hitch, *Islands in Transition*, pp. 73–82.

45. Perkins, *Denial of Empire*, pp. 81–4.

46. Sumner J. La Croix and Price Fishback, "Migration, Labor Market Dynamics, and Wage Differentials in Hawaiʻi's Sugar Industry, 1901–1915," in Kyle D. Kauffman, ed., *New Frontiers in Agricultural History* (Stamford, 2000), pp. 54–7.

47. Jon Thares Davidann, ed., *Hawaiʻi at the Crossroads of the U.S. and Japan before the Pacific War* (Honolulu, 2008), which also deals with the causes of Japanese emigration after the Meiji Restoration in 1868.

48. La Croix and Fishback, "Migration, Labor Market Dynamics, and Wage Differentials," pp. 56–7.

49. MacLennan, *Sovereign Sugar*, ch. 8; Hitch, *Islands in Transition*, pp. 82–7; Barnes Riznik, "From Barracks to Family Homes: A Social History of Labor Housing Reform on Hawai'i's Sugar Plantations," *Hawaiian Journal of History*, 33 (1999), pp. 119–57.

50. Sumner J. La Croix and Price V. Fishback, "Firm-Specific Evidence on Racial Wage Differentials and Workforce Segregation in Hawai'i's Sugar Industry," *Explorations in Economic History*, 26 (1989), pp. 403–23.

51. Tucker, *Insatiable Appetite*, pp. 84–5.

52. This is one of numerous versions of the song.

53. Ronald Tanaki, *Pau Hana: Plantation Life and Labor in Hawai'i, 1835–1920* (Honolulu, 1983), pp. 153–64.

54. Masayo U. Duus, *The Japanese Conspiracy: The O'ahu Sugar Strike of 1920* (Berkeley, 1999); John E. Reinecke, *Feigned Necessity: Hawai'i's Attempts to Obtain Chinese Contract Labor, 1921–1933* (San Francisco, 1979).

55. Reinecke, *Feigned Necessity*.

56. John E. Reinecke, *The Filipino Piecemeal Sugar Strike of 1924–1925* (Honolulu, 1996).

57. Reinecke, *Feigned Necessity*, pp. 28–30, 35; Moon-Kie Jung, "Symbolic and Physical Violence: Legitimate State Coercion of Filipino Workers in Prewar Hawai'i," *American Studies*, 45 (2004), pp. 107–37.

58. Reinecke, *Feigned Necessity*, pp. 135–8.

59. Perkins, *Denial of Empire*, 79–80.

60. John J. Stephan, *Hawai'i under the Rising Sun: Japan's Plans for Conquest after Pearl Harbor* (Honolulu, 1984), ch. 2; Jon T. Davidann, ed., *Hawai'i at the Crossroads of the U.S. and Japan before the Pacific War* (Honolulu, 2008); Evelyn N. Glenn, *Unequal Freedom: How Race and Gender Shaped American Citizenship and Labour* (Cambridge, 2002), treats Hawai'i as one of three case studies, the others being the American South and Southwest.

61. Jonathan Y. Okamura, *Ethnicity and Inequality in Hawai'i* (Philadelphia, 2008), traces the emergence of an intricate racial hierarchy held together by economic necessity and mutual antagonism. On the Korean community, which appears to have been disliked by everyone, see Yong-ho Ch'oe, ed., *From the Land of the Hibiscus: Koreans in Hawai'i, 1903–1950* (Honolulu, 2007).

62. Geoffrey Robinson, *The Dark Side of Paradise: Political Violence in Bali* (Ithaca, 1995).

63. Reinecke, *Feigned Necessity*, pp. 129–30.

64. William J. Puette, *The Hilo Massacre: Hawai'i's Bloody Monday, August 1, 1938* (Honolulu, 1988); Kent, *Hawai'i: Islands under the Influence*, pp. 87–8.

65. Hitch, *Islands in Transition*, pp. 127–31. The labor history of the period is covered by Edward D. Beechert, *Working in Hawai'i: A Labor History* (Honolulu, 1985).

66. Reinecke, *Feigned Necessity*, pp. 129–30.

67. Perkins, *Denial of Empire*, pp. 91–4 also deals with the notorious Massie case, which turned Washington's attention to the administration of justice in Hawai'i.

68. Bell, *Last Among Equals*, pp. 40–55, 59–62.

69. The quota was revised in 1937, but Hawai'i's allocation was still well below pre-1934 levels: Kent, *Hawai'i: Islands under the Influence*, p. 106.

70. Bell, *Last Among Equals*, pp. 63–73.

71. The literature on the attack on Pearl Harbor is vast but fortunately largely irrelevant to the present study. John R. Murnane provides a helpful introduction in "Japan's Monroe Doctrine? Reframing the Story of Pearl Harbor," *History Teacher*, 40 (2007), pp. 503–20.

72. Bell, *Last Among Equals*, ch. 3; Hitch, *Islands in Transition*, pp. 135–9. The fullest account is now Harry N. and Jane L. Scheiber, *Bayonets in Paradise: Martial Law in Hawai'i during World War II* (Berkeley, 2016).

73. Hitch, *Islands in Transition*, pp. 135–42.

74. Beth Baily and David Farber, "The 'Double-V' Campaign in World War II: Hawai'i, African-Americans, Racial Ideology and Federal Power," *Journal of Social History*, 26 (1993), pp. 817–43.

75. Hitch, *Islands in Transition*, pp. 151–2. In 1946, the U.S. Supreme Court ruled that the military takeover of civilian rule had been illegal.

76. Hitch, *Islands in Transition*, p. 144.

77. Jonathan Y. Okamura, "Race Relations during World War II: The Non-Internment of Japanese Americans," *Amerasia Journal*, 26 (2000), pp. 117–42.

78. Bell, *Last Among Equals*, pp. 80–82; Hitch, *Islands in Transition*, pp. 145–6.

79. Hitch, *Islands in Transition*, records some contrasting anecdotes on pp. 84 and 147.

80. President William McKinley, "Proclamation," 21 December 1898, at www.historywiz .com/primary sources/benevolent assimilation.htm.

81. The noted zoologist, Dean C. Worcester, was the guru of the moment and his views of Filipinos confirmed the racial expectations of incoming U.S. colonial officials. See Mark D. VanElls, "Assuming the White Man's Burden: The Seizure of the Philippines, 1898–1902," *Philippine Studies*, 43 (1995), pp. 607–22.

82. McKinley appointed Jacob G. Schurman, President of Cornell University, to chair the Commission (formally known as the First Philippine Commission). The second commission, led by William H. Taft, is commonly referred to as the Taft Commission. Vicente L. Rafael, provides a perceptive account of the census in "White Love: Census and Melodrama in the United State Colonization of the Philippines," *History & Anthropology*, 8 (1994), pp. 265–87.

83. *Census of the Philippines, Bulletin 1* (Washington, DC, 1904), tables 1 and 2.

84. Michael Cullinane, *Ilustrado Politics: Filipino Elite Responses to American Rule, 1898–1908* (Quezon City, 2003).

85. Major General Wood was exceptional in requiring his officers to learn a local language during the era of military rule in Mindanao.

86. The importance of this subject has been signaled by María Dolores Elizalde y Josep M. Delgardo, eds., *Filipinas: un país entre dos imperios* (Barcelona, 2011). I am especially indebted here to Paul Kramer's contribution, "Historias transimperiales: raíces españolas del estado colonial estadounidense en Filipinas," ibid., ch. 5.

87. Josep M. Delgardo, "*In God We Trust*. La administración colonial americana y el conflicto religioso en Filipinas," in Elizalede and Delgado, *Filipinas, un país entre dos imperios*, pp. 145–64.

88. Quoted in Perkins, *Empire of Denial*, p. 199. Thomas R., Metcalf, "From One Empire to Another: The Influence of the British Raj on American Colonialism in the Philippines," *Ab Imperio*, 3 (2012), pp. 25–41, explores the mixture of British and homegrown influences that shaped U.S. colonial rule. So, too, Patrick M. Kirkwood, "'Lord Cromer's Shadow': Political Anglo-Saxonism and the Egyptian Protectorate: A Model in the American Philippines," *Journal of World History*, 27 (2016), pp. 1–26.

89. Geoffrey Seed, "British Views of American Policy in the Philippines Reflected in Journals of Opinion," *Journal of American Studies*, 2 (1968), pp. 49–64.

90. Macario Sakay y de Léon (1870–1907) was a leading figure in the wars against Spain and the United States. He was tricked into surrendering by a piece of egregious duplicity authorized by the U.S. Governor.

91. Andrew Bacevich, "Disagreeable Work: Pacifying the Moros, 1903–1906," *Military Review*, 62 (1982), pp. 49–61; Joshua Gedacht, "'Mohammedan Religion Made It Necessary to Fire': Massacres on the American Imperial Frontier from South Dakota to the Southern Philippines," in Alfred W. McCoy and Francisco A. Scarano, eds., *Colonial Crucible: Empire in the Making of the Modern American State* (Madison, 2009), pp. 397–409.

92. Michael Cullinane, "Bringing in the Brigands: The Politics of Pacification in the Colonial Philippines, 1902–1907," *Philippine Studies*, 57 (2009), pp. 49–76, offers two case studies—one in Luzon and the other in Cebu (Visayas).

93. Michael Adas, "Improving on the Civilising Mission? Assumptions of United States Exceptionalism in the Colonisation of the Philippines," *Itinerario*, 22 (1998), pp. 44–66; Metcalf, "From One Empire to Another."

94. This paragraph draws particularly on Patricio N. Abinales, *Making Mindaneo: Cotabato and Daveo in the Formation of the Philippine Nation State* (Quezon City, 2000); Abinales, "The U.S. Army as an Occupying Force in Muslim Mindanao, 1899–1913," in McCoy and Scarano, *Colonial Crucible*, pp. 410–20; Michael Salman, *The Embarrassment of Slavery: Controversies over Bondage and Nationalism in the American Colonial Philippines* (Berkeley, 2001).

95. Jack C. Lane, *Armed Progressive: General Leonard Wood* (San Rafael, 1978); and the more recent account by Jack McCallum, *Leonard Wood: Rough Rider, Surgeon, Architect of American Imperialism* (New York, 2005).

96. Julian Go, "Colonial Reception and Cultural Reproduction: Filipino Elites and United States Tutelary Rule," *Journal of Historical Sociology*, 12 (1999), p. 357. For a discussion of these terms see Cullinane, *Ilustrado Politics*, ch. 1.

97. A point made powerfully by Ileto, *Knowing America's Colony*.

98. I owe a great deal here to Paul D. Hutchcroft's illuminating study, "Colonial Masters, National Politicos, and Provincial Lords: Central Authority and Local Autonomy in the American Philippines, 1900–1913," *Journal of Asian Studies*, 59 (2000), pp. 277–307. Manuel Luis Quezon y Molina (1878–1944), elected Governor of Tayabas in 1906; President of the Commonwealth of the Philippines, 1935–1944.

99. Paul D. Hutchcroft, "The Hazards of Jeffersonianism," in McCoy and Scarano, eds., *Colonial Crucible*, pp. 375–89.

100. Perkins, *Denial of Empire*, p. 202.

101. Quoted in Pratt, *America's Colonial Experiment*, p. 299. See also Hutchcroft, "Colonial Masters," pp. 294–5. Political scientists have long debated the character of the ensuing relationship, especially for the period after independence. I follow Paul D. Hutchcroft's adaptation of Weberian categories in *Booty Capitalism: The Politics of Banking in the Philippines* (Ithaca, 1998); Hutchcroft, "Oligarchs and Cronies in the Philippine State: The Politics of Patrimonial Plunder," *World Politics*, 43 (1991), pp. 414–50; Hutchcroft, "Colonial Masters." See also Nathan G. Quimpo, "Oligarchic Patrimonialism, Bossism, Electoral Clientism, and Contested Democracy in the Philippines," *Comparative Politics*, 37 (2005), pp. 229–50. Comparative references include Jean-Claude Willaume, *Patrimonialism and Political Change in the Congo* (Stanford, 1972); H. E. Chehabi and Juan J. Linz, eds., *Sultantistic Regimes* (Baltimore, 1998).

102. Rene R. Escalante, *The Bearer of the Pax Americana: The Philippine Career of William H. Taft, 1900–1903* (Quezon City, 2007).

103. Paul Kramer, "Reflex Actions: Colonialism, Corruption, and the Politics of Technocracy in the Early Twentieth-Century U.S.," in Bevan Seward and Scott Lucas, eds., *Challenging U.S. Foreign Policy: America and the World in the Long Twentieth Century* (London, 2011), pp. 14–35.

104. This paragraph draws on Perkins, *Denial of Empire*, pp. 220–21; Teodoro A. Agoncillo and Oscar M. Alfonso, *History of the Filipino People* (Quezon City, 2nd ed., 1967), p. 340; Michael Cullinane, "Implementing the 'New Order': The Structure and Supervision of Local Government during the Taft Era," in Norman G. Owen, ed., *Compadre Colonialism: Studies on the Philippines under American Rule* (Ann Arbor, 1971), pp. 13–75; Benedict Anderson, "Cacique Democracy and the Philippines: Origins and Dreams," *New Left Review*, 169 (1988), pp. 11–12; Hutchcroft, "Oligarchs and Cronies," pp. 420–24, 450; Hutchcroft, "Cacique Democracy."

105. Francis Burton Harrison (1873–1957) was Governor-General from 1913 to 1921. He was exceptional among colonial governors in having a strong commitment to the Philippines: he married a Filipino, was involved in the country in several important capacities in the 1930s and 1940s, and was buried in Luzon. He published an account of his tenure

as governor-general under the title *The Corner-Stone of Philippine Independence: A Narrative of Seven Years* (New York, 1922). He is a tempting subject for a full biography if sufficient documentation has survived.

106. Cullinane, *Ilustrado Politics*, chs. 2–7; Hutchcroft, "Colonial Masters."

107. Sergio Osmeña (1878–1961), President of the Philippines, 1944–1946.

108. Quoted in Cullinane, *Ilustrado Politics*, p. 1. William C. Forbes (1870–1959) was Commissioner of Police (1904–1908), Vice-Governor (1908–1909), Governor-General (1908–1913), and Ambassador to Japan, 1930–1932.

109. This paragraph draws on Alfred W. McCoy, *Policing America's Empire: The United States, the Philippines, and the Rise of the Surveillance State* (Madison, 2009), which is one of the truly original studies in the field of U.S. imperial history.

110. Frank L. Jenista, "Problems of the Colonial Civil Service: An Illustration from the Career of Manuel L. Quezon," *Southeast Asia: An International Quarterly*, 3 (1973), pp. 809–29, provides examples.

111. Ibid., p. 188.

112. Formally the Philippine Autonomy Act of 1916: Perkins, *Denial of Empire*, pp. 221–30.

113. Perkins, *Denial of Empire*, p. 228.

114. Ibid., p. 227, quoting Cardinal (James) Gibbons.

115. Taft's estimate of the time needed before the Philippines was ready for independence varied from "at least one generation" to three generations: Perkins, *Empire in Denial*, pp. 202–3, and pp. 218–19 for similar assessments.

116. On Taft's conversion to empire and Roosevelt's retreat from it, see Adam D. Burns, "Adapting to Empire: William H. Taft, Theodore Roosevelt, and the Philippines, 1900–08," *Comparative American Studies*, 11 (2013), pp. 418–33.

117. Wong Kwok Chu, "The Jones Bills, 1912–16: A Reappraisal of Filipino Views on Independence," *Journal of South-East Asian Studies*, 13 (1982), pp. 252–69.

118. Frank H. Golay, "The Search for Revenues," in Peter H. Stanley, ed., *Reappraising an Empire: New Perspectives on Philippine-American History* (Cambridge, MA, 1984), p. 252; Golay, " 'Manila Americans' and Philippine Policy: The Voice of American Business," in Norman G. Owen, ed., *The Philippine Economy and the United States: Studies in Past and Present Interactions* (Ann Arbor, 1983), pp. 6–8.

119. Golay, "The Search for Revenues," pp. 232–58.

120. Richard Hooley, "American Economic Policy in the Philippines, 1902–1940: Exploring a Dark Age in Colonial Statistics," *Journal of Asian Economics*, 16 (2005), p. 472.

121. According to one estimate, the military accounted for as much as three-quarters of government expenditure between 1899 and 1940: Catherine Porter, "The Philippines as an American Investment," *Far Eastern Survey*, 9 (1940), p. 220.

122. Greg Bankoff, "Breaking New Ground? Gifford Pinchot and the Birth of 'Empire Forestry' in the Philippines, 1900–1905," *Environment & History*, 15 (2009), pp. 369–93; Brendan Luyt, "Empire Forestry and Failure in the Philippines," *Journal of Southeast Asian Studies*, 47 (2016), pp. 66–87; Norman G. Owen, "Philippine Economic Development and American Policy: A Reappraisal," in Owen, *Compadre Colonialism*, p. 105. Ileto, *Knowing America's Colony*, pp. 32–7, examines the counterproductive consequences of U.S. policy toward cholera; Brendan Luyt, "Empire Forestry and Its Failure in the Philippines, 1901–1941," *Journal of Southeast Asian Studies*, 47 (2016), pp. 66–87.

123. Hooley, "American Economic Policy," p. 467.

124. Golay, "The Search for Revenues," p. 260.

125. Willem G. Wolters, "From Silver Currency to the Gold Standard in the Philippine Islands," *Philippine Studies*, 51 (2003), pp. 375–404; Yoshiko Nagano, "The Philippine Currency System during the American Colonial Period: Transformation from the Gold Exchange Standard to the Dollar Exchange Standard," *International Journal of Asian Studies*, 7 (2010), pp. 29–50. Allan E. S. Lumba, "Imperial Standards, Colonial Currencies, Racial Capacities, and Economic Knowledge during the Philippine-American War,"

Diplomatic History, 39 (2015), pp. 603–28, emphasizes Charles Conant's influence on colonial currency reform.

126. Abaca benefited from free entry into the United States from 1913 to 1935, when it was adversely affected by the quota system. Norman G. Owen, *Prosperity without Progress: Manila Hemp and Material Life in the Colonial Philippines* (Berkeley and Los Angeles, 1984), pp. 161, 179.

127. Luzviminda B. Francisco and Jonathan S. Fast, *Conspiracy for Empire: Big Business, Corruption and the Politics of Imperialism in America, 1876–1907* (Quezon City, 1985), pp. 258–60.

128. Pedro H. Abelarde, *American Tariff Policy Towards the Philippines, 1898–1946* (New York, 1947), pp. 1–36; Pratt, *America's Colonial Experiment*, pp. 168, 292.

129. Hooley, "American Economic Policy in the Philippines," p. 72.

130. Ibid.

131. Norman G. Owen, "Philippine Economic Development and American Policy: A Reappraisal," in Owen, *Compadre Colonialism*, pp. 103–28; Yoshiko Nagano, "Intra-Asian Trade at the Turn of the Century," in Florentino Rodao and Felice Noelle Rodriguez, eds., *The Philippine Revolution of 1896: Ordinary Lives in Extraordinary Times* (Quezon City, 2001), pp. 266–7, 274–5; John A. Larkin, *Sugar and the Origins of Modern Philippine Society* (Berkeley and Los Angeles, 1993), pp. 47–53, 249–52.

132. See the subsection titled "A Greater England with a Nobler Destiny," in chapter 11 of this text.

133. Porter, "The Philippines as an American Investment," pp. 219–25.

134. Golay, "Manila Americans."

135. Florentino Rodeo, "De colonizadores a residentes. Los españoles ante la transición imperial en Fillipinas," in Elizalde and Delgado, *Filipinas: un país entre dos imperios*, ch. 9.

136. Perkins, *Denial of Empire*, p. 211.

137. William Gervase Clarence-Smith, "The Impact of 1898 on Spanish Trade and Investment in the Philippines," in Charles Macdonald and Guillermo M. Pesignan, eds., *Old Ties and New Solidarities: Studies on Philippine Communities* (Manila, 2000), pp. 234–68.

138. Yoshiko Nagano has now consolidated a series of articles on this subject in *State and Finance in the Philippines, 1898–1941: The Mismanagement of an American Colony* (Singapore, 2015). See also Larkin, *Sugar and the Origins of Modern Philippine Society*, pp. 57–9, 113, 155–7.

139. Concepción had been one of Aguinaldo's generals during the struggles against Spain and the United States.

140. Nagano, *State and Finance*, works out this argument in detail.

141. Maurer, *The Empire Trap*, pp. 33–52. See also Francisco and Fast, *Conspiracy for Empire*, chs. 24, 29.

142. Adam D. Burns, "A New Pacific Border: William H. Taft, the Philippines, and Chinese Immigration, 1898–1903," *Comparative American Studies*, 9 (2011), pp. 309–254.

143. The failure of the United States to achieve far-reaching land reform is discussed by Noel Maurer and Lakshmi Iyer, "The Cost of Property Rights: Establishing Institutions on the Philippines Frontier Under American Rule, 1898–1918," NBER *Working Paper*, 14298 (2008).

144. Pratt, *America's Colonial Experiment*, pp. 295, 300.

145. Ronald K. Edgerton, "Americans, Cowboys, and Cattlemen on the Mindanao Frontier," in Peter W. Stanley, ed., *Reappraising and Empire: New Perspectives on Philippine-American History* (Cambridge, MA, 1984), pp. 171–97.

146. A. G. Hopkins, *An Economic History of West Africa* (London, 1973), pp. 210–12. William H. Lever (1851–1925), founder of Lever Bros. (now part of Unilever) was elevated to the peerage as Lord Leverhulme in 1917.

147. Larkin, *Sugar and the Origins of Modern Philippine Society*.

148. Ibid., pp. 87–93.

149. Calculated from Larkin, *Sugar*, pp. 69–70.

150. Alfred W. McCoy, "Sugar Barons: Formation of a Native Planter Class in the Colonial Philippines," *Journal of Peasant Studies*, 19 (1992), pp. 106–41; Larkin, *Sugar*, ch. 4.

151. This paragraph relies heavily on Albert J. Nyberg, "Growth in the Philippine Coconut Industry, 1901–1966," *Philippine Economic Journal*, 7 (1968), pp. 42–52; and Owen, *Prosperity without Progress*, pp. 174–80.

152. Coconuts, like palms, yield joint products: meat and oil (kernels and oil in the case of palms). The composition, processing, and marketing of the two products are different. The implications of the differences are essential for understanding the industry—from farming to consumption, as the history of coconuts in the Philippines will surely make clear—when it is written.

153. Nyberg, "Growth in the Philippine Coconut Industry," p. 51.

154. Scholars are greatly indebted to Owen's pioneering work, *Prosperity without Progress*. Nevertheless, his regional study (of southeast Luzon) needs to be complemented by additional research on the Visayas and Mindanao. For a history of abaca as a global commodity, see Elizabeth Potter Sievert, *The Story of Abaca* (Quezon City, 2009), and the Philippines in particular, pp. 79–88.

155. Owen, *Prosperity without Progress*, pp. 268–9.

156. Patricio N. Abinales, "Davao-kuo: The Political Economy of a Japanese Settler Zone in Philippine Colonial Society," *Journal of American-East Asian Relations*, 6 (1997), pp. 59–83.

157. Kimberly A. Alidio, "Between Civilizing Mission and Ethnic Assimilation: Racial Discourse, United States Colonial Education and Filipino Ethnicity, 1901–1946," University of Michigan Ph.D. dissertation, 2001.

158. Paul A. Kramer, *The Blood of Government: Race, Empire, the United States, and the Philippines* (Chapel Hill, 2006), pp. 28–32, 89, 185–6, 192.

159. Babette P. Resurrección, "Engineering the Philippine Uplands: Gender, Ethnicity, and Scientific Forestry in the American Colonial Period," *Bulletin of Concerned Asian Scholars*, 31 (1999), pp. 13–30.

160. David C. Dorward, "The Development of the British Colonial Administration among the Tiv, 1900–1949," *African Affairs*, 68 (1969), pp. 316–33.

161. Mariano C. Apilado, *Revolutionary Spirituality: A Study of the Protestant Role in the American Colonial Rule of the Philippines, 1898–1928* (Quezon City, 1999).

162. Nestor D. Bunda, "Philippines' Baptist Centennial History," in H. Agrarian, F. N. Jalandoon, and C. Vallejo, eds., *Faith and Challenges Learn to Be Qualified* (Manila, 2002).

163. Matthew T. Herbst, "Regime Change, Occupation, and Aggressive Christianity: The Detroit Annual Conference of the Methodist Episcopal Church and the U.S. Occupation of the Philippines (1898–1903)," *Methodist History*, 43 (2005), pp. 297–308.

164. Kenton J. Clymer, *Protestant Missionaries in the Philippines, 1898–1916: An Inquiry into the American Colonial Mentality* (Urbana, 1986); John N. Schumacher, "Foreign Missionaries and the Politico-Cultural Orientations of the Roman Catholic Church, 1910–70," *Philippine Studies*, 38 (1990), pp. 151–65.

165. Anne L. Foster, "Prohibition as Superiority: Policing Opium in South-East Asia, 1898–1925," *International History Review*, 22 (2000), pp. 253–73.

166. Michael Salman, *The Embarrassment of Slavery: Controversies over Bondage and Nationalism in the American Colonial Philippines* (Berkeley, 2001). Salman's valuable study should be read with that of one of the pioneers of the indigenous (and Spanish) history of the Philippines: William H. Scott, *Slavery in the Spanish Philippines* (Manila, 1991).

167. For example: Jeffrey Ayala Milligan, "Democratization or Neocolonialism? The Education of Muslims under U.S. Military Occupation, 1903–20," *History of Education*, 33 (2004), pp. 451–67.

168. Hooley, "American Economic Policy," p. 471, quotes a literacy rate of 84 percent by 1940, which seems hardly credible. All such figures are highly dependent on the basic data and the criteria for determining literacy.

169. Florentino Rodao, "Spanish Language in the Philippines, 1900–1940," *Philippine Studies*, 45 (1997), pp. 94–107. Rafael, *The Promise of the Foreign*, explores the way Spanish was seen as an agent both of national unity and colonial subordination.

170. Board of Education Survey, *A Survey of the Educational System of the Philippine Islands* (Manila, 1925). The Survey was led by Professor Paul Monroe, an educationalist at Columbia University and an advocate of standardized tests, which critics called "mechanical education." The Commission halted industrial training but also antagonized the islands' private schools. Roman Catholics in particular held that the Commission's purpose was to favor Protestants and to enhance the power of the state.

171. Anne Paulet, "To Change the World: The Use of American Indian Education in the Philippines," *History of Education Quarterly*, 47 (2007), pp. 173–202. I am grateful to Dr. Paulet for discussing her work with me.

172. Nationalist reactions to these priorities can be followed through the work of Renato Constantino. See especially *The Miseducation of the Filipino* (Manila, 1966).

173. Glenn Anthony May, "The Business of Education in the Colonial Philippines, 1909–30," in McCoy et al., *Colonial Crucible*, pp. 151–62.

174. Gerald R. Gems, *The Athletic Crusade: Sport and American Cultural Imperialism* (Lincoln, 2006), ch. 4.

175. Harrison's account is given in his book, *The Corner-Stone of Philippine Independence* (New York, 1922).

176. Megan C. Thomas, "K Is for De-Kolonization: Anti-Colonial Nationalism and Orthographic Reform," *Comparative Studies in Society & History*, 49 (2007), pp. 938–67; Andrew B. Gonzales, *Language and Nationalism: The Philippine Experience Thus Far* (Quezon City, 1980); and the commentary by Robert C. Kaplan, "Language and Nationalism," *Philippine Studies*, 30 (1982), pp. 120–48. After a long battle with Spanish and English, Tagalog was declared the national language in 1937, though it was not established effectively until the 1980s.

177. Gerald E. Wheeler, "Republican Philippine Policy, 1921–1933," *Pacific Historical Review*, 28 (1959), pp. 377–90.

178. Perkins, *Denial of Empire*, pp. 233–43, notes that Osmeña and Quezon also had reservations about premature independence.

179. Quoted in Wheeler-Bennett, "Thirty Years of American-Filipino Relations," p. 515.

180. Larkin, *Sugar and the Origins of Modern Philippine Society*, pp. 169–73.

181. Ibid., pp. 169–70, 172–4, 210–18; McCoy, "Sugar Barons."

182. Pratt, *America's Colonial Experiment*, pp. 301–3.

183. Thomas B. Pepinsky, "Trade Competition and American Decolonization," *World Politics*, 67 (2015), pp. 403–4, 409–12, 414–18.

184. Before 1934, Filipinos were treated as neither citizens nor aliens, but as nationals (Malays). The inglorious story of Filipino immigrants in the United States (principally in California) is well told by Rick Baldoz, *The Third Asiatic Invasion: Empire and Migration in Filipino America 1898–1946* (New York, 2011). See also Alidio, "Between Civilizing Mission and Ethnic Assimilation," which is especially informative on the fortunes of Filipino migrants in the United States.

185. James A. Tyner, "The Geopolitics of Eugenics and the Exclusion of Philippine Immigrants from the United States," *Geographical Review*, 89 (1999), pp. 54–73.

186. Theodore Roosevelt, Jr., *Colonial Policies of the United States* (New York, 1937), p. 187.

187. The essence of this story, though much elaborated by later writers, is well told by Pratt, *America's Colonial Experiment*, chs. 6–7; and Perkins, *Denial of Empire*, ch. 7.

188. Maurer, *The Empire Trap*, pp. 249–41.

189. Hoover was also influenced by Manuel Roxas and Sergio Osmeña, who judged that the Philippines lacked the viability needed for independence to be successful. Maurer, *The Empire Trap*, pp. 240–41.

190. Owen, "Philippine-American Economic Interactions," pp. 183–4; Larkin, *Sugar and the Origins of Modern Philippine Society*, pp. 161–3; Maurer, *The Empire Trap*, p. 240.

191. Maurer, *The Empire Trap*, pp. 236–40.

192. Hooley, "American Economic Policy in the Philippines," pp. 473–4.

193. Quoted in H. W. Brands, *Bound to Empire: The United States and the Philippines, 1890–1990* (New York, 1992), p. 163.

194. Maurer, *The Empire Trap*, p. 241.

195. Manila serves as a proxy for many of the general trends of the period. See Daniel F. Doeppers, *Manila, 1900–1941: Social Change in a Late Colonial Metropolis* (New Haven, 1984).

196. For an example of a series of four strikes in the major sugar port of Iloilo, see Alfred W. McCoy, "The Iloilo General Strike: Defeat of a Proletariat in a Philippine Colonial City," *Journal of Southeast Asian Studies*, 15 (1984), pp. 330–64.

197. Owen, *Prosperity without Progress*, pp. 124, 129, 150–52, 156–7; Gareth Austin, "The Emergence of Capitalist Relations in South Asante Cocoa-Farming, c. 1916–1933," *Journal of African History*, 28 (1987), pp. 259–72.

198. Larkin, *Sugar and the Origins of Modern Philippine Society*, pp. 187–200, 219–23.

199. Motoe Terami-Wada, "The Sakdal Movement, 1930–34," *Philippine Studies*, 36 (1988), pp. 131–50; Terami-Wada, "Benigno Ramos and the Sakdal Movement," *Philippine Studies*, 36 (1988), pp. 427–42; Joseph R. Hayden, *The Philippines: A Study in National Development* (New York, 1942), chs. 15–16.

200. David R. Sturtevant, "Sakdalism and Philippine Radicalism," *Journal of Asian Studies*, 21 (1962), pp. 19–213.

201. McCoy, *Policing America's Empire*, pp. 359–62.

202. Lewis E. Gleeck, "The Putsch that Failed," *Bulletin of the American Historical Collection*, 26 (1998), pp. 35–45.

203. Quezon and Osmeña repeated their double success in 1941. Rolando M. Gripaldo, "The Quezon-Osmeña Split of 1922," *Philippine Studies*, 39 (1991), pp. 158–75.

204. Larkin, *Sugar and the Origins of Modern Philippine Society*, pp. 165–6, 170, 201–10, 214–18, 236.

205. Ibid., p. 201.

206. Dean Kotlowski, "Independence or Not? Paul V. McNutt, Manuel Quezon, and the Re-Examination of Philippine Independence, 1937–9," *International History Review*, 32 (2010), pp. 501–31. The point was first made by Nicholas Tarling, "Quezon and the British Commonwealth," *Australian Journal of Politics & History*, 23 (1977), pp. 182–206.

207. Perkins, *Denial of Empire*, pp. 246–7.

208. McNutt (1891–1955) was High Commissioner from 1937 to 1939.

209. Baldoz, *The Third Asiatic Invasion*.

210. Pratt, *America's Colonial Experiment*, p. 310.

211. Vicente Angel S. Ybiernas, "The Philippine Commonwealth Government: In Search of a Budgetary Surplus," *Philippine Studies*, 51 (2003), pp. 96–124.

212. Anderson, "Cacique Democracy in the Philippines," p. 11, n. 26.

213. Grant K. Goodman, "Japan and Philippine Commonwealth Politics," *Philippine Studies*, 52 (2004), pp. 208–23.

214. These oscillations have been described authoritatively by Akira Iriye, *Across the Pacific: An Inner History of American-East Asian Relations* (New York, 1967); Iriye, *Pacific Estrangement: Japanese and American Expansion, 1897–1911* (Cambridge, MA, 1972).

215. Porter, "The Philippines as an American Investment," p. 219.

216. Brian McAllister Lin, *Guardians of Empire: The U.S. Army and the Pacific, 1902–1949* (Chapel Hill, 1997).

217. On the complex constitutional situation during the war, see Rolando M. Grimaldo, "The Presidential Succession of 1943," *Philippine Studies*, 38 (1990), pp. 301–15.
218. Yoshiko Nagano, "Philippines Cotton Production under Japanese Rule, 1942–1945," *Philippine Studies*, 46 (1998), pp. 313–39; Francis. K. Danquah, "Japan's Food Farming Policies in Wartime Southeast Asia: The Philippine Example, 1942–1944," *Agricultural History*, 64 (1990), pp. 60–80; Danquah, "Reports on Philippine Industrial Crops in World War II from Japan's English-Language Press," *Agricultural History*, 79 (2005), pp. 74–96.
219. Quezon's attitude toward independence remains controversial. Flexibility seems to have been his maxim. Discussions include Michael Paul Onorato, "Quezon and Independence: A Reexamination," *Philippine Studies*, 37 (1989), pp. 221–39; Bonifacio S. Salamanca, "Quezon, Osmeña and Roxas, and the American Presence in the Philippines," *Philippine Studies*, 37 (1989), pp. 301–16.
220. Charles V. Hawley, "You're a Better Filipino than I Am, John Wayne: World War II, Hollywood, and U.S.-Philippines Relations," *Pacific Historical Review*, 71 (2002), pp. 389–414; Camilla Fojas, "Foreign Domestics: The Filipino 'Home Front' in World War II Hollywood," *Comparative American Studies*, 8 (2010), pp. 3–21. Emily S. Rosenberg's *A Date that Will Live: Pearl Harbor in American Memory* (London, 2003) is also relevant.
221. The film was reissued in 1942 under the title *A Yank in the Philippines*, but later withdrawn when it became clear that the "savage" Moros had become allies. Appropriately, the screen's first Tarzan, Elmo Lincoln, had a small part in the film.
222. Gary Wills, *John Wayne's America: The Politics of Celebrity* (New York, 1997) shows how Wayne symbolized what Americans wanted to be. Wayne himself, however, did not volunteer for military service, unlike James Stewart, Henry Fonda, and Clark Gable, and his career prospered during World War II, when he made 13 movies.
223. From "Bayan Ko" (My Country), *kundiman* protest song and unofficial national anthem.
224. On this theme see the perceptive commentary by Ileto, *Knowing America's Colony*.
225. Ku'ualoha Ho'omanawanui, "This Land Is Your Land, This Land Is My Land," in Fujikane and Okamura, *Asian Settler Colonialism*, p. 129. The recovery of these sources is very much a work in progress. Much credit should go to Amy Ku'uleialoha Stillman. See, for example: "History Reinterpreted in Song: The Case of the Hawaiian Counter-Revolution," *Hawaiian Journal of History*, 23 (1989), pp. 1–30; "Aloha 'Aina': New Perspectives on 'Kaulana Na Pua,'" *Hawaiian Journal of History*, 33 (1999), pp. 83–99; "Of the People Who Love the Land: Vernacular History in the Poetry of Modern Hawaiian Hula," *Amerasia*, 28 (2002), pp. 85–108. Elizabeth Buck, *Paradise Remade: The Politics of Culture and History in Hawai'i* (Philadelphia, 1993), provides an introduction to the subject.
226. Francisco Santiago (1889–1947) is regarded as the founder of modern patriotic music in the Philippines. The device of containing a semi-coded message within a straightforward human story is familiar where political subordination constrains free expression. On Filipino music, see R. C. Banas, *Musika: An Essay on Philippines Ethnic Music* (Manila, 1992); Christi-Anne Castro, *Musical Renderings of the Philippine Nation* (New York, 2011).
227. "Bayan Ko" has multiple origins. Adaptations of the Spanish version appeared during the wars against Spain and the United States. The poet José Corazón de Jesús (1896–1932) popularized the lyrics in Tagalog in 1929; Constancio de Guzman set them to music. Numerous versions are available, as are adaptations made in other countries and languages.
228. The classic statement is Hla Myint, *The Economics of the Developing Countries* (London, 1964).
229. See, for example, Warren Zimmermann, "Jingoes, Goo-Goos, and the Rise of America's Empire," *Wilson Quarterly*, 22 (1998), p. 63.
230. This is also the claim advanced in Stanley Karnow's book, *In Our Image: America's Empire in the Philippines* (New York, 1989), which won a Pulitzer Prize. See Ileto's critical

comments in *Knowing America's Colony*, pp. 42–5; and the incisive essay by Michael Salman, "In Our Orientalist Imagination: Historiography and the Culture of a Colonialism in the United States," *Radical History Review*, 50 (1991), pp. 221–32.

231. Two bold attempts have been made to measure the economic progress of the Philippines under U.S. rule: Hooley, "American Economic Policy"; and Anne Booth, "Measuring Living Standards in Different Colonial Systems: Some Evidence from South East Asia, 1900–1942," *Modern Asian Studies*, 46 (2012), pp. 1145–81. Both studies rely heavily on calculations of GDP, which necessarily raise questions about the solidity of the conclusions drawn. Yoshiko Nagano of Kanagawa University, Tokyo, is currently managing a project designed to produce national accounts for the Philippines during the period of U.S. rule. I am most grateful to Professor Booth for some illuminating exchanges on this subject.

CHAPTER 14: "THE TWILIGHT OF CONFUSED COLONIALISM"

1. Rexford Tugwell, *The Stricken Land: The Story of Puerto Rico* (New York, 1947), pp. 81–2. The specific reference was to the inadequate control exercised by Acting Governor Guy J. Swope, who "labored in futility" in 1941.
2. Theodore Roosevelt, Jr., *Colonial Policies of the United States* (New York, 1937), p. 189. Roosevelt was a former Governor of Puerto Rico and Governor-General of the Philippines.
3. Tugwell, *Stricken Land*, pp. 81–2.
4. Roosevelt, *Colonial Policies of the United States*, p. 189.
5. Odd Arne Westad, "The Cold War and International History in the Twentieth Century," in Melvyn Leffler and Odd Arne Westad, eds., *Cambridge History of the Cold War*, I (2010), pp. 1–19, appeals for a global approach, though the format of the Cambridge volumes, perhaps inevitably, takes a segmented view of the subject. Only two chapters in volumes 1 and 2 deal explicitly with decolonization. Cary Fraser, "Decolonization and the Cold War," in Richard Immerman and Petra Goedde, eds., *Oxford Handbook of the Cold War* (Oxford, 2013), ch. 27, sets the subject in an appropriately global context.
6. Odd Arne Westad, *The Global Cold War: Third World Interventions and the Making of Our Times* (Cambridge, 2006); and the case study by Mark Atwood Lawrence, "Universal Claims, Local Uses: Reconceptualizing the Vietnam Conflict, 1945–60," in A. G. Hopkins, ed., *Global History: Interactions Between the Universal and the Local* (Basingstoke, 2006), ch. 8.
7. On the content of the Russian civilizing mission before the Revolution, see Alexander Morrison, "Peasant Settlers and the 'Civilising Mission' in Russian Turkestan, 1865–1917," *Journal of Imperial & Commonwealth History*, 43 (2015), pp. 387–417.
8. On the Soviet Union as an imperial power, see Vladislav M. Zubok, *A Failed Empire: The Soviet Union in the Cold War from Stalin to Gorbachev* (Chapel Hill, 2007), and the discussion in *h-diplo*, 9 (2008), pp. 1–41.
9. Rana Mitter, *China's War with Japan, 1937–45: The Struggle for Survival* (London, 2013).
10. Andrew J. Rotter, *The Path to Vietnam: Origins of the American Commitment to Southeast Asia* (Ithaca, 1987). An accessible survey is Mark Atwood Lawrence, *The Vietnam War: A Concise International History* (Oxford, 2008).
11. Robert McMahon, *Colonialism and Cold War: The United States and the Struggle for Indonesian Independence, 1945–1949* (Ithaca, 1981); McMahon, *The Limits of Empire: The United States and Southeast Asia since World War II* (New York, 1999).
12. Yoav Di-Capua, "Arab Existentialism: An Invisible Chapter in the Intellectual History of Decolonization," *American Historical Review*, 117 (2012), pp. 1061–91.
13. The long view is explored in Greg Grandin and Gilbert M. Joseph, eds., *A Century of Revolution: Insurgent and Counterinsurgent Violence During Latin America's Long Cold War* (Durham, 2010).

14. Two valuable and concise surveys are Mark Philip Bradley, "Decolonization, the Global South, and the Cold War, 1919–1962," in Leffler and Westad, *Cambridge History of the Cold War*, 2, ch. 22; and Fraser, "Decolonization and the Cold War."

15. Central Intelligence Agency, "The Break-up of the Colonial Empires and Its Implications for US Security," September 3, 1948, in Michael Warner, ed., *The CIA under Harry Truman* (Washington, DC, 1994), p. 234.

16. Harry S. Truman, "Presidential Address," 5 October 1947.

17. See, for example, the otherwise valuable essays in David Ryan and Victor Pungong, eds., *The United States and Decolonization: Power and Freedom* (New York, 2000); and the admirable specialized studies by McMahon, *Colonialism and the Cold War*; Andrew J. Rotter, *Comrades at Odds: The United States and India, 1947–1964* (Ithaca, 2000); Jason C. Parker, *Brother's Keeper: The United States, Race, and Empire in the British Caribbean, 1937–1962* (New York, 2008); Anne Foster, *The United States and Europe in Colonial Southeast Asia, 1919–1941* (Durham, 2010); and the vast literature on the United States and French Indo-China.

18. Robert J. McMahon, "Eisenhower and Third World Nationalism: A Critique of the Revisionists," *Political Science Quarterly*, 101 (1986), pp. 453–73, remains persuasive on this subject.

19. A full study would need to trace the origins of the Civil Rights movement to the Revolution of 1917 and the radical commitment generated by the Depression of 1930s. On these topics see Glenda Elizabeth Gilmore, *Forgotten Revolutionaries: How Southern Communists, Socialists and Expatriates Paved the Way for Civil Rights* (New York, 2008).

20. William Inboden, *Religion and American Foreign Policy, 1945–1960: The Soul of Containment* (Cambridge, 2008). For a more assertive argument along these lines, see Ira Chernus, *Apocalypse Management: Eisenhower and the Discourse of National Insecurity* (Palo Alto, 2008), and the perceptive review by Campbell Craig in the *Journal of Military History*, 73 (2009), pp. 1011–12. Andrew Preston, "Peripheral Visions: American Mainline Protestants and the Global Cold War," *Cold War History*, 13 (2013), pp. 109–30, draws attention to the role of liberal, ecumenical Protestants who advocated decolonization and dialogue with the Soviet Union.

21. Hal M. Friedman, "The Open Door in Paradise? The United States Strategic Security and Economic Policy in the Pacific Islands, 1945–1947," *Pacific Studies*, 20 (1997), pp. 63–87. Japan reclaimed sovereignty over Okinawa in 1972. Most of Micronesia had been passed from Germany to Japan as mandates after World War I.

22. Cary Fraser, *Ambivalent Anti-Colonialism: The United States and the Genesis of West Indian Independence, 1940–1964* (Westport, 1994); Parker, *Brother's Keeper*. Spencer Mawby, *Ordering Independence: The End of Empire in the Anglophone Caribbean, 1947–89* (Basingstoke, 2012), traces the inglorious final years of British rule, including the ill-fated Federation of the West Indies (1958–1962).

23. Jonathan Y. Okamura explores the intricacies of race relations in *Ethnicity and Inequality in Hawai'i* (Philadelphia, 2008).

24. Elizabeth Borgwardt, *A New Deal for the World: America's Vision for Human Rights* (Cambridge, MA, 2005), traces the process to the Atlantic Charter.

25. Hanne Hagtvedt Vik, "How Constitutional Concerns Framed the US Contribution to the International Human Rights Regime from Its Inception, 1947–53," *International History Review*, 34 (2012), pp. 887–909.

26. Mark Mazower, *No Enchanted Palace: The End of Empire and the Ideological Origins of the United Nations* (Princeton, NJ, 2009).

27. Charter of the United Nations, ch. 11; Mary L. Dudziak, *Cold War Civil Rights: Race and the Image of American Democracy* (Princeton, 2000); Carol Anderson, *Eyes Off the Prize: The United Nations and the African American Struggle for Human Rights, 1944–1955* (New York, 2003), ch. 3.

28. Anderson, *Eyes Off the Prize*, pp. 3–4, 131–7; and, more generally, Mary Ann Glendon, *A World Made New: Eleanor Roosevelt and the Universal Declaration of Human Rights* (New York, 2001).

29. A.W.B. Simpson, *Human Rights and the End of Empire: Britain and the Genesis of the European Convention* (Oxford, 2001), chs. 6, 16–20, shows that Britain's initiative resulted from muddle as well as design. Simpson's approach derives from a critical appraisal of the efficacy of common law in colonial settings, on which see David Campbell's penetrating essay, "Human Rights and the Critique of the Common Law," *Cardozo Law Review*, 26 (2005), pp. 791–835.

30. Rosemary Foot, "The Cold War and Human Rights," in Leffler and Westad, *Cambridge History of the Cold War*, 2, ch. 21.

31. Anderson, *Eyes Off the Prize*, p. 3.

32. Gunnar Myrdal, *An American Dilemma: The Negro Problem and Modern Democracy* (New York, 1944). On internal colonialism see Michael Hechter, *Internal Colonialism: The Celtic Fringe in British National Development* (London, 1975; 2nd ed., 1998).

33. Anderson's admirable study identifies and emphasizes this development: *Eyes Off the Prize*, pp. 1–7.

34. Beth Tompkins Bates, "A New Crowd Challenges the Agenda of the Old Guard in the NAACP, 1933–1941," *American Historical Review*, 102 (1997), pp. 340–77; Carol Anderson, "Rethinking Radicalism: African Americans and the Liberation Struggles in Somalia, Libya, and Eritrea, 1945–1949," *Journal of the Historical Society*, 11 (2011), pp. 385–423.

35. Carol Anderson, "International Conscience, The Cold War, and Apartheid: The NAACP's Alliance with the Reverend Michael Scott for South-West Africa's Liberation, 1946–1951," *Journal of World History*, 19 (2008), pp. 297–325. Curiously, the NAACP failed to support its short-lived branch in Hawai'i: Albert S. Broussard, "The Honolulu NAACP and Race Relations in Hawai'i," *Hawaiian Journal of History*, 39 (2005), pp. 115–33.

36. Charles H. Martin, "Internationalizing the 'American Dilemma': The Civil Rights Congress and the 1951 Genocide Petition to the United Nations," *Journal of American Ethnic History*, 16 (1997), pp. 35–61.

37. Anderson, *Eyes Off the Prize*, pp. 48–51. Dudziak, *Cold War Civil Rights*, pp. 24–27.

38. Truman's own military service during World War I had given him a sincere commitment to end segregation in the armed forces, notwithstanding his own racial assumptions. The navy and air force fell into line, but the army resisted desegregation until the Korean War.

39. Anderson, *Eyes Off the Prize*, p. 157.

40. Thomas Borstelmann, *Apartheid's Reluctant Uncle: The United States and Southern Africa in the Early Cold War* (Oxford, 1993).

41. Azza Salama Layton, *International Politics and Civil Rights Policies in the United States, 1941–1960* (Cambridge, 2000); Anderson, *Eyes Off the Prize*, pp. 201–2, 275–6.

42. Manfred Berg, "Black Rights and Liberal Anti-Communism: The NAACP in the Early Cold War," *Journal of American History*, 94 (2007), pp. 75–96.

43. Quoted in Thomas Borstelmann, *The Cold War and the Color Line: American Race Relations in the Global Arena* (Cambridge, MA, 2003), p. 77.

44. I use the term "American Indian" in this chapter because the literature on the period after World War II prefers it to "Native American," which has wider currency among historians who deal with earlier periods.

45. Laurence M. Hauptman, "Africa View: John Collier, the British Colonial Service, and American Indian Policy, 1933–1945," *Historian*, 48 (1986), pp. 559–74. See also the subsection titled "A Greater England with a Nobler Destiny," in chapter 11 of this text.

46. Donald L. Fixico, *Termination and Relocation: Federal Indian Policy, 1945–1960* (Albuquerque, 1986); Kenneth R. Philp, *Termination Revisited: American Indians on the Trail to Self-Determination, 1933–1953* (Lincoln, 1999). It is worth pointing out that the

policy aroused uncertainty as well as hostility; a segment of American Indian opinion thought, at least initially, that it might bring benefits.

47. Daniel M. Cobb, *Native Activism in Cold War America: The Struggle for Sovereignty* (Lawrence, 2008), emphasizes activity before the late 1960s, which has been well-publicized.

48. For one example, see Tracey Banivanua Mar, *Decolonisation and the Pacific: Indigenous Globalisation and the Ends of Empire* (Cambridge, 2016), though this study does not cover the Philippines and touches on Hawai'i only briefly.

49. Roger Bell, *Last Among Equals: Hawaiian Statehood and American Politics* (Honolulu, 1984), pp. 84–91. Bell's admirable study deserves appreciation for incorporating indigenous viewpoints and for its analysis, which has stood the test of time. See also Brian Ireland, *The U.S., Military in Hawai'i: Colonialism, Memory and Resistance* (Basingstoke, 2011).

50. Moon-Ki Jung, *Reworking Race: The Making of Hawai'i's Interracial Labor Movement* (New York, 2006), chs. 4–5.

51. Bell, *Last Among Equals*, pp. 139–40.

52. Ines M. Miyares, "Expressing 'Local Culture' in Hawai'i," *Geographical Review*, 98 (2008), pp. 513–31.

53. Bell, *Last Among Equals*, pp. 264–65.

54. Richard P. Tucker, *Insatiable Appetite: The United States and the Ecological Degradation of the Tropical World* (Berkeley and Los Angeles, 2000), pp. 86–95.

55. Ibid., p. 96.

56. Gretchen Heefner, "'A Symbol of the New Frontier': Hawaiian Statehood, Anti-Colonialism, and Winning the Cold War," *Pacific Historical Review*, 74 (2005), pp. 545–74.

57. Mililani B. Trask, "Hawai'i and the United Nations," in Candace Fujikane and Jonathan Y. Okamura, eds., *Asian Settler Colonialism* (Honolulu, 2008), pp. 67–70.

58. Bell, *Last Among Equals*, pp. 55–75, 87; Whitney T. Perkins, *Denial of Empire: The United States and Its Dependencies* (Leiden, 1962), pp. 95–102.

59. (New Orleans, 1957). See Ann K. Ziker, "Segregationists Confront American Empire: The Conservative White South and the Question of Hawaiian Statehood, 1947–1959," *Pacific Historical Review*, 76 (2007), pp. 439–65.

60. Giles Scott-Smith, "From Symbol of Division to Cold War Asset: Lyndon Johnson and the Achievement of Hawaiian Statehood in 1959," *History*, 89 (2004), p. 264.

61. Ziker, "Segregationists Confront American Empire," p. 455.

62. Perkins, *Denial of Empire*, pp. 97–99.

63. Gerald Horne, "Race from Power: U.S. Foreign Policy and the General Crisis of 'White Supremacy,'" *Diplomatic History*, 23 (1999), pp. 437–62.

64. Bell, *Last Among Equals*, pp. 139–41, 143, 149–61.

65. (Washington, 1945).

66. For a summary of the state of the colony at the end of the war, see Nick Cullather, *Illusions of Influence: The Political Economy of United States-Philippines Relations, 1942–1960* (Stanford, 1994), pp. 33–4.

67. American Historical Association, "What Lies Ahead," p. 1.

68. Cullather, *Illusions of Influence*, pp. 37, 183–4, 192.

69. For example: William J. Pomeroy, *An American Tragedy: Neo-Colonialism & Dictatorship in the Philippines* (New York, 1974); Stephen Rosskamm Shalom, *The United States and the Philippines: A Study of Neo-Colonialism* (Philadelphia, 1981).

70. Quoted in Shalom, *The United States and the Philippines*, p. 52.

71. On this distinction, see Susan Strange, *States and Markets* (London, 1988), ch. 2; and for an application, A. G. Hopkins, "Informal Empire in Argentina: An Alternative View," *Journal of Latin American Studies*, 26 (1994), pp. 469–84.

72. Shalom, *The United States and the Philippines*, ch. 2.

73. These events are well covered by Shalom, *The United States and the Philippines*, ch. 1; and Cullather, *Illusions of Influence*, chs. 1–2.

74. Shalom, *The United States and the Philippines*, pp. 5–7, 12–13, 17–22, 28–9, 48; Cullather, *Illusions of Influence*, pp. 45–7, 34.

75. Collaboration, it should be noted, was a complex issue. Some nationalists collaborated with the Japanese to secure independence; others collaborated with the United States to expel the Japanese. Michael J. Houlahan, "Reflections on Patriotism and Collaboration: The Philippines during World War II," *Bulletin of the American Historical Collection*, 31 (2003), pp. 49–63, explores individual cases.

76. Hukbalahap is itself an acronym derived from Tagalog words referring to the People's Army against the Japanese.

77. Keith Thor Carlson, "Born Again of the People: Luis Taruc and Peasant Ideology in Philippine Revolutionary Politics," *Social History*, 41 (2008), pp. 417–58, provides a portrait of one of the leading figures, who died in 2005 at age 91.

78. The standard work is Benedict J. Kerkvliet, *The Huk Rebellion: A Study of Peasant Revolt in the Philippines* (Berkeley, 1977); Eduardo Lachica, *The Huks: Philippine Agrarian Society in Revolt* (New York, 1971), also remains valuable.

79. John A. Larkin, "Philippine History Reconsidered: A Socio-Economic Perspective," *American Historical Review*, 87 (1982), p. 626; also Norman G. Owen, *Prosperity without Progress: Manila Hemp and Material Life in the Philippines* (Berkeley, 1984), pp. 124, 156–7, 220–22, who shows that Kabikolan, a declining center of the abaca industry on Luzon, provided support for militant populism during and after World War II. Vina A. Lanzona, *Amazons of the Huk Rebellion: Gender, Sex, and Revolution in the Philippines* (Madison, 2009), ch. 3.

80. The best accounts are Shalom, *The United States and the Philippines*, pp. 7–9, 21–32, 55–57, 68–88; Cullather, *Illusions of Influence*, pp. 64, 70–73, 79–84, 89–91, 100–106, 184–5.

81. Acheson to Truman, 20 April 1950. Quoted in Cullather, *Illusions of Influence*, p. 83.

82. Dennis Merrill, "Shaping Third World Development: U.S. Foreign Aid and Supervision in the Philippines, 1948–53," *Journal of American-East Asian Relations*, 3 (1993), pp. 137–59.

83. Rexford Guy Tugwell, *The Stricken Land* (New York, 1946), p. 668.

84. Quoted in Perkins, *Denial of Empire*, p. 140. Tydings sponsored the bill that came to Congress but it failed to attract sufficient support.

85. Ibid., pp. 135–6.

86. James Dietz, *Economic History of Puerto Rico: Institutional Change and Capitalist Development* (Princeton, 1986), pp. 204–5. Dr. Dietz's pioneering study is indispensable to the study of Puerto Rico in the twentieth century.

87. Tugwell, *The Stricken Land*, chs. 31–33, for an account of his long-running wrestling match with Washington.

88. César J. Ayala and Rafael Bernabe, *Puerto Rico in the American Century: A History since 1898* (Chapel Hill, 2007), pp. 105–10, summarizes the literature on this controversial figure.

89. Ramón Bosque-Pérez and José Javier Colón, eds., *Puerto Rico under Colonial Rule: Political Persecution and the Quest for Human Rights* (Albany, 2006), make it clear that the word "benign" does not apply to U.S. rule in Puerto Rico. Also Joel A. Blanco-Rivera, "The Forbidden Files: Creation and Use of Surveillance Files against the Independence Movement in Puerto Rico," *American Archivist*, 68 (2005), pp. 297–311. The Gag Law was instantly unpopular but survived until 1957, when it was repealed.

90. On the character of Puerto Rican politics, see the subsection titled "Puerto Rico: 'Into History as a Picnic,'" in chapter 9 of this text, and "Puerto Rico: 'An Example of the Best Methods of Administering Our Insular Possessions,'" in chapter 12 of this text.

91. Gabriel Villaronga, *Towards a Discourse of Consent: Mass Mobilization and Colonial Politics in Puerto Rico, 1932–1948* (Westport, 2004); Carlos R. Zapata Oliveras, *De independentista a autonomista: la transformación del pensamiento político de Luis Muñoz Marín (1931–1949)* (San Juan, 2003), covers the transition in detail.

92. Perkins, *Denial of Empire*, pp. 149–59.

93. Ayala and Bernabe, *Puerto Rico in the American Century*, pp. 184–7.

94. Ibid., ch. 10.

95. David A Rezvani, "The Basis of Puerto Rico's Constitutional Status: Colony, Compact or Federacy?" *Political Science Quarterly*, 122 (2007), pp. 115–40.

96. Surenda Bhana, *The United States and the Development of the Puerto Rican Status Question, 1936–1968* (Lawrence, 1975).

97. Quoted in Perkins, *Empire in Denial*, p. 153. Charles A. Hallack (1900–86) was Majority Leader in 1946 and 1952, and Minority Leader in 1959–1964.

98. The most illuminating narrative account of this period remains Hugh Thomas, *Cuba: A History* (London, 1971; revised with a new Afterword, 2001), chs. 53–82. Historiographical surveys include Kate Quinn, "Cuban Historiography in the 1960s: Revisionists, Revolutionaries and the Nationalist Past," *Bulletin of Latin American Research*, 26 (2007), pp. 378–98; Antoni Kapcia, "Does Cuba Fit Yet or Is It Still Exceptional?" *Journal of Latin American Studies*, 40 (2008), pp. 627–50.

99. See the subsection titled "Cuba: 'That Infernal Little Republic,'" in chapter 12 of this text.

100. Juan C. Santamarina, "The Cuba Company and Eastern Cuba's Economic Development, 1900–1959," *Essays in Business & Economic History*, 19 (2001), pp. 83–4.

101. Kirby Smith and Hugo Llorens, "Renaissance and Decay: A Comparison of Socioeconomic Indicators in Pre-Castro and Current-Day Cuba," in Association for the Study of the Cuban Economy, *Cuba in Transition*, 8 (Miami, 1998), pp. 247–59; Mary Speck, "Democracy in Cuba: Principles and Practice, 1902–1952," in M. Font, ed., *Cuba Futures: Historical Perspectives* (Bildner Center for Western Hemisphere Studies, City University, New York, 2011), pp. 1–28, especially pp. 18–25. I am grateful to Dr. Speck for allowing me to see her important and original research before it was published. Antonio Santamaría García reaches a similar conclusion over a longer period: "El crecimiento económico de Cuba republicana (1902–1959): una revisión y nuevas estimaciones en perspectiva comparada (problación, inmigración golondrina, ingreso no azucarero y producto nacional bruto)," *Revista de Indias*, 60 (2000), pp. 505–45.

102. The period of PA rule, long neglected, has been rescued from obscurity by Charles D. Ameringer, *The Cuban Democratic Experience: The Auténtico Years, 1944–1952* (Gainesville, 2000), who shows that, for all their weaknesses, the politicians of the day were much more than pawns of Washington.

103. Vanni Pettinà, "A Preponderance of Politics: The *Auténtico* Governments and US-Cuban Economic Relations, 1945–1951," *Journal of Latin American Studies*, 46 (2014), pp. 723–53. I am grateful to Dr. Rory Miller for this reference.

104. Thomas, *Cuba*, chs. 57–9.

105. Brenden Marino Carbonell, "Cuban Capitalism: Batista's Three-Year Plan and a Nation Betrayed," in Font, *Cuba Futures*, pp. 29–52.

106. Morris H. Morley, *Imperial State and Revolution: The United States and Cuba, 1952–1986* (New York, 1987), contains valuable information on this theme but is handicapped by its assumptions about relations between the state and capitalism.

107. Thomas, *Cuba*, pp. 507–8.

108. Georges-Henri Abtour, "L'URSS et l'Amérique latine pendant la guerre froide: présence soviétique et action communiste dans un continent en révolutions, 1944–1964," *Revue d'Histoire d'Outre-Mers*, 95 (2007), pp. 9–22; Vanni Pettinà, "The Shadows of Cold War over Latin America: The U.S. Reaction to Fidel Castro's Nationalism, 1956–59," *Cold War History*, 11 (2011), pp. 317–39.

109. Much to the alarm of the British. See Geoffrey Warner, "Anglo-American Relations and the Cold War in 1950," *Diplomacy & Statecraft*, 22 (2011), pp. 44–60.
110. Scholarly interest in Bandung has long since faded. Jamie Mackie, *Bandung 1955: Non-Alignment and Afro-Asian Solidarity* (New York, 2005) is a short account; Seng Tan and Amitav Acharya, eds., *Bandung Revisited: The Legacy of the 1955 Asian-African Conference for International Order* (Singapore, 2009), provide an assessment of the outcomes.
111. Akira Iriye, *Global Community: The Role of International Organizations in the Making of the Contemporary World* (Berkeley, 2002).
112. Quoted in Martin Evans, "Whatever Happened to the Non-Aligned Movement?" *History Today*, 57 (2007), p. 49. Richard Nathaniel Wright (1908–1960), novelist, poet, and playwright, is noted especially for *Uncle Tom's Children* (New York, 1938), and *Black Boy* (New York, 1945). He published *The Colour Curtain: A Report on the Bandung Conference*, in 1956.
113. Evans, "Whatever Happened to the Non-Aligned Movement?" p. 49. On the long-standing links between African Americans and India, see Gerald Horne, *The End of Empire: African Americans and India* (Philadelphia, 2008).
114. Pang Yang Hue, "The Four Faces of Bandung: Detainees, Soldiers, Revolutionaries, and Statesmen," *Journal of Contemporary Asia*, 39 (2009), pp. 63–86.
115. Laura Elizabeth Wong takes an unusual approach to this familiar theme in "Relocating East and West: UNESCO's Major Project on the Mutual Appreciation of Eastern and Western Cultural Values," *Journal of World History*, 19 (2008), pp. 349–74.
116. For an example of the latter, see Mark Philip Bradley, "Making Revolutionary Nationalism: Vietnam, America, and the August Revolution of 1945," *Itinerario*, 23 (1999), pp. 23–51.
117. Dean J. Kotlowski, "With All Deliberate Delay: Kennedy, Johnson and School Desegregation," *Journal of Policy History*, 17 (2005), pp. 155–92.
118. Anderson, *Eyes Off the Prize*, chs. 4–5.
119. In the 1950s, Money had a cotton gin and a population of about 400; today it has sunk further into poverty and has less than 100 inhabitants. Ironically, the only money to venture into Money since Till's death occurred when the perpetrators, Roy Bryant and his half-brother J. W. Milum, sold their story to a magazine. Bryant and Milum had been found not guilty by an all-white jury and so were free to tell their version of the event. See William Bradford Huie, "The Shocking Story of Approved Killing in Mississippi," *Look*, January 1956.
120. Written by Abel Meeropol in 1939 and recorded most famously by Billie Holliday in that year (and subsequently).
121. Extract from "The Death of Emmett Till" (1962). Perhaps the most moving of the many poems on this subject is James A. Emanuel's "Emmett Till," which is written with memorable simplicity and precision.
122. 24 September 1957. Quoted in Dudziak, *Cold War Civil Rights*, p. 131; see also the confirmatory comments on pp. 132–6.
123. Cary Fraser, "Crossing the Color Line in Little Rock: the Eisenhower Administration and the Dilemma of Race for U.S. Foreign Policy," *Diplomatic History*, 24 (2000), pp. 233–64; Dudziak, *Cold War Civil Rights*, pp. 130–31.
124. Scott-Smith, "From Symbol of Division to Cold War Asset," pp. 266–9.
125. Dudziak, *Cold War Civil Rights*, ch. 6.
126. There is one scholarly study: Nancy J. Weiss, *Whitney M. Young, Jr., and the Struggle for Civil Rights* (Princeton, NJ, 1989).
127. Malcolm X was assassinated in 1965; Stokely Carmichael left the United States for Guinea in 1969; membership of the Black Panthers peaked in 1969 and dwindled rapidly in the 1970s.
128. Interestingly, Medicare and Medicaid were two of the measures that have survived subsequent attacks on governmental welfare provision.

129. Cobb, *Native Activism in Cold War America.*

130. Paul C. Rosier, *Serving their Country: American-Indian Politics and Patriotism in the Twentieth Century* (Cambridge, MA, 2009); Cobb, *Native Activism in Cold War America.*

131. Dean J. Kotlowski, "Alcatraz, Wounded Knee and Beyond: The Nixon and Ford Administrations Respond to Native American Protest," *Pacific Historical Review*, 27 (2003), pp. 201–27. Alcatraz (on an island in San Francisco Bay) had been taken over briefly by "urban Indians" in 1964 and 1969 before the large, extended occupation took place.

132. Peter Mathiessen, *In the Spirit of Crazy Horse: The FBI's War against the American Indian Movement* (New York, 1983, 1992). Aspects of this book became highly controversial. For a balanced assessment, see the review by Alan M. Dershowitz, the noted authority on constitutional law and civil rights, in the *New York Times*, 6 March 1983.

133. Thomas Clarkin, *Federal Indian Policy in the Kennedy and Johnson Administrations, 1961–1969* (Albuquerque, 2001), ch. 3.

134. For subsequent developments, see Roberta Ulrich, *American Indian Nations from Termination to Restoration, 1953–2006* (Lincoln, 2010).

135. Scott-Smith, "From Symbol of Division to Cold War Asset"; Bell, *Last Among Equals*, chs. 8–9, remains the fullest and best source. John S. Whitehead, *Completing the Union: Alaska, Hawai'i, and the Battle for Statehood* (Albuquerque, 2005), is also valuable, though the general interpretation (completing the colonial mission) has not found favor with specialists.

136. Bell, *Last Among Equals*, p. 267.

137. Scott-Smith, "From Symbol of Division to Cold War Asset," p. 260. Eisenhower had grasped the point with respect to Hawai'i but had not extended it to the United States. See also Gretchen Heefner, "'A Symbol of the New Frontier': Hawaiian Statehood, Anti-Colonialism, and Winning the Cold War,'" *Pacific Historical Review*, 74 (2005), pp. 545–74.

138. Trask, "Hawai'i and the United Nations."

139. Quoted in Scott-Smith, "From Symbol of Division to Cold War Asset," p. 260. Inouye (1924–2012) will no doubt attract the full biography his extraordinary life merits.

140. The revisionist interpretation summarized here borrows from Cullather, *Illusions of Influence*, ch. 4. Also Shalom, *The United States and the Philippines*, chs. 3–4.

141. Cullather, *Illusions of Influence*, p. 108.

142. *Time Magazine*, 23 November 1953, quoted in Shalom, *The United States and the Philippines*, p. 92. The term was later applied to Ferdinand Marcos. See James Hamilton-Paterson, *America's Boy: A Century of United States Colonialism in the Philippines* (New York, 1999).

143. Paul D. Hutchcroft and Joel Rocamora, "Strong Demands and Weak Institutions: The Origins and Evolution of the Democratic Deficit in the Philippines," *Journal of East Asian Studies*, 3 (2003), pp. 268, 270–74.

144. Benedict Anderson, "Cacique Democracy and the Philippines: Origins and Dreams," *New Left Review*, 169 (1988), pp. 3–33.

145. Cullather, *Illusions of Influence*, p. 98.

146. Ibid., chs. 4–5.

147. Ibid., p. 148.

148. Ibid., pp. 85–9, 92–5, 124, 145, 178.

149. For an admirable study of strong families in a weak state, see Alfred M. McCoy, ed., *An Anarchy of Families: State and Family in the Philippines* (Madison, 1993).

150. Cullather, *Illusions of Influence*, ch. 6.

151. As Cullather points out (ibid., p. 176), official U.S. grants and loans to the Philippines far exceeded private investment.

152. Carlo R. Zapata-Oliveras, "International Recognition of the Commonwealth of Puerto Rico," *Horizontes*, 32 (1988), pp. 71–95.

153. Dietz, *Economic History of Puerto Rico*, remains the authoritative source.

154. Ayala and Bernabe, *Puerto Rico in the American Century*, ch. 7.

155. Perkins, *Empire in Denial*, pp. 138–9, 149; Dietz, *Economic History of Puerto Rico*, pp. 143–58, 198–9, 213–14; Ismael Carcia-Colón, "Playing and Eating Democracy: The Case of Puerto Rico's Land Distribution Program, 1940s–1960s," *Centro Journal*, 18 (2006), pp. 166–89.

156. Tugwell, *The Stricken Land*, p. 547.

157. Ibid., p. 668.

158. José Teodoro Moscoso Mora (1910–1992).

159. Dietz, *Economic History of Puerto Rico*, pp. 213–17, 220–21. Alex W. Maldonado, *Teodoro Moscoso and Puerto Rico's Operation Bootstrap* (Gainesville, 1977), provides a fascinating firsthand account, if also one that is inclined to endow its subject with heroic qualities.

160. Dietz, *Economic History of Puerto Rico*, pp. 185–6, 207–17.

161. Dennis Merrill, "Negotiating Cold War Paradise: U.S. Tourism, Economic Planning, and Cultural Modernity in Twentieth-Century Puerto Rico," *Diplomatic History*, 25 (2001), pp. 179, 203.

162. Ayala and Barnabe, *Puerto Rico in the American Century*, p. 195; Dietz, *Economic History of Puerto Rico*, p. 255.

163. Perkins, *Empire in Denial*, p. 162.

164. Dietz, *Economic History of Puerto Rico*, pp. 286–8; Ayala and Bernabe, *Puerto Rico in the American Century*, p. 181, for dramatic increases in wages in manufacturing.

165. Perkins, *Denial of Empire*, p. 165; Ayala and Bernabe, *Puerto in the American Century*, pp. 202–4.

166. Merrill, "Negotiating Cold War Paradise," pp. 201–2.

167. W. W. Rostow, *The Stages of Growth: A Non-Communist Manifesto* (Cambridge, 1960).

168. Ayala and Bernabe, *Puerto Rico in the American Century*, pp. 192–7.

169. Guy Rexford Tugwell, *The Art of Politics as Practiced by Three Great Americans: Franklin Delano Roosevelt, Luis Muñoz Marín, and Fiorello H. La Guardia* (New York, 1958), p. 38.

170. See especially Julia Sweig, *Inside the Cuban Revolution: Fidel Castro and the Urban Underground* (Cambridge, MA, 2002).

171. Jorge Renato Ibarra Guitart, *El Fracaso de los moderados en Cuba: Las alternativas reformistas de 1957-1958* (Havana, 2000).

172. There is a vast literature on the Revolution. The best narrative account remains Thomas, *Cuba*, chs. 60–78. See also Thomas G. Patterson, *Contesting Castro: The United States and the Triumph of the Cuban Revolution* (Oxford, 1994); Sweig, *Inside the Cuban Revolution*.

173. Biographies in English include: Robert Quirk, *Fidel Castro* (New York, 1993); Leycester Coltman, *The Real Fidel Castro* (New York, 2003); Thomas M. Leonard, *Fidel Castro: A Biography* (Westport, 2004); Volka Skierka, *Fidel Castro: A Biography* (Cambridge, 2006).

174. John Paul Rathbone, *The Sugar King of Havana: The Rise and Fall of Julio Lobo, Cuba's Last Tycoon* (New York, 2010).

175. Thomas, *Cuba*, pp. 484–5, 551–2, 585, 600, 619, 633, and appendixes 3 and 4. The price data in appendix 4 appear to be in current dollars.

176. Ibid.

177. Jorge I. Dominguez, "Culture: Is It the Key to the Troubles in U.S.-Cuban Relations?" *Diplomatic History*, 25 (2001), pp. 511–16.

178. For example, Patterson, *Contesting Castro*. For a reaffirmation of the importance of nationalism, see Philip Brenner, "The Power of Metaphor: Explaining U.S. Policy Toward Cuba," *Diplomatic History*, 34 (2010), p. 444.

179. What follows draws on Alan Dye and Richard Sicotte's important and ingenious study, "The U.S. Sugar Program and the Cuban Revolution," *Journal of Economic History*, 64 (2004), pp. 673–704.

180. Morley, *Imperial State and Revolution*.

181. Luis Martinez-Fernandez, "Sugar and Revolution, 1952–2002," in Font, *Cuba Futures*, pp. 75–99.

182. Quoted in Alan Dye and Richard Sicotte, "U.S-Cuban Trade Co-operation and Its Unraveling," *Business & Economic History*, 28 (1999), p. 28.

183. Ibid., pp. 698–9.

184. Lars Schoultz, *That Infernal Little Cuban Republic: The United States and the Cuban Revolution* (Chapel Hill, 2009), contains a good deal of information on this and allied matters.

185. On the evolution of the military from being a "modernizing elite" to becoming another special interest, see Louis A. Pérez, Jr., *Army Politics in Cuba, 1898–1958* (Pittsburgh, 1976), pp. 168–73.

186. Louis A. Pérez, Jr., *Cuba in the American Imagination: Metaphor and the Imperial Ethos* (Chapel Hill, 2008), is the definitive treatment of this subject.

187. Patterson, *Contesting Castro*, pp. 4–7.

188. On the persistence of these views, even after the Revolution, see Matt Jacobs, "Meeting the Neighbors: Fidel Castro's April 1959 Trip to the United States," in Font, *Cuba Futures*, pp. 215–37.

189. The quotation is from Dominguez, "Culture," p. 516.

190. Maurer, *The Empire Trap*, pp. 317–27, has been particularly helpful in forming this paragraph, as has Dr. Maurer himself, who responded with exceptional generosity to my appeal for guidance on the intricacies of the crisis in U.S.-Cuban relations. Vanni Pettinà, *Cuba y Estados Unidos (1933–1959). Del compromiso nacionalista al conflicto* (Madrid, 2011), pp. 211–71, underlines the incompetence that marked U.S. policy at this time as well as the failings of Cuba's postwar governments.

191. Abtour, "L'URSS et l'Amérique latine pendant la guerre froide"; Pettinà, "The Shadows of Cold War over Latin America"; Pettinà, *Cuba y Estados Unidos (1933–1959)*.

192. Jacobs, "Meeting the Neighbors," pp. 219–20.

193. Geoffrey Warner, "Eisenhower and Castro: U.S.-Cuban Relations, 1958–60," *International Affairs*, 75 (1999), pp. 803–17.

194. The U.S. pressed its European allies to cooperate in isolating Cuba. The British dodged and hedged but eventually compromised by halting sales of arms while continuing to trade in other goods. See Daniel Rubiera Zim, "Straining the Special Relationship: British and U.S. Policies Toward the Cuban Revolution, 1959–1961," *Cuban Studies*, 33 (2002), pp. 71–94; Chris Hull, "Our Arms in Havana: British Military Sales to Batista and Castro, 1958–59," *Diplomacy & Statecraft*, 18 (2007), pp. 593–616; Hull, "Parallel Spheres: Anglo-American Cooperation over Cuba, 1959–61," *Cold War History*, 12 (2012), pp. 51–68.

195. The alliance with the Soviet Union had consequences that extended far beyond the island itself. Cuba's revolution was regarded as a beacon throughout Latin America; Castro's foreign policy carried the ideal of liberation into Africa. See Piero Gleijeses, "Cuba and the Cold War, 1950–1980," in Leffler and Westad, *Cambridge History of the Cold War*, 2, ch. 16.

196. President Dwight D. Eisenhower, "State of the Union Message to Congress," 5 January 1956. Quoted in Scott-Smith, "From Symbol of Division to Cold War Asset," p. 259.

197. For an appeal for unification see A. G. Hopkins, "Rethinking Decolonization," *Past & Present*, 200 (2008), pp. 211–47.

198. Marilyn Lake and Henry Reynolds, *Drawing the Colour Line: White Men's Countries and the International Challenge of Racial Equality* (Cambridge, 2008).

199. For admirable summaries of different perspectives, see Anders Stephanson, "Cold War Degree Zero," and Odd Arne Westad, "Exploring the Histories of the Cold War: A Pluralist Approach," both in Joel Isaac and Duncan Bell, eds., *Uncertain Empire: American History and the Ideology of the Cold War* (New York, 2012), chs. 1 and 2.

200. Quoted in Evans, "Whatever Happened to the Non-Aligned Movement?" p. 49.

201. Ronald Robinson, "The Moral Disarmament of African Empire, 1919–1947," *Journal of Imperial and Commonwealth History*, 8 (1979), pp. 86–104; Stuart Ward, "The European Provenance of Decolonization," *Past & Present*, 230 (2016), pp. 227–60, traces the intellectual origins of the term to the 1930s.

202. Peter Clegg, "Independence Movements in the Caribbean: Withering on the Vine?" *Commonwealth & Comparative Politics*, 50 (2012), pp. 422–38.

203. John Quincy Adams, "Oration," 4 July 1793, p. 9, University of Missouri Special Collections.

CHAPTER 15: DOMINANCE AND DECLINE IN THE POSTCOLONIAL AGE

1. Oscar Wilde, "The Critic as Artist," in Wilde, *Intentions* (London, 1891; 1913), p. 129.

2. Some readers might find it helpful to relate this summary to the statement of intent in chapter 1. A fuller account of these phases, though with reference to Britain, appears in P. J. Cain and A. G. Hopkins, *British Imperialism, 1688–2015* (London, 3rd ed. 2016), pp. 706–17.

3. The global character of Euro-settlement is well covered by John C. Weaver, *The Great Land Rush and the Making of the Modern World, 1650–1900* (Montreal and Kingston, 2003); and James Belich, *Replenishing the Earth: The Settler Revolution and the Rise of the Anglo-World, 1783–1939* (Oxford, 2009).

4. As noted in chapter 1 (n. 111), the influence of postmodernism has led to the use of "postcolonial" to describe the period after the beginning of colonialism. This conflation merges two different and established phases: colonial (the period of formal colonial rule) and postcolonial (the period after the termination of formal rule). The traditional use is followed here.

5. A. G. Hopkins, "Macmillan's Audit of Empire, 1957," in Peter Clarke and Clive Trebilcock, eds., *Understanding Decline: Perceptions and Realities; Essays in Honour of Barry Supple* (Cambridge, 1997), pp. 234–60.

6. See, for example, Gunnar Myrdal's influential (and now largely unread) study, *Asian Drama: An Inquiry into the Poverty of Nations* (3 vols.; London, 1968).

7. See particularly A.W.B. Simpson, *Human Rights and the End of Empire: Britain and the Genesis of the European Convention* (Oxford, 2001); Roland Burke, *Decolonisation and the Evolution of International Human Rights* (Philadelphia, 2010); Rosemary Foot, "The Cold War and Human Rights," in Melvyn Leffler and Odd Arne Westad, eds., *Cambridge History of the Cold War*, 1 (Cambridge, 2010), ch. 21; Barbara Keys and Roland Burke, "Human Rights," in Richard Immerman and Petra Goedde, eds., *The Oxford Handbook of the Cold War* (Oxford, 2013), ch. 28; Samuel Moyne, *The Last Utopia: Human Rights in History* (Cambridge, MA, 2010). Specialists will be aware that the position taken here is more in accord with Burke than with Moyne.

8. Akira Iriye, Petra Goedde, and William I. Hitchcock, eds., *The Human Rights Revolution: An International History* (Oxford, 2012), provides full details. See also, Or Rosenboim, *The Emergence of Globalism: Visions of World Order in Britain and the United States, 1939–1950* (Princeton, NJ, 2017).

9. Paul Kennedy, *The Rise and Fall of the Great Powers: Economic Change and Military Conflict from 1500 to 2000* (New York, 1987), gave currency to the idea, which is the subject of continuing assessments.

10. A. G. Hopkins, "Rethinking Decolonisation," *Past & Present*, 200 (2008), pp. 211–47; Hopkins, "Globalisation and Decolonisation," *Journal of Imperial & Commonwealth History*, 45 (2017), pp. 729–45; and the relevant chapters in Phillip Buckner, ed., *Canada and the British Empire* (Oxford, 2008); and Deryck Schreuder and Stuart Ward, eds., *Australia's Empire* (Oxford, 2008).

11. See chapter 14 of this text. For other ways of dissecting the subject, see Joel Isaac and Duncan Bell, eds., *Uncertain Empire: American History and the Idea of the Cold War* (New York, 2012).

12. "Integration and Growth of the World Economy in Historical Perspective," *American Economic Review*, 54 (1964), pp. 1–22, at p. 3. Haberler (1900–1995) was a noted Austrian American economist specializing in international trade and one of a generation of economists (including W. A. Lewis and W. W. Rostow) who could take an informed long view because he had also been trained in historical studies.

13. Data are drawn mainly from Angus Maddison, *The World Economy*, 2 vols. (Paris, 2006); Alfred E. Eckes and Thomas W. Zeiler, *Globalization and the American Century* (Cambridge, 2003); and Michael Graff, A. G. Kenwood, and A. L. Lougheed, *Growth of the International Economy, 1820–2015* (Abingdon, Oxon, 5th ed. 2014). I am grateful to Professor Graff for clarifying some questions about the database.

14. Graff et al., *Growth of the International Economy*, pp. 279–81.

15. Ibid., p. 279.

16. This is a complex and controversial subject. A full analysis would need to treat "colonial" exports on a case-by-case basis and also include the income and factoral terms of trade. For a recent discussion of an old debate see David Colman, "Agriculture's Terms of Trade: Issues and Implications," *Agricultural Economics*, 41 (2010), pp. 1–15.

17. The BRICS: Brazil, Russia, India, China, and South Africa (which was added in 2010). The group was formed in 2001 and held its first summit in 2009.

18. The pioneering account is Akira Iriye, *Global Community: The Role of International Organizations in the Making of the Contemporary World* (Berkeley, 2002).

19. Elaine Bernard, "What's the Matter with NAFTA?" *Radical America*, 25 (1994), pp. 19–31.

20. Examples of the reassertion of the local are given in A. G. Hopkins, ed., *Global History: Interactions between the Universal and the Local* (Basingstoke, 2006).

21. See the discussion in Robert J. Holton, *Globalisation and the Nation-State* (2nd ed. Basingstoke, 2011).

22. The EU allowed the former British and French colonies a period of transition before applying protective tariffs.

23. Robert Cooper, "The Post-Modern State," in Mark Leonard, ed., *Reordering the World: The Long-Term Implications of September 11th* (London, 2002), ch. 2; Jeanne Morefield, *Empires without Imperialism: Anglo-American Decline and the Politics of Deflection* (Oxford, 2014) explores the intellectual strategies for making illiberal actions appear as liberal policies.

24. Louise Fawcett and Yezid Sayigh, eds., *The Third World Beyond the Cold War: Continuity and Change* (Oxford, 1999), take a different view, though diversification is one of the main themes of their book.

25. Paul Collier, *The Bottom Billion: Why the Poorest Countries Are Failing and What Can Be Done about It* (Oxford, 2006). Collier estimates that about 70 percent of the world's poorest people live in Africa.

26. For the persistence of the "classic" exchanges on the eve of World War II, see Graff et al., *Growth of the International Economy*, pp. 197–204.

27. Negotiations over the possible closure of the plant were handled by Sajid Javid, the Secretary of State for Business, Conservative M.P., and son of a Pakistani bus driver. For more on this topic, see the characteristically incisive essay by Ambrose Evans-Pritchard, "Britain Sacrifices Steel Industry to Curry Favour with China," *Telegraph*, March 31, 2016.

28. Roger Hart, "Universals of Yesteryear: Hegel's Modernity in an Age of Globalization," in Hopkins, *Global History*, ch. 3.

29. See chapter 10 of this text. For the view that the American "Century" will not meet the full qualification, see Andrew J. Bacevich, ed., *The Short American Century: A Postmortem* (Cambridge, MA, 2012).

30. Modernization theory is discussed in chapter 11 of this text.

31. Their complexity is also an obstacle to easy generalization: the debt crisis of the 1980s and policies of structural adjustment had consequences that varied globally; transnational corporations acquired commitments to the host country by participating in manufacturing and creating what has been termed "new dependency."

32. John A. Thomson, *A Sense of Power: The Roots of America's Global Role* (Ithaca, 2015), ch. 6, provides a judicious account of U.S. motives in engaging with Europe after 1945.

33. Christopher J. Sandars, *America's Overseas Garrisons: The Leasehold Empire* (Oxford, 2000), p. 5, estimates that the United States built 433 bases throughout the world during World War II, and retained most of them during the Cold War. Kent E. Calder, *Embattled Garrisons: Comparative Base Politics and American Globalism* (Princeton, 2007), argues that the bases were stabilizing influences.

34. Alan S. Milward, *The European Rescue of the Nation State* (Berkeley and Los Angeles, 1992).

35. As Chiarella Esposito, *America's Feeble Weapon: Funding the Marshall Plan in France and Italy, 1948–1950* (Westport, 1994), shows in the case of the so-called counterpart funds. Diane Kunz's admirable study examines the complementary relationship between economic and political aspects of U.S. strategy in *Butter and Guns: America's Cold War Economic Diplomacy* (New York, 1997).

36. Alan Dobson, "The Special Relationship and European Integration," *Diplomacy & Statecraft*, 2 (1991), pp. 79–102.

37. The British Ambassador to South Vietnam, 1966. Quoted in Wm. Roger Louis, "The Dissolution of the British Empire in the Era of Vietnam," *American Historical Review*, 107 (2002), p. 19. On the episode as a whole, see Jonathan Colman, *A "Special Relationship"? Harold Wilson, Lyndon B. Johnson and Anglo-American Relations "at the Summit," 1964–68* (Manchester, 2004).

38. Earl F. Ziemke, *The U.S. Army in the Occupation of Germany, 1944–1946* (Washington, DC, 1975; 1990), provides an exhaustive account.

39. Frances M. B. Lynch, *France and the International Economy: From Vichy to the Treaty of Rome* (London, 1997); William I. Hitchcock, *France Restored: Cold War Diplomacy and the Quest for Leadership in Europe, 1944–1954* (Chapel Hill, 1998).

40. Press conference, 15 May 1962. Quoted in Daniel J. Mahoney, *De Gaulle, Statesmanship, Grandeur, and Modern Democracy* (New Brunswick, 1996; 2000), p. 133. In case some readers may have forgotten, Volupük was an international language created in 1879–1880 by a German priest in response to divine inspiration. It was overtaken by Esperanto in the twentieth century.

41. Frances M. B. Lynch, "Resolving the Paradox of the Monnet Plan: National and International Planning in French Reconstruction," *Economic History Review*, 37 (1984), pp. 229–43. Bronson Long, *No Easy Occupation: French Control of the German Saar, 1944–1957* (New York, 2015).

42. James Ellison, "Separated by the Atlantic: The British and de Gaulle, 1958–1967," *Diplomacy & Statecraft*, 17 (2006), pp. 853–70. General de Gaulle's gloriously patronizing speech, "French President Charles de Gaulle's Veto on British Membership of the EEC," is available online at http://www.isn.ethz.ch/Digital-library/Publications/Detail/?lang=en&id=125401. Readers who are unfamiliar with the intricacies attending the evolution of European integration after 1945 need know only that the EEC was the precursor of the present EU.

43. Angela Romano, "Untying Cold War Knots: The EEC and Eastern Europe in the Long 1970s," *Cold War History*, 14 (2014), pp. 153–73.

44. See especially Alan S. Milward, *The Reconstruction of Western Europe, 1945–1951* (Berkeley, 1984). For a reassertion of the traditional view, see John Killick, *The United States and European Reconstruction, 1945–1960* (Edinburgh, 1997). In the case of Britain, it has been argued that aid was used to support the empire rather than to modernize the

economy. See Correlli Barnett, *The Audit of War: The Illusion and Reality of Britain as a Great Nation* (London, 1986; 2001); Barnett, *The Lost Victory: British Dreams, British Realities, 1945–1950* (London, 1995).

45. Commentators in the United States were particularly concerned that Britain was spending aid on "socialist experiments," notably the National Health Service. The dispute that followed contributed to Britain's decision to cancel Marshall Aid in 1951. Daniel M. Fox, "The Administration of the Marshall Plan and British Health Policy," *Journal of Policy History*, 16 (2004), pp. 191–211.

46. Douglas A. Irwin, "The GATT's Contribution to Economic Recovery in Post-War Western Europe," in Barry Eichengreen, ed., *Europe's Post-War Recovery* (Cambridge, 1995), ch. 5.

47. Piers Ludlow, "The Emergence of a Commercial Heavyweight: The Kennedy Round Negotiations and the European Community of the 1960s," *Diplomacy and Statecraft*, 18 (2007), pp. 351–687, argues that the negotiations resulted from pressure exerted by the EEC on the United States; Francine McKenzie, "The GATT-EEC Collision: The Challenge of Regional Trade Blocs to the General Agreement on Tariffs and Trade, 1950–67," *International History Review*, 32 (2010), pp. 229–52.

48. Graf et al., *Growth of the International Economy*, pp. 276–80, tables 20.1–20.5.

49. Ibid., p. 281, table 20.7.

50. Lucia Coppolaro, "U.S. Policy on European Integration during the GATT Kennedy Round Negotiations (1963–67): The Last Hurrah of America's Europeanists," *International History Review*, 33 (2011), pp. 409–29.

51. In a speech given on 23 April 1973. Thomas Robb, "Henry Kissinger, Great Britain, and the 'Year of Europe': The Tangled Skein," *Contemporary British History*, 24 (2010), pp. 297–318.

52. Keith Hamilton, "Britain, France, and America's Year of Europe, 1973," *Diplomacy & Statecraft*, 17 (2006), pp. 871–95.

53. Colin Crouch, "Models of Capitalism," *New Political Economy*, 10 (2005), pp. 439–56, provides a valuable survey. See, more generally, Peter A. Hall and David Soskice, eds., *Varieties of Capitalism: The Institutional Foundations of Comparative Advantage* (London, 2000).

54. Michael H. Hunt and Steven I. Levine, *Arc of Empire: America's Wars in Asia from the Philippines to Vietnam* (Chapel Hill, 2012), makes a unifying theme of four wars fought to advance U.S. interests in the region.

55. The fullest and most accessible account is John W. Dower, *Embracing Defeat: Japan in the Wake of World War II* (New York, 1999).

56. Masako Shibata, *Japan and Germany under the U.S. Occupation: A Comparative Analysis of Post-War Education Reform* (Lanham, 2005), shows that Japan welcomed the new program because it was a means of gaining access to the Western world, whereas Germany believed that its system of education had little to learn from the United States.

57. Aaron Forsberg, *America and the Japanese Miracle: The Cold War Context of Japan's Postwar Economic Revival, 1950–1960* (Chapel Hill, 2000), assigns much of the credit to U.S. policy.

58. Yoneyuki Sugita, *Pitfall or Panacea: The Irony of US Power in Occupied Japan, 1945–1952* (London, 2003).

59. R. Taggart Murphy, *Japan and the Shackles of the Past* (New York, 2015), argues that quasi-feudal relations continue to characterize Japan's political economy.

60. Tim Weiner, "C.I.A. Spent Millions to Support Japanese Right in 50s and 60s," *New York Times*, October 9, 1994.

61. Sayuri Shimizu, *Creating People of Plenty: The United States and Japan's Economic Alternatives, 1950–1960* (Kent, 2001).

62. Gregg A. Brazinski, *Nation-Building in South Korea: Koreans, Americans, and the Making of Democracy* (Chapel Hill, 2009).

63. Bruce Cumings, *Korea's Place in the Sun, A Modern History* (New York, 1997).

64. Lyong Choi, "The First Nuclear Crisis in the Korean Peninsula, 1975–76," *Cold War History*, 14 (2014), pp. 71–90; Jooyoung Lee, "Forming a Democratic Society: South Korean Responses to U.S. Democracy Promotion, 1953–1960," *Diplomatic History*, 39 (2015), pp. 844–75.

65. Kim Chong Min, "The United States' Economic Disengagement Policy and Korea's Industrial Transformation: Implications of the Textile Disputes (1969–1971) for the Quasi Alliance in East Asia," *Seoul Journal of Korean Studies*, 27 (2014), pp. 115–36.

66. Cumings, *Korea's Place in the Sun*, ch. 6.

67. Robert McMahon, *Colonialism and the Cold War: The United States and the Struggle for Indonesian Independence, 1945–49* (Ithaca, 1981).

68. Noel Maurer, *The Empire Trap: The Rise and Fall of U.S. Intervention to Protect American Property Overseas, 1893–2013* (Princeton, NJ, 2013), pp. 338–43.

69. H. W. Brands, "The Limits of Manipulation," *Journal of American History*, 76 (1989), pp. 785–808; David Easter, "'Keep the Indonesian Pot Boiling': Western Covert Intervention in Indonesia, October 1965–March 1966," *Cold War History*, 5 (2005), pp. 55–73; John Roosa, *Pretext for Mass Murder: The September 30th Movement and Suharto's Coup d'Etat in Indonesia* (Madison, 2006). Sukarno remained the nominal head of state until 1967.

70. Bradley R. Simpson's outstanding study, *Economists with Guns: Authoritarian Development and U.S.-Indonesian Relations, 1960–1968* (Stanford, 2008), traces the process and its endorsement by academics.

71. Mark Atwood Lawrence, *The Vietnam War: A Concise International History* (New York, 2008), provides a lucid guide to a vast literature. A fuller account, which includes the author's expertise on Indonesia, is Robert McMahon, *The Limits of Power: The United States and Southeast Asia Since World War II* (New York, 1999).

72. Alan P. Dobson and Steve Marsh, *U.S. Foreign Policy since 1945* (London, 2nd ed., 2007), pp. 97, 104; available online at www.veteranshour.com/vietnam_war_statistics.htm

73. Andrew Preston, "Monsters Everywhere: A Genealogy of National Security," *Diplomatic History*, 38 (2014), pp. 477–500.

74. As the C.I.A.'s "secret history" has confirmed. See James Risen, "Secrets of History: The C.I.A. in Iran," *New York Times*, 16 April 2000; Tim Walker, "The Truth about the CIA and Iran," *Independent*, August 20, 2013.

75. Michael B. Stoff, *Oil, War, and American Security: The Search for a National Policy on Foreign Oil, 1941–1947* (New Haven, 1980), traces the shift from government to private interests as tools of policy.

76. Robert Vitalis, *America's Kingdom: Mythmaking on the Saudi Oil Frontier* (Stanford, 2007). Aramco was the largest U.S. company operating abroad in the 1950s.

77. A perspective revealed by Roham Alvandi, *Nixon, Kissinger, and the Shah: The United States and Iran in the Cold War* (New York, 2014).

78. Andrew Scott Cooper, *The Oil Kings: How the U.S., Iran and Saudi Arabia Changed the Balance of Power in the Middle East* (New York, 2011).

79. Tore T. Petersen, *Richard Nixon, Great Britain and the Anglo-American Alignment in the Persian Gulf and Arabian Peninsula: Making Allies out of Clients* (Brighton, Sussex, 2008), pp. 31, 43, argues a stronger case that Nixon and Kissinger helped to engineer the price rise.

80. Cooper, *The Oil Kings*, chs. 10–12.

81. Chalmers Johnson, "Blowback," *National Interest*, October 15, 2001. Johnson, *Blowback: The Costs and Consequences of American Empire* (London, 2000; 2002). These remarkably prescient studies were neglected in the United States when they first appeared, and were taken up only after 9/11.

82. For one example, see Sami E. Baroudi, "Countering U.S. Hegemony: The Discourse of Salim al-Hoss and other Arab Intellectuals," *Middle Eastern Studies*, 44 (2008), pp. 105–29.

83. Petersen, *Richard Nixon*, pp. 43, 93.

84. Simon C. Smith, *Ending Empire in the Middle East: Britain, the United States and Post-War Decolonization, 1945–73* (London, 2012); Helene von Bismarck, *British Policy in the Persian Gulf, 1961–1968* (Basingstoke, Hants, 2013), emphasizes Britain's commitment down to 1968, when the government decided that it would end its military presence east of Suez in 1971. Spencer Mawby, *British Policy in Aden and the Protectorates, 1955–67: Last Outpost of a Middle East Empire* (London, 2015), shows how Britain's determination to hold Aden ultimately helped radicals to replace moderates in the region.

85. Smith, *Ending Empire*. Previous differences between the two powers in the region are well covered by Steven G. Galpern, *Money, Oil, and Empire in the Middle East: Sterling and Post-war Imperialism, 1944–1971* (New York, 2009).

86. Elizabeth Schmidt, *Foreign Intervention in Africa: From the Cold War to the War on Terror* (Cambridge, 2013), provides an overview. James P. Hubbard presents a full but conventional account from the perspective of international diplomacy: *The United States and the End of the British Empire in Africa, 1941–1968* (Jefferson, 2010).

87. Stephen R Weissman, "An Extraordinary Rendition," *Intelligence & National Security*, 25 (2010), pp. 198–222; Weissman, "What Really Happened in the Congo: The C.I.A., the Murder of Lumumba, and the Rise of Mobutu," *Foreign Affairs*, 93 (2014), pp. 14–24. Britain's MI6 assisted the CIA.

88. Irwin Wall, *France, the United States and the Algerian War* (Berkeley, 2001); Wall, "France in the Cold War," *Journal of European Studies*, 38 (2008), pp. 121–39. U.S. policy toward Tunisia was similar, but conditions there favored a swifter move to independence (1956). It was far harder for governments in Paris to give up Algeria, which had many more French settlers and was constitutionally part of France. See Roy Ikeda, *The Imperialism of French Decolonisation* (Cambridge, 2015), pp. 209–19.

89. Matthew Connelly, *A Diplomatic Revolution: Algeria's Fight for Independence and the Origins of the Post-Cold War Era* (Oxford, 2002), provides an Algerian viewpoint that emphasizes the importance of the moral case for ending colonial rule.

90. Witney W. Schneiderman, *Engaging Africa: Washington and the Fall of Portugal's Colonial Empire* (New York, 2004).

91. Lidwien Kapteijns, "Test-Firing the 'New World Order' in Somalia: The US/UN Military Humanitarian Intervention of 1992–1995," *Journal of Genocide Research*, 15 (2013), pp. 412–42. Intervention arose after the end of the Cold War, but followed from events in the 1980s that were part of it.

92. David N. Gibb, "Political Parties and International Relations: The United States and the Decolonization of Sub-Saharan Africa," *International History Review*, 17 (1995), pp. 306–27.

93. John Kent, "United States' Reaction to Empire, Colonialism, and Cold War in Black Africa," *Journal of Imperial & Commonwealth History*, 33 (2005), pp. 195–220.

94. Tony Chafer, "Chirac and 'La Françafrique': No Longer a Family Affair," *Modern & Contemporary France*, 13 (2005), pp. 7–23.

95. Gordon Martel, "Decolonization after Suez: Retreat or Rationalisation?" *Australian Journal of Politics & History*, 46 (2000), pp. 403–17. For a case study, see L. J. Butler, "Britain, the United States, and the Demise of the Central African Federation, 1959–63," *Journal of Imperial & Commonwealth History*, 28 (2000), pp. 131–51.

96. Robin Renwick, Britain's Ambassador to South Africa at the time, offers a fascinating account of Margaret Thatcher's complex thinking in *The End of Apartheid: Diary of a Revolution* (London, 2015).

97. Max Paul Friedman, "Retiring the Puppets, Bringing Latin America Back In: Recent Scholarship on United States–Latin American Relations," *Diplomatic History*, 27 (2003), pp. 621–36, reveals the limits of approaches that cast one party as the "hegemon" and the other as the "victim."

98. Serge Ricard, "The Roosevelt Corollary," *Presidential Studies Quarterly*, 36 (2006), pp. 17–26.

99. Greg Grandin, *Empire's Workshop: Latin America, the United States and the Rise of New Imperialism* (New York, 2006); Greg Grandin and Gilbert M. Joseph, eds., *A Century of Revolution: Insurgent and Counter-Insurgent Violence during Latin America's Long Cold War* (Durham, 2010).

100. On this episode and its consequences, see Peter Winn, "The Furies of the Andes: Violence and Terror in the Chilean Revolution and Counterrevolution," in Grandin and Gilbert, *A Century of Revolution*, pp. 239–75.

101. Jeffrey Taffet, *Foreign Aid as Foreign Policy: The Alliance for Progress in Latin America* (New York, 2007).

102. Brian Loveman, ed., *Addicted to Failure: U.S. Security Policy in Latin America and the Andean Region* (Lanham, 2006). Mark T. Hove, "The Arbenz Factor: Salvador Allende, U.S.-Chilean Relations, and the 1954 U.S. Intervention in Guatemala," *Diplomatic History*, 31 (2007), pp. 623–63, shows how intervention in Guatemala provoked reactions elsewhere, notably in Chile.

103. Peter M. Sanchez, "Bringing the International Back In: U.S. Hegemonic Maintenance and Latin America's Democratic Breakdown in the 1960s and 1970s," *International Politics*, 40 (2003), pp. 223–47. For two of many examples, see William Michael Schmidli, *The Fate of Freedom Elsewhere: Human Rights and U.S. Cold War Policy Toward Argentina* (Ithaca, 2013); Thomas, C. Field, Jr., *From Development to Dictatorship: Bolivia and the Alliance for Progress in the Kennedy Era* (Ithaca, 2014).

104. Greg Grandin, "Your Americanism and Mine: Americanism and Anti-Americanism in the Americas," *American Historical Review*, 111 (2006), pp. 1042–66; Kathryn Sikkink, *Mixed Signals: U.S. Human Rights Policy and Latin America* (Ithaca, 2004); Alan P. Dobson, "The Dangers of U.S. Interventionism," *Review of International Studies*, 28 (2002), pp. 577–87, compares Panama and Bosnia.

105. Carlos M. Vilas, "Turning to the Left? Understanding Some Unexpected Events in Latin America," *Journal of Diplomacy & International Relations*, 9 (2008), pp. 115–28.

106. Peter Hakim, "Is Washington Losing Latin America?' *Foreign Affairs*, 85 (2006), pp. 39–53.

107. Sherrie L. Baver, "Environmental Justice and the Cleanup of Vieques," *Centro Journal*, 18 (2006), pp. 90–107 (and other articles on this subject in vol. 18, issue 1).

108. The base was reopened for use by the U.S. Air Force in 2012, when anxiety about China's ambitions prompted Washington to revise its assessment of the strategic value of its former Pacific colony.

109. Noelani Goodyear-Ka'Opua, Ikaika Hussey, and Kahunawaika'ala Wright, eds., *A Nation Rising: Hawaiian Movements for Life, Land, and Sovereignty* (Durham, 2014).

110. Anne Feder Lee, "Hawaiian Sovereignty," *Publius*, 27 (1997), pp. 167–86.

111. Most of Hawai'i's sugar plantations had ceased operations by 1995. See Carol A. MacLennan, *Sovereign Sugar: Industry and Environment in Hawai'i* (Honolulu, 2014), pp. 275–82.

112. Dennis Merrill, *Negotiating Paradise: U.S. Tourism and Empire in Twentieth-Century Latin America* (Chapel Hill, 2009).

113. Zachary Abuza, "The Moro Liberation Front at 20: State of the Revolution," *Studies in Conflict & Terrorism*, 28 (2005), pp. 453–79. The Moro National Liberation Front (1972) made peace with the Philippine government in 1996. A splinter group, the Moro Islamic Liberation Front (1984), continued the struggle until 2012, when a negotiated peace was agreed. Tom McKenna, "Saints, Scholars and the Idealized Past in Philippine Muslim Separatism," *Pacific Review*, 15 (2002), pp. 539–53, traces the ideological roots of the movement.

114. Michael S. Billig, *Barons, Brokers, and Buyers: The Institutions and Cultures of Philippine Sugar* (Honolulu, 2003), chs. 3–6, provides a full assessment of changes in the sugar industry.

115. Donald W. Bray and Marjorie Woodford, "The Cuban Revolution and World Change," *Latin American Perspectives*, 36 (2009), pp. 16–30; John Foran, "Theorizing the Cuban Revolution," *American Perspectives*, 36 (2009), pp. 16–30.

116. President Trump has announced that he intends to halt the initiative President Obama took to improve relations between the two countries. See Martina Kunovic, "Five Things You Need to Know about Trump's Cuba Policy," *Washington Post*, June 22, 2017.

117. Heather Gillers and Nick Timiraos, "Puerto Rico Defaults on Constitutionally Guaranteed Debt," *Wall Street Journal*, July 1, 2016. Ironically, emigration, which had once benefited the economy, had reached the point where it contributed to the problem. For subsequent developments, see Tatiana Darie, "Puerto Rico's New Governor Takes Over as Debt Crisis Reaches Climax," *Bloomberg News*, January 3, 2017; John Dizard, "Hedge Funds Slug It Out Over Puerto Rico, *Financial Times*, January 13, 2017; Andrew Scurria, "Puerto Rico Creditors Open Checkbooks in Debt Negotiations," *Wall Street Journal*, January 23, 2017.

118. Frances Stonor-Saunders, *Who Paid the Piper: The CIA and the Cultural Cold War* (London, 1999); Volker T. R. Berghahn, *America and the Intellectual Cold Wars in Europe* (Princeton, NJ, 2001).

119. George C. Herring, *From Colony to Superpower: U. S. Foreign Relations since 1776* (Oxford, 2008), p. 917.

120. J. Richard Stevens, *Captain America: Masculinity & Violence: The Evolution of a National Icon* (Syracuse, 2015); Mark D. White, *Virtues of Captain America: Modern-Day Lessons on Character from a World War II Superhero* (New York, 2014), explores the philosophical basis of the Captain's expressed principles, but assumes that American values are universally valid. Captain America is not alone: *American Sniper*, Clint Eastwood's movie (2015), stands with him.

121. For some of the complexities of the transition, see, Mike S. Dubose, "Holding Out for a Hero: Reaganism, Comic Book Vigilantes, and Captain America," *Journal of Popular Culture*, 40 (2007), pp. 915–35.

122. Marc Levinson, *An Extraordinary Time: The End of the Postwar Boom and the Return of the Ordinary Economy* (New York, 2016); Charles S. Maier, *Among Empires: American Ascendancy and Its Predecessors* (Cambridge, MA, 2006), provides an illuminating commentary on these developments in chs. 5–6.

123. Alfred E. Eckes, Jr., and Thomas W. Zeiler, *Globalization and the American Century* (Cambridge, 2003), p. 209.

124. Peter H. Lindert, "U.S. Foreign Trade and Trade Policy in the Twentieth Century," in Stanley L. Engerman and Robert F. Gallman, eds., *Cambridge Economic History of the United States*, vol. 3 (Cambridge, 2000), ch. 7. Amid what is now a vast literature, special mention must be made of the exceptional contribution made by David P. Calleo, who has devoted the greater part of his long career to this subject. *Follies of Power: America's Unipolar Fantasy* (Cambridge, 2009), provides a guide to his work.

125. Maier, *Among Empires*, figures 1, p. 256; 2, p. 259; 3, p. 260; 4, p. 262; tables 1–2, pp. 298–9.

126. Barry Eichengreen, *Exorbitant Privilege: The Rise and Fall of the Dollar and the Future of the International Monetary System* (Oxford, 2011). The phrase derives from the French finance minister, Valéry Giscard d'Estaing, whose view was also shared by General de Gaulle.

127. The mood of the moment was captured by Paul Kennedy's best-selling book, *The Rise and Fall of the Great Powers; Economic Change and Military Conflict from 1500 to 2000* (New York, 1988). Bruce Cumings provides an engaging and incisive commentary: "Still the American Century," in Michael Cox, Ken Booth, and Tim Dunne, eds., *The Interregnum: Controversies in World Politics, 1989–1999* (Cambridge, 1999).

128. Rosemary Foot and Andrew Walter, "Whatever Happened to the Pacific Century?" *Journal of International Studies*, 25 (1999), pp. 245–69. The origins of modern Western

perceptions of Japan are dealt with in fascinating detail in Rotem Kowner, " 'Lighter than Yellow, But Not Enough': Western Discourse on the Japanese 'Race,' 1854–1904," *Historical Journal* 43 (2000), pp. 103–31.

129. Frances Fukuyama, *The End of History and the Last Man* (New York, 1992), expanded from an essay published in 1989. The fact that Fukuyama first supported the neoconservatives and the overthrow of Saddam Hussein and then rejected both positions says much for his integrity but places a question mark over his powers of prediction. See Fukuyama, *After the Neo Cons: Where the Right Went Wrong* (London, 2006). On the Soviet Union as an imperial power, see Vladislav M. Zubok, *A Failed Empire: The Soviet Union in the Cold War from Stalin to Gorbachev* (Chapel Hill, 2007), and the discussion in *h-diplo*, 9 (2008), pp. 1–41.

130. Stephen D. Krasner, *Sovereignty: Organized Hypocrisy* (Princeton, NJ, 1999).

131. C. Bradley Thompson with Yaron Brook, *Neoconservativism: An Obituary for an Idea* (New York, 2010), provides an overview but may well exaggerate the death of deep-seated ideas of the American mission to the world.

132. The assertion was a key element in what became known as the "Bush Doctrine," which was set out in *The National Security Strategy of the United States* (September 2002).

133. U.S. Army Command and General Staff College, *The Philippine-American War: A Model for Declaring Victory* (self-published, 2014), shows how history can be used to achieve the desired result, namely victory. Jack Fairweather, *The Good War: The Battle for Afghanistan, 2006–14* (London, 2014), provides a sober alternative.

134. A fuller account of the context surrounding the invasion of Iraq is in A. G. Hopkins, "Capitalism, Nationalism and the New American Empire," *Journal of Imperial & Commonwealth History*, 35 (2007), pp. 95–117.

135. Jamilo Anerlini, "UK Move to Join Asia Bank Startled Even Beijing," *Financial Times*, March 28, 2015.

136. The value of global foreign exchange held in U.S. dollars had already fallen from just over half the total in 2001 to about one-third in 2013. Liam Halligan, "The Dollar Is Currently Boosted by Being a Reserve Currency," *Daily Telegraph*, July 19, 2014. In 2016, the federal debt amounted to 25 percent of GDP, which was higher than at any time since 1950. Debt service will become increasingly difficult when interest rates rise from their current low levels. See, for example, Robert J. Samuleson, "Are We Ready for the Financial Crisis?" *Washington Post*, October 17, 2016; Paul A. Volker and Peter G. Peterson, "Ignoring the Debt Problem," *New York Times*, October 21, 2016; Landon Thomas, Jr., "Hearing Echoes of the Financial Crisis," *New York Times*, October 26, 2016; Paul Krugman, "Deficits Matter Again," *New York Times*, January 9, 2017.

137. Gideon Rachman, "Is America's New Declinism for Real," *Financial Times*, November 25, 2008.

138. Joseph S. Nye, "Fear Factor: The Illusion of American Decline," *World Politics Review*, October 9, 2012; Nye, *Is the American Century Over?* (London, 2015), ch. 4 deals with China; Joseff Joffe, *The Myth of America's Decline: Politics, Economics and a Half Century of False Promises* (New York, 2014); Ambrose Evans-Pritchard, "Writing Off America Was Foolish . . . Now It's on the Brink of a Golden Age," *Telegraph*, 24 April 2014; Martin Wolf, "On Top of the World," *Financial Times*, May 3, 2014.

139. Andrew Bacevich, *The Limits of Power: The End of American Exceptionalism* (New York, 2008); Martin Jacques, *When China Rules the World: The Rise of the Middle Kingdom and the End of the Western World* (London, 2009); David Pilling, "China Is Already Changing the World," *Financial Times*, May 3, 2014.

140. Nick Bisley, *Great Powers in the Changing International Order* (Boulder, 2012), advances a case for thinking that Western liberalism will not be carried forward by non-Western powers in the twenty-first century.

141. Patricia Cohen, "A Bigger Economic Pie, but a Smaller Slice for Half of the United States," *New York Times*, December 6, 2016; David Leonhardt, "The American Dream,

Quantified at Last," *New York Times*, December 8, 2016; Jeremy Ashkenas, "Nine New Findings about Inequality in the United States," *New York Times*, December 16, 2016. These articles deal with the research of Thomas Piketty and his colleagues.

142. BREXIT is an amalgam of Britain and exit.

143. Michael H. Hunt and James L. Huskey, *In a Time of Troubles: Big Picture History and the Specter of U.S. Decline* (forthcoming), ch. 4. I am grateful to Dr. Hunt for allowing me to see the drafts of his new book and for many illuminating exchanges on the subject of hegemony, empires, and the legacy of illusions they bequeath.

144. Quoted in Nigel John Ashton, "Harold Macmillan and the 'Golden Days' of Anglo-American Relations Revisited," *Diplomatic History*, 29 (2005), pp. 691–732 [online] at p. 15. See also Alex Danchev, "The Cold War 'Special Relationship' Revisited," *Diplomacy & Statecraft*, 17 (2006), pp. 579–95.

145. Dante, *The Inferno*, Canto XX.

146. Max Dublin, *Future Hype: The Tyranny of Prophecy* (New York, 1989); William A. Sheridan, *The Fortune Sellers: The Big Business of Buying and Selling Predictions* (New York, 1998).

147. Willard van Orman Quine, "On Simple Theories of a Complex World," *Synthese*, 15 (1963), pp. 103–6.

148. The phrase, launched in 1998, is still in (controversial) use. See Micah Zenko, "The Myth of the Indispensable Nation," *Foreign Policy*, November 6, 2014. Simon Reich and Richard Ned Lebow provide a trenchant critique of the idea of hegemonic supremacy in *Good-Bye Hegemony!: Power and Influence in the Global System* (Princeton, NJ, 2014).

149. See, for example, John G. Ikenberry, *Liberal Leviathan: The Origins, Crisis, and Transformation of the American World Order* (Princeton, NJ, 2011). On the ties between academia and government, see Ron Robin, *The Making of the Cold War Enemy: Culture and Politics in the Military-Intellectual Complex* (Princeton, NJ, 2001), which traces the link between behavioralism and the Defense Department from the 1940s to the 1960s.

150. Theodore Roosevelt, Jr., *Colonial Policies of the United States* (New York, 1937), p. 83.

151. Zachary Lockman provides a depressing set of repeated misperceptions of the Middle East in *Contending Visions of the Middle East: The History and Politics of Orientalism* (Cambridge, 2004); as does Michael B. Oram, *America in the Middle East, 1776 to the Present* (New York, 2006). Seth Jacobs, *The Universe Unraveling: American Foreign Policy in Cold War Laos* (Ithaca, 2012), argues that the misplaced belief that Laotians were lazy and cowardly inclined Washington to support the supposedly more energetic and upright Vietnamese.

EPILOGUE: LESSONS OF LIBERATION:
IRAQ, 2003–2011

1. Brian Turner, *Here, Bullet* (Farmington, 2005), p. 18. Turner was a sergeant and team leader with the Third Stryker Brigade Combat Team, Second Infantry Division, U.S. Army, and served in Iraq in 2003–2004. See also his second collection of poems, *Phantom Noise* (Tarset, Northumberland, 2010), and a memoir, *My Life as a Foreign Country* (New York, 2014).

2. Quoted in Charles Sennott, "The Imperial Imperative," *Boston Globe*, February 8, 2004. I am grateful to Mr. Sennott for an exchange of letters on the subject of his excellent article.

3. Humvee: the acronym for a High Mobility Multipurpose Wheeled Vehicle, or HMMWV, a light truck favored for its mobility but criticized for its vulnerability to road-side bombs. Evnin's Humvee carried three others: Sergeant Major David Howell, Staff Sergeant Dino Moreno (sniper), and John Koopman, an embedded reporter.

4. Mark Asher Evnin (10 May 1981–3 April 2003). I am indebted to John Koopman, *McCoy's Marines: Darkside to Baghdad* (St. Paul, 2004; 2009), especially chs. 6–7 and pp. 244, 297, 304. Koopman's book also contains photos of Mark, his mother, and his com-

rades. Additional information is available online at: http://www.thefallen.militarytimes
.com/marine-cpl-mark-a-evnin/25655; http://www.fallenheroesmemorial.com/oif
/profiles/evninmarka.html; https://www.youtube.com/watch?v=hepIGPIQIKE; http://
www.vpr.net/news_detail/68846/corporal-mark-evnin-mourned-in-burlington/.

5. The fact that the term became familiar during the First Gulf War (1990–1991) appears
   not to have influenced planning in 2003.

6. Christopher Cooper, "How a Marine Lost His Command in Race to Baghdad," *Wall
   Street Journal*, April 5, 2004; Thomas E. Ricks, "With Little Explanation, Marines Relieve Commander," *Washington Post*, April 5, 2003.

7. For reasons of space I am confining my references to the U.S. high command to General Mattis. His deputy, Brigadier General John F. Kelly, the Assistant Divisional Commander, was also involved in the decision-making.

8. Cooper, "How a Marine Lost His Command," quoting an official Marine account.

9. According to one source, "the Iraqi units did not take the bait." See Ricks, "With Little
   Explanation," quoting a Marine officer. For an alternative view, quoting General Mattis,
   see Evan Wright, "The Killer Elite," *Rolling Stone*, June 2003. President Donald Trump
   appointed General Mattis to the position of Secretary of Defense in 2017.

10. Dowdy was then relieved of his command: the episode, which was essentially a dispute
    over the priorities of "men or mission," ended his career. See n. 6.

11. Quoted in Peter Maass, "Good Kills," *New York Times*, April 20, 2003.

12. "Remembering Spring 2003 from the Iraqi Side of the Battle," *New York Times*, May 1,
    2008, is a rare example of events in the vicinity of Kut seen from the viewpoint of an
    Iraqi soldier.

13. Those things we know we do not know. Donald Rumsfeld, Secretary of Defense (2001–
    2006), Department of Defense News Briefing, February 12, 2002. More worryingly, there
    were also underestimated "unknown unknowns"—those things we do not know. For
    some of the mistaken assumptions, see Carla Anne Robbins, Greg Jaffe, and Michael M.
    Phillips, "Battle with Elite Guard Is Viewed as a Pivotal Juncture in the Conflict," *Wall
    Street Journal*, March 25, 2003.

14. Richard Sanders, "The Myth of Shock and Awe," *Telegraph*, March 19, 2013.

15. Nevertheless, in the absence of the Republican Guard in significant numbers, the bat-
    tle remained on a small scale. U.S. forces counted one dead, twelve wounded, and
    thirty prisoners, and estimated casualties among Iraqi troops at 150–200 killed and up to
    1,000 wounded.

16. Koopman, *McCoy's Marines*, pp. 158–9. Koopman points out that the sheep were mis-
    taken for Iraqi soldiers in the dark of night.

17. Ibid., pp. 159–67.

18. Ibid., p. 160.

19. Amtrac or Amtrak: an amphibious tracked personnel carrier that attracted criticism
    during the Second Gulf War because of the vulnerability of its armor.

20. Koopman, *McCoy's Marines*, p. 162.

21. Maass, "Good Kills."

22. Koopman, *McCoy's Marines*, ch. 8.

23. The crossing became controversial because it caused civilian deaths. See Koopman,
    McCoy's Marines, ch. 8; Maass, "Good Kills."

24. Koopman, *McCoy's Marines*, ch. 9.

25. Ibid., p. 205.

26. Ibid., p. 211.

27. Oil exports did not regain 2003 levels until 2011.

28. Koopman, *McCoy's Marines*, p. 212.

29. See the *Prologue* to this text.

30. See also the interview, ten years after the event, with the Iraqi who initiated the destruc-
    tion of the statue: Peter Beaumont, "Saddam's Statue and the Bitter Regrets of Iraq's

Sledgehammer Man," *Guardian*, March 9, 2013. "Then," Kadom al-Jabouri said, "we had only one dictator. Now we have hundreds."

31. Andrew Preston, "The Iraq War as Contemporary History," *International History Review*, 30 (2008), pp. 796–808, assesses ten studies that agree on the failings of U.S. policy down to 2006.

32. "Every morning the war arrives . . . The slain fill the wilderness and the guns howl forever." Fadhil al-Azzawi, prolific novelist and poet, was born in Kirkuk in 1940, spent three years in an Iraqi jail (having offended the Ba'athist regime), and took exile in Germany, where he still lives.

33. Major assessments of the record of the United States in Iraq include George Packer, *Assassins' Gate: America in Iraq* (New York, 2005); Anthony Shadid, *Night Draws Near: Iraq's People in the Shadow of America's War* (New York, 2005); Thomas E. Ricks, *Fiasco: The American Military Venture in Iraq* (New York, 2006); Rajiv Chandrasekaran, *Imperial Life in the Emerald City: Inside Iraq's Green Zone* (New York, 2006); Dexter Filkins, *The Forever War* (New York, 2008).

34. Vice President Cheney: "Now, I think things have gotten so bad inside Iraq, from the standpoint of the Iraqi people, my belief is we will, in fact, be greeted as liberators." NBC News, *Meet the Press*, March 16, 2003. The Deputy Defense Secretary, Paul Wolfowitz, made a similar claim before Congress in the previous month. For General Maude's declaration in 1917, see the Prologue to this text.

35. This realization led specialists to advocate alternative strategies for managing the occupation. For a critique of one of them (the "oil-spot" strategy), see A. G. Hopkins, "The 'Victory Strategy': Grand Bargain or Grand Illusion?" *Current History*, 105 (2006), pp. 14–19.

36. As catalogued by David Ryan and Patrick Kiely, eds., *America and Iraq: Policy-Making, Intervention and Regional Politics* (Abingdon, 2009); and Toby Dodge, *Iraq—From War to a New Authoritarianism* (London, 2013).

37. Franz Rosenthal, ed., Ibn Khaldun (1332–1406), *The Muqaddimah: An Introduction to History* (2nd ed. Princeton, NJ, 1967).

38. Gore Vidal, *The United States of Amnesia* (New York, 2004).

39. It is instructive to note how even sober and respected commentators (including David Brooks and Thomas Friedman) suspended disbelief and became advocates of war once emotional appeals to "patriotism" took hold. Subsequently, but too late to influence policy, some admitted error, though few with the degree of public soul-searching shown by Michael Ignatieff, "Getting it Wrong," *New York Times*, August 5, 2005. Not all commentators softened their stance: Sarah Baxter, "Neocon 'Godfather' Norman Podhoretz Tells Bush: Bomb Iran," *Times*, September 30, 2007.

40. Thomas Harding, "Former US Commander: West Is Only Halfway There in Afghanistan," *Daily Telegraph*, October 7, 2011. For an admirable account of the lessons unlearned, see Jack Fairweather, *The Good War: The Battle for Afghanistan, 2006–14* (London, 2014).

41. Walter J. Fishel, trans. and ed., *Ibn Khaldun and Tamerlane: Their Historic Meeting in Damascus, 1401 AD (803 AH)* (Berkeley and Los Angeles, 1952).

42. The outcome for the defenders was far less favorable. The amnesty Ibn Khaldun hoped to negotiate did not hold. Damascus was captured and virtually destroyed. Most of its citizens were slaughtered. Ibn Khaldun was robbed on his way home but returned to Egypt safely. Not even a philosopher and historian of his stature could be expected to hold a psychopath to his word.

43. Muhsin Mahdi, *Ibn Khaldun's Philosophy of History* (Chicago, 1964), p. 289.

INDEX

Italic pages refer to figures and tables.

abaca (hemp): alternatives to, 621–22; falling prices of, 350, 408, 719; foreign competition and, 618; Philippines and, 347, 350, 388, 406, 408, 411, 516, *608*, 617–18, 621–22, 631, 653, 673, 719, 906n126; quotas on, 653; tariffs and, 616; trade liberalization and, 406; World War I era and, 631
Aborigines, 598
Abyssinia, 466
Acheson, Dean, 656, 875n141
Act of Union, 67, 70, 767n47
Adams, John, 130
Adams, John Quincy, 142, 152, 154, 168, 177, 190, 687
Addams, Jane, 305–6
Aden, 482, 499
Adolphus, Gustavus, 48
Adventures of Huckleberry Finn, The (Twain), 329
Adventures of Tom Sawyer, The (Twain), 329
Afghanistan, 88, 233, 266, 453, 724, 737
Africa, 841n58, 879n209, 888n119; colonialism and, 640–42, 645, 647–48, 666, 684–85; forgotten empire and, 498, 503, 529, 531, 535–38; imperialism and, 37, 261, 264–69, 272, 277, 280, 284–85, 349, 450–51, 454, 461, 466–67, 470–72, 474, 476, 478–86, 489, 491, 596, 620; independence and, 144, 292, 334; intrusion and, 384, 394, 418, 433, 437–40; military-fiscal state and, 67, 85, 88–89; partitioning of, 384; postcolonialism and, 700, 705, 710, 714, 716–17; revolution and, 96, 98, 138–39; South, 89, 194, 205, 207, 210, 258, 263, 266, 285, 291, 312, 320, 418, 451, 454–55, 461–62, 476, 480, 484–85, 596,
645, 647–48, 684, 717; wars of incorporation and, 194, 197–99, 205, 207, 210, 235; West, 96, 267, 280, 483, 620–21, 647
African Americans: Afro-Cubans and, 572; Black Panthers and, 667; Carmichael and, 667; citizenship for, 227; civil rights and, 40, 647–48, 665, 667; Civil Rights Congress (CRC) and, 647–48; colonialism and, 665, 668–69; discrimination and, 380, 506, 645–47; forgotten empire and, 506; Hawai'i and, 605; imperialism and, 370, 380, 466; independence and, 143, 149, 181–83, 292, 308, 320, 323; Jim Crow and, 182, 292, 320; Korean War and, 663; Ku Klux Klan and, 290, 647–48; Malcolm X and, 667; minstrelsy and, 181–82, 329; NAACP and, 647–48; opposition to integration and, 665–66; *Plessy v. Ferguson* and, 320; riots and, 466; segregation and, 292, 320, 341–42, 506, 645, 665; slavery and, 341 (*see also* slavery); Tarzan and, 440; as under-people, 181–82; voting rights and, 292, 667; wars of incorporation and, 210, 218–19, 226–29
African Church, 411
African Survey, An (Hailey), 463
Afrikaners, 184, 198, 320, 485, 566
Afro-Cubans and, 572
Age of Democratic Revolutions (Palmer), 90
Age of Jackson, 143
Aglipay, Gregorio, 629, 859n177
agriculture: agrarian ideal and, 196–97, 219, 596; Caribbean and, 557, 568, 578–80, 586, 590; colonialism and, 656, 676, 681; dirt farmers and, 341; exports and, 121, 133, 154 (*see also* exports); Farmers' Alliance and, 297, 817n156; forgotten empire

agriculture (*continued*)
and, 500, 516, 529, 535; imperialism and, 241–44, 247, 250, 269, 275–80, 284, 339, 344–45, 368, 375, 452, 458, 478; imports and, 36 (*see also* imports); independence and, 154, 159, 161, 163, 168–71, 187–88, 293, 299, 303, 307–9, 336; intrusion and, 399, 407, 417–418, 427; military-fiscal state and, 54, 56, 82, 90, 94; Pacific and, 598, 600, 604, 606, 616, 619, 635–37; planter elite and, 121; postcolonialism and, 697–98, 701, 704, 725; proto-globalization and, 34; slavery and, 121 (*see also* slavery); wars of incorporation and, 196, 205, 221, 227. *See also* specific crop

Aguinaldo, Emilio Famy, 383, 413–15, 630–31

Alaska, 15, 198, 205, 237, 432, 523, 526, 529, 599, 651, 670

Albizu Campos, Pedro, 536, 554–58, 657–59, 700

alcohol, 322, 405, 598

Aldrich, Nelson, 360–61, 520

Alexander II, Tzar of Russia, 238

Alger, Horatio, 195

Alger, Russell A., 369

Algeria, 74, 84, 259, 261–62, 280, 418, 462, 476, 481–82, 489, 510, 596, 684, 698, 700, 716, 926n89

Alien and Sedition Acts, 130

Allende, Salvador, 717

Alliance for Progress, 717–18

al-Nasir Faraj, 737

Amalgamated Association of Iron and Steel Workers, 300

American Academy of Political and Social Science, 365

American & Foreign Power Company (AFP), 584–85

American Century, 38, 443–46, 492–93, 707, 723, 726

American Commonwealth, The (Bryce), 252

American Dream, 194, 726

American Federation of Labor (AFL), 297, 300, 321, 367, 425, 626

American Historical Association, 365, 652–53

American Indian Movement (AIM), 668–69

American Indians, 648–49, 665–66, 668–69, 794n37, 749n110. *See also* Native Americans

American Railway Union, 297, 300

American Revolution: causes of success of, 52–53; Declaration of Independence and, 54, 110, 123, 199; declining expectations and, 107–23; emerging global order and, 95–98; federal government issues and, 129–35; France and, 52; George Washington and, 95; global perspective on, 46; Glorious Revolution and, 126, 140; Harry Washington and, 95–98; independence and, 176–77, 307, 335; indissoluble union and, 123–29; loyalists and, 78, 96, 99, 116, 120, 124, 199, 207, 347, 394, 402, 487, 544, 709; military-fiscal state and, 8, 46, 52, 67, 70, 78, 87, 91; minutemen and, 120; postcolonialism and, 693, 698; as project of an empire, 135–41; rhetoric vs. reality of, 146–58; Second, 307; Second Great Awakening and, 176–77; Spain and, 52; Treaty of Paris and, 121, 199, 404, 414–415, 514, 618, 845n132; wars of incorporation and, 199

American Spelling Book (Webster), 179

American Sugar Refining Company. *See* Sugar Trust

American System, 160, 162, 169, 196, 296

American tobacco, 305

Amery, Leopold, 471

anarchy: authoritarianism and, 32; Caribbean and, 569; divided sovereignty and, 66; hegemony and, 6; imperialism and, 250, 256, 276–77, 281–82, 344, 363; independence and, 297, 300–302, 306; international system and, 31; intrusion and, 410, 440; liberty and, 32; military-fiscal state and, 66, 76, 87; revolution and, 120, 135; violence and, 37; wars of incorporation and, 203, 207, 219, 234

Angell, Norman, 254, 282, 811n61

Anglican Church, 61, 64, 67, 70, 79, 109, 177–78, 231, 411

Anglicization, 174–75

Anglo-Dutch War, 52

Anglo-Normans, 175, 218

Anglophilia, 178, 789n203

Anglophobia, 152, 165, 178, 252, 289, 317, 319, 455, 470, 476, 785n132

Anglo-Saxons: American melting pot and, 173; architecture and, 181; Caribbean and, 545, 551; colonialism and, 652, 664; cosmopolitan nationalism and, 316–32; cultural independence and, 186; Democrats and, 289; forgotten empire and, 495, 505, 514; imperialism and, 251–53, 264, 273,

342, 356, 363–66, 374, 379, 380, 455, 467, 470; intrusion and, 422, 425, 429, 438–40; Jefferson and, 161; as legitimating ideology, 183; Longfellow and, 180; mythology of, 174–75, 183; Pacific and, 592–93; Protestantism and, 133; race theory and, 251–53, 317, 319; Republicans and, 289; social Darwinism and, 251; spread of racism and, 292, 315–34; wars of incorporation and, 194, 210, 218–19
Anglo-South African War, 236, 258, 263, 285, 312, 320, 455
Anti-Corn Law League, 82
anti-Federalists, 128, 132, 141, 144
Anti-Imperialist League, 263–68, 367, 849n217
Anti-Slavery Association, 72–73, 88
Anti-Trust Act, 302
anti-trust legislation, 302, 305, 360, 521, 827n100
Apaches, 198, 200
apartheid, 292, 480, 484, 648, 684, 717
Arabian American Oil Company (ARAMCO), 715
Arab-Israeli War, 710, 715
Archenholz, Johann, 54
architecture, 181, 248, 331
Area Studies, 13
Arnold, Matthew, 328
Around the World in Eighty Days (Verne), 245
Aryanism, 89
assimilation policy: benevolent, 501, 513, 531–32, 559, 609; Caribbean and, 551, 559–60, 571; colonialism and, 27, 29, 39, 145, 186, 189, 198, 347, 452, 479, 498–504, 507, 509–13, 529–34, 572, 609–13, 637, 648, 669; constitutional issues and, 509–12; equality and, 27; forgotten empire and, 498–504, 507, 509–13, 529–34; imperialism and, 347, 452, 473, 479; independence and, 145, 173–74, 184, 186, 189, 317, 320, 322, 324–25, 332; intrusion and, 383, 412; Pacific and, 592, 603, 609–13, 622–24, 638; postcolonialism and, 719; wars of incorporation and, 198–201, 210, 237
Association of Southeast Asian Nations (ASEAN), 703
association policy, 39, 237, 452, 473, 498, 500–501, 503, 510, 514, 534, 558. *See also* assimilation policy
Atlantic Charter, 469

Atlas, Charles, 447
Attlee, Clement, 472
Australia: British claim on, 86; colonialism and, 641, 684; cultural cringe and, 180; federation of, 139; free trade and, 703; imperialism and, 250, 253, 258, 266, 451, 454, 477, 480, 487–88; independence and, 292, 298; "mateship" and, 195; military-fiscal state and, 86, 89; Pacific and, 596, 598; postcolonialism and, 700, 703; slavery and, 96; voting rights to women and, 196; wars of incorporation and, 195–98, 205; White Australia policy of, 684
Austria, 37, 73–75, 183, 230, 233–34, 249, 270
authoritarianism: anarchy and, 32; Caribbean and, 556, 560, 586, 588; colonialism and, 642, 649, 661, 674, 677, 682; independence and, 153, 178; military-fiscal state and, 62, 71, 73, 78; Pacific and, 605; postcolonialism and, 712, 718–20; revolution and, 96–97, 102, 122, 141
autonomy: Caribbean and, 545–46, 552, 555, 561, 575; Civil War and, 7; colonialism and, 659–60; forgotten empire and, 516; imperialism and, 352, 361, 381, 454, 488; independence and, 289; intrusion and, 394, 399, 402–3, 411–12, 416, 431, 433; Pacific and, 604, 628; postcolonialism and, 719; revolution and, 109, 114; spiritual, 109; wars of incorporation and, 217
Ayala Corporation, 407

Babbage, Charles, 244
Back to Bataan (movie), 632
Baden-Powell, Robert, 266
Baghdad, 2, 4, 731–34
Balzac, Honoré de, 73
bananas, 449, 540, 621, 869n27
Bandung Conference, 487, 663–64, 698, 702, 917n110
Bank Act, 270
Bank Charter Act, 272
Bank of England, 59, 63, 128, 164, 169, 257, 272, 298, 312, 812n66
Bank of Hawai'i, 599
Bank of New York, 311
Bank of Portugal, 269
Bank of Spain, 269
Bank of the United States, 59, 131, 151, 156, 168, 781n70
bankruptcies, 61, 64, 91, 107, 170, 222, 258, 304, 346, 396, 449, 552, 568, 577, 656

Bantustans, 200, 321
Baptists, 175, 177, 265, 366, 623
Barbados, 569
Baring, Alexander, 76, 209
Baring, Francis, 86
Baring Brothers, 165–66
Baring Crisis, 258
baseball, 330–31, 571–72
Basra, 1–2
Bates, John C., 611
Batista, Fulgencio, 537, 582–88, 661–62, 677–85, 700
Battle of Gettysburg, 335
Battle of Plassey, 105
Battle of Trenton, 373
Battle of Waterloo, 73, 77
Baudelaire, Charles, 243
Beard, Charles A., 16, 130, 378–79, 774n183
Beardslee, Lester, 384
Becker, Carl L., 123–24, 772n145
Belgium, 74, 261, 267, 269, 382, 451, 457, 467, 503, 619, 716
Benson, Arthur, 266
Bentham, Jeremy, 65, 89, 454
beriberi, 409
Berlin Wall, 723
Beveridge, Albert, 339, 343, 363, 365, 372–73, 472, 495, 497, 539, 593, 846n142
Bevin, Ernest, 474
Bierce, Ambrose, 187, 193, 793n14
Big Five, 599–605, 618, 649–52, 670
big government, 128, 144, 153, 155, 253, 294, 296, 307, 503, 643
Big Men, 291, 525, 609, 611, 634, 637, 672
Bill of Rights, 61, 126, 147–48
bimetallism, 260, 273–74, 293–94, 297–98, 301–3, 311–12, 350, 356, 362, 375, 831n169
Bismarck, 250–51, 295
Black Panthers, 667
Blackstone, William, 60, 66, 137
Blaine, James G., 295, 357, 396, 421–22, 429, 863n236
Bloch, Marc, 16
Bolsheviks, 451, 507
Bonifacio, Andrés, 411–13
Booth, William, 264
Borinqueña, La (Rodríguez de Tió), 588, 899n228
Bose, Subhas Chandra, 555
Boston Tea Party, 115–16
Bowring, John, 88
Boxer uprisings, 285

boycotts, 118, 585
Boy Scouts, 266
Brains Trust, 526, 529
Brazil, 72, 84, 220, 389, 446, 456, 547, 549, 717
Brazza, Pierre de, 263
Bread-Winners, The: A Social Study (Hay), 364
"Breaking of Nations, The" (Hardy), 254
Bretton Woods Agreements, 460, 474–75, 703, 708, 722
BREXIT, 726–27, 930n142
BRICS (Brazil, Russia, India, China, South Africa), 702, 725
Briggs, Charles, 623
Bright, John, 271, 377, 817n147
British East India Company, 29, 57, 61–62, 67–68, 79, 83, 86, 105–6, 115, 135, 271, 526
British Empire: Anglo-Japanese alliance and, 446–47; Augustan Age of, 47; Australia and, 86; BREXIT and, 726–27, 930n142; Caribbean and, 572; City of London and, 56, 60, 62, 80, 83, 106, 121–22, 139, 164–70, 215, 232, 275, 278, 284, 293, 299, 302, 310–12, 334, 375, 382, 420, 458–59, 467, 470, 474, 484; Colonial Development & Welfare Act and, 675–76; colonialism and, 18, 648 (see also colonialism); English Civil War and, 135; evolution of, 57, 60–64; exceptionalism and, 16, 754n71; exports and, 57 (see also exports); forgotten empire and, 522; George I and, 62; George III and, 53, 57, 100, 112, 116, 122, 137, 167, 183; globalization and, 27, 31; Glorious Revolution and, 46, 53–62, 68, 70, 90, 100, 103, 113, 122, 126, 137, 140; Home Counties and, 46; imperialism and, 263, 364, 451, 453, 467–72, 476, 480, 492 (see also imperialism); imports and, 58, 131 (see also imports); independence and, 143, 169, 178, 295, 330; India and, 1–4; Iraq and, 5–6, 736; James II and, 55–56, 59, 61, 70, 90; John Bull and, 99–100, 271, 334; Lend-Lease Agreement and, 469, 471; loyalists and, 78, 96, 99, 116, 120, 124, 199, 207, 347, 394, 402, 487, 544, 709; military-fiscal state and, 57, 60–65, 83–94; Navigation Acts and, 57; new global order and, 64–70; New World and, 18, 58, 76, 84, 91, 97–98, 112, 133, 136–41, 146, 175, 191, 195, 209–12, 218, 233, 245, 277, 328, 337, 374, 385, 387, 432, 445, 472, 474,

609, 671, 694, 706; noble destiny and, 497–504; Ottoman Empire and, 27, 36; Parliament Act and, 509; Pax Britannica and, 25, 283, 736; pound sterling and, 59, 81, 255, 272; reassertion of control by, 644; revolution and, 100, 105, 109, 112, 123, 135, 141; Royal Air Force and, 453; Royal Navy and, 88, 127–28, 160, 167, 186, 193, 208, 333, 354; Russia and, 702; socialism and, 924n45; as super-power, 47, 84, 92, 100, 243, 355, 378; Tories and, 55–56, 61–62, 77, 79, 81, 86, 93, 100–101, 103, 112, 130, 137; Town-shend and, 1–6, 730–32, 735, 737, 740n21, 740n24, 741n28; Union Jack and, 69, 285, 294; as union of permanence and change, 76–83; unitary government of, 509–10; vastness of, 83–90; voting rights to women and, 196; War of 1812 and, 77, 123, 127, 152, 160, 166–67, 178, 191, 193, 199, 210, 212–13, 232, 234, 335; wars of incorporation and, 192, 196, 213, 218–19, 236; West Indies and, 121 (*see also* West Indies); Whigs and, 55–56, 61–64, 70, 77, 86, 92–93, 100–103, 106, 112, 127, 130–37, 157, 160–61, 169, 189, 214–16, 223, 224, 234–35; William III and, 55; William of Orange and, 56; World War II era and, 465 (*see also* World War II era)

British Labor Party, 250

Brookings Institution, 543

Brooks, Elbridge S., 372

Brooks Adams, Henry, 325, 364

Brooks Adams, Peter, 248, 252–53, 318, 364, 440, 590–91, 833n215

Brown, Alexander, 164

Brown, William, 164–65

brownfield uprising, 80

Brown Shipley, 164

Brunel, Isambard Kingdom, 90

Bryan, William Jennings, 301–3, 367, 369, 495

Bryce, James, 194, 252, 289, 305

Buchanan, James, 222, 803n207

Budget, The (Hartley), 99

Bull, John, 99–100, 271, 334

Bull Run, 229

Bureau of Indian Affairs, 523, 668

Bureau of Insular Affairs, 523, 526–27, 589

Burgess, John W., 366, 422–23

Burke, Edmund, 66–67, 103

Burma, 480

Burnett, Frances Hodgson, 327

Burroughs, Edgar Rice, 437–40, 866n2

Bute, Lord, 100, 106

Butler, Samuel, 245

Buy British campaign, 702

Byng, John, 100

Byron, Lord, 72, 225, 283, 352, 591

caciques, 344, 374, 611, 613, 620, 634, 672, 840n35, 851n25, 857n121

Cánovas, Antonio del Castillo, 399, 855n83

Calhoun, John C., 219

Call of the Wild, The (London), 195, 793n24

Calvinists, 109

Camillo, Count of Cavour, 276

Canada, 796n86; annexation of, 295; as British territory, 86, 164; emigration and, 120; federation of, 139; imperialism and, 250, 260, 266, 273, 357–58, 447, 454, 477, 480–81, 487, 489, 596; indigenous people of, 89, 598; intrusion and, 394, 398, 402; NAFTA and, 703–4; NATO and, 475; Ottawa Agreements and, 458; peaceful frontier of, 797n92; postcolonialism and, 700, 703; Quezon and, 630; race patriotism and, 139; reciprocity and, 357; Shawnee and, 210; Treaty of Ghent and, 209; U.S. investment in, 312; voting rights to women and, 196; wars of incorpora-tion and, 194–98, 205, 207, 209–11, 232, 235–37

Candide (Voltaire), 254

Canning, George, 76, 85

capitalism: Caribbean and, 548–49, 558, 560, 569, 587, 590; colonialism and, 17, 22, 38, 647, 652, 659, 674, 676, 681; ex-cesses of, 38; forgotten empire and, 507, 520–21, 526–27, 529; Great Depression and, 456–65; imperialism and, 22, 250, 259, 262, 280–83, 339–40, 347, 355, 362, 364, 379–82, 451, 459, 463, 465; indepen-dence and, 150, 161, 164, 171–72, 177, 184, 291, 296–97, 301, 305, 314, 324, 332–33, 335; intrusion and, 390, 402; labor and, 37, 223, 233, 242, 248, 283, 288, 300, 305, 375, 390, 426, 695; military-fiscal state and, 54, 56, 88; Pacific and, 619, 636–37; postcolonialism and, 689, 699, 707, 711–12, 714, 717, 725–26; Rhenish version of, 711–12, 726; revolution and, 121–22; Viet-nam War and, 714; wars of incorporation and, 220, 226; Wisconsin School and, 17, 340–41, 360

Captain America, 721–22, 728–29
Captain America Civil War (movie), 728–29
Carey, Henry, 160–61, 238
Carey, Mathew, 160
Caribbean, 7; agriculture and, 557, 568, 578–80, 586, 590; anarchy and, 569; Anglo-Saxons and, 545, 551; assimilation and, 551, 559–60, 571; authoritarianism and, 556, 560, 586, 588; autonomy and, 545–46, 552, 555, 561, 575; British Empire and, 572; capitalism and, 548–49, 558, 560, 569, 587, 590; Catholicism and, 539, 541, 545, 551, 573; citizenship and, 545–46; civilizing mission and, 541, 543, 549, 580; coercion and, 657–62; collaboration in, 657–62; communism and, 581; conservatives and, 544, 557, 572, 575–77, 582–83; contrasts in, 674–83; Cuba and, 559–88 (*see also* Cuba); declaration of independence and, 122; decolonization and, 657–62, 674–83; democracy and, 543, 546, 565–66, 574, 576, 584, 586; Democrats and, 556, 557, 561, 576, 578, 584, 586; entrepreneurs and, 550, 567, 568; expansionism and, 543, 584; exports and, 544, 547–50, 560–61, 564, 567–70, 577–81, 587–91; Foraker Act and, 545–62, 566; free trade and, 548, 553, 568, 590; globalization and, 570; home rule and, 545; immigration and, 557, 578, 582; imports and, 564, 568, 586, 590; insular empire and, 39, 543–59, 566, 568, 570, 575–76, 580, 587, 589; labor and, 540, 548, 550, 558, 569, 578–79, 585, 587, 589; liberalism and, 586; liberty and, 543, 546, 574–75; lobbies and, 548–50, 564, 579–81, 587, 589; manufacturing and, 557–58, 568, 578–80, 588; McKinley and, 547, 561–63, 588; mercantilism and, 572, 590; monopolies and, 548, 599–600; national identity and, 541, 551–52, 570–72; nationalism and, 546, 554–64, 572–75, 577–79, 582–90; Netherlands and, 542; oligarchy and, 574, 579, 582, 585, 589; patriotism and, 541; plantations and, 387, 391–92, 394, 400; as pleasure islands, 539–43; populism and, 582, 585–86, 588–89; poverty and, 543, 547, 552, 558, 574, 581; progressives and, 556; protectionism and, 547–48, 564, 579–80, 587; Protestantism and, 545, 551, 571, 572–73; Puerto Rico and, 543–59 (*see also* Puerto Rico); raw materials and, 579; reciprocity and, 389–90, 396, 401, 408, 417, 419–24, 430,

436, 564–69, 573; reconstruction and, 556–57; Republicans and, 546–47, 554, 561, 578–80; self-determination and, 552, 555, 574, 577; slavery and, 120–22, 539, 541, 547; sovereignty and, 559–61; Spain and, 539–40, 544–47, 552, 561, 569–74, 590; sugar and, 386–402, 406–8, 411, 417–29, 434, 544, 547–54, 557, 560–69, 575, 577–82, 586–90; tariffs and, 547–49, 558, 564, 568–70, 578–81, 586–90; tourism and, 524, 539–40, 590–93; unemployment and, 550, 553, 558, 576, 581; wars of choice and, 427–36; World War I era and, 547, 552, 555–56, 568, 577, 580, 582, 588–89
Carlos I, King of Portugal, 269
Carlton, Guy, 95–96
Carlyle, Thomas, 17, 231, 328
Carmichael, Stokely, 667
Carnegie, Andrew, 314–16, 367, 455, 495, 832nn196, 197, 199, 202
Carnegie, William, 314
Castlereagh, Lord, 163
Castro, Fidel, 678–79, 682–83
Castro, Raúl, 678
Catalan Revolt, 74
Cathay, 702, 706
Catholicism: Caribbean and, 539, 541, 545, 551, 573; colonialism and, 658, 672; forgotten empire and, 502; imperialism and, 265–66, 279, 281, 345, 366–67; independence and, 174, 184, 301, 319, 322–23; intrusion and, 393, 406, 427, 430, 434; military-fiscal state and, 63, 69–70; Pacific and, 595, 609, 615, 619, 623; revolution and, 113
caudillos, 238, 569, 573–74, 589, 780n54
Cavaliers, 175, 220
Cavour, Camillo Benso, Count, 75, 276
centrales, 541, 550, 567, 629
Central Intelligence Agency (CIA), 643, 672, 674, 682–83, 713–17
Central Powers, 2
Cervantes, Miguel de, 48, 352, 750n6, 843n77
Céspedes, Carlos Manuel, 392
Ceylon, 480
Chadbourne Plan, 586
Chalmers, Thomas, 77
Chamberlain, Joseph, 273, 566
Chamberlain, Neville, 377, 466–68
Chardón, Carlos, 557
Charles X, King of France, 84

Chartism, Chartists, 80–81, 189, 281, 315, 761n198

Chateaubriand, François-René de, 243–44, 460, 709

Cherokees, 199, 795n53

Chiang Kai-shek, 536

Chile, 717

China, 11, 582; annexation of Manchuria and, 465–66; Bandung Conference and, 487, 663–64, 698, 702; Boxer uprisings in, 285; colonialism and, 23, 27, 641–44, 656, 663, 673–74, 685; as economic superpower, 725; foreign subordination of, 641–42; forgotten empire and, 534, 536; free trade and, 703, 706–7; imperialism and, 253, 262, 267, 280, 284–85, 357, 366, 443, 446, 448, 456, 465, 481, 483; independence and, 322; intrusion and, 387, 392–93, 403, 407–9, 412–13, 420, 424, 426, 434–36; Japanese invasion of, 465–66; Long March of, 711; mandate from heaven and, 6; Mao and, 450, 536; military-fiscal state and, 49–51, 57, 65, 79, 86, 88–90, 93; New Development Bank and, 725; Pacific and, 601, 603, 613, 619, 626, 633; postcolonialism and, 698, 700, 702–3, 706–7, 711–18, 721–22, 725–26; revolution and, 642, 656, 663, 711, 718; sugar and, 858n153; wars of incorporation and, 231–32

China Sea, 266, 347, *608*

Chinese Exclusion Act, 424

Chinese Revolution, 642, 656, 663, 711, 718

cholera, 4, 409, 415

Christian and Missionary Alliance, The (journal), 366

Christianity: colonialism and, 652; forgotten empire and, 512–13; imperialism and, 246, 248–49, 264–66, 363, 366–67, 381, 443, 472, 492; independence and, 175–76, 181, 183, 304, 316–17, 323–25; intrusion and, 402, 411, 429, 434; Japan and, 711–12; military-fiscal state and, 77–79, 83, 87–88; Native Americans and, 181; Pacific and, 595, 598, 610–11, 622–23; postcolonialism and, 711–12, 719; revolution and, 109; sports and, 815n120; wars of incorporation and, 207, 219

Christian Science Church, 323

Christmas, 315, 656

Churchill, Randolph, 326

Churchill, Winston, 469–70, 482–83

citizenship: Caribbean and, 545–46; forgotten empire and, 500, 513–15; imperialism and, 479, 487; Pacific and, 606; postcolonialism and, 703; wars of incorporation and, 196, 200–201, 227

City Bank of New York, 449

civilizing mission, 25; Caribbean and, 541, 543, 549, 580; colonialism and, 641, 657, 683; forgotten empire and, 496, 500–501, 508–9, 512–13, 519, 525, 531–36; historical perspective on, 7; imperialism and, 259, 262, 280, 444, 453, 472, 477, 490; intrusion and, 386, 416, 436; military-fiscal state and, 71, 88; Pacific and, 594, 610, 622–24, 630, 636–37; political progress and, 39; postcolonialism and, 719; revolution and, 106; social engineering and, 29; wars of incorporation and, 198, 237

civil rights, 912n19; African Americans and, 40, 647–48, 665; colonialism and, 645, 647–48, 650–51, 665–71; Democrats and, 645, 651, 666–67; Eisenhower and, 666; extension of, 667–68; FBI and, 648; Ickes and, 528; imperialism and, 493; independence and, 288, 332; Johnson and, 666–68; Kennedy and, 667; NAACP and, 647–48; Native Americans and, 40, 665, 668–69; opposition to integration and, 665–66; pluralism and, 332; postcolonialism and, 699; Red Scare and, 648; Republicans and, 666; Southern states and, 648; Supreme Court and, 665; United Nations and, 528, 699; Vietnam War era and, 493

Civil Rights Act, 667, 669, 671

Civil Rights Congress (CRC), 647–48

Civil War, American: Britain's neutrality and, 193–94, 227–34; Bull Run and, 229; Confederacy and, 219, 225–33, 238, 788n184, 801n166, 804n232, 804n234, 805n246, 823n34, 829n136; cosmopolitan nationalism and, 316–32; death toll of, 236; division of common nationalism and, 184–85; Emancipation Proclamation and, 227, 230, 392; fall of New Orleans and, 229; far-reaching effects of, 234–38; forgotten empire and, 515, 518; Fort Sumpter and, 225; Grant and, 212, 225; imperialism and, 243, 269, 285, 338, 344, 353, 356, 362, 367, 369–70, 380; independence and, 37, 149, 152, 155, 161, 163, 171–72, 184, 186–87, 190, 287–302, 306–11, 316, 320, 322, 326–35; industrialization after, 338;

Civil War, American (*continued*)
   intrusion and, 392, 400, 418–19, 431; as
   irrepressible conflict, 217–27; King Cotton
   and, 187, 193, 228, 232, 236; Lee and,
   225, 804n230; legitimacy claims and, 218;
   Lincoln and, 219–30, 234, 238, 326, 335,
   515; military-fiscal state and, 45–47, 53,
   55, 94; nation building and, 35–36; new
   conflicts after, 288; Northern concessions and, 596; Northern Congress and,
   307–8; peace settlement after, 288–90;
   reconstruction and, 237; revolution and,
   98, 129, 135, 139; as search for autonomy,
   7; Trent Affair and, 228; Union and, 186,
   210, 214, 216, 219–35, 287–93, 371; wars
   of incorporation and, 191, 193, 200, 203,
   211, 217–34, 217–38; white political economy and, 565
Clark Air Field, 718
Clarkson, Thomas, 96
Clay, Henry, 160–63, 169, 196, 214, 219, 296,
   781n69
Clayton, William, 440, 471
clergymen, 231, 402, 410
Cleveland, Grover, 290, 263, 294–99, 303,
   319, 353, 356, 360, 367, 369, 421–23, 429
Clive, Robert, 105–7
Cobbett, William, 196, 776n210
Cobden, Richard, 82, 88–90, 233–34, 254,
   262–63, 281–85, 294–95, 367, 377, 381,
   823n35
Cobden Club, 294–95
coconuts, 417, 457, 608, 617–18, 621–22, 626,
   672–73, 907n152
Cody, William (Buffalo Bill), 202, 321
Coercive Acts, 114
coffee, 65, 102, 193, 295, 347, 350, 388, 391,
   401–402, 406, 428, 457, 516, 547–49, 553,
   891n35
Cold War, 663; academic patriotism and, 18;
   Anglophobia and, 476; CIA and, 643,
   672, 674, 682, 713–17; colonialism and,
   640–46, 651, 657, 661, 668, 672–75, 684–
   86; Cuba and, 661; decolonization and,
   640, 642, 646, 651, 657, 661, 668, 672, 675,
   683–86; Evil Empire and, 560; forgotten
   empire and, 496, 531; France and, 714;
   Gaddis on, 24; Great Depression and,
   644; high politics and, 640; human rights
   and, 646–47; imperialism and, 460, 476,
   480, 483, 487–89, 492; Middle East and,
   714–16; national unity and, 644; perceived

end of, 723; postcolonialism and, 698–
   700, 705, 709–15, 718, 721, 723; power
   drain of, 709; Puerto Rico and, 657; U.S.
   global role and, 31, 40; Vietnam War and,
   529, 668, 714
Coleridge, Samuel Taylor, 90
Collet, Mark, 164–65
Collier, John, 503, 529, 648
Colonial Development & Welfare Act,
   477–78
colonialism: Adam Smith and, 110; Africa
   and, 640–42, 645, 647–48, 666, 684–85;
   African Americans and, 665, 668–69; agriculture and, 656, 676, 681; American
   Way and, 683–87; Anglo-Saxons and, 652,
   664; assimilation and, 27, 29, 39, 145,
   186, 189, 198, 347, 452, 479, 498–504,
   507, 509–13, 529–34, 571, 609–13, 638,
   648, 669; authoritarianism and, 642,
   649, 661, 674, 677, 682; autonomy and,
   659–60; capitalism and, 17, 22, 38, 647,
   652, 659, 674, 676, 681; Caribbean and,
   7 (*see also* Caribbean); Catholicism and,
   658, 672; China and, 23, 27, 641–44, 656,
   663, 673–74, 685; Christianity and, 652;
   civilizing mission and, 641, 657, 683; civil
   rights and, 645, 647–48, 650–51, 665–71;
   Cold War and, 640–46, 651, 657, 661,
   668, 672–75, 684–86; communism and,
   642–48, 652, 655, 659, 662, 667, 670,
   674, 678, 681, 683; conservatives and,
   642, 668, 670, 673, 684; Cuba and, 639,
   642–43, 650, 660–62, 676–86; decolonization and, 7 (*see also* decolonization);
   democracy and, 17–18, 25, 39, 639, 644,
   647, 652, 656, 664–65, 670, 672, 682;
   Democrats and, 39, 645, 648, 650–52, 656,
   666, 669–71, 681, 684; dialectical forces
   and, 32, 34, 38–40; direct rule and, 4, 71,
   503–4, 588–89, 611; empire-building and,
   13; Enlightenment and, 641; exceptionalism and, 8, 15–21, 641; expansionism and,
   18, 20; exports and, 110, 114–21, 133, 139,
   649–50, 653, 656–57, 660–61, 673–76,
   679–80, 684; forgotten empire and, 494–
   538 (*see also* forgotten empire); France
   and, 642, 644, 663, 669, 684; free trade
   and, 34, 36, 656; Germany and, 644; globalization and, 39–40, 640–43, 685; Great
   Depression and, 463–64; Hawai'i and,
   639, 645–46, 649–52, 662, 666, 669–71,
   674, 683–85; hegemony and, 6, 15, 18, 22,

24, 26, 30–32, 41; holding on, 643–49; home rule and, 659; human rights and, 646–48, 660, 666–68, 685; imperialism and, 530 (*see also* imperialism); imports and, 657, 673; India and, 1, 46, 67, 96, 98, 142, 618, 641, 647, 655, 663; indirect rule and, 71, 404, 452, 463–64, 472, 503–4, 525, 529, 534, 541, 598, 610–11, 622, 648, 669, 884n36; insular empire and, 8, 639–46, 649, 660, 684–86; international relations and, 645, 649, 685; Japan and, 639, 642, 644, 650, 652–53, 655, 663, 670–71; Korea and, 453; labor and, 29, 37, 39, 650, 652, 655, 659, 677, 680, 684; landowners and, 654; liberalism and, 661; liberation and, 483–89; liberty and, 17–18, 25, 32–33, 641, 645, 664–65, 682; lobbies and, 649, 651, 653, 673, 681; manufacturing and, 641, 659, 672–77; Marx and, 655, 672, 679; modernization and, 676, 682; monopolies and, 654; moving on, 662–69; nationalism and, 640–46, 655, 657–59, 662, 670, 673–74, 678, 680, 682–86; nation-building and, 35, 37; new colony system and, 98–105; New World and, 18, 58, 76, 84, 91, 97–98, 112, 133, 136–41, 146, 175, 191, 195, 209–12, 218, 233, 245, 277, 328, 337, 374, 385, 387, 432, 445, 472, 474, 609, 671, 694, 706; noble destiny and, 497–504; oligarchy and, 673–74; Ottoman Empire and, 642; Pacific and, 7 (*see also* Pacific); patriotism and, 644, 679; Philippines and, 634, 645, 652–56, 659, 662, 669–74, 684–85; populism and, 642, 655, 670, 684; poverty and, 668–69, 675–77, 686; property rights and, 677; protectionism and, 30, 681; Puerto Rico and, 639, 657–59, 662, 674–77, 684–86; raw materials and, 38, 40, 641; reconstruction and, 667; Republicans and, 645, 649–52, 660, 666–69, 671, 684; retaining authority and, 639–41; second occupation and, 470–83; segregation and, 499, 684; self-determination and, 641, 643, 647, 664–65, 668–69, 675, 685–86; slavery and, 685 (*see also* slavery); South Africa and, 89, 645, 647–48, 684; sovereignty and, 641, 659, 668, 682, 686; sugar and, 646, 649–50, 653, 657, 660–61, 670–83; surrendering authority and, 639–41; Taft and, 639; tariffs and, 639, 657, 660, 673, 676–77, 680; taxes and, 29, 34, 670, 673, 676–77, 697, 722–23, 726;

technology and, 664; terrorism and, 662; unemployment and, 36–37, 657, 676–77; United Nations and, 645–46, 664, 675; white settlers and, 653, 684; World War I era and, 642; World War II era and, 558, 591, 639–46, 649, 653, 660, 663, 668, 671

Colonial Systems of the World, The (U.S. Treasury), 498

colonos, 550, 569, 579, 581, 587, 626, 659

Columbus Day, 335

Comanches, 200, 213

Comity Agreements, 551, 571

Commissioner for Indian Affairs, 503, 529, 648

Commons, John, 529

Commonwealth, British, 445, 460, 473, 477–79, 481, 490, 630, 703; of the Philippines, 614, 628–630, 631, 654, 718; of Puerto Rico, 545, 557–58, 657, 659, 674, 685

communism, 39; Bolsheviks and, 451, 507; Castro and, 682–83; Caribbean and, 581; colonialism and, 642–48, 652, 655, 659, 662, 667, 670, 674, 678, 681, 683; Cuba and, 682–83; imperialism and, 449, 460, 462, 473, 475–76, 491, 493; Indonesia and, 713–14; Japan and, 712; Lenin and, 22, 262, 267, 450, 465; McCarthy era and, 648; Pacific and, 628; postcolonialism and, 711–13, 717–18, 720; Southern states and, 652; Stalin and, 663

Company of Scotland Trading to Africa, 67

Compromise of 1850, 224

Conant, Charles Arthur, 259, 847n165

Concepción, Venancio, 619

condominiums, 498, 883n18

Condorcet, Nicholas de, 127, 776n209

Confederacy: agricultural basis of, 227; Carlyle and, 231; Clay on, 219; Davis and, 804n230, 804n234; finances of, 226–27, 804n232, 804n234, 829n136; Fort Sumter and, 225; Gladstone and, 231; Lee and, 225, 804n230; Lewis and, 230; Lincoln and, 228–29; Russell and, 231–32; Southern states and, 219, 225–33, 238, 788n184, 801n166, 804n232, 804n234, 805n246, 823n34, 829n136

confederation, 72, 123, 125–26, 197, 235, 373

Congo, 382, 620

Congregationalists, 366, 623

Connecticut Yankee in King Arthur's Court, A (Twain), 329

Conolly, Patrick, 70
Conolly, William, 70
conservatives: Caribbean and, 544, 557, 572, 575–77, 582–83; colonialism and, 642, 668, 670, 673, 684; forgotten empire and, 500, 506, 528; imperialism and, 241, 249–50, 260, 263, 266, 271, 273, 275, 279, 283, 344–46, 352, 356, 362, 364, 367, 374–76, 444, 450, 452, 462, 464, 480, 483, 485; independence and, 144, 148, 150, 166, 188–89, 299, 313, 317, 333; intrusion and, 394–95, 398, 401–2, 406, 439; military-fiscal state and, 47, 55, 71, 73–82, 86, 93; Pacific and, 625; postcolonialism and, 683–84, 711–12, 723–24; progressives and, 35; reformers and, 8, 34; revolution and, 100–101, 103, 106–7, 112, 122, 135, 137–41; Spain and, 345–46; wars of incorporation and, 218, 233, 238
Constant, Benjamin, 77, 89, 282
Constantinople, 4
Conway, Henry Seymour, 103, 767n37
Cook, James, 417
Cooke, Jay, 256–57, 311
Coolidge, Albert, 336
Coolidge, Calvin, 109, 625
Cooper, Gary, 632
Corn Laws, 81–83, 87–88, 209, 246
Cortés, Hernán, 216
Cosmos (von Humboldt), 65
Costa Rica, 449
cotton, 822n17; Britain and, 167–68; independence and, 157, 162–63, 167–69, 186–87, 291, 308–9; as King, 187, 193, 228, 232, 236; military-fiscal state and, 80–81, 84–85; Philippines and, 626; postcolonialism and, 697; price collapse of, 168–69; slavery and, 220; Southern states and, 35–36, 129, 157, 162–63, 167, 186–87, 193, 213, 228, 232, 236; wars of incorporation and, 193, 213, 220–23, 227–32, 236, 238
cotton gins, 163, 917n119
Council of Foreign Bondholders, 258
counterculture, 145, 172, 187, 288, 317, 334, 591, 837n310
Crazy Horse, 202
Crèvecoeur, Hector St. John de, 194
cricket, 330–31, 572
Crimean War, 170, 326
criollos, 348, 387, 394, 395, 400, 402–3, 407, 410, 436, 544
Crispi Francesco, 276–77

Cromer, Lord, 507, 577
Crowder, Enoch H., 577–78, 584
Cuba, 164, 546, 920n194; AFP and, 584–85; annexation of, 384, 433–34; arbitrary rule and, 677–78; austerity measures and, 577–78; baseball and, 571–72; Batista and, 537, 582–88, 661–62, 677–85, 700; Cánovas and, 399; Castro and, 678–79, 682–83; Céspedes and, 293; Chadbourne Plan and, 586; Cold War and, 661; collaboration with, 660–62; colonialism and, 639, 642–43, 650, 660–62, 676–86; Comity Agreements and, 571; communism and, 581–82, 682–83; Constitution of, 560, 563–65, 576, 586, 589; dance of the millions and, 625; department stores in, 571; elitism and, 574–75; as Ever-Faithful Isle, 395; Evil Empire and, 560; Foraker Act and, 561–62, 566; Fordney-Mccumber Tariff and, 578; foreign capital and, 567; forgotten empire and, 494, 499–501, 504, 510, 515–21, 534–38; Foster-Cánovas Treaty and, 396–97; Franklin D. Roosevelt and, 559, 564, 584, 586–87, 589; global depression and, 579–80; globalization and, 594; Great Depression and, 579, 582; Guantánamo Bay and, 588, 718, 899n227; Guevara and, 678–79; *Guys and Dolls* and, 572; Haitian Revolution and, 391; image of, 539–40, 559–88; imperialism and, 266, 337, 345–51, 355, 358–62, 366–71, 376, 381, 447, 449; incorporation of, 561–62; as infernal little republic, 559–88; informal influence over, 588–89; intrusion and, 383, 386–402, 408–14, 423, 428–36, 851n14; invasion of, 337; Jenks on, 21; Jones-Costigan Act and, 587; Lee and, 431; Liberation Army and, 432–33; Lobo and, 678–80; Machado and, 536; Martí and, 383, 397–98, 403, 413, 540–41, 565, 574–75, 576; martial law and, 581–82; McKinley and, 396, 413, 431, 561–63; men on the spot in, 589; Mexican investments and, 567; Miami and, 572; militant tradition of, 635; modernity for, 572; music of, 572; national debt and, 433; negotiating skills of, 575; new relevance for, 588–91; occupation of, 576–77; Partido Auténtico and, 661–62; Partido Independiente de Color and, 576; Partido Revolucionario Cubano and, 397, 563, 563–65; Permanent Army and, 576; plantations and, 391–92, 394, 400, 520, 566–67, 569, 571, 578, 678;

Platt Amendment and, 447, 561, 563–66, 573, 577, 582, 586; as pleasure island, 539–43; population growth in, 680; post-colonialism and, 695–96, 700, 716–20; as protectorate, 15, 37, 499, 515–16, 559, 660, 686, 700, 882n8; quotas and, 681–82; Reciprocity Treaty and, 564–65, 568, 573; revolution and, 519, 585, 678–79, 682, 717, 719–20; rival religions and, 571; Root and, 563–64; Rough Riders and, 611; sacrifice of, 639; self-government and, 410; Smoot-Hawley Tariff and, 579–80, 587; Southern states and, 391, 393; Soviet Union and, 682–83; Spain and, 37, 84, 214, 238, 544, 635; Spanish language as national identity and, 572; standard of living in, 719–20; sugar and, 517, 547, 550, 553, 561–70, 575–82, 586–88, 590, 601, 621, 626, 650, 660–61, 677–83, 719, 897n164; Teller Amendment and, 433, 561; Ten Years' War and, 349, 392–97, 401, 430; Theodore Roosevelt and, 564–65, 569, 576; tourism and, 571, 679, 719–20; uprising of 1895 and, 345–46; *USS Maine* and, 345, 354, 360, 368, 370, 372, 399, 415, 431–32, 539, 724; Verdeja Act and, 579, 586; voting rights and, 519, 575–76; war effects on, 574; wars of incorporation and, 213–14, 220, 237; Wilson and, 577; Wood and, 539, 563, 564–66, 569, 572, 576–78, 589, 611; Woodford and, 431–32
Cuba Cane Sugar Company, 570
Cuba Company, 563, 563, 566–67
Cuba Libre, 573–74
Cuban-American Treaty, 563
Cuban Liberation Army, 399, 432–33, 565
Cuban National Party, 565
cultural uplift, 178, 304, 323, 325, 332–33, 513, 572, 609, 624, 789n210
Cunard, Samuel, 90
Currency Act, 114, 116
Curzon, Lord, 507
Custer, George Armstrong, 199, 202
Czarnikow-MacDougall, 570
Czolgosz, Leon, 303–5

Dante (Dante Alighieri), 709, 727
Darwin, Charles, 251
Darwish, Mukhtar, 730
Daughters of the American Revolution, 335
Davenport, Charles B., 253
Davis, Bette, 679

Davis, Dwight, 617
Dawes Act, 200, 321, 502, 504
Dawes Plan, 446, 448
Day, William R., 416
Debs, Eugene, 300
Declaration of Human Rights, 660
declaration of independence: American football and, 330; Bandung Conference and, 698; British, 471; Caribbean and, 122; Monroe Doctrine and, 211; Philippines and, 413; tariffs and, 161; Texas and, 214–15
Declaration of Independence (American), 54, 110, 112, 123, 199
Decline and Fall of the Roman Empire (Gibbon), 54, 104
Decline of the West, The (Spengler), 254
declinism, 723
decolonization, 7, 840n30; American way and, 683–97; Caribbean and, 657–62, 674–83; Cold War and, 640, 642, 646, 651, 657, 661, 668, 672, 675, 683–86; conventional studies of, 640–41; empire-building and, 13; forgotten empire and, 497, 499, 507, 525, 531; formal, 35; globalization and, 641; holding on and, 643–49; imperialism and, 261–62, 445, 471, 479–80, 485, 487, 491–92; independence and, 19, 144–48, 153, 185, 187, 190, 288, 330; insular empire and, 40; Korea and, 712; military-fiscal state and, 72, 84, 91, 94; moving on and, 662–69; Pacific and, 631, 649–56, 669–74; postcolonialism and, 696, 700; postponed, 39; revolution and, 98, 112, 124, 138–41; surrendering authority and, 639–41; trajectory of, 640; wars of incorporation and, 235
deflation: forgotten empire and, 494; gold standard and, 255–58; great deflation and, 255–61; imperialism and, 255–61, 349, 375, 379, 457; independence and, 168, 288, 293–94, 296, 316, 318, 336; international dimensions of, 824n56; military-fiscal state and, 36–37; revolution and, 114, 116, 118; Seven Years' War and, 114; Spain and, 349–50
deglobalization, 459
Delamere, Hugh, 453
Delgado, Emilio, 541
democracy: cacique, 672; Caribbean and, 543, 546, 565–66, 574, 576, 584, 586; colonialism and, 17–18, 25, 39, 639, 644, 647, 652, 656, 664–65, 670, 672, 682; forgotten empire and, 519; Free World and, 39, 460,

democracy (*continued*)
475, 487–88, 491–92, 646, 663, 675, 684, 698, 713, 716, 723; imperialism and, 246, 276, 282, 344, 369, 443, 491–92; independence and, 143, 148–49, 153, 158, 176, 180–81, 189, 305, 313–15, 322, 328, 335; Iraq and, 734; liberty and, 7–8, 17–18, 25, 97, 143, 148, 176, 195, 218–19, 282, 335, 369, 543, 546, 574, 597, 605, 607, 665, 682, 694, 715, 721, 724; military-fiscal state and, 79, 88; Pacific and, 597, 600, 603, 605, 607, 609, 613–15, 627, 631; postcolonialism and, 694, 712–25, 729; revolution and, 97, 125, 133–34; Tocqueville and, 88, 149, 182, 281, 305; voting rights and, 344; wars of incorporation and, 195, 217–19, 231, 234

Democratic Alliance, 654, 656

Democratic Vistas (Whitman), 328

Democrats, 824n46; Anglo-Saxons and, 289; Bourbons and, 292, 296; Caribbean and, 556, 558, 561, 576, 578, 584, 586; colonialism and, 39, 645, 648, 650–52, 656, 666, 669–71, 681, 684; forgotten empire and, 495, 507, 511–14, 518–21, 524–28; imperialism and, 338, 354, 356, 360–61, 368–69, 375–76, 379, 448, 455; independence and, 148–49, 152–58, 162, 189, 288–306, 312, 322, 328, 332; intrusion and, 390, 422; Jackson, 148, 154, 162, 215; military-fiscal state and, 90; Pacific and, 598, 610, 613–14, 625, 627, 630; postcolonialism and, 712, 716; wars of incorporation and, 214, 216, 222–26

Denmark, 73–75, 232, 272, 455

Department of Commerce and Labor, 305

Dependent Pension Act, 295

despotism, 5, 33, 66, 89, 91, 125, 161, 206, 220, 248, 251, 282, 353, 362, 367, 448, 655

Development Bank, 558

Dewey, George, 403, 416, 860n192

Dewey, John, 306, 367–68

dialectical forces: Adam Smith and, 34; colonialism and, 32, 34, 38–40; globalization and, 6–7, 12, 32, 38–40, 139, 457, 693; imperialism and, 379, 457; Montesquieu and, 32–34, 40, 53, 91, 124–25, 133, 136, 140–41, 282, 336, 693, 707, 727; postcolonialism and, 693; revolution and, 97, 139

Dicey, Albert, 252

Dickens, Charles, 364

Dickinson, Emily, 328–29, 837n286

Dictionary (Johnson), 53

Dictionary (Webster), 179

Dictionary (Worcester), 179

Diderot, Denis, 66, 89

Dien Bien Phu, 663

Dilke, Charles, 194, 377, 435

Dillingham Commission, 321–22

Dingley Tariff, 361, 423

direct rule, 4, 71, 503–4, 588–89, 611

discrimination: African Americans and, 380, 506, 645–47; Chinese immigrants and, 435; ethnicity and, 173, 175, 218, 236, 289, 342, 375, 410, 430, 605; Freetown and, 96; French radicalism and, 87; Irish exports and, 70; mercantilism and, 151, 273, 348, 435, 447, 518; *Plessy v. Ferguson* and, 320; racial, 221, 292, 323, 487, 506, 555, 602, 623, 645–47, 650, 661, 664, 667, 684, 700, 723; religious, 69, 113, 174; Spanish caste system and, 397; tariffs and, 151, 273, 348, 518; Voting Rights Act and, 667

Dismal Swamp Company, 95

Division of Territories and Insular Possessions, 589

d'Octon, Paul Vigné, 263

Dole, James D., 599

Dole, Sanford B., 422, 599–600, 603

Dollar Diplomacy (Nearing), 21

Dominican Republic, 449

Dostoyevsky, Fyodor, 75

Dowdy, Joseph D., 731–32

Dow Jones index, 723

Dred Scott case, 222, 224

Du Bois, W. E. B., 648

Dulles, John Foster, 489, 666

Dundas, Henry, 86

Dundas, Lawrence, 67

Dunmore, Lord, 95, 120

Dutch East India Company, 52

Dutch Republic, 59, 139

Dvorak, Anton, 331

Dylan, Bob, 665–66

dysentery, 265, 409, 415

Étienne, Eugène, 280

Eddy, Mary Baker, 323

Eden, Anthony, 484

Egypt, 45–46, 71, 258, 264, 453–56, 482, 504, 563, 577, 619, 716, 737, 894n107

Eisenhower, Dwight D., 305, 313, 643–45, 651, 663, 666, 671, 673, 676, 682–83

El Salvador, 717

Emerson, Ralph Waldo, 175, 179–80

empire, 5, 11–12; Adam Smith and, 135; British Empire and, 83–90 (*see also* British Empire); colonialism and, 13 (*see also* colonialism); concept of, 21–26; as epithet, 19; forgotten, 494–538; globalization and, 25–32 (*see also* globalization); informal, 15, 22–23, 27, 65, 188, 216, 262, 284, 385, 429, 430, 450, 471, 686, 699; insular, 383 (*see also* insular empire); intrusion and, 385, 388, 426–27; new global order and, 64–70; official tuition and, 521–30; political juggernaut and, 383–86; project of, 135–41; Seven Years' War and, 33, 45, 52, 57–58, 61–64, 83, 99, 105, 112, 114, 118–19, 122, 140; technology and, 6, 28; wars of incorporation and, 209; World War II era and, 465–70. *See also* imperialism

Engels, Friedrich, 69, 81, 679

English Civil War, 135

English Traits (Emerson), 180

Enlightenment: colonialism and, 641; independence and, 176–77, 184; intrusion and, 412; military-fiscal state and, 64–65, 71, 78, 87, 89; new global order and, 64–70; optimism of, 6; postcolonialism and, 698; revolution and, 103, 126, 132; Scottish, 103, 132; wars of incorporation and, 210

entrepreneurs: Caribbean and, 550, 567, 568; imperialism and, 350; independence and, 157, 314; intrusion and, 386, 394, 401, 422; military-fiscal state and, 48–49, 55, 67–68; Pacific and, 599, 620

Episcopalians, 366

Era of Good Feelings, 143, 152, 209, 210

Erewhon (Butler), 245

"Essay on Criticism, An" (Pope), v

Estrada Palma, Tomás, 564–65, 575

ethnicity, 173, 175, 218, 236, 289, 342, 375, 410, 430, 605

"Ethnogenesis" (Timrod), 225

eugenics, 253, 318, 438, 505

European Convention on Human Rights, 646

European Defense Community, 710

European Economic Community (EEC), 487, 710

European Union (EU), 703–4

Evangelical Alliance, 324

Evnin, Mark, 730–33, 735

Evnin, Mindy, 731

exceptionalism, 754n71; colonialism and, 8, 15–21, 641, 644, 743nn15, 16, 744nn20–22, 29; foreign policy and, 317; forgotten empire and, 525, 884n43; Glorious Revolution and, 53–60; independence and, 787n174; military-fiscal state and, 53–60, 753n44, 754n71; national psyche and, 530; normality and, 535; Pacific and, 904n93; postcolonialism and, 929n139; providential, 641; revolution and, 775n193; supranational forces and, 492; United States and, 15–21, 157, 335, 492, 530; wars of incorporation and, 796n77; Wilson and, 335

expansionism: American Century and, 38, 443–46, 492–93, 707, 723, 726; Caribbean and, 543, 584; colonialism and, 18, 20; desire for land and, 193, 410; economic optimism and, 245–49; forgotten empire and, 500–501, 521; Free World and, 39, 460, 475, 487–88, 491–92, 646, 663, 675, 684, 698, 713, 716, 723; Great Depression and, 561–62; gunboat diplomacy and, 88–89, 237, 536; imperialism and, 261–62, 270, 339, 354–65, 368, 370, 376–77; independence and, 295; intrusion and, 386, 393, 421, 430, 433–36; irresistible tendency to, 355–62; isolationism and, 17; manifest destiny and, 114, 148, 176, 191, 195, 214–15, 325, 365–66, 492, 508; Mexico and, 212–17; monopolies and, 136; official tuition and, 521–30; Pacific and, 595–96, 600, 605–6, 627, 631, 634; property rights and, 194–207; Soviet Union and, 713; Texas and, 215; Treaty of Ghent and, 209; wars of incorporation and, 192–93, 203, 212–16, 237

Expansionists of 1898 (Pratt), 20

exports: Caribbean and, 544, 547–50, 560–61, 564, 567–70, 577–81, 587–91; coffee and, 65, 102, 193, 295, 347, 350, 388, 391, 401–402, 406, 428, 457, 516, 547–49, 553; colonialism and, 110, 114–21, 133, 139, 649–50, 653, 656–57, 660–61, 673–76, 679–80, 684; crops and, 29, 38–39, 88, 261, 388, 406, 409, 499, 517, 536, 544, 549, 560, 595, 625; forgotten empire and, 499, 516–20, 526, 535–38; imperialism and, 250, 256–61, 274–80, 284, 342, 347–51, 356–60, 375–75, 381, 447–48, 458–59, 462, 477–78, 482; independence and, 151, 154, 162–64, 167–68, 170–71, 186–89, 293–96, 308–10, 323, 334; intrusion and,

exports (*continued*)
  385–96, 399–401, 404–11, 418–27, 433,
    436, 852n32; Jeffersonians and, 133;
    military-fiscal state and, 57–59, 69, 74–75,
    85, 88–89, 93; overseas trade growth and,
    57–58; Pacific and, 595, 598–606, 615,
    616–21, 625–30, 634–37; postcolonialism
    and, 697, 701–4, 708–13, 719, 722; sugar
    and, 39 (*see also* sugar); tobacco and, 58,
    110, 117–19, 162, 305, 308, 347, 388, 391–
    92, 397, 401, 405, 408, 544, 547–53, 582;
    Townshend Duties and, 114–15, 117; wars
    of incorporation and, 196, 208, 213, 222,
    227–29, 232; West Indies and, 58, 110, 164

Farmers' Alliance, 297, 817n156
fascism, 449, 460, 470, 491
Faubus, Orval, 666
Federal Bureau of Investigation (FBI), 250,
    648, 658, 718
Federalists, 128–35, 141, 144, 150–52, 155,
    157, 208, 224, 613, 773n150
Federal Reserve Bank, 312
Fenimore Cooper, James, 180
Ferdinand VII, King of Spain, 73–74
Ferguson, Adam, 103
Ferrara, Colonel Orestes, 569
Ferry, Jules, 280
FIDES, 477–78
Fiji, 504
financial crisis of 2008, 725–26, 728
Firestone, Harvey S., 619–20
First Continental Congress, 122–23
First National Bank, 165
First Peoples, 197, 207, 598, 648, 668, 719
Fish, Hamilton, 419
Fiske, John, 365–66
Flanders, 99
Flynn, Errol, 202
Fontaine, Joan, 679
food shortages, 63, 631
football, 330–31
Foraker Act, 545–49
Foraker Amendment, 561, 563, 566
Forbes, William C., 613–14
Fordney-McCumber Act, 518, 578–79
foreign aid, 229–30, 400, 464, 703, 722
foreign direct investment (FDI), 447, 459,
    701–2
Foreign Service Act, 522
forgotten empire, 39; Africa and, 498, 503,
    529, 531, 535–38; African Americans
    and, 506; agriculture and, 500, 516, 529,
    535; Anglo-Saxons and, 495, 505, 514;
    assimilation and, 498–504, 507, 509–13,
    529–34; autonomy and, 516; British
    Empire and, 522; buyer's remorse and,
    494–597; capitalism and, 507, 520–21,
    526–27, 529; Catholicism and, 502; China
    and, 534, 536; Christianity and, 512–13;
    citizenship and, 500, 513–15; civilizing
    mission and, 496, 500–501, 508–9, 512–13,
    519, 525, 531–36; Civil War and, 515, 518;
    Cold War and, 496, 531; conservatives
    and, 500, 506, 528; constitutional issues
    and, 509–12; Cuba and, 494, 499–501,
    504, 510, 515–21, 534–38; decolonization
    and, 497, 499, 507, 525, 531; deflation
    and, 494; democracy and, 519; Dem-
    ocrats and, 495, 507, 511–14, 518–21,
    524–28; empire-building and, 497, 531;
    expansionism and, 500–501, 521; exports
    and, 499, 516–20, 526, 535–38; France
    and, 500, 503, 508, 510–13, 525, 531–33,
    536–37; free trade and, 514, 520; French
    Revolution and, 526; Germany and, 507,
    535; globalization and, 535; Hawai'i and,
    494, 499–501, 504, 510, 515, 517, 519, 521,
    523, 526, 531, 533–38; immigration and,
    507, 534; imports and, 505, 516, 518; India
    and, 498, 503, 505, 529, 536–38; Insular
    Cases and, 515, 520; international rela-
    tions and, 496, 507; Italy and, 535; Japan
    and, 495, 507, 535, 538; Jefferson and,
    500; labor and, 508, 525–26, 534, 536;
    liberalism and, 505; liberty and, 505–7,
    512–21; lobbies and, 500, 512–21; man-
    ufacturing and, 536; McKinley and, 501,
    523; mercantilism and, 516; Mexico and,
    531; modernization and, 504–9; monopo-
    lies and, 520–21, 527; Muslims and, 504;
    Napoleon and, 526; national identity and,
    507; nationalism and, 496, 524, 527–32,
    536–37; nation-building and, 504, 509,
    523; New Left and, 513; official tuition
    and, 521–30; oil and, 495; oligarchy and,
    519, 537; Philippines and, 494–506, 511,
    517, 518–20, 523–38; plantations and,
    499; populism and, 519; poverty and, 528;
    progressives and, 506, 508, 521, 526; pro-
    tectionism and, 516, 519; Protestantism
    and, 513; Puerto Rico and, 494, 499–501,
    504, 509, 511, 515, 517, 520, 522–30, 534,
    536–38; raw materials and, 535; reciproc-
    ity and, 518, 520; reconstruction and, 523;
    Republicans and, 494–95, 507, 511–12,

514, 518, 520–21, 524–28, 536; Russia and, 507; Schurman Commission and, 497–98; self-determination and, 534, 538; slavery and, 516; sovereignty and, 516; Spain and, 494–95, 502, 532–33; Spanish-American War and, 501, 505, 507, 520–22; Taft and, 495, 502, 506, 512, 531; tariffs and, 514–21, 535; taxes and, 520; technology and, 508, 521; terrorism and, 494; Theodore Roosevelt and, 495, 506, 508, 512; unemployment and, 537; white man's burden and, 494; white settlers and, 537; Winks and, 496–97, 530–34; World War I era and, 507, 518, 536; World War II era and, 504, 508, 510, 512, 531, 537

Fort Knox, 471

Fortune magazine, 443

Foster, John W., 422

Foster-Cánovas Treaty, 396–97, 408

Founding Fathers, 17, 94, 153, 174, 183, 185, 192, 316, 363, 446, 509, 565

Fox, Charles James, 103

France: Bourbons and, 74; Cold War and, 714; colonialism and, 642, 644, 663, 669, 684; de Gaulle and, 479, 709–10; exceptionalism and, 16; FIDES and, 477–78; forgotten empire and, 500, 503, 508, 510–13, 525, 531–33, 536–37; Fourth Republic and, 479; Godless revolution in, 508; Greater France and, 473; imperialism and, 38, 246–47, 250, 253–54, 259–81, 285, 345–46, 355, 375, 445, 449–51, 457–59, 463–64, 468–83, 488–92; independence and, 160, 166–67, 173, 177, 189–90, 289, 327; Indo-China and, 267, 280, 409, 471, 476, 481, 483, 642, 656, 663, 714; intrusion and, 391, 397, 403; Méline Tariff and, 279; Michelet and, 16; military-fiscal state and, 46, 48, 51–53, 58, 62, 65–78, 84, 91; Ministry of Overseas France and, 881n245; Mitterand and, 481; Monnet Plan and, 709–10; Napoleon and, 57, 71–75, 78, 84, 92, 185, 188, 218, 228, 344, 526, 679; Napoleon III and, 230, 233, 278; Palmer and, 3; Paris Commune and, 279; postcolonialism and, 697, 709–10, 713–14, 716; reassertion of control by, 644; reconstruction in, 709–10; Reign of Terror and, 134–35, 662; restructuring of, 37; revolution and, 99–101, 106, 113–14, 123, 138; Robespierre and, 135; Suez Canal and, 716–17; Third Republic and, 279; tourism and, 478; War of 1812 and, 211;

wars of incorporation and, 192, 210, 213, 230–33; World War II era and, 471 (*see also* World War II era)

Francisco Sugar Company, 570

Franc Zone, 473–74, 476, 877n175

Franklin, Benjamin, 102, 112, 123, 303

Franz Ferdinand, Archduke of Austria, 270

Franz Joseph I, Emperor of Austria, 233

Frederick the Great, 48

free soilers, 157, 223

Freetown, 96

free trade: American System and, 160, 162, 169, 196, 296; Carey and, 160–61, 238; Caribbean and, 548, 553, 568, 590; China and, 706–7; colonialism and, 34, 36, 656; differential consequences of, 813n91; economic optimism and, 245–49; forgotten empire and, 514, 520; imperialism and, 245–46, 254–55, 257, 260–62, 272–74, 283, 347–48, 356, 358, 362, 375, 458; independence and, 155–70, 186, 188, 291–95, 302, 309, 332–33; intrusion and, 391, 396–97, 400, 402, 406, 422, 427, 435; liberals and, 273–74; military-fiscal state and, 47, 55–56, 67, 70, 74, 77–83, 86–88, 93; NAFTA and, 703–4; Pacific and, 616–17, 627–28; postcolonialism and, 703, 706; Reciprocity Act and, 163; revolution and, 131, 133, 137; Southern states and, 35; Suez Canal and, 347, 435, 482; sugar and, 406 (*see also* sugar); textile industry and, 167–68; wars of incorporation and, 196, 210, 220, 222, 226, 229, 231–32, 238

Free World, 39, 460, 475, 487–88, 491–92, 646, 663, 675, 684, 698, 713, 716, 723

French Revolution: as example for other countries, 134–35; Federalists and, 134; forgotten empire and, 526; imperialism and, 241, 346; independence and, 148, 177; military-fiscal state and, 47, 70, 78, 92; Tocqueville and, 114

French Wars: imperialism and, 241, 249; independence and, 151, 168; military-fiscal state and, 52–53, 57–59, 71–72, 77–83; revolution and, 126; wars of incorporation and, 208, 211–12

friars: lands of, 404, 410, 619, 859n158; Philippines and, 387, 404, 409–10, 611, 619, 851n24, 851n25, 857n121

Fries's Rebellion, 130

Fugitive Slave Act, 75, 224

Fuller, George A., 331

Gaddis, John Lewis, 24

Gage, Thomas, 119–20

Gag Law, 658

Gallagher, John, 23, 471

Galton, Francis, 253, 318

Gandhi, Mohandas, 148, 450, 461, 463, 469, 486, 536, 552, 667

García, Carlos Político, 674

García Menocal, Mario, 569, 577

Garibaldi, Giuseppe, 72, 75, 229, 238, 275, 682

Garrison, William Lloyd, 72–73, 88, 218

Gaulle, Charles de, 479, 709–10

gender, 13, 249, 266, 341–43, 699

General Agreement on Trade and Tariffs (GATT), 708, 710

General Electric, 314, 584

Genocide Convention, 646

George I, King of Great Britain and Ireland, 62

George III, King of Great Britain and Ireland, 53, 57, 100, 112, 116, 122, 137, 167, 183

George, Henry, 313

Germany: Battle of El Alamein and, 470; Berlin Wall and, 723; colonialism and, 644; denazification and, 709; forgotten empire and, 507, 535; imperialism and, 247, 250, 260–61, 267, 269–81, 285, 352, 354, 365–66, 375, 381, 446, 449–50, 457, 465–69, 472, 489–90; independence and, 288, 308, 313, 332; intrusion and, 416; military-fiscal state and, 72; Pacific and, 625; postcolonialism and, 709–13; reconstruction in, 709; self-determination and, 37; Teutonic qualities and, 251–52, 318, 366, 423; unification and, 37; World War II era and, 465 (*see also* World War II era)

Gibbon, Edward, 48, 54, 66, 86, 104, 122, 252, 750n7, 794n35

Gilded Age, 287, 297, 313, 317, 329, 362, 382, 520

Gilded Age, The (Twain and Warner), 313, 329, 808n7

Giolitti, Giovanni, 251

Gladstone, William, 79, 231, 253, 264, 271, 293, 295, 464, 522

globalization: balance of payments and, 702; British Empire and, 27, 31; Caribbean and, 570; colonialism and, 39–40, 640–43, 685; concept of, 25–32; Cuba and, 594; current interest in, 12–13; decolonization and, 641–43; deglobalization and, 459; dialectical forces and, 6–7, 12,

32, 457, 693; economic optimism and, 244–49; empires as agents of, 6; financial crisis of 2008 and, 725–26, 728; forgotten empire and, 535; global turn and, 11, 17, 49; Hawai'i and, 633; heterogeneity and, 11; homogeneity and, 11; hostility toward, 11; imperialism and, 6–7, 25–32, 241–49, 252, 254, 256, 260–68, 281–85, 337, 344, 352, 375, 444–45, 459–61; independence and, 190, 292, 296, 298, 301, 325–26, 332, 336; intrusion and, 38, 386, 409–10, 426–27, 436; Johnstones and, 68–69; military-fiscal state and, 45, 47, 68, 71, 91, 94, 693; modern, 32, 36, 94, 241, 243–49, 261, 268, 281–85, 336, 344, 352, 374, 426–27, 444–45, 492, 594, 636, 640, 691, 694–95, 725; modernization and, 241–49; multiple origins of, 32; new imperialism and, 261–67; Pacific and, 594, 633, 636; postcolonialism and, 8, 40, 689, 691–707, 718, 725–27; postwar environment and, 721–29; proto-globalization and, 7, 32, 34, 47, 71, 91, 94, 98, 139, 190, 241, 344, 426–27, 693; Puerto Rico and, 594; rapid institutional growth and, 702–3; revolution and, 98, 139; technology and, 29–30; three phases of, 7, 12; transfer of power and, 19; wars of choice and, 427–36

global turn, 11, 17, 49

Glorious Revolution: American Revolution and, 126, 140; British Empire and, 46, 53–62, 68, 70, 90, 100, 103, 113, 122, 126, 137, 140; exceptionalism and, 53–60; military-fiscal state and, 53–60; Spain and, 392

Gobineau, Count Joseph-Arthur de, 89

Goethe, Johann Wolfgang von, 248, 709

Gold Coast, 483

gold standard, 871n76; deflation and, 255–58; imperialism and, 255–60, 269, 272, 274, 278–79, 283–84, 350, 355–56, 362, 375, 381, 450, 456–57; independence and, 291–94, 298–99, 302–3, 310–11, 318, 333; military-fiscal state and, 80–81; Philippines and, 616; return to, 291

Gold Standard, The (Adams), 318

Goltz, Wilhelm Leopold Colmar von der, 2, 740n12

Gómez, José Miguel, 569, 575–76

Gompers, Samuel, 367

Good Neighbor policy, 449, 556, 584–85

Gordon, Charles, 202, 272

Gordon Riots, 53

Gore, Robert H., 524

Goulart, João, 717
Government of India Act, 454, 464, 631
Grand Army of the Republic, 335
Grangers, 296, 321
Grant, Ulysses S., 212, 225, 256, 419
Grau San Martin, Ramón, 582–86, 661
Great Awakening, 64, 78, 109, 175–76, 184, 264, 322–23, 334
Great Depression, 517, 812n67; catastrophic impact of, 456–65; causes of, 456–57; civil rights and, 668; Cold War and, 644; colonialism and, 463–64; Cuba and, 579–80, 582; deglobalization and, 459; expansionism and, 561–62; imperialism and, 256, 456–64; increasing specialization and, 457–58; Keynes and, 463, 471–72; manufacturing and, 463–64; nationalism and, 461; Ottawa Agreements and, 458; preconditions for, 456–58; rural society and, 461; Smoot-Hawley Tariff and, 458, 579; stock market crash of 1929 and, 456; urbanization and, 561–62
Great Exhibition, 244–45
Great Illusion, The (Angell), 254
Great Imperial Novel, 263
Great Railroad Strike, 299
Great Reform Act, 45, 78–79
Great Sioux War, 199–200
Great Society, 305, 668
Greece, 25, 30, 72, 225
green uprising, 80, 144, 148–49, 153, 189, 298, 461, 479, 537, 554, 582, 642
Grenville, George, 99–100, 106, 346
Gresham, Walter, 422
Gross Domestic Product (GDP), 171, 247, 257–58, 272, 278, 308, 681, 722
Gross National Product (GNP), 307–8
Gruening, Ernest, 527–29, 556–57, 889n144, 893n75, 893n76, 893n83
Guam, 494, 499, 504, 523, 526–28, 538, 838n2
Guantanamera (Cuban song), 541
Guantánamo Bay, 588, 718, 899n227
Guatemala, 449, 717
guerrillas, 72, 284, 415, 469, 482, 538, 631, 655–56, 677–78
Guevara, Che, 678–79
Guggenheim, Harry, 581
gunboat diplomacy, 88–89, 237, 536
Guys and Dolls (movie), 572

Haberler, Gotfried, 701
Habsburgs, 344

Hailey, Lord, 463
Haiti, 97, 148, 391–92, 449, 585
Hall, Robert, 482–83
Hamilton, Alexander: Beard and, 130; British model and, 132, 141; Carey and, 160–61; Clay and, 160; federal power and, 132; Fichte and, 782n87; First Bank of the United States and, 131; on French influence, 135; industrialization and, 161; Jeffersonians and, 146–59, 173, 189, 379; List and, 318, 363; national debt and, 131; "Report on Manufactures" and, 159; Republicans and, 293, 333; rhetoric of Revolution and, 146–47, 150–58; as Secretary of the Treasury, 130–31; state as bounded entity and, 173; tariffs and, 160; War of 1812 and, 160
Hancock, John, 112
Hancock, W. K., 499
Hanna, Marcus, 302, 369
Hanotaux, Gabriel, 280
Hanoverian rulers, 61, 98–101, 122, 136
Harding, Warren, 524, 625
Hardy, Thomas, 254
Hare-Hawes-Cutting Act, 627–29
Harper, Congressman Robert, 177
Harper's Weekly journal, 300
Harrison, Benjamin, 421–22
Harrison, Francis, 525, 613, 614, 625, 888n122, 904n105, 908n175
Harrison, William Henry, 169, 327, 421–22, 786n151, 831n171, 863nn235, 236, 238
Hartley, David, 99
Havana Casino Orchestra, 539–40
"have" and "have not" powers, 465, 466, 468, 487, 491, 643, 646, 663, 665, 686, 874n122
Havemeyer, Henry, 302, 360–61, 425, 513–14, 519–21, 547, 549, 564, 566, 619
Havemeyer, Horace, 549
Hawai'i: African Americans and, 605, 645; agrarian ideal and, 596; Aleutians and, 864n247; annexation of, 37, 215, 337, 361, 383–84, 417, 421–28, 645, 864n258; Big Five and, 599–605, 618, 649–52, 670; bombing of, 639; canoe transport and, 417; Chinese Exclusion Act and, 424; Civil Rights Act and, 671; Cleveland and, 421, 425; colonialism and, 639, 645–46, 649–52, 662, 666, 669–71, 674, 683–85 Committee of Safety and, 421–22; Cook and, 417; cultural resistance in, 593; dark side of, 417, 602–3; Dingley Tariff and, 423; diseases of, 418; economic viability

Hawai'i (*continued*)
of, 418–19; emigration and, 550; expansionism and, 605–6; as first foothold in Pacific, 633; forgotten empire and, 494, 499–501, 504, 510, 515, 517, 519, 521, 523, 526, 531, 533–34, 536; Franklin D. Roosevelt and, 604; Home Rule Party and, 597–98; image of, 539, 592, 594–606, 899n3; Immigration Act and, 603; imperialism and, 267, 337, 349–51, 353, 357–58, 361, 366, 370, 376, 468; incorporation and, 598–99, 718; independence and, 417–19, 635; International Longshore & Warehouse Union (ILWU) and, 604, 606, 650, 652; intrusion and, 383–84, 386–90, 408, 428–31, 435, 436, 851n14; Iraq and, 421; as island of peace, 417, 594–606; Japanese and, 601–6; Jones-Costigan Act and, 605; Kaho'olawe, 718, Kalākaua, 419–21, 425; Kalaniana'ole and, 598; Kamehameha and, 417–19; Kaua'i, 599, 862n209; labor strikes in, 602–4; lack of discrimination in, 645–46; Lana'i, 600, 862n209; land reform in, 418; languages of, 598; Lili'uokalani and, 421, 425, 429–30; material precedent of, 594–95; Matson Navigation Line and, 599–600; Maui, 600, 604, 862n209; McKinley and, 383–84, 421, 423, 425; Moloka'i, 862n209; music and, 634; Northern states and, 596; O'ahu, 599–600, 862n209, 862n210; Pearl Harbor and, 191, 353, 419, 421, 430, 468–69, 538, 595, 605, 631, 902n71; as people passing away, 417–25; pineapples and, 422, 599–601, 606, 650–51, 719; plantations and, 386, 418, 423, 534, 536, 596, 599–603, 606; population demographics of, 15, 596–97; postcolonialism and, 696, 700, 718–20; postwar economics of, 558; progress in, 669–71, 674; protection in, 649–53; resistance to foreigners and, 635; retrospective view on, 635–38; Root and, 601; segregation and, 670–71; self-government and, 544, 597; as settler colony, 596–97; Song of the Islands and, 899n3; Southern states and, 596, 646, 650–51, 684; specialized studies of, 863n230; Spreckels and, 419–20, 426; statehood and, 430, 510, 515, 519, 521, 531, 548, 597, 604–5, 622, 649–53, 662, 669–71, 683–85; Stevens and, 421–22, 428, 431; sugar and, 349–51, 386–90, 408, 417–25, 429, 517, 521, 534, 536, 567, 598–606, 626, 633, 646, 649–51, 670; Taft and, 601; Theodore Roosevelt and, 600–601; tourism and, 417, 592, 598, 602, 719; traditions and, 593; treaty with, 419–22; as tropical Eden, 417; voting rights and, 196; vulnerability of, 605; wars of incorporation and, 196, 205, 214, 237; white oligarchy of, 596; Wilson-Gorman tariff and, 423
Hawaiian Homes Commission Act, 600–601
Hawaiian Pineapple Company, 599–600
Hay, John, 364, 435, 447, 449
Hayden, Joseph R., 502–3, 527–28
Hayes, Rutherford B., 256
Haymarket Riots, 299
Hegel, Georg Wilhelm Friedrich, 6, 71, 175, 253, 318, 366, 707
hegemony, 748n87, 927n103; anarchy and, 6; colonialism and, 6, 15, 18, 22, 24, 26, 30–32, 41; imperialism and, 6, 15, 18, 22, 24, 26, 30–32, 41, 376, 450; Iraq and, 736; postcolonialism and, 692, 696, 699–700, 707–21, 723, 727
hemp. *See* abaca (hemp)
Henty, G. A., 263–64, 502, 815n113, 815n114
Herder, Johann Gottfried, 89
Hernández Marín, Rafael, 553
Hispanism, 551
History of the Peloponnesian War, The (Thucydides), 31
Hoar, George F., 371
Hobson, J. A., 6, 259, 367
Ho Chi Minh, 450, 536, 683, 714
Hofstadter, Richard, 341
holidays, 315, 335, 656
home rule: Caribbean and, 545; colonialism and, 659; imperialism and, 352, 370, 380; intrusion and, 394, 397–98, 402, 429, 431–434, 436; Pacific and, 597–98, 609, 628; revolution and, 122–24
Home Rule Party, 597–98
Homestead Act, 222, 293, 829n134
Honduras, 449
Hong Kong, 409, 413, 435, 618, 860n192
Hoover, Herbert, 449, 580–81, 627, 909n189
Hoover, J. Edgar, 648
House Banking and Currency Committee, 312
House of Brown, 164
House of Savoy, 276
Howe, Richard, 123
Hugo, Victor, 73, 75, 238, 397, 759n153, 807n288

Hukbalahaps (Huks), 615, 655–56, 672, 684, 699–700

hula, 593, 632, 634

Hull, Cordell, 470, 876n150

human rights, 913n29; colonialism and, 646–48, 660, 666–68, 685; imperialism and, 460; independence and, 145; natural rights as, 145; postcolonialism and, 698–99, 705–6, 718; postwar concept of, 105; wars of incorporation and, 219, 231, 237

Humboldt, Alexander von, 65

Hume, David, 33, 66, 89, 103–4, 125

Huskisson, William, 81

Hussein, Saddam, 733–34, 931n30

Hutcheson, Francis, 104–5

Ibero Pancho, 552

Ibn Khaldun, 735, 737–38, 932n42

Ickes, Harold L., 527–28, 553, 604

ilustrados, 403, 410, 504, 607, 611–13, 616, 620, 628, 633

immigration: Anglo-Saxon assimilation and, 317–21; Caribbean and, 557, 578, 582; disruption from, 329; ethnic diversity and, 184; foreign capital and, 333; forgotten empire and, 507, 534; imperialism and, 253, 338, 349, 363–64, 367, 375, 448; intrusion and, 408; labor issues and, 288 (see also labor); Northern states and, 292; Pacific and, 597, 601, 603, 626, 635, 908n184; population growth and, 110, 307; social unrest and, 203; urbanization and, 288, 292, 324, 338; wars of incorporation and, 193, 203–4, 214

Immigration Act, 507, 603, 626

Immigration Restriction League, 253, 321–22

imperialism: Adam Smith and, 244–46, 261, 273, 284–85, 344, 457; Africa and, 37, 261, 264–69, 272, 277, 280, 284–85, 349, 450–51, 454, 461, 466–67, 470–72, 474, 476, 478–86, 489, 491, 596, 620; African Americans and, 370, 380, 466; agriculture and, 241–44, 247, 250, 269, 275–80, 284, 339, 344–45, 368, 375, 452, 458, 478; American Century and, 38, 443–46, 492–93, 707, 723, 726; anarchy and, 250, 256, 276–77, 281–82, 344, 363; Anglo-Saxons and, 251–53, 264, 273, 342, 356, 363–66, 374, 379, 380, 455, 467, 470; anti-imperialism and, 105, 263, 303, 367–68, 372, 379, 461, 464, 470, 479, 494,

501, 508, 532, 561, 564, 584, 624, 639, 680, 713–14, 720, 814n106; assimilation and, 347, 452, 473, 479; Australia and, 250, 253, 258, 266, 451, 454, 477, 480, 487–88; autonomy and, 352, 361, 381, 454, 488; British Empire and, 36, 263, 364, 451, 453, 467–72, 476, 480, 492; Canada and, 250, 260, 266, 273, 357–58, 447, 454, 477, 480–81, 487, 489, 596; capitalism and, 22, 250, 259, 262, 280–83, 339–40, 347, 355, 362, 364, 380–82, 451, 459, 463, 465; Catholicism and, 265–66, 279, 281, 345, 366–67; China and, 253, 262, 267, 280, 284–85, 357, 366, 443, 446, 448, 456, 465, 481, 483; Christianity and, 246, 248–49, 264–66, 443, 472, 492; citizenship and, 479, 487; civilizing mission and, 259, 262, 280, 444, 453, 472, 477, 490; civil rights and, 493; Civil War and, 243, 269, 285, 338, 344, 353, 356, 362, 367, 369–70, 380; Cold War and, 460, 476, 480, 483, 487–89, 492; communism and, 449, 460, 462, 473, 475–76, 491, 493; conservatives and, 241, 249–50, 260, 263, 266, 271, 273, 275, 279, 283, 344–46, 352, 356, 362, 364, 367, 374–76, 444, 450, 452, 462, 464, 480, 483, 485; Cuba and, 266, 337, 345–51, 355, 358–62, 366–71, 376, 381, 447, 449; decolonization and, 261–62, 445, 471, 479–80, 485, 487, 491–92; deflation and, 255–61, 349, 375, 379, 457; democracy and, 246, 276, 282, 344, 369, 443, 491–92; Democrats and, 338, 354, 356, 360–61, 368–69, 375–76, 379, 448, 455; dialectical forces and, 379, 457; empire-building and, 241, 261, 268, 280, 369, 371, 380; empire studies and, 5, 11–12; entrepreneurs and, 350; expansionism and, 261–62, 270, 339, 354–65, 368, 370, 376–77; exports and, 250, 256–61, 274–80, 284, 342, 347–51, 356–60, 375, 381, 447–48, 458–59, 462, 477–78, 482; financial crisis and, 456–64; forgotten empire and, 494–538; France and, 38, 246–47, 250, 253–54, 259–81, 285, 345–46, 355, 375, 445, 449–51, 457–59, 463–64, 468–83, 488–92; free trade and, 245–46, 254–55, 257, 260–62, 272–74, 283, 347–48, 356, 358, 362, 375, 458; French Revolution and, 241, 346; French Wars and, 241, 249; Germany and, 247, 250, 260–61, 267, 269–81, 285, 352, 354, 365–66, 375, 381, 446, 449–50, 457, 465–69, 472, 489–90;

imperialism (*continued*)

globalization and, 6–7, 25–32, 241–49, 252, 254, 256, 260–68, 281–85, 337, 344, 352, 374, 444–45, 459–61; gold standard and, 255–60, 269, 272, 274, 278–79, 283–84, 350, 355–56, 362, 375, 381, 450, 456–57; Good Neighbor policy and, 449, 556, 584–85; Great Depression and, 256, 456–64; Hawai'i and, 267, 337, 349–51, 353, 357–58, 361, 366, 370, 376, 468; hegemony and, 6, 15, 18, 22, 24, 26, 30–32, 41, 376, 450; historical treatments of, 10–15; home rule and, 352, 370, 380; human rights and, 460; immigration and, 253, 338, 349, 363–64, 367, 375, 448; imports and, 256, 260, 275, 348, 351, 357, 375, 447, 458–59, 482; India and, 33, 245, 262, 274, 344, 450, 453–55, 461–64, 469–72, 475, 479–81, 486, 489 (*see also* India); industrialization and, 29, 56, 59, 221, 244, 248, 269, 272, 277, 281–82, 346, 584; insular empire and, 267, 339, 341, 349, 361, 455, 492; international relations and, 18, 20, 23, 39–41, 263, 443; Ireland and, 326; isolation and, 242, 271, 353, 377, 443, 446–50, 468; Italy and, 242, 247, 261, 267–70, 275–80, 344, 380, 451, 465–66; Japan and, 261, 266–67, 269, 381, 446, 451, 455–56, 465–72, 487; labor and, 242, 244, 247–48, 250, 256, 261, 263, 271, 281, 283, 347, 349, 351, 359, 363, 367, 375, 449, 452, 458, 460, 462, 471–72, 474, 478, 482, 487; liberalism and, 281, 352, 460; liberty and, 243, 251, 282, 354, 361, 363, 369, 375–77, 381, 444; lobbies and, 279–80, 353, 359, 361, 368, 380, 425–26, 448; manifest destiny and, 114, 148, 176, 191, 195, 215, 325, 365–66, 492, 508; manufacturing and, 244, 260–61, 268, 273–77, 284, 341, 345, 348–51, 357–62, 375–76, 380, 382, 444, 447, 457–58, 462–64, 482, 484; Marx and, 245, 247, 250, 255, 259, 262, 279, 282, 344, 374, 378, 381, 491; McKinley and, 252, 343, 355–61, 364, 369–73, 381, 440; mercantilism and, 23, 34, 246, 271, 347, 458; Mexico and, 346–47, 358, 372, 448–49; modernization and, 247, 268–71, 274–75, 282–83, 479; monopolies and, 247, 261, 269, 278, 356, 405–7, 434; Napoleon and, 344; national identity and, 271, 274, 368, 375, 382; nationalism and, 344–47, 352, 355–56, 363–64, 371, 444, 446, 449–56,

460–61, 463, 465–66, 470–71, 479–83, 486, 488, 491–92; nation-building and, 242, 249, 253, 266, 281–84, 344, 366, 374, 380, 486; Netherlands and, 267, 270–72, 451, 457, 483; new, 261–67; New Left and, 340–41, 360, 446; noble destiny and, 497–504; Northern states and, 276, 288–92; oil and, 449, 456–57, 478, 482; oligarchy and, 248, 276, 344; Ottoman Empire and, 258, 262, 280, 284, 451; patriotism and, 254, 264, 353, 362, 367, 369, 372, 376, 381, 454; Philippines and, 267, 337, 342, 347–51, 355, 367, 372, 376, 381, 455, 573; populism and, 250, 271, 345, 356, 367, 369, 489; poverty and, 252, 347, 358, 488; progressives and, 248, 250, 260, 339–40, 352; property rights and, 248, 283, 356, 376; protectionism and, 265, 273, 276, 284, 348, 351, 379, 448, 458–60; Protestantism and, 265–66, 272, 366–67, 377, 381, 405, 422, 425, 429–30, 433–434; Prussia and, 254, 270, 278; Puerto Rico and, 337, 347, 350–51; raw materials and, 265, 274, 277, 447, 457, 473, 477; reciprocity and, 356–58, 375, 379; reconstruction and, 246–47, 491; Recuperation of the West and, 11, 640, 726; Republicans and, 263, 338, 354–64, 368–70, 374–76, 379–80, 448; return to normality and, 450–56; Rise of the West and, 11, 640, 726; Russia and, 247–51, 256, 260, 266–67, 278, 285, 475, 490; self-determination and, 249, 451, 460, 469, 491; slavery and, 26, 265, 276, 284, 341, 345, 347–49, 351, 373; South Africa and, 451, 454–55, 461–62, 476, 480, 484–85; sovereignty and, 19, 22–23, 27, 40, 262, 276, 373, 479; Spain and, 316, 337–55, 359, 366, 369, 371–77, 381; Spanish-American War and, 264, 337, 353, 362, 364, 455; sugar and, 347–51, 354, 357, 360–62, 381, 457, 513–21, 534, 536; Taft and, 449; tariffs and, 246, 260, 273–74, 279, 284, 348, 351, 354–62, 369, 375, 381, 446, 449, 458–59, 473; taxes and, 244, 253, 268, 270, 274, 276, 278, 282, 346–48, 354, 358, 361, 381, 452, 462, 467, 473, 478, 489; technology and, 242, 263, 273, 283; terrorism and, 250, 483, 491; textile industry and, 273, 277; Theodore Roosevelt and, 343, 354, 363–65, 368–71, 382; unemployment and, 256–61, 271, 275, 379, 456–57, 462, 467; United

Nations and, 460, 491; U.S. Constitution and, 367; voting rights and, 242; wars of 1898 and, 38, 243, 267, 337, 339–43, 346, 378, 386, 502, 560, 568; West Indies and, 463, 469, 483; white settlers and, 453, 479; Wilson and, 455; World War I era and, 38, 245, 248, 254, 265, 274, 352, 372, 443–46, 449–56, 465–66, 490; World War II era and, 445, 454, 460–92

imports: Boston and, 115; Caribbean and, 564, 568, 586, 590; colonialism and, 657, 673; Currency Act and, 118; foreign exchange and, 110; forgotten empire and, 505, 516, 518; Hamiltonians and, 131; imperialism and, 256, 260, 275, 348, 351, 357, 375, 447, 458–59, 482; increase in consumer, 111; independence and, 163, 168, 299, 309–10, 333; intrusion and, 388, 390, 393, 396, 400, 406, 420–21; military-fiscal state and, 58, 81–82; overseas trade growth and, 57–58; Pacific and, 603–4, 617, 626; postcolonialism and, 712, 722–23; slavery and, 129 (*see also* slavery); tariffs and, 151 (*see also* tariffs); tax reform and, 128; Townshend Duties and, 114–15, 117; wars of incorporation and, 222, 226, 232

independence: Africa and, 144, 292, 334; African Americans and, 143, 149, 181–83, 292, 308, 320, 323; agriculture and, 154, 159, 161, 163, 168–71, 187–88, 293, 299, 303, 307–9, 336; American Revolution and, 176–77, 307, 335; American System and, 160, 162, 169, 196, 296; anarchy and, 297, 300–302, 306; assimilation and, 145, 173–74, 184, 186, 189, 317, 320, 322, 324–25, 332; Australia and, 292, 298; authoritarianism and, 153, 178; autonomy and, 289; British Empire and, 143, 169, 178, 295, 330; capitalism and, 150, 161, 164, 171–72, 177, 184, 291, 296–97, 301, 305, 314, 324, 332–33, 335, 647, 652, 659, 674, 676, 681; Catholicism and, 174, 184, 301, 319, 322–23; China and, 322; Christianity and, 175–76, 181, 183, 304, 316–17, 323–25, 363, 366–67, 381; civil rights and, 288, 332; Civil War and, 149, 152, 155, 161, 163, 171–72, 184, 186–87, 190, 287–302, 306–11, 316, 320, 322, 326–35; conservatives and, 144, 148, 150, 166, 188–89, 299, 313, 317, 333; cosmopolitan nationalism and, 271, 293, 316–32; cotton industry and, 157, 162–63, 167–69, 186–87, 291, 308–9; cultural continuities and, 172–85; declaration of, 54, 110, 112, 122–23, 161, 199, 209, 211, 214–15, 330, 413, 471, 698; decolonization and, 19, 144–48, 153, 185, 187, 190, 288; deflation and, 168, 288, 293–94, 296, 316, 318, 336; democracy and, 143, 148–49, 153, 158, 176, 180–81, 189, 305, 313–15, 322, 328, 335; Democrats and, 148–49, 152–58, 162, 189, 288–306, 312, 322, 328, 332; development dilemmas of, 158–72; effective, 19; Enlightenment and, 176–77, 184; entrepreneurs and, 157, 314; expansionism and, 295; exports and, 151, 154, 162–64, 167–68, 170–71, 186–89, 293–96, 308–10, 323, 334; France and, 148, 160, 166–67, 173, 177, 189–90, 289, 327; free trade and, 155–70, 186, 188, 291–95, 302, 309, 332–33; French Wars and, 151, 168; Germany and, 288, 308, 313, 332; globalization and, 190, 241–49, 252, 254, 256, 260–68, 281–85, 292, 296, 298, 301, 325–26, 332, 336; gold standard and, 291–94, 298–99, 302–3, 310–11, 318, 333; Hawai'i and, 417–19, 635; imports and, 163, 168, 299, 309–10, 333; India and, 142, 146, 190, 291, 309, 641, 878n201; insular empire and, 143, 174, 185, 187; international relations and, 144; Ireland and, 326; Italy and, 253–54, 288, 328, 332; Japan and, 322; Jefferson and, 143, 146–61, 166–67, 169, 173–79, 189, 293, 297, 302–3; labor and, 147, 157–58, 163, 169, 171, 288–91, 297, 300–308, 319–22, 335; landowners and, 154, 181, 308; liberalism and, 148; liberty and, 142–43, 146, 148, 156, 174, 176, 179, 185–90, 301, 316, 335; Marx and, 300–301; manufacturing and, 146, 157, 159–63, 167–72, 186–88, 293–95, 299–303, 307–12, 334; McKinley and, 295, 299, 301–4; mercantilism and, 151, 159–60, 163, 169, 186–88; Mexico and, 312, 346; modernization and, 154, 305; monopolies and, 159, 167, 290, 294, 296, 322, 333; Monroe Doctrine and, 209, 211–12, 333, 370, 447, 516, 717; Napoleon and, 185, 188; national debt and, 151, 154, 156, 161, 165, 188; national identity and, 145, 172, 183, 187, 289, 319, 336; nationalism and, 145, 152, 157, 159, 175, 177, 182, 184–85, 189, 293, 304, 306, 316–24, 330, 333; nation-building and, 145, 172–73, 185,

independence (*continued*)
288–91, 321, 335; oil and, 302, 305, 314; oligarchy and, 149; patriotism and, 180, 182, 287, 289, 294, 300, 319, 326, 330; Philippines and, 531, 584, 638, 639, 686; populism and, 144, 148, 153–54, 183, 189, 296, 298, 301, 303–4, 321, 332; poverty and, 142, 144, 152, 308, 313, 315, 321–22, 329; progressives and, 304, 312–13, 324, 330, 333; property rights and, 166, 177, 291; protectionism and, 144, 157, 161, 163, 168, 293; Protestantism and, 173–78, 183, 289, 317–18, 322–24, 334; Puerto Rico and, 635, 657–58, 686, 699; raw materials and, 186, 295, 334; reciprocity and, 163, 295, 301; reconstruction and, 287, 290–91, 320, 332; Republicans and, 157, 160–61, 170, 189, 288–306, 310–11, 314, 319, 322, 329, 332–33; Russia and, 189; slavery and, 147–63, 168, 170–71, 173–74, 176, 181, 184–89, 289–91, 297, 308, 317, 320; South Africa and, 292, 312, 320; sovereignty and, 19, 145–46, 177, 185, 187, 321, 340; sugar and, 290, 295, 302; tariffs and, 151, 154–56, 160–63, 169–71, 186, 189, 291, 293–96, 299, 301–4, 307, 312, 314, 332–33; taxes and, 148, 151, 156, 162, 167, 188–89, 291, 303, 312–13; technology and, 316, 329; terrorism and, 290, 304; unemployment and, 144, 168–70, 300, 303–4, 317, 322; U.S. Constitution and, 146–49, 166–67, 170, 173–74, 177, 185, 290; War of 1812 and, 208–12; white settlers and, 145, 147, 321; World War II era and, 504–5

India: annexation and, 33, 65; Bandung Conference and, 487, 663–64, 698, 702; colonialism and, 1, 35, 46, 67, 96, 98, 142, 618, 641, 647, 655, 663; cotton and, 232; forgotten empire and, 498, 503, 505, 529, 536–38; Gandhi and, 148, 450, 461, 463, 469, 486, 536, 552, 667; Government of India Act and, 454, 464, 631; imperialism and, 245, 262, 274, 344, 450, 453–55, 461–64, 469–72, 475, 479–81, 486, 489; independence and, 142, 146, 190, 291, 309, 641, 878n201; military-fiscal state and, 46, 51, 54, 57, 65, 67–68, 79, 83–88, 93, 755n77; Mughals and, 49–50, 105–7; Natal Indian Congress and, 461; nationalism and, 455; Nehru and, 142, 146, 190, 480–81, 486, 664; New Development Bank and, 725; partitioning of, 190, 475, 481, 704; Peace of Paris and, 101; postcolonialism and, 698, 704–7, 721, 725; Quit India and, 469–70; railroads and, 245; revolution and, 98, 101–8, 111–15, 121–22, 135, 137; subsistence farming and, 628; trade issues and, 231–32; wars of incorporation and, 198, 231–32, 235–36

Indian Army, 1–4, 475, 736
Indian Citizenship Act, 201, 793n29
Indian Civil Rights Act, 669
Indian Mutiny, 505
Indian National Army, 469–70
Indian National Congress, 537
Indian Ocean, 347, 404
Indian Reorganization Act, 503
Indian Self-Determination and Education Act, 669
Indian Wars, 39, 173, 193, 197, 203, 237, 353, 372, 611
indigo, 110
indirect rule, 71, 404, 452, 463–64, 472, 503–4, 525, 529, 534, 541, 598, 610–11, 622, 648, 669, 884n36
Indo-China, 14, 267, 280, 409, 471, 476, 481, 483, 642, 656, 663, 714
Indonesia, 617, 713–14
industrialization: after Civil War, 338; imperialism and, 244, 248, 269, 277, 281–82; modernization and, 7, 36, 54, 94, 139, 244, 248, 269, 277, 281–82, 313, 322, 338, 364, 367, 374, 394, 555, 676, 695
Industrial Revolution, 29, 56, 59, 221, 272, 346, 584
Industry and Empire (Hobsbawm), 90
inflation, 80, 114, 151, 227, 450, 467, 602
Influence of Sea Power upon History, The (Mahan), 354
Innu, 598
Inouye, Daniel K., 671
Insular Cases, 515, 520
insular empire, 8, 13; administration of Puerto Rico and, 543–59; Bureau of Insular Affairs and, 523, 526–27, 589; Caribbean and, 39, 543–59, 566, 568, 570, 575, 580, 587, 589; colonialism and, 639–46, 649, 660, 684–86; decolonialization and, 40; as forgotten empire, 31, 494–538; historiographical tradition and, 15–16; imperialism and, 267, 339, 341, 349, 361, 455, 492; independence and, 143, 174, 185, 187; intrusion and, 383–442 (*see also* intrusion); Iraq and, 736; Pacific and, 39,

594, 617, 635–38; postcolonialism and, 699–700, 718; Progressives and, 20; retrospective view on, 635–38; U.S. Supreme Court and, 515–16, 520

interest rates, 59, 169, 247, 309–10

International Bank for Reconstruction and Development (IBRD), 703

International Longshore & Warehouse Union (ILWU), 604, 606, 650, 652

International Monetary Fund (IMF), 474, 703, 718, 725

International Non-Governmental Organizations (INGOs), 88, 266

international relations: colonialism and, 645, 649, 685; forgotten empire and, 496, 507; hegemony and, 18; imperialism and, 18, 20, 23, 39–41, 263, 443; independence and, 144; Iraq and, 737; postcolonialism and, 721, 723; revolution and, 124; wars of incorporation and, 192, 219

International Sugar Agreement, 681

Interstate Commerce Act, 296

intrusion: Africa and, 384, 394, 418, 433, 437–40; agriculture and, 399, 407, 417–18, 426–27; anarchy and, 410, 440; Anglo-Saxons and, 422, 425, 429, 438–40; assimilation and, 383, 412; autonomy and, 394, 399, 402–3, 411–12, 416, 431, 433–34; Canada and, 394, 399, 402; capitalism and, 390, 402; Catholicism and, 393, 406, 427, 430, 434; China and, 387, 392–93, 403, 407–9, 412–13, 420, 424, 426, 434–36; Christianity and, 402, 410, 429, 433–434; civilizing mission and, 386, 416, 436; Civil War and, 392, 400, 418–19, 431; conservatives and, 394–95, 398, 401–2, 406, 439; Cuba and, 383, 386–402, 408–14, 423, 428–36; Democrats and, 390, 422; empire-building and, 385, 388, 426; Enlightenment and, 412; entrepreneurs and, 386, 394, 401, 422; expansionism and, 386, 393, 421, 429, 433–36; exports and, 385–96, 399–401, 404–11, 418–27, 433, 436; France and, 391, 397, 403; free trade and, 391, 396–97, 400, 402, 406, 422, 427, 435; Germany and, 416; globalization and, 38, 386, 409–10, 427, 436; Hawai'i and, 383–84, 386–90, 408, 428–31, 435, 436; home rule and, 394, 397–98, 402, 429, 431–34, 436; immigration and, 408; imports and, 388, 390, 393, 396, 400, 406, 420–21; Japan and, 413, 416, 420, 426–27,

429; Jefferson and, 420, 429; labor and, 387, 390–94, 401, 404–5, 407, 411, 417, 420, 425–26; landowners and, 392, 401, 411; liberalism and, 410; liberty and, 383, 386, 397, 411, 417, 425, 434; manufacturing and, 396, 406; McKinley and, 383, 396, 416, 421, 423, 425–27, 431–36, 440, 588; mercantilism and, 390, 401, 406; Mexico and, 391, 403, 405; modernization and, 395, 427, 436; national identity and, 416, 427, 430; nationalism and, 383, 394–96, 405, 406, 408–14, 419–20, 423–25, 430, 435–36; oligarchy and, 387; Ottoman Empire and, 436; patriotism and, 395; Philippines and, 383–84, 387–89, 403–16, 430, 434–35, 633, 851n14; political juggernaut and, 383–86; populism and, 424; poverty and, 401; property rights and, 402, 425; protectionism and, 396, 435; Puerto Rico and, 383, 386, 388–89, 399–403, 428–29, 430, 433–34, 436; reciprocity and, 389–90, 396, 401, 408, 417, 419–24, 430, 436; reconstruction and, 394; Republicans and, 390, 416, 432, 435–36; Russia and, 432, 440; self-determination and, 387, 397; slavery and, 387, 390–95, 400–404, 405, 407, 413; South Africa and, 418; sovereignty and, 384, 403, 420, 429, 433; Spain and, 384–416, 423, 427–28, 430–36; Spanish-American War and, 385, 399; sugar and, 386–96, 400–402, 406–8, 411, 417–29, 434, 852n32; tariffs and, 385, 388–90, 393, 396–98, 401, 406, 417, 420–28, 435; taxes and, 391–92, 396–97, 404–8, 418, 424; technology and, 392, 406, 418; unemployment and, 396; wars of choice and, 427–36; white settlers and, 384–86, 400, 418, 429; World War I era and, 435, 438

Inuit, 529, 598, 668

Iran, 456, 714–15

Iraq: Baghdad, 2, 4, 731–34; British Empire and, 5–6, 456, 736; democracy and, 734; hegemony and, 736; Hussein and, 733–34, 931n30; insular empire and, 736; international relations and, 737; Kut and, 1–8, 730–34, 739n9, 740n14, 741n27; lessons of liberation and, 1–9, 730–38; Mesopotamia and, 1–2, 4, 731; oil and, 2, 734; nationalism and, 735; Operation Iraqi Freedom and, 731–38; Ottoman Empire and, 4; Philippines and, 416; preemptive strike on, 724; Republican Guard and, 732, 931n15;

Iraq (*continued*)
self-determination and, 736; Townshend and, 1–6, 730–32, 735, 737; weapons of mass destruction and, 734, 736; withdrawal from, 725

Ireland: conquest of, 67, 69; home government and, 35; House of Commons of, 70; imperialism and, 326; independence and, 326; military-fiscal state and, 60–61, 64–70, 92; Navigation Acts and, 70; Revenue Commissioner of, 70; revolution and, 103–4, 107, 140; terrorism and, 250; Viceroy of, 69–70; wars of incorporation and, 217

Irish Free State, 453–54

Irvine, Robert, 815n111

Isabella II, Queen of Spain, 293

Ismay, Lord, 475

isolationism: imperialism and, 242, 271, 353, 377, 443, 446–50, 468; informal expansion and, 17; integration and, 446–50; proto-globalization and, 91; splendid, 228, 271, 727

Italy: Battle of El Alamein and, 470; Crispi and, 276–77; forgotten empire and, 535; Greater, 277; imperialism and, 242, 247, 261, 267–70, 275–80, 344, 380, 451, 465–66; independence and, 253–54, 288, 328, 332; invasion of Abyssinia and, 466; Kingdom of, 275–76; military-fiscal state and, 72–73; Risorgimento and, 72, 231, 275–76, 344; self-determination and, 36; unification and, 37; wars of incorporation and, 232, 234; World War II era and, 465 (*see also* World War II era)

Ivy League, 178

Jackson, Andrew: Age of Jackson and, 143; agrarian ideal and, 196–97, 596; background of, 152–53; Clay and, 169, 196, 781n69; East Coast elites and, 153, 298; Gandhi and, 148; as King Andrew, 154; national debt and, 156–57, 165; policies of, 143, 148, 150, 152–58, 161–62, 165, 168–69, 178, 188–89, 298; populism and, 189; ruling style of, 127; Second Bank of the United States and, 156; Southern states and, 162; tariffs and, 154–56; Van Buren and, 150, 152–53, 155–57, 169; voting rights and, 153; wars of incorporation and, 194, 196, 199, 210, 212, 215

Jackson Democrats, 148, 154, 162, 215

Jacobites, 46, 62–63, 67–69, 78

Jamaica, 233, 464, 569, 585

James II, King of England; King of Scotland as James VII, 55–56, 59, 61, 70, 90

James, Henry, 327–28

James, William, 367–68

Japan: Anglo-Japanese alliance and, 446–47; annexation of Manchuria and, 465–66; appropriation of Korea by, 267, 455; as bulwark of West, 711; cartels of, 711–12; Christianity and, 711–12; colonialism and, 16, 37, 639, 642, 644, 650, 652–53, 655, 663, 670–71; communism and, 712; cultural identity of, 16; exceptionalism and, 16; forgotten empire and, 495, 507, 535, 538; free trade and, 703; Hawai'i and, 601–6; imperialism and, 261, 266–67, 269, 381, 446, 451, 455–56, 465–72, 487; independence and, 322; intrusion and, 413, 416, 420, 426–27, 429; invasion of China and, 465–66; invasion of Singapore and, 469; Korean expulsion and, 642; Liberal Democratic Party (LDP) and, 712; Meiji Restoration and, 269; nuclear bomb attacks on, 708; Pacific and, 601–6, 615, 622, 625, 627, 630–31; Pearl Harbor and, 191, 353, 419, 421, 430, 468–69, 538, 595, 605, 631, 902n71; Perry and, 237; Philippines and, 538, 630–31, 639, 653; postcolonialism and, 697, 701, 703, 708, 711–13, 722–23, 924n56; restructuring of, 37; textile industry and, 713; wars of incorporation and, 237; World War II era and, 465 (*see also* World War II era); zaibatsu of, 712

Jaurès, Jean, 263

Jay's Treaty, 159

Jefferson, Thomas, 780n41; agrarian ideal and, 219, 596; Anglo-Saxons and, 161; entangling alliances and, 167; forgotten empire and, 500; independence and, 143, 146–61, 166–67, 169, 173–79, 189, 293, 297, 302–3; intrusion and, 420, 429; Lewis and Clark expedition and, 151; Native Americans and, 199; Pacific and, 596, 601, 612; physiocracy and, 783n111; revolution and, 118–19, 130–35, 143, 150, 158; War of 1812 and, 208; wars of incorporation and, 196, 199–200, 208–11, 219, 223

Jeffersonian Revolution, 143, 150, 158

Jehovah's Witnesses, 323

Jenks, Leland, 21

Jews, 319, 464

jíbaro, 539–40, 899n234

Jim Crow, 182, 292, 320

jingoism, 236, 243–44, 271, 367
Johnson, Andrew, 843n82
Johnson, Lyndon, 666–68
Johnson, Dr. Samuel, 53, 122
Johnstone family, 68–69
Jones, Arthur Creech, 478
Jones Act, 546, 615, 624–25
Jones-Costigan Act, 519, 553, 586–87, 604, 628
Journey to the Centre of the Earth, A (Verne), 245
Juárez, Benito, 233
Jungle, The (Sinclair), 438

Kalākaua, 419–21, 425
Kalaniana'ole, Jonah Kōhiō, 597–98
Kamehameha, 417–19
Kansas-Nebraska Act, 224
Kant, Immanuel, 66, 89, 254
Katipunan, 413
Kennedy, John F., 667, 676–77, 685, 717
Kenya, 453, 482, 485, 697
Keynes, John Maynard, 463, 471–72, 871n74
Khaled, Emir, 450, 536
Khalil Pasha, 4, 741n25
Kidd, Benjamin, 253
King, Martin Luther, 667
King Cotton, 187, 193, 228, 232, 236
King Mob, 53
Kipling, Rudyard, 1, 263, 476, 494, 524–25, 739n1, 882n2
Kissinger, Henry, 710
Klondike, 195
Knights of Labor, 297, 321
Koopman, John, 732–34, 930n4
Korea, 685; African American troops in, 663; colonialism and, 453; decolonization and, 712; expulsion of Japanese from, 642; free trade and, 703; industrialization of, 713; Japanese appropriation of, 267, 455; Liberal Party and, 712; postcolonialism and, 712–13, 722; Rhee and, 712–13
Korean War, 484, 656, 663, 680, 711–12, 714
Kossuth, Lajos, 73, 75, 225, 283
Kraus, Karl, 270
Kruger, Paul, 206, 566
Krupp, Alfred, 709
Ku Klux Klan, 290, 647–48
Kut, 1–8, 730–34

labor: Amalgamated Association of Iron and Steel Workers and, 300; American Federation of Labor (AFL) and, 297, 300, 321, 367, 425, 626; American Railway Union and, 297, 300; capital and, 37, 223, 233, 242, 248, 283, 288, 300, 305, 3, 390, 426, 695; Caribbean and, 540, 548, 550, 558, 569, 578, 585, 587, 589; Carnegie's war with, 315; cheap, 39, 244, 320, 424, 601, 677; colonialism and, 29, 37, 39, 650, 652, 655, 659, 677, 680, 684; crisis of over-production and, 81; Czolgosz and, 303–5; Department of Commerce and Labor and, 305; family, 117, 621–22; Farmers' Alliance and, 297, 817n156; forgotten empire and, 508, 525–26, 534, 536; free, 158, 220, 222, 349; immigration and, 288 (*see also* immigration); imperialism and, 242, 244, 247–48, 250, 256, 261, 263, 271, 281, 283, 347, 349, 351, 359, 363, 367, 374, 449, 452, 458, 460, 462, 471–72, 474, 478, 482, 487; independence and, 147, 157–58, 163, 169, 171, 288–91, 297, 300–308, 319–22, 335; intrusion and, 387, 390–94, 400, 404–5, 407, 410, 417, 420, 424–25; Knights of Labor and, 297, 321; market issues and, 222, 392, 425, 597, 603; mestizos and, 348, 387, 404, 407, 410, 412–13, 436, 607, 613, 626; military-fiscal state and, 54–56, 83; organizational strength of, 825n67; Pacific and, 596–97, 600–606, 616, 620–21, 626, 633; postcolonialism and, 695, 702, 705, 724; real wages and, 246–47, 813n75; revolution and, 117, 121; sharecroppers and, 308, 351, 407, 411, 622; slavery and, 117 (*see also* slavery); Socialist Labor Party (SLP) and, 297; strikes and, 299–300, 602–4; unemployment and, 36–37, 63 (*see also* unemployment); unions and, 585, 603, 652, 659, 684; United Mine Workers and, 297; wage, 220, 308, 393, 400, 462, 550, 621–22; Wagner Act and, 605; wars of incorporation and, 193, 195–96, 219–20, 223, 233
labor camps, 4
Labor Party, 271
LaFeber, Walter, 341
Lamento Borincano (Hernández Marín), 553
landowners: colonialism and, 654; independence and, 154, 181, 308; intrusion and, 392, 401, 411; military-fiscal state and, 55, 61–63, 67, 69, 80, 82, 92; Pacific and, 600; revolution and, 112, 131; wars of incorporation and, 234, 247, 279
Lascelles family, 121

Lavigerie, Charles Martial, 265, 513, 816n125
Law of Civilization and Decay, The (Adams), 318
Lawrence, T. E., 5
League of Nations, 4, 446, 451, 460, 466
Leaves of Grass (Whitman), 328, 800n161
Lee, Fitzhugh, 431
Lee, Robert E., 225, 804n230
Lend-Lease Agreement, 469, 471
Lenin, Vladimir, 22, 262, 267, 450–51, 465
Leopold II, King of Belgium, 269
Leroy-Beaulieu, Pierre Paul, 259, 499, 883n22
Lever, W. H., 620
Lévy-Bruhl, Lucien, 451–52
Lewis, George Cornewall, 230
Lewis and Clark expedition, 151
liberalism: Caribbean and, 586; colonialism and, 661; forgotten empire and, 505; imperialism and, 281, 352, 460; independence and, 148; intrusion and, 410; military-fiscal state and, 77, 92; postcolonialism and, 695, 728; rise of, 34; secular, 77; Spain and, 345–46; wars of incorporation and, 220
Liberal Party, 263, 273–74
liberty: anarchy and, 32; Caribbean and, 543, 546, 574–75; colonialism and, 17–18, 25, 32–33, 641, 645, 664–65, 682; democracy and, 7–8, 17–18, 25, 97, 143, 148, 176, 195, 218–19, 282, 335, 369, 543, 546, 574, 597, 605, 607, 665, 682, 694, 715, 721, 724; ethnicity and, 173, 175, 218, 236, 289, 342, 376, 410, 430, 605; forgotten empire and, 505–7, 512–21; imperialism and, 243, 251, 282, 354, 361, 363, 369, 375–77, 381, 444; independence and, 142–43, 146, 148, 156, 174, 176, 179, 185–90, 301, 316, 335; intrusion and, 383, 386, 397, 410, 417, 425, 434; lobbies and, 521–21; military-fiscal state and, 54, 63, 66, 71–72, 82–83, 87, 89; Montesquieu and, 32–34, 40, 53, 91, 124–25, 133, 136, 140–41, 282, 336, 693, 707, 727; Pacific and, 594, 597, 605, 607; postcolonialism and, 694, 715, 721, 724; property rights and, 109; revolution and, 95–98, 101, 109, 116, 128–31, 135, 141; wars of incorporation and, 195, 211, 215, 218–19, 237
Life magazine, 443
Liga Filipina, 412
Lili'uokalani, Queen of Hawai'i, 421, 424–425, *424*, 429–30, 863n233
Lincoln, Abraham, 685, 804n230; assassination of, 178; Carey and, 161; Civil War and, 220–30, 234, 238, 326, 335, 515; Emancipation Proclamation and, 227, 230, 392; Garibaldi and, 229; Hay and, 364; military-fiscal state and, 73, 75; money power and, 313; "plain man" of, 305
Linnaeus, Carl, 65
List, Friedrich, 169, 318, 363
Liszt, Franz, 331
literacy, 248, 440–41, 486, 598, 624, 676
Little Lord Fauntleroy (Burnett), 327
Liverpool, Lord, 77, 80–81
Livingstone, David, 265, 272, 513
Lloyd George, David, 451, 456
lobbies: annexation and, 425–26, 433, 448, 564–65, 620; business interests and, 39, 86, 121, 222, 279–80, 296–97, 353, 359, 361, 379, 425–26, 500, 512, 516–21, 548–50, 564, 580–81, 587, 590, 617, 620, 627, 634, 637, 653, 673, 681; Caribbean and, 548–50, 564, 580–81, 587, 590; colonialism and, 649, 651, 653, 673, 681; East India Company and, 86; forgotten empire and, 500, 512–21; imperialism and, 279–80, 353, 359, 361, 368, 380, 425–26, 448; Interstate Commerce Act and, 296–97; liberty and, 512–21; log-rolling and, 579; Native Americans and, 749; naval, 353; Pacific and, 617, 620, 627, 637, 651; Paris Peace Treaty and, 361; religion and, 512–13; Southern states and, 222; tariffs and, 39; venture capitalists and, 121
Lobo y Olavarría, Julio, 678–80
Lodge, Henry Cabot, 201–2, 363, 365, 369, 372, 16, 440, 864n257
London, Jack, 195, 793n24
Longfellow, Henry Wadsworth, 180, 624, 790n228
Lorca, Federico García, 352, 843n78
Loti, Pierre, 263
Louis XIV, King of France, 48
Louis XV, King of France, 53
Louis XVIII, King of France, 73
Louisiana Purchase, 150, 166, 184, 198, *204*
loyalists, 78, 96, 99, 116, 120, 124, 199, 207, 347, 394, 402, 487, 544, 709
Luce, Clare Boothe, 528
Luce, Henry Robinson, 443, 445–46, 450, 490, 492–93
Lugard, Frederick J. D., 503, 648, 884n36
Lyautey, Louis Hubert Gonzalve, 503, 522
lynchings, 320, 507, 648, 665, 832n234

Maass, Peter, 733, 797n100, 798n102, 931nn11, 21, 23
MacArthur, Douglas, 654–55, 672
Macartney, Lord, 94
Macaulay, Thomas Babbington, 86–87, 763n232
Macaulay, Zachary, 98, 765nn8, 13
Macdonald, John A., 196–97
MacDonald, Malcolm, 463, 873n110
Machado, Gerardo, 536, 579, 581–82, 584
Macmillan, Harold, 484–85
Macmillan, William, 463
Madison, James, 33, 125–26, 129, 132, 134, 139, 149, 151, 160, 174, 208, 210, 235–36
Magsaysay, Ramón del Fierro, 672–74, 685, 700
Mahan, Alfred Thayer, 354–55, 363–65, 378, 440
Maine, Henry James Sumner, 6, 25, 505, 884n46
Maistre, Joseph de, 281–82
malaria, 265, 409
Malaya, 481–83, 610
Malcolm X, 667, 917n127
Malta, 482, 499
Malthusianism, 86
Malvar, Miguel, 415–16
Manchuria, 465–66
manifest destiny: desire for land and, 193, 410; imperialism and, 114, 148, 176, 191, 195, 215, 325, 365–66, 492, 508; wars of incorporation and, 191, 195, 215
Manisero, El (The Peanut Vendor) (Havana Casino Orchestra), 539–40
manufacturing: American System and, 160, 162, 169, 196, 296; Caribbean and, 557–58, 568, 578–80, 588; colonialism and, 463–64, 641, 659, 672–77; forgotten empire and, 536; imperialism and, 244, 260–61, 268, 273–77, 284, 341, 345, 348–51, 357–62, 375–76, 380, 382, 444, 447, 457–58, 462–64, 482, 484; independence and, 146, 157, 159–63, 167–72, 186–88, 293–95, 299–303, 307–12, 334; intrusion and, 396, 406; military-fiscal state and, 47, 50, 54–58, 67, 81–90, 92; Pacific and, 596, 622, 626, 637; postcolonialism and, 695–98, 701–2, 706, 708, 710, 722, 725; raw materials and, 38, 40, 85, 186, 220, 265, 274, 277, 295, 334, 447, 457, 477, 535, 579, 641, 697, 701, 706; revolution and, 100, 103, 110, 115, 117, 129, 131, 136; Spain and,

347–48; wars of incorporation and, 196, 220–22, 231–32
Maori, 196–98, 598, 668
Mao Tse-tung, 450, 536
Marchand, Jean-Baptiste, 265
Marín, Luis Muñoz, 383, 554–58, 628, 658–59, 675, 677, 685, 700
market revolution, 143–44, 171, 176, 221, 307, 333
marriage, 68–69, 118, 121, 186, 320, 325–27, 335, 346, 364, 376, 438–39, 489, 551, 634, 648, 651
Marseille, Jacques, 280–81, 459, 820n209
Marshall, Alfred, 155, 333
Marshall, Sir William, 4
Marshall Plan, 475, 708, 710
Martí, José, 383, 397–98, 403, 413, 540–41, 565, 574–75, 576, 854n77
Marx, Karl: colonialism and, 655, 672, 679; crisis of overproduction and, 81; dependency thesis and, 10; Engels and, 69, 81, 679; imperialism and, 245, 247, 250, 255, 259, 262, 279, 282, 344, 374, 378, 381, 491; independence and, 300–301; Johnstones and, 69; postcolonialism and, 707, 717; revolution and, 107; societal achievement and, 6; Southern plantocracy and, 219, 220; wars of incorporation and, 219, 220
materialism, 96–97, 107, 182, 317, 323
Matson Navigation Line, 599–600
Mattis, James, 731–32
Maude, Sir Stanley, 4–5, 734, 741n29, 932n34
Mau Mau rebellion, 482
Maxim, Hiram, 90
May, Ernest R., 377
Mazzini, Giuseppe, 72–73, 75, 238, 249, 254, 275–76
McCarthy, Joseph, 648
McChrystal, Stanley, 737
McCoy, Bryan P., 732–34
McDowell, Edward Alexander, 331, 837n305
McKinley, William: assassination of, 252, 303–5; benevolent assimilation and, 501; Bryan and, 301–3; Caribbean and, 547, 561–63, 588; Cuba and, 396, 413, 430–31, 561–63; Czolgosz and, 303–5; economic growth and, 303; forgotten empire and, 501, 523; Hawai'i and, 383–84, 421, 423, 425–26; imperialism and, 252, 343, 355–61, 364, 369–73, 381, 440; independence and, 295, 299, 301–4; intrusion and, 383, 396, 416, 421, 423, 425–27, 431–36, 440, 588;

McKinley, William (*continued*)
lack of international expertise of, 369–70; Monroe Doctrine and, 370; National Association of Manufacturers and, 301–2; Pacific and, 607, 609; Philippines and, 304, 434–36, 563, 607, 609; Protestantism and, 381; Puerto Rico and, 547–48; pulse of the nation and, 440; Schurman and, 903n82; Spanish-American War and, 369–74; Tariff of, 295, 299, 356, 358, 360, 396, 421, 423, 425–26, 826n79; *USS Maine* and, 370; Wilson-Gorman tariff and, 423

McNutt, Paul, 524, 631, 654–55
Méline Tariff, 279
Mellon, Andrew, 314
Melville, Herman, 180, 417
Memorial Day, 315, 656
Menace of Hawaiian Statehood, The (Smith), 651
Mendelian genetics, 318
Mendieta, Carlos, 585
Menzies, Robert, 480
mercantilism: Adam Smith and, 56, 114–15; Caribbean and, 572, 590; coffee and, 65, 102, 193, 295, 347, 350, 388, 391, 401–402, 406, 428, 457, 516, 547–49, 553; crisis of overproduction and, 81; discrimination and, 151, 273, 348, 435, 447, 518; exports and, 29 (*see also* exports); forgotten empire and, 516; Hayden and, 502–3; imperialism and, 23, 34, 246, 271, 347, 458; imports and, 58 (*see also* imports); independence and, 151, 159–60, 163, 169, 186–88; intrusion and, 390, 401, 406; military-fiscal state and, 47, 55–59, 62, 80–85, 88, 91–93; Northern states and, 188–89; Pacific and, 637; raw materials and, 38, 40, 85, 186, 220, 265, 274, 277, 295, 334, 447, 457, 477, 535, 579, 641, 697, 701, 706; revolution and, 104, 113–15, 137, 139; Spain and, 347–48; Suez Canal and, 347, 435, 482; sugar and, 39 (*see also* sugar); tariffs and, 35 (*see also* tariffs); tea and, 114–16, 295; tobacco and, 58, 110, 117–19, 162, 305, 308, 347, 388, 391–92, 397, 401, 405, 408, 544, 547–53, 582; wars of incorporation and, 220; Wilson and, 625
Merivale, Herman, 86–87
Mesopotamia, 1–8, 731–34, 739n8
"Mesopotamia" (Kipling), 1
mestizos, 348, 387, 404, 407, 410, 412–13, 436, 607, 613, 620, 626, 851n22, 859n168

Methodists, 64, 175, 177, 323, 381, 623
Metternich, Klemens Furst von, 73
Mexican-American War, 157, 166, 170, 184, 191, 193, 212, 217
Mexico, 97, 807n275; civil war in, 233; Comanche and, 213; Cortés and, 216; Cuban investments and, 567; forgotten empire and, 531; imperialism and, 346–47, 358, 372, 448–49; independence and, 312, 346; intrusion and, 391, 404, 405; invasion of, 212–17; lost territories of, 212; NAFTA and, 703–4; NATO and, 475; revolution and, 552; Spain and, 84; Texas and, 214–17; Treaty of Guadalupe Hidalgo and, 217; wars of incorporation and, 191, 193, 212–16, 220, 230, 233–34, 237
Michelet, Jules, 16
Michels, Robert, 248
Micronesia, 645
Miles, Nelson Appleton, 403
military-fiscal state: Adam Smith and, 56–57, 66, 68–69, 77, 84, 89, 92; Africa and, 67, 85, 88–89; agriculture and, 54, 56, 82, 90, 94; American Revolution and, 8, 46, 52, 67, 70, 78, 87, 91; anarchy and, 66, 76, 87; Australia and, 86, 89; authoritarianism and, 62, 71, 73, 78; British Empire and, 60–65, 83–94; capitalism and, 54, 56, 88; Catholicism and, 63, 69–70; causes of, 45–47; China and, 49–51, 57, 65, 79, 86, 88–90, 93; Christianity and, 77–79, 83, 87–88; chronological perspective on, 45–47; civilizing mission and, 71, 88; Civil War and, 45–47, 53, 55, 94; conservatives and, 47, 55, 71–82, 86, 93; cotton and, 80–81, 84–85; decolonization and, 72, 84, 91, 94; deflation and, 36–37; demise of, 808n11; democracy and, 79, 88; Democrats and, 90; Enlightenment and, 64–65, 71, 78, 87, 89; entrepreneurs and, 48–49, 55, 67–68; exceptionalism and, 53–60; exports and, 57–59, 69, 74–75, 85, 88–89, 93; France and, 46, 48, 51–53, 58, 62, 65–78, 84, 91; free trade and, 47, 55–56, 67, 70, 74, 77–83, 86–88, 93; French Revolution and, 47, 70, 78, 92; French Wars and, 52–53, 57–59, 71–72, 77–83, 344; Germany and, 232, 234; globalization and, 45, 47, 68, 71, 91, 94, 693; Glorious Revolution and, 53–60; gold standard and, 80–81; great convergence and, 48–53; imports and, 58, 81–82; India and, 46, 51, 54, 57, 65, 67–68, 79, 83–88, 93,

755n77; Ireland and, 60–61, 64–70, 92; Italy and, 72–73; labor and, 54–56, 83; landowners and, 55, 61–63, 67, 69, 80, 82, 92; liberalism and, 77, 92; liberty and, 54, 63, 66, 71–72, 82–83, 87, 89; manufacturing and, 47, 50, 54–58, 67, 81–90, 92; mercantilism and, 47, 55–59, 62, 80–85, 88, 91–93; modernization and, 55–56, 59, 714, 721; monopolies and, 48, 57, 61–62, 67, 79, 83, 86–87; Napoleon and, 57, 71–75, 78, 84, 92; national debt and, 52, 59, 61, 64, 70, 80, 91–92; nationalism and, 72–73, 93; nation-building and, 93; Netherlands and, 52–53, 72–75, 84; new global order and, 64–70; New Left and, 21; oligarchy and, 46, 56, 58, 61, 63, 90, 92; Ottoman Empire and, 49, 88, 93; patriotism and, 78, 83; postcolonialism and, 693–95; progressives and, 73; property rights and, 67; protectionism and, 81–82; Protestantism and, 55, 66–67, 69–71; Prussia and, 48, 54, 72–74; raw materials and, 85; reconstruction and, 71–76, 87; reform and, 71–76; Republicans and, 73, 76; Russia and, 74–75, 84; Scotland and, 60–61, 64–70, 92; self-determination and, 72, 74–75; Seven Years' War and, 45, 52, 57–58, 61–64, 83; slavery and, 68, 72–73, 75–76, 79, 86–89; sovereignty and, 66, 91; sugar and, 58, 68, 79, 82; tariffs and, 55, 57–58, 81–82, 85–86; taxes and, 48–53, 58–65, 68, 70, 74, 80, 91–92; technology and, 48–51, 65; terrorism and, 75; textile industry and, 80–81, 85; unemployment and, 36–37, 63, 80–81, 86; war and, 71–76; West Indies and, 58, 61, 64, 79, 86; World War I era and, 36, 73; World War II era and, 85

Mill, John Stuart, 46, 89, 194, 231, 234, 248–49, 281, 344, 505, 807n280, 809n20

Minorca, 100

minstrelsy, 181–82, 329

minutemen, 120

Mississippi Constitutional Convention, 422

Missouri Crisis, 210, 218, 224

Missouri Line, 213

Missouri Territory, 150

Mitchell, Wesley, 529

Mitterand, François, 481

Moby-Dick (Melville), 180

modernization: ahistorical theory of, 10; colonialism and, 676, 682; dependency thesis and, 26; economic optimism and, 244–49; fiscal effects of, 241–42; forgotten empire and, 504–9, 884n47; globalization and, 241–49; imperialism and, 247, 268–71, 274–75, 282–83, 479; independence and, 154, 305; Indian Mutiny and, 505; industrialization and, 7, 36, 54, 94, 139, 244, 248, 269, 277, 281–82, 313, 322, 338, 364, 367, 374, 394–95, 555, 676, 695; intrusion and, 395, 427, 436; Maine and, 505; military-fiscal state and, 55–56, 59, 714, 721, 754n71; modernists and, 92, 243, 749n11, 836n284; modernity and, 16, 49, 60, 189, 202, 217, 220, 227, 242, 243, 283, 308, 321, 323, 329, 374, 382, 550–51, 571–73, 574, 607, 641, 707, 755n74, 776n209, 802n190, 866n1, 919n161, 922n28; post–Civil War era and, 200; postcolonialism and, 7–8, 708, 714–15, 721; predictability and, 26; revolution and, 135; Spanish-American War and, 504; urbanization and, 244, 249, 252, 282, 288, 292, 324, 336, 338, 695; wars of incorporation and, 200, 217, 221, 224; Weber and, 374, 505

molasses, 295

Monnet Plan, 709–10

monopolies: Adam Smith on, 57; bossism and, 356; Caribbean and, 548, 599–600; colonialism and, 654; expansionism and, 136; forgotten empire and, 520–21, 527; imperialism and, 247, 261, 269, 278, 356, 405–7, 434; independence and, 159, 167, 290, 294, 296, 322, 333; James II and, 61; Matson Navigation Line and, 599–600; military-fiscal state and, 48, 57, 61–62, 67, 79, 83, 86–87; Pacific and, 599; postcolonialism and, 704, 712

Monroe, James, 151–52

Monroe Doctrine, 209, 211–12, 333, 370, 447–50, 516, 717

Montagu-Chelmsford reforms, 454

Montesquieu, Charles-Louis Secondat, 32–34, 40, 53, 91, 124–25, 133, 136, 140–41, 282, 336, 693, 707, 727

Montgomery, Bernard, 470

Moody, Dwight L., 323

Moon, Parker T., 20

Morgan, J. P., 302, 310–15, 831n166

Mormons, 184

Morocco, 483, 503

Morrill Tariff Act, 228, 293

Morris, William, 245, 248

Morse, Samuel, 184–85

Mosca, Gaetano, 247

Moscoso, José Teodoro, 676

Mossaddegh, Mohammad, 714–15
Mott, John R., 366
Mughals, 49–51, 105–7
Muhammad, 5
mulatos, 387, 391–92, 395, 851n23
Muqaddimah, The (Ibn Khaldun), 735
Murphy, Frank, 524
music, 372; Caribbean, 539–41, 553, 572, 588; classical, 331; jíbaro, 539–40, 899n234; minstrelsy, 181–82, 329; Pacific, 384, 634; ponoi, 384; popular, 332
Muslims, 642; anti-capitalism and, 726; forgotten empire and, 504; fundamentalist, 726; Moro Islamic Liberation Front and, 927n113; Muhammad and, 5; Philippines and, 406, 609–10, 622–23; postcolonialism and, 719, 726
Myrdal, Gunnar, 647, 913n32, 921n6

NAACP, 647–48
nabobs, 68–69, 121, 758n131
Nagano, Yoshiko, 906n138, 910n218
Napoleon Bonaparte: Battle of Waterloo and, 73; forgotten empire and, 526; imperialism and, 344; independence and, 185, 188; military-fiscal state and, 57, 71–75, 78, 84, 92; postcolonialism and, 679; wars of incorporation and, 228
Napoleon III, Emperor of France, 230, 233, 278
Nasser, Gamal Abdel, 664
National Association of Manufacturers, 301–2
National Bank Acts, 310–11
National City Bank of New York, 449
National Congress of American Indians (NCAI), 649, 668
national debt: Adam Smith and, 135; Cold War and, 723; Cuba and, 433; as government credit card, 136; Hamilton and, 131; independence and, 151, 154, 156, 161, 165, 188; India and, 106; military-fiscal state and, 52, 59, 61, 64, 70, 80, 91–92; Pitt and, 101; U.S. Constitution and, 128
national identity: Anglo-Saxons and, 173 (*see also* Anglo-Saxons); Caribbean and, 541, 551–52, 570–72; cultural continuities and, 172–85; forgotten empire and, 507; imperialism and, 271, 274; independence and, 145, 172, 183, 187, 289, 319, 336; intrusion and, 416, 427, 430; military-fiscal state and, 87; revolution and, 117, 127, 138–39; wars of incorporation and, 209

National Interest, The (journal), 23
nationalism, 15; Caribbean and, 546, 554–64, 572–75, 577–79, 582–90; colonialism and, 640–46, 655, 657–59, 662, 670, 673–74, 678, 680, 682–86; cosmopolitan, 271, 293, 316–32; credit and, 306–16; economic, 306–16; forgotten empire and, 496, 524, 527–32, 536–37; Great Depression and, 461; imperialism and, 344–47, 352, 355–56, 363–64, 371, 444, 446, 449–56, 460–61, 463, 465–66, 470–71, 479–83, 486, 488, 491–92; independence and, 145, 152, 157, 159, 175, 177, 182, 184–85, 189, 293, 304, 306, 316–24, 330, 333; intrusion and, 383, 394–96, 405, 406, 408–14, 419–20, 423–25, 430, 435–36; Iraq and, 735; military-fiscal state and, 72–73, 93; Pacific and, 593–94, 598, 607, 610, 614, 617, 623, 625, 629, 632, 636, 637; postcolonialism and, 697–99, 704, 711–18, 724, 726; revolution and, 105, 120, 134, 138; Spain and, 345–46; wars of incorporation and, 219–20, 225, 245, 249, 254, 263, 271, 274, 283; World War I era and, 38
National Rifle Association, 266
nation-building, 7; colonialism and, 35, 37; forgotten empire and, 504, 509, 523; imperialism and, 242, 249, 253, 266, 281–84, 344, 366, 374, 380, 486; independence and, 145, 172–73, 185, 288–91, 321, 335; military-fiscal state and, 93; Pacific and, 635; postcolonialism and, 694–95, 704, 718–19; revolution and, 126, 128; wars of incorporation and, 192
Native Americans: American Indian Movement (AIM) and, 668–69; American Revolution and, 120–21; Amerindian ancestry and, 582; Apache, 198, 200; attempts at assimilation of, 624; Bureau of Indian Affairs and, 523, 668; Cherokee, 199, 795n53; Christianity and, 181; citizenship and, 200–201; civil rights and, 40, 665, 668–69; Comanche, 200, 213; Commissioner for Indian Affairs and, 503, 529, 648; Crazy Horse, 202; Dawes Act and, 502, 504; declaration of independence and, 199, 209; electorate of, 649; First Peoples and, 197, 207, 598, 648, 668, 719; Indian Citizenship Act and, 201, 793n29; Indian Civil Rights Act and, 669; Indian Mutiny and, 505; Indian Reorganization Act and, 503; Indian Self-Determination and Education Act

and, 669; Indian Wars and, 39, 173, 193, 197, 203, 237, 353, 372, 611; intertribal alliances and, 198–99; Jackson and, 153; Jefferson and, 199; lobbies and, 749; Lodge on, 201–2; Longfellow on, 180–81; Louisiana Purchase and, 198; Mississippi and, 321; National Congress of American Indians (NCAI) and, 649, 668; national saga and, 143; Ojibwe, 200; Oregon Cession and, 198; Pontiac's War and, 119; postcolonialism and, 693–94; property rights and, 198–201, 236–37; as savages, 199; segregation and, 648–49; Seminole, 198–200; Shawnee, 95, 210; Sioux, 199–202, 265, 321; Sitting Bull, 202; taming of, 181; terminology of, 749n110; Theodore Roosevelt on, 201–2; Trail of Broken Treaties and, 668; voting rights and, 133, 149, 196, 200; wars of incorporation and, 199–203, 209, 237; Washington on poor settlers and, 111; westward expansion and, 125, 147, 151, 192, 206, 208–9, 236, 380; white-American identity and, 173, 289, 320–21, 506, 514
natural resources, 50, 196, 288, 616, 619, 654
Naval War College, 353–54, 365
Navigation Acts, 57, 70, 82
Nearing, Scott, 21
Nehru, Jawaharlal, 142, 146, 190, 480–81, 486, 664
Nepomuceno, José, 625
Netherlands: Caribbean and, 542; French Wars and, 53; imperialism and, 267, 270–72, 451, 457, 483; military-fiscal state and, 52–53, 72–75, 84; postcolonialism and, 713; revolution and, 115
Newcastle, Duke of, 113
new colony system, 98–105
New Deal, 250, 287, 491, 526–29, 532, 537, 556, 557, 586, 589, 645, 675, 695, 698
New Development Bank, 702, 725
New England, 63, 109–12, 115, 132, 167, 175, 181, 194, 196, 220–21, 291, 362
Newgate Prison, 53
new global order, 64–70
New Left: capitalism and, 17, 340–41, 360; forgotten empire and, 513; imperialism and, 340–41, 360, 446; military-fiscal state and, 21; Wisconsin School and, 17, 340–41, 360
New York Stock Exchange, 165, 299, 311

New Zealand, 89, 196–98, 205, 245, 250, 266, 298, 451, 454, 477, 487, 571, 700, 703
Nicaragua, 449, 717
Nicholas I, Tzar of Russia, 73
Nietzsche, Friedrich, 254, 282
Niven, David, 632
Nixon, Sir, John Eccles, 2, 739n6, 740n10
Nixon, Richard M., 669
Nkrumah, Kwame, 486, 659, 664
Norman, Montagu Collet, 165
North, Lord, 100
North American Free Trade Agreement (NAFTA), 703–4
North American Review journal, 211
North Atlantic Treaty Organization (NATO), 475, 708, 710–11
Northern Pacific Railroad, 256
Northern Securities Trust, 305
Northern states: Anglo-Saxons and, 175 (*see also* Anglo-Saxons); Civil War and, 307 (*see also* Civil War); class warfare and, 301; corrupt court interests and, 156; financial interests of, 156–57, 171, 301–5, 334; Hawai'i and, 596; Immigration Act and, 507; imperialism and, 276, 288–92; Know Nothings and, 803n219; Memorial Day and, 335; mercantilism and, 188–89; political economy of, 356; protective tariffs and, 35; robber barons and, 314; slavery and, 181–82, 291; Spain and, 381; sports and, 330; terminology of, 774n176; Union and, 186, 210, 214, 216, 219–35, 287–93, 371; wars of incorporation and, 213, 216–29, 234
Norway, 73
Norweb, Henry, 559
Nova Scotia, 96
nuclear power, 485, 708, 710
Nullification Crisis, 155
Nuremberg trials, 646

oil: coconut, 620, 626, 907n152; cottonseed, 626; forgotten empire and, 495; imperialism and, 449, 456–57, 478, 482; importance of, 35; independence and, 302, 305, 314; Iran and, 714–15; Iraq and, 2, 734; Morgan and, 302; OPEC and, 710–11, 715; palm, 620–21, 907n152; postcolonialism and, 701, 710, 714–15, 719; Standard Oil and, 302, 305, 314; wars of incorporation and, 236
Ojibwe, 200

oligarchy: Caribbean and, 574, 579, 582, 585, 589; colonialism and, 673–74; forgotten empire and, 519, 537; imperialism and, 248, 276, 344; independence and, 149; intrusion and, 387; military-fiscal state and, 46, 56, 58, 61, 63, 90, 92; Pacific and, 596–97, 603, 606, 612–15, 628, 633; postcolonialism and, 712, 719; revolution and, 106, 122, 135; wars of incorporation and, 227–28

Olive Branch Petition, 123

"Ominous Decade," 74

Operation Bootstrap, 676–77, 700, 717

Operation Iraqi Freedom, 731–38

Opium Wars, China, 231, 347

Oregon Cession, 198

Organization of Petroleum Exporting Countries (OPEC), 710–11, 715

Osmeña, Sergio, 536, 613, 615, 625, 628–29, 654, 909n189

O'Sullivan, John L., 191, 792n2

Ottawa Agreements, 458

Ottoman Empire: British Empire and, 27, 36; Central Powers and, 2; colonialism and, 642; imperialism and, 258, 262, 280, 284, 451; intrusion and, 436; Iraq and, 4; military-fiscal state and, 49, 88, 93

Ottoman Public Debt Administration, 258

Our Country: Its Possible Future and Its Present Crisis (Strong), 324

Oxnard, Henry T., 354, 425

Pacific: agriculture and, 598, 600, 604, 606, 617, 620, 635–37; Anglo-Saxons and, 592–93; assimilation and, 592, 603, 609–13, 621–24, 638; Australia and, 596, 598; authoritarianism and, 605; autonomy and, 604, 628; Beardslee and, 384; capitalism and, 620, 637; Catholicism and, 595, 609, 615, 619, 623; China and, 601, 603, 613, 619, 626, 633; Christianity and, 595, 598, 610–11, 621–23; citizenship and, 606; civilizing mission and, 594, 610, 622–24, 630, 636–37; communism and, 628; conservatives and, 625; constitutions and, 900n16; decolonization and, 631, 649–56, 669–74; democracy and, 597, 600, 603, 605, 607, 609, 627, 630–31; Democrats and, 598, 610, 613–14, 625, 627, 630; entrepreneurs and, 599, 620; expansionism and, 595–96, 600, 627, 630–31, 634; exports and, 595, 598–606, 615, 617–22, 625–30, 634–37; free trade and, 616–17, 628; Germany and, 625; globalization and, 594, 633, 636; Hawai'i and, 632–33 (*see also* Hawai'i); home rule and, 597–98, 609, 628; immigration and, 597, 601, 603, 626, 635, 908n184; imports and, 603–4, 618, 626; insular empire and, 39, 594, 618, 635–38; Japan and, 601–6, 615, 622, 625, 627, 630–31; Jefferson and, 596, 601, 612; Jones Act and, 546, 615, 624–25; labor and, 596–97, 600–606, 616, 619–22, 626, 633; landowners and, 600; liberty and, 594, 597, 605, 607; lobbies and, 617, 620, 627, 637, 651; manufacturing and, 596, 622, 626, 637; Matson Navigation Line and, 599–600; McKinley and, 607, 609; mercantilism and, 637; monopolies and, 599; nationalism and, 593–94, 598, 607, 610, 614, 617, 623, 625, 629, 632, 636, 637; nation-building and, 635; oligarchy and, 596–97, 603, 606, 612–15, 628, 633; patriotism and, 634; Philippines and, 434–35 (*see also* Philippines); populism and, 636; progress in, 669–74; progressives and, 623; protectionism and, 617–18, 649–57; Protestantism and, 623–24, 644, 651; reciprocity and, 389–90, 396, 401, 408, 417, 419–24, 430, 436, 595; reconstruction and, 625; Republicans and, 597–98, 610, 615, 625, 630; Schurman Commission and, 497–98, 502, 607, 609; self-determination and, 615, 625; slavery and, 594, 611, 624, 635; sovereignty and, 598, 611, 630, 638; Spain and, 49, 595, 607, 609, 611, 618–19, 627, 634–35, 636; sugar and, 386–402, 406–8, 411, 417–29, 434, 595, 598–608, 615–21, 625–29, 633; Taft and, 592, 601, 607, 612–19, 625, 632; tariffs and, 598–601, 615–17, 621, 625–26, 627, 629–30, 636–38; taxes and, 615–17, 628; technology and, 612; tourism and, 524, 539–40, 592–93, 598; unemployment and, 606, 626, 630, 637; voting rights and, 601, 603, 605, 670; wars of choice and, 427–36; white settlers and, 596–97, 603, 635; World War I era and, 592, 599, 602–3, 625–26, 631; World War II era and, 602, 631, 638

Pacific Railroad Bill, 222

Páez, José Antonio, 154

Pahlavi, Mohammad Reza, 715

Pakistan, 51, 235–36, 704

Palestine, 456, 480, 482, 526

Palmer, Robert, 3, 90, 740n19, 740n20

Palmerston, Lord, 215, 228–31

Panama, 164, 237, 838n2

Papists, 324

Pareto, Vilfredo, 247

Parliament Act, 509

Parsons, Talcott, 6

patriotism, 18; Caribbean and, 541; colonialism and, 644, 679; imperialism and, 254, 264, 353, 362, 367, 369, 372, 376, 381, 454; independence and, 180, 182, 287, 289, 294, 300, 319, 326, 330; intrusion and, 395; military-fiscal state and, 78, 83; Pacific and, 634; race, 139, 395, 454; revolution and, 139; September 11, 2001, attacks and, 724–25

Pax Americana, 25, 128

Pax Britannica, 25, 283, 736

Payne-Aldrich Tariff, 617

Peace of Paris, 101, *108*, 119, 496

Pearl Harbor, 191, 353, 419, 421, 430, 468–69, 538, 595, 605, 631, 902n71

Pearson, Charles, 253

Pearson, Karl, 318

Peel, Robert, 81–82, 656

Peirce, Henry A., 419, 863n226

Pelham, Henry, 113

peninsulares, 387, 392, 394–95, 400–402, 410, 544, 547

Pennsylvania Railroad Company, 314

People's Party. *See* populism

Perkins, Whitney, 20–21

Permanent Court of International Justice, 446

Perry, Matthew, 237

Peterloo Massacre, 78

Peters, Carl, 263, 429

Peter the Great, 48

Pettit, Charles, 130

Philippine Church, 410

Philippine Independent Church, 629

Philippine National Bank, 619, 625

Philippine Rehabilitation Act, 654–56

Philippines, 888n137; abaca (hemp) and, 347, 350, 388, 406, 408, 411, 516, *608*, 617–18, 621–22, 631, 653, 673, 719, 906n126; Aguinaldo and, 413–15; alcohol and, 405; annexation of, 384, 434–35, 645; arbitrary rule and, 607–32; Ayala Corporation and, 407; Bayan Ko and, 634, 910n227; Bell Act and, 653–54; beriberi and, 409; Bonifacio and, 412–13; Cavite mutiny and, 409; cholera and, 409; Clark Air Base and, 654; coffee and, 406; colonialism and, 635, 645, 652–56, 659, 662, 669–74, 684–85; as colony of trade, 618; communism and, 628; cotton and, 626; covert policing and, 546; cultural resistance in, 593–94; Dawes Act and, 504; declaration of independence and, 413; Democratic Alliance and, 654, 656; Dewey and, 403, 416; dysentery and, 409; early history of, 403–5; education and, 624; Eisenhower and, 673; expansionism and, 543; familiarity of, 556; Federalistas and, 613; Filipino First movement and, 674; First Republic of, 411, 414, 436; forgotten empire and, 494–506, 511, *517*, 518–20, 523–38; Foster-Cánovas Treaty and, 408; Franklin D. Roosevelt and, 524, 627; Friar lands and, 404, 410, 619; gold standard and, 617; Hare-Hawes-Cutting Act and, 627–29; hemp and, 406, 621; Hollywood portrayal of, 632; Hukbalahaps Rebellion and, 615, 655–56, 672, 684, 699–700; ilustrados and, 403, 410, 504, 607, 611–13, 616, 620, 628, 634; image of, 539, 592–93; Immigration Act and, 626; imperialism and, 267, 337, 342, 347–51, 355, 367, 371, 376, 381, 455, 573; independence and, 531, 584, 637–38, 686; intrusion and, 383–84, 387–89, 403–16, 430, 434–36, 851n14; invasion of, 337; Iraq and, 416; island culture and, 539; Japan and, 538, 630–31, 639, 653; Jones Act and, 546, 615, 624–25; languages of, 607; Liberation Army and, 414; as little brown brothers, 592, 632, 639; MacArthur and, 654–55, 672; Magsaysay and, 672–74, 685, 700; malaria and, 409; Malvar and, 415–16; Manila Americans and, 386, 434, 618, 627; Marín and, 554; McKinley and, 304, 435–36, 561–63, 607, 609; militant tradition of, 635; Moro Province and, 610–11; Muslims and, 405, 609–10, 622–23, 719; Nacionalistas and, 613, 674; negotiating skills of, 575; Payne-Aldrich Tariff and, 617; plantations and, 404, 520, 620, 622, 634; population growth and, 15, 409; postcolonialism and, 696, 699–700, 712, 718–19; postwar economics of, 558; progress in, 669–74; protection in, 652–56; provincialism and, 416; regional diversity and, 411; retrospective view on, 635–38; rewards system for, 546; rinderpest and, 409; Rizal and, 411–13; Root and, 612, 625; Roxas and, 407, 654–56, 659, 672;

Philippines (*continued*)
Schurman Commission and, 497–98, 502, 607, 609; smallpox and, 409; socialism and, 628; Spain and, 37, 84, 618, 627; sprawling size of, 633; as stepping stone to Asia, 434; stunted growth and, 409; sugar and, 347, 349–51, 381, 403, 406–8, 411, 434, 517, 518–20, 534, 536, 547, 550, 566–67, 581, 601–2, 604, 615–21, 625, 628, 629–30, 653, 672–74, 719; Taft and, 502, 531, 592, 607, 612–19, 625–26, 633, 639; Tagalog and, 410–15, 593, 610, 625, 634, 673; Tayabas rebellion and, 410; Theodore Roosevelt and, 436, 495, 531, 576, 610–11, 615, 627; tobacco and, 405, 408; tourism and, 524, 539–40, 593; Treaty of Paris and, 404, 416–417; Tydings-McDuffie Act and, 627–28, 629–30; tyranny of distance and, 592–93; unofficial national anthem for, 634; vulnerability of, 605; wars of incorporation and, 203; Wilson and, 615; Wood and, 536, 611, 625
Philippines, The: A Study in National Development (Hayden), 528
Piave, Francesco Maria, 254
Pierce, Franklin, 237
Pilgrims, 175, 331, 438, 591
pineapples, 422, 599–601, 606, 650–51, 719
Pitt, William, the Elder, 66, 99–103, 106–7, 137, 777n218
Pitt, William, the Younger, 58, 77–78
plantations: Cuba and, 391–92, 394, 400, 520, 567, 569, 571, 578, 678; forgotten empire and, 499; Hawai'i and, 386, 418, 423, 534, 536, 596, 599–603, 606; Philippines and, 403, 520, 620, 622, 634; Puerto Rico and, 399–400, 520, 659; slavery and, 68, 112, 121, 147, 157, 168, 171, 182, 188, 203, 214, 220–22, 226–27, 290–91, 321, 391–94, 400, 404, 418, 423, 548–49, 567, 569, 571, 578, 596, 599–603, 606, 619, 621, 633, 659, 678; Southern states and, 112, 121, 147, 157, 168, 171, 182, 188, 203, 214, 220–22, 226–27, 290–91, 321
Plato, 461
Platt Amendment, 447, 561, 563–66, 573, 577, 582, 586
Playfair, William, 104
Pledge of Allegiance, 335
Plessy v. Ferguson, 320
pluralism, 145, 322, 332, 503, 507, 648

plutocracy, 62, 297, 301, 305, 313–16, 333, 364, 439, 658
Polk, James Knox, 170, 210, 212, 214, 216, 800n154
Pontiac's War, 119
Pope, Alexander, v, 749n112
population growth, 81, 92, 110, 152, 171, 206, 213, 244, 249, 307, 345, 409, 550
populism: absolutism and, 71; British green uprising and, 80; Caribbean and, 582, 585–86, 588–89; colonialism and, 642, 655, 670, 684; forgotten empire and, 519; imperialism and, 250, 271, 345, 356, 367, 369, 489; independence and, 144, 148, 153–54, 183, 189, 296, 298, 301, 303–4, 321, 332; intrusion and, 424–25; Napoleon and, 71; Pacific and, 636; postcolonialism and, 697, 724, 726; Republicans and, 37; revolution and, 101–3, 116, 125, 135, 138; Sons of Liberty and, 116; Wilkes and, 101, 101–3
Portugal, 72, 74, 84, 267–70, 404, 451, 467, 483, 678, 702
postcolonialism, 749n111; Adam Smith and, 707; Africa and, 700, 705, 710, 714, 716–17; agriculture and, 697–98, 701, 704, 725; American Revolution and, 693, 698; assimilation and, 719; Australia and, 700, 703; authoritarianism and, 712, 718–20; autonomy and, 719; balance of payments and, 702; Canada and, 700, 703; capitalism and, 689, 699, 707, 711–12, 714, 717, 725–26; China and, 698, 700, 702–3, 706–7, 711–18, 721–22, 725–26; Christianity and, 711–12, 719; citizenship and, 703; civilizing mission and, 719; civil rights and, 699; Cold War and, 698–700, 705, 709–15, 718, 721, 723; communism and, 711–13, 717–18, 720; conservatives and, 683–84, 711–12, 723–24; cotton and, 697; Cuba and, 695–96, 700, 716–20; decolonization and, 696, 700; democracy and, 694, 712–25, 729; Democrats and, 712, 716; dialectical forces and, 693; diversification and, 702; dominance/decline in, 691–729; Enlightenment and, 698; exports and, 697, 701–4, 708–13, 719, 722; France and, 697, 709–10, 713–14, 716; free trade and, 703, 706; Germany and, 709–13; globalization and, 8, 40, 689, 691–707, 718, 725–27; Hawai'i and, 696, 700, 718–20; hegemony and, 692, 696, 699–700, 707–21, 723,

727; human rights and, 698–99, 705–6, 718; imports and, 712, 722–23; India and, 698, 704–7, 721, 725; insular empire and, 699–700, 718; international relations and, 721, 723; Japan and, 697, 701, 703, 708, 711–13, 722–23, 924n56; Korea and, 712–13, 722; labor and, 695, 702, 705, 724; liberalism and, 695, 728; liberty and, 694, 715, 721, 724; manufacturing and, 695–98, 701–2, 706, 708, 710, 722, 725; Marx and, 707, 717; military-fiscal state and, 693–95; modernization and, 7–8, 714–15, 721; monopolies and, 704, 712; Muslims and, 719, 726; Napoleon and, 679; nationalism and, 697–99, 704, 711–18, 724, 726; nation-building and, 694–95, 704, 718–19; Native Americans and, 693–94; Netherlands and, 713; oil and, 701, 710, 714–15, 719; North American Free Trade Agreement (NAFTA) and, 703–4; oligarchy and, 712, 719; Philippines and, 696, 699–700, 712, 718–19; populism and, 697, 724, 726; poverty and, 699, 720, 723; progressives and, 693–94; protectionism and, 713; Puerto Rico and, 696, 699–700, 717–18, 720, 728; rapid institutional growth and, 702–3; raw materials and, 697, 701, 706; reconstruction and, 7–9, 697, 703, 713; rewriting history and, 691–92; self-determination and, 698, 706, 713–14, 720; South Africa and, 717; Southern United States and, 238, 291, 308; sovereignty and, 695–96, 703–5, 708; Spain and, 695; sugar and, 719; Taft and, 719; tariffs and, 705, 708; technology and, 693, 701, 727; terrorism and, 724, 728; tourism and, 719; unemployment and, 695, 698, 719–20, 723–25; United Nations and, 698–99, 703, 728, 734; World War I era and, 698; World War II era and, 692, 695–98, 701–3, 706–8, 713–14, 720–21
postmodernism, 10, 12, 703, 728
Poujade, Pierre, 489
pound sterling, 59, 81, 255, 272
poverty, 19; Caribbean and, 543, 547, 552, 558, 574, 581; colonialism and, 668–69, 675–77, 686; forgotten empire and, 528; imperialism and, 252, 347, 358, 488; independence and, 142, 144, 152, 308, 313, 315, 321–22, 329; intrusion and, 401; postcolonialism and, 699, 720, 723; revolution and, 112; wars of incorporation and, 195, 200, 226

Powell, Enoch, 480
Prairie School, 331
Pratt, Julius, 20, 844n110, 845n115
Presbyterians, 60, 175, 366, 623
Price, Richard, 102
Priestley, Joseph, 102, 176
Prince of Wales, 178
Prío Socarrás, Carlos, 661, 679
Privy Council, 119
Proclamation Line, 119–20
Progress and Poverty (George), 313
Progressives, 16; Caribbean and, 556; conservatives and, 35; demographics of, 828n116; forgotten empire and, 506, 508, 521, 526; imperialism and, 248, 250, 260, 352; independence and, 304, 312–13, 324, 330, 333; insular empire and, 20; military-fiscal state and, 73; Pacific and, 623; postcolonialism and, 693–94; wars of incorporation and, 233, 238
Progressive School, 339, 339–40
Project for the New American Century, 723
property rights: American Dream and, 194, 726; colonialism and, 677; conflict over land rights and, 198–99; exclusive rights and, 194–207; expansionism and, 194–207; frontier societies and, 195–96, 203, 429; Homestead Bill and, 222, 293; imperialism and, 248, 283, 356, 376; independence and, 166, 177, 291; indigenous peoples and, 29, 197–99; intrusion and, 402, 425; land policy and, 194–207; liberty and, 109; military-fiscal state and, 67; Native Americans and, 198–201, 237; permanent land transfers and, 28; revolution and, 109, 126, 132; voting rights and, 63, 133; wars of incorporation and, 194–207; women and, 623
protectionism: American System and, 160, 162, 169, 196, 296; Caribbean and, 547–48, 564, 579–80, 587; colonialism and, 30, 681; forgotten empire and, 516, 519; imperialism and, 265, 273, 276, 284, 348, 351, 379, 448, 458–60; independence and, 144, 157, 161, 163, 168, 293; intrusion and, 396, 435; military-fiscal state and, 81–82; Pacific and, 617–18; postcolonialism and, 713; tariffs and, 55, 58, 131, 151, 154, 161, 260, 279, 284, 291, 293, 296, 304, 307, 333, 355, 358, 375, 390, 435, 473, 521, 570, 579, 590; wars of incorporation and, 197
Protestantism: Caribbean and, 545, 551, 571, 572–73; forgotten empire and, 513;

Protestantism (*continued*)
imperialism and, 265–66, 272, 366–67, 377, 381, 405, 422, 425, 428–29, 434–35; independence and, 173–78, 183, 289, 317–18, 322–24, 334; McKinley and, 381; military-fiscal state and, 55, 66–67, 69–71; Pacific and, 623–24, 644, 651; revolution and, 100, 105, 111, 113, 133, 135; wars of incorporation and, 194, 207, 219
providentialism, 15–16, 176, 641
provincialism, 416
Prussia: imperialism and, 254, 270, 278; military-fiscal state and, 48, 54, 72–74; revolution and, 100; wars of incorporation and, 232–33
Puerto Rico, 915n89; Albizu Campos and, 536, 554–58, 657–59, 700; annexation of, 384; autonomistas and, 402; Campos and, 536; as Caribbean miracle, 677; caudillos and, 573–74; coffee and, 350; Cold War and, 657; colonialism and, 639, 657–59, 662, 674–77, 684–86; Comity Agreements and, 551; Commonwealth of, 545, 558, 657, 659, 674–75, 685, 718; debt default of, 720, 928n117; Development Bank and, 558; direct rule and, 589; economic distress in, 552–54; education in, 657; electoral system for, 547; elitism and, 544–45; Foraker Act and, 545–62, 566; forgotten empire and, 494, 499–501, 504, 509, 511, 515, 517, 520, 522–30, 534, 536–38; Franklin D. Roosevelt and, 556, 589; globalization and, 594; Hispanism and, 551; Ibero Pancho and, 552; identity and, 551–52; image of, 539–43, 547, 554; imperialism and, 337, 347, 350–51; independence and, 635, 657–58, 686, 699; Industrial Development Company and, 558; insular empire and, 543–99; intrusion and, 383, 386, 388–89, 399–403, 428–29, 430, 433–34, 436, 851n14; invasion of, 337; jíbaro music and, 539–40; Jones Act and, 546; Jones-Costigan Act and, 553; lack of militant tradition in, 635; Law 53 and, 658; Liberal Party and, 434; McKinley and, 547–48; Miles and, 399, 403; modernity for, 572; Muñoz Marín and, 383, 554–58, 628, 658–59, 675, 677, 685, 700; Muñoz Rivera and, 402–3, 545–46, 554; negotiating skills of, 575; new relevance for, 588–91; Operation Bootstrap and, 676–77, 700; Partido Nacionalista and, 554, 657–59; Partido Popular Democrático and, 554, 556, 558, 658–59, 674–75, 685; Partido Republicano and, 546–47, 554; Partido Socialista and, 554; Partido Unión and, 546–47, 554; peaceful revolution in, 675; plantations and, 400–401, 520, 548–49, 659; as pleasure island, 539–40; population of, 15; postcolonialism and, 696, 699–700, 717–18, 720, 728; postwar economics of, 558; poverty and, 676–77; rewards system for, 546; rival religions and, 571; Root and, 539, 543–47, 556; self-government and, 410, 544; Spanish-American War and, 399; Spanish language as national identity and, 531; sugar and, 347, 386, 388–89, 400–402, 428, 434, 517, 520, 547–50, 553–54, 557, 567, 569, 581, 586, 588, 590, 604, 657, 675, 677; Theodore Roosevelt and, 530, 543; tobacco and, 401; tourism and, 676, 720; Tugwell and, 509, 522, 529–30, 556–58, 639, 657, 675–77; tuition of officials and, 545; U.S. Constitution and, 545; Vieques, 718; *West Side Story* and, 572; Wilson and, 555; Works Projects Administration and, 553
Puerto Rico Reconstruction Administration (PRRA), 556
Pullman Palace Car Company, 300
Puritans, 109, 112, 175, 218

Quai d'Orsay, 455
Quesnay, François, 33
Quezon, Manuel, 536, 612, 614–15, 628–32, 910n219
Quinn, Anthony, 202, 632, 796n75
Quirino, Elpidio Rivera, 672
Quit India movement, 469–70

race patriotism, 139, 395, 454
race theory, 251–53, 317, 319
railroads, 29, 148, 163–66, 175, 199, 222, 229, 244–45, 256, 264, 293–99, 307, 310–11, 314, 334, 364, 391, 393, 457, 544, 562, 567, 827n102
raw materials: Caribbean and, 579; colonialism and, 38, 40, 641; forgotten empire and, 535; imperialism and, 265, 274, 277, 447, 457, 473, 477; independence and, 186, 295, 334; military-fiscal state and, 85; postcolonialism and, 697, 701, 706; wars of incorporation and, 220
Reagan, Ronald, 25, 717
Real Glory, The (movie), 632
real wages, 246–47, 813n75

reciprocity: Caribbean and, 389–90, 396, 401, 408, 417, 419–24, 430, 436, 564–68, 573; forgotten empire and, 518, 520; imperialism and, 356–58, 375, 379; independence and, 163, 295, 301; intrusion and, 389–90, 396, 401, 408, 417, 419–24, 430, 436; Pacific and, 389–90, 396, 400, 408, 417, 419–24, 430, 436, 595

Reciprocity Act, 163

reconstruction, 923n44; Caribbean and, 556–57; challenges to, 290–91; Civil War and, 237; Colonial Development & Welfare Act and, 477–78; colonialism and, 667; FIDES and, 477–78; forgotten empire and, 523; imperialism and, 246–47, 491; independence and, 287, 290–91, 320, 332; intrusion and, 394; Marshall Plan and, 475, 708, 710; military-fiscal state and, 71–76, 87; one-party states and, 291–92; Pacific and, 625; postcolonialism and, 7–9, 697, 703, 713; reform and, 71–76; revolution and, 123; second colonial occupation and, 470–83; wars of incorporation and, 233, 237

Reconstruction Act, 246

Red Scare, 648, 652

Reign of Terror, 134–35, 662

Reily, Emmet M., 524

religiosity, 79, 110, 175, 376

"Report on Manufactures" (Hamilton), 159

Republican Guard, 732, 931n15

Republicans: Anglo-Saxons and, 289; Caribbean and, 546–47, 554, 561, 578–80; Cobdenite lobby and, 823n35; colonialism and, 645, 649–52, 660, 666–69, 671, 684; forgotten empire and, 494–95, 507, 511–12, 514, 518, 520–21, 524–28, 536; imperialism and, 263, 338, 354–64, 368–70, 374–76, 379–80, 448; independence and, 157, 160–61, 170, 189, 288–306, 310–11, 314, 319, 322, 329, 332–33; intrusion and, 390, 416, 432, 435; Jefferson and, 132; Madison and, 132; military-fiscal state and, 73, 76; Mugwumps and, 292, 296; Pacific and, 597–98, 610, 615, 625, 630; populism and, 37; postcolonialism and, 716, 724; revolution and, 132, 134; tariffs and, 39; wars of incorporation and, 219, 224, 226

revisionists, 19, 31, 55, 97, 192, 197, 220, 457, 465, 476, 560, 640

revolution: Adam Smith and, 117; Africa and, 96, 98, 138–39; American Revolution and, 107 (see also American Revolution);

anarchy and, 120, 135; authoritarianism and, 96–97, 102, 122, 141; autonomy and, 109, 114; British Empire and, 100, 105, 109, 112, 123, 135, 141; capitalism and, 121–22; Catalan Revolt and, 74; China and, 642, 656, 663, 711, 718; Christianity and, 109; civilizing mission and, 106; Civil War and, 98, 129, 135, 139; conservatives and, 100–101, 103, 106–7, 112, 122, 135, 137–41; contention and, 129–35; Cuba and, 519, 585, 678–79, 682, 717, 719–20; declining expectations and, 107–23; decolonization and, 98, 112, 124, 138–41; deflation and, 114, 116, 118; democracy and, 97, 125, 133–34; dialectical forces and, 97, 139; emerging global order and, 95–98; Enlightenment and, 103, 126, 132; France and, 99–101, 106, 113–14, 123, 138; free trade and, 131, 133, 137; French Wars and, 126; globalization and, 98, 139; Glorious Revolution and, 46, 53–62, 68, 70, 90, 100, 103, 113, 122, 126, 137, 140, 392; home rule and, 122–24; India and, 98, 101–8, 111–15, 121–22, 135, 137; indissoluble union of the states and, 123–29; international relations and, 124; Ireland and, 103–4, 107, 140; Jacobites and, 46, 62–63, 67–69, 78; Jefferson and, 118–19, 130–35; labor and, 117, 121; landowners and, 112, 131; liberty and, 95–98, 101, 109, 116, 128–31, 135, 141; manufacturing and, 100, 103, 110, 115, 117, 129, 131, 136; Marx and, 107; mercantilism and, 104, 113–15, 137, 139; Mexico and, 552; modernization and, 135; national identity and, 117, 127, 138–39; nationalism and, 105, 120, 134, 138; nation-building and, 126, 128; Netherlands and, 115; new colony system and, 98–105; oligarchy and, 106, 122, 135; patriotism and, 139; populism and, 101–3, 116, 125, 135, 138; poverty and, 112; Proclamation Line and, 119–20; property rights and, 109, 126, 132; Protestantism and, 100, 105, 111, 113, 133, 135; Prussia and, 100; reconstruction and, 123; Republicans and, 132, 134; Russia and, 507, 552; Scotland and, 10–13, 107, 111, 124, 140; Seven Years' War and, 99, 105, 112, 114, 118–19, 122, 140; slavery and, 95–96, 117–22, 125, 128–29, 133, 141; sovereignty and, 98, 122, 124, 135, 137; taxes and, 95–103, 106–10, 114–15, 118–19, 123–25, 128–40; terrorism and, 134–35; Tocqueville and,

revolution (*continued*)
107, 114, 140, 491, 768n65, 790nn221, 237, 238; Treaty of Paris and, 121, 199, 404, 415–16, 514, 618; unemployment and, 111; U.S. Constitution and, 98, 124–31, 134, 139; West Indies and, 96

Revolution of 1688, 55–56, 59–60, 63, 90, 98, 100, 122, 126

Reynolds, Joshua, 179

Rhee, Syngman, 712–13

Rhenish capitalism, 711–12, 726

Rhodes, Cecil, 16, 429

Rhodesia, 454

rice, 110, 162, 182, 357, 409, 411, 419, 617

Rice, Thomas, 182

Riggs, Francis E., 556–57, 557

rinderpest, 409

Rionda, Manuel, 569–70

Risorgimento, 72, 231, 275–76, 344

Rivera, Luis, Muñoz, 402–3, 545–46, 554

River Tigris, 2

Rizal, José, 411–13

robber barons, 314

Robertson, William, 66, 103

Robespierre, 135

Robinson, Ronald, 23, 471

Rockefeller, John D., 314

Rockingham, Marquis of, 103

Rodríguez de Tió, Lola, 588

Romanovs, 49

Rome, 25

Roosevelt, Eleanor, 646

Roosevelt, Franklin D., 773n164; Atlantic Charter and, 469; Brains Trust and, 526, 529; Chamberlain and, 467–68; Cuba and, 559, 564–65, 584, 586–87, 589; economic nationalism and, 306; Good Neighbor policy and, 449, 556, 584–85; Hawai'i and, 604; Hoover and, 449; Ickes and, 528–29; Indian protests and, 470; MacArthur and, 655; "new brooms" of, 527; New Deal and, 250, 287, 491, 526–29, 532, 537, 556, 557, 586, 589, 645, 675, 695, 698; Pearl Harbor and, 468; Philippines and, 524, 627; Puerto Rico and, 556, 589; Tugwell and, 557; Winship and, 556

Roosevelt, Theodore, 638; Addams and, 306; America's civilizing mission and, 512, 683, 719; Boy Scouts and, 266; Burroughs and, 438, 440; buyer's remorse and, 495; Corollary to Monroe Doctrine and, 447, 449–50, 516, 717; Cuba and, 564–65, 569,

576; on defeating Spain, 427; Department of Commerce and Labor and, 305; foreign policy and, 304–5, 333; forgotten empire and, 495, 506, 508, 512; Hawai'i and, 600–601; high status of United States and, 336; honor of duty and, 343; imperialism and, 343, 354, 363–65, 368–71, 382; masculinity and, 323–24, 331, 343; McKinley and, 523; Native Americans and, 201–2; naval expertise of, 354, 427; Philippines and, 436, 495, 531, 576, 610–11, 615, 627; Platt Amendment and, 565; public health and, 323–24, 331; Puerto Rico and, 530, 543; reform and, 305; Rough Riders and, 266, 364, 379–82, 399, 438, 564; Secret Service and, 250; sports and, 331; Strong and, 324; Turkey and, 427; U.S. Navy and, 363

Roosevelt, Theodore, Jr., 511, 525, 528, 543, 627, 639, 728

Root, Elihu, 360, 369; Cuba and, 563–64; forgotten empire and, 503, 506, 511–12, 520, 522–25; Hawai'i and, 601; Philippines and, 612, 625; Puerto Rico and, 539, 543–47, 556

Rosas, Juan Manuel de, 154

Roscher, Wilhelm, 259

Rotary Club, 513

Rough Riders, 266, 364, 379–82, 399, 438, 564

rounders, 330

Roundheads, 220

Rousseau, Jean-Jacques, 89, 506

Rouvier, Maurice, 280

Roxas, Manuel Acuña, 654–56, 659, 672, 909n189, 910n219

Roxas y Ureta, Domingo, 407, 858n139

Royal Air Force, 453

Royal Commission on the Depression in Trade and Industry, 256

Royal Navy, 88, 127–28, 160, 167, 186, 193, 208, 333, 354

rugby, 330

Rumsfeld, Donald, 732

Ruskin, John, 248, 461

Russell, Lord, 228, 231, 805n248

Russia, 648; divinity of state and, 16; expansionism and, 2; forgotten empire and, 507; Hungary and, 666; imperialism and, 247–51, 256, 260, 266–67, 278, 285, 475, 490; independence and, 189; intrusion and, 432, 440; Japan and, 507; military-fiscal state and, 74–75, 84; *Narodniki*

and, 189; Peter the Great and, 48; postcolonialism and, 702; revolution and, 507,
552; wars of incorporation and, 234. *See
also* Soviet Union

Saint Simon, Henri de, 77
Sakdalistas, 628
Salisbury, Lord, 256, 466
Samoa, 353, 494, 499, 504, 523, 527–28,
838n2
Santa Cecilia Sugar Company, 581
Santayana, George, 322, 835n246
Sargent, John Singer, 331
Saudi Arabia, 456, 715–16
Schumpeter, Joseph, 463
Schurman Commission, 497–98, 502, 607,
609, 903n82
Scotland: Act of Union and, 67; home gov-
ernment and, 35; military-fiscal state and,
60–61, 64–70, 92; revolution and, 10–13,
107, 111, 124, 140; Union of the Kingdoms
and, 67
Scott, Walter, 180, 219, 328, 364
Scott, Winfield, 216
Scottish Enlightenment, 103, 132
Second Seminole War, 199–200
Secret Service, 250
Seeley, John, 262, 498
segregation, 913n38; African Americans
and, 292, 320, 341–42, 506, 645, 665;
apartheid and, 292, 480, 484, 648, 684,
717; armed forces and, 647; civil rights
and, 671 (*see also* civil rights); colonialism
and, 499, 684; foreign policy effects of,
666; Hawai'i and, 670–71; Native Americans and, 648–49; *Plessy v. Ferguson* and,
320; Southern states and, 292, 645, 665,
684; U.S. Supreme Court and, 665; wars
of incorporation and, 198, 237; WASP
leadership and, 507; White Australia policy and, 684
self-determination: Caribbean and, 552, 555,
574, 577; colonialism and, 641, 643, 647,
664–65, 668–69, 675, 685–86; demands
for, 40; forgotten empire and, 534, 538;
Germany and, 37; imperialism and, 249,
451, 460, 469, 491; individual rights and,
36; intrusion and, 387, 397; Iraq and, 736;
Italy and, 36–37; military-fiscal state and,
72, 74–75; Pacific and, 615, 625; postcolonialism and, 698, 706, 713–14, 720; wars
of incorporation and, 218–19, 225–31

self-help, 195, 229, 296, 582
Seminoles, 198–200, 199
September 11, 2001, attacks, 23, 25, 724–25,
737, 925n81
Settlement House, 306
Seven Years' War: empire and, 33, 45, 52,
57–58, 61–64, 83, 99, 105, 112, 114, 118–19,
122, 140; military-fiscal state and, 45, 52,
57–58, 61–64, 83; revolution and, 99, 105,
112, 114, 118–19, 122, 140; wars of incorpo-
ration and, 199
Seward, William H., 145–46, 217, 237, 432
Shah of Iran, 715
Shakespeare, William, 178, 328–29
sharecroppers, 308, 351, 407, 411, 622
Sharp, Granville, 96
Shawnee, 95, 210
Shelley, Percy Bysshe, 72, 759n148
Sherman Act, 305, 827n107
Siam, 617
Sierra Leone Company, 96
silver currency, 294, 350–51. *See also*
bimetallism
Silver Purchase Act, 299
Sinclair, Upton, 438, 867n6
Singapore, 469, 482, 499, 618
Sioux, 199–202, 265, 321
Sitting Bull, 202
slavery: abolition of, 73, 75, 79, 86–88, 96,
122, 157–58, 181–84, 188, 213, 215, 219–32,
290–91, 345, 376, 391–92, 395, 400, 547,
624, 685, 698, 799n138; Anti-Slavery Association and, 72–73, 88; Australia and,
96; Caribbean and, 120–22, 539, 541, 547;
Civil War and, 237 (*see also* Civil War);
Compromise of 1850 and, 222–24; Dred
Scott case and, 222, 224; Emancipation
Proclamation and, 227, 230, 392; forgotten empire and, 516; Fugitive Slave Act
and, 75; George Washington and, 95–96;
imperialism and, 26, 265, 276, 284, 341,
345, 347–49, 351, 372; independence and,
147–63, 168, 170–71, 173–74, 176, 181, 184–
89, 289–91, 297, 308, 317, 320; intrusion
and, 387, 390–95, 400–401, 405, 407, 413;
Kansas-Nebraska Act and, 224; Lincoln
and, 75; Merivale on, 86–87; Mexico and,
214; military-fiscal state and, 68, 72–73,
75–76, 79, 86–89; Northern states and,
181–82, 291; Pacific and, 386–402, 406–8,
411, 417–29, 434, 594, 611, 624, 635; plantations and, 68, 112, 121, 147, 157, 168,

slavery (*continued*)
171, 182, 188, 203, 214, 220–22, 226–27, 290–91, 321, 391–92, 394, 400, 404, 418, 423, 548–49, 566–67, 569, 571, 578, 596, 599–603, 606, 620, 622, 634, 659, 678; return of escaped slaves and, 95–96; revolution and, 95–96, 117–22, 125, 128–29, 133, 141; Southern states and, 39, 75, 121, 125, 129, 149–50, 153, 158, 160, 171, 185, 193, 203, 210–15, 219–29, 290–91, 320, 391, 393, 685; Spain and, 347; Texas and, 184, *204*, 214; Turner revolt and, 218; U.S. Supreme Court and, 149, 224; voting rights and, 133, 149, 290; wars of incorporation and, 193, 196–97, 203, 208, 210, 212–32, 237–38; West Indies and, 215; women and, 87

smallpox, 409

Smiles, Samuel, 195

Smith, Adam, 66; colonialism and, 110; commercial society and, 103; cost of empire and, 135; dialectical forces and, 34; imperialism and, 244–46, 261, 273, 284–85, 344, 457; mercantilism and, 56, 114–15; military-fiscal state and, 56–57, 68–69, 77, 84, 89, 92; national debt and, 135; postcolonialism and, 707; revolution and, 117; trade and, 33; wars of incorporation and, 205; *The Wealth of Nations* and, 54, 135–36

Smith, Drew L., 651

Smith, Goldwyn, 194

Smoot, Reed, 580–81

Smoot-Hawley Tariff, 446, 449, 458, 519, 579–80, 586–87

smuggling, 63, 115, 344, 348, 411, 413, 770n103

Smuts, Jan Christian, 472, 646

soccer, 330–31

social Darwinism, 251, 365–66

Social Gospel, 324

socialism, 203, 251, 259, 265, 276, 279–82, 297, 314–15, 382, 490, 586, 662, 666, 924n45

Socialist-Labor Party (SLP), 297

Society for the Abolition of the Slave Trade, 122

"Song of Hiawatha, The" (Longfellow), 180–81, 624

Sons of Liberty, 116

Sons of the American Revolution, 335

South Africa, 794n45; colonialism and, 89, 645, 647–48, 684; imperialism and, 258, 263, 266, 285, 451, 454–55, 461–62, 476, 480, 484–85, 596; independence and, 292, 312, 320; intrusion and, 418; postcolonialism and, 717; wars of incorporation and, 194, 205, 207, 210

Southern Democrats, 149, 648, 651–52, 666

Southern states: Adams and, 152; Anglo-Normans of, 175; Bible Belt of, 323; civil rights and, 648; Civil War and, 302 (*see also* Civil War); communism and, 652; Confederacy and, 219, 225–33, 238, 788n184, 801n166, 804n232, 804n234, 805n246, 823n34, 829n136; Cuba and, 391, 393; Emancipation Proclamation and, 227, 230, 392; free trade and, 35; grand estates of, 181; Hawai'i and, 596, 646, 650–51, 684; Home Rule and, 380; Immigration Act and, 507; intellectual thought in, 788n194; Jackson and, 153, 155, 157–58, 162; Jefferson and, 132; Kennedy and, 667, 685; Ku Klux Klan and, 290, 647; landed interests and, 93; Lee and, 225, 804n230; lobbies and, 222; minstrelsy and, 182; Missouri Territory and, 150; modernization and, 200; new South and, 308–9; Northern liberation army in, 290; plantations and, 112, 121, 147, 157, 168, 171, 182, 188, 203, 214, 220–22, 226–27, 290–91, 321; segregation and, 292, 665, 684; slavery and, 39, 75, 121, 125, 129, 149–50, 153, 158, 160, 171, 185, 193, 203, 210–15, 219–29, 290–91, 320, 391, 393, 685; sports and, 330; Supreme Court judges and, 149; tariffs and, 85; terminology of, 774n176; textile industry and, 308, 334; wars of incorporation and, 193, 200, 203, 210, 212–29, 234

South Porto Rico Sugar Company, 548–49

sovereignty: Caribbean and, 559–62; colonialism and, 641, 659, 668, 682, 686; declaration of independence and, 54, 110, 112, 122–23, 161, 199, 209, 211, 214–15, 330, 414, 471, 698; forgotten empire and, 516; Free World and, 39, 460, 475, 487–88, 491–92, 646, 663, 675, 684, 698, 713, 716, 723; imperialism and, 19, 22–23, 27, 40, 262, 276, 374, 479; independence and, 19, 145–46, 177, 185, 187, 321, 340; intrusion and, 384, 403, 420, 429, 433; military-fiscal state and, 66, 91; new supranational organizations and, 708–9; Pacific and, 598, 611, 630, 638; postcolonialism and,

695–96, 703–5, 708; postwar European power and, 708–10; protectorates and, 15, 37, 217, 455, 498–99, 515–16, 559, 613, 660, 686, 700, 709, 882n8; revolution and, 98, 122, 124, 135, 137; wars of incorporation and, 200, 216, 219, 231

Soviet Union, 920n195; Bolsheviks and, 451, 507; Cold War and, 31 (*see also* Cold War); colonialism and, 641, 644, 646, 663, 667, 683, 686; Cuba and, 682–83; expansionism and, 713; Ho Chi Minh and, 714; imperialism and, 466, 474; Kremlin's Pied Pipers and, 663; Lenin and, 22, 262, 267, 450, 465; postcolonialism and, 699, 705, 713–14, 716, 719–21; Stalin and, 663

Spain, 17; American Revolution and, 52; Basque Country and, 345; Caribbean and, 539–40, 544–47, 552, 561, 569–74, 590; Catalonia and, 74, 345; crisis of transition of, 349; conservatives and, 345–46; Cuba and, 37, 84, 213–14, 238, 544, 635; declining influence of, 343–52; deflation and, 349–50; exceptionalism and, 16; Ferdinand VII and, 73; forgotten empire and, 494–95, 502, 532–33; French Wars and, 53, 72, 344; Glorious Revolution and, 392; imperialism and, 316, 337–55, 359, 366, 369, 371–77, 381; intrusion and, 384–416, 423, 427–28, 430–36; liberals and, 345–46; manufacturing and, 347–48; McKinley and, 303; mercantilism and, 347–48; mestizos and, 348, 387, 404, 407, 410, 412–13, 436, 607, 613, 620, 626; Mexico and, 212–17, 346 (*see also* Mexico); nationalism and, 345–46; naval lobby and, 353–54; Northern states and, 381; Pacific and, 49, 595, 607, 609, 611, 617–18, 627, 634–35, 636; Peninsula of, 345; peso depreciation and, 350–51; Philippines and, 37, 84, 618, 627; postcolonialism and, 695; Puerto Rico and, 37, 84, 347; Queen Isabella and, 293; silver and, 350–51; slavery and, 347; stereotypes of, 752n33; sugar and, 350–51; Ten Years' War and, 349, 392–97, 401, 430; Third Carlist War and, 269; War of 1812 and, 210; wars of choice and, 427–36; wars of incorporation and, 192

Spanish-American War, 7, 338; Anglo-Saxon alliance and, 455; Beveridge and, 373; expansionism and, 237; forgotten empire and, 501, 505, 507, 520–22; as great aberration, 19–20; imperialism and, 264,

337, 353, 362, 364, 455; intrusion and, 385, 399; McKinley and, 369–74; military improvements after, 306; modernization and, 504; structure/agency causation for, 373–74; transition and, 337; *USS Maine* and, 345, 354, 360, 368, 370, 372, 399, 415, 431–32, 539, 724; war fever for, 370–73; wars of incorporation and, 237; Wilson and, 373; Winship and, 556

Spencer, Herbert, 6, 247, 251, 313, 317–18, 366, 381, 505

Spengler, Oswald, 254

Spirit of the Laws, The (Montesquieu), 33

spoils system, 144, 153–54, 353, 363, 521, 613

sports, 266, 325, 330–31, 335, 513, 571–72, 624, 731, 815n120

Spreckels, Claus, 419–20, 425–26

Stalin, Joseph, 663

Stamp Act, 103, 114, 117

Standard Oil, 302, 305, 314

Stanley, Henry Morton, 263, 265

Stead, William, 327, 334

steamships, 64, 164, 244, 264, 349, 386, 391, 406, 410, 420, 457

Stephen, James, 248

Sterling Area, 474, 476, 483

Stevens, John L., 421–22, 429, 431

Stevenson, Robert Louis, 263, 417, 567

Stimson, Henry L., 625

St. John, Henry, Viscount Bolingbroke, 62–63, 101, 132, 219

stock market, 10, 58–59, 116, 131, 156, 165, 175, 231, 299, 310–11, 359, 409, 416, 456, 681, 723

Stratemeyer, Edward, 372

Stricken Land, The: The Story of Puerto Rico (Tugwell), 529–30

Strong, Josiah, 264, 323–25, 440, 513

Suez Canal, 347, 435, 482, 716–17, 880n224

sugar, 39; beets and, 295, 349, 354, 361, 388–90, 394, 396, 399, 424–26, 516–21, 547–48, 552, 577–78, 579–80, 587, 590, 617, 620, 626, 646, 681; Caribbean and, 386–402, 406–8, 411, 417–29, 434, 544, 547–54, 557, 561–70, 575, 577–82, 586–90; China and, 858n153; colonialism and, 646, 649–50, 653, 657, 660–61, 670–83; Cuba and, 517, 547, 550, 553, 561–70, 575–82, 586–88, 590, 620, 626, 650, 660–61, 677–83, 719, 897n164; Fordney-McCumber Act and, 518, 578–79; Foster-Cánovas Treaty and, 396–97; Hawai'i and, 349–51, 386–90, sugar (*continued*)

408, 417–25, 430, *517*, 521, 534, 536, 567, 598–606, 626, 633, 646, 649–51, 670; imperialism and, 347–51, 354, 357, 360–62, 381, 457, *513*–21, 534, 536; independence and, 290, 295, 302; International Sugar Agreement and, 681; intrusion and, 386–96, 400–402, 406–8, 411, 417–29, 434, 825n32; Jones-Costigan Act and, 519, 553, 586–87, 604, 628; log-rolling and, 579–80; military-fiscal state and, 58, 68, 79, 82; molasses and, 295; Pacific and, 595, 598–608, 615–21, 625–29, 633; Philippines and, 347, 349–51, 381, 388–89, 403, 406–8, 411, 434, *517*, 518–20, 534, 536, 547, 550, 566–67, 580, 601–2, 604, 615–21, 625–26, 628, 629–30, 653; plantations and, 386, 896n134 (*see also* plantations); postcolonialism and, 719; Puerto Rico and, 347, 386, 388–89, 399–402, 428–29, 433–34, *517*, 520, 547–50, 553–54, 557, 567, 569, 580, 586, 588, 590, 604, 657, 675, 677; quotas and, 681–82; Rionda and, 569–70; Spreckels and, 419–20, 425–26; tyranny of distance and, 570; West Indies and, 110

Sugar Act, 114, 116

Sugar Duties Act, 82

Sugar Trust, 302, 360, 425, 513, 519–21, 547–48, 564, 566, 617

Suharto, Muhammed, 713–14

Sukarno, 713–14

Summer Welles, Benjamin, 584

Sumner, William Graham, 313, 371, 377, 865n260

Sweden, 48, 51, 72, 73

Swift, Jonathan, 104, 359

Switzerland, 272

Taft, William H., 21, 905n116; colonialism and, 639; forgotten empire and, 495, 502, 506, 512, 531; Hawai'i and, 601; imperialism and, 449; "little brown brothers" and, 592, 632, 639; Philippines and, 502, 531, 592, 607, 612–19, 625, 632, 639; postcolonialism and, 719

Tagalog, 410–15, 593, 610, 625, 673

Tamerlane, 737, 738

Tariff of Abominations, 155

tariffs: Caribbean and, 547–49, 558, 564, 568–70, 578–81, 586–90; colonialism and, 639, 657, 660, 673, 676–77, 680; as declaration of independence, 161; discriminatory, 151, 273, 348, 518; Fordney-McCumber Act and, 518, 578–79; forgotten empire and, 514–21, 535; General Agreement on Trade and Tariffs (GATT) and, 708; Hamilton and, 130–31, 160; imperialism and, 246, 260, 273–74, 279, 284, 348, 351, 354–62, 369, 375, 381, 446, 449, 458–59, 473; independence and, 151, 154–56, 160–63, 169–71, 186, 189, 291, 293–96, 299, 301–4, 307, 312, 314, 332–33; intrusion and, 385, 388–90, 393, 396–98, 401, 406, 417, 420–28, 435; Jackson and, 154–56; McKinley and, 295, 299, 356, 358, 360, 396, 421, 423, 425–26; military-fiscal state and, 55, 57–58, 81–82, 85–86; Pacific and, 598–601, 615–17, 620, 625–26, 627, 629–30, 636–38; postcolonialism and, 705, 708; protectionism and, 35, 55, 58, 131, 151, 154, 161, 260, 279, 284, 291, 293, 296, 304, 307, 333, 355, 358, 375, 390, 435, 473, 521, 570, 579, 590; Republicans and, 39; rival lobbies and, 39; Southern states and, 85; Townshend Duties and, 114–15, 117; Tyler and, 169; wars of incorporation and, 210, 222, 226, 228

Tartars, 201

Tarzan, 437–40, 447

Taussig, Frank W., 358

Tax Britannica, 128

taxes: colonialism and, 29, 34, 670, 673, 676–77, 697, 722–23, 726; forgotten empire and, 520; imperialism and, 244, 253, 268, 270, 274, 276, 278, 282, 346–48, 354, 358, 361, 381, 452, 462, 467, 473, 478, 489; independence and, 148, 151, 156, 162, 167, 188–89, 291, 303, 312–13; intrusion and, 391–92, 396–97, 404–8, 418, 424; military-fiscal state and, 48–53, 58–65, 68, 70, 74, 80, 91–92; Pacific and, 615–17, 628; Pitt and, 58, 66, 77–78, 99–103, 106–7, 137; revolution and, 95–103, 106–10, 114–15, 118–19, 123–25, 128–40; wars of incorporation and, 195, 200, 226

tea, 114–16, 295

technology: Babbage's analytical engine and, 244; colonialism and, 664; empire and, 6, 28; forgotten empire and, 508, 521; globalization and, 29–30; imperialism and, 242, 263, 273, 283; independence and, 316, 329; Industrial Revolution and, 29, 56, 59, 221, 272, 346, 584; intrusion and, 392, 406, 419; military, 352–53; military-fiscal state and, 48–51, 65; Pacific and, 612; postcolonialism and, 693, 701, 727; railroads, 29, 148, 163–66, 175, 199, 222, 229, 244–45, 256, 264, 293–99, 307, 310–11, 314, 334, 364, 391, 393, 457, 544, 562, 567; steamships, 64, 164, 244, 264, 349, 386, 391, 406, 410, 420, 457; superpowers and, 6; telegraphs, 64, 185–86, 244, 308, 391, 406, 451; telephones, 406, 451, 460, 578, 664; wars of incorporation and, 206

telegraphs, 64, 185–86, 244, 308, 391, 406, 451

telephones, 406, 451, 460, 578, 664

Teller, Henry, 433, 561

Tennyson, Lord (Alfred), 244–45, 328

Ten Years' War, 349, 392–97, 401, 430

terrorism: colonialism and, 662; forgotten empire and, 494; imperialism and, 250, 483, 491; independence and, 290; Iraq and, 724; Ireland and, 250; military-fiscal state and, 75; postcolonialism and, 724, 728; Reign of Terror and, 134–35, 662; revolution and, 134–35; September 11, 2001, attacks and, 23, 25, 725, 737, 925n81; war on, 724

Teutonic qualities, 251–52, 318, 366, 423

Texas, 327, 426; annexation of, 157, 170, 214–15, 216; debt of, 216; declaration of independence and, 214–15; incorporation of, 215; Mexico and, 212–17; as republic, 214; slavery and, 184, 214; statehood for, 214; Treaty of Guadalupe Hidalgo and, 217; war fever in, 370

Texas to Bataan (movie), 632

textile industry, 111; cotton and, 291 (*see also* cotton); free trade and, 167–68; imperialism and, 273, 277; Japan and, 713; mechanization of, 314; military-fiscal state and, 80–81, 85; Southern states and, 308, 334; wars of incorporation and, 228, 232–33

Thanksgiving, 335

Theory of Business Enterprise (Veblen), 256

They Were Expendable (movie), 632

Third Carlist War, 269

Thoreau, Henry David, 461

Thucydides, 31

Thurston, Lorrin A., 422

Till, Emmett, 665

Tillman, Benjamin, 302, 367

Time magazine, 443

Timrod, Henry, 225, 804n225

tobacco, 58, 110, 117–19, 162, 305, 308, 347, 388, 391–92, 397, 401, 405–8, 544, 547–53, 582

Tocqueville, Alexis de, 179, 764n254, 791n263; American love of money and, 182; democracy and, 88, 149, 182, 281, 305; French imperialism and, 89; independence and, 287–89, 305, 334, 821n1; instinctive sense of narrative by, 287; Marx and, 491; Mill and, 248 religion and, 182; revolution and, 107, 114, 140, 491, 768n65, 790nn221, 237, 238; U.S. decentralization and, 147; wars of incorporation and, 806n260, 807n280

Tolstoy, Leo, 461

Tories, 55–56, 61–62, 77, 79, 81, 86, 93, 100–103, 112, 130, 137, 776n208

Torrens, Robert, 81

torture, 415, 623, 861n199

tourism: Cuba and, 571, 679, 719–20; France and, 478; Hawai'i and, 417, 592, 598, 602, 719; Pacific and, 598; Philippines and, 524, 593; postcolonialism and, 719; Puerto Rico and, 676, 720

Townshend, Charles Vere Ferrers: career of, 1–2; India and, 1; Iraq and, 1–6, 730–32, 735, 737, 739n3, 740n21, 740n24; 741n28; as Lucky, 1

Townshend Acts, 114–15, 117

Toynbee, Arnold, 463

Toynbee Hall, 306

Tragedy of Pudd'nhead Wilson, The (Twain), 329

Trail of Broken Treaties, 668

Trans-Jordan, 456

Transvaal, 566

Treasure Island (Stevenson), 567

Treasury bills, 58

Treaty of Aix la-Chapelle, 99

Treaty of Ghent, 209

Treaty of Guadalupe Hidalgo, 217

Treaty of Paris, 121, 199, 404, 415–16, 514, 618, 845n132

Treaty of Washington, 209

Trent Affair, 228

Trinidad, 464, 545

Trotsky, Leon, 451

Truman, Harry S., 470–71, 475, 528, 643–48, 651, 656, 658, 661, 663, 913n38

Trump, Donald, 726, 928n116

Trust Territories, 645

Tugwell, Rexford Guy, 889n146, 919n169; benevolent assimilation and, 513; foreign empire and, 509, 513, 527–30; Puerto Rico and, 509, 522, 529–30, 556–58, 639, 657, 675–77; Roosevelt Brains Trust and, 529, 557

Tunisia, 483
Turkey, 2–4, 284, 427, 436
Turner, Brian, 730
Turner, Frederick Jackson, 194, 203, 252, 363, 508
Turner, Nat, 218
Twain, Mark, 263, 313, 329–30, 367, 417, 808n7
Twenty Thousand Leagues under the Sea (Verne), 245
Twin Towers, 724
Tydings, Millard, 557, 657
Tydings-McDuffie Act, 627, 629–30
Tyler, John, 169, 214

Umberto I, King of Italy, 276–77
unemployment: Caribbean and, 550, 553, 558, 576, 581; colonialism and, 36–37, 657, 676–77; forgotten empire and, 537; imperialism and, 256–61, 271, 275, 379, 456–57, 462, 467; independence and, 144, 168–70, 300, 303–4, 317, 322; intrusion and, 396; military-fiscal state and, 36–37, 63, 80–81, 86; Pacific and, 606, 626, 630, 637; postcolonialism and, 695, 698, 719–20, 723–25; revolution and, 111; wars of incorporation and, 214, 232
Union (Civil War), 186, 210, 214, 216, 219–35, 287–93, 371
Union française, 445, 473, 703, 877n170
Union of the Kingdoms, 67
Union of the Two Crowns, 67
United Mine Workers, 297
United Nations, 660; big four powers and, 491; civil rights and, 528; colonialism and, 645–46, 664, 675; General Assembly and, 664; imperialism and, 460, 491; League of Nations and, 4, 446, 451, 460, 466; postcolonialism and, 698–99, 703, 728, 734; Security Council and, 664; UNESCO, 460
United States: American Century and, 38, 443–46, 492–93, 707, 723, 726; American Revolution and, 8 (*see also* American Revolution); American way and, 501, 571, 609, 675, 683–97; Anglo-Japanese alliance and, 446–47; as aspiring hegemon, 707–21; Baghdad and, 2, 4, 731–34; Bill of Rights and, 61, 126, 147–48; Bureau of Indian Affairs and, 523, 668; Captain America and, 721–22, 728–29; CIA and, 643, 672, 674, 682, 713–17; civilizing mis-

sion of, 7; Civil War and, 7 (*see also* Civil War); Cold War and, 31 (*see also* Cold War); Commissioner for Indian Affairs and, 503, 529, 648; continuing power of, 721–29; Declaration of Independence and, 54, 110, 112, 123, 199; decolonization and, 683–87; exceptionalism and, 15–21, 157, 335, 492, 530; financial crisis of 2008 and, 725–26, 728; First Continental Congress and, 122–23; Founding Fathers of, 17, 94, 153, 174, 183, 185, 192, 316, 363, 446, 509, 565; Good Neighbor policy and, 449, 556, 584–85; historical treatments for, 10–15; imperialism and, 337 (*see also* imperialism); imports and, 163 (*see also* imports); Indian Mutiny and, 505; Indian Reorganization Act and, 503; Indian Wars and, 39, 173, 193, 197, 203, 237, 353, 372, 611; isolation and, 446–50; Korean War and, 484, 656, 663, 680, 711–12, 714; Lend-Lease Agreement and, 469, 471; manifest destiny and, 114, 148, 176, 191, 195, 215, 325, 365–66, 492, 508; Marshall Plan and, 475, 708, 710; Mexican-American War and, 170, 184, 191, 193, 212; NAFTA and, 703–4; Native Americans and, 503 (*see also* Native Americans); NATO and, 475, 710–11; New England, 63, 109–12, 115, 132, 167, 175, 181, 194, 196, 220–21, 291, 362; new supranational organizations and, 708–9; New World and, 18, 58, 76, 84, 91, 97–98, 112, 133, 136–41, 146, 175, 191, 195, 209–12, 218, 233, 245, 277, 328, 337, 374, 385, 387, 432, 445, 472, 474, 609, 671, 694, 706; Northern states and, 301 (*see also* Northern states); Operation Iraqi Freedom and, 730–38; peak power of, 707–8; Pearl Harbor and, 191, 353, 419, 421, 430, 468–69, 538, 595, 605, 631, 902n71; postcolonialism and, 689–729; postwar environment and, 708–10, 721–29; postwar power of, 447, 490–93; Spanish-American War and, 7, 19 (*see also* Spanish-American War); as superpower, 6, 11, 18, 97, 471, 644, 696, 721, 723, 736–37; Vietnam War and, 450, 493, 529, 536, 663, 668, 682–83, 685, 709, 714, 722; voting rights to women and, 196; War of 1812 and, 77, 123, 127, 152, 160, 166–67, 178, 191, 193, 199, 210–13, 232, 234–35, 335, 786n151; wars of choice and, 427–36; World War I era and, 7, 20 (*see also* World

War I era); World War II era and, 465, 708 (*see also* World War II era)

United States Steel Corporation, 314

Universal Declaration of Human Rights, 646

uranium, 648, 879n209

urbanization, 244, 249, 252, 282, 288, 292, 324, 336, 338, 561–62, 695

U.S. Army, 130, 199, 353, 415, 434, 523, 555, 606–7, 623, 632, 655, 663, 721, 724, 732

U.S. Constitution: benevolent assimilation and, 609; Bill of Rights and, 126, 147–48; Fourteenth Amendment and, 200; imperialism and, 367; independence and, 146–49, 166–67, 170, 173–74, 177, 185, 290; Madison and, 33; national debt and, 128; Preamble of, 124; Puerto Rico and, 545; revolution and, 98, 124–31, 134, 139; Second Amendment and, 201, 795n65; state peace pact of, 125; Thirteenth Amendment and, 230; wars of incorporation and, 201, 213, 218, 220, 235–36

U.S. Department of Agriculture, 556, 600, 681

U.S. Food Administration, 602

U.S. Foreign Service, 353, 522

U.S. Marines, 353, 422, 577, 584, 731–34

U.S. Navy, 333, 353–54, 365, 384, 416, 419, 435, 559

U.S.-Philippine Trade Act, 653–54

USS Maine, 345, 354, 360, 368, 370, 372, 399, 415, 431–32, 539, 724

U.S. Supreme Court: business interests and, 302; Dred Scott case and, 222, 224; Foraker Act and, 545–62, 566; income tax and, 312; Insular Cases and, 515–16, 520; Jones Act and, 546, 615, 624–25; Northern representation on, 290; *Plessy v. Ferguson* and, 320; segregation and, 665; slavery and, 149, 224; Voting Rights Act and, 667

U.S. Treasury, 312, 390, 498, 722

Valera, Eamon de, 555

Valéry, Paul, 16

Van Buren, Martin, 150, 152–53, 155–57, 169

Veblen, Thorstein, 8, 256, 313, 382, 832n191

Vega Sugar Company, 569

Venezuela, 319, 333, 542, 678, 719

Verdeja Act, 579, 586

Verdi, Giuseppe, 253

Verne, Jules, 245

Versailles Treaty, 446

Vico, Giambattista, 6, 742n40

Victor Emmanuel II, King of Italy, 234, 276

Victoria, Queen of the United Kingdom of Great Britain and Ireland, 178, 252, 321

Vietnam War, 450, 493, 529, 536, 663, 668, 682–83, 685, 709, 714, 722

Voltaire, François-Marie Arouet de, 53, 138, 254

voting rights, 344; African Americans and, 149, 292; Chartist movement and, 80; Cuba and, 519, 575–76; imperialism and, 242; Jackson and, 153; Missouri Crisis and, 210; Native Americans and, 149, 196, 200; Pacific and, 601, 603, 605, 670; property rights and, 133; slavery and, 149, 290; Walpole and, 63; women and, 133, 149, 196, 210, 551, 582, 586, 711

Voting Rights Act, 667

wage labor, 220, 308, 393, 400, 462, 550, 621–22

Wagner, Richard, 331

Wagner Act, 605

Wakefield, Edward Gibbon, 86, 196

Walker Tariff, 170

Wall, Max, 731

Wall Street, 311, 334, 356, 362

Walpole Sir Robert, 62–64, 98–100, 113

Warner, Charles Dudley, 313, 808n7

Warning from the West Indies (Macmillan), 463

War of 1812: France and, 210; Jefferson embargo and, 208; as second war of independence, 208–12; Spain and, 210; Treaty of Ghent and, 209; United States and, 77, 123, 127, 152, 160, 166–67, 178, 191, 193, 199, 210–13, 232, 234–35, 335, 786n151; wars of incorporation and, 207–12

War of the Austrian Succession, 99, 101

wars of 1898, 38, 243, 267, 337, 339–43, 346, 378–79, 386, 502, 560–61, 568

wars of incorporation: Adam Smith and, 205; Africa and, 194, 197–99, 205, 207, 210, 235; African Americans and, 210, 218–219, 226–29; agriculture and, 196, 205, 221, 227; American Revolution and, 199; anarchy and, 203, 207, 219, 234; Anglo-Saxons and, 194, 210, 218–19;

wars of incorporation (*continued*)
assimilation and, 198–201, 210, 237; Australia and, 195–98, 205; autonomy and, 217; British Empire and, 192, 196, 213, 218–19, 236; Canada and, 194–98, 205, 207, 209–11, 232, 235–37; capitalism and, 220, 225; China and, 231–32; Christianity and, 207, 219; citizenship and, 196, 200–201, 227; civilizing mission and, 198, 237; Civil War and, 191, 193, 200, 203, 211, 217–38; conservatives and, 218, 233, 238; cotton and, 193, 213, 220–23, 227–32, 236, 238; Cuba and, 213–14, 220, 238; decolonization and, 235; democracy and, 195, 217–19, 231, 234; Democrats and, 214, 216, 222–26; desire for land and, 193, 410; empire-building and, 209; Enlightenment and, 210; expansionism and, 192–93, 203, 212–16, 237; exports and, 196, 208, 213, 222, 227–29, 232; France and, 192, 210, 214, 230–33; free trade and, 196, 210, 220, 222, 226, 229, 231–32, 238; French Wars and, 208, 211–12; futurity and, 191–94; Germany and, 232, 234; Hawai'i and, 196, 205, 214, 237; human rights and, 219, 231, 237; immigration and, 193, 203–4, 214; imports and, 222, 226, 232; India and, 198, 232, 235–36; international relations and, 192, 219; Ireland and, 217; Italy and, 232, 234; Jackson and, 194, 196, 199, 210, 212, 215; Japan and, 237; Jefferson and, 196, 199–200, 208–11, 219, 223; labor and, 193, 195–96, 219–20, 222–23, 233; landowners and, 233, 247, 279; liberalism and, 220; liberty and, 195, 211, 215, 218–19, 237; manifest destiny and, 191, 195, 215; manufacturing and, 196, 220–22, 231–32; Marx and, 219, 220; mercantilism and, 220; Mexico and, 191, 193, 212–17, 220, 230, 234, 237; modernization and, 200, 217, 221, 224; Napoleon and, 228; national identity and, 209; nationalism and, 219–20, 225, 245, 249, 254, 263, 271, 274, 283; nation-building and, 192; Native Americans and, 199–203, 210, 237; Northern states and, 213, 216–29, 234; oil and, 236; oligarchy and, 227–28; Philippines and, 203; poverty and, 195, 200, 226; progressives and, 233, 238; property rights and, 194–207; protectionism and, 197; Protestantism and, 194, 207, 219; Prussia and, 232–33; reconstruction and, 233, 237; Republicans and, 219, 224, 226; Russia and, 234; segregation and, 198, 237; self-determination and, 218–19, 225–31; Seven Years' War and, 199; slavery and, 193, 196–97, 203, 208, 210, 212–32, 237–38; South Africa and, 194, 205, 207, 210; Southern states and, 193, 200, 203, 210, 212–29, 233–34; sovereignty and, 200, 216, 219, 231; Spain and, 192; Spanish-American War and, 237; tariffs and, 210, 222, 226, 229; taxes and, 195, 200, 226; technology and, 206; textile industry and, 228, 232; unemployment and, 214, 232; U.S. Constitution and, 201, 213, 218, 220, 235–36; War of 1812 and, 208–12; West Indies and, 215, 232, 235, 237; white settlers and, 192, 214
Washington, George, 721; Farewell Address of, 190, 192; independence and, 152, 166–67, 174, 190; Native Americans and, 200; revolution and, 95, 111, 118–19, 123–24, 128, 130; slavery and, 95–96; wars of incorporation and, 192, 200
Washington, Harry, 95–98, 120, 141
Washington, Jenny, 96
Washington, John, 95
Wayne, John, 632, 638, 910n222
Wealth of Nations, The (Smith), 54, 135–36
Weber, Max, 247–48, 306, 374, 505, 522–23, 887n107, 904n101
Webster, Daniel, 209
Webster, Noah, 179, 181, 785n215, 789n214
Webster-Ashburton Treaty, 209
Wedgwood, Josiah, 167
Wellington, Duke of, 76, 79–80, 272, 761n185
Wells, H. G., 254–55, 812n64
West Indies, 383, 538, 873n111; American Civil War and, 232; exports and, 58, 110, 164; federation and, 139, 235; imperialism and, 463, 469, 483; loyalty to Britain by, 121; Macmillan and, 463; military-fiscal state and, 58, 61, 64, 79, 86; Mill on, 46; revolution and, 96; slavery and, 215; wars of incorporation and, 215, 232, 235, 237
West Side Story (movie), 572
Weyler, Valeriano, 412
Wheeler, Joseph, 370
Whigs: independence and, 157, 160–61, 169, 189, 782n79, 786n151; military-fiscal state and, 55–56, 61–64, 70, 77, 86, 92–93; revo-

lution and, 100–103, 106, 112, 127, 130–37, 772n136, 776n208; wars of incorporation and, 214–16, 223, 224, 235

Whiskey Rebellion, 128

Whistler, James McNeil, 331

"white man's burden," 494

White Papers, 485

white settlers, 13; colonialism and, 653, 684; forgotten empire and, 537; imperialism and, 453, 479; independence and, 145, 147, 321; intrusion and, 384–86, 400, 418, 429; Pacific and, 596–97, 603, 635; wars of incorporation and, 192, 214; as worthless, 111

white supremacy, 40, 142, 198, 201, 291–92, 320–21, 506–7, 513, 641

Whitman, Walt, 178–80, 202, 212, 217, 241, 243, 285–86, 328–29, 790n228, 800n161, 807n1, 807n2, 808n6, 836n281

Wilberforce, William, 77, 96

Wilde, Oscar, 217, 651, 691

Wilhelm I, Emperor of Germany, 234

Wilkes, John, 101–3

William I, King of the Netherlands, 73–75, 232, 272, 455, 760n168

William III (William of Orange), 55–56, 73

Williams, Esther, 679

Williams, William Appleman, 341, 741n26, 746n58, 782n86, 868n10

Wilshire, H. Gaylord, 367

Wilson, Sir Arnold, 1, 4–5

Wilson, Woodrow, 290; Committee on Public Information and, 451–52; Cuba and, 577; dispersion of authority and, 521–22; exceptionalism and, 335; imperialism and, 343, 363, 374, 449, 451–52, 455; official tuition and, 521–22; Philippines and, 615, 625; Progressives and, 304–5, 333; Puerto Rico and, 546, 555; self-determination and, 451–52, 664; Spanish-American War and, 373

Wilson-Gorman Act, 299, 423

Winks, Robin, 496–97, 530–34, 882n9, 882n10

Winship, Blanton C., 556

Winthrop, John, 141

Wisconsin School, 17, 340–41, 360, 838n7

Wollstonecraft, Mary, 102

Woman's Christian Temperance Union (WCTU), 323, 835n252

women: citizenship for, 227; Dickinson and, 328; fashion and, 327; foreign service and, 522; gender issues and, 13, 249, 266, 341–43, 699; independence and, 143; labor strikes and, 554; in military, 655; opportunities for, 407, 411, 572; property rights and, 623; religion and, 183; rights of, 176, 342; slavery and, 87; voting rights and, 133, 149, 196, 210, 551, 582, 586, 711; working, 554, 578–79, 582, 606

Wood, Leonard, 501, 539, 563, 564–66, 569, 572, 576–78, 589, 611, 625

Woodford, Stewart L., 431–32

Worcester, Joseph, 179, 181

Wordsworth, William, 624, 760n178, 764n257

Works Projects Administration, 553

World Bank, 336, 474, 707–8, 718, 725

World Health Organization (WHO), 460

World War I era, 287; American Century and, 443–44; anti-German feeling and, 507–8; Caribbean and, 547, 552, 555–56, 568, 577, 580, 582, 588–89; colonialism and, 642; forgotten empire and, 507, 518, 536; imperialism and, 38, 245, 248, 254, 265, 274, 352, 371–72, 443–46, 449–56, 465–66, 490; international relations and, 20; intrusion and, 435, 438; Lenin and, 465; military-fiscal state and, 36, 73; Pacific and, 592, 599, 602–3, 625–26, 631; postcolonialism and, 698; return to normality and, 450–56

World War II era, 18, 20, 731; American Century and, 445–46; Battle of El Alamein and, 470; breaking/remaking of empires and, 465–70; Caribbean and, 558, 591; civil rights and, 40; colonialism and, 639–46, 649, 653, 660, 663, 668, 671; debt collection and, 258; decolonialization and, 235; devastation from, 39, 708; eugenics and, 318; forgotten empire and, 504, 508, 510, 512, 531, 537; Hollywood portrayal of, 632; human rights and, 105; imperialism and, 445, 454, 460–65, 468, 472, 477, 486, 490–92; indigenization decrees and, 311; Lend-Lease Agreement and, 469, 471; liberation and, 483–89; Marshall Plan and, 475, 708, 710; military-fiscal state and, 85; modernization and, 504–5; NATO and, 475, 710–11; neglected study of, 7; Nuremberg trials and, 646; Pacific and, 602, 631, 638; Pearl Harbor and, 191, 353, 419, 421,

World War II era (*continued*)
430, 468–69, 538, 595, 605, 631, 902n71;
postcolonialism and, 692, 695–98, 701–3,
706–8, 713–14, 720–21; postwar environment and, 721–29; principles of natural
rights and, 145; reconstruction and, 708–
11; second colonial occupation and, 470–
83; U.S. power after, 490–93
Wright, Frank Lloyd, 331
Wyvill, Christopher, 102

Yorkshire Association, 102
Young, Samuel, 433
Young, Whitney, 668
Young Men's Christian Association (YMCA),
323–24
Young Plan, 448
Young Women's Christian Association
(YWCA), 323–24, 513

Zayas, Alfredo, 577

ALSO IN THE SERIES

David Ekbladh, *The Great American Mission: Modernization and the Construction of an American World Order*

Martin Klimke, *The Other Alliance: Student Protest in West Germany and the United States in the Global Sixties*

Andrew Zimmerman, *Alabama in Africa: Booker T. Washington, the German Empire, and the Globalization of the New South*

Ian Tyrrell, *Reforming the World: The Creation of America's Moral Empire*

Rachel St. John, *Line in the Sand: A History of the Western U.S.–Mexico Border*

Thomas Borstelmann, *The 1970s: A New Global History from Civil Rights to Economic Inequality*

Donna R. Gabaccia, *Foreign Relations: American Immigration in Global Perspective*

Jürgen Osterhammel, *The Transformation of the World: A Global History of the Nineteenth Century*

Jeffrey A. Engel, Mark Atwood Lawrence, and Andrew Preston, eds., *America in the World*

Adam Ewing, *The Age of Garvey: Global Black Politics in the Interwar Era*

Kiran Klaus Patel, *The New Deal: A Global History*